Women's Lives

Multicultural Perspectives

Fifth Edition

Gwyn Kirk

Margo Okazawa-Rey

 **Higher Education**

Boston   Burr Ridge, IL   Dubuque, IA   New York   San Francisco   St. Louis
Bangkok   Bogotá   Caracas   Kuala Lumpur   Lisbon   London   Madrid   Mexico City
Milan   Montreal   New Delhi   Santiago   Seoul   Singapore   Sydney   Taipei   Toronto

Mc Graw Hill Higher Education

Published by McGraw-Hill, an imprint of The McGraw-Hill Companies, Inc., 1221 Avenue of the Americas, New York, NY 10020.

This book is printed on acid-free paper.

1 2 3 4 5 6 7 8 9 0 FGR/FGR 0 9

ISBN: 978-0-07-351230-3
MHID: 0-07-351230-3

Editor in Chief: *Michael Ryan*
Publisher: *Frank Moritmer*
Sponsoring Editor: *Gina Boedeker*
Development Editor: *Kate Scheinman*
Editorial Assistant: *Jordan Killam*
Marketing Manager: *Leslie Oberhuber*
Production Editor: *Alison Meier*
Media Project Manager: *Ron Nelms*
Design Coordinator: *Allister Fein*
Cover Design: *Elise Lansdon*
Photo Research: *Brian J. Pecko*
Production Supervisor: *Tandra Jorgensen*
Composition: *9/11 Palatino by Laserwords*
Printing: *45# New Era Matte, Quebecor World, Inc.*

Cover image: Hand-made crazy quilt with Woman's Relief Corps (WRC) ribbons (back view). Ca. 1930 (ribbons date from 1894–1930). Washington State Historical Society, Tacoma, Washington State, U.S.A. © Washington State Historical Society/Art Resource, NY
Credits: The credits section for this book begins on page C-1 and is considered an extension of the copyright page.

Library of Congress Cataloging-in-Publication Data

Kirk, Gwyn.
    Women's lives : multicultural perspectives / Gwyn Kirk and Margo Okazawa-Rey. — 5th ed.
        p. cm.
    Includes bibliographical references and index.
    ISBN-13: 978-0-07-351230-3 (alk. paper)
    ISBN-10: 0-07-351230-3 (alk. paper)
    1. Women—United States—Social conditions. 2. Women—United States—Economic conditions.
3. Feminism—United States. I. Okazawa-Rey, Margo. II. Title.
    HQ1421.K573 2009
    305.420973—dc22   2008042519

www.mhhe.com

To those who connect us to the past,
our mothers,
who birthed us, raised us,
taught us, inspired us, and took no nonsense from us
Edwina Davies, Kazuko Okazawa, Willa Mae Wells
and to those who connect us to the future
Charlotte Elizabeth Andrews-Briscoe
Gabrielle Raya Clancy-Humphrey
Jesse Simon Cool
Issac Kana Fukumura-White
Akani Kazuo Ai-Lee James
Ayize Kimani Ming Lee James
Hansoo Lim
Uma Talpade Mohanty
Camille Celestina Stovall-Ceja
Aya Sato Venet

Brief Contents

Contents

READINGS

CHAPTER TWO

Theories and Theorizing: Integrative Frameworks for Understanding   51

READINGS

CHAPTER THREE

◆◆◆

Identities and Social Locations: Who Am I? Who Are My People?   91

◆ PART TWO ◆

OUR BODIES, OURSELVES

CHAPTER FOUR

◆◆◆

Women's Sexuality   149

CHAPTER FIVE

◆◆◆

Women's Bodies, Women's Health   207

Health as Wellness   221

    Limits of the U.S. Medical Industry   221

    A More Holistic Health System   222

Questions for Reflection   223

Finding Out More on the Web   223

Taking Action   224

READINGS

25. Rosemarie Garland Thomson, "Feminist Theory, the Body, and the Disabled Figure"   224

26. Jean Kilbourne, "'The More You Subtract, the More You Add': Cutting Girls Down to Size"   231

27. Joy Harjo, "Three Generations of Native American Women's Birth Experience"   239

28. Asian Communities for Reproductive Justice, "Reproductive Justice: Vision, Analysis, and Action for a Stronger Movement"   242

29. Emma Bell and Luisa Orza, "Understanding Positive Women's Realities"   247

30. bell hooks, "Living to Love"   250

CHAPTER SIX

◆◆◆

Violence Against Women   257

What Counts as Violence Against Women?   257

The Incidence of Violence Against Women   260

    Intimate Partner Violence   260

    Rape and Sexual Assault   261

    Effects of Race, Class, Nation, Sexuality, and Disability   263

Explanations of Violence Against Women   264

    Micro-Level Explanations   264

    Macro-Level Explanations   265

Ending Violence Against Women   267

    The Importance of a Political Movement   267

    Providing Support for Victims/Survivors   268

◆ PART THREE ◆
WOMEN'S PLACES: HOME AND WORK IN A
GLOBALIZING WORLD

CHAPTER SEVEN

Making a Home, Making a Living   301

CHAPTER EIGHT

◆◆◆

Living in a Globalizing World   371

◆ PART FOUR ◆

SECURITY AND SUSTAINABILITY

CHAPTER NINE

◆◆◆

Women, Crime, and Criminalization   443

CHAPTER TEN

◆◆◆

Women and the Military, War, and Peace   493

CHAPTER ELEVEN

◆◆◆

Women and the Environment   535

◆ PART FIVE ◆

ACTIVISM AND CHANGE

CHAPTER TWELVE

◆◆◆

Creating Change: Theory, Vision, and Action   583

Preface

An introductory course is perhaps the most challenging women's studies course to conceptualize and teach. Depending on their overall goals for the course, instructors must make difficult choices about what to include and what to leave out. Students come into the course for a variety of reasons and with a range of expectations and prior knowledge, and most will not major in women's studies. The course may fulfill a distribution requirement for them, or it may be a way of taking one women's studies course during their undergraduate education out of a personal interest in women's lives. For women's studies majors and minors, the course plays a very different role, offering a foundation for their area of study.

Women's studies programs continue to build their reputations in terms of academic rigor and scholarly standards. Women's studies scholarship is on the cutting edge of many academic disciplines, especially in the arts, humanities, and social sciences. At the same time, women's studies occupies a marginal position within academia, challenging male-dominated knowledge and pedagogy, with all the tensions that entails. Women's studies faculty and our allies live with these tensions personally and professionally. Outside the academy, government policies and economic changes have made many women's lives more difficult in the United States—a loss of factory and office work as jobs continue to be moved overseas or become automated; government failure to introduce a health-care system that benefits everyone or to provide an adequate system of child care; cuts in welfare programs; greater restriction of government support to immigrants and their families; a dramatic increase in the number of women now incarcerated compared with twenty years ago; and vast expenditures on war and preparations for war.

In the past decade, the political climate for women's studies on campuses and in the wider society has become more challenging as conservative viewpoints have gained ground through political rhetoric, the narrow range of public discourse, changes in law and policy, and the "disappearing" of information regarding women's lives from government Web sites and publications (see, e.g., National Council for Research on Women 2004; National Women's Law Center 2004). In addition, a questioning of academic freedom on campuses has made many teachers' lives more difficult. Moreover, the inequalities U.S. women still face, borne out by the data presented in this book, mean that women's studies teachers are often in the position of bearing "bad news."

This text started out as two separate readers that we used in our classes at Antioch College (Gwyn Kirk) and San Francisco State University (Margo Okazawa-Rey) in the mid-1990s. Since then, we have learned a lot about teaching an introductory women's studies course, and the book has grown and developed as a result. We completed this revision before the November 2008 election, amid much debate about which candidates would get into office and what policy changes they would initiate. Even with the most favorable political scenario, there is much to do to improve women's lives and to reverse the trends of the past ten years or more, both in the U.S. and many other countries.

What We Want in an Introductory Women's Studies Book

As teachers, we want to present a broad range of women's experiences to our students in terms of class, race, culture, national origin, disability, age, and sexuality. We want teaching materials that do justice to the diversity of women's lives in this country. We also want materials that address the location of the United States in a globalizing world. In our introductory courses, we included some discussion of theory because a basic understanding of theoretical frameworks is a powerful tool not only for women's studies courses but also for other courses students take. We also emphasized women's activism. As women's studies has become more established and professionalized, it has tended to grow away from its roots in women's liberation movements, a trend that troubled us. Discussing our own lives, it was clear that we both value our long-standing involvements in political movements and projects. This activism has provided us with vital communities in which to learn, grow, and make a contribution to issues we care about. There are many women's activist and advocacy projects across the country, but students often do not know about them. Much of the information that students learn in women's studies concerning the difficulties of women's lives may be discouraging, but knowing about women's activism can be empowering, even in the face of sometimes daunting realities. This knowledge reinforces the idea that current inequalities and problems are not fixed but have the potential to be changed.

Linking Individual Experiences to National and Transnational Trends and Issues

We are both trained in sociology. We noted that students coming into our classes were much more familiar with psychological explanations for behaviors and experiences than they were with structural explanations. They invariably enjoyed first-person accounts of women's experiences, but a series of stories—even wonderfully insightful stories—are not enough to understand the complex circumstances and forces that women face and that shape our lives. Accordingly, we provide a broader context for the selected readings in the overview essays that open each chapter.

We recognize that many U.S. women—especially those in higher socio-economic groups—have greater opportunities for self-expression, for earning a living, and for engagement in the wider world compared with the past. However, we are concerned about the challenges facing women and

men in the twenty-first century: challenges regarding work and livelihood, personal and family relationships, violence on many levels, and the mounting pressures on the fragile physical environment. These issues raise major questions about personal and societal values, the distribution of resources, and what constitutes everyday security and sustainability. How is our society going to provide for its people in the years to come? What are the effects of the increasing polarization between rich and poor in the United States and between richer and poorer nations? These themes of security and sustainability provide the wider framework for this book and have influenced our choices about materials to include and topics to address.

As teachers we have been concerned with students' knowledge and understanding, and beyond that, with their aspirations, hopes, and values. One of our goals for this book is to provide a series of lenses that will help students understand their own lives and the lives of others. A second goal is that, through this understanding, they will be able to participate in some way in the creation of a genuinely secure and sustainable future.

New to the Fifth Edition

This fifth edition of *Women's Lives* relies on the analyses, principles, and style of earlier editions, but with major additions and changes:

- A new chapter, "Women's Rights, Women's Liberation, Women's Studies," provides a history of U.S. women's movements and women's studies.

- A revised chapter, "Women's Bodies, Women's Health," combines two earlier chapters and views body issues as a matter of public heath.

- A revised chapter, "Making a Home, Making a Living," combines two earlier chapters to reduce duplication.

- An expanded chapter, "Living in a Globalizing World," adds women's experiences of cross-border identities, families, and communities to our earlier emphasis on the global economy.

- Updated statistics are included throughout, and new readings on the history of U.S. women's movements; transgender issues and experiences; community responses to gender violence; women's experiences of immigration, prison, and the military; gender and climate change; and transnational feminist organizing.

- In each chapter there is a greater emphasis on the transnational.

- A revised and updated password-protected Instructor's Manual—including alternative Tables of Contents for flexible use of the book—is available on our companion Web site at www.mhhe.com/kirk5.

A number of considerations, sometimes competing or contradictory, have influenced the decisions we made to ensure this edition meets our goals. Since the beginning, we have been committed to including the work of established scholars and lesser-known writers from a range of racial and ethnic backgrounds and with differences in ability, age, class, culture, national origin, and sexuality. As in previous editions, we have looked for writers who, implicitly or explicitly, integrate several levels of analysis (micro, meso, macro, and global) in their work. Students we have talked with, including those in our own classes, love first person accounts because this kind of writing helps to draw them into more theoretical discussions. Teachers invariably want more theory, more history, and more research-based pieces. As we searched for materials, we have found much more theoretical work by white women than by women of color. We assume this is because there are fewer women of color in the academy, because white women scholars and writers have greater access to publishers, and because prevailing ideas about what theory is and what form it should take tend to exclude work by women of color. This can give the misleading impression that, aside from a few notable exceptions, women of color are not theorists. This raises the question of what theory is and who can theorize, which we take up in the second chapter. We have tried hard not to reproduce this bias in our selection, but we note this structural problem here to make this aspect of our process visible. We include personal essays and narratives that make theoretical points, what scholar and writer Gloria Anzaldúa (2002, p. 578) called "autohistoria-teoria"—a genre of writing about one's personal and collective history that may use fictive elements and that also theorizes. In a similar vein, people living in the United States have limited access to writings by and about women from countries of the global South, whether personal accounts, academic research, journalists' reports, policy recommendations, or critiques of policies imposed by countries of the North. A few scholars and fiction writers, working in English, are published widely. Again, structural limitations of the politics of knowledge affect who has access to book publishers or Web sites and whose work may be translated for English-language readers.

This new edition represents our best effort to balance these considerations as we sought to provide information, analysis, and inspiration concerning the myriad daily experiences, opportunities, limitations, oppressions, hopes, joys, and satisfactions that make up women's lives. As before, our focus is on women in the United States, but also, in each chapter, we have a broader reach and give attention to the many ways that U.S. women are tied to and part of a globalizing world.

Acknowledgments

Many people—especially our students, teachers, colleagues, and friends—made it possible for us to complete the first edition of this book over a decade ago. We are grateful to everyone at Mayfield Publishing who worked to put our manuscript between covers: Franklin Graham, our editor, whose confidence in our ideas never wavered and whose light hand on the steering wheel and clear sense of direction got us into print; also Julianna Scott Fein, production editor; the production team; and Jamie Fuller, copyeditor extraordinaire. For the second edition we were fortunate to have the support of Hamilton College as Jane Watson Irwin Co-Chairs in Women's Studies (1999–2001). Women's studies colleagues, other faculty members, and librarians welcomed and supported us. Again we acknowledge the Mayfield team: Serina Beauparlant, our editor; Julianna Scott Fein, production editor; the production team; and Margaret Moore, a wonderful copyeditor.

McGraw-Hill published the third edition. We benefited from support of the Women's Leadership Institute at Mills College and the DataCenter, an Oakland-based nonprofit, providing research and training to grassroots social justice organizations across the country. We greatly appreciate our editors Beth Kaufman and Sherith Pankratz and the work of Jean Mailander, Jen Mills, Karyn Morrison,

Amy Shaffer, and April Wells-Hayes. For edition four, our editors were Kate Scheinman and Sherith Pankratz, with Cathy Iammartino, Jason Huls, Alex Ambrose, and Laurie Entringer on the production team.

As before, this fifth edition builds on the accumulated work, help, and support of many people. Particular thanks go to Grace Chang, Piya Chatterjee, Marghi Dutton, Yoko Fukumura, Annie Fukushima, Aileen Hernandez, Albie Miles, and Barbara Nielsen for providing leads to new material, information, and insights. We thank the feminist scholars and activists whose work we have reprinted and all those whose research and writing not only have informed our work but have shaped the field of women's studies. We appreciate the independent bookstores and small presses that keep going thanks to dedicated staff and loyal readers. We also rely on other feminist "institutions": the *Women's Review of Books, Ms.,* scholarly journals, and WMST-L, ably "mastered" by Joan Korenman. We have benefited enormously from discussions on this list and suggestions for readings and classroom activities generously shared by teachers.

We acknowledge the encouragement, enthusiasm, and skills of our editors, Kate Scheinman and Gina Boedeker, and the work of the entire book team: Alison Meier, Allister Fein, Brian Pecko, and Tandra Jorgensen. Once again we benefited from the insights and advice of reviewers:

Lucille A. Adkins, La Roche College

Anita Anantharam, University of Florida

Rebecca Dingo, University of Missouri, Columbia

Sheila Hassell Hughes, University of Dayton

Piyasuda Pangsapa, University at Buffalo (SUNY)

Michele Ren, Radford University

The United States continues to gain brilliant young feminist writers, teachers, organizers, and artists—some of whose work is included here. Some years ago we began to acknowledge the groundbreaking contributions of older feminists who were passing on. This time we honor and remember Paula Gunn Allen, Native American writer and scholar, and Del Martin, pioneer for lesbian/gay rights and co-founder of the groundbreaking lesbian organization, Daughters of Bilitis, in 1995, who died while this manuscript was in preparation.

Lastly, we acknowledge our friendship over these past sixteen years, which provides a deep foundation for our shared understandings and our work together. We continue to be inspired by the cultural work of Sweet Honey in the Rock, a national living treasure whose blend of music and politics touches the head, heart, and hands, and also by the "sociological imagination"—C. Wright Mills's concept—that draws on the need for complex social analysis in order to make change.

To everyone, very many thanks.

—Gwyn Kirk and Margo Okazawa-Rey

We have chosen each other
and the edge of each other's battles
the war is the same
if we lose
someday women's blood will congeal
upon a dead planet
if we win
there is no telling
we seek beyond history
for a new and more possible meeting.

— AUDRE LORDE

1

◆◆◆

Women's Rights, Women's Liberation, Women's Studies

The Focus and Challenge of Women's Studies

The early 1970s saw the start of many women's studies programs across the United States building on the insights, energies, and activist commitments of the vibrant women's liberation movements of the times. Early courses had titles like "Women's Liberation," "The Power of Patriarchy," or "Sexist Oppression and Women's Empowerment." Texts often included mimeographed articles from feminist newsletters and pamphlets because there was so little appropriate material in books. By contrast, women's studies is now an established academic field with extensive bodies of literature and hundreds of programs in the United States and around the world, including master's and Ph.D. programs. Women's studies graduates are employed in business, education, electoral politics, feminist advocacy projects, filmmaking, health, international policy, journalism, law, library work, publishing, and social and human services (Luebke and Reilly 1995; Stewart 2007). Students

have reported that women's studies courses are informative and empowering; they provide a perspective on one's own life and on other college courses in ways that are often life changing.

Women's studies seeks new ways of understanding—more comprehensive than those offered by traditional academic disciplines. The discipline started as a critique of scholarship that ignored women's lives or treated women in stereotypical ways. Women's studies sought to provide missing information, new theoretical perspectives, and new ways of teaching. Most women's studies teachers do not use what Brazilian educator Paulo Friere called the "banking method" of education, common in many fields, where students are like banks and teachers deposit information—historical facts, dates, definitions—and withdraw it in quizzes and exams. Regardless of its relevance for other subjects, this method is not appropriate for women's studies where students come into class with experience, opinions, and theories about many of the topics discussed. Students are familiar with perspectives on issues that are circulating in the media, for example. They know where their spiritual community stands on matters they care about. In a women's studies class, students are encouraged to share and reflect on their experiences and to relate the readings and discussions to their own lives. Women's studies focuses on critical reading and critical thinking, which is a new way of learning for many students, especially those just starting college. It requires us all to synthesize information and integrate diverse points of view, which are significant academic and workplace skills.

Women's studies courses provide data that are often absent in the rest of the curriculum. Students may be challenged to rethink some of their assumptions and experiences as well as their positions on complex issues. This kind of study can evoke strong emotional reactions because everyone may be deeply affected by issues under discussion. Women's studies sometimes generates anger in students at the many forms of women's oppression, at other students' ignorance or lack of concern, at being female in a male-dominated world, and at the daunting nature of the issues and problems faced by women (Boxer 1998; Howe 2000). These aspects of women's studies have given rise to criticisms that the discipline is too "touchy-feely" or that it is an extended gripe session against men. We discuss these criticisms later in this chapter.

For several generations, the goals that dominated U.S. women's education concerned equality: to study alongside men, to have access to the same curriculum, and to be admitted to male professions. Women's studies called into question the gendered nature of knowledge itself with its focus on white, male, middle-class perspectives that are deemed to be universal, as we discuss in the following chapter. Forty years later, women's studies programs continue to build their reputations in terms of scholarly work and academic rigor. They continue to occupy a contradictory position within academia, challenging male-dominated knowledge and pedagogy. Women's studies scholars are under pressure from the university system to undertake research and writing that meets "scholarly standards." This has meant that much published work is overly abstract and inaccessible to most readers. Also, as women's studies has become more established and professionalized, it has tended to grow away from its movement roots.

The data we present show significant gains and some serious setbacks for women in the United States over the past forty years or so. Some of the information and analysis is discouraging. At the same time, however, important changes have taken place—including the very existence of women's studies and the wealth of women's writing and organizing that we draw on in this collection.

Tangling with the "F" Word

Whether or not students consider themselves feminists as a matter of personal identity, in women's studies they will study feminist perspectives and theories because these seek to understand and explain gender. In a nutshell, *feminism* concerns the liberation of women and girls from discrimination based on gender. The goal of feminist theory and practice is women's self-determination. For some feminists this means securing equal rights for women within existing institutions—from marriage and the family to government policies and laws. For others it means fundamentally changing these institutions. Gender subordination is linked to discrimination based on other systems of power and inequality, such as race, class, sexuality, age, ability, and national origin; we emphasize these links through selected readings and in our introductions to each chapter. In addition, we note that feminism can also liberate men from limitations imposed by gender hierarchy and inequality.

For some, feminism is a positive and empowering term. For others it conjures up negative images of white women, "mannish" women, women who do not wear makeup or don't shave their legs or underarms, and women who are said to be lesbians or man-haters. Mainstream newspapers and magazines often trivialize and distort feminist goals and perspectives. According to Erica Jong (1998), *Time* magazine published no less than 119 articles from the early 1970s to the mid 1990s that criticized feminism. Its June 1998 cover story, "Is Feminism Dead?" argued that feminism had become "a whole lot of stylish fluff" (p. 56).

When women talk of gender-based violence—battering, incest, rape, sexual abuse, and harassment—or racism, or living in poverty, or aging without health insurance, detractors describe them as "victim" feminists, or perhaps worse, "feminazis"—antisex, no fun, whining critics who are out to destroy men and the male establishment. This is part of what Pulitzer Prize-winning writer Susan Faludi (1991) meant when she wrote of a backlash against feminism, also compounded by government policies, which have eroded some of the gains made for and by women. In our society, women are socialized to care for men and to spare their feelings, but recognizing and discussing institutional inequalities between women as a group (with all their diversity) and men as a group are very different from "man-bashing." This garbled, trivializing media framework contributes to the many myths and misunderstandings about feminism and women's studies. We consider three of these myths here.

Myth 1: Feminism Is Ideological

Some people assume that women's studies is not "real" scholarship but, instead, is feminist propaganda. Yet feminist inquiry, analysis, and activism have arisen from real problems experienced by real women, from well-researched inequalities and discrimination. For instance, data recorded for more than one hundred years show that, on average, U.S. women's wages for full-time year-round work have never risen above 77 percent of what men earn on average; that is, on average, women earn 77 cents for every dollar earned by men. And the situation is worse for women of color (70 cents for African American women and 58 cents for Latinas, compared to all working men). Women's studies arose out of feminist theorizing and activism and values scholarly work that is relevant to activist concerns. Women's studies courses and projects seek to link intellectual, experiential, and emotional forms of knowing with the goal of improving women's lives. Women's studies is a rigorous endeavor, but its conception of rigor differs from that of much traditional scholarship, which values abstract, in-depth knowledge, narrowly defined, as discussed in Chapter 2. By contrast, women's studies scholarship places a high value on breadth and connectedness. This kind of rigor requires broad understandings grounded in a range of experiences and the ability to make connections between knowledge and insights from different fields of study. Knowledge is never neutral, and in women's studies this is made explicit.

To some students and scholars, feminism is something to believe in because it provides perspectives that make sense of the world and is personally empowering. But students who blithely blame everything on "rich white men" or "the patriarchy" without taking the trouble to read and think critically are anti-intellectual; they limit their own understanding and inadvertently reinforce the notion that women's studies is anti-intellectual.

Myth 2: Feminism Is a White, Middle-Class Thing

Many notable scholars, writers, and activists of color identify as feminists, among them Julia Alvarez, Gloria Anzaldúa, Sandra Cisneros, Combahee River Collective, Patricia Hill Collins, bell hooks, Aurora Levins Morales, Audre Lorde, Chandra Talpade Mohanty, Mitsuye Yamada, and others included in this anthology. Their approach to feminism links analyses of gender with race, class, and other systems of power and inequality.*

Since the writings of Aphra Behn in the early 1600s, some U.S. white women have been concerned with race and class as well as gender. White feminists worked against slavery in the nineteenth century, organized against lynching and the activities of the Ku Klux Klan, and participated in the civil rights movements of the 1950s and 1960s. Accounts of the diversity of U.S. women's movements in the 1960s and 1970s also explode this myth (see Reading 7; also Baxandall and Gordon 2000; Moraga and Anzaldúa 1981; Roth 2003; Springer 2005). African American critic and writer bell hooks (2000) argues that "there should be billboards; ads in magazines; ads on buses, subways, trains; television commercials spreading the word, letting the world know more about feminism," because "feminism is for everybody" (p. x).

----

*Recognizing the social construction of racial categories, we want to reflect this in our language. We capitalize Black to affirm this usage by Black writers and scholars as a small antiracist move for respect in a racist society. We capitalize white only to refer to White supremacy; otherwise, we use lowercase white. Although Black/White are stylistic counterparts, they are not political equivalents. Also, we use the term *white* rather than European American. The former refers to power and position conferred by whiteness in a racially stratified society; the latter refers to ethnicity and suggests analogy between European American and African American that does not exist due to the effects of institutionalized racism.

Milestones in U.S. History: Institutionalizing and Challenging Social Inequalities

1565	Spanish settlers established the first European colony in St. Augustine in what is now the state of Florida.
1584	Walter Raleigh founded Virginia, an English colony, at Roanoke Island.
1605	A Spanish settlement was established at Santa Fe, in what is now New Mexico.
1607	Captain Christopher Newport of the London Company established an English colony at Jamestown, Virginia.
1619	A Dutch "man of war" sailed into Jamestown harbor with 20 Africans on board; the captain sold his human cargo to the colonists.
1691	The first legal ban on interracial marriages was passed in Virginia. Subsequently, other states prohibited whites from marrying Blacks; marriages between whites and Native Americans, Filipinos, Asians, and Indians were forbidden specifically.
1776	The Second Continental Congress adopted the *Declaration of Independence*, written mostly by Thomas Jefferson, and asserting: "all men are created equal."
1787	The Constitution of the United States was sent to the states for ratification. Slaves were to be counted as 3/5 of a person in determining population and allocating numbers of representatives to Congress for each state; Indians were not to be counted or taxed; limitation on the slave trade was prohibited until 1808.
1820	Missouri entered the Union as the twelfth slave state "balanced" by Maine as the twelfth free state. Slavery was banned in the Louisiana Territory (purchased from France in 1803 for approximately $15 million) north of latitude 36°30'.
1830	At the request of President Andrew Jackson, Congress passed a law moving all Indian tribes from the southeastern United States to land west of the Mississippi River and granting them rights to these new lands "in perpetuity."
1834	The Department of Indian Affairs was established within the War Department to monitor the creation of reservations for Indian tribes. The Department was later transferred to the Department of

Myth 3: Feminism Is Narrowly Concerned with Women's Issues

Women's studies seeks to understand and explain women's diverse experiences and the significance of gender in the ordering of society, but we do not see this as catering to narrow "special interests." On the contrary, feminist analyses provide a series of lenses to examine many topics and academic disciplines, including anthropology, cultural studies, economics, environmental studies, ethnic studies, film and media studies, history, human biology, law, literature, national income accounting, philosophies of science, physics, political science, psychology, and sociology. Feminist scholarship is on the cutting edge of many of these fields and raises crucial questions about teaching and learning, research design and methodologies, and theories of knowledge. Far from narrow, women's studies is concerned with thinking critically about the world in all its complexity.

It is important to acknowledge that women's studies students include a growing number of men. We are mindful that our readership includes male students, and in places we pose questions and offer specific suggestions to them. There are many ways that men can contribute to and support wider opportunities for women—as sons, brothers, fathers, partners, friends, coworkers, supervisors, labor organizers, spiritual leaders, teachers, doctors, lawyers, police officers, judges, and legislators. Sociologist Michael Kimmel the Interior as the Bureau of Indian Affairs.

1848   The Treaty of Guadalupe Hidalgo ended the Mexican-American War (begun in 1846). It established the Rio Grande as the international boundary; ceded Texas to the United States together with Arizona, California, Nevada, and New Mexico; and guaranteed existing residents their land, language, culture, and U.S. citizenship.

The first Women's Rights Convention was held in Seneca Falls, New York. Delegates issued a *Declaration of Sentiments*, listing inequities faced by women and urging that women be given the right to vote (see Readings 2, 3, and 4).

1857   In *Dred Scott v. Sandford*, the Supreme Court argued, that, as an enslaved man, Dred Scott was not a citizen, and, therefore, had no standing to sue his master for his freedom although he had been living in free territory for four years. To grant Scott's petition, the Court argued, would deprive his owner of property without compensation, violating the fifth amendment. This invalidated states' rights to determine whether slavery should be banned.

1863   Abraham Lincoln issued the Emancipation Proclamation freeing slaves in Alabama, Arkansas, Florida, Georgia, Louisiana, Mississippi, North Carolina, South Carolina, Tennessee, Texas, and Virginia.

1864   U.S. military forces terrorized Indian nations. Navajo people endured the "long walk" to imprisonment at Fort Sumner (New Mexico Territory). U.S. troops massacred Cheyenne warriors (supported by Kiowa, Apache, Comanche, and Arapahoe warriors) at Sand Creek (see Readings 12 and 33).

1865   Following the assassination of Abraham Lincoln, the Civil War was ended. Congress established the Freedmen's Bureau, responsible for relief to former slaves and those made destitute by the war. The thirteenth amendment to the Constitution officially ended slavery and involuntary servitude.

calls for pro-feminist men to be cheerleaders, allies, and foot soldiers; "and we must be so in front of other men, risking our own fears of rejection, our own membership in the club of masculinity, confronting our own fears of other men" (in Kimmel and Messner 1998, p. 68). There is a long history of men's support for women's equality in the United States (see Reading 3; Digby 1998; Kimmel and Mosmiller 1992; Movement for a New Society 1983; Tarrant 2007), and training in women's studies can provide a powerful basis for this. In Chapter 6, readings by John Stoltenberg and Mimi Kim give examples of men refusing to be bystanders to acts of violence against women.

Women cannot achieve the changes we discuss in this book without male allies. And, we also assume that masculinity is socially constructed and highly constrained in our society and that there is something for men in this whole project, beyond being allies to women (see, e.g., Johnson 2005; Tarrant 2007). We believe that those in dominant positions on any social dimension (gender, race, class, age, ability, and so forth) are also limited by these structures of power and inequality. Despite its obvious benefits, privilege separates people and makes us ignorant of important truths. To be able to look others in the eye openly and completely, to join together to create a secure and sustainable future for everyone, we have to work to end systems of inequality. This repudiation of privilege, we believe, is not a sacrifice but rather the possibility of entering into genuine community where we can all be more truly human.

Feminist Legacies and Perspectives

Women's studies draws on rich and complex legacies of theorizing and activism, which we outline briefly below. Among several possible paths into these histories, we chose Paula Gunn Allen's article

1869	The first transcontinental railroad was completed. Chinese workers, allowed into the country to work on the railroad, experienced increased discrimination and "anti-Oriental" hysteria.
1870	Congress ratified the fifteenth amendment, which enfranchised Black men but permitted states to deny the vote to all women.
	Julia Ward Howe issued a *Mother's Day Proclamation* for peace (Reading 65).
1877	Ordered off their land in Oregon, the Nez Percé tribe attempted to flee to Canada, a trek of 1,600 miles, to avoid war with U.S. troops. They were forced to surrender 40 miles short of the border and sent to Oklahoma, where many died.
1887	Congress passed the Dawes Severalty Act, providing for the dissolution of Indian tribes and division of tribal holdings among the members. Over the next 50 years, white settlers took nearly two-thirds of Indian land holdings by deceit and intimidation (Reading 12).
1896	In *Plessy v. Ferguson*, the Supreme Court validated a Louisiana law requiring Blacks and whites to ride in separate railroad cars. The law had been challenged as a violation of the fourteenth amendment's right of equal protection, but the majority opinion held that "separate but equal" satisfied the constitutional requirement. This decision led to a spate of segregation laws in southern states. From 1870–1900, twenty-two Black men served in Congress. With the introduction of literacy tests, poll taxes, grandfather clauses, and white primaries, none were left by 1901.
1898	The U.S. declared war on Spain and acquired former Spanish colonial territories: the Philippines, Guam, Puerto Rico, and Cuba, including a military base at Guantanamo Bay, Cuba. Congress also approved U.S. annexation of the Hawaiian Islands.
1919	Suffragists were arrested in Washington, D.C. for blocking sidewalks during a

about the "red roots of white feminism," which she grounded in the centuries-old practice that gave Native American women policy-making power in the Iroquois Confederation, especially the power to decide matters of peace and war (Reading 1). She notes that the old council house where the Iroquois women met was very close to Seneca Falls, New York, site of the 1848 founding convention chosen by white suffragists.

Many histories divide decades of activism for women's rights into three periods signified by the labels first-wave, second-wave, and third-wave. Defining historical periods is a selective process, focusing attention on certain events or perspectives and masking others. We use this shorthand formulation here, despite its limitations, because these labels often occur in feminist writings. The wave metaphor suggests both continuity and discontinuity with the past as women shaped theoretical understandings for their generation, circumstances, and time

in history. Note, however, that these terms make complex, powerful, transformative movements with their divergent and overlapping strands seem much neater, more unitary, and more static than the reality. Karen Brodkin Sacks (1976) argued that the nineteenth-century U.S. women's movement was, in fact, three movements: a movement of women workers in the New England textile mills, a Black women's movement against racism and for economic improvement, and a white middle-class movement for legal equality. It is this third movement that many feminist activists and scholars have in mind when they speak of "the first wave."

The "First Wave": 1830s to 1920s

In 1840, two middle-class white women from the United States, Lucretia Mott and Elizabeth Cady Stanton, met at the World Anti-Slavery Convention in London. Both passionately opposed to slavery,

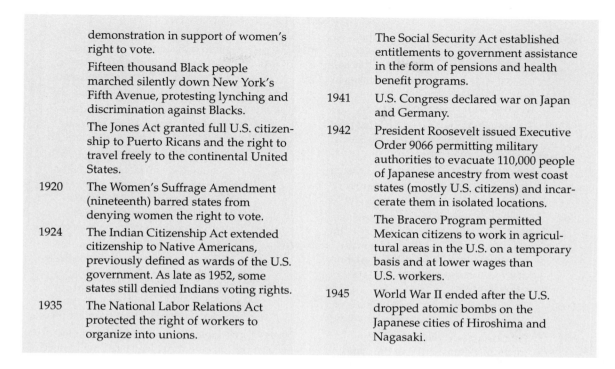

demonstration in support of women's right to vote.

Fifteen thousand Black people marched silently down New York's Fifth Avenue, protesting lynching and discrimination against Blacks.

The Jones Act granted full U.S. citizenship to Puerto Ricans and the right to travel freely to the continental United States.

1920　The Women's Suffrage Amendment (nineteenth) barred states from denying women the right to vote.

1924　The Indian Citizenship Act extended citizenship to Native Americans, previously defined as wards of the U.S. government. As late as 1952, some states still denied Indians voting rights.

1935　The National Labor Relations Act protected the right of workers to organize into unions.

The Social Security Act established entitlements to government assistance in the form of pensions and health benefit programs.

1941　U.S. Congress declared war on Japan and Germany.

1942　President Roosevelt issued Executive Order 9066 permitting military authorities to evacuate 110,000 people of Japanese ancestry from west coast states (mostly U.S. citizens) and incarcerate them in isolated locations.

The Bracero Program permitted Mexican citizens to work in agricultural areas in the U.S. on a temporary basis and at lower wages than U.S. workers.

1945　World War II ended after the U.S. dropped atomic bombs on the Japanese cities of Hiroshima and Nagasaki.

they were shocked to find that women delegates were excluded from the convention on the basis of gender (Schneir 1994). The irony of working against the system that enslaved people of African descent while experiencing discrimination as women gave them the impetus to work for women's rights. Eight years later they called a Women's Rights Convention at Seneca Falls, New York, where Stanton lived. The chapel where this historic gathering occurred is now part of the Women's Rights National Historical Park. Mott and Stanton led a small group in drafting the Seneca Falls *Declaration of Sentiments and Resolutions* (Reading 2), modeled on the *Declaration of Independence*. This document, which was read out and adopted at the convention, rallied women and men to the cause of women's equality. Frederick Douglass, a formerly enslaved man, attended the Convention and supported women's suffrage in *The North Star,* an abolitionist newspaper he edited (Reading 3). The issue was fiercely debated in newspaper editorials and public meetings. At an 1851 convention in Akron, Ohio, several Christian ministers opposed women's rights, arguing that Christ

was male, that women were not as intelligent as men, that they were weak, tainted with Eve's sin, and so forth (Schneir 1994, p. 94). Sojourner Truth, a formerly enslaved woman who had become a frequent speaker in anti-slavery circles, rebutted these arguments by referring to both her experience of hard physical labor and the fact that she had borne thirteen children, asking "And ain't I a woman?" (Reading 4).

Three amendments to the U.S. constitution allowing all men the right to vote were passed following the Civil War. The thirteenth amendment (1865) formally ended slavery and involuntary servitude. The fourteenth amendment (1868) defined citizens as those born or naturalized in the United States, with equal protection of law. The fifteenth amendment (1870) prohibited states from denying the right to vote to any citizen because of race, color, or previous condition of servitude. It enfranchised Black men, but still permitted states to deny the vote to women of all races. In 1869, controversy over passage of the fifteenth amendment, which awarded suffrage to Black men but not to women, caused a split in the women's

1954	In *Brown v. Board of Education,* the Supreme Court reversed its *Plessy v. Ferguson* decision and declared that segregated schools were inherently unequal. In 1955 it ordered the desegregation of schools "with all deliberate speed."	1973	The Rehabilitation Act (Section 504) prohibited discrimination against people with disabilities in programs that receive federal financial assistance.
1963	The Equal Pay Act mandated that men and women doing the same work must receive the same pay.	1975	The Individuals with Disabilities Education Act guaranteed children with disabilities a free, appropriate public education in the least restrictive environment.
	250,000 people participated in a March on Washington to gain public support for a comprehensive civil rights law.	1982	The Equal Rights Amendment failed. It was ratified by 35 states, rather than the required minimum of 38 states. Subsequent efforts to revive this campaign have not been successful.
1964	Congress passed the most comprehensive Civil Rights Act in the history of the nation. Under Title VII, employment discrimination was prohibited on the basis of race, color, religion, sex, or national origin.	1990	The Americans with Disabilities Act prohibited discrimination on the basis of disability by employers, public accommodations, state and local governments, public and private transportation, and in telecommunications.
1965	The Voting Rights Act ended the use of literacy tests as a prerequisite for voting.		
1972	Congress passed the Equal Rights Amendment and sent it to the states for ratification. It had been introduced in every session since 1923.	1994	The Violent Crime Control and Law Enforcement Act legislated mandatory life imprisonment for persons convicted in federal court of a "serious violent

movement. Lucy Stone and Julia Ward Howe were among those who founded the American Woman Suffrage Association, which worked for passage of the fifteenth amendment. Elizabeth Cady Stanton and Susan B. Anthony instead formed the National Woman Suffrage Association and redoubled their efforts for a constitutional amendment granting votes for women. The American Woman Suffrage Association adopted a state-by-state strategy, and Wyoming was the first territory to give women the right to vote in 1869. In 1920, the Women's Suffrage Amendment (nineteenth amendment) barred states from denying women the right to vote. This was seventy-two years after the Seneca Falls Convention, and ended a long campaign that included intense lobbying demonstrations, civil disobedience actions, arrests, and hunger strikes.

This campaign for women's rights grew out of **liberalism,** a theory about individual rights, freedom, choice, and privacy with roots in seventeenth-century European political ideas (e.g., the writings

of political philosopher John Locke). Liberalism has been a major part of U.S. political discourse since the founding of the nation, although political and legal rights were originally limited to white men who owned land and property. It has been a long, uneven process—marked by hard work, gains, and setbacks—to achieve greater equality among people in this country (see Milestones in U.S. History Box starting on p. 6). Far from complete, this process continues to this day.

Liberal feminism explains the oppression of women in terms of unequal access to existing political, economic, and social institutions (e.g., Eisenstein 1981; Friedan 1963; Steinem 1983). Liberal feminists are concerned with equal rights for women and men and that women have equal access to opportunities within existing economic and social structures. From the time of the Seneca Falls Convention, much feminist organizing in the United States has been based on this perspective. Many people hold liberal feminist opinions though they may not felony" and who had two or more prior convictions in federal or state courts, at least one of which was a "serious violent felony" (the "three strikes" law). The other prior offense may be a "serious drug offense." States adopted similar laws.

1996   The Personal Responsibility and Work Opportunity Reconciliation Act replaced families' entitlement to government assistance with Temporary Assistance for Needy Families, a time-limited work-based program.

The Defense of Marriage Act forbade the federal government from recognizing same-sex or polygamous marriages under any circumstances and stipulated that no state, city, or county is required to recognize a marriage between persons of the same sex even if the marriage is recognized in another state.

2001   Uniting and Strengthening America by Providing Appropriate Tools Required to Intercept and Obstruct Terrorism

Act (USA Patriot Act) greatly increased law enforcement agencies' powers of detention, search, and surveillance. It permitted

- detention of non-citizens if the attorney general has "reasonable grounds to believe" that they endanger national security;

- definition of domestic groups as terrorist organizations;

- interception of "wire, oral, and electronic communications relating to terrorism";

- easier FBI access to records about a person that are maintained by a business;

- expanded use of secret searches;

- financial institutions to monitor daily transactions and academic institutions to share information about students.

Primary source: Aileen Hernandez (1975, 2002).

Also see *A Timeline of Key U.S. Immigration Law and Policy* (Chapter 3).

realize it. Despite the disclaimer, "I'm not a feminist. . ." the comment "but I *do* believe in equal pay" is a liberal feminist position. Liberal feminism can be criticized because it accepts existing institutions as they are, only seeking access for women within them. This objective should not be underestimated, however, given the strength of patriarchy and White-supremacy as systems of power.

After U.S. women won the vote, Alice Paul of the National Women's Party drafted an amendment to the U.S. constitution that was introduced to the Senate in 1923. It stated: "men and women shall have equal rights throughout the United States" and became known as the Equal Rights Amendment. It would take another 50 years and a renewed upsurge of feminist activity before this amendment was approved by two-thirds of the Congress and sent to the states for ratification in 1972.

Meanwhile, national attention shifted, first to the dire effects of the Great Depression of the late

1920s and the early 1930s when the economy collapsed and many thousands were suddenly destitute. The government saw the need to intervene in the labor market to shield people from the worst effects of the booms and slumps inherent in a market economy. It initiated "New Deal" programs to provide economic relief for workers who had lost their livelihoods, and established Social Security and Medicare programs under the Social Security Act of 1935. Then in 1941, the U.S. entered World War II against Germany and Japan. Like all U.S. institutions at the time, the military was segregated along racial lines. Based on their contradictory experiences of fighting on behalf of people in Europe and Asia while being treated as second-class citizens within the military and in civilian life back home, men of color in the military agitated against this inequality.

After World War II, the first major social movement in the United States was for the civil rights of people of color, especially African Americans. Among many young women involved in the civil rights movement, Barbara Omolade (1994) took Ella Baker, executive secretary of the Southern Christian Leadership Conference, as her mentor and role model. She honored Baker's courage, strength, vision, organizing skills, and support for young people in the movement. Omolade noted that **Black nationalism** provided a powerful liberatory vision for many young African American activists. Women worked alongside men but gradually became disillusioned with sexism in the civil rights movement and Black power organizations. For women of color and white women, this struggle for racial equality was "midwife to a feminist movement" (Evans 1980, p. 24), as had happened in the nineteenth-century anti-slavery and women's rights movements.

The "Second Wave": 1960s to 1980s

The feminist organizing that flourished in the 1960s and '70s was a powerful force for change as well as a transforming experience for those involved (see, e.g., Brenner 1996; F. Davis 1991; DuPlessis and Snitow 1998; Rosen 2000). Women identified sexism in every area of life, including personal relationships, traditional gender roles, children's play, language, and symbolic events like the Miss America pageant. They used their own life experiences to theorize about patriarchy and to envision women's liberation. Some drew on liberal feminist ideas as the suffragists had done and challenged women's exclusion from higher education, the media, and well-paying jobs in blue-collar trades and professions like law and medicine. They also sought to increase pay and improve conditions for jobs based on women's traditional roles. They campaigned to elect more women to political office at city, state, and federal levels in the belief that this would change law and policy to benefit women. This included a ten-year nationwide campaign to ratify the Equal Rights Amendment, which required approval of a minimum of 38 states. When the June 30, 1982, deadline expired only 35 states had ratified the ERA, and it has not been adopted.

Other women developed a **radical feminism** that focused on men's control of women's sexuality and reproduction. This manifests itself in gender roles, family relationships, heterosexuality, and male violence against women, as well as the wider male-dominated world of work, education, government, religion, and law (e.g., Bell and Klein 1996; Daly 1976; Echols 1989; Harne and Miller 1996; Koedt, Levine, and Rapone 1973; Rhodes 2005). For radical feminists, women's liberation requires the eradication of patriarchy and the creation of women-centered ways of living. White lesbians were particularly influential in developing this strand of feminist thought and creating alternative women's institutions, including women's health centers, publishing projects, bookstores, coffee houses, writing circles, poetry readings, recording studios, music festivals, and women-owned land projects. Some of these flourished for a while; others are still active today.

In emphasizing their subordination as women, many white middle-class feminists glossed over their privilege on other dimensions, notably race, class, and sexuality. Feminists of color, working-class women, women with disabilities, lesbians and bisexual women, and feminists from outside the United States all criticized this assumption of "sisterhood" that ignored differences among women. The Combahee River Collective, a group of Black feminists active in the Boston area in the 1970s, provided an integrated analysis of interlocking systems of oppression based on race, class, gender, sexuality, and so forth (Reading 5). They noted that "Black, other Third World, and working women have been involved in the feminist movement" but had been obscured by racism and elitism within it and by the media, which focused on white feminist leaders like Betty Friedan and Gloria Steinhem. They argued that Black women have inherent value: "our liberation is a necessity not as an adjunct to somebody else's but because of our need as human persons for autonomy." The *Black Feminist Statement* reprinted here came out of a three-year process, from 1974 to 1977, of sharing ideas, working in various movements and organizations, reflecting on this activism, and generating a shared analysis over time. Group members identified themselves as **socialists** who believed that "work must be organized for the collective benefit of those who do the work and create the products, and not for the profit of the bosses."

Socialist feminism sees the oppression of women in terms of two interconnected and reinforcing systems, patriarchy and capitalism, and are particularly concerned with the economic aspects of women's lives (e.g., Eisenstein 1979; Hartmann 1981;

Hennessy and Ingraham 1997; Radical Women 2001; Roberts and Mizuta 1993; Smith 2005). Socialist feminists link capitalist exploitation of labor, expounded by German philosophers Frederick Engels and Karl Marx during the 1840s (contemporary with the Seneca Falls *Declaration of Sentiments and Resolutions*), to inequality based on gender. Zillah Eisenstein (1998) noted that "the language of socialism" seems foreign these days in the United States due to the break up of the former Soviet Union and the discrediting of the political philosophy of socialism along with it. She argued that an anti-capitalist, feminist politics is still of great relevance given the increasing integration of the world economic system, a point we take up in later chapters. Starting with an emphasis on race and gender, the Combahee River Collective went on to critique **capitalism** and **imperialism,** reflecting their solidarity with national liberation struggles then being waged in formerly colonized nations of Africa, Asia, and Central America. As feminists and lesbians they found white radical feminism too focused on male domination at the expense of oppressions based on race and class. Collective members also found lesbian **separatism,** advocated by some white lesbians, too limiting theoretically and in practice.

Also drawing on activist experiences during the 1970s, writer and educator Mitsuye Yamada traces Asian Pacific American women's histories, critiques commonplace stereotypes of Asian American women, and expresses her frustrations (echoed by many women of color) at white women's lack of understanding of the scope, depth, and ongoing nature of racism in the United States (Reading 6). Readings 5 and 6 show how feminists of color "provided a crucial challenge to the limits and exclusions of white feminist theory" (Stacey 1993, p. 61).

By the 1990s, the most visible signs of the 1970s women's movements were national organizations like the Fund for a Feminist Majority, the National Abortion Rights Action League (NARAL, now NARAL Pro-Choice America), the National Organization of Women (NOW), and the National Women's Political Caucus. They were associated with white, middle-class women who had been able to attract the resources and media coverage that helped to maintain these organizations over the years. Some women of color have tended to write off second-wave feminism as a white middle-class

movement that is irrelevant to them. Sociologist Becky Thompson constructs a very different history that describes a multiracial feminism, in contrast to what Chela Sandoval has called "hegemonic feminism" that focuses on sexism at the expense of race, class, and sexuality (Reading 7). The readings show the importance of documenting and recording women's perspectives and projects to create nuanced and accurate histories.

Theoretical perspectives that integrate gender with other systems of inequality, like that of the Combahee River Collective, have become known by the shorthand term, **intersectionality.** For African American women, especially, this idea has a long history, though the term is much more recent. Public speakers and writers in the nineteenth century, such as Frances E. W. Harper, Maria Stewart, and Sojourner Truth, explicitly linked oppression based on race and gender from the 1830s onward (Guy-Sheftall 1995). Writing in 1892, Anna Julia Cooper commented: "The colored woman of today occupies . . . a unique position in this country. . . . She is confronted by both a woman question and a race problem, and is as yet an unknown or unacknowledged factor in both" (quoted in Guy-Sheftall 1995, p. 45). Organizer and writer Linda Burnham noted that

> numerous Black feminist theorists have advanced the view that Black women's experience as women is indivisible from their experiences as African Americans. They are always "both/and," so analyses that claim to examine gender while neglecting a critical stance towards race and class inevitably do so at the expense of African American women's experiences.   *(Burnham 2001, p. 1)*

Burnham (2001, p. 1) acknowledged "the invaluable work of university-based theorists" but argued that too many people "assume that the core concepts of Black feminism were born in the academy." She traced the development of Black feminist thinking in the late 1960s and early 1970s from "the emergence of gender consciousness among Black women activists in the Student Non-Violence Coordinating Committee (SNCC)" through to organizations such as the Third World Women's Alliance and the Combahee River Collective. Her purpose is to show "the struggle for social transformation as a powerful generator of theoretical insight" (Burnham 2001, p. 4).

An integrative perspective that emphasizes intersectionality is not only the prerogative of women of color, though fewer white women have developed this kind of analysis. Becky Thompson notes significant shifts in understanding among some white feminists who, often learning from women of color, drew on anti-racist and anti-imperial perspectives, and who became allies to women of color (Reading 7; also Bush 2004; Frankenberg 1993; Pratt 1984; Rich 1986c; Segrest 1994; Spelman 1988).

Increasingly in the 1980s and 1990s, academic feminists were drawn to **feminist postmodernism,** which emphasizes the particularity of women's experiences in specific cultural and historical contexts and seeks to account for differences among women based on age, race, culture, national origin, ability, and other attributes (see, e.g., Alcoff 1988; Nicholson 1990; Scott 1988). Feminist philosopher Jane Flax (1986, p. 193) noted that some feminists and postmodern theorists shared "a profound skepticism regarding universal . . . claims about the existence, nature and powers of reason, progress, science, language and the 'subject/self.'" Sociologist Jackie Stacey noted that this "focus on difference between women has been an important redress in a movement that built its momentum on a falsely universalistic understanding of women's oppression" (1993, p. 63).

Indeed, some feminists asked whether it is meaningful to talk of women as a group, when there are so many differences among women (Weedon 1987). They emphasized the fluidity of all social categories depending on historical time, place, and cultural context. Thus, "woman" as a category "is regarded as a constantly shifting signifier of multiple meanings" (Stacey 1993, p. 64). An analysis of subjectivity is central to feminist postmodernism, meaning "the ways we understand ourselves as subjects positioned by discourses or ideologies" (Stacey 1993, p. 64) and constrained by power structures and institutions. Deconstructing the category "woman," Stacey (1993, p. 68) argued, means pulling "apart the ways in which the different meanings of femininity have been cemented together" to expose how femininity has been constructed by patriarchal cultures. An emphasis on difference also raises the question as to whether women can engage in collective action, something that first- and second-wave feminists took for granted. Note that the Combahee River Collective were both concerned with particularities of their experiences and with collective action to resist oppression and to improve women's lives.

The "Third Wave": 1990s to ?

Mainstream media depictions and facile stereotypes of feminists have deterred many younger women from embracing this term, even though they often support feminist ideas. Some challenge or reject what they know of the feminism associated with their mothers' generation as no longer relevant. A growing literature identified as **third-wave feminism** emphasizes multiple identities, ambiguities, and contradictions (see, e.g., Baumgardner and Richards 2000; Dicker and Piepmeier 2003; Findlen 1995; Heywood and Drake 1997; Walker 1995b; Zita 1997). Jee Yeun Lee (1995, p. 211) called for "recognition of the constructed racial nature of *all* experiences of gender"; that "heterosexual norms do not oppress solely lesbians, bisexuals, and gay men but affect all of our choices and non-choices"; that "issues posed by differently-abled women question our basic assumptions about body image, health care, sexuality, and work"; and so forth. Vivien Labaton and Dawn Lundy Martin, who are among the founders of the Third Wave Foundation, also emphasized the centrality of an integrated, intersectional perspective for many young feminists. They remarked:

> One of the luxuries that our generation has enjoyed is that we've reaped the benefits of all the social justice movements that have come before us; we have come of age in a world that has been shaped by feminism, queer liberation movements, antiracist movements, labor movements, and others. Consequently, many young women and men not only have an understanding of the interconnection of social justice issues but also see them as inextricable from one another.   *(2004, pp. xxv–xxvi)*

They noted that "woman" as a primary identity category has ceased to be the entry point for many young women's activist work. Instead, it has become one of the many investigatory means used to affect a broad range of issues and cultural analyses, including critiques of hip-hop, creation of independent media, and campaigns opposing oppressive immigration policies, police brutality, sweatshops, militarism, incarceration, and globalization (Labaton and Lundy Martin 2004).

Theories are refined and adapted as understanding grows and as experiences and events shed new light on issues or problems. Theory is, thus, continually evolving, and we continue this discussion in the following chapter and throughout this book. Now we turn to our approach to women's studies and the framework for this book.

The Framework for This Book: Collective Action for a Sustainable Future

This book is concerned with women in the United States and the rich diversity of our life experiences. As writers and editors, a big challenge for us has been to choose effective writings and salient facts from the vast wealth of material available. There has been a groundswell of women's writing and publishing in the past forty years, as well as a proliferation of popular and scholarly books and journals on issues of interest to women's studies students. When opinion polls, academic studies, government data, public debates, and grassroots research, available in print and through electronic media, are added, it is easy to be swamped with information and opposing viewpoints. In making our selections, we have filtered this wealth of material according to a number of principles—our particular road map.

A Matrix of Oppression and Resistance

Underlying our analysis is the concept of oppression, which we see as a group phenomenon, regardless of whether individuals in a group think they are oppressed or want to be in dominant positions. Men, as a group, are advantaged by sexism, for example, whereas women, as a group, are disadvantaged. Every form of oppression—for instance, **sexism, racism, classism, heterosexism, anti-Arabism, anti-Semitism, able-bodyism**—is rooted in social institutions, such as the family, education, religion, government, law, and the media. Oppression, then, is systemic, and it is systematic. It is used consistently by one group of people—those who are dominant in this society—to rule, control, and exploit (to varying degrees) another group—those who are subordinate—for the benefit of the dominant group.

Oppression works through systems of power and inequality, as well as the dominance of certain values, beliefs, and assumptions about people and how society should be organized. Members of dominant groups generally have built-in economic, political, and cultural power and benefits regardless of whether they are aware of, or even want, these advantages. This process of accruing benefits is often referred to as privilege. Those most privileged are often least likely to be aware of it or to recognize it (McIntosh 1988).

Oppression involves **prejudice,** which we define as unreasonable, unfair, and hostile attitudes toward people, and **discrimination,** differential treatment favoring those who are in positions of dominance. But oppression reaches beyond individual bigotry or good intentions; it is promoted by every social institution we encounter and are part of and cannot be fully changed without fundamental changes in institutional practices and **ideologies,** the ideas, attitudes, and values that institutions embody and perpetuate. Our definition of oppression assumes that everyone is socialized to participate in oppressive practices, thereby helping to maintain them. People may be involved as direct perpetrators or passive beneficiaries, or they may direct **internalized oppression** at members of their own group. Oppression results in appropriation and the loss—both voluntary and involuntary—of voice, identity, and agency of oppressed peoples.

It is important to think about oppression as an intricate system, at times blatantly obvious and at others subtly nuanced, rather than an either/or dichotomy of privileged/disadvantaged or oppressor/oppressed. Allan Johnson discusses this in relation to the system of patriarchy in Reading 9. We use the term **matrix of oppression and resistance** to describe the interrelatedness of various forms of oppression. People can be privileged in some respects (race or gender, for example) and disadvantaged in others (class or sexual orientation, for example). Negative ascriptions may provide powerful sources of resistance based on shared identities.

Linking the Personal and the Global

Throughout this book we use the terms **micro level** (personal or individual), **meso level** (community, neighborhood, or school, for example), **macro level** (national or institutional), and **global level.** To understand people's experiences or the complexity of a particular issue, it is necessary to look at all these levels and how they interconnect. For instance, a personal relationship might be thought to operate on a micro level. However, both partners bring all of themselves to the relationship. Thus, in addition to personal factors such as looks, generosity, or determination not to repeat the mistakes of one's parents' relationships, there are meso-level factors—such as our connections to people of other faiths or races—and macro-level factors—such as the obvious or hidden ways in which men or white people are privileged in this society. As editors we have made connections between these levels of analysis in our overview essays and looked for writings that also make these links.

We recognize the racial and ethnic diversity of this country; many people in the United States were not born here and come with hopes for a better future, but they also may have no illusions about inequalities here. We argue that people in the United States need to understand the significance of this country's pre-eminence in the world. This manifests culturally through the dominance of the English language and in widespread distribution of U.S. movies, news media, TV shows, music, books, and magazines. It manifests economically though the power of the dollar as an international currency and the impact of U.S.-based corporations abroad. It manifests militarily through the global reach of U.S. foreign policy, troops, and bases. People in the United States need to understand the significance of the globalization of the economy and connections between U.S. domestic policies like health care, child care, or welfare, and foreign policy issues such as military expenditures and foreign aid. Although this is not a book about global feminism, we examine the global context within which the United States exercises power culturally, economically, politically, and militarily. We consider the consequences of U.S. policies on people in other nations: the flow of people, jobs, capital, and popular culture across national borders and the factors that facilitate, require, or prohibit such movements. We explore what it means in terms of identity, culture, family, and community to live in a globalizing world.

A Sustainable and Secure Future

We see sustainability and security as central issues for the twenty-first century, which raises questions about the direction of future economic development and the distribution of wealth, both within the United States and among richer and poorer countries. Another major concern is the rapid deterioration of the physical environment on our overburdened planet. In many chapters security is an underlying theme. This includes the individual security of knowing who we are; having sturdy family relationships; living in freedom from threats, violence, or coercion; having adequate income or livelihood; and enjoying health and well-being. It also involves security for communities, nations, and the planet, and includes issues like crime, militarism, and environmental destruction. We see structural inequalities based on race, class, gender, and nation as a major threat to long-term security because they create literal and metaphorical walls, gates, and fences that separate people and maintain hierarchies among us. We argue that creating a more sustainable future means rethinking materialism and consumerism and finding new ways to distribute wealth so that everyone has the basics of life. These issues affect not only women, of course, and are not solely women's responsibility, but women are actively involved in community organizing and movements for economic and environmental justice in the United States and many other countries, often in greater numbers than men.

An Activist Approach

Women and men worldwide face a range of serious problems in the years ahead if we are to sustain our lives, the lives of our children, our children's children, and the environment that supports all life forms. Although some women in the U.S. have benefited from greater opportunities for education and wage earning, many are now working harder or working longer hours than their mothers did under pressure to keep a job and to juggle waged work with family responsibilities. Over the past thirty years, various economic changes and government policies have made many women's lives more difficult. Examples include a loss of factory and office work as jobs have been moved overseas or become automated; government failure to introduce an adequate system of child care or a health care system that benefits everyone; cuts in welfare programs; greater restrictions of government support to immigrants and their families; and a dramatic increase in the number of women incarcerated compared with the number from thirty years ago. While the U.S. military budget consumed a massive 54 percent of federal income taxes (for fiscal year 2009), according to the War Resisters League (2008), and some states spend more public money on incarceration than on higher education, thousands of people are homeless, inner-city schools lack basic resources, and funding for a range of services from preschool programs to the Veteran's Administration has been cut back. Individual women and men are personally affected by such changes and policies as they negotiate personal relationships, raise children, and make a living for themselves and their families.

We see collective action for progressive social change as a major goal of scholarly work, and thus, in the face of these economic and political trends, we take a deliberately activist approach in this book. We mention many projects and organizations to give students a sense of how much activist work is going on that is often not visible in the mainstream media. We suggest that students find out more about these projects and organizations on the Web and also take action themselves. Throughout our discussion we emphasize the diversity of women's experiences. These differences have often divided women. We assume no easy "sisterhood" across lines of race, class, nation, age, or sexual orientation, for example, but we do believe that alliances built on the recognition and understanding of such differences can make effective collective action possible.

The Scope of This Book

This book is concerned with theorizing about the oppressive conditions facing women today and the long-term work of transforming those conditions. In Part 1 (Chapters 1–3), we discuss the development of women's studies in the United States, theorizing about women's lives and the significance of gender and the role of identity and social location as standpoints for generating knowledge and understanding. Part 2 (Chapters 4–6) explores women's experiences of our bodies, sexuality, health, and gender violence. In Part 3 (Chapters 7–8), we look at what is involved in making a home and making a living, and how global factors affect particular groups. In Part 4 (Chapters 9–11), we discuss U.S. women's experiences of crime and criminalization, the military, and the environment. We end, in Part 5 (Chapter 12), by examining the importance of theories, visions, and action for creating change.

In each chapter, we present data and theoretical perspectives, drawing from personal narratives, government reports, journalists' accounts, and nonprofit research and advocacy organizations. Our goal is to provide some historical and contemporary context for the readings, selected to exemplify key points. Our overall argument is that improving the lives of women in the United States also means directing ourselves, our communities, this society, and the wider world toward a more sustainable future.

◆◆◆

Questions for Reflection

As you read and discuss the readings in this chapter, think about these questions:

1. What is your ancestry—biologically, culturally, and intellectually? How would you answer Paula Gunn Allen's question: Who is your mother?

2. How can you learn more about the history of women's lives and women's movements? Who will be your teachers? Your sources?

3. What has changed for U.S. women since the Seneca Falls Convention of 1848? What has not changed?

4. What was new to you in this chapter? How does knowledge of history affect your understanding of contemporary issues?

5. How can learning about women's lives contribute to the creation of a secure and sustainable future for everyone?

Finding Out More on the Web

1. In Reading 5, the writers mention Dr. Kenneth Edelin, Joan Little, and Inéz Garcia. Who were these people? Why were they significant?

2. In Reading 7, Becky Thompson mentions Hijas de Cuauhtemoc, Women of All Red Nations, and the National Black Feminist Organization. Find out more about their perspectives, strategies, and activities.

3. How many Black men held seats in the U.S. Congress in 2000 compared to 1900?

Taking Action

1. Learn more about the history of women's participation in your college or university— for example, as students, faculty, administrators, trustees, staff, and professors' wives.

2. Interview professors or staff of your campus women's center to learn about the beginnings of women's studies at your college or university.

3. Talk with older people in your family or community about their involvement in women's movements (or movements for workers' rights, civil rights of people of color, LGBT rights, immigrant rights, etc.).

4. Join a women's organization or support a campaign on an issue you care about.

O N E

Who Is Your Mother? Red Roots of White Feminism (1986)

Paula Gunn Allen

Paula Gunn Allen (1939—2008) was a poet, novelist, essayist, and literary critic of Laguna, Sioux, Lebanese, and Scottish ancestry who grew up on the Laguna Pueblo (New Mexico). She taught literature, creative writing, and Native American Studies. Among many awards, she received a Pulitzer Prize nomination for *Pocahontas: Medicine Woman, Spy, Entrepreneur, Diplomat* (2004), a Lifetime Achievement Award from the Native Writer's Circle of the Americas (2001), and the American Book Award from the Before Columbus Foundation for *Spider Woman's Granddaughters: Traditional Tales and Contemporary* Writing (1990).

At Laguna Pueblo in New Mexico, "Who is your mother?" is an important question. At Laguna, one of several of the ancient Keres gynocratic societies of the region, your mother's identity is the key to your own identity. Among the Keres, every individual has a place within the universe—human and nonhuman—and that place is defined by clan membership. In turn, clan membership is dependent on matrilineal descent. Of course, your mother is not only that woman whose womb formed and released you—the term refers in every individual case to an entire generation of women whose psychic, and consequently physical, "shape" made the psychic existence of the following generation possible.

But naming your own mother (or her equivalent) enables people to place you precisely within the universal web of your life, in each of its dimensions: cultural, spiritual, personal, and historical.

Among the Keres, "context" and "matrix" are equivalent terms, and both refer to approximately the same thing as knowing your derivation and place. Failure to know your mother, that is, your position and its attendant traditions, history, and place in the scheme of things, is failure to remember your significance, your reality, your right relationship to earth and society. It is the same as being lost—isolated, abandoned, self-estranged, and alienated from your own life. This importance of tradition in the life of every member of the community is not confined to Keres Indians; all American Indian Nations place great value on traditionalism.

The Native American sense of the importance of continuity with one's cultural origins runs counter to contemporary American ideas: in many instances, the immigrants to America have been eager to cast off cultural ties, often seeing their antecedents as backward, restrictive, even shameful. Rejection of tradition constitutes one of the major features of American life, an attitude that reaches far back into American colonial history and that now is validated by virtually every cultural institution in the country. Feminist practice, at least in the cultural artifacts the community values most, follows this cultural trend as well.

The American idea that the best and the brightest should willingly reject and repudiate their origins leads to an allied idea—that history, like everything in the past, is of little value and should be forgotten as quickly as possible. This all too often causes us to reinvent the wheel continually. We find ourselves discovering our collective pasts over and over, having to retake ground already covered by women in the preceding decades and centuries. The Native American view, which highly values maintenance of traditional customs, values, and perspectives, might result in slower societal change and in quite a bit less social upheaval, but it has the advantage of providing a solid sense of identity and lowered levels of psychological and interpersonal conflict.

Contemporary Indian communities value individual members who are deeply connected to the traditional ways of their people, even after centuries of concerted and brutal effort on the part of the American government, the churches, and the corporate system to break the connections between individuals and their tribal world. In fact, in the view of the traditionals, rejection of one's culture—one's traditions, language, people—is the result of colonial oppression and is hardly to be applauded. They believe that the roots of oppression are to be found in the loss of tradition and memory because that loss is always accompanied by a loss of a positive sense of self. In short, Indians think it is important to remember, while Americans believe it is important to forget.

The traditional Indians' view can have a significant impact if it is expanded to mean that the sources of social, political, and philosophical thought in the Americas not only should be recognized and honored by Native Americans but should be embraced by American society. If American society judiciously modeled the traditions of the various Native Nations, the place of women in society would become central, the distribution of goods and power would be egalitarian, the elderly would be respected, honored, and protected as a primary social and cultural resource, the ideals of physical beauty would be considerably enlarged (to include "fat," strong-featured women, gray-haired, and wrinkled individuals, and others who in contemporary American culture are viewed as "ugly"). Additionally, the destruction of the biota, the life sphere, and the natural resources of the planet would be curtailed, and the spiritual nature of human and nonhuman life would become a primary organizing principle of human society. And if the traditional tribal systems that are emulated included pacifist ones, war would cease to be a major method of human problem solving.

Re-membering Connections and Histories

The belief that rejection of tradition and of history is a useful response to life is reflected in America's amazing loss of memory concerning its origins in the matrix and context of Native America. America does not seem to remember that it derived its wealth, its values, its food, much of its medicine, and a large part of its "dream" from Native America. It is ignorant of the genesis of its culture in this Native American land, and that ignorance helps to perpetuate the longstanding European and Middle Eastern monotheistic, hierarchical, patriarchal cultures' oppression of women, gays, and lesbians, people of color, working class, unemployed people, and the elderly. Hardly anyone in America speculates that the constitutional system of government might be as much a product of American Indian ideas and practices as of colonial American and Anglo-European revolutionary fervor.

Even though Indians are officially and informally ignored as intellectual movers and shapers in the United States, Britain, and Europe, they are peoples with ancient tenure on this soil. During the ages when tribal societies existed in the Americas largely untouched by patriarchal oppression, they developed elaborate systems of thought that included science, philosophy, and government based on a belief in the central importance of female energies, autonomy of individuals, cooperation, human dignity, human freedom, and egalitarian distribution of status, goods, and services. Respect for others, reverence for life and, as a by-product, pacifism as a way of life; importance of kinship ties in the customary ordering of social interaction; a sense of the sacredness and mystery of existence; balance and harmony in relationships both sacred and secular were all features of life among the tribal confederacies and nations. And in those that lived by the largest number of these principles, gynarchy was the norm rather than the exception. Those systems are as yet unmatched in any contemporary industrial, agrarian, or postindustrial society on earth.

As we have seen in previous essays, there are many female gods recognized and honored by the tribes and Nations. Femaleness was highly valued, both respected and feared, and all social institutions reflected this attitude. Even modern sayings, such as the Cheyenne statement that a people is not conquered until the hearts of the women are on the ground, express the Indians' understanding that without the power of woman the people will not live, but with it, they will endure and prosper.

Indians did not confine this belief in the central importance of female energy to matters of worship. Among many of the tribes (perhaps as many as 70 percent of them in North America alone), this belief was reflected in all of their social institutions. The Iroquois Constitution or White Roots of Peace, also called the Great Law of the Iroquois,

codified the Matrons' decision-making and economic power:

> The lineal descent of the people of the Five Fires [the Iroquois Nations] shall run in the female line. Women shall be considered the progenitors of the Nation. They shall own the land and the soil. Men and women shall follow the status of their mothers. (Article 44)
>
> The women heirs of the chieftainship titles of the League shall be called Oiner or Otinner [Noble] for all time to come. (Article 45)
>
> If a disobedient chief persists in his disobedience after three warnings [by his female relatives, by his male relatives, and by one of his fellow council members, in that order], the matter shall go to the council of War Chiefs. The Chiefs shall then take away the title of the erring chief *by order of the women in whom the title is vested.* When the chief is deposed, the women shall notify the chiefs of the League . . . and the chiefs of the League shall sanction the act. The women will then select another of their sons as a candidate and the chiefs shall elect him. (Article 19) (Emphasis mine)[1]

The Matrons held so much policy-making power traditionally that once, when their position was threatened they demanded its return, and consequently the power of women was fundamental in shaping the Iroquois Confederation sometime in the sixteenth or early seventeenth century. It was women

> who fought what may have been the first successful feminist rebellion in the New World. The year was 1600, or thereabouts, when these tribal feminists decided that they had had enough of unregulated warfare by their men. Lysistratas among the Indian women proclaimed a boycott on lovemaking and childbearing. Until the men conceded to them the power to decide upon war and peace, there would be no more warriors. Since the men believed that the women alone knew the secret of childbirth, the rebellion was instantly successful.
>
> In the Constitution of Deganawidah the founder of the Iroquois Confederation of Nations had said: "He caused the body of our mother, the woman, to be of great worth and honor. He purposed that she shall be endowed

and entrusted with the birth and upbringing of men, and that she shall have the care of all that is planted by which life is sustained and supported and the power to breathe is fortified: *and moreover that the warriors shall be her assistants."*

The footnote of history was curiously supplied when Susan B. Anthony began her "Votes for Women" movement two and a half centuries later. Unknowingly the feminists chose to hold their founding convention of latter-day suffragettes in the town of Seneca [Falls], New York. The site was just a stone's throw from the old council house where the Iroquois women had plotted their feminist rebellion. (Emphasis mine)[2]

Beliefs, attitudes, and laws such as these became part of the vision of American feminists and of other human liberation movements around the world. Yet feminists too often believe that no one has ever experienced the kind of society that empowered women and made that empowerment the basis of its rules of civilization. The price the feminist community must pay because it is not aware of the recent presence of gynarchical societies on this continent is unnecessary confusion, division, and much lost time.

The Root of Oppression Is Loss of Memory

An odd thing occurs in the minds of Americans when Indian civilization is mentioned: little or nothing. As I write this, I am aware of how far removed my version of the roots of American feminism must seem to those steeped in either mainstream or radical versions of feminism's history. I am keenly aware of the lack of image Americans have about our continent's recent past. I am intensely conscious of popular notions of Indian women as beasts of burden, squaws, traitors, or, at best, vanished denizens of a long-lost wilderness. How odd, then, must my contention seem that the gynocratic tribes of the American continent provided the basis for all the dreams of liberation that characterize the modern world.

We as feminists must be aware of our history on this continent. We need to recognize that the same forces that devastated the gynarchies of Britain and the Continent also devastated the ancient African civilizations, and we must know that those same materialistic, antispiritual forces are presently engaged in wiping out the same gynarchical values, along with the peoples who adhere to them, in Latin America. I am convinced that those wars were and continue to be about the imposition of patriarchal civilization over the holistic, pacifist, and spirit-based gynarchies they supplant. To that end the wars of imperial conquest have not been solely or even mostly waged over the land and its resources, but they have been fought within the bodies, minds, and hearts of the people of the earth for dominion over them. I think this is the reason traditionals say we must remember our origins, our cultures, our histories, our mothers and grandmothers, for without that memory, which implies continuance rather than nostalgia, we are doomed to engulfment by a paradigm that is fundamentally inimical to the vitality, autonomy, and self-empowerment essential for satisfying, high-quality life.

The vision that impels feminists to action was the vision of the Grandmothers' society, the society that was captured in the words of the sixteenth-century explorer Peter Martyr nearly five hundred years ago. It is the same vision repeated over and over by radical thinkers of Europe and America, from François Villon to John Locke, from William Shakespeare to Thomas Jefferson, from Karl Marx to Friedrich Engels, from Benito Juarez to Martin Luther King, from Elizabeth Cady Stanton to Judy Grahn, from Harriet Tubman to Audre Lorde, from Emma Goldman to Bella Abzug, from Malinalli to Cherrie Moraga, and from Iyatiku to me. That vision as Martyr told it is of a country where there are "no soldiers, no gendarmes or police, no nobles, kings, regents, prefects, or judges, no prisons, no lawsuits . . . All are equal and free," or so Friedrich Engels recounts Martyr's words.[3]

Columbus wrote:

> Nor have I been able to learn whether they [the inhabitants of the islands he visited on his first journey to the New World] held personal property, for it seemed to me that whatever one had, they all took shares of . . . They are so ingenuous and free with all they have, that no one would believe it who has not seen it; of anything that they possess, if it be asked of them, they never say no; on the contrary, they invite you to share it and show as much love as if their hearts went with it.[4]

At least that's how the Native Caribbean people acted when the whites first came among them; American Indians are the despair of social workers, bosses, and missionaries even now because of their deeply ingrained tendency to spend all they have, mostly on others. In any case, as the historian William Brandon notes,

> the Indian *seemed* free, to European eyes, gloriously free, to the European soul shaped by centuries of toil and tyranny, and this impression operated profoundly on the process of history and the development of America. Something in the peculiar character of the Indian world gave an impression of classlessness, of propertylessness, and that in turn led to an impression, as H. H. Bancroft put it, of "humanity unrestrained . . . in the exercise of liberty absolute."[5]

A Feminist Heroine

Early in the women's suffrage movement, Eva Emery Dye, an Oregon suffragette, went looking for a heroine to embody her vision of feminism. She wanted a historical figure whose life would symbolize the strengthened power of women. She found Sacagawea (or Sacajawea) buried in the journals of Lewis and Clark. The Shoshoni teenager had traveled with the Lewis and Clark expedition, carrying her infant son, and on a small number of occasions acted as translator.[6]

Dye declared that Sacagawea, whose name is thought to mean Bird Woman, had been the guide to the historic expedition, and through Dye's work Sacagawea became enshrined in American memory as a moving force and friend of the whites, leading them in the settlement of western North America.[7]

But Native American roots of white feminism reach back beyond Sacagawea. The earliest white women on this continent were well acquainted with tribal women. They were neighbors to a number of tribes and often shared food, information, child care, and health care. Of course little is made of these encounters in official histories of colonial America, the period from the Revolution to the Civil War, or on the ever-moving frontier. Nor, to my knowledge, has either the significance or incidence of intermarriage between Indian and white or between Indian and Black been explored. By and

large, the study of Indian-white relations has been focused on government and treaty relations, warfare, missionization, and education. It has been almost entirely documented in terms of formal white Christian patriarchal impacts and assaults on Native Americans, though they are not often characterized as assaults but as "civilizing the savages." Particularly in organs of popular culture and miseducation, the focus has been on what whites imagine to be degradation of Indian women ("squaws"), their equally imagined love of white government and white conquest ("princesses"), and the horrifyingly misleading, fanciful tales of "bloodthirsty, backward primitives" assaulting white Christian settlers who were looking for life, liberty, and happiness in their chosen land.

But, regardless of official versions of relations between Indians and whites or other segments of the American population, the fact remains that great numbers of apparently "white" or "Black" Americans carry notable degrees of Indian blood. With that blood has come the culture of the Indian, informing the lifestyles, attitudes, and values of their descendents. Somewhere along the line—and often quite recently—an Indian woman was giving birth to and raising the children of a family both officially and informally designated as white or Black—not Indian. In view of this, it should be evident that one of the major enterprises of Indian women in America has been the transfer of Indian values and culture to as large and influential a segment of American immigrant populations as possible. Their success in this endeavor is amply demonstrated in the Indian values and social styles that increasingly characterize American life. Among these must be included "permissive" childrearing practices, for as noted in an earlier chapter ("When Women Throw Down Bundles"), imprisoning, torturing, caning, strapping, starving, or verbally abusing children was considered outrageous behavior. Native Americans did not believe that physical or psychological abuse of children would result in their edification. They did not believe that children are born in sin, are congenitally predisposed to evil, or that a good parent who wishes the child to gain salvation, achieve success, or earn the respect of her or his fellows can be helped to those ends by physical or emotional torture.

The early Americans saw the strongly protective attitude of the Indian people as a mark of their "savagery"—as they saw the Indian's habit of bathing frequently, their sexual openness, their liking for scant clothing, their raucous laughter at most things, their suspicion and derision of author-itarian structures, their quick pride, their genuine courtesy, their willingness to share what they had with others less fortunate than they, their egalitari-anism, their ability to act as if various lifestyles were a normal part of living, and their granting that women were of equal or, in individual cases, of greater value than men.

Yet the very qualities that marked Indian life in the sixteenth century have, over the centuries since contact between the two worlds occurred, come to mark much of contemporary American life. And those qualities, which I believe have passed into white culture from Indian culture, are the very ones that fundamentalists, immigrants from Europe, the Middle East, and Asia often find the most reprehensi-ble. Third- and fourth-generation Americans indulge in growing nudity, informality in social relations, egalitarianism, and the rearing of women who value autonomy, strength, freedom, and personal dignity—and who are often derided by European, Asian, and Middle Eastern men for those qualities. Contempo-rary Americans value leisure almost as much as tribal people do. They find themselves increasingly unable to accept child abuse as a reasonable way to nurture. They bathe more than any other industrial people on earth—much to the scorn of their white cousins across the Atlantic, and they sometimes en-joy a good laugh even at their own expense (though they still have a less developed sense of the ridicu-lous than one might wish).

Contemporary Americans find themselves more and more likely to adopt a "live and let live" attitude in matters of personal sexual and social styles. Two-thirds of their diet and a large share of their medications and medical treatments mirror or are directly derived from Native American sources. Indianization is not a simple concept, to be sure, and it is one that Americans often find themselves resisting; but it is a process that has taken place, re-gardless of American resistance to recognizing the source of many if not most of American's vaunted freedoms in our personal, family, social, and politi-cal arenas.

This is not to say that Americans have become Indian in every attitude, value, or social institution. Unfortunately, Americans have a way to go in learning how to live in the world in ways that im-prove the quality of life for each individual while do-ing minimal damage to the biota, but they have adapted certain basic qualities of perception and cer-tain attitudes that are moving them in that direction.

An Indian-Focused Version of American History

American colonial ideas of self-government came as much from the colonists' observations of tribal gov-ernments as from their Protestant or Greco-Roman heritage. Neither Greece nor Rome had the kind of pluralistic democracy as that concept has been un-derstood in the United States since Andrew Jackson, but the tribes, particularly the gynarchical tribal con-federacies, did. It is true that the *oligarchic* form of government that colonial Americans established was originally based on Greco-Roman systems in a number of important ways, such as its restriction of citizenship to propertied white males over twenty-one years of age, but it was never a form that Americans as a whole have been entirely comfortable with. Poli-tics and government in the United States during the Federalist period also reflected the English common law system as it had evolved under patriarchal feu-dalism and monarchy—hence the United States' retention of slavery and restriction of citizenship to propertied white males.

The Federalists did make one notable change in the feudal system from which their political system derived on its Anglo side. They rejected blooded aristocracy and monarchy. This idea came from the Protestant Revolt to be sure, but it was at least rein-forced by colonial America's proximity to American Indian nonfeudal confederacies and their concourse with those confederacies over the two hundred years of the colonial era. It was this proximity and concourse that enabled the revolutionary theorists to "dream up" a system in which all local polities would contribute to and be protected by a central governing body responsible for implementing poli-cies that bore on the common interest of all. It should also be noted that the Reformation followed Columbus's contact with the Americas and that his and Martyr's reports concerning Native Americans' free and easy egalitarianism were in circulation by the time the Reformation took hold.

The Iroquois federal system, like that of several in the vicinity of the American colonies, is remark-ably similar to the organization of the federal sys-tem of the United States. It was made up of local, "state," and federal bodies composed of executive, legislative, and judicial branches. The Council of Matrons was the executive: it instituted and determined general policy. The village, tribal (several villages), and Confederate councils determined and implemented policies when they did not conflict with the broader Council's decisions or with theological precepts that ultimately determined policy at all levels. The judicial was composed of the men's councils and the Matron's council, who sat together to make decisions. Because the matrons were the ceremonial center of the system, they were also the prime policymakers.

Obviously, there are major differences between the structure of the contemporary American government and that of the Iroquois. Two of those differences were and are crucial to the process of just government. The Iroquois system is spirit-based, while that of the United States is secular, and the Iroquois Clan Matrons formed the executive. The female executive function was directly tied to the ritual nature of the Iroquois politic, for the executive was lodged in the hands of the Matrons of particular clans across village, tribe, and national lines. The executive office was hereditary, and only sons of eligible clans could serve, at the behest of the Matrons of their clans, on the councils at the three levels. Certain daughters inherited the office of Clan Matron through their clan affiliations. No one could impeach or disempower a Matron, though her violation of certain laws could result in her ineligibility for the Matron's council. For example, a woman who married *and took her husband's name* could not hold the title Matron.

American ideas of social justice came into sharp focus through the commentaries of Iroquois observers who traveled in France in the colonial period. These observers expressed horror at the great gap between the lifestyles of the wealthy and the poor, remarking to the French philosopher Montaigne, who would heavily influence the radical communities of Europe, England, and America, that "they had noticed that in Europe there seemed to be two moities, consisting of the rich 'full gorged' with wealth, and the poor, starving 'and bare with need and povertie.' The Indian tourists not only marveled at the division, but marveled that the poor endured 'such an injustice, and that they took not the others by the throte, or set fire on their house.'"[8] It must be noted that the urban poor eventually did just that in the French Revolution. The writings of Montaigne

and of those he influenced provided the theoretical framework and the vision that propelled the struggle for liberty, justice, and equality on the Continent and later throughout the British empire.

The feminist idea of power as it ideally accrues to women stems from tribal sources. The central importance of the clan Matrons in the formulation and determination of domestic and foreign policy as well as in their primary role in the ritual and ceremonial life of their respective Nations was the single most important attribute of the Iroquois, as of the Cherokee and Muskogee, who traditionally inhabited the southern Atlantic region. The latter peoples were removed to what is now Oklahoma during the Jackson administration, but prior to the American Revolution they had regular and frequent communication with and impact on both the British colonizers and later the American people, including the African peoples brought here as slaves.

Ethnographer Lewis Henry Morgan wrote an account of Iroquoian matriarchal culture, published in 1877,[9] that heavily influenced Marx and the development of communism, particularly lending it the idea of the liberation of women from patriarchal dominance. The early socialists in Europe, especially in Russia, saw women's liberation as a central aspect of the socialist revolution. Indeed, the basic ideas of socialism, the egalitarian distribution of goods and power, the peaceful ordering of society, and the right of every member of society to participate in the work and benefits of that society, are ideas that pervade American Indian political thought and action. And it is through various channels—the informal but deeply effective Indianization of Europeans, and christianizing Africans, the social and political theory of the confederacies feuding and then intertwining with European dreams of liberty and justice, and, more recently, the work of Morgan and the writings of Marx and Engels—that the age-old gynarchical systems of egalitarian government found their way into contemporary feminist theory.

When Eva Emery Dye discovered Sacagawea and honored her as the guiding spirit of American womanhood, she may have been wrong in bare historical fact, but she was quite accurate in terms of deeper truth. The statues that have been erected depicting Sacagawea as a Matron in her prime signify an understanding in the American mind, however unconscious, that the source of just government, of right ordering of social relationships, the dream of "liberty and justice for all" can be gained only by following the Indian Matrons' guidance. For, as Dr. Anna Howard Shaw said of Sacagawea at the National American Woman's Suffrage Association in 1905:

> Forerunner of civilization, great leader of men, patient and motherly woman, we bow our hearts to do you honor! . . . May we the daughters of an alien race . . . learn the lessons of calm endurance, of patient persistence and unfaltering courage exemplified in your life, in our efforts to lead men through the Pass of justice, which goes over the mountains of prejudice and conservatism to the broad land of the perfect freedom of a true republic; one in which men and women together shall in perfect equality solve the problems of a nation that knows no caste, no race, no sex in opportunity, in responsibility or in justice! May 'the eternal womanly' ever lead us on![10]

NOTES

1. The White Roots of Peace, cited in *The Third Woman: Minority Women Writers of the United States,* ed. Dexter Fisher (Boston: Houghton Mifflin, 1980), p. 577. Cf. Thomas Sanders and William Peek, eds., *Literature of the American Indian* (New York: Glencoe Press, 1973), pp. 208–239. Sanders and Peek refer to the document as "The Law of the Great Peace."

2. Stan Steiner, *The New Indians* (New York: Dell, 1968), pp. 219–220.

3. William Brandon, *The Last Americans: The Indian in American Culture* (New York: McGraw-Hill, 1974), p. 294.

4. Brandon, *Last Americans,* p. 6.

5. Brandon, *Last Americans,* pp. 7–8. The entire chapter "American Indians and American History" (pp. 1–23) is pertinent to the discussion.

6. Ella E. Clark and Margot Evans, *Sacagawea of the Lewis and Clark Expedition* (Berkeley: University of California Press, 1979), pp. 93–98.

7. The implications of this maneuver did not go unnoticed by either whites or Indians, for the statues of the idealized Shoshoni woman, the Native American matron Sacagawea, suggest that American tenure on American land, indeed, the right to be on this land, is given to whites by her. While that implication is not overt, it certainly is suggested in the image of her that the sculptor chose: a tall, heavy woman, standing erect, nobly pointing the way westward with upraised hand. The impression is furthered by the habit of media and scholar of referring to her as "the guide." Largely because of the popularization of the circumstances of Sacagawea's participation in the famed Lewis and Clark expedition, Indian people have viewed her as a traitor to her people, likening her to Malinalli (La Malinche, who acted as interpreter for Cortés and bore him a son) and Pocahontas, that unhappy girl who married John Rolfe (not John Smith) and died in England after bearing him a son. Actually none of these women engaged in traitorous behavior. Sacagawea led a long life, was called Porivo (Chief Woman) by the Commanches, among whom she lived for more than twenty years, and in her old age engaged her considerable skill at speaking and manipulating white bureaucracy to help in assuring her Shoshoni people decent reservation holdings.

8. Brandon, *Last Americans,* p. 6.

9. Lewis Henry Morgan, *Ancient Society or Researches in the Lines of Human Progress from Savagery Through Barbarism to Civilization* (New York, 1877).

10. Clark and Evans, *Sacagawea,* p. 96.

T W O

◆◆◆

Declaration of Sentiments and Resolutions, Seneca Falls (1848)

The Seneca Falls *Declaration of Sentiments and Resolutions* was adopted at a founding convention of nineteenth-century suffragists, called to consider the "social, civil, and religious conditions and rights of woman," held at the Wesleyan Chapel, Seneca Falls, New York, on July 19, 1848 (Schneir 1994, p. 76). Elizabeth Cady Stanton, Lucretia Mott, and others in their circle drafted this document, using the *Declaration of Independence* as a model. (1848)

When, in the course of human events, it becomes necessary for one portion of the family of man to assume among the people of the earth a position different from that which they have hitherto occupied, but one to which the laws of nature and of nature's God entitle them, a decent respect to the opinions of mankind requires that they should declare the causes that impel them to such a course.

We hold these truths to be self-evident: that all men and women are created equal; that they are endowed by their Creator with certain inalienable rights; that among these are life, liberty, and the pursuit of happiness; that to secure these rights governments are instituted, deriving their just powers from the consent of the governed. Whenever any form of government becomes destructive of these ends, it is the right of those who suffer from it to refuse allegiance to it, and to insist upon the institution of a new government, laying its foundation on such principles, and organizing its powers in such form, as to them shall seem most likely to effect their safety and happiness. Prudence, indeed, will dictate that governments long established should not be changed for light and transient causes; and accordingly all experience hath shown that mankind are more disposed to suffer, while evils are sufferable, than to right themselves by abolishing the forms to which they were accustomed. But when a long train of abuses and usurpations, pursuing invariably the same object evinces a design to reduce them under absolute despotism, it is their duty to throw off such government, and to provide new guards for their future security. Such has been the patient sufferance of the women under this government, and such is now the necessity which constrains them to demand the equal station to which they are entitled.

The history of mankind is a history of repeated injuries and usurpations on the part of man toward woman, having in direct object the establishment of an absolute tyranny over her. To prove this, let facts be submitted to a candid world.

He has never permitted her to exercise her inalienable right to the elective franchise.

He has compelled her to submit to laws, in the formation of which she had no voice.

He has withheld from her rights which are given to the most ignorant and degraded men—both natives and foreigners.

Having deprived her of this first right of a citizen, the elective franchise, thereby leaving her without representation in the halls of legislation, he has oppressed her on all sides.

He has made her, if married, in the eye of the law, civilly dead.

He has taken from her all right in property, even to the wages she earns.

He has made her, morally, an irresponsible being, as she can commit many crimes with impunity, provided they be done in the presence of her husband. In the covenant of marriage, she is compelled to promise obedience to her husband, he becoming, to all intents and purposes, her master—the law giving him power to deprive her of her liberty, and to administer chastisement.

He has so framed the laws of divorce, as to what shall be the proper causes, and in case of separation, to whom the guardianship of the children shall be given, as to be wholly regardless of the happiness of women—the law, in all cases, going upon a false supposition of the supremacy of man, and giving all power into his hands.

After depriving her of all rights as a married woman, if single, and the owner of property, he has taxed her to support a government which recognizes her only when her property can be made profitable to it.

He has monopolized nearly all the profitable employments, and from those she is permitted to follow, she receives but a scanty remuneration. He closes against her all the avenues to wealth and distinction which he considers most honorable to himself. As a teacher of theology, medicine, or law, she is not known.

He has denied her the facilities for obtaining a thorough education, all colleges being closed against her.

He allows her in Church, as well as State, but a subordinate position, claiming Apolstolic authority for her exclusion from the ministry, and, with some exceptions, from any public participation in the affairs of the Church.

He has created a false public sentiment by giving to the world a different code of morals for men and women, by which moral delinquencies which exclude women from society, are not only tolerated, but deemed of little account in man.

He has usurped the prerogative of Jehovah himself, claiming it as his right to assign for her a sphere of action, when that belongs to her conscience and to her God.

He has endeavored, in every way that he could, to destroy her confidence in her own powers, to lessen her self-respect, and to make her willing to lead a dependent and abject life.

Now, in view of this entire disfranchisement of one-half the people of this country, their social and religious degradation—in view of the unjust laws above mentioned, and because women do feel themselves aggrieved, oppressed, and fraudulently deprived of their most sacred rights, we insist that they have immediate admission to all the rights and privileges which belong to them as citizens of the United States.

In entering upon the great work before us, we anticipate no small amount of misconception, misrepresentation, and ridicule; but we shall use every instrumentality within our power to effect our object. We shall employ agents, circulate tracts, petition the State and National legislatures, and endeavor to enlist the pulpit and the press in our behalf. We hope this Convention will be followed by a series of Conventions embracing every part of the country.

Resolutions

WHEREAS, The great precept of nature is conceded to be, that "man shall pursue his own true and substantial happiness." Blackstone in his Commentaries remarks, that this law of Nature being coeval with mankind, and dictated by God himself, is of course superior in obligation to any other. It is binding over all the globe, in all countries and at all times; no human laws are of any validity if contrary to this, and such of them as are valid, derive all their force, and all their validity, and all their authority, mediately and immediately, from this original; therefore,

Resolved, That such laws as conflict, in any way, with the true and substantial happiness of woman, are contrary to the great precept of nature and of no validity, for this is "superior in obligation to any other."

Resolved, That all laws which prevent woman from occupying such a station in society as her conscience shall dictate, or which place her in a position inferior to that of man, are contrary to the great precept of nature, and therefore of no force or authority.

Resolved, That woman is man's equal—was intended to be so by the Creator, and the highest good of the race demands that she should be recognized as such.

Resolved, That the women of this country ought to be enlightened in regard to the laws under which they live, that they may no longer publish their degradation by declaring themselves satisfied with their present position, nor their ignorance, by asserting that they have all the rights they want.

Resolved, That inasmuch as man, while claiming for himself intellectual superiority, does accord to woman moral superiority, it is pre-eminently his duty to encourage her to speak and teach, as she has an opportunity, in all religious assemblies.

Resolved, That the same amount of virtue, delicacy, and refinement of behavior that is required of woman in the social state, should also be required of man, and the same transgressions should be visited with equal severity on both man and woman.

Resolved, That the objection of indelicacy and impropriety, which is so often brought against woman when she addresses a public audience, comes with a very ill-grace from those who encourage, by their attendance, her appearance on the stage, in the concert, or in feats of the circus.

Resolved, That woman has too long rested satisfied in the circumscribed limits which corrupt customs and a perverted application of the Scriptures have marked out for her, and that it is time she should move in the enlarged sphere which her great Creator has assigned her.

Resolved, That it is the duty of the women of this country to secure to themselves their sacred right to the elective franchise.

Resolved, That the equality of human rights results necessarily from the fact of the identity of the race in capabilities and responsibilities.

Resolved, therefore, That, being invested by the Creator with the same capabilities, and the same consciousness of responsibility for their exercise, it is demonstrably the right and duty of woman, equally with man, to promote every righteous cause by every righteous means; and especially in regard to the great subjects of morals and religion, it is self-evidently her right to participate with her brother in teaching them, both in private and in public, by writing and by speaking, by any instrumentalities proper to be used, and in any assemblies proper to be held; and this being a self-evident truth growing out of the divinely implanted principles of human nature, any custom or authority adverse to it, whether modern or wearing the hoary sanction of antiquity, is to be regarded as a self-evident falsehood, and at war with mankind.

[At the last session Lucretia Mott offered and spoke to the following resolution:]

Resolved, That the speedy success of our cause depends upon the zealous and untiring efforts of both men and women, for the overthrow of the monopoly of the pulpit, and for the securing to woman an equal participation with men in the various trades, professions, and commerce.

◆◆◆

THREE

Editorial from *The North Star* (July 28, 1848)

Frederick Douglass

Frederick Douglass (1817–1895) was born into slavery in Maryland but later became a free man and edited a weekly abolitionist newspaper, *The North Star*, in Rochester, New York. He attended the 1848 Seneca Falls convention on women's rights and spoke strongly in favor of women's right to vote. In contrast to many newspapers, which opposed women's rights with ridicule and abuse, Douglass printed the following supportive editorial in *The North Star* on July 28, 1848 (Schneir 1994, p. 83).

One of the most interesting events of the past week, was the holding of what is technically styled a Woman's Rights Convention at Seneca Falls. The speaking, addresses, and resolutions of this extraordinary meeting were almost wholly conducted by women; and although they evidently felt themselves in a novel position, it is but simple justice to say that their whole proceedings were characterized by marked ability and dignity. No one present, we think, however much he might be disposed to differ from the views advanced by the leading speakers on that occasion, will fail to give them credit for brilliant talents and excellent dispositions. In this meeting, as in other deliberative assemblies, there were frequent differences of opinion and animated discussion; but in no case was there the slightest absence of good feeling and decorum. Several interesting documents setting forth the rights as well as grievances of women were read. Among these was a Declaration of Sentiments, to be regarded as the basis of a grand movement for attaining the civil, social, political, and religious rights of women. We should not do justice to our own convictions, or to the excellent persons connected with this infant movement, if we did not in this connection offer a few remarks on the general subject which the Convention met to consider and the objects they seek to attain. In doing so, we are not insensible that the bare mention of this truly important subject in any other than terms of contemptuous ridicule and scornful disfavor, is likely to excite against us the fury of bigotry and the folly of prejudice. A discussion of the rights of animals would be regarded with far more complacency by many of what are called the *wise* and the *good* of our land, than would be a discussion of the rights of women. It is, in their estimation, to be guilty of evil thoughts, to think that woman is entitled to equal rights with man. Many who have at last made the discovery that the negroes have some rights as well as other members of the human family, have yet to be convinced that women are entitled to any. Eight years ago a number of persons of this description actually abandoned the anti-slavery cause, lest by giving their influence in that direction they might possibly be giving countenance to the dangerous heresy that woman, in respect to rights, stands on an equal footing with man. In the judgment of such persons the American slave system, with all its concomitant horrors, is less to be deplored than this *wicked* idea. It is perhaps needless to say, that we cherish little sympathy for such sentiments or respect for such prejudices. Standing as we do upon the watchtower of human freedom, we can not be deterred from an expression of our approbation of any movement, however humble, to improve and elevate the character of any members of the human family. While it is impossible for us to go into this subject at length, and dispose of the various objections which are often urged against such a doctrine as that of female equality, we are free to say that in respect to political rights, we hold woman to be justly entitled to all we claim for man. We go farther, and express our conviction that all political rights which it is expedient for man to exercise, it is equally so for woman. All that distinguishes man as an intelligent and accountable being, is equally true of woman; and if that government only is just which governs by the free consent of the governed, there can be no reason in the world for denying to woman the exercise of the elective franchise, or a hand in making and administering the laws of the land. Our doctrine is that "right is of no sex." We therefore bid the women engaged in this movement our humble Godspeed.

FOUR

◆◆◆

Ain't I a Woman? (1851)

Sojourner Truth

Sojourner Truth (1795–1883), a formerly enslaved woman born in New York State, gained her freedom in 1827 when the state emancipated its slaves. Dropping her slave name, Isabella, she took the symbolic name of Sojourner Truth when she started to speak out publicly against slavery. She identified herself with rights for women and was the only Black woman to attend the First National Women's Rights Convention in Worcester, Massachusetts, in 1850. The following year she spoke at a woman's convention in Akron, Ohio. Several delegates tried to dissuade the chair, Frances D. Gage, from allowing her to speak, believing that she would harm their cause. The speech reprinted here was not officially recorded; it survives because Frances Gage wrote it down, although this version does not use the "heavy dialect" in which Gage recorded it (Schneir 1994, pp. 93–4).

Well, children, where there is so much racket there must be something out of kilter. I think that 'twixt the negroes of the South and the women at the North, all talking about rights, the white men will be in a fix pretty soon. But what's all this here talking about?

That man over there says that women need to be helped into carriages, and lifted over ditches, and to have the best place everywhere. Nobody ever helps me into carriages, or over mud-puddles, or gives me any best place! And ain't I a woman? Look at me! Look at my arm! I have ploughed and planted, and gathered into barns, and no man could head me! And ain't I a woman? I could work as much and eat as much as a man—when I could get it—and bear the lash as well! And ain't I a woman? I have borne thirteen children, and seen them most all sold off to slavery, and when I cried out with my mother's grief, none but Jesus heard me! And ain't I a woman?

Then they talk about this thing in the head; what's this they call it? [Intellect, someone whispers.] That's it, honey. What's that got to do with women's rights or negro's rights? If my cup won't hold but a pint, and yours holds a quart, wouldn't you be mean not to let me have my little half-measure full?

Then that little man in black there, he says women can't have as much rights as men, 'cause Christ wasn't a woman! Where did your Christ come from? Where did your Christ come from? From God and a woman! Man had nothing to do with Him.

If the first woman God ever made was strong enough to turn the world upside down all alone, these women together ought to be able to turn it back, and get it right side up again! And now they is asking to do it, the men better let them.

Obliged to you for hearing me, and now old Sojourner ain't got nothing more to say.

Sojourner Truth

FIVE

A Black Feminist Statement (1977)

Combahee River Collective

> Active in the mid to late seventies, the **Combahee River Collective** was a Black feminist group in Boston whose name came from the guerrilla action led by **Harriet Tubman** that freed more than 750 slaves and is the only military campaign in U.S. history planned and led by a woman.

We are a collective of Black feminists who have been meeting together since 1974. During that time we have been involved in the process of defining and clarifying our politics, while at the same time doing political work within our own group and in coalition with other progressive organizations and movements. The most general statement of our politics at the present time would be that we are actively committed to struggling against racial, sexual, heterosexual, and class oppression and see as our particular task the development of integrated analysis and practice based upon the fact that the major systems of oppression are interlocking. The synthesis of these oppressions creates the conditions of our lives. As Black women we see Black feminism as the logical political movement to combat the manifold and simultaneous oppressions that all women of color face.

We will discuss four major topics in the paper that follows: (1) the genesis of contemporary Black feminism; (2) what we believe, i.e., the specific province of our politics; (3) the problems in organizing Black feminists, including a brief herstory of our collective; and (4) Black feminist issues and practice.

1. The Genesis of Contemporary Black Feminism

Before looking at the recent development of Black feminism we would like to affirm that we find our origins in the historical reality of Afro-American women's continuous life-and-death struggle for survival and liberation. Black women's extremely negative relationship to the American political system (a system of white male rule) has always been determined by our membership in two oppressed racial and sexual castes. As Angela Davis points out in "Reflections on the Black Woman's Role in the Community of Slaves," Black women have always embodied, if only in their physical manifestation, an adversary stance to white male rule and have actively resisted its inroads upon them and their communities in both dramatic and subtle ways. There have always been Black women activists—some known, like Sojourner Truth, Harriet Tubman, Frances E. W. Harper, Ida B. Wells Barnett, and Mary Church Terrell, and thousands upon thousands unknown—who had a shared awareness of how their sexual identity combined with their racial identity to make their whole life situation and the focus of their political struggles unique. Contemporary Black feminism is the outgrowth of countless generations of personal sacrifice, militancy, and work by our mothers and sisters.

A Black feminist presence has evolved most obviously in connection with the second wave of the American women's movement beginning in the late 1960s. Black, other Third World, and working women have been involved in the feminist movement from its start, but both outside reactionary forces and racism and elitism within the movement itself have served to obscure our participation. In 1973 Black feminists, primarily located in New York, felt the necessity of forming a separate Black feminist group. This became the National Black Feminist Organization (NBFO).

Black feminist politics also have an obvious connection to movements for Black liberation, particularly those of the 1960s and 1970s. Many of us were active in those movements (civil rights, Black nationalism, the Black Panthers), and all of our lives were greatly affected and changed by their ideology, their goals, and the tactics used to achieve their goals. It was our experience and disillusionment within these liberation movements, as well as experience on the periphery of the white male left, that led to the need to develop a politics that was antiracist, unlike those of white women, and antisexist, unlike those of Black and white men.

There is also undeniably a personal genesis for Black feminism, that is, the political realization that comes from the seemingly personal experiences of individual Black women's lives. Black feminists and many more Black women who do not define themselves as feminists have all experienced sexual oppression as a constant factor in our day-to-day existence. As children we realized that we were different from boys and that we were treated differently. For example, we were told in the same breath to be quiet both for the sake of being "ladylike" and to make us less objectionable in the eyes of white people. As we grew older we became aware of the threat of physical and sexual abuse by men. However, we had no way of conceptualizing what was so apparent to us, what we *knew* was really happening.

Black feminists often talk about their feelings of craziness before becoming conscious of the concepts of sexual politics, patriarchal rule, and most importantly, feminism, the political analysis and practice that we women use to struggle against our oppression. The fact that racial politics and indeed racism are pervasive factors in our lives did not allow us, and still does not allow most Black women, to look more deeply into our own experiences and, from that sharing and growing consciousness, to build a politics that will change our lives and inevitably end our oppression. Our development must also be tied to the contemporary economic and political position of Black people. The post–World War II generation of Black youth was the first to be able to minimally partake of certain educational and employment options, previously closed completely to Black people. Although our economic position is still at the very bottom of the American capitalistic economy, a handful of us have been able to gain certain tools as a result of tokenism in education and employment which potentially enable us to more effectively fight our oppression.

A combined antiracist and antisexist position drew us together initially, and as we developed politically we addressed ourselves to heterosexism and economic oppression under capitalism.

2. What We Believe

Above all else, our politics initially sprang from the shared belief that Black women are inherently valuable, that our liberation is a necessity not as an adjunct to somebody else's but because of our need as human persons for autonomy. This may seem so obvious as to sound simplistic, but it is apparent that no other ostensibly progressive movement has ever considered our specific oppression as a priority or worked seriously for the ending of that oppression. Merely naming the pejorative stereotypes attributed to Black women (e.g., mammy, matriarch, Sapphire, whore, bulldagger), let alone cataloguing the cruel, often murderous, treatment we receive, indicates how little value has been placed upon our lives during four centuries of bondage in the Western Hemisphere. We realize that the only people who care enough about us to work consistently for our liberation are us. Our politics evolve from a healthy love for ourselves, our sisters and our community which allows us to continue our struggle and work.

This focusing upon our own oppression is embodied in the concept of identity politics. We believe that the most profound and potentially the most radical politics come directly out of our own identity, as opposed to working to end somebody else's oppression. In the case of Black women this is a particularly repugnant, dangerous, threatening, and therefore revolutionary concept because it is obvious from looking at all the political movements that have preceded us that anyone is more worthy of liberation than ourselves. We reject pedestals, queenhood, and walking ten paces behind. To be recognized as human, levelly human, is enough.

We believe that sexual politics under patriarchy is as pervasive in Black women's lives as are the politics of class and race. We also often find it difficult to separate race from class from sex oppression because in our lives they are most often experienced simultaneously. We know that there is such a thing as racial-sexual oppression which is neither solely racial nor solely sexual, e.g., the history of rape of Black women by white men as a weapon of political repression.

Although we are feminists and lesbians, we feel solidarity with progressive Black men and do not advocate the fractionalization that white women who are separatists demand. Our situation as Black people necessitates that we have solidarity around the fact of race, which white women of course do not need to have with white men, unless it is their negative solidarity as racial oppressors. We struggle together with Black men against racism, while we also struggle with Black men about sexism.

We realize that the liberation of all oppressed peoples necessitates the destruction of the political-economic systems of capitalism and imperialism as well as patriarchy. We are socialists because we believe the work must be organized for the collective benefit of those who do the work and create the products, and not for the profit of the bosses. Material resources must be equally distributed among those who create these resources. We are not convinced, however, that a socialist revolution that is not also a feminist and antiracist revolution will guarantee our liberation. We have arrived at the necessity for developing an understanding of class relationships that takes into account the specific class position of Black women who are generally marginal in the labor force, while at this particular time some of us are temporarily viewed as doubly desirable tokens at white-collar and professional levels. We need to articulate the real class situation of persons who are not merely raceless, sexless workers, but for whom racial and sexual oppression are significant determinants in their working/economic lives. Although we are in essential agreement with Marx's theory as it applied to the very specific economic relationships he analyzed, we know that his analysis must be extended further in order for us to understand our specific economic situation as Black women.

A political contribution which we feel we have already made is the expansion of the feminist principle that the personal is political. In our consciousness-raising sessions, for example, we have in many ways gone beyond white women's revelations because we are dealing with the implications of race and class as well as sex. Even our Black women's style of talking/testifying in Black language about what we have experienced has a resonance that is both cultural and political. We have spent a great deal of energy delving into the cultural and experiential nature of our oppression out of necessity because none of these matters has ever been looked at before. No one before has ever examined the multilayered texture of Black women's lives. An example of this kind of revelation/conceptualization occurred at a meeting as we discussed the ways in which our early intellectual interests had been attacked by our peers, particularly Black males. We discovered that all of us, because we were "smart" had also been considered "ugly," i.e., "smart-ugly." "Smart-ugly" crystallized the way in which most of us had been forced to develop our intellects at great cost to our "social" lives. The sanctions in the Black and white communities against Black women

thinkers are comparatively much higher than for white women, particularly ones from the educated middle and upper classes.

As we have already stated, we reject the stance of lesbian separatism because it is not a viable political analysis or strategy for us. It leaves out far too much and far too many people, particularly Black men, women, and children. We have a great deal of criticism and loathing for what men have been socialized to be in this society: what they support, how they act, and how they oppress. But we do not have the misguided notion that it is their maleness, per se—i.e., their biological maleness—that makes them what they are. As Black women we find any type of biological determinism a particularly dangerous and reactionary basis upon which to build a politic. We must also question whether lesbian separatism is an adequate and progressive political analysis and strategy, even for those who practice it, since it so completely denies any but the sexual sources of women's oppression, negating the facts of class and race.

3. Problems in Organizing Black Feminists

During our years together as a Black feminist collective we have experienced success and defeat, joy and pain, victory and failure. We have found that it is very difficult to organize around Black feminist issues, difficult even to announce in certain contexts that we *are* Black feminists. We have tried to think about the reasons for our difficulties, particularly since the white women's movement continues to be strong and to grow in many directions. In this section we will discuss some of the general reasons for the organizing problems we face and also talk specifically about the stages in organizing our own collective.

The major source of difficulty in our political work is that we are not just trying to fight oppression on one front or even two, but instead to address a whole range of oppressions. We do not have racial, sexual, heterosexual, or class privilege to rely upon, nor do we have even the minimal access to resources and power that groups who possess any one of these types of privilege have.

The psychological toll of being a Black woman and the difficulties this presents in reaching political consciousness and doing political work can never be underestimated. There is a very low value placed upon Black women's psyches in this society, which is both racist and sexist. As an early group member once said, "We are all damaged people merely by virtue of being Black women." We are dispossessed psychologically and on every other level, and yet we feel the necessity to struggle to change the condition of all Black women. In "A Black Feminist's Search for Sisterhood," Michele Wallace arrives at this conclusion:

> We exist as women who are Black who are feminists, each stranded for the moment, working independently because there is not yet an environment in this society remotely congenial to our struggle—because, being on the bottom, we would have to do what no one else has done: we would have to fight the world.[1]

Wallace is pessimistic but realistic in her assessment of Black feminists' position, particularly in her allusion to the nearly classic isolation most of us face. We might use our position at the bottom, however, to make a clear leap into revolutionary action. If Black women were free, it would mean that everyone else would have to be free since our freedom would necessitate the destruction of all the systems of oppression.

Feminism is, nevertheless, very threatening to the majority of Black people because it calls into question some of the most basic assumptions about our existence, i.e., that sex should be a determinant of power relationships. Here is the way male and female voices were defined in a Black nationalist pamphlet from the early 1970s.

> We understand that it is and has been traditional that the man is the head of the house. He is the leader of the house/nation because his knowledge of the world is broader, his awareness is greater, his understanding is fuller and his application of this information is wiser . . . After all, it is only reasonable that the man be the head of the house because he is able to defend and protect the development of his home . . . Women cannot do the same things as men—they are made by nature to function differently. Equality of men and women is something that cannot happen even in the abstract world. Men are not equal to other men, i.e., ability, experience or

even understanding. The value of men and women can be seen as in the value of gold and silver—they are not equal but both have great value. We must realize that men and women are a complement to each other because there is no house/family without a man and his wife. Both are essential to the development of any life.[2]

The material conditions of most Black women would hardly lead them to upset both economic and sexual arrangements that seem to represent some stability in their lives. Many Black women have a good understanding of both sexism and racism, but because of the everyday constrictions of their lives cannot risk struggling against them both.

The reaction of Black men to feminism has been notoriously negative. They are, of course, even more threatened than Black women by the possibility that Black feminists might organize around our own needs. They realize that they might not only lose valuable and hard-working allies in their struggles but that they might also be forced to change their habitually sexist ways of interacting with and oppressing Black women. Accusations that Black feminism divides the Black struggle are powerful deterrents to the growth of an autonomous Black women's movement.

Still, hundreds of women have been active at different times during the three-year existence of our group. And every Black woman who came, came out of a strongly-felt need for some level of possibility that did not previously exist in her life.

When we first started meeting early in 1974 after the NBFO first eastern regional conference, we did not have a strategy for organizing, or even a focus. We just wanted to see what we had. After a period of months of not meeting, we began to meet again late in the year and started doing an intense variety of consciousness-raising. The overwhelming feeling that we had is that after years and years we had finally found each other. Although we were not doing political work as a group, individuals continued their involvement in Lesbian politics, sterilization abuse and abortion rights work, Third World Women's International Women's Day activities, and support activity for the trials of Dr. Kenneth Edelin, Joan Little, and Inéz García. During our first summer, when membership had dropped off considerably, those of us remaining devoted serious discussion to the possibility of opening a refuge for battered women in a Black community. (There was no refuge in Boston at that time.) We also decided around that time to become an independent collective since we had serious disagreements with NBFO's bourgeois-feminist stance and their lack of a clear political focus.

We also were contacted at that time by socialist feminists, with whom we had worked on abortion rights activities, who wanted to encourage us to attend the National Socialist Feminist Conference in Yellow Springs. One of our members did attend and despite the narrowness of the ideology that was promoted at that particular conference, we became more aware of the need for us to understand our own economic situation and to make our own economic analysis.

In the fall, when some members returned, we experienced several months of comparative inactivity and internal disagreements which were first conceptualized as a Lesbian-straight split but which were also the result of class and political differences. During the summer those of us who were still meeting had determined the need to do political work and to move beyond consciousness-raising and serving exclusively as an emotional support group. At the beginning of 1976, when some of the women who had not wanted to do political work and who also had voiced disagreements stopped attending of their own accord, we again looked for a focus. We decided at that time, with the addition of new members, to become a study group. We had always shared our reading with each other, and some of us had written papers on Black feminism for group discussion a few months before this decision was made. We began functioning as a study group and also began discussing the possibility of starting a Black feminist publication. We had a retreat in the late spring which provided a time for both political discussion and working out interpersonal issues. Currently we are planning to gather together a collection of Black feminist writing. We feel that it is absolutely essential to demonstrate the reality of our politics to other Black women and believe that we can do this through writing and distributing our work. The fact that individual Black feminists are living in isolation all over the country, that our own numbers are small, and that we have some skills in writing, printing, and publishing makes us want to carry out these kinds of projects as a means of organizing Black feminists as we continue to do political work in coalition with other groups.

4. Black Feminist Issues and Projects

During our time together we have identified and worked on many issues of particular relevance to Black women. The inclusiveness of our politics makes us concerned with any situation that impinges upon the lives of women, Third World and working people. We are of course particularly committed to working on those struggles in which race, sex, and class are simultaneous factors in oppression. We might, for example, become involved in workplace organizing at a factory that employs Third World women or picket a hospital that is cutting back on already inadequate health care to a Third World community, or set up a rape crisis center in a Black neighborhood. Organizing around welfare and daycare concerns might also be a focus. The work to be done and the countless issues that this work represents merely reflect the pervasiveness of our oppression.

Issues and projects that collective members have already worked on are sterilization abuse, abortion rights, battered women, rape and health care. We have also done many workshops and educationals on Black feminism on college campuses, at women's conferences, and most recently for high school women.

One issue that is of major concern to us and that we have begun to publicly address is racism in the white women's movement. As Black feminists we are made constantly and painfully aware of how little effort white women have made to understand and combat their racism, which requires among other things that they have a more than superficial comprehension of race, color, and Black history and culture. Eliminating racism in the white women's movement is by definition work for white women to do, but we will continue to speak to and demand accountability on this issue.

In the practice of our politics we do not believe that the end always justifies the means. Many reactionary and destructive acts have been done in the name of achieving "correct" political goals. As feminists we do not want to mess over people in the name of politics. We believe in collective process and a nonhierarchical distribution of power within our own group and in our vision of a revolutionary society. We are committed to a continual examination of our politics as they develop through criticism and self-criticism as an essential aspect of our practice. In her introduction to *Sisterhood Is Powerful,* Robin Morgan writes:

> I haven't the faintest notion what possible revolutionary role white heterosexual men could fulfill, since they are the very embodiment of reactionary-vested-interest-power.

As Black feminists and Lesbians we know that we have a very definite revolutionary task to perform

and we are ready for the lifetime of work and struggle before us.

NOTES

1. Michele Wallace, "A Black Feminist's Search for Sisterhood," *The Village Voice,* 28 July 1975, pp. 6–7.
2. Mumininas of Committee for Unified Newark, *Mwanamke Mwananchi (The Nationalist Woman),* Newark, N.J., © 1971, pp. 4–5.

Asian Pacific American Women and Feminism (1981)

Mitsuye Yamada

Mitsuye Yamada is a writer and former professor of English at Cypress College where she worked from 1968 to 1989. A celebrated poet, she wrote her first book, *Camp Notes and Other Poems,* during and just after her internment at Camp Mindoka in Idaho during World War II, but it remained unpublished until 1976. Her most recent book is *Three Asian American Writers Speak Out on Feminism* with Nellie Wong and Merle Wu.

Most of the Asian Pacific American women I know agree that we need to make ourselves more visible by speaking out on the condition of our sex and race and on certain political issues which concern us. Some of us feel that visibility through the feminist perspective is the only logical step for us. However, this path is fraught with problems which we are unable to solve among us, because in order to do so, we need the help and cooperation of the white feminist leaders, the women who coordinate programs, direct women's buildings, and edit women's publications throughout the country. Women's organizations tell us they would like to have us "join" them and give them "input." These are the better ones; at least they know we exist and feel we might possibly have something to say of interest to them, but every time I read or speak to a group of people about the condition of my life as an Asian Pacific woman, it is as if I had never spoken before, as if I were speaking

to a brand new audience of people who had never known an Asian Pacific woman who is other than the passive, sweet, etc., stereotype of the "Oriental" woman.

When Third World women are asked to speak representing our racial or ethnic group, we are expected to move, charm or entertain, but not to educate in ways that are threatening to our audiences. We speak to audiences that sift out those parts of our speech (if what we say does not fit the image they have of us), come up to shake our hands with "That was lovely my dear, just lovely," and go home with the same mind set they come in with. No matter what we say or do, the stereotype still hangs on. I am weary of starting from scratch each time I speak or write, as if there were no history behind us, of hearing that among the women of color, Asian women are the least political, or the least oppressed, or the most polite. It is too bad not many people remember that one of the two persons in Seattle who stood up to contest the constitutionality of the Evacuation Order in 1942 was a young Japanese American woman. As individuals and in groups, we Asian Pacific women have been (more intensively than ever in the past few years) active in community affairs and speaking and writing about our activities. From the highly political writings published in *Asian Women* in 1971 (incisive and trenchant articles, poems, and articles), to more recent voices from the Basement Workshop in New York to

Unbound Feet in San Francisco, as well as those Asian Pacific women showcased at the Asian Pacific Women's Conferences in New York, Hawaii, and California this year, these all tell us we *have* been active and vocal. And yet, we continue to hear, "Asian women are of course traditionally not attuned to being political," as if most other women are; or that Asian women are too happily bound to their traditional roles as mothers and wives, as if the same cannot be said of a great number of white American women among us.

When I read in *Plexus* recently that at a Workshop for Third World women in San Francisco, Cherríe Moraga exploded with "What each of us needs to do about what we don't know is to go look for it," I felt like standing up and cheering her. She was speaking at the Women's Building to a group of white sisters who were saying, in essence, "it is *your* responsibility as Third World women to teach *us*." If the majority culture know so little about us, it must be *our* problem, they seem to be telling us; the burden of teaching is on us. I do not want to be unfair; I know individual women and some women's groups that have taken on the responsibility of teaching themselves through reaching out to women of color, but such gestures by the majority of women's groups are still tentatively made because of the sometimes touchy reaction of women who are always being asked to be "tokens" at readings and workshops.

Earlier this year, when a group of Asian Pacific American women gathered together in San Francisco poet Nellie Wong's home to talk about feminism, I was struck by our general agreement on the subject of feminism *as an ideal*. We all believed in equality for women. We agreed that it is important for each of us to know what it means to be a woman in our society, to know the historical and psychological forces that have shaped and are shaping our thoughts which in turn determine the directions of our lives. We agreed that feminism means a commitment to making changes in our own lives and a conviction that as women we have the equipment to do so. One by one, as we sat around the table and talked (we women of all ages ranging from our early twenties to the mid-fifties, single and married, mothers and lovers, straight women and lesbians), we knew what it was we wanted out of feminism, and what it was supposed to mean to us. For women to achieve equality in our society, we

agreed, we must continue to work for a common goal.

But there was a feeling of disappointment in that living room toward the women's movement as it stands today. One young woman said she had made an effort to join some women's groups with high expectations but came away disillusioned because these groups were not receptive to the issues that were important to her as an Asian woman. Women in these groups, were, she said "into pushing their own issues" and were no different from the other organizations that imposed opinions and goals on their members rather than having them shaped by the needs of the members in the organizations. Some of the other women present said that they felt the women's organizations with feminist goals are still "a middle-class women's thing." This pervasive feeling of mistrust toward the women in the movement is fairly representative of a large group of women who live in the psychological place we now call Asian Pacific America. A movement that fights sexism in the social structure must deal with racism, and we had hoped the leaders in the women's movement would be able to see the parallels in the lives of the women of color and themselves, and would "join" *us* in our struggle and give *us* "input."

It should not be difficult to see that Asian Pacific women need to affirm our own culture while working within it to change it. Many of the leaders in the women's organizations today had moved naturally from the civil rights politics of the 60s to sexual politics, while very few of the Asian Pacific women who were involved in radical politics during the same period have emerged as leaders in these same women's organizations. Instead they have become active in groups promoting ethnic identity, most notably ethnic studies in universities, ethnic theater groups, or ethnic community agencies. This doesn't mean that we have placed our loyalties on the side of ethnicity over womanhood. The two are not at war with one another; we shouldn't have to sign a "loyalty oath" favoring one over the other. However, women of color are often made to feel that we must make a choice between the two.

If I have more recently put my energies into the Pacific Asian American Center (a job center for Asians established in 1975, the only one of its kind in Orange County, California) and the Asian Pacific Women's Conferences (the first of its kind in our history), it is because the needs in these areas are so great. I have thought of myself as a feminist first, but my ethnicity cannot be separated from my feminism.

Through the women's movement, I have come to truly appreciate the meaning of my mother's life and the lives of immigrant women like her. My mother, at nineteen years of age, uprooted from her large extended family, was brought to this country to bear and raise four children alone. Once here, she found that her new husband who had been here as a student for several years prior to their marriage was a bachelor-at-heart and had no intention of changing his lifestyle. Stripped of the protection and support of her family, she found the responsibilities of raising us alone in a strange country almost intolerable during those early years. I thought for many years that my mother did not love us because she often spoke of suicide as an easy way out of her miseries. I know now that for her to have survived "just for the sake" of her children took great strength and determination.

If I digress, it is because I, a second generation Asian American woman who grew up believing in the American Dream, have come to know who I am through understanding the nature of my mother's experience; I have come to see connections in our lives as well as the lives of many women like us, and through her I have become more sensitive to the needs of Third World women throughout the world. We need not repeat our past histories; my daughters and I need not merely survive with strength and determination. We can, through collective struggle, live fuller, and richer lives. My politics as a woman are deeply rooted in my immigrant parent's and my own past.

Not long ago at one of my readings a woman in the audience said she was deeply moved by my "beautifully tragic but not bitter camp poems which were apparently written long ago,"[1] but she was distressed to hear my poem "To A Lady." "Why are you, at this late date, so angry, and why are you taking it so personally?" she said. "We need to look to the future and stop wallowing in the past so much." I responded that this poem *is not* at all about the past. I am talking about what is happening to us right now, about our nonsupport of each other, about our noncaring about each other, about not seeing connections between racism and sexism in our lives. As a child of immigrant parents, as a woman of color in a white society and as a woman in a patriarchical society, what is personal to me *is* political.

These are the connections we expected our white sisters to see. It should not be too difficult, we feel, for them to see why being a feminist activist is more dangerous for women of color. They should be able to see that political views held by women of color are often misconstrued as being personal rather than ideological. Views critical of the system held by a person in an "out group" are often seen as expressions of personal angers against the dominant society. (If they hate it so much here, why don't they go back?) Many lesbians I know have felt the same kind of frustration when they supported unpopular causes regarded by their critics as vindictive expressions to "get back" at the patriarchical system. They too know the disappointments of having their intentions misinterpreted.

In the 1960s when my family and I belonged to a neighborhood church, I became active in promoting the Fair Housing Bill, and one of my church friends said to me, "Why are you doing this to us? Haven't you and your family been happy with us in our church? Haven't we treated you well?" I knew then that I was not really part of the church at all in the eyes of this person, but only a guest who was being told I should have the good manners to behave like one.

Remembering the blatant acts of selective racism in the past three decades in our country, our white sisters should be able to see how tenuous our position in this country is. Many of us are now third and fourth generation Americans, but this makes no difference; periodic conflicts involving Third World peoples can abruptly change white Americans' attitudes towards us. This was clearly demonstrated in 1941 to the Japanese Americans who were in hot pursuit of the great American Dream, who went around saying, "Of course I don't eat Japanese food, I'm an American." We found our status as true-blooded Americans was only an illusion in 1942 when we were singled out to be imprisoned for the duration of the war by our own government. The recent outcry against Iranians because of the holding of American hostages tells me that the situation has not changed since 1941. When I hear my students say "We're not against the Iranians here who are minding their own business. We're just against those ungrateful ones who overstep our hospitality by demonstrating and badmouthing our government," I know they speak about me.

Asian Pacific American women will not speak out to say what we have on our minds until we feel secure within ourselves that this is our home too and until our white sisters indicate by their actions that they want to join us in our struggle because it is theirs also. This means a commitment to a truly communal education where we learn from each other because we want to learn from each other, the kind of commitment we do not seem to have at the present time. I am still hopeful that the women of color in our country will be the link to Third World women throughout the world, and that we can help each other broaden our visions.

NOTE

1. *Camp Notes and Other Poems* by Mitsuye Yamada (San Francisco: Shameless Hussy Press) 1976.

S E V E N

Multiracial Feminism
Recasting the Chronology of Second Wave Feminism (2002)
Becky Thompson

Becky Thompson is the author of several books, most recently *When the Center is on Fire: Passionate Social Theory for Our Times* (co-author, Diane Harriford) and *A Promise and A Way of Life: White Antiracist Activism*. She co-edited *Fingernails Across the Chalkboard: Poetry and Prose on HIV from the Black Diaspora*, an anthology adapted into a play that premiered in New York City in 2008. She teaches sociology and African American Studies at Simmons College in Boston.

In the last several years, a number of histories have been published that chronicle the emergence and contributions of Second Wave feminism.[1] Although initially eager to read and teach from these histories, I have found myself increasingly concerned about the extent to which they provide a version of Second Wave history that Chela Sandoval refers to as "hegemonic feminism."[2] This feminism is white led, marginalizes the activism and world views of women of color, focuses mainly on the United States, and treats sexism as the ultimate oppression. Hegemonic feminism deemphasizes or ignores a class and race analysis, generally sees equality with men as the goal of feminism, and has an individual rights-based, rather than justice-based vision for social change.

Although rarely named as hegemonic feminism, this history typically resorts to an old litany of the women's movement that includes three or four branches of feminism: liberal, socialist, radical, and sometimes cultural feminism.[3] The most significant problem with this litany is that it does not recognize the centrality of the feminism of women of color in Second Wave history. Missing too, from normative accounts is the story of white antiracist feminism which, from its emergence, has been intertwined with, and fueled by the development of, feminism among women of color.[4]

Telling the history of Second Wave feminism from the point of view of women of color and white antiracist women illuminates the rise of multiracial feminism—the liberation movement spearheaded by women of color in the United States in the 1970s that was characterized by its international perspective, its attention to interlocking oppressions, and its support of coalition politics.[5] Bernice Johnson Reagon's naming of "coalition politics"; Patricia Hill Collins's understanding of women of color as "outsiders within"; Barbara Smith's concept of "the simultaneity of oppressions"; Cherríe Moraga and Gloria Anzaldúa's "theory in the flesh"; Chandra Talpade Mohanty's critique of "imperialist feminism"; Paula Gunn Allen's "red roots of white feminism"; Adrienne Rich's "politics of location"; and Patricia Williams's analysis of "spirit murder" are all theoretical guideposts for multiracial feminism.[6] Tracing the rise of multiracial feminism raises many questions about common assumptions made in normative versions of Second Wave history. Constructing

a multiracial feminist movement time line and jux-
taposing it with the normative time line reveals
competing visions of what constitutes liberation
and illuminates schisms in feminist consciousness
that are still with us today.

The Rise of Multiracial Feminism

Normative accounts of the Second Wave feminist
movement often reach back to the publication of
Betty Friedan's *The Feminine Mystique* in 1963, the
founding of the National Organization for Women in
1966, and the emergence of women's consciousness-
raising (CR) groups in the late 1960s. All signaled a
rising number of white, middle-class women unwilling to be treated like second-class citizens in the
boardroom, in education, or in bed. Many of the
early protests waged by this sector of the feminist
movement picked up on the courage and forth-
rightness of 1960s' struggles—a willingness to stop
traffic, break existing laws to provide safe and accessible abortions, and contradict the older generation. For
younger women, the leadership women had demonstrated in 1960s' activism belied the sex roles that had
traditionally defined domestic, economic, and political relations and opened new possibilities for action.

This version of the origins of Second Wave history is not sufficient in telling the story of multiracial feminism. Although there were Black women
involved with NOW from the outset and Black and
Latina women who participated in CR groups, the
feminist work of women of color also extended beyond women-only spaces. In fact, during the 1970s,
women of color were involved on three fronts—
working with white-dominated feminist groups;
forming women's caucuses in existing mixed-
gender organizations; and developing autonomous
Black, Latina, Native American, and Asian feminist
organizations.[7]

This three-pronged approach contrasts sharply
with the common notion that women of color feminists emerged in reaction to (and therefore later
than) white feminism. In her critique of "model
making" in Second Wave historiography, which has
"all but ignored the feminist activism of women of
color," Benita Roth "challenges the idea that Black
feminist organizing was a later variant of so-called
mainstream white feminism."[8] Roth's assertion—
that the timing of Black feminist organizing is

roughly equivalent to the timing of white feminist
activism—is true about feminist activism by Latinas,
Native Americans, and Asian Americans as well.

One of the earliest feminist organizations of the
Second Wave was a Chicana group—Hijas de
Cuauhtemoc (1971)—named after a Mexican women's
underground newspaper that was published during
the 1910 Mexican Revolution. Chicanas who formed
this *femenista* group and published a newspaper
named after the early-twentieth-century Mexican
women's revolutionary group, were initially involved in the United Mexican American Student Organization which was part of the Chicano/a student
movement.[9] Many of the founders of Hijas de
Cuauhtemoc were later involved in launching the
first national Chicana studies journal, *Encuentro
Feminil.*

An early Asian American women's group,
Asian Sisters, focused on drug abuse intervention
for young women in Los Angeles. It emerged in
1971 out of the Asian American Political Alliance, a
broad-based, grassroots organization largely fueled
by the consciousness of first-generation Asian
American college students. Networking between
Asian American and other women during this period
also included participation by a contingent of 150
Third World and white women from North America
at the historic Vancouver Indochinese Women's
Conference (1971) to work with Indochinese women
against U.S. imperialism.[10] Asian American women
provided services for battered women, worked as
advocates for refugees and recent immigrants, produced events spotlighting Asian women's cultural
and political diversity, and organized with other
women of color.[11]

The best-known Native American women's
organization of the 1970s was Women of All Red
Nations (WARN). WARN was initiated in 1974 by
women, many of whom were also members of the
American Indian Movement, which was founded in
1968 by Dennis Banks, George Mitchell, and Mary
Jane Wilson, an Anishinabe activist.[12] WARN's activism included fighting sterilization in public
health service hospitals, suing the U.S. government
for attempts to sell Pine Ridge water in South
Dakota to corporations, and networking with indigenous people in Guatemala and Nicaragua.[13]
WARN reflected a whole generation of Native
American women activists who had been leaders in
the takeover of Wounded Knee in South Dakota in

1973, on the Pine Ridge reservation (1973–76), and elsewhere. WARN, like Asian Sisters and Hijas de Cuauhtemoc, grew out of—and often worked with—mixed-gender nationalist organizations.

The autonomous feminist organizations that Black, Latina, Asian, and Native American women were forming during the early 1970s drew on nationalist traditions through their recognition of the need for people of color–led, independent organizations.[14] At the same time, unlike earlier nationalist organizations that included women and men, these were organizations specifically for women.

Among Black women, one early Black feminist organization was the Third World Women's Alliance which emerged in 1968 out of the Student Nonviolent Coordinating Committee (SNCC) chapters on the East Coast and focused on racism, sexism, and imperialism.[15] The foremost autonomous feminist organization of the early 1970s was the National Black Feminist Organization (NBFO). Founded in 1973 by Florynce Kennedy, Margaret Sloan, and Doris Wright, it included many other well-known Black women including Faith Ringgold, Michelle Wallace, Alice Walker, and Barbara Smith. According to Deborah Gray White, NBFO "more than any organization in the century . . . launched a frontal assault on sexism and racism."[16] Its first conference in New York was attended by 400 women from a range of class backgrounds.

Although the NBFO was a short-lived organization nationally (1973–75), chapters in major cities remained together for years, including one in Chicago that survived until 1981. The contents of the CR sessions were decidedly Black women's issues—stereotypes of Black women in the media, discrimination in the workplace, myths about Black women as matriarchs, Black women's beauty, and self-esteem.[17] The NBFO also helped to inspire the founding of the Combahee River Collective in 1974, a Boston-based organization named after a river in South Carolina where Harriet Tubman led an insurgent action that freed 750 slaves. The Combahee River Collective not only led the way for crucial antiracist activism in Boston through the decade, but it also provided a blueprint for Black feminism that still stands a quarter of a century later.[18] From Combahee member Barbara Smith came a definition of feminism so expansive that it remains a model today. Smith writes that "feminism is the political theory and practice to free *all* women: women

of color, working-class women, poor women, physically challenged women, lesbians, old women, as well as white economically privileged heterosexual women. Anything less than this is not feminism, but merely female self-aggrandizement."[19]

These and other groups in the early and mid-1970s provided the foundation for the most far-reaching and expansive organizing by women of color in U.S. history. These organizations also fueled a veritable explosion of writing by women of color, including Toni Cade's pioneering *The Black Woman: An Anthology* in 1970, Maxine Hong Kingston's *The Woman Warrior* in 1977, and in 1981 and 1983, respectively, the foundational *This Bridge Called My Back: Writings by Radical Women of Color* and *Home Girls: A Black Feminist Anthology.*[20] While chronicling the dynamism and complexity of a multidimensional vision for women of color, these books also traced for white women what is required to be allies to women of color.

By the late 1970s, the progress made possible by autonomous and independent Asian, Latina, and Black feminist organizations opened a space for women of color to work in coalition across organizations with each other. During this period, two cohorts of white women became involved in multiracial feminism. One group had, in the late 1960s and early 1970s, chosen to work in anti-imperialist, antiracist militant organizations in connection with Black Power groups—the Black Panther Party, the Black Liberation Army—and other solidarity and nationalist organizations associated with the American Indian, Puerto Rican Independence, and Chicano Movements of the late 1960s and early 1970s. These women chose to work with these solidarity organizations rather than work in overwhelmingly white feminist contexts. None of the white antiracist feminists I interviewed (for a social history of antiracism in the United States) who were politically active during the civil rights and Black Power movements had an interest in organizations that had a single focus on gender or that did not have antiracism at the center of their agendas.

Militant women of color and white women took stands against white supremacy and imperialism (both internal and external colonialism); envisioned revolution as a necessary outcome of political struggle; and saw armed propaganda (armed attacks against corporate and military targets along with public education about state crime) as a possible tactic in revolutionary struggle. Although some of these women avoided or rejected the term "feminist" because of its association with hegemonic feminism, these women still confronted sexism both within solidarity and nationalist organizations and within their own communities. In her autobiographical account of her late-1960s' politics, Black liberation movement leader Assata Shakur writes: "To me, the revolutionary struggle of Black people had to be against racism, classism, imperialism and sexism for real freedom under a socialist government."[21] During this period, Angela Davis was also linking anticapitalist struggle with the fight against race and gender oppression.[22] Similarly, white militant activist Marilyn Buck, who was among the first women to confront Students for a Democratic Society (SDS) around issues of sexism, also spoke up for women's rights as an ally of the Black Liberation Army.

Rarely, however, have their stories—and those of other militant antiracist women—been considered part of the Second Wave history. In her critique of this dominant narrative, historian Nancy MacLean writes: "Recent accounts of the rise of modern feminism depart little from the story line first advanced two decades ago and since enshrined as orthodoxy. That story stars white middle-class women triangulated between the pulls of liberal, radical/cultural, and socialist feminism. Working-class women and women of color assume walk-on parts late in the plot, after tendencies and allegiances are already in place. The problem with this script is not simply that it has grown stale from repeated retelling. It is not accurate. . . ."[23]

The omission of militant white women and women of color from Second Wave history partly reflects a common notion that the women's movement followed and drew upon the early civil rights movement and the New Left, a trajectory that skips entirely the profound impact that the Black Power movement had on many women's activism. Omitting militant women activists from historical reference also reflects a number of ideological assumptions made during the late 1960s and early 1970s—that "real" feminists were those who worked primarily or exclusively with other women; that "women's ways of knowing" were more collaborative, less hierarchical, and more peace loving than men's; and that women's liberation would come from women's deepening understanding that "sisterhood is powerful."

These politics were upheld by both liberal and radical white feminists. These politics did not, however, sit well with many militant women of color and white women who refused to consider sexism the primary, or most destructive, oppression and recognized the limits of gaining equality in a system that, as Malcolm X had explained, was already on fire. The women of color and white militant women who supported a race, class, and gender analysis in the late 1960s and 1970s often found themselves trying to explain their politics in mixed-gender settings (at home, at work, and in their activism), sometimes alienated from the men (and some women) who did not get it, while simultaneously alienated from white feminists whose politics they considered narrow at best and frivolous at worst.

By the late 1970s, the militant women who wanted little to do with white feminism of the late 1960s and 1970s became deeply involved in multiracial feminism. By that point, the decade of organizing among women of color in autonomous Black, Latina, and Asian feminist organizations led militant antiracist white women to immerse themselves in multiracial feminism. Meanwhile, a younger cohort of white women, who were first politicized in the late 1970s, saw feminism from a whole different vantage point than did the older, white, antiracist women. For the younger group, exposure to multiracial feminism led by women of color meant an early lesson that race, class, and gender were inextricably linked. They also gained vital experience in multiple organizations—battered women's shelters, conferences, and health organizations—where women were, with much struggle, attempting to uphold this politic.[24]

From this organizing came the emergence of a small but important group of white women determined to understand how white privilege had historically blocked cross-race alliances among women, and what they, as white women, needed to do to work closely with women of color. Not surprisingly, Jewish women and lesbians often led the way among white women in articulating a politic that accounted for white women's position as both oppressed and oppressor—as both women and white.[25] Both groups knew what it meant to be marginalized from a women's movement that was, nevertheless, still homophobic and Christian biased. Both groups knew that "there is no place like home"—among other Jews and/or lesbians—and the limits of that home if for

Jews it was male dominated or if for lesbians it was exclusively white. The paradoxes of "home" for these groups paralleled many of the situations experienced by women of color who, over and over again, found themselves to be the bridges that everyone assumed would be on their backs.

As the straight Black women interacted with the Black lesbians, the first-generation Chinese women talked with the Native American activists, and the Latina women talked with the Black and white women about the walls that go up when people cannot speak Spanish, white women attempting to understand race knew they had a lot of listening to do. They also had a lot of truth telling to reckon with, and a lot of networking to do, among other white women and with women of color as well.

Radicals, Heydays, and Hot Spots

The story of Second Wave feminism, if told from the vantage point of multiracial feminism, also encourages us to rethink key assumptions about periodization. Among these assumptions is the notion that the 1960s and early 1970s were the height of the radical feminist movement. For example, in her foreword to Alice Echols's *Daring to Be Bad: Radical Feminism in America, 1967–1975,* Ellen Willis asserts that by the mid-1970s, the best of feminism had already occurred.[26] In her history of the women's liberation movement, Barbara Ryan writes that the unity among women evident in the early 1970s declined dramatically by the late 1970s as a consequence of divisions within the movement.[27]

Looking at the history of feminism from the point of view of women of color and antiracist white women suggests quite a different picture. The fact that white women connected with the Black Power movement could rarely find workable space in the early feminist movement crystalized for many of them with the 1971 rebellion at Attica Prison in New York State in response to human rights abuses.[28] For antiracist activist Naomi Jaffe, who was a member of SDS, the Weather Underground, and WITCH (Women's International Terrorist Conspiracy from Hell), attempts to be part of both early Second Wave feminism and an antiracist struggle were untenable. The Attica rebellion, which resulted in the massacre by state officials of thirty-one prisoners and nine guards, pushed Jaffe to decide between the two. She vividly remembers

white feminists arguing that there was no room for remorse for the "male chauvinists" who had died at Attica. Jaffe disagreed vehemently, arguing that if white feminists could not understand Attica as a feminist issue, then she was not a feminist. At the time, Black activist and lawyer Florynce Kennedy had said: "We do not support Attica. We ARE Attica. We are Attica or we are nothing." Jaffe claimed: "That about summed up my feelings on the subject."[29] With this consciousness, and her increasing awareness of the violence of the state against Black Panthers, antiwar protesters, and liberation struggles around the world. Jaffe continued to work with the Weather Underground. She went underground from 1970 to 1978.

Naomi Jaffe, like other white women working with the Black Power movement, were turned off by a feminism that they considered both bourgeois and reductionist. They stepped out of what antiracist historian Sherna Berger Gluck has termed "the master historical narrative," and they have been written out of it by historians who have relied upon a telling of Second Wave feminism that focused solely on gender oppression. Although the late 1960s and early 1970s might have been the "heyday" for white "radical" feminists in CR groups, from the perspective of white antiracists, the early 1970s were a low point of feminism—a time when many women who were committed to an antiracist analysis had to put their feminism on the back burner in order to work with women and men of color and against racism.

Coinciding with the frequent assumption that 1969 to 1974 was the height of "radical feminism," many feminist historians consider 1972 to 1982 as the period of mass mobilization and 1983 to 1991 as a period of feminist abeyance.[30] Ironically, the years that sociologists Verta Taylor and Nancy Whittier consider the period of mass mobilization for feminists (1972–82) are the years that Chela Sandoval identifies as the period when "ideological differences divided and helped to dissipate the movement from within."[31] For antiracist women (both white and of color), the best days of feminism were yet to come when, as Barbara Smith explains, "Those issues that had divided many of the movement's constituencies—such as racism, anti-Semitism, ableism, ageism, and classism—were put on the table."[32]

Ironically, the very period that white feminist historians typically treat as a period of decline within the movement is the period of mass mobilization among antiracist women—both straight and lesbian. The very year that Taylor and Whittier consider the end of mass mobilization because the ERA failed to be ratified, 1982, is the year that Gluck rightfully cites as the beginning of a feminism far more expansive than had previously existed. She writes: "By 1982, on the heels of difficult political struggle waged by activist scholars of color, ground-breaking essays and anthologies by and about women of color opened a new chapter in U.S. feminism. The future of the women's movement in the U.S. was reshaped irrevocably by the introduction of the expansive notion of feminisms."[33] Angela Davis concurs, citing 1981, with the publication of *This Bridge Called My Back,* as the year when women of color had developed as a "new political subject," due to substantial work done in multiple arenas.[34]

In fact, periodization of the women's movement from the point of view of multiracial feminism would treat the late 1960s and early 1970s as its origin and the mid-1970s, 1980s, and 1990s as a height. A time line of that period shows a flourishing multiracial feminist movement. In 1977, the Combahee River Collective Statement was first published; in 1979, *Conditions: Five,* the Black women's issue, was published, the First National Third World Lesbian Conference was held, and Assata Shakur escaped from prison in New Jersey with the help of prison activists.[35] In 1981, Byllye Avery founded the National Black Women's Health Project in Atlanta; Bernice Johnson Reagon gave her now-classic speech on coalition politics at the West Coast Women's Music Festival in Yosemite; and the National Women's Studies Association held its first conference to deal with racism as a central theme, in Storrs, Connecticut, where there were multiple animated interventions against racism and anti-Semitism in the women's movement and from which emerged Adrienne Rich's exquisite essay, "Disobedience and Women's Studies."[36] Then, 1984 was the year of the New York Women against Rape Conference, a multiracial, multiethnic conference that confronted multiple challenges facing women organizing against violence against women—by partners, police, social service agencies, and poverty. In 1985, the United Nations Decade for Women conference in Nairobi, Kenya, took place; that same year, Wilma Mankiller was

named the first principal chief of the Cherokee Nation. In 1986, the National Women's Studies Association conference was held at Spelman College. The next year, 1987, the Supreme Court ruled that the Immigration and Naturalization Service must interpret the 1980s' Refugee Act more broadly to recognize refugees from Central America, a ruling that reflected the work on the part of thousands of activists, many of whom were feminists, to end U.S. intervention in Central America.

In 1991, Elsa Barkley Brown, Barbara Ransby, and Deborah King launched the campaign called African American Women in Defense of Ourselves, within minutes of Anita Hill's testimony regarding the nomination of Clarence Thomas to the Supreme Court. Their organizing included an advertisement in the *New York Times* and six Black newspapers which included the names of 1,603 Black women. The 1982 defeat of the ERA did not signal a period of abeyance for multiracial feminism. In fact, multiracial feminism flourished in the 1980s, despite the country's turn to the Right.

Understanding Second Wave feminism from the vantage point of the Black Power movement and multiracial feminism also shows the limit of the frequent assignment of the term "radical" only to the white antipatriarchal feminists of the late 1960s and early 1970s. Many feminist historians link the development of radical feminism to the creation of several antipatriarchy organizations— the Redstockings, Radicalesbians, WITCH, and other CR groups. How the term "radical" is used by feminist historians does not square, however, with how women of color and white antiracists used that term from the 1960s through the 1980s. What does it mean when feminist historians apply the term "radical" to white, antipatriarchy women but not to antiracist white women and women of color (including Angela Davis, Kathleen Cleaver, Marilyn Buck, Anna Mae Aquash, Susan Saxe, Vicki Gabriner, and Laura Whitehorn) of the same era whose "radicalism" included attention to race, gender, and imperialism and a belief that revolution might require literally laying their lives on the line? These radical women include political prisoners— Black, Puerto Rican, and white—some of whom are still in prison for their antiracist activism in the 1960s and 1970s. Many of these women openly identify as feminists and/or lesbians but are rarely included in histories of Second Wave feminism.

What does it mean when the term "radical" is only assigned to white, antipatriarchy women when the subtitle to Cherríe Moraga and Gloria Anzaldúa's foundational book, *This Bridge Called My Back*, was "Writings by *Radical* Women of Color"?[37] To my mind, a nuanced and accurate telling of Second Wave feminism is one that shows why and how the term "radical" was itself contested. Recognizing that there were different groups who used the term "radical" does not mean that we then need an overarching definition of "radical feminism" that includes all these approaches. It does mean understanding that white feminists of the "daring to be bad period" (from 1967 to 1975) do not have exclusive rights to the term.[38] An expansive history would emphasize that Second Wave feminism drew on the civil rights movement, the New Left, *and* the Black Power movement which, together, helped to produce three groups of "radical" women.

Principles of a Movement

Although analysis of the feminist movement that accounts for competing views of what it means to be "radical" is a step forward in developing a complex understanding of Second Wave history, what most interests me about comparing normative feminist history with multiracial feminism are the contestations in philosophy embedded in these coexisting frameworks. Both popular and scholarly interpretations of Second Wave feminism typically link two well-known principles to the movement— "Sisterhood Is Powerful" and the "Personal Is Political." From the point of view of multiracial feminism, both principles are a good start but, in themselves, are not enough.

Conversations and struggles between women of color and white women encouraged white women to think about the limits of the popular feminist slogan "Sisterhood Is Powerful." There were many reasons why the editors of *This Bridge Called My Back* titled one of the sections of the book, "And When You Leave, Take Your Pictures with You: Racism in the Women's Movement." Lorraine Bethel's poem, "What Chou Mean *We*, White Girl? or the Cullud Lesbian Feminist Declaration of Independence" ("Dedicated to the proposition that all women are not equal, i.e., identical/ly oppressed"), clarifies that "we" between white and Black is provisional, at best.[39] Anthropologist Wendy Rose's critique of "white shamanism"—white people's attempt to

become native in order to grow spiritually—applies as well to white feminists who treat Native American women as innately spiritual, as automatically their spiritual mothers.[40]

Cross-racial struggle made clear the work that white women needed to do in order for cross-racial sisterhood to *really* be powerful. Among the directives were the following: Don't expect women of color to be your educators, to do all the bridge work. White women need to be the bridge—a lot of the time. Do not lump African American, Latina, Asian American, and Native American women into one category. History, culture, imperialism, language, class, region, and sexuality make the concept of a monolithic "women of color" indefensible. Listen to women of color's anger. It is informed by centuries of struggle, erasure, and experience. White women, look to your own history for signs of heresy and rebellion. Do not take on the histories of Black, Latina, or American Indian women as your own. They are not and never were yours.

A second principle associated with liberal and radical feminism is captured in the slogan "The Personal Is Political," first used by civil rights and New Left activists and then articulated with more depth and consistency by feminist activists. The idea behind the slogan is that many issues that historically have been deemed "personal"—abortion, battery, unemployment, birth, death, and illness—are actually deeply political issues.

Multiracial feminism requires women to add another level of awareness—to stretch the adage from "The Personal Is Political" to, in the words of antiracist activist Anne Braden, "The Personal Is Political and the Political Is Personal."[41] Many issues that have been relegated to the private sphere are, in fact, deeply political. At the same time, many political issues need to be personally committed to—whether you have been victimized by those issues or not. In other words, you don't have to be part of a subordinated group to know an injustice is wrong and to stand against it. White women need not be victims of racism to recognize it is wrong and stand up against it. Unless that is done, white women will never understand how they support racism. If the only issues that feminists deem political are those they have experienced personally, their frame of reference is destined to be narrowly defined by their own lived experience.

The increasing number of antiracist white women who moved into mixed-gender, multi-issue organizations in the 1980s and 1990s after having helped to build women's cultural institutions in the 1970s and 1980s may be one of the best examples of an attempt to uphold this politic. Mab Segrest, perhaps the most prolific writer among lesbian antiracist organizers, provides the quintessential example of this transition in her move from working on the lesbian feminist journal, *Feminary,* in the late 1970s and early 1980s, to becoming the director of North Carolinians against Racist and Religious Violence in the 1980s. A self-reflective writer, Segrest herself notes this transition in the preface to her first book, *My Mama's Dead Squirrel: Lesbian Essays on Southern Culture.* Segrest writes: "In the first [essay] I wrote, `I believe that the oppression of women is the first oppression.' Now I am not so sure. Later I wrote, `Relationships between women matter to me more than anything else in my life.' Now what matters most is more abstract and totally specific: the closest word to it, justice. . . . During the early years the writing comes primarily out of work with other lesbians; later on, from work where I am the only lesbian."[42] The book opens with autobiographical essays about her family and women's writing, but the last essays chronicle the beginning of her organizing against the Klan—essays that became the backdrop of her second book, *Memoir of a Race Traitor.* In Segrest's view, by 1983, her work in building lesbian culture—through editing *Feminary* and her own writing—"no longer seemed enough, it seemed too literary." Segrest found herself both "inspired by and frustrated with the lesbian feminist movement." Segrest recalls that she

> had sat in many rooms and participated in many conversations between lesbians about painful differences in race and class, about anti-Semitism and ageism and ablebodiedism. They had been hard discussions, but they had given me some glimpse of the possibility of spinning a wider lesbian movement, a women's movement that truly incorporates diversity as its strength. But in all those discussions, difficult as they were, we had never been out to kill each other. In the faces of Klan and Nazi men—and women—in North Carolina I saw people who would kill us all. I felt I needed to shift from perfecting consciousness to putting consciousness to the continual test of action.

I wanted to answer a question that had resonated through the lesbian writing I had taken most to heart: "What will you undertake?"[43]

This, I believe, remains a dogged and crucial question before us and one that requires us to move beyond litanies ultimately based on only a narrow group's survival.

The tremendous strength of autonomous feminist institutions—the festivals, conferences, bookstores, women's studies departments, women's health centers—were the artistic, political, and social contributions activists helped to generate. All of these cultural institutions required women to ask of themselves and others a pivotal question Audre Lorde had posited: Are you doing your work? And yet, by the mid-1980s, the resurgence of the radical Right in the United States that fueled a monumental backlash against gays and lesbians, people of color, and women across the races led multiracial feminists to ask again: Where and with whom are you doing your work? Many antiracist feminists who had helped to build the largely women-led cultural institutions that left a paper trail of multiracial feminism moved on, into mixed-gender, multiracial grassroots organizations, working against the Klan, in support of affirmative action and immigrant rights, and against police brutality and the prison industry. It is in these institutions that much of the hard work continues—in recognizing that "sisterhood is powerful" only when it is worked for and not assumed and that the "personal is political" only to the extent that one's politics go way beyond the confines of one's own individual experience.

Blueprints for Feminist Activism

There are multiple strategies for social justice embedded in multiracial feminism: a belief in building coalitions that are based on a respect for identity-based groups; attention to both process and product but little tolerance for "all-talk" groups; racial parity at every level of an organization (not added on later but initiated from the start); a recognition that race can not be seen in binary terms; a recognition that racism exists in your backyard as well as in the countries the United States is bombing or inhabiting economically; and a recognition of the limits of pacifism when people in struggle are up against the most powerful state in the world. Multiracial feminism is not just another brand of feminism that can be taught alongside liberal, radical, and socialist feminism. Multiracial feminism is the heart of an inclusive women's liberation struggle. The race-class-gender-sexuality-nationality framework through which multiracial feminism operates encompasses and goes way beyond liberal, radical, and socialist feminist priorities—and it always has. Teaching Second Wave feminist history requires chronicling how hegemonic feminism came to be written about as "the" feminism and the limits of that model. Teaching Second Wave history by chronicling the rise of multiracial feminism challenges limited categories because it puts social justice and antiracism at the center of attention. This does not mean that the work done within hegemonic feminism did not exist or was not useful. It does mean that it was limited in its goals and effectiveness.

Although the strategies for multiracial feminism were firmly established in the 1970s and 1980s, I contend that these principles remain a blueprint for progressive, feminist, antiracist struggle in this millennium. These are principles we will need in order to build on the momentum begun in Seattle (as activist energy shocked the World Trade Organization out of its complacency) while we refuse to reproduce the overwhelmingly white composition of most of the groups involved in that protest. We will need the principles introduced by multiracial feminism to sustain a critique of the punishment industry that accounts for the increasing number of women caught in the penal system. These are principles we will need to nurture what critical race theorist Mari Matsuda has named a "jurisprudence of antisubordination." Matsuda writes: "A jurisprudence of antisubordination is an attempt to bring home the lost ones, to make them part of the center, to end the soul-killing tyranny of inside/outside thinking. Accountability revisited. I want to bring home the women who hate their own bodies so much that they would let a surgeon's hand cut fat from it, or a man's batter and bruise it. I want to bring home the hungry ones eating from the trash bins; the angry ones who call me names; the little ones in foster care."[44] The principles of antisubordination embedded in multiracial feminism, in antiracism feminism, are a crucial piece of this agenda.

Because written histories of social movements are typically one generation behind the movements themselves, it makes sense that the histories of the feminist movement are just now emerging. That timing means that now is the time to interrupt normative accounts before they begin to repeat themselves, each time, sounding more like "the truth" simply because of the repetition of the retelling. This interruption is necessary with regard to Second Wave feminism as well as earlier movements.

In her retrospective account of Black nationalism of the late 1960s and early 1970s, Angela Davis describes how broad-based nationalism has dropped almost completely out of the frame of reference in popular representations of the Black Power movement. This nationalism included alliances between Black and Chicano studies, in which students in San Diego were demanding the creation of a college called Lumumba-Zapata, and Huey Newton was calling for an end to "verbal gay bashing, urging an examination of black male sexuality, and calling for an alliance with the developing gay liberation movement." Davis writes: "I resent that the legacy I consider my own—one I also helped to construct—has been rendered invisible. Young people with 'nationalist' proclivities ought, at least, to have the opportunity to choose which tradition of nationalism they will embrace. How will they position themselves en masse in defense of women's rights, in defense of gay rights, if they are not aware of the historical precedents for such positionings?"[45]

In a parallel way, I want young women to know the rich, complicated, contentious, and visionary history of multiracial feminism and to know the nuanced controversies within Second Wave feminism. I want them to know that Shirley Chisholm ran for president in 1972; that Celestine Ware wrote a Black radical feminist text in the 1970s which offered an inspiring conception of revolution with a deep sense of humanity; that before Mab Segrest went to work for an organization against the Klan in North Carolina, she and others published an independent lesbian journal in the 1970s that included some of the most important and compelling race-conscious writing by white women and women of color to date.[46] I want people to know that there are antiracist feminist women currently in prison for their antiracist activism in the 1960s and since.[47] Among them is Marilyn Buck, a poet, political prisoner and, in her words, "a feminist with a small 'f,'" who is serving an eighty-year sentence in California.[48] Her poems, including "To the Woman Standing Behind Me in

Line Who Asks Me How Long This Black History Month Is Going to Last," eloquently capture why Buck must be included in tellings of multiracial feminism.[49] She writes:

the whole month
even if it is the shortest month
a good time in this prison life

you stare at me
and ask why I think February is so damned fine

I take a breath
prisoners fight for February
African voices cross razor wire
cut through the flim-flam
of Amerikkan history
call its cruelties out
confirm the genius of survival
creation and
plain ole enduring

a celebration!

***

The woman drops her gaze
looks away and wishes
she had not asked
confused that white skin did not guarantee
a conversation she wanted to have
she hasn't spoken to me since
I think I'll try to stand
in line with her
again

Marilyn Buck's poems and the work of other multiracial feminist activists help show that the struggle against racism is hardly linear, that the consolidation of white-biased feminism was clearly costly to early Second Wave feminism, and that we must dig deep to represent the feminist movement that does justice to an antiracist vision.

NOTES

The author thanks several people for their generous help on this article, especially Monisha Das Gupta, Diane Harriford, and two *Feminist Studies* anonymous reviewers.

1. For examples of histories that focus on white feminism, see Sheila Tobias, *Faces of Feminism: An Activist's Reflections on the Women's Movement* (Boulder: Westview Press, 1997); Barbara Ryan, *Feminism and the Women's Movement: Dynamics of Change in Social Movement Ideology and Activism* (New York: Routledge, 1992); Alice Echols, *Daring to Be Bad: Radical Feminism in America, 1967–1975,* (Minneapolis: University of Minnesota Press, 1989).

2. Chela Sandoval, *Methodology of the Oppressed* (Minneapolis: University of Minnesota Press, 2000), 41–42.

3. Of these branches of feminism (liberal, socialist, and radical), socialist feminism, which treats sexism and classism as interrelated forms of oppression, may have made the most concerted effort to develop an antiracist agenda in the 1970s. For example, "The Combahee River Collective Statement" was first published in Zillah Eisenstein's *Capitalist Patriarchy and the Case for Socialist Feminism* (New York: Monthly Review Press, 1979), 362–72, before it was published in Barbara Smith's *Home Girls: A Black Feminist Anthology* (New York: Kitchen Table, Women of Color Press, 1983). *Radical America,* a journal founded in 1967 and whose contributors and editors include many social feminists, consistently published articles that examined the relationship between race, class, and gender. The 1970s' socialist feminist organization, the Chicago Women's Liberation Union, which considered quality public education, redistribution of wealth, and accessible child care key to a feminist agenda, also made room for a race analysis by not privileging sexism over other forms of oppression. However, the fact that socialist feminist organizations were typically white dominated and were largely confined to academic and/or middle-class circles limited their effectiveness and visibility as an antiracist presence in early Second Wave feminism. For early socialist feminist documents, see Rosalyn Baxandall and Linda Gordon, eds., *Dear Sisters: Dispatches from the Women's Liberation Movement* (New York: Basic Books, 2000).

4. For an expanded discussion of the contributions and limitations of white antiracism from the 1950s to the present, see Becky Thompson, *A Promise and a Way of Life: White Antiracist Activism* (Minneapolis: University of Minnesota Press, 2001).

5. For a discussion of the term "multiracial feminism," see Maxine Baca Zinn and Bonnie Thornton Dill, "Theorizing Difference from Multiracial Feminism," *Feminist Studies* 22 (summer 1996): 321–31.

6. Bernice Johnson Reagon, "Coalition Politics: Turning the Century," in *Home Girls*, 356–69; Patricia Hill Collins, *Black Feminist Thought: Knowledge, Consciousness, and the Politics of Empowerment* (Boston: Unwin Hyman, 1990), 11; Barbara Smith, introduction, *Home Girls*, xxxii; Cherríe Moraga and Gloria Anzaldúa, eds., *This Bridge Called My Back: Writings by Radical Women of Color* (New York: Kitchen Table, Women of Color Press, 1981); Chandra Talpade Mohanty, "Under Western Eyes: Feminist Scholarship and Colonial Discourses," in *Third World Women and the Politics of Feminism*, eds., Chandra Talpade Mohanty, Ann Russo, and Lourdes Torres (Bloomington: Indiana

University Press, 1991), 51–80; Paula Gunn Allen, "Who Is Your Mother? Red Roots of White Feminism," in her *The Sacred Hoop: Recovering the Feminine in American Indian Traditions* (Boston: Beacon Press, 1986), 209–21; Adrienne Rich, *Blood, Bread, and Poetry* (New York: Norton, 1986); Patricia Williams, *The Alchemy of Race and Rights* (Cambridge: Harvard University Press, 1991).

7. Here I am using the term "feminist" to describe collective action designed to confront interlocking race, class, gender, and sexual oppressions (and other systemic discrimination). Although many women in these organizations explicitly referred to themselves as "feminist" from their earliest political work, others have used such terms as "womanist," "radical women of color," "revolutionary," and "social activist." Hesitation among women of color about the use of the term "feminist" often signaled an unwillingness to be associated with white-led feminism, but this wariness did not mean they were not doing gender-conscious, justice work. The tendency not to include gender-conscious activism by women of color in dominant versions of Second Wave history unless the women used the term "feminist" fails to account for the multiple terms women of color have historically used to designate activism that keeps women at the center of analysis and attends to interlocking oppressions. Although the formation of a women's group—an Asian women's friendship group, a Black women's church group, or a Native American women's arts council—is not inherently a feminist group, those organizations that confront gender, race, sexual, and class oppression, whether named as "feminist" or not, need to be considered as integral to multiracial feminism.

8. Benita Roth, "The Making of the Vanguard Center: Black Feminist Emergence in the 1960s and 1970s," in *Still Lifting, Still Climbing: African American Women's Contemporary Activism,* ed., Kimberly Springer (New York: New York University Press, 1999), 71.

9. Sherna Berger Gluck, "Whose Feminism, Whose History? Reflections on Excavating the History of (the) U.S. Women's Movement(s)," in *Community Activism and Feminist Politics: Organizing across Race, Class, and Gender,* ed., Nancy A. Naples (New York: Routledge, 1998), 38–39.

10. Miya Iwataki, "The Asian Women's Movement: A Retrospective," *East Wind* (spring/summer 1983): 35–41; Gluck, 39–41.

11. Sonia Shah, "Presenting the Blue Goddess: Toward a National Pan-Asian Feminist Agenda," in *The State of Asian America: Activism and Resistance in the 1990s,* ed., Karin Aguilar-San Juan (Boston: South End Press, 1994), 147–58.

12. M. Annette Jaimes with Theresa Halsey, "American Indian Women: At the Center of Indigenous Resistance in Contemporary North America," in *The State of Native America: Genocide, Colonization, and Resistance,* ed., M. Annette Jaimes (Boston: South End Press, 1992), 329.

13. Stephanie Autumn, ". . . This Air, This Land, This Water—If We Don't Start Organizing Now, We'll Lose It," *Big Mama Rag* 11 (April 1983): 4, 5.

14. For an insightful analysis of the multidimensionality of Black nationalism of the late 1960s and early 1970s, see Angela Davis, "Black Nationalism: The Sixties and the Nineties," in *The Angela Davis Reader,* ed., Joy James (Malden, Mass: Blackwell, 1998), 289–96.

15. Ibid., 15, 314.

16. Deborah Gray White, *Too Heavy a Load; Black Women in Defense of Themselves* (New York: Norton, 1999), 242.

17. Ibid., 242–53.

18. Combahee River Collective, "The Combahee River Collective Statement," in *Home Girls,* 272–82.

19. See Moraga and Anzaldúa.

20. Toni Cade, ed., *The Black Woman: An Anthology* (New York: Signet, 1970); Maxine Hong Kingston, *The Woman Warrior* (New York: Vintage Books, 1977); Moraga and Anzaldúa; Smith.

21. Assata Shakur, *Assata: An Autobiography* (Chicago: Lawrence Hill Books, 1987), 197.

22. Angela Davis, *Angela Davis: An Autobiography* (New York: Random House, 1974).

23. Nancy MacLean, "The Hidden History of Affirmative Action: Working Women's Struggles in the 1970s and the Gender of Class," *Feminist Studies* 25 (spring 1999): 47.

24. As a woman who was introduced to antiracist work through the feminist movement of the late 1970s—a movement shaped in large part by women of color who called themselves "womanists," "feminists," and "radical women of color"—I came to my interest in recasting the chronology of Second Wave feminism especially hoping to learn how white antiracist women positioned themselves vis-à-vis Second Wave feminism. I wanted to learn how sexism played itself out in the 1960s and how antiracist white women responded to Second Wave feminism. And I wanted to find out whether the antiracist baton carried in the 1960s was passed on or dropped by feminist activists.

One of the most compelling lessons I learned from white women who came of age politically before or during the civil rights and Black Power movements was how difficult it was for many of them to relate to or embrace feminism of the late 1960s and early 1970s. White antiracist women resisted sexism in SDS and in militant organizations. As they talked about the exclusions they faced in the 1960s' organizations and criticized early feminist organizing that considered gender oppression its main target, I realized how much different the feminist movement they saw in the early 1970s was from what I was introduced to in the late 1970s. By then, there was a critical mass of seasoned feminists who were keeping race at the center of the agenda. They were teaching younger feminists that race, class, gender, and sexuality are inextricably connected and that it is not possible to call oneself a feminist without dealing with race.

25. Several key Jewish feminist texts that addressed how to take racism and anti-Semitism seriously in feminist activism were published during this period and included Evelyn Torton Beck, ed., *Nice Jewish Girls: A Lesbian Anthology* (Trumansburg, N.Y.: Crossing Press, 1982); Melanie Kaye/Kantrowitz and Irena Klepfisz, eds., *The Tribe of Dina: A Jewish Women's Anthology* (Boston: Beacon Press, 1989), first published as a special issue of *Sinister Wisdom*, nos. 29/30 (1986); Melanie Kaye/Kantrowitz, *The Issue Is Power: Essays on Women, Jews, Violence, and Resistance* (San Francisco: Aunt Lute, 1992); Irena Klepfisz., *Periods of Stress* (Brooklyn, N.Y.: Out & Out Books, 1977); and *Keeper of Accounts* (Watertown, Mass: Persephone Press, 1982).

For key antiracist lesbian texts, see Adrienne Rich, *On Lies, Secrets, and Silence: Selected Prose, 1966–1978* (New York: Norton, 1979); Joan Gibbs and Sara Bennett, *Top Ranking: A Collection of Articles on Racism and Classism in the Lesbian Community* (New York: Come! Unity Press, 1980); Mab Segrest, *My Mama's Dead Squirrel: Lesbian Essays on Southern Culture* (Ithaca, N.Y.: Firebrand Books, 1985); Elly Bulkin, Minnie Bruce Pratt, and Barbara Smith, *Yours in Struggle: Three Feminist Perspectives on Anti-Semitism and Racism* (Brooklyn, N.Y.: Long Haul Press, 1984).

26. Ellen Willis, foreword to *Daring to Be Bad,* vii.

27. Barbara Ryan.

28. Howard Zinn, *A People's History of the United States* (New York: HarperPerennial, 1990), 504–13.

29. For a published version of Florynce Kennedy's position on Attica and Naomi Jaffe's perspective, see Barbara Smith, "'Feisty Characters' and 'Other People's Causes,'" in *The Feminist Memoir Project:Voices from Women's Liberation,* eds. Rachel Blau DuPlessis and Ann Snitow (New York: Three Rivers Press), 479–81.

30. Verta Taylor and Nancy Whittier, "The New Feminist Movement," in *Feminist Frontiers IV,* eds., Laurel Richardson, Verta Taylor, and Nancy Whittier (New York: McGraw-Hill, 1997), 544–45.

31. Chela Sandoval, "Feminism and Racism: A Report on the 1981 National Women's Studies Association Conference," in *Making Face, Making Soul: Haciendo Caras: Creative and Critical Perspectives by Women of Color,* eds., Gloria Anzaldúa (San Francisco: Aunt Lute, 1990), 55.

32. Smith, "'Feisty Characters,'" 470–80.

33. Gluck, 32.

34. James, 313.

35. Activists who helped Assata Shakur escape include political prisoners Marilyn Buck, Sylvia Baraldini, Susan Rosenberg, and Black male revolutionaries.

36. Adrienne Rich, "Disobedience and Women's Studies," *Blood, Bread, and Poetry* (New York: Norton, 1986), 76–84.

37. Moraga and Anzaldúa.

38. I am borrowing that phrase from Alice Echol's chronicling of white radical feminist history.

39. Lorraine Bethel, "What Chou Mean *We*, White Girl?" in *Conditions: Five* (1979): 86.

40. Wendy Rose, "The Great Pretenders: Further Reflections on Whiteshamanism," in *The State of Native America,* 403–23.

41. Thompson. See also Anne Braden, *The Wall Between* (Knoxville: University of Tennessee Press, 1999); Anne Braden, "A Second Open Letter to Southern White Women," *Southern Exposure* 6 (winter 1977): 50.

42. Segrest, *My Mama's Dead Squirrel,* 12.

43. Mab Segrest, "Fear to Joy: Fighting the Klan," *Sojourner: The Women's Forum* 13 (November 1987): 20.

44. Mari Matsuda, "Voices of America: Accent, Antidiscrimination Law, and a Jurisprudence for the Last Reconstruction," *Yale Law Journal* 100 (March 1991): 1405.

45. Davis, "Black Nationalism," 292.

46. See *Feminary: A Feminist Journal for the South Emphasizing Lesbian Visions.* Schlesinger Library at the Radcliffe Institute for Advanced Study at Harvard University has scattered issues of *Feminary.* Duke University Rare Book, Manuscript, and Special Collection Library has vols. 5–15 from 1974–1985. For analysis of the import of working on this journal on Mab Segrest's consciousness and activism, see Jean Hardisty, "Writer/Activist Mab Segrest Confronts Racism," *Sojourner: The Women's Forum* 19 (August 1994): 1–2; Segrest, *My Mama's Dead Squirrel.*

47. Marilyn Buck, Linda Evans, Laura Whitehorn, and Kathy Boudin are among the white political prisoners who are either currently in prison or, in the case of Laura Whitehorn and Linda Evans, recently released, serving sentences whose length and severity can only be understood as retaliation for their principled, antiracist politics.

48. Marilyn Buck is in a federal prison in Dublin, California, for alleged conspiracies to free political prisoners, to protest government policies through the use of violence, and to raise funds for Black liberation organizations. [See Reading 50]

49. Marilyn Buck's poem, "To the Woman Standing Behind Me in Line Who Asks Me How Long This Black History Month Is Going to Last," is reprinted with written permission from the author.

2

Theories and Theorizing: Integrative Frameworks for Understanding

People have sought to understand themselves, their home environments, and the wider world since the beginning of time. Using skills of observation, reasoning, and trial-and-error experimentation, women have contributed significant knowledge and insight to the care of infants and children, selective breeding of wild grains, the domestication of animals, production of handicrafts, knowledge of the medicinal properties of plants, and theories of health and illness. With literacy, women observed and analyzed their social worlds in poetry, novels, and essays that conveyed their understandings, feelings, and beliefs.

Some asked feminist questions: Why are women in a subordinate position in our society? What are the origins of this subordination, and how is it perpetuated? How can it be changed?

Why are girls in the United States generally better at creative writing than at math? Has this always been so? Is this difference inevitable? Is rape about sexuality? Power? Both? Or neither? What is pornography? Is it the same as erotica? Do lesbians really want to be men? Why do so many marriages end in divorce? Why are so many children in the United States brought up in poverty? Why are more women going to jail than ever before?

In this chapter we examine theory and theory-making in general terms and continue the discussion of feminist theoretical frameworks we started in Chapter 1. As preparation for understanding the material presented in the rest of the book, we explore various ways in which knowledge is created and validated. People often say that facts speak for themselves. On the contrary, we argue that facts are always open to interpretation. How you think about women's situations and experiences affects what you see and what you understand by what you see.

What Is a Theory?

Consider the following assertion about poverty that many people in our society make: Poor people are poor because they are lazy. Think about the following questions:

1. What is the purpose of this statement?

2. What are the underlying assumptions on which it is based?

3. Who came up with this idea, under what circumstances, and when?

4. How did this idea become popular?

5. If the statement were true, what would it imply about action that should be taken? If the statement were not true, what ideological purpose might it serve?

6. What would you need to know to decide whether this statement is really true?

The preceding statement is a theory. It is one explanation of poverty. It is built on a set of assumptions, or certain factors taken for granted. For example, this theory assumes there are well-paying jobs for all who want to work and that everyone meets the necessary requirements for those jobs, such as education, skills, or a means of providing for child care. These factors are proposed as facts or truths. This explanation of poverty takes a moral perspective. A psychological explanation of poverty may argue that people are poor because they have low self-esteem, lack self-confidence, and take on self-defeating behaviors. A sociological explanation might conclude that structures in our society, such as the educational and economic systems, are organized to exclude certain groups from being able to live above the poverty line. Each theory explicitly or implicitly suggests how to address the problem, which could then lead to appropriate action. If the problem is defined in terms of laziness, a step to ending poverty might be to punish people who are poor; if it is defined in psychological terms, assertiveness training or counseling might be suggested; and if it is defined in terms of structural inequality, ending discrimination would be the answer.

Theories may also have ideological purposes. The term *ideology* refers to an organized collection of ideas applied to public issues. Dominant ideologies—the ideas that represent the foundational values of a particular society—often appear neutral, whereas alternative ideologies are seen as radical, regardless of their content. Putting forward particular ideologies for society, including the role of government, political organizations, lobbyists, and media reporting, is a fundamental part of politics. Societal institutions, such as education and criminal justice, help to support and perpetuate dominant ideologies. People in advantaged groups and disadvantaged groups may accept dominant ideologies although these may not be in their best interests. Even for scientists, who advance knowledge by challenging existing beliefs, the power of dominant ways of thinking may block new theories (Kuhn 1962).

Creating Knowledge: Epistemologies, Values, and Methods

Feminist philosopher Sandra Harding (1987) identified three elements that are basic to the process of creating knowledge:

1. *Epistemology*—a theory about knowledge, who can know, and under what circumstances.

2. *Methodology*—the researcher's values and choices about how to carry out research. Researchers can pose questions, collect evidence, and analyze information in different ways based on assumptions about what knowledge is and how the process of creating it is best undertaken.

3. *Method*—or techniques for gathering and analyzing information, whether from observation, listening to personal stories, conducting interviews, reading documents, undertaking media analysis, statistical analysis, and so on.

Virtually everyone thinks up explanations for their experiences; that is, they create theory. For instance, we analyze the causes of poverty, anorexia, or obesity in our communities; the impact of immigration on the state we live in; or the experience of rape. Theories generated by ordinary people, however, are usually not regarded as worthy of consideration beyond their own spheres of influence, among friends or coworkers, for example. Historically, Western, university-educated men from the upper classes and their theories, which are supported by societal institutions such as education and government, have had the greatest impact on how human beings and social phenomena are explained and understood. In the following sections, we discuss how certain kinds of theories have been legitimized in this society and suggest another way of theorizing and developing knowledge.

Dominant Perspectives

From the perspective of the **dominant culture**—the values, symbols, means of expression, language, and interests of the people in power in this society—only certain types of theories have authority. Generally, the authoritativeness of a theory about human beings and society is evaluated along two dimensions. One is its degree of formality, which is determined according to how closely its development followed a particular way of theorizing, the so-called scientific method, the basics of which most of us learned in high school science classes. The second is the scope and generality of the theory.

Although in practice there are several variations of the scientific method, key elements must be present for a theory to fit in this category. The scientific method, originally devised by natural scientists, rests on the presumption of **objectivity**, "an attitude, philosophy, or claim . . . independent of the individual mind [through emotional detachment and social distance] . . . verified by a socially agreed-upon procedure such as those developed in science, mathematics, or history" (Kohl 1992, p. 84).

Objectivity is seen as both a place to begin the process of theorizing and the outcome of that process. It has been long argued that "if done properly, [science] is the epitome of objectivity" (Tuana 1989, p. xi). Therefore, theories developed correctly using the scientific method are held out as value-free and neutral. The method is also empirical. That is, for something to be a fact, it must be physically observable, countable, or measurable. This proposition is extended to include the notion that something is either true or not true, fact or not fact. Last, the experimental method, commonly used in science, "attempts to understand a whole by examining its parts, asking how something works rather than why it works, and derives abstract formulas to predict future results" (Duff 1993, p. 51). In summary, these elements add up to research methods that

> generally require a distancing of the researcher from her or his subjects of study; . . . absence of emotions from the research process; ethics and values are deemed inappropriate in the research process, either as the reason for scientific inquiry or as part of the research process itself; . . . adversarial debates, whether written or oral, become the preferred method of ascertaining truth: the arguments that can withstand the greatest assault and survive intact become the strongest truth.   *(Collins 1990, p. 205)*

The scientific method was adopted by scholars in the social sciences as a way to validate and legitimate social scientific knowledge beginning in the late nineteenth century, as disciplines such as psychology and sociology were being developed. Indeed, French philosopher Auguste Comte, credited with coining the term *sociology*, put forward a version of empirical science, which he called **positivism**, to be applied to social as well as physical phenomena. In Comte's view, the only authentic knowledge is scientific knowledge, and such knowledge can only come from positive affirmation of theories through strict scientific method. Since that time, academic disciplines like education, nursing, and social work have also adopted the scientific method as the primary way through which to develop new knowledge in their fields, furthering the dominance or **hegemony** of this approach.

The second dimension for evaluating and judging theory is concerned with its scope and generality. The range is from the most specific explanation with the narrowest scope and most limited generality to the other end of the continuum, the general theory, which is the most abstract and is assumed to have the most general application. Many general theories have been promoted and accepted as being universally applicable. One of them, **biological determinism,** holds that a group's biological or genetic makeup shapes its social, political, and economic destiny. In mainstream society, biology is often assumed to be the basis of women's and men's different roles, especially women's ability to bear children. Most social scientists and feminist theorists see behavior as socially constructed and learned through childhood socialization, everyday experience, education, and the media, as argued by sociologist Judith Lorber (Reading 8). They explain differences in women's and men's roles in these terms and argue that variations in gender roles from one society to another provide strong evidence for **social constructionism.**

Critiques of Dominant Perspectives

Evaluating and judging theories according to the scientific method has come under heavy criticism from feminist theorists who have exposed fallacies, biases, and harmful outcomes of that way of creating knowledge (e.g., Bleier 1984; Collins 1990; Duran 1998; and Shiva 1988). The primary criticisms are that knowledge created by the scientific method is not value-free, neutral, or generalizable to the extent it is claimed to be. Science, as with other academic disciplines, is "a cultural institution and as such is structured by the political, social, and economic values of the culture within which it is practiced" (Tuana 1989, p. xi). As biologist Ruth Hubbard (1989) argued

> To be believed, scientific facts must fit the worldview of the times. Therefore, at times of tension and upheaval . . . some researchers always try to prove that differences in the social, political, and economic status of women and men, blacks and whites, poor people and rich people, are inevitable because they are the results of people's inborn qualities and traits. Such scientists have tried to "prove" that blacks are innately less intelligent than whites, or that women are innately weaker, more nurturing, less good at math than men.   *(p. 121)*

Rather than being neutral, all knowledge is value-laden and biased and reflects and serves the interests

of the culture that produced it, in this case the dominant culture.

The problem is not that theories are value-laden but that the values and biases of many theories are hidden under the cloak of "scientific objectivity." Moreover, there is the assumption that "if the science is 'good,' in a professional sense [following closely the rules of scientific method], it will also be good for society" (Hubbard 1989, p. 121). Sociologists Margaret Andersen and Patricia Hill Collins (1998) argued that much of what has passed for social knowledge in the United States has been based on exclusionary thinking that "does not reveal the intricate interconnections that exist between the different groups comprising American society" (p. 12). By contrast, inclusive thinking "shifts our perspective from the white, male-centered forms of thinking that have characterized much of Western thought, helping us better understand the intersections of race, class, and gender in the experiences of all groups, including those with privilege and power" (p. 13).

Many theories are applied by scholars, policy makers, and commentators not only to the United States but also to the rest of the world, often without acknowledgment that they primarily serve the interests of the dominant group in the United States. They use these theories to justify the inequalities in our society as well as differences and inequalities between the United States and other countries. An example of this can be found in theories of modernization, which assume that the economic development of Western Europe and North America is the path that all other nations should and will follow.

We argue that theorizing is a political project, regardless of whether this is acknowledged. Social theories—explaining the behavior of human beings and society—may serve to support the existing social order or can be used to challenge it. For those who are interested in progressive social change, the political work of theorizing is to generate knowledge that challenges conventional wisdom and those formal theories that do not explain the experiences of marginalized people, provide satisfactory solutions to their difficulties, or lead to their liberation.

The Role of Values

Director of the Center for Women's Global Leadership, Rutgers University, Charlotte Bunch (1987) recommended an effective four-step way to think about theory: describing what exists, analyzing why that reality exists, determining what should exist, and hypothesizing how to change what is to what should be.

"Determining what should exist," the third part of this model, is clearly a matter of values and beliefs. It involves being able to envision (if only vaguely) another way of organizing society, free from discrimination and oppression. Feminism is concerned with values by definition: the liberation of women and girls from discrimination based on gender, race, class, sexuality, nationality, and so on. Values do not come from facts or from the analysis of a situation but rather from people's beliefs in principles like fairness, equality, or justice. We may learn such principles from our families and communities, or through organized religion or a more personal sense of spirituality. We may think of them in terms of fundamental human rights (e.g., Agosín 2001; Bunch and Carillo 1991; Bunch and Reilly 1994; Kerr 1993). Whatever the source, feminist work invariably involves values whether stated explicitly or implied. Notice the value positions in the readings throughout this book. Several writers draw on spirituality (bell hooks, Reading 30), progressive secularism (Melanie Kaye/Kantrowitz, Reading 14), or an explicitly faith-based perspective that informs their view of the world and their sense of life purpose (Christina Leaño, Reading 16). Others show how religious traditions and values restrict and oppress women (Readings 19 and 35). At the individual and community level, spirituality is a source of comfort, connection, inspiration, and meaning for many women. They play a key role in teaching their children spiritual beliefs and practices and are respected for this in their families and communities. The world's major religions are all patriarchal, although this plays out in different ways in different traditions. Sacred texts are often open to divergent interpretations and are sometimes much more supportive of women than organized religious practice. At the institutional level, organized religions have a mixed record, at best, in supporting women's agency and empowerment. Religious leaders and representatives of international women's organizations who met in Chiang Mai, Thailand, in 2004, called for a commitment to women's human rights on the part of all religions (Reading 35).

Socially Lived Theorizing

We argue that theorizing is not the sole domain of elites. Feminist legal scholar Catharine MacKinnon (1991) wrote about the importance of "articulating the theory of women's practice—resistance, visions, consciousness, injuries, notions of community, experiences of inequality. By practic[e], I mean socially lived" (p. 20).

In the 1960s and 1970s, feminists popularized the slogan "the personal is political" to validate individual women's experiences as a starting point for recognizing and understanding discrimination against women as a group. This promoted the practice of "starting from one's own experience" as a legitimate way to theorize and create new knowledge. This practice was also useful in counteracting the dominant view of theorizing that personal experience, along with emotions and values, contaminates the "purity" of the scientific method.

We argue for a theoretical framework that allows us to see the diversity of women's lives and the structures of power, inequality, and opportunity that shape our experiences. Judith Lorber (Reading 8) contends that gender differences are not natural or biological but learned from infancy. Gender differences are maintained by key social institutions such as education, marriage, popular culture, news media, organized religion, government, and law. The implication of her argument is that gender arrangements are not fixed or inevitable but can be changed.

Sociologist Jackie Stacey (1993) noted that the concept of **patriarchy,** meaning "the systematic organization of male supremacy" (p. 53), is one that many feminist theorists have found useful. In Reading 9, sociologist Allan Johnson argues that patriarchy is not just a collection of individuals but a system whose core values are control and domination. Everyone is involved and implicated in this system, but we can choose *how* we participate. This emphasis on a wider system is crucial. Without it, as Johnson shows, our thinking and discussion get reduced to the personal level and bogged down in accusations, defensiveness, and hurt feelings.

First-person stories are compelling ways to learn about others, and we include several articles by writers who reflect on their experience in order to examine social processes and institutions, that is, to open a window onto a wider world. Abra Fortune

Chernik (Reading 68) discusses her struggle with an eating disorder and the process of overcoming it. Moving beyond her own experience, she asked "why society would reward my starvation and encourage my vanishing"? She examined psychological, sociological, and feminist theories for answers to this question. In Reading 37, Ann Filemyr uses her standpoint as a white lesbian to reflect on the insights she gained when she "crossed the color line" to live with her partner, Essie. She learned about racism by talking with Essie's grandmother and co-parenting Essie's son. She came to see how much she had taken for granted earlier, including her friendships and family relationships.

Different social and historical situations give rise to different experiences and theories about those experiences, hence the importance of **situated knowledge** (see, e.g., Belenky, Clinchy, Goldberger, and Tarnle 1986; Collins 1990) and **standpoint theory** (Harding 2004; Hartsock 1983) for understanding women's lives.

Standpoint Theory

Sandra Harding (1998) identified four elements that contribute to constructing a standpoint as a place to generate knowledge:

1. *Physical location*—including geographical location, bodily experiences, gendered activities, and the effects of race/ethnicity, class, and nation that "place" people differently.

2. *Interests*—different locations generate different interests.

3. *Access to discourses* that provide tools for making sense of specific experiences.

4. *Social organization of knowledge production*—being situated in a university, working for a women's nonprofit organization, or talking informally with friends and coworkers all facilitate the creation of some kinds of knowledge and obstruct others.

By definition, standpoints are grounded and limited. Our discussion of intersectionality in Chapter 1 provides an example. Many academics cite a groundbreaking paper by critical legal scholar Kimberlé Crenshaw (1993) as the source of this concept. Organizer and writer Linda Burnham (2001) argued that Black women in organizations such as the Combahee River Collective and the Third World Women's Alliance wrote about this idea some twenty years earlier. Beverley Guy-Sheftall (1995, p. 45), a women's studies scholar dedicated to African American women's issues and writings, pointed out that Black women in the United States were talking publicly about the intersection of race and gender as early as the 1830s, though not using this term. Each of these formulations utilizes a different standpoint, which offers different resources for making sense of the intertwining of race and gender in the lives of African American women—indeed, all women. Poet, writer, and teacher Minnie Bruce Pratt (1984) wrote about the process of becoming aware of her advantaged position and her fear of losing her familiar place as she became more conscious of privilege based on race. She noted the positive side of widening her standpoint:

> I learn a way of looking at the world that is more accurate, complex, multi-layered, multi-dimensioned, more truthful. . . . I've learned that what is presented to me as an accurate view of the world is frequently a lie. . . . So I gain truth when I expand my constricted eye, an eye that has only let in what I have been taught to see. *(p. 17)*

Sociologist Dorothy Smith saw a standpoint "as a strategic choice in doing research—a place from which to start" (Sprague 2005, p. 67). We chose to open this book on U.S. women's lives with Paula Gunn Allen's essay on the "red roots of white feminism" rather than with feminist writings generated in Europe. Allen's standpoint opens up a different history and a more critical view of first-wave feminism.

Many scholars assume that a standpoint is a point of view, something that individuals or groups think or say, often based on their identity or personal experience. Some argue that this means there is no basis for choosing among competing explanations of any social phenomenon. Others "privilege accounts offered by members of oppressed groups" (Sprague 2005, p. 57) on the grounds that people in dominant positions are taken in by their own ideologies, and those in less powerful positions have no interest in supporting ideologies that justify their oppression.

Sociologist Joey Sprague argues that a standpoint should not be read in terms of subjectivity. She cites political scientist Nancy Hartsock (1983), who distinguished a standpoint from the spontaneous consciousness of a particular group. Sociologist Patricia Hill Collins also maintained that standpoint is not about individual experiences but about "historically shared, group-based experiences" (1997, p. 375). As a sociology professor raised in an African American community, Hill Collins draws on these two very different standpoints in her discussion of Black feminist thought (Reading 10). She argues that traditional creators of Black feminist thought were not recognized as theorists by university-based Eurocentric masculinist epistemologies. Such thinkers included "blues singers, poets, autobiographers, storytellers, and orators validated by everyday Black women as experts on a Black woman's standpoint." As African American women have gained advanced degrees and academic positions some have chosen to "make creative use of their outsider-within status" in resisting the hegemonic nature of white male patterns of thinking and theorizing. Because Black women's standpoint exists in a context of domination, Hill Collins refers to Black women's thought as **subjugated knowledge.**

Many of us may have sat in class listening to a teacher or other students and have kept quiet when we knew what was being said did not match our experience. The fact that some women's experiences are not included in texts or class discussions is a result of partial standpoints used to explain or generalize. Sprague (2005) notes that knowledge produced in U.S. universities has changed as more women, men of color, and LGBT scholars have gained academic positions. She is quick to point out that it is not their identity that is responsible for this but their standpoints. Typically, academic researchers work in settings that separate them from most other people. They have socioeconomic privilege, access to libraries and labs, and opportunities to discuss their work with students and colleagues. They may receive research grants from the university, private foundations, corporations, or government agencies. The priorities of their universities and academic disciplines affect their interests and what is considered legitimate research. Not all women scholars are interested in contributing to feminist theorizing; conversely, some white male scholars are producing new understandings of race and gender. To see beyond the standpoint of their professional location, Sprague (2005) suggests that feminist researchers can "work to compensate for the limitations by

actively working to cross boundaries" (p. 73). Scholars who have access to standpoints that are marginalized by the academy, like Patricia Hill Collins, may cross such boundaries on a daily basis.

In Reading 11, antiracist, feminist educator and scholar Chandra Talpade Mohanty lays out aspects of her genealogy—her standpoint as a South Asian in the United States and a nonresident Indian. She notes that this telling is "interested, partial, and deliberate" and comments: "The stories I recall, the ones I retell and claim as my own, determine the choices and decisions I make in the present and the future." As a South Asian woman studying in the United States, one of these choices was to anchor herself here through the analytic and political lenses of racism and sexism. She made a significant shift in her sense of self, her interests, and the alliances she wanted to forge when she began to think of herself as a student of color rather than a foreign student. These new understandings also challenged her to rethink her place in Indian society. Mohanty draws on a **postcolonial feminism,** extending analysis of gender, race, and class to include nation and the complex long-term effects of Western colonialism; "the 'post' in post colonialism does not indicate that colonialism is over, but rather that colonial legacies continue to exist" (Mack-Canty 2004, p. 164; also see Alexander and Mohanty 1997; Cooper and Stoler 1997; McClintock 1995; Spivak 1988).

Challenges to Situated Knowledge and Standpoint Epistemology

Critiques of situated knowledge and standpoint epistemology emphasize the self-centeredness of **subjectivity,** "in which knowledge and meaning [are] lodged in oneself and one's own experiences" (Maher and Tétreault 1994, p. 94). This leads to comments such as "I can only know my own experience," "I can only speak for myself," or "What does all this have to do with *me?*"

Historian Joan Scott (1993) examined the authority of personal experience in creating theory. She acknowledged the value of theorizing from experience, especially if this has been ignored, denied, or silenced in dominant systems of knowledge-production, but noted that, in much writing of history, experience has been taken as the "the bedrock of evidence on which explanation is built"

(p. 399). Yet, as mentioned earlier, facts do not simply speak for themselves; historians construct an interpretation of their material, "a selective ordering of information" (p. 404), as shown by Becky Thompson in her account of second-wave feminism (Reading 7). Scott (1993) warned that assuming experience to be an authoritative source of knowledge may preclude questions about the constructed nature of experience, how one's vision is also structured, as noted earlier by Minnie Bruce Pratt. Scott argued that different experiences may be taken as "evidence for the fact of difference, rather than a way of exploring how difference is established, how it operates, how and in what ways it constitutes subjects who see and act in the world" (pp. 399–400). Scott concluded that experience should not be "the origin of our explanation, but that which we want to explain" (p. 412).

Following Sprague (2005), we argue that standpoint methodology is not based on individual experiences but on what Patricia Hill Collins called "historically shared, group-based experiences" (1997, p. 375). Moreover, researchers and theorists can recognize and address differences among standpoints by considering different perspectives on an issue, thus contributing to broader-based knowledge.

A second critique of situated knowledge involves **relativism.** Situated knowledge is taken as authoritative because it is someone's or some group's real experience. From a relativist perspective, each group's thought is equally valid, and "anything goes." As a result, others may think they have no basis on which to question or challenge it and no right to do so. Thus, the White Supremacist views of Ku Klux Klan members might be considered equally as valid as those held by anti-racist activists, or a New York judge could invoke "cultural difference" to justify sentencing a Chinese immigrant man who killed his wife to a mere five years' probation (Yen 1989).

Patricia Hill Collins notes that, "relativism represents the opposite of scientific ideologies of objectivity" (Reading 10). She argues that Black feminist thought offers a specific and partial perspective on domination that "allows African American women to bring a Black women's standpoint to larger epistemological dialogues concerning the nature of the matrix of domination." The

ideas that are validated by other oppressed groups based on their own distinctive, but overlapping, standpoints become the most "objective" truths.

For students of women's studies, it is important to take a stand on complex issues after thinking carefully about them and drawing on many standpoints. This is not the same as universalizing from one's own experience or telling other people what to think, what to know, or what to do. Many people's experiences and agency have been excluded or erased by dominant theoretical perspectives, and we do not want to replicate that way of knowing. We argue that standpoint methodology allows students and researchers to build bridges among overlapping standpoints, which can provide a solid place to stand on contentious issues. This generates shared truths that form the basis of what Chandra Talpade Mohanty (2003) has called a "common context of struggle" where people of diverse situations and standpoints can combine their perspectives and use these overlapping understandings to work together.

Purposes of Socially Lived Theorizing

We argue that knowledge should be used for the purposes of helping to transform the current social and economic structures of power and inequality into a sustainable world for all. As Catharine MacKinnon (1991) remarked, "It is common to say that something is good in theory but not in practice. I always want to say, then it is not such a good theory, is it?" (p. 1).

Margaret Andersen and Patricia Hill Collins (1998) argued for inclusive theorizing by putting "at the center of our thinking the experiences of groups who have formerly been excluded" (p. 12). They noted that partial knowledge "leads to the formation of bad social policy . . . that then reproduces, rather than solves, social problems" (Andersen and Collins 1998, p. 13).

For Chandra Talpade Mohanty, the wider goal is **transnational feminism,** or feminism without borders. Like Hill Collins, Mohanty argues that the creation of knowledge must avoid false universalisms and should involve ethical and caring dialogue across differences, divisions, and conflicts, to generate more broad-based understandings.

Such dialogues should strive to be "noncolonized" and anchored in equality and respect to avoid reproducing power dynamics and inequalities among feminists that parallel those inherent in colonization.

Socially lived theorizing requires what Brazilian educator Paulo Freire (1989) calls **conscientization,** or gaining a critical consciousness, "learning to perceive social, political, and economic contradictions . . . and to take action against oppressive elements of this reality" (p. 19). This is challenging, as most of us have had little opportunity to engage in honest dialogue with others—both people like ourselves and those from different backgrounds—about important issues. Honest, thoughtful dialogue and asking critical questions move us beyond excessive subjectivity because we are compelled to see and understand many different sides of the same subject. Creating theory for social change—something that will advance human development and create a better world for all—gives us a basis for evaluating facts and experiences. This in turn provides a framework for deciding where to draw the line on cultural relativism. Through ongoing, detailed discussion and conscientious listening to others, we can generate a carefully thought-out set of principles that lead to greater understanding of issues and of acceptable actions in a given situation.

In writing about the Holocaust—the mass murder primarily of Jewish people but also of Roma people, people with disabilities, and gay people in Europe during World War II—philosopher Alan Rosenberg (1988) made an important distinction between knowing and understanding something. According to Rosenberg, knowing is having the facts about a particular event or condition. We know the Holocaust happened: Eight million people were murdered, and countless others were tortured, raped, and otherwise devastated; the Nazis, under the leadership of Adolf Hitler, were the perpetrators; others, both inside and outside Germany, including the United States initially, were unable or refused to help; the result was the slaughter of 6 million Jewish people. Traditional educational practices, epitomized by the scientific method, teach us primarily to know. For Rosenberg, knowing is the first step to understanding, a much deeper process that, in the case of the Holocaust, involves not only comprehending its significance and longer-term effects but also trying to discover how to prevent similar injustices in the future.

> Knowing . . . refers to factual information or the process by which it is gathered. Understanding refers to systematically grasping the significance of an event in such a way that it becomes integrated into one's moral and intellectual life. Facts can be absorbed without their having any impact on the way we understand ourselves or the world we live in;

facts in themselves do not make a difference.
It is the understanding of them that makes a
difference.   *(Rosenberg 1988, p. 382)*

Many assume that the scientific method involves authoritativeness and rigor. We believe this
alternative way of theorizing redefines rigor by demanding the engagement of our intellectual, emotional, and spiritual selves. It compels us to think
systematically and critically, requires us to face the
challenges of talking about our differences, and ob-
ligates us to consider the real implications and consequences of our theories. Knowledge created in
this way helps us "to systematically grasp . . . the
significance of an event in such a way that it becomes
integrated into [our] moral and intellectual life," also
a form of rigor (Rosenberg 1988, p. 382).

Media Representations and the Creation of Knowledge

A major source of our understanding of our own
lives is our ability to reflect on our experiences and
to compare them to the experiences of others. We
learn about people from other groups through our,
often limited, interactions with them and through
many kinds of media representations.

We opened this chapter with a brief discussion
of theorizing about poverty. We chose this topic
because it has dropped out of mainstream discourse in the United States even though inequalities of wealth and income are becoming more
marked in this country as well as in others. Worldwide, approximately 1 billion people live on the
equivalent of $1 a day, and another billion live on
the equivalent of $2 dollars a day. Many people in
the United States are struggling financially, yet
relatively few elected representatives, academics,
journalists, or nonprofit organizations concern
themselves with poverty. This fact is an example
of the political nature of knowledge, discussed
earlier. Political interests backed by media reporting influence what people pay attention to.

It is a truism to say that we live in a media-
saturated culture with constant access to the Internet, TV and radio stations broadcasting 24 hours a
day, daily newspapers, weekly magazines, new
movies coming out all the time, and so on. This

list shows the plurality of media sources. From
opinion polls to academic research, media studies
evaluate the role of media in creating opinions, attitudes, and knowledge. Onnesha Roychouduri
(2007) argued

> The daily news is composed of articles by writ-
> ers who string together the handful of facts they
> have obtained in their research. They call it a
> "story" for good reason. Every day they are ex-
> pected to produce a cohesive article on an issue.
> There are bound to be mistakes and oversights.
> But we rarely stop to consider this because the
> end product is so seductively authoritative.

The line between information and entertainment is blurred as TV shows take up serious issues
and U.S. news reporting often focuses on the flip,
titillating, and controversial. The repetition of facts
and images also shapes our view of events and of
history (Morrow 1999). The mainstream media are
owned and controlled by mega-corporations like
Disney/ABC and Time Warner/Turner. One of the
media's main functions is to round up an audience
for advertisers, and advertisers exert considerable
influence concerning media content, especially in
television. From time to time they threaten to pull
advertising if they think the content of a show will
"turn off" their intended audience, and editors
and directors are usually forced to toe the line.

Mainstream media reporters, writers, editors,
and corporate sponsors are all involved in the creation of knowledge. They employ their own theories of who is a credible "authority" on an issue
and their methodologies are shaped by their values
and assumptions regarding what constitutes a
"good story" and what "the public wants to hear."
Thus, media outlets have their own standpoints:
their physical and social locations, interests, and
access to particular discourses; they are in powerful
positions in the social organization of knowledge
production.

Media scholars, critics, and some leading journalists are increasingly concerned about the
"unasked" and "unanswered" questions in much
contemporary journalism (e.g., Alterman 2003;
Borjesson 2002; Cohen 2005; Hamilton 2004), and
often attribute this to corporate media ownership,
characterized by Robert McChesney (2004) as
"hyper-commercialism."

As consumers of media, we develop sophisticated skills in "reading" media texts, whether they are ads, sitcoms, or documentaries. Media audiences bring their experiences, values, and beliefs—their standpoints—to what they watch, read, and hear, just as students bring their standpoints into the classroom. The more we know about particular people, the more we are able to judge the accuracy of media representations and to notice whether they reproduce myths and stereotypes, and romanticize or exoticize people, as discussed by Diane Raymond (Reading 22; also Carilli and Campbell 2005).

Women have been marginalized in media portrayals, as have people of color and working-class people. "Blatantly stereotypical images dominated the earlier years of mass media" (Croteau and Hoynes 1997, p. 147). Women on television, for example, are still mainly shown in the context of entertainment, sport, home, and personal relationships. Media analyst and radio reporter Laura Flanders (1997) noted that in the news media, women and girls are usually represented in "human interest" stories. Media representations serve to reinforce ideological notions of women's roles, women's bodies, and sexuality, while also giving complex and sometimes contradictory messages. A study undertaken by the Project for Excellence in Journalism (2005) found that "despite rising numbers of women in the workforce and in journalism schools, the news . . . still largely comes from a male perspective." This study examined 16,800 news stories across 45 news outlets during 20 randomly selected days in a nine-month period and found that "more than three quarters of all stories contain male sources, while only a third of stories contain even a single female source." Women are more likely to be included if the reporter is female, or in "lifestyle" pieces as opposed to "hard" news, business, or sports. Women are least likely to be quoted in stories about foreign affairs, giving the impression that there are no women with expertise in this area. *The Nation* columnist Katha Pollitt noted that white men's voices are assumed to be authoritative and neutral: ". . . a woman's opinion about Iraq or the budget is seen as a woman's opinion. The same for a black person . . ." (quoted in Zimmerman 2003, p. 5). Moreover, the faculty and administrators "who run the nation's journalism and mass communication schools are overwhelmingly white, and

How to Watch TV News

1. **In encountering a news show, you must come with a firm idea of what is important.** TV news is highly selective. Your values and beliefs are essential in judging what it is that really matters in the reporting of an event.

2. **In preparing to watch a TV news show, keep in mind that it is called a "show."** A TV news show is a successful business enterprise as well as a form of entertainment and a public service.

3. **Never underestimate the power of commercials.** They tell a great deal about our society. Note contradictory messages as you compare commercials and the news.

4. **Learn something about the economic and political interests of those who run TV stations.** This is relevant to judging what they say and don't say.

5. **Pay special attention to the language of newscasts.** Film footage and visual imagery claim our attention on TV news shows, but it is what newscasters *say* that frames the pictures and tells us how to interpret them.

———

(Adapted from Postman and Powers 1992, pp. 160–68.)

two-thirds of them are male," even though about two-thirds of their students are women (University of Maryland 2007).

Given the central importance of advertising, media representations, and popular culture in shaping knowledge and opinions, we include several articles on these topics in relation to the influence of advertising on girls' confidence and self esteem (Reading 26), queer representation in TV sitcoms (Reading 22), the killing of Brandon Teena (Reading 24), media reactions to men dealing with date rape on a college campus (Reading 33), women in the global sex trade (Reading 45), newspaper reports on Muslim Americans and Arab Americans (Reading 55), and the increasing militarization of U.S. culture (Reading 55).

Ariel Dougherty, co-founder of Women Make Movies, mentioned a 1970s radical feminist comment "No women's media; no women's progress" (Donna Allen and Dana Densmore 1977, quoted in Dougherty 2006, p. 25). We note the significance of alternative media of many kinds, disseminated through magazines, newsletters, and electronically (see, e.g., Breitbart and Nogueira 2004). This includes alternative and critical sources of news (e.g., www.womensenews.org; www.alternet.org; www.dollarsandsense.org), girls' media production (see Bleyer 2004; Kearney 2006), as well as feminist blogs (e.g., www.barnard.edu/sfonline/blogs; www.blogher.com) and materials posted on YouTube. An example of news reporting that countered CNN's dominance is the weblog produced by Riverbend (2005, 2006, http://riverbendblog.blogspot.com), an Iraqi woman in Baghdad, who described her family's experiences of war and occupation, as well as her comments on mainstream news reporting of events (see Reading 59).

International women's groups and networks also distribute information through Web sites, newsletters, radio shows, and community theater (Allen, Rush, and Kaufman 1996; Byerly and Ross 2006). Examples include Federation of African Media Women,

Feminist International Radio Endeavor (www.fire.or.cr/indexing.htm), FEMPRESS (Chile), ISIS International-Manila (www.isiswomen.org), Women's Feature Service (India), and feminist organizations and networks we cite in other chapters.

To summarize, in this chapter we argue that facts are always open to interpretation and that everyone makes theory in trying to understand their experiences. Feminist theories that seek to explain women's lives involve clear value positions and constitute a critique of the dominant view that sees theory as "objective" or "value-free." Socially lived theorizing is essential for women's studies. It creates knowledge that reflects the points of view and interests of a broad range of people. It is visionary and can lead to social change. Socially lived theorizing requires collective dialogue, careful listening to other people's theories, and sophisticated skills in "reading" media texts so that we do not draw stereotypical notions of others into our theory making.

This chapter may seem abstract in the beginning, and you may want to return to it as you work with the material in this book. It is also a good idea to review it at the end of your course. Or, you can study this chapter after you have read some of the thematic chapters that follow.

❖❖❖

Questions for Reflection

As you read and discuss the readings in this chapter, think about these questions:

1. How do *you* explain poverty? In the U.S.? Worldwide? How are these linked?

2. How do you explain inequality between women and men in this country? Between white people and people of color in this country?

3. What does it take for a member of a dominant group (e.g., a white male) to be willing to learn from and value the experiences of someone from another group (e.g., a Native American woman)?

4. What standpoints help to give full and cogent explanations of issues such as obesity and global warming?

5. Consider people and events that have affected the development of your thinking. How did this happen?

6. Have spiritual beliefs and religious institutions influenced your values and perspectives? If so, how?

7. How do you know what you know? How is this connected to your genealogy and standpoint?

Finding Out More on the Web

1. Explore the Web site of a women's organization. What can you learn about the organization's theoretical framework? How does this inform its activities? Here are some examples to get you started:

   Center for Women's Global Leadership: **www.cwgl.rutgers.edu**

   Fund for a Feminist Majority: **http://feminist.org**

   Global Fund for Women: **www.globalfundforwomen.org**

   Global Women's Strike: **www.globalwomenstrike.net**

   International Community of Women Living with HIV/AIDS: **www.icw.org**

   National Organization for Women: **www.now.org**

   Third Wave Foundation: **www.thirdwavefoundation.org**

   Women for Genuine Security: **www.genuinesecurity.org**

   Women Living Under Muslim Laws: **www.wluml.org/English**

   Women of Color Resource Center: **www.coloredgirls.org**

   Women's International League for Peace & Freedom: **www.wilpf.org/International**

2. Compare editorial perspectives and news coverage of an issue you care about in progressive magazines, Web logs, foreign newspapers online, or WomenseNews (**www.womensenews.org**) with those of mainstream U.S. reporting.

Taking Action

1. Analyze what happens when you get into an argument with a friend, classmate, or teacher about an issue that matters to you. Are you both using the same assumptions? Do you understand the other person's argument? Do you have compatible understandings of the issue? Can you explain your position more clearly, or do you need to rethink it? Are facts enough to convince someone who is skeptical of your views? Use what you have learned from this chapter to express your views.

2. Pay attention to the theoretical ideas incorporated into TV news reports. When the presenter says, "Now for the stories behind the headlines," whose stories are these? Who is telling them? What, if anything, is missing from these accounts? What else do you need to know in order to have a full explanation? How can you incorporate the ideas from this chapter into your "readings" of mass media?

3. Look critically at media representations of people like you and people in other groups. How are they portrayed? What is left out of these representations? What stereotypes do they reinforce?

4. Read a novel like Gerd Brantenberg's *Egalia's Daughters* or Marge Piercy's *Woman on the Edge of Time* that redefines gender roles and stereotypes. What do you learn about your assumptions?

E I G H T

The Social Construction of Gender (1991)

Judith Lorber

Judith Lorber is Professor Emerita of Sociology and Women's Studies at Brooklyn College and The Graduate School, City University of New York, and the author of numerous books and articles on gender, feminism, and women's health. In 1996 she received the American Sociological Association Jessie Bernard Career Award for her contribution to feminist scholarship.

Talking about gender for most people is the equivalent of fish talking about water. Gender is so much the routine ground of everyday activities that questioning its taken-for-granted assumptions and presuppositions is like thinking about whether the sun will come up. Gender is so pervasive that in our society we assume it is bred into our genes. Most people find it hard to believe that gender is constantly created and re-created out of human interaction, out of social life, and is the texture and order of that social life. Yet gender, like culture, is a human production that depends on everyone constantly "doing gender" (West and Zimmerman 1987).

And everyone "does gender" without thinking about it. Today, on the subway, I saw a well-dressed man with a year-old child in a stroller. Yesterday, on a bus, I saw a man with a tiny baby in a carrier on his chest. Seeing men taking care of small children in public is increasingly common—at least in New York City. But both men were quite obviously stared at—and smiled at, approvingly. Everyone was doing gender—the men who were changing the role of fathers and the other passengers, who were applauding them silently. But there was more gendering going on that probably fewer people noticed. The baby was wearing a white crocheted cap and white clothes. You couldn't tell if it was a boy or a girl. The child in the stroller was wearing a dark blue T-shirt and dark print pants. As they started to leave the train, the father put a Yankee baseball cap on the child's head. Ah, a boy, I thought. Then I noticed the gleam of tiny earrings in the child's ears, and as they got off, I saw the little flowered sneakers and lace-trimmed socks. Not a boy after all. Gender done.

Gender is such a familiar part of daily life that it usually takes a deliberate disruption of our expectations of how women and men are supposed to act to pay attention to how it is produced. Gender signs and signals are so ubiquitous that we usually fail to note them—unless they are missing or ambiguous. Then we are uncomfortable until we have successfully placed the other person in a gender status; otherwise, we feel socially dislocated. In our society, in addition to man and woman, the status can be *transvestite* (a person who dresses in opposite-gender clothes) and *transsexual* (a person who has had sex-change surgery). Transvestites and transsexuals construct their gender status by dressing, speaking, walking, gesturing in the ways prescribed for women or men—whichever they want to be taken for—and so does any "normal" person.

For the individual, gender construction starts with assignment to a sex category on the basis of what the genitalia look like at birth. Then babies are dressed or adorned in a way that displays the category because parents don't want to be constantly asked whether their baby is a girl or a boy. A sex category becomes a gender status through naming, dress, and the use of other gender markers. Once a child's gender is evident, others treat those in one gender differently from those in the other, and the children respond to the different treatment by feeling different and behaving differently. As soon as they can talk, they start to refer to themselves as members of their gender. Sex doesn't come into play again until puberty, but by that time, sexual feelings and desires and practices have been shaped by gendered norms and expectations. Adolescent boys and girls approach and avoid each other in an elaborately scripted and gendered mating dance. Parenting is gendered, with different expectations for mothers and for fathers, and people of different genders work at different kinds of jobs. The work adults do as mothers and fathers and as low-level workers and high-level bosses, shapes women's and men's life experiences, and these experiences produce different feelings, consciousness, relationships, skills—ways of being that we call feminine or masculine. All of these processes constitute the social construction of gender.

Gendered roles change—today fathers are taking care of little children, girls and boys are wearing unisex clothing and getting the same education, women and men are working at the same jobs. Although many traditional social groups are quite strict about maintaining gender differences, in other social groups they seem to be blurring. Then why the one-year-old's earrings? Why is it still so important to mark a child as a girl or a boy, to make sure she is not taken for a boy or he for a girl? What would happen if they were? They would, quite literally, have changed places in their social world.

To explain why gendering is done from birth, constantly and by everyone, we have to look not only at the way individuals experience gender but at gender as a social institution. As a social institution, gender is one of the major ways that human beings organize their lives. Human society depends on a predictable division of labor, a designated allocation of scarce goods, assigned responsibility for children and others who cannot care for themselves, common values and their systematic transmission to new members, legitimate leadership, music, art, stories, games, and other symbolic productions. One way of choosing people for the different tasks of society is on the basis of their talents, motivations, and competence—their demonstrated achievements. The other way is on the basis of gender, race, ethnicity—ascribed membership in a category of people. Although societies vary in the extent to which they use one or the other of these ways of allocating people to work and to carry out other responsibilities, every society uses gender and age grades. Every society classifies people as "girl and boy children," "girls and boys ready to be married," and "fully adult women and men," constructs similarities among them and differences between them, and assigns them to different roles and responsibilities. Personality characteristics, feelings, motivations, and ambitions flow from

these different life experiences so that the members of these different groups become different kinds of people. The process of gendering and its outcome are legitimated by religion, law, science, and the society's entire set of values.

Gender as Process, Stratification, and Structure

As a social institution, gender is a process of creating distinguishable social statuses for the assignment of rights and responsibilities. As part of a stratification system that ranks these statuses unequally, gender is a major building block in the social structures built on these unequal statuses.

As a *process,* gender creates the social differences that define "woman" and "man." In social interaction throughout their lives, individuals learn what is expected, see what is expected, act and react in expected ways, and thus simultaneously construct and maintain the gender order: "The very injunction to be a given gender takes place through discursive routes: to be a good mother, to be a heterosexually desirable object, to be a fit worker, in sum, to signify a multiplicity of guarantees in response to a variety of different demands all at once" (J. Butler 1990, 145). Members of a social group neither make up gender as they go along nor exactly replicate in rote fashion what was done before. In almost every encounter, human beings produce gender, behaving in the ways they learned were appropriate for their gender status, or resisting or rebelling against these norms. Resistance and rebellion have altered gender norms, but so far they have rarely eroded the statuses.

Gendered patterns of interaction acquire additional layers of gendered sexuality, parenting, and work behaviors in childhood, adolescence, and adulthood. Gendered norms and expectations are enforced through informal sanctions of gender-inappropriate behavior by peers and by formal punishment or threat of punishment by those in authority should behavior deviate too far from socially imposed standards for women and men.

Everyday gendered interactions build gender into the family, the work process, and other organizations and institutions, which in turn reinforce gender expectations for individuals. Because gender is a process, there is room not only for modification and variation by individuals and small groups but also for institutionalized change (J. W. Scott 1988, 7).

As part of a *stratification* system, gender ranks men above women of the same race and class. Women and men could be different but equal. In practice, the process of creating difference depends to a great extent on differential evaluation. As Nancy Jay (1981) says: "That which is defined, separated out, isolated from all else is A and pure. Not-A is necessarily impure, a random catchall, to which nothing is external except A and the principle of order that separates it from Not-A" (45). From the individual's point of view, whichever gender is A, the other is Not-A; gender boundaries tell the individual who is like him or her, and all the rest are unlike. From society's point of view, however, one gender is usually the touchstone, the normal, the dominant, and the other is different, deviant, and subordinate. In Western society, "man" is A, "woman" is Not-A. (Consider what a society would be like where woman was A and man Not-A.)

The further dichotomization by race and class constructs the gradations of a heterogeneous society's stratification scheme. Thus, in the United States, white is A, African American is Not-A; middle class is A, working class is Not-A, and "African American women occupy a position whereby the inferior half of a series of these dichotomies converge" (P. H. Collins 1989, 70). The dominant categories are the hegemonic ideals, taken so for granted as the way things should be that white is not ordinarily thought of as a race, middle class as a class, or men as a gender. The characteristics of these categories define the Other as that which lacks the valuable qualities the dominants exhibit.

In a gender-stratified society, what men do is usually valued more highly than what women do because men do it, even when their activities are very similar or the same. In different regions of southern India, for example, harvesting rice is men's work, shared work, or women's work: "Wherever a task is done by women it is considered easy, and where it is done by [men] it is considered difficult" (Mencher 1988, 104). . . . Conversely, because they are the superior group, white men do not have to do the "dirty work," such as housework;

the most inferior group does it, usually poor women of color (Palmer 1989). . . .

Societies vary in the extent of the inequality in social status of their women and men members, but where there is inequality, the status "woman" (and its attendant behavior and role allocations) is usually held in lesser esteem than the status "man." Since gender is also intertwined with a society's other constructed statuses of differential evaluation—race, religion, occupation, class, country of origin, and so on—men and women members of the favored groups command more power, more prestige, and more property than the members of the disfavored groups. Within many social groups, however, men are advantaged over women. The more economic resources, such as education and job opportunities, are available to a group, the more they tend to be monopolized by men. In poorer groups that have few resources (such as working-class African Americans in the United States), women and men are more nearly equal, and the women may even outstrip the men in education and occupational status (Almquist 1987).

As a *structure*, gender divides work in the home and in economic production, legitimates those in authority, and organizes sexuality and emotional life (Connell 1987, 91–142). As primary parents, women significantly influence children's psychological development and emotional attachments, in the process reproducing gender. Emergent sexuality is shaped by heterosexual, homosexual, bisexual, and sadomasochistic patterns that are gendered—different for girls and boys, and for women and men—so that sexual statuses reflect gender statuses.

When gender is a major component of structured inequality, the devalued genders have less power, prestige, and economic rewards than the valued genders. In countries that discourage gender discrimination, many major roles are still gendered; women still do most of the domestic labor and child rearing, even while doing full-time paid work; women and men are segregated on the job and each does work considered "appropriate"; women's work is usually paid less than men's work. Men dominate the positions of authority and leadership in government, the military, and the law; cultural productions, religions, and sports reflect men's interests. . . .

Gender inequality—the devaluation of "women" and the social domination of "men"—has social functions and social history. It is not the result of sex, procreation, physiology, anatomy, hormones, or genetic predispositions. It is produced and maintained by identifiable social processes and built into the general social structure and individual identities deliberately and purposefully. The social order as we know it in Western societies is organized around racial, ethnic, class, and gender inequality. I contend, therefore, that the continuing purpose of gender as a modern social institution is to construct women as a group to be the subordinates of men as a group.

The Paradox of Human Nature

To say that sex, sexuality, and gender are all socially constructed is not to minimize their social power. These categorical imperatives govern our lives in the most profound and pervasive ways, through the social experiences and social practices of what Dorothy Smith calls the "everday/evernight world" (1990, 31–57). The paradox of human nature is that it is *always* a manifestation of cultural meanings, social relationships, and power politics; "not biology, but culture, becomes destiny" (J. Butler 1990, 8). Gendered people emerge not from physiology or sexual orientation but from the exigencies of the social order, mostly, from the need for a reliable division of the work of food production and the social (not physical) reproduction of new members. The moral imperatives of religion and cultural representations guard the boundary lines among genders and ensure that what is demanded, what is permitted, and what is tabooed for the people in each gender is well known and followed by most (C. Davies 1982). Political power, control of scarce resources, and, if necessary, violence uphold the gendered social order in the face of resistance and rebellion. Most people, however, voluntarily go along with their society's prescriptions for those of their gender status, because the norms and expectations get built into their sense of worth and identity as . . . [the way we] think, the way we see and hear and speak, the way we fantasy, and the way we feel.

There is no core or bedrock in human nature below these endlessly looping processes of the social production of sex and gender, self and other, identity and psyche, each of which is a "complex cultural construction" (J. Butler 1990, 36). *For humans, the social is the natural.* Therefore, "in its feminist senses, gender cannot mean simply the cultural appropriation of biological sexual difference. Sexual difference is itself a fundamental—and scientifically contested—construction. Both 'sex' and 'gender' are woven of multiple, asymmetrical strands of difference, charged with multifaceted dramatic narratives of domination and struggle" (Haraway 1990, 140).

REFERENCES

Almquist, Elizabeth M. 1987. "Labor market gendered inequality in minority groups," *Gender & Society* 1:400–14.

Butler, Judith. 1990. *Gender Trouble: Feminism and the Subversion of Identity.* New York and London: Routledge.

Collins, Patricia Hill. 1989. "The social construction of black feminist thought," *Signs* 14:745–73.

Connell, R. [Robert] W. 1987. *Gender and Power: Society, the Person, and Sexual Politics.* Stanford, Calif.: Stanford University Press.

Davies, Christie. 1982. "Sexual taboos and social boundaries," *American Journal of Sociology* 87:1032–63.

Haraway, Donna. 1990. "Investment strategies for the evolving portfolio of primate female," in Jacobus, Mary, Evelyn Fox Keller, and Sally Shuttleworth (eds.). *Body/politics: Women and the Discourse of Science.* New York and London: Routledge.

Jay, Nancy. 1981. "Gender and dichotomy," *Feminist Studies* 7:38–56.

Mencher, Joan. 1988. "Women's work and poverty: Women's contribution to household maintenance in South India," in Daisy Dwyer and Judith Bruce (eds.). *A Home Divided: Women and Income in the Third World.* Stanford, Calif.: Stanford University Press.

Palmer, Phyllis. 1989. *Domesticity and Dirt: Housewives and Domestic Servants in the United States, 1920–1945.* Philadelphia: Temple University Press.

Scott, Joan Wallach. 1988. *Gender and the Politics of History.* New York: Columbia University Press.

Smith, Dorothy E. 1990. *The Conceptual Practices of Power: A Feminist Sociology of Knowledge.* Toronto: University of Toronto Press.

West, Candace, and Don Zimmerman. 1987. "Doing gender," *Gender & Society* 1:125–51.

NINE

Patriarchy, the System (1997)
An It, Not a He, a Them, or an Us

Allan G. Johnson

Allan G. Johnson is a sociologist, author, and public speaker with thirty years of teaching experience exploring the issues of privilege, oppression, and social inequality. His books include *The Forest and the Trees: Sociology as Life, Practice, and Promise* and *The Gender Knot: Unraveling Our Patriarchal Legacy.* http://www.agjohnson.us.

"When you say patriarchy," a man complained from the rear of the audience, "I know what you *really* mean—me!" A lot of people hear "men" whenever someone says "patriarchy," so that criticism of male privilege and the oppression of women is taken to mean that all men—each and every one of them—are oppressive people. It's enough to prompt many men to take it personally, bristling at what they often see as a way to make them feel guilty. And some women feel free to blame individual men for patriarchy simply because they're men. Some of the time, men feel defensive because they identify with patriarchy and its values and don't want to face the consequences these produce or the prospect of giving up male privilege. But defensiveness can also reflect a common confusion about the difference between patriarchy as a kind of society and the people who participate in it. If we're ever going to work toward real change, it's a confusion we'll have to clear up.

To do this, we have to realize that we're stuck in a model of social life that views everything as beginning and ending with individuals. Looking at things in this way, the tendency is to think that if bad things happen in the world, it's only because there are bad people who have entered into some kind of conspiracy. Racism exists, then, because white people are racist bigots who hate members of racial and ethnic minorities and want to do them harm. The oppression of women happens because men want and like to dominate women and act out hostility toward them. There is poverty and class oppression because people in the upper classes are greedy, heartless, and cruel. The flip side of this individualistic model of guilt and blame is that race, gender, and class oppression are actually not oppression at all, but merely the sum of individual failings on the part of blacks, women, and the poor, who lack the right stuff to compete successfully with whites, men, and others who know how to make something of themselves.

What this kind of thinking ignores is that we are all participating in something larger than ourselves or any collection of us. On some level, most people are familiar with the idea that social life involves us in something larger than ourselves, but few seem to know what to do with that idea. Blaming everything on "the system" strikes a deep chord in many people. But it also touches on a basic misunderstanding of social life, because blaming "the system" (presumably society) for our problems, doesn't take the next step to understanding what that might mean. What exactly *is* a system, for example, and how could it run our lives? Do *we* have anything to do with shaping *it*, and if so, how? How, for example, do we participate in patriarchy, and how does that link us to the consequences? How is what we think of as "normal" life related to male privilege, women's oppression, and the hierarchical, control-obsessed world in which everyone's lives are embedded?

Without asking such questions, we can't understand gender fully and we avoid taking responsibility either for ourselves or for patriarchy. Instead, "the system" serves as a vague, unarticulated catchall, a dumping ground for social problems, a scapegoat that can never be held to account and that, for all the power we think it has, can't talk back or actually *do* anything.

. . . But we can't have it both ways. If society is a powerful force in social life, as it surely is, then we have to understand it and how we are connected to it. To do this, we have to change how we think about it, because how we think affects the kinds of questions we ask. The questions we ask in turn shape the kinds of answers and solutions we'll come up with.

If we see patriarchy as nothing more than men's and women's individual personalities, motivations, and behavior, for example, then it probably won't even occur to us to ask about larger contexts—such as institutions like the family, religion, and the economy—and how people's lives are shaped in relation to them. From this kind of individualistic perspective, we might ask why a particular man raped, harassed, or beat a woman. We wouldn't ask, however, what kind of society would promote persistent *patterns* of such behavior in everyday life, from wife-beating jokes to the routine inclusion of sexual coercion and violence in mainstream movies. We'd be quick to explain rape and battery as the acts of sick or angry men, but we'd rarely take seriously the question of what kind of society would produce so much male anger and pathology or direct it toward sexual violence rather than something else. We'd rarely ask how gender violence might serve other more "normalized" ends such as male control and domination. We might ask why a man would like pornography that objectifies, exploits, and promotes violence against women, or debate whether the Constitution protects an individual's right to produce and distribute it. But it'd be hard to stir up interest in asking what kind of society would give violent and degrading visions of women's bodies and human sexuality such a prominent and pervasive place in its culture to begin with.

. . . We need to see and deal with the social roots that generate and nurture the social problems that are reflected in and manifested through the behavior of individuals. We can't do this without realizing that we all participate in something larger than ourselves, something we didn't create but that we have the power to affect through the choices we make about *how* to participate.

Some readers have objected to "participate" as a way to describe women's relation to patriarchy. This is based on the idea that participation is something voluntary, freely chosen, entered into as equals, and it therefore makes little sense to suggest that women can participate in their own oppression. But that is not my meaning here, nor is it a necessary interpretation of the word. To *participate*

is simply to have a *part* in what goes on, to do something (or *not*) and to have the choice affect the consequences, regardless of whether it is conscious or unconscious, coerced or not. Of course, the *terms* of women's participation differ dramatically from those that shape men's, but it is participation, nonetheless.

This concept is similar to the participation of workers in the system of capitalism. They do not participate as equals to the capitalists who employ them or on terms they would choose if they could. Nevertheless, without them, capitalism cannot function as a system that oppresses them.

The importance of participation can be seen in the great variety of ways that women and working-class people respond to oppression—all the forms that fighting back or giving in can take. To argue that women or workers do not participate is to render them powerless and irrelevant to patriarchy's and capitalism's past and future, for it is only as participants that people can affect anything. . . .

The something larger we all participate in is patriarchy, which is more than a collection of individuals (such as "men"). It is a system, which means it can't be reduced to the people who participate in it. If you go to work in a corporation, for example, you know the minute you walk in the door that you've entered "something" that shapes your experience and behavior, something that isn't just you and the other people you work with. You can feel yourself stepping into a set of relationships and shared understandings about who's who and what's supposed to happen and why, and all of this limits you in many ways. And when you leave at the end of the day you can feel yourself released from the constraints imposed by your participation in that system. You can feel the expectations drop away and your focus shift to other systems such as family or a neighborhood bar that shape your experience in different ways.

To understand a system like a corporation, we have to look at more than people like you, because all of you aren't the corporation, even though you make it run. If the corporation were just a collection of people, then whatever happened to the corporation would by definition also happen to them, and vice versa. But clearly this isn't so. A corporation can go bankrupt or cease to exist altogether without any of the people who work there going bankrupt or disappearing. Or everyone who works for a corporation could quit, but that wouldn't necessarily mean the end of the corporation, only the arrival of a new set of participants. We can't understand a system, then, just by looking at the people who participate in it, for it is something larger and has to be understood as such.

Even more so, we cannot understand the world and our lives in it without looking at the dynamic relationship between individual people and social systems. Nor can we understand the countless details—from sexual violence to patterns of conversation to unequal distributions of power—that make up the reality of male privilege and the oppression of women.

As the accompanying figure shows, this relationship has two parts. The arrow on the right side represents the idea that as we participate in social systems, we are shaped as individuals. Through the process of *socialization,* we learn how to participate in social life—from families, schools, religion, and the mass media, through the examples set by parents, peers, coaches, teachers, and public figures—a continuing stream of ideas and images of people and the world and who we are in relation to them.

Through all of this, we develop a sense of personal identity—including gender—and how this positions us in relation to other people, especially in terms of inequalities of power. As I grew up watching movies and television, for example, the message was clear that men are the most important people on the planet because they're the ones who supposedly do the most important things as defined by patriarchal culture. They're the strong ones who build, the heroes who fight the good fight, the geniuses, writers and artists, the bold leaders, and even the evil—but always interesting—villains. Even God is gendered male.

Among the many consequences of such messages is to encourage in men a sense of entitlement in relation to women—to be tended to and taken care of, deferred to and supported no matter how badly they behave. In the typical episode of the television sitcom, *Everybody Loves Raymond,* for example, Ray Barone routinely behaves toward his wife, Debra, in ways that are insensitive, sexist, adolescent, and downright stupid, but by the end of each half hour we always find out why she puts up with it year after year—for some reason that's never made clear, she just loves the guy. This sends the message that it's reasonable for a heterosexual man to expect to "have" an intelligent and beautiful woman who will love him and stay with him in spite of his behaving badly toward her a great deal of the time.

Invariably, some of what we learn through socialization turns out not to be true and then we may have to deal with that. I say "may" because powerful forces encourage us to keep ourselves in a state of denial, to rationalize what we've learned in order to keep it safe from scrutiny, if only to protect our sense of who we are and ensure our being accepted by other people, including family and friends. In the end, the default is to adopt the dominant version of reality and act as though it's the only one there is.

In addition to socialization, participation in social systems shapes our behavior through *paths of least resistance,* a concept that refers to the conscious and unconscious choices we make from one moment to the next. When a man hears other men tell sexist jokes, for example, there are many things he *could* do, but they vary in how much social resistance they're likely to provoke. He could laugh along with them, for example, or remain silent or ignore them or object. And, of course, there are millions of other things he could do—sing, dance, go to sleep, scratch his nose, and so on. Most of these possibilities won't even occur to him, which is one of the ways that social systems limit our options. But of those that do occur to him, usually one will risk less resistance than all the rest. The path of least resistance is to go along, and unless he's willing to deal with greater resistance, that's the choice he's most likely to make.

Our daily lives consist of an endless stream of such choices as we navigate among various possibilities in relation to the path of least resistance in each social situation. Most of the time, we make choices unconsciously without realizing what we're doing. It's just what seems most comfortable to us, most familiar, and safest. The more aware we are of what's going on, however, the more likely it is that we can make conscious, informed choices, and therein lies our potential to make a difference.

This brings us to the arrow on the left side of the figure, which represents the fact that human beings are the ones who make social systems happen. . . . Because people make systems happen, then people can also make systems happen differently. And when systems happen differently, the consequences are different as well. In other words, when people step off the path of least resistance, they have the potential not simply to change other people, but to alter the way the system itself happens. Given that systems shape people's behavior, this kind of change has enormous potential. When a man objects to a sexist joke, for example, it can shake other men's perception of what's socially acceptable and what's not so that the next time they're in this kind of situation, their perception of the social environment itself—not just of other people as individuals, whom they may or may not know personally—may shift in a new direction that makes old paths (such as telling sexist jokes) more difficult to choose because of the increased risk of social resistance.

The model in the figure represents a basic sociological view of the world at every level of human experience, from the global capitalist economy to sexual relationships. Patriarchy fits this model as a social system in which women and men participate. As such, it is more than a collection of women and men and can't be understood simply by understanding *them*. We are not patriarchy, no more than people who believe in Allah *are* Islam or Canadians *are* Canada. Patriarchy is a kind of society organized around certain kinds of social relationships and ideas that shape paths of least resistance. As individuals, we participate in it. Paradoxically, our participation both shapes our lives and gives us the opportunity to be part of changing or perpetuating it. But *we are not it*, which means patriarchy can exist without men having "oppressive personalities" or actively conspiring with one another to defend male privilege.

To demonstrate that gender privilege and oppression exist, we don't have to show that men are villains, that women are good-hearted victims, that women don't participate in their own oppression, or that men never oppose it. If a society is oppressive, then people who grow up and live in it will tend to accept, identify with, and participate in it as "normal" and unremarkable life. That's the path of least resistance in any system. It's hard not to follow it, given how we depend on society and its rewards and punishments that hinge on going along with the status quo. When privilege and oppression are woven into the fabric of everyday life, we don't need to go out of our way to be overtly oppressive for a system of privilege to produce oppressive consequences, for, as Edmund Burke tells us, evil requires only that good people do nothing.

"The System"

. . .

The crucial thing to understand about patriarchy or any other social system is that it's something people participate in. It's an arrangement of shared understandings and relationships that connect people to one another and something larger than themselves. In some ways, we're like players who participate in a game. Monopoly, for example, consists of a set of ideas about things such as the meaning of property and rent, the value of competition and accumulating wealth, and various rules about rolling dice, moving around a board, buying, selling, and developing property, collecting rents, winning, and losing. It has positions—player, banker, and so on— that people occupy. It has material elements such as the board, houses and hotels, dice, property deeds, money, and "pieces" that represent each player's movements on the board. As such, the game is something we can think of as a social system whose elements cohere with a unity and wholeness that distinguish it from other games and from nongames.[1] Most important, we can describe it as a system without ever talking about the personal characteristics or motivations of the individual people who actually play it at any given moment.

If we watch people play Monopoly, we notice certain routine patterns of feeling and behavior that reflect paths of least resistance inherent in the game itself. If someone lands on a property I own, for example, I collect the rent (if I happen to notice); and if they can't pay, I take their assets and force them from the game. The game encourages me to feel good about this, not necessarily because *I'm* greedy and merciless, but because the game is about winning, and this is what winning consists of in Monopoly. Since everyone else is also trying to win by driving me out of the game, each step I take toward winning protects me and alleviates some anxiety about landing on a property whose rent *I* can't pay.

Because these patterns are shaped by the game far more than by the individual players, we can find ourselves behaving in ways that might seem disturbing in other situations. When I'm not playing Monopoly, I behave quite differently, even though I'm still the same person. This is why I don't play Monopoly anymore—I don't like the way it encourages me to feel and behave in the name of "fun," especially toward people I care about. The reason we behave differently outside the game doesn't lie in our personalities but in the *game's* paths of least resistance, which define certain behavior and values as appropriate and expected. When we see ourselves as Monopoly players, we feel limited by the rules and goals the game defines, and experience it as something external to us and beyond our control.

It's important to note how rarely it occurs to people to simply change the rules. The relationships, terms, and goals that organize the game aren't presented to us as ours to judge or alter. The more attached we feel to the game and the more closely we identify ourselves as players, the more likely we are to feel helpless in relation to it. If you're about to drive someone into bankruptcy, you can excuse yourself by saying, "I've got to take your money, those are the rules," but only if you ignore the fact that you could choose not to play or could suggest a change in the rules. Then again, if you can't imagine life without the game, you won't see many alternatives to doing what's expected.

If we try to explain patterns of social behavior only in terms of individual people's personalities and motives—people do greedy things, for example, because they *are* greedy—then we ignore how behavior is shaped by paths of least resistance found in the systems people participate in. The "profit motive" associated with capitalism, for example, is typically seen as a psychological motive that explains capitalism as a system: Capitalism exists because there are people who want to make a profit. But this puts the cart before the horse by avoiding the question of where wanting to make a profit comes from in the first place. We need to ask what kind of world makes such wants possible and encourages people to organize their lives around them, for although we may pursue profit as we play Monopoly or participate in real-world capitalism,

the psychological profit motive doesn't originate with us. We aren't born with it. It doesn't exist in many cultures and was unknown for most of human history. The profit motive is a historically developed aspect of market systems in general and capitalism in particular that shapes the values, behavior, and personal motives of those who participate in it.

To argue that managers lay off workers, for example, simply because managers are heartless or cruel ignores the fact that success under capitalism often depends on this kind of competitive, profit-maximizing, "heartless" behavior. Most managers probably know in their hearts that the practice of routinely discarding people in the name of profit and expedience is hurtful and unfair. This is why they feel so bad about having to be the ones to carry it out, and protect their feelings by inventing euphemisms such as "downsizing" and "outplacement." And yet they participate in a system that produces these cruel results anyway, not because of cruel personalities or malice toward workers, but because a capitalist system makes this a path of least resistance and exacts real costs from those who stray from it.

To use the game analogy, it's a mistake to assume that we can understand players' behavior without paying attention to the game they're playing. We create even more trouble by thinking we can understand the *game* without ever looking at it as something more than what goes on inside the people who play it. One way to see this is to realize that systems often work in ways that don't reflect people's experience and motivations. . . .

In spite of all the good reasons to not use individual models to explain social life, doing so constitutes a path of least resistance because personal experience and motivation are what we know best. As a result, we tend to see something like patriarchy as the result of poor socialization through which men learn to act dominant and masculine and women learn to act subordinate and feminine. While there is certainly some truth to this, it doesn't work as an explanation of patterns like privilege and oppression. It's no better than trying to explain war as simply the result of training men to be warlike, without looking at economic systems that equip armies at huge profits and political systems that organize and hurl armies at one another. It's like trying to understand what happens during

Monopoly games without ever talking about the game itself and the kind of society in which it would exist. Of course, soldiers and Monopoly players do what they do because they've learned the rules, but this doesn't tell us much about the rules themselves and why they exist to be learned in the first place. Socialization is merely a process, a mechanism for training people to participate in social systems. Although it tells us how people learn to participate, it doesn't illuminate the systems themselves. As such, it can tell us something about the *how* of a system like patriarchy, but very little about the *what* and the *why*.

. . .

We can't find a way out of patriarchy or imagine something different without a clear sense of what patriarchy is and what it's got to do with us. . . .

We need to see more clearly what patriarchy is about as a system. This includes cultural ideas about men and women, the web of relationships that structure social life, and the unequal distribution of power, rewards and resources that underlies privilege and oppression. We need to see new ways to participate by forging alternative paths of least resistance; for the system doesn't simply "run us" like hapless puppets. It may be larger than us, it may not *be* us, but it doesn't happen except *through* us. And that's where we have power to do something about it and about ourselves in relation to it.

Patriarchy

. . .

Patriarchy's defining elements are its male-dominated, male-identified, male-centered, and control-obsessed character, but this is just the beginning. At its core, patriarchy is based in part on a set of symbols and ideas that make up a culture embodied by everything from the content of everyday conversation to literature and film. Patriarchal culture includes ideas about the nature of things, including women, men, and humanity, with manhood and masculinity most closely associated with being human and womanhood and femininity relegated to the marginal position of "other." It's about how social life is and how it's supposed to be, about what's expected of people and about how they feel. It's about standards of feminine beauty and masculine toughness, images of feminine vulnerability

and masculine protectiveness, of older men coupled with younger women, of elderly women alone. It's about defining women and men as opposites, about the "naturalness" of male aggression, competition, and dominance and of female caring, cooperation, and subordination. It's about the valuing of masculinity and maleness and the devaluing of femininity and femaleness. It's about the primary importance of a husband's career and the secondary status of a wife's, about child care as a priority in women's lives and its secondary importance in men's. It's about the social acceptability of anger, rage, and toughness in men but not in women, and of caring, tenderness, and vulnerability in women but not in men.

Above all, patriarchal culture is about the core value of control and domination in almost every area of human existence. From the expression of emotion to economics to the natural environment, gaining and exercising control is a continuing goal. Because of this, the concept of power takes on a narrow definition in terms of "power over"—the ability to control others, events, resources, or one's self in spite of resistance—rather than alternatives such as the ability to cooperate, to give freely of oneself, or to feel and act in harmony with nature. To have power over and to be prepared to use it are culturally defined as good and desirable (and characteristically "masculine"), and to lack such power or to be reluctant to use it is seen as weak if not contemptible (and characteristically "feminine"). This is a major reason that patriarchies with the means to do so are often so quick to go to war. Studies of the (mostly) men who formulate U.S. military strategy, for example, show that it is almost impossible to lose standing by advocating an excessive use of force in international relations (such as the U.S. response to terrorism and the 2003 invasion of Iraq). But anyone—especially a man—who advocates restraint in the use of force, runs the serious risk of being perceived as less than manly and, therefore, lacking credibility.

The main use of any culture is to provide symbols and ideas out of which to construct a sense of what is real. As such, language mirrors social reality in sometimes startling ways. In contemporary usage, for example, the words *crone, witch, bitch,* and *virgin* describe women as threatening, evil, or heterosexually inexperienced and thus incomplete. In prepatriarchal times, however, these words evoked far different images. The crone was the old woman whose life experience gave her insight, wisdom, respect, and the power to enrich people's lives. The witch was the wise-woman healer, the knower of herbs, the midwife, the link joining body, spirit, and Earth. The bitch was Artemis-Diana, goddess of the hunt, most often associated with the dogs who accompanied her. And the virgin was merely a woman who was unattached, unclaimed, and un-owned by any man and therefore independent and autonomous. Notice how each word has been trans-formed from a positive cultural image of female power, independence, and dignity to an insult or a shadow of its former self so that few words remain to identify women in ways both positive and powerful.

Going deeper into patriarchal culture, we find a complex web of ideas that define reality and what's considered good and desirable. To see the world through patriarchal eyes is to believe that women and men are profoundly different in their basic natures, that hierarchy is the only alternative to chaos, and that men were made in the image of a masculine God with whom they enjoy a special relationship. It is to take as obvious the idea that there are two and only two distinct genders; that patriarchal heterosexuality is "natural" and same-sex attraction is not; that be-cause men neither bear nor breast-feed children, they cannot feel a compelling bodily connection to them; that on some level every woman, whether heterosex-ual or lesbian, wants a "real man" who knows how to "take charge of things," including her; that females can't be trusted, especially when they're menstruat-ing or accusing men of sexual abuse. In spite of all the media hype to the contrary, to embrace patriarchy still is to believe that mothers should stay home and that fathers should work outside the home, regard-less of men's and women's actual abilities or needs. It is to buy into the notion that women are weak and men are strong, that women and children need men to support and protect them, all in spite of the fact that in many ways men are not the physically stronger sex, that women perform a huge share of hard physical labor in many societies (often larger than men's), that women's physical endurance tends to be greater than men's over the long haul, that women tend to be more capable of enduring pain and emotional stress.[2] And yet, as Elizabeth Janeway notes, such evidence means little in the face of a pa-triarchal culture that dictates how things *ought* to be and, like all cultural mythology, "will not be argued down by facts. It may seem to be making

straightforward statements, but actually these con-ceal another mood, the imperative. Myth exists in a state of tension. It is not really describing a situation, but trying by means of this description *to bring about* what it declares to exist."[3]

To live in a patriarchal culture is to learn what's expected of men and women—to learn the rules that regulate punishment and reward based on how indi-viduals behave and appear. These rules range from laws that require men to fight in wars not of their own choosing to customary expectations that mothers will provide child care. Or that when a woman shows sex-ual interest in a man or merely smiles or acts friendly, she gives up her right to say no and to control her own body. And to live under patriarchy is to take into ourselves ways of feeling—the hostile contempt for femaleness that forms the core of misogyny and pre-sumptions of male superiority, the ridicule men direct at other men who show signs of vulnerability or weakness, or the fear and insecurity that every woman must deal with when she exercises the right to move freely in the world, especially at night and by herself in public places.

Such ideas make up the symbolic sea we swim in and the air we breathe. They are the primary well from which springs how we think about ourselves, other people, and the world. As such, they provide a taken-for-granted everyday reality, the setting for our interactions with other people that continually fash-ion and refashion a sense of what the world is about and who we are in relation to it. This doesn't mean that the ideas underlying patriarchy determine what we think, feel, and do, but it does mean they define what we'll have to deal with as we participate in it.

The prominent place of misogyny in patriarchal culture, for example, doesn't mean that every man and woman consciously hates all things female. But it does mean that to the extent that we don't feel such hatred, it's *in spite of* paths of least resistance con-tained in our culture. Complete freedom from such feelings and judgments is all but impossible. It is cer-tainly possible for heterosexual men to love women without mentally fragmenting them into breasts, but-tocks, genitals, and other variously desirable parts. It is possible for women to feel good about their bodies, to not judge themselves as being too fat, to not abuse themselves to one degree or another in pursuit of im-possible male-identified standards of beauty and sex-ual attractiveness. All of this is possible, but to live in patriarchy is to breathe in misogynist images of women as objectified sexual property valued primarily for their usefulness to men. This finds its way into everyone who grows up breathing and swimming in it, and once inside of us it remains, however unaware of it we may be. So, when we hear or express sexist jokes and other forms of misogyny, we may not recognize it, and even if we do, we may say nothing rather than risk other people thinking we're "too sensitive" or, especially in the case of men, "not one of the guys." In either case, we are involved, if only by our silence.

The symbols and ideas that make up patriarchal culture are important to understand because they have such powerful effects on the structure of social life. By *structure,* I mean the ways privilege and oppression are organized through social relationships and unequal distributions of power, rewards, opportunities, and resources. This appears in countless patterns of everyday life in family and work, religion and politics, community and education. It is found in family divisions of labor that exempt fathers from most domestic work even when both parents work outside the home and in the concentration of women in lower-level pink-collar jobs and male predominance almost everywhere else. It is in the unequal distribution of income and all that goes with it, from access to health care to the availability of leisure time. It is in patterns of male violence and harassment that can turn a simple walk in the park or a typical day at work or a lovers' quarrel into a life-threatening nightmare. More than anything, the structure of patriarchy is found in the unequal distribution of power that makes male privilege possible, in patterns of male dominance in every facet of human life, from everyday conversation to global politics. By its nature, patriarchy puts issues of power, dominance, and control at the center of human existence, not only in relationships between men and women, but among men as they compete and struggle to gain status, maintain control, and protect themselves from what other men might do to them. . . .

The System in Us in the System

One way to see how people connect with systems is to think of us as occupying social positions that locate us in relation to people in other positions. We connect to families, for example, through positions such as "mother," "daughter," and "cousin"; to economic

systems through positions such as "vice president," "secretary," or "unemployed"; to political systems through positions such as "citizen," "registered voter," and "mayor"; to religious systems through positions such as "believer" and "clergy." How we perceive the people who occupy such positions and what we expect of them depend on cultural ideas—such as the belief that mothers are naturally better than fathers at child care. Such ideas are powerful because we use them to construct a sense of who we and other people are. When a woman marries, for example, how people (including her) perceive and think about her changes as cultural ideas about what it means to be a wife come into play—ideas about how wives feel about their husbands, what's most important to wives, what's expected of them, and what they may expect of others.

From this perspective, *who* we and other people think we are has a lot to do with *where* we are in relation to social systems and all the positions we occupy in them. We wouldn't exist as social beings if it weren't for our participation in one social system or another. It's hard to imagine just who we'd be and what our existence would consist of if we took away all our connections to the symbols, ideas, and relationships that make up social systems. Take away language and all that it allows us to imagine and think, starting with our names. Take away all the positions that we occupy and the roles that go with them—from daughter and son to occupation and nationality—and with these all the complex ways our lives are connected to other people. Not much would be left over that we'd recognize as ourselves.

We can think of a society as a network of interconnected systems within systems, each made up of social positions and their relations to one another. To say, then, that I'm white, male, college educated, nondisabled, and a writer, sociologist, U.S. citizen, heterosexual, middle-aged, husband, father, grandfather, brother, and son identifies me in relation to positions which are themselves related to positions in various social systems, from the entire world to the family of my birth. In another sense, the day-to-day reality of a society only exists through what people actually do as they participate in it. Patriarchal culture, for example, places a high value on control and maleness. By themselves, these are just abstractions. But when men and women actually talk and men interrupt women more than women interrupt men, or men ignore topics introduced by women in favor of their own or in other ways control conversation, or when men use their authority to harass women in the workplace, then the reality of patriarchy as a kind of society and people's sense of themselves as female and male within it actually happen in a concrete way.

In this sense, like all social systems, patriarchy exists only through people's lives. . . . This has two important implications for how we understand patriarchy. First, to some extent people experience patriarchy as external to them. But this doesn't mean that it's a distinct and separate thing, like a house in which we live. Instead, by participating in patriarchy we are *of* patriarchy and it is *of* us. Both exist *through* the other and neither can exist without the other. Second, patriarchy isn't static. It's an ongoing *process* that's continuously shaped and reshaped. Since the thing we're participating in is patriarchal, we tend to behave in ways that create a patriarchal world from one moment to the next. But we have some freedom to break the rules and construct everyday life in different ways, which means that the paths we choose to follow can do as much to change patriarchy as they can to perpetuate it.

We're involved in patriarchy and its consequences because we occupy social positions in it, which is all it takes. Because patriarchy is, by definition, a system of inequality organized around gender categories, we can no more avoid being involved in it than we can avoid being female or male. *All* men and *all* women are therefore involved in this oppressive system, and none us can control *whether* we participate, only *how*. As Harry Brod argues, this is especially important in relation to men and male privilege:

We need to be clear that there is no such thing as giving up one's privilege to be "outside" the system. One is always in the system. The only question is whether one is part of the system in a way which challenges or strengthens the status quo. Privilege is not something I take and which I therefore have the option of not taking. It is something that society gives me, and unless I change the institutions which give it to me, they will continue to give it, and I will continue to have it, however noble and egalitarian my intentions.[4]

NOTES

1. Although the game analogy is useful, social systems are quite unlike a game in important ways. The rules and other understandings on which social life is based are far more complex, ambiguous, and contradictory than those of a typical game and much more open to negotiation and "making it up" as we go along.
2. See, for example, Rosalyn Baxandall, Linda Gordon, and Susan Reverby, eds., *America's Working Women: A Documentary History—1600 to the Present* (New York: Vintage Press, 1976); Ashley Montagu, *The Natural Superiority of Women* (New York: Collier, 1974); Robin Morgan, ed., *Sisterhood Is Global* (New York: Feminist Press, 1996); and Marilyn Waring, *If Women Counted: A New Feminist Economics* (San Francisco: HarperCollins, 1990).
3. Elizabeth Janeway, *Man's World, Woman's Place: A Study in Social Mythology* (New York: Dell, 1971), 37.
4. Harry Brod, "Work Clothes and Leisure Suits: The Class Basis and Bias of the Men's Movement," in *Men's Lives*, edited by Michael S. Kimmel and Michael A. Messner (New York: Macmillan, 1989), 280.

T E N

◆◆◆

Black Feminist Thought: Knowledge, Consciousness, and the Politics of Empowerment (1990)—Excerpt

Patricia Hill Collins

Patricia Hill Collins is an award-winning writer and social theorist. Her books include *Black Feminist Thought: Knowledge, Consciousness and the Politics of Empowerment* and *Black Sexual Politics: African Americans, Gender, and the New Racism*. She has held editorial positions with professional journals and acted as a consultant for community organizations. She is a professor of sociology at the University of Maryland.

Knowledge, Consciousness, and the Politics of Empowerment

Black feminist thought demonstrates Black women's emerging power as agents of knowledge. By portraying African-American women as self-defined, self-reliant individuals confronting race, gender, and class oppression, Afrocentric feminist thought speaks to the importance that knowledge plays in empowering oppressed people. One distinguishing feature of Black feminist thought is its insistence that both the changed consciousness of individuals and the social transformation of political and economic institutions constitute essential ingredients for social change. New knowledge is important for both dimensions of change. . . .

Epistemological Shifts: Dialogue, Empathy, and Truth

Black Women as Agents of Knowledge Living life as an African-American woman is a necessary prerequisite for producing Black feminist thought because within Black women's communities thought is validated and produced with reference to a particular set of historical, material, and epistemological conditions. African-American women who adhere to the idea that claims about Black women must be substantiated by Black women's sense of our own experiences and who anchor our knowledge claims in an Afrocentric epistemology have produced a rich tradition of Black feminist thought.

Traditionally such women were blues singers, poets, autobiographers, storytellers, and orators validated by everyday Black women as experts on a Black women's standpoint. Only a few unusual African-American feminist scholars have been able to defy Eurocentric masculinist epistemologies and explicitly embrace an Afrocentric feminist epistemology. Consider Alice Walker's description of Zora Neale Hurston:

> In my mind, Zora Neale Hurston, Billie Holiday, and Bessie Smith form a sort of unholy trinity. Zora *belongs* in the tradition of black women singers, rather than among "the literati." . . . Like Billie and Bessie she followed her own road, believed in her own gods, pursued her own dreams, and refused to separate herself from "common" people. (Walker 1977, xvii–xviii)

Zora Neale Hurston is an exception for prior to 1950, few African-American women earned advanced degrees and most of those who did complied with Eurocentric masculinist epistemologies. Although these women worked on behalf of Black women, they did so within the confines of pervasive race and gender oppression. Black women scholars were in a position to see the exclusion of African-American women from scholarly discourse, and the thematic content of their work often reflected their interest in examining a Black women's standpoint. However, their tenuous status in academic institutions led them to adhere to Eurocentric masculinist epistemologies so that their work would be accepted as scholarly. As a result, while they produced Black feminist thought, those African-American women most likely to gain academic credentials were often least likely to produce Black feminist thought that used an Afrocentric feminist epistemology.

An ongoing tension exists for Black women as agents of knowledge, a tension rooted in the sometimes conflicting demands of Afrocentricity and feminism. Those Black women who are feminists are critical of how Black culture and many of its traditions oppress women. For example, the strong pronatal beliefs in African-American communities that foster early motherhood among adolescent girls, the lack of self-actualization that can accompany the double-day of paid employment and work in the home, and the emotional and physical abuse that many Black women experience from their fathers, lovers, and husbands all reflect practices opposed by African-American women who are feminists. But these same women may have a parallel desire as members of an oppressed racial group to affirm the value of that same culture and traditions (Narayan 1989). Thus strong Black mothers appear in Black women's literature, Black women's economic contributions to families is lauded, and a curious silence exists concerning domestic abuse.

As more African-American women earn advanced degrees, the range of Black feminist scholarship is expanding. Increasing numbers of African-American women scholars are explicitly choosing to ground their work in Black women's experiences, and, by doing so, they implicitly adhere to an Afrocentric feminist epistemology. Rather than being restrained by their both/and status of marginality, these women make creative use of their outsider-within status and produce innovative Afrocentric feminist thought. The difficulties these women face lie less in demonstrating that they have mastered white male epistemologies than in resisting the hegemonic nature of these patterns of thought in order to see, value, and use existing alternative Afrocentric feminist ways of knowing.

In establishing the legitimacy of their knowledge claims, Black women scholars who want to develop Afrocentric feminist thought may encounter the often conflicting standards of three key groups. First, Black feminist thought must be validated by ordinary African-American women who, in the words of Hannah Nelson, grow to womanhood "in a world where the saner you are, the madder you are made to appear" (Gwaltney 1980, 7). To be credible in the eyes of this group, scholars must be personal advocates for their material, be accountable for the consequences of their work, have lived or experienced their material in some fashion, and be willing to engage in dialogues about their findings with ordinary, everyday people. Second, Black feminist thought also must be accepted by the community of Black women scholars. These scholars place varying amounts of importance on rearticulating a Black women's standpoint using an Afrocentric feminist epistemology. Third, Afrocentric feminist thought within academia must be prepared to confront Eurocentric masculinist political and epistemological requirements.

The dilemma facing Black women scholars engaged in creating Black feminist thought is that a knowledge claim that meets the criteria of adequacy for one group and thus is judged to be an acceptable knowledge claim may not be translatable into the terms of a different group. Using the example of Black English, June Jordan illustrates the difficulty of moving among epistemologies:

> You cannot "translate" instances of Standard English preoccupied with abstraction or with nothing/nobody evidently alive into Black English. That would warp the language into uses antithetical to the guiding perspective of its community of users. Rather you must first change those Standard English sentences, themselves, into ideas consistent with the person-centered assumptions of Black English. (Jordan 1985, 130)

Although both worldviews share a common vocabulary, the ideas themselves defy direct translation.

For Black women who are agents of knowledge, the marginality that accompanies outsider-within status can be the source of both frustration and creativity. In an attempt to minimize the differences between the cultural context of African-American communities and the expectations of social institutions, some women dichotomize their behavior and become two different people. Over time, the strain of doing this can be enormous. Others reject their cultural context and work against their own best interests by enforcing the dominant group's specialized thought. Still others manage to inhabit both contexts but do so critically, using their outsider-within perspectives as a source of insights and ideas. But while outsiders within can make substantial contributions as agents of knowledge, they rarely do so without substantial personal cost. "Eventually it comes to you," observes Lorraine Hansberry, "the thing that makes you exceptional, if you are at all, is inevitably that which must also make you lonely" (1969, 148).

Once Black feminist scholars face the notion that, on certain dimensions of a Black women's standpoint, it may be fruitless to try and translate ideas from an Afrocentric feminist epistemology into a Eurocentric masculinist framework, then other choices emerge. Rather than trying to uncover universal knowledge claims that can withstand the translation from one epistemology to another (initially, at least), Black women intellectuals might find efforts to rearticulate a Black women's standpoint especially fruitful. Rearticulating a Black women's standpoint refashions the concrete and reveals the more universal human dimensions of Black women's everyday lives. "I date all my work," notes Nikki Giovanni, "because I think poetry, or any writing, is but a reflection of the moment. The universal comes from the particular" (1988, 57). bell hooks maintains, "my goal as a feminist thinker and theorist is to take that abstraction and articulate it in a language that renders it accessible—not less complex or rigorous—but simply more accessible" (1989, 39). The complexity exists; interpreting it remains the unfulfilled challenge for Black women intellectuals.

Situated Knowledge, Subjugated Knowledge, and Partial Perspectives
"My life seems to be an increasing revelation of the intimate face of universal struggle," claims June Jordan:

You begin with your family and the kids on the block, and next you open your eyes to what you call your people and that leads you into land reform into Black English into Angola leads you back to your own bed where you lie by yourself, wondering if you deserve to be peaceful, or trusted or desired or left to the freedom of your own unfaltering heart. And the scale shrinks to the size of a skull: your own interior cage. (Jordan 1981, xi)

Lorraine Hansberry expresses a similar idea: "I believe that one of the most sound ideas in dramatic writing is that in order to create the universal, you must pay very great attention to the specific. Universality, I think, emerges from the truthful identity of what is" (1969, 128). Jordan and Hansberry's insights that universal struggle and truth may wear a particularistic, intimate face suggest a new epistemological stance concerning how we negotiate competing knowledge claims and identify "truth."

The context in which African-American women's ideas are nurtured or suppressed matters. Understanding the content and epistemology of Black women's ideas as specialized knowledge requires attending to the context from which those ideas emerge. While produced by individuals, Black feminist thought as situated knowledge is embedded in the communities in which African-American women find ourselves (Haraway 1988).

A Black women's standpoint and those of other oppressed groups is not only embedded in a context but exists in a situation characterized by domination. Because Black women's ideas have been suppressed, this suppression has stimulated African-American women to create knowledge that empowers people to resist domination. Thus Afrocentric feminist thought represents a subjugated knowledge (Foucault 1980). A Black women's standpoint may provide a preferred stance from which to view the matrix of domination because, in principle, Black feminist thought as specialized thought is less likely than the specialized knowledge produced by dominant groups to deny the connection between ideas and the vested interests of their creators. However, Black feminist thought as subjugated knowledge is not exempt from critical analysis, because subjugation is not grounds for an epistemology (Haraway 1988).

Despite African-American women's potential power to reveal new insights about the matrix of domination, a Black women's standpoint is only one angle of vision. Thus Black feminist thought represents a partial perspective. The overarching matrix of domination houses multiple groups, each with varying experiences with penalty and privilege that produce corresponding partial perspectives, situated knowledges, and, for clearly identifiable subordinate groups, subjugated knowledges. No one group has a clear angle of vision. No one group possesses the theory of methodology that allows it to discover the absolute "truth" or, worse yet, proclaim its theories and methodologies as the universal norm evaluating other groups' experiences. Given that groups are unequal in power in making themselves heard, dominant groups have a vested interest in suppressing the knowledge produced by subordinate groups. Given the existence of multiple and competing knowledge claims to "truth" produced by groups with partial perspectives, what epistemological approach offers the most promise?

Dialogue and Empathy   Western social and political thought contains two alternative approaches to ascertaining "truth." The first, reflected in positivist science, has long claimed that absolute truths exist and that the task of scholarship is to develop objective, unbiased tools of science to measure these truths. But Afrocentric, feminist, and other bodies of critical theory have unmasked the concepts and epistemology of this version of science as representing the vested interests of elite white men and therefore as being less valid when applied to experiences of other groups and, more recently, to white male recounting of their own exploits. Earlier versions of standpoint theories, themselves rooted in a Marxist positivism, essentially reversed positivist science's assumptions concerning whose truth would prevail. These approaches suggest that the oppressed allegedly have a clearer view of "truth" than their oppressors because they lack the blinders created by the dominant group's ideology. But this version of standpoint theory basically duplicates the positivist belief in one "true" interpretation of reality and, like positivist science, comes with its own set of problems.

Relativism, the second approach, has been forwarded as the antithesis of and inevitable outcome of rejecting a positivist science. From a relativist perspective all groups produce specialized thought and each group's thought is equally valid. No group can claim to have a better interpretation of the "truth" than another. In a sense, relativism represents the opposite of scientific ideologies of objectivity. As epistemological stances, both positivist science and relativism minimize the importance of specific location in influencing a group's knowledge claims, the power inequities among groups that produce subjugated knowledges, and the strengths and limitations of partial perspective (Haraway 1988).

The existence of Black feminist thought suggests another alternative to the ostensibly objective norms of science and to relativism's claims that groups with competing knowledge claims are equal. In this volume I placed Black women's subjectivity in the center of analysis and examined the interdependence of the everyday, taken-for-granted knowledge shared by African-American women as a group, the more specialized knowledge produced by Black women intellectuals, and the social conditions shaping both types of thought. This approach allowed me to describe the creative tension linking how sociological conditions influenced a Black women's standpoint and how the power of the ideas themselves gave many African-American women the strength to shape those same sociological conditions. I approached Afrocentric feminist thought as situated in a context of domination and not as a system of ideas divorced from political and economic reality. Moreover, I presented Black feminist thought as subjugated knowledge in that African-American women have long struggled to find alternative locations and techniques for articulating our own standpoint. In brief, I examined the situated, subjugated standpoint of African-American women in order to understand Black feminist thought as a partial perspective on domination.

This approach to Afrocentric feminist thought allows African-American women to bring a Black women's standpoint to larger epistemological dialogues concerning the nature of the matrix of domination. Eventually such dialogues may get us to a point at which, claims Elsa Barkley Brown, "all people can learn to center in another experience, validate it, and judge it by its own standards without need of comparison or need to adopt that framework as their own" (1989, 922). In such dialogues, "one has no need to 'decenter' anyone in order to center someone else; one has only to constantly, appropriately, 'pivot the center'" (p. 922).

Those ideas that are validated as true by African-American women, African-American men, Latina lesbians, Asian-American women, Puerto Rican men, and other groups with distinctive standpoints, with each group using the epistemological approaches growing from its unique standpoint, thus become the most "objective" truths. Each group speaks from its own standpoint and shares its own partial, situated knowledge. But because each group perceives its own truth as partial, its knowledge is unfinished. Each group becomes better able to consider other groups' standpoints without relinquishing the uniqueness of its own standpoint or suppressing other groups' partial perspectives. "What is always needed in the appreciation of art, or life," maintains Alice Walker, "is the larger perspective. Connections made, or at least attempted, where none existed before, the straining to encompass in one's glance at the varied world the common thread, the unifying theme through immense diversity" (1983, 5). Partiality and not universality is the condition of being heard; individuals and groups forwarding knowledge claims without owning their position are deemed less credible than those who do.

Dialogue is critical to the success of this epistemological approach, the type of dialogue long extant in the Afrocentric call-and-response tradition whereby power dynamics are fluid, everyone has a voice, but everyone must listen and respond to other voices in order to be allowed to remain in the community. Sharing a common cause fosters dialogue and encourages groups to transcend their differences.

Existing power inequities among groups must be addressed before an alternative epistemology such as that described by Elsa Barkley Brown or Alice Walker can be utilized. The presence of subjugated knowledges means that groups are not equal in making their standpoints known to themselves and others. "Decentering" the dominant group is essential, and relinquishing privilege of this magnitude is unlikely to occur without struggle. But still the vision exists, one encompassing "coming to believe in the possibility of a variety of experiences, a variety of ways of understanding the world, a variety of frameworks of operation, without imposing consciously or unconsciously a notion of the norm" (Brown 1989, 921).

REFERENCES

Brown, Elsa Barkely. 1986. *Hearing Our Mothers' Lives.* Atlanta: Fifteenth Anniversary of African-American and African Studies, Emory University. (unpublished)

———. 1989. "African-American Women's Quilting: A Framework for Conceptualizing and Teaching African-American Women's History." *Signs* 14(4): 921–29.

Foucault, Michel. 1980. *Power/Knowledge: Selected Interviews and Other Writings 1972–1977,* edited by Colin Gordon. New York: Pantheon.

Giovanni, Nikki. 1988. *Sacred Cows . . . and Other Edibles.* New York: Quill/William Morrow.

Gwaltney, John Langston. 1980. *Drylongso, A Self-Portrait of Black America.* New York: Vintage.

Hansberry, Lorraine. 1969. *To Be Young, Gifted and Black.* New York: Signet.

Haraway, Donna. 1988. "Situated Knowledges: The Science Question in Feminism and the Privilege of Partial Perspective." *Feminist Studies* 14(3): 575–99.

hooks, bell. 1989. *Talking Back: Thinking Feminist, Thinking Black.* Boston: South End Press.

Jordan, June. 1985. *On Call.* Boston: South End Press.

Narayan, Uma. 1989. "The Project of Feminist Epistemology: Perspectives from a Nonwestern Feminist." In *Gender/Body/Knowledge: Feminist Reconstructions of Being and Knowing,* edited by Alison M. Jaggar and Susan R. Bordo, 256–69. New Brunswick, NJ: Rutgers University Press.

Walker, Alice. 1977. "Zora Neale Hurston: A Cautionary Tale and a Partisan View." Foreword to *Zora Neale Hurston: A Literary Biography,* by Robert Hemenway, xi–xviii. Urbana: University of Illinois Press.

———. 1983. *In Search of Our Mothers' Gardens.* New York: Harcourt Brace Jovanovich.

ELEVEN

Genealogies of Community, Home, and Nation (1993/2003)

Chandra Talpade Mohanty

Chandra Talpade Mohanty is a professor of women's studies at Syracuse University. Her widely acclaimed scholarly work, most recently *Feminism Without Borders: Decolonizing Theory, Practicing Solidarity,* focuses on transnational feminist theory, cultural studies, and antiracist education.

. . . At a time when globalization (and monoculturalism) is the primary economic and cultural practice to capture and hold hostage the material resources and economic and political choices of vast numbers of the world's population, what are the concrete challenges for feminists of varied genealogies working together? Within the context of the history of feminist struggle in the United States, the 1980s were a period of euphoria and hope for feminists of color, gay and lesbian, and antiracist, white feminists. Excavating subjugated knowledges and histories in order to craft decolonized, oppositional racial and sexual identities and political strategies that posed direct challenges to the gender, class, race, and sexual regimes of the capitalist U.S. nation-state anchored the practice of antiracist, multicultural feminisms.

At the start of this century, however, I believe the challenges are somewhat different. Globalization, or the unfettered mobility of capital and the accompanying erosion and reconstitution of local and national economic and political resources and of democratic processes, the post–cold war U.S. imperialist state, and the trajectories of identity-based social movements in the 1980s and 1990s constitute the ground for transnational feminist engagement in the twenty-first century. Multicultural feminism that is radical, antiracist, and nonheterosexist thus needs to take on a hegemonic capitalist regime and conceive of itself as also crossing national and regional borders. Questions of "home," "belonging," "nation," and "community" thus become profoundly complicated.

One concrete task that feminist educators, artists, scholars, and activists face is that of historicizing and denaturalizing the ideas, beliefs, and values of global capital such that underlying exploitative social relations and structures are made visible. This means being attentive not only to the grand narrative or "myth" of capitalism as "democracy" but also to the mythologies that feminists of various races, nations, classes, and sexualities have inherited about one another. I believe one of the greatest challenges we (feminists) face is this task of recognizing and undoing the ways in which we colonize and objectify our different histories and cultures, thus colluding with hegemonic processes of domination and rule. Dialogue across differences is thus fraught with tension, competitiveness, and pain. Just as radical or critical multiculturalism cannot be the mere sum or coexistence of different cultures in a profoundly unequal, colonized world, multicultural feminism cannot assume the existence of a dialogue among feminists from different communities without specifying a just and ethical basis for such a dialogue.

Undoing ingrained racial and sexual mythologies within feminist communities requires, in Jacqui Alexander's words, that we "become fluent in each other's histories." It also requires seeking "unlikely coalitions" (Davis 1998, 299)[1] and, I would add, clarifying the ethics and meaning of dialogue. What are the conditions, the knowledges, and the attitudes that make a noncolonized dialogue possible? How can we craft a dialogue anchored in equality, respect, and dignity for all peoples? In other words, I want to suggest that one of the most crucial challenges for a critical multicultural feminism is working out how to engage in ethical and caring dialogues (and revolutionary struggles) across the divisions, conflicts, and individualist identity formations that interweave feminist communities in the United States. Defining genealogies is one crucial element in creating such a dialogue.

Just as the very meaning and basis for dialogue across difference and power needs to be analyzed and carefully crafted, the way we define genealogies also poses a challenge. Genealogies that not only specify and illuminate historical and cultural differences but also envision and enact common political and intellectual projects across these differences constitute a crucial element of the work of building critical multicultural feminism.

To this end I offer a personal, anecdotal meditation on the politics of gender and race in the construction of South Asian identity in North America. My location in the United States is symptomatic of large numbers of migrants, nomads, immigrants, workers across the globe for whom notions of home, identity, geography, and history are infinitely complicated in the twenty-first century. . . .

Emotional and Political Geographies of Belonging

On a TWA flight on my way back to the United States from a conference in the Netherlands, the white professional man sitting next to me asks which school I go to and when I plan to go home—all in the same breath. I put on my most professorial demeanor (somewhat hard in crumpled blue jeans and cotton T-shirt) and inform him that I teach at a small liberal arts college in upstate New York and that I have lived in the United States for over twenty years. At this point, my work is in the United States, not in India. (This is no longer entirely true—my work is also with feminists and grassroots activists in India, but he doesn't need to know this.) Being "mistaken" for a graduate student seems endemic to my existence in this country: few Third World women are granted professional (i.e., adult) and/or permanent (one is always a student) status in the United States, even if we exhibit clear characteristics of adulthood such as gray hair and facial lines. The man ventures a further question: what do I teach? On hearing "women's studies," he becomes quiet and we spend the next eight hours in polite silence. He has decided that I do not fit into any of his categories, but what can you expect from a feminist (an Asian one) anyway? I feel vindicated and a little superior, even though I know he doesn't really feel "put in his place." Why should he? He claims a number of advantages in this situation: white skin, maleness, and citizenship privileges. Judging by his enthusiasm for expensive "ethnic food" in Amsterdam, and his J. Crew clothes, I figured class difference (economic or cultural) wasn't exactly a concern in our interaction. We both appeared to have similar social access as "professionals."

I have been asked the "home" question (when are you going home?) periodically for twenty years now. Leaving aside the subtly racist implications of the question (go home, you don't belong), I am still not satisfied with my response. What is home? The place I was born? Where I grew up? Where my parents live? Where I live and work as an adult? Where I locate my community, my people? Who are "my people"? Is home a geographical space, a historical space, an emotional, sensory space? Home is always so crucial to immigrants and migrants—I even write about it in scholarly texts (perhaps to avoid addressing it, as an issue that is also very personal?). What interests me is the meaning of home for immigrants and migrants. I am convinced that this question—how one understands and defines home—is a profoundly political one.

Since settled notions of territory, community, geography, and history don't work for us, what does it really mean to be "South Asian" in the United States? Obviously, I was not South Asian in India: I was Indian. What else could one be but "Indian" at a time when a successful national independence struggle had given birth to a socialist democratic nation-state? This was the beginning of the decolonization of the Third World. Regional geography (South Asia) appeared less relevant as a mark of identification than citizenship in a postcolonial independent nation on the cusp of economic and political autonomy. However, in North America, identification as South Asian (in addition to Indian, in my case) takes on its own logic. "South Asian" refers to folks of Indian, Pakistani, Sri Lankan, Bangladeshi, Kashmiri, and Burmese origin. Identifying as South Asian rather than Indian adds numbers and hence power within the U.S. state. Besides, regional differences among those from different South Asian countries are often less relevant than the commonalities based on our experiences and histories of immigration, treatment, and location in the United States.

Let me reflect a bit on the way I identify myself, and the way the U.S. state and its institutions categorize me. Perhaps thinking through the various labels will lead me to the question of home and identity. In 1977, I arrived in the United States on an F1 visa (a student visa). At that time, my definition of myself—a graduate student in education at the University of Illinois—and the "official" definition of me (a student allowed into the country on an F1 visa) obviously coincided. Then I was called a "foreign student" and expected to go "home" (to India, even though my parents were in Nigeria at the time) after

getting my Ph.D. This is the assumed trajectory for a number of Indians, especially the postindependence (my) generation, who come to the United States for graduate study.

However, this was not to be my trajectory. I quickly discovered that being a foreign student, and a woman at that, meant being either dismissed as irrelevant (the quiet Asian woman stereotype), or treated in racist ways (my teachers asked if I understood English and if they should speak slower and louder so that I could keep up—this in spite of my inheritance of the Queen's English and British colonialism) or celebrated and exoticized ("You are so smart! Your accent is even better than that of Americans"— a little Anglophilia at work here, even though all my Indian colleagues insist we speak English the Indian way).

The most significant transition I made at that time was the one from "foreign student" to "student of color." Once I was able to "read" my experiences in terms of race, and to read race and racism as they are written into the social and political fabric of the United States, practices of racism and sexism became the analytic and political lenses through which I was able to anchor myself here. Of course, none of this happened in isolation: friends, colleagues, comrades, classes, books, films, arguments, and dialogues were constitutive of my political education as a woman of color in the United States.

In the late 1970s and early 1980s feminism was gaining momentum on American campuses: it was in the air, in the classrooms, on the streets. However, what attracted me wasn't feminism as the mainstream media and white women's studies departments defined it. Instead, it was a very specific kind of feminism, the feminism of U.S. women of color and Third World women, that spoke to me. In thinking through the links among gender, race, and class in their U.S. manifestations, I was for the first time able to think through my own gendered, classed, postcolonial history. In the early 1980s, reading Audre Lorde, Nawal el Sadaawi, Angela Davis, Cherríe Moraga, bell hooks, Gloria Joseph, Paula Gunn Allen, Barbara Smith, Merle Woo, and Mitsuye Yamada, among others, generated a sort of recognition that was intangible but very inspiring. A number of actions, decisions, and organizing efforts at that time led me to a sense of home and community in relation to women of color in the

United States: home, not as a comfortable, stable, inherited, and familiar space but instead as an imaginative, politically charged space in which the familiarity and sense of affection and commitment lay in shared collective analysis of social injustice, as well as a vision of radical transformation. Political solidarity and a sense of family could be melded together imaginatively to create a strategic space I could call "home." Politically, intellectually, and emotionally I owe an enormous debt to feminists of color—especially to the sisters who have sustained me over the years. . . .

For me, engagement as a feminist of color in the United States made possible an intellectual and political genealogy of being Indian that was radically challenging as well as profoundly activist. Notions of home and community began to be located within a deeply political space where racialization and gender and class relations and histories became the prism through which I understood, however partially, what it could mean to be South Asian in North America. Interestingly, this recognition also forced me to reexamine the meanings attached to home and community in India.

What I chose to claim, and continue to claim, is a history of anticolonialist, feminist struggle in India. The stories I recall, the ones that I retell and claim as my own, determine the choices and decisions I make in the present and the future. I did not want to accept a history of Hindu chauvinist (bourgeois) upward mobility (even though this characterizes a section of my extended family). We all choose partial, interested stories/histories—perhaps not as deliberately as I am making it sound here, but, consciously or unconsciously, these choices about our past(s) often determine the logic of our present.

Having always kept my distance from conservative, upwardly mobile Indian immigrants, to whom the South Asian world in the United States was divided into green card holders and non-green card holders, the only South Asian links I allowed and cultivated were with South Asians with whom I shared a political vision. This considerably limited my community. Racist and sexist experiences in graduate school and after made it imperative that I understand the United States in terms of its history of racism, imperialism, and patriarchal relations, specifically in relation to Third World immigrants. After all, we were then into the Reagan-Bush years, when the neoconservative backlash made it impossible to ignore the rise of racist, antifeminist, and homophobic attitudes, practices, and institutions. Any purely culturalist or nostalgic sentimental definition of being "Indian" or "South Asian" was inadequate. Such a definition fueled the "model minority" myth. And this subsequently constituted us as "outsiders/foreigners" or as interest groups that sought or had obtained the American dream.

In the 1980s, the labels changed: I went from being a "foreign student" to being a "resident alien." I have always thought that this designation was a stroke of inspiration on the part of the U.S. state, since it accurately names the experience and status of immigrants, especially immigrants of color. The flip side of "resident alien" is "illegal alien," another inspired designation. One can be either a resident or illegal immigrant, but one is always an alien. There is no confusion here, no melting pot ideology or narratives of assimilation: one's status as an "alien" is primary. Being legal requires identity papers. (It is useful to recall that the "passport"—and by extensions the concept of nation-states and the sanctity of their borders—came into being after World War I.)

One must be stamped as legitimate (that is, not gay or lesbian and not communist) by the Immigration and Naturalization Service. The INS is one of the central disciplinary arms of the U.S. government. It polices the borders and controls all border crossings, especially those into the United States. In fact, the INS is also one of the primary forces that institutionalizes race differences in the public arena, thus regulating notions of home, legitimacy, and economic access to the "American dream" for many of us. For instance, carrying a green card documenting resident alien status in the United States is clearly very different from carrying an American passport, which is proof of U.S. citizenship. The former allows one to enter the United States with few hassles; the latter often allows one to breeze through the borders and ports of entry of other countries, especially countries that happen to be trading partners (much of Western Europe and Japan, among others) or in an unequal relationship with the United States (much of the noncommunist Third World). At a time when notions of a capitalist free-market economy is seen (falsely) as synonymous with the values attached to democracy, an American passport can open many doors. However, just carrying an American passport is no insurance against racism and unequal and unjust treatment within the United States.

A comparison of the racialization of South Asian immigrants to second-generation South Asian Americans suggests one significant difference between these two generations: experiencing racism as a phenomenon specific to the United States, versus growing up in the ever-present shadow of racism in the case of South Asians born in the United States. This difference in experience would suggest that the psychic effects of racism would also be different for these two constituencies. In addition, questions of home, identity, and history take on very different meanings for South Asians born in North America. But this comparison requires a whole other reflection that is beyond the scope of this chapter.

Home/Nation/Community: The Politics of Being NRI (Nonresident Indian)

Rather obstinately, I refused to give up my Indian passport and chose to remain a resident alien in the United States for many years.[2] This leads me to reflect on the complicated meanings attached to holding Indian citizenship while making a life for myself in the United States. In India, what does it mean to have a green card or U.S. passport, to be an expatriate? What does it mean to visit Mumbai (Bombay) every two to four years and still call it home? Why does speaking in Marathi (my mother tongue) become a measure and confirmation of home? What are the politics of being a part of the majority and the "absent elite" in India, while being a minority and a racialized "other" in the United States? And do feminist politics, or advocating feminism, have the same meanings and urgencies in these different geographical and political contexts?

Some of these questions hit me smack in the face during a visit to India in December 1992, after the infamous destruction of the Babri Masjid in Ayodhya by Hindu fundamentalists on 6 December 1992. (Horrifically, these deadly clashes between Hindus and Muslims took a new turn in March 2002, with Muslims burning a train full of Hindus returning from Ayodhya, inaugurating yet another continuing bloodbath.) In my earlier, rather infrequent visits (once every four or five years was all I

could afford), my green card designated me as an object of envy, privilege, and status within my extended family. Of course, the same green card has always been viewed with suspicion by leftist and feminist friends, who (quite understandably) demand evidence of my ongoing commitment to a socialist and democratic India. During my 1992 visit, however, with emotions running high within my family, my green card marked me as an outsider who couldn't possibly understand the "Muslim problem" in India. I was made aware of being an "outsider" in two profoundly troubling shouting matches with my uncles, who voiced the most hostile sentiments against Muslims. Arguing that India was created as a secular state and that democracy had everything to do with equality for all groups (majority and minority) got me nowhere. The very fundamentals of democratic citizenship in India were/are being undermined and redefined as "Hindu."

Mumbai was one of the cities hardest hit with waves of communal violence following the events of Ayodhya. The mobilization of Hindu fundamentalists, even paramilitary organizations, over the last century and especially since the mid-1940s, had brought Mumbai to a juncture at which the most violently racist discourse about Muslims seemed to be woven into the fabric of acceptable daily life. Racism was normalized in the popular imagination such that it became almost impossible to raise questions in public about the ethics or injustice of racial/ethnic/religious discrimination. I could not assume a distanced posture toward religion anymore. Too many injustices were being committed in my name.

Although born into a Hindu family, I have always considered myself a nonpracticing Hindu—religion had always felt rather repressive when I was growing up. I enjoyed the rituals but resisted the authoritarian hierarchies of organized Hinduism. However, the Hinduism touted by fundamentalist organizations like the RSS (Rashtriya Swayamsevak Sangh, a paramilitary Hindu fundamentalist organization founded in the 1930s) and the Shiv Sena (a Maharashtrian chauvinist, fundamentalist, fascist political organization that has amassed a significant voice in Mumbai politics and government) was one that even I, in my ignorance, recognized as reactionary and distorted. But this discourse was real—hate-filled rhetoric against

Muslims appeared to be the mark of a "loyal Hindu." It was heart-wrenching to see my hometown become a war zone, with streets set on fire and a daily death count to rival any major territorial border war. The smells and textures of my beloved Mumbai, of home, which had always comforted and nurtured me, were violently disrupted. The scent of fish drying on the lines at the fishing village in Danda was submerged in the smell of burning straw and grass as whole *bastis* (*chawls*) were burned to the ground. The very topography, language, and relationships that constituted "home" were exploding. What does community mean in this context?

December 1992 both clarified as well as complicated for me the meanings attached to being an Indian citizen, a Hindu, an educated woman feminist, and a permanent resident in the United States in ways that I have yet to resolve. After all, it is often moments of crisis that make us pay careful attention to questions of identity. Sharp polarizations force one to make choices (not in order to take sides, but in order to accept responsibility) and to clarify one's own analytic, political, and emotional topographies.

I learned that combating the rise of Hindu fundamentalism was a necessary ethical imperative for all socialists, feminists, and Hindus of conscience. Secularism, if it meant absence of religion, was no longer a viable position. From a feminist perspective, it became clear that the battle for women's minds and hearts was very much center stage in the Hindu fundamentalist rhetoric and social position of women. (Two journals, the *Economic and Political Weekly of India* and *Manushi,* are good sources for this work.)

Religious fundamentalist constructions of women embody the nexus of morality, sexuality, and nation—a nexus of great importance for feminists. As in Christian, Islamic, and Jewish fundamentalist discourses, the construction of femininity and masculinity, especially in relation to the idea of the nation, are central to Hindu fundamentalist rhetoric and mobilizations. Women are not only mobilized in the "service" of the nation, but they also become the ground on which discourses of morality and nationalism are written. For instance, the RSS mobilizes primarily middle-class women in the name of a family-oriented Hindu nation, much as the Christian Right does in the United States. But discourses of morality and nation are also embodied in the normative policing of women's sexuality (witness the surveillance and control of women's dress in the name of morality by the contemporary Iranian state and Taliban-ruled Afghanistan). Thus, one of the central challenges Indian feminists face at this time is how to rethink the relationship of nationalism and feminism in the context of religious identities. In addition to the fundamentalist mobilization that is tearing the country apart, the recent incursions of the International Monetary Fund and the World Bank, with their structural adjustment programs that are supposed to "discipline" the Indian economy, are redefining the meaning of postcoloniality and of democracy in India. Categories such as gender, race, caste/class are profoundly and visibly unstable at such times of crisis. These categories must thus be analyzed in relation to contemporary reconstructions of womanhood and manhood in a *global* arena increasingly dominated by religious fundamentalist movements, the IMF, the World Bank, and the relentless economic and ideological colonization of much of the world by multinationals based in the United States, Japan, and Europe. In all these global economic and cultural/ideological processes, women occupy a crucial position.

In India, unlike most countries, the sex ratio has declined since the early 1900s. According to the 1991 census, the ratio was 929 women to 1,000 men, one of the lowest sex ratios in the world. Women produce 70 to 80 percent of all the food in India and have always been the hardest hit by environmental degradation and poverty. The contradictions between civil law and Hindu and Muslim personal laws affect women but rarely men. Horrific stories about the deliberate genocide of female infants as a result of sex determination procedures such as amniocentesis and recent incidents of *sati* (self-immolation by women on the funeral pyres of their husbands) have even hit the mainstream American media. Gender and religious (racial) discrimination are thus urgent, life-threatening issues for women in India. Over the last decade or so, a politically conscious Indian citizenship has necessitated taking such fundamentally feminist issues seriously. In fact, these are the very same issues South Asian feminists in the United States need to address. My responsibility to combat and organize against the regressive and violent repercussions of Hindu fundamentalist mobilizations in India extends to my life in North America. After all, much of the money that sustains the fundamentalist movement is raised and funneled through organizations in the United States.

On Race, Color, and Politics: Being South Asian in North America

It is a number of years since I wrote the bulk of this chapter,[3] and as I reread it, I am struck by the presence of the journeys and border-crossings that weave into and anchor my thinking about genealogies. The very crossing of regional, national, cultural, and geographical borders seems to enable me to reflect on questions of identity, community, and politics. In the past years I have journeyed to and lived among peoples in San Diego, California; Albuquerque, New Mexico; London, England; and Cuttack, India. My appearance as a brown woman with short, dark, graying hair remained the same, but in each of these living spaces I learned something slightly different about being South Asian in North America; about being a brown woman in the midst of other brown women with different histories and genealogies.

I want to conclude with a brief reflection on my journeys to California and New Mexico since they complicate further the question of being South Asian in North America. A rather obvious fact, which had not been experientially visible to me earlier, is that the color line differs depending on one's geographical location in the United States. Having lived on the East Coast for many years, my designation as "brown," "Asian," "South Asian," "Third World," and "immigrant" has everything to do with definitions of "blackness" (understood specifically as African American). However, San Diego, with its histories of immigration and racial struggle, its shared border with Mexico, its predominantly brown (Chicano and Asian-American) color line, and its virulent anti-immigrant culture unsettled my East Coast definitions of race and racialization. I could pass as Latina until I spoke my "Indian" English, and then being South Asian became a question of (in)visibility and foreignness. Being South Asian here was synonymous with being alien, non-American.

Similarly, in New Mexico, where the normative meanings of race and color find expression in the relations between Native American, Chicano, and Anglo communities, being South Asian was a matter of being simultaneously visible and invisible as a brown woman. Here, too, my brownness and facial structure marked me visibly as sometimes Latina, sometimes Native American (evidenced by being hailed numerous times in the street as both). Even being Asian, as in being from a part of the world called "Asia," had less meaning in New Mexico, especially since "Asian" was synonymous with "East Asian": the "South" always fell out. Thus, while I could share some experiences with Latinas and Native American women, for instance, the experience of being an "alien"—an outsider within, a woman outside the purview of normalized U.S. citizenship—my South Asian genealogy also set me apart. Shifting the color line by crossing the geography and history of the American West and Southwest thus foregrounded questions about being South Asian in a space where, first, my brownness was not read against blackness, and second, Asian was already definitively cast as East Asian. In this context, what is the relation of South Asian to Asian American (read: East Asian American)? And why does it continue to feel more appropriate, experientially and strategically, to call myself a woman of color or Third World woman? Geographies have never coincided with the politics of race. And claiming racial identities based on history, social location, and experience is always a matter of collective analysis and politics. Thus, while geographical spaces provide historical and cultural anchors (Marathi, Mumbai, and India are fundamental to my sense of myself), it is the deeper values and strategic approach to questions of economic and social justice and collective anticapitalist struggle that constitute my feminism. Perhaps this is why journeys across the borders of regions and nations always provoke reflections of home, identity, and politics for me: there is no clear or obvious fit between geography, race, and politics for someone like me. I am always called on to define and redefine these relationships—"race," "Asianness," and "brownness" are not embedded in me, whereas histories of colonialism, racism, sexism, and nationalism, as well as of privilege (class and status) are involved in my relation to white people and people of color in the United States.

Let me now circle back to the place I began: defining genealogies as a crucial aspect of crafting critical multicultural feminist practice and the meanings I have come to give to home, community, and identity. By exploring the relationship between being a South Asian immigrant in America and an expatriate Indian citizen (NRI) in India, I have tried, however partially and anecdotally, to clarify the complexities of home and community for this particular feminist of color/South Asian in North America. The genealogy I have created for myself here is partial and deliberate. It is a genealogy that I find emotionally and politically enabling—it is part of the genealogy that underlies my self-identification as an educator involved in a pedagogy of liberation. Of course, my history and experiences are in fact messier and not at all as linear as this narrative makes them sound. But then the very process of constructing a narrative for oneself—of telling a story—imposes a certain linearity and coherence that is never entirely there. That is the lesson, perhaps, especially for us immigrants and migrants: that home, community, and identity all fit somewhere between the histories and experiences we inherit and the political choices we make through alliances, solidarities, and friendships.

One very concrete effect of my creating this particular space for myself has been my involvement in two grassroots organizations, one in India and the other in the United States. The former, an organization called Awareness, is based in Orissa and works to empower the rural poor. The group's focus is political education (similar to Paolo Friere's notion of "conscientization"), and its members have also begun very consciously to organize rural women. The U.S. organization I worked with is Grassroots Leadership of North Carolina. It is a multiracial group of organizers (largely African American and white) working to build a poor and working people's movement in the American South. While the geographical, historical, and political contexts are different in the case of these two

organizations, my involvement in them is very similar, as is my sense that there are clear connections to be made between the work of the two organizations. In addition, I think that the issues, analyses, and strategies for organizing for social justice are also quite similar. This particular commitment to work with grassroots organizers in the two places I call home is not accidental. It is very much the result of the genealogy I have traced here. After all, it took me over a decade to make these commitments to grassroots work in both spaces. In part, I have defined what it means to be South Asian by educating myself about, and reflecting on, the histories and experiences of African American, Latina, West Indian, African, European American, and other constituencies in North America. Such definitions and understandings do provide a genealogy, but a genealogy that is always relational and fluid as well as urgent and necessary.

NOTES

1. Davis, Angela, and Elizabeth Martinez. 1998. "Coalition Building Among People of Color: A Discussion with Angela Davis and Elizabeth Martinez." In *The Angela Davis Reader,* edited by Joy James. Boston: Blackwell.
2. I became a U.S. citizen in 1998, in order to adopt my daughter Uma Talpade Mohanty from Mumbai. Now I no longer hold an Indian passport, although of course my designation as NRI (Nonresident Indian) remains the same.
3. An earlier version of this chapter, entitled "Defining Genealogies: Feminist Reflections on Being South Asian in North America," was published in Women of South Asian Descent Collective (1993). This chapter is dedicated to the memory of Lanubai and Gauribai Vijaykar, my maternal grandaunts, who were single, educated, financially independent, and tall (over six feet), at a time when it was against the grain to be any one of these things; and to Audre Lorde, teacher, sister, friend, whose words and presence continue to challenge me.

3

◆◆◆

Identities and Social Locations:
Who Am I? Who Are My People?

Our identity is a specific marker of how we define ourselves. Discovering and claiming our unique identity is a process of growth, change, and renewal throughout our lifetime. One's identity may seem tangible and fixed at any given point. Over the life span, however, identity is more fluid. For example, an able-bodied woman who suddenly finds herself confined to a wheelchair after an automobile accident, an assimilated Jewish woman who begins the journey of recovering her Jewish heritage, an immigrant woman from a traditional Guatemalan family "coming out" as a lesbian in the United States, or a young, middle-class college student, away from her sheltered home environment for the first time and becoming politicized by an environmental justice organization on campus, will probably find herself redefining who she is, what she values, and what "home" and "community" mean to her.

Identity formation is the result of a complex interplay among a range of factors: individual decisions and choices, particular life events, community recognition and expectations, societal categorization, socialization, and key national or international events. It is an ongoing process that involves several key questions:

Who am I? Who do I want to be?

Who do others think I am and want me to be?

Who and what do societal and community institutions, such as schools, religious institutions, the media, and the law, say I am?

Where/what/who are my "home" and "community"?

Which social group(s) do I want to affiliate with?

Who decides the answers to these questions, and on what basis?

The *American Heritage Dictionary* (1993) defines *identity* as

> the collective aspect of the set of characteristics by which a thing is definitely known or recognizable;
>
> a set of behavioral or personal characteristics by which an individual is recognizable as a member of a group;
>
> the distinct personality of an individual regarded as a persisting entity;
>
> individuality.

The same dictionary defines *to identify* as "to associate or affiliate (oneself) closely with a person or group; to establish an identification with another or others."

These definitions point to the connections between us as individuals and how we are perceived by other people and classified by societal institutions. They also involve a sense of individual agency and choice regarding affiliations with others. Gender, race, ethnicity, class, nationality, sexuality, age, religion, dis/ability, and language are all significant social categories by which people are recognized by others. Indeed, on the basis of these categories alone, others often think they know who we are and how we should behave. Personal decisions about our affiliations and loyalties to specific groups are also shaped by these categories. For example, in communities of color, women may struggle over the question of race versus gender. Is race a more important factor than gender in shaping their lives? If a Latina speaks out publicly about sexism within the Latino community, is she betraying her people? This separation of categories, mirrored by our segregated social lives, tends to set up false dichotomies in which people often feel that they have to choose one aspect of their identity over another. It also presents particular difficulties for mixed-race, bisexual, or transgender people who do not fit neatly into such narrow categories, and reinforces the need for an intersectional framework as we argued in Chapter 1.

In order to understand the complexity and richness of women's experiences, we must examine them from the micro, meso, macro, and global levels of social relations. Each level involves the standards— beliefs, behaviors, customs, and worldview—that people value. But it is important to emphasize that in a society marked by serious social and economic inequality, such as the United States, people in subordinate positions rarely see their values reflected in the dominant culture. Indeed, this absence is an important aspect of their oppression. For example, writing about her family, whom she describes as "the ungrateful poor," Dorothy Allison (Reading 13) states: "My family's lives were not on television, not in books, not even comic books. There was a myth of the poor in this country; but it did not include us, no matter how hard I tried to squeeze us in."

Critically analyzing the issue of identity at all these levels will allow us to see that identity is much more than an individual decision or choice about who we are in the world. Rather, it is a set of complex and often contradictory and conflicting psychological, physical, geographical, political, cultural, historical, and spiritual factors.

Being Myself: The Micro Level

At the micro level, individuals usually feel the most comfortable as themselves. Here one can say, for example, "I am a woman, heterosexual, middle class, Buddhist, with a movement disability; but I am also much more than those categories." At this level we define ourselves and structure our daily activities according to our needs and preferences. At the micro level we can best feel and experience the process of identity formation, which includes naming specific forces and events that shape our identities. At this level we also seem to have more control of the process, although there are always interconnections between events and experiences at this level and the other levels.

Critical life events, such as entering kindergarten, losing a parent through death or divorce, or the onset of puberty, may all serve as catalysts for a shift in how we think about ourselves. A five-year-old Vietnamese American child may experience the first challenge to her sense of identity when her kindergarten teacher admonishes her to speak only in English. A white, middle-class professional woman who thinks of herself as "a person" and a "competent attorney" may begin to give more weight to the significance of gender if she witnesses younger, less experienced male colleagues in her law office passing her by for promotions. A woman who has been raped who attends her first meeting of a women's campus group feels the power of connection with other rape survivors and their allies. An eighty-year-old woman, whose partner of fifty years has just died, must face the loss of her life-time companion, friend, and lover. Such experiences shape each person's ongoing formulation of self, whether or not the process is conscious, deliberate, reflective, or even voluntary.

Identity formation is a lifelong process that includes discovery of the new; recovery of the old, forgotten, or appropriated; and synthesis of the new and old, as illustrated by several writers in this chapter who reflect on how their sense of identity has developed over the course of their lives. At especially important junctures during the process, individuals mark an identity change in tangible ways. An African American woman may change her name from the anglicized Susan to Aisha, with roots in Islamic and African cultures. A Chinese immigrant woman, on the other hand, may adopt an anglicized name, exchanging Nu Lu for Yvonne Lu as part of becoming a U.S. citizen. Another way of marking and effecting a shift in identity is by altering your physical appearance: changing your wardrobe or makeup; cutting your hair very short, wearing it natural rather than permed or pressed, dyeing it purple, or letting the gray show after years of using hair coloring. More permanent changes might include having a tattoo, having your body pierced, having a face lift or tummy tuck, or, for Asian American women, having eye surgery to "Europeanize" your eyes. Transsexuals—female to male and male to female—have surgery to make their physical appearance congruent with their internal sense of self. Other markers of a change in identity include redecorating your home, setting up home for the first time, or relocating to another neighborhood, another city, or another part of the country in search of a new home.

For many people, home is where we grow up until we become independent, by going to college, for example, or getting married; where our parents, siblings, and maybe grandparents are; where our needs for safety, security, and material comfort are met. In reality, what we think of as home is often a complicated and contradictory place where some things we need are present and others are not. Some people's homes are comfortable and secure in a material sense but are also places of emotional or physical violence and cruelty. Some children grow up in homes that provide emotional comfort and a sense of belonging, but

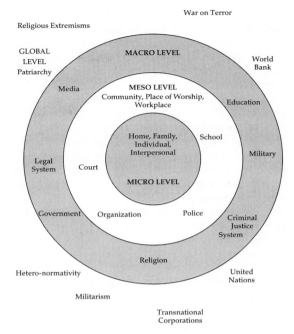

FIGURE 3.1 Levels of Analysis and Interaction (*Source:* Margo Okazawa-Rey)

as they grow older and their values diverge from those of their parents, home may become a source of discomfort and alienation. Children who have been adopted across lines of race, culture, and nation may never feel very comfortable in their adoptive homes. An important step in integrating the different parts of their identities may be to find their birth mothers, to trace their biological ancestry, or to gain the support and friendship of other transracial adoptees (see Simon and Roorda 2000; Trenka, Oparah, and Shin 2006).

Regardless of such experiences, or perhaps because of them, most people continue to seek places of comfort and solace and others with whom they feel they belong and with whom they share common values and interests. Home may be a geographic, social, emotional, and spiritual space where we hope to find safety, security, familiarity, continuity, acceptance, love, and understanding, and where we can feel and be our best, whole selves. Home may be in several places at once or in different places at different times of our lives. Some women may have a difficult time finding a home, a place that feels comfortable and familiar, even if they know what it is. Finally, this process may involve not only searching outside ourselves but also piecing together in some coherent way the scattered parts of our identities—an inward as well as an outward journey.

In the readings that follow, women offer us a view of their identities. An emphasis on the micro level helps us to understand them, to empathize, and to see their humanity, all an important corrective to the distorted representations and stereotyping often found in the mainstream media. Also crucial, these articles are not only about individual experiences but go beyond the micro level to include insights regarding the author's community and the macro-level factors that shape community history and experience.

Community Recognition, Expectations, and Interactions: The Meso Level

It is at the meso level—at school, in the workplace, in the neighborhood, or on the street—that people most frequently ask "Who are you?" or "Where are you from?" in an attempt to categorize us and determine their relationship to us. Moreover, it is here that people experience the complexities, conflicts, and contradictions of multiple identities, which we consider later.

The single most visible signifier of identity is physical appearance. How we look to others affects their perceptions, judgments, and treatment of us. Questions such as "Where do you come from?" and questioning behaviors, such as feeling the texture of your hair or asking if you speak a particular language, are commonly used to interrogate people whose physical appearances especially, but also behaviors, do not match the characteristics designated as belonging to established categories. At root, we are being asked, "Are you one of us or not?" These questioners usually expect simple and straightforward answers, assuming that everyone will fit existing social categories, which are conceived of as undifferentiated and unambiguous. Among people with disabilities, for example, people wanting to identify each other may expect to hear details of another's disability rather than the

fact that the person being questioned also identifies equally strongly as, say, a woman who is white, working class, and bisexual.

Community, like home, may be geographic and emotional, or both, and provides a way for people to express group affiliations. "Where are you from?" is a commonplace question in the United States among strangers, a way to break the ice and start a conversation, expecting answers like "I'm from Tallahassee, Florida," or "I'm from the Bronx." Community might also be an organized group like Alcoholics Anonymous, a religious group, or a political organization like the African American civil rights organization, the National Association for the Advancement of Colored People (NAACP). Community may be cultural or religious as discussed by Melanie Kaye/Kantrowitz (Reading 14), Christina Leaño (Reading 16), and Julia Alvarez (Reading 17), or something more abstract, as in "the women's community" or "the queer community," where there is presumed to be an identifiable group. In these examples there is an assumption of shared values, interests, culture, or language sometimes thought of as essential qualities that define group membership and belonging. This can lead to **essentialism,** where complex identities get reduced to specific qualities deemed to be essential for membership of a particular group: being Muslim or gay, for example.

At the community level, individual identities and needs meet group standards, expectations, obligations, responsibilities, and demands. You compare yourself with others and are subtly compared. Others size up your clothing, accent, personal style, and knowledge of the group's history and culture. You may be challenged directly, "You say you're Latina. How come you don't speak Spanish?" "You say you're working class. What are you doing in a professional job?" These experiences may both affirm our identities and create or highlight inconsistencies and contradictions in who we believe we are, how we are viewed by others, our role and status in the community, and our sense of belonging. In Reading 17, writer Julia Alvarez examines the significance of the quinceañera coming-of-age ceremony for Latina girls, their families, and communities as a way of affirming cultural identities and traditions that are, paradoxically, made—and remade—in the United States. This formerly upper-class celebration has become a rite of passage for U.S.-born daughters of immigrant families with very modest incomes. It incorporates traditions from Mexico, Central America, and the Caribbean, enlarged by U.S. cosumerism. Also, these North American ways of celebrating the quinceañera, Alvarez notes, are being exported "back home."

Some individuals experience **marginality** if they can move in two or more worlds and, in part, be accepted as insiders (Stonequist 1961). Examples include bisexuals, mixed-race people, and immigrants, who all live in at least two cultures. Margaret, a white, working-class woman, for instance, leaves her friends behind after high school graduation as she goes off to an elite university. Though excited and eager to be in a new setting, she often feels alienated at college because her culture, upbringing, and level of economic security differ from those of the many upper-middle-class and upper-class students. During the winter break, she returns to her hometown where she discovers a gulf between herself and her old friends who remained at home and took full-time jobs. She notices that she is now speaking a slightly different language from them and that her interests and preoccupations are different from theirs. Margaret has a foot in both worlds. She has become sufficiently acculturated at college to begin to know that community as an insider, and she has retained her old community of friends, but she is not entirely at ease or wholly accepted by either community. Her identity is complex, composed of several parts.

Dorothy Allison (Reading 13) describes her experience of marginality in high school and in college. First-generation immigrants invariably experience marginality, as described by Chandra Talpade Mohanty (Reading 11), Julia Alvarez (Reading 17), and Shailja Patel (Reading 43). The positive effect of marginality—also mentioned by writers in this chapter—is the ability to see both cultures more clearly than people who are embedded in only one context. This gives bicultural people a broader range of vision, a broader standpoint, and allows them to see the complexity and contradictions of both cultural settings. It also helps them to be cultural interpreters and bridge builders, especially at the micro and meso levels (Chiawei O'Hearn 1998; Kich 1992; Okazawa-Rey 1994; Root 1996; Walker 2001).

Social Categories, Classifications, and Structural Inequality: Macro and Global Levels

Classifying and labeling human beings, often according to real or assumed physical, biological, or genetic differences, is a way to distinguish who is included and who is excluded from a group, to ascribe particular characteristics, to prescribe social roles, and to assign status, power, and privilege. People are to know their places. Thus social categories such as gender, race, and class are used to establish and maintain a particular kind of social order. The classifications and their specific features, meanings, and significance are socially constructed through history, politics, and culture. The specific meanings and significance were often imputed to justify the conquest, colonization, domination, and exploitation of entire groups of people, and although the specifics may have changed over time, this system of categorizing and classifying remains intact. For example, Native American people were described as brutal, uncivilized, and ungovernable savages in the writings of early colonizers on this continent. This justified the near-genocide of Native Americans by white settlers, public officials, and the U.S. military, as well as the breaking of treaties between the U.S. government and Native American tribes (Zinn 1995). Today, Native Americans are no longer called savages but are often thought of as a vanishing species, or a nonexistent people already wiped out, thereby rationalizing their neglect by the dominant culture and erasing their long-standing and continuing resistance. Frederica Y. Daly speaks to the oppression of Native American people, as well as their success in retaining traditional values and the cultural revival they have undertaken (Reading 12). Paula Gunn Allen (Reading 1) and Andy Smith (Reading 31) also provide perspectives on Native American history and contemporary life that are pertinent here. Note how this macro-level process of classification and labeling has affected Arabs, Arab Americans, and "people who look like Muslims," especially after the attacks of September 11, 2001 (Reading 53). Dorothy Allison points out that a "horror of class stratification, racism, and prejudice is that some people begin to believe that the security of their families and community depends on the oppression of others, that for some to have good lives others must have lives that are mean and horrible" (Reading 13).

These social categories are the foundation of the structural inequalities present in our society. Those in dominant positions are deemed superior and legitimate and those relegated—whether explicitly or implicitly—to subordinate positions are deemed inferior and illegitimate. Of course, individuals are not simply in dominant or subordinate positions. A college-educated, Arab American heterosexual man has privilege in terms of gender, class, and sexuality, but is considered subordinate in terms of race and culture. Depending on context, these aspects of his identity will contribute to his experience of privilege or disadvantage. Self-awareness involves recognizing and understanding the significance of our identities, which are often complex and contradictory. For white people descended from European immigrants to this country, the advantages of being white are not always fully recognized or acknowledged. In Reading 15, Mary C. Waters describes how, at the macro level, this country's racial hierarchy benefits European Americans who can choose to claim an ethnic identity as, for example, Irish Americans or Italian Americans. These symbolic identities are individualistic, she argues, and do not have serious social costs for the individual compared with racial and ethnic identities of people of color in the United States. As a result, white people in the United States tend to think of all identities as equal: "I'm Italian American, you're Polish American. I'm Irish American, you're African American." This assumed equivalence ignores the very big differences between an individualist symbolic identity and a socially enforced and imposed racial identity. Note that Europeans were not considered equal when they immigrated to the United States in the nineteenth and early twentieth centuries. Scots, Irish, French, Italian, Polish, and Russian Jewish people, for example, were differentiated in a hierarchy based on skin color, culture, language, and their histories in Europe. In Reading 14, Melanie Kaye/Kantrowitz writes about the complex social location of Jews in the United States, and her conviction that privilege can and should be deployed to bring about equality and justice.

Sociologist Melanie Bush (2004) explored white students' perceptions of identity, privilege, democracy, and intergroup relations. She identified what she called "cracks in the wall of whiteness"— circumstances that can foster understanding about systemic racialized patterns of inequality—and argued that such understandings can provide a springboard for change.

Maintaining Systems of Structural Inequality

Maintaining systems of inequality requires ongoing objectification and dehumanization of subordinated peoples. Appropriating their identities is a particularly effective method of doing this, for it defines who the subordinated group/person is or ought to be. This happens in several ways:

Using the values, characteristics, features of the dominant group as the supposedly neutral standard against which all others should be evaluated. For example, men of a particular racial/ethnic group are generally physically larger and stronger than women of that group. Many of the clinical trials for new pharmaceutical drugs have been conducted using men's bodies and activities as the standard. The results, however, have been applied equally to both men and women. Women are often prescribed the same dosage of a medication as men are even though their physical makeup is not the same. Thus women, as a distinct group, do not exist in this research.

Using terms that distinguish the subordinate from the dominant group. Terms such as "non-white" and "minority" connote a relationship to another group, white in the former case and majority in the latter. A non-white person is the negative of the white person; a minority person is less than a majority person. Neither has an identity on her or his own terms.

Stereotyping. Stereotyping involves making a simple generalization about a group and claiming that all members of the group conform to it. Stereotypes are behavioral and psychological attributes; they are commonly held beliefs about groups rather than individual beliefs about individuals; and they persist in spite of contradictory evidence. Lesbians hate men. Latinas are dominated by macho Latinos. Women with physical disabilities are asexual. Fat women are good-humored but not healthy. As philosopher Judith Andre (1988) asserted, "A 'stereotype' is pejorative; there is always something objectionable in the beliefs and images to which the word refers" (p. 260).

Exoticizing and romanticizing. These two forms of appropriation are particularly insidious because on the surface there is an appearance of appreciation. For example, Asian American women are described as personifying the "mysterious Orient," Native American women as "earth mothers" and the epitome of spirituality, and Black women as perpetual towers of strength. In all three cases, seemingly positive traits and cultural practices are identified and exalted. This "positive" stereotyping prevents people from seeing the truth and complexity of who these women are.

Another aspect of romanticization may be **cultural appropriation,** where, for example, white people wear cowrie shells, beaded hairstyles, cornrows and dreadlocks, or claim to have been Native American in a former life (Smith 1991). Joanna Kadi (1996) argued that cultural appropriation reinforces imperialist attitudes and constitutes a form of cultural genocide. She urged people to think carefully about their right to wear "exotic" clothing or to play musical instruments from other cultures. Our intentions, our knowledge of those cultures, and authentic connections with people from different groups are all part of moving from cultural appropriation to what Kadi called "ethical cultural connections."

Images that are circulated and popularized about a group may also contribute to their "exoticization" or romanticization. How are various groups of women typically depicted in this society? The fundamental problem with the representation of women, as with all oppressed peoples, is that "they do not have central control over the production of images about themselves" (McCarthy and Crichlow 1993, p. xvii). The four processes of identity appropriation described above are used to project images of women that generally demean, dehumanize, denigrate, and otherwise violate their basic humanity. In Chapter 2, we noted the importance of independent media with reports and images produced by a diversity of women who speak the truths of their own lives.

In the face of structural inequalities, the issue of identity and representation can literally and metaphorically be a matter of life and death for members of subordinated groups for several reasons. They are reduced to the position of the "other"—that is, fundamentally unlike "us"—made invisible, misunderstood, misrepresented, and often feared. Equally significant, designating a group as "other" justifies its exploitation, its exclusion from whatever benefits the society may offer, and the violence and, in extreme cases, genocide committed against it. Therefore, at the macro and global levels, identity is a matter of collective well-being and survival. Individual members of subordinate groups tend to be judged by those in dominant positions according to negative stereotypes. If any young African American women, for example, are poor single mothers, they merely reinforce the stereotype the dominant group holds about them. When young African American women hold advanced degrees and are economically well off, they are regarded as exceptional by those in the dominant group, who rarely let disconfirming evidence push them to rethink their stereotypes.

Given the significance of identity appropriation as an aspect of oppression, it is not surprising that many liberation struggles have included projects and efforts aimed at changing identities and taking control of the process of positive identity formation and representation. Oppressed people often use the same terminology to name themselves as the dominant group uses to label them. One crucial aspect of liberation struggles is to get rid of pejorative labels and use names that express, in their own terms, who people are in all their humanity. Thus, groups may change the name they use to refer to themselves to fit their evolving consciousness. As with individual identity, naming ourselves collectively is an important act of empowerment. One example of this is the evolution of the names African Americans have used to identify themselves, moving from Colored to Negro to Black to Afro-American, and African American. Similarly, Chinese Americans gradually rejected the derogatory label "Chink" preferring to be called Orientals and now Chinese Americans or Asian Americans. These terms are used unevenly, perhaps according to the age and

Young Latinas at a rally for immigration rights.

political orientation of the person or the geographic region, where one usage may be more popular than another. Among the very diverse group of people connected historically, culturally, and linguistically to Spain, Portugal, and their former colonies (parts of the United States, Mexico, the Caribbean, and Central and South America), some use more inclusive terms such as Latino or Hispanic; others prefer more specific names such as Chicano, Puerto Rican, Nicaraguan, Cuban, and so on.

Colonization, Immigration, and the U.S. Landscape of Race and Class

Global-level factors affecting people's identities include colonization and immigration. Popular folklore would have us believe that the United States has welcomed "the tired, huddled masses yearning to breathe free" (Young 1997). This ideology that the United States is "a land of immigrants" obscures several important issues excluded from much mainstream debate about immigration: Not all Americans came to this country

voluntarily. Native American peoples and Mexicans were already here on this continent, but the former experienced near-genocide and the latter were made foreigners in their own land. African peoples were captured, enslaved, imported to this country, and forced to labor and bear children. All were brutally exploited and violated—physically, psychologically, culturally, and spiritually—to serve the interests of those in power. The relationships between these groups and this nation and their experiences in the United States are fundamentally different from the experiences of those who chose to immigrate here, though this is not to negate the hardships the latter may have faced. These differences profoundly shaped the social, cultural, political, and economic realities faced by these groups throughout history and continue to do so today.

Robert Blauner (1972) makes a useful analytical distinction between colonized minorities, whose original presence in this nation was involuntary, and all of whom are people of color, and immigrant minorities, whose presence was voluntary. According to Blauner, colonized minorities faced insurmountable structural inequalities, based primarily on race, that have prevented their full participation in social, economic, political, and cultural arenas of U.S. life. Early in the history of this country, for example, the Naturalization Law of 1790 (which was repealed as recently as 1952) prohibited peoples of color from becoming U.S. citizens, and the Slave Codes restricted every aspect of life for enslaved African peoples. These laws made race into an indelible line that separated "insiders" from "outsiders." White people were designated insiders and granted many privileges while all others were confined to systematic disadvantage. See (*A Timeline of Key U.S. Immigration Law and Policy* on page 100). As Mary C. Waters points out in Reading 15, the stories that European Americans learn of how their grandparents and great-grandparents triumphed in the United States "are usually told in terms of their individual efforts." The role of labor unions, community organizations, and political parties, as well as the crucial importance of racism, is usually left out of these accounts, which emphasize individual effort and hard work.

Studies of U.S. immigration "reveal discrimination and unequal positioning of different ethnic groups" (Yans-McLaughlin 1990, p. 6), challenging the myth of equal opportunity for all. According to political scientist Lawrence Fuchs (1990), "Freedom and opportunity for poor immigrant whites in the seventeenth and eighteenth centuries were connected fundamentally with the spread of slavery" (p. 294). It was then that diverse groups of European immigrants, such as Irish, Polish, and Italian people, ranked according to a European hierarchy began to learn to be white (Roediger 1991). Whiteness in the United States was constructed in relation to blackness (Morrison 1992). Acclaimed novelist and essayist James Baldwin (1984) commented: "no one was white before he/she came to America" and "it took generations, and a vast amount of coercion, before this became a white country." Thus the common belief among descendants of European immigrants that the successful **assimilation** of their foremothers and forefathers against great odds is evidence that everyone can "pull themselves up by the bootstraps" if they work hard enough does not take into account the racialization of immigration that favored white people. In Reading 14, Melanie Kaye/Kantrowitz discusses Jewish assimilation in the United States, and notes that despite its benefits, this process has been accompanied by extreme cultural loss—of language, history, literature, music, cultural diversity, and experience of rich Jewish traditions.

On coming to the United States, immigrants are drawn into the racial landscape of this country. In media debates and official statistics, this is still dominated by a Black/white polarization, sometimes with the addition of "Hispanics" as a non-white third category. Demographically, the U.S. population is much more diverse but often characterized in binary terms: people of color or white people. Immigrants generally identify themselves according to nationality—for example, as Cambodian or Guatemalan. Once in the United States, they may adopt the term *people of color* as an aspect of their identity here. Chandra Talpade Mohanty notes her transition from "foreign student" to "student of color" in the United States. "Racist and sexist experiences in graduate school and after made it imperative that I understand the U.S. in terms of its history of racism, imperialism, and patriarchal relations, specifically in relation to Third World immigrants" (Reading 11).

This emphasis on race tends to mask differences based on class, an important distinction among immigrant groups. For example, the Chinese and Japanese people who came in the nineteenth century and early twentieth century to work on plantations in Hawaii, as loggers in Oregon, or building roads and railroads in several western states were poor and from rural areas of China and Japan. The 1965 immigration law made way for "the second wave" of Asian immigration (Takaki 1987). It set preferences for professionals, highly skilled workers, and members of the middle and upper-middle classes, making this group "the most highly skilled of any immigrant group our country has ever had" (quoted in Takaki 1987, p. 420). The first wave of Vietnamese refugees who immigrated between the mid-1970s and 1980 were from the middle and upper classes, including many professionals; by contrast, the second wave of immigrants from Vietnam was composed of poor and rural people. The class backgrounds of immigrants affect not only their sense of themselves and their expectations but also how they can succeed as strangers in a foreign land. For example, a poor woman who arrives with no literacy skills in her own language will have a more difficult time learning to become literate in English than one who has formal schooling in her country of origin that may have included basic English.

A Timeline of Key U.S. Immigration Law and Policy*

U.S. immigration laws and policies seek to balance a concern for national security with the fact that immigrants contribute greatly to the U.S. economy. Tens of millions of newcomers have made their way to the United States throughout the nation's history, and the United States has resettled more refugees on a permanent basis than any other industrialized country. Immigration law changes in response to economic shifts, political concerns, and perceived threats to national security.

1790   The Naturalization Law of 1790, which was not repealed until 1952, limited naturalization to "free white persons" who had resided in the United States for at least two years. Slave Codes restricted every aspect of life for enslaved African peoples.

1875   The Immigration Act of 1875 denied admission to individuals considered "undesirable," including revolutionaries, prostitutes, and those carrying "loathsome or dangerous contagious diseases."

1882   The Chinese Exclusion Act, one of the most racist immigration laws in U.S. history, was adopted and subsequently upheld by the U.S. Supreme Court; variations were enforced until 1943. The act was a response to fear of the large numbers of Chinese laborers brought to the United States to lay railroads and work in mines.

1917   Congress banned immigration from Asia except Japan and the Philippines.

1921   The Immigration Act of 1921 set an overall cap on the number of immigrants admitted each year and established a nationalities quota system that strongly favored northern Europeans at the expense of immigrants from southern and eastern Europe and Asia.

1924   The Immigration Act of 1924 based immigration quotas on the ethnic composition of the U.S. population in 1920; it also prohibited Japanese immigration.

_____

* Thanks to Wendy A. Young for providing material.

Second- and third-generation immigrants raised in the United States often want to learn more about the country of their ancestry. Christina Leaño describes her decision to live in the Philippines after she graduated from college, seeking an opportunity to get to know her extended family there (Reading 16). She used her hybrid Filipina American identity as a resource in her work with communities affected by environmental contamination of former U.S. military bases. Some immigrants retain strong ties to their country of origin and may travel back and forth regularly, maintaining family and community connections in more than one place, as described by Julia Alvarez (Reading 17). In Chapter 8, we discuss patterns of migration, geographical and cultural displacement, and increasing cultural standardization related to economic globalization.

Multiple Identities, Social Location, and Contradictions

The social features of one's identity incorporate individual, community, societal, and global factors. **Social location** is a way of expressing the core of a person's existence in the social and political world. It places us in particular relationships to others, to the dominant culture of the United States, and to the rest of the world. It determines the kinds of power and privilege we have access to and can exercise, as well as situations in which we have less power and privilege.

Because social location is where all the aspects of one's identity meet, our experience of our own complex identities is sometimes contradictory and paradoxical. We live with multiple identities that

1945	President Harry Truman issued a directive after World War II allowing for the admission of 40,000 refugees.
1946	The War Brides Act permitted 120,000 foreign wives and children to join their husbands in the United States.
1948	The Displaced Persons Act of 1948 permitted entry to an additional 400,000 refugees and displaced persons as a result of World War II.
1952	The Immigration and Nationality Act of 1952 was a response to U.S. fear of communism and barred the admission of anyone who might engage in acts "prejudicial to the public interest, or that endanger the welfare or safety of the United States." It allowed immigration for all nationalities, however, and established family connections as a criterion for immigrant eligibility.
1953	The Refugee Relief Act of 1953 admitted 200,000 people, including Hungarians fleeing communism and Chinese emigrating after the Chinese revolution.
1965	The Immigration Act of 1965 established an annual quota of 120,000
	immigrants from the Eastern Hemisphere, which increased the number of Asian immigrants, especially middle-class and upper-middle-class people.
1980	The Refugee Act of 1980 codified into U.S. law the 1951 United Nations Convention Relating to the Status of Refugees and its 1967 Protocol; it defines a refugee as a person outside her or his country of nationality who has a well-founded fear of persecution on account of race, religion, nationality, political opinion, or membership in a particular social group.
1986	The Immigration Reform and Control Act of 1986 was intended to control the growth of illegal immigrants through an "amnesty" program to legalize undocumented people resident in the United States before January 1, 1982, and imposing sanctions against employers who knowingly employ undocumented workers.
1990	The Immigration Act of 1990 affirmed family reunification as the basis for most immigration cases; redefined employment-based immigration; created a new system to diversify the nationalities

can be both enriching and contradictory and that push us to confront questions of loyalty to individuals and groups. This is discussed by Chandra Talpade Mohanty (Reading 11), Dorothy Allison (Reading 13), and Melanie Kaye/Kantrowitz (Reading 14). It is through the complexity of social location that we are forced to differentiate our inclinations, behaviors, self-definition, and politics from how we are classified by larger societal institutions. An inclination toward bisexuality, for example, does not mean that one will necessarily act on that inclination. Defining oneself as working class does not necessarily lead to activity in progressive politics based on a class consciousness.

Social location is where we meet others socially and politically. Who are we in relation to people who are both like us and different from us? How do we negotiate the inequalities in power and privilege? How do we both accept and appreciate who we and others are and grow and change to meet the challenges of a multicultural world? In the readings that follow, the writers note significant changes in the way they think about themselves over time. Some mention difficulties in coming to terms with who they are and the complexities of their contradictory positions. They also write about the empowerment that comes from a deepening understanding of identity, enabling them to claim their place in the world.

The concept of social location overlaps with three concepts we introduced in Chapter 2 in our discussion of theory-making: intersectionality, standpoint, and subjugated knowledge. Paula immigrating to the United States, ostensibly to compensate for the domination of Asian and Latin American immigration since 1965; and created new mechanisms to provide refuge to those fleeing civil strife, environmental disasters, or political upheaval in their homelands.

1996   The Illegal Immigration Reform and Immigrant Responsibility Act targeted legal and illegal immigration. It provided for increased border controls and penalties for document fraud; changes in employer sanctions; restrictions on immigrant eligibility for public benefits, including benefits for those lawfully in the United States; and drastic streamlining of the asylum system.

The Personal Responsibility and Work Opportunity Reconciliation Act mainly dealt with changes in the welfare system and made legal immigrants ineligible for various kinds of federal assistance. In 1997, Congress restored benefits for some immigrants already in the country when this law took effect. There is a five-year waiting period before noncitizens can receive Medicaid or Temporary Assistance for Needy Families.

2001   Uniting and Strengthening America by Providing Appropriate Tools Required to Obstruct Terrorism Act (USA Patriot Act) was signed into law

following the attacks on the World Trade Center and the Pentagon on September 11. It significantly enhances the government's powers of detention, search, and surveillance. See *Milestones in U.S. History* (Chapter 1).

The "pull" factors drawing immigrants to the United States include the possibility of better-paying jobs, better education—especially for children—and greater personal freedom. "Push" factors include poverty, wars, political upheaval, authoritarian regimes, and fewer personal freedoms in the countries they have left. Immigration will continue to be a thorny issue in the United States as the goals of global economic restructuring, filling the country's need for workers, and providing opportunities for family members to live together are set against the fears of those who see continued immigration as a threat to the country's prosperity and security and to the dominance of European Americans.

Airport security has been tightened nationwide. The U.S.–Mexico border has become increasingly militarized with armed guards, infrared night-vision scopes, low-light TV cameras, motion sensors, helicopters, and all-terrain vehicles that patrol day and night. Immigration and Customs Enforcement (ICE) has stepped up raids on homes, schools, and workplaces in many towns and cities (see Reading 52). At the same time, immigrant communities have asserted their presence by taking to the streets in huge demonstrations.

Gunn Allen (Reading 1) and Chandra Talpade Mohanty (Reading 11) address the importance of knowing one's genealogy, which they both define broadly to include family, culture, and history. An ability to reflect on one's social location contributes to the generation of knowledge. Remember that Patricia Hill Collins argues that standpoint is not about individual experiences or identities but about "historically shared, group-based experiences" (1997, p. 375), the meso- and macro-aspects of identity. In the readings that follow, notice how the writers use their particular standpoints to locate their families and communities in the wider society. Note, too, that some writers' standpoints represent subjugated knowledges, deriving from their domination by other groups.

Questions for Reflection

As you read and discuss the readings in this chapter, think about these questions:

1. Who are you? How do you figure out your identity? Has your identity changed? If so, when and how did it change?

2. Which parts of your identity do you emphasize? Which do you underplay? Why? How does a particular context shape your identity?

3. Who are your "people"? Where or what are your "home" and "community"?

4. How many generations have your family members been in the United States? What was their first relationship to it? Under what conditions did they become a part of the United States?

5. What do you know of your family's culture and history before it became a part of the United States?

6. What is your social location?

7. Which of the social dimensions of your identity provide power and privilege? Which provide less power and disadvantage?

8. How do people with privilege contribute to eliminating the systems of privilege that benefit them? Why might they want to do this?

Finding Out More on the Web

1. Find out about women who are very different from you (in terms of culture, class, race/ethnicity, nationality, or religion) and how they think about their identities.

2. Research identity-based organizations. Why did they form? Who are their members? What are their purposes and goals? Did/do they have a vision of justice and equality?

3. Frederica Y. Daly mentioned the "trail of tears." What was it? Why is it famous?

4. Mary C. Waters mentions the "one drop rule." What is it? Why is it significant?

Taking Action

1. Take some action to affirm an aspect of your identity.

2. Talk to your parents or grandparents about your family history. How have they constructed their cultural and racial/ethnic identities?

TWELVE

Perspectives of Native American Women on Race and Gender (1994)

Frederica Y. Daly

Frederica Y. Daly taught psychology at Howard University, the State University of New York, and the University of New Mexico. She also practiced as a clinical psychologist for many years. In retirement she writes poetry and is engaged in genealogical research into her African and Indian ancestries.

. . .Native Americans constitute well over five hundred recognized tribes, which speak more than two hundred (mostly living) languages. Their variety and vital cultures notwithstanding, the official U.S. policy unreflectively, and simply, transforms them from Indians to "Americans" (Wilkinson 1987). Some consideration will be given to their unifying traditions, not the least of which are their common history of surviving genocide and their strong, shared commitment to their heritage.

Any discussion of Indian people requires a brief review of the history of the violent decimation of their populations as well as the massive expropriation of their land and water holdings, accomplished with rare exception with the approval of American governments at every level. To ignore these experiences prevents us from understanding the basis for their radical and profound desire for self-determination, a condition they enjoyed fully before the European incursions began. . . .

Historical Overview

Indian history, since the European invasion in the early sixteenth century, is replete with incidents of exploitation, land swindle, enslavement, and murder by the European settlers. The narration includes well-documented, government-initiated, biological warfare, which included giving Indians clothing infected with smallpox, diphtheria, and other diseases to which Indians were vulnerable. Starvation strategies were employed, with forced removal from their lands and the consequent loss of access to basic natural resources, [for] example, the Cherokee and Choctaw experiences in the famous "trail of tears."

Wilkinson as well as Deloria and Lytle (1983) assert that Indian history is best understood when presented within a historical framework established by four major, somewhat overlapping, periods. The events dominate federal policy about Indians, subsequent Indian law, and many of the formational forces described in Indian sociology, anthropology, and culture.

Period 1: 1532–1828

This period is described by Europeans as one of "discovery" and is characterized by the conquest of Indians and the making of treaties. The early settlers did not have laws or policies governing their relationships with the indigenous tribes until the sixteenth-century theologian Francisco de Vitorio advised the king of Spain in 1532 that the tribes should be recognized "as legitimate entities capable of dealing with the European nations by treaty." As a result, writes Deloria, treaty making became a "feasible method of gaining a foothold on the continent without alarming the natives" (1970, 3). Deloria explains further that inherent in this decision was the fact that it encouraged respect for the tribes as societies of people and, thus, became the workable tool for defining intergroup relationships. By 1778 the U.S. government entered into its first treaty, with the Delaware Indians, at which point the tribe became, and remains, the basic unit in federal Indian law. . . .

Period 2: 1828–87

The second period, beginning . . . a few decades before the Civil War, witnessed massive removal of Indians from their ancestral lands and subsequent relocation, primarily because of their resistance to mainstream assimilation and the "missionary efforts" of the various Christian sects.

Early in his presidency Andrew Jackson proposed voluntary removal of the Indians. When none of the tribes responded, the Indian Removal Act of 1830 was passed. The act resulted in the removal of the tribes from the Ohio and Mississippi valleys to the plains of the West. "Nearly sixteen thousand Cherokees walked from Georgia to Eastern Oklahoma . . . the Choctaws surrendered more than ten million acres and moved west" (Deloria and Lytle 1983, 7). Soldiers, teachers, and missionaries were sent to reservations for policing and proselytizing purposes, activities by no means mutually exclusive and which represented the full benefit of the act as far as the tribes were concerned. Meanwhile, discovery of gold (especially "strikes" on or near Indian land) in the West, coupled with the extension of the railroad, once again raised the "Indian Problem." But at this point, with nowhere else to be moved, Indian tribes were even more in jeopardy, setting the basis for the third significant period.

Period 3: 1887–1928

During the final years of the nineteenth century, offering land allotments seemed to provide a workable technique for assimilating Indian families into the mainstream. The Dawes Act of 1887 proposed the formula for allotment. "A period of twenty-five years was established during which the Indian owner [of a specified, allotted piece of reservation property] was expected to learn proper methods of self-sufficiency, e.g., business or farming. At the end of that period, the land, free of restrictions against sale, was to be delivered to the allottee" (Deloria and Lytle 1983, 9). At the same time, the Indian received title to the land and citizenship in the state.

The Dawes Act and its aftermath constitute one of the most sordid narratives in American history involving tribal peoples. Through assimilation, swindling, and other forms of exploitation, more than ninety million acres of allotted land were transferred to non-Indian owners. Furthermore, much of the original land that remained for the Indians was in the "Great American Desert," unsuitable for farming and unattractive for any other kind of development. During this same period, off-reservation boarding schools began to be instituted, some in former army barracks, to assist in the overall program of assimilation, and the Dawes Act also made parcels of reservation land available to whites for settlement. The plan to assimilate the Indian and thereby eradicate the internal tribal nations caused immense misery and enormous economic loss. But as we know, it failed. Phyllis Old Dog Cross, a nurse of the North Dakota Mandan Tribe, mordantly puts it, "We are not vanishing" (1987, 29).

Period 4: 1928–Present

The fourth period is identified by Wilkinson especially as beginning just before the Depression in 1928. It is characterized by reestablishment of tribes as separate "sovereignties" involving moves toward formalized self-government and self-determination, and cessation, during World War II, of federal assistance to the tribes.

Prucha (1985) reminds us that, with the increased belief in the sciences in the 1920s and the accompanying beliefs that the sciences could solve human problems, attitudes toward Indians hardened. At this point the professional anthropologist began to be sent and be seen on the reservations to study and live with the people, alongside the missionaries. The changing attitudes continued into the 1930s with the Roosevelt administration. It was during this period that John Collier became commissioner of Indian Affairs, and the reforms of the Indian Reorganization Act of 1934 invalidated the land allotment policies of the Dawes Act, effectively halting the transfer of Indian land to non-Indians. As Deloria indicates, the Reorganization Act provided immense benefits, including the establishment and reorganization of tribal councils and tribal courts.

After about a decade of progress, the budgetary demands of World War II resulted in deep reductions in domestic programs, including assistance to the tribes. John Collier resigned in 1945 under attack from critics and amid growing demands in Washington to cancel federal support for Indians. . . .

Deloria writes that Senator Watkins of Utah was "firmly convinced that if the Indians were freed from federal restrictions, they would soon prosper by learning in the school of life those lessons that a cynical federal bureaucracy had not been able to instill in them" (1970, 18). He was able to implement his convictions during the Eisenhower administration into the infamous Termination Act of 1953, in consequence of which several tribes in at least five states were eliminated. In effect, as far as the government was concerned, the tribes no longer existed and could make no claims on the government. Contrary to its original intent as a means of releasing the tribes from their status as federal wards under BIA [Bureau of Indian Affairs] control, the Termination Act did just the opposite, causing more loss of land, further erosion of tribal power, and literally terrorizing most of the tribes with intimidation, uncertainty, and, worst of all, fear of the loss of tribal standing.

Deloria quotes HR Doc. 363 in which, in 1970, President Nixon asserted, "Because termination is morally and legally unacceptable, because it produces bad practical results, and because the mere threat of termination tends to discourage greater self-sufficiency among Indian groups, I am asking the Congress to pass a new concurrent resolution which would expressly renounce, repudiate, and repeal the termination policy" (1970, 20). This firm repudiation by Nixon of the termination policy earned him the esteem of many Indian people, in much the same way that presidents Kennedy and Johnson are esteemed by many African Americans for establishing programs designed to improve their socioeconomic conditions.

From the Nixon administration through the Carter administration, tribal affairs were marked by strong federal support and a variety of programs aimed at encouraging tribal self-determination. The Indian Child Welfare Act of 1978, which gave preference to Indians in adoptions involving Indian children and authorized establishment of social services on and near reservations, was one of the major accomplishments of this period.

Prucha believes that the tribes' continued need for federal programs is an obstacle to their sovereignty . . . (1985, 97). Deloria insists that Indians are citizens and residents of the United States and of the individual states in which they live and, as such, "are entitled to the full benefits and privileges that are offered to all citizens" (246). . . .

Contemporary Native American Women and Sexism

I have just presented a very abbreviated statement of the general, post-European influx historical experiences of Indians in America, drawing from the research and insights of lawyers and social scientists. Without this introduction it would be difficult to understand Native American women and their contemporary experiences of sexism and racism.

Although many tribes were matrilineal, Indian women were seldom mentioned prominently in the personal journals or formal records of the early settlers or in the narratives of the westward movement. They were excluded from treaty-making sessions with federal government agents, and later ethnologists and anthropologists who reported on Indian women frequently presented distorted accounts of their lives, usually based on interviews with Christianized women, who said what they believed would be compatible with the European worldview. Helen Carr, in her essay in Brodzki and Schenck's *Life-Lines: Theorizing Women's Autobiographies,* offers some caveats about the authenticity of contemporary autobiographies of Indian women, when they are written in the Euro-American autobiographical tradition. She cautions that, in reading the autobiographies collected by early anthropologists, we need to be "aware that they have been structured, consciously or unconsciously, to serve particular 'white' purposes and to give credence to particular white views" (1988, 132).

Ruby Leavitt, writing in Gornick and Moran's *Women in Sexist Society,* states: "Certainly the status of women is higher in the matrilineal than the patrilineal societies. Where women own property and pass it on to their daughters or sisters, they are far more influential and secure. Where their economic role is important and well defined . . . they are not nearly so subject to male domination, and they have much more freedom of movement and action" (1972, 397).

We do not learn from social scientists observing Indian communities that women also were the traders in many tribes. With this history of matrilinealism and economic responsibilities, it is not surprising that some Indian women deny the existence of an oppressed, nonparticipatory tribal female role. Yet just as other North American women, they are concerned with child care needs, access to abortion, violence against women, and the effects of alcoholism on the family, all symptomatic of sexism experiences. They are also aware of these symptoms as prevalent throughout our society in the United States; they do not view them as specifically Indian related.

Bea Medicine, Lakota activist, anthropologist, and poet, as quoted in the preface of *American Indian Women—Telling Their Lives,* states "Indian women do not need liberation, they have always been liberated within their tribal structure" (1984, viii). Her view is the more common one I have encountered in my readings and in conversations with Native American women. In the middle 1970s, Native American women who were in New York City to protest a U.S. treaty violation, in a meeting to which they had invited non-Indian women, were adamant that they did not need the "luxury of feminism." Their focus, along with that of Indian men, concerned the more primary needs of survival.

The poet Carol Sanchez writes in *A Gathering of Spirit,* "We still have Women's societies, and there are at least thirty active woman-centered Mother rite cultures existing and practicing their everyday life in that manner on this continent" (1984, 164). These groups are characterized by their "keeping of the culture" activities.

Medicine and Sanchez concur about the deemphasis of the importance of gender roles in some tribes as reflected in the "Gia" concept. *Gia* is the word in the Pueblo Tewa language which signifies the earth. It is also used to connote nurturance and biological motherhood. The tribal core welfare role, which can be assumed by a male or a female, is defined by the tribe in this Gia context. To be a nurturing male is to be the object of much respect and esteem, although one does not act nurturing to gain group approval. Swentzell and Naranjo, educational consultant and sociologist, respectively, and coauthors, write, "The male in the gia role is a person who guides, advises, cares, and universally loves and encompasses all." The authors describe the role, saying, "The core gia was a strong, stable individual who served as the central focus for a large number of the pueblo's members . . . [for example], 'she' coordinated large group activities such as marriages, feast days, gathering and preparing of food products, even house building and plastering" (1986, 37). With increasing tribal governmental concerns the role of core group Gia has lessened, "so that children are no longer raised by the core group members" (39). Interestingly, the Gia concept is being used currently by social ecologists. For them it parallels the notion of Mother Earth and corresponds with the increasingly widespread understanding of the earth as a living organism.

Charles Lange, in *Cochiti—A New Mexico Pueblo, Past and Present,* says: "Among the Cochiti, the woman is boss; the high offices are held by men, but in the households and in the councils of the clans, woman is supreme. . . . She has been arbiter of destinies of the tribe for centuries" (1959, 367). The important role performed by the "Women's Society," Lange continues, includes "the ceremonial grinding of corn to make prayer meal" (283). Compatible with women's having spiritual role assignments is the fact that in some tribes the gods are women—for example, in the matrifocal Cherokee and Pueblo nations, Corn Mother is a sacred figure.

A Cheyenne saying reflects the tribe's profound regard for women: "A nation is not conquered until the hearts of its women are on the ground. Then it is done, no matter how brave its warriors, nor how strong its weapons" (Kutz 1988, 143–58). Historically, in some tribes women were warriors and participated in raiding parties. The Apache medicine woman and warrior Lozen lived such a role and was the last of the women warriors (Kutz 1988, 143–58). Paula Gunn Allen, in *The Sacred Hoop* (1986), notes that "traditional tribal lifestyles are more often gynocratic . . . women are not merely doomed victims of Western progress; they are also the carriers of the dream. . . . Since the first attempts at colonization . . . the invaders have exerted every effort to remove Indian women from every position of authority, to obliterate all records pertaining to gynocratic social systems and to ensure that no Americans . . . would remember that gynocracy was the primary social order of Indian America" (2–3). Later she alludes to the regeneration of these earlier roles: "Women migrating to the cities are regaining self-sufficiency and positions of influence they had held in earlier centuries" (31). "Women's traditions," she says, "are about continuity and men's are about change, life maintenance/risk, death and transformation" (82).

When Indian women deny having experienced sexism they seem mainly to be referring to their continuing historical roles within their tribes, in which they are seen as *the keepers of the culture.* There exists a general consensus that the powerful role of tribal women, both traditionally and contemporarily, is not paralleled in the non-Indian society. Additionally, they allude to the women serving in various tribes as council members, and they point to such prominent, well-known leaders as Wilma Mankiller, chief of the Oklahoma Cherokee Nation; Verna Williamson, former governor of Isleta Pueblo; and Virginia Klinekole, former president of the Mescalero Apache Tribal Council.

Contemporary Native American Women and Racism

The relentless system of racism, in both its overt and covert manifestations, impacts the lives of Indian women; most are very clear about their experiences of it, and they recognize it for what it is. Although many are reticent about discussing these experiences, a growing number of Native American women writers are giving voice to their encounters with racism.

Elizabeth Cook-Lynn, a poet and teacher with combined Crow, Creek, and Sioux heritage, writes about an editor who questioned her about why Native American poetry is so incredibly sad. Cook-Lynn describes her reaction . . . : "Now I recognize it as a tactless question asked out of astonishing ignorance. It reflects the general attitude that American Indians should have been happy to have been robbed of their land and murdered" (1987, 60–61).

In the same anthology Linda Hogan, from the Chickasaw Tribe in Oklahoma, writes with concern about the absence of information about Native American people throughout the curricula in our educational systems: "The closest I came to learning what I needed was a course in Labor Literature, and the lesson there was in knowing there were writers who lived similar lives to ours. . . . This is one of the ways that higher education perpetuates racism and classism. By ignoring our lives and work, by creating standards for only their own work" (1987, 243). Earlier she had written that "the significance of intermarriage between Indian and white or between Indian and black [has not] been explored . . . but the fact remains that great numbers of apparently white or black Americans carry notable degrees of Indian blood" (216). And in Brant's *A Gathering of Spirit* Carol Sanchez says, "To be Indian is to be considered 'colorful,' spiritual, connected to the earth, simplistic, and disappointing if not dressed in buckskin and feathers" (1984, 163).

These Indian women talk openly about symptoms of these social pathologies, [for] example, experiencing academic elitism or the demeaning attitudes of employees in federal and private, nonprofit Indian agencies. Or they tell of being accepted in U.S. society in proportion to the lightness of skin color. The few who deny having had experiences with racism mention the equality bestowed upon them through the tribal sovereignty of the Indian nations. In reality the tribes are not sovereign. They are controlled nearly completely by the U.S. Department of Interior, the federal agency that, ironically, also oversees animal life on public lands.

Rayna Green, a member of the Cherokee nation, in her book *That's What She Said* (1984), makes a strong, clear statement about racism and sexism: "The desperate lives of Indian women are worn by poverty, the abuse of men, the silence and blindness of whites. . . . The root of their problem appears attributable to the callousness and sexism of the Indian men and white society equally. They are tightly bound indeed in the double bind of race and gender. Wasted lives and battered women are part of the Indian turf" (10). It is not surprising to find some Indian men reflecting the attitudes of the white majority in relating to Indian women. This is the psychological phenomenon found in oppressed people, labeled as identification with the oppressor.

Mary Tallmountain, the Native Alaskan poet, writes in *I Tell You Now* (1987) that she refused to attend school in Oregon because her schoolmates mocked her "Indianness": "But, I know who I am. Marginal person, misfit, mutant; nevertheless, I am of this country, these people" (12). Linda Hogan describes the same experience, saying, "Those who are privileged would like for us to believe that we are in some way defective, that we are not smart enough, not good enough" (237). She recalls an experience with her former employer, an orthodontist, whom she says, "believed I was inferior because I worked for less than his wife's clothing budget or their liquor bill . . . and who, when I received money to attend night school and was proud, accused me of being a welfare leech and said I should be ashamed" (242). In her poem "Those Who Thunder," Linda translated the experience into verse:

> *Those who are timid are sagging in the soul,*
> *And those poor who will inherit the earth*
> *already work it*
> *So take shelter you*
> *because we are thundering and beating on floors*
> *And this is how walls have fallen in other cities.*
>
> (242)

In the United States we do not know one another, except from the stereotypes presented in the media. As a result, there is the tendency to view people of a differing group vicariously, through the eyes of media interpreters.

Louise Erdrich and Michael Dorris, both Indian and both university professors and eminent writers, reported in Bill Moyers's *World of Ideas* (1989): "We had one guy come to dinner, and we cleaned our house and made a nice dinner, and he looks and says, kind of depressed, 'Do you always eat on the table?'" (465). They used the example to demonstrate how people "imagine" (as distinguished from "know") Indians on the basis of movie portrayals, usually as figures partially dressed or dressed in the fashion of the nineteenth century and typically eating while seated on the ground. It is difficult to form accurate perceptions of the people and worldview of another group. Carol Sanchez seems to challenge us to do just that when she asks us not to dismiss Native Americans and then asks, "How many Indians do you know?" (163). . . .

Sanchez charges non-Indians with the wish to have Indians act like whites, so they will be more acceptable to whites, another example of accommodation, assimilation. She is describing the attitude cited by the young child care worker who said to me, "They like our food, our drum music, our jewelry, why don't they like us!?" Activist Winona La Duke, of the Ojibwa Tribe and by profession an economist, asserts in her offering in *A Gathering of Spirit:* "As far as the crises of water contamination, radiation, and death to the natural world and her children are concerned, respectable racism is as alive today as it was a century ago . . . a certain level of racism and ignorance has gained acceptance . . . in fact respectability . . . we either pick your bananas or act as a mascot for your football team . . . in this way, enlightened people are racist. They are arrogant toward all of nature, arrogant toward the children of nature, and ultimately arrogant toward all of life" (65–66). . . .

Continuing Tensions

That since the sixteenth century the history of Native Americans is one of racist oppression has become an integral part of contemporary historical understanding. Indian women are speaking with increasing frequency and force about their experiences of the double jeopardy of racism and sexism. I wish now to consider three factors that continue to contribute to serious tensions within the tribes and between the tribes and the so-called dominant culture. . . .

Tensions Within the Indian Community   Indian People who wish to retain their identity and culture by continuing reservation life have constantly to struggle with choices regarding adaptation to the dominant culture. They realize that extremism in either direction will result in destruction of their ways of life. Those who resist any adaptation will be made to do so involuntarily, and those who accept "white men's ways" completely and without modification by that very fact forgo their heritage. For well over a century, governmental policy favored assimilation and the concomitant dissolution of Indian tribal existence. Real estate value and greed for precious natural resources were crucial motivating factors throughout the period. Indians simply were in the way of the invaders' efforts to amass money. . . .

At the Flathead reservation in Montana, attempts are under way to "revive the traditional Salish culture and preserve the rugged land from development" (Shaffer 1990, 54). Attempts to protect the Indian land for future generations are buttressed by the traditional, nearly universal Indian belief that we do not own the land, that we are simply caretakers of it and will pass it on to future generations. Thus, how the land is used can become an issue of deep tension between strict traditionalists and those who want to assimilate contemporary economic development thinking into tribal life and institutions. Likewise, nearly universally held precepts include the prevailing rights of the tribe over individual rights and the discouragement of aggression and competitiveness, which are seen as threats to tribal harmony and survival. Phyllis Old Dog Cross, a Sioux and a nurse, speaking at a health conference in Denver in 1987, stated: "The need not to appear aggressive and competitive within the group is still seen among contemporary Indians . . . even quite acculturated Indians tend to be very unobtrusive. . . . [If not,] they receive strong criticism . . . also anything that would seem to precipitate anger, resentment, jealousy was . . . discouraged, for it is believed that tribal group harmony is threatened" (1987, 20).

Acknowledging their need for self-sufficiency as reductions in federal funding continue, the tribes are searching intensively for economic solutions. Some have introduced organized gambling onto the reservations and the leasing of land to business corporations; others are considering storage on reservation land of toxic wastes from federal facilities. Many of these measures are resisted, especially by traditionalists within the tribes, who see them as culturally destructive.

Erosion of Tribal Life: Cultural Marginality

Cultural marginality is increasingly experienced by Indian people because of the confusion resulting from ambiguities about what defines Indian identity, individually and tribally. The questions "Who is an Indian?" and "What is a tribe?" no longer permit neat unequivocal answers.

Different tribes have different attitudes toward people of mixed heritage. In some a person with white blood may be accepted, while a person with some African-American blood may or may not be identified as Indian. Indian women, if they marry non-Indians, may or may not be identified within their tribes as Indians. To be a member of a tribe, a person must meet that tribe's requirements. Many tribes require proof of a person's being one-sixteenth or one-quarter or more of Indian descent to receive tribal affiliation. . . .

A group or an individual may qualify as an Indian for some federal purposes but not for others. A June 1977 statement by the U.S. Department of Labor on American Indian Women reads: "For their 1970 Census, the Bureau included in their questionnaire the category 'American Indian,' persons who indicated their race as Indian. . . . In the Eastern U.S., there are certain groups with mixed white, Negro, and Indian ancestry. In U.S. censuses prior to 1950, these groups had been variously classified by the enumerators, sometimes as Negro and sometimes as Indian, regardless of the respondent's preferred racial identity." LeAnne Howe, writing in Paula Gunn Allen's *Spider Woman's Granddaughters*, says, "Half-breeds live on the edge of both races . . . you're torn between wanting to kill everyone in the room or buying them all another round of drinks" (1989, 220).

Paula Gunn Allen, of the Laguna Pueblo tribe and a professor of literature, in her essay in *I Tell You Now*, writes: "Of course I always knew I was an Indian. I was told over and over, 'Never forget that you're an Indian.' My mother said it. Nor did she say, 'Remember you're part Indian'" (1987, 144).

Conflicts Between Tribal and Other Governmental Laws

The Bureau of Indian Affairs, which has specific oversight responsibilities for the reservations, has played, at best, an ambivalent role, according to its very numerous critics. There have been many rumors of mishandled funds, especially of failure of funds to reach the reservations. It is the source of endless satire by Indian humorists, who, at their kindest, refer to it as the "Boss the Indian Around" department. By federal mandate the BIA is charged with coordinating the federal programs for the reservations. Originally, it was a section of the War Department, but for the last century and a half it has operated as part of the Department of the Interior.

Continuing skirmishes occur over violations of reservation land and water rights. Consequently, the tribes continue to appeal to the Supreme Court and to the United Nations for assistance in redressing federal treaty violations. When these cases are made public, they become fodder for those who continue to push for the assimilation of Indians into the dominant society as well as for the ever-present cadre of racial bigots.

Federal law and policy have too often been paternalistic, detrimental, and contrary to the best interests of the Indian people. Further, the federal dollar dominance of the tribes has a controlling interest on Indian life. Levitan and Johnston conclude that "for Indians, far more than for any other group, socioeconomic status is a federal responsibility, and the success or failure of federal programs determines the quality of Indian lives" (1975, 10).

To receive eligibility for government services requires that the person live on or near a reservation, trust, or restricted land or be a member of a tribe recognized by the federal government. To be an Indian in America can mean living under tribal laws and traditions, under state law, and under federal laws. The situation can become extremely complex and irksome, for example, when taxes are considered. The maze and snarl of legalese over such questions as whether the Navajo tribe can tax reservation mineral developments without losing its "trust status" and accompanying federal benefits would defeat, and does, the most ardent experts of jurisprudence. And the whole question of income tax for the Indian person living on a reservation and working in a nearby community requires expertise that borders on the ridiculous.

University of New Mexico law professor Fred Ragsdale, describing the relationship of reservation Indians with the federal government, compares it to playing blackjack: "Indians play with their own money. They can't get up and walk away. And the house gets to change the rules any time it wants" (1985, 1).

The outlawing of certain Indian religious practices occurred without challenge until the 1920s, when the laws and policies prohibiting dancing and ceremonies were viewed as cultural attacks. With the passage of the Indian Civil Rights Act in 1964, Indians have been able to present court challenges to discrimination based on their religious practices. Members of the North American Church use peyote, a psychoactive drug, in their ceremonies. Many consider their religion threatened by the . . . Supreme Court ruling that removes First Amendment protection of traditional worship practiced by Native Americans.

The negative impact of the 1966 Bennett freeze, a federally attempted solution to the bitter Navajo-Hopi land dispute, continues to cause pain to the Hopi, who use this 1.5-million-acre land mass for grazing, and to the Navajo, many of whom have resided on this land for generations. Sue Ann Presley, a *Washington Post* reporter, describes the area as being among the poorest in the nation and notes that the people living there are prohibited by law from participating in federal antipoverty programs. She reports that 90 percent of the homes have neither electricity nor indoor plumbing, and home repairs are not permitted. She quotes Navajo chair, Peterson Zah: "There are many Navajos who want to live in what we call the traditional way. But that does not mean they want to live with inadequate sewers, unpaved roads, no running water or electricity and under the watchful eye of the Hopi Tribe" (1993, B1). The forced removal of some of the Navajos from this area to border town housing caused a tremendous increase in the number of people who sought mental health treatment for depression and other disorders, according to the clinical observations of Tuba City, Arizona, psychologist Martin Topper. . . .

Conclusions

. . . Studies showing the impact of the privileged culture and dominant race on the development of Native Americans deserve continued exposure and extended development. We need medical research that investigates the health conditions and illnesses of minorities, including Native American women, whose general health status has to be among the worst in America. . . .

The development of new theories must include appropriate, representative definitions of the total population, free of gender bias and not derived disproportionately from the observation of middle-class white men and women. Curriculum offerings with accurate and comprehensive historical data about gender-specific Native American experiences are needed. . . .

As a country, we have failed to acknowledge our despicable treatment of the Indians. . . . It is hoped that the Indian quest for self-determination and proper respect will be realized, and with it will come our healing as a nation as well. There exists a tremendous need to help the U.S. public begin to understand the real significance of Indian history. . . .

REFERENCES

Allen, P. G. 1986. *The Sacred Hoop.* Boston: Beacon Press.

———. 1987. "The Autobiography of a Confluence." In *I Tell You Now,* ed. B. Swann and A. Krupat. Lincoln: University of Nebraska Press, 141–54.

———. ed. 1989. *Spider Woman's Granddaughters.* Boston: Beacon Press.

Bataille, G., and K. Sands. 1984. *American Indian Women—Telling Their Lives.* Lincoln: University of Nebraska Press.

Bergman, R. 1971. "Navajo Peyote Use: Its Apparent Safety." *American Journal of Psychiatry* 128:6.

Canby, W. C. 1981. *American Indian Law.* St. Paul, Minn.: West Publishing.

Carr, H. 1988. "In Other Words: Native American Women's Autobiography." In *Life-Lines: Theorizing Women's Autobiographies,* ed. Bella Brodzki and Celeste Schenck. Ithaca, N.Y.: Cornell University Press, 131–53.

Cook-Lynn, E. 1987. "You May Consider Speaking about Your Art." In *I Tell You Now,* ed. B. Swann and A. Krupat. Lincoln: University of Nebraska Press, 55–63.

Deloria, V. 1970. *We Talk, You Listen.* New York: Dell Publishing.

Deloria, V., and C. Lytle. 1983. *American Indians, American Justice.* Austin: University of Texas Press.

Erdrich, L., and M. Dorris. 1989. "Interview." In *Bill Moyers: A World of Ideas*, ed. B. S. Flowers. New York: Doubleday, 460–69.

Gornick, V., and B. Moran, eds. 1972. *Women in Sexist Society*. New York: Signet.

Green, R. 1984. *That's What She Said*. Bloomington: University of Indiana Press.

Hogan, L. 1987. "The Two Lives." In *I Tell You Now*, ed. B. Swann and A. Krupat. Lincoln: University of Nebraska Press, 231–49.

Howe, L. 1989. "An American in New York." In *Spider Woman's Granddaughters*, ed. P. G. Allen. Boston: Beacon Press, 212–20.

Kutz, J. 1988. *Mysteries and Miracles of New Mexico*. Corrales, N.M.: Rhombus Publishing.

La Duke, W. 1988. "They Always Come Back." In *A Gathering of Spirit*, ed. B. Brant. Ithaca, N.Y.: Firebrand Books, 62–67.

Lange, C. 1959. *Cochiti—A New Mexico Pueblo, Past and Present*. Austin: University of Texas Press.

Levitan, S., and W. Johnston. 1975. *Indian Giving*. Baltimore: Johns Hopkins University Press.

Old Dog Cross, P. 1987. "What Would You Want a Caregiver to Know about You?" *The Value of Many Voices Conference Proceedings*, 29–32.

Presley, S. 18 July 1993. "Restrictions Force Deprivations on Navajos." *The Washington Post*, G1–G2.

Prucha, F. 1985. *The Indians in American Society*. Berkeley: University of California Press.

Ragsdale, F. 1985. Quoted in Sherry Robinson's "Indian Laws Complicate Development." *Albuquerque Journal*, 1.

Sanchez, Carol. 1984. "Sex, Class and Race Intersections: Visions of Women of Color." In *A Gathering of Spirit*, ed. B. Brant. Ithaca, N.Y.: Firebrand Books.

Shaffer, P. January/February 1990. "A Tree Grows in Montana." *Utne Reader*, 54–63.

Swentzell, R., and T. Naranjo. 1986. "Nurturing the Gia." *El Palacio* (Summer–Fall): 35–39.

Tallmountain, M. 1987. "You Can Go Home Again: A Sequence." In *I Tell You Now*, ed. B. Swann and A. Krupat. Lincoln: University of Nebraska Press, 1–13.

Wilkinson, C. 1987. *American Indians, Time, and the Law*. New Haven, Conn.: Yale University Press.

THIRTEEN

❖❖❖

A Question of Class (1993)

Dorothy Allison

> **Dorothy Allison** authored the critically acclaimed novel, *Bastard Out of Carolina*, a finalist for the 1992 National Book Award, which became an award-winning movie. Other titles include *Trash; Skin: Talking About Sex, Class and Literature;* and *Cavedweller*. She has won many awards, including the 2007 Robert Penn Warren Award for Fiction. She describes herself as a feminist, a working-class storyteller, a Southern expatriate, a sometime poet, and a happily born-again Californian.

. . . My people were not remarkable. We were ordinary, but even so we were mythical. We were the *they* everyone talks about, the ungrateful poor. I grew up trying to run away from the fate that destroyed so many of the people I loved, and having learned the habit of hiding, I found that I also had learned to hide from myself. I did not know who I was, only that I did not want to be *they*, the ones who are destroyed or dismissed to make the real people, the important people, feel safer. By the time I understood that I was queer, that habit of hiding was deeply set in me, so deeply that it was not a choice but an instinct. Hide, hide to survive, I thought, knowing that if I told the truth about my life, my family, my sexual desire, my real history, then I would move over into that unknown territory, the land of *they*, would never have the chance to name my own life, to understand it or claim it.

Why are you so afraid? my lovers and friends have asked me the many times when I have suddenly seemed to become a stranger, someone who would not speak to them, would not do the things they believed I should do, simple things like applying for a job, or a grant, or some award they were sure I could acquire easily. Entitlement, I have told them, is a matter of feeling like *we*, not *they*. But it has been hard for me to explain, to make them understand. You think you have a right to things, a place in the world, I try to say. You have a sense of entitlement I don't have, a sense of your own importance. I have explained what I know over and over again, in every possible way I can, but I have never been able to make clear the degree of my fear, the extent to which I feel myself denied, not only that I am queer in a world that hates queers but that I was born poor into a world that despises the poor. The need to explain is part of why I write fiction. I know that some things must be felt to be understood, that despair can never be adequately analyzed; it must be lived. . . .

I have known I was a lesbian since I was a teenager, and I have spent a good twenty years making peace with the effects of incest and physical abuse. But what may be the central fact of my life is that I was born in 1949 in Greenville, South Carolina, the bastard daughter of a poor white woman from a desperately poor family, a girl who had left the seventh grade the year before, who worked as a waitress and was just a month past fifteen when she had me. That fact, the inescapable impact of being born in a condition of poverty that this society finds shameful, contemptible, and somehow deserved, has dominated me to such an extent that I have spent my life trying to overcome or deny it. I have learned with great difficulty that the vast majority of people pretend that poverty is a voluntary condition, that the poor are different, less than fully human, or at least less sensitive to hopelessness, despair, and suffering.

The first time I read [Jewish writer] Melanie Kaye/Kantrowitz's poems, I experienced a frisson of recognition. It was not that my people had been "burned off the map" or murdered as hers had. No, we had been erased, encouraged to destroy ourselves, made invisible because we did not fit the myths of the middle class. Even now, past forty and stubbornly proud of my family, I feel the draw of that mythology, that romanticized, edited version of the poor. I find myself looking back and wondering what was real, what true. Within my family, so much was lied about, joked about, denied or told with deliberate indirection, an undercurrent of humiliation, or a brief pursed grimace that belies everything that has been said—everything, the very nature of truth and lies, reality and myth. What was real? The poverty depicted in books and movies was romantic, a kind of backdrop for the story of how it was escaped. The reality of self-hatred and violence was either absent or caricatured. The poverty I knew was dreary, deadening, shameful.

My family was ashamed of being poor, of feeling hopeless. What was there to work for, to save money for, to fight for or struggle against? We had generations before us to teach us that nothing ever changed, and that those who did try to escape failed.

My mama had eleven brothers and sisters, of whom I can name only six. No one is left alive to tell me the names of the others. It was my grandmother who told me about my real daddy, a shiftless pretty man who was supposed to have married, had six children, and sold cut-rate life insurance to colored people out in the country. My mama married when I was a year old, but her husband died just after my little sister was born a year later. When I was five, Mama married the man she lived with until she died. Within the first year of their marriage Mama miscarried, and while we waited out in the hospital parking lot, my stepfather molested me for the first time, something he continued to do until I was past thirteen. When I was eight or so, Mama took us away to a motel after my stepfather beat me so badly it caused a family scandal, but we returned after two weeks. Mama told me that she really had no choice; she could not support us alone. When I was eleven I told one of my cousins that my stepfather was molesting me. Mama packed up my sisters and me and took us away for a few days, but again, my stepfather swore he would stop, and again we went back after a few weeks. I stopped talking for a while, and I have only vague memories of the next two years.

My stepfather worked as a route salesman, my mama as a waitress, laundry worker, cook, or fruit packer. I could never understand how, since they both worked so hard and such long hours, we never had enough money, but it was a fact that was true also of my mama's brothers and sisters, who worked in the mills or the furnace industry. In fact, my parents did better than anyone else in the family, but eventually my stepfather was fired and we hit bottom—nightmarish months of marshals at the door, repossessed furniture, and rubber checks. My parents worked out a scheme so that it appeared my stepfather had abandoned us, but instead he went down to Florida, got a new job, and rented us a house. In the dead of night, he returned with a U-Haul trailer, packed us up, and moved us south.

The night we left South Carolina for Florida, my mama leaned over the back seat of her old Pontiac and promised us girls, "It'll be better there." I don't know if we believed her, but I remember crossing Georgia in the early morning, watching the red clay hills and swaying gray blankets of moss recede through the back window. I kept looking back at the trailer behind us, ridiculously small to contain everything we owned. Mama had, after all, packed nothing that wasn't fully paid off, which meant she had only two things of worth, her washing and sewing machines, both of them tied securely to the trailer walls. Through the whole trip, I fantasized an accident that would burst that trailer, scattering old clothes and cracked dishes on the tarmac.

I was only thirteen. I wanted us to start over completely, to begin again as new people with nothing of the past left over. I wanted to run away completely from who we had been seen to be, who we had been. That desire is one I have seen in other members of my family, to run away. It is the first thing I think of when trouble comes, the geographic solution. Change your name, leave town, disappear, and make yourself over. What hides behind that solution is the conviction that the life you have lived, the person you are, are valueless, better off abandoned, that running away is easier than trying to change anything, that change itself is not possible, that death is easier than this life. Sometimes I think it is that conviction—more seductive than alcoholism or violence and more subtle than sexual hatred or gender injustice—that has dominated my life, and made real change so painful and difficult.

Moving to central Florida did not fix our lives. It did not stop my stepfather's violence, heal my shame, or make my mother happy. Once there our lives became dominated by my mother's illness and medical bills. She had a hysterectomy when I was about eight and endured a series of hospitalizations for ulcers and a chronic back problem. Through most of my adolescence she superstitiously refused to allow anyone to mention the word cancer. (Years later when she called me to tell me that she was recovering from an emergency mastectomy, there was bitter fatalism in her voice. The second mastectomy followed five years after the first, and five years after that there was a brief bout with cancer of the lymph system which went into remission after prolonged chemotherapy. She died at the age of fifty-six with liver, lung, and brain cancer.) When she was not sick, Mama, and my stepfather, went on working, struggling to pay off what seemed an insurmountable load of debts.

By the time I was fourteen, my sisters and I had found ways to discourage most of our stepfather's sexual advances. We were not close but we united against our stepfather. Our efforts were helped along when he was referred to a psychotherapist after losing his temper at work, and was prescribed psychotropic drugs that made him sullen but less violent. We were growing up quickly, my sisters moving toward dropping out of school, while I got good grades and took every scholarship exam I could find. I was the first person in my family to graduate from high school, and the fact that I went on to college was nothing short of astonishing.

Everyone imagines her life is normal, and I did not know my life was not everyone's. It was not until I was an adolescent in central Florida that I began to realize just how different we were. The people we met there had not been shaped by the rigid class structure that dominated the South Carolina Piedmont. The first time I looked around my junior high classroom and realized that I did not know who those people were—not only as individuals but as categories, who their people were and how they saw themselves—I realized also that they did not know me. In Greenville, everyone knew my family, knew we were trash, and that meant we were supposed to be poor, supposed to have grim low-paid jobs, have babies in our teens, and never finish school. But central Florida in the 1960s was full of runaways and immigrants, and our mostly white working-class suburban school sorted us out, not by income and family background, but by intelligence and aptitude tests. Suddenly I was boosted into the college-bound track, and while there was plenty of contempt for my inept social skills, pitiful wardrobe, and slow drawling accent, there was also something I had never experienced before, a protective anonymity, and a kind of grudging respect and curiosity about who I might become. Because they did not see poverty and hopelessness as a foregone conclusion for my life, I could begin to imagine other futures for myself.

Moving into that new world and meeting those new people meant that I began to see my family from a new vantage point. I also experienced a new level of fear, a fear of losing what before had never been imaginable. My family's lives were not on television, not in books, not even comic books. There was a myth of the poor in this country, but it did not include us, no matter how hard I tried to squeeze us in.

There was an idea of the good poor—hard-working, ragged but clean, and intrinsically noble. I understood that we were the bad poor, the ungrateful: men who drank and couldn't keep a job; women, invariably pregnant before marriage, who quickly became worn, fat, and old from working too many hours and bearing too many children; and children with runny noses, watery eyes, and bad attitudes. My cousins quit school, stole cars, used drugs, and took dead-end jobs pumping gas or waiting tables. We were not noble, not grateful, not even hopeful. We knew ourselves despised.

But in that new country, we were unknown. The myth settled over us and glamorized us. I saw it in the eyes of my teachers, the Lions' Club representative who paid for my new glasses, and the lady from the Junior League who told me about the scholarship I had won. Better, far better, to be one of the mythical poor than to be part of the *they* I had known before. *Don't let me lose this chance,* I prayed, and lived in fear that I might suddenly be seen again as what I knew I really was.

As an adolescent, I thought that the way my family escaped South Carolina was like a bad movie. We fled like runaway serfs and the sheriff who would have arrested my stepfather seemed like a border guard. Even now, I am certain that if we had remained in South Carolina, I would have been trapped by my family's heritage of poverty, jail, and illegitimate children—that even being smart, stubborn, and a lesbian would have made no difference. My grandmother died when I was twenty and after Mama went home for the funeral, I had a series of dreams in which we still lived up in Greenville, just down the road from where Granny had died. In the dreams I had two children and only one eye, lived in a trailer, and worked at the textile mill. Most of my time was taken up with deciding when I would finally kill my children and myself. The dreams were so vivid, I became convinced they were about the life I was meant to have had, and I began to work even harder to put as much distance as I could between my family and me. I copied the dress, mannerisms, attitudes, and ambitions of the girls I met in college, changing or hiding my own tastes, interests, and desires. I kept my lesbianism a secret, forming a relationship with an effeminate male friend that served to shelter and disguise us both. I explained to friends that I went home so rarely because my stepfather and I fought too much

for me to be comfortable in his house. But that was only part of the reason I avoided home, the easiest reason. The truth was that I feared the person I might become in my mama's house.

It is hard to explain how deliberately and thoroughly I ran away from my own life. I did not forget where I came from, but I gritted my teeth and hid it. When I could not get enough scholarship money to pay for graduate school, I spent a year of blind rage working as a salad girl, substitute teacher, and maid. I finally managed to get a job by agreeing to take any city assignment where the Social Security Administration needed a clerk. Once I had a job and my own place far away from anyone in my family, I became sexually and politically active, joining the Women's Center support staff and falling in love with a series of middle-class women who thought my accent and stories thoroughly charming. The stories I told about my family, about South Carolina, about being poor itself, were all lies, carefully edited to seem droll or funny. I knew damn well that no one would want to hear the truth about poverty, the hopelessness and fear, the feeling that nothing you do will make any difference, and the raging resentment that burns beneath the jokes. Even when my lovers and I formed an alternative lesbian family, sharing all our resources, I kept the truth about my background and who I knew myself to be a carefully obscured mystery. I worked as hard as I could to make myself a new person, an emotionally healthy radical lesbian activist, and I believed completely that by remaking myself I was helping to remake the world.

For a decade, I did not go home for more than a few days at a time.

It is sometimes hard to make clear how much I have loved my family, that every impulse to hold them in contempt has sparked in me a countersurge of stubborn pride. . . . I have had to fight broad generalizations from every possible theoretical viewpoint. Traditional feminist theory has had a limited understanding of class differences or of how sexuality and self are shaped by both desire and denial. The ideology implies that we are all sisters who should turn our anger and suspicion only on the world outside the lesbian community. It is so simple to say the patriarchy did it, that poverty and social contempt are products of the world of the fathers. How often I felt a need to collapse my sexual history into what I was willing to share of my class background, to pretend that both my life as a lesbian and my life as a working-class escapee were constructed by the patriarchy. The difficulty is that I can't ascribe everything that has been problematic or difficult about my life simply and easily to the patriarchy, or even to the invisible and much-denied class structure of our society. . . .

One of the things I am trying to understand is how we internalize the myths of our society even as we hate and resist them. Perhaps this will be more understandable if I discuss specifically how some of these myths have shaped my life and how I have been able to talk about and change my own understanding of my family. I have felt a powerful temptation to write about my family as a kind of moral tale with us as the heroes and the middle and upper classes as the villains. It would be within the romantic myth, for example, to pretend that we were the kind of noble Southern whites portrayed in the movies, mill workers for generations until driven out of the mills by alcoholism and a family propensity to rebellion and union talk. But that would be a lie. The truth is that no one in my family ever joined a union. Taken as far as it can go, the myth of the poor would make my family over into union organizers or people broken by the failure of the unions. The reality of my family is far more complicated and lacks the cardboard nobility of the myth.

As far as my family was concerned, union organizers, like preachers, were of a different class, suspect and hated as much as they might be admired for what they were supposed to be trying to achieve. Serious belief in anything—any political ideology, any religious system, or any theory of life's meaning and purpose—was seen as unrealistic. It was an attitude that bothered me a lot when I started reading the socially conscious novels I found in the paperback racks when I was eleven or so. I particularly loved Sinclair Lewis's novels and wanted to imagine my own family as part of the working man's struggle. But it didn't seem to be that simple.

"We were not joiners," my Aunt Dot told me with a grin when I asked her about the union. My cousin Butch laughed at that, told me the union charged dues and said, "Hell, we can't even be persuaded to toss money in the collection plate. An't gonna give it to no fat union man." It shamed me that the only thing my family wholeheartedly believed in was luck, and the waywardness of fate. They held the

dogged conviction that the admirable and wise thing to do was to try and keep a sense of humor, not to whine or cower, and to trust that luck might someday turn as good as it had been bad—and with just as much reason. Becoming a political activist with an almost religious fervor was the thing I did that most outraged my family and the Southern working-class community they were part of.

Similarly, it was not my sexuality, my lesbianism, that was seen by my family as most rebellious; for most of my life, no one but my mama took my sexual preference very seriously. It was the way I thought about work, ambition, and self-respect that seemed incomprehensible to my aunts and cousins. They were waitresses, laundry workers, and counter girls. I was the one who went to work as a maid, something I never told any of them. They would have been angry if they had known, though the fact that some work was contemptible was itself a difficult notion. They believed that work was just work, necessary, that you did what you had to do to survive. They did not believe so much in taking pride in doing your job as they did in stubbornly enduring hard work and hard times when you really didn't have much choice about what work you did. But at the same time they did believe that there were some forms of work, including maid's work, that were only for black people, not white, and while I did not share that belief, I knew how intrinsic it was to how my family saw the world. Sometimes I felt as if I straddled cultures and belonged on neither side. I would grind my teeth at what I knew was my family's unquestioning racism but still take pride in their pragmatic endurance, but more and more as I grew older what I truly felt was a deep estrangement from the way they saw the world, and gradually a sense of shame that would have been completely incomprehensible to them.

"Long as there's lunch counters, you can always find work," I was told by both my mother and my aunts, and they'd add, "I can always get me a little extra with a smile." It was obvious that there was supposed to be nothing shameful about it, that needy smile across a lunch counter, that rueful grin when you didn't have rent, or the half-provocative, half-begging way my mama could cajole the man at the store to give her a little credit. But I hated it, hated the need for it and the shame that would follow every time I did it myself. It was begging as far as I was concerned, a quasi-prostitution that I despised even while I continued to use it (after all, I needed the money). But my mother, aunts, and cousins had not been ashamed, and my shame and resentment pushed me even further away from them.

"Just use that smile," my girl cousins used to joke, and I hated what I knew they meant. After college, when I began to support myself and study feminist theory, I did not become more understanding of the women of my family but more contemptuous. I told myself that prostitution is a skilled profession and my cousins were never more than amateurs. There was a certain truth in this, though like all cruel judgments made from the outside, it ignored the conditions that made it true. The women in my family, my mother included, had sugar daddies, not johns, men who slipped them money because they needed it so badly. From their point of view they were nice to those men because the men were nice to them, and it was never so direct or crass an arrangement that they would set a price on their favors. They would never have described what they did as prostitution, and nothing made them angrier than the suggestion that the men who helped them out did it just for their favors. They worked for a living, they swore, but this was different.

I always wondered if my mother had hated her sugar daddy, or if not *him* then her need for what he offered her, but it did not seem to me in memory that she had. Her sugar daddy had been an old man, half-crippled, hesitant and needy, and he treated my mama with enormous consideration and, yes, respect. The relationship between them was painful because it was based on the fact that she and my stepfather could not make enough money to support the family. Mama could not refuse her sugar daddy's money, but at the same time he made no assumptions about that money buying anything she was not already offering. The truth was, I think, that she genuinely liked him, and only partly because he treated her so well.

Even now, I am not sure whether or not there was a sexual exchange between them. Mama was a pretty woman and she was kind to him, a kindness he obviously did not get from anyone else in his life, and he took extreme care not to cause her any problems with my stepfather. As a teenager with an adolescent's contempt for moral failings and sexual complexity of any kind, I had been convinced that Mama's relationship with that old man was contemptible and also

that I would never do such a thing. The first time a lover of mine gave me money, and I took it, everything in my head shifted. The amount she gave me was not much to her, but it was a lot to me and I needed it. I could not refuse it, but I hated myself for taking it and I hated her for giving it to me. Worse, she had much less grace about my need than my mama's sugar daddy had displayed toward her. All that bitter contempt I had felt for my needy cousins and aunts raged through me and burned out the love I had felt. I ended the relationship quickly, unable to forgive myself for *selling* what I believed should only be offered freely—not sex but love itself.

When the women in my family talked about how hard they worked, the men would spit to the side and shake their heads. Men took real jobs—hard, dangerous, physically daunting work. They went to jail, not just the hard-eyed, careless boys who scared me with their brutal hands and cold eyes, but their gentler, softer brothers. It was another family thing, what people expected of my mama's family, my people. "His daddy's that one was sent off to jail in Georgia, and his uncle's another. Like as not, he's just the same," you'd hear people say of boys so young they still had their milk teeth. We were always driving down to the county farm to see somebody, some uncle, cousin, or nameless male relation. Shaven-headed, sullen, and stunned, they wept on Mama's shoulder or begged my aunts to help. "I didn't do nothing, Mama," they'd say and it might have been true, but if even we didn't believe them, who would? No one told the truth, not even about how their lives were destroyed. . . .

By 1975, I was earning a meager living as a photographer's assistant in Tallahassee, Florida, but the real work of my life was my lesbian feminist activism, the work I did with the local Women's Center and the committee to found a Feminist Studies Department at Florida State University. Part of my role as I saw it was to be a kind of evangelical lesbian feminist, and to help develop a political analysis of this woman-hating society. I did not talk about class, more than by giving lip service to how we all needed to think about it, the same way I thought we all needed to think about racism. I was a serious and determined person, living in a lesbian collective, studying each new book that purported to address feminist issues and completely driven by what I saw as a need to revolutionize the world. . . .

The idea of writing fiction or essays seemed frivolous when there was so much work to be done, but everything changed when I found myself confronting emotions and ideas that could not be explained away or postponed for a feminist holiday. The way it happened was simple and completely unexpected. One week I was asked to speak to two completely divergent groups: an Episcopalian Sunday School class and a juvenile detention center. The Episcopalians were all white, well-dressed, highly articulate, nominally polite, and obsessed with getting me to tell them (without their having to ask directly) just what it was that two women did together in bed. The delinquents were all women, eighty percent black and Hispanic, dressed in green uniform dresses or blue jeans and work shirts, profane, rude, fearless, witty, and just as determined to get me to talk about what it was that two women did together in bed.

I tried to have fun with the Episcopalians, teasing them about their fears and insecurities, and being as bluntly honest as I could about my sexual practices. The Sunday School teacher, a man who had assured me of his liberal inclinations, kept blushing and stammering as the questions about my growing up and coming out became more detailed. When the meeting was over, I stepped out into the sunshine angry at the contemptuous attitude implied by all their questions, and though I did not know why, also so deeply depressed that I couldn't even cry. The delinquents were different. Shameless, they had me blushing within the first few minutes, yelling out questions that were partly curious and partly a way of boasting about what they already knew.

"You butch or femme?" "You ever fuck boys?" "You ever want to?" "You want to have children?" "What's your girlfriend like?" I finally broke up when one very tall confident girl leaned way over and called out, "Hey girlfriend! I'm getting out of here next weekend. What you doing that night?" I laughed so hard I almost choked. I laughed until we were all howling and giggling together. Even getting frisked as I left didn't ruin my mood. I was still grinning when I climbed into the waterbed with my lover that night, grinning right up to the moment when she wrapped her arms around me and I burst into tears.

It is hard to describe the way I felt that night, the shock of recognition and the painful way my thoughts turned. That night I understood suddenly everything that happened to my cousins and me, understood it from a wholly new and agonizing perspective, one that made clear how brutal I had been to both my family and myself. I understood all over again how we had been robbed and dismissed, and why I had worked so hard not to think about it. I had learned as a child that what could not be changed had to go unspoken, and worse, that those who cannot change their own lives have every reason to be ashamed of that fact and to hide it. I had accepted that shame and believed in it, but why? What had I or my cousins really done to deserve the contempt directed at us? Why had I always believed us contemptible by nature? I wanted to talk to someone about all the things I was thinking that night, but I could not. Among the women I knew there was no one who would have understood what I was thinking, no other working-class women in the women's collective where I was living. I began to suspect that we shared no common language to speak those bitter truths.

In the days after that I found myself . . . thrown back into my childhood, into all the fears and convictions I had tried to escape. Once again I felt myself at the mercy of the important people who knew how to dress and talk, and would always be given the benefit of the doubt while I and my family would not.

I felt as if I was at the mercy of an outrage so old I could not have traced all the ways it shaped my life. I understood again that some are given no quarter, no chance, that all their courage, humor, and love for each other is just a joke to the ones who make the rules, and I hated the rule makers. Finally I also realized that part of my grief came from the fact that I no longer knew who I was or where I belonged. I had run away from my family, refused to go home to visit, and tried in every way to make myself a new person. How could I be working-class with a college degree? As a lesbian activist? I thought about the guards at the detention center, and the way they had looked at me. They had not stared at me with the same picture-window emptiness they turned on the girls who came to hear me, girls who were closer to the life I had been meant to live than I could bear to examine. The contempt in their eyes was contempt for me as a lesbian, different and the same, but still contempt. . . .

In the late 1970s, the compartmentalized life I had created burst open. It began when I started to write and work out what I really thought about my family. . . . I went home again. I went home to my mother and my sisters, to visit, talk, argue, and begin to understand.

Once home I saw that, as far as my family was concerned, lesbians were lesbians whether they wore suitcoats or leather jackets. Moreover, in all that time when I had not made peace with myself, my family had managed to make a kind of peace with me. My girlfriends were treated like slightly odd versions of my sisters' husbands, while I was simply the daughter who had always been difficult but was still a part of their lives. The result was that I started trying to confront what had made me unable to really talk to my sisters for so many years. I discovered that they no longer knew who I was either, and it took time and lots of listening to each other to rediscover my sense of family, and my love for them.

It is only as the child of my class and my unique family background that I have been able to put together what is for me a meaningful politics, gained a sense of why I believe in activism, why self-revelation is so important for lesbians, reexamining the way we are seen and the way we see ourselves. There is no all-purpose feminist analysis that explains away all the complicated ways our sexuality and core identity are shaped, the way we see ourselves as parts of both our birth families and the extended family of friends and lovers we invariably create within the lesbian community. For me the bottom line has simply become the need to resist that omnipresent fear, that urge to hide and disappear, to disguise my life, my desires, and the truth about how little any of us understand—even as we try to make the world a more just and human place for us all. Most of all I have tried to understand the politics of *they*, why human beings fear and stigmatize the different while secretly dreading that they might be one of the different themselves. Class, race, sexuality, gender, all the categories by which we categorize and dismiss each other need to be examined from the inside.

The horror of class stratification, racism, and prejudice is that some people begin to believe that the security of their families and community depends on the oppression of others, that for some to have good lives others must have lives that are mean and horrible. It is a belief that dominates this culture; it is what made the poor whites of the South so determinedly racist and the middle class so contemptuous of the poor. It is a myth that allows some to imagine that they build their lives on the ruin of others, a secret core of shame for the middle class, a goad and a spur to the marginal working class, and cause enough for the homeless and poor to feel no constraints on hatred or violence. The power of the myth is made even more apparent when we examine how within the lesbian and feminist communities, where so much attention has been paid to the politics of marginalization, there is still so much exclusion and fear, so many of us who do not feel safe even within our chosen communities.

I grew up poor, hated, the victim of physical, emotional, and sexual violence, and I know that suffering does not ennoble. It destroys. To resist destruction, self-hatred, or lifelong hopelessness, we have to throw off the conditioning of being despised, the fear of becoming that *they* that is talked about so dismissively, to refuse lying myths and easy moralities, to see ourselves as human, flawed and extraordinary. All of us—extraordinary.

FOURTEEN

Jews in the U.S. (1994/5755)
The Rising Costs of Whiteness

Melanie Kaye/Kantrowitz

Melanie Kaye/Kantrowitz teaches literature, Women's Studies, and Jewish Studies. She is also a long-time activist for social justice, was founding director of Jews for Economic and Racial Justice, and former Director of Queens College/CUNY Worker Education Extension Center. Her published work includes *The Issue Is Power: Essays on Women, Jews, Violence, and Resistance* and *The Colors of Jews: Racial Politics and Radical Diasporism.*

Before America No One Was White

In 1990 I had returned to New York City to do antiracist work with other Jews, when a friend sent
me an essay by James Baldwin. "No one was
white before he/she came to America," Baldwin
had written:

> It took generations, and a vast amount of coer-
> cion, before this became a white country. . . . It
> is probable that it is the Jewish community—or
> more accurately, perhaps, its remnants—that in
> America has paid the highest and most ex-
> traordinary price for becoming white. For the
> Jews came here from countries where they were
> not white, and they came here in part because
> they were not white, and incontestably—in the
> eyes of the Black American (and not only in those
> eyes) American Jews have opted to become
> white. . . .[1]

Everything I think about Jews, whiteness, racism,
and contemporary U.S. society begins with this
passage. What does it mean: *Jews opted to become
white.* Did we opt? Did it work? Was it an illusion?
Could we have opted otherwise? Can we still?

Rachel Rubin, a college student who's been in-
terning at Jews for Racial and Economic Justice,
where I'm the director, casually mentions: when she
was eight, a cross was burned on her lawn in
Athens, Georgia. I remember the house I moved
into Down East Maine in 1979. On the bedroom
door someone had painted a swastika in what
looked like blood. I think about any cross-country
drive I've ever taken, radio droning hymn after
Christian hymn, 2000 miles of heartland.

On the other hand, I remember the last time I
was stopped by cops. It was in San Francisco. I was
getting a ride home after a conference on Jews and
multiculturalism. In the car with me were two
other white Jews. My heart flew into my throat, as
always, but they took a quick look at the three of
us and waved us on—*We're looking for a car like
this, sorry.* I remember all the stories I've heard
from friends, people of color, in which a quick
look is not followed by a friendly wave and an
apology. Some of these stories are about life and
death. . . .

Where is *Jewish* in the race/class/gender grid?
Does it belong? Is it irrelevant? Where do those
crosses and swastikas fit in?

Race or Religion?

"Race or religion?" is how the question is usually
posed, as though this doublet exhausts the possibilities. Christians—religiously observant or not—
usually operate from the common self-definition of
Christianity, a religion any individual can embrace
through belief, detached from race, peoplehood,
and culture.

But I have come to understand this detachment
as false. Do white Christians feel kinship with
African American Christians? White slaveowners,
for example, with their slaves? White Klansmen
with their black neighbors? Do white Christians feel
akin to Christians converted by colonialists all over
the globe? Doesn't Christianity really, for most
white Christians, imply *white?* And for those white
Christians, does *white* really include *Jewish?* Think
of the massive Christian evasion of a simple fact:
Jesus Christ was not, was never, a Christian. He was
a Jew. What did he look like, Jesus of Nazareth, 2000
years ago? Blond, blue-eyed?

Of course Jewish is not a race,[2] for Jews come in
all races. Though white-identified Jews may skirt
the issue, Jews are a multiracial people. There are
Ethiopian, Indian, Chinese Jews. And there are people
of every race who choose Judaism, were adopted, or
born into it from mixed parents. The dominant conception of "Jewish"—European, Yiddish-speaking—
is in fact a subset, Ashkenazi. Estimated at 85–97%
of Jews in the U.S. today, Ashkenazi Jews are those
whose religious practice and diaspora path can be
traced through Germany.[3] The huge wave of Jewish
immigration from Eastern Europe was Ashkenazi
(as was the earlier, much smaller, highly assimilated
community of German Jews, who looked with dread
upon the arrival of—from their perspective—an
impoverished, Yiddish-babbling, superstitious
horde). Ashkenazi Jews also migrated to the far
points of the globe—to South America, Australia,
Africa, Asia. They may be very fair or very dark.

Sephardic Jews are those whose mother tongue
is/was Ladino (Judeo-Español) and whose religious practice and diaspora path can be traced at
some point through the Iberian Peninsula (Spain
and Portugal), where they flourished, unghet-
toized, contributing along with Muslims to Spanish culture, until the Inquisition (read, *torture*)
forced conversion or expulsion from Spain of all
non-Christians. Sephardim migrated to, and lived

for generations and even centuries, in Holland, Germany, Italy, France, Greece, the Middle East, and the Americas. The first Jews in the New World were Sephardim: 1492 marks not only Columbus's voyage but also the expulsion of the Jews from Spain. Some Sephardi consider themselves the aristocrats of the Jews, and look with contempt upon the Ashkenazi history of ghettoization and persecution. They may also be quite fair or quite dark.

Mizrachi Jews are those who lived in the Arab world and Turkey (basically, what was once the Ottoman Empire), as minorities in Muslim rather than Christian culture. Their mother tongue often is/was Judeo-Arabic. *Mizrachi* means "Eastern," commonly translated as "Oriental," and is used by and about Israelis, often interchangeably with *Sephardi*. Spanish Sephardim sometimes resent the blurring of distinctions between themselves and Mizrachim, reacting with pride in their history and with Eurocentric bias against non-Europeans, referring to themselves as "true" or "pure" Sephardim.[4] The confusion between the categories is only partly due to Ashkenazi ignorance/arrogance, lumping all non-Ashkenazi together. Partly it's the result of Jewish history: some Jews never left the Middle East, and some returned after the expulsion from Spain, including to Palestine. Some kept Ladino, some did not. I imagine there was intermarriage. Mizrachim, though they may also range from fair to dark, are usually defined as people of color.

The point is, categories of white and color don't correspond neatly to Jewish reality. (What does correspond is Ashkenazi cultural hegemony: in the U.S., where they are dominant by numbers, and in Israel, where Sephardi/Mizrachi Jews make up about two-thirds of the Jewish population and strongly contest this hegemony.) Jewish wanderings have created a people whose experience eludes conventional categories of race, nationality, ethnicity, geography, language—even religion. Cataclysm and assimilation have depleted our store of common knowledge.

No, Jews are not a single race. Yet there is confusion here, and subtext. Confusion because we have so often been racialized, hated *as if* we were a race. Ethnic studies scholars have labored to document the process of racialization, the fact that race is not biological, but a socio-historically specific phenomenon. Observing Jewish history, Nancy Ordover has noted, offers an opportunity to break

down this process of racialization, because by leaving Europe, Jews "changed" our "race," even as our skin pigment remained the same.[5]

> For the Jews came here from countries where they were not white, and they came here in part because they were not white. . .

Confusion, too, because to say someone *looks Jewish* is to say something both absurd (Jews look a million different ways) and commonsense communicative.

When I was growing up in Flatbush (in Brooklyn, NY), every girl with a certain kind of nose—sometimes named explicitly as a Jewish nose, sometimes only as "too big"—wanted a nose job, and if her parents could pay for it, often she got one. I want to be graphic about the euphemism "nose job." A nose job breaks the nose, bruises the face and eye area like a grotesque beating. It hurts. It takes weeks to heal.

What was wrong with the original nose, the Jewish one? Noses were discussed ardently in Flatbush, this or that friend looking forward to her day of transformation.[6] My aunts lavished on me the following exquisite praise: *look at her, a nose like a shiksa* (gentile woman). This hurt my feelings. Before I knew what a *shiksa* was, I knew I wasn't it, and, with that fabulous integrity of children, I wanted to look like who I was. But later I learned my nose's value, and would tell gentiles this story so they'd notice my nose.

A Jewish nose, I conclude, identifies its owner as a Jew. Nose jobs are performed so that a Jewish woman does not look like a Jew.

Tell me again Jewish is just a religion.

Yet Nazi racial definitions have an "only a religion" response. Even earlier, the lure of emancipation (in Europe) and assimilation (in the U.S.) led Jews to define Judaism as narrowly as possible, as religion only: "a Jew at home, a man in the streets,"[7] a private matter, taken care of behind closed doors, like bathing.

Judaism, the religion, does provide continuity and connection to Jews around the globe. There is something powerful even for atheists about entering a synagogue across the continent or the ocean, and hearing the familiar service.

But to be a Jew, one need not follow religious practice; one need not believe in god—not even to become a rabbi, an element of Judaism of which I am especially fond.[8] Religion is only one strand of being Jewish. It is ironic that it is precisely this century's depletion of Jews and of Jewish identity, with profound linguistic and cultural losses—continuing as Yiddish[9] and Ladino speakers age and die—that makes imaginable a Jewishness that is *only a religion*—only now, when so much else has been lost. But to reduce *Jewishness* to *Judaism* is to forget the complex indivisible swirl of religion/culture/language/history that *was* Jewishness until, in the 18th century, Emancipation began to offer some Jews the possibility of escaping from a linguistically/culturally/economically isolated ghetto into the European "Enlightenment." To equate Jewishness with religion is to forget how even the contemporary, often attenuated version of this Jewish cultural swirl is passed down *in the family*, almost like genetic code.

Confusion and subtext. *Jewish* is often trivialized as something you choose, a preference, like tea over coffee. In contrast with visible racial identity, presumptions of choice—as with gayness—are seen as minimizing one's claim to attention, sympathy, and remedy. As a counter to bigotry, *I was born like this* strategically asserts a kind of victim status, modeled on race, gender, and disability: if you can't help yourself, maybe you're entitled to some help from others. . . .

What happens if, instead, I assert my right to choose and not suffer for it. To say, *I choose:* my lesbianism and my Jewishness.[10] Choose to come out, be visible, embrace both. I could live loveless or sexless or in the closet. I could have kept the name *Kaye,* and never once at Christmas—in response to the interminable "what are you doing for . . .? have you finished your shopping?"—never once answer, "I don't celebrate Christmas. I'm a Jew." I could lie about my lover's gender. I could wear skirts uncomfortably. I could bleach my hair again, as I did when I was fifteen. I could monitor my speech, weeding out the offensive accent, as I was taught at City College, along with all the other first and second generation immigrants' children in the four speech classes required for graduation, to teach us not to sound like ourselves. I could remain silent when queer or anti-Semitic jokes are told, when someone says "you know how *they* are." I could endure the pain in the gut, the hot shame. I could scrunch up much, much smaller.

In the U.S., *Christian*, like *white*, is an unmarked category in need of marking.[11] Christianness, a majority, dominant culture, is not only about religious practice and belief, any more than Jewishness is. As *racism* names the system that normalizes, honors, and rewards whiteness, we need a word for what normalizes, honors and rewards Christianity. Jews designate the assumption of Christianity-as-norm, the erasure of Jews, as "anti-Semitic." In fact, the erasure and marginalization of non-Christians is not just denigrating to Jews. We need a catchier term than *Christian hegemony*, to help make visible the cultural war against all non-Christians.

Christianism? Awkward, stark, and kind of crude—maybe a sign that something's being pushed. *Sexism* once sounded stark and kind of crude. Such a term would help contextualize Jewish experience as an experience of marginality shared with other non-Christians. Especially in this time of rising Christian fundamentalism, as school prayer attracts support from "moderates," this contextualization is critical for progressive Jews, compelling us to seek allies among Muslims and other religious minorities.

I also want to contextualize Jews in a theoretical framework outside the usual bipolar frame of black/white—to go beyond dualism; to distinguish race from class, and both from culture; to understand "whiteness" as the gleaming conferral of normality, success, even survival; to acknowledge who owns what in whose neighborhood; to witness how money does and does not "whiten."

> For in the eyes of the Black American (and not only in those eyes) American Jews have opted to become white. . . .

To begin to break out of a polarity that has no place for Jews, I survey the range of color in the U.S. People of color, a unity sought and sometimes forged, include a vast diversity of culture and history, forms of oppression and persecution. Contemporary white supremacists hate them all, but define some as shrewd, evil, inscrutable, sexually exotic, and perverse, and others as intellectually inferior, immoral, bestial, violent, and sexually rapacious. If it is possible to generalize, we can say that the peoples defined as shrewd and evil tend to be better off economically—or at least perceived as better off economically—than those defined as inferior and violent, who tend to remain in large numbers stuck at the bottom of the economic ladder (and are assumed by the dominant culture, to be stuck there), denied access to decent jobs and opportunities, systematically disadvantaged and excluded by the educational system.

In other words, among the creeping fearsome dark ones are, on one hand, those who exploit, cheat, and hoard money they don't deserve, and, on the other, those (usually darker) who, not having money, threaten to rob and pillage hard-working tax-paying white Christians. In this construct, welfare fits as a form of robbery, the women's form; the men are busy mugging. Immigrant-bashing— whether street violence or political movements like "English-only" . . . —becomes a "natural" response to "robbery."

It is easier now to see where Jews fit: we are so good with money. Our "darkness" may not show, and this ability to pass confers protection and a host of privileges. But we are the model money-grubbing money-hoarding scapegoats for an increasingly punitive economic system. Jews, Japanese, Koreans, Arabs, Indians, and Pakistanis—let's face it: *interlopers* are blamed for economic disaster; for controlling the economy or making money on the backs of the poor; for raising the price of oil; for stealing or eliminating jobs by importing goods or exporting production.

At the same time, those defined as inferior and violent are blamed for urban crime and chaos, for drugs, for the skyrocketing costs and failures of social programs. This blame then justifies the oppression and impoverishment of those brought here in chains and the peoples indigenous to this continent. Add in the darker, poorer immigrants from Latin America and the Caribbean, and recent immigrants from China and Southeast Asia. Media codes like "inner-city crime" and "teen gangs" distort and condense a vast canvas of poverty, vulnerability, and exploitation into an echoing story of some young men's violent response to these conditions. Thus those who are significantly endangered come to be defined as inherently dangerous.

That is, one group is blamed for capitalism's crimes; the other for capitalism's fallout. Do I need to point out who escapes all blame?

When a community is scapegoated, members of that community are most conscious of how they feel humiliated, alienated, and endangered. But the other function of scapegoating is at least as pernicious. It is to protect the problem which scapegoats are drafted to conceal: the vicious system of profit and exploitation, of plenty and scarcity existing side by side.

The Cost of Whiteness

Aryan ideology aside, Jews are often defined as white, though this wipes out the many Jews who are by anyone's definition people of color, and neglects the role of context: many Jews who look white in New York City look quite the opposite in the South and Midwest. Radicals often exclude the category *Jewish* from discussion, or subsume us into *white*, unless we are by *their* definition also people of color, in which case they subsume us as *people of color*.

The truth is, Jews complicate things. *Jewish* is both a distinct category and an overlapping one. Just as homophobia is distinct from sexism yet has everything to do with sexism, anti-Semitism in this country is distinct from racism yet has everything to do with racism. It's not that a Jew like myself should "count" as a person of color, though I think sometimes Jews do argue this because the alternative seems to be erasure. But that means we need another alternative. The problem is a polarization of white and color that excludes us. We need a more complex vision of the structure of racism, one that attends to the sick logic of white supremacists. We need a more complex understanding of the process of "whitening."

> It is probable that it is the Jewish community— or more accurately, perhaps, its remnants—that in America has paid the highest and more extraordinary price for becoming white.

Every time I read this passage, at the word "remnants," my hand moves to the hollow at the base of my throat, to help me breathe. *Remnants.*

What have we paid?

How many of us speak or read Yiddish or Ladino or Hebrew? How many of us have studied Jewish history or literature, recognize the terms that describe Jewish experience, are familiar with the Jewish calendar, can sing more than three or four Jewish songs, know *something* beyond matzoh balls or stuffed grape leaves? Many of us—especially secular Jews, but also those raised in some suburban synagogues where spirituality took a back seat to capital construction, where Jewish pride seemed like another name for elitism—many of us have lost our culture, our sense of community. Only anti-Semitism reminds us who we are, and we have nothing to fight back with—no pride and no knowledge—only a feeble, embarrassed sense that hatred and bigotry are wrong. I have even heard Jews, especially, "progressives," justify anti-Semitism: maybe we really are "like that," rich and greedy, taking over, too loud, too pushy, snatching up more than our share, ugly and parasitical, Jewish American Princesses, Jewish landlords, Jewish bosses, emphasis on *Jewish.* Maybe we really deserve to be hated. . . .

Do we even know the history of which we, Jewish radicals, are a part? As Trotsky's master biographer Isaac Deutscher explained "the non-Jewish Jew" to the World Jewish Congress in 1958:

> The Jewish heretic who transcends Jewry belongs to a Jewish tradition. . . . Spinoza, Heine, Marx, Rosa Luxemburg, Trotsky, and Freud . . . all went beyond the boundaries of Jewry. They all found Jewry too narrow, too archaic, and too constricting. . . . Yet I think that in some ways they were very Jewish indeed. . . . as Jews they dwelt on the borderlines of various civilizations, religions, and national cultures.[12]

. . . It is frustrating that those Jews best equipped to grasp what it means to choose *not to be white*—not to blend, pass, or mute one's differences—are the Hasidim (ultra-orthodox).[13] But because they are also separatist, and by ideology and theology do not value encounters with diversity, the Hasidim have rarely forged alliances around diversity and against bigotry. Instead, they tend to protect their individual communities and to blame urban chaos on their neighbors, often people of color, with law-and-order rhetoric and actions both racist and quintessentially American.[14]

The response of other Jews toward the Hasidim is instructive. Embarrassment, exposure, shame, rage; *why do they have to be so blatant?*—including *so blatantly Jewish* and *so blatantly racist*—as opposed to the discreet liberal norm of moving out of the neighborhood or sending the kids to private schools faintly integrated by race but starkly segregated by class. And somewhere, for Jews who care about Jewish identity, the Hasidim also represent a kind of courage: they dare to walk around looking Jewish.

Progressive Jews need to reconstruct an authentically American progressive Jewish identity, choosing from the vast storehouse of history/culture/religion which pieces we want to reclaim, which will enable us to be out as Jews with our own brand of Jewish courage. It's not that most Jews in the U.S. will endure the same unsheddable visual vulnerability as most people of color, though buttons and t-shirts, the *kipah* (skullcap worn by observant men)) and the *magen david* (Star of David—"Jewish star") may draw us into street visibility. But Jews, like all other people, make political choices. With whose interests will we identify and stake our future? With the dominant and privileged few—white, Christian, and rich, ensuring that poverty remains part of the American landscape, leaving bigotry unchallenged, to feed on the local minority of choice?

. . . Many Jews who work against racism and on various progressive issues do this work as progressives, as women, as workers, as queers, as whites, as people of color. We are invisible *as Jews,* while Jewish political conservatives are highly visible. We relinquish to the Jewish right wing the claim to represent the Jewish community, though the sheer number of Jews involved with progressive politics is stunning. We abandon Jewish culture to the religious orthodox: we think they are the "real Jews" and we are not. We neglect the powerful tradition of Jewish radicalism, a potential source of instruction, inspiration, and courage. Committed as progressives to the survival of people's culture, we stand, unseeing and uncaring, at the edge of a chasm opened by assimilation and infinitely deepened by the Holocaust. We facilitate the dwindling of the Jewish community—*to remnants.*

Is It Coming Again?

How can I concern myself with progressive coalitions and alliances when everyone—including progressives—hates Jews? When I speak in the Jewish community, people say this to me all the time. And they have a point. Look at the July 1994 bombing of the Jewish Community Center in Buenos Aires. The center had housed libraries, cemetery records, archives of 100 years of Yiddish theater, Yiddish newspapers, services of all kinds. Among the 95 killed, the hundreds wounded, were workers at the Center, students doing research in the library, and poor people in need of the services dispensed on Mondays, when the bombing took place. One of the oldest Jewish communities in South America was devastated. . . .

At a recent Jews for Racial and Economic Justice meeting, in a discussion which begins with the Buenos Aires bombing, we talk about how anti-Semitism is often used as a counterweight to progressive values, and how this use makes it hard to establish or sometimes even to feel solidarity with other Jews. We are often so busy reminding the mainstream Jewish community that Palestinians are killed all the time. . . .

Several people note the difference between New York City and the rest of the country; here Jews are hardly a minority, and most benefit from the privileges of white skin, while "in the Diaspora" at least one person present has been confronted with the question, *where are your horns?* Another says, "People are always asking me, *what are you?* They don't know I'm Jewish, but they know I'm *something*.". . . Someone remarks that in the South and Northwest, Jews and people of color join to fight white supremacist groups as a matter of course. We agree that focusing on the seriousness and connectedness of right wing activity—racist, anti-Semitic, homophobic, and anti-abortion— helps us reach out to other Jews.

I am writing this at Rosh Hashonah, the Jewish New Year opening year 5755 of the Jewish calendar. We call the ten days following Rosh Hashonah *Yamim Noraim,* the Days of Awe, the most solemn time of our year, culminating in Yom Kippur, the Day of Atonement. If a Jew steps foot inside a synagogue once a year, Yom Kippur is the day. I am thinking about the danger, in this time of increased attacks on Jews, of stepping inside visibly Jewish spaces packed with Jews. At this time of heightened danger I feel intensely, paradoxically, the need to be among Jews in a Jewish space.

Elsewhere I have written, "to be a Jew is to tangle with history."[15] In the U.S. people tend to be both ahistorical and insulated from the impact of international events. From this tunnel perspective, Jews have it good. What are we worried about? And we *do* have it good. And we do worry. Jews have a history of nearly 6000 recorded years of repeated cycles of calm, then chaos: periods of relative safety and prosperity disrupted by persecution, brutal oppression, murder, and expulsion or exile for the surviving remnant to a strange land where the cycle begins again. Grace Paley reports her immigrant mother's succinct comment on Hitler's rise to power: "It's coming again."[16]

In the U.S. much of the bias against Jews has been mitigated by the development of some institutionalized Jewish power. This should be a cause for celebration. Instead it makes us nervous. Jewish success is often used against us, as evidence of our excessive control, power, and greed, evidence which could at any moment topple us from the calm and, for many Jews, prosperous phase of the cycle into danger and chaos.

Besides, Jewish success—like any other U.S. success—has been achieved inside a severe class structure, and Jews, like many other ethnic and racial minorities, have benefitted in concrete ways from racism against African Americans. Karen Sacks' brilliant investigation, "How Did Jews Become White Folks?" describes how "federal programs which were themselves designed to assist demobilized GIs and young families systematically discriminated against African Americans," and functioned as "affirmative action . . . [which] aimed at and disproportionately helped male, Euro-origin GIs."[17] Thus she convincingly explains post-World War II Jewish upward mobility.

History. In 1492 the Inquisition forced thousands of us to convert to Christianity or flee Spain and Portugal. Some of us ended up in the Americas and were forced to convert anyway. But many of us maintained our Jewishness secretly. . . .

Passing. I get to choose when to disclose I'm a Jew. It doesn't show, at least not blatantly or automatically. If I need to, I can hide. Clearly, this applies to some Jews and not others, a benefit something like that "enjoyed" by the conventionally feminine-looking lesbian vis-à-vis the stone butch; or by the lighter skin, English-speaking Chicana. In other words, Jews benefit from not looking Jewish.[18] That many Jews walk safely down the streets of North America because our Jewishness is not visible is a fact, but not necessarily a comforting one. Many of us would prefer to be both visible and safe. Sometimes it's hard to find each other (why confirmed atheists like me, when we live rurally or outside large Jewish communities—join synagogues; how else would we find the Jews?). Passing/invisibility has a double edge.

Yet any time I feel whiny about passing's double edge, I picture myself in a car, any car, with a cop pulling up alongside. I think of all the times I didn't get followed around stores with someone assuming I was about to rip them off, even when I *was* about to rip them off.

I also think of my father changing his name from Kantrowitz to Kaye before I was born, pressured by the exigencies of being a Jew in the forties, even in New York. "It was easier," he'd explain, "people always called me Mr. K. anyway, they couldn't pronounce or remember it." (But when have you heard of a Gloucester, a Leicester, a McLoughlin changing his name?) When he died, in 1982, I took back Kantrowitz. I just didn't like the name going out of the world, and a certain incident weighed on me: a white gentile lesbian who knew my writing exclaimed upon meeting me, "Oh! I expected you to be tall and blond." I knew if my name were Melanie Kantrowitz, no one would ever expect me to be tall and blond.

But I have recognized in some situations exactly how I need to stiffen my spine to say (and then spell, though it is perfectly phonetic) *Kantrowitz. Kantrowitz. Kantrowitz.* And sometimes when I just don't have the *koyekh* (strength), I say *Kaye,* and feel grimly close to my dead ghetto-raised father.

To Discover Water

My father. *My father loved all things Jewish,* I wrote after he died in a poem I called *Kaddish,* which is the Jewish prayer for the dead.[19] My father who changed his name. My father *who loved the sound of Yiddish but would not speak it.* And my mother: hates bagels, hates matzoh balls, never went to *shul,* is careful to distinguish herself from *those others,* has spent her lifetime hating her nose, her Jewish nose. Yet says, repeatedly, *scratch a goy* (non-Jew) *you'll find an anti-Semite.*

My grandparents immigrated from Russia and Poland early in this century. My father, a teenager in Brownsville (a poor Jewish ghetto in Brooklyn) during the Depression, joined the Young Communist League; as an adult his major hero remained his friend Aaron, a communist who had spoken on street corners and died fighting in the second World War. My mother had circulated petitions against the Korean War, walking up to people on the streets of Flatbush during peak McCarthy period, and she had been spat on.

. . . This was my Jewish upbringing, as much as the candles we lit for Hanukkah, or the seders where bread and matzoh shared the table. My father had been raised observant, my mother, not. But to us breaking religious observance was progressive, the opposite of superstitious. When we ate on Yom Kippur, it never occurred to me that this was unJewish. I knew I was a Jew. I knew Hitler had been evil. I knew Negroes—we said then—had been slaves and that was evil too. I knew prejudice was wrong, stupid. I knew Jews believed in freedom and justice (the screaming arguments at extended family gatherings never challenged my belief that we, the un-prejudiced, were the "real" Jews). My parents' attachment to Adlai Stevenson was such that I grew up sort of assuming he was Jewish, while a photograph of FDR hung on our living room wall, surrounded by reverence, god in modern drag. When Eisenhower-Nixon ran against Stevenson in 1952, I noticed Nixon's dark, wavy hair, like my father's, and said, "He looks like Daddy." "Nothing like him, *nothing,* how could you think such a thing," my mother snapped. She then explained in detail how Nixon got elected to congress only by redbaiting Helen Gahagan Douglas (the liberal Congresswoman). I was seven years old.

I remember my mother crying when the Rosenbergs were executed, and I was terrified, because I knew they were good people, like my parents, with children the same age as my sister and me. *Who would take care of their children?* Soon we would get our first TV, so my mother (and I) could watch the McCarthy hearings. I knew the whole fate of humanity hinged on these hearings, as surely as I knew McCarthy and his people had killed the Rosenbergs. It literally did not occur to me that real people, people I might meet, people who had children and went to work, hated the Rosenbergs or liked McCarthy. Not did it occur to me that there were people who thought unions were bad, people who did not know you never cross a picket line, did not know prejudice was wrong and stupid. I could not even conceive of someone voting for Eisenhower: *how had he won?*

That this set of principles was Jewish never occurred to me. Around me was Flatbush, a swirling Jewish ghetto/community of first and second generation immigrants, including Holocaust survivors; . . . there were clerks, trade unionists, salespeople, plumbers, small business people, radio and TV repairmen, people like my parents (small shopkeepers) "in the middle," apartment dwellers where the kids shared a room, and fathers worked 60–70 hours a week; and people poorer than us, who lived in apartments where kitchen smells lingered on the stairs, someone slept in the living room, and summers the kids swam in underwear instead of bathing suits. There were teachers and even doctors who were rich and lived in what we called "private houses" in the outreaches of the neighborhood at the point where not everyone was Jewish.

But where I lived, everyone was, or almost. Jewish was the air I breathed, nothing I articulated, everything I took for granted.

Not-Jewish meant, for the most part, Catholic. Catholics were plentiful and scary: if you married them they would demand your children, and the pope could tell you what not to read. My high school, Erasmus Hall, the oldest and largest in the country, in theory integrated, was so severely tracked that the mostly Jews, Italians, and African Americans who attended rarely had classes together. As for WASPs, I knew they were the majority somewhere, but where? I knew *Jones* and *Smith* were someone's idea of an ordinary dime-a-dozen name, but I never met one: my idea of the commonest name on earth was *Susan Goldberg.*

I was 17 and a high school graduate before I met privileged WASPs, and that was in the Civil Rights Movement in Harlem. Before Harlem, I barely thought consciously about either whiteness or Jewishness (though I straightened my hair and performed unspeakable obscenities on my eyebrows). In Harlem the world divided up into white and black and there was no question what I was. I barely registered the large proportion of Jews among white people working in the Civil Rights Movement.[20] Nor in years of activism on the left did I note the extent of Jewish participation as something to take pride in, or understand that my rebellion against traditionalism had been enacted simultaneously by thousands of young Jews. Not until the early seventies when I moved to Oregon and encountered

white Christian anti-Semites, did I even understand that to them I was not white: I was a Jew.

In 1972, I had just moved to Portland, Oregon, and was attending a feminist conference, talking with a woman while we waited for the elevator. I have forgotten the context for what she said: that she did not like Jews. Jews were loud and pushy and aggressive. This was the first time I had heard someone say this outright. I was stunned, didn't know what to say—"no, they're not?"—and I couldn't believe she didn't know that I was Jewish. My voice came out loud and flat: "I'm Jewish." To this day I can't remember how she responded or what I did next.

In Portland, I heard for the first time the habitual use of *Christian* interchangeably with *virtuous: Act like a Christian.* Even among leftists, it was tricky: liberation theology was sometimes a contemporary version of *Christian* equals *good.* As for feminists, the one thing they knew about Jews was that Jewish men thank god every morning for not making them a woman (this prayer exists, but is hardly a core ritual). . . .

And *my* Jewishness? I had never articulated it. I began to think about it.

That first year in Portland, I read Hannah Arendt's *Eichmann in Jerusalem,* and realized something I had somehow up to this point managed not to notice: I would have been killed. My family, everyone I grew up around, practically, would have been killed. Random family tidbits clicked into place: my grandparents' families *had* been killed. . . .

What is clear is this: the more outside of a Jewish ambience I was, the more conscious I became of Jewishness. Like Marshall McLuhan's perhaps apocryphal remark: *I don't know who discovered water, but I'm sure it wasn't a fish.* Inside a Jewish environment, where I could take for granted a somewhat shared culture, an expectation about Jewish survival, where my body type and appearance were familiar, my voice ordinary, my laughter not too loud but hearty and normal, above all, normal . . . in this environment, I did not know what it meant to be a Jew, only what it meant to be a *mentsh.* I did not know that *mentsh* was a Jewish word in a Jewish language.

To Create Solidarity

The more conscious I became, the more I thought and talked and came to write about it and act visibly and politically as a Jew, the more I encountered both blankness and kinship, anti-Semitism and solidarity—the more I came to locate myself in a tradition of Jewish women.

Initially I felt most connected to women like myself, with thick dark eyebrows, sturdy legs, full mouths, big teeth, wild hair, skin full of oil glands for the desert. Secular, Ashkenazi, from Eastern Europe. English modelled on Yiddish inflection. Laughter explosive and frequent. We interrupt. We argue. We take for granted that the work of this lifetime is to seek justice; that if you're not a *mentsh*, you're a *shanda* (shame).

Emma Goldman lectured frequently in Yiddish. Clara Lemlich, at sixteen, cut short the speechifying at the famous Cooper Union garment workers meeting by calling for a strike vote (it passed). Rose Schneiderman first spoke the demand for bread *and* roses adopted by second wave feminism (could feminists have noticed *this* as Jewish, along with that obscure prayer?). Pauline Newman, Mary Dreier, Lillian Wald were open lesbians and important labor activists and social reform advocates. Anzia Yezierska wrote in Yiddish-inflected English about the struggles of immigrant women for education, independence and love. Lil Moed and Naomi Kies devoted their lives to the struggle for Palestinian rights and peace between Israel and Palestine. Grace Paley and Vera Williams create wildly original stories and continue to slog along in the trenches of social justice.[21]

But the list goes on, to encompass the women *not* "like me"—rabbis and theologians whose critiques of traditional Judaism, or fights to include women in a transformed Judaism, have made it possible for a secularist like myself to go to *shul*. Scholars Judith Plaskow and Susannah Heschel demand the presence of women in the Jewish religion. Rabbi Julie Greenberg reinterprets Jewish practice and, as a single mother and a lesbian, raises her three joyfully-chosen children. Rabbi Susan Talve leads her St. Louis congregation into justice-seeking partnership with an African American church. Poet/translator Marcia Falk creates highly evolved feminist blessings and prayers, using traditional imagery but taking back the source of divinity, the power to bless.[22]

. . . And what is this new Jewish tradition we are creating and which, in turn, creates us? I once heard Judith Plaskow respond to someone's discomfort with new prayers reformed to eliminate male god language—"Those aren't the prayers I grew up with," the woman said, "I don't feel comfortable with them." And Plaskow responded, "We're not the generation that gets to feel comfortable. We're the generation that gets to create a tradition so the next generation grows up in it, and for them it will be the authentic tradition, and they will feel comfortable." No, we are not the generation that gets to feel comfortable. But we are the generation that sometimes gets to feel whole.

On the evening of Election Day, 1992, I was driving down from Seattle to Portland, Oregon, where Measure 9, the most vitriolic of the homophobic hate measures, was on the ballot. Measure 9 would have sanctioned discrimination explicitly and violence implicitly; would have banned from public libraries and schools books that deal positively with gay and lesbian experience; would have blocked funding of any public institutions that aided gays and lesbians—for example, AIDS counselling.

. . . As I pulled into my friend's neighborhood, Northeast Portland, a neighborhood mixed by income and by race—not especially gay—I saw signs on every lawn—NO ON 9. I started to cry, and I realized I had no concept of allies. Even though the friend I was going to stay with was heterosexual, and I knew she'd been working very hard on this issue, I had still somewhere assumed that no one would stand with us—that we would be fighting alone. And I knew this came from my history as a Jew.

I had heard about the escalation of violence against Oregon lesbians and gays. But I still was not prepared for what I found. I saw antigay propaganda that copied actual Nazi cartoons which showed Jews controlling the economy, substituting gays instead. Powell's Bookstore, which had been featuring displays of books endangered by 9, had received bomb threats, as had individuals working against 9. House and car windows had been smashed, cars tampered with. Physical attacks on lesbians and gays had skyrocketed, and in Salem a black lesbian and a white gay man had been murdered. . . .

I heard bits and pieces of this struggle: how some people in Portland or Salem didn't want to bother organizing rurally, how some white people did not understand the need to build coalitions with communities of color. Yet despite some reluctance and ignorance, a vast broad coalition was created. People told me not about the ease of creating this coalition but about the clarity and desperation and drive. . . . Out of something ugly and outrageous has come something astonishing and inspiring, a model for the rest of the country, for the continued struggle against hatred—for survival.

A model for Jews as well. Oregon's Jews stood unanimously against Measure 9: every synagogue, every community organization and institution, every rabbi. . . . Here is an excerpt from the Oregon Jews' statement, deeply informed by Jewish history, and by Jewish recognition of the intolerably high cost and inevitable slippage of any safety based on "whiteness":

> [The Holocaust] began with laws exactly like Ballot Measure 9. Those laws first declared groups of people to be sub-human, then legalized and finally mandated discrimination against them. Comparisons to the Holocaust must be limited. But clearly, this is the start of hatred and persecution that must stop now.

At the victory rally the night after the election, all the coalition partners spoke to celebrate, warn, rage, and comfort. There were representatives from the Jewish community, African American community, Native American community, labor. . . . Two voices especially stand out in my memory. One was a Chicano organizer from the Farmworkers Union, who said, "In this, we were there for you. Now we're organizing our strike, and I need to ask you to be there for us." The other voice was a white lesbian activist, who answered the farmworker: *"Su lucha es mi lucha." Your struggle is my struggle.*

I may be secular, but I know holiness when I hear it. One of its names is solidarity, the opposite of "whiteness." The more you claim it, honor it, and fight for it, the less it costs.

NOTES

I thank Esther Kaplan, Roni Natov, and Nancy Ordover for substantial critical feedback. Sections of this essay are drawn from earlier writings published in *The Issue Is Power: Essays on Women, Jews, Violence and Resistance* (San Francisco: Aunt Lute, 1992).

1. "On Being 'White'. . . and Other Lies," *Essence* (April, 1984).

2. On the other hand, Karen Sacks, "How Did Jews Become White Folks?" in *Race*, eds., Steven Gregory and Roger Sanjek (New Brunswick: Rutgers University Press, 1994), points to "a 1987 Supreme Court ruling that Jews and Arabs could use civil rights laws to gain redress for discrimination against them . . . on the grounds that they are not racial whites."

3. *Ashkenazi* comes from the word for Germany; *Sephardi*, from Spain.

4. For Sephardi in the former Ottoman Empire, see Interview with Chaya Shalom in *The Tribe of Dina: A Jewish Women's Anthology*, eds., Melanie Kaye/Kantrowitz and Irena Klepfisz (Boston: Beacon Press, 1989: 1st pub., *Sinister Wisdom*, 1986), pp. 214–226.

5. Nancy Ordover, oral critique, December, 1994.

6. See Aisha Berger's poem, "Nose is a country . . . I am the second generation," in *The Tribe of Dina*. pp. 134–138. One of Berger's many illuminating images: "this unruly semitic landmass on my face." The era of Jewish nose jobs is not over, though Barbra Streisand broke the spell that mirrored Jewish noses as inherently ugly.

7. First expressed by Moses Mendelssohn (1729–86), the central figure in the German Jewish *Haskalah* (Enlightenment), as the ideal of Jewish assimilation.

8. One is, however, hard put to be a Jew without Jewish community. Even in religious practice, the unit of prayer is not the individual but the *minyan*, at least ten adult Jews, the Jewish quorum—in Orthodox Judaism, ten men.

9. There is painful irony in the fact that Yiddish, the beloved *mame-losbn* of Jewish socialists, is dwindling to a living language only for the ultra-orthodox Hasidim.

10. In this discussion I am indebted to Nancy Ordover, "Visibility, Alliance, and the Practice of Memory." *Socialist Review*. 25, no. 1 (1995): 119–134.

11. Ruth Frankenberg's *White Women/Race Matters* (Minneapolis: University of Minnesota, 1993) offers useful insight on whiteness as an unmarked racial category. But Frankenberg misses opportunities to note the significance of *Jewish* as a category, although she and a disproportionate number of the white anti-racist activists she interviewed are Jews.

12. Isaac Deutscher, "The Non-Jewish Jew," in *The Non-Jewish Jew and Other Essays* (London: Oxford University Press, 1968). pp. 26–27.

13. In appearance, immediately identifiable as Jews because of distinct dress (black hats and coats for the men, arms and legs fully covered for the women) and hair (*peyes*—unshorn sideburns—for the men; hair cropped and covered by a *sheytl*—wig—or headscarf for the women), the Hasidim are magnets for anti-Semitism. Similarly, anti-Semitic graffiti, vandalism, and bombing of synagogues demonstrate that identifiable Jewish places are also vulnerable.

14. Though the Hasidim are vulnerable as individuals to acts of bigotry and violence, in New York City the

Hasidic communities (Lubovitcher, in Crown Heights, and Satmar, in Williamsburg) wield influence. This is not a function of numbers; the Hasidim comprise a tiny percent of the world's Jews. Nor is it a function of wealth; indeed, a great many families in the Hasidic communities are poor, partly due to family size (as in all fundamentalist religions, the use of birth control is prohibited). Hasidic influence is a function of social organization: Hasidic leaders can deliver votes in an election and bodies in a demonstration. . . . Here is a lesson for progressive Jews about the need for *progressive* Jewish visibility and organization.

15. In "The Issue Is Power: Some Notes on Jewish Women and Therapy," *The Issue Is Power: Essays on Women, Jews, Violence and Resistance* (San Francisco: Aunt Lute, 1992).

16. Grace Paley, "Now and Then." *Tikkun* (May/June 1989), p. 76. In particular, European medieval and Renaissance history from a Jewish perspective reads like a disaster chronicle: expelled from here, massacred there, forced conversions someplace else. Occasionally there is a bright spot: "Jews return to Worms" (from which they had been expelled the year before); "Jews allowed to settle in England" (from which they had been expelled some centuries earlier). The late nineteenth and early twentieth century, especially in Eastern Europe, presents a similar wave of persecution, dwarfed only by the magnitude of what followed. Grievous official and unofficial oppression of Jews was a common feature of modern pre-Holocaust Europe.

17. Karen Sacks, in *Race*, eds. Steven Gregory and Roger Sanjek.

18. Jews who could pass as gentile, because they looked less Jewish and could speak the dominant language fluently, were more likely to survive the various swings of anti-Semitism. Thus to tell a survivor of the European Holocaust "you don't look Jewish" is to probe a painful truth—had the person looked more Jewish, s/he would probably be dead.

19. "Kaddish," in *Nice Jewish Girls: A Lesbian Anthology*, ed., Evelyn Torton Beck (Boston: Beacon Press, 1989), pp. 107–11; first published in *Sinister Wisdom* 25 (1984).

20. See Melanie Kaye/Kantrowitz, "Stayed on Freedom: Memories of a Jew in the Civil Rights Movement." in *Narrow Bridge: Jews and Multiculturalism*, ed. Maria Brettschneider (New Brunswick: Rutgers, University Press, 1996).

21. See *The Tribe of Dina*, tribute to Naomi Kies: interviews with Lil Moed and Grace Paley.

22. Judith Plaskow, *Standing Again At Sinai* (San Francisco: HarperSanFrancisco, 1990); Susannah Heschel, *On Being a Jewish Feminist* (New York: Schocken, 1983); Marcia Falk, *The Book of Blessings: Re-Creation of Jewish Prayer* (San Francisco: HarperSanFrancisco, 1994); for Julie Greenberg, "Seeking a Feminist Judaism," and Susan Talve, "Sarika." see *The Tribe of Dina.*

FIFTEEN

◆◆◆

Optional Ethnicities (1996)
For Whites Only?

Mary C. Waters

Mary C. Waters is the M.E. Zukerman Professor of Sociology at Harvard University and a distinguished scholar specializing in the study of immigration, intergroup relations, the formation of racial and ethnic identity among the children of immigrants, and the challenges of measuring race and ethnicity. Her many books include *Black Identities: West Indian Immigrant Dreams and American Realities; Inheriting the City: The Second Generation Comes of Age* (co-author); and *The New Americans: A Guide to Immigration Since 1965* (co-author).

. . . What does it mean to talk about ethnicity as an option for an individual? To argue that an individual has some degree of choice in their ethnic identity flies in the face of the commonsense notion of ethnicity many of us believe in—that one's ethnic identity is a fixed characteristic, reflective of blood ties and given at birth. However, social scientists who study ethnicity have long concluded that while ethnicity is based in a *belief* in a common ancestry, ethnicity is primarily a *social* phenomenon, not a biological one (Alba 1985, 1990; Barth 1969; Weber [1921] 1968, p. 389). The belief that members of an ethnic group have that they share a common ancestry may not be a fact. There is a great deal of change in ethnic identities across generations through intermarriage, changing allegiances, and changing social categories. There is also a much larger amount of change in the identities of individuals over their life than is commonly believed. While most people are aware of the phenomenon known as "passing"—people raised as one race who change at some point and claim a different race as their identity—there are similar life course changes in ethnicity that happen all the time and are not given the same degree of attention as "racial passing."

White Americans of European ancestry can be described as having a great deal of choice in terms of their ethnic identities. The two major types of options White Americans can exercise are (1) the option of whether to claim any specific ancestry, or to just be "White" or American (Lieberson [1985] called these people "unhyphenated Whites"), and (2) the choice of which of their European ancestries to choose to include in their description of their own identities. In both cases, the option of choosing how to present yourself on surveys and in everyday social interactions exists for Whites because of social changes and societal conditions that have created a great deal of social mobility, immigrant assimilation, and political and economic power for Whites in the United States. Specifically, the option of being able to not claim any ethnic identity exists for Whites of European background in the United States because they are the majority group—in terms of holding political and social power, as well as being a numerical majority. The option of choosing among different ethnicities in their family backgrounds exists because the degree of discrimination and social distance attached to specific European backgrounds has diminished over time.

The Ethnic Miracle

When European immigration to the United States was sharply curtailed in the late 1920s, a process was set in motion whereby the European ethnic groups already in the United States were for all intents and purposes cut off from any new arrivals. As a result, the composition of the ethnic groups began to age generationally. The proportion of each ethnic group made up of immigrants or the first generation began to gradually decline, and the proportion made up of the children, grandchildren, and eventually great-grandchildren began to increase. Consequently, by 1990 most European-origin ethnic groups in the United States were composed of a very small number of immigrants, and a very large proportion of people whose link to their ethnic origins in Europe was increasingly remote.

This generational change was accompanied by unprecedented social and economic changes. The very success of the assimilation process these groups experienced makes it difficult to imagine how much the question of the immigrants' eventual assimilation was an open one at the turn of the century. At the peak of immigration from southern and central Europe, there was widespread discrimination and hostility against the newcomers by established Americans. Italians, Poles, Greeks, and Jews were called derogatory names, attacked by nativist mobs, and derided in the press. Intermarriage across ethnic lines was very uncommon—castelike in the words of some sociologists (Pagnini and Morgan 1990). The immigrants and their children were residentially segregated, occupationally specialized, and generally poor.

After several generations in the United States, the situation has changed a great deal. The success and social mobility of the grandchildren and great-grandchildren of that massive wave of immigrants from Europe has been called "The Ethnic Miracle" (Greeley 1976). These Whites have moved away from the inner-city ethnic ghettos to White middle-class suburban homes. They are doctors, lawyers, entertainers, academics, governors, and Supreme Court justices. But contrary to what some social science theorists and some politicians predicted or hoped for, these middle-class Americans have not completely given up ethnic identity. Instead, they have maintained some connection with their immigrant ancestors' identities—becoming Irish American doctors, Italian American Supreme Court justices, and Greek American presidential candidates. In the tradition of cultural pluralism, successful middle-class Americans in the late twentieth century maintain some degree of identity with their ethnic backgrounds. They have remained "hyphenated Americans." So, while social mobility and declining discrimination have created the option of not identifying with any European ancestry, most White Americans continue to report some ethnic background.

With the growth in intermarriage among people of European ethnic origins, increasingly these people are of mixed ethnic ancestry. This gives them the option of which ethnicity to identify with. The U.S. census has asked a question on ethnic ancestry in the 1980 and 1990 censuses. In 1980, 52 percent of the American public responded with a single ethnic ancestry, 31 percent gave multiple ethnic origins (up to three were coded, but some individuals wrote in more than three), and only 6 percent said they were American only, while the remaining 11 percent gave no response. In 1990 about 90 percent of the population gave some response to the ancestry question, with only 5 percent giving American as a response and only 1.4 percent reporting an uncodeable response such as "don't know" (McKenney and Cresce 1992; U.S. Bureau of the Census 1992).

Several researchers have examined the pattern of responses of people to the census ancestry question. These analyses have shown a pattern of flux and inconsistency in ethnic ancestry reporting. For instance, Lieberson and Waters (1986, 1988, p. 93) have found that parents simplify children's ancestries when reporting them to the census. For instance, among the offspring in situations where one parent reports a specific single White ethnic origin and the other parent reports a different single White origin, about 40 percent of the children are not described as the logical combination of the parents' ancestries. For example, only about 60 percent of the children of English-German marriages are labeled as English-German or German-English. About 15 percent of the children of these parents are simplified to just English, and another 15 percent are reported as just German. The remainder of the children are either not given an ancestry or are described as American (Lieberson and Waters 1986, 1993).

In addition to these intergenerational changes, researchers have found changes in reporting ancestry that occur at the time of marriage or upon leaving home. At the ages of eighteen to twenty-two, when many young Americans leave home for the first time, the number of people reporting a single as opposed to a multiple ancestry goes up. Thus while parents simplify children's ancestries when they leave home, children themselves tend to report less complexity in their ancestries when they leave their parents' homes and begin reporting their ancestries themselves (Lieberson and Waters 1986, 1988; Waters 1990).

These individual changes are reflected in variability over time in the aggregate numbers of groups determined by the census and surveys. Farley (1991) compared the consistency of the overall counts of different ancestry groups in the 1979 Current Population Survey, the 1980 census, and the 1986 National Content Test (a pretest for the 1990 census). He found much less consistency in the numbers for northern European ancestry groups whose immigration peaks were early in the nineteenth century—the English, Dutch, Germans, and other northern European groups. In other words, each of these different surveys and the census yielded a different estimate of the number of people having this ancestry. The 1990 census also showed a great deal of flux and inconsistency in some ancestry groups. The number of people reporting English as an ancestry went down considerably from 1980, while the number reporting German ancestry went up. The number of Cajuns grew dramatically. This has led officials at the Census Bureau to assume that the examples used in the instructions strongly influence the responses people give. (Cajun was one of the examples of an ancestry given in 1990 but not in 1980, and German was the first example given. English was an example in the 1980 instructions, but not in 1990.)

All of these studies point to the socially variable nature of ethnic identity—and the lack of equivalence between ethnic ancestry and identity. If merely adding a category to the instructions to the question increases the number of people claiming that ancestry, what does that mean about the level of importance of that identity for people answering the census? Clearly, identity and ancestry for Whites in the United States, who increasingly are from mixed backgrounds, involve some change and choice.

Symbolic Ethnicities for White Americans

What do these ethnic identities mean to people, and why do they cling to them rather than just abandoning the tie and calling themselves American? My own field research with suburban Whites in California and Pennsylvania found that later-generation descendants of European origin maintain what are called "symbolic ethnicities." Symbolic ethnicity is a term coined by Herbert Gans (1979) to refer to ethnicity that is individualistic in nature and without real social cost for the individual. These symbolic identifications are essentially leisure-time activities, rooted in nuclear family traditions and reinforced by the voluntary enjoyable aspects of being ethnic (Waters 1990). Richard Alba (1990) also found later-generation Whites in Albany, New York, who chose to keep a tie with an ethnic identity because of the enjoyable and voluntary aspects to those identities, along with the feelings of specialness they entailed. An example of symbolic ethnicity is individuals who identify as Irish, for example, on occasions such as Saint Patrick's Day, on family holidays, or for vacations. They do not usually belong to Irish American organizations, live in Irish neighborhoods, work in Irish jobs, or marry other Irish people. The symbolic meaning of being Irish American can be constructed by individuals from mass media images, family traditions, or other intermittent social activities. In other words, for later-generation White ethnics, ethnicity is not something that influences their lives unless they want it to. In the world of work and school and neighborhood, individuals do not have to admit to being ethnic unless they choose to. And for an increasing number of European-origin individuals whose parents and grandparents have intermarried, the ethnicity they claim is largely a matter of personal choice as they sort through all of the possible combinations of groups in their genealogies.

Individuals can choose those aspects of being Italian, for instance, that appeal to them, and discard those that do not. Or a person whose father is Italian, and mother part Polish and part French, might choose among the three ethnicities and present herself as a Polish American. For instance, a nineteen-year-old college student, interviewed in California in 1986, told me he would have answered Irish on the 1980 census form that asked about ethnic ancestry. These are his reasons:

Q: Why would you have answered that?
A: Well, my Dad's name is Kerrigan and my mom's name is O'Leary, and I do have some German in me, but if you figure it out, I am about 75 percent Irish, so I usually say I am Irish.
Q: You usually don't say German when people ask?
A: No, no, I never say I am German. My dad just likes being Irish. . . . I don't know I just never think of myself as being German.
Q: So your dad's father is the one who immigrated?

A: Yes. On his side is Irish for generations. And then my grandmother's name is Dubois, which is French, partly German, partly French, and then the rest of the family is all Irish. So it is only the maternal grandmother who messes up the line.
(Waters 1990, p. 10)

Thus in the course of a few questions, this man labeled himself Irish, admitted to being part German but not identifying with it, and then as an afterthought added that he was also part French. This is not an unusual case. With just a little probing, many people will describe a variety of ancestries in their family background, but do not consider these ancestries to be a salient part of their own identities. Thus the 1990 census ancestry question, which estimated that 30 percent of the population is of mixed ancestry, most surely underestimates the degree of mixing among the population. My research, and the research of Richard Alba (1990), shows that many people have already sorted through what they know of their ethnic ancestries and simplified their responses before they ever answer a census or survey question (Waters 1990).

But note that this freedom to include or exclude ancestries in your identification to yourself and others would not be the same for those defined racially in our society. They are constrained to identify with the part of their ancestry that has been socially defined as the "essential" part. African Americans, for example, have been highly socially constrained to identify as Blacks, without other options available to them, even when they know that their forebears included many people of American Indian or European background. Up until the mid-twentieth century, many state governments had specific laws defining one as Black if as little as one-thirty-second of one's ancestors were defined as Black (Davis 1991; Dominguez 1986; Spickard 1989). Even now when the one drop rule has been dropped from our legal codes, there are still strong societal pressures on African Americans to identify in a particular way. Certain ancestries take precedence over others in the societal rules on descent and ancestry reckoning. If one believes one is part English and part German and identifies in a survey as German, one is not in danger of being accused of trying to "pass" as non-English and of being "redefined" English by the interviewer. But if one were part African and part German, one's self identification as German would be highly suspect and probably not accepted if one "looked" Black according to the prevailing social norms.

This is reflected in the ways the census collects race and ethnic identity. While the ethnic ancestry question used in 1980 and 1990 is given to all Americans in the sample regardless of race and allows multiple responses that combine races, the primary source of information on people defined racially in the United States is the census race question or the Hispanic question. Both of these questions require a person to make a choice about an identity. Individuals are not allowed to respond that they are both Black and White, or Japanese and Asian Indian on the race question even if they know that is their background. In fact, people who disobey the instructions to the census race question and check off two races are assigned to the first checked race in the list by the Census Bureau.

In responding to the ancestry question, the comparative latitude that White respondents have does not mean that Whites pick and choose ethnicities out of thin air. For the most part, people choose an identity that corresponds with some element of their family tree. However, there are many anecdotal instances of people adopting ethnicities when they marry or move to a strongly identified neighborhood or community. For instance, Micaela di Leonardo (1984) reported instances of non-Italian women who married into Italian American families and "became Italian." Karen Leonard (1992) describes a community of Mexican American women who married Punjabi immigrants in California. Some of the Punjabi immigrants and their descendants were said to have "become Mexican" when they joined their wives' kin group and social worlds. Alternatively she describes the community acknowledging that Mexican women made the best curry, as they adapted to life with Indian-origin men.

But what do these identities mean to individuals? Surely an identity that is optional in a number of ways—not legally defined on a passport or birth certificate, not socially consequential in terms of societal discrimination in terms of housing or job access, and not economically limiting in terms of blocking opportunities for social mobility—cannot be the same as an identity that results from and is nurtured by societal exclusion and rejection. The choice to have a symbolic ethnicity is an attractive and widespread one despite its lack of demonstrable content, because having a symbolic ethnicity combines individuality with feelings of community. People reported to me that they liked having an ethnic identity because it gave them a uniqueness and feeling of being special. They often contrasted their own specialness by virtue of their ethnic identities with "bland" Americanness. Being ethnic makes people feel unique and special and not just "vanilla" as one of my respondents put it. For instance, one woman describes the benefits she feels from being Czech American:

> I work in an office and a lot of people in there always talk about their background. It's weird because it is a big office and people are of all different backgrounds. People are this or that. It is interesting I think to find out. Especially when it is something you do not hear a lot about. Something that is not common like Lithuania or something. That's the good part about being Czech. People think it is something different.   *(Waters 1990, p. 154)*

Because "American" is largely understood by Americans to be a political identity and allegiance, and not an ethnic one, the idea of being "American" does not give people the same sense of belonging that their hyphenated American identity does. When I asked people about their dual identities—American and Irish or Italian or whatever—they usually responded in a way that showed how they conceived of the relationship between the two identities. Being an American was their primary identity; but it was so primary that they rarely, if ever, thought about it—most commonly only when they left the country. Being Irish American, on the other hand, was a way they had of differentiating themselves from others whom they interacted with from day to day—in many cases from spouses or in-laws. Certain of their traits—being emotional, having a sense of humor, talking with their hands—were understood as stemming from their ethnicity. Yet when asked about their identity as Americans, that identity was both removed from their day-to-day consciousness and understood in terms of loyalty and patriotism. Although they may not think they behave or think in a certain way because they are American, being American is something they are both proud of and committed to.

Symbolic ethnicity is the best of all worlds for these respondents. These White ethnics can claim to be unique and special, while simultaneously finding the community and conformity with others that they also crave. But that "community" is of a type that will not interfere with a person's individuality. It is not as if these people belong to ethnic voluntary organizations or gather as a group in churches or neighborhoods or union halls. They work and reside within the mainstream of American middle-class life, yet they retain the interesting benefits—the "specialness"—of ethnic allegiance, without any of its drawbacks.

It has been suggested by several researchers that this positive value attached to ethnic ancestry, which became popular in the ethnic revival of the 1970s, is the result of assimilation having proceeded to an advanced stage for descendants of White Europeans (Alba 1985; Crispino 1980; Steinberg 1981). Ironically, people celebrate and embrace their ethnic backgrounds precisely because assimilation has proceeded to the point where such identification does not have that much influence on their day-to-day life. Rather than choosing the "least ethnic" and most bland ethnicities, Whites desire the "most ethnic" ones, like the once-stigmatized "Italian," because it is perceived as bringing the most psychic benefits. For instance, when an Italian father is married to an English or a Scottish or a German mother, the likelihood is that the child will be reported to the census with the father's Italian ancestry, rather than the northern European ancestries, which would have been predicted to have a higher social status. Italian is a good ancestry to have, people told me, because they have good food and a warm family life. This change in the social meaning of being Italian American is quite dramatic, given that Italians were subject to discrimination, exclusion, and extreme negative stereotyping in the early part of the twentieth century.

Race Relations and Symbolic Ethnicity

However much symbolic ethnicity is without cost for the individual, there is a cost associated with symbolic ethnicity for the society. That is because symbolic ethnicities of the type described here are confined to White Americans of European origin. Black Americans, Hispanic Americans, Asian Americans, and American Indians do not have the option of a symbolic ethnicity at present in the United States. For all of the ways in which ethnicity does not matter for White Americans, it does matter for non-Whites. Who your ancestors are does affect your choice of spouse, where you live, what job you have, who your friends are, and what your chances are for success in American society, if those ancestors happen not to be from Europe. The reality is that White ethnics have a lot more choice and room to maneuver than they themselves think they do. The situation is very different for members of racial minorities, whose lives are strongly influenced by their race or national origin regardless of how much they may choose not to identify themselves in terms of their ancestries.

When White Americans learn the stories of how their grandparents and great-grandparents triumphed in the United States over adversity, they are usually told in terms of their individual efforts and triumphs. The important role of labor unions and other organized political and economic actors in their social and economic successes are left out of the story in favor of a generational story of individual Americans rising up against communitarian, Old World intolerance and New World resistance. As a result, the "individualized" voluntary, cultural view of ethnicity for Whites is what is remembered.

One important implication of these identities is that they tend to be very individualistic. There is a tendency to view valuing diversity in a pluralist environment as equating all groups. The symbolic ethnic tends to think that all groups are equal; everyone has a background that is their right to celebrate and pass on to their children. This leads to the conclusion that all identities are equal and all identities in some sense are interchangeable—"I'm Italian American, you're Polish American. I'm Irish American, you're African American." The important thing is to treat people as individuals and all equally. However, this assumption ignores the very big difference between an individualistic symbolic ethnic identity and a socially enforced and imposed racial identity.

My favorite example of how this type of thinking can lead to some severe misunderstandings between people of different backgrounds is from the *Dear Abby* advice column. A few years back a person wrote in who had asked an acquaintance of Asian background where his family was from. His acquaintance answered that this was a rude question and he would not reply. The bewildered White asked Abby why it was rude, since he thought it was a sign of respect to wonder where people were from, and he certainly would not mind anyone asking HIM about where his family was from. Abby asked her readers to write in to say whether it was rude to ask about a person's ethnic background. She reported that she got a large response, that most non-Whites thought it was a sign of disrespect, and Whites thought it was flattering:

Dear Abby,
I am 100 percent American and because I am of Asian ancestry I am often asked "What are you?" It's not the personal nature of this question that bothers me, it's the question itself. This query seems to question my very humanity. "What am I? Why I am a person like everyone else!"

Signed, A REAL AMERICAN

Dear Abby,
Why do people resent being asked what they are? The Irish are so proud of being Irish, they tell you before you even ask. Tip O'Neill has never tried to hide his Irish ancestry.

Signed, JIMMY

In this exchange, JIMMY cannot understand why Asians are not as happy to be asked about their ethnicity as he is, because he understands his ethnicity and theirs to be separate but equal. Everyone has to come from somewhere—his family from Ireland, another's family from Asia—each has a history and each should be proud of it. But the reason he cannot understand the perspective of the Asian American is that all ethnicities are not equal; all are not symbolic, costless, and voluntary. When White Americans equate their own symbolic ethnicities with the socially enforced identities of non-White Americans, they obscure the fact that the experiences of Whites and non-Whites have been qualitatively different in the United States and that the current identities of individuals partly reflect that unequal history. . . .

Institutional Responses

Our society asks a lot of young people [on college campuses]. We ask young people to do something that no one else does as successfully on such a wide scale—that is to live together with people from very different backgrounds, to respect one another, to appreciate one another, and to enjoy and learn from one another. The successes that occur every day in this endeavor are many, and they are too often overlooked. However, the problems and tensions are also real, and they will not vanish on their own. We tend to see pluralism working in the United States in much the same way some people expect capitalism to work. If you put together people with various interests and abilities and resources, the "invisible hand" of capitalism is supposed to make all the parts work together in an economy for the common good.

. . . There is a lot to be said for the idea that bringing people who belong to different ethnic or racial groups together in institutions with no interference will have good consequences. Students from different backgrounds will make friends if they share a dorm room or corridor, and there is no need for the institution to do any more than provide the locale. But like capitalism, the invisible hand of pluralism does not do well when power relations and externalities are ignored. When you bring together individuals from groups that are differently valued in the wider society and provide no guidance, there will be problems. In these cases the "invisible hand" of pluralist relations does not work, and tensions and disagreements can arise without any particular individual or group of individuals being "to blame." On college campuses in the 1990s some of the tensions between students are of this sort. They arise from honest misunderstandings, lack of a common background, and very different experiences of what race and ethnicity mean to the individual.

The implications of symbolic ethnicities for thinking about race relations are subtle but consequential. If your understanding of your own ethnicity and its relationship to society and politics is one of individual choice, it becomes harder to understand the need for programs like affirmative action, which recognize the ongoing need for group struggle and group recognition, in order to bring about social change. It also is hard for a White college student to understand the need that minority students feel to band together against discrimination. It also is easy, on the individual level, to expect everyone else to be able to turn their ethnicity on and off at will, the way you are able to, without understanding that ongoing discrimination and societal attention to minority status makes that impossible for individuals from minority groups to do. The paradox of symbolic ethnicity is that it depends upon the ultimate goal of a pluralist society, and at the same time makes it more difficult to achieve that ultimate goal. It is dependent upon the concept that all ethnicities mean the same thing, that enjoying the traditions of one's heritage is an option available to a group or an individual, but that such a heritage should not have any social costs associated with it.

As the Asian Americans who wrote to *Dear Abby* make clear, there are many societal issues and involuntary ascriptions associated with non-White identities. The developments necessary for this to change are not individual but societal in nature. Social mobility and declining racial and ethnic sensitivity are closely associated. The legacy and the present reality of discrimination on the basis of race or ethnicity must be overcome before the ideal of the pluralist society, where all heritages are treated equally and are equally available for individuals to choose or discard at will, is realized.

REFERENCES

Alba, Richard D. 1985. *Italian Americans: Into the Twilight of Ethnicity.* Englewood Cliffs, NJ: Prentice-Hall.

———. 1990. *Ethnic Identity: The Transformation of White America.* New Haven, CT: Yale University Press.

Barth, Frederik. 1969. *Ethnic Groups and Boundaries.* Boston: Little, Brown.

Crispino, James. 1980. *The Assimilation of Ethnic Groups: The Italian Case.* Staten Island, NY: Center for Migration Studies.

Davis, Floyd James. 1991. *Who Is Black? One Nation's Definition.* University Park: Pennsylvania State University Press.

di Leonardo, Micaela. 1984. *The Varieties of Ethnic Experience: Kinship, Class and Gender among Italian Americans.* Ithaca, NY: Cornell University Press.

Dominguez, Virginia. 1986. *White by Definition: Social Classification in Creole Louisiana.* New Brunswick, NJ: Rutgers University Press.

Farley, Reynolds. 1991. "The New Census Question about Ancestry: What Did It Tell Us?" *Demography* 28:411–29.

Gans, Herbert. 1979. "Symbolic Ethnicity: The Future of Ethnic Groups and Cultures in America." *Ethnic and Racial Studies* 2:1–20.

Greeley, Andrew M. 1976. "The Ethnic Miracle." *Public Interest* 45 (Fall): 20–36.

Leonard, Karen. 1992. *Making Ethnic Choices: California's Punjabi Mexican Americans.* Philadelphia: Temple University Press.

Lieberson, Stanley. 1985. "Unhyphenated Whites in the United States." *Ethnic and Racial Studies* 8:159–80.

Lieberson, Stanley, and Mary Waters. 1986. "Ethnic Groups in Flux: The Changing Ethnic Responses of American Whites." *Annals of the American Academy of Political and Social Science* 487:79–91.

———. 1988. *From Many Strands: Ethnic and Racial Groups in Contemporary America.* New York: Russell Sage.

———. 1993. "The Ethnic Responses of Whites: What Causes Their Instability, Simplification, and Inconsistency?" *Social Forces* 72(2): 421–50.

McKenney, Nampeo R., and Arthur R. Cresce. 1992. "Measurement of Ethnicity in the United States: Experiences of the U.S. Census Bureau." Paper presented at the Joint Canada–United States Conference on the Measurement of Ethnicity, Ottawa, Canada, April 1–3.

Pagnini, Deanna L., and S. Philip Morgan. 1990. "Intermarriage and Social Distance among U.S. Immigrants at the Turn of the Century." *American Journal of Sociology* 96(2): 405–32.

Spickard, Paul R. 1989. *Mixed Blood.* Madison: University of Wisconsin Press.

Steinberg, Stephen. 1981. *The Ethnic Myth: Race, Ethnicity, and Class in America.* Boston: Beacon Press.

U.S. Bureau of the Census. 1992. *Census of Population and Housing, 1990: Detailed Ancestry Groups for States.* Supplementary Reports CP-S-1–2. Washington, DC: U.S. Government Printing Office.

Waters, Mary C. 1990. *Ethnic Options: Choosing Identities in America.* Berkeley and Los Angeles: University of California Press.

Weber, Max. 1921. *Economy and Society: An Outline of Interpretive Sociology,* edited by Guenther Roth and Claus Wittich, translated by Ephraim Fischoff. New York: Bedminster Press.

SIXTEEN

Listening to the Voices of My Spiritual Self (2001)

Christina Leaño

A second-generation Filipina American, **Christina Leaño** is a founding member and founding director of Filipino/American Coalition for Environmental Solidarity. She has worked with Pace e Bene, Malaya, an experiment in the liberating possibilities of the intersection of faith, spirituality, and social justice as well as California Interfaith Power and Light, an environmental organization focused on engaging the religious community on climate change issues.

We are not human beings on a spiritual journey, but spiritual beings on a human journey.

—Pierre Teilhard de Chardin, Jesuit priest and paleontologist (1881–1955)

My whole life has been driven by voices. Tiny, inner voices that have emerged from some unknown depths and have guided me (during those times I was willing) to unexpected places. They have taunted me with questions like "What does it mean to be Filipina? Where is God in your life? Why are you doing this social justice work?" until the friction from their words was too uncomfortable to ignore.

During my junior year in college, I was in Kenya participating in a semester abroad program. I was amazed by the vibrancy of the people and the richness of Kenyan culture, yet something inside me was awry. The colorful markets, tropical forests, and reality of daily struggle were foreign and at the same time strangely familiar. I realized that Kenya reminded me of what I had seen in the Philippines during my only visit as a child. This revelation was nudged by one of those prodding voices: "Your experience in Kenya is beautiful. Can you imagine the richness if it were a culture of your own blood? You need not go any further than your own heritage to find cultural treasure. Go, explore that."

This voice spoke from a void within me—this disconnect between my culture and myself. For most of my twenty-one years I did not see myself as a Filipina. Growing up in a white, upper-middle-class suburb and attending a private college preparatory in Florida gave me little opportunity to claim my brownness. There were even times when my color (and my relatives' color) shamed me, as I tried to keep my white friends from seeing our darkness. I had always thought that I was just an average kid with a flat nose and shiny, black hair.

Yet, when that voice emerged within me, I was filled with fear. It was like waking up and realizing that the ground below me was but a mist I was about to slip through. How was it that I did not know my Filipino heritage? What is my history, my culture? Who are my ancestors? Where are my roots? This voice led me from fear toward a hunger that was waiting to be filled. And I realized that I would have to answer those questions before I could move on with my life. How else would I find the ground to walk upon? So I decided that my next destination after college would be the Philippines.

After graduating, I signed up with the Mennonite Central Committee for three years as a volunteer in the Philippines. I chose a Christian organization, because another emerging voice was calling me to explore my spirituality. It frightened the heck out of me, being a "missionary," as I knew the damage that missionaries had done in the Philippines in the past, first during Spanish colonization and then during the American occupation. But there were enough signs—a volunteer placement that fit my exact interests (with the People's Task Force for Bases Cleanup, which dealt with environmental justice issues, the subject of my college thesis) and with people who gave me the support I needed—to show me that my decisions were in line with the Universe's. All I had to do was take a deep breath and trust.

That decision led to a whirlwind of adventure, transformation, and growth. Being in the Philippines gave me an opportunity to learn Tagalog, to get to know tens of cousins, aunts, uncles, grandparents, and to embrace my Filipino-ness that I hardly knew existed. This seed sprouted and bloomed as soon as I swallowed my first drop of Philippine water. Qualities and values that had been passed on to me by my parents—the importance of smooth interpersonal relationships and the centrality of family, faith, and education—were revealed as legacies embedded within the culture. I was Filipina without even realizing it.

Most important, I realized that my identity as a Filipina American was self-defined. I worked in a campaign demanding U.S. responsibility for cleaning up toxic contamination left behind in their former military bases in the Philippines. Thus my passion and desire as a Filipina for justice for the communities around the bases, and my anger at what my government had left behind, provided an opportunity to bridge my two identities. I could use my Filipino heart and my American citizenship for social change in the Philippines that addressed the huge inequities in the hundred-year relationship between the two nations. There was no choosing. I am both.

After two-and-a-half years, I came back to the United States to work in Washington, D.C. as director of a newly launched organization, FACES (Filipino/American Coalition for Environmental Solutions), the U.S. counterpart of the Philippines clean-up campaign. Although there were times of incredible joy and growth, after a year I was overwhelmed with fatigue, sadness, and doubt. I was working too much (isn't 25 too young to burn out?), I was not taking care of my physical, emotional, and spiritual needs, and I was not quite sure why I was doing this social justice work. My good side wanted to assure me that it was because of the enormous injustice resulting from the negligence of the U.S. government. But then there was another side of me, the ego side, which was focused on me trying to make a difference.

Working at FACES, I was still supported by the Mennonite Central Committee and was surrounded by folks who were able to articulate their commitment to social and environmental justice in terms of their faith. They could pull out Bible verses this way and that, while me, with my Catholic non-Bible upbringing, had to tediously search the thin pages for the right lines. How I longed to be able to translate my Catholic faith into a justice-making language.

I also thought that most of my difficulties, such as relating to Congressional aides or public speaking, were rooted in the spiritual. I could not name it, but I sensed that if I was grounded in my faith, tapped into the power of God, I couldn't fail. Most of all, the fatigue and weight of the work I was experiencing felt so wrong. I was depending too much on myself instead of allowing the creative power of God to step in, but how could I let go? That, more than not knowing my ethnic identity, was frightening. But the weeks of crying and being so tired even when I got enough sleep broke me down. My spiritual director labeled my tears "grace," as they provided me an opening to listen to those voices asking me hard questions: "What does it mean to be a child of God? How can you truly ground your social justice work and activism in your faith?"

Next thing I knew, I was flying out to California to study at the Graduate Theological Union in Berkeley. . . . I thought I might be able to take a break from activism while studying, but I have learned that my activism is actually part of my "spiritual practice" and not a distraction from it. I became involved with the San Francisco Bay Area chapter of FACES as co-chair and the work has been non-stop. In the last year and a half, we have marched in rallies, filed a lawsuit against the U.S. military, hosted several cultural events, and given presentations to numerous colleges and organizations.

One of my greatest learnings from studying theology and engaging in movement work is realizing that the great divide between spirituality and activism, contemplation and action, is a false one. My spirituality and contemplation invite me further into my activism, and my activism further into my spirituality and contemplation. Meditation and prayer provide the space for me to get in touch with the suffering of others, to keep myself accountable to the Divine within and around me, and to be honest about my human limitations and needs. Activism allows me to transform the connectedness with others' suffering into action and to live out my beliefs through my relationships with others. Thus, spirituality and activism, contemplation and action are but two sides of the same coin of compassion and love.

It has been quite a journey, and I know there is more to come, thanks to the persistence of those voices. For a while I did not really name them. I now realize that they are the voices of my True Self, the God-self, urging me to follow the map imprinted in my heart, carved by the Life Source herself. To know myself is to peel back all the layers of identity that have been given to me on this earth—as a Filipina, as an American, as a woman, as a lover of justice and peace, and as a Christian—to get to my core as a child of the Universe, the Divine, God. Trusting this process, creating the space, and allowing myself to be led, I have found my true power and a sense of peace. Don't get me wrong, even amidst this happiness, I still seem to be wearing earplugs most of the time, listening to my own beat and rhythm. Thank goodness those voices are loud. May they continue to haunt me, until I claim them as my own.

S E V E N T E E N

Once Upon a Quinceañera (2007)—Excerpt
Coming of Age in the U.S.A.

Julia Alvarez

> Born in New York City and raised in the Dominican Republic, **Julia Alvarez** has published essays, collections of poetry, books for children, and five books of fiction, including *How the García Girls Lost Their Accents.* With her husband she founded Alta Gracia, a sustainable farm in the Dominican Republic that produces organic coffee and serves as a literacy center. She is a writer in residence at Middlebury College, Vermont.

You are dressed in a long, pale pink gown, not sleek and diva-ish, but princessy, with a puffy skirt of tulle and lace that makes you look like you're floating on air when you appear at the top of the stairs. Your court of fourteen couples has preceded you, and now they line up on the dance floor, forming a walkway through which you will pass to sit on a swing with garlanded ropes, cradling your last doll in your arms. Your mami will crown you with a tiara recessed in a cascade of curls the hairstylist spent most of the afternoon sculpting on your head. Then your papi will replace the flats you are wearing with a pair of silver heels and lead you out to the dance floor, where you will dance a waltz together.

No, you are not Miss America or a princess or an actress playing Cinderella in a Disney movie. In fact, you are not exceptionally beautiful or svelte and tall, model material. Your name is María or Xiomara or Maritza or Chantal, and your grandparents came from Mexico or Nicaragua or Cuba or the Dominican Republic. Your family is probably not rich; in fact, your mami and papi have been saving since you were a little girl or they've mortgaged the house or lined up forty godparents to help sponsor this celebration, as big as a wedding. If challenged about spending upward of five thousand dollars—the average budget—on a one-night celebration instead of investing in your college education or putting aside the money for their own mortgage payments, your parents will shake their heads knowingly because you do not understand: this happens only once.

What is going on?

You are having your quinceañera . . .

A "quinceañera" (the term is used interchangeably for the girl and her party) celebrates a girl's passage into womanhood with an elaborate, ritualized fiesta on her fifteenth birthday. (Quince años, thus quinceañera, pronounced: *keen-seah-gneer-ah.*) In the old countries, this was a marker birthday: after she turned fifteen, a girl could attend adult parties; she was allowed to tweeze her eyebrows, use makeup, shave her legs, wear jewelry and heels. In short, she was ready for marriage. . . . Even humble families marked a girl's fifteenth birthday as special, perhaps with a cake, certainly with a gathering of family and friends at which the quinceañera could now socialize and dance with young men. Upper-class families, of course, threw more elaborate parties at which girls dressed up in long, formal gowns and danced waltzes with their fathers.

Somewhere along the way these fancier parties became highly ritualized. In one or another of our

Latin American countries, the quinceañera was crowned with a tiara; her flat shoes were changed by her father to heels; she was accompanied by a court of fourteen damas escorted by fourteen chambelanes, who represented her first fourteen years; she received a last doll, marking both the end of childhood and her symbolic readiness to bear her own child. And because our countries were at least nominally Catholic, the actual party was often preceded by a Mass or a blessing in church or, at the very least, a priest was invited to give spiritual heft to the fiesta. These celebrations were covered in the newspapers, lavish spreads of photos I remember poring over as a little girl in the Dominican Republic, reassured by this proof that the desire to be a princess did not have to be shed at the beginning of adulthood, but could in fact be played out happily to the tune of hundreds upon thousands of Papi's pesos.

In the late sixties, when many of our poor headed to el Norte's land of opportunity, they brought this tradition along, and with growing economic power, the no-longer-so-poor could emulate the rich back home. The spin-offs grew (quinceañera cruises, quinceañera resort packages, quinceañera videos and photo shoots); stories of where this quinceañera custom had come from proliferated (an ancient Aztec tradition, an import from European courts); further elaborations were added (Disney themes, special entrances, staged dance routines à la Broadway musicals); and in our Pan-Hispanic mixing stateside, the U.S. quinceañera adopted all the little touches of specific countries to become a much more elaborate (and expensive) ceremony, exported back to our home countries. But rock-bottom, the U.S. quinceañera is powered by that age-old immigrant dream of giving the children what their parents had never been able to afford back where they came from.

In fact, . . . many of us older, first-generation Latinas never had a quinceañera. There was no money back when we were fifteen, or we had recently arrived in the United States and didn't want anything that would make us stand out as other than all-American. Or we looked down our noses at such girly-girl fuss and said we didn't want a quince because we didn't understand that this was not just about us.

These cultural celebrations are also about building community in a new land. Lifted out of the context of our home cultures, traditions like the quinceañera become malleable; they mix with the traditions of other cultures that we encounter here; they become exquisite performances of our ethnicities within the larger host culture while at the same time reaffirming that we are not "them" by connecting us if only in spirit to our root cultures. In other words, this tradition tells a larger story of our transformation into Latinos, a Pan-Hispanic group made in the USA, now being touted as the "new Americans."

It's that story which intrigues me. Why, when I was invited by an editor to write a book about quinceañeras, I welcomed the opportunity to follow the tradition wherever it might lead me. . . .

. . .I traveled to various Latino communities in the United States: Dominican-Americans in Lawrence, Massachusetts, and Queens, New York; Cuban Americans in Miami; Mexican Americans in San Antonio and Los Angeles. . . .

I also spoke with dozens of girls and their families and members of their courts, with events providers and photographers, with parish priests and youth ministers and choreographers. I talked to Latinas my age and older, Latinas in academia and in businesses catering to the quinceañera market, who observed that the quinceañera has become an even bigger deal stateside than it had ever been back home.

With that elaboration and expense, a certain entitlement has set in. Many of the Latina girls I interviewed who responded in writing often termed the celebration "my right of passage." Given that spell-check would not have picked up this transposition, this was an understandable orthographical mistake, but it also seemed an apt description of what happens to traditions in the United States. Rites become rights. New generations feel entitled to what older first generations struggled to obtain for them.

By the same token, this entitlement ethic does not seem to shield our young Latina population from failure. As I read the research, I was alarmed by how our teen Latinas are topping the charts for all sorts of at-risk behaviors: from teen pregnancy to substance abuse to dropping out of high school. What is going on? We are crowning them princesses, and meanwhile the statistics are showing a large number of our young girls headed for poverty and failure! Are these the same girls, I wonder?

So, what began as the study of a tradition became a journey of exploration rife with questions and misgivings. I admit that the disjunction between this grand Latina debut and the reality of their lives, the enormous cost of the celebration to struggling families, made me initially skeptical about the tradition. And yet, time and time again as I attended these celebrations I felt deeply moved by something at the heart of the tradition, a desire to empower our young women, a need to ritually mark their passage into adulthood, remind them of their community and its past, and by doing so give them and ourselves hope. Who could argue with that?

. . . Our exported tradiciones mix and combine with those of other Latin American and Caribbean countries stateside and become more elaborate, more expensive, more traditional than they ever were back home.

In fact, to have a full-blown traditional quinceañera in our Pan-Hispanic United States is to have adopted every other Latino group's little traditions and then some. So that now, Cuban quinceañeras in Miami are hiring Mexican mariachis to sing the traditional "Las Mañanitas." The full court of fourteen damas and chambelanes, "each couple representing a year of the quinceañera's life," a mostly Mexican practice, is now a traditional must. As is the changing of the shoes to heels, which seems to originally have been a Puerto Rican embellishment. From the Puerto Ricans as well, though some say from the Mexicans, came the tradition of la última muñeca, a "last doll" dressed exactly like the quinceañera, which the girl cradles to symbolize the "end of her childhood" or "the child that she herself will be having in the not-too-distant future" (both explanations given to me by different events planners). The quinceañera might keep this last doll as a keepsake or give it away to a younger member of the family. In one celebration, perhaps inspired by the wedding bouquet, the quinceañera threw her last doll over her shoulder to be caught by a screaming group of little girls, anticipating their own future quinceañeras.

This symbol of bygone childhood is also mirrored in a Central American or Puerto Rican custom (I've heard both) of having a very little girl dress up in a minuscule version of the quinceañera's dress and be "the symbol of innocence." Sometimes she is accompanied by a little escort, though the tradition has now been further elaborated so that "the symbol of innocence" as well as a little prince and princess (slightly older) are part of a full traditional court.

There is also always some sort of photo session to commemorate the event . . . there are whole albums of the young lady in different outfits, in different locations, a practice that seems to have started with the Cuban community in Miami, where girls sometimes just have the photo shoot and forego the party. Many girls also have videos made, recounting their lives since birth, with still shots and footage of themselves at different ages and credits rolling as if this were a real movie with the quinceañera playing the lead and her parents starring as "padre" and "madre" and Julio Iglesias's "De Niña a Mujer" as the score, of course. . . .

The tradition of crowning the young girl is often ascribed to the Mexicans, who seem to be the group that has most ritualized the ceremony. But here in America, every quinceañera gets her tiara. The bouquet the quinceañera carries to put at the Virgin Mary's statue at the Mass is also part of the Mexican and Central American tradition, as is the Mass, which our more hedonistic Caribbean party-cultures dispensed with back home. But now the Mass and the Virgin's bouquet have become part of our Dominican and Puerto Rican and Cuban "tradition" in the United States. . . .

"Today, it's all about supersizing," Nina Diaz, the executive producer of *My Super Sweet 16,* told *U.S. News & World Report.* (The price tag for a recent quince party featured in one of the episodes was $180,000.) One quince site I happened upon in cruising the Web for Q-lore—just Google "quinceañera" and you will get 8,230,000 hits (if you put the tilde over the "n") or 4,220,000 hits (if you dispense with the tilde)—urged providers to register with their site. "The Hispanic population's buying power is expected to reach $300 billion by 2006. Timing is prime to begin your Sweet 16 and Quinceanera advertising campaign. The demand for more vendors that cater to Latinos is of epic proportions." . . .

At Disneyland, Denny Nicholas, manager of corporate and wedding sales, says he has seen anything from a modest $5,000 to $50,000 for a quinceañera, the average nowadays being about $12,000 to $15,000. When I ask Denny if he doesn't find this *average* shocking given that the poverty threshold for a family of three is $15,277, he laughs. "By the time families come to me, they've already made the decision that this is what they want. All I do is provide the elements they need to make their dreams come to life." . . .

Trying to track down the origins of the quinceañera tradition is a little like playing that old party game, telephone. A whispers some news in B's ear, B then recounts the news to C, all the way around the circle. By the time the news has come back to A, and is pronounced out loud, it has morphed into a skewed version of whatever it was that A claims to have originally said.

Many books, articles, and Web sites state that the roots of the quinceañera tradition lie in an ancient Aztec rite. Sometimes the origin is given as Mayan as well as Aztec, and sometimes more generally described as "indigenous." I don't know if it's because the phrase "an ancient Aztec tradition" has a phony ring to it—an alliterative angling for authenticity in ancientness. But when I repeatedly read this claim in too many articles, I begin to search the bibliographies (in the few cases where one is provided) to see what I can find.

Most folks quote as their source Michele Salcedo's *Quinceañera!*, an informative, well-written guide, the best in its genre. Through a series of e-mails, I finally track down Michele Salcedo at the *South Florida Sun-Sentinel,* where she is assistant city editor. She tells me how about a decade ago, she took a year off from her reporting job to study the quinceañera tradition and write a planner-slash-background book. She is gracious and generous with her time but understandably cannot cite chapter and verse for the source of a detail in a book she wrote more than fifteen years ago. She does recall getting some of her material on origins from "a nun's book." This has to be one of Sister Angela's many manuals where I, too, have read about this ancient Aztec and Mayan tradition.

And so I e-mail Sister Angela trying not to sound like the doubting Thomas I am, and she sends me to some books—Sylvanus Morley's *The Ancient Maya* and Victor Von Hagen's *Los Aztecas: Hombre y Tribu.* I end up inside the compendious *Florentine Codex,* which was assembled back in the 1560s by a Spanish priest, Fray Bernardino de Sahagún, from testimonies given forty years earlier to a mission of Franciscan monks by twelve high priests of the Aztec empire about their traditions. (Think again of the telephone game: a conquered nation as understood by Catholic priests interviewed four decades later by another Franciscan.) Whatever "facts" we know about the Aztecs are several critical removes from a true and living practice.

But Sister Angela is absolutely right that our indigenous American ancestors did indeed acknowledge the passage of young girls into womanhood. What is uncertain is the age at which the ritual took place. We do know that the Aztec maiden was ready for marriage at the age of fifteen. Presumably at an earlier juncture there was a ceremony of some sort. The *Codex* cites long ceremonial speeches in which fathers and mothers publicly admonished their daughters, probably as part of some ritual. The speeches themselves are quite moving to read. The tenderness is palpable. The father describes his daughter's coming-of-age in heart-tugging words:

> It is as if thou wert an herb, a plant which hath propagated, sprouted, blossomed. It is also as if thou hadst been asleep and hadst awakened

Meanwhile, the mother warns "my dove, my little one, my child, my daughter" that life is dangerous and she must be careful. (So my own mami's dire warnings were not so off the mark. It seems a traditional task of mothers to terrify their daughters into good behavior.) "Behold the road thou art to follow," the mother advises:

> On earth we live, we travel along a mountain peak. Over here there is an abyss, over there is an abyss. If thou goest over here, or if thou goest over there, thou wilt fall in. Only in the middle doth one go, doth one live. Place this word, my daughter, dove, little one, well within the chambers of thy heart. Guard it well.

This is a far cry from Mami crowning her daughter with a rhinestone tiara or Papi dancing with her as Julio Iglesias sings "De Niña a Mujer." But in both cases there is a transmission going on, an acknowledgment that womanhood is upon her and a life of perils and possibilities is about to begin.

Mayans, too, celebrated the onset of puberty with an elaborate ceremony. Again, the age given by sources varies. Part of the female ceremony involved the mother cutting off a red shell that had been tied around her daughter's waist as a child. Presumably the girl was now considered ripe for marriage and childbearing. We can, of course, stretch the comparison and find in the cutting off of the red shell of virginity a parallel to the casting off of the last doll of childhood. But why belabor the point? Down through the generations the human family has celebrated passages in our mortal lives with rites that use the symbols and signs of our moment in time. We don't have to prove the legitimacy of these rites. They are what they are, part of our human legacy.

This push to legitimize the quinceañera by connecting it with an indigenous past is a fairly recent thing. Back in our home countries in the fifties, elite families would have blanched at any suggestion that their presentation parties had any connection at all to an "Indian" rite. "Indigenous heritage was played down in favor of European and North American culture," writes Valentina Napolitano in *Migration, Mujercitas, and Medicine Men*. Instead, "the fifteenth-birthday celebration used the symbology of European culture (for example, waltzes, performances of classical music, maids of honor, and pages)." It was only with the democratizing of the tradition stateside that the supposed Aztec connection began to be talked about. The desire for native credentials demonstrates both a yearning to reconnect with something forever lost as well as what Renato Rosaldo calls in *Culture & Truth* "imperialist nostalgia," a nostalgia for a culture you have dominated, a people you have destroyed.

More traceable are the courtly elements of the quinceañera tradition. "The first elaborate quinceañeras were balls staged by families of means who liked to pride themselves on their Spanish ancestry and manners," writes Maricel Presilla in an article in the *Miami Herald*. Michele Salcedo cites that its origin might have come from a practice of the Duchess of Alba in eighteenth-century Spain in which she would "invite girls on the cusp of womanhood to the palace, where she would dress them and make them up as adults for the first time." The Empress Carlotta of Mexico, a century later, also "invited the daughters of members of her court to be presented as young ladies eligible for marriage." Interestingly, though its origin might have been these courtly presentations, the quinceañera is unknown in Spain . . . the quinceañera has changed from a celebration for daughters of the elite to a fiesta for all classes. "When I was your age, only rich girls had quinceañeras," Estrella's mother tells her in *Estrella's Quinceañera,* one of the young adult novels . . . that centers on this tradition.

Most historians trace this shift to the 1960s and the beginning of vast migrations to el Norte's land of opportunity; the tradition soon became an option for middle and lower classes, both here in the USA and back home. Cross-fertilization knows no borders, and influences travel without visa or green card. In fact, even in present-day Cuba, the quinceañera is seeing a revival, as Cuban girls dream of parties like their Cuban-American cousins enjoy in Miami. Many stateside families send their old quinceañera gowns and tiaras along with dollars and medicines to their needy relatives.

Certainly the quinceañera found welcome soil in the American consumer culture, where businesses stood to gain from the expensive elaborations of the ceremony. In fact, when the Los Angeles archdiocese issued guidelines back in January 1990 to try to curtail the growing commercialization and expense of quinceañeras, the outcry came not from the parishioners but from Grupo Latino Por Nuestras Tradiciones, which despite its name was made up of many small-business owners. The group's president, Luis Yanez, declared that "for the church, quinceañeras are not important, but for us they are one of the few traditions we have left," and in the same breath he complained that his shop, which supplies everything from the dresses to the headpieces and artificial bouquets and monogrammed cups, had seen a drastic decline from fifty quinceañeras to five since the guidelines were issued.

And so, while the quinceañera is touted as a marker of ethnicity, it is in many ways an ethnicity with a label that reads MADE IN THE USA (or "Remade in the USA," if you will). Even as the younger generations assimilate in every other way to a mainstream culture, they are holding on to this old-country tradition, which is actually being created here. Odd. Or is it?

In fact, this creation of a past that never was turns out to be a common enough social phenomenon. In his book *The Invention of Tradition*, Eric Hobsbawm coins the term "invented traditions" to describe both traditions actually invented from whole cloth (Kwanzaa, the Bat Mitzvah, just to mention a couple) as well as traditions that "emerge in a less easily traceable manner within a brief and datable period, establishing themselves with great rapidity." These invented traditions are likely to appear when a group is undergoing transformation, and they serve as a way to legitimize and galvanize its members by establishing continuity with a past that may be largely fictitious.

This is not to dismiss them as bogus, Hobsbawm is quick to point out. Instead, they are interesting hot spots in a group's evolution where adaptation and self-creation and legitimization are in progress, as well as moving testimonies toward cohesion just as the winds of dispersal are blowing us hither and yon. . . .

And so, it makes perfect sense for Mr. Ramos to want his daughter to hold on to her roots by doing something that comes to him from a past that never was—at least not for his working-class family prior to 1960. As his daughters grow up in the USA, speaking spotty Spanish and celebrating their quinces at sixteen, this is the one thing he can give them that might remind them of who they are. *One of the few traditions we have left.* A last Latin spin with his little girl because who knows where she'll end up?

"It used to be that you could give your daughter a wedding. But you don't know anymore if she's going to get married or if she's going to live with her boyfriend first like they do here, or if she's going to get divorced and get remarried several times," Mr. Ramos explained to me, a sentiment echoed by many parents. . . .

Twenty-five-year-old Maurice Mompoint, . . . based in Miami, represents a younger generation of quinceañera business entrepreneurs. His Web site, yourquinces.com, is allied with his mother's Happy Holidays Travel Agency, which does a large volume of the crucero business.

. . . "I give it ten years," he says cryptically, and for a moment I think he's talking about how long he can last at his job. But he says that in ten years, quinces will be a thing of the past. "The next generation growing up, their parents will all have been born and raised here. A lot of them won't even speak Spanish that well. There isn't going to be that grandparent or parent from the old country pushing for the quinceañera." Is he worried about this? Not really. "In ten years, a lot of these girls are going to be getting married. I've been building my database, and with a couple of switches, I can turn yourquinces.com into a wedding site."

I wondered about Maurice's prognosis. Are quinceañeras on a culturally endangered list? Higinio Muñoz, who is part of the Muñoz dynasty of photographers that for three generations has been snapping quinces in Cuba and now in south Florida, does not think so at all. "For the last forty years of this business, you think, oh, the tradition is going to end with the next generation, but I've now got second- and third-generation girls, and the tradition is not waning. In fact, it's growing. I have Haitian quinceañeras and African American quinceañeras and American girls wanting quinceañeras." He has a point. At www.quinceañera.us.com, where you can register your quinceañera, there are mothers registering little girls who will be turning fifteen in 2015!

But history would seem to be on Maurice's side. After all, generations of immigrants have trod the assimilation path in America, shedding most of their ethnic past, with maybe only a parade left to commemorate those roots, a green cardigan on St. Patrick's Day, a polka night at the Polish-American club. . . .

On the other hand, America is now seeing a new kind of immigrant whose ties to a homeland are never completely severed. In his rousing and passionate book *Living in Spanglish: The Search for Latino Identity in America,* Ed Morales explains that the old idea of "Americanization" involved the loss of contact with people from the old country. "But the continuing migration of Latinos to the north has the effect of reinforcing the Latin culture that we would otherwise have lost."

And the travel is not just north but back and forth. In fact, the whole concept of nation-states with set borders you cross and leave behind is not the way the world really works anymore, according to Michael Dear, head of the Geography Department at the University of Southern California. In "Postborder Cities/Postborder World?" he notes how people, money, communication, and culture are all moving in new currents and combinations. Globalization is creating a new kind of mobile and mutating world citizenry. . . .

Quinces definitely have the potential of introducing a new story into the imagination of the next generation, one that might indeed help them live happier, more productive lives.

Why else would companies like Maggi and Kern's Nectar choose the quinceañera as the target tradition at which to aim their public relations campaigns? They know a powerful cultural icon when they see one.

But others are drawn to the tradition not as an advertising tool but as an opportunity to truly empower young people to believe that their dreams for their lives can come true.

Enter the fairy godmothers.

Isabella Martínez Wall . . . dispensing advice from her Web site, bellaquinceañera.com, and committed to making each girl feel like the queen of her life; Priscilla Mora, organizing expos to educate Latinas on financially responsible and culturally meaningful quinceañeras; Sister Angela, using the tradition as a teachable moment for Catholic youth, boys and girls, Latino or not. A fourth fairy godmother, Ana Maria Schachtell, founded the Stay-in-School Quinceañera Program, which could well become a model for such programs elsewhere. In Idaho, of all places. . . .

. . . "We start in January, twice a week, one school night and then one Saturday, thirty to forty fourteen-year-old girls and boys," Ana Maria explains. "We have them until the end of school in June. Most of them have just started high school or are going to start in the fall." She figures she has a small window in which to make a difference about how their lives are going to go. "Most of these kids come from poor migrant families. Their parents haven't had much education. They need to hear it can be done. So, we bring in teachers from the high school to talk about what to expect there. We bring in community leaders to encourage them to think about their future and make them proud of their past, their roots, their traditions. Judge Gutierrez, our only Hispanic judge in Idaho, has come to talk to them, and this last year we brought in Loretta Sanchez!" This is obviously a big fish, and I'm embarrassed not to know who she is. Later I Google her and find out she is a congresswoman from California. . . .

According to Ana Maria, the kids have a lot of fun—"or they wouldn't keep coming back, week after week." Much of that fun comes from doing things that affirm their sense of pride in their culture. "They learn old cerámica techniques. We brought in an eighty-nine-year-old woman to teach the girls how to make their traditional coronas out of wax flowers, a Mexican handiwork that is being lost because of the cheap plastic crowns around. And for the boys, we bring in a charro, that's the original American cowboy. A lot of people don't know that. The charro tradition represents the best of machismo, how to be a real hombre, responsible to your familia and community. The boys eat it up."

I bet they do. How could they not, with Ana Maria cheering them on? The whole program culminates in a gala night, a fundraiser for the Hispanic Cultural Center. The center has a stock of thirty gowns for the girls, and it rents tuxedos for the boys. The governor comes, the senators, the mayor. (The Hispanic population of the state is growing at four times the rate of the non-Hispanic population. No doubt, these elected officials have done the numbers.)

What is inspiring about Ana Maria's program, which is now in its eighth year, is that it takes the tradition of the quinceañera, acknowledging its power as a coming-of-age ceremony, but recasts it with new content, including a strong emphasis on education. What does it mean to be a man, un hombre, un charro, in this new country? What does it mean to be una mujer who knows her tradiciones, can make the old-country wax flowers for a corona but can also run for Congress? In other words, the Stay-in-School program takes the occasion of the quinceañera to revise the limited narrative the rite has traditionally endorsed. . . .

But the fact that these old restrictive narratives about womanhood persist in our young Latina girls speaks to the need for retooling. And the quinceañera tradition—as a number of fairy godmothers have discovered—can provide that amazing learning opportunity. . . .

4

◆◆◆

Women's Sexuality

The body is the place where biological sex, socially constructed gender, and sexuality come together. Sexual attitudes and behaviors vary considerably from society to society and across historical time periods (Caplan 1987; Lancaster and di Leonardo 1997). Sexuality is both instinctive and also learned mainly from our families, our peers, sex education in school, popular culture, negotiations with partners, and listening to our own bodies. Much is learned from what is not said as well as what is made explicit. In this society, sexuality is a source of intimacy and pleasure, vulnerability and danger. There is a heavy emphasis on sexuality in advertising, news reporting, and popular culture sometimes characterized as "pornification" of media culture (Paasonen, Nikunen, and Saarenmaa 2008). At the same time, there is a dearth of accurate information about women's sexuality, and there are many constraints on it. Over the course of our lives, sexuality may take different forms and take on different degrees of significance.

This chapter focuses on women's experiences of sexuality, the meso- and macro-level forces that shape these experiences, and the ways that women are defining sexuality for themselves. As you read this chapter, think also about the social construction of male sexuality.

The Erotic as Power

The late Black lesbian poet, teacher, and activist Audre Lorde discussed the power of the erotic in the broadest way in her now classic essay (Reading 18). She described the erotic "as our most profoundly creative source," noting that women have been "taught to separate the erotic . . . from most vital areas of our lives other than sex." By contrast, she wrote: "When I speak of the erotic . . . I speak of it as an assertion of the life-force of women: of that creative energy empowered, the knowledge and use of which we are now reclaiming in our language, our history, our dancing, our loving, our work, our lives." Lorde saw the distortion and suppression of the erotic as one of the ways that women are oppressed under patriarchal institutions and cultures, and concluded: "Recognizing the power of the erotic in our lives can give us the energy to pursue genuine change within our world."

As Audre Lorde argued, dominant U.S. culture takes a limited and distorted view of the erotic, reducing it to sexuality, and restricted notions of sexuality at that. By foregrounding her perspective in this chapter we make this disparity explicit. Sexuality can be a source of restriction and vulnerability for women. This may be true for those who challenge or repudiate patriarchal norms and women whose sexual activities and identities fit patriarchal expectations. Also, sexuality can be a source of power, affirmation, and self-definition for women, and many are claiming the right to sexual pleasure on their own terms, despite the distortions, contradictions, and double standards of patriarchal cultures regarding women's sexuality.

Stereotypes, Contradictions, and Double Standards

In advertising images and popular culture, sexuality is the prerogative of the young, slender, and able-bodied. Many of these images portray white women. Melba Wilson (1993) noted that racism and sexism converge in mainstream stereotypes of women of color as "exotic creatures of passion" (p. 66). Asian and Asian American women are stereotyped as "exotic flowers," overly promiscuous and at the same time submissive, sexually accommodating and focused on serving men. A 1957 novel, *The World of Suzie Wong,* also adapted for stage, film, and ballet, reinforced racist and sexist stereotypes of Asian women in its tale of a young English artist in Hong Kong and a bar girl working in a hotel catering to British and U.S. sailors. Suzie Wong also personified another stereotype: the hooker with a heart of gold. The film *Slaying the Dragon* (1988; distributed by Women Make Movies) provides an excellent critique of such stereotypes. Sociologist Patricia Hill Collins (2004, p. 30) argued that ideas of pure white womanhood, developed as part of European national identity, "required a corresponding set of ideas about hot-blooded Latinas, exotic Suzy Wongs, wanton jezebels." She continued:

> Civilized nation-states required uncivilized and backward colonies for their national identity to have meaning, and the status of women in both places was central to this endeavor. In this context, Black women became icons of hypersexuality.

These powerful stereotypes continue to be reinforced in media representations.

By contrast, women with disabilities and older women of all racial groups are stereotyped as sexless.

According to the late Barbara Waxman Fiduccia, an advocate for reproductive rights for people with disabilities, and Marsha Saxton, a teacher of disability studies, women with disabilities have been socially isolated and discouraged from expressing their sexuality. In their *Disability Feminism: A Manifesto* (1997), they wrote: "We want our sexuality accepted and supported with accurate information" (p. 60). Lillian Gonzales Brown, of the Institute on Disability Culture (Honolulu, Hawaii), noted the influence of the disability rights movement on changing attitudes for people with disabilities. There has been a shift from feeling shame, then wanting to assimilate, to disability pride. In workshops on sexuality for women with disabilities, she urges participants to explore their sexuality and to see themselves as sexual beings (L. G. Brown, personal communication, October 1996; see also Kaufman, Silverberg, and Odette 2003).

Ads that use women's bodies to sell products also sell ideas of heterosexuality, as discussed by Jean Kilbourne (Reading 26). As sex objects, women are commonly portrayed as child-like or doll-like playthings. These images flow from and reinforce macro-level patriarchal constructions of gender and sexuality based on the following assumptions: Heterosexuality is prescribed or natural for women and men, men are the initiators in heterosexual encounters, and men's sexuality is assertive and in need of regular release. Women are expected to be modest and virtuous, to look beautiful, and, simultaneously, to lure men and to fend them off. Traditionally, a woman has been expected to remain a virgin until marriage, untouched except by her husband, and this attitude is still strong in some communities in the United States and around the world. Nancy Kurshan notes that women who committed "moral" offenses were imprisoned in reformatories in the early part of the twentieth century (Reading 49). Men's sexual activity is assumed and accepted; after all, "Boys will be boys." Girls may easily get a "bad reputation" and be condemned as "sluts." Writers Leonora Tanenbaum (2000) and Emily White (2002) found many reasons that girls are labeled this way: they may be early developers, victims of rape, outsiders to the community, or targets of revenge. Some may be sexually active, but many are not. In response to the "nice girl" stereotype, however, some young women have reclaimed "slut" as a positive identification that emphasizes independence and sexual agency while others have written of their own sexual experimentation (see, e.g., Johnson 2002; Walker 1995; Wolf 1997).

This fundamental contradiction between encouraging men's sexuality and expecting women to be chaste results in the construction of two categories of women: "good" women and "bad" women, virgins and whores—the women men marry and the women they fool around with. This double standard controls women's sexuality and autonomy, and serves to divide women from each other. Growing up in a Mexican American community, Sandra Cisneros (Reading 19) writes that *la Virgen de Guadalupe* was the model held up to girls. The boys "were fornicating like rabbits," she writes, "while the Church ignored them and pointed us women towards our destiny—marriage and motherhood. The other alternative was *puta*hood," being defined a whore. Writer and literature professor Gloria Wade-Gayles (1993) learned the same double standard, but women in her Memphis neighborhood also divided men into two categories: good men who cared for their wives and families, and "dogs" who "only want one thing." This latter category included white men who cruised through the neighborhood "in search of Black women who, they assumed, were naturally sensuous, sexually superior, and easy" (p. 84).

Traditional cultural limitations on women's sexuality and sexual expression can divide younger women and older women in immigrant communities, as described by human rights activist Surina A. Khan who struggled for many years to reconcile her queer and Pakistani identities (Reading 21). Mother and daughter, psychologist Shamita das Dasgupta and pediatrician Sayantani DasGupta, wrote:

> As Asian women of two different generations, we attest to the politically divisive and psychologically unbearable situation in which we have been placed. As daughters, we are faced with the choice of rejecting our community and culture or destroying our sexual selves. As mothers, we can be exiled as destroyers of community culture or be our daughters' prison guards. *(1996, p. 240)*

They understand the South Asian communities' control of women's sexuality as an attempt to resist cultural erasure in the United States and as a response to the racism of this society, as well as a result of patriarchal control within their own communities. They endorse Indian women's activism (against violence against women, and for gay, lesbian, and bisexual rights) as a way of creating a progressive South Asian space to "define our private selves as public and discover our collective power" (p. 241).

It is important to note that many girls and women experience sexual coercion and abuse—in childhood, as adults, or both (see Chapter 6). Some women struggle for many years with the devastating effects of sexual abuse on their confidence, trust, sexuality, and sense of themselves in the world. In Reading 32, Aurora Levins Morales refers to her childhood experience of sexual abuse and her path toward reclaiming "the wounded erotic." At the core of that process, she writes, is "blazing and untarnished aliveness."

What Is Women's Autonomous Sexuality?

In the 1960s and 1970s there was much talk of a sexual revolution in the United States, partly made possible by the availability of contraceptive pills for the first time. Women "on the pill" could be sexually active with men without the same fear of pregnancy as in the past. In practice, many feminists argued that this "revolution" was very much on men's terms (Segal 1994), but more recently there has been increasing discussion of women's own sexual needs and preferences (see, e.g., Boston Women's Health Book Collective 2005; Cox 1999; Ehrenreich, Hess, and Jacobs 1986; Ensler 1998; hooks 1993; Johnson 2002; Muscio 1999; Rose 2003). Women's health advocate Rebecca Chalker (1995) described this process as a "real woman-friendly sexual revolution in progress" (p. 52). Women's magazines have provided one forum for this discourse, as well as women's erotica (e.g., Blank 2001; Bright 2000; Bruce 2001; Slugocki and Wilson 2000) and images of stars like Beyonce and Britney Spears, who revel in their sexuality in public. Eve Ensler, a playwright and screenwriter, has performed her Obie-winning show, *The Vagina Monologues*, in many parts of the country. Ensler (1998) noted that, for many women, the word *vagina* is associated with shame, embarrassment, silencing, and violation. Starting in 1998, students, staff, and faculty from hundreds of U.S. colleges and universities have

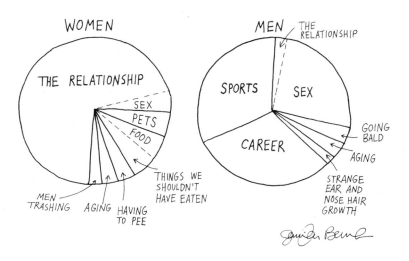

THOUGHT FREQUENCY AS PIE CHARTS

WOMEN — THE RELATIONSHIP, SEX, PETS, FOOD, MEN TRASHING, AGING, HAVING TO PEE, THINGS WE SHOULDN'T HAVE EATEN

MEN — THE RELATIONSHIP, SPORTS, SEX, CAREER, GOING BALD, AGING, STRANGE EAR AND NOSE HAIR GROWTH

performed Ensler's script as part of the V-Day College Initiative, a nationwide project to celebrate women and to oppose sexual violence.

Sexuality is one of the few recognized ways in this society for people to make intimate connections, especially for men, who, typically, are not socialized to express emotions easily. Shere Hite has conducted extensive surveys of men's and women's sexual experiences and preferences. In her groundbreaking research into women's and men's attitudes to sexuality and love, she found that, for male respondents, dating and marriage were primarily about sex, and they often shopped around for varied sexual experiences (Hite 1994). For the female respondents, expressing emotion through sexual intimacy and setting up a home were usually much more important than they were for men. Hite attributed much of the frustration in heterosexual relationships to these very different approaches. Also, she saw women as "revolutionary agents of change" in relationships, working with men to renegotiate this intimate part of their lives. The following questions, from one of Hite's surveys, were written for women, but they are also relevant for men:

Is sex important to you? What part does it play in your life?

Who sets the pace and style of sex—you or your partner or both? Who decides when it's over?

Do you think your genital area and vagina are ugly or beautiful?

If you are sexually active, do you ever fake orgasms? Why?

What are your best sex experiences? What would you like to try that you never have?

What is it about sex that gives you the greatest pleasure? Displeasure?

Have you chosen to be celibate at any point? What was/is that like for you?

In the best of all possible worlds, what would sexuality be like?

Do you know as much as you'd like to know, about your own body? Orgasm? Conception and pregnancy? Safe sex?

Do your partners know about your sexual desires and your body? If not, do you ask for it or act yourself to get it?

(Hite 1994, pp. 17–22)

To discover what is sexually empowering for us, ideally women need a safe place and freedom from worries about being attractive and the risk of pregnancy or sexually transmitted infections. In addition, we need information on safer sex, access to reliable contraception, and open discussion with sexual partners.

For many teens, sex is a "rite of passage," an essential part of growing up. How "sex" is defined can vary; for example, many sexually active heterosexual teens do not count oral sex as sex. Magazine editor Susannah Indigo (2000) interviewed girls about their experience with sex play including masturbation, phone sex, and oral sex, which they jokingly referred to as "outercourse," as opposed to "real sex" or intercourse. Some young people pledge virginity before marriage but do not necessarily rule out sex play. Lee Che Leong (2004, p. 37), Director of the Teen Health Initiative at the New York Civil Liberties Union, commented that "The ranks of those 'saving themselves' by being blowjob queens are increasing as oral sex is on the rise" among teens of all racial groups.

Leong discussed the effects of federal funding criteria on sex education programs. According to the Department of Health and Human Services, to qualify for funding, a program must teach that "abstinence from sexual activity is the only certain way to avoid out-of-wedlock pregnancy, sexually transmitted diseases, and other associated health problems"; that "a mutually faithful monogamous relationship in the context of marriage is the expected standard of human sexual activity"; and that "sexual activity outside of the context of marriage is likely to have harmful psychological and physical effects" (quoted by Leong 2004, pp. 36, 37).

Researcher Heather Boonstra (2007), a policy associate at the Alan Guttmacher Institute, reviewed compelling evidence that abstinence-only programs do not stop—or even delay—teen sex. In 2007 these programs were funded at a level of $176 million annually and made up 35 percent of U.S. sex education programs. In contrast, there was no comparable federal program to support sex education that included information about abstinence as well as contraceptive use. Currently, one in three U.S. teens get no education about birth control. Improved contraceptive use, not teens abstaining from sex, is responsible for 86 percent of recent declines in teen pregnancy. Despite declines, the United States has the highest teen pregnancy rate among industrialized nations.

This discussion relates to the question of sexual agency. Is sex play and "hooking up" for casual sex

empowering for girls and women? Are women valued only for their sexual skills? Are they allowing themselves to be used by boys and men, or is the issue more complicated? Psychologist Lynn Phillips (2000) found young women "flirting with danger" and struggling to negotiate and make sense of power differences around sexuality, and in some cases, sexual abuse and violation. Journalist Paula Kamen (2000) argued that outercourse is an important part of women's pleasure. She saw young women choosing to be in sexual relationships—or not—very much on their own terms. For those who choose to have sex with men, attitudes about condoms and women's ability to influence their partners to use them are important aspects of safer sex practices. New Zealand psychologists Nicola Gavey, Kathryn McPhillips, and Marion Doherty found that power dynamics between women and men, women's assumptions about assertiveness and what it means to be a "good lover," together with their ideals of giving and sharing, may be in conflict with their desire for safer sex (Reading 20). Emma Bell and Luisa Orza, staff members of the International Community of Women Living with HIV/AIDS, discuss sexuality for women who are HIV-positive (Reading 29).

Challenging Sex/Gender Binaries

Our society constructs sex as a dichotomy: female or male. Geneticist and professor of biology Anne Fausto-Sterling (1993; 2000) has shown how intersexual people challenge these categories in a fundamental way. Fausto-Sterling (2000) reported on the frequency of intersexual births from an extensive review of medical literature and estimated that for every 1,000 children, 17 are intersexual, in the sense that they represent "chromosomal, anatomical, and hormonal exceptions to the dimorphic ideal." She estimated that "the number of intersexuals who might, potentially, be subject to surgery as infants is smaller—probably between one in 1,000 and one in 2,000 live births." Fausto-Sterling does not consider intersexed or transgender people as "living midway between the poles of male and female" but sees sex and gender as "points in a multidimensional space." She comments that the medical and scientific communities "have yet to adopt a language that is capable of describing such diversity," a point that has been reiterated by intersex people, some of whom underwent extremely clumsy surgeries as infants at the hands of medical professionals (see, e.g., Colligan 2004; May 2005).

Sexuality, too, has been defined in binary terms. According to Jonathan Katz (1995), a historian of sexuality, the concept of heterosexuality developed in parallel with the concept of homosexuality, and both date from the end of the nineteenth century. The word *heterosexuality* was first used in the 1890s, an obscure medical term applied to nonprocreative sex—that is, sex for pleasure. At the time, this was considered a deviant idea, showing "abnormal or perverted appetite toward the opposite sex" (p. 86). Webster's dictionary did not include the word *heterosexuality* until 1934, and it gradually came into common usage in the United States as a "stable sign of normal sex" (p. 40). As with other dominant dimensions of systems of power such as whiteness, wealth, and masculinity, heterosexuality has been much less scrutinized than homosexuality. Sociologist Chrys Ingraham (2004) explored the nature of heterosexuality as a dominant institution with cultural, economic, social, and political dimensions.

Lesbians and gay men have long challenged the legitimacy and "normalcy" of heterosexuality (see, e.g., Allen 1986; Boswell 1994; Cavin 1985; Duberman, Vicinus, and Chauncey 1989; Faderman 1981; Grahn 1984; History Project 1998). Bisexual people express and argue for greater fluidity in sexual desire and behaviors, what Kathleen Bennett (1992) called "a both/and option for an either/or world" (see also Anderlini-D'Onofrio 2003; Hutchins and Ka'ahumanu 1991; Ochs and Rowley 2005; Storr 1999; Weise 1992). Lisa Orlando (1991) noted that stereotypes about bisexuality have grown out of the fact that bisexuals are poised between what "appear as two mutually exclusive sexual cultures" and from a common assumption "that homosexual and heterosexual desires exclude each other." Eridani (1992) argued that many women are probably bisexual and do not fit into a gay/straight categorization. She suggested that sexual orientation, meaning a "deeply rooted sense . . . that serious relationships are possible only with persons of the opposite sex or the same sex" (p. 174), is itself a masculinist perspective. On the basis of research into the sexual lives of nearly 100 young women over a 10-year period, psychologist Lisa Diamond (2008) came to see women's sexuality as a dynamic process characterized by fluidity, openness to variation, and a capacity to act on varying attractions and desires. Riki Anne Wilchins (1997) noted the limited notion of the erotic entailed in hetero-homo dualism: "an entire Geography of the Absent—body parts that aren't named, acts one mustn't do, genders one can't perform—because they are outside the binary box" (p. 167). The late June Jordan, poet, essayist, and scholar, urged bisexuality and sexual freedom as part of a wider struggle for freedom and justice. She wrote

> If you are free, you are not predictable and you are not controllable. To my mind, that is the keenly positive, politicizing significance of bisexual affirmation: . . . to insist upon the equal validity of all the components of social/sexual complexity.   *(1992, p. 193)*

who refuse to tailor their looks and actions to traditional categories—for example, butch lesbians, cross-dressers, drag kings and queens, and those described by writer and activist Leslie Feinberg (1996) as "transgender warriors"—are involved in something profoundly challenging and transformative. Drag, for example, has a long history in European culture (see Bullough and Bullough 1993, 1997; Garber 1992; Halberstam and Volcano; Lorber 1994). It plays with the idea of appearance as an illusion, mimics and parodies conventions and raises questions as to who the person is in terms of outside appearance and inner identity. During the 1980s and 1990s, younger people reclaimed the word *queer,* which for many older lesbians and gay men was a hateful and oppressive word (Bernstein and Silberman 1996). This is a broadening of queerness, with an emphasis on experimentation and playfulness, and includes all who challenge heteronormativity (Gage, Richards, and Wilmot 2002; Nestle, Howell, and Wilchins 2002; Rodríguez 2003). What was defined forty years ago as a gay/lesbian movement has grown enormously in size, complexity, and visibility. The most inclusive current term may be LGBTQQI—lesbian, gay, bisexual, transgender, queer, questioning, and intersex. In the past fifteen years or so TV shows featuring LGBTQQI people such as *Queer as Folk, The L Word,* and *Queer Eye for the Straight Guy* have attracted significant audiences. TV shows have also included gay and lesbian characters, discussed by Diane Raymond, professor of philosophy and women's studies (Reading 22; also Walters 2001). Raymond argues that there are many ways to "read" these shows depending on viewers' own perspectives, and that, ironically, these queer representations may reinforce the "normalcy" of heterosexism. In 2000, a watershed year for the representation of transgender characters and themes in feature films, filmmaker Pedro Almodóvar won an Oscar for *All About My Mother,* as did Hilary Swank for her portrayal of Brandon Teena in *Boys Don't Cry* (see Reading 24).

Philosopher and queer theorist Judith Butler (1990) considered "the binary framework for both sex and gender" to be "regulatory fictions" that consolidate and naturalize the power of masculine and heterosexist oppression (p. 33). Her conception of gender as performative allows and requires us to think of gender and sexuality more fluidly than

rigid categories permit. It also opens the possibility that, under less repressive circumstances, people would have a much wider repertoire of behaviors than most currently do. At the same time, Butler noted that people "who fail to do their gender right" by standards held to be appropriate in specific contexts, may be punished for it, through name calling, discrimination, hate, and outright violence (p. 140). In Reading 23, Leslie Feinberg describes an occasion when this happened to *hir* in a hospital emergency room. Preferring gender-neutral pronouns, *sie* writes:

> I am a human being who unnerves some people. As they look at me, they see a kaleidoscope of characteristics they associate with both males and females. I appear to be a tangled knot of gender contradictions. . . . I'm a female who is more masculine than those prominently portrayed in mass culture. . . . My life only comes into focus when the word *transgender* is added to the equation.

In Reading 24, Judith Halberstam examines the life and execution-style killing of Brandon Teena, a young female-born transgender person who was living as a man and dating women. Halberstam refers to two films about Brandon's death: a documentary, *The Brandon Teena Story,* and a feature film, *Boys Don't Cry.* Both implicate rural homophobia in Brandon's killing, though his girlfriends described him as a "dream guy." Halberstam examines research and theorizes about queer experiences in small towns, pointing out that much gay/queer theorizing is centered in metropolitan areas like New York and San Francisco, giving rise to a "metrosexual" norm, and emphasizing migration from rural to urban areas as part of the process of "coming out." She calls for nuanced stories of queer people's lives in small towns and rural areas as a counterweight to this city-based knowledge and urban assumptions of rural areas as homophobic, racist, and intolerant. She constructs a many-layered story of gender variance, race, and small-town culture, creating a Brandon archive that is "simultaneously a resource, a productive narrative, a set of representations, a history, a memorial, and a time capsule. It literally records a moment in the history of twentieth-century struggles around the meaning of gender categories."

In Chapter 3, we noted that renaming and getting rid of pejorative labels is an important factor in liberation struggles. Transgender people have developed new language to describe themselves rather than the clinical terminology of medical reports and psychotherapy. York University researcher Krista Scott-Dixon (2006) uses the broad term "trans" to include people who have been described as transsexual, pre- or post-operative, transgender, transvestite, and so on; she uses "non-trans" for everyone who does not identity as trans. In her *Transfeminist Manifesto,* Emi Koyama (2003), founder and director of the Intersex Initiative in Portland, Oregon, urged trans women—"individuals who identify, present, or live more or less as women despite their sex assignment at birth"—to speak out about their lives (p. 245). Or, to write about them. Most published materials about trans people are the work of researchers and commentators replete with their assumptions, imposed definitions, and attributed feelings, hence the importance of trans people writing for themselves (see, e.g., Namaste 2000; Scott-Dixon 2006; Serano 2007).

Theorizing Sexuality

Medical anthropologist Carole Vance (1984) summed up the contradictions of sexuality for women:

> Sexuality is simultaneously a domain of restriction, repression, and danger as well as a domain of exploration, pleasure, and agency. To focus only on pleasure and gratification ignores the patriarchal structure in which women act, yet to speak only of sexual violence and oppression ignores women's experience with sexual agency and choice. *(p. 1)*

Feminists have engaged in heated argument about women's sexuality and the possibility of genuine sexual agency in patriarchal cultures (see, e.g., Jaggar 1994; Snitow, Stansell, and Thompson 1983; Vance 1984). Philosopher Marilyn Frye (1992) noted that "the word *virgin* did not originally mean a woman whose vagina was untouched by any penis, but a free woman, one not betrothed, not married, not bound to, not possessed by any man. It meant a female who is sexually and hence socially her own person" (p. 133). Frye argued that radical feminist

lesbians have created ways of living out this ki virginity. Is this also possible for heteros women? As Frye put it: "Can you fuck witho ing your virginity?" (p. 136). She concludes th is unlikely, but conceded it may be possible if v are willing to be wild and undomesti sexually, socially, and politically.

Naomi Wolf (1992) noted that "all over t try, millions of feminists have a secret ind By day they fight gender injustice; by ni sleep with men. . . . Is sleeping with a man, with the enemy'?" (p. 29). She resolved es tion by advocating what she called "radi sexuality." To achieve this, women w teed financial independence, marriage wou ve to be very different, and both women and r vould have to give up their "gender beefits. cholo gist Lynne Segal (1994) and sociolo Pepper Schwartz (1994) described how some rosexual couples are negotiating sex to make it e egalitar ian. Schwartz noted that in U.S. culture e is a com monly held feeling that 'male leadersh nd control is inherently erotic," th role differes between women and men and "t mystery of knowing each other" make for a nre exciting life (p. 70). But only some men, Schwartz wrote "paps those with strong mothers, or wh a great rest for com petence and intelligence, nd equality mpelling and sexy" (p. 78). And not women "rse to be an instrument in male orchestation" (p. 7 She com mented that sexual passion is Western ial for mar riage, although research shows that passi decreases over the length of a relationhip. A lonterm **peer marriage,** which is intentically egabrian, she noted, may be better at proviing romce and re spect than providing passion as currently lefined.

Writer and activist Suzann Pharr (988) made an important link between eminist and anti homophobic work in her analyis of hmophobia as a weapon of sexism. She commentd that "as long as the word lesbian can srike far in any woman's heart, then work on bhalf of women can be stopped; the only successtl work against sexism must include work against honophobia" (p. 26). The term *homophobia,* meaning ear of ho mosexuals, masks the power and privlege of het erosexuality as a system. Note the dsparity in language compared to that used for othe: systems of power. People do not say *colorphobia* or *working-classphobia,* but racism or classism. We use the

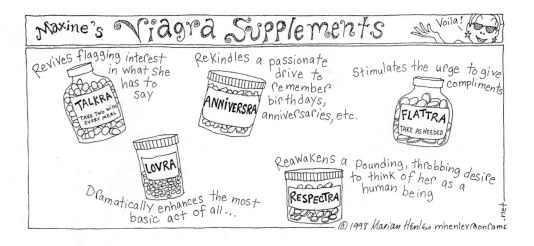

Maxine's Viagra Supplements — Voila!

Revives flagging interest in what she has to say — TALKRA TAKE TWO WITH EVERY MEAL

ReKindles a passionate drive to remember birthdays, anniversaries, etc. — ANNIVERSRA

Stimulates the urge to give compliments — FLATTRA TAKE AS NEEDED

Dramatically enhances the most basic act of all... — LOVRA

Reawakens a pounding, throbbing desire to think of her as a human being — RESPECTRA

© 1998 Marian Henley mhenley@onramp.net

terms *heterosexism* or *heteronormativity* rather than homophobia.

Many feminists have focused on sexual violence —both theoretically and through active participation in rape crisis centers and shelters for battered women—and understand that sexuality can be a source of profound vulnerability for women. The late writer and activist Andrea Dworkin (1987), for example, argued that intercourse is inherently repressive for women, partly for anatomical reasons, but more because of unequal power relations between women and men. As a way of repudiating the eroticization of inequality, some feminists have argued that women's sexuality should be based on sexual acts that are safe, loving, and intimate, in the context of a caring, monogamous relationship. Others have seen this as a new—feminist—restriction on women's freedom of expression (see, e.g., Duggan and Hunter 1995; Jaggar 1994; Johnson 2002; Leidholdt and Raymond 1990). Gayle Rubin (1984) noted two strains of feminist thought concerning sexuality: one criticizing "restrictions on women's sexual behavior," denouncing "the high costs imposed on women for being sexually active," and calling for "a sexual liberation that would work for women as well as for men"; the other considering "sexual liberation to be inherently a mere extension of male privilege" (p. 301). Heated feminist debate about sexuality, power, and violence has continued for many years, especially with regard to issues like prostitution/sex work and pornography (see, e.g., Califia 2000; Cornell 2000; Dworkin 1993; Feminist Anti-Censorship Task Force 1992; Jeffreys 1997; Johnson 2002; Kempadoo and Doezema 1998; Nagel 1997; Queen 2002; Russell 1993; Stan 1995; Strossen 2000; Whisnant and Stark 2004).

In her now-classic essay, award-winning poet and writer Adrienne Rich (1986a) discussed how social institutions like law, religion, philosophy, official kinship, and popular culture support what she termed compulsory heterosexuality. She argued that patriarchy *demands* heterosexuality to keep women serving masculinist interests. For Rich, what needs to be explained is not why women identify as lesbians, but how and why so many women are heterosexual, since, typically, we first experience the intimacy of emotional caring and physical nurture with women—our mothers or other female caregivers. In many cultural settings, women and girls spend time together, care for, and depend on one another, and enjoy each other's friendship—often passionately. Why would women ever redirect that search, Rich asks. As you read this chapter, consider Rich's question: What are "the societal forces that wrench women's emotional and erotic energies away from themselves and other women" (p. 35), and which seek to teach us to see men as appropriate partners?

After the Stonewall Riots (New York) in 1969, a gay rights movement flourished, drawing on feminist ideas as well as "strands of sex research that did not treat homosexuality as pathological and on an urban gay subculture that had been expanding since the end of World War II" (Lancaster and di Leonardo 1997, p. 3).

With varying degrees of success and through struggles that continue today, gay and lesbian activists have publicly championed all that is positive, pleasurable, and creative in same-sex desire while opposing the obvious sources of antigay oppression: police harassment, social stigma, religious bigotry, psychiatric persecution, and sodomy laws. In the process, these concrete struggles have revealed the less obvious heteronormative premises deeply embedded in law, science, philosophy, official kinship, and vernacular culture.

(Lancaster and di Leonardo 1997, p. 3)

Lisa Orlando (1991) hypothesized that desire involves "some kind of interaction between a more or less shapeless biological 'drive' and a combination of individual experiences and larger social forces." She noted that the very notion of sexual identity is specific to our culture and time in history.

Economic changes such as industrialization, the development of the factory system, and the spread of wage labor had a profound impact on family life. Gradually, families stopped producing the goods they needed and supported themselves through wage labor. Children, who had been an economic advantage to their families by contributing to household production, became an expense. The U.S. birthrate dropped dramatically during the twentieth century as a result. Further, developments like the contraceptive pill, alternative insemination, in vitro fertilization, and other reproductive technologies have made possible the separation of intercourse and procreation. Heterosexual women can be sexually active without becoming pregnant, and any woman can become pregnant without having intercourse. Historian John D'Emilio (1984) argued that these trends have created conditions "that allow some men and women to organize a personal life around their erotic/emotional attraction to their own sex" (p. 104). They have "made possible the formation of urban communities of lesbians and gay men, and more recently, of a politics based on a sexual identity" (p. 104). On this analysis, sexual identity has a basis in macrolevel circumstances as much as personal factors (D'Emilio and Freedman 1997), although cultural acceptance of lesbians and gay men does not always follow (see, e.g., Anzaldúa 1987; Eng and Hom 1998; Leong 1996; Rodríguez 2003; Smith 1998; Trujillo 1991). D'Emilio (1984) accepted that there have been same-sex partnerships for generations, as claimed by Adrienne Rich (1986a) and many other authors and researchers cited above. He complicated this claim, however, by differentiating homosexual *behavior* from homosexual *identity* and argued that only under certain economic conditions are homosexual identity and community possible. Clare Hemmings (2002) noted that such communities both generate and require supportive locations to survive and flourish, in her discussion of Northampton, Massachusetts, and San Francisco as cities with strong LGBTQQI communities. Judith Halberstam (2005) elaborates on the relationship between queer identity and place in Reading 24.

This links to the experience of Surina A. Khan (Reading 22). Despite the fact that images of same-sex couples have been part of the history of South Asia for hundreds of years, she notes that most people from South Asia do not have words for homosexuality and regard it as a Western phenomenon. This apparent paradox is exactly what D'Emilio's distinction between behavior and identity helps to explain. Further, it may be useful to think of four distinctive categories: inclination, behavior, identity, and politics. One may have sexual inclinations but may decide not to act on them. One may engage in certain sexual behaviors but not adopt LGBTQQI identity. One may identify as a lesbian or transgendered woman but not act on that identity in a political way.

Gay and lesbian activism and theorizing led to the development of queer theory and queer studies (see, e.g., Alcoff 1988; Fuss 1991; Jeffreys 2003; Stein 1997; Sullivan 2003), which take sexuality as the main category of analysis. Queer theorist Eve Sedgwick's (1990) Axiom #2 distinguished queer theory from feminist theory: "The study of sexuality is not coextensive with the study of gender; correspondingly, antihomophobic inquiry is not coextensive with feminist inquiry" (p. 27). Trans writers and activists have also critiqued feminist theories. Emi Koyama (2003) argued that second-wave feminists' separation

of biological sex from socially constructed gender was useful for breaking down compulsory gender roles. It was also limited, "avoiding the question of the naturalness of essential female and male sexes" (p. 249). She argued for the reconnection of sex and gender and recognition that these intertwined systems are both socially constructed. Krista Scott-Dixon (2006) noted that, in general, feminist theorists have given scant attention to trans people and issues, while some have been openly hostile. She suggested several common themes and concerns of interest to feminist and trans scholars and activists (pp. 25–28):

- a focus on the operations of sex/gender systems of power and privilege
- the importance of self-definition and self-naming
- the value of intersectional perspectives
- a concern for shelter that is free from violence
- the right to bodily integrity and freedom of sexual expression
- collaborative organizing principles and methods
- speaking out against discrimination

Like Scott-Dixon and Koyama, Leslie Feinberg (1998) and Kate Bornstein (1995, 1998) have argued that transgender people are creating a broader space for everyone to express their diverse genders and sexualities (see also Boylan 2003; Halberstam 1998, 2005). Whether transgenderism as a movement can deal with inequalities of power raises the question of how personal freedoms, played out through the construction of sexuality and the body, are connected to other political issues and other progressive groups in society.

Activism and Sexuality

A number of online educational and activist organizations provide information for young people about sexuality and health (e.g., Go Ask Alice, Scarleteen, Teenwire, and Youth Resource). Many informal networks, local groups, and national organizations support and advocate for lesbians, bisexuals, transgender people, and gay men, especially in urban areas. Some are primarily social group; others are support groups that provide information and social connections. Still others focus on particular issues like LGBTQQI health, HIV/AIDS, parenting, community, police violence, religious oppression, or the situation of gays in the military. Others run journals, magazines, newsletters, bookstores, presses, churches, bars, coffeehouses, bands, sports teams, and theater companies; support political candidates for local, state, or national office; oppose city and state ordinances designed to limit LGBTQQI rights; or raise funds for LGBTQQI organizations. These various networks and organizations span a broad political spectrum. Some are overtly feminist; others are more closely aligned with queer politics. Examples include BiNet USA (Arlington, VA), the Boston Bisexual Women's Network, the Detroit Women's Coffeehouse, Old Lesbians Organizing for Change (Houston, Texas), Trikone: Lesbian, Gay, Bisexual, and Transgendered South Asians (San Francisco), New York Association for Gender Rights Advocacy, the National Gay and Lesbian Taskforce (Washington, D.C.), Unid@s: the National Latino/a LGBT Human Rights Organization (Washington, D.C.), Gender Education and Advocacy (www.gender.org), and the International Gay and Lesbian Human Rights Commission (New York, Buenos Aires, and Johnnesburg). In addition, women who identify as lesbian, bisexual, queer, or transgender are active in antiracist organizing, rape crisis centers, shelters for battered women, labor unions, antimilitarist organizations, and women's studies programs where they link their knowledge and experiences of oppression based on sexuality with other oppressions.

Questions for Reflection

As you read and discuss the readings that follow, consider the questions raised by Shere Hite, listed on p. 152.

Finding Out More on the Web

1. Review the information about sexuality and health given on one of the online sites mentioned in this chapter.

2. The World Wide Web is a significant new tool in the commodification of women. Type "Philippine women" or "Asian women" into your search engine and see what comes up. Also look at www.asianwomenonline.com—where Asian women are reclaiming cyberspace and breaking stereotypical portrayals.

3. Research an organization mentioned in this chapter. What are its goals, strategies, and activities?

4. Research the history of transgender experience in the United States. The following site has a useful glossary of terms: www.thefword.org.uk/features/2008/03/trans_101

Taking Action

1. Write in your journal or have a candid conversation with a friend about your ideas about sexuality. How do you recognize the power of the erotic as Audre Lorde describes it?

2. Analyze the way women's magazines and men's magazines discuss women's sexuality.

3. Look critically at the way women's sexuality is portrayed in movies, on TV, and in ads. What is being represented?

4. However you define your sexuality, participate in campus or community events to commemorate National Coming-Out Day (usually in October) or Gay Pride (usually in June).

EIGHTEEN

Uses of the Erotic (1984)
The Erotic as Power

Audre Lorde

> **Audre Lorde** (1934–1992) was an acclaimed writer and educator whose books included *Sister Outsider, The Cancer Journals,* and *Zami: A New Spelling of My Name.* She held many teaching positions and toured the world as a lecturer, founding a sisterhood in South Africa and the St. Croix Women's Coalition. She published ten volumes of poetry, numerous essays, and won awards and honors, including being named New York State's Poet Laureate. She co-founded Kitchen Table: Women of Color Press.

There are many kinds of power, used and unused, acknowledged or otherwise. The erotic is a resource within each of us that lies in a deeply female and spiritual plane, firmly rooted in the power of our unexpressed or unrecognized feeling. In order to perpetuate itself, every oppression must corrupt or distort those various sources of power within the culture of the oppressed that can provide energy for change. For women, this has meant a suppression of the erotic as a considered source of power and information within our lives.

We have been taught to suspect this resource, vilified, abused, and devalued within western society. On the one hand, the superficially erotic has been encouraged as a sign of female inferiority; on the other hand, women have been made to suffer and to feel both contemptible and suspect by virtue of its existence.

It is a short step from there to the false belief that only by the suppression of the erotic within our lives and consciousness can women be truly strong. But that strength is illusory, for it is fashioned within the context of male models of power.

As women, we have come to distrust that power which rises from our deepest and nonrational knowledge. We have been warned against it all our lives by the male world, which values this depth of feeling enough to keep women around in order to exercise it in the service of men, but which fears this same depth too much to examine the possibilities of it within themselves. So women are maintained at a distant/inferior position to be psychically milked, much the same way ants maintain colonies of aphids to provide a life-giving substance for their masters.

But the erotic offers a well of replenishing and provocative force to the woman who does not fear its revelation, nor succumb to the belief that sensation is enough.

The erotic has often been misnamed by men and used against women. It has been made into the confused, the trivial, the psychotic, the plasticized sensation. For this reason, we have often turned away from the exploration and consideration of the erotic as a source of power and information, confusing it with its opposite, the pornographic. But pornography is a direct denial of the power of the erotic, for it represents the suppression of true feeling. Pornography emphasizes sensation without feeling.

The erotic is a measure between the beginnings of our sense of self and the chaos of our strongest feelings. It is an internal sense of satisfaction to which, once we have experienced it, we know we can aspire. For having experienced the fullness of this depth of feeling and recognizing its power, in honor and self-respect we can require no less of ourselves.

It is never easy to demand the most from ourselves, from our lives, from our work. To encourage excellence is to go beyond the encouraged mediocrity of our society. To go beyond the encouraged mediocrity of our society is to encourage excellence. But giving in to the fear of feeling and working to capacity is a luxury only the unintentional can afford, and the unintentional are those who do not wish to guide their own destinies.

This internal requirement toward excellence which we learn from the erotic must not be misconstrued as demanding the impossible from ourselves nor from others. Such a demand incapacitates everyone in the process. For the erotic is not a question only of what we do; it is a question of how acutely and fully we can feel in the doing. Once we know the extent to which we are capable of feeling that sense of satisfaction and completion, we can then observe which of our various life endeavors bring us closest to that fullness.

The aim of each thing that we do is to make our lives and the lives of our children richer and more possible. Within the celebration of the erotic in all our endeavors, my work becomes a conscious decision—a longed-for bed, which I enter gratefully and from which I rise up empowered.

Of course, women so empowered are dangerous. So we are taught to separate the erotic demand from most vital areas of our lives other than sex. And the lack of concern for the erotic root and satisfactions of our work is felt in our disaffection from so much of what we do. For instance, how often do we truly love our work even at its most difficult?

The principal horror of any system that defines the good in terms of profit rather than in terms of human need or that defines human need to the exclusion of the psychic and emotional components of that need—the principal horror of such a system is that it robs our work of its erotic value, its erotic power and life appeal and fulfillment. Such a system reduces work to a travesty of necessities, a duty by which we earn bread or oblivion for ourselves and those we love. But this is tantamount to blinding a painter and then telling her to improve her work and to enjoy the act of painting. It is not only next to impossible; it is also profoundly cruel.

As women, we need to examine the ways in which our world can be truly different. I am speaking here of the necessity for reassessing the quality of all the aspects of our lives and of our work and of how we move toward and through them.

The very word *erotic* comes from the Greek word *eros*, the personification of love in all its aspects—born of Chaos and personifying creative power and harmony. When I speak of the erotic, then, I speak of it as an assertion of the lifeforce of women, of that creative energy empowered, the knowledge and use of which we are now reclaiming in our language, our history, our dancing, our loving, our work, our lives.

There are frequent attempts to equate pornography and eroticism, two diametrically opposed uses of the sexual. Because of these attempts, it has become fashionable to separate the spiritual (psychic and emotional) from the political, to see them as contradictory or antithetical. "What do you mean, a poetic revolutionary, a meditating gunrunner?" In the same way, we have attempted to separate the spiritual and the erotic, thereby reducing the spiritual to a world of flattened affect, a world of the ascetic who aspires to feel nothing. But nothing is farther from the truth. For the ascetic position is one of the highest fear, the gravest immobility. The severe abstinence of the ascetic becomes the ruling obsession. And it is one not of self-discipline but of self-abnegation.

The dichotomy between the spiritual and the political is also false, resulting from an incomplete attention to our erotic knowledge. For the bridge which connects them is formed by the erotic—the sensual—those physical, emotional, and psychic expressions of what is deepest and strongest and richest within each of us, being shared: the passions of love in its deepest meanings.

Beyond the superficial, the considered phrase, "It feels right to me," acknowledges the strength of the erotic into a true knowledge, for what that means is the first and most powerful guiding light toward any understanding. And understanding is a handmaiden, which can only wait upon, or clarify, that knowledge, deeply born. The erotic is the nurturer or nursemaid of all our deepest knowledge.

The erotic functions for me in several ways, and the first is in providing the power that comes from sharing deeply any pursuit with another person. The sharing of joy, whether physical, emotional, psychic, or intellectual, forms a bridge between the sharers, which can be the basis for understanding much of what is not shared between them and lessens the threat of their difference.

Another important way in which the erotic connection functions is the open and fearless underlining of my capacity for joy. In the way my body stretches to music and opens into response, hearkening to its deepest rhythms, so every level upon which I sense also opens to the erotically satisfying experience, whether it is dancing, building a bookcase, writing a poem, examining an idea.

That self-connection shared is a measure of the joy that I know myself to be capable of feeling, a reminder of my capacity for feeling. And that deep and irreplaceable knowledge of my capacity for joy comes to demand from all of my life that it be lived within the knowledge that such satisfaction is possible and does not have to be called *marriage,* nor *god,* nor *an afterlife.*

This is one reason why the erotic is so feared and so often relegated to the bedroom alone when it is recognized at all. For once we begin to feel deeply all the aspects of our lives, we begin to demand from ourselves and from our life-pursuits that they feel in accordance with that joy that we know ourselves to be capable of. Our erotic knowledge empowers us, becomes a lens through which we scrutinize all aspects of our existence, forcing us to evaluate those aspects honestly in terms of their relative meaning within our lives. And this is a grave responsibility, projected from within each of us, not to settle for the convenient, the shoddy, the conventionally expected, nor the merely safe.

During World War II, we bought sealed plastic packets of white, uncolored margarine, with a tiny, intense pellet of yellow coloring perched like a topaz just inside the clear skin of the bag. We would leave the margarine out for a while to soften, and then we would pinch the little pellet to break it inside the bag, releasing the rich yellowness into the soft pale mass of margarine. Then taking it carefully between our fingers, we would knead it gently back and forth, over and over, until the color had spread throughout the whole pound bag of margarine, thoroughly coloring it.

I find the erotic such a kernel within myself. When released from its intense and constrained pellet, it flows through and colors my life with a kind of energy that heightens and sensitizes and strengthens all my experience.

We have been raised to fear the *yes* within ourselves, our deepest cravings. But, once recognized, those which do not enhance our future lose their power and can be altered. The fear of our desires keeps them suspect and indiscriminately powerful, for to suppress any truth is to give it strength beyond endurance. The fear that we cannot grow beyond whatever distortions we may find within ourselves keeps us docile and loyal and obedient, externally defined, and leads us to accept many facets of our oppression as women.

When we live outside ourselves, and by that I mean on external directives only rather than from our internal knowledge and needs, when we live away from those erotic guides from within ourselves, then our lives are limited by external and alien forms, and we conform to the needs of a structure that is not based on human need, let alone an individual's. But when we begin to live from within outward, in touch with the power of the erotic within ourselves, and allowing that power to inform and illuminate our actions upon the world around us, then we begin to be responsible to ourselves in the deepest sense. For as we begin to recognize our deepest feelings, we begin to give up, of necessity, being satisfied with suffering and self-negation and with the numbness which so often seems like their only alternative in our society. Our acts against oppression become integral with self, motivated and empowered from within.

In touch with the erotic, I become less willing to accept powerlessness or those other supplied states of being which are not native to me, such as resignation, despair, self-effacement, depression, self-denial.

And yes, there is a hierarchy. There is a difference between painting a back fence and writing a poem, but only one of quantity. And there is, for me, no difference between writing a good poem and moving into sunlight against the body of a woman I love.

This brings me to the last consideration of the erotic. To share the power of each other's feelings is different from using another's feelings as we would use a kleenex. When we look the other way from our experience, erotic or otherwise, we use rather than share the feelings of those others who participate in the experience with us. And use without consent of the used is abuse.

In order to be utilized, our erotic feelings must be recognized. The need for sharing deep feeling is a human need. But within the European-American tradition, this need is satisfied by certain proscribed erotic comings-together. These occasions are almost always characterized by a simultaneous looking away, a pretense of calling them something else, whether a religion, a fit, mob violence, or even playing doctor. And this misnaming of the need and the deed gives rise to that distortion which results in pornography and obscenity—the abuse of feeling.

When we look away from the importance of the erotic in the development and sustenance of our power, or when we look away from ourselves as we satisfy our erotic needs in concert with others, we use each other as objects of satisfaction rather than share our joy in the satisfying, rather than make connection with our similarities and our differences. To refuse to be conscious of what we are feeling at any time, however comfortable that might seem, is to deny a large part of the experience and to allow ourselves to be reduced to the pornographic, the abused, and the absurd.

The erotic cannot be felt secondhand. As a Black lesbian feminist, I have a particular feeling, knowledge, and understanding for those sisters with whom I have danced hard, played, or even fought. This deep participation has often been the forerunner for joint concerted actions not possible before.

But this erotic charge is not easily shared by women who continue to operate under an exclusively European-American male tradition. I know it was not available to me when I was trying to adapt my consciousness to this mode of living and sensation.

Only now, I find more and more women-identified women brave enough to risk sharing the erotic's electrical charge without having to look away and without distorting the enormously powerful and creative nature of that exchange. Recognizing the power of the erotic within our lives can give us the energy to pursue genuine change within our world rather than merely settling for a shift of characters in the same weary drama.

For not only do we touch our most profoundly creative source, but we do that which is female and self-affirming in the face of a racist, patriarchal, and anti-erotic society.

N I N E T E E N

◆◆◆

Guadalupe the Sex Goddess (1996)

Sandra Cisneros

Sandra Cisneros is an award-winning fiction and poetry writer whose first book, *House on Mango Street*, sold over 2 million copies. Her writing has earned her numerous honors, including the prestigious MacArthur Foundation Fellowship. She is the president and founder of the Macondo Foundation, an association of socially engaged writers working to advance creativity, and Writer-in-Residence at Our Lady of the Lake University in San Antonio (Texas).

In high school I marveled at how white women strutted around the locker room, nude as pearls, as unashamed of their brilliant bodies as the Nike of Samothrace. Maybe they were hiding terrible secrets like bulimia or anorexia, but, to my naive eye then, I thought of them as women comfortable in their skin.

You could always tell us Latinas. We hid when we undressed, modestly facing a wall, or, in my case, dressing in a bathroom stall. We were the ones who still used bulky sanitary pads instead of tampons, thinking ourselves morally superior to our white classmates. *My mama said you can't use tampons till after you're married.* All Latina mamas said this, yet how come none of us thought to ask our mothers why they didn't use tampons *after* getting married?

Womanhood was full of mysteries. I was as ignorant about my own body as any female ancestor who hid behind a sheet with a hole in the center when husband or doctor called. Religion and our culture, our culture and religion, helped to create that blur, a vagueness about what went on "down there." So ashamed was I about my own "down there" that until I was an adult I had no idea I had another orifice called the vagina; I thought my period would arrive via the urethra or perhaps through the walls of my skin.

No wonder, then, it was too terrible to think about a doctor—a man!—looking at you down there when you could never bring yourself to look yourself. *¡ Ay, nunca!* How could I acknowledge my sexuality, let alone enjoy sex, with so much guilt? In the guise of modesty my culture locked me in a double chastity belt of ignorance and *vergüenza,* shame.

I had never seen my mother nude. I had never taken a good look at myself either. Privacy for self-exploration belonged to the wealthy. In my home a private space was practically impossible; aside from the doors that opened to the street, the only room with a lock was the bathroom, and how could anyone who shared a bathroom with eight other people stay in there for more than a few minutes? Before college, no one in my family had a room of their own except me, a narrow closet just big enough for my twin bed and an oversized blond dresser we'd bought in the bargain basement of *el Sears.* The dresser was as long as a coffin and blocked the door from shutting completely. I had my own room, but I never had the luxury of shutting the door.

I didn't even see my own sex until a nurse at the Emma Goldman Clinic showed it to me—*Would you like to see your cervix? Your os is dilating. You must be ovulating. Here's a mirror; take a look.* When had anyone ever suggested I take a look or allowed me a speculum to take home and investigate myself at leisure!

I'd only been to one other birth control facility prior to the Emma Goldman Clinic, the university medical center in grad school. I was 21 in a strange town far from home for the first time. I was afraid and I was ashamed to seek out a gynecologist, but I was more afraid of becoming pregnant. Still, I agonized about going for weeks. Perhaps the anonymity and distance from my family allowed me finally to take control of my life. I remember wanting to be fearless like the white women around me, to be able to have sex when I wanted, but I was too afraid to explain to a would-be lover how I'd only had one other man in my life and we'd practiced withdrawal. Would he laugh at me? How could I look anyone in the face and explain why I couldn't go see a gynecologist?

One night, a classmate I liked too much took me home with him. I meant all along to say something about how I wasn't on anything, but I never quite found my voice, never the right moment to cry out—*Stop, this is dangerous to my brilliant career!* Too afraid to sound stupid, afraid to ask him to take responsibility too, I said nothing, and I let him take me like that with nothing protecting me from motherhood but luck. The days that followed were torture, but fortunately on Mother's Day my period arrived, and I celebrated my nonmaternity by making an appointment with the family planning center.

When I see pregnant teens, I can't help but think that could've been me. In high school I would've thrown myself into love the way some warriors throw themselves into fighting. I was ready to sacrifice everything in the name of love, to do anything, even risk my own life, but thankfully there were no takers. I was enrolled at an all-girls' school. I think if I had met a boy who would have me, I would've had sex in a minute, convinced this was love. I have always had enough imagination to fall in love all by myself, then and now.

I tell you this story because I am overwhelmed by the silence regarding Latinas and our bodies. If I, as a graduate student, was shy about talking to anyone about my body and sex, imagine how difficult it must be for a young girl in middle school or high school living in a home with no lock on the bedroom door, perhaps with no door, or maybe with no bedroom, no information other than misinformation from the girlfriends and the boyfriend. So much guilt, so much silence, and such a yearning to be loved; no wonder young women find themselves having sex while they are still children, having sex without sexual protection, too ashamed to confide their feelings and fears to anyone.

What a culture of denial. Don't get pregnant! But no one tells you how not to. This is why I was angry for so many years every time I saw a *la Virgen de Guadalupe,* my culture's role model for brown women like me. She was damn dangerous, an ideal so lofty and unrealistic it was laughable. Did boys have to aspire to be Jesus? I never saw any evidence of it. They were fornicating like rabbits while the Church ignored them and pointed us women toward our destiny—marriage and mother-hood. The other alternative was *puta*hood.

In my neighborhood I knew only real women, neither saints nor whores, naive and vulnerable *huerquitas* like me who wanted desperately to fall in love, with the heart and soul. And yes, with the *panocha* too.

As far as I could see, *la Lupe* was nothing but a Goody Two-Shoes meant to doom me to a life of un-happiness. Thanks, but no thanks. Motherhood and/or marriage were anathema to my career. But being a bad girl, that was something I could use as a writer, a Molotov cocktail to toss at my papa and *el Papa,* who had their own plans for me.

Discovering sex was like discovering writing. It was powerful in a way I couldn't explain. Like writ-ing, you had to go beyond the guilt and shame to get to anything good. Like writing, it could take you to deep and mysterious subterranean levels. With each new depth I found out things about myself I didn't know I knew. And, like writing, for a slip of a moment it could be spiritual, the cosmos pivoting on a pin, could empty and fill you all at once like a Ganges, a Piazzolla tango, a tulip bending in the wind. I was no one, I was nothing, and I was every-thing in the universe little and large—twig, cloud, sky. How had this incredible energy been denied me!

When I look at *la Virgen de Guadalupe* now, she is not the Lupe of my childhood, no longer the one in my grandparents' house in Tepeyac, nor is she the one of the Roman Catholic Church, the one I bolted the door against in my teens and twenties. Like every woman who matters to me, I have had to search for her in the rubble of history. And I have found her. She is Guadalupe the sex goddess, a god-dess who makes me feel good about my sexual power, my sexual energy, who reminds me that I must, as Clarissa Pinkola Estés so aptly put it, "[speak] from the vulva . . . speak the most basic, honest truth," and write from my *panocha.*

In my research of Guadalupe's pre-Columbian an-tecedents, the she before the Church desexed her, I found Tonantzin, and inside Tonantzin a pantheon of other mother goddesses. I discovered Tlazolteotl, the goddess of fertility and sex, also referred to as Totzin. Our Beginnings, or Tzinteotl, goddess of the rump. *Putas,* nymphos, and other loose women were known as "women of the sex goddess." Tlazolteotl was the patron of sexual passion, and though she had the power to stir you to sin, she could also forgive you and cleanse you of your sexual transgressions via her priests who heard confession. In this aspect of confes-sor Tlazolteotl was known as Tlaelcuani, the filth eater. Maybe you've seen her; she's the one whose im-age is sold in the tourist markets even now, a statue of a woman squatting in childbirth, her face grimacing in pain. Tlazolteotl, then, is a duality of maternity *and* sexuality. In other words, she is a sexy mama.

To me, *la Virgen de Guadalupe* is also Coatlicue, the creative/destructive goddess. When I think of the Coatlicue statue in the National Museum of Anthropology in Mexico City, so terrible it was unearthed and then reburied because it was too frightening to look at, I think of a woman enraged, a woman as tempest, a woman *bien berrinchuda,* and I like that. *La Lupe as cabrona.* Not silent and passive, but silently gathering force.

Most days, I too feel like the creative/destructive goddess Coatlicue, especially the days I'm writing, ca-pable of fabricating pretty tales with pretty words, as well as doing demolition work with a volley of *palabrotas* if I want to. I am the Coatlicue-Lupe whose square column of a body I see in so many Indian women, in my mother, and in myself each time I check out my thick-waisted, flat-assed torso in the mirror.

Coatlicue, Tlazolteotl, Tonantzin, *la Virgen de Guadalupe.* They are each telescoped one into the other, into who I am. And this is where *la Lupe* in-trigues me—not the Lupe of 1531 who appeared to Juan Diego, but the one of the 1990s who has shaped who we are as Chicanas/*mexicanas* today, the one in-side each Chicana and *mexicana.* Perhaps it's the Tlazolteotl-Lupe in me whose *malcriada* spirit inspires me to leap into the swimming pool naked or dance on a table with a skirt on my head. Maybe it's my Coatlicue-Lupe attitude that makes it possible for my mother to tell me, "No wonder men can't stand you." Who knows? What I do know is this: I am obsessed with becoming a woman comfortable in her skin.

I can't attribute my religious conversion to a flash of lightning on the road to Laredo or anything like that. Instead, there have been several lessons learned subtly over a period of time. A grave depres-sion and near suicide in my thirty-third year and its subsequent retrospection. Vietnamese Buddhist monk Thich Nhat Hanh's writing that has brought out the Buddha-Lupe in me. My weekly peace vigil for my friend Jasna in Sarajevo. The writings of Glo-ria Anzaldúa. A crucial trip back to Tepeyac in 1985 with Cherríe Moraga and Norma Alarcón. Drives across Texas, talking with other Chicanas. And research for stories that would force me back inside the Church from where I'd fled.

My *Virgin de Guadalupe* is not the mother of God. She is God. She is a face for a god without a face, an *indigena* for a god without ethnicity, a female deity for a god who is genderless, but I also understand that for her to approach me, for me to finally open the door and accept her, she had to be a woman like me.

Once watching a porn film, I saw a sight that terrified me. It was the film star's *panocha*—a tidy, elliptical opening, pink and shiny like a rabbit's ear. To make matters worse, it was shaved and looked especially childlike and unsexual. I think what startled

me most was the realization that my own sex has no resemblance to this woman's. My sex, dark as an orchid, rubbery and blue-purple as *pulpo*, an octopus, does not look nice and tidy, but otherworldly. I do not have little rosette nipples. My nipples are big and brown like the Mexican coins of my childhood.

When I see *la Virgen de Guadalupe* I want to lift her dress as I did my dolls, and look to see if she comes with *chones* and does her *panocha* look like mine, and does she have dark nipples too? Yes, I am certain she does. She is not neuter like Barbie. She gave birth. She has a womb. *Blessed art thou and blessed is the fruit of thy womb. . . .* Blessed art thou, Lupe, and, therefore, blessed am I.

T W E N T Y

◆◆◆

"If It's Not On, It's Not On"—Or Is It? (2001)
Discursive Constraints on Women's Condom Use

Nicola Gavey, Kathryn McPhillips, and Marion Doherty

Nicola Gavey is Associate Professor of psychology at the University of Auckland in New Zealand whose research and writing focuses on gender, power, and sexuality. **Kathryn McPhillips** is a psychologist and clinical manager at the Auckland Sexual Abuse Help Foundation. **Marion Doherty** contributed to the research and writing of this article as a graduate student in the psychology department, University of Auckland.

"If it's not on, it's not on!" Slogans such as these exhort women not to have sexual intercourse with a man unless a condom is used. Health campaigns targeting heterosexuals with this approach imply that it is women who should act assertively to control the course of their sexual encounters to prevent the spread of HIV/AIDS and other sexually transmitted infections (STIs). Researchers and commentators, too, have sometimes explicitly concluded that it is women in particular who should be targeted for condom promotions on the basis of assumptions such as "the disadvantages of condom use are fewer for girls" (Barling and Moore 1990). . . .

Aside from the obvious question of whether women *should* be expected to take greater responsibility for sexual safety, this approach relies on various assumptions that deserve critical attention. For example, what constraints on women's abilities to unilaterally control condom use are overlooked in these messages? What assumptions about women's sexuality are embedded in the claim that the disadvantages of condoms are fewer for women? That is, is safer sex simply a matter of women deciding to use condoms at all times and assertively making this happen, or do the discursive parameters of heterosex work to subtly constrain and contravene this message? Moreover, are condoms as unproblematic for women's experiences of sex as the logic offered for targeting women implies? These questions demand further investigation given that research has repeatedly shown the reluctance of heterosexuals to consistently use condoms despite clear health messages about their importance.

There is now a strong body of feminist research suggesting that condom promotion in Western societies must compete against cultural significations of condom-*less* sexual intercourse as associated with commitment, trust, and "true love" in relationships (e.g., Holland et al. 1991; Kippax et al. 1990; Willig 1995; Worth 1989; see also Hollway 1989). Here, we contribute to this body of work, which collectively highlights how women's condom use needs to be understood in relation to some of the complex gender dynamics that saturate heterosexual encounters. In particular, we critically examine (1) the concept of women's control over condom use that is tacitly assumed in campaigns designed to promote safer sex and condoms to women and (2) the foundational assumption of such campaigns that condoms are relatively unproblematic for women's sexual experiences. . . .

The Study

In-depth interviews were conducted by the first author with 14 predominantly Pakeha women (two women had mixed ethnic backgrounds but primarily identified as Pakeha). Pakeha are non-Maori New Zealanders of European descent, who form approximately 80 percent of the New Zealand population (Statistics New Zealand 2001). Our group of participants does not, therefore, represent the cultural and ethnic diversity of New Zealand. The women's ages ranged from 22 to 43 years, and 12 of the women were between 27 and 37 years old. They came from diverse work situations and educational backgrounds but could be described as generally middle class. They all had experience of heterosexual relationships and at least some experience with condoms. The women were recruited through word of mouth. . . . All participants either chose or were given pseudonyms to protect their anonymity.

Interviews were semistructured to the extent that all women were questioned about the same broad range of topics, including their past and current experiences with condoms, their heterosexual relationships and practices more generally where relevant, their personal views of condoms, and how they thought others regarded condoms. We were interested in women's condom use or intended use for both contraceptive purposes and the prevention of sexually transmitted infections. An interview schedule was used as a guide, although the style of the interviews was more conversational than a question-answer format. . . .

Assertion, Identity, and Control

Either your partner uses a condom or you don't have sex. If a women doesn't look out for herself, who will? We must learn how to say no to a partner who won't use condoms. It's either that or abstinence.   *(Sack 1992, 118)*

Public sexual health education fervently promotes the rights of women to demand condom use by male partners. Against a backdrop of implied male aversion to condoms, both the Planned Parenthood Federation of America (1988–2001) and the Family Planning Association (2000) in New Zealand offer mock scripts that despite an air of gender neutrality suggest ways women can assert their right to insist on a condom being used for sexual intercourse. In this section, we consider what these kinds of hard-line "calls to assertiveness" might look like in practice. The excerpt below is taken from the interview with Rose, a young woman in her early 20s. At the very beginning of the interview, in response to a question about her "current situation, in terms of your relationships," she said, "My last experience was fairly unpleasant and so I thought I'll really try and um devote myself to singledom for a while before I rush into anything." In this one-night stand, approximately three weeks prior to the interview, Rose did manage to successfully insist that her partner use a condom. Her account of this experience is particularly interesting for the ways in which it graphically demonstrates the kinds of interactional barriers that a woman might have to overcome to be assertive about using a condom; moreover, it demonstrates how even embodiments of the male sex drive discourse that are not perceived to be coercive can act out levels of sexual urgency that provide a momentum that is difficult to stop. Although the following quote is unusually long, we prefer to present it intact to convey more about the flavor of the interaction she describes. We will refer back to it throughout this article and want to keep the story intact.

Nicola: So were condoms involved at all in that—

Rose: Yeah um, actually that's quite an interesting one because we were both very drunk, but I still had enough sense to make it a priority, you know, and I started to realize that things were getting to the point where he seemed to be going ahead with it, without a condom, and I was— had to really push him off at one point and— cause I kept saying sort of under my breath, are you going to get a condom now, and—and he didn't seem to be taking much notice, and um—

Nicola: So you were actually saying that?

Rose: Yeah. I was—

Nicola: In a way that was audible for him to—

Rose: Yeah. (Nicola: Yeah) And um—at least I think so. (Nicola: Yeah) And—and it got to the point where [laughing] I had to push him off, and I think I actually called him an arsehole and—I just said, look fuck, you know, and—and so he did get one then but it seemed—

Nicola: He had some of his own that he got?

Rose: Yeah. (Nicola: Yeah) Yeah it was at his flat and he had them. In fact that was something I'd never asked beforehand. I presumed he would have some. And um he did get one and then you know—and that was okay, but it was sort of like you know if I hadn't demanded it, he might've gone ahead without it. And I am fairly sure that he's pretty, um—you know he has had a pretty dubious past, and so that worried me a bit, I know he was very drunk and out of control and, um—otherwise the whole situation would never have occurred I'm sure, but still I had it together enough, thank God, to demand it.

Nicola: And you actually had to push him off?

Rose: Yeah, I think—I'm pretty sure that I did, you know it's—it's all quite in a bit of a haze, [laughing] (Nicola: laughing) but um, it wasn't that pleasant, the whole experience. It was—he was pretty selfish about the whole thing. And um— yeah.

Nicola: How much old—how—You said that he was a bit older than you.

Rose: Ohh, he's only twenty-eight or nine, but that's quite a big difference for me. I usually see people that are very much in my own age-group. Mmm.

Nicola: And um, you said that it was kind of disappointing sexually and otherwise and he was quite selfish, (Rose: laughter) like at the point where you know you were saying, do you want to get— are you going to get a condom, at that point were you actually wanting to have sexual intercourse?

Rose: Um, mmm, that's good question. I can't remember the whole thing that clearly. And I seem to remember that I was getting um—I was just getting sick of it, or—[laughing] or—I might

have been, but my general impression was that it was quite a sort of fumble bumbled thing, and— and it was quite—he just didn't—he didn't have it together. He wasn't—he possibly would've been better if he was less drunk, but he was just sort of all over the place and um—and I was just thinking, you know, I want to get this over and done with. Which is not the [laughing] best way to go into—into that sort of thing and um—yeah I—I remember at points—just at points getting into it and then at other points it just being a real mess. Like he couldn't—he wasn't being very stimulating, he was trying to be and bungling it 'cause he was drunk. And being too rough and just too brutish, just yeah. And um—

Nicola: When you say he was trying to [laughing] be, what do you—

Rose: Ohh, he was just like you know, trying to use his hands and stuff and just it—it was just like a big fumble in the dark (Nicola: Right) type thing. I mean I'm sure h—I hope he's not usually that bad it was just like—I was in—sometimes— most of the time in fact I was just saying, look don't even bother. [laughing] You obviously haven't got it together to make it pleasurable. So in some ways—

Nicola: You—you said you were thinking that or you said that?

Rose: I just sort of—I did push his hand away and just say, look don't bother. Because—and I thought at that point that probably penetration would be, um more pleasurable, yeah. But— and then—yeah. And I think I was actually wanting to just go to sleep and I kept—I think I um mentioned that to him as well and said, you know why don't we—we're not that capable at the moment, why don't we leave it. But he wasn't keen on [laughing] that idea.

Nicola: What did he—is that from what he said, or just the fact that he didn't—

Rose: I think he just said, ohh no, no, no we can't do that. It was kind of like we had to put on this big passionate spurt but um it just seemed quite farcical, considering the state we were both in. And um, so I—yeah I thought if—yeah I thought it would probably be the best idea to [laughing] just get into it and like as I—as I presumed—ohh, actually I don't know what I expected, but he didn't last very long at all, which was quite a relief and he was quite—he was sort of a bit apologetic and like ohh you know, I shouldn't have come so soon. And I was just thinking, oh, now I can go to sleep. [laughing] Yes, so I just um—since then I've just been thinking, um one-night stands ahh don't seem to be the way to go. They don't seem to be much fun and [laughing] I'm not that keen on the idea of a relationship either at the moment. So I don't know. Who—I—it's hard to predict what's going to happen but—mmmm.

This unflattering picture of male heterosexual practice painted by Rose's account classically illustrates two of the dominant organizing principles of heterosexual sex—a male sex drive discourse and a coital imperative. The male sex drive discourse (see Hollway 1984, 1989) holds that men are perpetually interested in sex and that once they are sexually stimulated, they need to be satisfied by orgasm. Within the terms of this discourse, it would thus not be right or fair for a woman to stop sex before male orgasm (normatively through intercourse). This discursive construction of male sexuality thus privileges men's sexual needs above women's; the absence of a corresponding discourse of female desire (see Fine 1988) or drive serves to indirectly reinforce these dominant perceptions of male sexuality.

The extent to which male behavior, as patterned by the male sex drive discourse, can constrain a woman's attempts to insist on condom use are graphically demonstrated in Rose's account. The man she was with behaved with such a sense of sexual urgency and unstoppability that although she was able to successfully ensure a condom was used, it was only as a result of particularly determined and persistent efforts. He was unresponsive to her verbal requests and did not stop proceeding with intercourse until Rose became more directly confrontational—calling him "an arsehole" and physically pushing him off. At this point, he eventually did agree to wear a condom and did not use his physical strength to resist and overcome her actions to retain or take control of the situation. We will come back to analysis of Rose's account later in this article.

Another participant, Anita, who was in her mid-20s, described a very similar experience:

Anita: This one friend and I—I mean I got quite drunk, I have to say, and we had penetrative sex without a condom but then—no I think we—I—

think we had sex without a condom and then I stopped, and 'cause I was like, no no no, you have to use a condom.

Nicola: What you mean after he'd ejaculated you stopped, or—

Anita: No no no, it was just—(Nicola: You stopped) we did—and like he did put his penis inside me, (Nicola: Right) we were just sort of having sex and I suddenly thought he hasn't got a condom on, (Nicola: Right) [laughing] 'cause I was really pissed. So was he. And I made him stop, and he said, "Ohh no, it's all right, I trust you." And I was [laughing] just floored. Fuck you arrogant— what a nerve, and stopped, at that point.

Nicola: What you mean you—you sort of physically stopped him?

Anita: Yeah, I pushed him off (Nicola: Yeah yeah yeah) and said, "That's not—that's you know— that's not okay, I can't believe you said that." And, um, I think he had sex with a condom after that.

Rose and Anita did indeed act in "Trojan woman fashion" (Chapman and Hodgson 1988, 104), but their accounts demonstrate how this can be anything but straightforward to do. For both, acting assertively necessitated strong physical resistance and verbal censure. The literature on women's heterosexual experiences (e.g., Holland et al. 1998), as well as our own interviews for this study, strongly suggests that this will not be an attractive or possible option for many, or even most, women. Indeed, we would argue that advice to women that simply encourages them to be assertive is deeply problematic, not because it is undesirable for women to act with strength and experience real choices in their sexual relationships with men but because these kinds of mottos deny the complex interpersonal and subjective constraints on achieving this. As we will see in later sections, the kind of assertiveness shown by Rose and Anita requires enacting attributes and an identity not compatible with traditional embodiments of female sexuality and thus not readily accessible to some women. Moreover, these kinds of assertive actions not only could expose women to danger (such as physical retaliation from the man) but also may jeopardize her chances of continuing with that particular heterosexual encounter (and, possibly, relationship)—a choice that may be undesirable if not impossible for many women to make. Indeed, Rosenthal, Gifford, and Moore (1998) have argued that some women and men regard "casual sex as a strategy for obtaining the possibility of 'love'" and that the use of condoms at such times may be seen to risk romance and the promise of love.

Pleasing a Man

The male sex drive discourse constructs masculinity in ways that directly affect women's heterosexual experiences as evidenced in the above descriptions of Rose's and Anita's experiences. However, as we alluded to above, this discursive framework can also constitute women's sexual subjectivity in complex and more indirect ways. For example, for some women situated within this discursive framework, their ability to "please a man" may be a positive aspect of their identity. In this sense, a woman can be recruited into anticipating and meeting a man's "sexual needs" (as they are constituted in this discursive framework) as part of her ongoing construction of a particular kind of identity as a woman.

Sarah reported not liking condoms. She said she did not like the taste of them; she did not like the "hassle" of putting them on, taking them off, and disposing of them; and that they interfered with her sexual pleasure. However, it seemed that her reluctance to use them was also related to her sexual identity and her taken-for-granted assumptions about men's needs, desires, and expectations of her during sex. Sarah traced some of her attitudes toward sex to her upbringing and her mother's attitudes in which the male sex drive discourse was strongly ingrained.[1] She directly connected the fact that "when I've started, I never stop" to her difficulty in imagining asking a man to use a condom. As she said in an ironic tone,

> If a man gets a hard-on, you've gotta take care of it because he gets sick. You know these are the mores I was brought up with. So you can't upset his little precious little ego by asking to use a condom, or telling if he's not a good lover.

Sarah explained her own ambivalence toward this male sex drive discourse by drawing on a psychoanalytic distinction between the conscious and unconscious mind:

I mean I've hopefully done enough therapy to have moved away from that, but it's still in your bones. You know there's my conscious mind can say, that's a load of bullshit, but my unconscious mind is still powerful enough to drive me in some of these moments, I would imagine.

Thus, despite having a rational position from which she rejected the male sex drive discourse, Sarah found that when faced with a man who wanted to have sex with her, her embodied response would be to acquiesce irrespective of her own desire for sex. Her reference to this tendency being "in [her] bones" graphically illustrates how she regarded this as a fundamental influence. It is evocative of Judith Butler's suggestion "that discourses do actually live in bodies. They lodge in bodies, bodies in fact carry discourses as part of their own lifeblood" (Meijer and Prins 1998, 282). Sarah recalled an incident where her own desire for sex ceased immediately on seeing the man she was with undress, but she explained that she would not be prepared to stop things there:

Sarah: He's the hairiest guy I ever came across. I mean—but no way I would stop. I mean, as soon as he took his shirt off I just kind of about puked [laughing], but I ain't gonna say—I mean having gone to all these convolutions to get this thing to happen there's no way I'm gonna back down at that stage.
Nicola: So when he takes his shirt off he's just about the most hairiest guy you've ever met, which you find really unappealing.
Sarah: Terribly.
Nicola: Um, but you'd rather go through with it?
Sarah: Well I wouldn't say rather, but I do it.

Sarah also described another occasion where she met a man at a party who said, "Do you want to get together?" and I said, "Well, you know, I just want to cuddle," and he said, "Well, that's fine, okay." She explained that it was very important to her to make her position clear before doing anything. However, they ended up having sexual intercourse, because as she said,

Sarah: I was the one. I mean we cuddled, and then I was the one that carried it further.
Nicola: And what was the reason for that?
Sarah: As I said, partly 'cause I want to and partly 'cause if ohh he's got a hard-on you have to.

For women like Sarah, it seemed that an important part of their identity involved being a "good lover." This required having sexual intercourse to please a man whenever he wanted it and, in Sarah's case, to the point of anticipating this desire on the basis of an erect penis. She implied that among people who know her, she would have a reputation as a woman who had enjoyed sex with a lot of men, and thus she would subconsciously expect a man to think she was silly if she suggested using a condom—"Why make the fuss, you know." Given these expectations, and her belief that most men do not like condoms, it is not surprising that she had developed an almost fatalistic attitude toward her own risk of contracting HIV, such that she could say, "There's a part of me that also says, as long as I'm clear and not passing it on, I'm not gonna worry. You know, and if I get it, hey, it was meant to be."

For understanding the actions of Sarah and women like her, the assertiveness model is not at all helpful. In these kinds of sexual encounters, Sarah's lack or possession of assertiveness skills is beyond the point. What stops her from acting assertively to avoid undesired sex are deeply inscribed features of her own identity—characteristics that are not related to fear of assertion so much as the production of a particular kind of self. Well before she gets to the point of acting or not acting assertively, she is motivated by other (not sexual) desires, about what kind of woman she wants to *be*.

In a similar way to Sarah, an important part of Sally's identity was having "integrity about sexuality." She explained her position in relation to not "leading somebody on" in terms of a desire for honesty:

> And so—and I—that really was clinched somehow that you didn't lead somebody on and so that's part of—that's one of the sort of ways in which I understand that contract notion, really. And so maybe that had something to do with how I see myself about being a person with a reasonable—with integrity about sexuality. I won't go into something with false promises kind of thing.

Prior to these comments, Sally talked about the origins of her beliefs about this kind of contractual notion where it was not possible to be physically intimate with someone unless you were prepared to have intercourse. She remembered feeling awful about touching a man's penis when she was younger.

> I had been unfair because of the—I suppose the feeling of sort of cultural value of—of the belief that men somehow you know it's tormenting to them to leave a cock unappeased (N: [laughter]) [laughing] basically or something like that.

Like Sarah, Sally too reflected on her experiences in a way that highlights the limitations of attempting to influence sexual behavior based on understandings of people as unitary rational actors. Sally discussed a six-month relationship with a past lover in which she had not used condoms. She said that she had made the decision not to use condoms because she already had an intrauterine device (IUD) and because they were seen to connote a more temporary rather than long-lasting relationship (a view ironically reinforced by the advice of a nurse at the Family Planning Clinic):

Sally: It's like condoms are about more casual kinds of encounters or I mean—I mean, I'm kind of—um they are kind of anti-intimacy at some level.
Nicola: And so, if you'd used condoms with him, that would've meant—
Sally: Maybe it would have underscored its temporariness or its—yeah, its lack of permanence. I don't understand that. What I've just said really particularly. It doesn't [seem] very rational to me. [laughter]
Nicola: [laughter] No it's very rational and I—
Sally: [indistinguishable] it seems to be coming out of you know, somewhere quite deeper about um—I think it goes back to that business about ideals stuff. And I think that's one of the things about not saying no, you know. And that the ideal woman and lover—the ideal woman is a good lover and doesn't say no. Something like that. And it is incredibly counterproductive [softly] at my present time in life. [sigh/laugh]

Sally's reference to the ideal woman who is a good lover (because) she does not say no implicitly recognizes the strength of male sex drive discourse and its effect on her sexual experiences. In a construction that is similar to Sarah's, Sally refers to this kind of influence as "deeper" than her "rational" views. She presents an appreciation of this kind of cultural ideal as internalized in some way that is capable of having some control over her behavior despite her assessment of this as "counterproductive."

Engaging in Unwanted Sex

Many of the women in this study recounted experiences of having sex with men when they did not really want to, for a variety of reasons. This now common finding (e.g., Gavey 1992) underscores the extent to which women's control of sex with men is limited by various discursive constraints in addition to direct male pressure, force, or violence. As Bronwyn said, it is part of "the job":

Nicola: You said that you enjoy intercourse up to a point. Um, beyond that point, um, what are your reasons for continuing, given that you're not enjoying it?

Bronwyn: Ohh I just think it's part of my function if you like [laughter] that sounds terribly cold-blooded, but it is, [laughing] you know, it's part of the job.

Nicola: The job of—

Bronwyn: Being a wife. A partner or whatever.

Rose's account of her confrontational one-night stand, discussed previously, can be seen to be influenced in complex and subtle ways by the discursive construction of normative heterosexuality in which male sexuality and desire are supreme. She described the encounter as being quite unpleasant and disappointing, both sexually and in the way that he treated her—with respect to condoms and more generally throughout the experience. She described his actions during the encounter as clumsy and not the least bit sexually arousing ("He wasn't being very stimulating, he was trying to be and bungling it because he was drunk. And being too rough and just too brutish"), and at one stage she suggested that they give up and go to sleep, but he rejected this idea very strongly. Despite the extremely unsatisfactory nature of the sexual interaction and despite Rose's demonstrated skills of acting assertively, she did continue with the encounter until this man had had an orgasm through vaginal intercourse. It is difficult to understand why she would have done this without appreciating the power of the male sex drive discourse and the coital imperative in determining the nature of heterosexual encounters.

Although she did not define herself as a victim of the experience, Rose's account also makes clear that somehow she did not feel it was an option to end sex unless he gave the okay:

> It was sort of like—and I guess in that case he didn't have my utmost respect by that point. But it was sort of like, um, you know, he'd—he seemed to be just going for it, and I really really—I was drunk and sort of dishevelled and—and pretty resigned to having a bit of loose un—and unsatisfactory time which I didn't have a lot of control over.

She partially attributed this lack of control over the situation to the fact that the encounter took place at his flat, but this seems to be reinforced by underlying assumptions about sexuality and the primacy of his desires:

> Um, but it was kind of like he had his idea of what was going to happen and um I sort of realized after a while that he was so intent on it and the best thing to do was to just comply I guess, and make it as pleasurable as possible. Try and get into the same frame of mind that he was in. And—and yeah. Mmm, get it over with. It sounds really horrible in retrospect, it wasn't that bad it was just lousy, you know. It was just sort of a poor display of [laughing] everything. I suppose. Of intelligence and—and good manners. [laughter]

Part of the reason for the ambivalent nature of her account (swinging from describing what happened in very negative terms to playing down the experience as a poor display of manners) can be argued to originate from her positioning within a kind of liberal feminist discourse about sex. She had made a point of saying that she did not think things went in stages and defining herself in opposition to a model of female sexuality as fragile and in need of protection. The result of the connection between this liberal discourse of sexuality and that of the male sex drive is that she is left with no middle ground from which to negotiate within a situation of this kind. The absence of an alternative discourse of active female sexuality leaves her in a position of no return once she has consented to heterosexual relations and when certain minimal conditions are fulfilled (for her, this was the use of condoms). If heterosexuality were instead discursively constructed in such a way that women's sexual pleasure was central rather than optional, it makes sense that Rose may have felt able to call an end to this sex—which was, after all, so unpleasant that it led to her resolve to "devote [herself] to singledom for a while."

The Question of Pleasure

"I'm probably atypical from what I read of women in the fact that I personally don't like condoms." Sarah made this comment in the first minutes of the interview, and then much later she shared her assumption about how men regard using condoms: "Most men hate it. I've never asked them, but . . . that's the feeling I have from what I've read or heard." Sarah's generalized views about how women and men regard condoms echo dominant commonsense stories in Western culture. That is, most men do not like condoms—a view shared by 80.5 percent of women in one large U.S. sample (Valdiserri et al. 1989), while women do not mind them. To explain her own dislike of condoms, Sarah was forced to regard herself as atypical. In the following section, we will discuss evidence that challenges the tacit assumption that condoms are relatively unproblematic for women.

Enforcers of the Coital Imperative: Condoms as Prescriptions for Penetration

Research on how men and women define what constitutes "real sex" has repeatedly found that a coital imperative exists that places penis-vagina intercourse at the center of (hetero) sex (Gavey, McPhillips, and Braun 1999; Holland et al. 1998; McPhillips, Braun, and Gavey 2001). The strength of this imperative was also reflected in the current research—as one woman explained, "I don't think I worked out a model of being with someone like naked intimate touching which doesn't have sex at the end of it" (Sally defined sex as penis-vagina intercourse during the interview). Although this coital imperative could be viewed as forming part of the male sex drive discourse examined above, it is addressed separately here as it has particular consequences for safer sex possibilities.

Condoms seem to reinforce the coital imperative in two interconnected ways, both in terms of their symbolic reinforcement of the discursive construction of sex as *coitus* and through their material characteristics that contribute at a more practical level to rendering sex as finished after coitus. In the analyses that follow, we will be attending to the material characteristics of condoms as women describe them. As discussed earlier, we adopt a realist reading of women's accounts here. What the women told us about the ways in which condoms help to structure the material practice of heterosex casts a shadow over the assumption that condoms are unproblematic for women's sexual experience. These accounts illuminate how the male sexual drive discourse can shape not only the ways people speak about and experience heterosex but also the ways in which a research lens is focused on heterosexual practice to produce particular ways of seeing that perpetuate commonsense priorities and silences (which, in this case, privilege men's pleasure above women's). That is, the ways in which condoms can interfere with a woman's sexual pleasure are relatively invisible in the literature, which tends, at least implicitly, to equate "loss of sexual pleasure" with reduced sensation in the penis, or disruption of desire and pleasure caused by the act of putting a condom on. As the following excerpts show, the material qualities of condoms have other particular effects on the course of sex. These effects are especially relevant both to the question of a woman's pleasure and to the way in which the coital imperative remains unchallenged as the definitive aspect of heterosex.

While many of the women said they like (sometimes or always) and/or expect sexual intercourse (i.e., penis-vagina penetration) when having sex with a man, many of the women noted how condoms operated to enforce intercourse as the finale of sex. Several women found this to be a disadvantage of condoms, in that they tend to limit what is possible sexually, making sex more predictable, less spontaneous, playful, and varied. That is, once the condom is on, it is there for a reason and one reason only—penile penetration. It signals the beginning of "the end." Women who identified this disadvantage tended to be using condoms for contraceptive purposes and so were comparing sex that involved condoms unfavorably to intercourse with some less obtrusive form of contraception such as the pill or an IUD, or with no contraception during a "safe" time of the month.

For example, Julie found that condoms prescribed penetration at a point where she could be more flexible if no condom was involved:

> That's what I mean about the condom thing. It's like this is *the act* you know, and you have to go through the whole thing. Whereas if you don't use condoms, you know, like he could put it in me and then we could stop and then put it in again, you know, you can just be a bit more flexible about the whole thing.

The interconnection between the material characteristics of condoms (its semen-containing properties require "proper use") and the discursive construction of the encounter (coitus is spoken about as *"the act"*) has the effect of constraining a woman's sexual choices and leaving this generally unspoken coital imperative unchallenged. The discursive centrality of coitus within heterosex is materially reinforced by the practical difficulties associated with condoms, as Deborah said,

> Once you've put on the condom . . . that limits you. Once you've got to the stage in sex that you put a condom on, you then—it's not that you can't change plans, but it's a hassle if you then decided that you might like to move to do um—you might like to introduce oral sex at this stage, as opposed to that stage, then you have to take it off, or you don't, or—

Similarly, Rose said,

> Well that's the one problem, I suppose with condoms, is that you've already had penetrative sex with one and you either decide to um stop that and go onto something else, or you've finished and maybe you want to start again later, is that, you know, it's got that—you can't have oral sex because of that horrible taste. Or you can, but it really—it really does taste quite yucky.

And Suzanne, commenting about the unpleasant smell and taste of condoms, said, "And so like once it's on you're sort of committed to penetration, in a way. Um, as you sex."

Thus, condoms not only signaled when penetration would take place, but their use served to reinforce the taken-for-granted axiom of heterosexual practice, that coitus is the main sexual act. Furthermore, one woman (Sally) described how the need for a man to withdraw his penis soon after ejaculation when using a condom disrupted the postcoital "close feeling" she enjoyed. These excerpts can be seen to represent a form of resistance to the teleological assumptions of the coital imperative; women's accounts of desiring different forms of sexual pleasure (including, but by no means limited to, emotional pleasures) may provide rich ground for exploring safer sex options. This potentially productive area has yet to be fully exploited by traditional health campaigns, which perhaps reflects the lack of acknowledgment given to discourses of female sexual desire and pleasure in Western culture in general (see also Fine 1988).

Some women also talked about the effect using condoms had on their sexual pleasure by using the language of interruption and "passion killing" more commonly associated with men. Sarah, who rarely used condoms, said that "it breaks the flow":

> I have a lot of trouble reaching an orgasm anyway, and it's probably one of the reasons I don't like something that's interrupting, because I do go off the boil very quickly. Um, once it's on and it's sort of decided that penetration tends to be what happens. I don't suppose it's a gold rule, but it seems to be the way it is. So you know there's no more warm-up.

Unlike health campaigns directed at the gay community, which have emphasized the range of possible sex acts carrying far less risk of HIV infection than penile penetration, campaigns aimed at heterosexuals have done little to challenge the dominant coital imperative. Health campaigns that promote condoms as the only route to safer sex implicitly reinforce this constitution of heterosexuality and the dominance of the male sex drive discourse. As the responses of the women in this study demonstrate, this reluctance to explore other safer sex possibilities may be a missed opportunity for increasing erotic possibilities for women at the same time as increasing opportunities for safer sex. The fact that all of these women spent some time talking about the ways in which condoms can operate to enforce the coital imperative or reduce their desire indicates the importance of taking women's pleasure into account when designing effective safer sex programs. That is, it may simply not be valid to assume that "the disadvantages of condom use are fewer for girls" (Barling and Moore 1990) if we expect women's sexual desires and pleasures to be taken as seriously as men's. Special effort may be required to ask different questions to understand women's experiences in a way that doesn't uncritically accept a vision of heterosex as inherently constrained through the lens of the coital imperative and male sex drive discourses.

Discussion

Research on sexual coercion has shown that women may have limited control over the outcome of (hetero) sex even in the absence of direct force or violence from their male partners (Gavey 1992). Discourses of normative heterosexuality, such as those discussed in this article, play an important role in maintaining power dynamics between men and women. In the context of safer sex, the same cultural scripts that serve to legitimize various levels of coercion also limit the ways in which women may control the course and outcomes of heterosexual encounters. As the accounts of the women in this research show, power is infused in discursive constructions of normative heterosexuality, organized around a male sex drive discourse and a coital imperative, in ways that limit women's control and safer sex options. Anecdotal reports suggest that some women have been beaten and raped because they have tried to negotiate safer sex (Read 1990). In the absence of direct force, however, identities can be discursively produced in ways that render us particular kinds of subjects (e.g., "good lovers"), for whom desires associated with being this kind of person can override any desire for condom use (where that would be incompatible with this particular type of personhood). The question of a woman being assertive, then, to ensure that her partner wears a condom, will not even arise if her own desire for a condom to be worn is exceeded by these other kinds of desires. More simply, the strong ethic of individualism that is reified within the concept of assertiveness (Crawford 1995) arguably runs counter to dominant constructions of femininity. Moreover, contemporary ideals of reciprocity (see Gilfoyle, Wilson, and Brown 1992), mutuality, sharing, and giving arguably render the whole notion of assertiveness a delicate achievement within the context of sexual relatedness (especially without recourse to an analysis of gendered power).

Achieving condom use is not a challenge of immense proportions for all women, however. Some of the women in this study demonstrated that they had embraced sentiments like the "If it's not on, it's not on" slogan as their own in ways that were strong and positive. Both Rose and Anita, for example, recalled situations in which they described themselves as being very "drunk," but it was nevertheless a high priority for them not to have sexual intercourse in such circumstances without a condom. These two women were seemingly able to act in these ways with relative ease; they were clear that they wanted the men to use condoms, they were clear about their rights to insist on this, they were clear they did not like what was happening, and they were apparently unafraid of acting physically and verbally to change this. The ability of these women to act from a position of strength and determination is perhaps cause for optimism about the discursive possibilities available to women. However, for a range of complex reasons, this sort of action is not easy for all women in all circumstances (Gavey 1992; Holland et al. 1998). Rose's and Anita's accounts also highlight both the limits and the possible consequences of enacting resistance to dominant constructions of heterosexuality. On one hand, their physical responses toward the men placed them in a position outside traditional notions of femininity, and their actions may have jeopardized future relations with their male partners. On the other hand, while the men they were with acted in ways that dramatically reduced their appeal, neither woman at that stage extricated herself from the ongoing sexual encounter. Less optimistically, then, it is perhaps only when casual sex is characterized by neither emotional nor physical pleasures that the conditions lend themselves to women asserting condom use. It is striking, for example, that the specter of romance is not particularly evident in the alcohol-facilitated one-night stands Rose and Anita described. As Warr (2001) and others have argued, romance can provide a context in which "even the self-interest of physical pleasure is often irrelevant" (243) to the attainment of other kinds of pleasures associated with love or "emotional intimacy and warmth" (243) and where "sex is figurative for an exchange of self" (242) in ways that contradict thinking about sex in terms of health risk (see also Rosenthal, Gifford, and Moore 1998).

Holland et al. (1998) have argued that heterosexual relations as they stand are premised on a construction of femininity that endangers women. Evidence for this position can be drawn from the current study as the interaction of discourses determining normative heterosexuality produces situations in which women are unable to always ensure their safety during sexual encounters. Holland et al. (1998) have argued that a refiguring of femininity is needed to ensure that women have a greater chance of safer heterosexual encounters. One of the prerequisites for change of this kind would be acknowledgment of the discourses of active female desire, which have traditionally been repressed (Fine 1988). Indeed, our research here suggests that the claim that condoms are "relatively unproblematic" for women is based on a continued relegation of the importance of women's sexual pleasure, relative to men's. Without challenging the gendered nature of dominant representations of desire, and more critically examining the coital imperative, condom promotion to women is likely to remain a double-edged practice. As both a manifestation and a reinforcement of normative forms of heterosex, it may be of limited efficacy in promoting safer heterosex.

Author's note: We gratefully acknowledge the women we interviewed for this study. We thank members of the University of Auckland Psychology Discourse Research Unit (Alison Towns, Fiona Cram, Kate Paulin, Peter Adams, Ray Naim, and Tim McCreanor) for critical feedback on an earlier draft of this article, Maree Burns for research assistance support, and our friend (nameless, to protect participants' anonymity) for help with recruiting participants. We also thank Christine Bose and two anonymous reviewers for helpful comments on the article. This research was supported, in part, by grants from the Health Research Council of New Zealand, the University of Auckland Research Committee, and by the Department of Psychology Summer Research Assistantship Programme.

NOTES

1. It should be emphasized that Sarah's mother's attitudes would have been in line with contemporary thought at the time. Take, for example, the advice of "A Famous Doctor's Frank, New, Step-by-Step Guide to Sexual Joy and Fulfilment for Married Couples" (on front cover of Eichenlaub 1961, 36), published when Sarah was nearly an adolescent:

Availability: If you want good sex adjustment as a couple, you must have sexual relations approximately as often as the man requires. This does not mean that you have to jump into bed if he gets the urge in the middle of supper or when you are dressing for a big party. But it does mean that a woman should never turn down her husband on appropriate occasions simply because she has no yearning of her own for sex or because she is tired or sleepy, or indeed for any reason short of a genuine disability. (Eichenlaub 1961, 36)

REFERENCES

Barling, N. R., and S. A. Moore. 1990. Adolescents' attitudes towards AIDS precautions and intention to use condoms. *Psychological Reports* 67:883–90.

Chapman, S., and J. Hodgson. 1998. Showers in raincoats: Attitudinal barriers to condom-use in high-risk heterosexuals. *Community Health Studies* 12:97–105.

Crawford, M. 1995. *Talking difference: On gender and language.* London: Sage.

Eichenlaub, J. E. 1961. *The marriage art.* London: Mayflower.

Family Planning Association. 2000. *Condoms* [Pamphlet]. Auckland, New Zealand: Family Planning Association. (Written and produced in 1999. Updated 2000.)

Fine, M. 1988. Sexuality, schooling, and adolescent families: The missing discourse of desire. *Harvard Educational Review,* 58:29–53.

Gavey, N. 1992. Technologies and effects of heterosexual coercion. *Feminism & Psychology* 2:325–51.

Gavey, N., K. McPhillips, and V. Braun. 1999. Interruptus coitus: Heterosexuals accounting for intercourse. *Sexualities* 2:37–71.

Gilfoyle, J., J. Wilson, and Brown. 1992. Sex, organs, and audiotape: A discourse analytic approach to talking about heterosexual sex and relationships. *Feminism & Psychology* 2:209–30.

Holland, J., C. Ramazonaglu, S. Scott, S. Sharpe, and R. Thomson. 1991. Between embarrassment and trust: Young women and the diversity of condom use. In *AIDS: Responses, interventions, and care,* edited by P. Aggleton, G. Hart, and P. Davies. London: Falmer.

Holland, J., C. Ramazonaglu, S. Sharpe, and R. Thomson. 1998. *The male in the head: Young people, heterosexuality and power.* London: The Tufnell.

Hollway, W. 1984. Gender difference and the production of subjectivity. In *Changing the subject: Psychology, social regulation and subjectivity,* edited by J. Henriques, W. Hollway, C. Urwin, and V. Walkerdine. London: Methuen.

———. 1989. *Subjectivity and method in Psychology: Gender, meaning, and science.* London: Sage.

Kippax, S. J. Crawford, C. Waldby, and P. Benton. 1990. Women negotiating heterosex: Implications for AIDS prevention. *Women's Studies International Forum* 13:533–42.

McPhillips, K., V. Braun, and N. Gavey. 2001. Defining heterosex: How imperative is the "coital imperative"?
Women's Studies International Forum 24:229–40.

Meijer, I. C., and B. Prins. 1998. How bodies come to matter: An interview with Judith Butler, *Signs: Journal of
Women in Culture and Society* 23:275–86.

Planned Parenthood Federation of America, Inc. 1998–2001.
Condoms. Retrieved 18 June 2001 from the World Wide
Web: http//www.plannedparenthood.org.

Read, V. 1990. Women and AIDS. *Australian Nurses Journal*
20:22–24.

Rosenthal, D., S. Gifford, and S. Moore. 1998. Safe sex or
safe love: Competing discourses? *AIDS Care* 10:35–47.

Sack, F. 1992. *Romance to die for: The startling truth about
women, sex and AIDS.* Deerfield Beach, FL: Health
Communications.

Statistics New Zealand. 2001. *Statistics and information about
New Zealand.* Retrieved 4 July 2001 from the World
Wide Web: http//www.stats.govt.nz/default.htm.

Valdiserri, R. O., V. C. Arena, D. Proctor, and F. A. Bonati.
1989. The relationship between women's attitudes
about condoms and their use: Implications for condom
promotion programs. *American Journal of Public Health*
79:499–501.

Warr, D. J. 2001. The importance of love and understanding: Speculation on romance in safe sex health
promotion. *Women's Studies International Forum*
24:241–52.

Willig, D. 1995. "I wouldn't have married the guy if I'd
have to do that." Heterosexual adults' accounts of
condom use and their implications for sexual practice. *Journal of Community and Applied Social Psychology* 5:75–87.

Worth, D. 1989. Sexual decision-making and AIDS: Why
condom promotion among vulnerable women is likely
to fail. *Studies in Family Planning* 20:297–307.

◆◆◆

The All-American Queer Pakistani Girl (1997)

Surina A. Khan

Surina Khan was born in Pakistan and came to the
United States as a child. A writer, researcher, and advocate, she served as Executive Director of the International Gay and Lesbian Human Rights Commission
for several years. Currently, Ms. Khan is Director of
Programs at the Women's Foundation of California
and serves on boards and advisory committees of
nonprofit organizations working on gender, LGBT,
and human rights issues.

I don't know if my grandmother is dead or alive. I
can't remember the last time I saw her—it must
have been at least ten years ago, when I was in Pakistan for a visit. She was my only living grandparent, and her health was beginning to fail. Every
once in a while, I think she's probably dead and no
one bothered to tell me.

I'm completely out of touch with my Pakistani
life. I can hardly speak Urdu, my first language; I certainly can't read or write it. I have no idea how many
cousins I have. I know my father comes from a large
family—eleven brothers and sisters—but I don't
know all their names. I've never read the Koran, and
I don't have faith in Islam.

As a kid, I remember being constantly reminded
that I was different—by my accent, my brown skin
color, my mother's traditional clothing, and the smell
of the food we ate. And so I consciously American-
ized myself. I spent my early childhood perfecting
my American accent, my adolescence affirming my
American identity to others, and my late teens rejecting my Pakistani heritage. Now, at the age of twenty-
seven, I'm feeling the void I created for myself.

Sometimes I think of what my life would be like
if my parents hadn't moved to Connecticut in 1973,
when I was five. Most of my family has since
moved back to Pakistan, and up until seven years
ago, when I came out, I went back somewhat regularly. But I never liked going back. It made me feel
stifled, constrained. People were always talking
about getting married. First it was, "You're almost
old enough to start thinking about finding a nice
husband," then, "When are you getting married?"
Now I imagine they'd say, with disappointment,
"You'll be an old maid."

My family is more liberal than most of Pakistani society. By American standards that translates into conservative (my mother raised money for George Bush). But I was brought up in a family that valued education, independence, integrity, and love. I never had to worry about getting pressured into an arranged marriage, even though several of my first cousins were—sometimes to each other. Once I went to a wedding in which the bride and groom saw each other for the first time when someone passed them a mirror after their wedding ceremony and they both looked into it at once. That's when I started thinking my family was "modern."

Unfortunately they live in a fundamentalist culture that won't tolerate me. I can't even bring myself to visit Pakistan. The last time I went back was seven years ago, for my father's funeral, and sometimes I wonder if the next time will be for my mother's funeral. She asks me to come visit every time I talk to her. I used to tell her I was too busy, that I couldn't get away. But three years ago I finally answered her truthfully. I told her that I didn't like the idea of traveling to a country that lashed lesbians one hundred times in public. More important, I didn't feel comfortable visiting when she and I had not talked about anything important in my life since I had come out to her.

Pakistan has always been my parents' answer to everything. When they found out my sisters were smoking pot in the late 1970s, they shipped all of us back. "You need to get in touch with the Pakistani culture," my mother would say. When my oldest sister got hooked on transcendental meditation and started walking around the house in a trance, my father packed her up and put her on a plane back to the homeland. She's been there ever since. Being the youngest of six, I wised up quickly. I waited to drop my bomb until after I had moved out of the house and was financially independent. If I had come out while I was still living in my parents' home, you can bet I'd have been on the next flight to Islamabad.

When I came out to my mother, she suggested I go back to Pakistan for a few months. "Just get away from it all," she begged. "You need some time. Clear your head." But I knew better. And when I insisted that I was queer and was going to move to Washington, D.C., to live with my girlfriend, Robin (now my ex-girlfriend, much to my mother's delight), she tried another scare tactic: "You and your lover better watch out. There's a large Pakistani community in D.C., and they'll find out about you. They'll break your legs, mutilate your face." That pretty much did it for me. My mother had just validated all my fears associated with Pakistan. I cut all ties with the community, including my family. *Pakistan* became synonymous with *homophobia.*

My mother disowned me when I didn't heed her advice. But a year later, when Robin and I broke up, my mother came back into my life. It was partly motivated by wishful thinking on her part. I do give her credit, though, not only for nurturing the strength in me to live by my convictions with integrity and honesty but also for eventually trying to understand me. I'll never forget the day I took her to see a lawyer friend of mine. She was on the verge of settling a lawsuit started by my father before he died and was unhappy with her lawyer. I took her to see Maggie Cassella, a lawyer/comedian based in Hartford, Connecticut, where I was again living. "I presume this woman's a lesbian," my mother said in the car on the way to Maggie's office. "Yes, she is," I replied, thinking, *Oh, no, here it comes again.* But my mother took me by surprise. "Well, the men aren't helping me; I might as well go to the dykes." I didn't think she even knew the word *dyke.* Now, *that* was a moment.

Her changing attitude about my lesbian identity was instilling in me a desire to reclaim my Pakistani identity. The best way to do this, I decided, would be to seek out other Pakistani lesbians. I barely knew any Pakistanis aside from my family, and I sure as hell didn't know, or even know of, any Pakistani lesbians. I was just naive enough to think I was the only one.

It wasn't easy for me even to arrive at the concept of a Pakistani lesbian. Having rejected my culture from a young age, I identified only as a lesbian when I came out, and in my zeal to be all-American, I threw myself into the American queer liberation movement. I did not realize that there is an active South Asian gay and lesbian community in the United States— and that many of us are here precisely because we're able to be queer and out in the Western world.

South Asian culture is rampant with homophobia—so much so that most people in South Asia literally don't have words for homosexuality, which is viewed as a Western phenomenon despite the fact that images of gays and lesbians have been a part of the subcontinent's history for thousands of years. In the temples of Khajuraho and Konarak in India, there are images of same-gender couples—male and female—in intimate positions. One temple carving depicts two women caressing each other, while another shows four women engaged in sexual play. There are also references to homosexuality in the *Kāma-sūtra*, the ancient Indian text on the diversities of sex. Babar, the founder of the Mughal dynasty in India, is said to have been gay, as was Abu Nawas, a famous Islamic poet. The fact is that homosexuality is as native to South Asia as is heterosexuality. But since the culture pressures South Asian women to reject our sexual identity, many South Asian queers living in the

United States reject South Asian culture in turn. As a result, we are often isolated from one another.

Despite the odds, I started my search for queer people from South Asia—and I found them, all across America, Canada, and England. Connecting with this network and talking with other queer South Asians has begun to fill the void I've been feeling. But just as it took me years to reject my Pakistani heritage, it will likely take me as long, if not longer, to reintegrate my culture into my life as it is now.

I'm not ready to go back to Pakistan. But I am ready to start examining the hostility I feel toward a part of myself I thought I had discarded long ago.

◆◆◆

Popular Culture and Queer Representation (2003)
A Critical Perspective
Diane Raymond

Diane Raymond is Professor of Philosophy and Women's Studies and Dean of the College of Arts and Sciences at Simmons College. Her teaching, research, and writing focus on feminist theory, critical race theory, and applied ethics and cultural studies, and include *Sexual Politics and Popular Culture* and *Looking at Gay and Lesbian Life* (co-author).

"Queer" is a category in flux. Once a term of homophobic abuse, recently the term has been reappropriated as a marker for some gay, lesbian, bisexual, transgender (glbt), and other marginalized sexual identities. In addition, "queer theory" has emerged in academic scholarship to identify a body of knowledge connected to but not identical with lesbian/gay studies. The term is itself open-ended, and its advocates argue that its fluidity is to be embraced rather than "fixed." Though there is no consensus on the term's meaning (and who is included and who excluded), there is general agreement that the "queer" is politically radical, rejects binary categories (like heterosexual/homosexual), embraces more fluid categories, and tends to be "universalizing" rather than "minoritizing," to use

literary theorist Eve Kosofsky Sedgwick's (1990) distinction. That is, queer theory reads queerness throughout the culture and not simply as a fixed, clearly demarcated category. . . .

Queer theory emerged as one of the many oppositional discourses of the 1960s and 1970s, including postcolonial, feminist, and multicultural theory. . . . Regardless of their specific differences, these marginalized views sought to move the "margins" to the "center": "This way of seeing affirmed otherness and difference, and the importance of attending to marginalized, minority, and oppositional groups and voices previously excluded from the cultural dialogue" (Kellner, 1995, p. 24). In addition, these theoretical perspectives tended . . . to reject any strict dichotomy between high and low culture and to reject any vision of popular culture that constructed it as monolithic and viewers as passive dupes. The relationship between viewers and cultural artifacts, including popular media, was, according to these postmodern views, more complex, culturally mediated, and open to a mix of possible "readings."

I want to look at three recurring patterns or tropes that I have identified in situation comedies. The first pattern—the increased appearance of glbt major or supporting characters—acknowledges the very real changes that have occurred in the constitution of the characters populating television's worlds. The remaining two tropes—that of the "gay pretender" and that of the "straight-mistaken-for-gay"—have less to do with the actual diversity of characters we see and more with how gayness itself is understood and metaphorized. All three offer the potential for subverting heterosexist norms and assumptions. I shall argue, however, that how these shows resolve tensions often results in a "reinscription" of heterosexuality and a "containment" of queer sexuality, that is, that the resolution these programs offer enables viewers to distance themselves from the queer and thereby to return to their comfortable positions as part of the dominant culture. Such a dynamic enables power to mask itself, making it all the harder to pin down and question. Thus, . . . my approach suggests how what might seem to be "queer" can come to be normalized in mainstream culture. . . .

I must insist here that my conclusions can be tentative at best and are meant to suggest more complex ways of reading rather than determinative readings themselves. . . . Further, given the truism that no social group is homogeneous and that even a single individual occupies multiple subject positions, I in no way mean to imply that my readings here are "queer," generalizable to any particular group or sort of person, or noncontroversial. To put the point more simply, there is no "correct" queer reading, no one queer reading, and no unchanging queer perspective. . . .

Despite the occasional mention of a drama, my focus here is on comedy, the arena where images of glbt people appear most frequently. To attempt to explain in any persuasive way why such is the case would take me far from my topic. But I might briefly conjecture two possible explanations. First, as traditional family comedies—along with the traditional family—began to disappear, space opened up for "alternative" sorts of narratives, including those of nontraditional "families." . . . For example, the oldest son in *Party of Five* becomes a surrogate father *and* mother to his younger siblings; married characters on popular shows like *Mary Tyler Moore* get divorced; in some cases married characters are never seen with their spouses; and holidays like Thanksgiving, traditionally

constructed as times for "family," get reconstructed on shows like *Friends*. These shifts in roles and viewer expectations clearly allowed for the appearance of nonheterosexual characters in major and supporting roles; cultural shifts linked to an increasingly visible gay and lesbian movement no doubt helped to buttress such changes. Finally, situation comedies—however "realistic" they might be—do not claim, like dramas, to be offering us "real life." That lack of seriousness may allow these programs to play with themes under cover of humor where those themes might be too volatile or even too didactic for another sort of audience. Such play and flexibility may also help to account for what may be a wider variety of possible readings. . . .

The Queering of Television

Until very recently, it was not unusual for glbt activists and scholars to bemoan their virtual absence in popular media, particularly television. For example, in 1995, Larry Gross used the term "symbolic annihilation" (p. 62) to describe the invisibility of gays and lesbians in mass media. . . .

Media critics pointed out that those rare depictions of glbt people tended both to dichotomize anyone glbt as victim or villain and to reinforce demeaning stereotypes and caricatures: gay men as effeminate and lesbians as unattractive man-haters, for example. According to Gross (1995), "Hardly ever shown in the media are just plain gay folks, used in roles which do not center on their deviance as a threat to the moral order which must be countered through ridicule or physical violence" (p. 65). . . .

Today's even casual television viewers, however, would find such critiques oddly out-of-date. Network programs are now full of gay/queer characters. . . . Forty-two million people watched the coming-out episode on *Ellen* on April 30, 1997, making it the highest-ranked show on television that year except for the Academy Awards. Though some argue that Ellen DeGeneres's sexuality led to the cancellation of her show in 1998, the queering of prime-time television since that time is without dispute.[1]

A . . . *Boston Globe* article notes there are at least two dozen gay television characters scattered throughout prime-time shows (Rothaus, 2000). Where once soap operas floated gay characters only to have them die of AIDS or leave town mysteriously, *All My Children* has introduced a new plot line in which a character who has grown up on the show comes out as a lesbian. According to the actress who plays the character, the story-line—about how an almost obsessively heterosexual mother deals with her daughter's lesbianism—is meant to be "accessible to everyone" (Rothaus, 2000) and, . . . makes a "concerted effort to show that a gay relationship is just like any other" (Rothaus, 2000). *Will and Grace,* two of whose four major characters are openly gay, is one of the most popular shows on television. Indeed, one might argue that television is light years ahead of mainstream film, whose "gay" characters still seem to be confined to psychopathic murderers (e.g., *Basic Instinct, The Talented Mr. Ripley, Silence of the Lambs, Braveheart, JFK, American Beauty,* etc.) or lonely, asexual best friends (e.g., *Silkwood, As Good as It Gets,* etc.);[2] for the most part, one needs to turn to independent films to see the "just plain gay folks" Gross seeks.

. . . Given that the majority viewing audience is heterosexual, programming sympathetic to glbt communities must appeal to mainstream liberal viewers who today most likely know someone gay in the workplace, the family, or among friends. Thus, where once glbt viewers had to resort to oppositional or subversive readings . . . —are Cagney and Lacey really lovers? Can one find a queer resonance in the films of Rock Hudson? and so forth—such readings seem quaint and tame by today's television standards when gayness is much discussed, gay sexual practices are the subject of comedic banter, and a range of appealing characters are openly gay or lesbian.

Albeit somewhat one-dimensional, these gay or lesbian television characters are attractive and professional—Will Truman is a lawyer, and the lesbians on *Friends* and the now-defunct but highly popular *Mad About You* are doctors, accountants, and mothers. They include younger characters—*Buffy the Vampire Slayer* has featured two teenaged girls in a budding lesbian relationship, and *Dawson's Creek* featured a main character's coming out in its story line. They are occasionally people of color—*Spin City* includes an African American gay man as part of the political team. Viewers have seen lesbian weddings, lesbian and gay parenting arrangements, gay therapists, gay seniors, and the angst

and humor of coming out. Such "main-streaming" seems likely to change popular perceptions and misperceptions about homosexuality. As Mohr (1997) points out, "Without demonization, it is hard, perhaps impossible, to conceptualize homosexuality as a vampire-like corruptive contagion, a disease that spreads itself to the pure and innocent by mere proximity" (p. 333).

Though there is no question that the majority of the viewing audience for these shows is heterosexual, these portrayals engage with viewers who see themselves as hip, nonjudgmental, mostly urban, and gay-friendly. *Will and Grace* is full of campy in-jokes (many referring back to popular culture itself) and sexual innuendo, and as viewers we are asked to feel superior to Jack's mother who fails to realize that he is gay. *Saturday Night Live* pokes fun at a Batman-and-Robin-like team of superheroes, the Ambiguously Gay Duo, in animated sketches full of phallic imagery and less-than-subtle references to anal intercourse. Smithers is clearly smitten with (and even has erotic dreams about) Mr. Burns in *The Simpsons,* and in one episode gay director John Waters is the voice of an antique dealer Homer idolizes until he discovers that the dealer is gay. We are amused that Jaimie's impossible-to-please mother-in-law in *Mad About You* prefers her lesbian daughter's lover to Jaimie. The stars of *Xena* discuss without defensiveness in mainstream periodicals the "lesbian subtext" of that long-running series. It is now homophobes, not gays and lesbians, who are vilified or ignored, and often the test of a character (e.g., the gay plotline in *Dawson's Creek*) comes down to how well he or she deals with a friend or family member's coming out.

This "queering" of television goes well beyond the presence of glbt characters. A . . . *New York Times* article references the growing number of gay television writers who are influencing shows even where there are no gay characters. The article suggests that "a gay sensibility has infiltrated American comedy, even when flying beneath the radar in an ostensibly heterosexual situation" (Kirby, 2001, p. 23). This phenomenon . . . allows for multiple readings of a character or situation, those readings dependent on the subject position of the viewer. Thus, *Frasier's* two brothers, but for the fact that they sleep with women, are stereotypically gay in their tastes and preferences; knowing more about Puccini than basketball, these brothers evidence a gay sensibility striking to all but the most naïve. Indeed, much of the humor emerges from their macho-cop father's vain attempts to make his sons more "butch." Further, Niles and Frasier's shared memories of the childhood trauma they experienced as a result of being fussy, intelligent, artistic, and averse to athletics resonate with the experiences of many glbt people who did not as youths conform to the dominant culture's gender codes.

These more subtle gestures may, as Danae Clark (1993) suggests in her discussion of advertising campaigns, serve a dual function: They avoid alienating gay audiences at the same time that they mask the gay content and retain majority viewers. Finally, in a number of cases, actors playing heterosexual characters are known to viewing audiences to be gay, lesbian, or bisexual. For example, David Hyde Pierce, who plays Frasier's brother Niles Crane, is openly gay; knowledgeable viewers, then, can play with multiple levels of reading performances such as Pierce's, even where the ostensible plot line involves, for example, his long-term obsession with Daphne, his father's live-in physical therapist. . . .

Though cultural studies critics have tended to look for so-called subversive moments in television and film as opportunities for resistant readings, my approach here adopts a different orientation to suggest how moments of apparently subversive potential are undermined and ultimately contained. . . .

Queering Theory and Representation

Ideology . . . constructs viewing positions and identities. Sexuality, at least in modern times, is one component of that ideology, a component whose regulation occurs both formally and informally. In a culture grounded in what Adrienne Rich (1980) has termed "compulsory heterosexuality," popular culture will tend to portray heterosexuality as if it were natural and inevitable and to position alternative forms of sexuality as "other." Compulsory heterosexuality (or what some have called "heteronormativity") functions to underline the fact that heterosexuality is an institution, a practice, with its own set of expectations, norms, and principles of conduct. If, however, heterosexuality is not a naturalized, innate state of being, then its existence is more fragile than is obvious at first glance. Given that fragility, heterosexuality cannot be taken as a given or presumed; in a culture framed by homophobia and heterosexism,

institutions both formal and informal—police behavior, boundaries, expectations, and values—a dynamic blend of incentives and disincentives function to channel desire in "appropriate" ways and to make invisible those practices falling outside its discursive domain.

Heterosexuality and homophobia organize the structures in which we are immersed, structures so pervasive as to become almost invisible. Sociologist Pierre Bourdieu (1990) has employed the notion of *habitus* to describe how what is constructed can come to seem inevitable and natural. Like the fish that does not feel the weight of the water, human beings live in a world of "social games embodied and turned into second nature" (p. 63). . . .

The mechanisms that serve to construct and regulate sexuality may not be obvious or even intentional; indeed, as Foucault (1990) puts it, "Power is tolerable only on condition that it mask a substantial part of itself. Its success is proportional to its ability to hide its own mechanisms" (p. 86). If ideology generally effaces itself, then even the very producers of popular culture—whatever their explicit political leanings, sexuality, or agenda—are immersed in that ideology. Further, power's ability to mask itself may mean that, ironically, the mechanisms of power produce pleasure. We don't have to go far to find such examples—Gothic romances, pornography, certain clothing styles, exercise regimens, gendered toys for children, and so forth—all function to produce pleasure as they disguise the ways that they reinforce norms relating to sexuality and, less obviously, race, age, and class. The question becomes, then, not whether queer (or straight) viewers find pleasure in the proliferation of these television images . . . but rather how one might read and understand such pleasure. Pleasure itself is never innocent or neutral and there is a danger in valorizing pleasure without looking at its context. Given that, I want to ask how the new representations of gays and lesbians circulate in culture.

If the homo/hetero schema is "written into the cultural organization of Western societies" (Epstein, 1987, p. 133), then the question of the homosexual/heterosexual matrix rather than the question of personal identity becomes primary. Such a perspective would suggest that what is at stake is less the question how many gay/queer characters populate television or even how sympathetically they are portrayed but rather about the ways desire and meaning are structured, even in the absence of such images. Thus, identity must be thought of as always in relation, never fixed or stable. As Fuss, Sedgwick, Butler, and others have noted, heterosexuality is a parasitic notion, dependent on that-what-it-is-not, namely, homosexuality. "Each is haunted by the other" (Fuss, 1991, p. 4), and the homosexual comes to represent the "terrifying [sexual] other" of the heterosexual. Yet popular television programming seems to belie this theoretical claim, bombarding us with images of gayness and far less threatening homosexuals who suggest the possibility of new normative understandings of sexual difference.

First, one should note that the appearance of *difference* per se is not necessarily subversive. . . . That heterosexuals now can, like tourists, visit glbt culture does not in itself guarantee social change. Further, capitalist systems need difference to create desire and to sell commodities. Kellner (1995) notes:

> Difference sells. Capitalism must constantly multiply markets, styles, fads, and artifacts to keep absorbing consumers into its practices and lifestyles. The mere valorization of "difference" as a mark of opposition can simply help market new styles and artifacts if the difference in question and its effects are not adequately appraised.   *(p. 40)*

[If] Stuart and Elizabeth Ewen (1992) are right that "novelty and disposability make up the backbone of the market" (p. 193), then the static is the enemy of popular media. Difference can also serve to provide one with a sense of uniqueness or individuality. As Jonathan Rutherford has quipped, "It's no longer about keeping up with the Joneses, it's about being different from them" (quoted in hooks, 1995, p. 157). Further, the promotion of gayness as a "lifestyle" tends to attach it to commodities rather than practices as an expression of the self. *Will and Grace*'s bitchy attention to fashion, weight, career, and popular media is exemplary in this respect.

In addition, Torres (1993) points to the ways visits from "real lesbians" may help to deflect the viewer's attention from the possibility that ongoing characters may harbor same-sex feelings. Especially in shows that feature all, or mostly, female troupes like *Kate and Allie*, *Designing Women*, *Cagney and Lacey*, and *Golden Girls*, for example, the introduction of lesbian and gay

characters may serve to reassure viewers that the same-sex groupings are purely platonic. Cultural unease with lesbianism may be tied to cultural unease with feminism, but it may also emerge from lesbianism's own murky boundaries. Obviously, my case would be much easier to make if these characters reflected negative or insulting stereotypes; yet, I have already suggested that the characters we see exhibit a range of personality types, interests, values, and flaws. But I want to look more closely for a moment at a dynamic in *Will and Grace* that may help to clarify how the subversive potential in these images is ultimately policed and contained.

It's Not Just the Numbers . . .

The dynamic I want to explore pervades this show, and its repetition suggests a certain ambivalence over sexuality, queer sexuality in particular. To illustrate this phenomenon more concretely, let's look at the montage that opens the show. In these brief scenes, we see the show's four main characters in a variety of poses and places. Yet, strikingly, we never see the two gay men together and the only times we see the women together occur when they are with at least one of the men. Instead, we are treated to a number of opposite-sex couplings. We see, in the first clip, Will and Grace dancing a tango, a dance which has come to epitomize sexual heat and romance. We see Jack and Karen frequently together in other scenes, including one where they bounce off each other's chests and another where they hug. In episodes of the show, we frequently see Will and Grace in bed together and, though Grace recently had and lost a boyfriend, Will's relationships are rare and end almost as soon as they begin. Will and Grace's behavior mirrors that of a traditional heterosexual husband and wife, and Karen is quick to point to Grace's neurotic attachment to Will (indeed, she often refers to Will as Grace's gay husband). Grace becomes the supremely neurotic fag hag par excellence who identifies with gay culture, surrounds herself with gay men, and is never guilty of even the mildest expression of homophobia. Will and Grace are comfortable physically with one another, they finish each other's sentences, and, though they briefly lived apart (across the hall from one another!), they soon came back together as roommates. Do we, like Grace, hope someday that the two will be united, that Will can be converted to the heterosexual partner that Grace desperately wants? Further, Jack's flamboyance and his stereotypical nature may suggest that Will is somehow less gay and therefore recuperable to heterosexuality.

As already noted, there is no question that the new glbt characters we see on television are an attractive group both morally and physically. In some cases, for example, *ER* and *Buffy,* shows allow a long-standing character to play with a same-sex attraction, even if the feelings/relationships are temporary. The famous "kisses"—one thinks back to the *Roseanne* show for one of the first—and the more recent kisses on *Friends* and *Ally McBeal*—occur during sweeps weeks and are unabashed strategies to increase the viewing audience. The fact that these episodes earn viewer warnings is noteworthy in itself. But even more noteworthy, it seems to me, is the fact that these episodes result in no change in diegesis or character evolution. These kisses come and go as if they were a dream; they are never incorporated into a character's understanding of his/her identity and sexuality, and the possibility of bisexuality, a more fluid sexual identity, or even a recurrence is rarely if ever entertained.

Indeed, fluidity seems to pose such a threat that its possibility is rarely if ever acknowledged. Thus, when "real" gay or lesbian characters tell their stories, their narratives tend almost always to reinscribe gayness as innate, and those who are gay as having no choice. Thus, we hear that Will has always loved Grace, but that he has never had any sexual feelings of any kind for her. When she is devastated to learn that he has had sex with another woman, he insists that it was merely to have the experience and that he had no real interest in the woman. The idea that Will's best friend Jack might have been attracted to a woman is so obviously ludicrous that the very idea earns a huge laugh. The noteworthy absence of bisexuals in these comedies suggests that the fluidity of a bisexual sexual identity may be too disruptive for such programming. . . .

Finally, an important strategy for learning to read popular texts like television sitcoms is to look for those moments where a moral voice seems to speak. Because these shows . . . are meant to be light and entertaining, they cannot afford to be overly didactic. But there is no question that moral ideology permeates these shows. In some cases, it is certain characters who seem to represent the voice of moral authority. In *Will and Grace* that character

seems to be Grace, who, despite her ditziness, often seems to be the moral voice of the show. . . . Grace's total absence of any vestiges of homophobia makes her a kind of model for the heterosexual viewer. . . . Grace is a dependable friend, a creative and dedicated professional, and enemy of oppression. In one episode, Grace is horrified to discover that Jack is not out to his mother. She urges him to come out and emphasizes the importance of being honest about his identity. In another episode . . . Grace refuses to speak to Will because he is willing to date someone who is in the closet. Grace repeatedly pushes on this issue and accuses Will of hypocrisy and self-loathing. The fact that the heterosexual woman on the show is the one to insist on being openly gay is itself worth noting. Even more striking, however, is the fact that the narrative vilifies those glbt people who, for a variety of powerful reasons, decide not to come out. Never acknowledging any costs to being openly gay, the moral message seems to be that all secrets are bad and the decision to stay in the closet is just another secret that one is never justified in keeping. Questions of power and subordination are thereby erased in the effort to homogenize all lies and secrets. Indeed, once Jack does tell his mother that he is gay, she immediately responds, "I have a secret too." The momentum switches away from Jack's confession and its possible implications to her announcement that the man who is Jack's biological father is not who he thinks he is.

Pretending to Be Gay . . .

My second theme, the trope of the gay pretender, has been a staple of situation comedies ever since Jack Tripper in *Three's Company* posed as gay so that his uptight landlord would let him live with two attractive women. . . . Martin, Frasier's dad, poses as gay in order to avoid having to date a woman he's not interested in. Kate and Allie, in that long-defunct series, pose as lesbians in order to curry favor (and a new lease) from their lesbian landladies. In *Three Sisters*, one sister's ex-husband convinced her that he was gay in order to get a quickie divorce. Klinger in *M.A.S.H.* was, we assume as viewers, a heterosexual man posing as gay or transvestite in order to secure a release from the military. Finally, . . . the soap opera *Days of Our Lives* introduced a new plotline where Jack "outs" himself to Greta so as not to hurt her feelings and confess that he is not attracted to her.

Readers no doubt will be able to come up with examples of their own, and the ease with which we are able to produce these examples suggests how common this trope is. How might one explain its recurrence? On the one hand, one reading suggests that these examples of gender and sexuality play may be consistent with a progressive queer agenda that suggests either that we're all queer or that there's a little queer in each of us. Sedgwick labels this approach to sexuality a "universalizing discourse," meaning that it views queerness/sexuality as nonbinary and more amorphous than is traditionally believed. . . . What makes for the humor in these situations is, at least partly, the fact that the viewer knows that the character's heterosexuality is never in doubt. Such certainty enables these characters to play with gay stereotypes without seeming to be homophobic—in *Frasier*, for example, Martin suddenly becomes limpwristed, interested in décor, and able to express his emotions. Certain mannerisms come to be coded as gay even though the character expressing them is not. The character we "know" is straight is positioned against the character we "know" is gay (interestingly, this trope seems to be rarely used with female characters; does this suggest that lesbians have fewer identifiable mannerisms?) and the comedy of errors and misreadings ensues.

Yet there is never any suggestion whatsoever of any temptation or questioning on the part of the "straight" character; that firmness of resolve serves once again not only to reinforce a strict binary of gay/straight but also to suggest that solid and impermeable boundaries frame one's sexuality. Thus, potentially oppositional discourses are subverted by naturalizing them within terms that make sense in the context of the dominant perspective.

In addition, the "gay pretender" trope implicitly creates a fantasy world where not only do gays and lesbians not experience cultural ostracism and legal discrimination; they also enjoy *more* power than heterosexuals. In addition, it is striking that sex and sexuality seem to be foregrounded in these dynamics. They are landlords who favor "their own kind"; they are released from the burdens of heterosexual dating and romance (and, indeed from having to tell the truth!); they do not have to serve in the military; and they are simply able to have more fun, as Karen in *Will and Grace* discovers, when posing as a lesbian

enables her to offer make-up tips and kiss cute women. This inversion results in humor and unanticipated consequences but it may also serve to mask the ways that power operates and to make the mechanisms of power even more covert.

I'm Not Gay but My Boyfriend Is . . .

Finally, the "straight-mistaken-for-gay" trope is common throughout comedy. This trope represents an almost total inversion of the tendency in earlier television audiences to ignore telltale signs of gayness in a television character or actor. To the less naïve viewer today, the flamboyance and campiness of a Liberace, Flip Wilson, or PeeWee Herman suggest a gay sensibility too obvious to be overlooked. But today's situation comedies manipulate signs of gayness to create humor and playfulness. For example, in a now-classic *Seinfeld* episode, Jerry and George are mistakenly identified as a gay couple by a college reporter who then outs them in her school newspaper. The refrain "not that there's anything wrong with it" serves in part to mock standard liberal attitudes toward homosexuality. . . . In *Third Rock From the Sun*, John Lithgow attempts to "come out" as an alien and is instead assumed to be coming out as gay. *Friends* often hints at the ways Chandler's affect positions him as gay. . . . Indeed, part of the humor in these episodes is that the heterosexual character's mannerisms come to be recoded as queer. Further, this trope suggests the ways that virtually any behavior can be reread as gay once the viewer's perspective is framed by that lens.

The "straight-mistaken-for-gay" trope, like the gay pretender, derives much of its humor from the audience's knowledge that the character(s) in question is/are *not* in fact gay. Such an epistemological advantage sets the audience member apart from the mistaken character and provides the audience member not only with a certain degree of distance but also with reinscribed boundaries between the gay and the straight. . . .

Queer theory embraces a kind of intellectual tension: where, on the one hand, the viewer insists that sexuality and the domain of the sexual are cultural inventions and not essential; on the other hand, it deploys sexuality as a (if not *the*) significant determinant of cultural and individual identity. If Doty (1993) is right that queerness should "challenge and confuse our understanding and uses of sexual and gender categories" (p. xvii), then the sorts of examples I've been describing and analyzing here represent failures.

Marginalized identities are not just oppressed by power; they are also, as Foucault points out, constructed by those very same power relations. Thus, there is no doubt that these new representations of glbt characters and of heterosexuality will give birth to new meanings and new signifiers attached to queer sexuality. But we must wait for that next episode.

NOTES

1. Indeed, fall 2001 premiered a new show starring DeGeneres, who plays an out lesbian who returns to her hometown. Unlike her earlier show, where it took years and much publicity for her to out herself, in this new show she is already out in the first episode and her sexuality is treated casually by her family and those she meets.

2. Unless the film deals explicitly with "gay issues" like AIDS (*Philadelphia, Long Time Companion*, etc.) or homophobic violence (e.g., *Boys Don't Cry*).

REFERENCES

Bourdieu, P. (1990). *In other words: Essays towards a reflexive sociology.* Cambridge, UK: Polity.

Butler, J. (1990). *Gender trouble: Feminism and the subversion of identity.* New York: Routledge.

Clark, D. (1993). Commodity lesbianism. In H. Abelove, M. Aina Barale, & D. M. Halperin (Eds.), *The lesbian and gay studies reader* (pp. 186–201). New York: Routledge.

Doty, A. (1993). *Making things perfectly queer: Interpreting mass culture.* Minneapolis: University of Minnesota Press.

Epstein, S. G. (1987). Gay politics, ethnic identity: The limits of social constructionism. *Socialist Review, 93/94.*

Ewen, S., & Ewen, E. (1992). *Channels of desire: Mass images and the shaping of American consciousness.* Minneapolis: University of Minnesota Press.

Foucault, M. (1990). *The history of sexuality* (Vol. 1, R. Hurley, Trans.). New York: Vintage Books.

Fuss, D. (1991). *Inside/out: Lesbian theories, gay theories.* New York: Routledge.

Gross, L. (1995). Out of the mainstream: Sexual minorities and the mass media. In G. Dines & J. M. Humez (Eds.), *Gender, race and class in media: A text-reader* (pp. 61–69). Thousand Oaks, CA: Sage.

hooks, b. (1995). *Killing rage: Ending racism.* New York: Henry Holt.

Kellner, D. (1995). *Media culture: Cultural studies, identity, and politics between the modern and the postmodern.* London: Routledge.

Kirby, D. (2001, June 17). The boys in the writers' room. *New York Times*, pp. 23, 33.

Mohr, R. (1997). A gay and straight agenda. In J. Corvino (Ed.), *Same sex: Debating the ethics, science, and culture of homosexuality* (pp. 331–344). Lanham, MD: Rowman & Littlefield.

Rich, A. (1980, Summer). Compulsory heterosexuality and lesbian existence. *Signs,* 5(4), 631–660.

Rothaus, S. (2000, December 30). Better reception for gay TV characters. *Boston Globe*, p. D26.

Sedgwick, E. K. (1990). *Epistemology of the closet.* Berkeley: University of California Press.

Torres, S. (1993). Television/feminism: *Heartbeat* and prime time lesbianism. In H. Abelove, M. Aina Barale, & D. M. Halperin (Eds.), *The lesbian and gay studies reader* (pp. 176–185). New York: Routledge.

TWENTY-THREE

◆◆◆

We Are All Works in Progress (1998)

Leslie Feinberg

Leslie Feinberg is a novelist, historian, and activist. Hir award-winning titles include *Stone Butch Blues; Transliberation: Beyond Pink or Blue; Transgender Liberation: A Movement Whose Time Has Come;* and *Drag King Dreams.* Sie writes a regular column, "Lavender and Red," in *Worker's World*, a socialist weekly newspaper.

The sight of pink-blue gender-coded infant outfits may grate on your nerves. Or you may be a woman or a man who feels at home in those categories. Trans liberation defends you both.

Each person should have the right to *choose* between pink or blue tinted gender categories, as well as all the other hues of the palette. At this moment in time, that right is denied to us. But together, we could make it a reality. . . .

I am a human being who would rather not be addressed as Ms. or Mr., ma'am or sir. I prefer to use gender-neutral pronouns like *sie* (pronounced like *"see"*) and *hir* (pronounced like *"here"*) to describe myself. I am a person who faces almost insurmountable difficulty when instructed to check off an "F" or an "M" box on identification papers.

I'm not at odds with the fact that I was born female-bodied. Nor do I identify as an intermediate sex. I simply do not fit the prevalent Western concepts of what a woman or man "should" look like. And that reality has dramatically directed the course of my life.

I'll give you a graphic example. From December 1995 to December 1996, I was dying of endocarditis—a bacterial infection that lodges and proliferates in the valves of the heart. A simple blood culture would have immediately exposed the root cause of my raging fevers. Eight weeks of 'round-the-clock intravenous antibiotic drips would have eradicated every last seedling of bacterium in the canals of my heart. Yet I experienced such hatred from some health practitioners that I very nearly died.

I remember late one night in December my lover and I arrived at a hospital emergency room during a snowstorm. My fever was 104 degrees and rising. My blood pressure was pounding dangerously high. The staff immediately hooked me up to monitors and worked to bring down my fever. The doctor in charge began physically examining me. When he determined that my anatomy was female, he flashed me a mean-spirited smirk. While keeping his eyes fixed on me, he approached one of the nurses, seated at a desk, and began rubbing her neck and shoulders. He talked to her about sex for a few minutes. After his pointed demonstration of "normal sexuality," he told me to get dressed and then he stormed out of the room. Still delirious, I struggled to put on my clothes and make sense of what was happening.

The doctor returned after I was dressed. He ordered me to leave the hospital and never return. I refused. I told him I wouldn't leave until he could tell me why my fever was so high. He said, "You have a fever because you are a very troubled person."

This doctor's prejudices, directed at me during a moment of catastrophic illness, could have killed me. The death certificate would have read: Endocarditis. By all rights it should have read: Bigotry.

As my partner and I sat bundled up in a cold car outside the emergency room, still reverberating from the doctor's hatred, I thought about how many people have been turned away from medical care when they were desperately ill—some because an apartheid "whites only" sign hung over the emergency room entrance, or some because their visible Kaposi's sarcoma lesions kept personnel far from their beds. I remembered how a blemish that wouldn't heal drove my mother to visit her doctor repeatedly during the 1950s. I recalled the doctor finally wrote a prescription for Valium because he decided she was a hysterical woman. When my mother finally got to specialists, they told her the cancer had already reached her brain.

Bigotry exacts its toll in flesh and blood. And left unchecked and unchallenged, prejudices create a poisonous climate for us all. Each of us has a stake in the demand that every human being has a right to a job, to shelter, to health care, to dignity, to respect.

I am very grateful to have this chance to open up a conversation with you about why it is so vital to also defend the right of individuals to express and define their sex and gender, and to control their own bodies. For me, it's a life-and-death question. But I also believe that this discussion will have great meaning for you. All your life you've heard such dogma about what it means to be a "real" woman or a "real" man. And chances are you've choked on some of it. You've balked at the idea that being a woman means having to be thin as a rail, emotionally nurturing, and an airhead when it comes to balancing her checkbook. You know in your guts that being a man has nothing to do with rippling muscles, innate courage, or knowing how to handle a chain saw. These are really caricatures. Yet these images have been drilled into us through popular culture and education over the years. And subtler, equally insidious messages lurk in the interstices of these grosser concepts. These ideas of what a "real" woman or man should be straightjacket the freedom of individual self-expression. These gender messages play on and on in a continuous loop in our brains, like commercials that can't be muted.

But in my lifetime I've also seen social upheavals challenge this sex and gender doctrine. As a child who grew up during the McCarthyite, Father-Knows-Best 1950s, and who came of age during the second wave of women's liberation in the United States, I've seen transformations in the ways people think and talk about what it means to be a woman or a man.

Today the gains of the 1970s women's liberation movement are under siege by right-wing propagandists. But many today who are too young to remember what life was like before the women's movement need to know that this was a tremendously progressive development that won significant economic and social reforms. And this struggle by women and their allies swung human consciousness forward like a pendulum.

The movement replaced the common usage of vulgar and diminutive words to describe females with the word *woman* and infused that word with strength and pride. Women, many of them formerly isolated, were drawn together into consciousness-raising groups. Their discussions—about the root of women's oppression and how to eradicate it—resonated far beyond the rooms in which they took place. The women's liberation movement sparked a mass conversation about the systematic degradation, violence, and discrimination that women faced in this society. And this consciousness-raising changed many of the ways women and men thought about themselves and their relation to each other. In retrospect, however, we must not forget that these widespread discussions were not just organized to *talk* about oppression. They were a giant dialogue about how to take action to fight institutionalized anti-woman attitudes, rape and battering, the illegality of abortion, employment and education discrimination, and other ways women were socially and economically devalued.

This was a big step forward for humanity. And even the period of political reaction that followed has not been able to overturn all the gains made by that important social movement.

Now another movement is sweeping onto the stage of history: Trans liberation. We are again raising questions about the societal treatment of people based on their sex and gender expression. This discussion will make new contributions to human consciousness. And trans communities, like the women's movement, are carrying out these mass conversations with the goal of creating a movement capable of fighting for justice—of righting the wrongs.

We are a movement of masculine females and feminine males, cross-dressers, transsexual men and women, intersexuals born on the anatomical sweep between female and male, gender-blenders, many other sex and gender-variant people, and our significant others. All told, we expand understanding of how many ways there are to be a human being.

Our lives are proof that sex and gender are much more complex than a delivery room doctor's glance at genitals can determine, more variegated than pink or blue birth caps. We are oppressed for not fitting those narrow social norms. We are fighting back.

Our struggle will also help expose some of the harmful myths about what it means to be a woman or a man that have compartmentalized and distorted your life, as well as mine. Trans liberation has meaning for you—no matter how you define or express your sex or your gender.

If you are a trans person, you face horrendous social punishments—from institutionalization to gang rape, from beatings to denial of child visitation. This oppression is faced, in varying degrees, by all who march under the banner of trans liberation. This brutalization and degradation strips us of what we could achieve with our individual lifetimes.

And if you do not identify as transgender or transsexual or intersexual, your life is diminished by our oppression as well. Your own choices as a man or a woman are sharply curtailed. Your individual journey to express yourself is shunted into one of two deeply carved ruts, and the social baggage you are handed is already packed.

So the defense of each individual's right to control their own body, and to explore the path of self-expression, enhances your own freedom to discover more about yourself and your potentialities. This movement will give you more room to breathe—to be yourself. To discover on a deeper level what it means to be your self.

Together, I believe we can forge a coalition that can fight on behalf of your oppression as well as mine. Together, we can raise each other's grievances and win the kind of significant change we all long for. But the foundation of unity is understanding. So let me begin by telling you a little bit about myself.

I am a human being who unnerves some people. As they look at me, they see a kaleidoscope of characteristics they associate with both males and females. I appear to be a tangled knot of gender contradictions. So they feverishly press the question on me: woman or man? Those are the only two words most people have as tools to shape their question.

"Which sex are you?" I understand their question. It sounds so simple. And I'd like to offer them a simple resolution. But merely answering woman or man will not bring relief to the questioner. As long as people try to bring me into focus using only those two lenses, I will always appear to be an enigma.

The truth is I'm no mystery. I'm a female who is more masculine than those prominently portrayed in mass culture. Millions of females and millions of males in this country do not fit the cramped compartments of gender that we have been taught are "natural" and "normal." For many of us, the words *woman* or *man, ma'am* or *sir, she* or *he*—in and of themselves—do not total up the sum of our identities or of our oppressions. Speaking for myself, my life only comes into focus when the word *transgender* is added to the equation.

Simply answering whether I was born female or male will not solve the conundrum. Before I can even begin to respond to the question of my own birth sex, I feel it's important to challenge the assumptions that the answer is always as simple as either-or. I believe we need to take a critical look at the assumption that is built into the seemingly innocent question: "What a beautiful baby—is it a boy or a girl?"

The human anatomical spectrum can't be understood, let alone appreciated, as long as female or male are considered to be all that exists. "Is it a boy or a girl?" Those are the only two categories allowed on birth certificates.

But this either-or leaves no room for intersexual people, born between the poles of female and male. Human anatomy continues to burst the confines of the contemporary concept that nature delivers all babies on two unrelated conveyor belts. So, are the birth certificates changed to reflect human anatomy? No, the U.S. medical establishment hormonally molds and shapes and surgically hacks away at the exquisite complexities of intersexual infants until they neatly fit one category or the other.

A surgeon decides whether a clitoris is "too large" or a penis is "too small." That's a highly subjective decision for anyone to make about another person's body. Especially when the person making the arbitrary decision is scrubbed up for surgery! And what is the criterion for a penis being "too small"? Too small for successful heterosexual intercourse.

Intersexual infants are already being tailored for their sexuality, as well as their sex. The infants have no say over what happens to their bodies. Clearly the struggle against genital mutilation must begin here, within the borders of the United States.

But the question asked of all new parents: "Is it a boy or a girl?" is not such a simple question when transsexuality is taken into account, either. Legions of out-and-proud transsexual men and women demonstrate that individuals have a deep, developed, and valid sense of their own sex that does not always correspond to the cursory decision made by a delivery-room obstetrician. Nor is transsexuality a recent phenomenon. People have undergone social sex reassignment and surgical and hormonal sex changes throughout the breadth of oral and recorded human history.

Having offered this view of the complexities and limitations of birth classification, I have no hesitancy in saying I was born female. But that answer doesn't clear up the confusion that drives some people to ask me, "Are you a man or a woman?" The problem is that they are trying to understand my gender expression by determining my sex—and therein lies the rub! Just as most of us grew up with only the concepts of *woman* and *man,* the terms *feminine* and *masculine* are the only two tools most people have to talk about the complexities of gender expression.

That pink-blue dogma assumes that biology steers our social destiny. We have been taught that being born female or male will determine how we will dress and walk, whether we will prefer our hair shortly cropped or long and flowing, whether we will be emotionally nurturing or repressed. According to this way of thinking, masculine females are trying to look "like men," and feminine males are trying to act "like women."

But those of us who transgress those gender assumptions also shatter their inflexibility.

So, why do I sometimes describe myself as a masculine female? Isn't each of those concepts very limiting? Yes. But placing the two words together is incendiary, exploding the belief that gender expression is linked to birth sex like horse and carriage. It is the social contradiction missing from Dick-and-Jane textbook education.

I actually chafe at describing myself as masculine. For one thing, masculinity is such an expansive territory, encompassing boundaries of nationality, race, and class. Most importantly, individuals blaze their own trails across this landscape.

And it's hard for me to label the intricate matrix of my gender as simply masculine. To me, branding individual self-expression as simply feminine or masculine is like asking poets: Do you write in English or Spanish? The question leaves out the possibilities that the poetry is woven in Cantonese or Ladino, Swahili or Arabic. The question deals only with the system of language that the poet has been taught. It ignores the words each writer hauls up, hand over hand, from a common well. The music words make when finding themselves next to each other for the first time. The silences echoing in the space between ideas. The powerful winds of passion and belief that move the poet to write.

That is why I do not hold the view that gender is simply a social construct—one of two languages that we learn by rote from early age. To me, gender is the poetry each of us makes out of the language we are taught. When I walk through the anthology of the world, I see individuals express their gender in exquisitely complex and ever-changing ways, despite the laws of pentameter.

So how can gender expression be mandated by edict and enforced by law? Isn't that like trying to handcuff a pool of mercury? It's true that human self-expression is diverse and is often expressed in ambiguous or contradictory ways. And what degree of gender expression is considered "acceptable" can depend on your social situation, your race and nationality, your class, and whether you live in an urban or rural environment.

But no one can deny that rigid gender education begins early on in life—from pink and blue color-coding of infant outfits to gender-labeling toys and games. And those who overstep these arbitrary borders are punished. Severely. When the steel handcuffs tighten, it is human bones that crack. No one knows how many trans lives have been lost to police brutality and street-corner bashing. The lives of trans people are so depreciated in this society that many murders go unreported. And those of us who have survived are deeply scarred by daily run-ins with hate, discrimination, and violence.

Trans people are still literally social outlaws. And that's why I am willing at times, publicly, to reduce the totality of my self-expression to

descriptions like masculine female, butch, bulldagger, drag king, cross-dresser. These terms describe outlaw status. And I hold my head up proudly in that police lineup. The word *outlaw* is not hyperbolic. I have been locked up in jail by cops because I was wearing a suit and tie. Was my clothing really a crime? Is it a "man's" suit if I am wearing it? At what point—from field to rack—is fiber assigned a sex?

The reality of why I was arrested was as cold as the cell's cement floor: I am considered a masculine female. That's a *gender* violation. My feminine drag queen sisters were in nearby cells, busted for wearing "women's" clothing. The cells that we were thrown into had the same design of bars and concrete. But when we—gay drag kings and drag queens—were thrown into them, the cops referred to the cells as bull's tanks and queen's tanks. The cells were named after our crimes: gender transgression. Actual statutes against cross-dressing and cross-gendered behavior still exist in written laws today. But even where the laws are not written down, police, judges, and prison guards are empowered to carry out merciless punishment for sex and gender "difference."

I believe we need to sharpen our view of how repression by the police, courts, and prisons, as well as all forms of racism and bigotry, operates as gears in the machinery of the economic and social system that governs our lives. As all those who have the least to lose from changing this system get together and examine these social questions, we can separate the wheat of truths from the chaff of old lies. Historic tasks are revealed that beckon us to take a stand and to take action.

That moment is now. And so this conversation with you takes place with the momentum of struggle behind it.

What will it take to put a halt to "legal" and extralegal violence against trans people? How can we strike the unjust and absurd laws mandating dress and behavior for females and males from the books? How can we weed out all the forms of transphobic and gender-phobic discrimination?

Where does the struggle for sex and gender liberation fit in relation to other movements for economic and social equality? How can we reach a point where we appreciate each other's differences, not just tolerate them? How can we tear down the electrified barbed wire that has been placed between us to keep us separated, fearful, and pitted against each other? How can we forge a movement that can bring about profound and lasting change—a movement capable of transforming society?

These questions can only be answered when we begin to organize together, ready to struggle on each other's behalf. Understanding each other will compel us as honest, caring people to fight each other's oppression as though it was our own.

TWENTY-FOUR

◆◆◆

The Brandon Archive (2005)

Judith Halberstam

Judith Halberstam is Professor of English and Gender Studies at the University of Southern California, specializing in cultural studies, queer theory, visual culture, and gender variance. Her books include *Female Masculinity*, *In a Queer Time and Place: Transgender Bodies, Subcultural Lives*, and *The Drag King Book* (co-author).

Hilary Swank plays Brandon Teena in Boys Don't Cry (1999)

Out There

. . . In December 1993, I remember reading a short story in the newspaper about an execution-style killing in rural Nebraska. The story seemed unremarkable except for one small detail buried in the heart of the report: one of the murder victims was a young female-bodied person who had been passing as a man. The murder of this young transgender person sent shock waves through queer communities in the United States and created fierce identitarian battles between transsexual activists and gay and lesbian activists, with each group trying to claim Brandon Teena as one of their own. . . .

The tragic facts in the case of the murder of Brandon Teena and his two friends are as follows: on December 31, 1993, three young people were shot to death, execution style, in Falls City in rural Nebraska. Ordinarily, this story would have evoked only mild interest from mainstream America and a few questions about the specific brutalities of rural America; one of the three victims, however, was a young white person who had been born a woman but who was living as a man and had been dating local girls. The other two victims, Brandon's friend Lisa Lambert, and her friend Philip DeVine, a disabled African

American man, appeared to have been killed because they were in the wrong place at the wrong time, although this too is debatable.

This chapter relates, explores, and maps the shape and the meaning of the remarkable archive that has developed in the aftermath of the slaying of Brandon Teena, Lisa, and Philip; the archive has created a new "Brandon." This new Brandon is the name that we now give to a set of comforting fictions about queer life in small-town America. The Brandon archive is simultaneously a resource, a productive narrative, a set of representations, a history, a memorial, and a time capsule. It literally records a moment in the history of twentieth-century struggles around the meaning of gender categories, and it becomes a guide to future resolutions. . . . I want to lay out the geopolitical ramifications of Brandon's murder by imagining the Brandon archive as made up of the insights and revelations allowed by a careful consideration of the many lives and social formations that Brandon's life and death sheds light on. If we think of the murder of Brandon as less of a personal tragedy that has been broadened out to create a symbolic event and more of a constructed memorial to the violence directed at queer and transgender lives, we will be better equipped to approach the geographic and class specificities of rural Nebraska.

The execution of Brandon, Lisa, and Philip was in fact more like an earthquake or a five-alarm fire than an individualized event: its eruption damaged more than just the three who died and the two who killed; it actually devastated the whole town, and brought a flood of reporters, cameras, and journalists into the area to pick through the debris and size up the import of the disaster. That media rush, in many ways, transformed the Brandon murders from a circumscribed event to an ever-evolving narrative. . . . among the magazine articles, talk shows, and other media that covered the case, an Oscar-winning feature film, *Boys Don't Cry,* was released about Brandon's death. . . . in this chapter on place, space, and regionality, I discuss the documentary film that greatly influenced *Boys Don't Cry: The Brandon Teena Story,* directed by Susan Muska and Greta Olafsdottir (1998). Like the feature film yet in different ways, *The Brandon Teena Story* tried to re-create the material conditions of Brandon's undoing, but like the feature film, it ultimately told a tall story about rural homophobia.

By designating the stories told about Brandon and his friends as "an archive". . . , I am tracing the multiple meanings of this narrative for different communities. Ann Cvetkovich theorizes queer uses of the term "archives" in her book *An Archive of Feelings:* "Understanding gay and lesbian archives as archives of emotion and trauma helps to explain some of their idiosyncrasies, or, one might say, their 'queerness'" (Cvetkovich 2003, 242). The Brandon archive is exactly that: a transgender archive of "emotion and trauma" that allows a narrative of a queerly gendered life to emerge from the fragments of memory and evidence that remain. When Brandon was shot to death by John Lotter and Thomas Nissen, his failure to pass as a man in the harsh terrain of a small town in rural North America prompted a national response from transgender activists. This response has been amplified and extended by other queers for different and conflicting reasons. Some queers use Brandon's death to argue for hate-crime legislation; others have made Brandon into a poster child for an emergent transgender community dedicated to making visible the plight of cross-identified youth . . . still others have pointed to Brandon's death as evidence of a continuing campaign of violence against queers despite the increasing respectability of some portions of the gay and lesbian community. But few of the responses have taken into consideration the specificity of Brandon's nonmetropolitan location, and few if any have used the murder and the production of activist and cultural activity that it has inspired as a way of reexamining the meaning of sexual identity in relation to a postmodern politics of place.

I use the Brandon material, then, to unpack the meaning of "local homosexualities" or transsexualities in the context of the United States. Like other narratives about nonmetropolitan sexuality, popular versions of this story posit a queer subject who sidesteps so-called modern models of gay identity by conflating gender and sexual variance. Indeed, in the popular versions of the Brandon narrative that currently circulate, like *Boys Don't Cry,* Brandon's promiscuity and liminal identity is depicted as immature. . . . When Brandon explores a mature and adult relationship with one woman who recognizes him as "really female," that film suggests, Brandon accedes to a modern form of homosexuality and is finally "free." Reconstituted now as a liberal subject, Brandon's death at the hands of local men can be read simultaneously as a true tragedy and an indictment of backward, rural communities. . . . By reading Brandon's story in and through postcolonial queer theory and queer geography, we can untangle the complex links that this narrative created for the urban consumers who were its most avid audience between modern queerness and the rejection of rural or small-town locations.

I believe that an extensive analysis of the Brandon murders can serve to frame the many questions about identification, responsibility, class, regionality, and race that trouble queer communities today. Not only does Brandon represent a martyr lost in the struggle for transgender rights to the brutal perpetrators of rural hetero-masculine violences, Brandon also serves as a marker for a particular set of late-twentieth-century cultural anxieties about place, space, locality, and metropolitanism. Fittingly, Brandon has become the name for gender variance, for fear of transphobic and homophobic punishment; Brandon also embodies the desire directed at nonnormative masculinities. Brandon represents other rural lives undone by fear and loathing, and his story also symbolizes an urban fantasy of homophobic violence as essentially midwestern. But violence wherever we may find it marks different conflictual relations in different sites; and homicide, on some level, always depicts the microrealities of other battles displaced from the abstract to the tragically material. While at least one use of any Brandon Teena project must be to connect Brandon's gender presentation to other counternarratives of gender realness, I also hope that Brandon's story can be a vehicle linked to the discussions of globalization, transnational sexualities, geography, and queer migration. On some level Brandon's story, while cleaving to its own specificity, needs to remain an open narrative—not a stable narrative of female-to-male transsexual identity nor a singular tale of queer bashing, not a cautionary fable about the violence of rural America nor an advertisement for urban organizations of queer community. Brandon's story permits a dream of transformation that must echo in the narratives of queer life in other nonmetropolitan locations.

Falls City, Nebraska: A Good Place to Die?

In *The Brandon Teena Story*, Muska and Olafsdottir attempt to place the narrative of Brandon's life and death firmly in the countryside of Nebraska, so much so that Nebraska takes on the role and the presence of a character in this drama. We see prolonged shots of the rolling Nebraska countryside, road signs welcoming the traveler to Nebraska's "good life," and scenes of everyday life and culture in small-town America. The filmmakers make it clear early on that their relationship to Falls City and its communities is ironic and distanced. They never appear in front of the camera even though about 75 percent of the documentary involves talking-head interviews with interviewees responding to questions from invisible interlocutors. In the few "local" scenes, the camera peers voyeuristically at the demolition derby and the line-dancing and karaoke bar, and in the interview sequences, the camera pushes its way rudely into the lives of the people touched by the Brandon story. . . . Interactions between the camera and its subjects register the filmmakers as outsiders to the material realities of the rural Midwest, mark the objects of the gaze as literally haunted by an invisible camera, and finally, place the viewer at a considerable distance from the actors on the screen. This distance both allows for the emergence of multiple versions of the Brandon story but also pins the narrative of violent homophobic and transphobic violence firmly to the landscape of white trash America, and forces modes of strenuous disidentification between the viewer and the landscape.

The landscape of Nebraska serves as a contested site on which multiple narratives unfold—narratives, indeed, that refuse to collapse into simply one story, "the Brandon Teena story." Some of these narratives are narratives of hate, or of desire; others tell of ignorance and brutality; still others of isolation and fear; some allow violence and ignorant prejudices to become the essence of poor, white, rural identity; and still others provoke questions about the deployment of whiteness and the regulation of violence. While the video itself encourages viewers to distance themselves from the horror of the heartlands and to even congratulate themselves for living in an urban rather than a rural environment, ultimately we can use Brandon's story as it emerges here to begin the articulation of the stories of white, working-class, rural queers, and to map the immensely complex relations that make rural America a site of horror and degradation in the urban imagination.

For queers who flee the confines of the rural Midwest and take comfort in urban anonymity, this video may serve as a justification of their worst fears about the violent effects of failing to flee; closer readings of Brandon's story, however, reveal the desire shared by many midwestern queers for a way of staying rather than leaving. While some journalists in the wake of Brandon's murder queried his decision to stay in Falls City, despite having been hounded by the police and raped by the men who went on to murder him, we must consider the condition of "staying put" as part of the production of complex queer subjectivities. . . . The danger of small towns as Willa Cather described it, also in reference to rural Nebraska, emerges out of a suffocating sense of proximity: "lives roll along so close to one another," she wrote in *Lucy Gayheart,* "loves and hates beat about, their wings almost touching" [Cather 1935, 167]. This beautiful, but scary image of rural life as a space all-too-easily violated depends absolutely on an opposite image— the image of rural life as wide open and free ranging, as "big sky" and open plains. Cather captures perfectly the contradiction of rural life as the contrast between wide-open spaces and sparse populations, on the one hand, and small-town claustrophobia and lack of privacy, on the other.

The life and death of Brandon provokes endless speculation about the specificities of the loves and hates that characterized his experiences in Falls City, and any straightforward rendering of his story remains impossible. Some viewers of *The Brandon Teena Story* have accused the filmmakers of an obvious class bias in their depictions of the people of Falls City; others have seen the film as an accurate portrayal of the cultures of hate and meanness produced in small, mostly white towns. Any attempt to come to terms with the resonances of Brandon's murder will ultimately have to grapple with both of these proposals. . . .

One way in which *The Brandon Teena Story* is able to grapple with the lives beneath the stereotypes (of white trash, of gender impersonation) is by allowing some of the women whom Brandon dated to explain themselves and articulate their own extraordinary desires. In the media rush to uncover the motivations behind Brandon's depiction of himself as a man, most accounts of the case have overlooked the fact that Brandon was actively chosen over more conventionally male men by the women he dated despite the fact that there were few social rewards for doing so. One girlfriend after another in the video characterizes Brandon as a fantasy guy, a dream guy, a man who "knew how a woman wanted to be treated." Gina describes him as romantic, special, and attentive, while Lana Tisdale calls him "every woman's dream." We might conclude that Brandon lived up to and even played into the romantic ideals that his girlfriends cultivated about masculinity. Brandon's self-presentation must be read, I believe, as a damaging critique of the white working-class masculinities around him; at the same time, however, his performance of courtly masculinity is a shrewd deployment of the middle-class and so-called respectable masculinities that represent an American romantic ideal of manhood. In the accounts that the women give of their relations with Brandon, we understand that he not only deliberately offered them a treatment they could not expect from local boys, but he also acknowledged the complexity of their self-understandings and desires.

In order to understand the kinds of masculinities with which Brandon may have been competing, we can turn to the representations of the murderers themselves. While some accounts of the Brandon case have attempted to empathize with the men who murdered Brandon—Lotter and Nissen—by revealing their traumatic family histories and detailing their encounters with abuse, the video tries to encourage the men to give their own reasons for their brutality. The conversations with Lotter and Nissen are fascinating for the way they allow the men to coolly describe rape and murder scenes, and also because Lotter in particular articulates an astute awareness of the violence of the culture into which he was raised. Nissen, however, shows little power of self-reflection; the video represents him as ultimately far more reprehensible than his partner in crime. For one second in the video, the camera focuses on a small tattoo on Nissen's arm, but does not allow the viewer to identify it. In Aphrodite Jones's book on the Brandon case, *All S/he Wanted,* she provides information that situates this tattoo as a symbol of white supremacy politics. Nissen, we learn, was involved off and on throughout his early life with the White American Group for White America (Jones 1996, 154). While Nissen's flirtation with brutally racist white supremacist groups need not surprise us, it does nonetheless flesh out the particular nexus of hate that came to focus on Brandon, Lisa, and Philip.

Nowhere in the documentary, however, nor in media coverage of the case, does anyone link Nissen's racial politics with either the brutalization of Brandon or the execution of the African American, Philip; indeed, the latter is always constructed as a case of "wrong place, wrong time," but Philip's situation needs to be explored in more detail. In *The Brandon Teena Story,* Philip's murder is given little airplay, and none of his relatives or family make an appearance in the video. While every other character in the drama, including Lisa, is carefully located in relation to Brandon and the web of relations among Brandon's friends, Philip alone is given only the most scant attention. No explanation is given for the nonappearance of his family and friends, and no real discussion is presented about his presence in the farmhouse the night of the murders.[1]

It is hard to detach the murder of Philip from the history of Nissen's involvement in white supremacist cults. Many accounts of white power movements in the United States connect them to small, all-white towns in the Midwest and to economically disadvantaged white populations. While one would not want to demonize poor, white, rural Americans as any more bigoted than urban or suburban white yuppie populations in the United States, it is nonetheless important to highlight the particular fears and paranoia that take shape in rural, all-white populations. Fear of the government, fear of the United Nations, and fear of Jews, blacks, and queers mark white rural masculinities in particular ways that can easily produce cultures of hate (Ridgeway 1995). In small towns where few people of color live, difference may be marked and remarked in relation to gender variance rather than racial diversity. As Newitz and Wray point out in their anatomy of white trash, some degree of specificity is necessary when we try to describe and identify different forms of homophobia and transphobia as they are distributed across different geographies.

In "Get Thee to a Big City: Sexual Imaginary and the Great Gay Migration," anthropologist Kath Weston begins a much-needed inquiry into the difference between urban and rural "sexual imaginaries" (Weston 1995). She comments on the rather stereotyped division of rural/urban relations that "locates gay subjects in the city while putting their presence in the countryside under erasure" (262). Weston also traces the inevitable disappointments that await rural queers who escape the country only to arrive in alienating queer urban spaces. As Weston proposes, "The gay imaginary is not just a dream of a freedom to be gay that requires an urban location, but a symbolic space that configures gayness itself by elaborating an opposition between urban and rural life" (274). She wants us to recognize that the distinction between the urban and the rural that props up the gay imaginary is a symbolic one, and as such, it constitutes a dream of an elsewhere that promises a freedom it can never provide. But it is also crucial to be specific about which queer subjects face what kinds of threats, from whom, and in what locations. While in the city, for example, one may find that the gay or transsexual person of color is most at risk for violence from racist cops; in rural locations, one may find that even the white queers who were born and raised there are outlawed when they disrupt the carefully protected homogeneity of white, family-oriented communities. One may also discover that while the brutalization of a transgender sex worker of color raises little outcry in the city from local queer activists, the murder of a white boy in rural North America can stir up an enormous activist response that is itself symbolic of these other imaginary divisions.

The material in the Brandon archive has led me to question my own interest in the case, and it has forced me to "know my place" in terms of the rural/urban divisions in queer communities that reactions to the story make visible. When I began thinking and writing about the Brandon murders in 1996, I approached the material with the bewilderment of a typical urban queer who wanted to know why Brandon, but also his African American friend Philip, did not pick up and leave Falls City as soon as they could, and furthermore, why they were there in the first place. Falls City, in all the literature, sounded like the last place in the United States where one would want to try to pass as a man while dating local girls; it was also clearly not a good place to be one of the few people of color in town and a black man dating a white woman. Deindustrialization and the farming crises of the 1970s and 1980s had made this town, like so many other midwestern small towns, a place of poverty and neglect where jobs were hard to come by. . . .

Having read much of the material on Brandon's short life and brutal murder and having viewed this documentary about the case, I quickly rationalized the whole episode as an inevitable case of a queer running afoul of the rednecks in a place one would not want to live in anyway. In fall 1996, I was invited up to Seattle to speak at a gay and lesbian film festival following the screening of *The Brandon Teena Story*. I would be joined as a discussant by Seattle-local transman and anthropologist Jason Cromwell and Los Angeles–based philosophy professor and transman Jacob Hale. We conferred briefly before the panel, and after sitting through the disturbing documentary, we went to the stage to discuss the film with the audience. The organizers of the conference seemed to assume that the debate likely to be motivated by the documentary would involve whether we should understand Brandon as a female-to-male transsexual without access to sex reassignment surgery or a transgender butch who had deliberately decided not to transition. My comments skimmed over this debate, which seemed beside the point, and went straight to the question of regionality, location, and rural existence. I remarked that Nebraska was not simply "anywhere" in this video, but that the documentary filmmakers had skillfully tried to situate the landscape as a character in this drama. The audience made noises of approval. Next, I went on to the topic of life in small, mostly white, midwestern towns, and suggested that many of these places were the breeding grounds for cultures of hate and meanness that had both homophobic and racist dimensions. The audience was quiet, too quiet.

The question-and-answer session began without controversy, and a few people testified to the difficulties they had encountered as female-to-male transsexuals or as partners of female-to-males. Others talked about the traumatic experience of watching the video and coming so close to the horrific details of Brandon's murder. Then something strange happened. A harmless question came my way: "What do you think of the documentary? Do you think it is good? Do you think the directors were at all condescending?" While I did have some real problems with the video and its representations of the people of Falls City, I felt that I had been invited to lead an even-handed discussion of *The Brandon Teena Story*, and so I shrugged off the implied criticism and said that I thought Muska and

Olafsdottir had done some amazing interviews. The next question went a bit deeper: "What did you think about the depiction in the video of rural life, and furthermore, what do you mean by small towns in the heartland being `cultures of hate and meanness?'" I tried to explain that I was describing the bigotry that resides in mostly white, nonurban constituencies. Then it got ugly. A woman stood up and denounced my comments as insensitive to those people present who may have come from small towns, and who, moreover, very much wanted to return to a small-town life and did not believe that the small town was an essentially racist or bigoted place. The audience broke out into spontaneous and sustained applause, and then one person after another stood up to testify that they too were from a small town or a rural background and that they too felt offended. Apart from a bruised ego (it is no fun to have an audience give a standing ovation to someone who has just told you that you are full of it), I left Seattle unscathed, but this experience forced me to reconsider what was at stake in the mythmaking that now surrounds Brandon's murder.[2] Confronted with my own urban bias, I decided that one could make use of the Brandon material to study urban attitudes toward queer rural life, and to examine more closely the essential links that have been made between urban life and queerness per se.

The murder of Brandon Teena, like the murder of Matthew Shepard some six years later, did in fact draw public attention to the peculiar vulnerabilities of queer youth (whether transgender or gay/lesbian) living in North America's heartland. In both cases, the victims became martyrs for urban queer activists fighting for LGBT rights, and they were mythologized in a huge and diverse array of media as extraordinary individuals who fell prey to the violent impulses of homophobic and transphobic middle-America masculinities. But while it is tempting to use the materials produced in the aftermath of the killings of both Brandon Teena and Matthew Shepard to flesh out the details of the lives and deaths of the subjects, it makes more sense to my mind to collect the details, the stories, the facts, and the fictions of the cases, and then to create deep archives for future analysis about the many rural lives and desires that were implicated in the lives ands deaths of these individuals. Here I do not mean simply a collection of data; rather, I use the word archive in a Foucauldian way to suggest a discursive field and a structure of thinking. The archive is an immaterial repository for the multiple ideas about rural life that construct and undergird urban identity in the twentieth and twenty-first centuries. In the case of Brandon, the archive that has posthumously developed contains vital information about racial and class constructions of identity and desire in rural areas, and it also provides some important details about the elaborate and complex desires of young women coming to maturity in nonurban areas; the young women who were drawn to Brandon's unconventional manhood must have lots to tell us about adolescent feminine fantasy. . . . all too often such girlish desires for boyish men are dismissed within a Freudian model of female sexuality as a form of immaturity and unrealized sexual capacity; the assumption that underpins the dismissal of adolescent female desires is that the young women who fall for a Brandon, a teen idol, or some other icon of youthful manhood, will soon come to full adulthood, and when they do, they will desire better and more authentic manhood. By reckoning only with Brandon's story, as opposed to the stories of his girlfriends, his family, and those other two teenagers who died alongside him, we consent to a liberal narrative of individualized trauma. For Brandon's story to be meaningful, it must be about more than Brandon.

Space and Sexuality in Queer Studies

In gay/lesbian and queer studies, there has been little attention paid to date to the specificities of rural queer lives. Indeed, most queer work on community, sexual identity, and gender roles has been based on and in urban populations, and exhibits an active disinterest in the productive potential of nonmetropolitan sexualities, genders, and identities. . . . And yet, at the same time that most theories of modern sexuality have made definitive links between the city and homosexuality, urban queers have exhibited an endless fascination for stories of gays, lesbians, and transgender people living outside the city. For example, we might explain the appeal of the case of Brandon to urban queers in terms of its ability to locate the continuing homophobic and transphobic violence directed at sex- and gender-variant people in the United States in spaces removed from urban life.

The deaths of Brandon and Matthew have sparked new considerations of the relationship between mainstream gay and lesbian rights movements and the harsh realities of lives lived far beyond the reach of rights-based policies. The response to these murders, in fact, suggests that they were, in the words of James C. Scott, "but a variant of affronts suffered systematically by a whole race, class, or strata" (Scott 1990). As Scott writes, "An individual who is affronted may develop a personal fantasy of revenge and confrontation, but when the insult is but a variant of affronts suffered systematically by a whole race, class, or strata, then the fantasy can become a collective cultural product" (9). . . . The Brandon archive is, in some ways, the "collective cultural product" that has responded to the affront of this brutal and phobic murder. And the archive reveals how little we actually know about the forms taken by queer life outside of metropolitan areas. The Brandon archive also makes historical and thematic links between the kinds of violences perpetrated against queer bodies and the documented violences against black bodies in lynching campaigns in the early twentieth century. Lisa Duggan has documented the ways in which lynching narratives and lesbian murder narratives in the 1890s mapped out overlapping histories of violence, and Duggan's powerful study of race, sex, and violence in her *Sapphic Slashers* makes these two seemingly distinct narratives tell a more complete story of the emergence of what she calls "twentieth century U.S. modernity" (Duggan 2000). Brandon's story, coupled as it is with the death of African American Philip DeVine, reminds us of the interchangeability of the queer and the racially other in the white American racist imagination.

Most theories of homosexuality within the twentieth century assume that gay culture is rooted in cities, that it has a special relationship to urban life, and that as Gayle Rubin comments in "Thinking Sex," erotic dissidents require urban space because in rural settings queers are easily identified and punished; this influential formulation of the difference between urban and rural environments was, in 1984 when Rubin's essay was first published, a compelling explanation for the great gay migrations of young queers from the country to the city in the 1970s (Rubin 1984). And since Rubin's essay was heavily committed to the project of providing a theoretical foundation for "sexual ethnographesis" or the ethnographic history of community, it made sense to contrast the sexual conformity of small towns to the sexual diversity of big cities; such a contrast made crystal clear the motivations of young white gay men who seemed to flock in droves in the 1970s from small towns in the Midwest, in particular, to urban gay centers like San Francisco and New York. So in theory, the distinction between rural repression and urban indulgence makes a lot of sense, but in actuality, as recent research has shown, we might find that rural and small-town environments nurture elaborate sexual cultures even while sustaining surface social and political conformity. . . .

Rural and small-town queer life is generally mythologized by urban queers as sad and lonely, or else rural queers might be thought of as "stuck" in a place that they would leave if they only could. Only of late has the rural/urban divide and binary begun to produce some interesting inquiries into life beyond the metropolitan center; in some recent work, the rural/urban binary reverberates in really productive ways with other defining binaries like traditional/modern, Western/non-Western, natural/cultural, and modern/postmodern. The editors of one anthology of queer writings on sexual geographies, for example, *De-centering Sexualities: Politics and Representations beyond the Metropolis,* suggest that rural or nonmetropolitan sites have been elided within studies of sexuality and space, which typically focus on either "sexualized metropolitan areas such as New York and Berlin or on differently sexualized, marginalized, and colonized spaces including the Orient and Africa" (Phillips et al. 2000). By comparison, "much less has been said about other liminal or in-between spaces including the small towns and rural parts of Europe, Australia and North America" (1). The volume as a whole points to the dominance of models of what David Bell in his "Eroticizing the Rural" terms helpfully "metrosexuality" and the concomitant representation of the rural as essentially either "hostile" or "idyllic" (Bell 2000).

The notion of metrosexuality as a cultural dominant in U.S. theorizing about gay/lesbian lives also gives rise to the term metronormativity. This term reveals the conflation of "urban" and "visible" in many normalizing narratives of gay/lesbian subjectivities. Such narratives tell of closeted subjects who "come out" into an urban setting, which in turn, supposedly allows for the full expression of the sexual self in relation to a community of other gays/lesbians/queers. The metronormative narrative maps a story of migration onto the coming-out narrative. While the story of coming out tends to function as a temporal trajectory within which a period of disclosure follows a long period of repression, the metronormative story of migration from "country" to "town" is a spatial narrative within which the subject moves to a place of tolerance after enduring life in a place of suspicion, persecution, and secrecy. Since each narrative bears the same structure, it is easy to equate the physical journey from small town to big city with the psychological journey from closet case to out and proud. As Howard [1999] comments in *Men Like That,* the rural is made to function as a closet for urban sexualities in most accounts of rural queer migration. But in actual fact, the ubiquity of queer sexual practices, for men at least, in rural settings suggests that some other epistemology than the closet governs sexual mores in small towns and wide-open rural areas. In reality, many queers from rural or small towns move to the city of necessity, and then yearn to leave the urban area and return to their small towns; and many recount complicated stories of love, sex, and community in their small-town lives that belie the closet model. . . .

In an illuminating essay that acknowledges the difference between the kind of inevitable model of global gay life that Dennis Altman [2001] proposes . . . Alan Sinfield notes that "the metropolitan gay model will be found in Johannesburg, Rio de Janeiro, and Delhi as well as New York and London in interaction with traditional local, nonmetropolitan, models" (Sinfield 2000, 21). In other words, Sinfield recognizes that a global gay model is always interacting with other, often nonmetropolitan sexual economies. . . . could it be possible that nonmetropolitan models also share certain characteristics cross-culturally? These shared characteristics might be attributed less to capitalist modalities like gay tourism on which the metropolitan model depends and more to the separation of localized sexual economies from the so-called gay global model. In other words, could there be some level of correspondence between a nonmetropolitan sexual system in rural Indonesia and one in rural Nebraska? And could both regions be considered other in relation to the dominant metropolitan model of gay male sexual exchange? . . . Calling for a "more serious engagement with postcoloniality as a category of analysis" within queer studies, Boellstorff [1999] argues that such an engagement "might improve our understanding of sexualities outside the 'West'" (478). But the full deployment of translocal analysis—by which Boellstorff means a way of moving beyond the local/global and sameness/difference binaries that have characterized much of the work on transnational sexualities—would presumably also potentially improve and indeed complicate our understanding of sexualities *within* the "West."

The kinds of sexual communities, identities, and practices that Howard describes in *Men Like That,* and that have been depicted and "discovered" in relation to narrative events like the murder of Brandon Teena, may indeed have less in common with the white gay and lesbian worlds associated with the Castro in San Francisco, West Hollywood in Los Angeles, and Chelsea in New York, and they may share some significant traits with the sexual and gender practices associated with *tombois* in Indonesia and Thailand, *travesti* in Brazil, and *bakla* in the Philippines (Morris 1994; Manalansan 1997; Donham 1998). Like other nonmetropolitan sex/gender systems, U.S. small-town and rural alternative sexual communities may often be characterized by distinct gender roles, active/passive sexual positioning, and passing practices; and like other nonmetropolitan models, they may exist in proximity to, rather than in distinction from, heterosexualities.

In the United States, rural populations are studied more often in relation to class or the formation known as white trash, and only rarely is the plight of the rural poor linked to other subaltern populations around the world. There are of course good reasons for not simply lumping all rural populations into one large subaltern formation: as George Lipsitz has documented, even working-class whites in the United States have a "possessive investment in whiteness" that situates them in often contradictory relations to power and dominant discourses (Lipsitz 1998). In the Midwest, moreover, the history of whiteness is linked to the early-twentieth-century Alien Land Laws, which restricted landownership only to those eligible for citizenship, thereby excluding, for example, Asian immigrants (Lowe 1996). As the federal government waged war on native populations in states like Nebraska, "white" immigrants from Scandinavia and other northern

European destinations were encouraged to settle in the Midwest by specific government policies aimed at recruiting "white" settlers (Lieberman 1998; Hietala 2003). White rural populations in the United States, particularly in the Midwest, must in fact be thought about through the racial project of whiteness and the historical construction of working-class "whiteness" as a place of both privilege and oppression. Because of this complex construction, we must avoid either romanticizing rural lives or demonizing them: rural queers in particular may participate in certain orders of bigotry (like racism or political conservatism) while being victimized and punished by others (like homophobia and sexism). If we turn to the case of Brandon's murder, we discover a developing archive for the further consideration of queer rural lives. In the narratives and accounts that have poured out of the tragic murder of a young transgender man and his two friends in rural Nebraska, we find an intricate knot of questions about how Brandon passed; the desire he elicited from local girls; his relationship to gay, lesbian, and transgender identities; the hate and violence his performance drew from two young white male friends; and the enduring legacy of the whiteness of the heartland.

One account of gay life in the Midwest that records the combination of privilege and oppression that characterizes the lives of the white gay men who live there, can be found in an oral history project called *Farm Boys* (Fellows 2001). In this volume, historian Will Fellows collected the memories and testimonies of a group of midwestern gay men, all of whom grew up on farms in Scandinavian American or German American families. The narratives presented by Fellows in *Farm Boys* were all submitted in response to a questionnaire that he circulated, and so the stories have an unfortunate generic quality that emphasizes the similarities rather than the differences between the life experiences of the men. In this stock format, each man speaks of his relationship with his father and brothers, describes some childhood sexual experiences, . . . and discusses his move from his rural hometown to the city and (sometimes) back again. But despite the repetitive and formulaic nature of these stories, some important features do emerge. Many of the men stress, for instance, the isolation and lack of queer community in rural settings. Their isolation has sometimes led to a lengthy delay in the man's coming-out process, and many take detours through unwanted marriages. Yet the isolation can, on occasion, also allow for an array of gay or queer identities since the men are not modeling themselves on one stereotypical narrative. The emergence of idiosyncratic formulations of sexual identity implies that if certain sex/gender categories are not presented as inevitable, other options may emerge. Howard claims as much in *Men Like That* "What is apparent is that gay identity in Mississippi (surely as elsewhere) existed alongside multiple queer desires that were not identity based or identity forging" (29).

Farm Boys also shows that rural settings and small towns may offer a reduced amount of contact between the queer person and the kinds of medical discourses that have been so influential on the lives of gays, lesbians, and transsexuals in the twentieth century (Terry 1999). Also, in climates where homosexual identity is not forbidden but simply unthinkable, the preadult sexual subject who pursues same-sex eroticism may do so without necessarily assuming that this sexual activity speaks the truth of one's identity. Furthermore, according to the male narrators of *Farm Boys*, same-sex sexual activity for them was not necessarily accompanied by noticeable degrees of effeminacy, and in fact, male effeminacy was actively discouraged within their communities less as a sign of homosexual tendencies and more because it did not fit with the heavy labor expected of boys in farm families. By the same logic, however, rural women were more likely to be characterized by gender inversion because masculinity in women seems not to have been actively discouraged. A masculine woman, in the context of a farm, is not automatically read as a lesbian; she is simply a hardworking woman who can take care of herself and her farm. Farm masculinities for men and women, then, result in an asymmetrical development of gay and lesbian identities in terms of their relations to gender-inversion models of sexual identity.

Many of the men in *Farm Boys* disassociated themselves from the metropolitan gay worlds that they discovered once they left their rural and small-town homes. Some were puzzled and disturbed by gay effeminacy in the cities, and others were annoyed by the equation of gay with "activist." This desire to have a sexual practice separate from an overt ideological critique of the state or heteronormativity

can be taken as one legacy of the history of whiteness that marks the communities the gay rural men left behind. Fellows makes no comment on the often reactionary political sentiments of these white gay men and his remarks focus instead on the importance of pluralistic accounts of gay life. As an oral historian, furthermore, who has actively solicited and shaped the responses of his informants, Fellows has left himself little room for critical commentary. His project points to the difficulties involved in taking account of rural gay lives, but it also charts the contradictory nature of rural queers who have been omitted from dominant accounts of queer life and yet must not be represented as a subaltern population.

As Fellows's volume argues, it is not always easy to fathom the contours of queer life in rural settings because, particularly in the case of gay men, queers from rural settings are not well represented in the literature that has been so much a hallmark of twentieth-century gay identity. Gay men and lesbians from rural settings tend not to be artists and writers in such great numbers, and so most of the coming-out stories that we read are written by people from cities or suburbs. As Eve Kosofsky Sedgwick's work has shown in compelling detail, the history of twentieth-century literature in an Anglo-American context has been indelibly marked and influenced by the contributions of white gay men; consequently, literature has been a powerful vehicle for the production and consolidation of gay identity (Sedgwick 1986, 1990). But again, little of this literature has anything at all to say about rural life, and most of it ties homosexual encounters to the rhythms of the city. Just a quick glance at some of the most influential high-culture texts of queer urban life would reveal gay guidebooks to Oscar Wilde's London, Jean Genet's Paris, Christopher Isherwood's Berlin, E. M. Forster's Florence, Thomas Mann's Venice, Edmund White's New York, John Rechy's Los Angeles, Allen Ginsberg's San Francisco, and so on. Canonized literary production by Euro-American lesbian writers like Radclyffe Hall, Djuna Barnes, Jeanette Winterson, and Gertrude Stein similarly focuses, although less obsessively, on urban locations like Paris, London, and New York. But in queer writing by women, we do find some of the themes that we might also expect to see in accounts of rural queer life like stories of isolation and numerous passing narratives.

While fictional narratives of queer rural life are quite hard to find, some ethnographic work and oral histories did emerge in the 1990s. Howard's *Men Like That* is an exemplary and unique history and ethnographic survey of the sexual practices and social mores of men who have sex with men in southern Mississippi. His book examines "sexual and gender nonconformity, specifically male homosexualities and male-to-female transgender sexualities in Mississippi from 1945–1985" (Howard 1999, xiv). Arguing that men "like that" in the rural South in the 1950s were "largely homebound, living in familial households," Howard shows that these men did travel nonetheless, but most did not migrate to big cities; instead, "queer movement consisted of circulation rather than congregation" (xiv). Most queers, he claims, found partners within their immediate vicinity, and in the 1950s, these men were able to escape state surveillance of their illicit activities and their queer sexual practices went undetected. By the supposedly liberal 1960s, however, a new discourse of perversion allowed for the large-scale harassment and arrest of large numbers of queer men. What Howard's book perhaps does not emphasize enough is the impunity from legal and moral scrutiny in Mississippi that was extended specifically to white men while the sexual activities of black men (gay or straight) were constantly watched by fretful white citizens. In fact, it is not *so* surprising that white patriarchs during the same period were able to have sex with boys, black men, and each other without incurring any kind of comment. Howard's book also has little to say about female sexual practices in rural areas, and we are left to wonder whether the histories of men like that can tell us anything at all about the women who were also homebound and yet had no opportunities for congregation or circulation.

While Brandon fits only nominally into the category of "woman" and while his complex story cannot at all be called "lesbian," Brandon's choices do give us some insight into what kinds of options may exist for cross-identified, female-born transgender people in rural settings. Many urban gays, lesbians, and transgender people responded to the murder of Brandon with a "what do you expect" attitude, as if brutality was an inevitable consequence of trying to pull off such a risky endeavor as passing for male in some godforsaken place. But what such a response ignores is the fact that Brandon had been passing for male with only mixed success in the city of Lincoln, Nebraska, since his early teenage years; indeed, it was only when he left the city and made a reverse migration to the small town of Falls City that he really pulled off a credible presentation as male. . . .

Brandon clearly knew what was possible in Falls City, Nebraska, and he seemed to know what limits might be imposed on his passing performance. He moved to Falls City not in order to be a stranger with no history but because he had friends there. . . . Brandon quite quickly developed a friendship network in Falls City, which included both his girlfriends and his killers, but he seemed to take a certain comfort in being known and in knowing everyone in town. By moving to a small town and setting up life as a young man, moreover, Brandon was operating within the long tradition of passing women in rural areas of North America that has been documented by historian Lisa Duggan among others. [Angelia] Wilson [2000] mentions at least one such narrative involving an "African American woman who lived as a man for 15 years" in Mississippi in the 1940s and 1950s. Jim McHarris/Annie Lee Grant lived in a small town called Kosciusko, working and dating women, and was only discovered when he was arrested by the local police for a traffic violation. After that, Jim left town and began his life as a man elsewhere.[3] . . .

The Brandon story brings to light at least three historiographical problems related to the topic of studying queer rural life. First, this narrative reveals how difficult transgender history has been to write in general, but also how there may be specific dimensions of transgender identity that are particular to a rural setting. Given that many gay, lesbian, and transgender people who grow up and live in small rural areas may not identify at all with these labels, the rural context allows for a different array of acts, practices, performances, and identifications. Second, the Brandon story suggests that too often minority history hinges on representative examples provided by the lives of a few extraordinary individuals. And so in relation to the complicated matrix of rural queer lives, we tend to rely on the story of a Brandon Teena or a Matthew Shepard rather than finding out about the queer people who live quietly, if not comfortably, in isolated areas or small towns all across North America. . . . much critical attention focuses on the individual, the formation and transformations of self, the psychology of desire, the drama of pathology and pathologization, the emergence of types, and even the biographies of famous representative individuals (like Radclyffe Hall, Oscar Wilde, and so on). Less time, as George Chauncey has pointed out, has been spent on considering the developments of queer communities, and the negotiations of desire and identity within communities that may be unified or disunified by other modes of identification (Chauncey 1989). Even less time has been spent in consideration of those subjects who remain outside the ambit of the medical and psychological productions of identity, and the reverse discourses that greet and shape their use. Precisely because queer history has been so preoccupied with individuals, it has been harder to talk about class and race, and it has seemed much more relevant to discuss gender variance and sexual practices. All too often, community models are offered only as a generalized model of many individuals rather than as a complex interactive model of space, embodiment, locality, and desire. The Brandon archive, then, needs to be read less in terms of the history of one extraordinary person, and more in terms of the constructions of community and self that it brings to light.

The third and final historiographical problem in relation to this case has to do with the stakes of authenticity. What is real? What is narrative? . . . queer genders profoundly disturb the order of relations between the authentic and the inauthentic, the original and the mimic, the real and the constructed. . . . there are no true accounts of "passing lives" but only fictions, and the whole story turns on the production of counterfeit realities that are so convincing that they replace and subsume the real. This case itself hinges on the production of a "counterfeit" masculinity that even though it depends on deceit and illegality, turns out to be more compelling, seductive, and convincing than the so-called real masculinities with which it competes.

Future Histories

Ultimately, the Brandon archive is not simply the true story of a young queer misfit in rural North America. It is also a necessarily incomplete and ever expanding record of how we select our heroes as well as how we commemorate our dead. James Baldwin, in his account of the 1979 Atlanta murders

of black children, calls our attention to the function of streamlining in the awful vicinity of violent erasure. In *The Evidence of Things Not Seen*, Baldwin writes: "The cowardice of this time and place—this era—is nowhere more clearly revealed than in the perpetual attempt to make the public and social disaster the result, or the issue of a single demented creature, or, perhaps, half a dozen such creatures, who have, quite incomprehensibly, gone off their rockers and must be murdered and locked up" (Baldwin 1995, 72). The desire, in other words, the desperate desire, to attribute hate crimes to crazy individuals and to point to the U.S. justice system as the remedy for unusual disturbances to the social order of things must be resisted in favor of political accounts of crime and punishment. In the end, we are not simply celebrating a Brandon Teena and denouncing a John Lotter or Thomas Nissen, nor should we be seeing love as the redemptive outcome to a tale of hate; the real work of collecting the stories of a Brandon Teena, a Billy Tipton, or a Matthew Shepard must be to create an archive capable of providing a record of the complex interactions of race, class, gender, and sexuality that result in murder, but whose origins lie in state-authorized formations of racism, homophobia, and poverty. Justice in the end lies in the unraveling of the crime not simply in its solution, and when we cease to unravel we become collaborators. "The author of a crime," notes Baldwin, "is what he is . . . but he who collaborates is doomed forever in that unimaginable and yet very common condition which we weakly call hell" (125). The stories we collect in the Brandon archive should stretch far beyond the usual tales of love and hate and the various narratives of accommodation; this archive lends us precisely the kind of evidence for things not seen that Baldwin sought, and in the end, if we read it right, it may tell us a different story about late-twentieth-century desire, race, and geography. With careful organization now, this archive may also become an important resource later for future queer historians who want to interpret the lives we have lived from the few records we have left behind.

NOTES

1. For more on the erasure of Philip and the downplaying of the racial narrative, see the debates about *Boys Don't Cry* in *Screen*, particularly the essay by Jennifer Devere Brody (2002).

2. I found out later that the filmmakers, Muska and Olafsdottir, had been present at an earlier screening of the film in Seattle where similar concerns had been raised and no satisfactory answers had been provided by the two directors. In some ways, I was fielding questions meant for Muska and Olafsdottir, but in other ways, I was being positioned as another "outsider" who seemed not to be able to comprehend the complexities of small-town life in the Midwest. . . .

3. According to Wilson (2000), this story was reported in *Ebony*, Nov. 10, 1954.

REFERENCES

Altman, D. 2001. The Globalization of Sexual Identities. In *Global Sex*. Chicago: University of Chicago Press.

Baldwin, J. 1995. *Evidence of Things Not Seen*. New York: Henry Holt.

Bell, D. 2000. Eroticizing the Rural. In *De-Centering Sexualities: Politics and Representations Beyond the Metropolis*, edited by R. Phillips, D. Watt, and D. E. Shuttleton, 83–101. London: Routledge.

Boellstorff, T. 1999. The Perfect Path: Gay Men, Marriage, Indonesia. *Gay Lesbian Quarterly*, no. 4: 475–510.

Brody, J. D. 2002. Boyz Do Cry: Screening History's White Lies. *Screen* 43, no. 1: 91–96.

Cather, W. 1935. *Lucy Gayheart*. New York: Knopf.

Chauncey, G. 1989. Christian Brotherhood or Sexual Perversion? Homosexual Identities and the Construction of Sexual Boundaries in the World War I Era. In *Hidden from History: Reclaiming the Gay and Lesbian Past*, edited by M. Vicinus, G. Chauncey, and M. B. Duberman, 294–317. New York: Meridian.

Cvetkovich, A. 2003. *An Archive of Feelings: Trauma, Sexuality and Lesbian Public Cultures*. Durham, NC: Duke University Press.

Donham, D. 1998. Freeing South Africa: The 'Modernization' of Male-Male Sexuality in Soweto. *Cultural Anthropology* 13, no. 1: 3–21.

Duggan. L. 2000. *Sapphic Slashers: Sex, Violence and American Modernity*. Durham, N.C.: Duke University Press.

Fellows, W. 2001. *Farm Boys: Lives of Gay Men from the Rural Midwest*. Madison: University of Wisconsin Press.

Hietala, T. 2003. *Manifest Design: American Exceptionalism and Empire*. Ithaca, NY: Cornell University Press.

Howard, J. 1999. *Men Like That: A Southern Queer History*. Chicago: University of Chicago Press.

Jones, A. 1996. *All S/he Wanted*. New York: Pocket Books.

Lieberman, R. C. 1998. *Shifting the Color Line: Race and the American Welfare State*. Cambridge, MA: Harvard University Press.

Lipsitz, G. 1998. *The Possessive Investment in Whiteness: How White People Profit from Identity Politics*. Philadelphia: Temple University Press.

Lowe, L. 1996. *Immigrant Acts: On Asian American Cultural Politics*. Durham, NC: Duke University Press.

Manalansan, M. 1997. In the Shadow of Stonewall: Examining Gay Transnational Politics and the Diasporic Dilemma. In *The Politics of Culture in the Shadow of Capital*, edited by L. Lowe and D. Lloyd, 485–505. Durham, NC: Duke University Press.

Morris, R. 1994. Three Genders and Four Sexualities: Redressing the Discourses on Sex and Gender in Contemporary Thailand, *Positions 2*, no. 1: 15–43.

Phillips, R., D. Watt, and D. E. Shuttleton, eds. 2000. *De-Centering Sexualities: Politics and Representations beyond the Metropolis*. London: Routledge.

Ridgeway, J. 1995. *Blood in the Face: The Ku Klux Klan, Aryan Nations, Nazi Skinheads, and the Rise of a New White Culture*. New York: Thunder's Mouth Press.

Rubin, G. 1984. Thinking Sex: Notes for a Radical Theory of the Politics of Sexuality. In *Pleasure and Danger: Exploring Female Sexuality*, edited by Carol Vance, 267–319. New York: Routledge.

Scott, J. C. 1990. *Domination and the Arts of Resistance: Hidden Transcripts*. New Haven,: Yale University Press.

Sedgewick, E. K. 1986. *Between Men: English Literature and Male Homosocial Desire*. New York: Columbia University Press.

Sinfield, A. 2000. The Production of Gay and the Return of Power. In *De-Centering Sexualities: Politics and Representations beyond the Metropolis*, edited by R. Phillips, D. Watt, and D. E. Shuttleton, 21–36. London: Routledge.

Terry, J. 1999. *An American Obsession: Science, Medicine, and the Place of Homosexuality in Modern Society*. Chicago: University of Chicago Press.

Wilson, A. T. 2000. Getting Your Kicks on Route 66: Stories of Gay and Lesbian Life in Rural America. In *De-Centering Sexualities: Politics and Representations beyond the Metropolis*, edited by R. Phillips, D. Watt, and D. E. Shuttleton, 199–216. London: Routledge.

5

***

Women's Bodies, Women's Health

Our bodies grow and develop from the first moments of life. Through them we experience sexuality, pain, healing, and the complex physical, hormonal, neurological, and emotional changes that come with menstruation and menopause, pregnancy, and aging. Many of us develop strength, agility, concentration, and coordination through exercise, dance, sports, martial arts, yoga, or outdoor activities. We show dexterity in handling tools, from kitchen knives to wrenches, hammers, and saws. Pregnancy and childbirth provide intense understanding of our bodies' elasticity and stamina, and the wonder of being able to sustain another body developing inside us. We have an awareness of our bodily rhythms throughout the day or through the menstrual cycle—the ups and downs of mental and physical energy, tiredness, stiffness, and cramps.

Although there are physiological, financial, and technological limits to how much we can shape them, up to a point our bodies are malleable. We may diet or exercise, use skin-lightening creams or tanning lotions, have a nose job or a tummy tuck, and adopt particular postures and body language. We may have surgeries to counteract disabilities; our bodies may be altered by mastectomy due to breast cancer; we may need to use reading glasses, wheelchairs, or hearing aids. We may have surgery to make our physical appearance congruent with our internal sense of self.

Health is a complex mix of physical, mental, emotional, and spiritual well-being, but Western medicine separates these connected aspects into distinctive specializations with different practitioners. Our subjective experiences of health and illness are negotiated with medical experts and, increasingly, mediated through technologies like mammograms and ultrasound. This chapter discusses body issues; the effects of age, race, and class on health disparities; reproductive health; and feminist approaches to wellness.

Women's Bodies and Health

Rosemarie Garland Thompson argues that, within Western thought, female bodies and disabled bodies are viewed as "deviant and inferior" (Reading 25). She grounds this association of femaleness and disability in Aristotle's discourse on the "normal and the abnormal," where he differentiated "the generic type" (read male) from "monstrosities," or deviations from this type (read female and disabled). Hierarchical thinking also separates body and mind, and considers organic, bodily processes (associated with femaleness) inferior to the mind (associated with maleness). She shows connections between feminist theorizing and disability discourse and argues that each can gain from perspectives of the other (also see National Women's Studies Association 2002; Smith and Hutchison 2004).

Dominant U.S. culture often reduces women to bodies, valuing us only as sex objects or as bearers of children. The advertising industry uses women's bodies to sell shampoo, soft drinks, beer, tires, cars, fax machines, chain saws, and gun holsters, as well as concepts of womanliness, manliness, and heteronormativity. The **objectification** and **commodification** of women in advertising pave the way for women's dismemberment (literal and figurative) in pornography.

A key part of liberation movements for women, LGBTQQI people, people of color, and people with disabilities has been the reclaiming of our bodies as strong and beautiful, with calls for ethnic pride, LGBTQQI pride, and disability pride. Many people with disabilities argue that they are more handicapped by the mental limitations of non-disabled people than by their own minds and bodies. From some cultural perspectives, disability is considered an act of God; other cultures blame women who birth children with disabilities. Thompson suggests that it is not meaningful to insist on a clear-cut boundary between the categories "disabled" and "non-disabled." Ynestra King (1993a) also emphasized the contingent nature of bodily experience:

> The common ground for the person—the human body—is a place of shifting sand that can fail us at any time. It can change shape and properties without warning; this is an essential truth of embodied existence. Of all the ways of becoming "other" in our society, disability is the only one that can happen to anyone in an instant, transforming that person's life and identity forever. *(p. 75)*

Beauty "Ideals" Can Make You Sick

Everyone needs nourishing food, clean drinking water, and adequate exercise in order to maintain health and vitality. The appropriate balance of food and exercise is somewhat subjective, depending on age, physical ability, personal tastes, and cultural preferences. Two examples of serious imbalance are eating disorders like anorexia and bulimia, often with a punishing exercise regime, and overeating, typically accompanied by too little exercise.

Much research, commentary, and concern has focused on the damaging health effects of obsessive dieting, which mainly affects young white middle-class women, exemplified by Abra Fortune Chernik who describes her experience with anorexia in Reading 68. Feminist scholars have analyzed the oppressive nature of ads and media representations that bombard women and girls with an ideal of beauty defined as thin, lean, tall, young, white, and heterosexual, with flawless skin and well-groomed hair (see, e.g., Bordo 1993; Brumberg 1997; Hesse-Biber 1996; Kilbourne 1999; Martin 2007; Wolf 1991). Where women of color are used, they are often light-skinned and conform to this same body type. This beauty standard is backed by a multi-billion-dollar beauty industry that sees women's bodies as a series of problems in need of correction. The aim is to promote insecurity, self-hatred, and distorted perceptions of size, appetite, and attractiveness, so that we will consume the countless products, diet plans, and cosmetic surgeries marketed to remedy our alleged deficiencies. Realty TV shows like *Extreme Makeover* and *America's Next Top Model* normalize this goal. To the extent that women internalize ideal beauty standards, what Kim Chernin (1994) called "the tyranny of slenderness," we set ourselves up to pursue a goal that is largely unattainable. Even the elite corps of full-time fashion models, "deployed in a way that keeps 150 million women in line" (Wolf 1991, p. 41), have their photos airbrushed and digitally enhanced (see, e.g., Collins 2008; Reaves et al. 2004). Jean Kilbourne describes the "toxic cultural environment" surrounding U.S. girls and shows how advertising images can severely undermine girls' self-confidence and sense of agency, which can lead to serious physical and emotional health problems (Reading 26).

Resisting Beauty Stereotypes

Ideal beauty standards are ableist, ageist, heterosexist, and racist, and many women and girls do their best to resist them. Women in their fifties, sixties, or older often feel that they have newfound confidence and purpose as they age (Bird 1995; Brice 2003). These years may be a time of self-definition and autonomy when they can resist earlier pressures to conform to dominant beauty standards. Writer Meridel Le Sueur (1982) used the word "ripening" to describe the development of her work over five decades and her satisfaction with her fulfilling life—a positive

Italian fashion designer Valentino and two supermodels who helped make his collection a success.

way of thinking about aging with an emphasis on "generativity, rather than decline" (Browne 1998, p. 68).

Noting that mainstream culture equates beauty and power for women, Silva Tenenbein (1998) reversed the beauty-power equation for lesbians. "For dykes it's not beauty which makes us powerful but power that makes us beautiful . . . our passion, our strength, and our courage to choose to be the 'other' . . . our adamant refusal to be deflected from what we want" (pp. 159, 160).

Large women of all racial/ethnic groups challenge weight-loss industry stereotypes and mainstream assumptions that they are sloppy, irresponsible, undisciplined, depressed, sexless, unwanted, or unhealthy (e.g., Lamm 1995). Many African American women say, "I don't want to be no skinny minny." Queen T'isha wrote:

Racism and sexism as practiced in America includes body hostilities. I didn't grow up with the belief that fat women were to be despised.

The women in my family were fat, smart, sexy, employed, wanted, married, and the rulers of their households.

(Quoted in Edison and Notkin 1994, p. 106)

And Elsie Matthesen argued,

We have a right to take up space. We have a right to stretch out, to be big, to be "too much to handle." To challenge the rest of the world to grow up, get on with it, and become big enough to "handle" us. . . .

(Quoted in Edison and Notkin 1994, p. 107)

Dora Dewey-McCracken confounded common assumptions about fatness with regard to health:

I've been diabetic since I was nineteen. . . . All my life I gained and lost at least sixty pounds each year. . . . I tried all diets, eating disorders, and fasts, only to gain the fat back, and more each time. I'm the fattest I've ever been, and

Overweight and Obesity: Social and Economic Factors

- *Access to nutritious food.* Eating well takes greater effort in low-income neighborhoods, which tend to have a preponderance of liquor and convenience stores rather than full-service supermarkets that carry fresh fruits and vegetables. Fast food restaurants are more prevalent in poorer neighborhoods than in middle-class areas; fast food is offered at a lower price relative to more healthy options (Morland et al. 2002).

- *Industrialized food processing* has made "energy-dense" snacks and desserts (with a high proportion of fat and sugar) extremely inexpensive (Brownell and Horgen 2004).

- *Costs for foods* such as milk, eggs, bread, vegetables, chicken, and beef have risen, mainly because of increased oil prices and the growing demand for food crops, such as corn and soybeans for alternative fuels like ethanol and biodiesel.

- *Time.* Women juggling responsibilities of waged-work and caring for their families may have difficulty finding time to shop for food, cook meals at home, or exercise.

- *Exercise.* Most people in the United States lead sedentary lives. Fewer girls than boys take up sports; many adult women have no regular exercise practice. Larger women feel self-conscious in gyms that mainly cater to young, thin women. Women do not want to walk—or allow their children to hang out—in unsafe neighborhoods (Yancey, Leslie, and Abel 2006).

- *Culture of self-care.* Many women have been socialized to take care of others in their families and communities rather than themselves (Beauboeuf-Lafontant 2007). They may prioritize their outward appearance and pay for clothes, hair-care, and nails rather than exercise programs or fitness classes.

- *Overeating.* Eating can be a significant source of comfort and pleasure; it is socially acceptable for women and a safer way to buffer pain than drugs or alcohol. Women may overeat as a way to cope with frustration, anger, anxiety, and sadness; physical, emotional, or sexual abuse; and the daily pain of sexism, racism, classism, and heterosexism (Thompson 1994).

yet my diabetic blood work is the best it's ever been. My doctor once told me, "As long as your disease is controlled and your blood chemistry is good, your fat is just a social issue." I'm extremely lucky to have this doctor; with most doctors, fat phobia is the rule, not the exception. They see the fat and their brains turn off.

(Quoted in Edison and Notkin 1994, p. 104)

Size Acceptance, Obesity, and Health

In response to discrimination and stigma experienced by women who are considered overweight, some feminists have welcomed the notion of "size acceptance" and view "fat as an aesthetic . . . issue" (Yancey, Leslie, and Abel 2006, p. 425), seeing obesity as a social construction. A growing number of organizations are working to counter fat oppression including Boston Area Fat Liberation (Cambridge, Mass.), the Council on Size and Weight Discrimination (Mount Marion, N.Y.), Largess—the Network for Size Esteem (New Haven, Conn.) and the National Association to Advance Fat Acceptance (Sacramento, Calif.). Photographers have also undertaken "full body" projects that celebrate women of all shapes and sizes (e.g., Edison and Notkin 1994; Nimoy 2007; Olson 2008).

Public health researchers Antronette Yancey, Joanne Leslie, and Emily Abel (2006) argued that women's studies teachers and scholars have tended to downplay the "accumulating data about the health consequences of the obesity epidemic," which they found "surprising and troubling" (p. 425). These writers endorsed government definitions of overweight as having a body mass index of 25 to 29.9, and obesity as an index of 30 or more. On this standard, 67 percent of U.S. adults are overweight or obese, and 34 percent are obese (National Center for Health Statistics 2007, p. 38). More women are overweight than men; 50 percent of Black women are defined as overweight compared with 32 percent of white women. Scholars and advocates concerned with the health of women of color have pointed out this disparity and underlined the links between obesity and illness, especially heart disease, diabetes, strokes, and joint problems (see, e.g., Avery 1990; hooks 1993; Lovejoy 2001; Thompson 1994; White 1991). Yancey, Leslie, and Abel (2006) argue that public health practitioners generally view obesity in terms of social and economic factors that contribute to an obesity-causing environment, which particularly affects low-income people of color (see Box). They advocate prevention policies and programs that address underlying causes as much more effective than urging individuals to lose weight.

The discourse of fat acceptance is in marked contrast with many health practitioners' views on obesity, which raises significant questions of where to draw the line in the interests of physical, emotional, and spiritual health. A range of micro- and meso-level factors are involved in being able to care for ourselves, as shown in this chapter. Also, attention to macro-level factors provides an understanding of the health disparities among women based on race, class, culture, sexuality, and nationality.

Reproductive Health

The ability to become pregnant and have a baby is a profound experience, usually with far-reaching consequences for the mother. A woman becomes pregnant for many reasons: she wants to have a child; she wants to experience pregnancy and childbirth; she wants to be recognized as a grown woman; she believes it will make her a "real" woman; she hopes it will keep her relationship together or make her partner happy. Some women plan to be pregnant; others get pregnant by accident; still others as a result of being raped. This deeply personal experience is also a public issue. For some women—especially teenagers, lesbians, and mothers receiving welfare—there may be a serious

tension between the personal event of pregnancy and societal attitudes to it. African American women have consistently tried to be self-determining in their reproductive lives despite having been used as breeders by slaveholders and despite subsequent systematic state interventions to control their fertility (Darling and Tyson 1999; Dula 1996; Hill Collins 2004; Roberts 1997; Ross 1993; Silliman et al. 2004; Taylor 1997). These include state-sponsored sterilization programs, chemical contraceptives like Depo-Provera and Norplant, and the chemical sterilizing agent, Quinacrine. Law professor and legal scholar Dorothy Roberts (1997) has referred to this phenomenon as nothing less than "killing the black body."

Controlling Fertility

Women's reproductive years span roughly half our lifetimes, from our teens to our forties. Many women in the United States want to control their fertility—to limit the number of children they have, to postpone pregnancy until they are older, to avoid pregnancy with a particular partner, or to avoid it altogether. Women also want the freedom to bear children. To do this we need sex education that is accurate and culturally appropriate; affordable and reliable birth control; safe, legal, affordable abortion; prenatal care and care through childbirth; health care for infants and children; and alternative insemination. In addition we need an adequate income, good general health care, and widespread cultural acceptance that we have a right to control our lives in this way. As argued by Rosemarie Garland Thompson (Reading 25), women with disabilities must also fight for the right to have children in the face of a dominant view that they are nonsexual beings who could not cope with being mothers (see also Finger 1990; Prilleltensky 2003; Saxton 1995; Wilkerson 2002).

Birth Control Barrier methods like condoms and diaphragms have been used for many years. In the 1960s the intrauterine device (IUD), often called the coil, was introduced despite severe unwanted side effects for some women, such as heavy bleeding, pain, and cramps. The pill, introduced around the same time—and the most popular form of contraception today for women under 30—was the first chemical contraceptive to be taken every day. It

NON SEQUITOR

affects the whole body continuously, as do newer methods like Depo-Provera (an injectable contraceptive that is effective for three months) and Norplant (implanted under the skin and effective for up to five years). Low-income African American and Native American women and Latinas are much more likely than white women to be encouraged to use these long-acting contraceptives. Official policy seeks to limit their pregnancies and assumes that these women would be unreliable using other methods, thereby continuing the long connection between birth control and **eugenics,** or selective breeding, often linked to racism and ableism, supposedly to create healthier and more intelligent people, to save resources, and to lessen human suffering (Roberts 1997; Ross 1993; Smith 2002). The Black Women's Health Network, the National Latina Health Organization, and other women's health advocates have called for the withdrawal of Depo-Provera as unsafe and also called attention to the fact that many women using Norplant had difficulty finding anyone to remove it. These methods compound many of the health problems that affect poor women of color, including hypertension, diabetes, and stress. In 1999 American Home Products Corporation, which sells Norplant, agreed to offer cash settlements to 36,000 women who filed suit claiming that they had not been adequately warned about possible negative effects of using Norplant (Morrow 1999a). These included excessive menstrual bleeding, headaches, nausea, dizziness, and depression.

Other birth-control methods include the female condom, a loosely fitting, polyurethane (not latex) pouch with a semiflexible plastic ring at each end that lines the vagina and fits over the vulva. It provides protection from sexually transmitted infections (STIs) as well as pregnancy, but is not as effective as the male condom. Emergency contraception that prevents fertilization is available over the counter to women 18 years and over, under the trade name Plan B. It can be used in the event of unprotected sex or if another form of contraception fails. This is a chemical method that involves taking oral contraceptives within 72 hours of unprotected sex, the sooner the better. The Food and Drug Administration delayed making this form of contraception available without a doctor's prescription although its Advisory Committee on Reproductive Health Drugs and Nonprescription Drugs voted for it overwhelmingly (Stein 2007). According to a *Washington Post* report, "surveys and anecdotal reports indicate that some pharmacies refuse to stock the drug," and "some pharmacists refuse to provide it to women" (Stein 2007). A popular over-the-counter contraceptive, the Today Sponge, came back on the market in 2003 but does not offer the same degree of protection as oral contraceptives (Zernike 2003).

Pharmaceutical companies have all but abandoned the field of contraceptive research in this country because of a decline in funding from the government, international sources, and private foundations, as well as political opposition.

Abortion   Attitudes toward abortion have varied greatly over time and from one society to another. Historically, the Catholic Church held the view that the soul did not enter the fetus for at least forty days after conception and allowed abortion up to that point. In 1869, however, Pope Pius IX declared that life begins at conception, and thus all abortion became murder in the eyes of the Church. In the United States up until the mid-nineteenth century, women were allowed to seek an abortion in the early part of pregnancy before they felt the fetus moving, a subjectively determined time, referred to as the quickening. After the Civil War more restrictive abortion laws were passed, partly to increase population and partly to shift authority over women's reproductive lives to the developing medical profession. By 1900 the only legal ground for an abortion was to save the life of the mother. Many women were forced to bring unwanted pregnancies to term in poverty, illness, or appalling personal circumstances. Thousands died trying to abort themselves or at the hands of "backstreet" abortionists. Some upper- and middle-class women found doctors to perform safe abortions for a high price; some doctors did abortions for poor women. The women and the doctors risked prosecution if they were found out, as described by Grace Paley (1998) in her short article, "The Illegal Days" (also see Joffe 1995; Miller 1993; Reagan 1997; Solinger 1994, 2000). Women with knowledge of herbs or medicine helped other women. The Janes organized a clandestine feminist abortion service in the Chicago area in the early 1970s (Arcana 2005; Kamen 2000; Kaplan 1995).

In 1973 the landmark case *Roe v. Wade* made abortion legal. It defined freedom of choice as a right to privacy, protected by the U.S. Constitution. It recognized that no one except the woman herself has the right to decide whether to have an abortion. Ever since this legislation was enacted, it has been contested. This began in 1977 with the Hyde Amendment that withdrew state funding for abortion for poor women. Subsequent measures included rules requiring waiting periods and parental consent for teens. Anti-choice organizations have staged violent protests at abortion clinics, bombed clinics, harassed patients, and killed doctors known to perform abortions as part of their practice (Baird-Windle and Bader 2001; Jaggar 1994). Women's health advocates have struggled to keep clinics open and lobbied for the Freedom of Access to Clinic Entrances Act 1994, which reduced harassment outside clinics. These legal restrictions, together with severe, ongoing harassment, have reduced the number of abortion providers, and,

by 2000, 87 percent of U.S. counties and 97 percent of rural counties had no abortion provider (Henshaw 2003). Fewer doctors are being trained to carry out the procedure, and many have stopped performing abortions because of the risks to themselves and their families.

In 2005, 19 out of every 1,000 women aged 15 to 44 had abortions, the lowest rate since 1975 (Guttmacher Institute 2008b). Factors assumed to be responsible for this decline include increased willingness to use contraception, reduced access to abortion, and negative attitudes toward abortion. Most women who had an abortion in 2005 were 25 or younger, white, and unmarried; 60 percent of the procedures were done in the first eight weeks of pregnancy, and 88 percent in the first twelve weeks. Proportionate to their numbers in the overall population, Black women were 4.8 times as likely as white women to have an abortion, and Latinas were 2.7 times as likely. In 2000, the Food and Drug Administration approved RU-486 (the "abortion pill," also called mifespristone). An increasing number of providers now offer medication abortions; in 2005 these accounted for 22 percent of all abortions before 9 weeks and 13 percent of all abortions (Guttmacher Institute 2008b).

Women's complex thoughts and feelings about abortion, about the profound responsibility of choosing to end a life, have been downplayed by pro-abortion activists as they focused on keeping abortion legal. Judith Arcana (1994) has argued that abortion is a motherhood issue, a decision a woman makes because she believes it is the best for herself and her baby. Like anti-choice activists, she called a fetus a baby. Unlike them, Arcana passionately defends a woman's right to abortion. She argued that the semantics of *"fetus or embryo"* used by pro-choice organizers skirts the central moral issue and has cost them potential support. It has conceded the space for anti-choice activists to excoriate women who have abortions as heartless and irresponsible monsters. She called for women to speak about our abortions "in open recognition of our joy or sadness, our regret or relief—in conscious acceptance of the responsibility for our choice" (see also Arcana 2005; Jacob 2002).

White feminists made abortion the centerpiece of reproductive rights activism in the 1980s and 1990s. By contrast, women of color have generally seen abortion as only one part of a wider reproductive-health agenda that includes health care for women and children and the freedom to have children (see, e.g., Nelson 2003; Ross et al. 2002; Silliman et al. 2004). Abortion advocates originally campaigned for women's *right* to abortion but have moved to a "softer" pro-choice framework. Rights apply to everyone; choice is only meaningful for those with resources. Thus, a pro-choice framework creates a hierarchy among women based on resources which are linked to race and class. Some women of color health advocates have developed the concept of **reproductive justice** that relates health and reproductive rights to broader issues of social and economic justice, as elaborated by Asian Communities for Reproductive Justice (Reading 28; Silliman et al. 2004; Smith 2005a). This offers a way of thinking about wellness for individuals, communities, and the wider society in terms of the eradication of systems of oppression and injustice. Historian Rickie Solinger (2005) argued that this is a long way off in the United States where the government and elites have always sought to control women's fertility through laws, attitudes, and social pressure. She cites current restrictions on abortion, beliefs that value the fetus over the mother, women prisoners' lack of reproductive control, and inadequate sex education as evidence that this continues.

Meanwhile, a whole generation of women has grown up, taking abortion rights for granted despite the wide and growing gap between legality and access. In April 2004, more than one million people from all walks of life, many of them young women, participated in the March for Women's Lives, in Washington, D.C., the largest protest march in U.S. history. Their main demand was for broad reproductive freedoms. According to national pollster Celinda Lake (2005) 56 percent of respondents polled nationwide favored keeping abortion legal in all or most cases, and 62 percent felt that the government should not interfere with a woman's access to abortion.

For the past thirty-five years, well-funded anti-abortion groups have worked strategically to undermine and overturn the right to abortion. They have used public education, mainstream media, protests, and direct action—including attacks on clinics and their staffs as mentioned earlier. They have financed and elected anti-choice political candidates at city, state, and congressional levels. Republican Congresspersons have introduced bills session after session to whittle away at the legality of abortion and elevate the unborn child, even as a "nonviable fetus," to the status of "personhood" with rights equal to or greater than those of the mother. In January 2005, on the 32nd anniversary of *Roe v. Wade,* President George W. Bush assured abortion-rights opponents, "This movement will not fail" (Associated Press 2005). If the Supreme Court overturns *Roe v. Wade,* legal jurisdiction will revert to the states, many of which are poised to ban abortion or to re-criminalize it (Guttmacher Institute 2008a). This issue is central to women's autonomy and will continue to be highly contentious (see, e.g., Feldt 2004; Nelson 2003; Petchesky 1990; Silliman et al. 2004; Smith 2005a; Solinger 1998, 2005).

Sterilization   Sterilization abuse, rather than the right to abortion, has been a concern of poor women, especially women of color, for many years. Sterilization, without women's full knowledge or under duress, has been a common practice in the United States for poor Latina, African American, and Native American women. By 1982, 24 percent of African American women, 35 percent of Puerto Rican women, and 42 percent of Native American women had been sterilized, compared with 15 percent of white women (Black Women's Health Project 1995; also see Davis 1983a; Jaimes and Halsey 1986; Lopez 1997; Nelson 2003; Silliman et al. 2004; Smith 2002). Currently, sterilization is federally funded under the Medicaid program and is free on demand to poor women. Quinacrine, a chemical sterilizing agent, is the newest method and has dangerous side effects.

Teen Pregnancy   Babies born to teens present a tremendous responsibility for young mothers and their families, and the U.S. has the highest rate of teen pregnancy of all industrialized countries. Analyzed by race and ethnicity, teen birthrates are highest for Latinas, African Americans, and Asian or Pacific Island teens. Government and community organizations have made major efforts to reduce the number of teen births from an all-time high of 62 births per 1,000 girls in 1991. The reduction in teen births is due to increased use of condoms or injectable and implant contraceptives

(Depo-Provera and Norplant) and changing teenage sexual activity. However, in 2006 the teen birthrate showed a 3 percent rise for girls aged 15–19, to 42 births per 1,000 girls (Hamilton, Martin, and Ventura 2007). As mentioned in Chapter 4, many health advocates criticize the limitations of federally funded sex education programs that emphasize "abstinence-only" (Boonstra 2007). School and community programs that do not receive federal funding can teach about contraception and may distribute condoms, which prevent pregnancy and the spread of sexually transmitted infections, including HIV/AIDS. These issues have been highly contentious for some parents, school boards, conservative religious groups, and Bush administration policy-makers. In 2007, Sister Song Women of Color Reproductive Health Collective organized a three-day conference, "Let's Talk About Sex," which included a workshop by teen mothers who are members of Sistas on the Rise. The presenters, young women of African American, Dominican, and Latino descent who have stayed in school and continued their education, discussed issues they faced and "presented a fresh perspective on birthing and parenting at a young age" (Counts 2007).

Sexually Transmitted Infections (STIs)   Sexually transmitted infections affect some 19 million people each year, almost half of them aged 15–24 (Centers for Disease Control and Prevention 2007b). The term STI refers to more than twenty-five diseases, including herpes, genital warts, pubic lice ("crabs"), chlamydia, gonorrhea, syphilis, and HIV. With the exception of syphilis, all STIs are increasing at an alarming rate. For women, STIs may not be noticeable or may be difficult to diagnose as women often do not have any symptoms or, if they do, the symptoms are mistaken for something else. Sexually transmitted infection can affect how a woman feels about her body and her partner and can lead to pelvic inflammatory disease or infertility. Knowing about safer sexual practices is important in reducing the risk of sexually transmitted infections, including HIV/AIDS. It is important to note that condoms (male or female) are the only form of birth control that also give some protection against sexually transmitted infections. But knowing this is not enough. In Reading 20, psychologists Nicola Gavey, Kathryn

McPhillips, and Marion Doherty note several factors that limit women's ability to influence their partners to use condoms. These include the power dynamics between women and men, women's assumptions about what it means to be a "good lover," and their ideals of giving and sharing. In Reading 29, Emma Bell and Luisa Orza, staff members of the International Community of Women Living with HIV/AIDS, discuss challenges faced by women diagnosed as HIV-positive, including stigma, intimate partnerships, and family relationships.

Medicalization of Reproductive Life

Childbirth   Before there were male gynecologists, midwives helped women through pregnancy and childbirth (Ehrenreich and English 1972, 2005). As medicine became professionalized in the nineteenth century, gynecology and obstetrics developed as an area of medical specialization. Doctors eroded the position of midwives and ignored or scorned their knowledge as "old wives' tales." Largely for the convenience of the doctor, women began to give birth lying on their backs, perhaps the hardest position in which to deliver a baby. Forceps and various painkilling medications were widely used. From the 1950s onward cesarean sections (C-sections) became more common, often for the doctors' convenience or from fear of malpractice suits. In 2005, 30 percent of births in the United States were C-sections, the highest rate in the world (Hamilton, Martin, and Ventura 2006). The past thirty-five years have seen a further extension of this medicalization process as doctors monitor pregnancy from the earliest stages with a battery of techniques such as amniocentesis, sonograms, and ultrasound. Although this technology allows medical practitioners, and through them, pregnant women, to know details about the health and condition of the fetus, as well as its sex, it also changes women's experiences of pregnancy and childbirth and can erode their knowledge of and confidence in their bodily processes. In Reading 27, Joy Harjo describes changes in Native American women's experiences of childbirth over three generations—her mother, her daughter, and herself. These included variations in their life circumstances, medical technology, and their treatment by hospital staff as Native American women. She notes the routine way she was offered the option of being sterilized and told that "the moment of birth was the best time to do it."

Reproductive Technologies   Technologies such as in vitro fertilization (IVF), in which a woman's eggs are fertilized by sperm outside her body and the fertilized embryo is then implanted into her womb, are an important development. They push the medicalization of pregnancy and childbirth one step further and hold out the hope that infertile couples or postmenopausal women will be able to have children. Bearing a child as a surrogate mother under contract to an infertile couple is one way a young woman can earn an estimated $15,000–20,000 plus medical expenses for nine months' "work." Ads specify attributes sought in the birth mother, including race, age, IQ, etc. Fertility clinics also need ovum donors and seek to harvest the eggs of young, college-educated women from a range of specified racial and ethnic groups. Infertility treatments so far have had a spectacularly low success rate and are very expensive. They are aimed at middle- and upper-middle-class women as a way of widening individual choice. Infertility may stem from a range of causes such as sexually transmitted infections, the effects of IUDs, delayed childbearing, and occupational and environmental factors. Infertility rates were lower in the 1990s than in previous decades, but this issue has a higher profile nowadays because of technological developments.

These reproductive technologies open up an array of economic, legal, and moral questions (Donchin and Purdy 1999; Ginsburg and Rapp 1995; Hubbard 1990; Ragone and Twine 2000; Teays and Purdy 2001). Are they liberating for women? For which women? And, at what costs? Some feminists have argued that women's biology and the ability to reproduce have been used to justify their social and economic subordination. In her now classic radical feminist text, Shulamith Firestone (1970), for example, was convinced that women's liberation requires freedom from biological reproduction and looked forward to developments in reproductive technology that would make it possible for a fetus to develop outside the womb. This is in stark contrast to sociologist Barbara Katz Rothman (1986) and the myriad women who believe that, if women lose their ability to reproduce, we lose a "quintessential female experience" (p. 111). Other feminist critics of reproductive technologies have focused on their invasiveness and consumers' lack of power over and knowledge about these methods, as compared with that of medical experts or "medocrats" (Arditti, Klein, and Minden 1984; Corea 1985, 1987; Lublin 1998; Morgan and Michaels 1999; Petchesky 1997; Stanworth 1987).

Menopause   This natural life process is increasingly treated as a disease rather than as a series of complex bodily and emotional changes. Many middle-aged women have been advised to take hormone-replacement therapy (HRT) to control the symptoms of menopause such as hot flashes, insomnia, and vaginal dryness (Klein and Dumble 1994; Komesaroff, Rothfield, and Daly 1997). A major study of 46,355 women conducted by the National Cancer Institute confirmed that long-term use of hormone replacement after menopause can increase the risk of breast cancer (Grady 2000).

Executive Director of National Women's Health Network, Cindy Pearson, "uses science to challenge science," opposing the biomedical "definition of older women's bodies as deficient" and proving that what is "lost" through menopause "does not need to be replaced in order for a woman to live out the rest of her life healthfully" (*NWSAction* 2004, p. 39; also see Worcester 2004).

Women and Illness

There is a rich and growing literature on women's experiences of illness, healing, and recovery, particularly in relation to breast cancer, chronic fatigue immune deficiency syndrome (CFIDS), and multiple sclerosis (e.g., Duff 1993; Griffin 1999; Lorde 1996; Mairs 1996; Rosenblum 1997; Sigler, Love, and Yood 1999). Counselor and writer Kat Duff (1993) noted that our society's "concepts of physical and psychological health have become one-sidedly identified with the heroic qualities most valued in our culture: youth, activity, productivity, independence, strength, confidence, and optimism" (p. 37). Illness challenges us to rethink our definition of self, our value and worth, in this ableist society, as these authors attest.

The World's Deadliest Disease Is Poverty

- Around ten million children worldwide die each year before their fifth birthday, mainly from malnutrition, malaria, acute respiratory infections, measles, diarrhea, and HIV/AIDS.

- Most of these conditions can be prevented or cured with improvements in sanitation, clean water supply, better housing, an adequate food supply, and general hygiene. The majority of deaths from infectious diseases can be prevented with existing, cost-effective measures including childhood vaccinations, bed nets and other malaria prevention treatments, oral rehydration therapy, and antibiotics.

- Poor nutrition and underweight affects an estimated 27 percent of all children under 5. This puts them at increased risk for infections like diarrhea and pneumonia. Underweight remains a pervasive problem in developing countries where poverty is a strong underlying determinant, contributing to household food insecurity, mothers' inadequate nutrition, unhealthy environments, and poor health care.

- Diseases linked to high blood pressure, cholesterol, tobacco, alcohol, and obesity have been most common in industrialized countries. They are now becoming more prevalent in countries of the global South, reflecting changes in living patterns, including diet, physical activity, the availability of tobacco and alcohol, and cultural upheavals.

Source: UNICEF 2007.

Health Disparities: Race, Class, and Gender

A growing literature evidences marked disparities in health among different groups in the United States (see, e.g., Barr 2008; Braveman 2006; Kawachi, Daniels, and Robinson 2005; LaVeist 2005; Schultz and Mullings 2005). This disparity is attributable to a mix of overlapping factors including income level, educational attainment, occupation, access to health services, neighborhood and work conditions, and so forth—factors linked to both race and class. Most government statistics are analyzed according to race/ethnicity in three undifferentiated categories: white, Black, and Hispanic—which includes Puerto Ricans, Cubans, Mexican Americans, and people from Central and South America. Some reports give details for Native Americans and Native Alaskans, or for Asians and Pacific Islanders—another very heterogeneous group. Data on many social issues are rarely analyzed according to socioeconomic class. Bear this in mind during this discussion, which suffers from limitations of the data available. Also note that some racial/ethnic and gender disparities in health persist even after controlling for the beneficial effects of education and economic well-being.

Taken as a whole, the health of white women and Asian American women is significantly better than that of African American women, Native American women, and Latinas (Ross et al. 2002). However, middle-class, educated women of all races are more likely than low-income women to know about mammograms as a screening procedure for the early detection of breast cancer and that they are recommended for women over 40. They are more likely to have insurance to cover mammograms and to be registered with a doctor who encourages having them. Late diagnosis of breast cancer is directly related to higher mortality rates. Among cancer patients, white women also get what the literature refers to as "more aggressive treatment" compared to African American women, who are often not told about all relevant treatment options, not given the full range of tests, and not always prescribed the most effective medications. Breast cancer affects one woman in nine nationwide, though there are much higher incidences in certain geographic areas. Science researchers Rita Arditti and Tatiana Schreiber (1998) argued that environmental factors are significant in explaining this discrepancy. The higher incidence is linked to race and class, as low-income women, especially women of color, often live in areas with poor physical environment.

Tuberculosis, an infectious disease associated with poverty and poor living conditions, was prevalent in the late nineteenth century and all but eradicated in the United States during the twentieth century. Compared with the general population, Native Americans are four times as likely to have tuberculosis. Frederica Daly (Reading 12) gives detailed historical, legal, and economic background for her brief discussion of Native American health, which is among the worst in the country. Hypertension, a major risk factor for heart disease and stroke, is much more prevalent among African American women than it is among white women. Public health researchers have attributed this difference, in part, to stress related to racism and poverty. More African American women die in their twenties compared to white women due to drug use, HIV/AIDS, homicide, and maternal mortality.

Another indicator of health disparities is found in data on infant mortality, the number of infants who die before their first birthday. Infant mortality for babies born in 2003, for example, showed the typical pattern in the United States. Asian and Pacific Islanders have the lowest rate (4.8 deaths per 1,000 live births), followed by white (5.7), Puerto Rican (8.2), American Indian (8.7), and African American infants (13.5) (National Center for Health Statistics 2007, Table 19). Infant mortality rates have steadily decreased over the past seventy years, but Black infants continue to die at more than twice the rate of white infants. Infant mortality rates are linked to personal factors such as smoking during pregnancy and macro-level factors like poverty. Mortality rates were higher for infants whose mothers did not have prenatal care in the first trimester, more common among Native American, Mexican American, and African American women, compared with Asian American women and white women. Biologist Sandra Steingraber (2001) discussed the complex process of fetal development and linked fetal and infant health to external environmental factors like contamination due to lead, chemical weed-killers, and other hazardous substances (Reading 62).

Gender has also been a significant factor in diagnosing women with HIV/AIDS (Goldstein and Manlowe 1997). Women have not been diagnosed as early as men because their symptoms are not so clear-cut and doctors were less likely to look for symptoms of HIV/AIDS in women. Also, because there were fewer women in clinical research trials, they did not receive the better treatment received by men who participated in such trials. Primary care internist Barbara Ogur (1996) has pointed out

that negative stereotypes of HIV-positive women (as drug users and women with multiple sex partners) have affected their visibility and care. Of the women in the United States who were living with HIV/AIDS in 2005, 64 percent were Black, 19 percent were white, 15 percent were Hispanic, 1 percent were Asian or Pacific Islander, and less than 1 percent were American Indian or Native Alaskan (Centers for Disease Control and Prevention 2007a). Far more women than men contract HIV through heterosexual contact (79 percent compared to 17 percent). Emma Bell and Luisa Orza work with the International Community of Women Living with HIV/AIDS, a nonprofit organization founded in 1992, and the only international network of HIV-positive women. In Reading 29, they discuss the policy framework established in various countries to support women with HIV/AIDS, and argue for improvements in services and changes in attitudes on the part of medical professionals and policy makers, especially regarding women's sexuality, pregnancy, and mothering.

Toxic workplaces are a serious health hazard, especially for women of color. Some companies have kept women out of the most hazardous work—often the highest paid among blue-collar jobs—or required that they be sterilized first, to avoid being sued if these workers later give birth to babies with disabilities. Women working in computer manufacturing, nursing, housecleaning, chicken processing, and the dairy industry are all exposed to chemicals as part of their work, as are manicurists and farm workers. We take up this issue of environmental contamination and health again in Chapter 11.

Women of all race and class groups who are beaten by their partners or suffer emotional violence or sexual abuse are subject to a significant health hazard (see Chapter 6).

Mental and Emotional Health

Many more women are classified as having some sort of mental illness compared to men, especially depression, and the proportion of women seeking help for personal or emotional problems is twice as high as it is for men. However, one cannot infer from this that everyone who "seeks help" does so voluntarily; sometimes seeing a counselor or therapist is required by a social service agency or is a condition of probation. Voluntarily seeking help for emotional problems is linked to one's ability to pay, finding a suitable therapist, and cultural attitudes toward this kind of treatment. Also, it is more socially acceptable for women to seek help for mental health concerns compared to men. Patients in mental hospitals represent a relatively small proportion of those who are suffering mentally and emotionally. In general, women are admitted to mental hospitals as inpatients in roughly the same numbers as men.

Many people of all classes and racial groups attempt to deal with the pain and difficulty of their lives through drugs and alcohol. Frederica Daly noted that rates of alcoholism, homicide, and suicide among Native Americans are significantly higher than the national rates (Reading 12). In the United States, drug addiction is often thought of as a crime rather than as a health issue. We discuss it further under the topic of crime and criminalization in Chapter 9, but we also see it as a symptom of stress brought on by the pressures of life, often caused by social and economic inequality. There are far fewer drug-treatment programs than required, and fewer for women than for men.

A number of feminist writers have argued that contemporary approaches to mental distress, as illness, can be harmful to women (Chesler 1972; Ehrenreich and English 2005; Lerman 1996; Russell 1995; Showalter 1987; Ussher 1991). Philosopher Denise Russell (1995) traced the history of definitions of madness from medieval Europe, where it was thought of as a combination of error and sin. During the seventeenth century, economic crises and rising unemployment in Europe prompted local officials to build houses of confinement for beggars, drunks, vagabonds, and other poor people and petty criminals, as well as for those who were thought mad. Through the eighteenth and nineteenth centuries, psychiatry gradually developed as a medical specialty and asylums in Europe and the United States were headed by doctors, who theorized that much mental distress experienced by women was due to their reproductive capacities and sexuality. Hysteria, thought to be due to a disturbance of the womb, became a catchall category to describe women's mental illness. (The English word *hysterical* comes from the Greek word *hysterikos,* meaning "of the womb.") Writer/literary critic Elaine Showalter (1987) and psychologist/ psychotherapist Phyllis Chesler (1972) showed how definitions of

madness had been used to suppress women's agency, creativity, education, and political involvement. Nineteenth-century white upper- and middle-class women who wanted to write, paint, travel, or speak out in public on issues of the day were assumed by their husbands—and by psychiatrists—to be insane. Charlotte Perkins Gilman's powerful fictional work *The Yellow Wallpaper,* for example, describes this experience and was written as a result of having lived through it. More recently, depression and premenstrual syndrome (PMS) have replaced "hysteria" as stock phrases used in describing mental illness in women.

Feminist writers offer scathing critiques of the alleged objectivity of much contemporary mental health theorizing and of the value judgments and blatant sexism involved in many diagnostic categories like depression, behavioral disorders, and personality disorders that affect women more than men. Symptoms for these disorders are often very general, vague, and overlapping, and, according to feminist philosopher, Denise Russell (1995), there is little agreement among practitioners as to what conditions are indicated by the symptoms. The American Psychological Association did not drop homosexuality from its list of mental disorders until 1973. Lesbianism was thought to be caused by dominant mothers and weak fathers or, conversely, by girls having exclusively male role models. Those who "came out" in the 1950s and 1960s risked being sent to psychiatrists or mental institutions for a "cure." Since the 1980s, women who do not conform to traditional gender roles may be diagnosed with "gender identity disorder" (Scholinski 1997; Stryker and Whittle 2006).

Russell questioned the assumption that there is a biological or neurological basis for mental distress and argues that drug therapies based on this assumption have very mixed results in practice. Rather, she points to many external factors affecting women's mental equilibrium, including childhood sexual abuse, rape, domestic violence, restricted educational or economic opportunities, and pressure to look beautiful, to be thin, to be compliant wives and long-suffering mothers, any of which could reasonably make women depressed or "crazy." Hopelessness and anger at such circumstances are not irrational reactions. Women's symptoms may seem vague to doctors, who may not really try to find out what is troubling them. Even

We men may have 99% of the world's property, earn 90% of the world's income and work ± as many hours as you, but.. you'll **LIVE** longer!

Is longevity a major cause for celebration under the circumstances?

when understood by doctors, such traumas and problems are not easy to cure.

Women have written powerful fiction and autobiographical accounts of mental illness and medical treatments (e.g., Danquah 1998; Kaysen 1994; Millet 1990; Plath 1971; Shannonhouse 2003; Slater 1998). In Reading 30, cultural critic bell hooks shows the serious long-term effects of racism and internalized oppression on African Americans' mental and spiritual health. She notes that slave narratives often emphasized the importance of Black people's capacity to repress feelings as a key to survival, and that this ingrained habit has been passed on through family experiences for several generations. As a result, she argues, "many black females have learned to deny our inner needs while we develop the capacity to cope and confront in public life." Sociologist Tamara Beauboeuf-Lafontant (2007) confirms this in her study of Black women and depression. She argues that "being strong" may be taken as a sign of emotional health for white women. However, "being strong" is a "culturally specific expectation placed on Black women," which "normalizes struggle, selflessness, and internalization strategies" that compromise Black women's health (p. 46).

Health and Aging

Women's average life expectancy in the United States is 80 years, compared to 75 years for men. On average, African American women die younger than white women (at age 76) but live longer than African American men, who have a life expectancy of 69 years (National Center for Health Statistics 2007, Table 27). Typically, Asian Americans of both sexes live longer than white people. Like men, U.S. women are most likely to die from heart disease or cancer, followed by strokes, diabetes, respiratory diseases, pneumonia, and accidents. Older women suffer higher rates of disabling diseases such as arthritis, Alzheimer's, cataracts, diabetes, deafness, broken bones, digestive conditions, and osteoporosis than do men. Women under 45 mostly use reproductive heath services. Women over 45 use hospitals less than men do, reflecting a basic health difference between the sexes: Men are more likely to have fatal diseases, whereas women have chronic conditions that worsen with age.

The health of women in middle age and later life is partly linked to how healthy they were when they were younger. The effects of stress, poor nutrition, smoking, or not getting enough exercise build up over time. Exposure to toxic chemicals, the physical and emotional toll of pregnancies, accidents, injuries, and caring for others all affect our health as we grow older.

Older women may have to accept the fact that they need support and care. They have to face their changed looks, physical limitations, and the loss of independence and loved ones, which calls on their emotional and spiritual resources, including patience, forbearance, courage, optimism, and religious faith (see, for example, Doress-Worters and Siegal 1994). Over 3 million women in the United States provide personal assistance to family members who are sick or disabled, and over 10 million women provide care to people outside their own households, usually their elderly parents and their husbands' elderly parents. This caretaking of elders may go on for as much as fifteen years and often overlaps with the women's other responsibilities—holding jobs, taking care of growing children, and managing homes. This regimen can be very trying; it involves physical and emotional stress and added expense and can seriously affect the quality of life and health for women in their middle years, who may have to give up opportunities for education, professional development, social life, or leisure-time activities. These women may be reluctant and resentful at times but accept their situation as part of what it means to be a good wife or daughter. It is important to recognize that women who care for others need support and respite themselves.

Shevy Healey (1997) argued that confronting ageism in society, as well as individual women's negative feelings about aging, is a must for women's mental health. Women's studies researchers Margaret Morganroth Gullette (2004) and Margaret Cruickshank (2003) both emphasized the social construction of aging. Cruickshank (2003) argued that "aging in America is shaped more by . . . beliefs, customs, and traditions than by bodily changes" and that "awareness of social constructions and resistance to them is crucial for women's comfortable aging" (p. ix). She critiqued the field of gerontology for the acceptance of a medical model of aging and proposed a new approach, gerastology, that emphasizes longevity, life changes, older women's needs, and research conducted by older women. Collette Browne (1998) faulted feminist theorists who, typically, have not focused on older women or the process of aging. She urged "a feminist age analysis that can document the strengths of older women, who . . . are trivialized and ignored by patriarchal society" (p. 109). Calasanti and Slevin (2006) also countered the cultural insistence on "successful aging" (p. 3) and the ways "the anti-aging industry operates to reinscribe gendered, ageist stereotypes onto the body" (quoted in Winterich 2007, p. 784).

Health as Wellness

Limits of the U.S. Medical Industry

The Western medical model focuses on illness and disease rather than on the wholeness of people's lives, often treating symptoms rather than causes. For example, though stressors generated by racism are a strong influence in the hypertension that disproportionately affects African Americans, the medical response is to treat the symptoms with medication, rather than to involve doctors, patients, and the wider society in combating racism. Similarly, many women are prescribed antidepressants rather than being empowered and supported in changing their life circumstances. This medical model also contributes to fantasies of immortality to be achieved by life-prolonging surgeries and drug treatments, as well as expensive cosmetic surgeries.

Because medical care is provided on a fee-paying basis in the United States, the medical industry has many of the characteristics of any business venture (see Chapter 8). The emphasis is on high-tech treatments, particularly drug therapies and surgery, as these are the most profitable for drug companies and manufacturers of medical equipment. Most people have benefited from vaccines and antibiotics, and the use of drugs and surgery may improve the lives of cancer patients, give relief from arthritic pain, or restore good vision to people with cataracts. However, this overall emphasis has severely skewed the range of treatments available. It has led to an overproduction of intensive care equipment, for example, while some people have little access to the most rudimentary medical services. This emphasis has also shaped public policy through the testing and use of new drugs, the routine use of mammograms in breast cancer screening, sonograms and amniocentesis in pregnancy, and the prevalence of hysterectomies and births by cesarean section.

The United States is the only industrialized country without a national health care system. Current provisions comprise a patchwork of government programs for those who are eligible with employment-based insurance for some workers. Many children, students, people with disabilities, immigrants, self-employed, and unemployed people fall through the cracks.

Although 70 percent of people in the United States have some kind of private medical insurance, this often covers only emergencies and hospitalization. Only 7 to 8 percent of participants in group plans are fully covered for hospital maternity charges. Fewer African American women and Latinas initiate prenatal care in the first trimester of pregnancy, at least in part because they lack insurance coverage; by contrast, 80 percent of white women seek early prenatal care. Women's Wellness programs are an important—and profitable—screening service provided by hospitals, though many insurance policies do not cover them or any kind of contraception.

For most people who have private medical insurance (62 percent), this is employment-related. Twenty-five percent of the population receive coverage through Medicaid or Medicare. More women than men are covered this way, reflecting Medicaid eligibility criteria that focus on mothers and children, and the greater numbers of women among the elderly who rely on Medicare. Cuts in Medicaid and Medicare over the past 10–15 years have meant that some people have lost medical coverage altogether or in part. States with large immigrant populations have the highest proportion of uninsured people: Arizona, California, Louisiana, New Mexico, and Texas (Mills and Bhandari 2003). Since the mid-1990s, changes in government policy have sought to bar undocumented people and some legal immigrants from public health-care services, including emergency care. There is sufficient confusion about eligibility to deter some eligible immigrant women from seeking services. Michael Moore's film, *Sicko*, exposed many of the inadequacies of the U.S. medical system. A growing number of doctors, nurses, elected officials, labor organizers, and community members argue for universal health care (e.g., www.healthcareforall.org; www.healthcare-now.org; www.pnhp.org).

Other barriers to people's use of medical services include fear of treatment, transportation difficulties, long waiting times, not being able to take time off work or losing pay for doing so, child-care responsibilities, language and cultural differences, and residential segregation, which may mean that there are few medical facilities in some communities. Most inner cities have large teaching hospitals that treat local people, predominantly people of color, in their emergency rooms, but this treatment may be slanted toward the educational needs of the hospital's medical students rather than to the health needs of the patients.

A More Holistic Health System

The United Nations World Health Organization defined health very broadly as "a state of complete physical, mental, and social well-being and not merely the absence of disease or infirmity" (WHO 1946). Health requires clean water and air, access to nutritious food, adequate housing, safety, healthy working conditions, emotional and material supports, as well as culturally appropriate and affordable health care services. The many newspaper and magazine articles that focus on individual lifestyle factors—diet, cigarette smoking, weight, exercise, and a positive attitude to coping with stress—urge us to take more personal responsibility for our health. Although this is valuable advice, lifestyle is only part of the story, as suggested by the data we presented earlier. Living in damp housing or near a busy freeway or polluted industrial area, working in hazardous factories and mines, being exposed to toxic pesticides in agricultural work, doing repetitive tasks all day, and sitting in the same position for long periods of time are all aspects of daily life that can compromise one's health.

Women's health has been a central concern for feminists for the past forty years (Avery 1990; Morgen 2002; Norsigian 1996; Nowrojee and Silliman 1997; Ross et al. 2002; Silliman et al. 2004; White 1990). Because many women's health needs are not met under the current system, feminist health practitioners and advocates urge a fundamental shift in emphasis toward a more holistic system of health care that recognizes that physical, emotional, and mental health are intimately connected.

Self-Education and Preventive Care   Preventing illness through self-education has had low priority in the United States, and beyond basic dietary guidelines, immunization for infants, and minimal sex education for teens, it has generally been left to interested practitioners, organizations like the American Cancer Society, or community health care projects. It involves learning to listen to our bodies and becoming more conscious of what they can tell us; learning to eat well and to heal common ailments with home remedies; taking regular exercise; getting enough sleep; quitting smoking; doing breast self-exams; and practicing safer sex. Self-education and preventive care also include various types of self-help programs. Many of these, like Alcoholics Anonymous, Al-Anon, Narcotics Anonymous, Workaholics Anonymous, and other twelve-step programs, have been successful in helping people change negative habits and attitudes, though they usually do not address macro-level factors like institutionalized racism, sexism, and heterosexism. A self-help approach also means taking a greater degree of personal responsibility for one's health and being able to make informed decisions about possible remedies and treatments, rather than simply consuming services. Finally, preventive care encompasses creative activities, like dancing, music, poetry, sports, and homemaking, that give us joy and make us feel alive.

Complementary and Alternative Therapies   Therapies such as acupuncture, homeopathy, chiropractic care, and massage may be highly beneficial for a range of complaints. They are considered "alternative" from the perspective of contemporary Western medicine with its emphasis on drugs and surgery but are rooted in much older systems of knowledge. Acupuncture, ayurvedic care, and Shiatsu massage, for example, are available in Asian American communities. Native American, Latino, Caribbean, and African American communities also include practitioners who know the medicinal properties of plants and long-standing traditions of herbal medicines. Many alternative therapies have been scorned as "unscientific" and "unproven" by the U.S. medical establishment but are being used more widely, sometimes in conjunction with Western medicine. Many are not covered by medical insurance.

Feminist Health Projects   Such projects have been active since the early 1970s. Examples include courses in women's health; informal self-health groups like the Bloomington Women's Health Collective (Bloomington, Ind.); women's health centers (e.g., in Concord, N.H., and Burlington, Vt.); campaigns for reproductive rights (e.g., NARAL Pro-Choice America and regional affiliates) or for public funding for breast cancer research and treatment (e.g., Women's Community Cancer Project, Cambridge, Mass.); community health campaigns (e.g., LGBT Health Access Project); and national organizations like Black Women's Health Imperative (Washington, D.C.), Lesbian Health Fund (San Francisco), the National Asian Women's Health Organization (San Francisco), the National Latina Health Organization (Oakland, Calif.), the National Women's Health Network (Washington, D.C.), and the Native American Women's Health and Education Resource Center (Lake Andes, S. Dak.). The Boston Women's Health Book Collective's ground-breaking book *Our Bodies, Ourselves* first started as mimeographed notes for a course in women's health and was later developed for publication. It has become an essential resource on women's health and sexuality for women of all ages and has been translated and adapted for use in many countries.

Questions for Reflection

As you read and discuss this chapter, consider these questions:

1. How do you feel about your own body? What makes you feel good about your body? How do you know when you're healthy? Sick?

2. What are the main health issues for women in your family, your community, or on your campus?

3. What theoretical frameworks and activist projects are associated with reproductive rights and reproductive justice? What are the strengths and weaknesses of these approaches?

4. Who should pay for health care? How? Why?

5. How much did you eat while reading this section? How much exercise did you do?

Finding Out More on the Web

1. Mobility International USA is involved with disability rights activists internationally (www.miusa.org). How are they improving the lives of women with disabilities?

2. In Spain, the Madrid Regional Government introduced regulations banning the thinnest models from participating in the 2006 Madrid fashion show; the Italian and British governments also urged fashion designers to present a healthy image of women's bodies. Use your search engine to find out whether such initiatives have developed and what their effects have been.

3. Visit the following websites to see how fashion photos are retouched:

   http://demo.fb.se/e/girlpower/retouch/

   http://glennferon.com

4. Find out about the history of *Roe v. Wade.* How and why did this piece of legislation gain support? What was the cultural and historical context? Who were some of the key players who helped to make it happen? What is its status now?

5. Find out more about the positions, arguments, and activities of anti-choice organizations (e.g., the Army of God, the Christian Coalition, Focus on the Family, Operation Rescue) and pro-choice organizations (e.g., Choice USA, Fund for a Feminist Majority, Planned Parenthood, NARAL Pro-Choice America). What did you learn from this?

◆◆◆

Taking Action

1. Make it your daily practice to affirm your body. List all the steps you take to care for yourself and any additional ones you could take.

2. Write to a TV station or magazine that shows positive (or negative) images of women and let them know what you think. Send examples of sexist ads to *Bitch* magazine or *Ms.* Magazine's "No Comment" section; participate in the Third Wave Foundation's "I Spy Sexism" campaign or Mind on the Media's "GirlCaught" campaign.

3. Find out more about your body by, for example, reading *Our Bodies, Ourselves: A New Edition for a New Era.*

4. Organize an activity on your campus or in your home community to draw attention to body issues for women and to challenge common stereotypes.

5. Find out more about what your family and community consider effective self-care practices. Where can women go to keep healthy or to get quality health care in your community?

TWENTY-FIVE

Feminist Theory, the Body, and the Disabled Figure (1997)

Rosemarie Garland Thomson

Rosemarie Garland Thomson is a professor of Women's Studies at Emory University where she teaches feminist theory, American literature, and disability studies. Author of *Staring: How We Look* and *Extraordinary Bodies: Figuring Physical Disability in American Literature and Culture,* she is devoted to developing the field of disability studies in women's studies and the humanities.

The Female Body and the Disabled Body

Many parallels exist between the social meanings attributed to female bodies and those assigned to disabled bodies. Both the female and the disabled body are cast within cultural discourse as deviant and inferior; both are excluded from full participation in public as well as economic life; both are defined in opposition to a valued norm which is assumed to possess natural corporeal superiority. Indeed, the discursive equation of femaleness with disability is common, sometimes in the service of denigrating women and sometimes with the goal of defending them. Examples abound, from Freud's understanding femaleness in terms of castration to late nineteenth-century physicians' defining menstruation as a disabling and restricting "eternal wound" to Thorstein Veblen's describing women in 1900 as literally disabled by feminine roles and costuming. Feminists today even often invoke negative images of disability to describe the oppression of women, as does Jane Flax—to cite a common example—in her assertion that women are "mutilated and deformed" by sexist ideology and practices.[1]

Perhaps, however, the founding association of femaleness with disability occurs in the fourth book of *Generation of Animals,* Aristotle's inaugural discourse of the normal and the abnormal in which he refines the Platonic concept of antinomies so that bodily variety translates into the hierarchies of the typical and the aberrant. "[A]nyone who does not take after his parents," Aristotle asserts, "is really in a way a monstrosity, since in these cases Nature has in a way strayed from the generic type. The first beginning of this deviation is when a female is formed instead of a male." Here the philosopher whom we might consider the founding father of Western taxonomy projects idealism onto corporeality to produce a definitive, seemingly neutral "generic type" along with its particularized antithesis, the "monstrosity," whose departure from such a "type" constitutes a profound "deviation.". . . Aristotle's choreography of bodies thus conjoins the "monstrosity"—whom we would today term "congenitally disabled"—and the female on a course leading away from the definitive norm. In Book Two, Aristotle also affirms his connection of disabled and female bodies by stating that "the female is as it were a deformed male" or—as it appears in other translations—"a mutilated male."[2]

More significant than his simple conflation of disability and femaleness is that Aristotle reveals here the source from which all otherness arises: the concept of a normative, "generic type" against which all corporeal variation is measured and found to be different, derivative, inferior, and insufficient. Not only does this definition of the female as a "mutilated male" inform later versions of woman as a diminished man, but it arranges somatic diversity into a hierarchy of value that assigns plenitude to some bodies and lack to others based on their configurations. Furthermore, by focusing on defining femaleness as deviant rather than the maleness he assumes to be essential, Aristotle also initiates the discursive practice of marking what is deemed aberrant while concealing the position of privilege by asserting its normativeness. Thus we witness perhaps the originary operation of the logic which has become so familiar in discussions of gender, race, or disability: male, white, or able-bodied superiority is naturalized, remaining undisputed and obscured by the ostensible problem of female, black, or disabled deviance. What this passage makes clearest, however, is that without the monstrous body to demarcate the borders of the generic, without the female body to distinguish the shape of the male, and without the pathological to give form to the normal, these taxonomies of bodily value that underwrite political, social, and economic arrangements would collapse.

Considering this persistent intertwining of disability with femaleness in Western discourse provides a fruitful context for explorations of social identity and the body. As Aristotle's pronouncement suggests, the social category of disability turns upon the significance accorded bodily functioning and configuration, just as the social category woman does. Placing disability studies in a feminist context allows feminist theory's . . . inquiries into gender as a category, the body's role in identity and selfhood, and the complexity of social power relations to be brought to bear on an analysis of disability. Moreover, applying feminist theory to disability analyses infuses it with feminism's politicized insistence on the relationship between the meanings attributed to bodies by cultural representations and the consequences of those meanings in the world. In viewing disability through a feminist lens, I hope at the same time to suggest how the category of disability might be inserted into feminist theory so that the bodily configurations and functioning we call "disability" will be included in all feminist examinations of culture and representation. This brief exploration aims then at beginning the work of altering the terms of both feminist and disability discourses.

Feminist Theory and Disability Discourse

. . . I want to extend in a fresh juxtaposition, then, the association of disability and femaleness with which I began this essay. Rather than simply conflating the disabled body with the female body, however, I want to theorize disability in the ways that feminism has theorized gender. Both feminism and the interrogation of disability I am undertaking challenge existing social relations; both resist interpretations of certain bodily configurations and functioning as deviant; both question the ways that particularity or difference is invested with meaning; both examine the enforcement of universalizing norms; both interrogate the politics of appearance; both explore the politics of naming; both participate in positive identity politics. Nevertheless, feminism has formulated the terms and probed the logic of these concerns much more thoroughly than has disability studies, at this point.[3]

Eve Sedgwick's distinction, for example, between a "minoritizing" and a "universalizing" view of difference can be applied usefully to disability discourse. One minoritizes difference, . . . by imagining its significance and concerns as limited to a narrow, specific, relatively fixed population or arena of inquiry. In contrast, a universalizing view sees issues surrounding a particularized form of difference as having "continuing, determinative importance in the lives of people across the spectrum of [identities].[4] . . . I would advocate for disability studies to be seen as a universalizing discourse. . . . Such a conceptualization makes possible, among other things, recognizing that disability (or gender or homosexuality) is a category that structures a wide range of thought, language, and perception not explicitly articulated as "disability" (or gender or homosexuality). Universalizing, then, names the impulse behind the attempt here to show how the unarticulated concept of disability informs such national ideologies as American liberal individualism and sentimentalism, as well as explorations of African-American and lesbian identities. Such semantics emerging from feminist theory can be enlisted to dislodge the persistent assumption that disability is a self-evident condition of bodily inadequacy and private misfortune whose politics concern only a limited minority—just as femaleness so easily seemed before feminism.

A universalizing disability discourse which draws on feminism's confrontation with the gender system requires asserting the body as a cultural text which is interpreted, inscribed with meaning, indeed *made*, within social relations of power. Such a perspective advocates political equality by denaturalizing disability's assumed inferiority, casting its configurations and functions as difference rather than lack. But while this broad constructionist perspective does the vital cultural work of destigmatizing gender or racial differences as well as the corporeal traits we call disability, it also threatens to obscure the material and historical effects of those differences and to destabilize the very social categories we analyze and, in many cases, claim as significant in our own and others' lives. . . .

. . . The kind of legally mandated access to public spaces and institutions which began for women in the nineteenth century and has accelerated since the 1960s was only fully launched for disabled people by the Americans with Disabilities Act of 1990, a broad civil rights bill that is only beginning to be implemented. And while race and gender are accepted generally as differences rather than deviances in the political moves toward equality, disability is still most often seen as bodily inadequacy or misfortune to be compensated for through a pity, rather than a civil rights, model. So, on the one hand, it is important to employ the constructionist argument to denaturalize the assumption that disability is bodily insufficiency and to assert instead that disability arises from the interaction of embodied differences with an unaccommodating physical and social environment. But, on the other hand, the particular, historical materiality of the disabled body that demands both accommodation and recognition must be preserved as well. Consequently, the embodied difference that using a wheelchair or being deaf makes should be claimed, but without casting that difference as lack.[5]

Both constructionism and essentialism, then, become theoretical strategies—framings of the body—invoked when useful to achieve specific ends in the political arena, to liberate psychologically subjects whose bodies have been narrated to them as defective, or to facilitate imagined communities from which a positive identity politics can emerge. Thus, a strategic constructionism destigmatizes the disabled body, locates difference relationally, denaturalizes normalcy, and challenges appearance hierarchies. A strategic essentialism, by contrast, validates experience and consciousness, imagines community, authorizes history, and facilitates self-naming. The identity "disabled" operates, then, as a pragmatic narrative, what Susan Bordo calls "a life-enhancing fiction," grounded in the materiality of a particular embodiment and perspective embedded in specific social and historical contexts.[6]

Imagining Feminist Disability Discourse

But if the category "disabled" is a useful fiction, the disabled body set in a world structured for the normative, privileged body is not. Disability, perhaps more than other forms of alterity, demands a reckoning with the messiness of bodily variegation, with literal individuation run amok. Because the embodiment we think of as disability exists not so much as a set of observable predictable traits—like racialized or gendered physical features—but rather as *any* departure from an unstated corporeal norm, disability foregrounds embodiment's specificity. In other words, the concept of disability unites a highly marked, heterogeneous collection of embodiments whose only commonality is being considered abnormal. As a departure from a norm made neutral by an environment created to accommodate it, disability becomes intense, extravagant, and problematic embodiment. It is the unorthodox made flesh. Occupying the province of the extraordinary, disability refuses to be normalized, neutralized, or homogenized. More important yet, in an era governed by the abstract principle of universal equality, disability signals the body that cannot be universalized. Unified only by exclusion, disability confounds any notion of a generalizable, constant corporeal subject by flaunting the vagaries of an embodiment shaped by history, defined by particularity, and at odds with its environment. The cripple before the stairs, the blind before the printed page, the deaf before the radio, the amputee before the typewriter, and the dwarf before the counter—all

testify with their particular bodies to the fact that the myriad structures and practices of material, daily life enforce the cultural expectation of a certain standard, universal subject before whom all others appear inferior.

Indeed, the identity category of disability can pressure feminist theory to acknowledge bodily particularity and history. Perhaps feminism's most useful concept for doing so is standpoint theory, which recognizes the local and complex quality of embodiment. Emphasizing the multiplicity of all women's identities, history, and embodiment, this theory of positionality recognizes that individual material situations structure the subjectivity from which particular women can speak and perceive with authority. . . . Standpoint theory and the feminist practice of explicitly situating oneself when speaking make way for complicating inflections such as disabilities or, more broadly, the category of corporeal configuration—as in such attributions as fat, disfigured, abnormal, ugly, or deformed—to be inserted into our considerations of identity and subjectivity. Such a dismantling of the unitary category woman has enabled feminist theory to encompass—although not without contention—such feminist differentiations as Patricia Hill Collins's "black feminist thought," for instance, or my own explorations of a "feminist disability studies."[7] . . .

I am suggesting, then, that a feminist political praxis for women with disabilities needs strategically to focus at times on the specificity and perhaps the ineluctability of the flesh and to find clarity in the identity it occasions. For example, in one of the inaugural explorations of the politics of self-naming, Nancy Mairs claims the appellation "cripple" because it demands that others acknowledge the singularity of her embodiment. "People . . . wince at the word 'cripple,'" Mairs contends. Even though she retains what has been a derogatory term, she insists on determining its significance herself: "Perhaps I want them to wince. I want them to see me as a tough customer, one to whom the fates/gods/viruses have not been kind, but who can face the brutal truth of her existence squarely. As a cripple, I swagger." Here Mairs is not so much rehabilitating the term of otherness as a celebration or as an attempt to reverse its contemptuous connotation; rather, she wants to call attention less to her oppression and more to the material reality of her crippledness, to her bodily difference her experience of it. For Mairs, the social constructionist argument risks neutralizing the difference of her pain and her struggle with an environment built for a body other than hers.[8]

The confrontation with bodily difference that disability provokes also places some disabled women at odds with several mainstream feminist assumptions that do not take into account disabled women's material situations. For example, while feminism quite legitimately decries the sexual objectification of women, disabled women often encounter what Harlan Hahn has called "asexual objectification," the assumption that sexuality is inappropriate in disabled people. One woman who uses a wheelchair and is at the same time quite beautiful reports, for example, that people often respond to her as if this combination of traits were a remarkable and lamentable contradiction. The judgment that the disabled woman's body is asexual and unfeminine creates what Michelle Fine and Adrienne Asch term "rolelessness," a kind of social invisibility and cancellation of femininity which sometimes prompts disabled women to claim an essential femininity which the culture denies them. For example, Cheryl Marie Wade insists upon a harmony between her disability and her womanly sexuality in a poem characterizing herself as "The Woman with Juice"[9] [see photo]. As Mairs's exploration of self-naming and Wade's assertion of sexuality suggest, a feminist disability politics would uphold the right for women to define their corporeal differences and their relationship to womanhood for themselves rather than acceding to received interpretations of their embodiment.

Wade's poem of self-definition echoes Mairs by maintaining firmly that she is "not one of the physically challenged," but rather she claims, "I'm the Gimp/I'm the Cripple/I'm the Crazy Lady." Affirming her body as at once sexual and different, she asserts, "I'm a French kiss with cleft tongue." Resisting the cultural tendency to erase not only her sexuality but the depreciated materiality of her embodiment, she characterizes herself as "a sock in the eye with gnarled fist." This image of the disabled body as a visual assault, as a shocking spectacle to the normative eye, captures a defining aspect of disabled experience. Whereas feminists claim that women are objects of the male gaze which demarcates their subjectivity, Wade's image of her body as "a sock in the eye" subtly reminds us that the disabled body is the object not of the appropriating gaze but of the stare. If the male gaze informs the normative female self as a sexual

Cheryl Marie Wade is an award-winning writer performer, poet, and activist, whose videos include *Body Talk* and *Vital Signs: Crip Culture Talks Back*.

spectacle, then the stare sculpts the disabled subject as a grotesque spectacle. The stare is the gaze intensified, framing her body as an icon of deviance. Indeed, as Wade's poem suggests, the stare is the material gesture that creates disability as an oppressive social relationship. And as every person with a visible disability knows intimately, managing, deflecting, resisting, or renouncing that stare is the daily business of life.

In addition to having to prove their sexuality, disabled women must sometimes defend as well against the assessment that their bodies are unfit for motherhood or that they are the infantilized objects upon which others exercise their virtue. Whereas motherhood is often seen as compulsory for women, disabled women are often denied access or discouraged from entrance to the arena of reproduction that some feminist thinkers have found oppressive. The controversial feminist ethic of care also has been criticized by feminist disability scholars as potentially threatening to symmetrical, reciprocal relations among disabled and nondisabled women as well as for suggesting that care is the sole responsibility of women. . . .

Perhaps more problematic yet, feminist abortion rationale seldom questions the prejudicial assumption that "defective" fetuses destined to become disabled people should be eliminated.[10] The concerns of older women, who are often disabled, tend also to be ignored by younger feminists, as well. One of the most pervasive feminist assumptions that undermines some disabled women's struggle is the ideology of autonomy and independence emanating from liberal feminism and the broader impulse toward female empowerment. By tacitly incorporating the liberal premise that levels individual particularities and differences in order to posit an abstract, disembodied subject of democracy, feminist practice often leaves no space for the needs and accommodations that disabled women's bodies require.[11] The angry and disappointed words prominent disability rights activist Judy Heumann spoke to me reflect an alienation not unlike that between some black women and some white feminists: "When I come into a room full of feminists, all they see is a wheelchair."[12] These conflicts testify that feminists, like everyone else, including disabled people themselves, have been acculturated to stigmatize those whose bodies are deemed aberrant.

Femininity and Disability

So while I want to insist on disabled women's particularity and identity even while questioning its sources and its production, I also want to suggest nevertheless that a firm boundary between "disabled" and "nondisabled" women cannot be meaningfully drawn—just as any absolute distinction between sex and gender must be problematized. Femininity and disability are inextricably entangled in Western culture, as Aristotle's equation of women and disabled men illustrates. Not only has the female body been represented as deviant, but historically the practices of femininity have configured female bodies in ways that duplicate the parameters of disability. Feminizing conventions such as Chinese foot binding, African scarification, clitoridectomy, and

Euroamerican corseting were (and are) socially accepted, encouraged, even compulsory, forms of female disablement that ironically constitute feminine social enablement, increasing a woman's value and status as a woman at a given moment in a particular society. Similarly, such conditions as anorexia, hysteria, and agoraphobia are in a sense standard feminine scripts writ large enough to become disabling conditions, blurring the line between normal feminine behavior and pathology.[13]

Feminine beauty's disciplinary regime often obscures the seemingly self-evident categories of the "normal" and the "pathological" as well. For example, the nineteenth-century Euroamerican prescription for upper-class feminine beauty precisely paralleled the symptoms of tuberculosis just as the cult of thinness promoted by the fashion industry approaches the appearance of disease. In another instance, the iconography and language of contemporary cosmetic surgery presented in women's magazines persistently casts the unreconstructed female body as having "abnormalities" that can be "corrected" by surgical procedures which "improve" one's appearance by producing "natural looking" noses, thighs, breasts, chins, and so on. This discourse casts women's unmodified bodies as unnatural and abnormal while the surgically altered bodies become normal and natural. Although cosmetic surgery is in one sense only the logical extension of beauty practices such as make-up, perms, relaxers, skin lighteners, and hair removal, it differs profoundly from these basically decorative forms of self-reconstruction because, like clitoridectomies and scarification, it involves mutilation, pain, and wounding that is definitive of many disabilities.

While all of these practices cannot, of course, be equated, each nevertheless transforms an infinitely plastic body in ways similar to the ways disability alters the body. The difference is that these changes are imagined to be choices that will sculpt the female body so it conforms to a feminine ideal. Disabilities, despite their affinities with beautification procedures, are imagined, in contrast, to be random transformations that move the body away from ideal forms. Within the visual economy in which appearance has come to be the primary index of value for women, feminizing practices normalize the female body, while disabilities abnormalize it. Feminization prompts the gaze, while disability prompts the stare. Feminization alterations increase a woman's cultural capital, while disabilities reduce it.[14]

But as Aristotle's equation of femaleness with mutilated males suggests, the normalized female body is abnormal in reference to the universally human male body. The normative female body—the figure of the beautiful woman—is a narrowly prescribed version of what the ideal male figure is not. If he is to be strong, active, hirsute, hard, and so on, then she must be his opposite—weak, passive, hairless, soft, and so on. The normative female body, then, occupies a dual and paradoxical cultural role: it is the negative term opposing the male body, but it is also simultaneously the privileged term in reference to the abnormalized female body.

For example, the nineteenth-century obsession with scientific quantification actually produced a detailed description of absolute beauty, laid out by Havelock Ellis, which posited a Darwinian ranking of beauty, determined entirely by corporeal characteristics and ranging from the "beautiful" European woman to what was considered to be her grotesque opposite, the African woman. Moreover, scientific discourse conceived this anatomical scale of beauty as simultaneously one of pathology. The further a female body departed from absolute beauty, the more "abnormal" it became as a female body. The markers of this indubitable pathology were traits such as dark skin and physical disability, or behaviors like prostitution, which were often linked to bodily characteristics. Within this scheme, all women are seen as deviant in their femaleness, but some women are imagined as doubly deviant. So the simple dichotomy of objectified feminine body and masculine subject is complicated, then, by other sets of binary oppositions that further clarify the original terms. Indeed, the unfeminine, unbeautiful body mutually constitutes the very shape of the feminine body. This other figure of woman has been identified variously in history and discourse as black, fat, lesbian, sexually appetitive, disabled, ugly, and so on. What is important for this study, however, is that her deviance and subsequent devaluation are always attributed to some visible bodily characteristic—a mark that can operate as an emblem of her difference—just as beauty has always been located in the body of the feminine woman. As one manifestation of the unbeautiful woman, the third term that disrupts a tidy pair of

antinomies, the figure of the disabled woman tends to complicate discourses announcing themselves as trafficking in oppositional paradigms.

As this discussion of normalized and abnormalized female bodies suggests, it is the cultural figure of the disabled woman, rather than the actual woman with a disability, that this essay focuses upon. Within the politics of representation I have explored here, the figure of the disabled woman is best apprehended as a product of a conceptual triangulation. She is a cultural third term, a figure constituted by the originary binary pair of the masculine figure and the feminine figure. Thus, the disabled female figure occupies an intragender position; that is, she is not only defined against the masculine figure, but she is imagined as the antithesis of the normative woman as well. . . .

NOTES

1. See Patricia Vertinsky, "Exercise, Physical Capability, and the Eternally Wounded Woman in Late Nineteenth-Century North America," *Journal of Sport History* 14, 1 (1987): 7–27, p. 7; Thorstein Veblen, *The Theory of the Leisure Class* (Boston: Houghton Mifflin, 1973); Jane Flax, *Thinking Fragments: Psychoanalysis, Feminism, and Postmodernism in the Contemporary West* (Berkeley: University of California Press, 1990), p. 136.

2. Aristotle, *Generation of Animals,* trans. A. L. Peck, (Cambridge: Harvard University Press, 1944) Book IV, 401 and Book II, 175.

3. Most theorists of disability either naturalize disability while protesting exclusion and oppression of disabled people or they adopt a strict social constructionist perspective in order to claim equality, while asserting difference for the purposes of establishing identity.

4. Eve Kosofsky Sedgwick, *Epistemology of the Closet* (Berkeley: University of California Press, 1990), p. 1.

5. See Joseph Shapiro, *No Pity: People with Disabilities Forging a New Civil Rights Movement* (New York: Times Books/Random House, 1993); Claire Liachowitz, *Disability as a Social Construct*; and Richard Scotch, *From Good Will to Civil Rights.*

6. Diana Fuss in *Essentially Speaking* examines this tension between constructionist and essentialist conceptions of identity, concluding that to deconstruct identity is not to deny categories, but rather to expose the fictionality of them even while claiming them for political purposes and to establish community and affinity. Benedict Anderson's concept of "imagined communities" is useful here to suggest the strategic aspect of such communities for political and psychological purposes; see *Imagined Communities: Reflections on the Origin and Spread of Nationalism* (New York: Verso, 1991).

7. See Collins, *Black Feminist Thought,* and Rosemarie Garland Thomson, "Redrawing the Boundaries of Feminist Disability Studies," *Feminist Studies* 20 (Fall 1994): 583–95.

8. Nancy Mairs, "On Being a Cripple," *Plaintext: Essays* (Tucson: University of Arizona Press, 1986), p. 90.

9. Michelle Fine and Adrienne Asch, "Disabled Women: Sexism without the Pedestal," *Women and Disability: The Double Handicap,* eds., Mary Jo Deegan and Nancy A. Brooks (New Brunswick, NJ: Transaction Books, 1985), 6–22, 12. Cheryl Marie Wade, MS II (3): 57.

10. For discussions of disability in relation to abortion and reproductive rights, see Ruth Hubbard, "Who Should and Should Not Inhabit the World," in Ruth Hubbard, ed., *The Politics of Women's Biology* (New Brunswick, NJ: Rutgers University Press, 1990); Marsha Saxton, "Born and Unborn: The Implications of Reproductive Technologies for People with Disabilities," in Rita Arditti, Renate Duell Klein, and Shelley Minden, eds., *Test-Tube Women: What Future for Motherhood?* (Boston: Pandora, 1984), 298–312; and Anne Finger, "Claiming All of Our Bodies: Reproductive Rights and Disability," in Arditti et al., ed., *Test-Tube Women,* pp. 281–96; Fine and Asch, eds., *Women with Disabilities,* esp. ch. 12 and 13; and Deborah Kaplan, "Disabled Women," in Alison Jaggar, ed., *Living with Contradictions: Controversies in Feminist Social Ethics* (Boulder: Westview Press, 1994).

11. Susan Bordo argues in a similar vein that the feminist search for equality has caused a flight from gender and, hence, from the body, that often masquerades as "professionalism." Disabled women's inability to erase the claims of their bodies or to be able to fit the standardized image of the "professional" often alienates them from feminists who enter the workplace on such terms. See Bordo, *Unbearable Weight: Feminism, Western Culture, and the Body* (Berkeley: University of California Press, 1993), 229–33, for a discussion of this point; also see Fine and Asch, eds., *Women with Disabilities,* 26–31.

12. Personal conversation, Society for Disability Studies Annual Meeting, June, 1991, Denver, CO.

13. The philosopher Iris Marion Young argues for the construction of femininity as disability, for example, by asserting that the cultural objectification of women is manifest in their tendency to be inhibited in using their bodies as unselfconscious agents of physical capability. "Women in a sexist society are physically handicapped," concludes Young in the essay that focuses on the phenomenon of "Throwing Like a Girl" (*Throwing Like a Girl,* 153).

14. Mary Russo's *The Female Grotesque: Risk, Excess, and Modernity* (New York: Routledge, 1994) observes what she calls "the normalization of feminism" which involves "strategies of reassurance" that encourage feminists to focus on standard forms of femininity and avoid the female sites she calls "the grotesque," which I might term the "abnormal."

TWENTY-SIX

◆◆◆

"The More You Subtract, the More You Add" (1999)
Cutting Girls Down to Size

Jean Kilbourne

Starting with *Killing Us Softly: Advertising's Image of Women,* public speaker, writer, and documentary filmmaker **Jean Kilbourne** became internationally recognized for her critiques of tobacco and alcohol advertising as well as images of women in advertising. She is the recipient of the 2000 Distinguished Publication Award from the Association for Women in Psychology, the 2006 Media Activist National Award, and many others.

. . . Adolescents are new and inexperienced consumers—and such prime targets. They are in the process of learning their values and roles and developing their self-concepts. Most teenagers are sensitive to peer pressure and find it difficult to resist or even to question the dominant cultural messages perpetuated and reinforced by the media. Mass communication has made possible a kind of national peer pressure that erodes private and individual values and standards, as well as community values and standards. As Margaret Mead once said, today our children are not brought up by parents, they are brought up by the mass media.[1]

Advertisers are aware of their role and do not hesitate to take advantage of the insecurities and anxieties of young people, usually in the guise of offering solutions. A cigarette provides a symbol of independence. A pair of designer jeans or sneakers convey status. The right perfume or beer resolves doubts about femininity or masculinity. All young people are vulnerable to these messages and adolescence is a difficult time for most people, perhaps especially these days. . . . But there is a particular kind of suffering in our culture that afflicts girls.

. . . Girls who were active, confident, feisty at the ages of eight and nine and ten often become hesitant, insecure, self-doubting at eleven. Their self-esteem plummets. As Carol Gilligan, Mary Pipher and other social critics and psychologists have pointed out . . . , adolescent girls in America are afflicted with a range of problems, including low self-esteem, eating disorders, binge drinking, date rape and other dating violence, teen pregnancy, and a rise in cigarette smoking.[2] . . .

It is important to understand that these problems go way beyond individual psychological development and pathology. Even girls who are raised in loving homes by supportive parents grow up in a toxic cultural environment, at risk for self-mutilation, eating disorders, and addictions. The culture, both reflected and reinforced by advertising, urges girls to adopt a false self, to bury alive their real selves, to become "feminine," which means to be nice and kind and sweet, to compete with other girls for the attention of boys, and to value romantic relationships with boys above all else. Girls are put into a terrible double bind. They are supposed to repress their power, their anger, their exuberance and be simply "nice," although they also eventually must compete with men in the business world and be successful. They must be overtly sexy and attractive but essentially passive and virginal. It is not surprising that most girls experience this time as painful and confusing, especially if they are unconscious of these conflicting demands.

Of course, it is impossible to speak accurately of girls as a monolithic group. The socialization that emphasizes passivity and compliance does not apply to many African-American and Jewish girls, who are often encouraged to be assertive and outspoken, and working-class girls are usually not expected to be stars in the business world. Far from protecting these girls from eating disorders and other problems, these differences more often mean

that the problems remain hidden or undiagnosed and the girls are even less likely to get help. Eating problems affect girls from African-American, Asian, Native American, Hispanic, and Latino families and from every socioeconomic background.[3] The racism and classism that these girls experience exacerbate their problems. Sexism is by no means the only trauma they face. . . .

Girls try to make sense of the contradictory expectations of themselves in a culture dominated by advertising. Advertising is one of the most potent messengers in a culture that can be toxic for girls' self-esteem. Indeed, if we looked only at advertising images, this would be a bleak world for females. Girls are extremely desirable to advertisers because they are new consumers, are beginning to have significant disposable income, and are developing brand loyalty that might last a lifetime. . . .

Seventeen, a magazine aimed at girls about twelve to fifteen, sells these girls to advertisers in an ad that says, "She's the one you want. She's the one we've got." The copy continues, "She pursues beauty and fashion at every turn" and concludes with, "It's more than a magazine. It's her life." In another similar ad, *Seventeen* refers to itself as a girl's "Bible." Many girls read magazines like this and take the advice seriously. Regardless of the intent of the advertisers, what are the messages that girls are getting? . . .

Primarily girls are told by advertisers that what is most important about them is their perfume, their clothing, their bodies, their beauty. Their "essence" is their underwear. "He says the first thing he noticed about you is your great personality," says an ad featuring a very young woman in tight jeans. The copy continues, "He lies." "If this is your idea of a great catch," says an ad for a cosmetic kit from a teen magazine featuring a cute boy, "this is your tackle box." Even very little girls are offered makeup and toys like Special Night Barbie, which shows them how to dress up for a night out. Girls of all ages get the message that they must be flawlessly beautiful and, above all these days, they must be thin.

Even more destructively, they get the message that this is possible, that, with enough effort and self-sacrifice, they can achieve this ideal. Thus many girls spend enormous amounts of time and energy attempting to achieve something that is not only trivial but also completely unattainable. The glossy images of flawlessly beautiful and extremely thin women that surround us would not have the impact they do if we did not live in a culture that encourages us to believe we can and should remake our bodies into perfect commodities. These images play into the American belief of transformation and ever-new possibilities, no longer via hard work but via the purchase of the right products. . . .

Women are especially vulnerable because our bodies have been objectified and commodified for so long. And young women are the most vulnerable, especially those who have experienced early deprivation, sexual abuse, family violence, or other trauma. Cultivating a thinner body offers some hope of control and success to a young woman with a poor self-image and overwhelming personal problems that have no easy solutions.

Although troubled young women are especially vulnerable, these messages affect all girls. A researcher at Brigham and Women's Hospital in Boston found that the more frequently girls read magazines, the more likely they were to diet and to feel that magazines influence their ideal body shape.[4] Nearly half reported wanting to lose weight because of a magazine picture (but only 29 percent were actually overweight). Studies at Stanford University and the University of Massachusetts found that about 70 percent of college women say they feel worse about their own looks after reading women's magazines.[5] Another study, this one of 350 young men and women, found that a preoccupation with one's appearance takes a toll on mental health.[6] Women scored much higher than men on what the researchers called "self-objectification." This tendency to view one's body from the outside in—regarding physical attractiveness, sex appeal, measurements, and weight as more central to one's physical identity than health, strength, energy level, coordination, or fitness—has many harmful effects, including diminished mental performance, increased feelings of shame and anxiety, depression, sexual dysfunction, and the development of eating disorders.

These images of women seem to affect men most strikingly by influencing how they judge the real women in their lives. Male college students who viewed just one episode of *Charlie's Angels,* the hit television show of the 1970s that featured three beautiful women, were harsher in their evaluations of the attractiveness of potential dates than were males who had not seen the episode.[7] In another study, male college students shown centerfolds from *Playboy* and *Penthouse* were more likely to find their own girlfriends less sexually attractive.

Adolescent girls are especially vulnerable to the obsession with thinness, for many reasons. One is the ominous peer pressure on young people. Adolescence is a time of such self-consciousness and terror of shame and humiliation. Boys are shamed for being too small, too "weak," too soft, too sensitive. And girls are shamed for being too sexual, too loud, too boisterous, too big (in any sense of the word), having too hearty an appetite. Many young women have told me that their boyfriends wanted them to lose weight. One said that her boyfriend had threatened to leave her if she didn't lose five pounds. "Why don't you leave him," I asked, "and lose 160?"

The situation is very different for men. The double standard is reflected in an ad for a low-fat pizza: "He eats a brownie . . . you eat a rice cake. He eats a juicy burger . . . you eat a low fat entree. He eats pizza . . . you eat pizza. Finally, life is fair." Although some men develop eating problems, the predominant cultural message remains that a hearty appetite and a large size is desirable in a man, but not so in a woman. . . .

Normal physiological changes during adolescence result in increased body fat for women. If these normal changes are considered undesirable by the culture (and by parents and peers), this can lead to chronic anxiety and concern about weight control in young women. A ten-year-old girl wrote to *New Moon,* a feminist magazine for girls, "I was at the beach and was in my bathing suit. I have kind of fat legs, and my uncle told me I had fat legs in front of all my cousins and my cousins' friends. I was so embarrassed, I went up to my room and shut the door. When I went downstairs again, everyone started teasing me."[8] Young women are even encouraged to worry about small fluctuations in their weight. "Sometimes what you wear to dinner may depend on what you eat for breakfast," says an ad for cereal that pictures a slinky black dress. In truth, daily and weekly and monthly fluctuations in weight are perfectly normal.

The obsession starts early. Some studies have found that from 40 to 80 percent of fourth-grade girls are dieting.[9] Today at least one-third of twelve- to thirteen-year-old girls are actively trying to lose weight, by dieting, vomiting, using laxatives, or taking diet pills.[10] One survey found that 63 percent of high-school girls were on diets, compared with only

16 percent of men.[11] And a survey in Massachusetts found that the single largest group of high-school students considering or attempting suicide are girls who feel they are overweight.[12] Imagine. Girls made to feel so terrible about themselves that they would rather be dead than fat. This wouldn't be happening, of course, if it weren't for our last "socially acceptable" prejudice—weightism.[13] Fat children are ostracized and ridiculed from the moment they enter school, and fat adults, women in particular, are subjected to public contempt and scorn. This strikes terror into the hearts of all women, many of whom, unfortunately, identify with the oppressor and become vicious to themselves and each other.

No wonder it is hard to find a woman, especially a young woman, in America today who has a truly healthy attitude toward her body and toward food. Just as the disease of alcoholism is the extreme end of a continuum that includes a wide range of alcohol use and abuse, so are bulimia and anorexia the extreme results of an obsession with eating and weight control that grips many young women with serious and potentially very dangerous results. Although eating problems are often thought to result from vanity, the truth is that they, like other addictions and compulsive behavior, usually have deeper roots—not only genetic predisposition and biochemical vulnerabilities, but also childhood sexual abuse.[14]

Advertising doesn't cause eating problems, of course, any more than it causes alcoholism. Anorexia in particular is a disease with a complicated etiology, and media images probably don't play a major role. However, these images certainly contribute to the body-hatred so many young women feel and to some of the resulting eating problems, which range from bulimia to compulsive overeating to simply being obsessed with controlling one's appetite. Advertising does promote abusive and abnormal attitudes about eating, drinking, and thinness. It thus provides fertile soil for these obsessions to take root in and creates a climate of denial in which these diseases flourish.

The influence of the media is strikingly illustrated in a . . . study that found a sharp rise in eating disorders among young women in Fiji soon after the introduction of television to the culture.[15] Before television was available, there was little talk of dieting in Fiji. "You've gained weight" was a traditional compliment and "going thin" the sign of a problem. In 1995 television came to the island. Within three years, the number of teenagers at risk for eating disorders more than doubled, 74 percent of the teens in the study said they felt "too big or too fat," and 62 percent said they had dieted in the past month. Of course, this doesn't prove a direct causal link between television and eating disorders. Fiji is a culture in transition in many ways. However, it seems more than coincidental that the Fiji girls who were heavy viewers of television were 50 percent more likely to describe themselves as fat and 30 percent more likely to diet than those girls who watched television less frequently. As Ellen Goodman says, "The big success story of our entertainment industry is our ability to export insecurity: We can make any woman anywhere feel perfectly rotten about her shape."[16]

Being obsessed about one's weight is made to seem normal and even appealing in ads for unrelated products, such as a scotch ad that features a very thin and pretty young woman looking in a mirror while her boyfriend observes her. The copy, addressed to him, says, "Listen, if you can handle 'Honey, do I look fat?' you can handle this." These two are so intimate that she can share her deepest fears with him—and he can respond by chuckling at her adorable vulnerability and knocking back another scotch. And everyone who sees the ad gets the message that it is perfectly normal for all young women, including thin and attractive ones, to worry about their weight. . . .

Not all of this is intentional on the part of the advertisers, of course. A great deal of it *is* based on research and *is* intended to arouse anxiety and affect women's self-esteem. But some of it reflects the unconscious attitudes and beliefs of the individual advertisers, as well as what Carl Jung referred to as the "collective unconscious." Advertisers are members of the culture too and have been as thoroughly conditioned as anyone else. The magazines and the ads deliberately *create* and intensify anxiety about weight because it is so profitable. On a deeper level, however, they *reflect* cultural concerns and conflicts about women's power. Real freedom for women would change the very basis of our male-dominated society. It is not surprising that many men (and women, to be sure) fear this.

"The more you subtract, the more you add," says an ad that ran in several women's and teen magazines in 1997. Surprisingly, it is an ad for clothing, not for a diet product. Overtly, it is a statement about minimalism in fashion. However, the fact that the girl in the ad is very young and very thin reinforces another message, a message that an adolescent girl constantly gets from advertising and throughout the popular culture, the message that she should diminish herself, she should be *less* than she is.

On the most obvious and familiar level, this refers to her body. However, the loss, the subtraction, the cutting down to size also refers to her sense of her self, her sexuality, her need for authentic connection, and her longing for power and freedom. I certainly don't think that the creators of this particular ad had all this in mind. They're simply selling expensive clothing in an unoriginal way, by using a very young and very thin woman—and an unfortunate tagline. It wouldn't be important at all were there not so many other ads that reinforce this message and did it not coincide with a cultural crisis taking place now for adolescent girls.

"We cut Judy down to size," says an ad for a health club. "Soon, you'll both be taking up less space," says an ad for a collapsible treadmill, referring both to the product and to the young woman exercising on it. *The obsession with thinness is most deeply about cutting girls and women down to size.* It is only a symbol, albeit a very powerful and destructive one, of tremendous fear of female power. Powerful women are seen by many people (women as well as men) as inherently destructive and dangerous. Some argue that it is men's awareness of just how powerful women can be that has created the attempts to keep women small.[17] Indeed, thinness as an ideal has always accompanied periods of greater freedom for women—as soon as we got the vote, boyish flapper bodies came into vogue. No wonder there is such pressure on young women today to be thin, to shrink, to be like little girls, not to take up too much space, literally or figuratively.

At the same time there is relentless pressure on women to be small, there is also pressure on us to succeed, to achieve, to "have it all." We can be successful as long as we stay "feminine" (i.e., powerless enough not to be truly threatening). One way to do this is to present an image of fragility, to look like a waif. This demonstrates that one is both in control and still very "feminine." One of the many double binds tormenting young women today is the need to be both sophisticated and accomplished, yet also delicate and childlike. Again, this applies mostly to middle- to upper-class white women.

The changing roles and greater opportunities for women promised by the women's movement are trivialized, reduced to the private search for the slimmest body. In one commercial, three skinny young women dance and sing about the "taste of freedom." They are feeling free because they can now eat bread, thanks to a low-calorie version. A commercial for a fast-food chain features a very slim young woman who announces, "I have a license to eat." The salad bar and lighter fare have given her freedom to eat (as if eating for women were a privilege rather than a need). "Free yourself," says ad after ad for diet products. . . .

Most of us know by now about the damage done to girls by the tyranny of the ideal image, weightism, and the obsession with thinness. But girls get other messages too that "cut them down to size" more subtly. In ad after ad girls are urged to be "barely there"—beautiful but silent. Of course, girls are not just influenced by images of other girls. They are even more powerfully attuned to images of women, because they learn from these images what is expected of them, what they are to become. And they see these images again and again in the magazines they read, even those magazines designed for teenagers, and in the commercials they watch.

"Make a statement without saying a word," says an ad for perfume. And indeed this is one of the primary messages of the culture to adolescent girls. "The silence of a look can reveal more than words," says another perfume ad, this one featuring a woman lying on her back. "More than words can say," says yet another perfume ad, and a clothing ad says, "Classic is speaking your mind (without saying a word)." An ad for lipstick says, "Watch your mouth, young lady," while one for nail polish says, "Let your fingers do the talking," and one for hairspray promises "hair that speaks volumes." In another ad, a young woman's turtleneck is pulled over her mouth. And an ad for a movie soundtrack features a chilling image of a young woman with her lips sewn together.

It is not only the girls themselves who see these images, of course. Their parents and teachers and doctors see them and they influence their sense of how girls should be. A 1999 study done at the University of Michigan found that, beginning in preschool, girls are told to be quiet much more often than boys.[18] Although boys were much noisier than girls, the girls were told to speak softly or to use a "nicer" voice about three times more often. Girls were encouraged to be quiet, small, and physically constrained. The researcher concluded that one of the consequences of this socialization is that girls grow into women afraid to speak up for themselves or to use their voices to protect themselves from a variety of dangers. . . .

"Score high on nonverbal skills," says a clothing ad featuring a young African-American woman, while an ad for mascara tells young women to "make up your own language." And an Italian ad features a very thin young woman in an elegant coat sitting on a window seat. The copy says, "This woman is silent. This coat talks." Girls, seeing these images of women, are encouraged to be silent, mysterious, not to talk too much or too loudly. In many different ways, they are told "the more you subtract, the more you add." In this kind of climate, a Buffalo jeans ad featuring a young woman screaming, "I don't have to scream for attention but I do," can seem like an improvement—until we notice that she's really getting attention by unbuttoning her blouse to her navel. This is typical of the mixed messages so many ads and other forms of the media give girls. The young woman seems fierce and powerful, but she's really exposed, vulnerable.

The January 1998 cover of *Seventeen* highlights an article, "Do you talk too much?" On the back cover is an ad for Express mascara, which promises "high voltage volume instantly!" As if the way that girls can express themselves and turn up the volume is via their mascara. Is this harmless wordplay, or is it a sophisticated and clever marketing ploy based on research about the silencing of girls, deliberately designed to attract them with the promise of at least some form of self-expression? Advertisers certainly spend a lot of money on psychological research and focus groups. I would expect these groups to reveal, among other things, that teenage girls are angry but reticent. Certainly the cumulative effect of these images and words urging girls to express themselves only through their bodies and through products is serious and harmful.

Many ads feature girls and young women in very passive poses, limp, doll-like, sometimes acting like little girls, playing with dolls, and wearing bows in their hair. One ad uses a pacifier to sell lipstick and another the image of a baby to sell Baby-Doll Blush Highlight. "Lolita seems to be a comeback kid," says a fashion layout featuring a woman wearing a ridiculous hairstyle and a baby-doll dress, standing with shoulders slumped and feet apart. In women's and teen magazines it is virtually impossible to tell the fashion layouts from the ads. Indeed, they exist to support each other.

As Erving Goffman pointed out in *Gender Advertisements,* we learn a great deal about the disparate power of males and females simply through the body language and poses of advertising.[19] Women, especially young women, are generally subservient to men in ads, through both size and position. . . .

Girls are often shown as playful clowns in ads, perpetuating the attitude that girls and women are childish and cannot be taken seriously, whereas even very young men are generally portrayed as secure, powerful, and serious. People in control of their lives stand upright, alert, and ready to meet the world. In contrast, females often appear off-balance, insecure, and weak. Often our body parts are bent, conveying unpreparedness, submissiveness, and appeasement. We exhibit what Goffman terms "licensed withdrawal"—seeming to be psychologically removed, disoriented, defenseless, spaced out.

Females touch people and things delicately, we caress, whereas males grip, clench, and grasp. We cover our faces with our hair or our hands, conveying shame or embarrassment. And, no matter what happens, we keep on smiling. "Just smiling the bothers away," as one ad says. This ad is particularly disturbing because the model is a young African-American woman, a member of a group that has long been encouraged to just keep smiling, no matter what. She's even wearing a kerchief, like Aunt Jemima. The cultural fear of angry women is intensified dramatically when the women are African-American. . . .

. . . As girls come of age sexually, the culture gives them impossibly contradictory messages. As the *Seventeen* ad says, "She wants to be outrageous. And accepted." Advertising slogans such as "because innocence is sexier than you think," "Purity, yes. Innocence never," and "Nothing so sensual was ever so innocent" place them in a double bind. "Only something so pure could inspire such unspeakable passion," declares an ad for Jovan musk that features a white flower. Somehow girls are supposed to be both innocent and seductive, virginal and experienced, all at the same time. As they quickly learn, this is tricky.

Females have long been divided into virgins and whores, of course. What is new is that girls are now supposed to embody both within themselves. This is symbolic of the central contradiction of the culture—we must work hard and produce and achieve success and yet, at the same time, we are encouraged to live impulsively, spend a lot of money, and be constantly and immediately gratified. This tension is reflected in our attitudes toward many things, including sex and eating. Girls are promised fulfillment both through being thin and through eating rich foods, just as they are promised fulfillment through being innocent and virginal and through wild and impulsive sex. . . .

The emphasis for girls and women is always on being desirable, not on experiencing desire. Girls who want to be sexually *active* instead of simply being the objects of male desire are given only one model to follow, that of exploitive male sexuality. It seems that advertisers can't conceive of a kind of power that isn't manipulative and exploitive or a way that women can be actively sexual without being like traditional men.

Women who are "powerful" in advertising are uncommitted. They treat men like sex objects: "If I want a man to see my bra, I take him home," says an androgynous young woman. They are elusive and distant: "She is the first woman who refused to take your phone calls," says one ad. As if it were a good thing to be rude and inconsiderate. Why should any of us, male or female, be interested in someone who won't take our phone calls, who either cares so little for us or is so manipulative?

Mostly though, girls are not supposed to have sexual agency. They are supposed to be passive, swept away, overpowered. "See where it takes you," says a perfume ad featuring a couple passionately embracing. "Unleash your fantasies," says another. "A force of nature." This contributes to the strange and damaging concept of the "good girl" as the one who is swept away, unprepared for sex, versus the "bad girl" as the one who plans for sex, uses contraception, and is generally responsible. A young woman can manage to have sex and yet in some sense maintain her virginity by being "out of control," drunk, or deep in denial about the entire experience.

No wonder most teenage pregnancies occur when one or both parties is drunk. Alcohol and other mind-altering drugs permit sexual activity at the same time that they allow denial. One is almost literally not there. The next day one has an excuse. I was drunk, I was swept away. I did not choose this experience.

In adolescence girls are told that they have to give up much of what they *know* about relationships and intimacy if they want to attract men. Most tragically, they are told they have to give up each other. The truth is that one of the most powerful antidotes to destructive cultural messages is close and supportive female friendships. But girls are often encouraged by the culture to sacrifice their relationships with each other and to enter into hostile competition for the attention of boys and men. "What the bitch who's about to steal your man wears," says one ad. And many ads feature young women fighting or glaring at each other.

Of course, some girls do resist and rebel. Some are encouraged (by someone—a loving parent, a supportive teacher) to see the cultural contradictions clearly and to break free in a healthy and positive way. Others rebel in ways that damage themselves. A young woman seems to have only two choices: She can bury her sexual self, be a "good girl," give in to what Carol Gilligan terms "the tyranny of nice and kind" (and numb the pain by overeating or starving or cutting herself or drinking heavily).[20] Or she can become a rebel—flaunt her sexuality, seduce inappropriate partners, smoke, drink flamboyantly, use other drugs. Both of these responses are self-destructive, but they begin as an attempt to survive, not to self-destruct. . . .

There are few healthy alternatives for girls who want to truly rebel against restrictive gender roles and stereotypes. The recent emphasis on girl power has led to some real advances for girls and young women, especially in the arenas of music and sports. But it is as often co-opted and trivialized. . . . Magazines like *New Moon, Hues,* and *Teen Voices* offer a real alternative to the glitzy, boy-crazy, appearance-obsessed teen magazines on the newsstands, but they have to struggle for funds since they take no advertising. There are some good zines and Websites for girls on the Internet, but there are also countless sites that degrade and endanger them. And Barbie continues to rake in two billion dollars a year . . . while a doll called "Happy to be me," similar to Barbie but much more realistic and down to earth, was available for a couple of years in the mid-1990s . . . and then vanished from sight.[21] Of course, Barbie's makers have succumbed to pressure somewhat and have remade her with a thicker waist, smaller breasts, and slimmer hips. As a result, according to Anthony Cortese, she has already lost her waitressing job at Hooter's and her boyfriend Ken has told her that he wants to start seeing other dolls.[22]

Girls who want to escape the stereotypes are viewed with glee by advertisers, who rush to offer them, as always, power via products. The emphasis in the ads is always on their sexuality, which is exploited to sell them makeup and clothes and shoes. . . . A demon woman sells a perfume called Hypnotic Poison. A trio of extremely thin African-American women brandish hair appliances and products as if they were weapons—and the brand is 911. A cosmetics company has a line of products called "Bad Gal." In one ad, eyeliner is shown in cartoon version as a girl, who is holding a dog saying, "grrrr," surely a reference to "grrrls," a symbol these days of "girl power" (as in cybergrrrl.com, the popular Website for girls and young women). Unfortunately, girl power doesn't mean much if girls don't have the tools to achieve it. Without reproductive freedom and freedom from violence, girl power is nothing but a marketing slogan. . . .

Of course, the readers and viewers of these ads don't take them literally. But we do take them in—another grain of sand in a slowly accumulating and vast sandpile. If we entirely enter the world of ads, imagine them to be real for a moment, we find that the sandpile has completely closed us in, and there's only one escape route—buy something. . . . "Hey girls, you've got the power of control" says an ad for . . . hairspray. "The possibilities are endless" (clothing). "Never lose control" (hairspray again). "You never had this much control when you were on your own" (hair gel). "Exceptional character" (a watch). "An enlightening experience" (face powder). "Inner strength" (vitamins). "Only Victoria's Secret could make control so sensual" (girdles). "Stronger longer" (shampoo). Of course, the empowerment, the enlightenment, is as impossible to get through products as is anything else—love, security, romance, passion. On one level, we know this. On another, we keep buying and hoping—and buying.

Other ads go further and offer products as a way to rebel, to be a real individual. "Live outside the lines," says a clothing ad featuring a young woman walking out of a men's room. This kind of rebellion isn't going to rock the world. And, no surprise, the young woman is very thin and conventionally pretty. Another pretty young woman sells a brand of jeans called "Revolt." "Don't just change . . . revolt," says the copy, but the young woman is passive, slight, her eyes averted.

"Think for yourself," says yet another hollow-cheeked young woman, demonstrating her individuality via an expensive and fashionable sweater. "Be amazing" (cosmetics). "Inside every woman is a star" (clothing). "If you're going to create electricity, use it" (watches). "If you let your spirit out, where would it go" (perfume). These women are all perfect examples of conventional "femininity," as is the young woman in a Halston perfume ad that says, "And when she was bad she wore Halston." What kind of "bad" is this? . . .

NOTES

1. In a speech at Richland College, Dallas, Texas, on February 24, 1977.

2. Gilligan, C. 1982. *In a different voice.* Cambridge, MA: Harvard University Press; Pipher, M. 1994. *Reviving Ophelia: Saving the selves of adolescent girls.* New York: Putnam; Sadker, M., and D. Sadker. 1994. *Failing at Fairness: How our schools cheat girls.* New York: Simon and Schuster.

3. Steiner-Adair, C., and A. Purcell. 1996. Approaches to mainstreaming eating disorders prevention. *Eating Disorders,* vol. 4, no. 4: 294–309.

4. Field, A.E., L. Cheung, A.M. Wolf, D.B. Herzog, S.L. Gortmaker, and G.A. Colditz. 1999. Exposure to the mass media and weight concerns among girls. *Pediatrics,* vol. 103, no. 3: 36–41.

5. Then, D. 1992. Women's magazines: Messages they convey about looks, men and careers. Paper presented at the annual convention of the American Psychological Association, Washington, DC; also Richins, M.L. 1991. Social comparison and idealized images of advertising. *Journal of Consumer Research,* 18: 71–83.

6. Fredrickson, B.L. 1998. *Journal of Personality and Social Psychology,* vol. 75. no. 1. Reported in *Media Report to Women,* 5.

7. Strasburger, V.C. 1989, Adolescent sexuality and the media. *Pediatric Clinics of North America,* vol. 36, no. 3, 747–73.

8. E-mail correspondence with Heather S. Henderson, editor-in-chief of *HUES* magazine, New Moon Publishing, March 22, 1999.

9. Stein, J. 1986 (October 29). Why girls as young as 9 fear fat and go on diets to lose weight. *Los Angeles Times,* 1, 10.

10. Rodriguez, C. 1998 (November 27). Even in middle school, girls are thinking thin. *Boston Globe,* B1, B9.

11. Rothblum, E.D. 1994. "I'll die for the revolution but don't ask me to diet": Feminism and the continuing stigmatization of obesity. In *Feminist Perspectives on Eating Disorders,* edited by P. Fallon, M.A. Katzman, and S.C. Wooley. New York: Guildford Press: 53–76.

12. Overlan, L. 1996 (July 2). "Overweight" girls at risk. *Newton Tab,* 15.

13. Steiner-Adair, C., and A. Purcell. 1996. Approaches to mainstreaming eating disorders prevention. *Eating Disorders,* vol. 4, no. 4: 294–309.

14. Smith K.A., C.G. Fairburn, and P.J. Cowen. 1999. Symptomatic relapse in bulimia nervosa following acute tryptophan depletion. *Journal of the American Medical Association,* vol. 56: 171–76. Also, Hsu, L.K. 1990. *Eating disorders.* New York: Guildford Press; Jonas, J.M. 1989. Eating disorders and alcohol and other drug abuse. Is there an association? *Alcohol Health & Research World,* vol. 13, no. 3: 267–71; Krahn, D.D. 1991. Relationship of eating disorders and substance abuse. *Journal of Substance Abuse,* vol. 3, no. 2: 239–53; Thompson, B.W. 1994. *A hunger so wide and so deep.* Minneapolis: University of Minnesota Press.

15. Becker, A.E., and R.A. Burwell. 1999. *Acculturation and disordered eating in Fiji.* Poster presented at the American Psychiatric Association Annual Meeting, Washington, DC, May 19, 1999.

16. Goodman, E. 1999 (May 27). The culture of thin bites Fiji teens. *Boston Globe,* A23.

17. Faludi, S. 1991. *Backlash.* New York: Crown; also Kilbourne, J. 1986. The child as sex object: Images of children in the media. In *The Educator's Guide to Preventing Child Sexual Abuse,* edited by M. Nelson and K. Clark. Santa Cruz, CA: Network Publications.

18. Martin, K.A. 1998. Becoming a gendered body: Practices of preschools. *American Sociological Review,* vol. 63, no. 4: 494–511.

19. Goffman, E. 1978. *Gender advertisements.* Cambridge, MA: Harvard University Press.

20. Brown, L.M., and C. Gilligan. 1992. *Meeting at the crossroads: Women's psychology and girls' development.* New York: Ballantine, 53.

21. Goldsmith, J. 1999 (February 10). A $2 billion doll celebrates her 40th without a wrinkle. *Boston Globe,* D3.

22. Cortese, A. 1999. *Provocateur: Women and minorities in advertising.* Lanham, MD: Rowman and Littlefield, 57.

TWENTY-SEVEN

Three Generations of Native American Women's Birth Experience (1991)

Joy Harjo

Poet, musician, and teacher **Joy Harjo** has published many award-winning poetry collections, most recently *How We Became Human: New and Selected Poems.* She is the Joseph M. Russo Professor in Creative Writing at the University of New Mexico and the recipient of numerous fellowships and awards including the American Indian Distinguished Achievement in the Arts Award and the William Carlos Williams Award of the Poetry Society of America. She performs her poetry and plays saxophone with her band, Poetic Justice.

It was still dark when I awakened in the stuffed back room of my mother-in-law's small rented house with what felt like hard cramps. At 17 years of age I had read everything I could from the Tahlequah Public Library about pregnancy and giving birth. But nothing prepared me for what was coming. I awakened my child's father and then ironed him a shirt before we walked the four blocks to the Indian hospital because we had no car and no money for a taxi. He had been working with another Cherokee artist silk-screening signs for specials at the supermarket and making $5 a day, and had to leave me alone at the hospital because he had to go to work. We didn't awaken his mother. She had to get up soon enough to fix breakfast for her daughter and granddaughter before leaving for her job at the nursing home. I knew my life was balanced at the edge of great, precarious change and I felt alone and cheated. Where was the circle of women to acknowledge and honor this birth?

It was still dark as we walked through the cold morning, under oaks that symbolized the stubbornness and endurance of the Cherokee people who had made Tahlequah their capital in the new lands. I looked for handholds in the misty gray sky, for a voice announcing this impending miracle. I wanted to change everything; I wanted to go back to a place before childhood, before our tribe's removal to Oklahoma. What kind of life was I bringing this child into? I was a poor, mixed-blood woman heavy with a child who would suffer the struggle of poverty, the legacy of loss. For the second time in my life I felt the sharp tug of my own birth cord, still connected to my mother. I believe it never pulls away, until death, and even then it becomes a streak in the sky symbolizing that most important warrior road. In my teens I had fought my mother's weaknesses with all my might, and here I was at 17, becoming as my mother, who was in Tulsa, cooking breakfasts and preparing for the lunch shift at a factory cafeteria as I walked to the hospital to give birth. I should be with her; instead, I was far from her house, in the house of a mother-in-law who later would try to use witchcraft to destroy me.

After my son's father left me I was prepped for birth. This meant my pubic area was shaved completely and then I endured the humiliation of an enema, all at the hands of strangers. I was left alone in a room painted government green. An overwhelming antiseptic smell emphasized the sterility of the hospital, a hospital built because of the U.S. government's treaty and responsibility to provide health care to Indian people.

I intellectually understood the stages of labor, the place of transition, of birth—but it was difficult to bear the actuality of it, and to bear it alone. Yet in some ways I wasn't alone, for history surrounded me. It is with the birth of children that history is given form and voice. Birth is one of the most sacred acts we take part in and witness in our lives. But sacredness seemed to be far from my lonely labor room in the Indian hospital. I heard a woman screaming in the next room with her pain, and I wanted to comfort her. The nurse used her as a bad example to the rest of us who were struggling to keep our suffering silent.

The doctor was a military man who had signed on this watch not for the love of healing or out of awe at the miracle of birth, but to fulfill a contract for medical school payments. I was another statistic to him; he touched me as if he were moving equipment from one place to another. During my last visit I was given the option of being sterilized. He explained to

me that the moment of birth was the best time to do it. I was handed the form but chose not to sign it, and am amazed now that I didn't think too much of it at the time. Later I would learn that many Indian women who weren't fluent in English signed, thinking it was a form giving consent for the doctor to deliver their babies. Others were sterilized without even the formality of signing. My light skin had probably saved me from such a fate. It wouldn't be the first time in my life.

When my son was finally born I had been deadened with a needle in my spine. He was shown to me—the incredible miracle nothing prepared me for—then taken from me in the name of medical progress. I fell asleep with the weight of chemicals and awoke yearning for the child I had suffered for, had anticipated in the months proceeding from his unexpected genesis when I was still 16 and a student at Indian school. I was not allowed to sit up or walk because of the possibility of paralysis (one of the drug's side effects), and when I finally got to hold him, the nurse stood guard as if I would hurt him. I felt enmeshed in a system in which the wisdom that had carried my people from generation to generation was ignored. In that place I felt ashamed I was an Indian woman. But I was also proud of what my body had accomplished despite the rape by the bureaucracy's machinery, and I got us out of there as soon as possible. My son would flourish on beans and fry bread, and on the dreams and stories we fed him.

My daughter was born four years later, while I was an art student at the University of New Mexico. Since my son's birth I had waitressed, cleaned hospital rooms, filled cars with gas (while wearing a mini-skirt), worked as a nursing assistant, and led dance classes at a health spa. I knew I didn't want to cook and waitress all my life, as my mother had done. I had watched the varicose veins grow branches on her legs, and as they grew, her zest for dancing and sports dissolved into utter tiredness. She had been born with a caul over her face, the sign of a gifted visionary.

My earliest memories are of my mother writing songs on an ancient Underwood typewriter after she had washed and waxed the kitchen floor on her hands and knees. She too had wanted something different for her life. She had left an impoverished existence at age 17, bound for the big city of Tulsa. She was shamed in a time in which to be even part

Indian was to be an outcast in the great U.S. system. Half her relatives were Cherokee full-bloods from near Jay, Oklahoma, who for the most part had nothing to do with white people. The other half were musically inclined "white trash" addicted to country-western music and Holy Roller fervor. She thought she could disappear in the city; no one would know her family, where she came from. She had dreams of singing and had once been offered a job singing on the radio but turned it down because she was shy. Later one of her songs would be stolen before she could copyright it and would make someone else rich. She would quit writing songs. She and my father would divorce, and she would be forced to work for money to feed and clothe four children, all born within two years of each other.

As a child growing up in Oklahoma, I liked to be told the story of my birth. I would beg for it while my mother cleaned and ironed. "You almost killed me," she would say. "We almost died." That I could kill my mother filled me with remorse and shame. And I imagined the push-pull of my life, which is a legacy I deal with even now when I am twice as old as my mother was at my birth. I loved to hear the story of my warrior fight for my breath. The way it was told, it had been my decision to live. When I got older, I realized we were both nearly casualties of the system, the same system flourishing in the Indian hospital where later my son Phil would be born.

My parents felt lucky to have insurance, to be able to have their children in the hospital. My father came from a fairly prominent Muscogee Creek family. *His* mother was a full-blood who in the early 1920s got her degree in art. She was a painter. She gave birth to him in a private hospital in Oklahoma City; at least that's what I think he told me before he died at age 53. It was something of which they were proud.

This experience was much different from my mother's own birth. She and five of her six brothers were born at home, with no medical assistance. The only time a doctor was called was when someone was dying. When she was born her mother named her Wynema, a Cherokee name my mother says means beautiful woman, and Jewell, for a can of shortening stored in the room where she was born.

I wanted something different for my life, for my son, and for my daughter, who later was born in a university hospital in Albuquerque. It was a bright summer morning when she was ready to begin her journey. I still had no car, but I had enough money saved for a taxi for a ride to the hospital. She was born "naturally," without drugs. I could look out of the hospital window while I was in labor at the bluest sky in the world. I had support. Her father was present in the delivery room—though after her birth he disappeared on a drinking binge. I understood his despair, but did not agree with the painful means to describe it. A few days later Rainy Dawn was presented to the sun at her father's pueblo and given a name so that she will always be recognized as a part of the people, as a child of the sun.

That's not to say that my experience in the hospital reached perfection. The clang of metal against metal in the delivery room had the effect of a tuning fork reverberating fear in my pelvis. After giving birth I held my daughter, but they took her from me for "processing." I refused to lie down to be wheeled to my room after giving birth; I wanted to walk out of there to find my daughter. We reached a compromise, and I rode in a wheelchair. When we reached the room I stood up and walked to the nursery and demanded my daughter. I knew she needed me. That began my war with the nursery staff, who deemed me unknowledgeable because I was Indian and poor. Once again I felt the brushfire of shame, but I'd learned to put it out much more quickly, and I demanded early release so I could take care of my baby without the judgment of strangers.

I wanted something different for Rainy, and as she grew up I worked hard to prove that I could make "something" of my life. I obtained two degrees as a single mother. I wrote poetry, screenplays, became a professor, and tried to live a life that would be a positive influence for both of my children. My work in this life has to do with reclaiming the memory stolen from our peoples when we were dispossessed from our lands east of the Mississippi; it has to do with restoring us. I am proud of our history, a history so powerful that it both destroyed my father and guarded him. It's a history that claims my mother as she lives not far from the place her mother was born, names her as she cooks in the cafeteria of a small college in Oklahoma.

When my daughter told me she was pregnant, I wasn't surprised. I had known it before she did, or at least before she would admit it to me. I felt despair, as if nothing had changed or ever would. She had run away from Indian school with her boyfriend, and they had been living in the streets of Gallup, a border town notorious for the suicides and deaths of Indian peoples. I brought her and her boyfriend with me because it was the only way I could bring her home. At age 16, she was fighting me just as I had so fiercely fought my mother. She was making the same mistakes. I felt as if everything I had accomplished had been in vain. Yet I felt strangely empowered, too, at this repetition of history, this continuance, by a new possibility of life and love, and I steadfastly stood by my daughter.

I had a university job, so I had insurance that covered my daughter. She saw an obstetrician in town who was reputed to be one of the best. She had the choice of a birthing room. She had the finest care. Despite this, I once again battled with a system in which physicians are taught the art of healing by dissecting cadavers. My daughter went into labor a month early. We both knew intuitively the baby was ready, but how to explain that to a system in which numbers and statistics provide the base of understanding? My daughter would have her labor interrupted; her blood pressure would rise because of the drug given to her to stop the labor. She would be given an unneeded amniocentesis and would have her labor induced—after having it artificially stopped! I was warned that if I took her out of the hospital so her labor could occur naturally my insurance would cover nothing.

My daughter's induced labor was unnatural and difficult, monitored by machines, not by touch. I was shocked. I felt as if I'd come full circle, as if I were watching my mother's labor and the struggle of my own birth. But I was there in the hospital room with her, as neither my mother had been for me, nor her mother for her. My daughter and I went through the labor and birth together.

And when Krista Rae was born she was born to her family. Her father was there for her, as were both her grandmothers and my friend who had flown in to be with us. Her paternal great-grandparents and aunts and uncles had also arrived from the Navajo Reservation to honor her. Something *had* changed.

Four days later, I took my granddaughter to the Saguaro forest before dawn and gave her the name I had dreamed for her just before her birth. Her name looks like clouds of mist settling around a sacred mountain as it begins to speak. A female ancestor approaches on a horse. We are all together.

TWENTY-EIGHT

◆◆◆

Reproductive Justice: Vision, Analysis, and Action for a Stronger Movement (2005)

Asian Communities for Reproductive Justice

Founded in 1989, **Asian Communities for Reproductive Justice** (Oakland, California) has been at the forefront of building a reproductive justice movement that places the reproductive health and rights of Asian women and girls within a social justice framework.

We believe reproductive justice is the complete physical, mental, spiritual, political, economic, and social well being of women and girls, and that it will be achieved when women and girls have the economic, social, and political power and resources to make healthy decisions about our bodies, sexuality, and reproduction for ourselves, our families and our communities. For this to become a reality, we need to make change on the individual, community, institutional, and societal levels.

Oppression and Reproduction

The fight for women's emancipation has been inextricably linked to control over reproduction. The reproductive health and reproductive rights agendas have largely focused on individual rights and solutions rather than structural societal changes. Many women at the margins of the movement have championed the need for greater analysis of oppressions in discussions of reproduction. As Dorothy Roberts stated, "Reproduction is not just a matter of individual choice. Reproductive health policy affects the status of entire groups. It reflects which people are valued in our society, who is deemed worthy to bear children and capable of making decisions for themselves. Reproductive decisions are made within a social context, including inequalities of wealth and power."[1] The focus on individualism neglects the broader societal context in which Asian and Pacific Islander (API) women live.

Repeatedly, economic, social, and institutional policies have severely affected women's choice to determine reproduction. The regulation and control of API women and girls' bodies, sexuality, and reproduction have played a key role in colonization and racial oppression, and in controlling API communities in the United States. Historically, the nation's immigrant exclusion laws targeted people from Asia and served as a form of population control. As early as 1870, in an attempt to limit the size of the Asian population in California, the state legislature passed a law that prohibited the immigration of Asian women, and in 1875 the United States Congress passed the Page Law to forbid entry of mostly "Chinese, Japanese and Mongolian" women. Current policies restricting immigration and access to social services also significantly prevent API women from truly being able to make reproductive choices.

In focusing on a narrow abortion agenda or even a broader reproductive health agenda, the mainstream reproductive health and reproductive rights movement typically neglects critical circumstances that many Asian and Pacific Islander women face. For example, API women who are immigrants or those with limited English proficiency have little power to negotiate interactions with reproductive health providers. Many queer API women face homophobia that deters them from accessing reproductive care. Reproductive health programs and service providers often focus on women as individuals and may adopt a paternalistic approach that oppresses and regulates women's reproduction. Although there is, currently, a movement to incorporate "cultural competence" and language access in health services, these interventions usually do not address power differentials in the patient-provider relationship. They do not empower API women to be partners with medical practitioners in making decisions. Also they usually do not incorporate or respect traditional health practices that API women value such as homeopathic medicine, herbal healing, or acupuncture. Moreover, numerous Asian cultures promote societal, community, and family decision-making that is incompatible with an individualistic approach to reproductive rights. API women often have to navigate social taboos and traditions within their cultures in making reproductive decisions, so that "choice" is not necessarily theirs to make.

Creation of the Women of Color Reproductive Justice Movement

In response to the limitations of mainstream frameworks in addressing their reality, women of color . . . have advocated for a broader reproductive justice analysis that addresses race, class, gender, sexuality, ability, generation, and immigration status.

Although some historians have tended to erase the contributions of women of color to the movement, women of color have been actively organizing for reproductive justice for many years. In the past two decades, this race and ethnic-based organizing has gained visibility and increasing success. The National Black Women's Health Project was formed in 1984 as the first women-of-color reproductive health organization, building a foundation for organizations representing the major ethnic groups. The Mother's Milk Project on the Akwesasne Reservation in New York was created in 1985, followed by the National Latina Health Organization in 1986. The Native American Women's Health Education and Resource Center was launched in 1988, and Asian Pacific Islanders for Choice (forerunner to ACRJ) in 1989. Since then, women of color have organized numerous conferences, collaborated with each other, and formed alliances with civil rights and women's rights organizations.

In November 1994, a Black women's caucus first coined the term *reproductive justice,* naming themselves "Women of African Descent for Reproductive Justice" at the Illinois Pro-Choice Alliance Conference. According to Loretta Ross, one of the caucus participants, "We were dissatisfied with the pro-choice language, feeling that it did not adequately encompass our twinned goals: To protect the right to have—and not to have—children. Nor did the language of choice accurately portray the many barriers African American women faced when trying to make reproductive decisions. We began exploring the use of the human rights framework in our reproductive rights activism in the United States, as many grassroots activists do globally. We sought a way to partner reproductive rights to social justice and came up with the term 'reproductive justice'."[2] Later, the SisterSong Women of Color Reproductive Health Collective was formed by 16 women-of-color organizations in 1997, with a focus on grassroots mobilization and public policy. In April 2004, SisterSong coordinated thousands of women in a "Women of Color for Reproductive Justice" contingent as part of the March for Women's Lives in Washington, D.C.

Attacking Reproductive Oppression: Asian Communities for Reproductive Justice (ACRJ)

At ACRJ we work towards a vision of the world where Asian women and girls have self-determination, power, and resources to make the decisions they need. Our Reproductive Justice Agenda illustrates our vision, solutions, and values for attacking the root causes of reproductive oppression (see Figure 1). In this Agenda we articulate our analysis based on the experiences, issues, and research carried out for and by Asian women and girls to develop a model that is at the nexus of the intersections of gender, race, class, sexuality, ability, generation, and immigration status. In our organizing work, we use popular education and community-based participatory research to develop the leadership of Asian women and girls to plan campaigns for specific and measurable gains at the local and state level. For instance, we worked in collaboration with environmental justice groups to shut down a toxic medical waste incinerator in Oakland, California, and have been working to pass and enforce state legislation that ensures comprehensive sex education in public high schools. And finally, we build and strengthen women of color and mainstream alliances for reproductive justice. We recognize the importance of broader inclusion and leadership of the most excluded groups of women. These include low-income women, queer women, women with disabilities, young women, immigrant and refugee women. Many are women of color; some white women are also excluded on account of their class position, sexuality, language competence, and so on. We believe that organized communities, particularly the most marginalized groups mentioned above, are key agents of change, and we focus on improving social conditions and changing power and access to resources on all levels. Figure 1 summarizes our approach.

ACRJ's Reproductive Justice Agenda (RJA) places reproductive justice at the center of the most critical social and economic justice issues facing our communities such as domestic safety, labor rights, environmental justice, queer rights, and immigrant rights. For example, under conditions of reproductive justice, we will live in homes free from sexual and physical violence; we will live and work without fear of sexual harassment; we will have safe work and home environments protected from corporate exploitation and environmental toxins; we will be free from hatred due to sexual identity; we will be valued for all the forms of work we do; we will earn equitable and livable wages; we will eat healthy and affordable food; we will have comprehensive health care for ourselves and our families. Moreover, the government and private institutions will support our decisions whether or not to have a child and we will receive the necessary support for our choices. In addition we will receive an education that honors and teaches the contributions of women, people of color, working class communities, and queer communities.

As illustrated in the Reproductive Justice Agenda, women's bodies, reproduction, and sexuality are often used as the excuse and the target for unequal treatment in the attempt to control

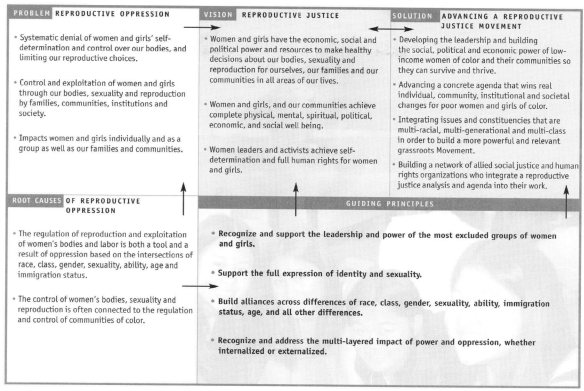

PROBLEM REPRODUCTIVE OPPRESSION	VISION REPRODUCTIVE JUSTICE	SOLUTION ADVANCING A REPRODUCTIVE JUSTICE MOVEMENT
• Systematic denial of women and girls' self-determination and control over our bodies, and limiting our reproductive choices. • Control and exploitation of women and girls through our bodies, sexuality and reproduction by families, communities, institutions and society. • Impacts women and girls individually and as a group as well as our families and communities.	• Women and girls have the economic, social and political power and resources to make healthy decisions about our bodies, sexuality and reproduction for ourselves, our families and our communities in all areas of our lives. • Women and girls, and our communities achieve complete physical, mental, spiritual, political, economic, and social well being. • Women leaders and activists achieve self-determination and full human rights for women and girls.	• Developing the leadership and building the social, political and economic power of low-income women of color and their communities so they can survive and thrive. • Advancing a concrete agenda that wins real individual, community, institutional and societal changes for poor women and girls of color. • Integrating issues and constituencies that are multi-racial, multi-generational and multi-class in order to build a more powerful and relevant grassroots Movement. • Building a network of allied social justice and human rights organizations who integrate a reproductive justice analysis and agenda into their work.

ROOT CAUSES OF REPRODUCTIVE OPPRESSION	GUIDING PRINCIPLES
• The regulation of reproduction and exploitation of women's bodies and labor is both a tool and a result of oppression based on the intersections of race, class, gender, sexuality, ability, age and immigration status. • The control of women's bodies, sexuality and reproduction is often connected to the regulation and control of communities of color.	• **Recognize and support the leadership and power of the most excluded groups of women and girls.** • **Support the full expression of identity and sexuality.** • **Build alliances across differences of race, class, gender, sexuality, ability, immigration status, age, and all other differences.** • **Recognize and address the multi-layered impact of power and oppression, whether internalized or externalized.**

FIGURE 5.1 ACRJ's Reproductive Justice Agenda

our communities. For example, some blame environmental degradation on the relatively high birth rates among women of color, both in the United States and in the Global South. We believe that by challenging patriarchal social relations and addressing the intersection of racism, sexism, xenophobia, homophobia, and class oppression within a women of color context, we will be able to build the collective social, economic, and political power of all women and girls to make choices that protect and contribute to our reproductive health and overall well being. From this vision, we have developed key strategies and projects. From the perspective of a Reproductive Justice framework, the key problem for women is lack of power, resources, and control. At ACRJ we organize to gain power and to make change on the grassroots, community, statewide, and national levels (see Figure 2).

Translating Vision into Action: ACRJ's Impact

Efforts to advance reproductive justice cannot be achieved by vision and analysis alone. In our work with Asian women and girls, we have translated our vision for reproductive justice into action.

Since 1998, ACRJ has instituted a youth organizing program that involves over 250 low-income Asian young women across California. ACRJ-trained youth leaders have won two campaigns, the School Safety Campaign and the Healthy Communities Campaign, protecting the reproductive health of Asian women. The School Safety Campaign resulted in six school-wide sexual harassment policy changes as well as a district-wide task force on school safety for girls in Long Beach, California. In collaboration with environmental justice groups, the Healthy Communities Campaign

FIGURE 5.2 Intersectionality of Reproductive Justice with Social Justice Issues

FIGURE 5.3 Intersectionality of ACRJ's Reproductive Justice Work with Social Justice Issues

increased the visibility of reproductive health issues related to toxic emissions and culminated in victory when one of the most toxic medical waste incinerators in the nation was forced to close in 2002. ACRJ has partnered with the ACLU of Northern California to pass and enforce state legislation that simplifies sex education guidelines and ensures that public school sex education is comprehensive, accurate, and free of bias. Also, in response to the wide body of evidence that shows the health hazards of beauty products, ACRJ has established POLISH, the Participatory Research, Organizing, and Leadership Initiative for Safety and Health. POLISH participants are currently researching the degree to which Asian women and girls and nail salon workers are exposed to toxic chemicals through both personal use and professional occupation. The results will fill major gaps in information, and the project will increase Asian girls' and women's capacity to identify reproductive justice problems and intervene in their community's health. Figure 3 illustrates how ACRJ's work fits into a Reproductive Justice Agenda.

The ultimate goal of our work is to build self-determination for individuals and communities. We believe that translating the vision of our Reproductive Justice Agenda into action will yield social change on all levels. For example,

1. An individual woman or girl will acquire skills, leadership ability, and commitment to furthering reproductive justice;

2. A community will change its norms to support women and girls as community leaders;

3. An institution such as a church, school/school district, business/workplace, or legislative body will make changes to stop reproductive oppression and protect reproductive justice for women and girls; and

4. Women and girls will gain complete self-determination.

NOTES

1. Roberts, Dorothy. "Race, Reproduction, and the Meaning of Liberty: Building A Social Justice Vision of Reproductive Freedom." Delivered 18 April 2000 at a Public Forum presented by The Othmer Institute.

2. Ross, Loretta. "Revisions to the ACRJ Reproductive Justice paper." E-mail to the author. 3 August 2005.

TWENTY-NINE

Understanding Positive Women's Realities (2006)

Emma Bell and Luisa Orza

Emma Bell and **Luisa Orza** are staff members at the London office of the International Community of Women Living with HIV/AIDS (ICW), a nonprofit organization founded in 1992 and the only international network of HIV-positive women. Emma Bell holds the position of Communications and Research Officer, and Luisa Orza, Monitoring and Evaluations Officer.

Despite growing recognition of the right of HIV-positive women to have healthy, fulfilling sexual lives and reproductive choices, there remain myriad factors that make such rights only a dream for most of them. The reasons women have sex and how they have it are influenced by various factors. It is widely known that violence, abandonment, and blame on disclosure can be major problems for positive women as are loss of land, livelihoods, and children. The fear thus created can be an even more pervasive influence on how HIV-positive women live their sexual lives, including whether or not they will talk openly to their partners about their sexual health and needs.

Then there are the very human desires of love, trust, and intimacy that make practicing ABC (Abstinence, Being faithful, Condom use) not as easy or desirable as it sounds. These often go unrecognized in sexual health programs, which tend to render sex sterile and pragmatic, rather than the expression of a complex mix of emotions, identity, and intimacy, which is what many people experience. "Messages are abstract and sterile. We need to bring love back into the whole thing," an International Community of Women Living with HIV/AIDS (ICW) member from Namibia said at a session entitled Love, Sex, and Abstinence at the International AIDS Conference (IAC) in Toronto held in August 2006.

For many women, an HIV diagnosis brings about significant changes in the way they enact their sexuality and how they feel about sexual relationships. There are many reasons why HIV-positive women continue to have sex or not. Some choose abstinence while others feel that abstinence is thrust upon them. For many, a period of time is needed before they discover that sexual relationships can still be a necessary and healing part of their lives. At the session in Toronto an ICW member from Zimbabwe said: "At the time of my diagnosis, I was in a good relationship with someone, and although we had always had protected sex, I could no longer have sex with him. I felt dirty, disgusting, used, defiled, and as far from sexy as humanly possible. The relationship ended, and I spent the next four years celibate." In some cases, HIV-positive women are able to use their status to negotiate safer sex. An ICW member from the United Kingdom said: "I grew to like condoms as there is no mess. And I felt as if I was in control and I wasn't prepared to let anybody have unsafe sex with me and throw it in my face. . . . So in some ways [HIV] has made me more assertive sexually."

Testing and Rights

HIV and sexual and reproductive health programmes and policies generally fail to recognize the complexity of people's lives and the contexts in which their sexual and reproductive choices are situated. Take for example the drive to test as many people as possible for HIV. It is as though programmers equate knowing one's status with being able to act on that knowledge to improve one's well-being and that of one's partners and children. For many, this is not the case, and services are not preparing people for the consequences of a positive result of an HIV test. In many cases, more women than men have access to voluntary counseling and testing services, and though testing is usually framed as voluntary, the power imbalance existing between service providers and service users is often not taken into account as the following testimony shows: "When I was pregnant and went for antenatal care, I was told to have a blood test. They did not tell me what the test was for . . . I realized it was the AIDS test when I received the results" (HIV-positive woman from Thailand).[1]

Testing, along with other HIV services, has to be carried out and projected within a sexual rights framework which takes into account the context of women's and men's daily realities. This should include their sexual realities and the appropriate support services to enable them to manage the complexities of their post-diagnosis lives. Voluntary, informed, confidential testing is the cornerstone of ICW's work in protecting the rights of people living with HIV. An example of good practice in this arena is the Liverpool Voluntary Counselling and Testing Project in Kenya. This project addresses HIV from a perspective of gender-based violence and their training addresses gender inequalities within relationships. Counsellors are trained to discuss women's experience of sexual power relations with clients and to provide them with strategies for sexual negotiation and disclosure.

Understanding Women's Realities

Many HIV-positive women have sexual desires and sexual relationships, and services need to recognize this by providing them with contraceptive advice and services, sexual health check-ups, and comprehensive advice on pre- and post-natal care for mother and child. There is need for service providers to understand that women's relationships impact on their ability to access treatment and other health services. Women's relationships also impact their ability to act on advice given to them by service providers. Partner control can prevent women from accessing treatment and can also impede their ability to adhere to treatment regimes.

A woman from Tanzania said during a treatment mapping meeting organized by ICW: "Most of us women living with HIV and who are using antiretrovirals (ARVs), we face a common problem that our husbands or partners tend to force us to give them our ARV dose while he has not tested for HIV and doesn't know his CD4 count. They do not want to go for testing while they show all HIV symptoms. Even if you refuse he will find out where you keep your medicine and steal them." Too often health care workers fail to recognize such pressures and label patients "difficult to manage" or feel that their advice is ignored.

The Right to Have Sex and Children

More problematic is that health care workers, under pressure themselves, often make harsh judgments concerning HIV-positive women's rights to have sex and children and pressure them into taking certain courses of action. HIV-positive women with children are frequently considered deviant in some way—to have made a mistake. Health care workers, community members, the media, even HIV activists have labeled HIV-positive women who get pregnant as irresponsible. In fact ICW members have reported that access to ARVs can sometimes be offered only to those who are on contraceptives; women in Lesotho and Namibia have reported that access to ARVs has been tied to use of certain types of contraceptives—either hormonal injections or IUDs, in both cases doctor-controlled methods, because it is believed that as HIV-positive women they should not get pregnant.[2] This is not only a violation of their reproductive rights but also places them in danger of re-infection and STIs as safer sex is often negotiated around contraceptive use.

Conversely, others have been denied contraceptives because it is believed that they should not be having sex, as one HIV-positive woman from Thailand learned: "I'd been to hospital and was told to have an IUD fitted. Then, when he checked my medical file and learned that I had HIV, they said 'Oh! This one was infected! The HIV-infected should not use it'."[3] Under such circumstances when HIV-positive women do become pregnant, the emphasis is on saving the life of the child, neglecting the health of the 'undeserving' mother, which not only reverses the impact of prevention of mother to child transmission but also denies women their right to health: "You are only important when you get pregnant; the baby becomes important; once you are separated you have to see to yourself."[4]

Balancing Fear, Security, and Desires

For many women, the balancing act requires them to manage the fear of abandonment from partners, fear of unwanted disclosure, fear of stigma, discrimination, and violence, and fear of infecting infants and partners, with the need for security, support, and the desire for intimacy, love, and possibly children. This can simply be too much to manage. "If you start using milk powder, everyone will know you must be HIV-positive. If you demand condom use, to stop repeated exposure, he will either hit you or just go off and have sex somewhere else and likely bring back other infections. So you just go on having unprotected sex and breast feeding even though you know you are doing exactly what they tell you you mustn't do. . . ."[5]

Women are often left to research treatment options for themselves, and only those who have access to and confidence in the relevant information are successful in accessing the treatment they require, especially around reproductive choices. "[The Support group] is run by an NGO, but if you get pregnant you have to go to the Federal AIDS Centre and they try to discourage you from having a child. . . . It is very much frowned upon for a woman with HIV to have a child and a sex life . . . at the Federal AIDS Centre you are told to have an abortion. You can get information [about prevention of mother-to-child transmission] from the support group . . . but the doctors will convince you that it's not effective. . . . If a woman does decide and insists on having a child they will help."[6]

Towards More Meaningful Involvement

The complexities of the lives and circumstances of women living with HIV require their involvement in policy and program design in order to effectively address these issues. More often than not, people living with HIV, and especially women, are still excluded from decision-making forums, and when they are invited to participate, it is still someone else who has set the agenda. Such situations can be intimidating and overwhelming, and many ICW members report having felt sidelined once they have delivered a personal testimony on how they became infected. Yet these same policy makers claim to embrace the principle of Greater Involvement of People living with HIV and AIDS. ICW actually prefers the term Meaningful Involvement of People living with HIV and AIDS—including HIV-positive women—in all decision making that affects their lives. This means that policy makers need to ensure that such inclusiveness is developed. At present the onus still lies with the people who are living with HIV to push for their own inclusion.

Challenging Stereotypes and Inequalities

Examples of good practice in the areas described here do not abound, but they do exist. An example is the Mother to Child Transition Plus Initiative in clinics in South Africa operated by Médecins Sans Frontières in Cape Town. The program involves HIV-positive women who have already been through the program to support new mothers and families entering the scheme. The initiative provides long-term follow-up care for HIV-positive mothers, their children, and their partners, fostering caring and healthy families in which the responsibility for childbearing and rearing is shared.

Programs need to be non-stigmatizing and reflect the realities people living with HIV already face rather than burdening them with a host of new ones. They need to challenge existing stereotypes and inequalities and, if possible, be led by women living with HIV. If not, then they need to involve HIV-positive women at every level—from planning and consultation to development of the budget, implementation, training, monitoring, and evaluation.

ICW's vision is a world where women have the right to make choices concerning their reproductive and sexual lives. This cannot be achieved through top-down calls for abstinence or fidelity or tokenistic, strategically-placed boxes of condoms but by changing the conditions of all women's lives. It also involves challenging the existing power relations between men and women and inequalities that influence these women's reproductive and sexual lives. Only then will HIV-positive women realize their sexual and reproductive rights.

NOTES

This article was produced by International Community of Women living with HIV/AIDS (ICW: www.icw.org) as part of Oxfam's Knowledge Infrastructure with and between Counterparts project (www.oxfamkic.org).

1. Quoted in S. Paxton, A. Welbourn, P. Kousalya, et al., *"Oh! This one is infected!" Women, HIV and Human Rights in the Asia-Pacific Region.* Paper prepared for UNHCHR, March 2004: www.icw.org/tiki-download_file.php?fileId579

2. J. Gatsi, *ICW treatment mapping project report,* Namibia, ICW: www.icw.org/node/218; and M. de Bruyn, 2005. *Reproductive rights for women affected by HIV/AIDS? A project to monitor Millennium Development Goals 5 and 6,* Chapel Hill, N.C.: Ipas,www.icw.org/tiki-download_file.php?fileId5185

3. S. Paxton, A. Welbourn, P. Kousalya, et al., *"Oh! This one is infected!" Women, HIV and Human Rights in the Asia-Pacific Region.*

4. ICW members from South Africa and Swaziland, interviews conducted during a policy development and training project in Durban, South Africa, 2005, report available from ICW.

5. Ibid.

6. ICW member from Russia, interviewed for *ICW News,* Issue 35, 2006: www.icw.org/files/English_35_Web.pdf

THIRTY

Living to Love (1993)

bell hooks

> **bell hooks** describes herself as a "black woman intellectual" and "revolutionary activist." She is an educator and popular public speaker whose work focuses on gender, race, culture, and media representations. A prolific writer, she has published over thirty books and numerous articles for scholarly and popular audiences.

Love heals. We recover ourselves in the act and art of loving. A favorite passage from the biblical Gospel of John that touches my spirit declares: "Anyone who does not love is still in death."

Many black women feel that we live lives in which there is little or no love. This is one of our private truths that is rarely a subject for public discussion. To name this reality evokes such intense pain that black women can rarely talk about it fully with one another.

It has not been simple for black people living in this culture to know love. Defining love in *The Road Less Traveled* as "the will to extend one's self for the purpose of nurturing one's own or another's personal growth," M. Scott Peck shares the prophetic insight that love is both an "intention and an action." We show love via the union of feeling and action. Using this definition of love, and applying it to black experience, it is easy to see how many black folks historically could only experience themselves as frustrated lovers, since the conditions of slavery and racial apartheid made it extremely difficult to nurture one's own or another's spiritual growth.

Notice, that I say, difficult, not impossible. Yet, it does need to be acknowledged that oppression and exploitation pervert, distort, and impede our ability to love.

Given the politics of black life in this white-supremacist society, it makes sense that internalized racism and self-hate stand in the way of love. Systems of domination exploit folks best when they deprive us of our capacity to experience our own agency and alter our ability to care and to love ourselves and others. Black folks have been deeply and profoundly "hurt," as we used to say down home, "hurt to our hearts," and the deep psychological pain we have endured and still endure affects our capacity to feel and therefore our capacity to love. We are a wounded people. Wounded in that part of ourselves that would know love, that would be loving. The choice to love has always been a gesture of resistance for African Americans. And many of us have made that choice only to find ourselves unable to give or to receive love.

Slavery's Impact on Love

Our collective difficulties with the art and act of loving began in the context of slavery. It should not shock us that a people who were forced to witness their young being sold away; their loved ones, companions, and comrades beaten beyond all recognition; a people who knew unrelenting poverty, deprivation, loss, unending grief, and the forced separation of family and kin; would emerge from the context of slavery wary of this thing called love. They knew firsthand that the conditions of slavery distorted and perverted the possibility that they would know love or be able to sustain such knowing.

Though black folks may have emerged from slavery eager to experience intimacy, commitment, and passion outside the realm of bondage, they must also have been in many ways psychologically unprepared to practice fully the art of loving. No wonder then that many black folks established domestic households that mirrored the brutal arrangements they had known in slavery. Using a hierarchical model of family life, they created domestic spaces where there were tensions around power, tensions that often led black men to severely whip black women, to punish them for perceived wrongdoing, that led adults to beat children to assert domination and control. In both cases, black people were using the same harsh and brutal methods against one another that had been used by white slave owners against them when they were enslaved. . . . We know that slavery's end did not mean that black people who were suddenly free to love now knew the way to love one another well.

Slave narratives often emphasize time and time again that black people's survival was often determined by their capacity to repress feelings. In his 1845 narrative, Frederick Douglass recalled that he had been unable to experience grief when hearing of his mother's death since they had been denied sustained contact. Slavery socialized black people to contain and repress a range of emotions. Witnessing one another being daily subjected to all manner of physical abuse, the pain of over-work, the pain of brutal punishment, the pain of near-starvation, enslaved black people could rarely show sympathy or solidarity with one another just as that moment when sympathy and solace was most needed. They rightly feared reprisal. It was only in carefully cultivated spaces of social resistance, that slaves could give vent to repressed feelings. Hence, they learned to check the impulse to give care when it was most needed and learned to wait for a "safe" moment when feelings could be expressed. What form could love take in such a context, in a world where black folks never knew how long they might be together? Practicing love in the slave context could make one vulnerable to unbearable emotional pain. It was often easier for slaves to care for one another while being very mindful of the transitory nature of their intimacies. The social world of slavery encouraged black people to develop notions of intimacy connected to expedient practical reality. A slave who could not repress and contain emotion might not survive.

Repressed Emotions: A Key to Survival

The practice of repressing feelings as a survival strategy continued to be an aspect of black life long after slavery ended. Since white supremacy and racism did not end with the Emancipation Proclamation, black folks felt it was still necessary to keep certain emotional barriers intact. And, in the worldview of many black people, it became a positive attribute to be able to contain feelings. Over time, the ability to mask, hide, and contain feelings came to be viewed by many black people as a sign of strong character. To show one's emotions was seen as foolish. Traditionally in Southern black homes, children were often taught at an early age that it was important to repress feelings. Often, when children were severely whipped, we were told not to cry. Showing one's emotions could lead to further punishment. Parents would say in the midst of painful punishments: "Don't even let me see a tear." Or if one dared to cry, they threatened further punishment by saying: "If you don't stop that crying, I'll give you something to cry about."

How was this behavior any different from that of the slave owner whipping the slave by denying access to comfort and consolation, denying even a space to express pain? And if many black folks were taught at an early age not only to repress emotions but to see giving expression to feeling as a sign of weakness, then how would they learn to be fully open to love? Many black folks have passed down from generation to generation the assumption that to let one's self go, to fully surrender emotionally, endangers survival. They feel that to love weakens one's capacity to develop a stoic and strong character.

"Did You Ever Love Us?"

When I was growing up, it was apparent to me that outside the context of religion and romance, love was viewed by grown-ups as a luxury. Struggling to survive, to make ends meet, was more important than loving. In that context, the folks who seemed most devoted to the art and act of loving were the old ones, our grandmothers and great grandmothers, our granddaddys and great granddaddys, the Papas and Big Mamas. They gave us acceptance, unconditional care, attention and, most importantly, they affirmed our need to experience pleasure and joy. They were affectionate. They were physically demonstrative. Our parents and their struggling-to-get-ahead generation often behaved as though love was a waste of time, a feeling or an action that got in the way of them dealing with the more meaningful issues of life.

When teaching Toni Morrison's novel *Sula*, I am never surprised to see black female students nodding their heads in recognition when reading a passage where Hannah, a grown black woman, asks her mother, Eva: "Did you ever love us?" Eva responds with hostility and says: "You settin' here with your healthy-ass self and ax me did I love you? Them big old eyes in your head would a been two holes of maggots if I hadn't." Hannah is not satisfied with this answer for she knows that Eva has responded fully to her children's material needs. She wants to know if there was another level of affection, of feeling and action. She says to Eva: "Did you ever, you know, play with us?" Again Eva responds by acting as though the question is completely ridiculous:

> Play? Wasn't nobody playin' in 1895. Just 'cause you got it good now you think it was always this good? 1895 was a killer girl. Things was bad. Niggers was dying like flies. . . . What would I look like leapin' round that little old room playin' with youngins with three beets to my name?

Eva's responses suggest that finding the means for material survival was not only the most important gesture of care, but that it precluded all other gestures. This is a way of thinking that many black people share. It makes care for material well-being synonymous with the practice of loving. The reality is, of course, that even in a context of material privilege, love may be absent. Concurrently, within the context of poverty, where one must struggle to make ends meet, one might keep a spirit of love alive by making a space for playful engagement, the

expression of creativity, for individuals to receive care and attention in relation to their emotional well-being, a kind of care that attends to hearts and minds as well as stomachs. As contemporary black people commit ourselves to collective recovery, we must recognize that attending to our emotional well-being is just as important as taking care of our material needs.

It seems appropriate that this dialogue on love in *Sula* takes place between two black women, between mother and daughter, for their interchange symbolizes a legacy that will be passed on through the generations. In fact, Eva does not nurture Hannah's spiritual growth, and Hannah does not nurture the spiritual growth of her daughter, Sula. Yet, Eva does embody a certain model of "strong" black womanhood that is practically deified in black life. It is precisely her capacity to repress emotions and do whatever is needed for the continuation of material life that is depicted as the source of her strength. . . .

If We Would Know Love

Love needs to be present in every black female's life, in all of our houses. It is the absence of love that has made it so difficult for us to . . . live fully. When we love ourselves we want to live fully. Whenever people talk about black women's lives, the emphasis is rarely on transforming society so that we can live fully, it is almost always about applauding how well we have "survived" despite harsh circumstances or how we can survive in the future. When we love ourselves, we know that we must do more than survive. We must have the means to live fully. To live fully, black women can no longer deny our need to know love.

If we would know love, we must first learn how to respond to inner emotional needs. This may mean undoing years of socialization where we have been taught that such needs are unimportant. Let me give an example. In her recently published book, *The Habit of Surviving: Black Women's Strategies for Life,* Kesho Scott opens the book sharing an incident from her life that she feels taught her important survival skills:

> Thirteen years tall, I stood in the living room doorway. My clothes were wet. My hair was mangled. I was in tears, in shock, and in need

of my mother's warm arms. Slowly, she looked me up and down, stood up from the couch and walked towards me, her body clenched in criticism. Putting her hands on her hips and planting herself, her shadow falling over my face, she asked in a voice of barely suppressed rage, "What happened?" I flinched as if struck by the unexpected anger and answered, "They put my head in the toilet. They say I can't swim with them." "They" were eight white girls at my high school. I reached out to hold her, but she roughly brushed my hands aside and said, "Like hell! Get your coat. Let's go."

. . . [Kesho] asserts: "My mother taught me a powerful and enduring lesson that day. She taught me that I would have to fight back against racial and sexual injustice." Obviously, this is an important survival strategy for black women. But Kesho was also learning an unhealthy message at the same time. She was made to feel that she did not deserve comfort after a traumatic painful experience, that indeed she was "out-of-line" to even be seeking emotional solace, and that her individual needs were not as important as the collective struggle to resist racism and sexism. Imagine how different this story would read if we were told that as soon as Kesho walked into the room, obviously suffering distress, her mother had comforted her, helped repair the damage to her appearance, and then shared with her the necessity of confronting (maybe not just then, it would depend on her psychological state whether she could emotionally handle a confrontation) the racist white students who had assaulted her. Then Kesho would have known, at age thirteen, that her emotional well-being was just as important as the collective struggle to end racism and sexism—that indeed these two experiences were linked.

Many black females have learned to deny our inner needs while we develop our capacity to cope and confront in public life. This is why we can often appear to be functioning well on jobs but be utterly dysfunctional in private. . . . I see this chaos and disorder as a reflection of the inner psyche, of the absence of well-being. Yet until black females believe, and hopefully learn when we are little girls, that our emotional well-being matters, we cannot attend to our needs. Often we replace recognition of inner emotional needs with the longing to control. When we deny

our real needs, we tend to feel fragile, vulnerable, emotionally unstable and untogether. Black females often work hard to cover up these conditions.

Let us return to the mother in Kesho's story. What if the sight of her wounded and hurt daughter called to mind the mother's deep unaddressed inner wounds? What if she was critical, harsh, or just downright mean, because she did not want to break down, cry, and stop being the "strong black woman"? And yet, if she cried, her daughter might have felt her pain was shared, that it was fine to name that you are in pain, that we do not have to keep the hurt bottled up inside us. What the mother did was what many of us have witnessed our mothers doing in similar circumstances—she took control. She was domineering, even her physical posture dominated. Clearly, this mother wanted her black female presence to have more "power" than that of the white girls.

A fictional model of black mothering that shows us a mother able to respond fully to her daughters when they are in pain is depicted in Ntozake Shange's novel *Sassafrass, Cypress and Indigo.* Throughout this novel, Shange's black female characters are strengthened in their capacity to self-actualize by a loving mother. Even though she does not always agree with their choices she respects them and offers them solace. Here is part of a letter she writes to Sassafrass who is "in trouble" and wants to come home. The letter begins with the exclamation: "Of course you can come home! What do you think you could do to yourself that I wouldn't love my girl?" First giving love and acceptance, Hilda later chastises, then expresses love again:

> You and Cypress like to drive me crazy with all this experimental living. You girls need to stop chasing the coon by his tail. And I know you know what I'm talking about . . . Mark my words. You just come on home and we'll straighten out whatever it is that's crooked in your thinking. There's lots to do to keep busy. And nobody around to talk foolish talk or experiment with. Something can't happen every day. You get up. You eat, go to work, come back, eat again, enjoy some leisure, and go back to bed. Now, that's plenty for most folks. I keep asking myself where did I go wrong? Yet I know in my heart I'm not wrong. I'm right. The world's going crazy and trying to take my

children with it. Okay. Now I'm through with all that. I love you very much. But you're getting to be a grown woman and I know that too. You come back to Charleston and find the rest of yourself. Love, Mama.

Loving What We See

The art and practice of loving begins with our capacity to recognize and affirm ourselves. That is why so many self-help books encourage us to look at ourselves in the mirror and talk to the image we see there. Recently, I noticed that what I do with the image I see in the mirror is very unloving. I inspect it. From the moment I get out of bed and look at myself in the mirror, I am evaluating. The point of the evaluation is not to provide self-affirmation but to critique. Now this was a common practice in our household. When the six of us girls made our way downstairs to the world inhabited by father, mother, and brother, we entered the world of "critique." We were looked over and told all that was wrong. Rarely did one hear a positive evaluation.

Replacing negative critique with positive recognition has made me feel more empowered as I go about my day. Affirming ourselves is the first step in the direction of cultivating the practice of being inwardly loving. I choose to use the phrase "inwardly loving" over self-love, because the very notion of "self" is so inextricably bound up with how we are seen by and in relation to others. Within a racist/sexist society, the larger culture will not socialize black women to know and acknowledge that our inner lives are important. Decolonized black women must name that reality in accord with others among us who understand as well that it is vital to nurture the inner life. As we examine our inner life, we get in touch with the world of emotions and feelings. Allowing ourselves to feel, we affirm our right to be inwardly loving. Once I know what I feel, I can also get in touch with those needs I can satisfy or name those needs that can only be satisfied in communion or contact with others.

Where is the love when a black woman looks at herself and says: "I see inside me somebody who is ugly, too dark, too fat, too afraid—somebody nobody would love, 'cause I don't even like what I see;" or maybe: "I see inside me somebody who is so hurt, who is just like a ball of pain and I don't want to look

at her 'cause I can't do nothing about that pain." The love is absent. To make it present, the individual has to first choose to see herself, to just look at that inner self without blame or censure. And once she names what she sees, she might think about whether that inner self deserves or needs love.

I have never heard a black woman suggest during confessional moments in a support group that she does not need love. She may be in denial about that need but it doesn't take much self-interrogation to break through this denial. If you ask most black women straight-up if they need love—the answer is likely to be yes. To give love to our inner selves we must first give attention, recognition and acceptance. Having let ourselves know that we will not be punished for acknowledging who we are or what we feel can name the problems we see. I find it helpful to interview myself, and I encourage my sisters to do the same. Sometimes it's hard for me to get immediately in touch with what I feel, but if I ask myself a question, an answer usually emerges.

Sometimes when we look at ourselves, and see our inner turmoil and pain, we do not know how to address it. That's when we need to seek help. I call loved ones sometimes and say, "I have these feelings that I don't understand or know how to address, can you help me?" There are many black females who cannot imagine asking for help, who see this as a sign of weakness. This is another negative debilitating world view we should unlearn. It is a sign of personal power to be able to ask for help when you need it. And we find that asking for what we need when we need it is an experience that enhances rather than diminishes personal power. Try it and see. Often we wait until a crisis situation has happened when we are compelled by circumstances to seek the help of others. Yet, crisis can often be avoided if we seek help when we recognize that we are no longer able to function well in a given situation. For black women who are addicted to being controlling, asking for help can be a loving practice of surrender, reminding us that we do not always have to be in charge. Practicing being inwardly loving, we learn not only what our souls need but we begin to understand better the needs of everyone around us as well.

Black women who are *choosing* for the first time (note the emphasis on choosing) to practice the art and act of loving should devote time and energy showing love to other black people, both people we know and strangers. Within white-supremacist capitalist patriarchy, black people do not get enough love. And it's always exciting for those of us who are undergoing a process of decolonization to see other black people in our midst respond to loving care. Just the other day T. told me that she makes a point of going into a local store and saying warm greetings to an older black man who works there. Recently, he wanted to know her name and then thanked her for the care that she gives to him. A few years ago when she was mired in self-hate, she would not have had the "will" to give him care. Now, she extends to him the level of care that she longs to receive from other black people when she is out in the world.

When I was growing up, I received "unconditional love" from black women who showed me by their actions that love did not have to be earned. They let me know that I deserved love; their care nurtured my spiritual growth.

Many black people, and black women in particular, have become so accustomed to not being loved that we protect ourselves from having to acknowledge the pain such deprivation brings by acting like only white folks or other silly people sit around wanting to be loved. When I told a group of black women that I wanted there to be a world where I can feel love, feel myself giving and receiving love, every time I walk outside my house, they laughed. For such a world to exist, racism and all other forms of domination need to change. To the extent that I commit my life to working to end domination, I help transform the world so that it is that loving place I want it to be.

Love Heals

Nikki Giovanni's "Woman Poem" has always meant a lot to me because it was one of the first pieces of writing that called out black women's self-hatred.

Published in the anthology, *The Black Woman,* edited by Toni Cade Bambara, this poem ends with the lines: "face me whose whole life is tied up to unhappiness cause it's the only for real thing i know." Giovanni not only names in this poem that black women are socialized to be caretakers, to deny our inner needs, she also names the extent to which self-hate can make us turn against those who are caring toward us. The black female narrator says: "how dare you care about me—you ain't got no good sense—cause i ain't shit you must be lower than that to care." This poem was written in 1968. Here we are, decades later, and black women are still struggling to break through denial to name the hurt in our lives and find ways to heal. Learning how to love is a way to heal.

I am empowered by the idea of love as the will to extend oneself to nurture one's own or another's spiritual growth because it affirms that love is an action, that it is akin to work. For black people it's an important definition because the focus is not on material well-being. And while we know that material needs must be met, collectively we need to focus our attention on emotional needs as well. There is that lovely biblical passage in "Proverbs" that reminds us: "Better a dinner of herbs, where love is, than a stalled ox and hatred therewith."

When we as black women experience fully the transformative power of love in our lives, we will bear witness publicly in a way that will fundamentally challenge existing social structures. We will be more fully empowered to address the genocide that daily takes the lives of black people—men, women and children. When we know what love is, when we love, we are able to search our memories and see the past with new eyes; we are able to transform the present and dream the future. Such is love's power. Love heals.

SAN FRANCISCO COMMISSION ON THE STATUS OF WOMEN

The sexiest thing you

can say to a woman is,

"Is this okay with you?"

Make sure she wants you as much as you want her - ask her first. There's a fine line between sexual pressure and sexual violence. And words can be a powerful way to prevent both. To find out more or help end the abuse in a relationship, call (415)647-7273 or (415)864-4722.

RESPECT IS WHAT'S SEXY

6

Violence Against Women

Gender violence affects women in all societies, all socioeconomic classes, all racial/ethnic groups, and it can occur throughout the life cycle (Heise, Pitanguy, and Germain 1994). Lori Heise (1989) commented: "This is not random violence; the risk factor is being female" (p. 13). In the United States, this includes battering, rape, child sexual abuse, stalking, hassles on the street, obscene phone calls, and sexual harassment at school or workplace. Underlying these incidents and experiences are systemic inequalities, also a kind of violence, that maintain women's second-class status—culturally, economically, and politically. This chapter focuses on violence against women in this country and the many efforts to stop it. This is a key issue and we refer to it in other chapters also with regard to relationships, family, and work (Chapter 7), regarding women in prison (Chapter 9), and in connection with the military (Chapter 10). We recognize that this is a tough issue for women and for many men. It may bring up memories or push you to rethink your own experiences. Support yourself by talking to a friend, a professor, members of your campus Women's Center or anti-rape group, or go to your campus counseling center.

What Counts as Violence Against Women?

Most women—heterosexual, queer, lesbian, or transgender—experience a certain amount of what could be defined as sexual violence as part of daily life. We experience hassles on the street, in parks, on public transit, or in cafés and bars. We put up with sexist comments from bosses or coworkers. We sometimes make compromises as part of maintaining intimate relationships, including going along with sex when we do not really want it, or tolerating "joking," put-downs, threats, and inconsiderate behavior. We may define some of these experiences as violence, and others not, and different women may define violence differently.

Researchers and writers use terms like *sexual assault, sexual abuse, battering,* or *domestic violence* but not in a standardized way. Differences of definition and terminology have led to marked discrepancies in reporting and have contributed to considerable confusion and debate about these issues, which should be borne in mind throughout this chapter.

The United Nations Declaration on Violence Against Women (General Assembly resolution

48/104) of December 20, 1993, defined such violence as "any act of gender-based violence that results in, or is likely to result in, physical, sexual or psychological harm or suffering to women, including threats of such acts, coercion or arbitrary deprivation of liberty whether occurring in public or private life" (quoted in Heise, Pitanguy, and Germaine 1994, p. 46). This includes physical acts like battering, rape, child sexual abuse, stalking, and inappropriate touching. It includes verbal and psychological violence against intimate partners like yelling, intimidation, and humiliation; inappropriate personal remarks made to coworkers or students; and offensive sexist "jokes." It also includes forced isolation, denial of support, and threats of violence or injury to women in the family. This broad definition implicitly recognizes that men as a group have power over women—the women they are close to and those they encounter in public places. Women may be physically smaller or weaker, they may be economically dependent on their partner, or they may need their boss's support to keep their jobs or to get a promotion or a pay raise. Thus, macro-level inequalities are present in violence at the micro level. An important element of this male power is that it is sexualized. This is a given in interactions between intimate partners. It is also often true of interactions that are violent or that border on violence between people who are not intimate but who are friends, coworkers, teachers and students, or complete strangers (see Figure 6.1).

LGBT people are also victims and perpetrators of intimate partner violence (Girshick 2002; Kaschak 2002; Renzetti 1992; Ristock 2002; Wingspan Domestic Violence Project 1998), as well as being subjected to intimidation, physical and verbal abuse, and hate crimes by people outside LGBT communities, as mentioned in Chapter 4 (see Readings 23 and 24).

Many researchers and commentators focus on specific physical acts that can be measured. Emotional violence and the fear of threats are impossible to quantify precisely. It is much easier to bring charges of violence if one can show clear evidence of physical coercion or harm. Indeed, the legal system demands demonstrable damage or there is nothing to claim. The problem with this kind of quantification is that one cannot see the interpersonal dynamics or the structural power relationships within which violence occurs.

At micro and meso levels, women can be violent as well as men. Women may abuse children, other family members, their peers, and people who work for them. Writer and cultural critic bell hooks (1984b) noted that women "may employ abusive measures to maintain authority in interactions with groups over whom they exercise power" (p. 119). Research shows that, in general, women hit children more than men do, but they also spend much more time with children and often shoulder the major responsibilities for raising children, even in two-parent families. Women may contribute to the dynamic of a violent relationship; they may provoke an argument or hit their partner first. Occasionally women kill abusive partners, seemingly the only way out of situations in which they believe they would be killed if they did not defend themselves (see Reading 51; Rennison 2003; Ritchie 1996). According to Bureau of Justice statistician Shannan Catalano, in 2005, 3 percent of male murder victims were killed by their wives or girlfriends compared to 33 percent of female murder victims who were killed by their husbands or boyfriends (Catalano 2008). Indeed, the vast majority of gender violence is violence against women. The chance of being victimized by an intimate is significantly greater for women (85 percent) than for men (15 percent) (Rennison 2003). We use the term *violence against women* as well as *gender-based violence* because it makes this inequality explicit.

The definition of violence against women can also be expanded beyond the United Nations definition quoted earlier. Psychologist Hussein Bulhan (1985), for example, proposed the following:

> Violence is any relation, process, or condition by which an individual or a group violates the physical, social, and/or psychological integrity of another person or group. From this perspective, violence inhibits human growth, negates inherent potential, limits productive living, and causes death.   *(p. 135)*

This would include colonization, poverty, racism, lack of access to education, health care, and negative media representations. These factors affect men as well as women. But women as a group are poorer than men; women's rights may be limited due to cultural factors; and women are systematically objectified and commodified in the media. We

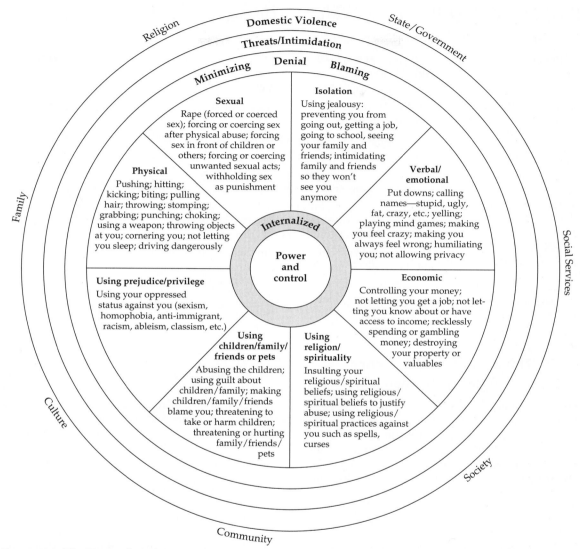

FIGURE 6.1 The Dynamics of Domestic Violence: Power and Control Wheel. (*Source:* Asian Women's Shelter, adapted from Domestic Abuse Intervention Project, Duluth, MN. Used with permission.)

argue that such macro-level factors jeopardize women's security and should be part of the broader discussion of violence.

Andy (Andrea) Smith, Native American scholar and cofounder of INCITE! Women of Color Against Violence, shows how sexualized violence was integral to European colonization of North America (Smith 2005b). She gives graphic examples of the dehumanization of Native American women by white settlers, a dimension of U.S. history that is rarely taught in U.S. schools and which persists into the present (Reading 31). Most acts of violence against Native American women are committed by men who are not Native American.

Gender Violence Worldwide, Throughout the Life Cycle

PHASE	TYPE OF VIOLENCE
Prebirth	Inadequate prenatal care due to poverty; battering during pregnancy (emotional and physical effects on the woman; effects on birth outcome); coerced pregnancy (for example, mass rape in war); and sex-selective abortion.
Infancy	Emotional and physical abuse; differential access to food and medical care for girl infants; and female infanticide.
Girlhood	Sexual abuse by family members and strangers; differential access to food and medical care; child prostitution; child marriage; and genital mutilation.
Adolescence	Dating and courtship violence; economically coerced sex; sexual abuse in the workplace; rape; sexual harassment; forced prostitution; trafficking in women.
Reproductive age	Abuse of women by intimate male partners; marital rape; partner homicide; psychological abuse; sexual abuse in the workplace; sexual harassment; rape; abuse of women with disabilities; dowry abuse and murders.
Elderly	Abuse of widows; elder abuse (in the United States, for example, elder abuse affects mostly women).

Source: Heise, Pitanguy, and Germain (1994), p. 5.

The Incidence of Violence Against Women

Domestic violence, rape, sexual abuse, and child sexual abuse are all illegal in the United States. The incidence of such violence is difficult to estimate accurately because of discrepancies in definition and terminology, limited research, and underreporting. We include several estimates, recognizing the limitations of available data.

Intimate Partner Violence

The idealized family is assumed to provide a secure home for its members, what historian Christopher Lasch (1977) called "a haven in a heartless world." For some this is generally true. For many women and children, however, home is not a safe place but one where they experience emotional or physical violence. For purposes of this discussion, intimate partners include current and former spouses, boyfriends, and girlfriends. The narrower term, *domestic violence,* used for many years, still appears in some government reports and academic studies.

According to the Family Violence Prevention Fund (1998), "Every year, as many as 4 million American women are physically abused by men who promised to love them" (p. 1). The U.S. Department of Justice (1997) reported that 37 percent of all women who sought care in hospital emergency rooms for violence-related injuries in 1997 were injured by intimate partners. Abuse-related injuries include bruises, cuts, burns and scalds, concussion, broken bones, penetrating injuries from knives, miscarriages, permanent injuries such as damage to joints, partial loss of hearing or vision, and physical disfigurement. There are also serious mental health effects of isolation, humiliation, and ongoing threats of violence. As mentioned earlier, some researchers do not take account of psychological and emotional dimensions of intimate partner violence because they are difficult to measure. They define it as physical assault only, which gives the impression that quantifiable acts of violence—kicking, punching, or using a weapon—tell the whole story.

Writing in an anthology of short stories about battering and resistance, Barbara Harman (1996) described how a woman in an abusive relationship is

always second-guessing and responding to an abusive partner in her attempts to avoid further violence:

> Don't raise your voice. Don't talk back. Don't say no to sex. Like whatever he does. Don't ask him to do anything he has not already done. Get up when he gets up. Go to bed when he goes to bed. Wait. Do what he wants to do. Never contradict him. Laugh at what he thinks is funny. Never ask for his time, attention, his money. Have your own money, but give it to him if he wants it. Never go out alone but do not expect him to go with you. If he is angry in the car, walk home. Be his friend except when he needs an enemy. Defend his family except when he hates them. Understand everything.   *(p. 287)*

One in five high school girls surveyed reported that she had been physically or sexually abused; the majority of these incidents occurred at home and happened more than once (Commonwealth Fund 1997). Girls ages 16 to 19 experience one of the highest rates of violence by an intimate partner (Rennison 2003). According to the government's Office on Violence Against Women, 20 percent of teenage girls and young women have experienced some form of dating violence, which can include physical, emotional, verbal, psychological, or sexual abuse (Office of Justice Programs 2007). June Larkin and Katherine Popaleni's (1997) interviews with young women revealed how young men use criticism, intimidation, surveillance, threats, and force to establish and maintain control over their girlfriends. The popularity of cell phones has increased the ease of informal "surveillance." Laura O'Toole and Jessica Schiffman (1997) noted that young women are vulnerable to abuse because they may feel that involvement in a personal relationship is necessary to fit in; they may be flattered by a dating partner who demands time and attention; and they lack experience negotiating affection and sexual behavior.

Rape and Sexual Assault

The legal definition of rape turns on force and nonconsent. Consent to sexual intercourse is not meaningful if given under the influence of alcohol, drugs, or prescription medication. Like domestic violence, rape is not always reported, and the true scope of the problem is difficult to assess. Rates of rape vary widely among studies according to how the crime is defined, who participates in the study, and what methodology is used. Between 1992 and 2000, an estimated 63 percent of completed rapes and 65 percent of attempted rapes were not reported to the police (Rennison 2002). Rape is defined as forced sexual intercourse—vaginal, anal, or oral penetration. Sexual assault includes attacks involving unwanted sexual contact; it may involve force and include grabbing or fondling, also verbal threats. The groups most at risk for sexual assault are 16- to 19-year-olds, then 20- to 24-year-olds. In contrast to popular ideas about rape committed by a stranger in a dark alley, 73 percent of women who reported that they had been raped or physically assaulted said that their partner or date committed the assault (Catalano 2008).

A study of acquaintance rape on campuses in the mid-1980s found that one in nine college women had been raped and that eight out of ten victims knew their attacker, although as few as 5 percent reported the crime (Koss 1988). One in twelve college men responding to the same survey admitted that they had committed acts that met legal definitions of rape (Koss, Dinero, and Seibel 1988). The FBI's Uniform Crime Report (compiled from over 16,000 law enforcement agencies covering 96 percent of the nation's population) estimated that one in four U.S. college women was a victim of rape or attempted rape, and this estimate is still widely used by academics, activists, and journalists. Skeptics counter that such figures are highly inflated and that many women who claim to have been raped blame their dates for their own poor judgement in having sex (see, e.g., Paglia 1990; Roiphe 1993). According to the U.S. Bureau of Justice, the most recent and methodologically rigorous studies show that sexual assault still occurs at rates similar to those identified more than 20 years ago when Koss, Giducz, and Wisiewski (1987) found that approximately 27.5 percent of college women reported experiences that met the legal criteria for rape (Office of Justice Programs 2007). Given the continued prevalence of rape, especially for young women, some advocates and commentators

describe the United States as having a "rape culture" (see e.g., Buchwald, Fletcher, and Roth 2005). Police consultant Rana Sampson (2002) reported that most rapes of college women are not date rapes, but rapes by acquaintances maybe at a party or while studying together in a dorm room. Ninety percent of college women who are victims of rape or attempted rape know their assailant, usually a classmate, friend, boyfriend, or ex-boyfriend (in that order) (Fisher, Cullen, and Turner 2000). College athletes are disproportionately reported to campus officers for acquaintance rape, and fraternities have been at the center of controversy for rapes and attempted rapes at fraternity house parties. Psychologists Stephen Humphrey and Arnold Kahn (2000) distinguished between fraternities and athletic teams that are high risk and low risk for rape, and found that college women correctly identified them, based on the type of parties they held. Under the 1990 Student Right-to-Know and Campus Security Act (updated as the 1998 Jeanne Cleau Disclosure of Campus Security Policy and Campus Crime Statistics Act), all colleges and universities that receive federal funding must spell out rape victims' rights and publish information on prevention programs. In Reading 33, John Stoltenberg, cofounder of Men Against Pornography, records a conversation with Duke University students in Men Acting for Change, a campus group working to confront sexual violence. The students discuss how violence against women affects their own lives and the value of a group like Men Acting for Change where they can talk and think together with peers and learn how to take their insights into conversations with other men on campus.

Female students are most at risk of acquaintance rape in the first few weeks of college. They often do not report a rape because of confusion, guilt, or fear, or because they feel betrayed; they may be ashamed to tell parents or college counselors; and they may not identify the experience as rape. However, the reporting of rape increased significantly on U.S. college campuses during the 1990s. The psychological effects of rape can be traumatic and long-lasting. They include feelings of humiliation, helplessness, anger, self-doubt, self-hate, and fear; and a student may become depressed and withdrawn and do poorly in school.

Effects of Race, Class, Nation, Sexuality, and Disability

Although these forms of violence occur across the board, women's experiences are complicated by race, class, national origin, sexual orientation, and disability.

Research The Bureau of Justice Statistics (1995) noted that domestic violence was consistent across racial and ethnic lines. Jody Raphael and Richard Tolman (1997) found that past and current victims of domestic violence were overrepresented among women on welfare and families with extremely low incomes. Bureau of Justice statistician Callie Marie Rennison (2002) found that, in 1999, African American women ages 20 to 24 experienced more intimate violence than white women of the same age. Official estimates of violence are limited by the fact that many cases are not reported, and research into this issue is limited by the scope of studies undertaken. Children and adolescents, prostituted women, homeless women, women with mental disabilities, institutionalized women, very poor women, and women in neighborhoods with high crime rates are rarely included in surveys. Women and girls with physical and mental disabilities are particularly vulnerable to physical, emotional, and sexual abuse from partners, caregivers, and service providers (Abramson et al. 2000; Young et al. 1997). The few studies that exist suggest that women with disabilities are between four and ten times as likely to be sexually assaulted as other women.

Reporting Although violence between intimate partners is illegal in this country, it is seriously under-reported because of confusion, shame, self-blame, loyalty to the abuser, lack of information, or fear of repercussions, including loss of a partner's income. Women may not believe that reporting violence to the police will do any good. Women of color, poor women, and prostituted women often have very negative experiences with the police. Women of color may decide not to report acts of violence or rape to avoid bringing more trouble on husbands, partners, friends, and acquaintances who already suffer discrimination based on race, as mentioned by Andy Smith (Reading 31) and Mimi Kim (Reading 34). In many communities of color the police are perceived not as helpful but, rather, as abusive, harassing, and violent. Women as well as men "bear the brunt of police indifference and abuse" and "men are frequently targeted for false arrest" (M. Smith 1997). Their community may expect women of color to maintain silence about sexual assault, to protect "family honor and community integrity" (Crenshaw 1993, p. 5). Melba Wilson (1993) discussed the conflicting pressures operating here and urged Black women to hold men accountable for sexual abuse of children. Elderly women may not report acts of violence committed by spouses, adult children, caregivers, relatives, and neighbors, because they fear being rejected, losing their caregiver, being placed in a nursing home, or losing their property—particularly their home or independent access to money. Immigrant women who are dependent on an abusive partner for their legal status may fear repercussions from ICE (Immigration and Customs Enforcement) if they report violence. In a very different subculture, some women have been reluctant to speak about abuse in lesbian or transgender relationships, not wanting to feed negative stereotypes circulating in the wider society (see, e.g., Kaschak 2002; Renzetti 1992; Ristock 2002).

Responses of the Police, Support Services, Medical and Legal Systems The response to reports of violence against women and the provision of services have greatly expanded over the last forty years as this issue has become recognized publicly. Police officers, judges, doctors, nurses, and emergency-room staff may undergo professional training, although much more still needs to be done in this regard.

During slavery times, the rape of Black women in the United States was legal and commonplace. They were chattel, the legal property of their masters, and available for anything and everything. Andy Smith notes that in "patriarchal thinking, only a 'pure' body can really be violated. The rape of bodies that are considered inherently impure simply does not count" (Reading 31). Currently, negative stereotypes about women of color, poor white women, prostituted women, lesbians, and transgender women all perpetuate the idea, in the wider society, that these women are not worthy of respect. They are less likely to be taken seriously if they report acts of violence. Law professor Kimberlé Crenshaw (1993) noted an early-1990s study of sentences given to convicted rapists in

Dallas: "The average sentence given to the rapist of a Black woman was two years . . . to the rapist of a Latina . . . five years, and . . . to the rapist of a white woman . . . ten years. Interviews with jurors revealed that the low conviction rate of men accused of raping Black women is based on ongoing sexual stereotypes about Black women" (p. 4) as mentioned in Chapter 4.

Similar pressures that keep lesbians, transgender women, and many heterosexual women of color from reporting acts of violence may also keep them from talking openly about this issue within their own communities. African American feminist academics Johnnetta Cole and Beverly Guy-Sheftall (2003) decided to share their personal experiences as part of an extended discussion with other prominent African American thinkers and writers regarding violence against women in African American families and communities. They took this step to show how the dehumanization of racism distorts and limits ideas of manhood and womanhood for many African Americans, and to honor those seeking to transform interpersonal and family relationships. Sociologist Patricia Hill Collins (2004) analyzed the micro-, meso-, and macro-level forces that affect African Americans' experiences of sexuality as well as violence. All three authors commented on the difficulty of "airing dirty linen in public" and the possibility that their work would be used to reinforce racist stereotypes. They decided to take this risk in order to strengthen relationships between African American men and women (also see Reading 30).

Explanations of Violence Against Women

Most explanations of violence against women are social theories. Before discussing some of these, we note the resurfacing of a biological explanation of rape. Randy Thornhill and Craig Palmer (2000) argued that rape evolved historically as a form of male reproductive behavior. These authors based their claims on studies of animal species from the scorpion fly to primates. As with other sociobiological theories, they make huge leaps between animal behavior and human life, they are not grounded in an analysis of social systems, and their claims are not borne out by the experience of women who have suffered acts of violence.

As in other chapters, we focus on social theories and separate micro- and macro-level explanations.

Micro-Level Explanations

Intimate partner violence, rape, and child sexual abuse are often explained in terms of an individual mental health problem, innate sexual craving, or personal dysfunction on the part of perpetrators. By contrast, Jean Grossholtz (1983), a professor of political science and women's studies, argued that research on rapists and batterers showed them to be "ordinary men, indistinguishable from nonrapists and nonbatterers" (p. 59). Another micro-level explanation for intimate partner violence is that the partners have an "unhealthy" relationship.

Three psychological syndromes have been advanced to explain violence against women: battered woman syndrome, rape trauma syndrome, and false memory syndrome.

Battered Woman Syndrome   Psychologist Lenore Walker (1979, 1984) put forward the notion of a "battered woman syndrome." She noted a pattern of behavior that she termed "learned helplessness," whereby women who are repeatedly battered "learn" it is impossible to escape. After an episode of violence, they are seduced back by the batterer with declarations of love and promises that he will change. These calm, loving episodes alternate with periods of accelerating violence, isolating the woman further and tying her closer to him. Attorneys have used a "battered woman syndrome" defense for women who kill violent partners by arguing that their clients' judgment was affected "in such a way as to make them honestly believe that they were in imminent danger and that the use of force was their only means of escape" (Gordon 1997, p. 25).

Rape Trauma Syndrome   This term is used by mental health and legal professionals to refer to women's coping strategies following rape. The focus is on women's reactions and responses rather than on the actions of the perpetrators or the prevalence of sexual violence in our society. Rape trauma syndrome has been used to explain women's supposedly "counterintuitive" reactions—such as not reporting a rape for days or even months, not remembering parts of the assault, appearing too calm, or expressing anger at their treatment by police, hospital staff, or the legal system—in terms of pathology (Stefan 1994, p. 1274). Women diagnosed with rape trauma syndrome—who are generally white and middle class—are given psychiatric treatment with the goal of recovery and resolution. Expert testimony concerning rape trauma syndrome in rape trials has improved the chances that a perpetrator would be convicted but at the cost of representing the woman as a pathetic victim. Susan Stefan (1994), an attorney and law professor, argued that the creation of this syndrome has depoliticized the issue of rape.

False Memory Syndrome   Childhood sexual abuse by parents, older siblings, stepparents, and other family members is another aspect of family life that has gradually become a public issue through the efforts of survivors, counselors, and feminist advocates. Many abused children block out memories of what happened to them, and these may not surface again until their adult years, perhaps through flashbacks, nightmares, panic attacks, or pain (Petersen 1991; White 1988). They then gradually piece together fragments of their experience that have been suppressed. Those who have been abused as children often experience confusion, shame, fear, or fear of being crazy. They may spend years thinking they were to blame. They may have feelings of not being worth much, or conversely, they may feel special. The child is invariably told that this special secret must never be spoken about. Healing from the effects of childhood sexual abuse takes time, courage, and support, as described by Aurora Levins Morales (Reading 32), and many families do not want to open up this can of worms (Bass and Davis 1988; Haines 1999; Herman 1992; Petersen 1991; E. C. White 1985; L. White 1988; Wilson 1993). False memory syndrome (FMS) has been invoked by parents who believe they "have been falsely accused [of incest] as a result of their adult children discovering 'memories' in the course of therapy" (Wasserman 1992, p. 18) and by lawyers acting on their behalf. According to FMS, the incest survivor is someone with impaired cognitive functioning. Memory is complex cognitively, and there are well-regarded psychologists on both sides of this issue.

These syndromes were developed for legal or therapeutic purposes. As explanations of violence against women, they are all inadequate. They pathologize women who experience acts of violence as helpless victims. As legal defenses in cases involving acts of violence, they are also highly problematic. A battered-woman-syndrome defense for women who have killed abusive partners represents battered women as impaired, rather than as "rational actors responding to perceived danger" (Gordon 1997, p. 25). Attorneys have tried to get courts to accept that the law of self-defense applies to battered women, but without much success. These syndromes all **blame the victim** for her situation. The advice that police departments often give to women for their safety also assumes that we bring assaults on ourselves: Do not go out alone late at night; do not wear "provocative" clothing; always walk purposefully; do not make eye contact with men on the street; park your car in a lighted area; have your keys ready in your hand before you leave the building; look into the back seat before getting in your car, and so on. This advice is well intentioned and may be helpful. However, it assumes that women are responsible for acts of violence against them, either directly "asking for it" by their dress or behavior or indirectly encouraging it by not being sufficiently cautious.

Macro-Level Explanations

Micro-level explanations of violence against women can be compelling if one focuses on specific personal interactions, but by themselves they cannot explain such a universal and systemic phenomenon. It is essential to analyze this issue at the meso and macro levels to understand it fully and to generate effective strategies to stop it.

Macro-level explanations focus on the cultural legitimation of male violence and the economic, political, and legal systems that marginalize, discriminate against, and disempower women.

Hussein Bulhan's (1985) very broad definition of violence mentioned earlier emphasized the structural nature of violence and rests on several assumptions:

> Violence is not an isolated physical act or a discrete random event. It is a relation, process, and condition undermining, exploiting, and curtailing the well-being of the victim. . . . Violence in any of the three domains—physical, social, or psychological—has significant repercussions in

the other two domains. Violence occurs not only between individuals, but also between groups and societies. Intention is less important than consequence in most forms of violence. Any relation, process, or condition imposed by someone that injures the health and well-being of others is by definition violent.   *(p. 135)*

Applying these ideas to violence against women may make it easier to see this violence in terms of inequalities of power under patriarchy, as argued by Allan Johnson (Reading 9, Chapter 2). In Reading 31, Andy Smith shows how sexual violence was part of U.S. colonization of Native Americans. Macro-level factors such as sexism, heterosexism, racism, economic opportunities, working conditions, unemployment, poverty, or loss of status and cultural roots that may accompany immigration also affect personal and family relationships from the outside. Lora Jo Foo (2007) mentions the severe cultural and economic disruptions and dislocations experienced by first-generation immigrants, which undoubtedly contribute to the incidence of domestic violence in these communities. Immigrants are often at the bottom of the U.S. job hierarchy; they may not speak or read English; the U.S. legal and political system is unfamiliar; and parents may have to rely on their children to negotiate and interpret the world outside home and family. This is not to excuse those who abuse their partners or children but, rather, to provide a wider context for understanding violence. Indeed, family violence is embedded in institutional roles and relationships, supported by cultural standards and expectations—meso- and macro-level factors.

The Cultural Legitimation of Male Violence   This includes cultural beliefs in male superiority and male control of women's behavior and of the family, which are supported by social institutions such as education, law, religion, and popular culture. War toys, competitive games, violent and aggressive sports, and violence on TV, in video games, and in movies are integral to children's socialization, especially that of boys. Popular culture, news media, and advertising all reinforce these cultural attitudes and contribute to the objectification and commodification of women. Jean Kilbourne discussed this "toxic culture" in relation to advertising (Reading 26). The music business, MTV, TV shows, and feature films all contribute to a culture of violence against women. At the meso level too, in various communities, cultural attitudes and religious beliefs support domestic violence as a husband's prerogative to "discipline" his wife. The old idea that a wife is the property of her husband still lingers in custom and in law. Wives are supposed to agree to sex, for example, as part of their wifely duty. Rape in marriage was made a crime in the United States as recently as 1993, but in thirty-three states there are varying exemptions from prosecuting husbands for rape, which indicates that rape in marriage is still treated as a lesser crime than other forms of rape. Another example of male control is street harassment, where women may be "touched, harassed, commented upon in a stream of constant small-scale assaults" (Benard and Schlaffer 1997, p. 395). The public street is defined as male space where women without male escorts may be considered "fair game." Cheryl Benard and Edith Schlaffer noted that women need to "plan our routes and our timing as if we are passing through a mine field" (p. 395).

The cultural legitimation of male superiority involves patterns of male and female socialization in the family and in schools, and the social construction of masculinity and of male sexuality (see Kimmel 1993; 2000, chap. 11; Kimmel and Messner 1995; Lefkowitz 1997; Messner 1992). In a White Supremacist society, men of color may be attracted to a construction of masculinity that derives from white patriarchal attitudes and behavior. Discussing violence against women in African American communities, bell hooks (1994) commented:

> Black males, utterly disenfranchised in almost every arena of life in the United States, often find that the assertion of sexist domination is their only expressive access to the patriarchal power they are told all men should possess as their gendered birthright.   *(p. 110)*

Economic Systems That Disempower Women   Women as a group earn less than men as a group. It may be difficult for a woman to leave a violent marriage or relationship if she is financially dependent on her partner. In the workplace, women may find it difficult to speak up about sexual harassment. Sociologist Michael Kimmel (1993) noted that sexual harassment "fuses two levels of power: the power of employers over employees and the power of men over women. Thus what may be said or intended as a man to a woman is also experienced in the context of superior and subordinate" (p. 130).

Legal Systems That Discriminate Against Women

This includes inadequate laws and practices concerning violence against women, and insensitive treatment of women by police and the courts. Martha Mahoney (1994) emphasized the narrowness of legal categories and procedures in dealing with violence against women. For instance, the "statute of limitations," a limit on the time period allowed for bringing a lawsuit for damages or criminal charges against a perpetrator, stops some women from using the law for redress in cases of rape or childhood sexual abuse. In the latter case, they may be in their twenties, and years past the time limit, before they recognize that they were abused as children and gain the personal strength to confront the perpetrator publicly. Jean Grossholtz (1983) argued that violence against women has not "simply been overlooked by the criminal justice system" (p. 67), but that this is part of the way patriarchal power compels women "through fear and endangerment, to submit to self-depreciation, heterosexuality, and male dominance in all spheres of life" (pp. 67–68).

Political Systems That Marginalize Women's Concerns

Women are still a minority in elected office in the United States, especially at the congressional level. Violence against women is often not taken seriously by policy makers or legislators. Compared to male voters, more women are concerned about gender-based violence. More women also favor meaningful gun control, an end to the international trade in arms, reductions in military spending, and disarmament, believing that such changes would greatly increase their security and the well-being of their communities (Ducat 2004; Gallagher 1993). We take up the issue of women in electoral politics in Chapter 12.

The levels of violence mentioned earlier are interconnected and reinforce each other. Debra Borkovitz (1995) argued that it is necessary to transform prevailing ideas of *domination,* whether of racism, imperialism, male violence against women, or same-sex battering. Similarly, bell hooks (1984b) argued that violence against women should be seen as part of a general pattern of violence between the powerful and the powerless stemming from the "notion of hierarchical rule and coercive authority that is the root cause of violence against women, of adult violence against children, of all violence between those who dominate and those who are dominated" (p. 118). She argued that feminists should oppose all forms of coercive domination rather than concentrating solely on male violence against women. Kimberlé Crenshaw (1993) pointed out that the anti-violence movement must be an anti-oppression movement.

Ending Violence Against Women

Women have made various efforts to stop gender-based violence. Historian Linda Gordon (1988, 1997) noted that U.S. feminists challenged wife-beating as part of antidrinking campaigns in the late nineteenth century, then again in the 1930s in campaigns for child custody and welfare for single mothers so that they could leave abusive men. Extremely important feminist work in the 1960s and 1970s broke through the prevailing silence on this subject (e.g., Brownmiller 1975; Griffin 1971; Russell 1975). Feminists reframed and politicized the issue of rape, exposing the myth that rape is about sex—a crime of "frustrated attraction, victim provocation, or uncontrollable biological urges, perpetrated only by an aberrant fringe" (Caputi and Russell 1990, p. 34). Rather, rape is about power and control—a "direct expression of sexual politics and an assertion of masculinist norms that reinforce and preserve the gender status quo" (Caputi and Russell 1990, p. 34). Feminist writers and organizers insisted that no woman deserves to be abused, or brings it on herself, or "asks for it."

The Importance of a Political Movement

Educator and organizer Judith Herman, M.D. (1992) argued that changing public consciousness about a traumatic issue like violence against women takes a concerted political movement. In her study of trauma and recovery connected to violence, she wrote that perpetrators of violence "ask bystanders to do nothing, simply to ignore the atrocity"; whereas "victims demand action, engagement, and remembering" (pp. 7–8). In Reading 34, Barbara describes preparing her son to intervene and stop acts of violence before allowing him to go to unsupervised teen parties. She had worked in a rape crisis center and a battered-women's program and comments that, although it is important to raise boys not to commit sexual violence, "it's just as important for them not to be bystanders."

To emphasize women's agency, feminist writers and workers in shelters and rape crisis projects often use the term *survivor* to refer to women who are coping with acts of violence, rather than calling them victims. Herman's use of the term *victim* in the following discussion is perhaps unfortunate, but her comments on the processes of denial and silencing that often surround violence against women are very insightful.

> In order to escape accountability for his crimes, the perpetrator does everything in his power to promote forgetting. Secrecy and silence are the perpetrator's first line of defense. If secrecy fails, the perpetrator attacks the credibility of his victim. If he cannot silence her absolutely, he tries to make sure that no one listens. To this end, he marshals an impressive array of arguments, from the most blatant denial to the most sophisticated . . . rationalization. After every atrocity one can expect to hear the same predictable apologies: it never happened; the victim lies; the victim exaggerates; the victim brought it upon herself; and in any case it is time to forget the past and move on. The more powerful the perpetrator, the greater is his prerogative to name and define reality, and the more completely his arguments prevail.   *(p. 8)*

Herman argued that to cut through the power of the perpetrators' arguments "requires a social context that affirms and protects the victim and that joins victim and witness in a common alliance" (p. 9). For the individual victim of violence, relationships with family and friends create this context. For the wider society, "the social context is created by political movements that give voice to the disempowered" (p. 9), a key example being feminist movements.

Philosopher Nadya Burton (1998) criticized second-wave feminists for using oversimplistic rhetoric in their attempts to break the silence and to get the issue of violence against women on the public agenda. They also emphasized fear, passivity,

and victimhood. While acknowledging the damage suffered as a result of violence, it is also important to see women as resistors and survivors, people who cope with violation, who are not defined by it and who often go on to thrive despite it. More recently, many feminists have emphasized women's agency—their ability to make decisions and to deal effectively with their circumstances. These perspectives sometimes result in a victim/agent dichotomy. The underlying issue is respect and dignity for people who have been violated—not pity, disbelief, judgment, do-goodism, or condescension. In wanting to avoid these responses, some feminist researchers and advocates have over-emphasized women's agency to the point where the real-life effects of trauma and violation are minimized. We argue that women may be both victims of violence and agents who can direct their lives. A person who has been violated can decide what kind of support s/he wants and ask for it; can choose if and when to speak out; can undertake the personal work that is part of healing; can decide to confront the perpetrator directly (with friends, family, or other community support), or press charges, or not deal with the perpetrator at all. We also agree with Judith Herman (1992) that deep healing from trauma often requires both individual transformative work by people who have been violated and collective responsibility to recognize and address the causes and impacts as an act of solidarity.

Feminist theorizing about the systemic nature of violence against women under patriarchy led to concerted efforts to provide supports for women who experienced such violence, to educate the wider society on the issue, and to change public policy.

Providing Support for Victims/Survivors

The first shelter for battered women in the United States opened in 1974. Now there are over 2,500 shelters and service programs nationwide, stretched to capacity. More shelters are needed, and those that exist need to be more accessible—physically and culturally—to women with disabilities, women of color, immigrant women, lesbians, and transgender women. Organizations that emphasize culturally relevant perspectives and services include the Asian Women's Shelter (San Francisco); Baitul Salaam (Atlanta); Black, Indian, Hispanic and Asian

Women in Action—BIHA (Minneapolis); Casa Myrna Vasquez (Boston); the Farmworker Women's Organizing and Gendered Grassroots Leadership Project (Pomona, Calif.); Hermanas Unidas (Washington, D.C.); the Korean American Family Service Center (New York); Sakhi (New York); and Uzuri (Minneapolis). They include an analysis and understanding of cultural factors, religious beliefs, economic issues, and the language and conceptual barriers facing their clients, in a way that many shelters organized by white women have not done, as mentioned in Readings 31 and 34.

Similarly, rape crisis centers operate in many cities throughout the country. Volunteers and paid staff answer emergency calls to crisis hotlines, give information, and refer women who have been raped to counseling, medical, and legal services. They may accompany a woman to the police or a doctor or advocate for her in court proceedings. Rape crisis centers often conduct public education and self-defense training for women, and many have peer counselors who are rape survivors. Over the years, some rape crisis projects that mainly served white women have become multicultural by broadening their perspectives to include antiracist work. Other organizations focus their efforts on the needs of women of color, lesbians, bisexuals, and transgender women.

Students and women's organizations continue to organize "Take Back the Night" marches and rallies on campuses and in their neighborhoods where women and men speak out about their experiences of sexual violence, some of them for the first time in a public setting. College women reporting rapes have often been blamed for putting themselves in compromising situations, especially if they have been drinking. In many cases, the men involved have been protected and punished lightly if at all, especially if they are university athletes. Some administrators have been concerned about the effects of alcohol and drug use and the role of fraternity parties in campus rapes. Others seem more concerned to protect their college's reputation. Campus materials and workshops on date rape for incoming students emphasize girls' and boys' different socialization and attitudes toward dating. The work of Students Active for Ending Rape (N.Y.) is notable among the efforts to deal with this issue, as is Antioch College's sexual offense policy, which expected students to talk through a sexual encounter step by step, giving verbal consent at each step (Gold and Villari 2000).

Men's projects that work on violence against women are making a crucial contribution to creating change on this issue. Examples include the National Organization for Men Against Sexism, Emerge (Cambridge, Mass.), Men Can Stop Rape (Washington, D.C.), Men Stopping Violence (Decatur, Ga.), and MOVE (Men Overcoming Violence, San Francisco). Men's campus groups offer educational programs in men-only settings, show films, bring speakers to campus, and participate in campus or community events. Examples include Haverford Men Against Sexism and Rape, Men Educating Men on the Prevention of Sexual Assault (Bowling Green, Ohio), Men Against Rape (Tulane), Men Against Rape and Sexual Violence (Yale), Western Men against Violence (Western Washington University), and Men Acting for Change (Duke; Reading 36).

Finally, an organization working with survivors of child sexual abuse is Generation Five (San Francisco), which has the goal of eliminating this devastating problem within five generations. In Reading 32, Aurora Levins Morales describes her journey to reclaim her sexuality and sense of integrity after experiencing sexual abuse as a child.

Public and Professional Education

Compared with a generation ago, there is now considerable public information and awareness about violence against women, including public service announcements, bumper stickers, and ads on billboards, buses, and TV. Increasingly, employers and labor unions recognize that domestic violence can interfere with a woman's ability to get, perform, or keep a job. Some corporations and labor unions have developed education and training programs on domestic violence for managers and workers. Others contribute financially to shelters.

There is a great deal of research as well as theoretical, therapeutic, and political writing on this subject (see, e.g., Bart and O'Brien 1993; Bass and Davis 1988; Bohmer and Parrot 1993; Buchwald, Fletcher, and Roth 2005; Fineman and Mykitiuk 1994; Herman 1992; Jones 1994b; Koss et al. 1994; NiCarthy 1987, 2004; Russell 1990; White 1985; Zambrano 1985). Public exhibitions like The Clothesline Project (East Dennis, Mass.) also make powerful public statements. In this project, women express their thoughts, feelings, and experiences of gender violence by decorating a T-shirt, which they hang on a clothesline as testimony to be viewed by others.

Another development has been the growth of professional education on violence against women for doctors, nurses, emergency-room staff, and other health-care providers, as well as social workers and teachers. Greater knowledge and understanding are also imperative for police officers, judges, and legislators. National-level organizations like the Family Violence Prevention Fund (Washington, D.C.; San Francisco), INCITE! Women of Color Against Violence, the National Coalition Against Domestic Violence (Washington, D.C.), National Domestic Violence Hotline (www.ndvh .org), National Latino Alliance for the Elimination of Domestic Violence (Arlington, Va.), the National Resource Center on Domestic Violence (Harrisburg, Pa.), the Network for Battered Lesbians and Bisexual Women (Boston), Rape Abuse and Incest National Network (Washington, D.C.), and V-Day (New York) provide visibility, public education, research, and expertise to local organizations, the news media, and policy makers at state and federal levels.

Policy and Legislative Initiatives

Forty years ago there were no U.S. laws concerning domestic violence. Now there is a growing, if uneven, body of law, mainly at the state level, including protection orders that prohibit the abuser from coming near or contacting the woman and her children. The rape laws have also been reformed because of pressure from feminists and rape survivors. This has been a piecemeal process and also varies from state to state. Nowadays, rape laws no longer require the corroboration of a victim's testimony; women are no longer required to have resisted their attackers; and the sexual histories of rape victims are no longer a subject for cross-examination, unless shown to be relevant.

On the federal level, the Violence Against Women Act (VAWA) was signed into law as part of the Violent Crime and Law Enforcement Act of 1994. It authorized $1.6 billion to be spent over six years to address and prevent violence against women. In 2000, VAWA was reauthorized with funds for the National Domestic Violence Hotline, battered women's shelters and community initiatives, training for judges and court personnel, improvements in arrest policies, and legal advocacy programs for victims. It also included provisions to deal with violence against women with disabilities and for elder abuse, neglect, and exploitation. In 2005, VAWA was reauthorized and will come up again in 2010. Lora Jo Foo (2007) provides a more detailed review of various laws and government policies that seek to address violence against women, especially immigrant women.

Contradictions in Seeking State Support to End Violence Against Women

An increase in government funding and increasing professionalization of work involving violence against women may be seen as major successes. A negative aspect of this development is the fact that shelters and rape crisis centers have come under closer official scrutiny, especially regarding workers' professional qualifications. Although there is still a vital role for volunteers, many leadership positions require a master's degree in social work (MSW) or a counseling qualification. This is linked to the current emphasis on individual services and therapeutic remedies compared to the more political approach of the 1970s and 1980s. Yet, as hard as women work to help particular individuals, there are always many more—seemingly an endless stream of women needing help. This can lead to burnout among workers who well understand the continuing strength of meso- and macro-level factors that perpetuate violence against women.

There is an inherent contradiction in looking to the government—the State—to solve this problem. The State is a patriarchal institution involved in the subordination of women through laws, public policy, judge's decisions, and police treatment (e.g., INCITE! Women of Color Against Violence 2006). Also, government employees, U.S. prison guards and border patrols rape and abuse women (Amnesty International 2000; Falcón 2006; Kurshan 1996; Martinez 1998). U.S. military personnel also commit acts of violence against women, including their colleagues, "enemy" women, and women involved in militarized prostitution (Enloe 1993a, 2000; Guenter-Schlesinger 1999; Morris 1999).

As described by Mimi Kim (Reading 34), participants at the Color of Violence conference, held at the University of California, Santa Cruz in April 2000, called for a re-politicization of work regarding violence against women and set up a new organization, INCITE! Women of Color Against Violence. In the opening keynote, activist, writer, and scholar Angela Davis (2001) highlighted a core contradiction in current anti-violence work that looks to the State for solutions:

> Given the racist and patriarchal patterns of the state, it is difficult to envision the state as the holder of solutions to the problem of violence against women. However, as the anti-violence movement has been institutionalized and professionalized, the state plays an increasingly dominant role in the way we conceptualize and create strategies to minimize violence against women. One of the major tasks of this conference, and of the anti-violence movement as a whole, is to address this contradiction, especially as it presents itself to poor communities of color. *(p. 13)*

Reporting on the conference, Andy (Andrea) Smith (2001) argued for the need to address personal violence and State violence at the same time: to ensure safety for women affected by violence, but without strengthening the criminal justice system that is "brutally oppressive toward communities of color" (p. 66). Mimi Kim notes that increased federal funding for anti-violence organizations under the Violence Against Women Act is "often tied to collaboration with the police, prosecutors or promotion of pro-arrest policies" (p. 46). Rather, she advocates the development of community-based approaches that address violence against women without increasing State violence against men (Reading 34). In Reading 31, Andy Smith gives examples of "anticolonial responses" currently being pursued in Native American communities in contrast to mainstream anti-violence organizations that are calling for longer prison sentences for batterers and rapists.

Women's Rights as Human Rights

Violence against women has engaged the attention, anger, and activist efforts of scholars, policy makers, and organizers around the world in response to the many forms of gender-based violence in all countries.

In December 1979, the United Nations adopted the Convention on the Elimination of All Forms of Discrimination Against Women (CEDAW), which includes violence against women. One hundred eighty-four countries have ratified CEDAW and adopted it as national policy, though often with many reservations so that implementation has been much more limited. More than thirty years later, U.S. women's organizations are still lobbying for the United States to ratify CEDAW.

Defining violence against women as a human rights issue has been a successful strategy to get this issue onto the international agenda (see, e.g., Agosín 2001; Beasley and Thomas 1994; Bunch and Carillo 1991; Kerr 1993). In June 1993, women from many countries organized the Global Tribunal on Violations of Women's Human Rights to coincide with the Non-Governmental Organization (NGO) Forum of the U.N. World Conference on Human Rights, held in Vienna (Bunch and Reilly 1994). In 1994 the U.N. Commission on Human Rights created a new position—the Special Rapporteur on Violence Against Women, Its Causes and Consequences—based in Geneva, Switzerland. The Center for Women's Global Leadership (Rutgers University) sponsors an annual 16 Days of Activism Against Gender Violence (Nov. 25 to Dec. 10). (See Box.) Initiated by activists from the global North and South, the campaign emphasizes that all forms of violence, whether in the public or private sphere, are a violation of human rights. The campaign links two days designated by the United Nations for public activities around related themes: International Day Against Violence Against Women (November 25th) and International Human Rights Day (December 10th).

The final reading in this chapter is a statement published by leaders of women's human rights organizations and religious leaders who came together in Chiang Mai (Thailand), in 2004, "to explore how the positive powers of religion could be engaged to advance the well-being of women" (Reading 35). Participants noted the "contradiction between the message of peace inherent in all religions and the absence of advocacy for peace in the home and society." They called for religious institutions to act on their commitment to human dignity, social justice, and human rights for all, with specific reference to violence against women.

As this chapter makes clear, there is an urgent need for many changes at micro, meso, macro,

Sixteen Days of Activism Against Gender Violence

The 16 Days of Activism Campaign, November 25–December 10, 2007, was celebrated with actions and events taking place in at least fifty-four countries.

- In Africa, groups working to end violence against women organized street theatre in Burundi, public demonstrations in the Democratic Republic of the Congo, activities in camps for internally displaced people in Uganda, lobbying for the fair implementation of the comprehensive peace agreement in Sudan, and public marches in South Africa.

- Activities in Asia included the launch of a TV and radio campaign to end gender-based violence in Sri Lanka, the launch of a worldwide campaign to free women human rights defenders in Burma, round table discussions to raise awareness of the impact of guns and small arms on women's lives in Papua New Guinea, and marches, rallies, and interactive blog sites hosted by the *Wake up Now* Campaign in Uttar Pradesh, India.

- In Europe, poster exhibitions sought to raise awareness on the effects of gender violence in Ireland. In Italy people hung white sheets from balconies of homes, offices, and public buildings to signify their solidarity with victims of violence. Events in Britain highlighted the use of sexual violence as a weapon of war in Darfur.

- Middle East organizations campaigned against acts of family violence that continue to be condoned by states. A feminist network, Women Living Under Muslim Laws, launched a worldwide *Stop Stoning and Killing Women* campaign in Istanbul, Turkey.

- Latin American activists hosted public rallies in Chile, highlighted the effects of armed conflict on women in Colombia and Peru, and held public events in Nicaragua focusing on the persecution of women political leaders. In Mexico City's Zocalo Square, people protested the Mexican government's neglect of the serial murders of women on the U.S.–Mexico border.

- Across the United States groups organized public events and workshops with the goal of shifting attitudes and behaviors that perpetuate violence against women. In San Francisco, women organized a creative healing ceremony in which girls, women, and elders of diverse cultures, including lesbian and transgender women, articulated a culture of respect for the sacredness of the female body and sexuality. The UNIFEM office in New York launched an ongoing online campaign featuring their Goodwill Ambassador Nicole Kidman and entitled *Say NO to Violence Against Women*. In Canada groups commemorated December 17 as a day to end violence against sex workers.

Sources: www.cwgl.rutgers.edu/16days/home.html
www.cwgl.rutgers.edu/globalcenter/proghigh.html

---

and global levels for women to be secure from violence including:

- the socialization and education of children and young people to respect and value each other;
- changes in social constructions of femininity and masculinity, and the abolition of cultural attitudes and systems of inequality that support male superiority;
- an end to the objectification and commodification of women;
- changes in women's work and wages, and support for community-based economic development to give women economic security and independence;
- changes in laws, court decisions, police practices, and political systems so that women's human rights are central; and
- continued collaboration among all who are working to end violence, and challenges to those who are not.

◆◆◆

Questions for Reflection

In reading and discussing this chapter, consider these questions:

1. What beliefs about rape are really myths? How would your life be different if rape and the threat of rape did not exist?

2. How do the intersections of gender, race, class, nation, sexuality, and so forth, affect violence against women?

3. How do boys in your community learn to respect women? To disrespect women?

4. How has abuse or violence affected your life? Your family? Your community?

5. What kinds of masculinity would help to create personal security for women and for men?

6. What are men's roles and responsibilities in ending violence against women?

Finding Out More on the Web

1. Research how the Web is used to support and reinforce beliefs about violence against women.

2. Research U.S. and international organizations mentioned in this chapter that are working to end violence against women. What are their goals, strategies, and activities? What theoretical frameworks shape their work? Additional organizations:

   Madre: www.madre.org/programs/pe/speakers_fall06.html

   Women Against Violence Europe: www.wave-network.org/start.asp?ID=22650

   Women Living Under Muslim Laws: www.wluml.org/english/index.shtml

◆◆◆

Taking Action

1. Talk about this issue with your peers, and initiate public discussion on your campus or in your community. Find out about your college's policy on sexual assault and how it is enforced (or not). Find out about rape crisis centers, shelters, and support groups in your area so that you can offer this information to someone who is coping with sexual assault.

2. Volunteer with a rape crisis project on campus or at a shelter for victims of domestic violence. Men students: Work with other men on this issue.

3. Support a campus or community event concerned with violence against women.

◆◆◆

Sexual Violence and American Indian Genocide (1999)

Andy Smith

Scholar, writer, and activist **Andrea (Andy) Smith** is cofounder of INCITE! Women of Color Against Violence, a national organization that utilizes critical dialogue, direct action, and grassroots organizing. She is an award-winning teacher, and has published widely including *Native Americans and the Christian Right: The Gendered Politics of Unlikely Alliances*, and *Conquest: Sexual Violence and American Indian Genocide*.

I once attended a conference where a speaker stressed the importance of addressing sexual violence within Native communities. When I returned home, I told a friend of mine, who was a rape survivor, about the talk. She replied, "You mean other Indian women have been raped?" When I said yes, she asked, "Well, why don't we ever talk about it?" Indeed, the silence surrounding sexual violence in Native communities—particularly the sexual assault of adult women—is overwhelming. Under Janet Reno, the Department of Justice poured millions of dollars into tribally-based sexual and domestic violence programs. Although domestic violence programs are proliferating, virtually no tribes have developed comprehensive sexual assault programs.

Native survivors of sexual violence often find no support when they seek healing and justice. When they seek help from non-Indian agencies, they are often told to disassociate themselves from their communities, where their abusers are. The underlying philosophy of the white-dominated anti-rape movement is implicit in Susan Brownmiller's statement: "[Rape] is nothing more or less than a conscious process of intimidation by which all men keep all women in a state of fear."[1] The notion that rape is "nothing more or less" than a tool of patriarchal control fails to consider how rape also serves as a tool of racism and colonialism. At the same time, when Native survivors of sexual violence seek healing within their communities, other community members accuse them of undermining Native sovereignty and being divisive by making their abuse

public. According to the Mending the Hoop Technical Assistance Project in Minnesota, tribally-based sexual assault advocates believe that a major difficulty in developing comprehensive programs to address sexual assault in tribal communities, particularly sexual violence against adult women, is that many community members believe that sexual violence is "traditional." Historical evidence suggests, however, that sexual violence was rare in Native communities prior to colonization, and that it has served as a primary weapon in the U.S. war against Native nations ever since. . . . Far from being traditional, sexual violence is an attack on Native sovereignty itself. As one elder stated at a conference I attended: "As long as we destroy ourselves from inside, we don't have to worry about anyone on the outside."

The Colonial Context of Sexual Violence

Ann Stoler argues that racism is a permanent part of the social fabric: "[R]acism is not an effect but a tactic in the internal fission of society into binary opposition, a means of creating 'biologized' internal enemies, against whom society must defend itself."[2] She notes that in the modern state, it is the constant purification and elimination of racialized enemies that ensures the growth of the national body. "Racism does not merely arise in moments of crisis, in sporadic cleansings. It is internal to the biopolitical state, woven into the web of the social body, threaded through its fabric."[3] Similarly, Kate Shanley notes that Native peoples are a permanent "present absence" in the U.S. colonial imagination, an "absence" that reinforces the conviction that Native peoples are vanishing and that the conquest of native lands is justified.[4] . . . This "absence" is effected through the metaphorical transformation of Native bodies into a pollution from which the colonial body must purify itself. In the 1860s, white Californians described Native people as "the dirtiest lot of human beings on earth." They wear "filthy rags, with their persons unwashed, hair uncombed and swarming with vermin."[5] An 1885 Proctor & Gamble ad for Ivory Soap also illustrates this equation between Indian bodies and dirt:

We were once factious, fierce and wild,
In peaceful arts unreconciled
Our blankets smeared with grease and stains
From buffalo meat and settlers' veins.
Through summer's dust and heat content
From moon to moon unwashed we went.
But IVORY SOAP came like a ray
Of light across our darkened way
And now we're civil, kind and good
And keep the laws as people should.
We wear our linen, lawn and lace
As well as folks with paler face
And now I take, where'er we go
This cake of IVORY SOAP to show
What civilized my squaw and me
And made us clean and fair to see.[6]

In the colonial imagination, Native bodies are also polluted with sexual sin. . . . In 1613, Alexander Whitaker, a minister in Virginia, wrote: "They live naked in bodie, as if their shame of their sinne deserved no covering: Their names are as naked as their bodie: They esteem it a virtue to lie, deceive and steale as their master the divell teacheth them."[7] Furthermore, according to Bernardino de Minaya: "Their [the Indians'] marriages are not a sacrament but a sacrilege. They are idolatrous, libidinous, and commit sodomy. Their chief desire is to eat, drink, worship heathen idols, and commit bestial obscenities."[8]

This understanding of Native peoples as dirty whose sexuality threatens U.S. security was echoed in the comments of one doctor in his attempt to rationalize the mass sterilization of Native women in the 1970s:

People pollute, and too many people crowded too close together cause many of our social and economic problems. These in turn are aggravated by involuntary and irresponsible parenthood. . . . We also have obligations to the society of which we are part. The welfare mess, as it has been called, cries out for solutions, one of which is fertility control.[9]

. . .

Because Indian bodies are considered "dirty," they are sexually violable and "rapable." In patriarchal thinking, only a "pure" body can really be violated. The rape of bodies that are considered inherently impure simply does not count. For instance, women in prostitution have an almost impossible time if they are raped because the dominant society considers a prostituted woman as lacking bodily integrity and violable at all times. Similarly, the history of mutilation of Indian bodies, both living and dead, makes it clear to Indian people that they are not considered to have bodily integrity. President Andrew Jackson, for instance, ordered the mutilation of approximately 800 Muscogee Indian corpses, cutting off their noses and slicing long strips of flesh from their bodies to make bridle reins.[10] Tecumseh's skin was flayed and made into razor-straps.[11] A soldier cut off the testicles of White Antelope to make a tobacco pouch. Colonel John Chivington led an attack against the Cheyenne and Arapahoe in which nearly all the victims were scalped, their fingers, arms, and ears amputated to obtain rings, necklaces, and other jewelry, and their private parts were cut out to be exhibited before the public in Denver.[12] Throughout the history of massacres against Indian people, colonizers attempted not only to defeat Indian people but to eradicate their very identity and humanity. They attempted to transform Indian people from human beings into tobacco pouches, bridle reins, or souvenirs—objects for white people's consumption.

As Stoler explains this process of racialized colonization, "[T]he more 'degenerates' and 'abnormals' [in this case, Native peoples] are eliminated, the lives of those who speak will be stronger, more vigorous, and improved. The enemies are not political adversaries, but those identified as external and internal threats to the population. Racism is the condition that makes it acceptable to put [certain people] to death in a society of normalization."[13] She further notes that "the imperial discourses on sexuality cast white women as the bearers of a racist imperial order."[14] By extension, as bearers of a counter-imperial order, Native women pose a supreme threat to the imperial order. Symbolic and literal control over their bodies is important in the war against Native people, as these examples attest:

When I was in the boat I captured a beautiful Carib woman. . . . I conceived desire to take pleasure. . . . I took a rope and thrashed her well, for which she raised such unheard screams that you would not have believed your ears. Finally we came to an agreement in such a manner that I can tell you that she seemed to have been brought up in a school of harlots.[15]

Two of the best looking of the squaws were lying in such a position, and from the appearance of the genital organs and of their wounds, there can be no doubt that they were first ravished and then shot dead. Nearly all of the dead were mutilated.[16]

One woman, big with child, rushed into the church, clasping the altar and crying for mercy for herself and unborn babe. She was followed, and fell pierced with a dozen lances . . . the child was torn alive from the yet palpitating body of its mother, first plunged into the holy water to be baptized, and immediately its brains were dashed out against a wall.[17]

The Christians attacked them with buffets and beatings. . . . Then they behaved with such temerity and shamelessness that the most powerful ruler of the island had to see his own wife raped by a Christian officer.[18]

I heard one man say that he had cut a woman's private parts out, and had them for exhibition on a stick. I heard another man say that he had cut the fingers off of an Indian, to get the rings off his hand. I also heard of numerous instances in which men had cut out the private parts of females, and stretched them over their saddlebows and some of them over their hats.[19]

Although the era of deliberate, explicit Indian massacres in North America is over, in Latin America the wholesale rape and mutilation of indigenous women's bodies has continued. . . . Many white feminists are correctly outraged by mass rapes in Bosnia, and have organized to instigate a war crimes tribunal against the Serbs. Yet one wonders why the mass rapes of indigenous women in Guatemala, Chiapas, or elsewhere in Latin America have not sparked the same outrage. Feminist legal scholar Catherine MacKinnon argues that in Bosnia, "the world has *never* seen sex used this consciously, this cynically, this elaborately, this openly, this systematically . . . as a means of destroying a whole people."[20] She seems to forget that she only lives on this land because millions of Native people

were raped, sexually mutilated and murdered. Is mass rape of European women "genocide," while mass rape of indigenous women is business as usual? Even in the white feminist imagination, are native women's bodies more rapable than white women's bodies?

The colonization of Native women's bodies continues today. In the 1980s, when I served as a nonviolent witness for the Chippewa spearfishers who were being harassed by white racist mobs, one white harasser carried a sign saying "Save a fish; spear a pregnant squaw." During the 1990 Mohawk crisis in Oka [Quebec], a white mob surrounded an ambulance taking a Native woman off the reservation because she was hemorrhaging after giving birth. She was forced to "spread her legs" to prove it. The police at the scene refused to intervene. An Indian man was arrested for "wearing a disguise" (he was wearing jeans), and was brutally beaten, with his testicles crushed. Two women from Chicago WARN (Women of All Red Nations, the organization I belong to) went to Oka to videotape the crisis. They were arrested and held in custody for eleven hours without being charged, and were told that they could not go to the bathroom unless the male police officers could watch. The place they were held was covered with pornographic magazines.

In 1982, this colonial desire to subjugate Indian women's bodies was quite apparent when Stuart Kasten marketed a new video, "Custer's Revenge," in which players get points each time they, in the character of Custer, rape an Indian woman. The slogan of the game is "When you score, you score." He describes the game as "a fun sequence where the woman is enjoying a sexual act willingly." According to the promotional material:

You are General Custer. Your dander's up, your pistol's wavin'. You've hog-tied a ravishing Indian maiden and have a chance to rewrite history and even up an old score. Now, the Indian maiden's hands may be tied, but she's not about to take it lying down, by George! Help is on the way. If you're to get revenge you'll have to rise to the challenge, dodge a tribe of flying arrows and protect your flanks against some downright mean and prickly cactus. But if you can stand pat and last past the strings and arrows—You can stand last. Remember? Revenge is sweet.[21]

Ironically, while enslaving women's bodies, colonizers argued that they were actually freeing Native women from the "oppression" they supposedly faced in Native nations. Thomas Jefferson, for example, argued that Native women "are submitted to unjust drudgery. This I believe is the case with every barbarous people. It is civilization alone which replaces women in the enjoyment of their equality."[22] The *Mariposa Gazette* similarly noted that when Indian women were safely under the control of white men, they "are neat, and tidy, and industrious, and soon learn to discharge domestic duties properly and creditably."[23] In 1862, a Native man in Conrow Valley was killed and scalped with his head twisted off; his killers said, "You will not kill any more women and children."[24] Apparently, Native women can only be free while under the dominion of white men, and both Native and white women have to be protected from Indian men, rather than from white men. . . .

. . . Although stereotypes of Native women as beasts of burden for their men prevail, prior to colonization Indian societies were not male-dominated for the most part. Women served as spiritual, political, and military leaders. Many societies were matrilineal and matrilocal. Although there was a division of labor between women and men, women's and men's labor was accorded similar status.[25] Thus, the historical record would suggest, as Paula Gunn Allen argues, that the real roots of feminism should be found in Native societies. . . .

Just as, historically, white colonizers who raped Indian women claimed that Indian men were the real rapists, white men who rape and murder Indian women often make this same claim today. In Minneapolis, a white man, Jesse Coulter, raped, murdered and mutilated several Indian women. He claimed to be Indian, adopting the name Jesse Sittingcrow, and emblazoning an AIM tattoo on his arm.[26] Similarly, Roy Martin, a full-blooded Native man, was charged with sexual assault. The survivor identified the rapist as white, about 25 years old, with a shag haircut. Martin was 35 with hair past his shoulders.[27] Although this case was eventually dismissed, the fact that it even made it to trial indicates the extent to which Native men are seen as the rapists of white women.

Of course, Indian men do commit acts of sexual violence. After years of colonialism and boarding-school experiences, violence has been internalized in Indian communities. However, this view of the Indian man as the "true" rapist serves to obscure who has real power in this racist and patriarchal society. The U.S. is indeed engaged in a "permanent social war" against Native bodies, particularly Native women's bodies, which threaten its legitimacy.[28] Colonizers evidently recognize the wisdom of the Cheyenne saying, "A Nation is not conquered until the hearts of the women [and their bodies as well] are on the ground."

Through this colonization and abuse of their bodies, Indian people have learned to internalize self-hatred. Body image is integrally related to self-esteem. When one's body is not respected, one begins to hate oneself.[29] For example, Anne, a Native boarding-school student, reflects on this process:

> You better not touch yourself. . . . If I looked at somebody . . . lust, sex, and I got scared of those sexual feelings. And I did not know how to handle them. . . . What really confused me was if intercourse was sin, why are people born? . . . It took me a really long time to get over the fact that . . . I've sinned: I had a child.[30]

As her words indicate, when the bodies of Indian people are inherently sinful and dirty, it becomes a sin just to be Indian. Thus, it is not a surprise that Indian people who have survived sexual abuse often say that they no longer wish to be Indian. The Menominee poet Chrystos writes in such a voice in her poem "Old Indian Granny."

You told me about all the Indian women you counsel
who say they don't want to be Indian anymore
because a white man or an Indian one raped them
or killed their brother
or somebody tried to run them over in the street
or insulted them or all of it
our daily bread of hate
Sometimes I don't want to be Indian either
But I've never said so out loud before
Since I'm so proud and political
I have to deny it now
Far more than being hungry
having no place to live or dance
no decent job no home to offer a Granny
It's knowing with each invisible breath
that if you don't make something pretty
they can hang on their walls or wear around their
    necks
you might as well be dead.[31]

The fact that many Native peoples will argue that sexual violence is "traditional" indicates the extent to which our communities have internalized self-hatred. . . . Then, as Michael Taussig notes, Native peoples are portrayed by the dominant culture as inherently violent, self-destructive and dysfunctional. For example, in 1990, Mike Whelan made the following statement at a zoning hearing in South Dakota, calling for the denial of a permit for a shelter to serve Indian women who have been battered:

> Indian Culture as I view it, is presently so mongrelized as to be a mix of dependency on the Federal Government and a primitive society wholly on the outside of the mainstream of western civilization and thought. The Native American Culture as we know it now, not as it formerly existed, is a culture of hopelessness, godlessness, of joblessness, and lawlessness. . . . Alcoholism, social disease, child abuse, and poverty are the hallmarks of this so-called culture that you seek to promote, and I would suggest to you that the brave men of the ghost dance would hang their heads in shame at what you now pass off as that culture. . . . I think that the Indian way of life as you call it, to me means cigarette burns in arms of children, double-checking the locks on my cars, keeping a loaded shotgun by my door, and car bodies and beer cans on the front lawn. . . . This is not a matter of race, it is a matter of keeping our community and neighborhood away from that evil that you and your ideas promote.[32]

Taussig comments on the irony of this logic: "Men are conquered not by invasion but by themselves. It is a strange sentiment, is it not, when faced with so much brutal evidence of invasion."[33]

Completing the destruction of a people involves the destruction of the integrity of their culture and spirituality that forms the matrix of Native women's resistance to sexual colonization. Native counselors generally agree that a strong cultural and spiritual identity is essential if Native people are to heal from abuse. This is because Native women's healing entails healing not only from any personal abuse she has suffered, but also from the patterned history of abuse against her family, her nation, and the environment in which she lives.[34] Because Indian spiritual traditions are holistic, they have the ability to restore survivors of abuse to the community, and to restore their bodies to wholeness. That is why the most effective programs for healing revolve around reviving indigenous spiritual traditions.

In the colonial discourse, however, Native spiritual traditions become yet another site for the commodification of Indian women's bodies. As part of the genocidal process, Indian cultures lose the means to restore wholeness and become objects of consumerism for the dominant culture. Haunani Kay Trask, a Native Hawai'ian activist, describes this process as "cultural prostitution." "Prostitution, in this context, refers to the entire institution which defines a woman (and by extension the 'female') as an object of degraded and victimized sexual value for use and exchange through the medium of money. . . . My purpose is not to exact detail or fashion a model but to convey the utter degradation of our culture and our people under corporate tourism by employing 'prostitution' as an analytical category. . . . The point, of course, is that everything in Hawai'i can be yours, that is, you the tourist, the non-tourist, the visitor. The place, the people, the culture, even our identity as a 'Native' people is for sale. Thus, Hawai'i, like a lovely woman, is there for the taking."[35] . . .

Meanwhile, the colonizing religion [of Native peoples], Christianity, which is supposed to "save" Native women from allegedly sexually exploitative traditional practices, has only made them more vulnerable to sexual violence. The large-scale introduction of sexual violence in Native communities is largely a result of the Christian boarding-school system, which began in the 1600s under Jesuit priests along the St. Lawrence River. The system was more formalized in 1870 when Congress set aside funds to erect school facilities to be run by churches and missionary societies.[36] Attendance was mandatory and children were forcibly taken from their homes for the majority of the year. They were forced to practice Christianity (native traditions were prohibited) and speak English only.[37] Children were subjected to constant physical and sexual abuse. Irene Mack Pyawasit, a former boarding-school resident from the Menominee reservation, testifies to her experience, which is typical of many:

> The government employees that they put into the schools had families, but still there were an awful lot of Indian girls turning up pregnant.

Because the employees were having a lot of fun, and they would force a girl into a situation, and the girl wouldn't always be believed. Then, because she came up pregnant, she would be sent home in disgrace. Some boy would be blamed for it, never the government employee. He was always scot-free. And no matter what the girl said, she was never believed.[38]

Even when teachers were charged with abuse, boarding schools refused to investigate. In the case of just one teacher, John Boone, at the Hopi school, FBI investigations found that he had sexually abused over 142 children, but the school principal had not investigated any allegations of abuse.[39] Despite the epidemic of sexual abuse in boarding schools, the Bureau of Indian Affairs did not issue a policy on reporting sexual abuse until 1987, and did not issue a policy to strengthen the background checks of potential teachers until 1989.[40]

Although all Native people did not view their boarding-school experiences as negative, it appears that abuse became endemic in Indian families after the establishment of boarding schools in Native communities. Randy Fred, a former boarding-school student, says that children in his school began to mimic the abuse they were experiencing.[41] After Father Harold McIntee from St. Joseph's residential school on the Alkali Lake reserve was convicted of sexual abuse, two of his victims were later convicted of sexual abuse charges.[42]

Anti-Colonial Responses to Sexual Violence

The struggle for Native sovereignty and the struggle against sexual violence cannot be separated. Conceptualizing sexual violence as a tool of genocide and colonialism leads to specific strategies for combatting it. Currently, the rape crisis movement has called for strengthening the criminal justice system as the primary means to end sexual violence. Rape crisis centers receive much state funding, and, consequently, their strategies tend to be state-friendly: hire more police, give longer sentences to rapists, etc. There is a contradiction, however, in relying upon the state to solve the problems it is responsible for creating. Native people *per capita* are the most arrested, most incarcerated, and most victimized by

police brutality of any ethnic group in the country.[43] Given the oppression Native people face within the criminal justice system, many communities are developing their own programs for addressing criminal behavior based on traditional ways of regulating their societies. However, as James and Elsie B. Zion note, Native domestic violence advocates are often reluctant to pursue traditional alternatives to incarceration for addressing violence against women.[44] Survivors of domestic and sexual violence programs are often pressured to "forgive and forget" in tribal mediation programs that focus more on maintaining family and tribal unity than on providing justice and safety for women. In his study of traditional approaches for addressing sexual/domestic violence on First Nations reserves in Canada, Rupert Ross notes that these approaches are often very successful in addressing child sexual abuse where communities are less likely to blame the victim for the assault. In such cases, the community makes a pro-active effort in holding perpetrators accountable so that incarceration is often unnecessary. When a crime is reported, the working team that deals with sexual violence talks to the perpetrator and gives him the option of participating in the program. The perpetrator must first confess his guilt and then follow a healing contract, or go to jail. The perpetrator can decline to participate in the program and go through the normal routes in the criminal justice system. Everyone affected by the crime (victim, perpetrator, family, friends, and the working team) is involved in developing the healing contract. Everyone also holds the perpetrator to his contract. One Tlingit man noted that this approach was often more difficult than going to jail.

> First one must deal with the shock and then the dismay on your neighbors' faces. One must live with the daily humiliation, and at the same time seek forgiveness not just from victims, but from the community as a whole. . . . [A prison sentence] removes the offender from the daily accountability, and may not do anything towards rehabilitation, and for many may actually be an easier disposition than staying in the community.[45]

Along similar lines, Elizabeth Barker notes that the problem with the criminal justice system is that it diverts accountability from the community to players in the criminal justice system. Perpetrators are taken away from their community and are further limited from developing ethical relationships within a community context.[46] Ross notes: "In reality, rather than making the community a safer place, the threat of jail places the community more at risk."[47] Since the Hollow Lake reserve adopted this approach, 48 offenders have been identified. Only five chose to go to jail, and only two who entered the program have repeated crimes (one of the re-offenders went through the program again and has not re-offended since). However, Ross notes, these approaches often break down in cases where the victim is an adult woman because community members are more likely to blame her instead of the perpetrator for the assault.[48]

Many Native domestic violence advocates I have interviewed note similar problems in applying traditional methods of justice to cases of sexual assault and domestic violence. One advocate from a tribally-based program in the Plains area contends that traditional approaches are important for addressing violence against women, but they are insufficient. To be effective they must be backed up by the threat of incarceration. She notes that medicine men have come to her program saying, "We have worked with this offender and we have not been successful in changing him. He needs to join your batterers' program." Traditional approaches to justice presume that the community will hold a perpetrator accountable for his crime. However, in cases of violence against adult women, community members often do not regard this violence as a crime and will not hold the offender accountable. Before such approaches can be effective, we must implement community education programs that will change community attitudes about these issues.

Another advocate from a reservation in the Midwest argues that traditional alternatives to incarceration might be more harsh than incarceration. Many Native people presume that traditional modes of justice focused on conflict resolution. In fact, she argues, penalties for societal infractions were not lenient. They included banishment, shaming, reparations, and sometimes death. This advocate was involved in an attempt to revise tribal codes by reincorporating traditional practices, but she found that it was difficult to determine what these practices were and how they could be made useful today. For example, some practices, such as banishment, would not have the same impact today.

Prior to colonization, Native communities were so close-knit and interdependent that banishment was often the equivalent of a death sentence. Today, however, Native peoples can simply leave home and join the dominant society. In addition, the elders with whom she consulted admitted that their memories of traditional penal systems were tainted with the experience of being in boarding school. Since incarceration is understood as punishment, this advocate believes that it is the most appropriate way to address sexual violence. She argues that if a Native man rapes someone, he subscribes to white values rather than Native values because rape is not an Indian tradition. If he follows white values, then he should suffer the white way of punishment.

However, there are a number of difficulties in pursuing incarceration as the solution for addressing sexual assault. First, so few rapes are reported that the criminal justice system rarely has the opportunity to address the problem. Among tribal programs I have investigated, an average of about two cases of rape are reported each year. Because rape is a major crime, rape cases are generally handed to the State's Attorney, who then declines the vast majority of cases. By the time tribal law-enforcement programs even see rape cases, a year might have passed since the assault, making it difficult for them to prosecute. Also, because rape is covered by the Major Crimes Act, many tribes have not developed codes to address it as they have for domestic violence. One advocate who conducted a training for southwestern tribes on sexual assault says that the participants said they did not need to develop codes because the "Feds will take care of rape cases." She asked how many rape cases had been federally prosecuted, and the participants discovered that not one case of rape had ever reached the federal courts. In addition, there is inadequate jail space in many tribal communities. When the tribal jail is full, the tribe has to pay the surrounding county to house its prisoners. Given financial constraints, tribes are reluctant to house prisoners for any length of time.

But perhaps most importantly, as sociologist Luana Ross (Salish) notes, incarceration has been largely ineffective in reducing crime rates in the dominant society, much less Native communities. "The white criminal justice system does not work for white people; what makes us think it's going to work for us?" she asks.

The criminal justice system in the United States needs a new approach. Of all the countries in the world, we are the leader in incarceration rates. . . . Society would profit if the criminal justice system employed restorative justice. . . . Most prisons in the United States are, by design, what a former prisoner termed "the devil's house." Social environments of this sort can only produce dehumanizing conditions.[49]

As a number of studies have demonstrated, more prisons and more police do not lead to lower crime rates.[50] For instance, the Rand Corporation found that California's three-strikes legislation, which requires life sentences for three-time convicted felons, did not reduce the rate of "murders, rapes, and robberies that many people believe to be the law's principal targets."[51] Changes in crime rates often have more to do with fluctuations in employment rates than with increased police surveillance or increased incarceration rates.[52] Steven Walker concludes: "Because no clear link exists between incarceration and crime rates, and because gross incapacitation locks up many low-rate offenders at a great dollar cost to society, we conclude as follows: gross incapacitation is not an effective policy for reducing serious crime."[53] Similarly, criminologist Elliot Currie found that "the *best* face put on the impact of massive prison increases, in a study routinely used by prison supporters to prove that 'prison works,' shows that prison growth seems not to have 'worked' at all for homicide or assault, barely if at all for rape. . . ."[54]

The premise of the justice system is that most people are law-abiding except for "deviants" who do not follow the law. However, given the epidemic rates of sexual and domestic violence . . . , it is clear that most men are implicated in our rape culture. It is not likely that we can send all of these men to jail. As Fay Koop argues, addressing rape through the justice system simply furthers the myth that rape/domestic violence is caused by a few bad men, rather than seeing most men implicated in such violence.[55] Thus, relying upon the criminal justice system to end violence against women may strengthen the colonial apparatus in tribal communities that furthers violence while providing nothing more than the illusion of safety to survivors of sexual and domestic violence. . . .

Sexual violence is a fundamental attack on Indian sovereignty, and both Native and non-Native communities are challenged to develop programs that address sexual violence from an anti-colonial, anti-racist framework so that we don't attempt to eradicate acts of personal violence by strengthening the apparatus of state violence. Nothing less than a holistic approach towards eradicating sexual violence can be successful. As Ines Hernandez-Avila states:

> We must imagine a world without rape. But I cannot imagine a world without rape, a world without misogyny, without imagining a world without racism, classism, sexism, homophobia, ageism, historical amnesia and other forms and manifestations of violence directed against those communities that are seen to be "asking for it." Even the Earth is presumably "asking for it." . . . What do I imagine then? From my own Native American perspective, I see a world where sovereign indigenous peoples continue to plunge our memories to come back to our originality, to live in dignity and carry on our resuscitated and ever-transforming cultures and traditions with liberty. . . . I see a world where native women find strength and continuance in the remembrance of who we really were and are . . . a world where more and more native men find the courage to recognize and honor— that they and the women of their families and communities have the capacity to be profoundly vital and creative human beings.[56]

NOTES

1. Susan Brownmiller, *Against our will* (Toronto: Bantam Books, 1986), p. 5.

2. Ann Stoler, *Race and the education of desire* (Durham, N.C.: Duke University Press, 1997), p. 59.

3. Ibid., p. 59.

4. Lecture, Indigenous Intellectual Sovereignties Conference. UC Davis, April 1998.

5. James Rawls, *Indians of California: The changing image* (Norman: University of Oklahoma Press, 1984), p. 195.

6. Andre Lopez, *Pagans in our midst* (Mohawk Nation: *Akwesasne Notes*), p. 119.

7. Robert Berkhofer, *The white man's Indian* (New York: Vintage, 1978), p. 19.

8. David Stannard, *American Holocaust: Columbus and the conquest of the New World* (New York: Oxford University Press, 1992), p. 211.

9. Oklahoma: Sterilization of native women charged to I.H.S., in *Akwesasne Notes*, mid Winter, p. 30.

10. Stannard, *American Holocaust*, p. 121.

11. David Wrone and Russell Nelson (eds.), *Who's the savage? A documentary history of the mistreatment of the Native North Americans* (Malabar: Robert Krieger Publishing, 1982), p. 82. Quote William James, *A full and correct account of the military occurrences of the late war between Great Britain and the United States of America* (2 vols., London: printed by the author, 1818), vol. 1, pp. 293–296.

12. John Terrell, *Land grab: The truth about the "winning of the West"* (New York: Doubleday, 1972), p. 13.

13. Stoler, p. 85.

14. Ibid., p. 35.

15. From Cuneo, an Italian nobleman, quoted in Kirkpatrick Sale, *The conquest of paradise: Christopher Columbus and the Columbian legacy* (New York: Knopf, 1990), p. 140.

16. Wrone and Nelson, *Who's the savage?* p. 123. Cite U.S. Commissioner of Indian Affairs, *Annual Report for 1871* (Washington, D.C.: Government Printing Office, 1871), pp. 487–488.

17. Ibid., p. 97. Cite LeRoy R. Haven (ed.), *Ruxton of the Rockies* (Norman: University of Oklahoma Press, 1950), pp. 46–149.

18. Las Casas, p. 33.

19. *The Sand Creek Massacre: A documentary history,* pp. 129–130. Quotes Lieutenant James D. Cannon from "Report of the Secretary of War," 39th Congress, Second Session, Senate Executive Document 26, Washington, D.C., 1867. New York: Sol Lewis, 1973.

20. Catherine MacKinnon, Turning rape into pornography: Postmodern genocide, in *Ms. Magazine*, 4, no. 1, p. 27 (emphasis added).

21. Undated promotional material from Public Relations: Mahoney/Wasserman and Associates, Los Angeles, Calif.

22. Quoted in Roy Harvey Pearce, *Savagism and civilization* (Baltimore: Johns Hopkins Press, 1965), p. 93.

23. Robert Heizer (ed.), *The destruction of California Indians* (Lincoln: University of Nebraska Press, 1993), p. 284.

24. James Rawls, *Indians of California*, p. 182.

25. See Annette Jaimes and Theresa Halsey, American Indian women: At the center of indigenous resistance in North America, in Annette Jaimes (ed.), *The state of Native America: Genocide, colonization, and resistance* (Boston: South End Press, 1992), pp. 311–344.

26. Mark Brunswick and Paul Klauda, Possible suspect in serial killings jailed in N. Mexico, in *Minneapolis Star and Tribune*, May 28, 1987, p. 1A.

27. Indian man being tried for rape with no evidence, in *Fargo Forum*, January 9, 1995.

28. Stoler, p. 69.

29. For further discussion on the relationship between bodily abuse and self-esteem, see *The courage to heal: A guide for women survivors of child sexual abuse*, edited by Ellen Bass and Laura Davis (New York: Harper & Row, 1988), esp. pp. 207–222; and Bonnie Burstow, *Radical feminist therapy* (London: Sage, 1992), esp. pp. 187–234.

30. Quoted in Celia Haig-Brown, *Resistance and renewal* (Vancouver: Tilacum, 1988), p. 108.

31. Chrystos, *Fugitive colors* (Vancouver: Press Gang, 1995), p. 41.

32. Native American Women's Health and Education Resource Center, *Discrimination and the double whammy* (Lake Andes, S. Dak.: Native American Women's Health and Education Resource Center, 1990), pp. 2–3.

33. Michael Taussig, *Shamanism, colonialism and the wild man* (Chicago: University of Chicago Press, 1987), p. 20.

34. Justine Smith (Cherokee), personal conversation, February 17, 1994.

35. Haunani Kay Trask, *From a native daughter: Colonialism and sovereignty in Hawai'i* (Monroe, Maine: Common Courage Press, 1993), pp. 185–194.

36. Jorge Noriega, American Indian education in the United States: Indoctrination for subordination to colonialism, in *State of Native America*, p. 380.

37. Frederick Binder and David M. Reimers (eds.), *The way we lived* (Lexington, Mass.: D. C. Heath, 1982), p. 59. Quotes U.S. Bureau of Indian Affairs, "Rules for Schools," Annual Report of the Commissioner of Indian Affairs, 1890, Washington, D.C., pp. cxlvi, cl–clii.

38. Fran Leeper Buss, *Dignity: Lower income women tell of their lives and struggles* (Ann Arbor: University of Michigan Press, 1985), p. 156. For further accounts of the widespread nature of sexual and other abuse in boarding schools, see Native Horizons Treatment Center, *Sexual abuse handbook* (Hagersville, Ont.), pp. 61–68; The end of silence, *Maclean's*, vol. 105, no. 37, September 14, 1992, pp. 14, 16; Jim deNomie, American Indian boarding schools: Elders remember, in *Aging News*, Winter 1990–91, pp. 2–6; David Wrone and Russell Nelson, *Who's the savage?* pp. 152–154, cite U.S. Congress, Senate, Subcommittee on Indian Affairs, *Survey of the conditions of the Indians in the United States*, Hearings before a subcommittee of the Committee on Indian Affairs, Senate, SR 79, 70th Congress, 2d session, 1929, pp. 428–429, 1021–1023, 2833–2835.

39. Goodbye BIA, Hello New Federalism, in *American Eagle*, vol. 2, no. 6, December 1994, p. 19. After the allegations of abuse became public, the BIA merely provided a counselor for the abused children who used his sessions with them to write a book.

40. Child sexual abuse in federal schools, in *The Ojibwe News*, January 17, 1990, p. 8.

41. Celia Haig-Brown, *Resistance and renewal*, pp. 14–15.

42. Native Horizons Treatment Center, *Sexual abuse handbook*, p. 66. Quotes *The Province*, July 19, 1989, and *Vancouver Sun*, March 17, 1990.

43. Troy Armstrong, Michael Guilfoyle, and Ada Pecos Melton, Native American delinquency: An overview of prevalence, causes, and correlates, in Marianne O. Nielsen and Robert A. Silverman (eds.), *Native Americans, crime, and justice* (Boulder, Colo.: Westview Press, 1996), p. 81.

44. James Zion and Elsie Zion, Hazho's Sokee'—Stay together nicely: Domestic violence under Navajo common law, in Nielsen and Silverman (eds.), *Native Americans, crime, and justice,* p. 106.

45. Rupert Ross, *Return to the teachings* (London: Penguin Books, 1997), p. 18.

46. Elizabeth Barker, The paradox of punishment in light of the anticipatory role of abolitionism, in Herman Bianchi and Rene van Swaaningern (eds.), *Abolitionism* (Amsterdam: Free University Press, 1986), p. 91.

47. Ross, *Return to the teachings,* p. 38.

48. Rupert Ross, Leaving our white eyes behind: The sentencing of native accused, in Nielsen and Silverman (eds.), *Native Americans, crime, and justice,* p. 168.

49. Luana Ross, *Inventing the savage: The social construction of Native American criminality* (Austin: University of Texas Press, 1998).

50. Steven Donziger, *The real war on crime* (New York: HarperCollins, 1996), pp. 42, 162; Samuel Walker, *Sense and nonsense about crime and drugs* (Belmont, Calif.: Wadsworth,

1998); Elliott Currie, *Crime and punishment in America* (New York: Metropolitan Books, 1998).

51. Quoted in Walker, *Sense and nonsense about crime and drugs,* p. 139.

52. Steve Box and Chris Hale, Economic crisis and the rising prisoner population in England and Wales, in *Crime and social justice,* 1982, vol. 17, pp. 20–35. Mark Colvin, Controlling the surplus population: The latent functions of imprisonment and welfare in late U.S. capitalism, in B. D. MacLean (ed), *The political economy of crime* (Scarborough: Prentice-Hall Canada, 1986). Ivan Jankovic, Labour market and imprisonment, in *Crime and social justice,* 1977, vol. 8 pp. 17–31.

53. Walker, *Sense and nonsense about crime and drugs,* p. 130.

54. Currie, *Crime and punishment in America,* p. 59.

55. Fay Honey Koop, On radical feminism and abolition, in *We who would take no prisoners: Selections from the Fifth International Conference on Penal Abolition* (Vancouver: Collective Press, 1993), p. 592.

56. Ines Hernandez-Avila, In praise of insubordination, or what makes a good woman go bad? In Emilie Buchwald, Pamela R. Fletcher, and Martha Roth (eds.), *Transforming a rape culture* (Minneapolis: Milkweed, 1993), pp. 388–389.

THIRTY-TWO

◆◆◆

Radical Pleasure (1998)
Sex and the End of Victimhood

Aurora Levins Morales

Aurora Levins Morales is a feminist historian, writer, and activist, who is both Puerto Rican and Jewish. Published work includes poetry, essays, and two books: *Getting Home Alive* and *Remedios.* Her poetry is aired regularly on the Pacifica Radio program *Flashpoints.*

1

I am a person who was sexually abused and tortured as a child. I no longer define myself in terms of my survival of this experience, but what I learned from surviving it is central to my political and spiritual practice. The people who abused me consciously and deliberately manipulated me in an attempt to break down my sense of integrity so they could make me into an accomplice to my own torture and that of others. They deliberately and consciously interfered with my sexuality as one method of accomplishing this. We are so vulnerable in our pleasures and desires. The fact they could induce physical pleasure in me against my will allowed them to shame me. It allowed them to persuade me that my sexuality was untrustworthy and belonged to others. It allowed them to persuade me that my desires were dangerous and were one of the causes of my having been abused. My sexuality has stuttered ever since, flaring and subsiding in ways I have not known how to manage, ricocheting from intense excitement to absolute numbness, from reckless trust to impenetrable guardedness. This place of wounded eroticism is one that is honored in survivor culture, evidence of blows inflicted and then denied by our abusers. When the skeptical ask us "Where are your scars?" we can point to the unsteady rhythms of fascination and disgust, obsession and revulsion through which we experience sex as evidence of what we know to be true.

2

"So why choose to reclaim sex?" This is the final question in a five-hour interview of me by my friend Staci Haines. We have been talking about the seductiveness of the victim role; about the thin satisfactions that come from a permanent attitude of outrage. About how having to resist too much, too young, locks us into rigid stances of resistance that interfere with intimacy, which ultimately requires vulnerability and surrender. About the seductiveness of an identity built on righteous indignation, and how close that stance actually lies to rampant self-pity. So when she asks me "Why reclaim sex?" I answer in layers.

Of course because it is part of aliveness. But among the many topics we've ranged over in our hours of conversation, the one that grabs me now is the need and obligation to leave victimhood behind. Staci and I share a somewhat taboo belief that as survivors we have an obligation to think about the healing of the perpetrators who are, after all, our kin—victims who survived in body but were unable to remain spiritually intact. So what comes to mind is the high price we pay when we settle for being wronged. Victimhood absolves us from having to decide to have good lives. It allows us to stay small and wounded instead of spacious, powerful and whole. We don't have to face up to our own responsibility for taking charge of things, for changing the world and ourselves. We can place our choices about being vulnerable and intimate and effective in the hands of our abusers. We can stay powerless and send them the bill.

But deciding not to heal fully, not to reclaim that place of intimate harm and make it flourish, is also unjust. By making the damage done to us

permanent and irreversible, we lock both ourselves and the perpetrators away from any hope of healing. We saddle them with an even bigger spiritual debt than they have already incurred, and sometimes the reason is revenge, as if our full recovery would let them off the hook and we must punish them by seeing to it that our victimhood is never diminished or challenged. But when we refuse healing for the sake of that rage, we are remaking ourselves in the image of those who hurt us, becoming the embodiment of the wound, forsaking both ourselves and the abandoned children who grew up to torment us.

3

The path of reclaiming the wounded erotic is neither placid nor boring. It is full of dizzying precipices, heady moments of release, crushing assaults of shame. But at its core is the real fire we are all after, that blazing and untarnished aliveness that lies within everything of value and spirit that we do. Right here in our bodies, in our defense of our right to experience joy, in the refusal to abandon the place where we have been most completely invaded and colonized, in our determination to make the bombed and defoliated lands flower again and bear fruit, here where we have been most shamed is one of the most radical and sacred places from which to transform the world. To shamelessly insist that our bodies are for our own delight and connection with others clearly defies the predatory appropriations of incestuous relatives and rapists; but it also defies the poisoning of our food and water and air with chemicals that give us cancer and enrich the already obscenely wealthy, the theft of our lives in harsh labor, our bodies used up to fill bank accounts already bloated, the massive abduction of our young people to be hurled at each other as weapons for the defense and expansion of those bank accounts—all the ways in which our deep pleasure in living has been cut off so as not to interfere with the profitability of our bodies. Because the closer I come to that bright, hot center of pleasure and trust, the less I can tolerate its captivity, and the less afraid I am to be powerful, in a world that is in desperate need of unrepentant joy.

THIRTY-THREE

◆◆◆

"I Am Not a Rapist!" (1998)

Why College Guys Are Confronting Sexual Violence

John Stoltenberg

Feminist activist and author, **John Stoltenberg** was a founder of "Men Against Pornography" in New York City. His books include *Refusing to Be a Man* and *The End of Manhood: Parables of Sex and Selfhood*. He is the managing editor of *AARP The Magazine*.

What follows is an emotionally charged conversation among members of a Duke University student organization called Men Acting for Change (MAC), one of many new men's groups at colleges and universities across the United States and Canada. Besides meeting regularly to talk personally, MAC members present programs about gender and sexuality, focusing on sexual violence and homophobia, to fraternities and other campus groups.

MAC came to national prominence in the United States when members appeared in a segment about pornography on the ABC newsmagazine program *20/20*. On January 28, 1993, millions of viewers heard these college-age males speak graphically about the negative effects of pornography, including *Playboy*, on their sex lives and their relationships with women.

A year earlier, Kate Wenner, an ABC producer, asked to pick my brains about how to do a pornography story that hadn't been done before. Over an amiable lunch at a café near Lincoln Center, I suggested she report how pornography has become a primary form of sex education for young men. She liked the idea and tracked down MAC. The resulting broadcast included footage of frank conversations among both female and male Duke students and was perhaps the most astute coverage of pornography's interpersonal effects yet to appear on network television.

After that *20/20* segment aired, MAC members were invited to appear on *Oprah, Donahue, Jerry Springer, Maury Povich,* and *Montel Williams,* but they declined to have their stories sensationalized. Meanwhile *Playboy* went ballistic and, in an apparent attempt at damage control, ridiculed them in print

as "the pointy-headed, wet-behind-the-scrotum boys at Duke."

In January 1994, curious to know what makes MAC tick, I traveled to Durham, North Carolina, to attend the third annual Student Conference on Campus Sexual Violence, to be held at Duke. The brochure promised "focus on student activism and involvement in the anti-rape movement" and quoted Jason Schultz, a conference organizer and *20/20* participant: "Through our work against rape, we take control of our future and generate the skills and perspectives that we need to help make it a better, safer place for both women and men." The afternoon before the conference opened, Jason arranged a private conversation in his home among five MAC members. They understood that I would sit in, ask questions, and try to get an edited transcript of their conversation published where it could contribute to more accurate understanding of the student movement against sexual violence.

As I listened, I realized that these young men had taken the meaning of sexual violence to heart in some intensely personal and generationally specific new ways. Everyone in the group knew friends who had been sexually assaulted. At one point I asked them to estimate how many. One said that one in five of his friends had told him this. Another said fifty. Another said that among his twenty to twenty-five friends who had been sexually assaulted, he also knew the perpetrator in half the cases.

At another point one told something he had never before shared with his fellow MAC members: he himself had been sexually molested in his youth. That dramatic moment was generationally specific too, I realized. Such a disclosure would never have occurred among college-age males even a decade before. The vocabulary and sense of social safety would simply not have existed.

I came to understand that what these college-age males had to say is historically unprecedented: they had each become aware, through personal experience, of their own stake in confronting sexual violence.

There is a newsworthy story here, I thought to myself, a trend to be watched. An extraordinary new student-based social-change movement has begun; yet no major news-gathering medium has thought to listen in to the generationally specific experience represented by these five members of MAC.[1] Although they spoke as individuals and from particular viewpoints—the group was a mix of straight, bi, and gay; white and black—they also seemed at times to speak on behalf of many more male agemates than themselves. Quite matter-of-factly, without any prompting, they each described an experience now so common that it may define their generation more profoundly than any war ever has: how it feels to be perceived by female peers as a potential rapist.

Ever since the women's movement began to bring sexual violence to light in the early 1970s, the extent of rape and the extent of women's fears of it have been trivialized, refuted, and ridiculed by mainstream media. Today the aspirations of campus activists to radical gender egalitarianism and eroticized equality are similarly distorted in the popular press. For example, in the early 1990s students at Antioch College developed a comprehensive, nine-page policy spelling out the meaning of consent in sexual contact and conduct; defining and prohibiting a list of offenses that included rape, sexual assault, "sexual imposition," and nondisclosure of a known HIV-positive status; and detailing fair hearing procedures and remedies in case of violation. This path-breaking, gender-neutral, ethically acute initiative was widely sneered at by media commentators who had never read it, never talked to the students who drafted and implemented it. During the 1960s and early 1970s, many "with it" magazine and book editors reveled in the ribald romance of covering the radical student antiwar movement in depth and at length. By contrast, today's middle-age male media decision makers act as if their journalistic radar screens got stuck in time along with the anachronistic sexual politics of their youth. Nostalgic for the 1960s "sexual revolution" days before feminism made "no" even an option for women—when, in the hustle of the time, "Girls say yes to [sex with] boys who say no [to the military]"—today's middle-age male media decision makers package smug blather about "date-rape hysteria" (a *New York* magazine cover story) or

"sexual correctness" (a *Newsweek* cover story) or "do-me feminism" (an *Esquire* cover story) and sign up execrably researched diatribes about "morning-after misgivings" (Katie Roiphe) or "the new Victorianism" (Rene Denfield). Today's middle-age male media decision makers just don't get it.

What this conversation reveals, however, is that a significant subset of young males have started to get it. Typical of a brand-new kind of self-selected peer group, they voice values that do not much resemble the sexual politics of most men their fathers' age. Within their transient, education-centered communities, the social and relational meaning of sexual violence to young women has become apparent to them as an everyday, lived reality. Never before have so many young males struggled to take this reality on board in their moral map of the world, and never before have so many known that others are doing so also.

In the student antiwar movement of the 1960s, many young women of conscience organized politically in behalf of young men whose bodies were then regarded as most at risk—deployable as cannon fodder in an immoral military operation. Today, more and more young men of conscience have begun to understand their vital role in the student movement against sexual violence, and this time it is they who have put their lives on the line in behalf of the women whose bodies are most at risk.

For older menfolk—especially those who hold jobs in academia and are therefore in a position to offer material support and substantive resources—this movement presents a classic challenge for teachers: to listen to and learn from students.

· · ·

Q: Why did you get involved in Men Acting for Change?

Warren Hedges *(30, Ph.D. candidate in English)*[2]: I got involved because of women I was close to and things they had survived. When I walk on campus at night and a woman in front of me sees I'm a man walking behind her, her shoulders tense up and she starts walking more quickly. Her keys come out of her pocket in case she needs them to defend herself from me. It wouldn't do any good to try and convince her I'm a nice guy or "enlightened." I'm perceived as something that doesn't fit with what I want to be, and the only way to change that is by

changing the broader social structure—laws and economic relations and things like that.

In our culture having a penis is supposed to be a package deal: You're supposed to have specific desires (for women) and pursue them in specific ways (aggressively, competitively), identify with men instead of women, have specific—and usually boring—sexual practices. There's this broad cultural discourse saying, "This is who you should be if you happen to have this particular organ." I can't create a space where I can express myself and be more upfront about my desires and my identifications and my practices and so forth without trying to change the larger social structures.

Andy Moose *(21, pre-law English major):* My reason for doing this came through a slow process, especially with MAC meetings, of having the space to really reflect about how I felt about a lot of emotional and personal issues that I hadn't spent much time as a man thinking about before. I'm in a fraternity and have seen a lot of abuses that go on within that system. I want to stay in there and work to improve the situation so that my fraternity brothers get to that process as well. I've felt it could help them, and also stop a lot of the abuses that were going on to other friends. It's personal for me, rather than seeing a great deal of violence and wanting to work towards stopping that. That's a major concern, but the bigger driving force for me is the personal gains that I see possible for people in working with these issues.

Carlton Leftwich *(25, premed):* I'm twenty-five years old and I have come to the realization that I've never had a healthy relationship with a woman. There's a lot of issues here that make me reflect on my opinion of women and how I treat them, how I deal with them, and how I could develop a healthy relationship with one. Healthy to me is looking at them and not saying, "Oh, that's a *woman's* point of view"—making everything that she says or feels inferior. I'd like to get on an even keel when discussing something with a woman and not just look at her and say, "She's a totally different kind of thing."

Erick Fink *(22, psych major and women's studies minor):* I took this intro to women's studies class and it hit me that this feminist stuff made a lot of sense. Like, even though you've never raped anyone or even thought about it, other men are doing that in your name and they're hurting people that you love in your name. All the pressure that men feel to act a certain way and do a certain thing and fit a certain mold—maybe it *used* to work, but it's not working now. And now I'm here, and I'm going to try to do something about it. I feel like I and people with penises have something to gain from the women's movement, a lot to gain: being able to be exactly who you are without having to be "a man" in the traditional sense.

I've felt very limited by patriarchy. My sense of masculinity mostly came from where everybody else's does, TV—"If you do this, chicks will dig you." That was what was masculine for me—how to attract the opposite sex. But I didn't want to be this macho guy. It's not that I didn't want to be; I just wasn't.

Carlton: I never could identify with what straight was—this rugby-playing kind of rough-and-tumble guy, always having to prove that I was macho—so I just automatically thought that I had to be gay, because I was very sensitive and I loved classical music. I was not a quote unquote normal young man, because I never liked football. And I always heard, "Well, all guys like football—if you don't play football you're a sissy."

Jason Schultz (*22, public policy major and women's studies minor*):   In high school I was one of the top ten in my class academically. The other nine were all girls. They were brilliant and they taught me—about math, physics, English. Learning from female peers really had a big influence. The culture tells you women are bimbos, don't know anything, and are ditzes, sex objects; but my reality was different. I had good relationships with women who were intellectual and spoke their mind and wouldn't let me get away with shit—in a very loving way. Not "Get the fuck out" but "You better change or *I'm* going to get the fuck out." When I got to college, the intelligent, assertive, self-confident women started calling themselves feminists, and these were the people I loved to hang out with—"Oh, sure I'll go to your meeting. Oh, that sounds like an interesting class"—and I started to get involved. But for me there was a piece missing. I went through fraternity rush, didn't find any men that I really liked

to hang out with, and felt really stupid. Women in women's studies classes were focusing on women's experience, women's perspective—which made a lot of sense, because it's left out of traditional academia—but nothing was speaking to me on a first-person level. At that time there were a couple other men on campus who wanted the same thing, and it was framed as men interested in confronting sexual violence. It was this group that I felt could look at the other component, the part that I needed to match—not to feel isolated as much as I was sometimes, not to feel like I had to speak for men.

Q: How have you personally been affected by sexual violence?

Jason: My first year in college, a good friend of mine, a female friend, was avoiding me. We weren't communicating; we didn't have the intimacy I enjoyed so much. And I'm like, "What's up with you? what's bugging you? did you flunk some test or something?" I knew that she had gone out with this guy, and I knew who he was, and she told me the story in brief detail: She was raped. And she was like, "That's why I don't feel comfortable around you—it's because I don't know who to trust anymore." I didn't blame her at all. I was pissed at him. I was *really* pissed at him. It made me angry that this guy had ruined a friendship of mine with somebody I cared about. Then when I saw this men-concerned-with-sexual-violence thing, it came together.

As a man doing this kind of work you get stories and stories—it's just exponential. I probably know fifty survivors personally—most of them through campus.

Warren: The first person who told me she had survived a rape—here on campus by another Duke student on Valentine's Day—was during my first year in graduate school. For me it was a real hard lesson learning that just me being sensitive is not enough. This sort of thing was happening to women and it was going to change the way they reacted to all or most men, especially initially. And that prompted me to get involved with this program in Durham with men who batter their wives.

Once it became known on campus that I was concerned about these issues, and once I had a chance to speak at a Take Back the Night march, the number of stories I heard from women just seemed to multiply. One reason

MAC has been so important to me is that I feel I've got an emotional support network now—not just feeling utterly overwhelmed by the number of stories that seemed to come flooding in. Probably one in five friends told me—attempted rapes and assaults, but usually rape.

Carlton: When I was growing up I was abused sexually. I just internalized everything and left it there. It was through MAC I could come in contact with people who had a rape encounter and see how they handled it, how they were surviving it, without actually having to admit that I was someone who had been raped also. That was really difficult for me. But to see women have the courage to pick up their lives and keep on going—it's really empowering. I can feel for women a lot more now that I know that it was something that I had no control over and that it wasn't my fault. I can understand that helplessness and that dirty feeling, the pain and sorrow.

Most guys are like, "Well, how do you rape a male?" There are a lot of ways to rape a male. And I would say to any other male survivor, "Don't be ashamed." Even if it happened ten, fifteen, twenty years ago, it still happened, and you're going to have to deal with it. You're going to have to address those feelings. It's not going to be easy, but try and hook up with a group of guys that can really feel for you and care about you. And by caring for women—I guess I took that assumption, that these guys care about women—then they're obviously going to care about my plight and respect me.

Erick: For the women I know that have been sexually assaulted or raped—I'd say twenty to twenty-five percent—it sticks with them; it changes their lives.

Carlton: Your sense of security is gone, and once you lose your sense of security you're never going to get it back.

Erick: There's an awful lot of fear out there—like if there's a woman sitting in a room with me alone, and we're sitting there talking, there's the chance that she is fearful of me.

Carlton: Sometimes I just want to shout, "I'm not going to hurt you!"

Jason: Holding up a sign: "not a rapist"?

Carlton: Yeah.

Andy: My first experience of sexual violence was from the other side, knowing the male who was being accused. During freshman year at Duke, I was faced with a rape case that was going to the Judi [Judicial] Board. This was a huge shock for me—becoming aware of the size of the problem and the frequency with which these acts were going on. It was something I was completely unaware of in high school. Having a very dear personal friend share with me that they were assaulted, coupled with knowing someone accused of the rape—those two things at the same time forced me to try to understand how this could happen. I couldn't just say, "Well, it's obvious these people are incredibly violent," because I wasn't seeing that. How could this happen around me every day and these people don't show me any signs of violent tendencies? How could this be happening with such frequency?

As you begin to get involved, a lot more people, a shocking number, tell you things. It takes you aback, the numbers—between twenty and twenty-five good friends, very close. Mostly women, ninety-some percent. I had one male friend share like that. And there were a number of stories where the male was someone I knew, probably a fourth of them. Actually more than that—probably half.

Talking with other people in MAC and doing programs on sexual violence helped me, because I felt I could do something. In a very basic way that feels good, to fight a situation that before you felt really helpless in. I have a little bit more understanding of how the event could happen—so it's not so much burning hatred towards that individual. I'm not so quick just to discard that person and say, "OK, he raped this woman so now I'm just going to not communicate with him any longer." I don't want to do that. There's definitely resentment and anger, a great deal of anger, and I try to suppress that as much as I can, because when you have these sorts of numbers around you, it's vital that you don't hate and cut that person off just because—. I mean, you become very lonely, obviously.

Q: How do you reach other men?

Jason: Standing up to them never seems to work. It seems to push them farther away, make them reactive. It's a balance of making them feel like I care what they say and being willing to sit down and listen to them for a long time, but then be willing to challenge them. Not saying, "Oh, you're a sexist pig—get the fuck outta here," but when the opportunity is there to say, "What you're saying really bothers me" or "I'd really like to talk to you about this because I'm learning where this is coming from."

Carlton: Don't make men feel like a minority. There are a lot of men out there who really want to understand themselves and their feelings a lot more, and you can really turn somebody off with that raw anger that seems to be associated with feminists. That's intimidating to men. I know it is to me.

Andy: A lot of the successes that I've been a part of talking with fraternity men came from catching them off guard. The minute some discussion on sexual violence comes up they become defensive. When they've gotten in these discussions with women or with non-Greek men, oftentimes it's led to an argument, they didn't feel very good about it, they don't want to talk about it, and so they don't deal with it. If there's something being discussed about a Greek function, they immediately assume that the fraternity men are going to be blamed, and they're going to defend themselves as not being a rapist or whatever. So a lot of the successes have come from surprise, when they realize there's a real conversation that's going to happen and it's not going to become some heated argument—because a lot of men haven't really thought about it much at all, and people really enjoy having an opportunity to reflect about their opinions, to recognize, "Wow, you know, I've thought about this and it really helped."

Erick: I was talking to a good friend and he said, "You know what I think date rape is? I think this woman has sex with this guy and the next morning she decides she shouldn't have done it, so she just screams rape." And I'm like, "Well, you know, I remember not long ago I felt the same way. But if you really think about it, things like that can happen. On a date maybe with somebody that you might know very well or have been seeing for a long time, you could get violent with that person, couldn't you?" And he said, "Uh, I don't know." And I'm like, "Well, have you ever gotten so angry or so frustrated with your girlfriend that you could just—" And he's like, "Sure, I guess so." And there was a relation there, where I could see how he was feeling,

and he could see how I was feeling too. I think if he had said that to a woman, she would be very offended—and rightfully so.

Andy: You have to have discussions for the potential rapist, but also focus on how people contribute to an environment or make it easier for a rape to happen. A lot of times they don't recognize how they in a much more subtle way contribute or make these sorts of things easier to happen, by a comment or a particular action in a situation.

Warren: Or by no action.

Andy: Right, exactly, because so quickly they say, "Well, **I'm** not a rapist." They don't think about what environment you're establishing when you're having a party or you're making some joke or you don't say anything in a particular situation. It's better to have dialogue about those issues.

Jason: A lot of men don't hear what feminists are actually saying when it's coming from women. Their words are so devalued, and we value men's words more. My experience has been that it takes some patience, because if somebody said something sexist like "Oh, she deserved to be raped, look at how she's dressed," there's an instinct to want to confront that. But what seems to be more beneficial is to ask questions, maybe let the story weave itself a little more, find a deeper belief system, and figure out what about that issue to confront. I think with some men you can definitely do that.

Warren: My formative experience thinking about male violence was working with men who beat their wives. They were ordered by the courts to attend. The men couldn't leave the program angry because they might go home and beat their partner. That was a real constraint on my need to be vindictive and self-righteous. There was a counselor who put it very well when he said, "Dealing with abusive men is like judo; you gotta grab ahold of their energy and move them someplace they don't expect to end up."

NOTES

1. I tried for two years to get this conversation into print. Among the publications that passed on it are *Cosmopolitan, Details, Elle, Glamour, Mademoiselle, Ms., On the Issues, Rolling Stone,* and the *Village Voice.*

2. Ages and academic concentrations are given as of the date of this conversation.

THIRTY-FOUR

Alternative Interventions to Violence: Creative Interventions (2006)

Mimi Kim

Mimi Kim is the Director of Creative Interventions, a nonprofit organization working on family and community solutions to interpersonal violence. She has worked at Asian Women's Center, co-founded Shimtuh: Korean Domestic Violence and Sexual Assault Program, and is a board member of the National Steering Committee of the Asian and Pacific Islander Institute on Domestic Violence.

Are the solutions to violence against women and children to be found via state interventions—through the police, prosecution and imprisonment? Or are alternative, grassroots, community-based responses required? These are questions being asked by many women of color in the USA. Creative Interventions is an organization based in Oakland, California, which seeks to empower families and communities to resolve family, intimate partner and other forms of interpersonal violence.[1] It is hoped that this piece will spark conversations about ways of supporting community initiatives to address violence against women. Practitioners and community members working on similar issues in other countries are invited to contribute their ideas and stories.

Anti-Violence Movement in the U.S.

My involvement in exploring creative interventions in relation to violence against women and children has a particular history. It is linked to two pathways—the work of social justice movements in the U.S. that have been led by people of color to address the concerns of our communities, and years of anti-violence work, primarily within Asian American immigrant communities.

These pathways of social justice movements and the anti-violence movement have not always run a parallel course. The anti-violence movement in the U.S. has strayed from the grassroots and radical origins of its nascent years in the 1970s. Indeed,

many would say that this can no longer be called a movement but rather a human service sector which has professionalized and legitimized itself into a provider of social service rather than as an agent of social change.

Throughout the 1980s and, particularly, the 1990s, government funding of anti-violence organizations in the U.S. increased significantly. This funding was often tied to collaboration with the police, prosecutors or promotion of pro-arrest policies. This funding trend both reflects and promotes the increasing reliance upon criminal legal interventions for domestic and sexual violence. As a long-time worker in anti-violence organizations, I witnessed this increase in federal and state funding, celebrated the availability of much-needed resources, and also came to recognize the short-term and long-term consequences these developments would have upon the very movement which fostered these gains.

During the ten years I worked within the Asian Women's Shelter with women who had been subjected to interpersonal violence, I embraced three key beliefs/principles of the mainstream anti-violence movement in the U.S.:

- that victims are a class of people distinct from perpetrators;
- that change for perpetrators is unlikely and, more often than not, not worth the effort; and
- that engagement with perpetrators is dangerous and therefore best left to the state.

While I understand the evolution of these beliefs/principles and am all too familiar with the victim-blaming, anti-woman myths from which these were a welcome departure, I also saw us walk into another sort of trap.

While the anti-violence movement originally challenged patriarchy within the family and the patriarchal state which protected it, successful attempts to lobby for changes to state policies and practices led to a shift towards a collaborative relationship. Furthermore, the anti-violence movement was primarily led by white women (who were becoming increasingly professionalized) who experienced this shift in relationship with the state as beneficial to abused women and children as well as to their organizations which gained legitimacy and, in some cases, increased funding due to this improved relationship. While the positions of women of color with regard to this shift can in no way be described as homogeneous, women of color have been much more likely to challenge this relationship between the anti-violence movement and the state.

In recent years, this challenge has escalated with the alarming rise in rates of incarceration particularly among people of color. Likewise, increasing anti-immigrant sentiment and policies in the U.S. have contributed to concern over the pro-criminalization approach supported by anti-violence advocates and the state. Many of us, already wary of the pro-arrest recommendations often offered to women seeking assistance from our own organizations, were particularly struck by earlier compromises represented in the passage of the Violence Against Women Act (VAWA) in 1994. This important act was the first piece of federal legislation regarding violence against women in the U.S. and the result of years of struggle from anti-violence and immigrant rights advocates. Among other measures, its passage led to significant increases in federal funding available to anti-violence organizations and allowed for critical gains for immigrant women facing domestic violence from their U.S. citizen or legal resident spouses. These were outcomes we all celebrated.

At the same time, however, VAWA was passed as a section of the Violent Crime Control and Law Enforcement Act of 1994 (1994 Crime Bill), the bill backed by President Clinton which significantly increased prison construction and legislated "three strikes you're out"—a mandate for automatic long-term sentencing for anyone convicted of three felony offenses. For many of us, this compromise symbolized the untenable position the mainstream anti-violence movement had reached with regard to the state and its embrace of criminalization as a primary intervention response.

On the ground, women experiencing domestic violence had been encouraged to seek safety through our services. Our help lines often advised women to call the police. When women reached our phone lines after hours, they were told to call 911 (the dial code for the police) in case of emergency.

While we were often skeptical of the response they might actually receive and spent time instructing women on how best to manage a police response, we failed to think of an alternative way to protect women and children and engage perpetrators of abuse.

Safety, we believed, was paramount. And safety was defined as devising a plan to leave the abuser and engage the police if necessary. Of course, we knew that women more often than not did not leave the relationships or when they left, they often returned at a later date. This is common for anyone involved in an abusive relationship. But for women in immigrant communities and communities of color there are additional concerns. For instance, the fear of an abusive partner may be matched by fear of the police. Immigrant women want violence to end, but they do not necessarily want their partner arrested, nor to go to a shelter, nor to leave their homes. Those concerned about their immigration status also risk exposure to deportation for themselves, their children, and for their abusive partners.

For those involved in abusive same-gender relationships or for the lesbian/gay/bi-sexual/transgender or queer community, fears in relation to the police or state involvement are heightened by knowledge that most conventional anti-violence programs will fail to understand them and their situations. Few anti-violence advocacy services actively target the queer community or have effective anti-homophobia policies and practices. And police response towards the queer community is known to range from insensitivity to brutal violence.

While advocate-led trainings about domestic violence, and the experience of immigrant communities and queer communities may have mitigated some of the most egregious aspects of police response and positively changed policies and practices within some parts of the criminal legal system, the system remains one based on separation, punishment, state definitions of crimes, and state control. Embedded in a criminal legal system which purports "blind" justice remain deep biases based upon class, race, gender, sexual orientation, immigration status, nationality, religion, and physical and mental ability which permeate the system on all levels. Since 9/11, changes in laws, policies and practices have had devastating effects on already oppressed groups.

Even the most ardent supporters of the current anti-violence intervention approach in the U.S. will admit these limitations. However, many fail to see an alternative. The basic assumptions that the best way to achieve safety is through the survivor leaving an abusive relationship and the best way to engage a perpetrator is through the criminal legal system remain. Other options are deemed too dangerous, too subject to the manipulation of the perpetrator, or simply unimaginable.

In recent years, those raising a critique of state interventions and demanding new alternative responses to challenge intimate violence and state violence have coalesced into a vocal and powerful force. In 2000, an organisation called *Incite! Women of Color Against Violence* was formed during the *Color of Violence* conference in Santa Cruz to name and respond to the complex intersection of forms of oppression facing women of color and communities of color. This organization has continued to articulate a new analysis of violence while creating spaces for alternative responses.

Incite! and *Critical Resistance,* a multi-racial national organization challenging the prison-industrial-complex, created a joint statement which acknowledged the uncharted territory between those trying to address state violence associated with prisons, and those in the anti-violence movement trying to address interpersonal violence against women and children. The preamble to the *Critical Resistance—Incite statement on gender violence and the prison industrial complex* articulates a joint commitment to work together:

> We call social justice movements to develop strategies and analysis that address both state AND interpersonal violence, particularly violence against women. Currently, activists/movements that address state violence (such as anti-prison, anti-police brutality groups) often work in isolation from activists/movements that address domestic and sexual violence. The result is that women of color, who suffer disproportionately from both state and interpersonal violence, have become marginalized within these movements. It is critical that we develop responses to gender violence that do not depend on a sexist, racist, classist, and homophobic criminal justice system. It is also important that we develop strategies that challenge the criminal justice system and that also provide safety for survivors of sexual and

domestic violence. To live violence-free lives, we must develop holistic strategies for addressing violence that speak to the intersection of all forms of oppression. (Incite! Women of Color Against Violence, 2006, p. 223)

Communities as Spaces of Possibility

Many of us within oppressed communities seek safety within the same collective spaces which hold those who perpetrate violence against us. Leaving violent situations may not seem possible because of potential persecution from those around us, not only abusive partners but family, faith communities, friends, community members, and leaders. These are attitudes which many of us in the anti-violence community are challenging in order to make it possible for those who have been subjected to violence to speak out about this, and to be embraced and supported rather than shunned or blamed. Leaving violent contexts may also expose us to new vulnerabilities, some of which may in the long run be less safe than the homes and communities from which we escape, i.e., poverty, racism, exposure to deportation, religious persecution, language barriers, cultural barriers, homophobia, transphobia, and so on. As anti-violence advocates and those committed to wider social justice, we are doing all we can to change these conditions.

However, despite conditions of violence, communities also offer multiple forms of safety: emotional safety; material resources; security of home and family; shared language, culture, history and religion; sense of belonging; and so on. These are important to most human beings. For members of oppressed communities, however, these are particularly scarce resources which may only be accessible within the sacred pockets of our intimate spaces. How can these treasures be salvaged? How can the positive benefits of community be nurtured? And, in situations of intimate violence, how can we rely upon these very community resources to lead the way towards safety and accountability—and not simply rely upon outside systems to "pull us out of danger" by removing us or those from within our communities who violate us?

The shortcomings of currently available intervention options and the need to develop new models for community-based responses to violence became painfully clear to me as I faced the violence in the relationship of my own long-time friends. When I learned what was happening, my instinct was to gather a collective group of our community together to form a system of response not only to support the survivor but also to engage her abusive partner. My professional training told me that this would be too dangerous. Going to a shelter, seeking refuge at a friend's home, calling the police—these were all familiar suggestions which were rejected outright by my friend. I had worked all these years in the anti-violence movement and, yet, the options we had to offer were so ineffective. This was not because a woman was not ready to make these difficult choices. This was because, for her, these choices were the wrong ones.

Creating Alternative Community-Based Interventions to Violence

Despite a growing critique of the limited intervention approaches available and despite the development of some proposed alternative frameworks (*Generation Five*, forthcoming; *Incite! Women of Color against Violence* 2005; Kim 2002; Mills 2003), on-the-ground implementation of alternative responses to violence in the U.S. has been surprisingly lacking. Restorative justice applications to intimate forms of violence have been attempted in only a few places (Bazemore & Earle 2002; Blagg 2002; Coker 1999, 2002; Kelly 2002; Pennell & Anderson 2005; Pranis 2002; Stubbs 1997, 2002), and most have been closely tied to the criminal legal system. Some anti-violence organizations have prioritized community organizing over a social service model (Asian and Pacific Islander Women & Family Safety Center 2001; Bhattacharjee 1997; Close to Home 2003; Das Dasgupta 2002; Fullwood 2002; Kim 2005; Mitchell-Clark & Autry 2004), but few have engaged the community to take a more active role in actually intervening in violence.

After researching existing programs and participating in local and national discussions confirming the need for alternative options, I decided to form an independent organization from which to nurture these alternative community-based interventions to violence. In 2004, with the support and inspiration of long-time visionaries in the anti-violence

movement, I established *Creative Interventions* in Oakland, California. I also knew of a handful of local and national anti-violence organizations which would be willing to work together collaboratively to explore these alternative options but which individually lacked the institutional resources to develop them.[2]

Creative Interventions begins with the assumption that those closest to and most impacted by violence have the greatest motivation to end that violence, i.e., survivors, friends, family and community members. And as these are often the people to whom survivors first turn, they are in a position to offer the most accessible and culturally-appropriate assistance at the earliest stages of violence. It also assumes that the intimate network is often already engaged with the perpetrator and may be in the best position to leverage their authority and connection to demand and support change. Thus the key to community-based interventions is not outside systems, but rather the intimate network. The missing pieces are the framework, knowledge, and resources to equip these intimate networks to offer effective, ethical, and sustainable intervention options.

Creating New Knowledge to Support Alternative Community-Based Interventions

The first project of Creative Interventions is a documentation project called the StoryTelling and Organizing Project which gathers stories from everyday people on successful and not-so-successful community-based interventions to violence. We have become so conditioned to think of our current system of shelters, police, and professional intervention programs for those who are violent, that many of us cannot even imagine what a community-based intervention would look like. Yet, I have found that when any group has discussed the topic, people invariably think of efforts that they or others have carried out. "Oh yes, I remember that my cousin and his friends helped this girl who was being beaten up by her dad. They went to his house and told him that they knew what was happening and he'd better not do it again." Stories like these contain rich information regarding community-based interventions. What we need to do is to recognize the value of these stories, seek them out, and then rigorously explore these often hidden stories for more information:

- Who decided to start the intervention?
- Why did you do this?
- Why then? What made you know that this was the time to do this?
- How did you decide to move forward?
- What skills were involved in taking this action?
- How did you learn how to do this?
- Who else did you involve?
- What effects did this have?
- Did it reduce or end the violence?
- How?
- What did you learn from this process?
- What advice would you give to others who are in a similar situation?

If these stories of courageous acts of everyday people can be collected in one place, documented, analyzed and then turned back to our communities, what further community interventions will be inspired?

Creative Interventions will also add to community knowledge through a second project, the Community-Based Intervention Project, which seeks to demonstrate ways of creating alternative community-based models of intervention. An alternative model which organizes collective responses to violence including support for survivors, engagement of perpetrators, and education for the community, is currently being developed among partner organizations primarily working within communities of color, immigrant, and queer communities in the San Francisco Bay Area. Upon completion of this pilot project and its evaluation, the model will be documented and disseminated widely.

These are our efforts to create new paradigms and tools to address and prevent violence. This organization and its collaborative projects represent just one of many efforts among women of color in the U.S. to create alternative responses to intimate forms of violence, while at the same time addressing the very real effects of state violence on our communities.

I will end this piece with Barbara's[3] story collected through the StoryTelling and Organizing Project in order to provide an example of how these stories can inspire and inform.[4]

Barbara's Story

I have three children; the oldest two are boys. I had them when I was still running a rape crisis center and a battered women's program/child sexual abuse program. And I remember panic about having boys: "How in the world am I going to love boys?" 'Cause in my view, men were responsible for much of what was wrong with the culture, and cultures in general, and that aggression and that violence that we were seeing happen in families and in communities. It was deeply life-transforming to *completely* love—love like I've never loved before—these two little boys. And watch them grow up, and shepherding their growth in a really racist, sexist, screwed-up world. And knowing that you could only do as good of a job as you can do.

When my oldest son was a freshman at high school, he was dying to go to these unsupervised parties that were actually being given by seniors when their parents were out of town. The good news is he was deeply honest and said, "I really want to go to these parties." And I'd say, "No, you can't go to these parties." And we had a running debate for half of the year.

He kept saying, "Mom, you know I'm not going to do anything terrible. And you know in yourself that at some point I'm going to experiment, but I'm not going to do more than that. What's the problem?" And I realize, as we talk about it, that the problem was I *knew* that at these parties—at some point—there'd be a young woman who would either have gotten too drunk or too high, or was too confused about the attention . . . of some powerful senior, to not end up upstairs in a bedroom, and that she would be raped. And I *knew*—I had no question—that my son would not be the person to do that. I had not an iota of doubt or worry.

But I couldn't bear the idea that he would be there and not stop it. And that he'd be part of a problem by not being able to stop it. So I said, "You're not going to be the problem. But somebody else is. And I don't know how I could bear you being present. So the only way you can go to this unsupervised party is if you can role-play with me—if you can strategize with me—what you're going to do, because you *have* to be able to stop it. And if that means putting your body in the way, or if it means calling the police and dealing with whatever trouble you might get for calling the authorities on the older boys, or gathering a group of your friends together to stop it in some way . . . you *have* to . . . I have to know that you will not allow it to happen because being on the side and not doing it yourself is not enough. You've got to be an active part of the solution." And we had long talks about this.

We talked through what he would do, how he would feel, what he would do if he had to call the police—how before he did it he'd have to know the address, he'd have to know how to describe it, he'd have to be willing to be there when they came so that they weren't turned away at the door . . . There were a million details that we had to walk through in order for me to feel confident. And in the end, right near the end of freshman year, he convinced me that he would be strong enough. And that whatever it was—if it took getting a posse of his friends together to stand in the way, . . . if it meant grabbing the girl and running off and getting her to safety—that he would do it. That was our agreement.

And then, I think it was a week before his senior graduation, he came to me one day and said, "Mom, do you remember those discussions we had my freshman year?" And I said, "You mean about the parties?" And he said, "Yeah." He said, "Mom, I did it." I said, "What are you saying?" And he said, "There was a party I was at and six guys led a girl upstairs and I watched that. And I ran upstairs and I stood in the doorway. And I grabbed her hand and I ran downstairs with her, and I told those young men they had to get out. And I took her home. And she was okay." And he didn't cry when he told me.

And actually, later that day, a girlfriend of his, and I don't know if she was the girl, or if she just knew the girl . . . she came to me and said, "Barbara, do you know what your son did?" And I said, "You mean at the party?" And she said, "Yes. He saved this girl." And she said, "Barbara, you should be really proud."

. . . So I think it's possible. You can raise boys. And it's important to raise them and know they won't do it. But it's just as important for them not to be bystanders—to raise them to be courageous and to have them understand that their job is far more than that; they have to stop it.

An Invitation to Contribute Your Own Stories

If you know of stories of grassroots community initiatives to address violence, Creative Interventions would be delighted to hear from you! Please contact us c/o stories@creative-interventions.org.

NOTES

1. See www.creative-interventions.org.

2. These include Generation Five, a San Francisco–based national organization committed to ending child sexual abuse through community organizing and leadership development, and local immigrant-specific domestic violence programs, including Shimtuh in the Korean community; Narika, which works in the South Asian community; and Asian Women's Shelter, a pan-Asian battered women's shelter which has been particularly interested in looking at alternatives for the Asian and Pacific Islander queer community. Other affiliated organizations include prison abolitionist organizations in the Bay Area including Critical Resistance and Justice Now, the latter organization advocating for women in prison, and DataCenter, a social justice research center.

3. Barbara gave permission for her first name to be shared publicly.

4. If you want to contribute stories of grassroots community initiatives to address violence, Creative Interventions would be delighted to hear from you. Contact stories@creative-interventions.org

REFERENCES

Asian & Pacific Islander Women & Family Safety Center 2001: *Organizing with passion: Domestic violence organizing strategies.* Seattle: Asian & Pacific Islander Women & Family Safety Center.

Bazemore, G. & Earle, T. H. 2002: 'Balance in the response to family violence: Challenging restorative principles'. In Strang, H. & Braithwaite, J. (eds), *Restorative justice and family violence*, pp. 153–177. Cambridge: Cambridge University Press.

Bhattacharjee, A. 1997: 'A slippery path: Organizing resistance to violence against women'. In Shah, S. (ed), *Dragon ladies*, pp. 29–45. Boston, MA: South End Press.

Blagg, H. 2002: 'Restorative justice and Aboriginal family violence: Opening a space for healing'. In Strang H. & Braithwaite, J. (eds), *Restorative justice and family violence*, pp. 191–205. Cambridge: Cambridge University Press.

Close to Home 2003: *Mobilizing family, friends, & neighbors to prevent domestic violence.* Dorchester, MA: Close to Home.

Coker, D. 1999: 'Enhancing autonomy for battered women: Lessons from Navajo peacemaking', *University of California Los Angeles Law Review*, 47:1.

Coker, D. 2002: 'Anti-subordination processes in domestic violence'. In Strang H. & Braithwaite, J. (eds), *Restorative justice and family violence*, pp. 128–152. Cambridge: Cambridge University Press.

Das Dasgupta, S. 2002: *Organizing communities to challenge violence against women.* Duluth, MN: Praxis International.

Fullwood, P. C. 2002: *Preventing family violence: Community engagement makes the difference.* San Francisco, CA: Family Violence Prevention Fund.

Generation Five 2006: *Transformative justice approaches to child sexual abuse: Challenges, principles, and applications.* San Francisco: Generation Five.

Incite! Women of Color Against Violence 2006: *The Incite! anthology.* Boston: South End Press.

Incite! Women of Color Against Violence 2005: *Gender oppression, abuse, violence: Community accountability within the people of color progressive movement.* Incite: Women of Color Against Violence.

Kelly, L. 2002: 'Using restorative justice principles to address family violence in Aboriginal communities'. In Strang, H. & Braithwaite, J. (eds), *Restorative justice and family violence,* pp. 206–222. Cambridge: Cambridge University Press.

Kim, M. 2002: *Innovative strategies to address domestic violence in Asian and Pacific Islander communities: Examining themes, models, and interventions.* San Francisco: Asian & Pacific Islander Institute on Domestic Violence.

Kim, M. 2005: *The community engagement continuum: Outreach, mobilization, organizing and accountability to address violence against women in Asian and Pacific Islander communities.* San Francisco: Asian & Pacific Islander Institute on Domestic Violence.

Mills, L. 2003: *Insult to injury: Rethinking our responses to intimate abuse.* Princeton: Princeton University Press.

Mitchell-Clark, K. & Autry, A. 2004: *Preventing family violence: Lessons from the Community Engagement Initiative.* San Francisco: Family Violence Prevention Fund with support from the Annie E. Casey Foundation.

Pennell, J. & Anderson, G. (eds). 2005: *Widening the circle: The practice and evaluation of family group conferencing with children, youths, and their families.* Washington, DC: NASW Press.

Pranis, K. 2002: 'Restorative values and confronting family violence'. In Strang H. & Braithwaite, J. (eds), *Restorative justice and family violence,* pp. 23–41. Cambridge: Cambridge University Press.

Stubbs, J. 1997: 'Shame, defiance and violence against women: A critical analysis of "communitarian conferencing"'. In Cook, S. & Bessant, J. (eds): *Women's encounters with violence: Australian experiences.* Thousand Oaks, CA: Sage Publishing.

Stubbs, J. 2002: 'Domestic violence and women's safety: Feminist challenges to restorative justice'. In Strang, H. and Braithwaite, J. (eds): *Restorative justice and family violence,* pp. 42–61. Cambridge: Cambridge University Press.

T H I R T Y - F I V E

◆◆◆

The Chiang Mai Declaration (2004)
Religion and Women: An Agenda for Change

International Committee for the Peace Council

The **International Committee for the Peace Council** is a diverse group of internationally known people of faith. Its mission is to demonstrate that effective interreligious collaboration to make peace is possible. This text was approved at the Peace Council's 2004 annual meeting in Chiang Mai, Thailand, which included a conference held jointly with leaders of international women's organizations.

the world. Their own relevance is at stake as they become more and more isolated from the values and needs of their members.

It is urgent that religions address these realities. Religions must be consonant with the cultural evolution in which we are all immersed. Religions must no longer tolerate violence against women. Women are alienated from religions that do. We are committed to working towards change, and we call on others, women and men, to join in this task.

Preamble

We, the participants in this conference on women and religion, recognize that contemporary realities have tragic consequences for women's lives. Without a commitment to women's human rights and to the resolution of these tragedies, religions are failing

I. Women and Globalization: Problem and Promise

We live in a time of rapid change which provides both challenges and opportunities. This change has profound effects on all our lives.

Our globalized world is ravaged by armed conflict, increasing economic disparity, the feminization of poverty, massive displacement of peoples, violence against women, the pandemic of HIV and AIDS, enduring racism, and extremisms—all of which generate a climate of deep fear and widespread insecurity.

Globalized capitalism has reduced everything to a commodity and everyone to a consumer and commodity. Nowhere is this more evident than in the lives of women:

- Women's and children's bodies are commodified, especially in sexual trafficking.
- Increasingly HIV and AIDS have a woman's face.
- Women and children disproportionately populate the camps of refugees and displaced persons.
- Women make up the greater proportion of exploited laborers.
- Pressures of the globalized economy have led to even greater violence against women and children.

Globalization, however, also bears the promise and possibilities of advancing women's human rights and well-being:

- More women in more places can be gainfully and justly employed.
- Information technology can enable women throughout the world to share strategies, successes, and hope.

II. Women and Religions: Problem and Promise:

Religions at their best celebrate the dignity of each human being and of all life as valuable parts of a sacred whole. They inspire and empower us to compassion and justice.

Religions, however, have not always been at their best. They have collaborated with dehumanizing values of cultural, economic and political powers. Thus they have contributed to the suffering of women:

- They have made women invisible by denying them religious education and excluding them from decision-making.

- They have been silent when patriarchal systems have legitimated the violence, abuse, and exploitation of women by men.
- This silence has been deafening in the face of such atrocities as rape, incest, female genital mutilation, sex selective abortion, and discrimination against sexual minorities.
- They have not recognized the conscience and moral agency of women, especially in relation to their sexuality and reproductive decisions.

But religions can and must do better. They must reclaim their core values of justice, dignity, and compassion and apply these values to women. We reached consensus that:

A. Within the Religions, Women's Religious Literacy Should Be Recognized and Fostered. Women Are:

- Students: Just as education of women is today understood to be critical in transforming the world, so providing women with religious education is critical in transforming religion. Women seek religious education at both basic and advanced levels. They should be welcomed.
- Scholars: In spite of obstacles, women have developed as religious scholars. That scholarship is an essential resource for the overall development of our understanding of religion. It should be promoted.
- Teachers: Male religious leaders and students have much to gain from exposure to women teachers of religion. Unless we work to change men, the ability of religions to progress in sensitivity to women is impossible.
- Leaders: Women should be full participants in the life and institutional leadership of their religious communities. Women are prepared to be decision-makers, and their gifts should be recognized and used to the fullest extent.

B. Within the World:

- Religions should apply their message of peace in order to oppose the daily reality of violence in family and society. There is a contradiction between the message of peace inherent in all religions and the absence of advocacy for peace in the home and society.

- Women are subjects, not objects, in their own lives. The right to choose any role, including motherhood, should be supported socially, economically, and politically.

- Religions should apply the message of social justice to women. The world's religions play a leadership role in seeking social justice, in the environment, against racism, and for the poor. But religions have been largely silent in response to critical issues of women's human rights, in the family and in the work place.

- This is nowhere more evident than in the area of women's sexuality and reproductive health. Given the moral concern about abortion and the range of stances toward it, the view of any particular religious tradition should not be imposed on the consciences of others. Decriminalization of abortion is a minimal response to this reality and a reasonable means of protecting the life and health of women at risk.

Conclusion

Our experience of coming together as women leaders and religious leaders has convinced us that the religious traditions and the aspirations of women are not in opposition. We are not enemies. On the contrary, we share the same commitment to human dignity, social justice, and human rights for all.

We therefore commit ourselves and call on other women and other religious leaders to reach out to each other to enhance mutual understanding, support, and cooperation. This can be done on the regional level to expand the consensus achieved here and at the national level to define concrete, joint activities toward advancing women's human rights and well-being.

We came together as women and men to explore how the positive powers of religion could be engaged to advance the well-being of women. Indeed, we believe that when women and religious traditions collaborate, a powerful force for advancing women's human rights and leadership will be created.

7

◆◆◆

Making a Home, Making a Living

Asking for support from family and friends, falling in love, moving in with a roommate, holding your newborn baby for the first time, breaking up with a partner of many years, struggling to understand a teenage son or daughter, or helping your mother die in peace are commonplace life events. These ties between us, as human beings, define the very texture of our personal lives. This chapter explores U.S. women's experiences of home, family, and making a living. We argue that personal and economic security are fundamental to women's well-being and to the security of our families and communities.

Intimate Relationships, Home, and Family

Personal and family relationships are central to individual development, as noted in Chapter 3. In the family, we learn about socially defined **gender roles**: what it means to be a daughter, brother, wife, or father, and what is expected of us. We learn about our cultural heritage, ideas of right and wrong, practical aspects of life, and how to negotiate the world outside the home. Family resources, including material possessions, emotional bonds, cultural connections, language, and status in the wider community, all contribute to our identity and sense of belonging. How parents and siblings treated us during childhood and our observation of adult relationships provide the early foundation for our own intimate relationships. Friends and family may offer rules for dating etiquette. Magazine features and advice columns coach us on how to catch a man or woman and how to keep him or her happy once we have.

Marriage and Domestic Partnership

Marriage is often thought to be an essential part of a woman's life. People may not refer to unmarried women as "old maids" or "on the shelf" as much as in the past, but there is still a stigma attached to being single in many cultural groups if a woman remains unmarried after a certain age. At the micro- and meso- levels marriage provides recognition, validation, and a sense of personal empowerment.

301

Grandmothers play an important role in passing on family history and cultural traditions.

It is the conventional and respected way of publicly affirming one's commitment to a partner and being supported in this commitment by family and friends as well as societal institutions. Also, there are macro-level material benefits in terms of taxes, health insurance, pension rights, ease of inheritance, and immigration status. In 1997, the U.S. General Accounting Office found no less than 1,049 federal laws in which benefits, rights, and privileges were contingent on marital status.

The ideal of a committed partnership seems to hold across sexual orientation—with many women looking for Mr. or Ms. Right—even though fewer U.S. women are marrying these days, and those who do are marrying later. Many women appear to be less interested in what sociologist Judith Stacey (1996) called "the patriarchal bargain." Jaclyn Geller (2001, Chapter 1) detailed the history of marriage as the institutionalization of inequalities between women and men. She viewed marriage as the paradigmatic institution that makes heterosexuality appear natural and "normal," and as a heterosexual woman she vehemently opposed it. Some lesbians, bisexual and transgender women, gay men, and heterosexual couples who have chosen not to marry have campaigned for the benefits of

"domestic partnership"—to be covered by a partner's health insurance, for example or to be able to draw the partner's pension if she or he dies. And increasing numbers of state and local governments, academic institutions, and major corporations offer domestic partnerships, though many firms still do not.

Demands for gay marriage in the interest of equal treatment for LGBT and heterosexual couples provide an interesting counterweight to feminist critiques of marriage as inherently patriarchal. Advocates argue that mixed-sex marriage laws are discriminatory and unjust, denying same-sex couples the many legal, economic, and social benefits that privilege heterosexual marriages. In Reading 36, Paula Ettelbrick argues against marriage for gay men and lesbians and contends that the goals of gay liberation must be much broader than the right to marry. Political science professor Mary Shanley (2004) also questioned the institution of marriage that same-sex couples seek to enter. She proposed various arrangements that would offer personal freedoms as well as supports for committed relationships—gay or straight—such as civil unions, universal care-giving partnerships, "nonconjugal relationships of economic and emotional interdependency," and polyamorous relationships

(Shanley 2004, p. 112). Not all lesbians or gay men want to marry; some have argued that "legalizing gay and lesbian marriage will not 'dismantle the legal structure of gender in every marriage'" (e.g., Polikoff 1993).

Belgium, Canada, the Netherlands, and Spain all allow gay marriage, and many other nations allow same-sex civil unions. In 2004, Massachusetts became the first state in the U.S. to legalize gay marriage (see Gozemba, Kahn, and Humphries 2007), with California following in May 2008. Connecticut, New Hampshire, Oregon, Vermont, and Washington allow same-sex partnerships; twenty-six states have passed constitutional amendments restricting marriage to a union between a man and a woman. In 1996 the U.S. Congress passed the Defense of Marriage Act that excludes same-sex couples from receiving federal protections and rights of marriage. Even if some states allow gay marriage, the Defense of Marriage Act blocks gay partners from receiving federal benefits.

That same year, Congress also passed the Personal Responsibility and Work Opportunity Reconciliation Act, which provides for Temporary Assistance to Needy Families (TANF) and which declared that "marriage is the foundation of a successful society" (quoted in Mink 2002). Given that two-parent families have higher incomes than single parents, apparently the framers of this policy reasoned that marriage would lift single mothers out of poverty. Accordingly, the federal government has provided millions of dollars to states for marriage promotion programs. TANF eligibility rules "can include mandatory enrollment in marriage classes and couples counseling" (Mink 2002). Additional incentives can be paid to mothers who marry. Moreover, states that reduce births to unmarried women without resorting to abortions can receive "illegitimacy bonuses." Mothers receiving welfare are subject to severe bureaucratic intrusion into their personal lives and their ability to make decisions for themselves and their families. They are required to disclose the identity of their child's father and to pursue a child support order against him, regardless of his circumstances or whether they want the men in their lives (see Kilty and Segal 2006).

The Ideal Nuclear Family

In much public debate, the nuclear family is touted as the centerpiece of American life. This idealized family, immortalized in the 1950s TV show, *Leave It to Beaver*, consists of a heterosexual couple, married for life, with two or three children. The father is the provider while the wife/mother spends her days running the home. This family is regularly portrayed in ads for food, cars, cleaning products, or life insurance, which rely on our recognizing—if not identifying with—this symbol of togetherness and care. Conservative politicians invoke this family in their

rhetoric on "traditional family values." Although this mythic family makes up only a small proportion of U.S. families today, the prevalence of this ideal has a strong ideological impact. It serves both to mask and delegitimize the diversity of family forms and gives no hint of family violence or the conflicts inherent in juggling paid work and caring for children. Sociologist Stephanie Coontz (1997) argued that nostalgia for the so-called traditional family is based on myths. Specifically, the post–World War II white, middle-class family was the product of a particular set of circumstances that were short-lived:

> Fewer women remained childless during the 1950s than in any decade since the late nineteenth century. The timing and spacing of children became far more compressed so that young mothers were likely to have two or more children in diapers at once. . . . the educational gap between middle-class women and men increased, while job segregation for working men and women seems to have peaked. . . . The result was that family life and gender roles became much more predictable, orderly, and settled in the 1950s than they were either twenty years earlier or would be twenty years later. *(p. 36)*

This ideal family, with its rigid gender-based division of labor, always applied more to white families than to families of color, and to middle-class families of all racial/ethnic groups. Cultural critic and writer bell hooks (1984a) argued that many women of color and working-class white women have always had to work outside the home. Moreover, families take many forms. Children are raised in multigenerational families, by divorced parents who have remarried, by adoptive parents, single parents (usually mothers), or grandparents. Eleanor Palo Stoller and Rose Campbell Gibson (1994) noted that "when children are orphaned, when parents are ill or at work, or biological mothers are too young to care for their children alone, other women take on child care, sometimes temporarily, sometimes permanently" (p. 162). Sociologist Barbara Omolade (1986) described strong female-centered networks linking African American families in which single mothers support one another in creating stable homes for their children. She challenged official characterization of this kind of family as "dysfunctional." Anthropologist Leith Mullings (1997) noted that women-headed households are an international phenomenon, shaped by global as well

Pam and Lisa Liberty-Bibbens with McKenzie and Brennan

as local factors like the movement of jobs from former industrialized nations to countries of the global South. An increasing number of families are split between countries through work, migration, or the dislocations of war (as discussed in Chapter 8).

Lesbians, gay men, and transgender people have established intimate partnerships and extensive networks of friends who function as families. According to the Family Pride Coalition, an umbrella organization for gay and lesbian family support groups, at least 2 million gay and lesbian parents in the United Sates are raising between 3 million and 5 million children, most of them from earlier heterosexual marriages. The National Adoption Information Clearinghouse, a federal agency, put the figures much higher (Lowy 1999). In Reading 37, writer and teacher Ann Filemyr describes "loving across the boundary," as a white woman in partnership with Essie, a woman of color; their family included Essie's son and her grandmother. Filemyr makes insightful connections between their personal experiences; other people's reactions to their caring, multiracial household; and the impacts of racism and heterosexism on their lives.

Defining Women's Work

All women in the world work. They are farmers, artists, craft workers, factory workers, businesswomen, maids, baby-sitters, engineers, secretaries, soldiers, teachers, nurses, sex workers, journalists, bus drivers, lawyers, therapists, waitpersons, prison guards, doctors, cashiers, airline pilots, executives, sales staff, professors, carpenters, dishwashers, filmmakers, mail carriers, dancers, homemakers, mothers, and wives. Many find satisfaction and challenge, even enjoyment in their work; for others it is a necessary drudgery.

Anthropologist Leith Mullings (1997) distinguished four kinds of women's work in the United States: paid work in the formal sector; reproductive work including housework and raising children, as well as paid work taking care of children, elderly people, or those who are sick; work in the informal sector, which may be paid under the table or in favors returned; and transformational work, volunteering in community organizations, professional groups, and clubs of all kinds.

According to dictionary definitions, the English word *economy* comes from two Greek words: *oikos,* meaning "house," and *nemo,* meaning "to manage." Thus, economy can be understood as managing the affairs of the household, and beyond that, the wider society. Modern-day economists make a distinction between "productive" and "unproductive" work, which is not implied in this original definition. So-called productive work—what Gloria Albrecht calls market-oriented work (Reading 38)—is done for money; unpaid work is defined as unproductive to the economy (Waring 1988). On this analysis a woman who spends her day making meals for her family, changing diapers, doing laundry, finding schoolbooks and football shoes, packing school lunches, making beds, washing the kitchen floor, waiting for the TV repair person, taking the toddler to the park, walking the dog, meeting older children after school, going to the doctor's office with her mother, planning a celebration for her mother-in-law's birthday, making calls for an upcoming PTA (Parent-Teacher Association) meeting, changing the cat litter, paying bills, or balancing her checkbook is not involved in productive work.

One effect of the **gendered division of labor** in the home has been a similar distinction between women's and men's waged work. In the past forty years, some women have broken into professions and blue-collar jobs that were once the preserve of men, but most women work in day-care centers, elder-care facilities, garment factories, food processing, retail stores, restaurants, laundries, and

Debby Tewa, solar electrician for the Hopi Foundation.

other women's homes. Even professional work is gendered: elementary school teachers, social workers, nurses, and health-care workers tend to be women. There is an emphasis on caring for and serving others in many women's jobs; some may also require being on display and meeting dominant beauty standards.

Natasha Josefowitz listed stereotypical ways supervisors and co-workers judge women and men as workers, dating from the late 1970s (see Box). Thirty years later, gendered double standards still apply. Women senior executives are advised: Take charge but don't get angry; Be nice but not too nice; Speak up but don't talk too much (Belkin, 2007). Journalist Lisa Belkin (2007) reported that women who focus on work relationships and express concern for other people's perspectives are considered less competent. However, if they behave in ways that are seen

He Works, She Works, but What Different Impressions They Make

The family picture is on HIS desk:
Ah, a solid, responsible family man.

HIS desk is cluttered:
He's obviously a hard worker and busy man.

HE'S talking with coworkers:
He must be discussing the latest deal.

HE'S not at his desk:
He must be at a meeting.

HE'S having lunch with the boss:
He's on his way up.

HE'S getting married.
He'll get more settled.

HE'S having a baby:
He'll need a raise.

HE'S leaving for a better job:
He recognizes a good opportunity.

HE'S aggressive.

HE'S careful.

HE loses his temper.

HE'S depressed.

HE follows through.

HE'S firm.

HE makes wise judgments.

HE is a man of the world.

HE isn't afraid to say what he thinks.

HE exercises authority.

HE'S discreet.

HE'S a stern taskmaster.

The family picture is on HER desk:
Hmm, her family will come before her career.

HER desk is cluttered:
She's obviously a disorganized scatterbrain.

SHE'S talking with coworkers:
She must be gossiping.

SHE'S not at her desk:
She must be in the ladies' room.

SHE'S having lunch with the boss:
They must be having an affair.

SHE'S getting married:
She'll get pregnant and leave.

SHE'S having a baby:
She'll cost the company in maternity benefits.

SHE'S leaving for a better job:
Women are undependable.

SHE'S pushy.

SHE'S picky.

SHE'S bitchy.

SHE'S moody.

SHE doesn't know when to quit.

SHE'S stubborn.

SHE reveals her prejudices.

SHE'S been around.

SHE'S opinionated.

SHE'S tyrannical.

SHE'S secretive.

SHE'S difficult to work for.

Source: Natasha Josefowitz, 1980.

as more "male"—such as acting assertively, focusing on the task, or displaying ambition—they are seen as "too tough" and "unfeminine." Researchers argue that awareness of such bias in perceptions and evaluations of women's work is an essential step toward reframing these perceptions and eliminating bias.

Balancing Home and Work

Despite the influx of relatively inexpensive consumer goods into the United States, especially clothing and electronic items from "global factories" around the world, it has become much harder for many U.S. families to make ends meet. Several factors have made it imperative that more and more women are income earners. Rents and housing payments, medical insurance, and the cost of college tuition, for example, have increased. Much manufacturing, such as car assembly work, which was relatively well paid and largely done by men, has been automated or moved out of the country, and, on average, men's wages have fallen. More than 75 percent of divorced mothers with custody of their children are employed. Many fathers (more than 50 percent by some estimates) pay little or no child support. In 2004, 60 percent of all U.S. women were in the paid workforce (U.S. Department of Labor Women's Bureau 2005). Juggling the conflicting demands of paid work and family responsibilities is a defining life experience for many women (see, e.g., Barnett and Rivers 1996; Douglas and Michaels 2004; Folbre 2001; Hochschild 1989, 1997; Stone 2007; Williams 2000).

Adrienne Rich (1986b) argued that it is not motherhood itself that is oppressive to women but the way our society constructs motherhood. She advocated thinking of pregnancy and childbirth, a short-term condition, quite separately from child rearing, a much longer term responsibility. Psychologists Nancy Chodorow (1978) and Dorothy Dinnerstein (1976) both advocated shared parenting as essential to undermining rigid gender roles under which many men are cut off, practically and emotionally, from the organic and emotional concerns of children, thus, dissociated from life processes. Two decades later, sociologists Pepper Schwartz (1994) and Barbara Risman (1998) made similar arguments. A contemporary media image of a young mother with immaculate hair and makeup, wearing a chic business suit, briefcase in one hand and toddler in the other, may define an ideal for some young women. But it also sets a standard that is virtually unattainable without causing the mother to come apart at the seams—especially if she does not have a generous budget for convenience foods, restaurant meals, work clothes, dry cleaning, hairdressing, and child care. Many women find joy and affirmation in motherhood, despite contradictions and challenges (see, e.g., Abbey and O'Reilly 1998; Blakely 1994; Gore and Lavendar 2001; Hays 1996; Jetter, Orlech, and Taylor 1997; Kline 1997; Meyers 2001). In the early 1990s, writer and editor Ariel Gore started the upbeat zine, *Hip Mama,* as her senior project in college; highlights from the first ten years provide hilarious and heart-wrenching essays "from the cutting edge of parenting" (Gore

2004; also see Sarah 2006). Women's studies professor Andrea O'Reilly writes about feminism and empowered mothering (2006).

The Second Shift

Most women employed outside the home still carry the main responsibility for housework and raising children, what sociologist Arlie Hochschild (1989) called a **second shift.** Although this is particularly acute for single parents, many women living with men also do more housework and child care than their partners (see Bianchi et al. 2002; Mainardi 1992). Undoubtedly, this pattern varies among couples and perhaps also at different stages in their lives. A 2003 time-use survey undertaken by the U.S. Department of Labor showed that "the average working woman spends more than twice as much time on household chores and child care than the average working man." In households where men are present, housework tends to be divided along gendered lines. Men take care of the car, do yard work and household repairs, and take out the trash. Women usually have major responsibility for food shopping, meals, laundry, and child care—tasks that have to be done every day and which take more time and emotional energy than "men's" tasks. However, Suzanne Bianchi and Colleagues (2002) reported significant changes in the gender division of household labor since the 1960s, with men taking on more responsibility as a result of wives devoting more time to waged work, and "changed attitudes about what is expected, reasonable and fair for men to contribute to the maintenance of their home" (p. 184). With so many women in waged work, families rely more on take-out meals; they do less cleaning, and far less ironing than in the past. Affluent households hire other women as cleaners, nannies, maids, and caregivers for elderly relatives—which helps to free upper-middle-class women from the stress and time crunch of balancing home and work.

Caring for Children

Child care is a major family expense. For some women who want to do waged work, the cost of child care is prohibitive, even if they can find suitable child-care providers. Federal and state governments, employers, and labor unions offer some assistance to parents and child-care providers in the form of tax credits, grants to child-care programs,

BABY BLUES

on-site care, provisions for child care as part of a benefits package, flextime, and leave for family emergencies. Taken overall these provisions are woefully inadequate. It is particularly difficult to obtain child care for the hours before and after school and during school vacations. Head Start programs, for example, which offer preschool education to low-income children, are usually available only for a half day and only one in seven children eligible for federal child-care assistance gets this support (Children's Defense Fund 2005).

Overall, 70 percent of U.S. mothers with children under 18 years of age are doing waged work. Black mothers are more likely to be in the paid workforce than white or Latina mothers. In 2006, 19 percent of families were maintained solely by women, with a wide disparity based on race: 46 percent of Black families, 23 percent of Latino families, 14 percent of white families, and 12 percent of Asian families were maintained by women (Cromartie 2007).

Another aspect of this issue is the working conditions of child-care workers, women who work in their own homes, other women's homes, or at child-care centers and preschool programs. Although parents may struggle to afford child care, child-care workers are poorly paid and many have no health insurance or retirement benefits. On average, child-care workers earn less than animal caretakers, parking lot attendants, or garbage collectors. Several scholars point to a "crisis of care" in the United States and other wealthy nations. High numbers of women from countries of the global South, including the Dominican Republic, El Salvador, and the Philippines, for example, are caring for children, elderly people, and

sick people in the United States (see Cancian et al. 2002; Ehrenreich and Hochschild 2003; Hondagneu-Sotelo 2001; Parreñas 2001; Tuominen 2003; Uttal 2002). In Reading 44, Rhacel Salazar Parreñas analyzes the situation of children in the Philippines whose parents are working overseas. Feminist ethicist Gloria Albrecht (2004, p. 139), a professor of religious studies, argued: "how a society organizes the necessary work of social reproduction (access to basic needs, the care of dependent persons, nurturance and socialization) in relationship to the work of material production is a matter of social justice." The data presented in this chapter attest to what Albrecht (2004, p. 139) called the "unjust pattern that this relationship takes in the United States." She calls attention to the fact that time has been redefined by a global market system at work twenty-four hours a day, seven days a week, and the implications this has for family life (Reading 38).

Flextime, Part-Time Work, Home Working, and the Mommy Track

The labor market is structured so that the best positions are reserved

> for those adults who have someone on call to handle the life needs of an always-available worker. Economist Randy Albelda calls these positions "jobs with wives."   *(Withorn 1999, p. 9)*

Many women need flexible work schedules so that they can look after children or aging parents. This may mean working jobs that allow some flextime, seeking part-time work, or working at home. Ann Withorn (1999), a professor of social policy, noted that part-time work is often a "devil's bargain," with low wages and no benefits, but 70 percent of part-time workers are women. Home working by telecommuting is touted for professional and corporate workers as a means to greater personal freedom and no stressful commute. For garment workers and child-care providers, who account for the majority of home workers, the pay is poor and there are no benefits. Garment workers on piecework rates put in long hours; they are also isolated from one another, which makes it much more difficult to improve their pay through collective bargaining (Albrecht 2004).

Another possible solution, put forward in the 1980s, was that firms adopt a "mommy track." Professional women, such as attorneys, who wanted career advancement comparable to that of men either would not have children or would somehow combine family life with working long hours, attending out-of-town meetings, taking little vacation time, and generally doing whatever the job demanded. Otherwise, they could "opt" for the mommy track and be recompensed accordingly. Law professor and legal scholar Joan Williams (2000) argued that professional women knew full well that this would mean being marginalized in their careers, and all but a few avoided the mommy track like the plague. Journalist and writer Ann Crittenden decided to leave her job at the *New York Times* for parenting and later calculated what this cost her in lost earnings (Reading 39). She estimated that, in her case, this discriminatory "mommy tax" amounted to "between $600,000 and $700,000, not counting the loss of a pension." She argues for new laws and policies to prevent discrimination against people with caregiving responsibilities as a way to improve a mother's lifetime earnings.

Families, Work, and Income

Before industrialization, home and work were not separated as happened under the factory system. Housework, which included growing vegetables and tending orchards and livestock, was directly productive in a home-based economy. In addition, women produced goods for home use and for sale— dyed cloth, finished garments, lace, netting, rope, furniture, and medicinal remedies. Adults could integrate child care with their daily tasks, activities in which children also participated. Indeed, childhood was a different phenomenon, with an emphasis on learning skills and responsibilities as part of a community, rather than on play or institutionalized schooling.

Economist Teresa Amott (1993) identified several economic systems in the United States before wage labor developed:

> family farming, the *hacienda* system of large ranches in the Southwest, plantation slavery in the South, the economies of different Native American nations, and the early capitalist industrial enterprises. *(p. 15)*

Teresa Amott and Julie Matthaei (1996) noted that race and ethnicity were central in determining who was assigned to each of these labor systems; gender and class determined what work people performed.

> In a very real sense, the lives of any one group of women have been dependent upon the lives of others. . . . Unfortunately, the ties which have joined us have rarely been mutual, equal, or cooperative; instead, our interdependence has been characterized by domination and exploitation. American Indian women's lost lands were the basis for European immigrant wealth. The domestic work of African American and poor European immigrant women, along with the labors of their husbands, sons, and daughters in factories, underwrote the lavish lifestyles of upper-class European American women. The riches enjoyed by the wives and children of Mexican American *hacienda* owners were created by the poverty of displaced and landless Indians and Chicanas. And U.S. political and economic domination of the Philippines and Puerto Rico allowed U.S. women to maintain higher standards of living, and encouraged the migration of impoverished Filipina and Puerto Rican women to U.S. shores. *(p. 3)*

This basic pattern of inequality and interdependence among women continues to this day, with ever more women involved in the global economic system, differentially placed, as workers and consumers (see Chapter 8).

Women's Wages: Gender, Race, Class, Disability, and Education

The best-paid jobs for U.S. women are as lawyers, physicians, engineers, computer analysts, and scientists, but many more women earn the minimum wage or not much more. According to the National Committee on Pay Equity (2007), on average, women who worked full time year round earned 77 cents for every dollar that men earned in 2006. For African American women the comparable figure was 70 cents, and 58 cents for Latinas (Murphy and Graff 2005; Pozner 2006). This gap has slowly narrowed since passage of the Equal Pay Act in 1963 when women workers, on average, earned 59 cents for men's dollar. This is partly because women's wages have improved but more because men's wages have fallen. The U.S. Census Bureau reported the following average annual earnings for full-time workers in 2006, with lower wage ratios for women, presumably because some women were not working year-round:

	Earnings ($)	Wage Ratio
All women	32,649	
White women	35,151	73.5
Black women	30,398	63.6
Latinas	24,738	51.7
All men	42,210	
White men	47,814	100
Black men	34,480	72.1
Latinos	27,490	57.5

Source: U.S. Census Bureau, *Current Population Survey, 2007. Annual Social and Economic Supplement.*

Education   The more education a woman has the more likely she is to be employed and the higher her earnings; college graduates earn nearly twice as much as high-school graduates, for example. Veronica Chambers emphasizes the importance of education for professional Black women (Reading 41); others emphasize education as a passport to greater opportunity (see, e.g., Dorothy Allison, Reading 13). This close relationship between educational attainment and higher wage levels is expected to continue in many jobs, often linked to developments in computer technology. Workers need to keep skills up to date, which requires access to opportunities to keep learning and a willingness to do so, as mentioned by Gloria Albrecht (Reading 38). Sociologist Johanna Shih compares the experiences of highly educated U.S.-born white women with those of Asian immigrant men and women engineers in Silicon Valley's hi-tech industry. She found that, by job-hopping and using their **social capital** based on ethnic and industry networks, these workers were able to mediate mechanisms of discrimination and contest organizational bias in this labor market (Reading 40).

A lack of educational qualifications is a key obstacle for many women, particularly those on welfare who need greater educational opportunity if they are to acquire meaningful work at sustainable wage levels. Women receiving welfare used to be able to attend college, and many were able to move out of poverty as a result, including Congresswoman Barbara Lee who graduated from Mills College (Oakland). The 1996 Personal Responsibility and Work Opportunity Reconciliation Act only allows short-term vocational training or "job readiness education" as work activity, not preparation for professional work. Several scholars and activists advocate for changes in this policy and for more academic institutions, community agencies, and foundations to provide academic, financial, and social support necessary for poor women's education (see, e.g., Adair 2004; Adair and Dahlberg 2003; Martinson and Strawn 2003; Marx 2002).

Women with disabilities generally have lower educational attainment than non-disabled women, which makes it difficult for many to find work. They may have missed a lot of school as children or may not have been provided with relevant special education programs. Vocational schools and rehabilitation programs for women who suffer a disability after completing their education tend to channel then into dependent roles within the family or to low-paying "women's work." Added to these limitations are the prejudices and ignorance of employers and coworkers and the ableist attitudes of mainstream culture. Women with disabilities may also have to make "significant and sometimes costly special arrangements" (Mudrick 1988, p. 246) to maintain their employment, such as transportation or extra help at home. Lisa Schur (2004), professor of labor studies, argued that high schools and colleges need to assist young women with disabilities in making the transition from school to work; advocates and self-help organizations should offer employment counseling to help women with disabilities find jobs; and women with disabilities need to be actively involved in developing programs to improve their job prospects.

Even with a college education, however, and equivalent work experience and skills, professional women are far less likely than men to get to the top of their professions or corporations. They are halted by unseen structural barriers, such as men's negative attitudes to senior women and perceptions of their leadership abilities and styles, their motivation, training, and skills. This barrier has been called a **glass ceiling.** Women can see what the senior positions in their company look like, but few women reach them (Morrison et al. 1992). In 2007, women were roughly 16 percent of corporate officers at Fortune 500 companies (Catalyst 2007). A related term, **sticky floor,** describes the structural limitations for women in low-paid, low-status jobs who cannot move up.

Organized Labor and Collective Action Workers usually make significant gains in wage levels and working conditions when they are members of a labor union. In 2007, women union members in full-time work earned 25 percent more than non-union women, and the differential was higher for African Americans (27 percent) and Latinas (33 percent) (U.S. Department of Labor, Bureau of Labor Statistics 2007). Union workers are also more likely to have health and pension benefits. Currently, women are joining unions at a faster rate than men, particularly hotel workers (HERE), service employees (SEIU), garment workers (UNITE), public employees (AFSCME), and communication workers (CWA). The United Farm Workers of America, founded by Cesar Chavez and Dolores Huerta, has pressured growers to sign union contracts to improve the pay and working conditions of its members, many of whom are migrant workers and immigrants to the United States whose health is routinely compromised by exposure to chemical pesticides.

The majority of women in the U.S. workforce are not union members. This is partly due to the decline of unions nationally in recent decades. Also, many women work in jobs that are hard to unionize, such as retailing or the fast-food business, where they are scattered at separate locations. The nation's largest employer, Wal-Mart, is strongly anti-union. Wal-Mart's stringent cost cutting—of prices, wages, and operating costs—has become legendary and is redefining corporate practice, summed up in the phrase: the "Wal-Mart-ing" of the economy. Increasingly Wal-Mart's competitors are adopting its model, making Wal-Mart not just an industry leader but an economy leader.

Working and Poor Organized labor calls attention to low wages. According to *Business Week* (2004) 63 percent of U.S. families below the official **poverty level** had one or more workers. In 2008, the federal poverty guideline was $17,600 a year for a family of three (U.S. Department of Health and Human Services 2008). Some advocates have campaigned for a "living wage" that reflects regional variations in the cost of living. Others use a "self-sufficiency standard" that "provides a measure of income needed to live at a basic level . . . without public or private assistance" (Women's Foundation 2002). More women than men make up the working poor, and women of color are more than twice as likely to be poor compared with white women. Policy researchers Peiyun She and Gina A. Livermore (2006) found that a majority of those in the working-age population who experience long-term poverty have a disability.

In public debate, poor people are usually assumed to be on welfare, masking the reality of life for many working poor people. Some people with very low incomes are working minimum-wage jobs; others work part time or seasonally. They may be involved in the informal economy as maids, baby-sitters, or gardeners, for example, doing home work for the garment trade, fixing cars, carrying and selling small amounts of drugs, getting money for sex, selling roses at off ramps. Still others work in sweatshops, discussed in the next chapter, which are also unregulated in terms of wages, hours, and conditions of work.

Income Supports: Pensions, Disability Payments, and Welfare For women who cannot work because of illness, age, or disability, and for those who are made redundant or who cannot leave their children, there is a complex patchwork of income-support measures and means-tested allowances provided by federal and state governments and

Economic Inequalities

- Between 1979 and 2005, the top 5 percent of U.S. families saw their real incomes increase by 81 percent. Over the same period, the lowest-income fifth saw their real incomes decline by 1 percent (U.S. Census Bureau 2006).

- The richest 1 percent of U.S. households owns 34 percent of the nation's private wealth, more than the combined wealth of the bottom 90 percent. The top 1 percent owns 37 percent of all corporate stock (Economic Policy Institute, *State of Working America 2006–07*, Table 5.1 & Fig. 5F).

- In 2006, the number of poor children under age 18 in the United Sates was 12.8 million (17.4 percent) or one child in six. For white children this was one in ten; for Latinos one in four; for Black children one in three (Children's Defense Fund 2008).

- The average CEO of a large U.S. company made roughly $10.8 million in 2006, or 364 times that of U.S. full-time and part-time workers, who made an average of $29,544 (Institute for Policy Studies and United for a Fair Economy, cited by Sahadi 2007).

- Top U.S. executives make about twice the pay of their counterparts in France, Germany, and Britain, and about four times that of Japanese and Korean corporate heads (Lucian Bebchuk, testimony before the House Financial Services Committee, March 8, 2007).

- In 2005, the top 10 percent of U.S. citizens received a total income equal to that of the poorest 2.2 billion people in the rest of the world (*Dollars and Sense* 2005, p. 14).

- The richest 20 percent of people worldwide consume 86 percent of everything that is sold for private consumption; the poorest 20 percent consume 1 percent of it. On average, a person in the U.S. buys 53 times as many products as someone in China, and consumes the same amount of resources as 35 people in India (Sierra Club cited by Oliver 2007).

private pension plans. Pensions are based on wage levels while the person was working and on the number of years in paid work. Women's pensions are significantly lower than those paid to men since, generally, women earn less than men, are more likely to work part time, and may move in and out of the workforce as they balance paid work with family responsibilities. Women make up 60 percent of Social Security pension beneficiaries. At least 40 percent of U.S. women aged 65 and over, and 60 percent of African American women and Latinas in this age group, are entirely dependent on these government pensions (Bethel 2005). Social Security benefits are guaranteed for life, which is important because of women's longer life span. Income support for people with disabilities is designed with the needs of working men in mind. As a result, fewer women with disabilities can claim Social Security Disability Insurance (DI) and must rely on the Supplemental Security Income program (SSI), which is subject to a means test for eligibility and greater bureaucratic scrutiny and is often demeaning.

Social Security and Social Security Disability Insurance allow individuals, considered to be "deserving," to draw from an insurance fund to which they have contributed during their working lives. Welfare payments, by contrast, are based on the concept of public assistance. In 1996, the federal government ended entitlements to assistance dating back to the 1935 Social Security Act and replaced them with block grants to states for Temporary Assistance for Needy Families (TANF). TANF is a work-based program with lifetime limits and an emphasis on marriage incentive programs, as mentioned earlier. Women are required to spend up to 40 hours a week in "work experience." States have flexibility to provide other benefits, such as health care, transportation, or child-care subsidies to cushion the transition from welfare to work. For employers, TANF has the advantage that—in place of wages—it is paid out of state funds.

Myths about welfare recipients abound in public discourse, stigmatizing those who need to rely on assistance and serving to erode the possibility of empathy by those who are better off for those who are poor. Women's Studies professor Gwendolyn Mink (2002) argued that single mothers are poor because their family care-giving work is not remunerated. Several welfare-rights organizations have redefined welfare as caregivers' income, including the Women's Committee of One Hundred, Every Mother Is a Working Mother Network, Quality Homecare Coalition in Los Angeles, and Welfare Warriors in Wisconsin (also see Nadasen 2005).

TANF rates are too low to live on, which means that recipients have to supplement their welfare checks in some way. Not reporting additional income to the welfare office may make women liable for criminal charges for perjury or fraud. Law professor Kaaryn Gustafson (2005) argued that poor families are penalized through "completely inadequate levels of support, through public shaming, and through intrusive administrative forays into their personal lives that none but the truly needy would tolerate" (p. 2). Law enforcement officials are allowed access to information contained in aid recipients' files. No one who is wanted by law enforcement officials for a felony or for violating the terms of parole or probation—which may be as little as missing a meeting—can receive any government benefits. Anyone found guilty of a drug-related felony is banned from receiving benefits for life. States can require drug tests, fingerprints, and photographs for those applying for benefits. Women who give birth to a child while on welfare are denied a financial increase despite the fact that they have another child to care for.

It is important to note here that many people in this society receive some kind of government support, be it through income-tax deductions for homeowners, medical benefits for those in the military, tax breaks for corporations, agricultural subsidies to farmers, government bailouts to savings and loans companies, or government funding for high-tech military-related research conducted by universities and private firms. This is often not mentioned in discussions of welfare, but it should be.

Feminist Approaches to Marriage, Family, and Women's Work

Many feminist scholars, policy makers, and activists have argued for shared parental responsibility for child care, payment of child support, and redrawing the terms of divorce so that both post-divorce households would have the same standard of living. Feminists have campaigned for good-quality child care subsidized by government and employers, on-site at big workplaces, and they have organized community child-care facilities and informal networks of parents who share child care. Although some of these efforts have been successful, there is still a great deal to be done if women are not to be penalized for having children.

Although policy makers and politicians often declare that children are the nation's future and greatest resource, parents are given little practical help in caring for them. Over fifteen years ago, the editors of *Mothering* magazine pulled no punches when they asked:

> Why is the United States the only industrial democracy in the world that provides no universal pre- or postnatal care, no universal health coverage; . . . has no national standards for child care; makes no provision to encourage at-home care in the early years of life; . . . has no explicit family policies such as child allowances and housing subsidies for all families?
>
> *(Quoted in Brennan, Winklepleck, and MacNee 1994, p. 424)*

Most European countries have instituted family policies (see Box). In the United States, family policy is still an unfamiliar term, and the few policies that support families, like welfare, unemployment assistance, and tax relief, are inadequate and uncoordinated.

Feminist researchers and policy analysts have long challenged inequities in pay between women and men. These inequities may be partly explained by differences in education, qualifications, and work experience, but part of this wage gap is simply attributable to gender. This has led to detailed discussion of the **comparable worth** of women's jobs when considered next to men's jobs requiring comparable levels of skill and knowledge. Advocates for comparable worth have urged employers to evaluate employees without regard to gender, race, or class, but in terms of knowledge and skills needed to perform the job, mental demands or decision making involved in the job, accountability or the degree of supervision involved, and working conditions, such as how physically safe the job is. Such calculations reveal many discrepancies in current rates of pay between women's work and men's work.

In addition to advocating for comparable worth in wage rates, feminist advocates have encouraged women to return to school to improve their educational qualifications, opposed sexual

Pro-family Policies for the United States

- Provide financial support for full-time child care.

- Create more jobs and stop assuming job-holders have a wife at home.

- Raise wages to a "living wage" level. Mandate equal pay for comparable work.

- Provide financial support to cover housing and health costs—the two major "family budget busters."

- Expand the safety net—through unemployment insurance, temporary disability insurance, or welfare payments.

- Provide affordable and accessible education and training for all.

- Promote community-based economic development.

- Introduce a fairer tax structure that benefits people in the lower tax brackets.

Source: Albelda and Tilly 1997, pp. 147–64.

harassment on the job, exposed the dangers of occupational injury and the health hazards of toxic work environments, and argued for women in senior positions in all fields. Examples of such organizations include the Institute for Women's Policy Research (Washington, D.C.), the National Organization for Women (Washington, D.C.), and 9 to 5 National Organization of Working Women (with chapters in several states). The "Take Our Daughters to Work Day" initiated by the Ms. Foundation exposes girls to jobs they may know little about and provides role models for them. Several organizations have worked to open up opportunities for women to enter well-paying trades such as carpentry and construction, including Hard Hatted Women (Cleveland, Ohio), Women in the Building Trades (Jamaica Plain, Mass.), Minnesota Women in the Trades, and Northern New England Tradeswomen (Essex Junction, Vt.). Many local groups help women to start small businesses, utilizing existing skills. The Women's Bean Project (Denver), Tierra Wools

(Los Ojos, N. Mex.), and the Navaho Weaving Project (Kykotsmovi, Ariz.) are group projects that promote self-sufficiency.

Feminist researchers have also pointed to the **feminization of poverty** (Abramovitz 1996; Dujon and Withorn 1996; Sidel 1996). The two poorest groups in the United States are women raising children alone and women over sixty-five living alone. *Poverty* is a complex term with economic, emotional, and cultural dimensions. One may be materially well-off but emotionally impoverished, for example, and vice versa. Poverty also needs to be thought about in the context of costs—for housing, food, transportation, health care, child care, and clothes needed to go to work—hence the value of a self-sufficiency standard. Poverty is also linked to social expectations of this materialist culture. Many poor children in the United States clamor for name-brand clothing, for example, in response to high-pressure advertising campaigns.

Understanding Class Inequalities

Class is a key concept in any discussion of work, income, and economic security. For Marxist theorists, a person's class is defined in relation to economic production—whether she or he must work for a living. The vast majority of people in the United States are workers, but most describe themselves as "middle class," a loose term that includes a very wide range of incomes, occupations, life situations, and levels of personal and economic security. As noted in Chapter 3, some people raised in a working-class community may have a middle-class education and occupation later in life and a somewhat mixed class identity as a result. In much U.S. public debate, class is more of a psychological concept rather than an economic one. Poverty is often explained as resulting from low self-esteem, laziness, or dysfunctional families, as we pointed out in Chapter 2. In Reading 13, Dorothy Allison notes the power of class stratification, racism, and prejudice whereby

> some people begin to believe that the security of their families and community depends on the oppression of others. . . . It is a belief that dominates this culture: it is what made the poor whites of the South so determinedly racist and the middle class so contemptuous of the poor.

In Reading 41, writer Veronica Chambers reports on the contradictions and challenges Black women professionals face as they balance the benefits of college education and material success with a sense of responsibility to family networks and the wider Black community.

In public discourse on inequality, race is invariably emphasized at the expense of class. As mentioned in Chapter 5, government studies and census data are analyzed for racial differences, which gives the impression that race is much more significant than class. Intersectional analysis makes class one facet of a person's or group's social location along with many others. In practice, race and class overlap, but greater attention to economic sources of inequality may provide a basis for alliances between people of color and white people along class lines. There is currently no politically accepted way for most people to make a livelihood except by working for it, and in this society work, in addition to being an economic necessity, also carries a strong moral overtone. Note that this principle is not applied to those among the very rich who live on unearned income from corporate profits, investments, trust funds, or rents.

Toward a Redefinition of Home and Work

On the basis of the data we cite in this chapter, we argue that elevating the ideal of the nuclear, two-parent family is a major contradiction in contemporary U.S. society. Regardless of its form, we believe that the family should

be able to care for family members emotionally and materially;

promote egalitarian relationships among the adults, who should not abuse their power over children;

share parenting between women and men so that it is not the province of either gender;

do away with a gendered division of labor;

teach children nonsexist, antiracist, and anticlassist attitudes and behavior and the values of caring and connectedness to others; and

pass on cultural heritage.

Economic security is also an important aspect of well-being. Low educational attainment, low wages, having children, and divorce all work against women's economic security, as do macro-level economic trends. If current trends continue, many young people in the United States—especially young people of color—will never be in regular, full-time employment in their lives. Changes in the economy, which include the continued impact of globalization on the availability of work and wage rates in the United States, force us to confront some fundamental contradictions that affect women's work and the way work is thought about generally:

What should count as work?

Does the distinction between "productive" and "unproductive" work make sense?

How should work be rewarded?

How should those without paid work, many of them women, be supported?

How can the current inequalities between haves and have-nots be justified?

Is the work ethic useful?

Is materialism the mark of success?

Years ago, pushed by the impact of the Great Depression of the 1930s, social commentators saw great potential for human development promised by (then) new technologies like telephones, Dictaphones, and washing machines, by means of which people could provide for their needs in a relatively short time each week. The British philosopher Bertrand Russell (1935), for example, favored such "idleness" as an opportunity to become more fully human, to develop oneself in many dimensions of life. Recognizing that this could not happen if material living standards had to keep rising, he put forth a modest notion of what people "need." He also understood that these kinds of changes would require political imagination and will if people were to be freed from unnecessary work. Two generations later, the pace and scale of production of consumer goods and services is unprecedented, and time has been redefined in market terms so that "all time and everyone's time is money" (Albrecht 2004, p. 129), which has put increasing strain on U.S. families. We discuss further implications of this reality in the following chapter, and again in Chapter 11, where we consider the environmental effects of current consumption patterns, and the ecofeminist argument that a sustainable future must be geared to biological rather than market time.

◆◆◆

Questions for Reflection

As you read and discuss this chapter, think about these questions:

1. What do you expect/hope for in an intimate relationship?

2. How do you define family? Whom do you consider your family?

3. What is at stake with regard to same-sex marriage? Where do you stand on this issue? Why?

4. What changes are necessary to involve more men in parenting? Look at the micro-, meso-, macro-, and global levels of analysis.

5. What have you learned through working? About yourself? About other people's lives? About the wider society? How did you learn it? Who were your teachers?

6. What have you wanted to change in your work situations? What would it take to make these changes? What recourse do you have as a worker to improve your conditions of work?

7. How do you justify differences in pay?

◆◆◆

Finding Out More on the Web

1. Find out more about the Defense of Marriage Act (1996). What assumptions is it based on?

2. Find out about family policies in western European countries (especially Denmark, Germany, the Netherlands, and Sweden). Why do you think these countries provide better supports for families than the United States?

3. Consult these Web sites for more information on the wage gap, poverty levels, and family and welfare policies in your state and nationally:

   9 to 5 National Association of Working Women: www.9to5.org

   Children's Defense Fund: www.childrensdefense.org

   Coalition of Labor Union Women: www.cluw.org

   Institute for Women's Policy Research: www.iwpr.org

   Moms Rising: www.momsrising.org

   National Jobs for All Coalition: www.njfac.org

   Economic Success Clearinghouse: www.financeproject.org

4. Compare the very low amounts the government spends on welfare with other federal expenditures. See:

   National Priorities Project: www.nationalpriorities.org

   War Resisters League: www.warresisters.org/pages/piechart.htm

Taking Action

1. Talk with your peers about your non-negotiables in a personal relationship. What are you willing to compromise on, if anything? Why?

2. Draw up a detailed budget of your needs, expenses, income, and savings. What did you learn by doing this?

3. Talk with your mother or grandmother (or women of their ages) about their experiences of marriage, parenting, family, and work. What opportunities did they have? What choices did they make? What similarities and differences do you notice between your own life and theirs at the same age?

4. Look critically at how magazines, ads, movies, and TV shows portray women in relationships and family and as workers. What is being promoted through these media?

THIRTY-SIX

Since When Is Marriage a Path to Liberation? (1989)

Paula Ettelbrick

Lawyer, educator, and civil rights activist **Paula L. Ettelbrick** is the Executive Director of the International Gay and Lesbian Human Rights Commission. She has written and lectured extensively on the civil and constitutional rights of lesbians and gay men.

"Marriage is a great institution, if you like living in institutions," according to a bit of T-shirt philosophy I saw recently. Certainly, marriage is an institution. It is one of the most venerable, impenetrable institutions in modern society. Marriage provides the ultimate form of acceptance for personal intimate relationships in our society, and gives those who marry an insider status of the most powerful kind.

Steeped in a patriarchal system that looks to ownership, property, and dominance of men over women as its basis, the institution of marriage long has been the focus of radical feminist revulsion. Marriage defines certain relationships as more valid than all others. Lesbian and gay relationships, being neither legally sanctioned or commingled by blood, are always at the bottom of the heap of social acceptance and importance.

Given the imprimatur of social and personal approval which marriage provides, it is not surprising that some lesbians and gay men among us would look to legal marriage for self-affirmation. After all, those who marry can be instantaneously transformed from "outsiders" to "insiders," and we have a desperate need to become insiders.

It could make us feel OK about ourselves, perhaps even relieve some of the internalized homophobia that we all know so well. Society will then celebrate the birth of our children and mourn the death of our spouses. It would be easier to get health insurance for our spouses, family memberships to the local museum, and a right to inherit our spouse's cherished collection of lesbian mystery novels even if she failed to draft a will. Never again would she have to go to a family reunion and debate about the correct term for introducing our lover/partner/significant other to Aunt Flora. Everything would be quite easy and very nice.

So why does this unlikely event so deeply disturb me? For two major reasons. First, marriage will not liberate us as lesbians and gay men. In fact, it will constrain us, make us more invisible, force our assimilation into the mainstream, and undermine the goals of gay liberation. Second, attaining the right to marry will not transform our society from one that makes narrow, but dramatic, distinctions between those who are married and those who are not married to one that respects and encourages choice of relationships and family diversity. Marriage runs counter to two of the primary goals of the lesbian and gay movement: the affirmation of gay identity and culture; and the validation of many forms of relationships.

When analyzed from the standpoint of civil rights, certainly lesbians and gay men should have a right to marry. But obtaining a right does not always result in justice. White male firefighters in Birmingham, Alabama have been fighting for their "rights" to retain their jobs by overturning the city's affirmative action guidelines. If their "rights" prevail, the courts will have failed in rendering justice. The "right" fought for by the white male firefighters, as well as those who advocate strongly for the "rights" to legal marriage for gay people, will result, at best, in limited or narrowed "justice" for those closest to power at the expense of those who have been historically marginalized.

The fight for justice has as its goal the realignment of power imbalances among individuals and classes of people in society. A pure "rights" analysis often fails to incorporate a broader understanding of the underlying inequities that operate to deny justice to a fuller range of people and groups. In setting our priorities as a community, we must combine the concept of both rights and justice. At this point in time, making legal marriage for lesbian and gay couples a priority would set an agenda of gaining rights for a few, but would do nothing to correct the power imbalances between those who are married (whether gay or straight) and those who are not. Thus, justice would not be gained.

Justice for gay men and lesbians will be achieved only when we are accepted and supported in this society *despite* our differences from the dominant culture and the choices we make regarding our relationships. Being queer is more than setting up house, sleeping with a person of the same gender, and seeking state approval for doing so. It is an identity, a culture with many variations. It is a way of dealing with the world by diminishing the constraints of gender roles which have for so long kept women and gay people oppressed and invisible. Being queer means pushing the parameters of sex, sexuality, and family, and in the process transforming the very fabric of society. Gay liberation is inexorably linked to women's liberation. Each is essential to the other.

The moment we argue, as some among us insist on doing, that we should be treated as equals because we are really just like married couples and hold the same values to be true, we undermine the very purpose of our movement and begin the dangerous process of silencing our different voices. As a lesbian, I am fundamentally different from non-lesbian women. That's the point. Marriage, as it exists today, is antithetical to my liberation as a lesbian and as a woman because it mainstreams my life and voice. I do not want to be known as "Mrs. Attached-To-Somebody-Else." Nor do I want to give the state the power to regulate my primary relationship.

Yet, the concept of equality in our legal system does not support differences, it only supports sameness. The very standard for equal protection is that people who are similarly situated must be treated equally. To make an argument for equal protection, we will be required to claim that gay and lesbian relationships are the same as straight relationships. To gain the right, we must compare ourselves to married couples. The law looks to the insiders as the norm, regardless of how flawed or unjust their institutions, and requires that those seeking the law's equal protection situate themselves in a similar posture to those who are already protected. In arguing for the right to legal marriage, lesbians and gay men would be forced to claim that we are just like heterosexual couples, have the same goals and purposes, and vow to structure our lives similarly. The law provides no room to argue that we are different, but are nonetheless entitled to equal protection.

The thought of emphasizing our sameness to married heterosexuals in order to obtain this "right" terrifies me. It rips away the very heart and soul of what I believe it is to be a lesbian in this world. It robs me of the opportunity to make a difference. We end up mimicking all that is bad about the institution of marriage in our effort to appear to be the same as straight couples.

By looking to our sameness and de-emphasizing our differences, we don't even place ourselves in a position of power that would allow us to transform marriage from an institution that emphasizes property and state regulation of relationships to an institution which recognizes one of many types of valid and respected relationships. Until the constitution is interpreted to respect and encourage differences, pursuing the legalization of same-sex marriage would be leading our movement into a trap; we would be demanding access to the very institution which, in its current form, would undermine *our* movement to recognize many different kinds of relationships. We would be perpetuating the elevation of married relationships and of "couples" in general, and further eclipsing other relationships of choice.

Ironically, gay marriage, instead of liberating gay sex and sexuality, would further outlaw all gay and lesbian sex which is not performed in a marital context. Just as sexually active non-married women face stigma and double standards around sex and sexual activity, so too would non-married gay people. The only legitimate gay sex would be that which is cloaked in and regulated by marriage. Its legitimacy would stem not from an acceptance of gay sexuality, but because the Supreme Court and society in general fiercely protect the privacy of marital relationships. Lesbians and gay men who did not seek the state's stamp of approval would clearly face increased sexual oppression.

Undoubtedly, whether we admit it or not, we all need to be accepted by the broader society. That motivation fuels our work to eliminate discrimination in the workplace and elsewhere, fight for custody of our children, create our own families, and so on. The growing discussion about the right to marry may be explained in part by this need for acceptance. Those closer to the norm or to power in this country are more likely to see marriage as a principle of freedom and equality. Those who are more acceptable to the mainstream because of race, gender, and economic status are more likely to want the right to marry. It is the final acceptance, the ultimate affirmation of identity.

On the other hand, more marginal members of the lesbian and gay community (women, people of color, working class, and poor) are less likely to see marriage as having relevance to our struggles for survival. After all, what good is the affirmation of our relationships (that is, marital relationships) if we are rejected as women, black, or working class?

The path to acceptance is much more complicated for many of us. For instance, if we choose legal marriage, we may enjoy the right to add our spouse to our health insurance policy at work, since most employment policies are defined by one's marital status, not family relationship. However, that choice assumes that we have a job *and* that our

employer provides us with health benefits. For women, particularly women of color who tend to occupy the low-paying jobs that do not provide healthcare benefits at all, it will not matter one bit if they are able to marry their women partners. The opportunity to marry will neither get them the health benefits nor transform them from outsider to insider.

Of course, a white man who marries another white man who has a full-time job with benefits will certainly be able to share in those benefits and overcome the only obstacle left to full societal assimilation—the goal of many in his class. In other words, gay marriage will not topple the system that allows only the privileged few to obtain decent health care. Nor will it close the privilege gap between those who are married and those who are not.

Marriage creates a two-tier system that allows the state to regulate relationships. It has become a facile mechanism for employers to dole out benefits, for businesses to provide special deals and incentives, and for the law to make distinctions in distributing meager public funds. None of these entities bothers to consider the relationship among people; the love, respect, and need to protect that exists among all kinds of family members. Rather, a simple certificate of the state, regardless of whether the spouses love, respect, or even see each other on a regular basis, dominates and is supported. None of this dynamic will change if gay men and lesbians are given the option of marriage.

Gay marriage will not help us address the systemic abuses inherent in a society that does not provide decent health care to all of its citizens, a right that should not depend on whether the individual (1) has sufficient resources to afford health care or health insurance, (2) is working and receives health insurance as part of compensation, or (3) is married to a partner who is working and has health coverage which is extended to spouses. It will not address the underlying unfairness that allows businesses to provide discounted services or goods to families and couples—who are defined to include straight, married people and their children, but not domestic partners.

Nor will it address the pain and anguish of an unmarried lesbian who receives word of her partner's accident, rushes to the hospital and is prohibited from entering the intensive ward or obtaining information about her condition solely because she is not a spouse or family member. Likewise, marriage will not help the gay victim of domestic violence who, because he chose not to marry, finds no protection under the law to keep his violent lover away.

If the laws change tomorrow and lesbians and gay men were allowed to marry, where would we find the incentive to continue the progressive movement we have started that is pushing for societal and legal recognition of all kinds of family relationships? To create other options and alternatives? To find a place in the law for the elderly couple who, for companionship and economic reasons, live together but do not marry? To recognize the right of a long-time, but unmarried, gay partner to stay in his rent-controlled apartment after the death of his lover, the only named tenant on the lease? To recognize the family relationship of the lesbian couple and the two gay men who are jointly sharing child-raising responsibilities? To get the law to acknowledge that we may have more than one relationship worthy of legal protection?

Marriage for lesbians and gay men still will not provide a real choice unless we continue the work our community has begun to spread the privilege around to other relationships. We must first break the tradition of piling benefits and privileges on to those who are married, while ignoring the real life needs of those who are not. Only when we de-institutionalize marriage and bridge the economic and privilege gap between the married and the unmarried will each of us

have a true choice. Otherwise, our choice not to marry will continue to lack legal protection and societal respect.

The lesbian and gay community has laid the groundwork for revolutionizing society's views of family. The domestic partnership movement has been an important part of this progress insofar as it validates non-marital relationships. Because it is not limited to sexual or romantic relationships, domestic partnership provides an important opportunity for many who are not related by blood or marriage to claim certain minimal protections.

It is crucial, though, that we avoid the pitfall of framing the push for legal recognition of domestic partners (those who share a primary residence and financial responsibilities for each other) as a stepping stone to marriage. We must keep our eyes on the goals of providing true alternatives to marriage and of radically reordering society's views of family.

The goals of lesbian and gay liberation must simply be broader than the right to marry. Gay and lesbian marriages may minimally transform the institution of marriage by diluting its traditional patriarchal dynamic, but they will not transform society. They will not demolish the two-tier system of the "haves" and the "have-nots." We must not fool ourselves into believing that marriage will make it acceptable to be gay or lesbian. We will be liberated only when we are respected and accepted for our differences and the diversity we provide to this society. Marriage is not a path to that liberation.

THIRTY-SEVEN

Loving Across the Boundary (1995)

Ann Filemyr

Writer, teacher, and artist **Ann Filemyr** is the Dean of the Center for Arts and Cultural Studies at the Institute of American Indian Arts in Santa Fe, New Mexico. Her poems have been twice nominated for a Pushcart Prize in Poetry. Her current research is on ecology, feminism, and the intersection of nature, culture, and identity.

Nubian, our puppy, scratches and whines at the bedroom door. Essie sits bolt upright in bed crying out: "What time is it?" Groggy, I squint at the clock, "Almost seven—"

"Granny was supposed to wake us up at six!"

"Maybe she forgot—" I hustle into my bathrobe at the insistent scratching on the door, "I've got to let Nubi out—"

"Granny never forgets to wake us," Essie mutters under her breath as she scrambles out of the tangled sheets.

I race down the stairs, "Granny! GRANNY!"

I find her body on the cold kitchen floor, but she is gone. I can feel her spirit lifting up and out into the golden morning light filtering through the grand old maples that surround the farmhouse. Despite the utter peace in the room, I panic.

"Essie! Essie Carol!" I scream up the stairs to my partner.

Granny's breath is gone, but her body remains. A line from the book *Daughters of Copper Woman* circles through my mind, *"And she left her bag of bones on the beach. . . ."* Sun crowds the kitchen and the golden maple leaves gleam in October light. Essie flies barefoot across cold linoleum, cradling Granny in her arms, the first sob rising in our throats. . . .

Granny had made her bed that morning. She was dressed and ready for her Monday morning walk. But instead of the familiar stroll, Granny had traveled where we could not follow. We shared a long, sad look. Essie's face crumpled in pain. . . .

In the hospital emergency room we wept, our heads bent over Granny's body. Stroking back her wavy black hair (even at 79 her hair had not turned white) we sighed and pleaded. Two years earlier in ICU the doctors had told us she was gone. Her heart would not hold a steady beat. They pointed to the monitor above her unconscious body to show us the erratic yellow line, the uneven blip across the screen. Only the machines kept her breathing. We said no. It was her second heart failure in three months that winter of 1991, but we had plans for our shared lives—Granny, Essie and me. We were anticipating spring. . . .

Granny regained her strength that time. But that was March 1991 and this was October 1993. The doctor nodded to us and spoke with her strong Pakistani accent, "She looks happy. She had a long life. She would die one day." Then she left us alone, but the nurse on duty asked us a million questions about "the body"—about funeral arrangements—about donating organs—about contacting "the family"—we could not respond.

We *are* the family—an elder with her two granddaughters. This is our story of love, though now we are the body of women weeping. Granny was ours to care for, we had taken her into our daily lives because we loved her, and now she is sleeping, and we cannot wake her.

Skin color marked Essie as the one who belonged to Granny. The nurse nodded and smiled at me, "It's so nice of you to stand by your friend at a time like this."

Where else would I be? Granny was my grandmother, too. She loved me like no one else in my life: she loved me fiercely. She knew I had stepped across the line in North America which is drawn across the center of our faces to keep us separate—to keep the great grandchildren of slavekeepers from the great grandchildren of slaves. When she met me as Essie's "friend" twelve years earlier, she had watched me closely, but then she accepted me into her household and into her family. As the elder, her acceptance meant acceptance. She recognized my love for her granddaughter and would say to me, "People talk, but you hold your head up. You walk tall. The Lord sees what you're doing for my granddaughter, how you help her with her son. He sees how you stick together and help each other out." As far as Granny was concerned it was the *quality of our caring* not our sexuality that mattered. In this she was far wiser than most.

For the past three years we had lived together in Yellow Springs, sharing meals and dishes. She would sometimes pull out her old photo albums and tell her stories, laughing at memories of wild times out dancing with her friends in the juke joint or riding horses with her cousin on her father's ranch or traveling cross country in the rig with her husband and his magical black cat when he worked as a truckdriver. Rich, warm memories, and I would sip my coffee and imagine her days and nights. What sustained her? Love—no doubt. Love and greens and cornbread—good food. That's what she craved. And the kitchen was her favorite room next to her bedroom.

She had been raised in the fields and farms of the south. When I was deciding whether or not to take the job in Ohio, Granny was part of the decision-making process. Moving back to the country after four decades in the city felt like coming full circle to her. She said she wanted to come with us. And it was here in Ohio that Granny and I had the luxury of time together to make our own relationship to each other. She would talk to me about "the things white folks do—" how they tend to "put themselves first like they better than other folks—" how foolish they looked on the TV talk shows "tellin' all their business—" or how much she had enjoyed some of the white friends she and her husband once had.

She spoke her mind without embarrassment or apology. I listened. She had survived the jim crow laws of the south. She had survived segregation and desegregation. She kept a gun under her pillow she called "Ole Betsy" in case someone would try to break in or "mess with her." Granny paid attention to details as a matter of survival. She prided herself on the subtle things she observed in watching how people acted and how they treated one another. She would interpret everything: tone of voice, a simple gesture, the hunch of someone's shoulders. She always knew when someone felt sad or tired. You didn't have to say anything. She comforted. She sympathized. She was extremely skilled at making others feel loved, feel noticed, feel good about themselves. But if Essie had not been in my life it is doubtful that I would have ever known this remarkable woman, her namesake, Essie (Granny) Hall.

When I moved in with Essie in 1982, my nomadic tendencies were pulling at me, urging me to convince Essie that it was a perfect time for us to relocate to another city. I had lived in Milwaukee for two and a half years, for me that was long enough. I'd found a new love, an important someone in my life. It seemed like the perfect time to move on with my new partner. But Essie's life was described and defined by different currents. She had roots. She had family. She told me, "I will be here as long as Granny needs me." I was shocked. My feet carried me freely; I fought against family attachments. Was this difference cultural? Personal? Both? But now I have grown to respect and appreciate this way of being, this way of belonging. Is it a middle-class white cultural tendency to break free, to move on, to move up, to move out? Certainly the bonds of family and of commitment were far stronger for Essie than for me. One of the greatest gifts in my life has been that she shared her son and grandmother with me.

I wanted to tell the emergency room nurse all of this. I held Essie Carol in my arms as she cried. I wanted to scream, "Here we are, can't you see us? Lovers and partners holding each other in a time of crisis—What do you need for proof?". . .

Sunday mornings Granny listened to gospel preachers on her old radio, rocking and clapping to the music. When we weren't home, she'd get up and dance through the rooms of the house, tears flowing freely as she sang out loud. We'd catch her and tease her. Once Granny hung a plastic Jesus in the bathroom; he had his hands folded in prayer and flowing blonde locks thrown back over his shoulders. Essie groaned, "A white man on the bathroom wall!" She took it down and tried to explain to Granny everybody did not worship the same way she did.

We were not only a multiracial household, but one that held different spiritual beliefs. Essie followed a path she had first been introduced to by Granny's mother, her great-grandmother, Caroline Kelly Wright, affectionately known as Ma. Ma wore her hair in long braids and had been called "the little Indian" most of her life. She had married a freed African slave, but she herself was Blackfoot. Ma smoked a pipe and prayed to the sun. Essie remembered as a child the whole family would gather in Ma's bedroom facing East. The dawn's pale light would begin to appear through the open window only a few city blocks from the enormous freshwater ocean called Lake Michigan. Everyone listened as Ma prayed aloud over the family, telling all secrets, opening up all stories, praying to Creator to provide answers, to help guide them to find their purpose in life and hold to it, to be strong. Everything was said on these Sunday mornings and tears fell as Ma blew her smoke toward the light of the rising sun.

Ma had delivered Essie during a wild January blizzard. Ma was a midwife, herbalist, neighborhood dream interpreter, the community sage and soothsayer. If the term had been as popular then as it is now, Ma would have been honored as a shaman. Essie remembers the Baptist preacher visiting their house and saying to Ma, "I'll pray for you, Miz Caroline," and Ma responding, "You can't pray for me, but I can pray for you."

At the age of eight after a preacher had singled her out to stand up and read the Bible as a punishment for something she hadn't even done, Essie told her great-grandmother that she did not want to attend church anymore. Ma agreed. So Essie had little patience for Granny's Christianity. She was especially offended by refrains such as the "Good Master" and would try to point out to Granny how Black Christian faith was a result of slavery, the product of an enforced cultural genocide. Essie would try to "educate" Granny about the ways slaves were punished for trying to hold on to older beliefs, such as the care and worship of the ancestors or relating to land and nature as an expression of the Sacred. Of course this didn't work, and I would try to negotiate peace settlements between the two generations, between the two Essies, between the centuries, between the ancestors and the youth. Neither one of them really listened to me. I would take the younger Essie aside and tell her, "Leave Granny alone. You're not going to change her." And the younger Essie would retort, "But she's trying to change me!". . .

[A]t the funeral the man in the black suit did his best. He tried to save us. He opened the doors of the church and urged us to enter. He forgot about the corpse in the casket behind him, and he called the stray flock home. White men and Black men held each other in the back row. White women held Black women in the front row. And in between were all shades of brown and pink, young and old, from four-week-old Jade, the last baby Granny had blessed, to Mrs. Cooper, Granny's phone buddy. They had spoken every day on the phone for a year. Granny adored "Cooper" as she called her, though they had never met in person. Here we sat in rows before an open casket: all colors, ages, sexualities, brought together by a mutual love for an exceptional person. As some of Essie's family members called out urgently, encouraging the preacher with *Amen* and *Yes, Lord* others ignored the eulogy, attending to their own prayers.

At the funeral we sat side by side in the front row in dark blue dresses. Essie's sister and son sat on the other side of her. We wept and held each other's hands. If Granny loved us for who we were, then we weren't going to hide our feelings here. Certainly there were disapproving glances from some family members, but not all. During the decade we lived in Milwaukee, we had shared childcare and holidays, made it through illnesses and the deaths of other beloved family members—what else qualifies someone as family? Yet despite this, I knew there were those who despised my presence for what I represented was the alien. I was the lesbian, and I was white. For some my presence was an inexcusable reminder of Essie's betrayal. She had chosen to be different, and I was the visible reminder of her difference. For some this was a mockery of all they valued, but she did not belong to them so they could control her identity. Granny knew this, and Granny loved her because she had the strength to be herself.

My family is liberal Democrat, yet my mother once said to me that my choice to love other women would make my life more difficult. She wanted to discourage me from considering it. She said, *I would tell you the same thing if you told me you loved a Black man.* I was then nineteen. It struck me as curious that to love someone of the same sex was to violate the same taboo as to love someone across the color line. In the end I chose to do both. Does this make me a rebel? Certainly if my attraction was based initially on the outlaw quality of it, that thrill would not have been enough to sustain the trauma of crossing the color line in order to share love. The rebellious young woman that I may have been could not make sense of the other story, the story of her darker-skinned sister, without a willingness to question everything I had been raised to accept as "normal," without an active analysis of the politics of racial subjugation and institutionalized white male supremacy. And without personal determination, courage, a refusal to be shamed, a sheer stubbornness based on our assumption that our lives held unquestionable worth as women, as women together, as women of different colors together, despite the position of the dominant culture—and even at times the position of the women's community—to diminish and deny us, we would not have been able to make a life together.

I have participated in and been witness to a side of American life that I would never have glimpsed if Essie had not been my partner. The peculiar and systematic practice of racial division in this country has been brought into sharp focus through many painful but revealing experiences. By sharing our lives, our daily survival, our dreams and aspirations, I have been widened and deepened. It has made me much more conscious of the privileges of being white in a society rigidly structured by the artificiality of "race."

One of the first awakenings came near the beginning of our relationship when her son came home with a note from the school librarian that said, "Your overdue books will cost 45 cents in fines. Irresponsible handling of school property can lead to problems later including prison." I was shocked—threatening a nine-year-old boy with prison because of overdue books? I couldn't imagine what that librarian was thinking. Did she send these letters home with little white boys and girls?

I wanted to call the school and confront her. Essie stopped me by telling me a number of equally horrifying stories about this school so we agreed to take Michael out.

We decided that Michael, who had been staying with Granny and Daddy Son and attending the school near their home during the week, should move in full-time with us. Essie worked first shift at the hospital, and I was a graduate student at the university. She left for work at 6 A.M., and I caught the North Avenue bus at 9:30. I would be able to help Michael get to school before I left for the day. We decided to enroll Michael in our neighborhood school.

The neighborhood we lived in was one of the few mixed neighborhoods in the city. It formed a border between the rundown urban center and the suburbs on the west side. The neighborhood school was across an invisible boundary, a line I did not see but would grow to understand. Somewhere between our house and this building, a distance of approximately six blocks, was a color line. A whites-only-no-Blacks-need-apply distinctly drawn and doggedly patrolled. We scheduled a visit with the principal, and when both of us appeared the next morning, we observed a curious reaction. Though polite, she was absolutely flustered. She could not determine who to direct her comments to. She looked from Essie's closely cropped black hair to my long loose wavy hair, from cream skin to chocolate skin, and stammered, "Who—who is the mother?"

"I am," said Essie.

"I'm sorry," was the reply. "We have already reached our quota of Black students in this school."

"Quota? We live in this neighborhood," I replied. "This is not a question of bussing a child in. He lives here."

She peered at the form we had filled out with our address on it. Then responded coldly, "We are full."

"That's ridiculous," I objected.

"Are you telling me that my child is not welcome to attend the fourth grade in your school?" Essie asked icily.

"We simply don't have room."

Essie stood up and walked out of the room without another word. I wanted to scream. I wanted to force the principal to change her mind, her politics, her preoccupation with the boundaries defined by color. I sat there staring at her. She refused to meet my eyes. I said slowly, "This will be reported to the Superintendent and to the school board," and walked out following Essie to the car.

We scheduled a meeting at the school administration to register a formal complaint and find Michael another school. I was furious. We were taxpayers. These are public schools. How can he be refused entrance? How can a child be denied because of some quota determined by an administrator somewhere? I was naive in matters of race.

I would have to say all white people are naive about the persistence of the color line. We prefer naiveté—in fact we insist on it. If we, as white people, actually faced the entrenched injustice of our socioeconomic system and our cultural arrogance, we might suffer tears, we might suffer the enormous weight of history, we might face the iceberg of guilt which is the underside of privilege. We might begin to glimpse our losses, our estrangement from others, our intense fear as the result of a social system that places us in the precarious position of the top. We might be moved to call out and protest the cruelty that passes for normal behavior in our daily lives, in our cities, and on our streets. . . .

Nothing in my life, my education, my reading, my upbringing, prepared me to straddle the color-line with Essie under the Reagan years in Milwaukee, a post-industrial city suffering economic decline and social collapse. The rigidly entrenched division of social power by race and the enormously draining limitations we faced on a daily basis began to tear at the fabric of our daily survival. I began to experience a kind of rage that left me feeling as sharp as broken glass. I was in this inner state when we finally arrived in the long quiet corridors of the central administration of Milwaukee Public Schools.

We were ushered into an office with a man in a suit sitting behind a desk. He could have been an insurance salesman, a loan officer, or any other briefcase-carrying decision-making tall white man in a position of power and control. We were two women of small build and modest dress, but we were carrying the larger presence—righteous anger. We sat down. I leaned across his desk and challenged him to explain to us why Michael had been refused admittance into the school of our choice. He back-pedaled. He avoided. He dodged. Essie suddenly said, "I am finished. I am taking my child out of school," and stood up.

I snapped my notebook closed, signaling the end of the conversation. The man had never asked me who I was. Did he assume I was a social worker? a family member? a friend? a lawyer? a journalist? Had it even crossed his mind that he was looking at a pair of lovers, at a family, at the two acting parents of this child? For the first time he looked worried, "I am sure we can find an appropriate school for your son. Tell me his interests. We'll place him in one of our specialty schools."

We hesitated.

"I'll personally handle his registration," he seemed to be pleading with us. He looked from Essie to me wondering who his appeal would reach first.

We settled on a school with a square of wild prairie, the environmental science specialty school. It was a half hour bus ride from our home. Michael liked the school, but we did not feel completely victorious. How could we? Though we had challenged the system, these policies and practices which place undue emphasis on the color of a child's skin had not been changed. The school system simply accommodated us, perhaps fearing our potential to cause widespread dissent by giving voice to the intense dissatisfaction of the African American community with the public school system. We compromised—perhaps exhausted by the constant fight against feeling invisible and powerless. It was not just that Michael was Black. It was also that his family consisted of a white woman and a Black woman, and regardless of our commitment to him, we were not perceived as a valid family unit though we functioned as a family. . . .

It is heartbreaking to raise an African American boy in the U.S. From an early age he is taught that others fear him. He is taught that he is less than. He is taught that his future is defined by certain streets in certain neighborhoods, or that the only way out is through musical or athletic achievement. Michael played basketball and football. He wrote raps and performed them to the punctuated beat of electronic keyboards and drum machines. When it was fashionable, he would breakdance on the living-room floor. He had a few good years in school, but by and large school did not satisfy his quest for knowledge, nor did it provide him with creative avenues for self-expression. . . .

There were so many things I could not do for Michael. I could not clothe him in transparent skin to prevent him from being prejudged by color-conscious teachers who would label him inferior. I could not surround him with safety on the street corner where he waited for his school bus. One grisly morning in November he came home shaking. He and a small boy had been shot at while waiting on a familiar corner two blocks from the house. It was 7:30 A.M. While he was preparing to attend school, boys his age were shooting guns out of car windows hoping to kill somebody in order to get into a gang so they could make money.

On that gray morning, the capitalist notion of success as the acquisition of material wealth appeared for what it is: an absolute perversion of human dignity. Yet white American culture persists in holding material affluence as the highest symbol of achievement. The way this plays out in the lives of people of color and those who love them can be summed up in one word: cruelty. We suffer for a lack of basic resources because of the hoarding, the feverish consumerism, and the complete lack of concern by people who have more than they will ever possibly need. Fashion crimes, ganking [gang violence targeting rival gang members or other young people], children beating and killing other children to acquire the stingy symbols of status in a society devoid of real meaning—this is what happens on the city streets of the richest nation in the world.

I could not keep Michael from the bullets. I could not move him out into the suburbs where another kind of violence would confront him daily, those who would question his presence and limit his right to move freely from one house to the next. I could not close his eyes to the terror he would see in his friends when death visited among them. I could not hold him against the rage he held inside. A rage that thundered through the house pulverizing everything in its path, terrifying me, tearing at his mother.

What could we say to him about how to live on the mean streets of a bully nation? We did not live on those same streets even though we lived in the same neighborhood. His experience, my experience, his mother's experience—we walked out of the front door into three separate worlds. Worlds we did not define or control except in how we would respond to them. Michael watched the hours I spent typing, writing, scratching out, rewriting. He watched the transformations his mother carried out with color on canvas, making lumps of cold clay into warm red altar bowls with her naked hands. He saw that we took our pain and rage, our grinding frustration and radiant hope, and made something out of it that gave us strength. Michael is still writing, making music, performing in his own music videos. He sees himself as an artist as we see ourselves; this is the thing that has carried us through.

The Westside where we bought a home had always been a working class neighborhood where people invested in their sturdy brick and wood frame houses planting roses in their green squares of grass. The neighborhood had been built in the teens and twenties by German immigrants who took a certain pride in quality. These homes had fireplaces and stained-glass windows, beautifully crafted built-in bookshelves and beveled mirrors. Only a few generations earlier, there was safety and prosperity here. Waves of immigrants—Greek, Polish, Hasidic Jews, African Americans coming North to work in the factories, shared these streets. I can remember walking into the corner bakery and the Greek woman behind the counter asked Essie and I if we were sisters. It was possible there at that time. Blood was shared. Love between the races happened. We laughed and nodded, "Yes—yes, we're sisters." In these moments we utterly and joyfully belonged together.

My friends who lived on the Eastside of the city rarely came to visit after I moved in with Essie. It was as if I had moved to the other side of the moon. . . . I trusted white women less and less as friends because they could not be counted on when things got tough. They tended to retreat. Race issues are ugly and hard, but if white women who want to fight male supremacy can't stand up to their own fears around the issue of color and simultaneously fight white supremacy, how can they really undertake the work of women's liberation? Certainly without an analysis and willingness to deal with race, there is no depth to the commitment. It is simply a get-ahead strategy for a particular middle class white female minority. Today I feel there is a greater commitment to address issues of racism within the feminist movement, but most of the voices I hear are still women of color. . . .

White women are conditioned to stay put, even rebellious daughters who love other women rarely cross the road that divides the races. Any woman who engages in a serious relationship—as friend or family, as lover, or mother to daughter—with a woman of a different shade of skin will find this relationship demanding a deeper vulnerability than any other as long as race relationships continue to be fraught with tension. But if we settle for a divided nation, we settle for social rigidity and police brutality, we settle for ignorance and stereotypes, we settle for emptiness and fear.

I am still learning how to confront racism when I see it, how to educate my friends without alienating them, how to ask for what I need in terms of support. It has been a rare occurrence, but a joyful one, for us to find other mixed-race lesbian couples. When we begin to talk about how difficult it is, we discover certain patterns and find solace that we are not alone. But why should we suffer for being ourselves and finding ourselves in the borderless culture between races, in the undefined space where wakefulness is necessary for survival, where honest communication and self-reflection must replace the simple recipes of romance. . . .

Few of us born in the Americas can trace our bloodline with impunity. So many of our ancestors have been erased or invented as need be. I know very few family names that have not gone without at least one attempt at revision—to anglicize it—simplify it—discard the ethnic or cultural baggage of a *ski* or *stein* or other markers of race/ethnic identity. One who is raised as part of an unwanted people will shift the identity to become acceptable. Note the number of Chippewa and Menominee people in Wisconsin with French last names. One Chippewa man explained to me how in every neighborhood his family adopted another identity: Mexican when living on the Southside, French on the Eastside. Only back up on the reservation could they say aloud their true names. . . .

How many of us are of African descent? Slavery was challenged in part because of the enormous outcry against the "white slave children." Children of enslaved African women who were the result of forced sex with slavemasters ended up on the auction block. Some of these children looked just like the "free" children of "free" European-American mothers. Obviously there was a tremendous outcry resulting from the confusion that the rationale for chattel slavery was based on a strict hierarchy of skin color as the basis of privilege. How could they justify selling these children that by all appearances looked white even if the mother was a light-skinned African American slave? White men in the South parented children on both sides of the yard: women they took as wives, and women who worked the fields. The brown and pale children were half-brothers and half-sisters related by blood through the father. This simple truth was denied, and these children were taught to never consider themselves as one family. There is no doubt that many of us have relatives we never considered before. Part of my work has been beginning to claim these un-named Ancestors as family.

The day after I wrote that paragraph, I visited my parents. It was a week before Christmas, and I was planning to spend the day with my two grandmothers and my parents. . . . While in my parents' home, I asked about an old photo album that I remembered from childhood. My mother commented that it had recently surfaced from the jumble of daily life and brought it into the kitchen. Tintypes and daguerreotypes, family photographs spanning 1850–1900. Fifty years of Walkers, my mother's father's family.

That night, back in the city, stretched across the guest bed at a friend's house, I slowly turned the pages. There are my Ancestors, among the first generation here from the British Isles. Aunt Mary and Uncle Tom Walker. By pulling the photographs out and inspecting the little leather and brass book, I discovered they settled in Clinton and Seaforth, Ontario. I knew these relatives had lived in Canada, but hadn't known they lived between Lakes Huron, Erie and Ontario! All of the faces were unfamiliar, stiff, caught in frozen poses over a century ago. A few of the photographs I remembered from my childhood, especially the sad-faced child in the unusual robe with straight cropped black hair and Asian eyes. For the first time it occurred to me that this could be the face of a native child—not European at all! Who is this child? Then a particularly striking face caught my attention. A young woman gazed confidently, intently, at what? Her hair hung around her wide face and high cheekbones in thick black ringlets, her full lips barely open, her strong chin—this is a woman of African descent. Who is she to me? She wore a gold hoop earring and a checkered bow over a satin dress. With one arm resting against an uphol-stered pillow, she posed proudly. Why had I never heard of her before?. . .

No one in my family seems to know much about these faces, these people, these lives, and how they relate to us. . . . If I am supposed to be a proud daughter of the colonizing English and the migrating Irish, why can't I also be a proud daughter of the Anishinabeg or Haudenausaunee, two of the indigenous peoples of this Great Lakes region, as well as a proud daughter of the African Diaspora? In America the idea of Europe was created, as if my English Ancestors weren't trying to dominate my Irish Ancestors. Why can't we talk about our truly diverse heritages? Nothing has been passed down in my family of these darker-skinned faces in my family's picture album. Is the refusal to see ourselves as something other than Northern European based in a fearful grasping after shreds of white-skinned privilege? What do we lose if we acknowledge our connection? What do we gain?

Granny kept a photo album. The pictures were important. Some were tattered and worn out, but they mattered. They held the faces of relatives—cousins, aunts, sisters—men in fine hats and women in silk dresses looking into the camera, into the future. In the album is a small square black and white snapshot of two plump white babies seated outdoors on a stuffed armchair. The Kelly boys. Irish. Part of the family. Essie remembers her great-grandmother telling her children, grandchildren and great-grandchildren, "These are your cousins." I bet those white boys don't show the dark faces of their cousins to their kin. . . .

The tight little boxes of identity defined by our society keep the building blocks of political and economic power in place. How can we gender-bend, race-cross, nature-bond, and love ourselves in our plurality enough to rebel against the dead-ening crush of conformity? Is it a crisis of the imag-ination which prevents us from extending compassion beyond the boundaries of limited per-sonal experience to listen *and be moved to action* by stories of injustice others suffer. How can we ex-tend the boundaries of our own identities so that they include "the other"? If we have any hope for the future of life, how can we expand our sense of self to include other people as well as beings in na-ture? The structure of our society is articulated by separation and difference. How do we challenge this by living according to a sense of connection not alienation?

For us, for Essie and I, the greatest challenge has been inventing ourselves as we went along for we could not find a path to follow. Where are our foremothers? Light and Dark women who held each other's hands through childbirth and child-raising? Who stood side by side and loved each other refusing to budge despite everybody's objections? Who pooled their measly resources together to make sure there was food and heat and light enough for everyone's needs? I want to know them. I want to hear their stories. I'll tell them mine. . . .

Despite the absence of role models, we share specific Ancestors, disembodied presences gliding through our lives like a sudden breeze teasing the candle flame on the altar; secret-keepers who come under guard of moonlight, carrying apple baskets full of fresh fruit which they drop into our sleeping; we wake up before dawn with the sweet taste on our lips of good dreams and lucky numbers. We have our shared Ancestors to thank, and we are fortunate to count Granny among them.

THIRTY-EIGHT

◆◆◆

Spending Time When Time Is Money (2002)

Gloria H. Albrecht

Gloria H. Albrecht is Professor of Religious Studies and Women's Studies at University of Detroit Mercy and the author of *Hitting Home: Feminist Ethics, Women's Work, and the Betrayal of "Family Values"* and *The Character of Our Communities: Toward an Ethic of Liberation for the Church.*

We are getting less than 40 hours of work from a large number of our K.C.-based EMPLOYEES. The parking lot is sparsely used at 8 A.M.; likewise at 5 P.M. As managers—you either do not know what your EMPLOYEES are doing; or you do not CARE. . . . In either case, you have a problem and you will fix it or I will replace you. . . . NEVER in my career have I allowed a team which worked for me to think they had a 40-hour job. I have allowed YOU to create a culture which is permitting this. NO LONGER.[1]

Thus read an e-mail memo sent by a CEO to his managers. The memo went on to list six potential punishments, including the lay-off of 5 percent of the work force if managers did not succeed in getting the parking lot full at 7:30 A.M. and at 6:30 P.M. and half full on Saturdays. The memo boomeranged. After it was leaked and posted on Yahoo!, the internet exploded with derisive comments. The business community chastised the CEO for using e-mail as a managerial memo. He was criticized for the tone of the e-mail. Many derogatory comments were directed at the idea of measuring productivity by counting cars in the parking lot.

The price of the company's stock dropped 22 percent in three days. However, in this blitz of opinions, one topic was absent—the issue of time. No one argued with the amount of time devoted to work that this CEO expected.

Controlling time, and changing people's sense of time, was central to the development of capitalism. "Lose no time: Be always employ'd in something useful: cut off all unnecessary Action," wrote Benjamin Franklin.[2] Consequently, one part of capitalism's story has been the success with which employers expanded the discipline of industrial hours over their work force.

The other part has been workers' resistance to that discipline—a resistance that finally resulted after World War II in what most Americans today consider a normal workweek: the eight-hour day and the five-day week. At that time observers of the American scene celebrated the leisure time enjoyed by many Americans, accompanied as it was by rising wages and rising productivity. One expert testified to a Senate subcommittee that by the 1990s, Americans would be enjoying "either a twenty-two hour week, a six-month work year, or a standard retirement age of thirty-eight."[3] So much for experts!

In the new economy, as the value of time increases, so does the conflict over time. There is just not enough time in any one day to go around. The traditional boundaries of time have disappeared. The basic rhythms of the day—waking and sleeping—have lost their meaning. Business hours are twenty-four/seven. Every moment is awake and every moment *works*. Engineering projects subcontracted to workers in India are transmitted before dawn into the still dark and quiet offices of U.S. companies. At any moment, somewhere in the world, a stock exchange is adding and subtracting wealth from portfolios that are always open. Money whisks electronically across continents. Risk and opportunity spar in each moment. There is no rest. There is no time for rest. Time is money. In hindsight, Franklin's horse-powered life of constant industry appears leisurely.

How much time *should* workers work at market-oriented activities? What tempo *should* guide the weave of productive work and family work into a full fabric of meaningful life? Does the assessment of this e-mail change if one imagines a woman as the CEO, women as the managers, or women as the employees from whom greater market-oriented work time is being demanded? How do gender assumptions fit into the tempo of globalized work? How should they?

Time's Discipline in the New Economy

Twenty-four/Seven

Work Force Flexibility   In the new economy flexibility is the new core value. Every moment must be met with rapid, just-in-time, response. Businesses must be able to transform themselves almost instantly to meet new demands as productively as possible. Companies are frequently hiring even as they are firing in a continuous process of tailoring labor to fit the available work. Flexibility means "that work tasks and work time can be constantly adapted to changing products, processes, and markets."[4]

. . .

In the United States, . . . one aspect of the demand for flexibility has been the demise of the traditional labor contract and its replacement by the new "employability" contract. Both the Clinton and the George W. Bush administrations encouraged the concept of free agency for employees, in which companies recognize a responsibility to improve the skills of workers rather than responsibility to provide job security.[5] Now that more employees are required to sign documents acknowledging that they are "employed at will," laying off employees is no longer regarded as a mark of disloyalty or greed. It is simply the new face of business.

In the surge of layoffs that characterized dot.coms at the end of the year 2000 and into 2001, skilled employees typically received no advance notice and often no severance pay.[6] Severance pay, when offered, was often linked to employees' willingness to sign agreements relinquishing their rights to sue their employer—suits, for example, that might be based on employees' suspicions that they were singled out for layoffs because of age or race. Amazon.com offered twelve weeks of severance pay to those who signed releases and only two weeks to those who did not. In 2001, Lucent Technologies paid no severance to laid-off employees unless they signed such a release.[7] Newly laid-off workers, especially those with families, faced a difficult choice between desperately needed income and the uncertain outcome of a legal claim, no matter how valid. In the new economy the flexibility needs of business reestablish the economy's control over workers and their families by abandoning responsibility for them.

Mandatory Overtime

While flexibility results in job loss for some, it results in too many hours at work for others. Nursing strikes in Flint, Michigan, and at Nyack Hospital in New York during the winter of 2000–2001 highlighted the problem of mandatory overtime.[8] Responding both to nursing shortages and to pressure for greater economic efficiencies, hospital administrators used mandatory overtime to handle fluctuations in patient census while maintaining a lean work force. The result was nurses with increased numbers of more critically ill patients under their care being asked to work well beyond the ten hours that most studies show to be the limit for effective nursing care. In Flint and at Nyack, nurses struck against mandatory overtime that required nurses to work two eight-hour shifts, back to back. In response to similar pressures, the Massachusetts Board of Registration in Nursing issued an advisory stating that the refusal to work overtime would not be considered "patient abandonment," for which a nurse can lose her license. Of course, the life and death context of the nursing practice usually results in public support when the issue is overtime. Workers in other occupations of service or production may not get as much sympathy from a harried public.

At the height of its success in the late 1990s, Amazon.com enforced mandatory overtime work of at least ten hours a week for its second-level customer-service representatives. These tier II workers were expected to work a minimum of fifty hours a week. The work pace was to be "at Amazon time," or on "uptime," terms meaning an intense work pace with minimal interruptions and maximum efficiency. Time pressures were part of the reason for some workers' attempt to unionize these college-educated, hourly-wage earners in the new economy.[9]

The millennial year saw eighty-five thousand telephone workers strike Verizon Communications. The issues included job security, benefits, unionizing of the lower-wage employees of the new economy, and time. One employee, Patricia Egan, wanted measures that would help reduce stress and the use of forced overtime.

> We generally work from 8 in the morning until 4, but often we're forced to work until 8 at night. It wreaks havoc. People go to school and they're forced to miss classes. Many workers are single parents, and this forced overtime is a nightmare. It creates serious problems for their child care arrangements.[10]

Mindy Fried describes this singular focus on work as a "culture of overtime." Fried studied ten large corporations, all of which were participants in a national organization focused on family and work issues. One large financial services corporation has at its corporate headquarters over seven thousand employees, two-thirds of whom are women. It has a large menu of family-oriented policies. Fried was studying, as she put it, the best-case scenario.[11] Yet, Fried found that while the company provided information about its policies, it did not promote them. In subtle ways the clearer message was that in a business crisis, the best employees were those who set all else aside for the sake of the company. A daily corollary to that message was the common-sense managerial view that the more time an employee gave to the job, the more productive she was. Employees who took family leave or who resisted overtime, men or women, were rated down in merit-pay evaluations because such evaluations were based on time-oriented measures of productivity. Recent experiences with layoffs had made employees fearful. In a business climate of mergers, outsourcing, and downsizing, each feared giving any impression that might make one seem to be the more "disposable" employee.

While this company's official thirty-seven-and-one-half-hour workweek looked good on paper, in actuality, its employees worked over forty hours a week. On paper, this company's generous parental leave policy included eight weeks of *paid* maternity leave. Yet, few managers, and no male managers, had used it between 1992 and 1995. Men did not even consider taking leave at the birth of a child. Even among nonprofessional employees, the culture of overtime was so internalized that those who took some leave returned as quickly as possible to their jobs in order to prove their commitment and loyalty, and to make up the time they had lost. Long hours at work, "face time," was viewed as necessary behavior to save one's job. Fried concludes that it is the workplace culture, not the work/family policies, that determine the use of leave time for family needs. She quotes a human resources manager:

> We work all the time. Whether you're working or not, you're here all the time. We're trying to shift this, but people feel, "I'm going to lose my job if I'm not here." People are afraid to go to a reduced schedule. "If I'm not here, what will happen?"[12]

Working Longer for Less

In 1991 Juliet Schor, an economist, caused a stir by announcing that the average American worker had added 164 more hours (a month's worth of work) to the work year between 1970 and 1990. She further estimated that a quarter of all full-time workers was working forty-nine or more hours per week.[13] American workers had surpassed the workers of all other industrialized nations, even Japan, in the amount of hours per year spent in employed work.

Almost a decade later, Schor's basic thesis of an overworked American labor force, which had not gone unchallenged, received new support.[14] The Economic Policy Institute estimated that in the decade from 1990 to 2000, each family had added three more hours of work a week to their yearly total—an addition of 156 hours.[15] The International

Labor Organization, a United Nations agency, confirmed that the 1,979 hours that U.S. workers worked in 2000, on average, is almost nine full weeks more than most European workers. It is about twelve-and-one-half weeks more a year than German workers, and three-and-one-half weeks more than Japanese workers.[16] Part of this increase in market-oriented work came at the expense of vacation time, holidays, and other forms of paid leave. In the decade of the 1980s, while European workers were securing their four-week, or more, paid vacations, U.S. workers actually lost paid time off per year.

The rest of the increase came from simply putting in more hours at the job. Louis Uchitelle, citing a 1999 Labor Department survey, states that at least 19 percent of the private-sector work force is working forty-nine hours per week or more.[17] Those who work on fixed salaries, he writes, are being stretched "off-the-clock" into many more hours at the workplace for no extra pay. Additional "off the clock" hours include the uncounted time that workers spend on their laptops, cell phones, home computers, and fax machines. Employees "work" in cars, planes, and trains, not to mention homes.

Schor and others argue that families pay the cost when members spend more hours at the job with less time for personal and domestic needs—like sleeping, eating, family provisioning, and attention to children, the ill, and the aged. A 1999 report from the Council of Economic Advisors states that since 1969 U.S. parents have twenty-two hours less each week to spend at home, on average, primarily because of the shift in mothers' time from work at home to employed work.[18] A study of how parents distributed household and market labor hours between 1971 and 1991 supports this contention. On the one hand, the study clearly shows the advantage to families' time when one job generates enough income to sustain a middle-income family life. As "traditional" male-earner families aged and children grew up, the total number of hours spent in all work declined. Husbands tended to decrease the number of hours spent in market labor while increasing substantially the number of hours spent in household labor; wives generally decreased the number of hours they spent in household labor as children became adults.

On the other hand, dual-earner families, particularly those in which wives contributed more than 25 percent of the family's income over the twenty-year period, added approximately six hundred hours of market labor and reduced their household labor by about five hundred hours. According to the authors of this study, the significant decrease experienced in the real earnings of men in these families had to be offset by a significant increase in wives' earnings. Fewer hours were spent in household labor overall because, while men increased their share, it was still far less than that once contributed by women. For most families, then, the cause of increased working hours is economic. As the real wages of men have remained relatively stagnant, "having a single wage earner becomes an increasingly untenable option for most families."[19]

Delaying Retirement

Even at the end of a long life of work, company time seems to be expanding. From the 1950s until the late 1980s, American workers retired at ever-younger ages in large part because of employment-related pensions and medical coverage offered by firms that were encouraging older, more expensive employees to retire. Today, a larger percentage of people over sixty-five are still employed than at any time since 1979 (12.8 percent in 2000). Why the change? Certainly the desire of healthy people to continue working is part of the reason. In addition, the tight labor market of the late 1990s made older workers attractive once more to employers. But, economists also point to the growing numbers of workers who simply cannot afford to retire.[20] A *New York Times* poll of 1,124 adults in February 2001, in the heat of a deep market downturn, found a large majority of respondents worried about whether they were setting aside enough money for retirement. The percentage of respondents who were planning to work beyond age sixty-five increased to 20 percent (from 14 percent in 1995) with most identifying finances as the reason.[21]

In the new economy's tightening of efficiencies, retirement benefits also have been cut. In 1980, 84 percent of full-time employees working for medium and large companies were covered by defined-benefit pension plans. In 1995 that figure had dropped to 52 percent. What has increased is the use of tax-deferred savings plans, like the 401(k). While these are portable, they are financed mostly by employee contributions out of current wages and carry with them the risks of the stock market. The collapse of the Enron Corporation in 2001 revealed the risk of 401(k)s that become too heavily invested in one company—a practice often encouraged, even required, by some companies' formulas for contributions. . . .

Moreover, the employee-financed system provides a good deal less for retirement. When added to Social Security, the traditional employer-financed plans provided a retirement income at age sixty-five of about 60 percent of the typical worker's pre-retirement pay. 401(k)s added to Social Security provide a typical pension that is less than 50 percent of pre-retirement pay to people who can expect to live longer than ever before. One economist estimates that to collect 60 percent of pre-retirement pay, and to collect it through age eighty-four, today's retiree needs to work four-and-one-half more years—to age sixty-nine-and-one-half. Thus, the new retirement age is somewhere between sixty-eight and seventy years of age.[22] While it is too soon to tell whether this is the beginning of a long-range trend, the total length of one's work life may be increasing for middle- and lower-wage workers.

Producing New Workers

Michael Novak described the change in time consciousness that capitalism required, the shift from sleepy agrarian time to capitalism's always-awake time, as part of a new spirit—the spirit of democratic capitalism. He wrote approvingly:

> Under the goal of a better future time came to exert a discipline over the natural rhythms of the body and the psyche. The pace of human life seemed to quicken. Economic activities were no longer oriented merely toward survival or sufficiency but toward a kind of spiritual goal. They acquired purposiveness. The new sense of time demanded abnegations of the body and the emotions not unlike the mortifications of the monks at their monastic "hours."[23]

As capitalism once replaced the sun with the clock and disciplined workers with its bell, so in the transition to the postindustrial, flexible, global form of capitalism, time is again being restructured. Time-as-money, in an ever-faster cycle, again reshapes the lives and virtues of workers. In this new environment, flexible workers are those who are agile in time and place. They absorb the cost of efficiency

by being capable of rapid response, longer hours, shorter job tenure, interfirm and intrafirm mobility, wired networking, and constant updating of skills. Pauline Borsook describes the successful entrepreneur who thrives in this economy as a personality

> which needs little downtime, which must be narrowly focused and not prone to self-doubt, which will do all and anything to succeed, which tirelessly and compulsively must act like the greatest salesman in the world, which by definition is workaholic, which risks (and maybe devalues) family life and health. . . .[24]

For most workers, the pressure to stay long hours comes from more intense competition, the new form of job instability under the employability contract, and the new packaging of work into "projects" with tight delivery times. One IBM manager described life in the 1990s:

> You couldn't get to your e-mails during the day, so you'd do them at night. It was like you didn't have a home life. IBM gave you a computer at home. That made it easy to work. I used to pride myself on thinking, I'm not going to complain. I can take it all on. I can do anything.[25]

As most of us can testify, a deeply ingrained psychological element accompanies our increasing hours at work. As the pace of employed work speeds up so does the rest of life's activities. A routine expectation develops that all those involved in meeting our needs should speed up as well. Many admit a growing impatience with slow service, slow computers, slow fax machines, slow traffic lights, and airport delays as expectations about time speed up. According to one labor economist, "We have incorporated the longer hour into our self-image and we have come to accept that to be really successful you have to work a lot of hours."[26]

At the same time, flexible workers must also be able to receive unfazed the pink slips that are now part of the normal work experience.[27] A recent edition of the *Harvard Business Review* displays the new respectability given to the decision to lay off workers as a standard business practice—not the last resort of previous times. At issue is simply the question of how to get workers to work harder. The older answer, represented by one article, stressed employee loyalty.[28] But the new business culture accepts layoffs as a first response. In this culture workers work hard not out of loyalty but out of their own self-interest that, with the constant threat of layoffs, is finely tuned. According to one economist, "Companies are finding that they can achieve their goals by maintaining a certain level of fear in the work force that leads people to work hard."[29]

According to management consultants Laurence J. Stybel and Maryanne Peabody, the promise to employees is freedom. Workers have been freed from the limitations imposed by company loyalty. Workers are now free to think primarily about their own success, to make those choices that enhance their own personal goals and develop their individualized portfolio of skills. Restraints of loyalty, of ties to a company, are replaced by commitment to one's self and one's success in achieving greater and greater employability. They write: "Do not allow yourself to develop the view that you are indispensable to your company or that company is family."[30] In his book *Only the Paranoid Survive,* Andrew Grove, CEO of Intel in the 1990s, agrees: "The sad news is, nobody owes you a career. Your career is literally your business. You own it as a sole proprietor. . . . It is your responsibility to protect this personal business of yours from harm. . . . "[31] Similarly Martin Carnoy argues that the requirements of the new economy shape a "new breed of young professional" who "is constantly on the lookout for a better job, and is ready to jump firms if he thinks there is any chance his present employer might downsize him out of work." Workers, according to Carnoy, become "increasingly autonomous in the work process."[32] This employment instability, that is, "freedom," also changes the nature of work relationships:

> The job and everything organized around the job—the group of friends in the company, the after-work hangouts, the trade union, and even the car pool—lost their social function. They are as "permanently temporary" as the work itself.[33]

In changing the nature of employment, the new economy creates the demand for a new moral character. Agility, taking risks, and a willingness to disconnect quickly triumph over loyalty and stability. Temporary relationships that add a new experience or a new skill are more valuable than long-lasting relationships. The new economy, as Carnoy bluntly states, is "a way of work and a way of life. Its core values are flexibility, innovation, and risk. . . . it infuses

old industrial cultures with these values."[34] Management gurus and the new outplacement industry join the chorus with a pleasing lyric celebrating the new free agency of employees: "What you offer is You Inc. . . . "[35]

Job insecurity and layoffs are what economists consider natural and inevitable. In the new economy, they are what corporations call "career-change opportunities," or "schedule adjustments," or "force management," or "releases of resources." For employees, however, what is sold as "freedom" is still unemployment, underemployment, and the loss of family stability that good work provides. It is what many workers describe as an assault, a living death, a label of shame.

> I used to work in engineering [as a] technician, I worked there for the last four years and last summer they were having a shakedown, what they were doing was getting ready to have another layoff, so they didn't want to lose me apparently, so they brought me back down into production into the tool room. They froze my pay and dropped me back two pay grades, two levels, and red circled my pay. It was like having to go back to fifth grade. And I'm not kidding you. I mean . . . it's just like somebody said, "You aren't capable of teaching so you've got to go and learn all over again." And this is just the way it feels to me.[36]

Nor have the effects on income of an involuntary job loss changed in the last two decades. In good times and bad, workers who are laid off average an 11 percent cut in earnings compared to what they would have been earning had they stayed in their original jobs.[37] Moreover, the promise of increased employability is hollow. Of those who lost their jobs between 1995 and 1997, about 40 percent of those who gained reemployment earned less than they had at their previous jobs. After reemployment 25 percent took more than a 20 percent cut in income. More experienced workers saw the greatest decline.[38]

Not everyone shares the managerial enthusiasm for the life and character of the new worker. One critical worker typed out this description of work in the high tech industry:

> the computer industry eats people, consumes them whole . . . their Dockers-and-button-down

clad minions push and push and push the people who do the actual work until stomachs writhe in the acid and sleep disappears and skin goes bad and teeth ache. . . . People who work eight hours a day then go home to families and lives are derided as not being "team players."[39]

As we have seen, this is not a condition confined to the high tech workplace. It is in the financial services corporation, the health care system, the white-collar sweatshop, the varieties of service occupations, and everywhere that more is expected to be done by fewer people who cannot afford to give and cannot expect to receive workplace loyalty. Most of those who have lamented the increase in "expressive individualism" among American women and men have pointed to the failings of civil society as the source of a growing emphasis on the self. But if people become what they must practice daily, if people pursue the characteristics that receive social acclaim, then the practices of the new economy provide a stronger explanation for the growth of "Me, Inc."

Whose Choices?

While her announcement of increased time spent in employed work received the most public attention, Schor was actually asking a deeper question: "Why has leisure been such a conspicuous casualty of prosperity?" This increase in working hours was not required, she argued. It was a choice. Schor claimed that increased worker productivity would allow the United States to produce a 1948 standard of living in less than half the time it took to be produced in 1948. We could choose to live in comfortable modern surroundings, particularly compared to most of the rest of the world, and still have a good deal of free time. A choice had been made. Of course, no one had asked most Americans to weigh the benefits and costs of the decision to produce more and more consumer products—and to try to consume them.

Perhaps it could be argued that American workers do prefer to work more hours in exchange for always-newer consumer goods. But multiple surveys do not sustain that argument. One survey of over one thousand employees between the ages of twenty-one and sixty-five, commissioned by the Radcliffe Public Policy Center, describes how increases in employed time impact people's real lives:

- One-third of these employees reported working forty hours a week; another 45 percent work more than forty hours a week.

- In families with a full-time worker whose spouse is also employed, 77 percent of the spouses are working forty hours per week or more.

- Only 27 percent of these workers get the recommended eight hours of sleep a night, or more. Forty percent said they needed more sleep.

- Forty-two percent agreed, or strongly agreed, that work–life balance is a problem.

- When asked to name what would help balance work and family needs, 70 percent cited flexible hours; 69 percent cited a four-day workweek; 56 percent wanted fewer hours in the workweek; and 50 percent named having an office at home or telecommuting.[40]

Despite the concerns of workers, it is very clear that reducing the accelerated pace of production in goods and services is not an option in the new economy. In 1989 Schor wrote a letter to three hundred business leaders advocating a shorter workweek. None saw this as a possibility. She quotes a typical response.

I cannot imagine a shorter work week. I can imagine a longer one both in school and at work if America is to be competitive in the first half of the next century.[41]

In a 1993 *Fortune* magazine survey, 77 percent of the CEOs polled believed that global success will require pushing managers even harder.[42] The experience of workers confirms that the philosophy of working harder while earning less shapes the lives of more and more workers. A technical writer at Intel, and a single father, describes his life:

Nominally, Intel has work hours, usually eight to five. . . . [But] life at Intel is intense. . . . incredibly hard work. I'd get the kids up, give them breakfast, then I'd take off. Get there about seven in the morning. Usually I'd leave right at five. [He would come home to prepare dinner and eat with his daughters.] Then I'd put them to bed at eight and come back to the office until about 1 A.M.[43]

Devotion to market-oriented work now shapes the dominant cultural sense of self and others. Borsook argues that the devaluing of any form of life outside market-oriented work is part of an entrenched worldview. It strengthens a strongly libertarian philosophy that disdains government, celebrates individualism, sees the absolute ownership of private property as the basis of individual liberty, and describes economic life in terms of a hostile, evolutionary climate in which only the strong survive. Working long hours at paid employment has become the primary sign of responsible citizenship. The question "What do you do?" has only one meaning. Teenagers who work after school and on weekends are applauded for their self-discipline and commitment to "work." Proclaiming the importance of developing a work ethic, business interests that employ young workers and those who benefit from teenage spending typically resist attempts to restrict student hours in employment.[44] Low-income single mothers who do not "work" are by definition lazy.[45] We have become a people justified by paid "work," regardless of its quality, its compliance with the demands of justice; and we are suspicious of leisure.

But our families are stretched too far, now that *no one* should be at home. Arlie Hochschild comments, "while the mass media so often point to global competition as the major business story of the age, it is easy to miss the fact that corporate America's fiercest struggle has been with its local rival—the family."[46] . . .

NOTES

1. Edward Wong, "A Stinging Office Memo Boomerangs," *New York Times,* 5 April 2001: C1, C13.

2. Benjamin Franklin, *The Autobiography of Benjamin Franklin* (New York: Washington Square Press, 1955), 103, cited in Michael Novak, *The Spirit of Democratic Capitalism* (Lanham, Md.: Madison Books, 1982, 1991), 97.

3. Cited in Juliet Schor, *The Overworked American: The Unexpected Decline of Leisure* (New York: Basic Books, 1991), 4.

4. Martin Carnoy, *Sustaining the New Economy: Work, Family, and Community in the Information Age* (New York: Russell Sage Foundation, 2000), 56.

5. Louis Uchitelle, "Pink Slip? Now, It's All in a Day's Work," *New York Times,* 5 August 2001: BU1, 11.

6. Jennifer Lee, "Discarded Dreams of Dot-Com Rejects," *New York Times,* 21 February 2001: C1, C8.

7. Jonathan D. Glater, "For Last Paycheck, More Workers Cede Their Right to Sue," *New York Times,* 24 February 2001: A1, B16.

8. Jane Slaughter, "Overtime Out: Nurses Strike to End Dangerously Long Shifts," *In These Times,* 10 February 2001: 10–11.

9. Mark Leibovich, "Not All Smiles Inside Amazon. com," *The Washington Post,* 25 November 1999; available at http://seattletimes.nwsource.com/news/technology/html98/amaz_19991125.html. Washington Alliance of Technology Workers, "Holiday in Amazonia," *Industry News,* 21 December 1998; available at www.washtech.org/roundup/news/amazon.html.

10. Steven Greenhouse, "Phone Workers Fight for Place in Wireless Era," *New York Times,* 31 July 2000: A1, A12.

11. Mindy Fried, *Taking Time: Parental Leave Policy and Corporate Culture* (Philadelphia: Temple University Press, 1998), 30.

12. Ibid., 39.

13. Schor, *The Overworked American,* 30–32.

14. For the argument that Americans have gained in leisure time since the 1960s, see John P. Robinson, Geoffrey Godbey, Anne Jacobson, *Time for Life: The Surprising Way Americans Use Their Time* (State College: Pennsylvania State University Press, 1999). For Schor's response to similar arguments, see Appendix B in *The Overworked American,* 168–69.

15. David Leonhardt, "Lingering Job Worries Amid a Sea of Plenty," *New York Times,* 29 August 2000: C1, C5.

16. Steven Greenhouse, "Report Shows Americans Have More 'Labor Days.'" *New York Times,* 1 September 2001: A6. See also Steven Greenhouse, "So Much Work, So Little Time," *New York Times,* 5 September 1999: 1WK, 4WK. Europeans' longer vacation times, four to six weeks, are protected by legislation. The higher productivity rate of the United States is tied to more hours, not to greater productivity per worker per hour.

17. Louis Uchitelle, "At the Desk, Off the Clock and Below Statistical Radar," *New York Times,* 18 July 1999: BU 4; Stephen S. Roach, "Working Better or Just Harder," *New York Times,* 14 February 2000: A27.

18. Institute for Women's Policy Research, *Network News* 8, no. 2 (June 1999): 1.

19. David H. Ciscel, David C. Sharp, and Julia A. Heath, "Family Work Trends and Practices: 1971 to 1991," *Journal of Family and Economic Issues* 21, no. 1 (Spring 2000): 27–28, 35; Jill Andresky Fraser, *White-Collar Sweatshop: The Deterioration of Work and Its Rewards in Corporate America* (New York: W.W. Norton, 2001), 119–20.

20. Mary Williams Walsh, "Reversing Decades-Long Trend, Americans Retiring Later in Life," *New York Times,* 26 February 2001: A1, A13.

21. John O'Neil and Marjorie Connelly, "As Savings Go Up, Worries Go Down (A Little)," *New York Times,* 21 March 2001: C1, C10. In another survey, only 22 percent of all workers surveyed said that they were "very confident" that they "will have enough money to live comfortably in retirement." Riva D. Atlas, "Why Juan Won't Save," *New York Times,* 20 June 2001: C1.

22. See Louis Uchitelle, "Workers Find Retirement Is Receding Toward 70," *New York Times,* 3 February 2002: BU 4.

23. Novak, *Spirit of Democratic Capitalism,* 101.

24. Paulina Borsook, *Cyberselfish: A Critical Romp through the Terribly Libertarian Culture of High Tech* (New York: Public Affairs, 2000), 41.

25. Fraser, *White-Collar Sweatshop,* 18–19.

26. Uchitelle, "At the Desk," BU 4; Roach, "Working Better," A27.

27. Yet, fewer than 30 percent of those who file for unemployment insurance receive it, and only 31 percent of unemployed women receive benefits compared to 37 percent of unemployed men. Unemployment insurance typically excludes people who work part-time, those recently hired into low-wage work (such as recent welfare recipients), those who quit their jobs (perhaps to care for a sick relative), and those who refuse a new shift or a geographical move for family reasons. Part-time workers pay unemployment insurance tax while working but do not receive unemployment benefits in most states. David Leonhardt, "Out of Work, and out of the Benefits Loop," *New York Times,* 17 October 2001: C1, C13; Robert B. Reich, "Lost Jobs, Ragged Safety New," *New York Times,* 12 November 2001: A23; Heidi Hartmann, "Placing Women First and Center: New Family and Economic Realities," Press Conference Comments, 2 November 2001, available at www.iwpr.org/comments.

28. Frederick F. Reichheld, "Lead for Loyalty," *Harvard Business Review* (July/August 2000); available at www.hbsp.harvard.edu/products/hbr.

29. Paul Osterman, cited in Louis Uchitelle, "These Days Layoffs Compete with Loyalty," *New York Times,* 19 August 2001: BU 4.

30. Laurence J. Stybel and Maryanne Peabody, "The Right Way to Be Fired," *Harvard Business Review* (July/August 2000); available at www.hbsp.harvard.edu/products/hbr. According to a Gallup survey conducted in 1999 with two million employees at seven hundred companies, 56 percent of employees believe that their company does not care about them or their careers, and 55 percent said that they have no strong loyalty to their company.

31. Andrew S. Grove, *Only the Paranoid Survive: How to Exploit the Crisis Points That Challenge Every Company and Career* (New York: Currency, Doubleday, 1996), 6, cited in Jill Andresky Fraser, *White-Collar Sweatshop,* 139. Intel changed the terms of its employment contract from "for cause" to "at will" in the early 1990s.

32. Carnoy, *Sustaining the New Economy,* 56–57.

33. Ibid.

34. Ibid., 1. Carnoy is assuming jobs that do in fact teach new skills. However, similar expectations of employee flexibility for the sake of efficiency are imposed upon service sector workers whose jobs provide no opportunity for skill enhancement. These workers are also expected to avoid contact and lasting relationships with fellow employees. Their need to feel a sense of relationship is manipulated toward their employer. See Barbara Ehrenreich, *Nickel and Dimed: On (Not) Getting By in America* (New York: Metropolitan Books, 2001).

35. Andrea G. Eisenberg, Managing Principal of Right Management Consultants, quoted in Uchitelle, "Pink Slip?": BU 11.

36. Margaret K. Nelson and Joan Smith, *Working Hard and Making Do: Surviving in Small Town America* (Berkeley: University of California Press, 1999), 158.

37. Thomas J. Cottle, *Hardest Times: The Trauma of Long Term Unemployment* (Westport, Conn.: Praeger, 2000). For the corporate spin on layoffs, see Fraser, *White-Collar Sweatshop,* chap. 9; David Leonhardt, "Yes, Layoffs Still Hurt, Even During Good Times," *New York Times,* 17 May 2001: BU 4.

38. Fraser, *White-Collar Sweatshop,* 53–57.

39. Ibid., 156.

40. Radcliffe Public Policy Center, *Life's Work: Generational Attitudes toward Work and Life Integration,* available at www.radcliffe.edu/pibpol. See summary in *The National Report on Work and Family,* 2000 Business Publishers, Inc., 13, no. 10 (16 May 2000): 81–82.

41. Schor, *The Overworked American,* 152; Jill Andresky Fraser, *White-Collar Sweatshop.* Of course, if competition demands it, firms may indeed cut hours. An interesting example occurred when the Charles Schwab Corporation, a brokerage firm, ordered half of its employees to *not* show up on three of the following five Fridays. The employees were expected to either use vacation time or unpaid leave. Either way the corporation wanted to reduce its compensation costs by $9 to $15 million in order to bolster its reported earnings for the quarter. Patrick McGeehan, "Schwab Tells Some Workers to Stay Home," *New York Times,* 31 January 2001: C1, C2.

42. Rosalind C. Barnett and Caryl Rivers, *She Works He Works: How Two-Income Families Are Happier, Healthier, and Better-Off* (San Francisco: Harper-SanFrancisco, 1996), 65.

43. Fraser, *White-Collar Sweatshop,* 21–22.

44. Of U.S. high school seniors 55 percent work three or more hours on a regular school day, compared to an 18 percent average for other nations. Negative effects seem to be associated with working more than fifteen hours a week: lower grades, absenteeism from school, alcohol and drug use, and the selection of less demanding courses. Richard Rothstein, "When After-School Jobs

Lead to Poor Performance in School," *New York Times*, 31 October 2001: A14.

45. See Michael B. Katz, *The Undeserving Poor: From the War on Poverty to the War on Welfare* (New York: Pantheon Books, 1989), esp. chaps. 1 and 4 for an account of how

poverty has been transformed from an economic problem to a problem of morality and culture.

46. Arlie Russell Hochschild, *The Time Bind: When Work Becomes Home and Home Becomes Work* (New York: Metropolitan Books, 1997), 203–4.

THIRTY-NINE

The Mommy Tax (2001)

Ann Crittenden

Ann Crittenden is a former reporter for *The New York Times, Fortune,* and *Newsweek.* Her widely published articles on economics and finances earned her a Pulitzer Prize nomination.

On April 7, 1999, the Independent Women's Forum, a conservative antifeminist organization, held a news conference at the National Press Club in Washington, D.C. Displayed in the corner of the room was a large green "check," made out to feminists, for ninety-eight cents. The point being made was that American women now make ninety-eight cents to a man's dollar and have therefore achieved complete equality in the workplace.

The sheer nerve of this little exercise in misinformation was astonishing. Upon closer examination, it turned out that the women who earn almost as much as men are a rather narrow group: those who are between the ages of twenty-seven and thirty-three and who have never had children.[1] The Independent Women's Forum was comparing young childless women to men and declaring victory for all women, glossing over the real news: that mothers are the most disadvantaged people in the workplace. One could even say that motherhood is now the single greatest obstacle left in the path to economic equality for women.

For most companies, the ideal worker is "unencumbered," that is, free of all ties other than those to his job. Anyone who can't devote all his or her energies to paid work is barred from the best jobs and has a permanently lower lifetime income. Not coincidentally, almost all the people in that category happen to be mothers.

What is the Value of Unpaid Labor?

1. Decide which non-market activities are work, e.g., cooking, cleaning, childcare, yard work, and repairs. If someone else could do these tasks they count as work.

2. Record how much time is spent on these activities.

3. Calculate the money value of that time.

   - Estimate what it would cost to hire someone to do all the jobs performed by a wife and mother—the "housekeeper wage" approach.

   - Estimate the cost of hiring different specialists for the various services, e.g., cleaners, cooks, childcare workers, etc.—the "specialist wage" approach.

   Both these methods underestimate the value of women's unpaid labor because they are based on the low wage rates for work traditionally done by women rather than the level of a middle manager or social worker.

   - Estimate the homemakers' "opportunity costs"—or the amount she would expect to earn outside the home. This gives much higher valuations for women who can command high rates of pay in the workforce.

Source: Crittenden (2001) pp. 79–80.

The reduced earnings of mothers are, in effect, a heavy personal tax levied on people who care for children, or for any other dependent family members. This levy, a "mommy tax," is easily greater than $1 million in the case of a college-educated woman.[2] For working-class women, there is increasing evidence both in the United States and worldwide that mothers' differential responsibility for children . . . is the most important factor disposing women to poverty.

. . . The much-publicized earnings gap between men and women narrowed dramatically in the 1980s and early 1990s. All a girl had to do was stay young and unencumbered. The sexual egalitarianism evident in so many television sit-coms, from *Friends* to *Seinfeld* to *Ally McBeal,* is rooted in economic reality. Young women don't need a man to pay their bills or take them out, any more than men need a woman to iron their shirts or cook

their dinner. Many childless women under the age of thirty-five firmly believe that all of the feminist battles have been won, and as far as they're concerned, they're largely right.

But once a woman has a baby, the egalitarian office party is over. I ought to know.

Million-Dollar Babies

After my son was born in 1982, I decided to leave the *New York Times* in order to have more time to be a mother. I recently calculated what that decision cost me financially.

I had worked full-time for approximately twenty years, eight of those at the *Times.* When I left, I had a yearly salary of roughly $50,000, augmented by speaking fees, freelance income, and journalism awards. Had I not had a child, I probably would have worked at least another fifteen years, maybe taking early retirement to pursue other interests. Under this scenario, I would have earned a pension, which I lost by leaving the paper before I had worked the requisite ten years to become vested. (The law has since changed to allow vesting after five years with one employer.)

My annual income after leaving the paper has averaged roughly $15,000, from part-time freelance writing. Very conservatively, I lost between $600,000 and $700,000, not counting the loss of a pension. Without quite realizing what I was doing, I took what I thought would be a relatively short break, assuming it would be easy to get back into journalism after a few years, or to earn a decent income from books and other projects. I was wrong. As it turned out, I sacrificed more than half of my expected lifetime earnings. And in the boom years of the stock market, that money invested in equities would have multiplied like kudzu. As a conservative estimate, it could have generated $50,000 or $60,000 a year in income for my old age.

At the time, I never sat down and made these economic calculations. I never even thought about money in connection with motherhood, or if I did, I assumed my husband would provide all we needed. And had I been asked to weigh my son's childhood against ten or fifteen more years at the *Times,* I doubt whether the monetary loss would have tipped the scales. But still, this seems a high price to pay for doing the right thing.

So then the Knight slew the dragon and married the beautiful princess and they both went to work for a major law firm and in addition to her job she had primary responsibility for the housework, and when the kids were home sick she . . .

Does this story have a happy ending?

The mommy tax I paid is fairly typical for an educated middle-class American woman. Economist Shirley Burggraf has calculated that a husband and wife who earn a combined income of $81,500 per year and who are equally capable will lose $1.35 million if they have a child. Most of that lost income is the wages forgone by the primary parent.[3] In a middle-income family, with one parent earning $30,000 per year as a sales representative and the other averaging $15,000 as a part-time computer consultant, the mommy tax will still be more than $600,000. Again, this seems an unreasonable penalty on the decision to raise a child, a decision that contributes to the general good by adding another productive person to the nation.

. . .

Those who care for elderly relatives also discover that their altruism will be heavily penalized. A small survey of individuals who provided informal, unpaid care for family members found that it cost them an average of $659,139 in lost wages, Social Security, and pension benefits over their lifetimes. The subjects reported having to pass up promotions and training opportunities, use up their sick days and vacations, reduce their workload to part-time, and in many cases even quit their paid jobs altogether. This exorbitant "caring tax" is being paid by an increasing number of people, three-quarters of them women.[4]

The mommy tax is obviously highest for well-educated, high-income individuals and lowest for poorly educated people who have less potential income to lose. All else being equal, the younger the mother, and the more children she has, the higher her tax will be, which explains why women are having fewer children, later in life, almost everywhere.

The tax is highest in the Anglo-Saxon countries, where mothers personally bear almost all the costs of caring, and lowest in France and Scandinavia, where paid maternity leaves and public preschools make it easier for mothers to provide care without sacrificing their income.

Most women never think about the mommy tax until they have an encounter with rude reality. Virginia Daley was an interior designer for Aetna Life & Casualty in Hartford, Connecticut. After almost ten years with the company, and consistently good performance reviews, raises, and promotions, Daley was fired in 1993 from her $46,640-a-year job. The dismissal occurred after she had had a baby and then tried to arrange a more flexible work week, in accordance with the company's stated policies.

Not only were her requests for flexibility denied, her workload was actually increased in the wake of a massive corporate downsizing. Already frustrated, Daley was furious to learn in late 1992 that Aetna's chairman Ronald Compton had been awarded a "Good Guy" award from the National Women's Political Caucus for his support of model family-leave programs. (Aetna also consistently made *Working Mother* magazine's annual list of best companies for employed mothers, and in 1992 was touted as one of the *four* "most family-friendly companies" in America by the Families and Work Institute.)

Daley dashed off a memo to Compton, charging that "when it comes to offering flexible family arrangements, Aetna's performance is far from award-winning." The memo concluded that "realistic options for Aetna employees to meet their family obligations without sacrificing their careers are not generally available today. To continue to represent to Aetna employees and the national media that these options are available is unconscionable."

Three months later Daley was terminated, on the grounds of poor performance.

She sued, and the case went to trial in 1997. Aetna maintained that Daley had lost her position because she wasn't able to handle the additional responsibilities that she was assigned after the downsizing (and the baby). The jury essentially agreed with Aetna. It also agreed with the company that Daley was not speaking out on a matter of public concern when she complained that numerous employees were being denied family-friendly schedules. Her memo to Compton was therefore not "protected speech," i.e., an important statement that entitles an employee to protection from retaliation. Daley lost the case, as well as subsequent appeal.

. . .

According to Daley's lawyer, Philip L. Steele, the jury foreman told him after the trial that although the panel was very sympathetic to Daley, its members felt she had probably "overextended" herself. "They believed it was just too hard for a woman to raise little kids and do a good job," Steele told me. "The thinking was, how can a woman do all that, not how could a company do that?"

The decision cost Daley dearly. She calculates that over the next five years following her departure from Aetna, her income as a part-time consultant was from \$90,000 to \$154,000 lower than if she had stayed at the company. And that doesn't include the loss of Aetna's annual contribution to her 401(K) retirement plan. "I figure that if I'd stayed at Aetna another ten years," Daley told me, "their contribution to my 401(K) alone would have been more than \$25,000. That could easily become more than six figures by the time I am retirement age. . . . People need to know that once you have a child you'll definitely be poorer."[5]

The Cost of Being a Mother

A small group of mostly female academic economists has added another twist to the story. Their research reveals that working mothers not only earn less than men, but also less per hour than childless women, even after such differences as education and experience are factored out. The pay gap between mothers and nonmothers under age thirty-five is now larger than the wage gap between young men and women.

. . .

. . . Jane Waldfogel at Columbia University . . . set out to assess the opportunity cost of motherhood by asking exactly how much of the dramatic wage gains made by women in the 1980s went to women without family responsibilities. How many of the female winners in the 1980s were people like Donna Shalala, Janet Reno, Elizabeth Dole, and Carole Bellamy, the director of UNICEF: childless women whose work patterns were indistinguishable from those of traditional males.

Back in the late 1970s, Waldfogel found, the difference between men's and women's pay was about the same for all women. Nonmothers earned only slightly higher wages. But over the next decade things changed.[6] By 1991, thirty-year-old American women without children were making 90 percent of men's wages, while comparable women with children were making only 70 percent. Even when Waldfogel factored out all the women's differences, the disparity in their incomes remained—something she dubbed the "family wage gap."[7]

Why do working mothers earn so much less than childless women? Academic researchers have worried over this question like a dog over a bone but haven't turned up a single, definitive answer.

Waldfogel argues that the failure of employers to provide paid maternity leaves is one factor that leads to the family wage gap in the United States. This country is one of only six nations in the world that does not require a paid leave. (The others are Australia, New Zealand, Lesotho, Swaziland, and Papua New Guinea.)[8] With no right to a paid leave, many American mothers who want to stay at home with a new baby simply quit their jobs, and this interruption in employment costs them dearly in terms of lost income. Research in Europe reveals that when paid maternity leaves were mandated, the percentage of women remaining employed rose, and women's wages were higher, unless the leaves lasted more than a few months.[9]

In the United States as well, women who are able to take formal paid maternity leave do not suffer the same setback in their wages as comparably placed women who do not have a right to such leaves. . . .

Paid leaves are so valuable because they don't seem to incur the same penalties that employers impose on even the briefest of unpaid career interruptions. A good example is the experience of the 1974 female graduates of the University of Michigan Law School. During their first fifteen years after law school, these women spent an average of only 3.3 months out of the workplace, compared with virtually no time out for their male classmates. More than one-quarter of the women had worked part-time, for an average of 10.1 months over the fifteen years, compared with virtually no part-time work among the men. While working full-time, the women put in only 10 percent fewer hours than full-time men, again not a dramatic difference.

But the penalties for these slight distinctions between the men's and women's work patterns were strikingly harsh. Fifteen years after graduation, the women's average earnings were not 10 percent lower, or even 20 percent lower, than the men's, but almost 40 percent lower. Fewer than one-fifth of the women in law firms who had worked part-time for more than six months had made partner in their firms, while more than four-fifths of the mothers with little or no part-time work had made partner.[10]

Another survey of almost 200 female M.B.A.s found that those who had taken an average of only 8.8 months out of the job market were less likely to reach upper-middle management and earned 17 percent less than comparable women who had never had a gap in their employment.[11]

Working-class women are also heavily penalized for job interruptions, although these are the very women who allegedly "choose" less demanding occupations that enable them to move in and out of the job market without undue wage penalties. The authors of one study concluded that the negative repercussions of taking a little time out of the labor force were still discernible after twenty years.[12] In blue-collar work, seniority decides who is eligible for better jobs, and who is "bumped" in the event of lay-offs. Under current policies, many women lose their seniority forever if they interrupt their employment, as most mothers do. Training programs, required for advancement, often take place after work, excluding the many mothers who can't find child care.[13]

Mandatory overtime is another handicap placed on blue-collar mothers. Some 45 percent of American workers reported in a recent survey that they had to work overtime with little or no notice.[14] . . . Where does that leave a woman who has to be home in time for dinner with the kids? Out of a promotion and maybe out of a job. Increasingly in today's driven workplace, whether she is blue- or white-collar, a woman who goes home when she is supposed to go home is going to endanger her economic well-being.

The fact that many mothers work part-time also explains some of the difference between mothers' and comparable women's hourly pay. About 65 percent of part-time workers are women, most of whom are mothers.[15] Employers are not required to offer part-time employees equal pay and benefits for equal work. As a result, nonstandard workers earn on average about 40 percent less an hour than full-time workers, and about half of that wage gap persists even for similar workers in similar jobs.

Many bosses privately believe that mothers who work part-time have a "recreational" attitude toward work, as one Maryland businessman assured me. Presumably, this belief makes it easier to justify their exploitation. But the working conditions they face don't sound very much like recreation. A recent survey by Catalyst, a research organization focused on women in business, found that more than half of the people who had switched to part-time jobs and lower pay reported that their workload stayed the same. Ten percent reported an increase in workload after their income had been reduced. Most of these people were mothers.[16]

Another factor in the family wage gap is the disproportionate number of mothers who operate their own small businesses, a route often taken by women who need flexibility during the child-rearing years. . . . In 1999, women owned 38 percent of all U.S. businesses, compared with only 5 percent in 1972, a remarkable increase that is frequently cited as evidence of women's economic success. One new mother noted that conversations at play groups "center as much on software and modems as they do on teething and ear infections."[17]

Less frequently mentioned is the fact that many of these women-owned businesses are little more than Mom-minus-Pop operations: one woman trying to earn some money on the side, or keep her career alive, during the years when her children have priority. Forty-five percent of women-owned businesses are home-based. And the more than one-third of businesses owned by women in 1996 generated only 16 percent of the sales of all U.S. businesses in that year.[18]

In 1997, although women were starting new businesses at twice the rate of men, they received only 2 percent of institutional venture capital, a principal source of financing for businesses with serious prospects for growth. Almost one-quarter of female business owners financed their operations the same way that they did their shopping: with their credit cards.[19]

Some researchers have suggested that mothers earn less than childless women because they are less productive. This may be true for some mothers who work at home and are subject to frequent interruptions, or for those who are exhausted from having to do most of the domestic chores, or distracted by creaky child-care arrangements. But the claim that mothers have lower productivity than other workers is controversial and unproven. . . .

It's Discrimination, Stupid

It is revealing that those occupations requiring nurturing skills, such as child care, social work, and nursing, are the most systematically underpaid, relative to their educational and skill demands.[20] These are also, of course, the occupations with the highest percentage of females. But men who are primary caregivers also pay a heavy price: a "daddy tax," if you will. This suggests that at least part of the huge tax on mothers' earnings is due to work rules and practices and habits of mind that discriminate against anyone, of either sex, who cannot perform like an "unencumbered" worker. In other words, discrimination against all good parents, male or female.

Surveys have found that wives may adore husbands who share the parenting experience, but employers distinctly do not. A majority of managers believe that part-time schedules and even brief parental leaves are inappropriate for men.[21] When Houston Oiler David Williams missed one Sunday game to be with his wife after the birth of their first child, he was docked $111,111.

A survey of 348 male managers at twenty Fortune 500 companies found that fathers from dual-career families put in an average of *two* fewer hours per week—or about 4 percent less—than men whose wives were at home. That was the only difference between the two groups of men. But the fathers with working wives, who presumably had a few more domestic responsibilities, earned almost 20 percent less. There it is again: a 20 percent family wage gap.[22]

"Face time still matters as much or more than productivity in many companies," Charles Rodgers, a management consultant in Boston, said. Rodgers told me about a man in a high-tech company who regularly came to work two hours early so that he could occasionally leave early for Little League games with his son. He was given a poor performance rating.[23]

. . .

Only eight states currently have laws prohibiting discrimination against parents in the workplace. Examples include taking a primary parent off a career track out of an assumption that the individual couldn't do the work; hiring someone without children over a more qualified person with children; forcing a primary parent to work overtime, or else; and refusing to hire a single parent, though the employer hires single, childless people. In the course of my reporting, I encountered numerous mothers who felt that their employer's refusal to arrange a shorter workweek, particularly after the birth of a second baby, amounted to career-destroying discrimination. . . .

How to Lower the Mommy Tax

Until now, narrowing the gender wage gap in the United States has depended almost entirely on what might be called the "be a man" strategy. Women are told to finish school, find a job, acquire skills, develop seniority, get tenure, make partner, and put children off until the very last minute. The longer a woman postpones family responsibilities, and the longer her "preparental" phase lasts, the higher her lifetime earnings will be.

Ambitious women of the baby-boom generation and younger have by and large tried to be a man in this way. A good example is Susan Pedersen, a historian who achieved tenure at Harvard in the mid-1990s. By that time, she was married and in her late thirties, but she had postponed having children until her academic career was secure. Motherhood was something she wanted very much, she commented during an interview, but it posed a serious threat to her professional dreams and had to be delayed.[24]

As Pedersen's success demonstrates, this strategy does work—for the very small number who are able to pull it off. And women who have their children later in life do have higher lifetime earnings and a wider range of opportunities than younger mothers. The advice dished out by writers like Danielle Crittenden—no relation—an antifeminist ideologue who has urged women to marry and have their babies young, ignores this, along with some other hard truths. Crittenden never tells her readers that young parents tend to separate and divorce much more frequently than older couples, leaving young mothers and children vulnerable to poverty. Large numbers of the women who end up on welfare are there because they have done exactly what she recommends: married and had children young and then been left to support them alone.[25]

But trying to be a man has its own risks. Many baby-boomer women postponed families only to discover that when they wanted to become pregnant, it was too late. . . . And millions of women don't feel that being a man is the way they want to live their lives. . . .

An alternative strategy is followed in countries like France and Sweden, where the government, private employers, and/or husbands share much more of the costs of raising children. This makes it far easier for women to be mothers and to work. In France, for example, families with two preschool-age children receive about $10,000 worth of annual subsidies, including free health care and housing subsidies and excellent free preschools.[26] As a result, child poverty is unusual, and the pay gap between mothers and others is much smaller in France than in the United States. . . .

Whenever Europe is singled out as a model, the usual response is that Americans would never support such generous social policies. But in fact, the United States already does have an extremely generous social welfare state. But unlike the welfare states of western Europe, the American government doesn't protect mothers; it protects soldiers.

Men who postpone or interrupt civilian employment for military service pay a tax on their lifetime earnings that is quite comparable to the mommy tax. White men who were drafted during the Vietnam War, for example, were still earning approximately 15 percent less in the early 1980s than comparable nonveterans.[27] This "warrior wage gap" is strikingly similar to the family wage gap, again indicating that mothers' lower earnings are not entirely attributable to gender discrimination.

But there is unquestionable discrimination in the way the government has responded to the financial sacrifices that soldiers and parents, particularly mothers, make. . . .

To illustrate this double standard, let's look at two men with identical characteristics. One works as a computer technician, is married to a woman in the same occupation, and has two children. He is a conscientious father, making sure to be home for dinner every night, even helping to cook it. He takes his kids to sporting events, attends teacher conferences, and tries to limit his travel and outside commitments.

This man is legitimately worried about what his dedication to family will do to his career. Let's say he does get fewer promotions and over the years earns 15 to 20 percent less than he would have had he not shared the family obligations. We can realistically say that he pays a significant daddy tax.

Now take a man with the same education and imagine that he spends three or four years in military service. He is worried that these years out of his active professional life will affect his economic future, and they might, although his boss believes that his service was good leadership training. But whatever career losses he suffers will be cushioned by the generous thanks that the nation pays to its ex-servicemen. He discovers that his warrior tax is lowered by these benefits, which are available to him even if he never got near a battlefield:

- He can stay in the military for twenty years as a *part-time reservist* and draw half pay for the rest of his life.[28]

- He will get special preference for government jobs. Extra points will be added to whatever civil service exams he may take, and some rules are written so that he will be chosen over closely ranked nonveterans. In government layoffs, he will have extra protection. Unlike mothers or fathers who find that after a few years out of the job market their credentials are downgraded, his are given a major boost by veterans' preferences.

- If he decides to go back to school for more education, he can qualify for thirty-six months of cash payments worth more than $17,000.

- He also qualifies for a government-guaranteed housing loan, financed at interest rates usually half a percentage point below the going market rate.

- He can make use of a hospital system costing the federal government $17 billion a year.

- He will have access to special low auto insurance rates, available only to individuals with some connection to the military. These come in especially handy when his teenage son begins to drive.

- As long as he remains in the military or works on a military base as a civilian, he can enjoy subsidized child care provided by the best day-care system in the country. For only $37 to $98 a week (in 1997), depending on his income, he can enroll his children in infant and toddler care and preschools staffed by expertly trained and licensed teachers. In the private sector, the fees would be two to four times higher, for often inferior care.

None of these benefits is contingent on service in combat. In 1990, 6.3 million of the 27 million veterans eligible for benefits served only during peacetime. Millions of ex-servicemen, who do not even have a hangnail to show for their harrowing experience in uniform, enjoy the same government largesse that flows to the veterans who were once put in the way of danger.

The benefits paid to military veterans are . . . second only to Social Security in terms of government payments to individuals. And they do an excellent job of reducing the warrior tax. The educational benefits in particular help veterans overcome many of the economic disadvantages they suffer by leaving the workplace for a few years.

A congressional study in the early 1990s concluded that the veterans of World War II who took advantage of the G.I. Bill to earn a college degree enjoyed incomes of up to 10 percent more than they might otherwise have earned. Society was also the beneficiary, for the additional taxes paid by the college-educated veterans during their working lives more than paid for the program.[29]

It hardly needs to be said that there is no G.I. Bill, no health care, no subsidized housing, and no job preferences for mothers. As things now stand, millions of women sacrifice their economic independence and risk economic disaster for the sake of raising a child. This says a lot about family values, the nation's priorities, and free riding.

A third way to reduce the mommy tax would be to expand the antidiscrimination laws to cover parents. Joan Williams, a law professor at American University's Washington College of Law, argues that the design of work around masculine norms can be reconceptualized as discrimination. As an example, Williams suggests that if a woman works full-time, with good job evaluations for a significant period, then switches to part-time because of family responsibilities and is paid less per hour than full-time employees doing similar work, she could claim discrimination under the Equal Pay Act. Williams believes that disparate-action suits could also be filed against employers whose policies (including routine and mandatory overtime, promotion tracks, resistance to part-time work) have a disparate impact on women, producing disproportionate numbers of men in top-level positions.[30]

The essential point is that existing laws, and new laws preventing discrimination against people with caregiving responsibilities, could go a very long way toward improving mothers' lifetime earnings.

The Ultimate Mommy Tax: Childlessness

The cost of children has become so high that many American women are not having children at all. One of the most striking findings of Claudia Goldin's survey of white female college graduates is their high degree of childlessness (28 percent). Now that the baby-boomer generation is middle-aged, it is clear that more than one-quarter of the educated women in that age group will never have children. Indeed, the percentage of all American women who remain childless is also steadily rising, from 8 to 9 percent in the 1950s to 10 percent in 1976 to 17.5 percent in the late 1990s.

Is this rising childlessness by choice? Goldin thinks not. She found that in 1978, while in their twenties, almost half of the college-educated boomers who would remain childless had said that they did want children. Goldin calculated that almost one-fifth of this entire generation (19 percent) of white college graduates was disappointed in not having a child. This is the ultimate price of the "be a man" strategy that has been forced on working women. For women in business, the price is staggering. A recent Catalyst survey of 1,600 M.B.A.s found that only about one-fifth of the women had children, compared with 70 percent of the men.

. . .

Americans have a hard time realizing that such deeply personal choices as when or whether to have a child can be powerfully circumscribed by broader social or economic factors. American women, in particular, are stunningly unaware that their "choices" between a career and a family are much more limited than those of women in many European countries, where policies are much more favorable to mothers and children.

. . .

In sum, an individual woman's decision whether to have a child or not, and whether to stay home or not, is heavily influenced by her country's willingness to help her bear the costs. In . . . the United States, the official message is *caveat mater,* or "mothers beware": you're on your own.

NOTES

1. This calculation was made by economist June O'Neill, using data from the National Longitudinal Survey of Youth. June O'Neill and Solomon Polachek, "Why the Gender Gap in Wages Narrowed in the 1980s," *Journal of Labor Economics* 11 (1993): 205–28. See also June O'Neill, "The Shrinking Pay Gap," *Wall Street Journal,* October 7, 1994.

2. The concept of the mommy tax was inspired by development economist Gita Sen, who has described the extra economic burden borne by women as a "reproduction tax."

3. Burggraf assumes that the more flexible parent's earnings average $25,750 a year, versus $55,750 for the primary breadwinner. She then multiplies $30,000 (the difference between what the two parents earn) by 45 (the years in a working lifetime) to get the $1.350 million. *The Feminine Economy and Economic Man*, p. 61.

4. The National Alliance for Caregivers estimates that the number of employed people who provide care for elderly family members will grow to 11 to 15.6 million in the first decade of the twenty-first century.

5. *Virginia V. Daley et al. v. Aetna Life & Casualty et al.*, August 12, 1994. Virginia Daley, personal communication, May 1996; Philip L. Steele, personal communication, October 2000.

6. Jane Waldfogel, "Women Working for Less: Family Status and Women's Pay in the US and UK," Malcolm Wiener Center for Social Policy Working Paper D-94-1, Harvard University, 1994.

7. Jane Waldfogel, "Understanding the 'Family Gap' in Pay for Women with Children," *Journal of Economic Perspectives* 12, no. 1 (winter 1998): 137–56. See also Waldfogel, "The Family Gap for Young Women in the United States and Britain," *Journal of Labor Economics* 11 (1998): 505–19.

8. Elizabeth Olson, "U.N. Surveys Paid Leave for Mothers," *New York Times*, February 16, 1998.

9. Christopher J. Ruhm, "The Economic Consequences of Parental Leave Mandates: Lessons from Europe," *Quarterly Journal of Economics* CXIII, no. 1 (1998): 285–317.

10. Wood, Corcoran, and Courant, "Pay Differentials," pp. 417–28.

11. This 1993 study was coauthored by Joy Schneer of Rider University's College of Business Administration and Frieda Reitman, professor emeritus at Pace University's Lubin School of Business.

12. Joyce Jacobsen and Arthur Levin, "The Effects of Intermittent Labor Force Attachment on Female Earnings," *Monthly Labor Review* 118, no. 9 (September 1995): 18.

13. For a good discussion of the obstacles to mothers' employment in relatively well-paying blue-collar work, see Williams, *Unbending Gender*, pp. 76–81.

14. This survey of 1,000 workers was conducted by researchers at the University of Connecticut and Rutgers University, and was reported in the *Wall Street Journal*, May 18, 1999.

15. A survey of more than 2,000 people in four large corporations found that 75 percent of the professionals working part-time were women who were doing so because of child-care obligations. Only 11 percent of the male managers surveyed expected to work part-time at some point in their careers, compared with 36 percent of women managers. *A New Approach to Flexibility: Managing the Work/Time Equation* (New York: Catalyst, 1997), pp. 25–26.

16. See Reed Abelson, "Part-Time Work for Some Adds Up to Full-Time Job," *New York Times*, November 2, 1998.

17. Tracy Thompson, "A War Inside Your Head," *Washington Post Magazine*, February 15, 1998, p. 29.

18. Information on women-owned businesses provided by the National Foundation for Women Business Owners in Washington, D.C., September 2000.

19. Noelle Knox, "Women Entrepreneurs Attract New Financing," *New York Times*, July 26, 1998.

20. See Paula England, George Farkas, Barbara Kilbourne, Kurt Beron, and Dorothea Weir, "Returns to Skill, Compensating Differentials, and Gender Bias: Effects of Occupational Characteristics on Wages of White Women and Men," *American Journal of Sociology* 100, no. 3 (November 1994): 689–719.

21. [One] study found that 63 percent of large employers thought it was inappropriate for a man to take *any* parental leave, and another 17 percent thought it unreasonable unless the leave was limited to two weeks or less. Martin H. Malin, "Fathers and Parental Leave," *Texas Law Review* 72 (1994): 1047, 1089; cited in Williams, *Unbending Gender*, p. 100.

22. This study, by Linda Stroh of Loyola University, was reported by Tamar Lewin, "Fathers Whose Wives Stay Home Earn More and Get Ahead, Studies Find," *New York Times*, October 12, 1994.

23. Charles Rodgers, personal communication, October 1993.

24. Susan Pedersen, personal interview, June 1996.

25. Being a young mother obviously worked for Crittenden, who was affluent enough to have purchased a $1.3-million home in Washington, D.C., while still in her midthirties. But not many mothers enjoy such options.

26. Barbara Bergmann, personal conversation, January 4, 1999.

27. Joshua D. Angrist, "Lifetime Earnings and the Vietnam Era Draft Lottery: Evidence from Social Security Administrative Records," *American Economic Review* 80, no. 3 (June 1990): 313–31.

28. The United States is the only country in the world that offers *full* retirement to military reservists. In 1993 the cost to taxpayers was $1.9 billion. See Congressional Budget Office, *Reducing the Deficit: Spending and Revenue Options*, Washington, D.C., 1995, p. 64.

29. David O'Neill, "Voucher Funding of Training Programs: Evidence from the G.I. Bill," *Journal of Human Resources* 12, no. 4 (fall 1977): 425–45; and Joshua D. Angrist, "The Effects of Veterans' Benefits on Education and Earnings," *Industrial and Labor Relations Review* 46, no. 4 (July 1993): 637–57.

30. Williams, *Unbending Gender*, pp. 101–10.

FORTY

Circumventing Discrimination (2006)
Gender and Ethnic Strategies in Silicon Valley
Johanna Shih

Johanna Shih is Assistant Professor of Sociology at Hofstra University. She contributed to research on care, family, and work at the Center for Working Families, University of California, Berkeley. Her research interests include gender and racial inequality in the labor market.

Silicon Valley's exponential growth and rapid pace in hi-tech product and service innovation captured worldwide attention in the 1990s. As "valley watchers" flocked to study the region, a pervasive discourse emerged about Silicon Valley, lauding its commitment to meritocracy as key to its success. Journalists wrote that "one of Silicon Valley's secret weapons is its openness to immigrants and to women" (Vital intangibles 1997) and reported that the region is "the quintessence of the American Dream. . . . People rarely care what school you attended, your ethnic background, or your family pedigree. They want proof of IQ" (Reinhardt and Hamilton 1997). Academics joined the praise as well, observing that "the single important criterion in determining success is work performance" (Rogers and Larsen 1984, 154). Even the region's billboards proclaimed that this was where "The Glass Ceiling Meets the Glass Cutter."

The claim of meritocracy is worth a closer look because women in general, as well as Asian men and women, are well represented in the high-skilled sector of this industry. While there has been significant research analyzing the experiences of Asian (male) immigrant engineers in Silicon Valley (Alarcon 1999; Dossani 2002; Saxenian 1999), the experiences of women engineers have been largely ignored (Hyde 2004). This is surprising for three reasons. First, the participation of women in science and engineering has been a long-standing concern (National Science Foundation 2000b) not only because of a U.S. labor shortage in these fields but also because previous studies have consistently documented mechanisms of gender inequality and bias. Second, although women still represent only a fraction of Silicon Valley's high-skill, hi-tech labor force, they constitute a critical mass in the region that is absent in other science and engineering industries. In 1990, both U.S.-born and foreign-born women represented approximately 17 percent of the engineering and scientist work force in the region (Alarcon 1999), in comparison to the nation overall, where women held 8 percent of engineering jobs in 1993 (Lal, Yoon, and Carlson 1999). When considering women in core information technology occupations, women are even better represented, composing 28 percent of this workforce (Ellis and Lowell 1999). Asians, in particular ethnic Chinese and Indian immigrants—in the region, 84 percent of the former and 98 percent of the latter are foreign born (Saxenian 1999)—are also well represented in the hi-tech work force. In 1990, they accounted for 21 percent of Silicon Valley's technical workforce (Alarcon 1999; Saxenian 1999), in comparison to 10 percent in the United States (National Science Foundation 2000b). Third, leading scholars of Silicon Valley have argued that the hi-tech industry's "regional advantage" (Saxenian 1994) stemmed from its economic structure of flexible specialization (Piore and Sabel 1984), identifying key characteristics in this mode of economic production that makes it well suited to adapt to the rapid demand fluctuations of global capitalism. Silicon Valley thus represents the shift from the Fordist era of mass production to production that is at least partly based on specialized firms interconnected through a dense web of networks (Piore and Sabel 1984). This poses the question of how the organizational mechanisms that produce gender and ethnic inequality are affected by the shift in economic structure.

To answer this question, I explore gender and ethnic inequality in the hi-tech industry through analysis of 54 in-depth interviews of white and Asian men and women engineers who work in Silicon Valley. I focus on the comparative experiences of U.S.-born white women on one hand and primarily foreign-born Asian men and Asian women on the other. While this categorization does injustice by collapsing the experiences of Asian immigrant women and Asian immigrant men, my analysis was guided by the accounts of these respondents. In particular, Asian immigrant women characterized their experiences and trajectories as primarily shaped by their ethnic status (and the attendant ethnic resources and networks) rather than their gender status.

In investigating the experiences of white women, Asian men, and Asian women, I identify two central characteristics of flexible specialization that potentially affect those who work in Silicon Valley. First, I show how the characteristic of job-hopping in the region serves as a useful strategy by which these groups could circumvent employers and firms that they viewed as discriminatory. Notwithstanding the regional discourse on meritocracy, white women, Asian women, and Asian men report facing forms of bias that are well documented in past studies, such as gender or ethnic typecasting and lack of access to firms' inner networks. However, they also report being able to turn the tables on biased employers by job-hopping to firms that they viewed as more egalitarian. Second, I show how the region's reliance on networks did not disadvantage white women, Asian men, and Asian women. This is counterintuitive because lack of access to key networks has been consistently identified as problematic in studies of work and organizations. However, because of the specific histories of these groups' entrance into Silicon Valley, respondents reported being able to create and tap into resource-rich, cross-rank, gender- and ethnic-based networks that could rival the utility of "old white boys' networks."

The comparative perspective reveals that while white women, Asian women, and Asian men used the same strategy of job-hopping, their network resources channeled them into divergent trajectories. White women reported using networks to locate jobs and firms that were women friendly and believed that they could or had achieved significant success in these more egalitarian firms. Two larger-scale studies on hi-tech firms have also suggested that women in hi-tech are tapped into the right networks for movement into mainstream firms (Baron, Hannan, and Burton 1999; Peterson, Saporta, and Seidel 2000). In contrast, Asian respondents (both men and women) reported job-hopping into co-ethnic-run firms, or

moving into entrepreneurship themselves, motivated partly from pessimism about overcoming ethnic typecasting in white majority firms and partly because they faced a different structure of opportunities. By 1988, Chinese and Indians were CEOs of 24 percent of hi-tech firms started since 1980, an impressive feat given that this was not ethnic entrepreneurship in the peripheral or secondary sectors but rather entrepreneurship in a sector that accounted for one-third of U.S. real economic growth from 1995 to 1997 (U.S. Department of Commerce 1999).

Ethnic and Gender Inequality in Organizations

Research on work organizations consistently documents the impact of race and gender on individuals' career mobility (Baldi and McBrier 1997; Bielby and Baron 1986; DiPrete and Soule 1988; Mueller, Parcel, and Tanaka 1989). Three interconnected mechanisms are consistently highlighted in the literature on organizational inequality. First, studies revealed how organizational mechanisms channel women and racial/ethnic minority men into less prestigious tracks that result in intra-organizational job segregation (Collins 1997; DiPrete and Soule 1988). Second, individuals in these groups can be "de-skilled" through differential access to training (Knoke and Ishio 1998; Mueller, Parcel, and Tanaka 1989; Nkomo and Cox 1990), thus truncating opportunities for mobility. Third, informal processes can exclude these groups from key networks and from mentoring relationships (Baldi and McBrier 1997; Kanter 1977), relegating them as outsiders to organizational culture. These informal processes differentiate between who gets ahead through a "sponsor" model (exemplified by Kanter's [1977] concept of "homosocial reproduction") and who gets ahead through a "contest" model that is based on formal criteria (Baldi and McBrier 1977; Mueller, Parcel, and Tanaka 1989). For these reasons, organizations with formal personnel guidelines are viewed as more egalitarian.

These mechanisms of organizational inequality have been identified in studies specific to science and engineering occupations. The findings with respect to women generally indicate that a consistent gender pay gap (Prokos and Padavic 2005) exists regardless of cohort status and that a glass ceiling may be present that poses obstacles to women's attaining positions of authority.[1] The National Science Foundation reports, for example, that while there has been an increase in women engineers, only 13 percent of women engineers reported management as primary work activity, versus 31 percent of men (1991, 6). Asian men and Asian women also face a race or immigrant disadvantage in the attainment of managerial positions (Fernandez 1998; Tang 1993). For example, analysis of the Survey of Social Scientists and Engineers data shows no income differences between Asian and non-Asian engineers but consistent differences in achieving managerial status and positions of authority (Tang 1993). Surprisingly, in investigating whether Asian women face "double jeopardy" in science and engineering, Tang (1997) finds that Asian women do better than other women (including white women), suggesting that race and gender are not additive disadvantages in these fields.

Ethnographic studies of scientists and engineers also found a gender or ethnic/racial disadvantage shaped by informal processes. Women engineers report that their male colleagues often have "patronizing" attitudes, treating them as they would a daughter or secretary (Carter and Kirkup 1990), and workplace settings where a "locker room culture" prevails (McIlwee and Robinson 1992). More broadly, researchers argued that engineering and mathematics is where "patriarchy got the moon" (Hacker 1990, 109) and where technical skill is equated with masculinity (Cockburn 1991).

Asian men and Asian women engineers face a different typecasting, as technical "workhorses" (Iwata 1993). In an analysis of the performance evaluations of 24 U.S. companies, DiTomaso and Smith (1996) found that Asian Ph.D. scientists had lower ratings in promotability despite high ratings in technical knowledge, and Tang (2000) found that Asian engineers had difficulties switching from technical tracks to managerial tracks. A survey study of Asian professionals in Silicon Valley (Iwata 1993) found that two-thirds of Asians perceive themselves as being disadvantaged in attaining managerial status, and 80 percent also believe that Asians were underrepresented at the highest levels of their companies. Respondents viewed exclusion from the inner circles of their companies as a key reason for unequal outcomes.

Flexible Specialization in Silicon Valley

A unifying theme in the mechanisms of inequality identified in these studies is that they focus primarily on intra-organizational processes, assuming that individuals' trajectories were contingent on mobility along an internal career ladder. Epitomized by Whyte's (1956) "organization man," this road to mobility reflected the large, hierarchical firms that dominated in the Fordist era of mass production. The economic structure of Silicon Valley, however, is better characterized as flexible specialization (Piore and Sabel 1984), a mode of production that is viewed as a response to a change in consumption patterns that arose with the improvement in the technologies of communication . . . and the globalization of capitalism. Given the more ephemeral tastes of consumers, mass production using expensive, rigid machinery became less profitable, especially within the context of rising international competition. In contrast, flexibly organized economies have a "regional advantage" (Saxenian 1994) because of the proliferation of small, specialized firms linked by dense networks, which is an organizational structure that is well suited to adapt quickly to the fluctuations of globalized capitalism.

Here, I highlight two characteristics of Silicon Valley's economic structure that affect high-skilled workers. First, the region has a "high velocity labor market" (Hyde 1997) as characterized by fluid organizational boundaries and by the norm of job-hopping in the region (Baron, Hannan, and Burton 2001; Carnoy, Castells, and Benner 1997; Hyde 1997).[2] A high-velocity labor market stems from the fact that corporations have relinquished responsibility for their workers (Harvey 1989; Kumar 1995) and also reflects the career mobility strategies of high-skilled workers. From the perspective of companies and employers, flexibility is partially achieved through the ability to quickly reshape workforce size in response to market fluctuations, and workers are thus expected to be accountable for their own careers. From the perspective of workers, job-hopping is a means by which one can maintain marketability by acquiring a breadth of experiences and skills. In this manner, workers with sought-after skills can potentially benefit from a high-velocity job market, because "flexibility represents a new form of entrepreneurship in which the individual worker markets his or her capital portfolio among various 'buyers' " (Carnoy, Castells, and Benner 1997, 30).

The second characteristic of note follows from the first: To survive in this situation of heightened instability, high-skilled workers must maintain extensive networks across the region that supply them with job-relevant information and contacts (Piore and Sabel 1984). Given the break in the implicit labor contract between employer and employee, individuals are charged with ensuring their own livelihood. Nardi, Whittaker, and Schwarz (2000, 2) write, "Rather than being nurtured by institutionalised group structures, we found that workers are increasingly thrown back on their own individual resources. . . . Access to labor and information comes through workers' own social networks—structures they must carefully propagate and cultivate themselves."

These two characteristics suggest to me a marked break from the assumptions of the previous literature on ethnic and gender inequality among high-skilled workers because it points to the relevance of *inter*organizational processes (the ability to move from organization to organization), and the factors that influence these processes (mainly network resources), as fundamental for understanding ethnicity and gender in economies such as Silicon Valley. While this reliance on networks is potentially problematic given past research, the fluidity of organizational boundaries suggests that workers are not trapped or held captive in facing organizational mechanisms of inequality, provided of course that they have the resources to achieve lateral mobility and that firms exist that have more egalitarian cultures and processes.

Data and Method

This study is based on 54 semistructured interviews of high-skilled, white and Asian men and women working in Silicon Valley. The interviews were conducted between March 1999 and January 2001; all interviewees worked in the hi-tech industry in Silicon Valley and were in engineering jobs or jobs that require engineering background at the time of the interview. With the exception of four interviews, the data were collected before the Internet bust of late 2000. Interviewees were chosen using a snowball

method. Initial respondents were located from a number of sources, including contacts garnered from attendance at specialized engineering society functions, solicitation of professors at major universities in Taiwan and India for referrals to graduates they sent abroad, an ad in an alumni magazine, and referrals from acquaintances. Interviews ranged from one to two hours and occurred primarily at interviewees' workplaces. They were audiotaped and fully transcribed.

One important limitation of the sampling scheme is that it yielded an overrepresentation of successful engineers. This stems from both the manner in which the initial contacts were obtained and the subsequent snowball sampling. In terms of the initial contacts, engineers who are leaders or vocal in networking organizations, who are likely to be referred by professors, or who volunteer to be interviewed are more likely to be successful and satisfied with their careers. The initial contacts then referred me to other members of their networks, who were subsequently also more likely to be successful. The argument of this article is that job-hopping and networking strategies were important to the career livelihoods of white women, Asian men, and Asian women. While these strategies were evident among my respondents, it is likely that the sampling scheme overlooked those for whom these strategies were not available.

All interviews were conducted by the author, who is a second-generation Chinese American woman. My gender and ethnic background were advantages during the interview process, facilitating rapport with the interviewees. It was my perception that white women engineers were willing to be open about their experiences with me at least partly because of my gender and it was common for Asian respondents to ask me about my ethnic background and generational status, which then served to create a bond between us. This was true of both Indian and Chinese respondents because their identity was not only shaped by their particular ethnic background but was also shaped in contrast to (white) "Americans," of which I was not seen as a member.

During each interview, respondents were first asked to give a detailed history of their careers. From this point, the interview schedule was designed to elicit information around three primary topics of interest. First, respondents were asked about their perceptions of meritocracy in Silicon Valley and what they viewed as the necessary criteria for mobility. Second, respondents were asked to explain the types of networks they were involved in, how they gained access to these networks, and what type of functions they served. Third, respondents were asked about the pace and structure of work and how this interacted with their personal and family lives.

All respondents had college degrees, and half had advanced graduate degrees. Thirty-two of the respondents were women. Nineteen of the respondents were Chinese/Taiwanese, 19 were white, 13 were Indian, 2 were Filipino, and 1 was Vietnamese. Twenty-four of the respondents were U.S. born (including all of the whites); the remainder were foreign born. The average age of the respondents was 36, which approximates the average age of high-skilled workers in Silicon Valley (Alarcon 1999). The respondents worked (or were entrepreneurs) at 39 different firms, representing both larger, well-established organizations and smaller firms or start-ups. However, the majority of the respondents had worked in the past for both established and newer firms, and almost all the respondents had worked for more than one company. The average number of years in the work force was 11.

Results

Job-Hopping: Strategies of Integration and Separation

While respondents viewed Silicon Valley as being more meritocratic than other industries or regions where they had worked, two-thirds of respondents also reported that they had experienced some form of gender or ethnic bias, describing experiences within organizations such as ethnic- or gender-based typecasting, hitting glass walls (job segregation) and ceilings, or being excluded from key old boys' networks. Among those who reported facing bias, most said that they used job-hopping as a strategy to circumvent these obstacles.

There were two discernible strategies of job-hopping. The first pattern, which was reported by mostly white women, was a strategy based on a careful search for more egalitarian workplace cultures and bosses. This is exemplified by Susan, who

is currently a senior vice president. She describes a situation in her past company where she believed she was being excluded from the most interesting and prestigious projects because her manager was uncomfortable working with women. She says,

> The boss, and this should have been a sign to me, was a retired army colonel with eight daughters! He had spent his entire career in what at that point in time was a male-dominated military, and his entire home life he was surrounded by women. . . . So I was a first-time manager, and he could walk and talk and say all the words and say there wasn't going to be a problem, but six months later, I realized that every really interesting project that would come along, he would never give it to me, so I went to see him again, and I gave him three more months, and then realized, This man is going to die before he gives anything to me. And that's fine, I'm not going to report him, but I'll find someone else to work for.

Susan felt that the gender bias of her boss limited her opportunities to be on the most innovative projects, and this was problematic because it would subsequently limit her ability to gain the experience, skills, and visibility she needed for career mobility. Her response is telling because she says she will not "report him," that is, file a formal complaint, which is the traditional avenue of recourse, but that she will simply find someone else to work for. Faced with what she saw was an insurmountable obstacle, Susan decided to job-hop, to leave the company, and she subsequently achieved significant success in her career in environments that she views as more women friendly.

Another respondent, Mary, talks about how a friend's continuous job-hopping allowed her to circumvent the glass walls that exist in many companies. From her perspective, women face constraints to lateral mobility within companies, for instance, moving from marketing to design engineering to research and development. This kind of variegated experience is necessary to enter the higher ranks in Silicon Valley. She says that while "the guys move around all the time," women are "channeled," less able to move around easily. Given this situation, she notes a friend's strategy to overcome the glass walls within companies: "[My friend was] moving from this company to another company, and then moving from this company to here, to broaden her scope, so she's available for this pool of executive management. She had to have experience here and here and here, and to get that she had to change companies, because she couldn't move through the walls in her company, but she could move into the arena in a different company. . . . So her company-hopping has allowed her I think to advance." As Mary's comments suggest, continuous job-hopping is a means by which women can circumvent glass walls within companies, to gain the experience needed to move into executive management.

In a final example of this type of job-hopping, Linda, who is a midlevel manager, job-hopped because she felt excluded by an old boys' network at her previous company. She says about this company's environment, "I definitely felt out of the loop. . . . I very much felt that that company was run by an old boys' network, and you had to be [a] certain kind of old boy, meaning not every guy was included. . . . Women in general were not embraced or sought after, and I saw women attempt to break through that with marginal success, so everybody came to the conclusion that they had to move elsewhere." The women at this company believed they were excluded from key circles, and consequently, many left the company in a case one could call mass job-hopping. Ironically, the company later folded, which, Linda laughed, seemed like "Justice!" When she switched companies, she looked for a place that had a higher proportion of women in general and within the executive levels, and she eventually ended up at a place that she had "heard" was friendly to women. She says, "A lot of people don't know that, they just wanted to work for the hottest companies. [My company] was good. . . . They had certain processes to make sure that the careers of certain groups of people were developed."

Of course one could argue that women could be simply job-hopping from one biased situation to another, but as I think is hinted by the examples, job-hopping is not blindly done. These women did not simply switch from company to company in the hopes of finding a less biased environment but rather engaged in a careful scrutiny of potential companies, which includes soliciting information and advice about which companies are more egalitarian and evaluating the prospective new companies. For example, a manager at a software company

mentioned that he knew exactly how many women managers were in his division because a candidate he had interviewed earlier in the day had asked this question.

This conscious strategy of evaluating the gender attitudes of a company is described by Susan, the engineer in the first example, who says,

> What I actually think is more important for a woman is shopping for a boss. And I say that, and people laugh, bosses shop for employees, but I mean that very seriously. You need to find a boss who trusts you, who you connect with, who is going to give you opportunities as they come along. . . . I did a significant amount of interviewing, and finally ended up going to work for somebody who more than anyone else has single-handedly been responsible for my having been included in major projects that I worked on that got me to be VP. And that's what it's all about. It's making the connection with people who will give you the opportunity and being comfortable with them as bosses. And it's true for big companies, start-ups, and anywhere else. And it's your responsibility for doing it. To really push that person you're interviewing, understand how comfortable they are, look around their organization, look who they are giving work to and what decisions are being made: Are there women there? Are they getting on good projects? Are they getting promoted? Because that's what's important.

Similarly, a midlevel manager who had experienced rapid promotions at her company says,

> I think it depends on the company. I think [my company] is the most integrated company I've seen in terms of gender in management. There are a fair number of women in significant management positions, and it also has a lot of couples; there are a lot of women in software, which is pretty much an open area for women. People who want to go into engineering should be real careful on where they want to do work. Right now there's a pretty good blend. There are some places where you run into some pockets where you probably are not going to see a woman manager.

Alexandra, an engineer who was early in her career, noted about her most recent job interview, "This time I was very specific, I learned a lot after I interviewed at [company] and took that job. I mean I think I didn't ask enough questions that time. In any interview, you think you are going to go in and you are supposed to be answering questions rather than asking them questions. But I learned a lot. So when possible I scan people. I was very specific about what will I be doing, what projects are there, who will I be responsible for, what are my day-to-day responsibilities." These examples illustrate a strategic form of job-hopping: These white women are seeking integration and mobility into women-friendly companies. Larger studies seem to suggest that technically skilled women are able to achieve this type of lateral mobility. In an analysis of the hiring practices of a large hi-tech company, Peterson, Saporta, and Seidel (2000) find that referrals are a key predictor to who gets hired and that white women surprisingly faced no disadvantages relative to white men in this regard. In contrast, Asian immigrants faced a disadvantage in hiring specifically because they were less likely to be referred to the job, suggesting that they lacked access to the "right" networks for integration into this large organization. Similarly, in a study of hi-tech start-ups, Baron, Hannan, and Burton's (1999, 554) research suggests that women "penetrate technology based start-ups through network based hiring," a finding that they note contrasts with the assumptions of previous studies on gender inequality in work organizations.

As may be foreshadowed by Peterson, Saporta, and Seidel's (2000) study, Asian immigrants were less likely to use their networks to move into mainstream firms but rather opted to job-hop into co-ethnic-owned startups or alternatively engaged in entrepreneurship themselves. This strategy of separation is particularly feasible for Asian immigrants because of the increasing rates of Chinese and Indian entrepreneurship in the late 1990s. Like the white women cited above, Asian immigrants' job-hopping is at least partially motivated by experiences of bias. Respondents reported that they felt typecast into technical roles rather than viewed as management material. Furthermore, as immigrants, they perceived themselves to be cultural outsiders, excluded from the inner circles and networks in mainstream companies.

Ping, a male, Chinese immigrant engineer who had worked for large, white-majority companies, for example, suggests that immigrants may not have the American culture necessary to move up, saying,

> There's a lot of overseas engineers coming in, [but they are not represented at the top levels, partly because] in order to be able to move up and be able to manage in this company, its not just the technology and the skills but also the culture, you need the culture as well, the communication skills, presentation skills . . . social interaction, all that comes into play. Also, [it] depends on what culture you come from, from people who come from Canada, very little, people from Europe a little, but people coming from Asia, there's a lot of difference. . . . I guess as you get [to] the higher level, the ones up there are very American.

In the same vein, Joyce, a Chinese immigrant software engineer says that she does think that ethnicity makes a difference at work because "the Chinese cultural background are different, more humble, quiet. . . . We're not as aggressive." From her point of view, this means that "we end up not being recognized by the manager. They know you are not a troublemaker, and so they don't give the attention, the [pay] raise to us. He always takes advantage. . . . I think most Chinese in San Jose feel the way I do, [the manager] gives white people more attention." Joyce's view of the obstacles she faces is characteristic of other Asian immigrant women I spoke to. They did not speak of their gender as an issue but rather viewed their ethnic or immigrant status as the source of their disadvantage.

One of the differences between U.S.-born women's accounts and Asian immigrants' accounts (both men's and women's) is that the latter report far greater pessimism about finding firms that do not typecast them, in part because this issue is tangled with potential language difficulties or cultural differences. Patterns in large hi-tech companies lend credence to this pessimism. Data obtained by the *San Francisco Chronicle* (Angwin and Castaneda 1998) on the ethnic breakdown of leading Silicon Valley companies suggests Asians are underrepresented at the managerial level. For example, at Intel, Asians compose 18 percent of the professional workforce but only 8 percent of managers and officials. Whites, in contrast, held 70 percent of professional jobs but 85 percent of managerial and official jobs.

Given Asian immigrants' perception of technical typecasting in larger firms, respondents say they are drawn to co-ethnic firms or to entrepreneurship, where they are allowed to develop a spectrum of skills. An example of this strategy is that employed by Lei, an engineer from China, who has recently joined as a director in a co-ethnic-run start-up. His previous employment had been in companies where whites predominated. In these companies, he was put solely into technical roles and not into other divisions or into management. Lei explained that usually, "when I put a tech hat on to look for jobs, no problem. [They are] looking for a bag of skill sets, they just see me as a body." However, when he looks to go beyond this "tech hat," he usually has difficulties. In comparison, he says about the co-ethnic start-up that he has joined, "I feel very excited because I can contribute on many fronts, not only on the technology side, but product management, marketing, sales."

In another example, Lin, a Taiwanese immigrant engineer who had been working for an established, large chip manufacturer, was persuaded by his department manager, who was also Chinese, to go with him to a co-ethnic-run start-up. When I ask Lin why he and his boss decided to move to this start-up, he explains that his manager had become frustrated and decided to leave to start his own company, taking most of the Chinese engineers in their department with him because he felt he was "always kicked around by some other guy. I think somehow he felt frustrated so he thought he might as well start his own company." When asked why his boss was frustrated, Lin seemed uncomfortable and cautiously answers, "He thinks, he thought [long pause], well in the company people play politics, and he is always the victim or something [laughs uneasily], so he asked us if we want to join him, and some of us decided to." While it is unspecified why Lin's boss felt unhappy, his action of leaving and taking only other Chinese engineers suggests that some of his dissatisfaction was related to his experiences as a Chinese immigrant. Similarly, the fact that most of the Chinese engineers agreed to leave with him suggests that they too might have been uncomfortable in that environment (this is reminiscent of the case above, where several women left a company). Lin himself mentions that he and the other Chinese engineers who

job-hopped with him were in the technical division of the previous company and that he felt that they would not have had the opportunity to develop any other skills and experiences.

As a last example, Chun also had recently left his job, at a semiconductor firm where he had worked for 10 years, to join a co-ethnic firm. As a senior manager at his past company, he was in charge of a 15-to-20-person research and development department that was almost entirely made up of immigrants. When the director left, he was not promoted, and he felt that he "basically hit my ceiling." When I ask him if he felt that there was a glass ceiling for him and other Asian immigrants, he says matter-of-factly, "Yeah, of course, that is obvious. . . . Glass ceiling is definitely there. . . . [To succeed] you need to be very, very good; if you are just marginally better, there is one Caucasian and one Chinese, and you are just a little bit better, then chance to be promoted to the position is not good." However, Chun did not decide to leave because of this. More important was the fact that his entire department had in effect been demoted due to an increase in subcontracting, and he felt that he would soon be told to lay off people who were primarily Asian immigrants. Chun explains that his decision to leave and become vice president of operations at a co-ethnic-owned company was a direct result of the fact that he felt angry that the division with mostly immigrants was being expended and that his efforts to change this were fruitless.

Building Resource-Rich, Gender- and Ethnic-Based Networks

While I have argued thus far that job-hopping in Silicon Valley became a viable strategy by which white women and Asian men and women could negotiate discrimination, I do not suggest that this is a strategy that is available to all groups, or at any time period. What is critical to the ability of these groups to job-hop is their access to resource-rich, gender- and ethnic-based networks that could challenge the utility of old white boys' networks. In Silicon Valley, this became a possibility because of the historical convergence of two trends—the growth of Silicon Valley's hi-tech industry on one hand and the increasing supply of technically trained white women, Asian men, and Asian women on the other. In tandem, this led to the ability of these groups to get a foot in the door of a growing industry, cultivating members in senior positions who became well positioned to help newcomers. In addition, for Asian immigrants, the global nature of the hi-tech industry changed the structure of opportunities because transnational ties became increasingly important.

The origins of Silicon Valley are rooted in the 1930s with the development of micro electronics followed by the growth of the semiconductor industry. However, the current incarnation of the hi-tech industry is a post-1970s phenomenon, first fueled by the development of the market for integrated circuits and microprocessors,[3] bolstered in the 1980s with networking technology, and exploding in the mid 1990s by the Internet boom (Henton 2000; Rogers and Larsen 1984). The exponential and unexpected growth of this industry led to a labor shortage of engineers and other technically trained workers. A report by Joint Venture Silicon Valley (2000) found that the workforce gap in Silicon Valley was 31 to 37 percent of the hi-tech industry demand, while the Computing Technology Industry Association found that 269,000 hi-tech jobs remained unfilled in 2000, costing U.S. businesses some $4.5 billion annually in production loss. Similarly, the National Science Foundation (2000b) projects that between the years 1998 and 2008, science and engineering occupations will increase by 51 percent, or four times the rate of all occupations. Eighty percent of this growth is attributable to computer-related occupations alone.

Clearly, strong growth in the region is good news for those with the right skills because it creates an "employees' market" where competition over well-trained employees is high. I was reminded of this when, chatting in an elevator with someone on my way up to meet a respondent in his office, I was suddenly asked, "You're not going to try and steal [respondent] away from us, are you?" As I assured him that was not my intent, he jovially responded, "Good good!" and then immediately asked if I was considering joining their company. Indeed, those whom I spoke with who were in charge of hiring confirmed the difficulties of finding qualified candidates. When I asked an engineering manager in charge of hiring at a well-established company about the labor shortage, he immediately exclaimed, "Oh! It's really hard. It's a nightmare to hire people. In the last two years, information technology has just exploded, and there is fundamentally not enough people in the U.S., people are not interested [in learning the skills]."

Given this labor market context, employers would find it difficult to satisfy any "tastes" for discrimination by excluding qualified women and/or immigrant engineers. This perspective is shared by respondents. A director at a company that manufactures chip-making equipment notes that the labor shortage impedes employers' ability to discriminate. She remarks, "I think the nature of hi-tech is that because the demand for resources is so high pressured it could not afford to eliminate or constrain one element of its work force. It just couldn't afford to do it; it has been growing too rapidly. I mean [my company] has grown tremendously just in the last 15 years, and if they tried to do that, constraining one element, they couldn't do it."

At the same time that the hi-tech expansion resulted in increasing labor shortages, the supply of technically trained women and Asian immigrants also grew. Science and engineering degrees granted to women increased from the 1970s, encouraged by the civil rights and women's liberation movements. Table 1 illustrates women's increasing representation in earned bachelor's degrees in math, computer

Table 1 Women's Share (In Percentages) of Bachelor's Degrees in Engineering, Mathematics, and Computer Science: 1954, 1985, 1990, and 1995

	1954	1985	1990	1995
Engineering	0.00 (65)	15 (11,246)	15 (9,973)	17 (10,950)
Mathematics	33 (1,368)	46 (7,094)	46 (6,811)	47 (6,491)
Computer sciences	NA	37 (14,431)	30 (8,374)	28.5 (7,063)

Source: Data adapted from Streeter (1993, Table 2) and National Science Foundation (2000, 28).

science, and engineering. Only 65 women earned engineering degrees in 1954, compared to 10,950 (17 percent of all engineering degrees) in 1995. In addition, women have represented a significant share of those receiving degrees in mathematics and computer science, degrees that are central to hi-tech. Both these trends meant that women were prepared to take the opportunities in Silicon Valley when they emerged.

Furthermore, the implementation of affirmative action programs in the 1970s and 1980s encouraged companies to diversify their workforces. Respondents noted that during this time, companies made active attempts to recruit women engineers in particular. A white woman engineer with a long-term perspective on Silicon Valley remarked, "Starting in the late 70s/early 80s, corporate America was highly motivated to support affirmative action efforts. . . . [They went by] demographics, during the 80s, late 70s. People were antsy. . . . Those were the days when they were really taking care of their employees. The joke was that they had everyone in there except white guys between the ages of 25 and 40. They were looking at women as a group, minorities as a group, people over 40 as a group. It really expanded the nonmainstream people they had."

National figures seem to confirm that women are increasingly represented at the managerial level because of affirmative action legislation. DiTomaso and Smith (1996, 90) note that from 1975 to 1993, women doubled their representation as officials and managers from 14.2 percent to 29.9 percent, according to data from the Equal Employment Opportunity Commission. They find that nonwhite representation also increased during this time period, from 5.4 percent to 10.8 percent.

The historical convergence that allowed the entry of women into hi-tech at its origins was critical, allowing women to get a foot in the door of an emerging industry and eventually entering senior positions. Mary, a white engineer in senior management, compares her experience in the construction industry with the hi-tech industry.

> Where [Silicon Valley is] unique is that they are a very young industry. . . . The number of women in the Silicon industry is extraordinarily higher than the traditional construction

engineering. . . . The Silicon industry came around and it was brand new, and it had been acceptable for women for close to 100 years, or marginally acceptable at least to major in mathematics. . . . The programming industry has a very mathematical side, a lot of math, a lot of logic, so there was a large pool, or a larger pool of women to draw from. . . . So the Silicon industry had a lot of women, and since they were already there, a lot of senior people who were available to take on projects were women, so when people started thinking about who am I going to hire, who am I going to hire, the fact that it was male or female didn't come into it at all.

According to Mary, hi-tech "works to women's advantage because the demand exceeds the supply, and that's a good thing for women. . . . We've been fortunate to grow with an industry that has always needed people, needed more people than it could find, which was true 10, 20 years ago."

Changes in immigration policies for Asians also coincided with the growth of hi-tech, leading to Asians' presence at the origins of the hi-tech expansion and allowing for a steady increase in their numbers through the present. First, the contours of Asian immigration were fundamentally changed by the 1990 Immigration Act, which increased threefold the number of immigrants admitted through skills, prioritizing workers with extraordinary abilities, professionals with advanced degrees, and skilled workers (Bagchi 2001). The 1990 restructuring of immigration categories fostered the migration of hi-tech, high-skilled workers. Of all scientists and engineers admitted in these visa categories in 1993, almost 58 percent were from Asian countries, with the People's Republic of China contributing 20 percent and India another 17 percent (Streeter 1993).

Second, the increase on the caps for H-1B temporary worker visas has directly shaped Asian presence in Silicon Valley.[4] The H-1B visa program is used heavily by hi-tech firms: Half of the petitions for H-1Bs are for computer-related occupations (U.S. Immigration and Naturalization Service 2000), and about a quarter of the top H-1B-using companies are in California (Lowell 2000). The third channel by which Asian scientists and engineers enter the United States is student visas (F-1).

Table 2   Percentage of Asians Receiving U.S. Bachelor's, Master's, and Doctoral Degrees in Engineering, Math, and Computer Science, 1997

	B.S.	M.S.	Ph.D.
Asian origin	10.7	9.6	11.2
Nonresident alien	7.3	34.1	38.4

Source: Recalculated data from National Science Foundation (2000a, detailed statistical tables).

As Table 2 shows, Asians represent a sizable percentage of those earning bachelor's, master's, and doctoral degrees in the field of science and engineering. "Nonresident alien" refers to those without U.S. citizenship or permanent residency; Asians represent 73 percent of this category (Hill 1997). Students may remain in the United States after graduation since F-1 visas can be converted to H-1B visas with employer sponsorship.

Finally, a fourth channel of immigration is worth noting in relation to the migration of skilled women. In a study of immigration patterns of professionals using Immigration and Naturalization Service data, Bagchi (2001) finds that professional women immigrants are much more likely to come through spousal admissions than men immigrants with the same qualifications, estimating that between 69 and 77 percent of women doctors, scientists, and engineers enter the United States through spousal sponsorship rather than employer sponsorship.

The result of these converging trends is a critical mass of technically skilled, U.S.-born women and Asian immigrants at both senior and junior levels of companies, which in turn enabled the formation of resource-rich, gender- and ethnic-based networks that functioned to facilitate job-hopping. However, as the following examples of a gender-based network and an ethnic-based network show, the resources of these networks channeled the groups differently, at least in part because of a change in the structure of opportunities afforded to Asian immigrants in the globalized hi-tech industry.

My first example is a network rooted in the Silicon Valley chapter of the Society of Women Engineers (SWE). This nationwide organization grew from 1,000 members in 1970 to more than 15,000 members in 2000 (representing about one-tenth of women engineers in the nation). The Silicon Valley chapter is active, hosting a variety of events ranging from social networking get-togethers to career-related training sessions. Based on observations of the functions I attended, this network appears to be primarily composed of white women, with a few women of other races who are U.S. born. Asian immigrant women were not a noticeable presence. This is likely to be attributable more to Asian immigrant women's reports that they "cannot melt in" with "Americans" because of language and cultural differences than to any racially exclusionary processes of SWE.

An underlying theme of the meetings is the importance of building networks to share advice, information, and referrals among women engineers. For example, at the close of one meeting, the organizer told the audience, "You've heard the backgrounds of the people here; maybe there's someone who can help you with someone, so network and establish your chain!"

Members viewed these networks as important because they believed that women in Silicon Valley are well positioned throughout the region and subsequently have valuable resources to share. One member, Gail, remarks about the information access of women engineers: "A good example of an old girls' network is the Society for Women Engineers. . . . If you look within the political structure of SWE, there are definitely old, established networks where no matter what was going on in a management and organization, people in the network had the information about what was going on, down to the significant amount of details, they know what's going on." The presence of "old girls' networks" functions to aid junior-level women, sharing resources cross-rank. Another member of SWE who is a senior-level manager talks about this relationship: "There are women all over the Valley and in every company, so these women supply information, and when they know you and what you are doing, they'll think of you when an opportunity comes up; they'll tell you informally, maybe because they worked with you on different projects where they saw your management skills. So getting to know who they are and building a relationship [is important]." Gender-based networks thus reflect a conscious strategy, developed from the awareness that the current labor market context provides a critical opportunity. . . .

The creation of gender-based networks, and the sharing of resources within them, is facilitated by the presence of an ethic of mentoring. Whether in the formal meetings of the SWE, where everyone is exhorted, "If you are a manager, you can be a mentor," or in more informal associations, women reported freely seeking and offering "backstage" information about which places or people to avoid, how to deal with projects, and how to find other job opportunities. This ethic is rooted in the experiences of women as minorities in engineering and in their belief that they share similar obstacles.

At a function that I attended designed to address the issues of women managers, a speaker encouraged members to help other women, saying that they definitely had the power to make a difference.

> I'm going to tell you my experience. I was in an organization with 800 engineers, and I hired about 250 engineers last year. [When I was hiring] for the first seven weeks, I saw not one woman that my staffing team had brought in, and I was part of a company that was known to be a great place to work. I ran the organization! And yet these women were not being brought in. . . . I still believe that there is a tendency to bring in people who are like you. My staffing organization, which I hadn't hired, were all white males, and they presented me with all, and I didn't say most, I said what, all white males. So I said, excuse me, I believe there are about 15 percent of women out there, and I would like to see them Thursday morning.

This ethic of helping other women is present in respondents' accounts as well, where women make comments such as, "I like the fact that I am helping other women engineers get jobs, so I try to share my experiences, or refer them to people I know at some companies, and it makes me feel good I guess."

In a sense, the mentoring that women engineers consciously engage in is what male engineers may take for granted through processes of what Kanter (1977) called "homosocial reproduction." This is reflected in the description of Angie, a senior-level engineer, who talks about the informal process by which she was mentored and then became a mentor. "There were several projects I was very successful on; the majority was when I worked for a woman, and she and I had very similar backgrounds—both our fathers were in the military and so on—and we had a common foundation. We worked very well together, not that we

always came up with the same answer, but we had a common understanding. . . . She thought of me [because she was three years my senior and therefore a step up] whenever she had to get a team together; she recounted, 'the first person I think of is you.'" When I asked her if she tried, in turn, to mentor other women she said,

> Yes, I try to be available to let them understand why things are the way they are. I was very surprised when I left [my last company]; one of the senior women in my client's organization . . . pulled me aside and said that she really appreciated the strong mentoring I'd given her. She credited the fact that she was not still just an engineer as some of the people who came in with her class were, with the fact that there was somebody put her name forward. . . . [I helped] her in the sense that I would say, "Hey, I put your name in for this, and if you want to talk about it we will." If she got into a tight spot we'd talk about it.

This type of informal mentoring that Angie describes can be understood as mobility via a sponsor model, a model that has typically excluded women.

If gender-based networks functioned through the "beachhead effect" created by senior members who share an ethic of mentoring, the networks of Asian men and Asian women immigrants tapped into a different structure of opportunities predicated by the groups' increasing rates of entrepreneurship and access to venture capital. The example that follows of an immigrant network of alumni from the Indian Institute of Technology (IIT) shows that Indian immigrants had opportunities unlike those of white women.

The IITs are a string of prestigious technology institutes in India, whose alumni have immigrated to the United States in large numbers during the post-1965 era. IIT-Mumbai (Bombay) has a particularly strong record of sending graduates abroad. In one study of IIT-Mumbai alumni, more than 60 percent of the top quartile of electrical engineering graduates of 1973 to 1977 immigrated (Sukhatme 1987). Even as India's software industry grows, IIT-Mumbai continues to send graduates abroad: In 1998, about 30 percent of the graduating class left for the United States (Rajghatta 1999). The IITs have become a well-established name in Silicon

Valley because of their rigorous entrance exam, and perhaps more important, because so many of their graduates in Silicon Valley have spawned successful startups.

The networks formed have yielded advantages to their members, as illustrated by the following story of Anil, who decided to come into the region in the 1980s. When he came, he first contacted two other graduates whom he had kept in touch with who had moved to Silicon Valley in the 1970s. They immediately sent him a long list of job opportunities, furnished by the network of IIT graduates they had in Silicon Valley, and he quickly got a job at a company where another IIT graduate worked. He and his family also easily transitioned into Silicon Valley because of the personal aid given to him by the IIT network. A few years later, as venture funding became more accessible to Indians in general and to IIT graduates in particular because of the growing prestige of their school, he and his friend became cofounders of their own start-up that became quite successful. They have since started other endeavors with other alumni and co-ethnics and acted as investors in other Indian-run start-ups.

Alumni from IIT share the mentoring ethic of SWE members, saying that they are committed to helping younger graduates, and see themselves as mentors because they view themselves as a "successful group of people who have grown in the valley and in a sense become influential in a lot of ways"; "we know what it took to get there, and we realize that we need to give back." Formalized networking meetings have brought in speakers who lecture on issues such as strategies in securing venture funding or developing a strong business plan. These meetings, which are common among a number of ethnic-based networks, are also designed to match investors with entrepreneurs with high-skilled talent.

The effect of these networks, which work to foster the growing reputation of immigrant entrepreneurs, is expressed by Vijaya, an IIT-Mumbai graduate, who was in the process of starting her own firm when we spoke. She says, "It's very easy right nowadays to find venture capital, for Indians anyway, because of networks; it really does help. Just talking to people, it's very easy to find, especially in the Bay Area, at least to get your story heard. I mean, I've had lots of rejections from venture capitalists, . . . but I don't take it very seriously

[laugh]. . . . So because you know somebody who has been through the process who knows somebody, or whatever, it's very easy." She also remarks that at a time when one of the greatest challenges of forming a start-up was labor shortage, she was able to tap into her alumni and co-ethnic networks to quickly find the necessary engineers.

Mashu, a repeat entrepreneur who has been in Silicon Valley since the 1970s, agrees with Vijaya's perception of Indians' access to venture capital but talks about this within a historical perspective. He says,

> In terms of funding kinds of stuff, it really has become significantly a lot easier. I remember in the `86 timeframe, we were looking for second funding for [his company], it was hard. . . . I think it's easier for two reasons. It's easier because now there are so many success stories, and also now the venture capitalists have more money, but there are so many success stories that this is now a well-understood model. . . . And second, then about the immigrant issue, again same issue, there are enough success models, that I don't think there is really *any* difference between immigrants and nonimmigrants trying to get money, which used to be the case 15 to 20 years ago.

As is suggested by these two comments, the opportunities for immigrants to start their own firms or to join co-ethnic firms increased in the 1990s.

The IIT case is not unique. Chinese immigrant respondents also reported using alumni networks to their advantage. Respondents' accounts are supported by a recent survey of 2,272 members of ethnic Chinese or Indian networking associations, which found that almost 15 percent of immigrants from China, 34 percent from Taiwan, and 43 percent from India were involved full-time in founding or running a start-up, with an additional 16 percent of each group involved part-time in these activities. Even more striking, when respondents were asked how many of their firms' founders were co-ethnics, only 18 percent from China, 20 percent from Taiwan, and 11 percent from India said none were co-ethnics. While sampling the membership of ethnic networks overestimates those engaged in co-ethnic businesses, the data remain suggestive.

The numbers of Asian immigrants involved in running or being employed in co-ethnic start-ups is directly linked to the global context of the hi-tech industry, where increasingly, the expansion and survival of Silicon Valley is reliant on foreign labor, foreign subcontractors, foreign consumers, and foreign investment (Saxenian 1999). This global context means that transnational ties and cultural know-how become valuable, for example, to make subcontracting agreements with companies in India or marketing agreements with companies in China, to recruit high-skilled labor from foreign institutions, or to seek foreign investment. Saxenian (1999) documents the extensive ties between immigrants in Silicon Valley and in the hi-tech regions of Taiwan, China, and India, arguing that the hardware industries of the former two countries and the software industry of the latter reflect the work of transnational relationships.

In this scenario, Asian immigrants' social capital from their homeland, as well as reconstituted ethnic ties in Silicon Valley, has become a convertible commodity. Put differently, immigrants are increasingly able to import forms of social and cultural capital from their homelands. This is different from the situation in the past, where immigrants have typically been unable to transport these forms of capital: it was either useless, as in the ubiquitous anecdotes of professionals who are now laborers in Chinatowns, for instance, or limited, as in the case of social capital within the confines of ethnic economies. This is a potentially significant consequence of the global nature of industries like hi-tech because it signals the ability of some Asian immigrants to reach outside the domestic structure of ethnic and race relations to access resources. The change in the structure of opportunities, that is, the increasing convertibility of transnational and co-ethnic ties, along with increased access to funding has made job-hopping into co-ethnic-owned firms or starting one's own firm a viable option that did not exist for the white women I interviewed. In this sense, the type of network resources each group had access to channeled their job-hopping.

Conclusion

This article compared the experiences of U.S.-born white women, Asian women, and Asian men engineers in Silicon Valley. The case study of Silicon Valley contributes to a more complete understanding of gender and ethnic inequality in organizations by underscoring the role that region, group, and historically specific contexts play in mediating mechanisms of discrimination and by examining how these contexts potentially enable traditionally disadvantaged groups to contest organizational bias.

Studies of work organizations have focused on gender and ethnic typecasting, segregation within organizations, and lack of access to networks and role models as key factors in explaining ethnic and gender inequality. While the respondents in this study confirmed the presence of these factors, they also indicated that they were able to employ successful strategies to counter discrimination. Simply put, when faced with bias in their workplace, they reported job-hopping into firms that they viewed as more egalitarian, and they reported having access to networks that facilitated this process.

The argument here is not that all women and ethnic minority men can use this strategy in any situation (or even that all women and ethnic minority men in Silicon Valley could do so). Rather, this case study suggests the pivotal role that contexts play in providing avenues for resistance. Three contexts were emphasized: the region's high-velocity labor market that made job-hopping normative, and the historical and group-specific contexts of Silicon Valley that enabled white women, Asian men, and Asian women to build and tap into resource-rich, gender- and ethnic-based networks that could challenge the old white boys' networks. The relevance of these contexts was clearly illustrated in the example of the old girls' network. The accounts of these members richly explain why quantitative studies have found that in contrast to expectations, white women in hi-tech are tapped into the "right networks" in mainstream firms (Baron, Hannan, and Burton 1999; Peterson, Saporta, and Seidel 2000).

This case study subsequently highlights the importance of studying the other side of discrimination. Research on work organizations too often focuses on mechanisms of discrimination without full consideration of what strategies may be employed to combat these mechanisms and what conditions are necessary for these strategies to have effect. This is clearly an incomplete picture, depicting workers as helpless against inexorable structures. By looking at the strategies of white women, Asian men, and Asian women in challenging bias, this study gives appropriate weight to both agency and the conditions that make agency possible, highlighting the interplay between the two. In relation, the two networks presented hint at the role of identities and ethics in facilitating the sharing and allocation of resources within networks. Members in both networks described an identity based on a disadvantaged status, coupled with a mentoring ethic. This meant that access to the most valuable network resources was not just the province of senior members but rather was shared with those who stand to benefit the most, creating an important ladder effect. In this sense, Silicon Valley may be meritocratic, as the public discourse is fond of suggesting, but meritocracy, when it exists, does not stem from the culture of the region but rather exists as an achieved outcome of the work of groups.

Finally, the comparison of white women with Asian immigrant women reflects the interaction of gender and ethnicity in shaping divergent (but not necessarily unequal) trajectories. While I noted earlier that Asian immigrant women spoke of their experiences in primarily ethnic or immigrant terms and similarly white women viewed their careers as shaped by gender rather than race, it is clear that each of these groups' outcomes were shaped by both statuses. For white women, the ability to locate firms they viewed as egalitarian was partly shaped by the fact that race or immigrant status was not a problematic issue. In addition, the social networks they reported clearly included white male engineers, indicating that they had access to some mixed-gender but primarily single-race networks. This is not to suggest that Asian immigrant women faced a double disadvantage. Instead, their experiences were filtered through and buffered by the Asian immigrant networks they were a part of, and while it is reasonably safe to assume that there are gender differences in access to these network resources, these networks still offered Asian immigrant women a different but no less effective set of resources.

NOTES

AUTHOR'S NOTE: This research was supported through dissertation grants from the Social Science Research Council International Migration Program, and from the Asian American Studies Center at UCLA. I am grateful to Lande Ajose, Horacio Enroque, Gil Eyal, John Horton, Shirley Hune, Roger Waldinger, and Min Zhou for their invaluable comments on earlier versions of this article and for the insightful guidance of three anonymous reviewers and editor Christine Williams.

1. There have been challenges to the glass ceiling hypothesis. Morgan (1995) has suggested that what had been seen as a glass ceiling effect can be understood as a cohort effect, with younger cohorts of women engineers experiencing negligible gender disadvantage. More recently, Prokos and Padaviv (2005) found a consistent gender pay gap (regardless of cohort) but no evidence of a glass ceiling.

2. Hyde (1997) estimates that the average job duration among hi-tech professionals is two years; Joint Venture Silicon Valley (2000) finds that the regional turnover rate was twice the national average; and Carnoy, Castells, and Benner (1997) find that human resources managers in hi-tech companies report annual turnover rates ranging from 15 percent to 25 percent.

3. For example, Intel produced its first microprocessor in 1971, while Apple Computer was formed in 1976. Cisco Systems, a leader in networking technology, was founded in 1984, and the first version of Netscape Communications emerged in 1994.

4. H-1B visas allow entrance through guest worker status for a maximum of six years (two three-year extensions). While a cap of 65,000 was instituted in 1990, annual numbers have exceeded this, with 137,000 workers admitted in 1999 alone. In response to lobbying by the hi-tech industry, Congress passed legislation in 1999 that increased the annual cap to 115,000 for three years.

REFERENCES

Alarcon, Rafael. 1999. Recruitment processes among foreign born engineers and scientists in Silicon Valley. *American Behavioral Scientist* 42 (9):1381–97.

Angwin, Julie, and Laura Castaneda. 1998. The digital divide: High-tech boom a bust for Blacks, Latinos. *San Francisco Chronicle*, 4 May.

Bagchi, Ann. 2001. Migrant networks and the immigrant professional: An analysis of the role of weak ties. *Population Research and Policy Review* 20:9–31.

Baldi, Stephanie, and Debra Branch McBrier. 1997. Do the determinants of promotion differ for Blacks and whites? *Work and Occupations* 24:478–97.

Baron, James N., Michael T. Hannan, and M. Diane Burton. 1999. Building the iron cage: Determinants of managerial intensity in the early years of organizations. *American Sociological Review* 64:527–47.

———. 2001. Labor pains: Change in organizational models and employee turnover in young high-tech firms. *American Journal of Sociology* 106 (4):960–1012.

Bielby, William, and James Baron. 1986. Men and women at work: Sex segregation and statistical discrimination. *American Journal of Sociology* 91:759–99.

Carnoy, Martin, Manuel Castells, and Chris Benner. 1997. Labor markets and employment practices in the age of flexibility: A case study of Silicon Valley. *International Labor Review* 136:27–48.

Carter, Ruth, and Gill Kirkup. 1990. *Women in engineering: A good place to be?* London: Macmillan.

Cockburn, Cynthia. 1991. *In the way of women: Men's resistance to sex equality in organizations.* Ithaca, New York: ILR.

Collins, Sharon. 1997. *Black corporate executives.* Philadelphia: Temple University Press.

DiPrete, Thomas, and Whitman Soule. 1988. Gender and promotion in segmented job ladder systems. *American Sociological Review* 53:26–40.

DiTomaso, Nancy, and Steven Smith. 1996. Race and ethnic minorities and white women in management: Changes and challenges. In *Women and minorities in American professions,* edited by Joyce Tang and Earl Smith, 87–110. New York: State University of New York Press.

Dossani, Rafiq. 2002. *Chinese and Indian engineers and their networks in Silicon Valley.* Stanford, CA: Asia/Pacific Research Center.

Ellis, Richard, and Lindsay Lowell. 1999. Foreign-origin persons in the U.S. information technology workforce. IT Workforce Data Project, report 3. New York: United Engineering Foundation.

Fernandez, Marilyn. 1998. Asian Indian Americans in the Bay Area and the glass ceiling. *Sociological Perspectives* 41:119–49.

Hacker, Sally. 1990. *Doing it the hard way: Investigations of gender and technology.* Boston: Unwin Hyman.

Harvey, David. 1989. *The conditions of post modernity.* Oxford, UK: Basil Blackwell.

Henton, Doug. 2000. A profile of the Valley's evolving structure. In *The Silicon Valley edge,* edited by Chong-Moon Lee, William Miller, Marguerite Hancock, and Henry Rowen, 456–58. Stanford, CA: Stanford University Press.

Hill, Susan T. 1997. *Science and engineering bachelor's degrees awarded to women increase overall but decrease in several fields.* NSF 97–326. Arlington, VA: National Science Foundation.

Hyde, Alan. 1997. Employee identity caucuses in Silicon Valley: Can they transcend the boundaries of the firm? *Labor Law Journal* August:491–97.

———. 2004. Employment discrimination in a high velocity labor market. *Faculty Papers* 13.

Iwata, Edwards, ed. 1993. *Qualified, but . . . A report on glass ceiling issues facing Asian Americans in Silicon Valley.* Report by Asian Americans for Community Involvement. Santa Clara, CA: Quick Silver.

Joint Venture Silicon Valley. 2000. *An analysis of the workforce gap in Silicon Valley, 2000.* Silicon Valley, CA: Joint Venture Silicon Valley Network.

Kanter, Rosabeth Moss. 1977. *Men and women of the corporation.* New York: Basic Books.

Knoke, David, and Yoshito Ishio. 1998. The gender gap in company job training. *Work and Occupations* 25:141–67.

Kumar, Krishan. 1995. *From post-industrial to post-modern society.* Oxford, UK: Blackwell.

Lal, Bhavya, Sam Yoon, and Ken Carlson. 1999. *How large is the gap in salaries of male and female engineers?* NSF 99–352. Arlington, VA: National Science Foundation.

Lowell, B. Lindsay. 2000. Information technology companies and U.S. immigration policy: Hiring foreign workers. Paper prepared for the Fourth International Metropolis Conference, Washington DC, 8–11 December.

McIlwee, Judith, and J. Gregg Robinson. 1992. *Women in engineering: Gender, power and workplace culture.* Albany: State University of New York Press.

Morgan, Laurie. 1998. The earnings gap for women engineers, 1982 to 1989. *American Sociological Journal* 63 (4): 479–93.

Mueller, Charles, Tony Parcel, and Kazuko Tanaka. 1989. Particularism in authority outcomes of Black and white supervisors. *Social Science Research* 18:1–20.

Nardi, Bonnie, Steve Whittaker, and Heinrich Schwarz. 2000. It's not what you know, it's who you know: Work in the information age. *First Monday* 5 (5):1–37.

National Science Foundation. 1991. *Women and minorities in science and engineering.* Washington, DC: National Science Foundation.

———. 2000a. *Science and engineering degrees by race/ethnicity of recipients, 1989–1997.* Washington, DC: National Science Foundation.

———. 2000b. *Science and engineering indicators, 2000.* Washington, DC: National Science Foundation.

Nkomo, Stella, and Taylor Cox Jr. 1990. Factors affecting the upward mobility of Black managers in private sector organizations. *Review of Black Political Economy* winter:39–57.

Peterson, Trond, Ishak Saporta, and Mark-David Seidel. 2000. Offering a job: Meritocracy and social networks. *American Journal of Sociology* 106 (3):763.

Piore, Michael, and Charles Sabel. 1984. *The second industrial divide: Possibilities for prosperity.* New York: Basic Books.

Prokos, Anastasia, and Irene Padavic. 2005. An examination of competing explanations for the pay gap among scientists and engineers. *Gender & Society* 19:523–43.

Rajghatta, Chidanand. 1999. Brain curry. *Express Xclusive,* 7 December.

Reinhardt, Andy, and Joan Hamilton. 1997. What matters is how smart you are: Silicon Valley, how it really works. *Business Week* 18 August:68–72.

Rogers, Everett, and Judith Larsen. 1984. *Silicon Valley fever.* New York: Basic Books.

Saxenian, Annalee. 1994. *Regional advantage.* Cambridge, MA: Harvard University Press.

———. 1999. *Silicon Valley's new immigrant entrepreneurs.* San Francisco: Public Policy Institute of California.

Streeter, Joanne. 1993. *Immigrant scientists, engineers and technicians*. NSF 96322. Arlington, VA: National Science Foundation.

Sukhatme, S. P. 1987. *Pilot study on the magnitude and nature of the brain drain of graduates of the Indian Institute of Technology, Bombay*. Bombay: Department of Science and Technology, Government of India.

Tang, Joyce. 1993. The career attainment of Caucasian and Asian engineers. *Sociological Quarterly* 34:467–96.

———. 1997. Evidence for and against the "double penalty" thesis in science and engineering fields. *Population Research and Policy Review* 16:337–62.

———. 2000. *The career attainment and mobility of Caucasian, Black, and Asian-American engineers*. Lanham, MD: Rowman & Littlefield.

U.S. Department of Commerce. 1999. *The emerging digital economy II*. Washington, DC: U.S. Department of Commerce.

U.S. Immigration and Naturalization Service. 2000. *Characteristics of specialty occupation workers (H-1B): October 1999 to February 2000*. Washington, DC: U.S. Immigration and Naturalization Service.

Vital intangibles. 1997. *The Economist*, 29 March:7–11.

Whyte, William, 1956. *The organization man*. New York: Simon and Schuster.

FORTY-ONE

♦♦♦

To Whom Much Is Given, Much Is Expected: Successful Women, Family, and Responsibility (2003)

Veronica Chambers

Former editor and writer at *Newsweek* and *New York Times Magazine*, **Veronica Chambers** is also a children's book author. Much of her work, including her awardwinning memoir *Mama's Girl* (1996), focuses on stories that reflect her African and Latina heritage. Other titles include *Having It All: Black Women and Success* and *Kickboxing Geishas: How Modern Japanese Women Are Changing Their Nation*.

To whom much is given, much is expected" was both personal and political to young black women in the 1970s. At the time, Walteen Grady-Truely was getting her undergraduate degree at Michigan State University. She remembers two things distinctly: the culture of black nationalism that permeated her campus and the sense of marriage panic that hung over her heart. "As I reflect over the atmosphere of the 70s, my decisions were overlaid by the sense that the revolution was going to happen tomorrow and that you had to choose sides," says Walteen. "If you didn't make the right choice, you could hurt the whole black community. It wasn't like I could have the luxury of finding myself. I had to choose the right side of the battle lines. . . . "

For those women who came of age right after the civil rights movement, life was a mixture of often contradictory rules. You were supposed to say it loud about being black and proud, but to assert your independence with black men was counter-revolutionary. Education was a key component to uplifting the race, but as Stokely Carmichael so famously put it, "the black woman's place in the movement is prone." Black men could, and would, date white women without losing their place in the black power movement. Yet, black women who chose to date white men were nothing more than self-deluded, voluntary chattel, ignorant of 200 years of rape and slavery.

At six-feet tall, with a short salt-and-pepper afro, Walteen is now in her late 40s. At the time of our first conversation she's recruiting mentors for at-risk teens as the Director of the New York Volunteer for Youth Campaign. She radiates a strong, calming presence. As we sit and talk at a Thai restaurant near her New York City office, she is in the process of divorcing her husband of 15 years. Her smooth, dark skin is unlined, but there is a definite furrow across her brow. She has been taking a memoir-writing course, she tells me, and it has helped her as she tries to assess the choices that she has made in her life; there are pieces of her younger self that she misses and that she hopes to recover.

Walteen spent her teenage years traveling with her family; her father was in the military. She lived in Nigeria for four years, attended a Swiss boarding school for another year, then graduated from a high school in Bangkok. One of the memories that her writing course has brought up is that in Thailand, as a high school senior, she asked a white classmate to the Sadie Hawkins dance. Returning to the United States to go to school, she would never have considered such a possibility. "When I went to college, there was such a strong era of nationalism," she remembers. "I felt that I didn't have the right not to marry a black man. I felt I had a responsibility to have a black child."

"I didn't have the right." "I felt I had a responsibility." Those are powerful words to use when discussing one's personal life. How did she end up shouldering so much guilt? "It's guilt and responsibility," Walteen corrects me. "I think the two things are very much entwined. No one ever told me that I could be true to myself and still carry out that sense of responsibility." Yet she is hardly alone in her generation of women, who allowed the politics of the black power movement to dictate who and how she loved.

Guilt was also a factor in how Walteen chose her life's work. "Oh absolutely!" she says emphatically. "I believe it is what drove me in almost all my career choices. I chose to go into education. Before that, I wanted to be a lawyer. It was always with an eye towards creating a world where there would be more people like me, where there would be more people who shared a quality educational background, who had the advantage of having access to the whole world, not just the neighborhood."

This was a powerful notion for Walteen, who felt it was her life's work to bridge the gaps between the blacks who were haves and those who were have-nots. Growing up as a middle-class black girl, Walteen remembers complaining to her parents about her sense of isolation. "I didn't have any friends like me," she says. "I wasn't meeting people. My mother used to say, 'Well, I've been lonely all my life.' I guess she thought that was comforting, but it wasn't." Her mother's comments are clearly a painful memory for Walteen. During our most recent interview, she had moved back home to the Poconos where she's an instructor of education and coordinator for the Learning Support Center at the local Penn State campus. She moved so her son could be near his grandmother and attend better schools, but she worries that while he is now thriving academically, he's also suffering from the same loneliness she once did. "I don't think it's new," she

says. "But there's a sense that if you're African American and on the cutting edge economically and educationally, there are not going to be other people like you. There are so few of us. I definitely have that feeling and my son has it, too."

Several years earlier, when she worked in Tribeca, she decided to register her son, Romare, at a nearby school. She knew it would be a marked improvement from the school he attended in their Fort Greene neighborhood. In an effort to ease the transition, she made it a point to continue Romare's play dates with his best friend, Rodney. The boys were both ten when Walteen overhead the following conversation. Rodney asked, "So what's your school like?" Romare said, "Oh, it's a school." Rodney paused, then asked, "Well, do you have gunshot holes in your windows?" It's a painful memory for Walteen, whose face, as she tells the story, displays a mixture of shame and hurt. "It just blew me away," she says. "It was almost as if we had to have a choice between having a community of black people and an environment that was very unsafe or having a safer environment physically and no community. It hurts me to see that repeated over and over again." Even in this day and age, a whole new generation of young people are being offered opportunities that aren't afforded the majority. As far as we have come, there is still a talented tenth—with all the weight of responsibility and guilt that comes along with it.

The Talented Tenth

In 1903, the great scholar W. E. B. DuBois published his masterwork, *The Souls of Black Folk.* DuBois's writing was an intellectual, improvisational pastiche of narrative fiction and social criticism, anthropology and state of the union address—it reads like highly developed literary jazz. In it, he famously declared "the problem of the 20th century is the problem of the color line." DuBois would be hailed as a visionary, again and again. His words resonated throughout almost all of the 20th century's great social struggles and tragedies. Whether it was the Turkish massacres of Armenians, the German slaughter of Jews, or the colonizers' ways with the colonized, it's remarkable how we've been driven again and again into war, massacre and upheaval by the power of racial difference. DuBois, who always meant his quote to address a far greater scale than racial politics in the United States, saw it coming.

DuBois's prophecy was marked not only by the eloquence of his words, but also by the breadth of his scope: what ambitious statesman—black or white—would look a hopeful people in the eye and tell them that racism would last not a decade or two, but 100 years? As bold as it was, his proclamation was hardly a news flash. Even Langston Hughes's fictional colored man on the corner, Jesse B. Semple, could have looked at the masses of sharecropping southerners and northern factory workers addled by poor working conditions and minimum pay and declared "Houston, we have a problem." Any uneducated black man or woman could have told you that Lincoln didn't solve the race problem as they cited the tyranny of hapless, random violence that was a constant threat to their lives. In those fragile years, as former slaves and their children tried to construct a place for themselves within the severe constraints of the northern-mandated freedom, *The Souls of Black Folk* could have been merely a preacher yapping at the choir.

DuBois, however, operated like a jazz musician. For the most part, his book wasn't aimed at black folks at all. Like other great race men and women before him, such as Frederick Douglass and Sojourner Truth, he sweetened the melody for the liberal white audience that he hoped would start swaying in beat to his cause. Yet he knew that blacks were listening and, in order not to lose their attention and support, he would sometimes curve a note in their direction. His theory of the Talented Tenth swung like that. DuBois's Tenth was the segment of the black community who had the wit, social skills and means to uplift the entire race. This Talented Tenth would be the leaders and architects of black achievement in America. Our shining glory.

From the beginning, the theory brewed controversy. At the turn of the century, the problem of entry into the upper echelons of black society was indeed the problem of the color line. Black elites monitored membership in the most prestigious black civic organizations, churches, fraternities and sororities with a paper bag test: anyone darker than a paper bag need not apply. Despite their own intraracism, these people considered themselves sanctioned by birth and skin color to lead the poorer black masses. They beamed with pride at DuBois's notion of the Talented Tenth because surely, they reasoned, he was talking about them.

Conversely, there were those who disagreed vehemently with DuBois. Some of them could care less about the colorism that plagued the black upper classes. These critics simply saw the idea of a Talented Tenth as being inherently divisive and problematic. How could we commit the wealth of our resources and energies to just one-tenth of our community? How could we be sure that once educated and anointed they would uplift our cause? And what happens, generation after generation, to those who are left behind? It's a question that black people struggle with to this day. Cheryl Mills, former deputy White House counsel and current Oxygen Media vice president, put it this way to Lynette Clemetson in a *Newsweek* article: "We're now getting to this place where we have the privilege to decide if we are all going to be on the same bus or whether or not we are going to get off the bus. I think the black community is finding itself now at this crossroads where it has to decide. Are we going to continue to be connected as a community or are the privilege levels and the progress we're seeing going to mean different things for different [people]?"[1]

Take, for example, an anecdote separated from the race issue altogether. Each year, a poor village has ten students that complete the modest lessons taught in its one-room schoolhouse. They pick one young man to continue his education in the big city. They pay for his schooling, his lodging, his expenses—everything, so he can focus on his studies and become a doctor. Obligation, and some might say guilt, would predicate that the young man returns to the village to open a practice, and perhaps one day, a hospital. But who's to say that the young man will? Maybe he will take a job at a research facility; maybe his destiny is not to cure colicky babies and ill farm animals, but to find the cure to some interminable disease. Maybe his aim or intention isn't even as noble as that. Maybe he takes a job with a big city hospital, gets rich and builds himself a big house. What happens to the village then? What good is their investment in the Talented Tenth? Maybe they should have sent two students to college, with partial scholarships each. Maybe they should have truly hedged their bets and sent three.

Shaking Off the Guilt: A Generational Shift

At 31, Angela Kyle feels much less anxious than Walteen Grady-Truely about finding a place in the black community. And she feels none of the guilt. It's the gift that women of Walteen's generation have given to the women of mine: we have the luxury to find ourselves without worrying that our actions are, as Walteen phrased it, "hurting the whole black community." Angela and I meet at the Bel Age Hotel in Los Angeles; she lives nearby in Beverly Hills. Angela is tall and thin with the kind of All-American freshness of a J. Crew model. Today, she's wearing a close-fitting T-shirt, slacks and has a cardigan tied around her hips. Angela's chestnut-colored skin is flawless, without a hint of makeup, and she wears her shoulder-length hair in a fashionable bob. She's just finished her second day in her new job as senior director of business development at Live Planet—a company often in the news because of its two co-founders, Ben Affleck and Matt Damon. The heart-throbs want to bring together old media (film and television) with new media (the Internet) in intriguing, profitable ways.

It's a high-stakes gambit. Other Internet-related companies led by such visionaries as Steven Spielberg and Ron Howard blew through millions of dollars, then failed. Ben and Matt have Hollywood convinced they'll do better. Angela's an anomaly in the office; the executive suite is largely a good young boys' network from Boston and their early days as struggling actors in L.A. She's an Ivy League graduate, with business degrees from Columbia University and the London School of Economics. She's a young, black woman in a business that could care less about affirmative action or the Talented Tenth or diversity. She's at Live Planet for one reason alone—to make deals and making deals is what she loves.

Angela remembers that growing up, "I lived in a predominantly white neighborhood and went to a predominantly white school. In order to balance the whole white thing, I went to a black church." It's interesting to me that even Angela's language is more flippant, more casual, than Walteen's pained confessions. By the late 1970s and early 1980s, "the whole white thing" was not a big deal at all. "I was really active in church stuff so I had a group of black girls my age," she says. "Then at school, I had white female friends. I never really tried to bridge the two or bring them together, I was comfortable with them being separate."

Later, at Brown University, Angela felt none of the social or political pressures that Walteen experienced at Michigan State. At Brown, she joined a group called OUAP, the Organization of United African Peoples. But this was hardly her social center. "I wanted to be in OUAP," she says. "I wasn't really active, but I was at least present and accounted for." The desire to be simply "present and accounted for" is a seismic shift from Walteen's college years when she felt weighed down by her obligations to the movement. . . . In contrast, Angela describes her experience with black groups at Brown to being similar to the way her Asian friends felt about Asian-American organizations. "We were all aware of what was going on in our respective communities," she says. "But what drove my experience was meeting people that I had things in common with. I was pretty comfortable forging this network of friends that was racially mixed."

Similarly, when Angela talks about her career in business development, race hardly enters the conversation at all. She's not pressured to find a black husband, hasn't even begun to think about kids. "My thought is that right now I can't get married and I can't have kids," she says. "For me, the ultimate success as an adult is career success, getting to the top of something, winning awards. This is the arena in which I feel like I'm making my mark on the world. I know that I can't balance my life with family in any way, shape or form so I haven't really tried."

In Angela's conversation, there are hints of so many things, especially the luxury of young black women today to put career first. . . . There may be so much talk in the public sphere about successful black women and the dearth of highly educated, high-income earning male counterparts, but there seems to be little realization that for women like Angela, marriage and family aren't a priority. She doesn't know or care if there are "enough" black men out there. She's not really looking. It's not that she doesn't value her black girlfriends or that she isn't interested in black men. It's just that right now she's having too much fun and is way too ambitious to worry.

"My friend Suzie was here last weekend," Angela mentions. "She was saying that sometimes it stresses her out to be in a group of all black women. She says that no matter where the conversation starts, be it on the topic of work or family, it always ends on men and how everyone's looking and can't find one. Blah. Blah. Blah. It's not so much that the fantasy of a Prince Charming doesn't apply to me as a black woman. It's more that I'm a workaholic and I have other issues." And on that note, Angela gets up to leave. Her company is throwing a party to announce the winner of a screenplay competition they've been running. It will be one of her first opportunities to get face time with the heads of her company. With a wave, she is off—to gather intelligence, to meet and greet, to make deals.

Even though they live on different sides of the country, I know that Walteen would be proud of Angela. That in some ways, Angela's attitude is something she is striving for herself. Both women represent a vision of DuBois's Talented Tenth, but they embody it in radically different ways. The last time we met, Walteen said that what she has always admired about my generation is that "You've always represented for me the right to have stuff, the right to carve our own space and not just be the banner carrier for the race. You feel a right to be yourself. This is the next level of black liberation: the right to be ourselves, the right to define our own successes. In the '60s, I might have defined success as the right to fight for my people. That was the pinnacle. You are part of a group of women who are enjoying their lives. That's the next frontier."

Who Do We Owe?

If the civil rights act of 1964 was our economic emancipation, the open sesame to access to the education and jobs that would level the playing field, then it is a relatively recent freedom. One of the markers of the black middle class is that, for the most part, its members are still closely tied to those in real poverty. The women I interviewed spoke of their concern for the black community in general. But they could also each point to a sibling or a cousin or other relatives who were struggling.

To a certain extent, the problem of the villager who goes off to medical school and feels an obligation to his community is one these women can relate to easily. On a Saturday afternoon in Hoboken, I got together with a group of 30-something and 40-something women. The walls of Tracie Howard's living room were painted a warn golden hue that

brought to mind the faded gilt of Renaissance Italy. The chandelier was a 1920s Art Deco find and framed photos of family and friends graced the surface of her baby grand piano. Paintings by prominent African-American artists hung on most walls, while a lighted breakfront displayed her collection of three-legged teacups from Limoges, Japan and Italy. In complete defiance of the old paper bag rule, the women were a rainbow mix from fair-skinned to very dark-skinned. All of them were members of the upper middle class and had ventured to Tracie's from their homes in New York City, Westchester and Greenwich, Connecticut.

The women talked animatedly about their passion for mentoring and community service. For them, it's more than doing a good deed. They see themselves in the young people that they are helping, they believe that their actions are improving the lot not of "poor black folks" but of "brothers and sisters." There's a big difference in the way these women speak about community service and the language their white society counterparts use. By doing good, they feel they are also "doing the right thing," as Spike Lee so aptly called it. Furthermore, their charitable efforts keep them in touch with a home they don't want to leave behind.

I probe a little deeper, and each woman admits that while community service is fulfilling, trying to meet the needs of poorer family members is almost always a losing battle. The women in their 40s have come to terms with the economic disparities in their own families. "No guilt," says one of the guests, an investment banker on Wall Street. Her simple declaration is followed by so many "Amens," the room is almost transformed into Sunday church. But these are women in their 40s, who've made the tough choices and don't take any mess off anyone. I found that among my peers, women in our 30s, there's not always the same confidence. We're not always sure that we don't owe the village every penny in our pockets.

Though I'm not a banker or Wall Street broker, my "Amen" was right there with the others. As the first person in my immediate family to graduate from college, I basked in the glow of achievement. I lived the dream deferred. A year after graduation, I was making more money than my mother was. My role as the family money store began. Siblings and other more distant relatives began to pull a guilt trip on me: I'd been "lucky" to get a scholarship, "lucky" to meet whites who mentored me and offered me jobs. They'd not been so lucky in life. Where they lived, life was hard—or had I forgotten?

Looking back, I could say that I was young and easily influenced. But I know that it was more than that. Despite the hefty student loan bill that I pay each month, I would not have been able to attend college at all had it not been for the largesse of a W. E. B. DuBois scholarship that handled a sizeable portion of my tuition every year. My school, Simon's Rock College, is in Great Barrington, Massachusetts: birth home of DuBois. My reading of *The Souls of Black Folk* at the age of 16 had a powerful impact on how I viewed race and its obligations. I would never have called myself part of the Talented Tenth, but I certainly took my place among its platoons of strivers.

When my summa cum laude degree was re-warded with one good job after another, I knew I had to give back. And as my family laid it out for me: charity begins at home. Throughout my 20s, I buckled under the guilt and pressure and gave out thousands of dollars in "loans" that could never, would never, be repaid. Even when lending money meant draining my savings account or giving away the next month's rent, I jumped at the desperate calls in the middle of the night and the wailing darkness of "I have nowhere else to turn." Like many profes-sional black women, I'm hardly wealthy by main-stream American standards. But compared to the poverty of those I love so dearly, the fact that I even had next month's rent in the bank meant that I was rich. Absolutely loaded. "We have extended family who think we're Rockefellers," says Robin Nelson Rice, a former pharmaceutical company executive now living in London. "We're not even Rock, forget Rockefeller! But from their viewpoint, it's 'Oh yes. Somebody comes and cleans your house. I need that job. I could be that. You could pay me that money.' They're always calculating. 'Oh, the nanny. Do you hear that? They've got a nanny.'"

For Tarin Washington, a 32-year-old finance ex-ecutive, earning an MBA roused the jealousy of old friends. As one male friend put it, "You think you're better than me because you're successful and moved out of the hood." It had been a bonanza year for Tarin: she'd recently completed her MBA and purchased a home in Connecticut as well as a used luxury model car. She says, "I realized that his perception of my having reached success was just

that, perception. I wasn't anywhere near the suc-cess that I have planned for myself. I still have a very long way to go. As a matter of fact, I was still living in the 'hood, just in a new development in a different city!" But like a lot of the women I spoke to, poorer relations and friends thought that the purchase of luxury items, an advanced degree and a healthy income meant that all of your problems were solved, forever and ever.

Soon after I graduated from college I read an arti-cle in *Money* magazine that struck a similar chord about the expectations of extended family on young black professionals. The headline of the piece was: "Hunting for the First House." The sub-head read: "Home-buying can be a financial and emotional chal-lenge for any couple. As African Americans looking in Chicago's white suburbs, Trish and Larry Harvey faced special hurdles—but overcame them."[2]

The story went on to introduce us to the Har-veys, ages 26 and 29. They were "both MBAs, with fast-track jobs and a combined income close to $100,000 a year." But the article showed this couple to be more than materialistic Buppies. Although childless themselves and still so young, they were raising Trish's 16-year-old niece, Raven. And their "carefully calculated budget" included not only money for rent and insurance, food and a vacation fund, but $500 a month toward assisting relatives. Money that, out of politeness, might be called a loan; but money the Harveys never expected to see again.

Who Is Giving? What Is Expected?

I can't remember the first time I heard the phrase, "to whom much is given, much is expected," though I suspect I was still in diapers. Nor can I tell you how often the phrase was repeated throughout my childhood; the number would have to be in the hundreds, if not the thousands. I heard it every Sun-day that I attended church and every Saturday when our family went visiting. I heard it from my teachers when I received high grades and heard it, underlined, when I brought home Cs. The parents of my friends uttered it during pep talks after school and old black ladies murmured it in my ear when I respectfully leaned forward to kiss their powdery cheeks. Along with the West Indian equiv-alent of "Walk good" and the also often-repeated

"Each one teach one," "to whom much is given, much is expected," was passed down as more than a platitude. It was the knight's code, a secret moral compass that would guide me should I make it through the woods, into the kingdom of higher education and on to the palaces of good fortune beyond.

Though I did not know it then, the reference is biblical. It's in the New Testament, Luke 12:48: "For unto whomsoever much is given, of him shall be much required: and to whom men have committed much, of him they will ask the more." The first sentence of the verse had been passed down in the black community (no doubt by savvy pastors who found their collection plates to be a little light). The second part of the verse may not have been uttered, but was certainly implied. I know that I'm not alone among middle-class women and men who have had to learn that you aren't a traitor to the people when you turn down a relative or a friend for a loan. I also know that as black women continue to outpace black men educationally and financially, more of the burden of helping falls upon us. We pay for our success not only financially, but emotionally as well.

In the work place, the "much is given, much is expected" motto can be a double-edged sword for successful black women. Clearly, our success provides an opportunity for service. "It's about taking ownership," one 30-something programmer . . . told me. "I love going out on recruiting trips and being able to reach out to young black kids. Even if they don't come and work for my company, I can give them the tools and tips they need to get ahead. I feel like I'm helping people."

At the same time, the expectation can be that our success means we should be ever grateful and behave accordingly. We are dealt our daily share of racism and sexism, yet our class—and the means by which we make our living—predicates that we must often bite our tongue or risk being labeled as "angry," "difficult," or even "racist.". . .

At home, the challenge can be equally painful. One need only look at the hit film *Soul Food,* the story of three sisters and their families in Chicago. The most successful one is a lawyer named Terry. As portrayed by Vanessa L. Williams, Terry is brittle, caustic and quick to criticize. The message the filmmakers send is that Terry's ambition has drained her soul. She's on her second marriage and, when husband number two commits adultery, it's Terry's fault for working so hard. Her sister

Maxine, in contrast, has no loot but a lot of love: she's been married to her husband for 11 years and the two still flirt shamelessly. Maxine has three beautiful kids, while Terry is trying, but childless. Maxine can also cook huge Sunday dinners, steeped in Southern tradition. Terry has no domestic skills, but a seemingly endless ability to write checks. The film sets her up as a bad guy, but I painfully recognized her plight. Who can blame her for being so cranky when she's the one who's got to pay her mother's hospital bills, fund her youngest sisters' business ventures and bail her brother-in-law out of jail? With not so much as a thank you, mind you. It's little wonder that when Terry explodes, she says, "As far as you know, I'm an ATM. It's always Automatically Terry's Money." My generation is getting better at shaking off the guilt, but for those of us who come from families that were born poor and have stayed poor, balancing the weight of expectation is never easy.

What We Owe Ourselves

As chair of the African-American studies program at Princeton University, Valerie A. Smith is a high-profile figure in a high-pressure job. She is the Woodrow Wilson Professor of Literature and the author of many critically acclaimed books, including *Self-Discovery and Authority in Afro-American Narrative* and *Representing Blackness: Issues in Film and Video.* Among certain passionate circles of Afro-Bohemia, she is known as the woman who brought Andrea Lee's *Sarah Phillips* back into print, a novel about race, class and identity that is now taught in hundreds of colleges nationwide. She is smart. She is powerful. But what I hear more than anything about Valerie Smith is that she is physically fit. I mean really fit. I begin to hear a rumor that while she was a professor at UCLA, she would only hold student conferences during her daily hour-and-a-half hike up Runyon Canyon. I hear that she is known for urging her black women colleagues, students and friends not to give so much of themselves that they don't take time for themselves. It's when this last comment drifts back to me that I decide I have to meet her.

We meet for tea, at 4:00 at Sally Lunn's in Princeton, an old-fashioned teashop that looks like a scene out of *Mary Poppins.* I ask Valerie, who is indeed fit and who looks barely old enough to buy alcohol, much less chair a university department, about her fitness journey. "In junior high school and high school, I really wasn't athletic at all," she tells me. "For a variety of reasons. Mostly I was this high-achieving academic kid, who couldn't get into competitive sports. Then I began running in graduate school. There was a group of us who got together and running was a social thing."

. . . I ask her about the student conferences held during grueling canyon hikes and she laughs out loud. "I'm notorious for that," she says, mischievously. "I'd get my grad students to have conferences with me during my 6:30 A.M. hike. I felt like I was sending a message: channel your anxiety into this exercise. I also felt like this was a way for them to have my full attention. They certainly were not going to get an hour and a half of my time while I was busy in my office." Not only did some of her students begin to exercise on their own, but a number of them also quit smoking. "They didn't have

enough wind to talk, going up those hills," Valerie says with a smile.

. . .

Smith believes that if we are going to continue to thrive as black women we need to take care of not only our minds and our spirits, but our bodies as well. The week before we meet, thousands of black women had mourned the death of the poet June Jordan. She was 65. For me, as for others, it had echoes of the deaths of Audre Lorde, Virginia Hamilton, Sherley Anne Williams. "We're beginning to see how many of our successful sisters are dying young or suffering from chronic illness," says Smith. "We've got to pay attention to what we eat, what we do physically. We take responsibility for so much. We've got to take responsibility for ourselves."

NOTES

1. Lynette Clemetson and Allison Samuels. "We Have the Power." *Newsweek,* September 18, 2000.
2. Bill Sheeline. "Hunting for the First House." *Money,* December 1993.

8

◆◆◆

Living in a Globalizing World

To understand the situations and experiences of women in the United States, it is important to know something of those of women worldwide and the ways we all participate in, and are affected by, an increasingly integrated global system. This chapter takes this wider angle of view, with nation as an additional analytical category together with gender, race, and class. We discuss personal experiences of home and family that cross national borders, patterns of migration and displacement, cultural diversity and homogenization, the movement of work across national borders, efforts to reduce global inequalities, and unsustainable patterns of consumption. Throughout this book we refer to the global level of analysis and interaction; in this chapter we emphasize the global and macro-level structures within which people organize their lives.

Locations, Circuits, and Flows

In Chapter 3, we noted that connections to people, communities, and home are important parts of our identities. For many people those connections may be in several places, as with some writers in this collection. Christina Leaño, for example, a second-generation immigrant born and raised in the United States, decided to live in the Philippines after graduating from college, to develop stronger ties to her extended family there and to learn firsthand about Filipino life and culture (Reading 16). This experience opened up new consciousness for her and a new sense of self and life purpose. Surina Khan was born in Pakistan and immigrated to the United States as a child. In Reading 21, she comments that, "Pakistan has always been my parents' answer to everything." As a young lesbian she rejected Pakistan as synonymous with homophobia but gradually sought out queer people from South Asia, which led her to examine a part of herself she thought she had discarded. In Reading 17, Julia Alvarez notes that some Latino/a immigrants retain strong ties to their countries of origin and may travel back and forth regularly, maintaining family and community connections in more than one place.

In this chapter, Gloria Anzaldúa traces the original migrations into what is now the United States, and the subsequent conquest and settlement of Mexico and the U.S. by Spanish and British colonizers, respectively. She writes as a mixed race person, a mestiza, located in more than one place, with more than one consciousness, who moves smoothly between two languages and who has learned "to be an Indian in Mexican culture and to be Mexican from an Anglo point of view" (1987, p. 79). The current U.S.–Mexico border was defined in the 1848 Treaty of Guadalupe Hidalgo that established the Rio Grande River as the international boundary and ceded Texas to the United States together with Arizona, California, Nevada, and New Mexico. Referring to this history, Mexican Americans often say: We didn't cross the border; the border crossed us. Anzaldúa describes the border as a place where "the Third World grates against the first and bleeds" and considers the challenges, benefits, and losses involved in border-crossing (Reading 42).

In Reading 45, Swiss filmmaker Ursula Biemann describes flows of women crisscrossing the globe in her video essay, *Remotely Sensed,* concerning the trafficking of women for the sex industry. She argues that they travel along ever-changing routes and trajectories shaped by economic hardship, cultures and laws that provide for men's sexual lives, and the immigration policies of receiving countries. We draw on this imagery of circuits and flows to visualize the world in terms of interconnected networks of people, homes, goods, information, work, money, and cultural productions like music and movies. Movement along global pathways is facilitated or impeded by specific conditions, rules, and assumptions about what should be traded, who should travel, and for what reasons. Notice the direction of these flows. Are they reciprocal? Are they mainly one way? Also note that such circuits operate at meso-, macro- and global levels.

People in the United States are dependent on the labor of myriad others who work both here and abroad. Economist Teresa Amott (1993) showed how race and ethnicity have been central in assigning people to specific kinds of work in the United States (see Chapter 7). This same basic principle holds true for the global system. The circuits and pathways that direct these patterns of movement are flexible in that they respond to changing opportunities and desires. Also, they are relatively predictable in how they sort and route particular groups of people toward specific destinations. Nation of origin—intersecting with class, gender, and race—shapes who goes where, for what purpose, under what circumstances, and for how long.

The current **neoliberal** economic policies and practices that frame people's life decisions and opportunities give corporations freedom to operate with relatively little interference from governments, international financial institutions, or labor unions (see Box). Spike Peterson emphasizes the significance of what she calls "the virtual economy" with almost instantaneous worldwide communication through Web and Internet systems (Reading 47). This has made possible current forms of **globalization,** by which the world's people are brought into an increasingly integrated system that is structured around a range of rules, institutions, and conditions.

International Institutions

While World War II still raged, 730 delegates from 44 allied nations met at Bretton Woods (New Hampshire) to discuss ways to rebuild and regulate the post-war international economic system. The **Bretton Woods Agreements** included the formation of the International Bank for Reconstruction and Development (now one of five institutions in the World Bank group) and the International Monetary Fund (IMF). Together with the World Trade Organization (WTO), the United Nations (UN), and international laws and treaties, these international financial institutions provide a framework of rules and agreements within which governments, banks, corporations, and non-profit organizations operate and interact. The WTO, established in 1995, adjudicates cases brought by nations regarding restraints on trade due to limiting factors in other nations' laws and regulations (see Box on international economic institutions and trade agreements).

All countries are involved in trade. Many pay more for imports than they earn in exports, leading to a balance of payments deficit. In order to take out additional loans, the World Bank and the IMF have required indebted nations to make stringent changes to their economies. The aim of such Structural Adjustment Programs is to increase the profitability of corporations on the grounds that this will benefit everyone. Required measures include:

- cutting back government spending on social services;

- abolishing price controls, particularly on food, fuel, and public transportation;

- adding new taxes and increasing existing taxes;

- selling nationalized industries, or at least a majority of the shares, to private corporations, often from outside the country;

Market Economies: Basic Operating Principles

Capitalism, also called a market system, is a cultural, economic, and political system in which the major means of production and distribution are privately held and operated for profit. Individuals, small businesses, and major corporations invest capital—money and property—in manufacturing, communications, or agriculture, for example. By producing goods and services, workers earn wages and increase the wealth of their employers.

A mixture of corporate and government decisions provide the framework for business operations. Governments and corporate elites share assumptions about what makes the economy successful, with variations in different countries. Governments provide infrastructure in the form of roads, railways, bridges, and airports; give tax breaks and financial incentives for investment; and sometimes waive environmental regulations to attract businesses.

Governments levy taxes that may be used to alleviate the social impacts of the booms and slumps and uneven development inherent in this system. In extreme circumstances, they may sanction the use of police or military force against workers who strike for better pay and working conditions or against communities who oppose privatization of resources. Specific principles include:

- *The profit motive.* Companies compete to sell services and products and stay in business as long as it is profitable or while governments are willing to subsidize them, as happens, for example, with agriculture and defense industries in the United States.

- *Consumerism and expansion.* Companies seek to produce more products, develop new products, and to find new markets and new needs to supply. Many of the things we think we need are not absolute necessities but are contrived needs generated by advertising or social pressures. Needs also depend on context. Currently cars are necessary in many parts of the United States that have little or no adequate public transportation.

- *Corporate responsibility.* Companies have little or no responsibility to workers left stranded, when, for example, car assembly plants close down in Detroit or Mattel moves its Barbie doll factory to Malaysia.

- *Short-term costs.* The business definition of costs—the short-term costs of raw materials, plant, payroll, and other operating expenses—is a narrow one. It does not include effects of production on workers' well-being, the surrounding community, or the wider environment.

Key International Economic Institutions and Trade Agreements

The World Bank

Headquartered in Washington, D.C., the World Bank was set up in 1944 to provide loans for reconstruction after the devastation of World War II and to promote development in countries of the global South, where the bank's emphasis has been on major, capital-intensive projects such as roads, dams, hydroelectric schemes, irrigation systems, and the development of large-scale, chemical-dependent, cash-crop production. The bank's investors are the governments of rich countries that make money on the interest on these loans. Because the World Bank assigns voting power in proportion to the capital provided by its shareholders, its decisions are dominated by the governments of the global North, and its policies are in line with their concerns.

International Monetary Fund (IMF)

Also based in Washington, the IMF is an international body with 184 member countries. It was founded at the same time as the World Bank to promote international trade and monetary cooperation. It makes loans to governments for development projects and in times of severe budget deficits. France, Germany, Japan, Britain, and the United States have over 50 percent of the votes, which are allocated according to financial contribution to the fund. If member countries borrow from the fund, they must accept a range of conditions, such as structural adjustment programs, and must put export earnings above any other goal for the country's economy.

Trade Agreements

The General Agreement on Tariffs and Trade (GATT) was started after World War II to regulate international trade; over a hundred nations, responsible for four-fifths of world trade, have participated in it. Starting in 1986, the agreement was changed significantly in response to transnational corporations' demand for fewer tariffs on the goods they move around the world—data, components, finished products, and foods.

The United States entered into specific free trade agreements with Mexico and Canada in 1994 (North American Free Trade Agreement—NAFTA); with Costa Rica, the Dominican Republic, El Salvador, Guatemala, Honduras, and Nicaragua, beginning in 2005 (Central America Free Trade Agreement—CAFTA); and with South Korea in 2007 (KORUS-FTA). These agreements reduce import tariffs, eliminate import quotas, and open up local resources to outside ownership and extraction. Proponents contend that free trade will result in increased prosperity. Opponents cite evidence of the effects of NAFTA, which included major job losses in the United States and even larger losses in Mexico. CAFTA and KORUS FTA were pushed through by all governments despite widespread popular opposition from labor unions, farmers, environmentalists, community organizers, and fair trade activists. As well as job losses, such trade agreements undermine local food production and food security in Mexico or South Korea, for example, because local farmers cannot compete with "cheap" U.S.-produced corn and rice, subsidized through the U.S. farm bill.

World Trade Organization (WTO)

This is an unelected international body over which member nations and their peoples have no democratic control. The WTO allows national governments to challenge each others' laws and regulations as violations of WTO rules against restraints to trade. Cases are decided by a panel of three trade experts. WTO tribunals are secret, binding on member states, and provide no outside appeal or review. Once a WTO ruling is issued, losing countries have a set time to change their laws to conform to WTO requirements, pay compensation to the winning country, or face trade sanctions (Working Group on the WTO 1999, p. 5).

Nations can challenge environmental laws as a constraint on trade, exemplified in the shrimp-turtle case, in which India, Malaysia, Pakistan, and Thailand challenged the U.S. Endangered Species Act that requires domestic and foreign shrimp fishers to catch shrimp by methods that do not kill endangered sea turtles. The WTO determined that this law violated WTO rules (Wallach and Sforza 2000; Wallach and Woodall 2004). It also ruled against the European Union in a case that challenged European nations' rights to give preference to bananas produced by small-scale farmers in Africa and the Caribbean who work their own farms rather than huge plantation production, which exploits labor and uses environmentally damaging techniques. Other examples include a challenge by the U.S., Canada, and Argentina to European Union restrictions on importing genetically modified foods and a challenge by Canada and Brazil to U.S. farm subsidies.

- improving profitability for corporations through wage controls, tax breaks, loans, and credit; or by building ports, better roads, or rail transportation; and
- increasing the output of cash crops for export.

Though not required to do so by the World Bank, successive U.S. administrations have adopted similar policies, including, for example, the deregulation of air transport, cuts in welfare and social services, the privatization of public utilities like water and electricity, as well as aspects of the prison industry and military contracting. Also with the goal of increasing business profitability, the United States has entered into free trade agreements with other nations on both American continents, as well as South Korea (see Box).

National and Local Governments

One of the roles of nation-states is to provide the social and political conditions that make it possible for business to operate. They may also seek to control corporate activities, though this is limited by shared assumptions about the central role of business in the current economic and political system as well as by their different resources. Governments of some small countries have operating budgets smaller than those of transnational corporations. Exxon-Mobil, General Motors, and Ford have higher revenues than the national budgets of all but seven countries: United States, Germany, Japan, China, Italy, Britain, and France. Some companies have more revenue than the budgets of their home governments (e.g., Shell/Netherlands and Daewoo/South Korea). Beyond this, global governance structures are provided by international financial institutions, which are unaccountable to people and local and national governments, as mentioned above. The logic of economic globalization entails a borderless world for capital and corporate activities. Indeed, national boundaries have become more porous with regard to capital but not with regard to all workers or people who migrate for other reasons. Many corporations recognize that effective global reach depends on becoming more deeply embedded in local economies, hence the term **glocalization.** The penetration of global rules and institutions means that nations, cities, and neighborhoods are affected by corporate decisions that may be made thousands of miles away. This is not to say that local and national institutions have no power, but that they exercise their powers within this global context.

Assumptions and Ideologies

The circuits and flows of the global system are defined by ideas about development and progress. Countries of the global South are often called developing countries, assuming that they will become industrialized like Canada, the U.S., and Western Europe. Constructing a continuum from "undeveloped" to "developed" suggests that this process is both linear and the best way for a nation to progress. This continuum masks the fact that so-called developing countries have thousands of years of traditional knowledge. Much of the wealth of developed nations has come from poorer ones; indeed this is a key reason for their lack of economic

You don't understand; the "econo-me" grew, not the "econo-you."

development. Vandana Shiva (1988), a scientist and writer on environment and development, used the term "devastated" instead of "undeveloped" economies to emphasize this connection.

Economic growth is often conflated with "progress"—a much more complex concept with social, moral, spiritual, and intellectual dimensions. This view of progress often leads people in a highly material society like the United States to value themselves primarily in terms of the money they make and the things they own or consume. At a national level, too, it leads to an emphasis on material success and material security with support for government policies that facilitate profit making regardless of social costs. Spike Peterson comments that, increasingly, "public provision of welfare is ideologically constructed as a luxury that viable (competitive) national economies cannot afford" (Reading 47).

People in dominant positions may justify inequalities among and within nations with reference to ideologies of racism, classism, sexism, and national superiority. Others argue that in principle, inequality is unjust. Some people's freedom and comfort should not be bought at the expense of other's people's oppression, degradation, and poverty. More pragmatically, inequality is an ongoing source of violence and conflict. On an international level it is a cause of war; on a community level it can lead to alienation, anger, violence, vandalism, and crime. Since its inception in 1948, the United Nations has developed an extensive body of protocols and agreements that provide standards for human rights, equality, and justice. Examples include the 1948 Universal Declaration of Human Rights, the 1951 Convention Relating to the Status of Refugees, the 1989 Convention on the Rights of the Child, and the 2000 UN Protocol to Prevent, Suppress, and Punish Trafficking in Persons, Especially Women and Children. Governments sign on to these documents and may ratify them to bring them into national law. The U.N. provides a forum for governments to be held accountable for their commitments and is the focus of organizing efforts by non-governmental organizations who seek to influence international policies.

Legacies of Colonization

Current disparities among nations are often based on older inequalities resulting from colonization. Former British colonies include India, Ghana, Hong Kong, Kenya, Nigeria, and Pakistan. France had colonial possessions in Algeria, Senegal, Togo, and Vietnam. Although the details varied from place to place and from one colonial power to another, several factors were central to this process:

- the imposition of legal and political institutions;
- cultural and spiritual devastation and replacement of language;
- transformation of social relations, including gender roles and ethnic and class stratification;
- psychological dimensions of ethnocentrism and racism, such as internalized racism and colorism rooted in whiteness and white supremacy; and
- distortions of the economy with dependence on a few agricultural products or raw materials for export.

Colonial powers extracted raw materials—timber, minerals, and cash crops—which were processed into manufactured goods in the colonial centers for consumption there and for export. During the second half of the twentieth century, virtually all colonies gained political independence, but many have remained tied to their colonizers politically, culturally, and linguistically. In terms of inhibiting self-determination, continuing economic ties may be the most devastating. This includes dependence on firms established during colonial times, the activities of transnational corporations, and loans from governments and banks of countries of the global North. These factors have led many commentators to characterize the continuing inequalities between richer and poorer countries in terms of **neocolonialism.**

Immigration Policies

Movements of people are facilitated and limited by immigration policies, which shift in response to economic booms and slumps, political concerns like support for refugees, relationships with allied nations, and perceived threats to national security. Overall, tens of millions of people have started new lives in the United States and have contributed greatly to the nation's economy and cultural diversity (see Chapter 3 for key immigration laws and policies). Johanna Shih notes the importance of work visas that allow highly qualified people from China, Taiwan, and India to take high-tech jobs in Silicon Valley (Reading 40).

Immigration is currently a highly contentious issue in the United States and in other receiving countries

such as Britain, France, and Germany. The U.S. government has strengthened and militarized the long border with Mexico in an attempt to stop undocumented immigrants from entering that way. Armed guards, infrared night-vision scopes, low-light TV cameras, motion sensors, helicopters, and all-terrain vehicles patrol the border fence day and night. Immigration and Customs Enforcement (ICE) has stepped up raids on homes, schools, and workplaces in many towns and cities. At the same time, immigrant communities have asserted their presence and the contributions they make to this nation, by taking to the streets in huge demonstrations. Race and class are significant factors in immigration policies, practices, and enforcement. People who hold Australian, Canadian, European, Japanese, and U.S. passports have relative freedom of travel, especially for short-term trips and vacations. By contrast, people from poorer countries, as well as countries identified by the government as "terrorist" or "hostile," need visas and are subject to greater scrutiny at borders.

Migrations and Displacements

Migration

Human migration is not a new phenomenon. Movements of ancient peoples within regions and across continents have been amply documented, with a general agreement that people of the Rift Valley in what is now Mozambique were among the first recorded to travel to Europe and then to other continents from around 1.5 million to 5,000 years before the Common Era (Koser 2007). Why and how people moved has varied during each wave of great migrations. The political and economic interests and aspirations of ancient empires and modern-day imperial powers have resulted in huge movements of people, mainly according to the needs and priorities of dominant or colonizing powers.

Perhaps the most important of these in modern memory took place during the eighteenth and nineteenth centuries and involved the transporting of some 12 million enslaved West Africans to the "New World," with others taken to the Mediterranean or across the Indian Ocean. After the ending of slavery in the United States, Chinese, Filipino, Indian, and Japanese workers were allowed to enter the country to meet the demand for labor (see *Immigration Timeline* in

Chapter 2). Also the rise of the United States as a major industrial power, together with weakening economies and political repression in Europe, led to massive European immigration to the U.S. starting in the mid-nineteenth century. More recent immigration has mainly involved people from Asia and Central America. Some are high-tech employees, as noted earlier, but most fill the "3D jobs"—dirty, difficult, and dangerous. They are underpaid and overworked, and employers can use their status as immigrants to exploit them further.

According to the International Organization for Migration, migration "is considered one of the defining global issues of the early twenty-first century" (IOM 2007). Consider the following data from 2005:

- There were an estimated 200 million migrants worldwide, up from 176 million in 2000. They included 9 million refugees.
- Migrants comprised 3 percent of the global population.

Categories of Migrants Recognized by the United Nations

Asylum seekers: People who file an application for asylum in a country other than their own and who remain in this status until their application is decided.

Contract migrant workers: People working in a country other than their own under contractual arrangements that limit the period of employment and the specific job held.

Diplomats and consular personnel: Foreigners working under diplomatic permits for foreign embassies or consulates in the receiving country. Also, citizens traveling on diplomatic passports to and from their country's embassies or consulates abroad.

Domestic employees: Foreigners admitted for the specific purpose of providing personal services to foreign diplomatic and consular personnel in the country.

Foreign retirees (as settlers): People beyond retirement age who are granted the right to stay over a long period or indefinitely in a State other than their own, provided that they have sufficient independent income and do not become a charge to that State.

Foreign students: People admitted by a country other than their own, usually under special permits or visas, for the purpose of following a particular course of study in an accredited institution of the receiving country.

Foreign tourists: People admitted under tourist visas (if required) for leisure, recreation, holiday, visits to friends or relatives, health or medical treatment, or religious pilgrimage.

Foreigners admitted for family formation or reunification: Immediate relatives of people residing in the receiving country or the foreign fiance(e)s or adopted children of citizens. The definition of immediate relatives varies but generally includes the spouse and minor children of the person concerned.

Internally displaced persons: People forced to flee from their homes as a result of or in order to avoid the effects of armed conflict, situations of generalized violence, violations of human rights, or natural or man-made disasters, and who have not crossed an internationally recognized State border.

Military personnel: Foreign military personnel, officials, and advisers stationed in the country. Dependents and domestic employees may be allowed to accompany them.

Refugees: Foreign persons granted refugee status and entering to be resettled in the receiving country or persons granted refugee status on a group basis.

Stateless persons: People who are not recognized as citizens of any State.

Trafficked persons: People who are illegally recruited, coerced, and/or forcibly moved within national or across national borders.

- Women accounted for 50 percent of global migrants.

- If the total number of migrants were a nation, it would be the fifth most populated country in the world (after China, India, the United States, and Indonesia).

The United Nations distinguishes several types of migrants (see Box). Personal dreams and decisions, community expectations and pressures, macro-level immigration policies, or global labor markets all influence who moves, where they move from and to, the conditions under which they relocate, and the situations they face at their destinations. As mentioned earlier, national origin, gender, race, class, religion, culture, language, and other significant aspects of structural power shape the circuits along which people move. Also, given a combination of opportunity, education, hard work, support, and luck, some people are able to go "off-track." Shailja Patel describes her parents' struggle to maneuver their daughters from the East African nation of Kenya to Britain and the United States (Reading 43). They confronted a succession of gatekeepers, including school principals, officials who evaluated visa applications, overseas examination boards, and immigration officers, while the exchange rate between Kenyan shillings and British pounds and U.S. dollars spiraled irreversibly upwards.

In her discussion of sex trafficking, Ursula Biemann opens up the question of what meanings women ascribe to their life decisions, how they understand the constraints within which they live and the opportunities available to them. She asks whether one can call these movements voluntary and, if so, in what sense. Enormous differences in living standards between the United States, Japan, and Europe compared to poorer countries are a source of continuing pressure for people to leave their families and homelands. Grace Chang and Kathleen Kim note the "coercive nature of most migration" given this reality (2007, p. 327). Other reasons that people are forced to move include religious or political persecution, armed conflict, or natural disasters.

Migration Patterns

Migration patterns include places of origin, transit, and destination. For example, movement often originates from a country in the global South with a Northern country as the final destination. A woman may leave her home and family in a rural area, move to a city in her country, then to a neighboring country, and finally **immigrate** to her intended destination. People who migrate voluntarily usually move to places where they have connections based on national, community, or family ties. For example, people from the Middle East, Afghanistan, Bosnia, and Southeast Asia have settled in Dearborn (Michigan), Fremont (California), Utica (New York), and Minneapolis (Minnesota), respectively.

Contemporary migration patterns are unique in two important ways. First, women constitute half the world's migrants, often as the primary breadwinners for their families. In Europe, Latin America, and the Caribbean, more migrants are women than men because of a greater demand for women as domestic workers, nurses' aides, home health care workers, as well as sex industry workers or mail-order brides (see, e.g., Chang 2000; Ehrenreich and Hochschild 2000; Perez 2003). We noted the crisis of care work in North America and Western Europe in the previous chapter, allowing—and needing—women from the Philippines, Central America, and the Dominican Republic to migrate for such jobs. Conditions in the sending countries are also key factors. The Philippines is an impoverished nation that exports people to work in Europe, North America, the Middle East, Hong Kong, and Japan. Rhacel Salazar Parreñas discusses the impact of this macro-level policy on Philippine families and communities when mothers undertake care work abroad (Reading 44; see also Heymann 2006; Zimmerman, Litt and Bose 2006). Similarly, Indonesia, the country with the largest population of Muslims in the world, exports women to work in Arab states such as Jordan and Lebanon because Muslim employers prefer Muslim household help. Jacquelyn Litt and Mary Zimmerman emphasize that the labor of women from poorer nations "serves as the infrastructure on which **First World** economic expansion depends" (2003, p. 157). In addition, immigration policies may extend rights for female family members to join their children and spouses who have settled abroad. Families, thus, become defined by where work is available.

A second feature of contemporary migration patterns is the blurring of boundaries between points of origin, transit, and destination. As a result, according to migration scholar Alejandro Portes, this has created transnational communities that are made up of dense networks across political borders created by immigrants in their quest for economic advancement and social recognition. Through these networks, an increasing number of people are able to live dual lives. Participants are often bilingual, move easily between cultures, frequently maintain homes in two countries, and pursue economic, political, and cultural interests that require presence in both.   *(1997, p. 812)*

These people include migrant workers who live in the United States and support their families and home communities in El Salvador or the Philippines, for example, by sending regular remittances or sponsoring schools or other community projects. It also includes professionals, corporate executives, and academics, whose families and professional lives straddle national borders. Chandra Talpade Mohanty discusses her relationship to "home" in the United States as well as India (Reading 11).

Although our focus here is on those who move, it is important to note that millions of people are prevented from moving or their movements are monitored and curtailed. Within the U.S., for example, it is very difficult for working-class and poor young people of color to move out from inner-city communities unless they join the military. Others who are restricted include Arab and Muslim people during this era of "war on terror," Palestinians in the West Bank and Jerusalem, and refugees in war-torn countries.

Transnational Adoptions, Tourism, and Trafficking

Briefly, we consider three types of movement within and across national borders: transracial/transnational adoption, tourism, and trafficking. Despite major differences, these examples share certain characteristics. They are each structured as industries that include recruiters and procurement agencies, businesses that apply for visas and deal with government bureaucracies, and the organization of transportation, including escorts and guides (see, e.g., Hübinette 2006).

Transracial/Transnational Adoptions   Children who are adopted across national boundaries constitute a particular case of migration, as heterosexual couples, single women, and lesbian/gay couples in countries of the global North expand their families this way (see Simon and Roorda 2000; Trenka, Oparah, and Shin 2006). Angelina Jolie and Madonna, for example,

have made headlines as fulfilled adoptive mothers of children born in the global South, exemplifying the consumption aspect of adoption, what Kim Park Nelson (2006) called "shopping for children in the international marketplace." Photos of these celebrity mothers and their adopted children depict an ideal family, with the children on their way to a new and privileged life in the States. These media images make transracial/transnational adoption seem unproblematic for the child, for the newly constituted family, and for the child's country of birth. Of course, at the micro-level, children need homes, love, and nurturing. Birth mothers decide, or are forced to give up their babies depending on their personal circumstances, which are affected by macro-level economic conditions, or policies like China's one child policy and cultural preference for sons. Others are sometimes tricked and deceived into surrendering their parental rights. Many transracial/transnational adoptions have involved children from South Korea in the 1950s and 1960s and more recently Vietnam, Cambodia, Guatemala, and Nicaragua, which were all devastated by wars. Transnational adoption may have been the best option at the time for the birth parents and the babies, but it also represents a loss to these children's home communities.

Adapting to their new home in the United States may not be easy for such children, especially if they are raised by white parents in a predominantly white community. Establishing a sense of identity and belonging is much more difficult across lines of race and culture. These adopted children have been cut off from their ancestry as well as their biological parents. As we noted in Chapter 3, they may need to reconnect with their family and culture of origin in some way as part of the process of resolving their hybrid identity. In the U.S., there is also a history of forced removal of Native American children to boarding schools and adoptive homes away from their home communities, with some parallels to transnational adoptions (Trenka, Oparah, and Shin 2006).

Tourism   Traveling abroad is something that many people in the United States want to do, whether this is through college programs, volunteering with nonprofit organizations, taking a tour, or enlisting in the military. Travel is fun, a chance to see new places and meet new people, though such "meetings" happen on artificial and unequal terms. By definition, tourists have leisure time and disposable income, which sets us apart from people who live and work in tourist destinations. In her classic essay, *Report from the Bahamas,* the late June Jordan (1980) noted with deep regret the social distance between herself—an African American university professor, poet, and writer—and the Black people staffing the hotel where she stayed. Jamaica Kincaid (1988) gave a caustic account of what tourists see, what they do not see, and how local people view them in the Caribbean island of Antigua. In Reading 65, attorney and activist Mililani Trask notes the negative effects of tourism on Hawaiian communities and the commodified, exoticized version of Hawaiian culture that is retailed to tourists. Although the tourist industry generates jobs, these may be seasonal and usually pay low wages; the most profitable businesses geared toward tourists are national and international chains, such as car rental agencies, hotels, and restaurants, which undercut local businesses. Tourism also competes with other forms of development; consumes scarce resources, including water, food supplies, and land; and generates considerable waste for local communities to absorb.

Trafficking   Organizers and advocates Lora Jo Foo, Gabriela Villareal, and Norma Timbang define human trafficking as "the recruitment, harboring, movement, or obtaining of a person by force, fraud, or coercion for the purpose of involuntary servitude, debt bondage, or slavery" (2007, p. 38). Electronic communications, poverty and inequality, demand for cheap labor, and increasingly restrictive immigration laws have all contributed to a rise in human trafficking. Both women and men are trafficked—into agriculture, domestic service, restaurants, hotels, manufacturing, construction, and the sex industry.

As mentioned earlier, structural adjustment policies instituted by the World Bank and IMF, and free trade agreements between richer and poorer nations have undermined subsistence economies, eliminated social services, and resulted in job losses and food crises in many poorer nations. Economic upheaval due to the break-up of the former Soviet Union left many thousands of people unemployed. Wars, crop failures, and other hardships are also "push" factors that compel people to risk emigration. Despite the difficulties and the possibilities for fraud and deception, when faced with responsibilities for their family's survival, women and men make the decision to travel abroad for work. People's experience of being trafficked may range from consent to coercion. A person may initially participate on the basis of 'knowledge and consent'; she "may later wish to leave the

work or particular employment site, yet be held captive by an employer" (Chang and Kim 2007, p. 327).

Trafficking can happen within a nation or across national borders. Typically, poorer countries are sending people. For example, men from Bangladesh are taken to work in sweatshops in South Korea; women from the former Soviet Union end up in Israel; people from China and Central America are brought to the United States; men from Turkey are taken to France; and women from Thailand are brought into Japan. Traffickers may use complex routes with transit points in a third country. They may change routes and destinations depending on changes in national laws, immigration policies and enforcement, and penalties for getting caught. Recruiters front the money for visas, transportation, guidance, and other services, so their clients are indebted to them from the beginning. Human trafficking is an important operation in the contemporary criminal underworld that investigative reporter Misha Glenny (2008) refers to as "McMafia," which he argues has flourished since the fall of the Soviet Union.

Ursula Biemann comments that women who travel for sex work enter "cross-border circuits, illegal and illicit networks as well as alternative circuits of survival." She comments that they often feel that agents who recruit them are providing a valuable service in helping them to achieve their desire to move to a richer country. She argues that women enter these migration circuits for many reasons and with varying expectations. In her video, the migrating women appear as data streams, scans, and X-rays portrayed over landscapes passing by. Their anatomical and demographic data are recorded; their routes appear in electronic travel schedules on the screen. They are the embodiment of the abstract financial flows that feed the global economy (Reading 45 and photo).

Trafficking of women always entails risk of sexual abuse and violation, and trafficking of girls and women into the sex industry is significant, for example, in Thailand, Cambodia, India, and the Philippines (see, e.g., Shih 2007; Tadiar 2003). Sex trafficking into the United States represents a minority of people who are trafficked. Non-governmental organizations and academic researchers estimate that from one-half to two-thirds of trafficking into the United States occurs in non-sex-related industries. For example, the Coalition to Abolish Slavery and Trafficking reported that clients trafficked to Los Angeles are subject to exploitation in many fields, including domestic work (40 percent), factory work (17 percent),

sex work (17 percent), restaurant work (13 percent), and servile marriage (13 percent) (cited in Chang and Kim 2007). This is in contrast to the U.S. government's conflation of human trafficking and prostitution, which has resulted in narrow application of the federal Trafficking Victims Protection Act to sex trafficking cases. Also, mass media reports have sensationalized stories of sex slaves who need to be rescued by law enforcement, reminiscent of historical conceptions of 'white sexual slavery' at the turn of the twentieth century.

Such perceptions of trafficking divert attention away from economic factors that drive trafficking; they also distort the profile of 'trafficking victim' to exclude many other migrant workers. Chang and Kim (2007) cite a range of advocates and service providers in the United States who seek to redefine trafficking as a labor migration issue. Paradoxically, although current U.S. policy seeks to clamp down on trafficking, U.S. economic and immigration policies are major factors causing the conditions that lead to it.

Consumption: Goods, Information, Popular Culture

Material Flows

Supermarkets and stores in countries of the global North source the products they sell from farms and factories worldwide (Figures 8.1 and 8.2). Wal-Mart, the world's biggest retailer, exemplifies this model. In 2004, the company bought products from 65,000 suppliers worldwide and sold to over 138 million consumers every week through its 1,300 stores in 10 countries (Oxfam International 2004, p. 4). Companies at the top of the global supply chains seek flexibility and the freedom to operate wherever it is most beneficial for them. This results in precarious conditions of employment for those at the bottom of the chain—whether in the global South, migrants to countries of the global North, or low-income people in richer countries. Subcontractors in the middle of the chain are pressured for low prices and speedy turnaround. They pass this on to their workers in

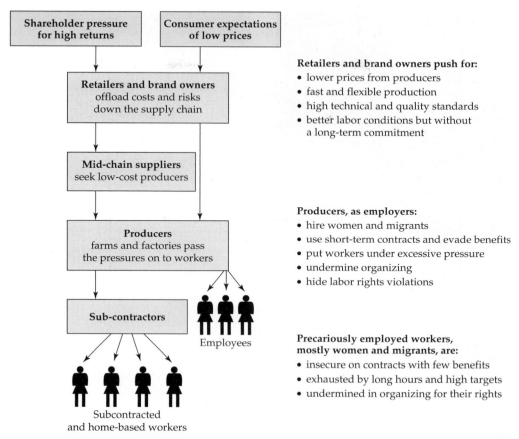

FIGURE 8.1 Supply chain pressures create precarious employment. (*Source:* Oxfam International (2004, 5).)

low wages, stressful quotas, and enforced overtime in the scramble to fill orders (Figure 8.3).

Worldwide, consumers have differential buying power, with most production destined for middle-class people in the global North. In Reading 47, Spike Peterson emphasizes the profusion of styles, changing fashions, and importance of brand names that are promoted through advertising and often valued mainly for what they say about the buyers' tastes and affluent lifestyles. Increasingly, identity is expressed through patterns of conspicuous consumption and conspicuous waste, terms coined by sociologist Thorsten Veblen (1899). As Peterson shows, current patterns of consumption are characterized by access to global supply chains, with shopping a major leisure time activity, especially for women who make most purchases, whether in person or through the

Internet. Also pertinent here is H. Patricia Hynes' discussion of unsustainable and unequal patterns of consumption expressed in terms of "ecological footprints" (see Reading 66). Aspirations of people in poorer nations to consume resources at the same rates as people in the U.S., Canada, Western Europe, or Japan would seem to be impossible. Commentators have estimated that this would require between two and seven additional planets to extract the necessary resources and to deposit the accumulated waste.

Information Flows

It is a commonplace to say that we live in an "information age." Spike Peterson discusses some of the implications of this in her analysis of how power operates in the global economy. Information is at the core of the

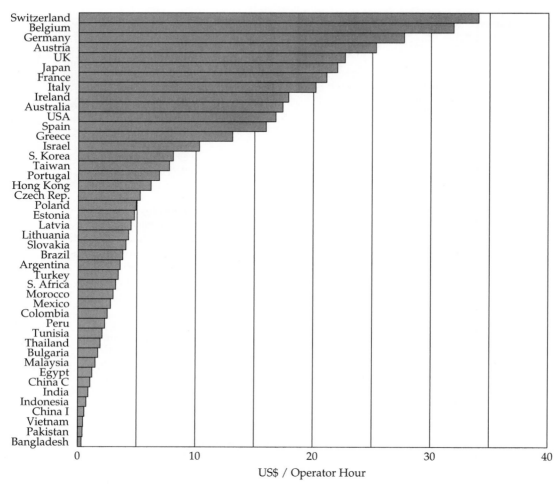

FIGURE 8.2 Labor Cost Comparisons in the Textile Industry (2008). (*Source:* Werner International Management Consultants.)

international financial system and has extended and transformed the speed of cross-border transactions. The information economy compresses both time and space, and redefines geographical distance. In some ways, physical location is immaterial—you can work anywhere as long as you have reliable Internet access. For example, computer support services have been outsourced to India (English speakers) and El Salvador (Spanish speakers). The script readers are "over there," but at the same time they are also "here," their voices coming through the phones in our hands as they talk us through what to do to fix our computers.

As hubs of financial trading, however, world centers like Tokyo, London, and New York are key locations.

Information workers participate in a fast-paced industry, as mentioned by Johanna Shih in her discussion of job opportunities in Silicon Valley (Reading 40). The industry demands a high degree of flexibility; work is organized in short-term contracts; workers are responsible for gaining experience and keeping their skills and networking contacts up to date, also mentioned by Gloria Albrecht (Reading 38). Johanna Shih notes the restructuring of U.S. immigration categories in 1990 that fostered the migration of hi-tech, high-skilled workers, and argues that their transnational ties and cultural know-how are a critical part of the expansion of Silicon Valley through subcontracting agreements, for example, with companies in India or marketing agreements with companies in China.

Information is not just a part of manufacturing or cultural production; increasingly information is what is traded. Although much assembly-line work has been outsourced from former industrial centers of the global North, the design of new products, decisions about style, market positioning, and finance are retained by company headquarters in the U.S. or Western Europe, and this work is increasingly centralized. Selling information, Peterson notes, is very different from selling material goods or services. Information can be sold to multiple buyers and still be retained by the seller; it increases in value the more people are "locked in" to particular products, and so forth (Reading 47).

Given this plethora of information and the rapid, unceasing innovation of the information economy, Peterson underscores the politics of knowledge creation, a point we introduced in Chapter 2 in our discussion of theories and theorizing. She asks:

> whose questions are pursued, whose concerns are silenced, whose health needs are prioritized, whose methods are authorized, whose paradigm is presumed, whose project is funded, whose findings are publicized, whose intellectual property is protected.

She comments that conventional distributions of power are reflected in and tend to be reproduced by the information economy. This economy is both diffused and concentrated in particular groups and locations. Peterson notes that decision makers in the global information economy are predominantly men.

Cultural Flows

Peterson also emphasizes the significance of mass communications at the global level. One aspect of this is the prevalence of large-scale corporate media, as mentioned in Chapter 2, such that U.S. news outlets like CNN and Fox News, and Britain's BBC, are sources of information worldwide. An example of news flowing "upstream" is the weblog written by Riverbend (2005, 2006), an Iraqi woman in Baghdad, who described her family's experiences of war and occupation, as well as commenting on mainstream news reporting of events (see Reading 59). Although nowhere near the scale of CNN and BBC, Al-Jazeera News, based in Doha, Qatar, is another example.

U.S.-produced music, movies, and TV series such as *Friends, Desperate Housewives,* and *Sex in the City;* reality shows like *Survivor* and *American Idol;* and talk shows featuring *Oprah Winfrey* or *Dr. Phil* are distributed worldwide. It is possible to travel to many places around the globe, especially metropolitan areas, and hear the voices of contemporary musicians—50 Cent, Christina Aguilera, Mariah Carey, Michael Jackson, and Garth Brooks, for example—as well as the range of voices that were part of the earlier U.S. and British popular music scenes, such as the Beatles, the Carpenters, Billy Joel, and "Motown Sound" performers like the Temptations. At the same time, musicians in many countries have adapted U.S. forms, most notably hip-hop, to their languages and, to some extent, their cultures. Musicians singing in Arabic, Japanese, Korean, and European languages are fusing their respective forms with hip-hop forms that originated in urban, African American youth culture (see, e.g., Condry 2006; Elam and Jackson 2005; Mitchell 2001). You may not understand the words, but you recognize the beat immediately as hip-hop. Some commercialized U.S. hip-hop is misogynist and homophobic, but fundamentally the form has been one of resistance and has been adopted this way outside the United States.

Spike Peterson discusses the effects of digitization on cultural diversity, **cultural homogenization,** and the commodification of culture. She argues that globalization does not only homogenize cultures; it also "celebrates novelty and the local," but decision-making power over what is selected as valuable is highly concentrated. Some see cultural merging as evidence that "the world has become one." Critics decry the loss of traditional or locally produced cultural forms and loss of cultural diversity. Vandana Shiva's (1993) term "monocultures of the mind," referring to the acceptance of homogenization, can be borrowed for this discussion. Cultural richness and variation is in danger of becoming flattened into a handful of uniformly recognizable symbols, representations, and icons. Some have referred to this as "McDonaldization," a term coined by sociologist George Ritzer (1993) to mean standardization, whether of french fries, burgers, and Coke, or high-ticket items.

The direction of flow of globalizing processes reflects the power imbalances among nations and regions. Hollywood-made films and music from the U.S. dominate global markets. How often do you hear Arabic, Japanese, Korean, or French popular music on your local radio station or at your music shop? How often do you see titles of films from Nigeria, China, or Chile displayed on the marquee of your local movie theater? The U.S. music industry differentiates various genres, including "world music." What does this term mean? Why is "classical music" in the United States usually taken to mean European classical composers though all cultures have classical music? Who controls the flow of cultural productions? Who benefits, who are disadvantaged, and in what ways? What are the longer-term impacts of "monocultures of the mind"?

Depictions of U.S. life in TV shows, replete with remodeled kitchens, color-coordinated furnishings, lavish meals, and different outfits from scene to scene, also serve to generate desires for consumer goods and an affluent lifestyle, which is a factor in people's decisions to migrate. Through popular culture, people are likely to be more aware of disparities in living standards among nations. U.S. movies and TV shows sell the idea of the "America Dream" and notions of U.S. superiority. They promote dominant beauty standards (see Chapter 5, Reading 26), and help to create a demand for hair straighteners and skin-lightening products. The "B" movies that are a staple of TV programming in many nations also sell ideas of individualism—hard, blue-eyed, white masculinity, tough Black gangstas, and long-legged, grasping women—in pursuit of greed, money, violence, killing, and sex. How people "read" these media productions depends on their perspectives and values. They may find them appealing or irrelevant, so far removed from local realities and values as to be ridiculous; or they may loathe and despise U.S. popular culture as cultural pollution awash with sleaze, crime, and degradation, what Spike Peterson calls "westoxification."

In order to counter mainstream media stereotypes and to provide alternative representations of women's lives, feminist projects in many countries are using media for social change, as mentioned in Chapter 2. A Woman's Place, in India, is one example of a feminist media collective with this goal. Filmmaker Paromita Vohra, who has worked closely with

Workers in a Reebok factory in China

this group, discusses the challenges of making feminist media representations that are sufficiently nuanced and complex and that also counter mainstream media stereotypes (Reading 46). She notes that media advocacy has followed three main paths: making alternative media such as documentary films, critiquing mainstream media, and making media tools available to people from subordinated groups to express themselves. She argues that the priorities and expectations of political movements, nonprofit organizations, and funders have contributed to the development of alternative media approaches that are formulaic and conformist. She raises complex questions about how to represent women's lives equitably, who can speak for whom, how to do justice to contradictions of women's lives and experiences, and the relationships between media-making and art.

Production: The Global Factory

The films *The Global Assembly Line* (distributed by New Day Films, www.newday.com) and *Life and Debt* (distributed by New Yorker Films, www. newyorkerfilms.com) are an excellent introduction to this topic, and students are urged to see them, if possible, in conjunction with reading this chapter.

As discussed earlier, many people move for work. In the past forty years, electronic communications and air transport have made it increasingly possible for corporations to move work to areas where they can pay lower wages, or where there are fewer constraints on their operations. Nike, Playtex, Dell, Apple, Mattel, and General Motors (based in the U.S.); East Asian companies like Sony, Panasonic, and Hyundai; and European companies like Nokia, Siemens, and Philips all have much of their manufacturing work done overseas—in, for example, Indonesia, China, Mexico, the Philippines, Guatemala, or Eastern Europe (see, e.g., Collins 2003; Enloe 1995; Greider 1997; Kamel 1990; Kamel and Hoffman 1999; Ross 1997). This organization of work results in inexpensive consumer goods for Australian, European, Japanese, Canadian, and U.S. markets, particularly clothing, toys, household appliances, and electronic equipment. The global assembly line also includes computer-based services done by women in the Caribbean, for example, who make hotel reservations for some U.S. and Canadian hotel chains (Freeman 2000), and computer support, as mentioned earlier. The fact

that standards of living and wage rates differ greatly from country to country means that the process of moving work around the world is likely to continue and to become increasingly complex (see Figure 8.2 showing comparative wage rates for the textile industry).

Note the significance of gender in the international division of labor and that this intersects with inequalities based on race, ethnicity, and national origin. Roughly 90 percent of the factory workers in offshore production are young women in their late teens and early twenties. Some countries, like the Philippines and China, have established Export Processing Zones (EPZs), where transnational corporations set up factories making products for export to Europe, the U.S., Canada,

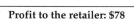

Profit to the retailer: $78
Large retail chains set the prices and the styles of garments.

Profit to the manufacturer: $33
Retailers purchase clothing from manufacturers, which design and register product lines and purchase the fabric. They then contract out the actual clothing production.

Profit to the contractor: $13
Receives orders from manufacturers, then often subcontracts the work out. Cutting, dyeing, and sewing clothing can be performed by different contractors.

Cost to the contractor: $33
Material: $20, Misc. Labor: $10, Seamstress: $3
Garment workers cut, stitch, and dye the clothing that consumers buy at the retail stores.

The skirt sells for $157.
You get paid $3.
Who gets the difference, and how do they spend it?

FIGURE 8.3 Markup of $157 skirt. (*Source: Los Angeles Herald Examiner* garment industry investigation.)

and Japan. In Mexico, this is done through *maquiladoras*—factories that make goods on contract to a "parent" company. There are over 3,000 *maquiladoras* in Mexico; the majority are owned by U.S. interests and located within thirty miles of the border.

Even in countries like Mexico, with protective labor and environmental laws, these regulations are often not strongly—if ever—enforced in relation to the operations of transnational corporations. Thus, workers experience oppressive working conditions, suffer stress from trying to make the assigned quotas, and contract illnesses from exposure to glues, solvents, and other toxic chemicals, or lint and dust in the case of textile factories. Women's eyesight deteriorates from hours spent at microscopes. They are subject to sexual harassment by male supervisors and have been required to undergo pregnancy tests as a condition of employment.

When workers complained and organized to protest such dire conditions, they were often threatened that the plants would close and move elsewhere; indeed, this has happened. For example, when women campaigned for better wages and working conditions, Nike moved some of its production from South Korea to Indonesia and China, pitting workers in one country against those in another, in what has been described as "a race to the bottom." Some years ago, global trade rules imposed a quota system that limited manufacturers' access to the U.S. clothing market. Korean and Taiwanese companies set up textile factories in Africa and parts of Asia purely as a way around the quotas, importing all machinery and materials to these production sites. When the rules changed in 2005, factories closed resulting in huge job losses in several countries including Cambodia, El Salvador, the Dominican Republic, Lesotho, and Mauritius (Earnest 2005). The current rules have opened up the global garment trade to increased competition. China has a major market share on account of its low wages and increasing technological sophistication. A new factor for manufacturers to contend with is a Chinese government plan to protect workers' rights and allow unions greater power in response to workers' protests over pay and poor working conditions and the widening income gap within the country (Barboza 2006).

Toward a Secure and Sustainable Future

As this chapter shows, the rules and conditions imposed by corporate and government decision-makers at all levels have resulted in increasing insecurity for many people worldwide. Alternative ways of organizing society, redistributing income and wealth, or generating everyday security and sustainability are often marginalized as "unrealistic." In this last section, we explore several changes underway that point toward the possibility of a more secure and sustainable future.

Understanding the Significance of Globalization and Transforming Consciousness

Women in the global North need to learn much more about the effects of "our" corporate and government policies on women in Asia, Africa, Latin America, and the Caribbean and to understand the connections between these women's situations and our own. In countries of the global South, thousands of workers' organizations, environmentalists, feminists, and religious groups have been campaigning for better pay and working conditions and for economic development that is environmentally sound. Increased consumer awareness and activism in the U.S., Canada, and Western Europe has brought about some changes in wages and working conditions for overseas workers. A major campaign against Nike, for example, protested inhumane working conditions in plants making Nike shoes in Vietnam and China (Greenhouse 1997; Sanders and Kaptur 1997). In 1997, North Olmsted, Ohio, a working-class suburb of Cleveland, became the first U.S. city to ban municipal purchases of sweatshop-made products. Students from over 100 U.S. colleges have called on their institutions to honor strict codes of conduct for overseas factories that make goods bearing college names (Featherstone 2002), and this campaign continues to expand. In addition, non-profit organizations have generated principles for ethical travel (e.g., Ethical Traveler, a project of Earth Island Institute).

An intersectional perspective is necessary for understanding globalization, with nation as a category of analysis, linked to gender, race, class, and so on. Scholarly feminist work in international relations, economics, and post-colonial theorizing provide useful perspectives. In the United States, we need much greater access to materials written by and about women in countries of the global South, including academic research, activist concerns, journalists' accounts, policy recommendations, and critiques of policies imposed by countries of the North. A few notable writers from the global South are published worldwide, including Vandana Shiva (Reading 48), and the Web opens up additional resources, but those with access tend to be U.S.-based NGOs who work with women overseas. Spike Peterson makes a related point about the politics of information in Reading 47. Our search for materials for this chapter was affected by these realities.

Fair Trade

Movements for fair trade have arisen in response to the negative effects of free trade on individuals and communities. Fair trade criteria include paying a fair wage in the local context; providing equal opportunities, especially for the most disadvantaged people; engaging in environmentally sustainable practices; providing healthy and safe working conditions; and being open to public accountability. A number of U.S. nonprofit organizations support fair trade between producers and craftspeople in the global South and consumers in the North. These include Equal Exchange (Cambridge, Mass.), Global Exchange (San Francisco Bay Area), Just Coffee (Madison, Wis.), Pachamama (San Rafael, Calif.), Pueblo to People (Houston, Tex.), and Ten Thousand Villages (Akron, Pa.), which all sell through stores and the Internet. Maquiladora Dignidad y Justicia (Dignity and Justice Maquiladora Company), a small worker-owned and operated business, was started by five members of Comite Fronterizo de Obrer@s (Border Committee of Women Workers) in Mexico in 2003. They took this initiative after being laid off when large *maquiladoras* closed down (Hernández and Flory 2005). In 2008, eight women were able to pay themselves double the standard wage in the *maquiladoras* and to determine the terms of their employment. Their 2008 product line included organic cotton T-shirts, sweatshirts, and tote bags. Such businesses are small seeds toward a more sustainable economy.

Addressing the issue of consumption, or overconsumption, in countries of the global North goes far beyond fair trade and will take huge changes in consciousness, priorities, and economic organization. We return to this issue in Chapter 11.

Debt Cancellation

For many poor countries, especially in Africa and Latin America, the burden of external debt is catastrophic. At times, some nations, including Mexico and Argentina, have announced that they would not repay their debts. Advocacy organizations worldwide support debt cancellation. They argue that much of the money borrowed has benefited only upper-class and professional elites or has gone into armaments, nuclear power plants, or luxuries such as prestige buildings, especially in urban areas. In some countries, large sums borrowed by governments were kept by corrupt politicians and business people and then reinvested in lender countries. It is an inescapable fact that the world's poorest countries will never be able to pay their international debts. With agreement of the leading industrialized nations, the governing boards of the IMF and World Bank adopted a debt-relief proposal in 1996 for the most heavily indebted nations, mostly in Africa. This was partly in response to major protests against world economic priorities and concerted lobbying by Jubilee 2000, a worldwide alliance of NGOs and religious groups, which urged debt cancellation. Several nations, including Britain, Canada, France, Italy, and Spain, have written off some debts, but much more has been promised than has been delivered. The Global Call to Action against Poverty, the world's largest anti-poverty coalition, continues to pressure the governments of richer countries to address global imbalances of wealth and power.

Self-Determination and Democratization

Despite political and economic limits to national and local decision-making processes, many individuals and communities are challenging international financial institutions or government policies that jeopardize their livelihood and security. Much grassroots community organizing in the United States is based on demands for community decision making and self-determination, as with the work of the Labor Community Strategy Center, a multiracial "think tank/act tank" in Los Angeles. In Reading 48, Vandana Shiva reports on a successful challenge to corporate plunder of water supplies by the Coca-Cola

Company. This was initiated by marginalized women in Kerala (southern India) who mobilized support from community officials, Kerala political leaders, notable writers, and internationally known activists with extensive contacts. This two-year campaign involved protest, scientific research, a lawsuit, lobbying, and actions taken by elected officials. The Kerala High Court argued in favor of protecting water supplies from excessive exploitation and ordered the Coca-Cola Company to stop using underground water. Further, local people used the energy generated by this campaign to start production of refreshing drinks from locally grown coconuts. In 2007, the state government of Kerala filed criminal charges against Coca-Cola for damages it has caused in the community of Plachimada.

Thousands of environmentalists, union members, indigenous people, feminists, and people of many faiths participated in workshops on economic and environmental issues, part of a major protest against the World Trade Organization (WTO) at its third ministerial conference, in Seattle in November 1999. This coordinated opposition was successful in stalling the "Seattle round" of talks aimed at further opening up global trade. Massive international protests continued at IMF, World Bank, and WTO meetings on all continents (see, e.g., Prokosch and Raymond 2002; Starhawk 2002b). A new form of international gathering, the World Social Forum, started in 2001 when 20,000 people from 117 countries came together in Porto Alegre (Brazil) under the slogan "Another World Is Possible." Such meetings have continued internationally, regionally, and locally and have given rise to new U.S.-based coalition efforts, like Grassroots Global Justice.

Citing historical evidence, activists and writers Mary Zepernick (1998a, 1998b) and Virginia Rasmussen (1998) have argued that corporate dominance is not inevitable. In the eighteenth and nineteenth centuries, U.S. city and state governments watched corporations closely and revoked or amended their charters if they harmed the general welfare or exceeded the powers granted to them by government. In 1843, for example, the Pennsylvania Legislature declared: "A corporation in law is just what the incorporation act makes it. It is the creature of the law and may be moulded to any shape or for any purpose the Legislature may deem most conducive for the common good" (quoted in Grossman 1998a). Corporate owners worked hard to change such limiting laws and perspectives. In

an 1886 decision, the U.S. Supreme Court declared corporations legal persons. Gradually they were given a long list of civil and political rights, such as free speech, property rights, and the right to define and control investment, production, and the organization of work (Grossman 1998b). This resulted in a gradual reversal of the sovereignty of the people over corporations—originally mere legal entities—and an undermining of democracy, for people who are subordinate to corporations are consumers not citizens. Zepernick and Rasmussen noted that corporations are *things;* they cannot care or be responsible. The Program on Corporations, Law, and Democracy (POCLAD) has shown the fundamental contradiction between democracy and corporate control (Ritz 2001). It advocates that city governments, for example, create policies and programs to ensure control over corporations that conduct business with the city as a step toward reclaiming people's power over corporate entities.

Self-determination also has strong cultural elements, as suggested by Gloria Anzaldúa (Reading 42; 1987), who drew on her ancestry and history to forge a visionary mestiza consciousness. In opposition to cultural homogenization of mass media, myriad projects worldwide sustain and celebrate living cultures. In immigrant communities in the United States, too, people speak many languages, play traditional instruments, perform and teach traditional dance, often adapting and reviving aspects of their traditional culture for current times and consciousness and as a foundation for their resistance to cultural homogenization.

Transnational Alliances

The worldwide mobility of capital calls for transnational labor movements to standardize wages and hold corporations accountable for working conditions. Indeed, the global economic situation has generated new alliances and organizations working across national borders. Examples include STITCH (Support Team International for Textileras), a network of women organizers in the United States and Guatemala, the Central American Network of Women in Solidarity with Maquila Workers (see Mendez 2002), and the Comite Fronterizo de Obrer@s (Border Committee of Women Workers) in Mexico, mentioned earlier, which works with the American Friends Service Committee. Leaders of women's human rights and religious organizations came together in Chiang Mai, Thailand, in 2004, for an international conference on women and religion. Noting the severe negative effects of globalization on women's lives and opportunities, they called on religious leaders and institutions to work to advance the well-being of women (Reading 35).

In the 1960s and 1970s, those active in U.S. movements for liberation and civil rights made theoretical and practical connections with anticolonial struggles in such countries as South Africa, Vietnam, Cuba, Angola, and Mozambique. In the twenty-first century, these international linkages are crucial, as scholar and activist Angela Davis (1997) remarked, not merely "as a matter of inspiration or identification, but as a matter of necessity," because of the impacts of globalization—positive and negative—on people's lives. We continue this discussion of security and sustainability in later chapters and also take up the issue of transnational alliances among women in Chapter 12.

Questions for Reflection

In thinking about the issues raised in this chapter, consider these questions:

1. What do you know about countries outside the United States? What are your sources of information?

2. Why does the impact of the globalization of the economy matter to people living in the United States? What does it tell us about structural privilege (which we may not know we have and may not want)? If some of this material is new to you, why do you think you have not learned it before?

3. How does global inequality reinforce sexism, racial prejudice, and institutionalized racism in the United States?

4. How do you define wealth, aside from material possessions? List all the ways you are enriched.

5. Does wealth equal political power? Are rich people always in the **power elite**— the group that influences political and economic decisions in the country? Who makes up the power elite in the United States?

6. How do people in elite positions justify the perpetuation of inequalities to others? To themselves? How are the ideologies of nationalism, racial superiority, male superiority, and class superiority useful here?

Finding Out More on the Web

1. Find examples of the influence of U.S. media abroad, for example, at a movie theater in Zurich, Switzerland: www.kitag.com

2. Study the maps on the following sites that show colonial histories and contemporary disparities among nations:

   www-personal.umich.edu/~mejn/cartograms/

   http://en.wikipedia.org/wiki/Image:World_1898_empires_colonies_territory.png

   http://www.worldmapper.org

3. The following Web sites have information about alternatives to globalization, including fair trade and debt relief:

   CorpWatch: www.corpwatch.org

   Global Exchange: www.globalexchange.org

Global Women's Strike: www.globalwomenstrike.net

Jubilee USA Network: www.jubileeusa.org

Net Aid: www.netaid.org

Sweatshop Watch: www.sweatshopwatch.org

World Social Forum: www.forumsocialmundial.org.br

4. Use your search engine to research organizations concerned with the global sex trade and trafficking such as

Coalition Against Trafficking in Women (CATW)

Global Alliance Against Trafficking of Women (GAATW)

Women's Education, Development, Productivity and Research Organization (WEDPRO)

Taking Action

1. Interview a person who immigrated to the United States to understand why they left their home country and how they got to where they are now.

2. Look at the labels in your clothes and on all products you buy. Where were they made? Look up these countries on a map if you don't know where they are.

3. Do you need all you currently own? List everything you need to sustain life. Which items do you need to buy? Which might you make yourself, share, or barter with others?

4. Find out who manufactures the clothing that bears your college's name, and whether there are sweatshops in your region.

5. Get involved with a campaign that is tackling the issue of sweatshop production or debt relief.

FORTY-TWO

The Homeland (1987)
Aztlán / El otro México

Gloria Anzaldúa

Gloria Anzaldúa (1942–2004) was a Chicana lesbian-feminist poet and fiction writer. With Cherríe Moraga, she co-edited the ground-breaking anthology *This Bridge Called My Back: Writings by Radical Women of Color*, winner of the Before Columbus Foundation American Book Award. She taught Chicano Studies, Feminist Studies, and creative writing at various universities. Her other books include *Borderlands: La Frontera—The New Mestiza* and *The Bridge We Call Home: Radical Visions for Transformation* (edited with Analouise Keating).

El otro México que acá hemos construido
el espacio es lo que ha sido
territorio nacional.
Esté el esfuerzo de todos nuestros hermanos
y latinoamericanos que han sabido
progressar.

—Los Tigres del Norte[1]

"The *Aztecas del norte* . . . compose the largest single tribe or nation of Anishinabeg (Indians) found in the United States today. . . . Some call themselves Chicanos and see themselves as people whose true homeland is Aztlán [the U.S. Southwest]."[2]

Wind tugging at my sleeve
feet sinking into the sand
I stand at the edge where earth touches ocean
where the two overlap
a gentle coming together
at other times and places a violent clash.

Across the border in Mexico
    stark silhouette of houses gutted by waves,
    cliffs crumbling into the sea,
        silver waves marbled with spume
            gashing a hole under the border fence.

                    Miro el mar atacar
                la cerca en Border Field Park
                con sus buchones de agua,
an Easter Sunday resurrection
of the brown blood in my veins.

Oigo el llorido del mar, el respiro del aire,
    my heart surges to the beat of the sea.
    In the gray haze of the sun
        the gulls' shrill cry of hunger,
            the tangy smell of the sea seeping into me.

            I walk   through the hole in the fence
                to the other side.
    Under my fingers I feel the gritty wire
    rusted by 139 years
        of the salty breath of the sea.

Beneath the iron sky
Mexican children kick their soccer ball across,
run after it, entering the U.S.

        I press my hand to the steel curtain—
        chainlink fence crowned with rolled barbed
        wire—
    rippling from the sea where Tijuana touches
    San Diego
        unrolling over mountains
                and plains
                    and deserts,
this "Tortilla Curtain" turning into *el río Grande*
    flowing down to the flatlands
        of the Magic Valley of South Texas
            its mouth emptying into the Gulf.

1,950 mile-long open wound
        dividing a *pueblo*, a culture,
            running down the length of my body,

staking fence rods in my flesh,
splits me   splits me
        me raja me raja

This is my home
this thin edge of
        barbwire.

But the skin of the earth is seamless.
The sea cannot be fenced,
el mar does not stop at borders.
To show the white man what she thought of his
            arrogance,
        Yemaya blew that wire fence down.

            This land was Mexican once,
                was Indian always
                    and is.
                And   will be again.

Yo soy un puente tendido
    del mundo gabacho al del mojado,
lo pasado me estirá pa' 'trás
    y lo presente pa' 'delante.
Que la Virgen de Guadalupe me cuide
Ay ay ay, soy mexicana de este lado.

The U.S.-Mexican border *es una herida abierta* where the Third World grates against the first and bleeds. And before a scab forms it hemorrhages again, the lifeblood of two worlds merging to form a third country—a border culture. Borders are set up to define the places that are safe and unsafe, to distinguish *us* from *them*. A border is a dividing line, a narrow strip along a steep edge. A borderland is a vague and undetermined place created by the emotional residue of an unnatural boundary. It is in a constant state of transition. The prohibited and forbidden are its inhabitants. *Los atravesados* live here: the squint-eyed, the perverse, the queer, the troublesome, the mongrel, the mulato, the half-breed, the half dead; in short, those who cross over, pass over, or go through the confines of the "normal." Gringos in the U.S. Southwest consider the inhabitants of the borderlands transgressors, aliens—whether they possess documents or not, whether they're Chicanos, Indians or Blacks. Do not enter, trespassers will be raped, maimed, strangled, gassed, shot. The only "legitimate" inhabitants are those in power, the whites and those who align themselves with whites. Tension grips the inhabitants of the borderlands like a virus. Ambivalence and unrest reside there and death is no stranger.

> In the fields, *la migra*. My aunt saying, *"No corran*, don't run. They'll think you're *del otro lado."* In the confusion, Pedro ran, terrified of being caught. He couldn't speak English, couldn't tell them he was fifth generation American. *Sin papeles*—he did not carry his birth certificate to work in the fields. *La migra* took him away while we watched. *Se lo llevaron.* He tried to smile when he looked back at us, to raise his fist. But I saw the shame pushing his head down, I saw the terrible weight of shame hunch his shoulders. They deported him to Guadalajara by plane. The furthest he'd ever been to Mexico was Reynosa, a small border town opposite Hidalgo, Texas, not far from McAllen. Pedro walked all the way to the Valley. *Se lo llevaron sin un centavo al pobre. Se vino andando desde Guadalajara.*

During the original peopling of the Americas, the first inhabitants migrated across the Bering Straits and walked south across the continent. The oldest evidence of humankind in the U.S.—the Chicanos' ancient Indian ancestors—was found in Texas and has been dated to 35000 B.C.[3] In the Southwest United States archeologists have found 20,000-year-old campsites of the Indians who migrated through, or permanently occupied, the Southwest, Aztlán—land of the herons, land of whiteness, the Edenic place of origin of the Azteca.

In 1000 B.C., descendants of the original Cochise people migrated into what is now Mexico and Central America and became the direct ancestors of many of the Mexican people. (The Cochise culture of the Southwest is the parent culture of the Aztecs. The Uto-Aztecan languages stemmed from the language of the Cochise people.)[4] The Aztecs (the Nahuatl word for people of Aztlán) left the Southwest in 1168 A.D.

> Now let us go.
>   *Tihueque, tihueque,*
> *Vámonos, vámonos.*
>   *Un pájaro cantó.*
> *Con sus ocho tribus salieron*
>   *de la "cueva del origen,"*
> *los aztecas siguieron al dios*
>   *Huitzilopochtli.*

Huitzilopochtli, the God of War, guided them to the place (that later became Mexico City) where an eagle with a writhing serpent in its beak perched on a cactus. The eagle symbolizes the spirit (as the sun, the father); the serpent symbolizes the soul (as the earth, the mother). Together, they symbolize the struggle between the spiritual/celestial/male and the underworld/earth/feminine. The symbolic sacrifice of the serpent to the "higher" masculine powers indicates that the patriarchal order had already vanquished the feminine and matriarchal order in pre-Columbian America.

At the beginning of the 16th century, the Spaniards and Hernán Cortés invaded Mexico and, with the help of tribes that the Aztecs had subjugated, conquered it. Before the Conquest, there were twenty-five million Indian people in Mexico and the Yucatán. Immediately after the Conquest, the Indian population had been reduced to under seven million. By 1650, only one-and-a-half-million pureblooded Indians remained. The *mestizos* who were genetically equipped to survive small pox, measles, and typhus (Old World diseases to which the natives had no immunity), founded a new hybrid race and inherited Central and South America.[5] *En 1521 nació una nueva raza, el mestizo, el mexicano* (people of mixed Indian and Spanish blood), a race that had never existed before. Chicanos, Mexican-Americans, are the offspring of those first matings.

Our Spanish, Indian, and *mestizo* ancestors explored and settled parts of the U.S. Southwest as early as the sixteenth century. For every gold-hungry *conquistador* and soul-hungry missionary who came north from Mexico, ten to twenty Indians and *mestizos* went along as porters or in other capacities.[6] For the Indians, this constituted a return to the place of origin, Aztlán, thus making Chicanos originally and secondarily indigenous to the Southwest. Indians and *mestizos* from central Mexico intermarried with North American Indians. The continual intermarriage between Mexican and American Indians and Spaniards formed an even greater *mestizaje*.

El destierro/The Lost Land

> *Entonces corré la sangre*
> *no sabe el indio que hacer,*
> *le van a quitar su tierra,*
> *la tiene que defender,*
> *el indio se cae muerto,*

y el afuerino de pie.
Levántate, Manquilef.

Arauco tiene una pena
más negra que su chamal,
ya no son los españoles
los que les hacen llorar,
hoy son los propios chilenos
los que les quitan su pan.
Levántate, Pailahuan.

—Violeta Parra, *"Arauco tiene una pena"*[7]

In the 1800s, Anglos migrated illegally into Texas, which was then part of Mexico, in greater and greater numbers and gradually drove the *tejanos* (native Texans of Mexican descent) from their lands, committing all manner of atrocities against them. Their illegal invasion forced Mexico to fight a war to keep its Texas territory. The Battle of the Alamo, in which the Mexican forces vanquished the whites, became, for the whites, the symbol for the cowardly and villainous character of the Mexicans. It became (and still is) a symbol that legitimized the white imperialist takeover. With the capture of Santa Anna later in 1836, Texas became a republic. *Tejanos* lost their land and, overnight, became the foreigners.

Ya la mitad del terreno
les vendió el traidor Santa Anna,
con lo que se ha hecho muy rica
la nación americana.

¿Qué acaso no se conforman
con el oro de las minas?
Ustedes muy elegantes
y aquí nosotros en ruinas.

—from the Mexican corrido,
"Del peligro de la Intervención"[8]

In 1846, the U.S. incited Mexico to war. U.S. troops invaded and occupied Mexico, forcing her to give up almost half of her nation, what is now Texas, New Mexico, Arizona, Colorado and California.

With the victory of the U.S. forces over the Mexican in the U.S.-Mexican War, *los norteamericanos* pushed the Texas border down 100 miles, from *el río Nueces* to *el río Grande*. South Texas ceased to be part of the Mexican state of Tamaulipas. Separated from Mexico, the Native Mexican-Texan no longer looked toward Mexico as home; the Southwest became our homeland once more.

The border fence that divides the Mexican people was born on February 2, 1848 with the signing of the Treaty of Guadalupe-Hidalgo. It left 100,000 Mexican citizens on this side, annexed by conquest along with the land. The land established by the treaty as belonging to Mexicans was soon swindled away from its owners. The treaty was never honored and restitution, to this day, has never been made.

> The justice and benevolence of God
> will forbid that . . . Texas should again
> become a howling wilderness
> trod only by savages, or . . . benighted
> by the ignorance and superstition,
> the anarchy and rapine of Mexican misrule.
> The Anglo-American race are destined
> to be forever the proprietors of
> this land of promise and fulfillment.
> Their laws will govern it,
> their learning will enlighten it,
> their enterprise will improve it.
> Their flocks range its boundless pastures,
> for them its fertile lands will yield . . .
> luxuriant harvests . . .
> The wilderness of Texas has been redeemed
> by Anglo-American blood & enterprise.
> —William H. Wharton[9]

The Gringo, locked into the fiction of white superiority, seized complete political power, stripping Indians and Mexicans of their land while their feet were still rooted in it. *Con el destierro y el exilo fuimos desuñados, destroncados, destripados*—we were jerked out by the roots, truncated, disemboweled, dispossessed, and separated from our identity and our history. Many, under the threat of Anglo terrorism, abandoned homes and ranches and went to Mexico. Some stayed and protested. But as the courts, law enforcement officials, and government officials not only ignored their pleas but penalized them for their efforts, *tejanos* had no other recourse but armed retaliation.

After Mexican-American resisters robbed a train in Brownsville, Texas, on October 18, 1915, Anglo vigilante groups began lynching Chicanos. Texas Rangers would take them into the brush and shoot them. One hundred Chicanos were killed in a matter of months, whole families lynched. Seven thousand fled to Mexico, leaving their small ranches and farms. The Anglos, afraid that the *mexicanos*[10] would seek independence from the U.S., brought in 20,000 army troops to put an end to the social protest movement in South Texas. Race hatred had finally fomented into an all out war.[11]

> My grandmother lost all her cattle,
> they stole her land.

"Drought hit South Texas," my mother tells me. *"La tierra se puso bien seca y los animales comenzaron a morrirse de se'. Mi papá se murío de un* heart attack *dejando a mamá* pregnant *y con ocho huercos,* with eight kids and one on the way. *Yo fuí la mayor, tenía diez años.* The next year the drought continued *y el ganado* got hoof and mouth. *Se calleron* in droves *en las pastas y el* brushland, *pansas blancas* ballooning to the skies. *El siguiente año* still no rain. *Mi pobre madre viuda perdió* two-thirds of her *ganado.* A smart *gabacho* lawyer took the land away *mamá* hadn't paid taxes. *No hablaba inglés,* she didn't know how to ask for time to raise the money." My father's mother, Mama Locha, also lost her *terreno.* For a while we got $12.50 a year for the "mineral rights" of six acres of cemetery, all that was left of the ancestral lands. Mama Locha had asked that we bury her there beside her husband. *El cemeterio estaba cercado.* But there was a fence around the cemetery, chained and padlocked by the ranch owners of the surrounding land. We couldn't even get in to visit the graves, much less bury her there. Today, it is still padlocked. The sign reads: "Keep out. Trespassers will be shot."

In the 1930s, after Anglo agribusiness corporations cheated the small Chicano landowners of their land, the corporations hired gangs of *mexicanos* to pull out the brush, chaparral and cactus and to irrigate the desert. The land they toiled over had once belonged to many of them or had been used communally by them. Later the Anglos brought in huge machines and root plows and had the Mexicans scrape the land clean of natural vegetation. In my childhood I saw the end of dryland farming. I witnessed the land cleared; saw the huge pipes connected to underwater sources sticking up in the air. As children, we'd go fishing in some of those canals when they were full and hunt for snakes in them when they were dry. In the 1950s I saw the land, cut up into thousands of neat rectangles and squares, constantly being irrigated. In the 340-day growth season, the seeds of any kind of fruit or vegetable had only to be stuck in the ground in order to grow. More big land corporations came in and bought up the remaining land.

To make a living my father became a sharecropper. Rio Farms Incorporated loaned him seed money and living expenses. At harvest time, my father repaid the loan and forked over 40% of the earnings. Sometimes we earned less than we owed, but always the corporations fared well. Some had major holdings in vegetable trucking, livestock auctions and cotton gins. Altogether we lived on three successive Rio farms; the second was adjacent to the King Ranch and included a dairy farm; the third was a chicken farm. I remember the white feathers of three thousand Leghorn chickens blanketing the land for acres around. My sister, mother and I cleaned, weighed and packaged eggs. (For years afterwards I couldn't stomach the sight of an egg.) I remember my mother attending some of the meetings sponsored by well-meaning whites from Rio Farms. They talked about good nutrition, health, and held huge barbeques. The only thing salvaged for my family from those years are modern techniques of food canning and a food-stained book they printed made up of recipes from Rio Farms' Mexican women. How proud my mother was to have her recipe for *enchiladas coloradas* in a book.

El cruzar del mojado/Illegal Crossing

> *"Ahora si ya tengo una tumba para llorar,"* dice Conchita, upon being reunited with her unknown mother just before the mother dies.
> —from Ismael Rodriguez' film, *Nosotros los pobres*[12]

La crisis. Los gringos had not stopped at the border. By the end of the nineteenth century, powerful landowners in Mexico, in partnership with U.S. colonizing companies, had dispossessed millions of Indians of their lands. Currently, Mexico and her eighty million citizens are almost completely dependent on the U.S. market. The Mexican government and wealthy growers are in partnership with such American conglomerates as American Motors, IT&T and Du Pont which own factories called *maquiladoras.* One-fourth of all Mexicans work at *maquiladoras;* most are young women. Next to oil, *maquiladoras* are Mexico's second greatest source of U.S. dollars. Working eight to twelve hours a day to wire in backup lights of U.S.

autos or solder miniscule wires in TV sets is not the Mexican way. While the women are in the *maquiladoras,* the children are left on their own. Many roam the street, become part of *cholo* gangs. The infusion of the values of the white culture, coupled with the exploitation by that culture, is changing the Mexican way of life.

The devaluation of the *peso* and Mexico's dependency on the U.S. have brought on what the Mexicans call *la crisis. No hay trabajo.* Half of the Mexican people are unemployed. In the U.S. a man or woman can make eight times what they can in Mexico. By March, 1987, 1,088 pesos were worth one U.S. dollar. I remember when I was growing up in Texas how we'd cross the border at Reynosa or Progreso to buy sugar or medicines when the dollar was worth eight *pesos* and fifty *centavos.*

La travesía. For many *mexicanos del otro lado,* the choice is to stay in Mexico and starve or move north and live. *Dicen que cada mexicano siempre sueña de la conquista en los brazos de cuatro gringas rubias, la conquista del país poderoso del norte, los Estados Unidos. En cada Chicano y mexicano vive el mito del tesoro territorial perdido.* North Americans call this return to the homeland the silent invasion.

> *"A la cueva volverán"*
> —El Puma *en la cancion "Amalia"*

South of the border, called North America's rubbish dump by Chicanos, *mexicanos* congregate in the plazas to talk about the best way to cross. Smugglers, *coyotes, pasadores, enganchadores* approach these people or are sought out by them. *"¿Qué dicen muchachos a echársela de mojado?"*

> "Now among the alien gods with
> weapons of magic am I."
> —Navajo protection song,
> sung when going into battle.[13]

We have a tradition of migration, a tradition of long walks. Today we are witnessing *la migración de los pueblos mexicanos,* the return odyssey to the historical/mythological Aztlán. This time, the traffic is from south to north.

El retorno to the promised land first began with the Indians from the interior of Mexico and the *mestizos* that came with the *conquistadores* in the 1500s. Immigration continued in the next three centuries, and, in this century, it continued with the *braceros* who helped to build our railroads and who picked our fruit. Today thousands of Mexicans are crossing the border legally and illegally; ten million people without documents have returned to the Southwest.

Faceless, nameless, invisible, taunted with "Hey cucaracho" (cockroach). Trembling with fear, yet filled with courage, a courage born of desperation. Barefoot and uneducated, Mexicans with hands like boot soles gather at night by the river where two worlds merge creating what Reagan calls a frontline, a war zone. The convergence has created a shock culture, a border culture, a third country, a closed country.

Without benefit of bridges, the *"mojados"* (wetbacks) float on inflatable rafts across *el río Grande,* or wade or swim across naked, clutching their clothes over their heads. Holding onto the grass, they pull themselves along the banks with a prayer to *Virgen de Guadalupe* on their lips: *Ay virgencita morena, mi madrecita, dame tu bendición.*

The Border Patrol hides behind the local McDonalds on the outskirts of Brownsville, Texas, or some other border town. They set traps around the river beds beneath the bridge.[14] Hunters in army-green uniforms stalk and track these economic refugees by the powerful nightvision of electronic sensing devices planted in the ground or mounted on Border Patrol vans. Cornered by flashlights, frisked while their arms stretch over their heads, *los mojados* are handcuffed, locked in jeeps, and then kicked back across the border.

One out of every three is caught. Some return to enact their rite of passage as many as three times a day. Some of those who make it across undetected fall prey to Mexican robbers such as those in Smugglers' Canyon on the American side of the border near Tijuana. As refugees in a homeland that does not want them, many find a welcome hand holding out only suffering, pain, and ignoble death.

Those who make it past the checking points of the Border Patrol find themselves in the midst of 150 years of racism in Chicano *barrios* in the Southwest and in big northern cities. Living in a no-man's-borderland, caught between being treated as criminals and being able to eat, between resistance and deportation, the illegal refugees are some of the poorest and the most exploited of any people in the U.S. It is illegal for Mexicans to work without green cards. But big farming combines, farm bosses and smugglers who bring them in make money off the "wetbacks'" labor—they don't have to pay federal minimum wages, or ensure adequate housing or sanitary conditions.

The Mexican woman is especially at risk. Often the *coyote* (smuggler) doesn't feed her for days or let her go to the bathroom. Often he rapes her or sells her into prostitution. She cannot call on county or state health or economic resources because she doesn't know English and she fears deportation. American employers are quick to take advantage of her helplessness. She can't go home. She's sold her house, her furniture, borrowed from friends in order to pay the *coyote* who charges her four or five thousand dollars to smuggle her to Chicago. She may work as a live-in maid for white, Chicano or Latino households for as little as $15 a week. Or work in the garment industry, do hotel work. Isolated and worried about her family back home, afraid of getting caught and deported, living with as many as fifteen people in one room, the *mexicana* suffers serious health problems. *Se enferma de los nervios, de alta presión.*[15]

La mojada, la mujer indocumentada, is doubly threatened in this country. Not only does she have to contend with sexual violence, but like all women, she is prey to a sense of physical helplessness. As a refugee, she leaves the familiar and safe home-ground to venture into unknown and possibly dangerous terrain.

> This is her home
> this thin edge of
> barbwire.

NOTES

1. Los Tigres del Norte is a *conjunto* band.

2. Jack D. Forbes, *Aztecas del Norte: The Chicanos of Aztlán* (Greenwich, CT: Fawcett Publications, Premier Books, 1973), 13, 183; Eric R. Wolf, *Sons of Shaking Earth* (Chicago, IL: University of Chicago Press, Phoenix Books, 1959), 32.

3. John R. Chávez, *The Lost Land: The Chicano Images of the Southwest* (Albuquerque, NM: University of New Mexico Press, 1984), 9.

4. Chávez, 9. Besides the Aztecs, the Ute, Gabrillino of California, Pima of Arizona, some Pueblo of New Mexico, Comanche of Texas, Opata of Sonora, Tarahumara of Sinaloa and Durango, and the Huichol of Jalisco speak Uto-Aztecan languages and are descended from the Cochise people.

5. Reay Tannahill, *Sex in History* (Briarcliff Manor, NY: Stein and Day/Publishers/Scarborough House, 1980), 308.

6. Chávez, 21.

7. Isabel Parra, *El Libro Major de Violeta Parra* (Madrid, España: Ediciones Michay, S.A., 1985), 156–7.

8. From the Mexican *corrido*, "*Del peligro de la Intervención.*" Vicente T. Mendoza, *El Corrido Mexicano* (México. D.F.: Fondo De Cultura Económica, 1954), 42.

9. Arnoldo De León, *They Called Them Greasers: Anglo Attitudes Toward Mexicans in Texas, 1821–1900* (Austin, TX: University of Texas Press, 1983), 2–3.

10. The Plan of San Diego, Texas, drawn up on January 6, 1915, called for the independence and segregation of the states bordering Mexico: Texas, New Mexico, Arizona, Colorado, and California. Indians would get their land back, Blacks would get six states from the south and form their own independent republic. Chávez, 79.

11. Jesús Mena, "Violence in the Rio Grande Valley," *Nuestro* (Jan/Feb. 1983), 41–42.

12. *Nosotros los pobres* was the first Mexican film that was truly Mexican and not an imitation European film. It stressed the devotion and love that children should have for their mother and how its lack would lead to the dissipation of their character. This film spawned a generation of mother-devotion/ungrateful-sons films.

13. From the Navajo "Protection Song" (to be sung upon going into battle). George W. Gronyn, ed., *American Indian Poetry: The Standard Anthology of Songs and Chants* (New York, NY: Liveright, 1934), 97.

14. Grace Halsell, *Los ilegales*, trans. Mayo Antonio Sánchez (Editorial Diana Mexica, 1979).

15. Margarita B. Melville, "Mexican Women Adapt to Migration," *International Migration Review,* 1978.

◆◆◆

FORTY-THREE

Shilling Love (2004)

Shailja Patel

Shailja Patel is a Kenyan poet, playwright, and performing artist who has appeared at the Lincoln Center (New York) and at venues across the United States and Europe. She presented her one-woman show, *Migritude*, in Vienna and Nairobi. Her work is featured in the International Museum of Women in San Francisco. *www.shailja.com*

Editors' note: In the late nineteenth century, British colonial administrators moved people from one place to another as needed. Men from India, for example, were taken to Kenya (East Africa) to build railroads and were used as a "buffer group" between the British elite and Kenyan Africans. After the railroads were completed, they were allowed to stay and go into business. By the 1970s, when Kenya gained political independence from Britain, many Kenyan Asian families were relatively prosperous. They were highly unpopular in independent Kenya on economic and cultural grounds and ultimately forced to leave, which threw families into personal, economic, and political crisis.

One

They never said / they loved us

Those words were not / in any language / spoken by my parents

I love you honey was the dribbled caramel / of Hollywood movies / Dallas / Dynasty / where hot water gushed / at the touch of gleaming taps / electricity surged / 24 hours aday / through skyscrapers banquets obscene as pornography / were mere backdrops / where emotions had no consequences words / cost nothing meant nothing would never / have to be redeemed

My parents / didn't speak / that / language

1975 / 15 Kenyan shillings to the British pound / my mother speaks battle

Storms the bastions of Nairobi's / most exclusive prep schools / shoots our cowering / six-year-old bodies like cannonballs / into the all-white classrooms / scales the ramparts of class distinction / around Loreto convent / where the president / sends his daughter / the government ministers, foreign diplomats / send their daughters / because my mother's daughters / will / have world-class educations

She falls / regroups / falls and re-groups / in endless assaults on visa officials / who sneer behind their bulletproof windows / at US and British consulates / my mother the general / arms her daughters / to take on every citadel

1977 / 20 Kenyan shillings to the British pound / my father speaks / stoic endurance / he began at 16 the brutal apprenticeship / of a man who takes care of his own / relinquished dreams of / fighter pilot rally driver for the daily crucifixion / of wringing profit from a small business / my father the foot soldier, bound to an honour / deeper than any currency / *you must / finish what you start you must / march until you drop you must / give your life for those / you bring into the world*

I try to explain love / in shillings / to those who've never gauged / who gets to leave who has to stay / who breaks free and what they pay / those who've never measured love / by every rung of the ladder / from survival / to choice

A force as grim and determined / as a boot up the backside / a spur that draws blood / a mountaineer's rope / that yanks / relentlessly / up

My parents never say / they love us / they save and count / count and save / the shilling falls against the pound / college fees for overseas students / rise like flood tides / love is a luxury / priced in hard currency / ringed by tariffs / and we devour prospectuses / of ivied buildings smooth lawns vast / libraries the way Jehovah's witnesses / gobble visions of paradise / because we know we'll have to be / twice as good three times as fast four times as driven / with angels powers and principalities on our side just / to get / on / the / plane

Thirty shillings to the pound forty shillings to the pound / my parents fight over money late in the night / my father pounds the walls and yells / *I can't—it's impossible—what do you think I am?* / My mother propels us through school tuition exams applications / locks us into rooms to study / keeps an iron grip on the bank books

1982 / gunfire / in the streets of Nairobi / military coup leaders / thunder over the radio / Asian businesses wrecked and looted Asian women raped / after / the government / regains control / we whisper what the coup leaders planned

Round up all the Asians at gunpoint / in the national stadium / strip them of whatever / they carry / march them 30 miles / elders in wheelchairs / babies in arms / march them 30 miles to the airport / pack them onto any planes / of any foreign airline / tell the pilots / down the rifle barrels / *leave* / *we don't care where you take them* / *leave*

I learn like a stone in my gut that / third-generation Asian Kenyan will never / be Kenyan enough / all my patriotic fervor / will never turn my skin black / as yet another western country / drops a portcullis / of immigration spikes / my mother straps my shoulders back with a belt / to teach me / to stand up straight

50 Kenyan shillings to the pound / we cry from meltdown pressure / of exam after exam where second place is never good enough / they snap / faces taut with fear / *you can't be soft* / *you have to fight* / *or the world will eat you up*

75 Kenyan shillings to the pound / they hug us / tearless stoic at airports / as we board planes for icy alien England / cram instructions into our pockets like talismans / *Eat proper meals so you don't get sick* / *cover your ears against the cold* / *avoid those muffathias* / *the students without*

purpose or values / *learn and study* / *succeed* / *learn and study* / *suceed* / *remember remember remember the cost of your life*

they never say / they love us

Two

I watch how I love / I admonish exhort / like a Himalayan guide I / rope my chosen ones / yank them remorselessly up / when they don't even want to be / on the frigging mountain

like a vigilante squad I / scan dark streets for threats I / strategize for war and famine I / slide steel down spines

I watch heat / steam off my skin / when Westerners drop / *I love you's* into conversation / like blueberries hitting / soft / muffin / dough / I convert it to shillings / and I wince

December 2000 / 120 shillings to the British pound / 90 Kenyan shillings to the US dollar / my sister Sneha and I / wait for our parents / at SFO's international terminal /

Four hours after / their plane landed / they have not emerged

And we know with the hopeless rage / of third-world citizens / African passport holders / that the sum of their lives and labour / dreams and sacrifice / was measured sifted weighted found / wanting / by the INS

Somewhere deep in the airport's underbelly / in a room rank with fear and despair / my parents / who have travelled / 27 hours / across three continents / to see their children / are interrogated / by immigration officials

My father the footsoldier / numb with exhaustion / is throwing away / all the years / with reckless resolve / telling them / *take the passports* / *take them* / *stamp them* / *no readmission EVER* / *just let me out to see my daughters*

My mother the general / dizzy with desperation / cuts him off shouts him down / demands *listen to me I'm the one* / *who filled in the visa forms* / in her mind her lip curls she thinks /

these Americans / call themselves so advanced so / modern but still / in the year 2000 / they think it must be the husband in charge / they won't let the wife speak

On her face a lifetime / of battle-honed skill and charm / turns like a heat lamp / onto the INS man until he / stretches / yawns / relents / he's tired / it's late / he wants his dinner / and my parents / trained from birth / to offer Indian / hospitality / open their bags and give their sandwiches / to this man / who would have sent them back / without a thought

Sneha and I / in the darkened lobby / watch the empty exit way / our whole American / dream-bought-with-their-lives / hisses mockery around our rigid bodies / we swallow sobs because / they raised us to be tough / they raised us to be fighters and into that / clenched haze / of not / crying

here they come

hunched / over their luggage carts our tiny / fierce / fragile / dogged / indomitable parents

Hugged tight they stink / of 31 hours in transit / hugged tighter we all stink / with the bravado of all the years / pain bitten down on gargantuan hopes / holding on through near-disasters / never ever / giving in / to softness

The stench rises off us / unbearable / of what / was never said

Something / is bursting the walls of my arteries something / is pounding its way up my throat like a volcano / rising / finally / I understand / why I'm a poet

Because I was born to a law / that states / before you claim a word you steep it / in terror and shit / in hope and joy and grief / in labour endurance vision costed out / in decades of your life / you have to sweat and curse it / pray and keen it / crawl and bleed it / with the very marrow / of your bones / you have to earn / its / meaning

FORTY-FOUR

◆◆◆

The Care Crisis in the Philippines (2003)
Children and Transnational Families in the New Global Economy

Rhacel Salazar Parreñas

Rhacel Salazar Parreñas is a professor of Asian American studies at the University of California, Davis. She is the author of *Children of Global Migration: Transnational Families and Gendered Woes; Engendering Globalization: Essays on Women, Migration and the Philippines;* and *Servants of Globalization: Women, Migration, and Domestic Work.*

A growing crisis of care troubles the world's most developed nations. Even as demand for care has increased, its supply has dwindled. The result is a care deficit,[1] to which women from the Philippines have responded in force. Roughly two-thirds[2] of Filipino migrant workers are women, and their exodus, usually to fill domestic jobs,[3] has generated tremendous social change in the Philippines. When female migrants are mothers, they leave behind their own children, usually in the care of other women. Many Filipino children now grow up in divided households, where geographic separation places children under serious emotional strain. And yet it is impossible to overlook the significance of migrant labor to the Philippine economy. Some 34 to 54 percent of the Filipino population is sustained by remittances from migrant workers.[4]

Women in the Philippines, just like their counterparts in postindustrial nations, suffer from a "stalled revolution." Local gender ideology remains a few steps behind the economic reality, which has produced numerous female-headed, transnational households.[5] Consequently, a far greater degree of anxiety attends the quality of family life for the dependents of migrant mothers than for those of migrant fathers. The dominant gender ideology, after all, holds that a woman's rightful place is in the home, and the households of migrant mothers present a challenge to this view. In response, government officials and journalists denounce migrating mothers, claiming that they have caused the Filipino family to deteriorate, children to be abandoned, and a crisis of care to take root in the Philippines. To end this crisis, critics admonish, these mothers must return. Indeed, in May 1995, Philippine president Fidel Ramos called for initiatives to keep migrant mothers at home. He declared, "We are not against overseas employment of Filipino women. We are against overseas employment at the cost of family solidarity."[6] Migration, Ramos strongly implied, is morally acceptable only when it is undertaken by single, childless women.

The Philippine media reinforce this position by consistently publishing sensationalist reports on the suffering of children in transnational families. These reports tend to vilify migrant mothers, suggesting that their children face more profound problems than do those of migrant fathers; and despite the fact that most of the children in question are left with relatives, journalists tend to refer to them as having been "abandoned." One article reports, "A child's sense of loss appears to be greater when it is the mother who leaves to work abroad."[7] Others link the emigration of mothers to the inadequate child care and unstable family life that eventually lead such children to "drugs, gambling, and drinking."[8] Writes one columnist, "Incest and rapes within blood relatives are alarmingly on the rise not only within Metro Manila but also in the provinces. There are some indications that the absence of mothers who have become OCWs [overseas contract workers] has something to do with the situation."[9] The same columnist elsewhere expresses the popular view that the children of migrants become a burden on the larger society: "Guidance counselors and social welfare agencies can show grim statistics on how many children have turned into liabilities to our society because of absentee parents."[10]

From January to July 2000, I conducted sixty-nine in-depth interviews with young adults who grew up in transnational households in the Philippines. Almost none of these children have yet reunited with their migrant parents. I interviewed thirty children with migrant mothers, twenty-six with migrant fathers, and thirteen with two migrant parents. The children I spoke to certainly had

endured emotional hardships; but contrary to the media's dark presentation, they did not all experience their mothers' migration as abandonment. The hardships in their lives were frequently diminished when they received support from extended families and communities, when they enjoyed open communication with their migrant parents, and when they clearly understood the limited financial options that led their parents to migrate in the first place.

To call for the return of migrant mothers is to ignore the fact that the Philippines has grown increasingly dependent on their remittances. To acknowledge this reality could lead the Philippines toward a more egalitarian gender ideology. Casting blame on migrant mothers, however, serves only to divert the society's attention away from these children's needs, finally aggravating their difficulties by stigmatizing their family's choices.

The Philippine media has certainly sensationalized the issue of child welfare in migrating families, but that should not obscure the fact that the Philippines faces a genuine care crisis. Care is now the country's primary export. Remittances—mostly from migrant domestic workers—constitute the economy's largest source of foreign currency, totaling almost $7 billion in 1999.[11] With limited choices in the Philippines, women migrate to help sustain their families financially, but the price is very high. Both mothers and children suffer from family separation, even under the best of circumstances.

Migrant mothers who work as nannies often face the painful prospect of caring for other people's children while being unable to tend to their own. One such mother in Rome, Rosemarie Samaniego,[12] describes this predicament:

> When the girl that I take care of calls her mother "Mama," my heart jumps all the time because my children also call me "Mama." I feel the gap caused by our physical separation especially in the morning, when I pack [her] lunch, because that's what I used to do for my children. . . . I used to do that very same thing for them. I begin thinking that at this hour I should be taking care of my very own children and not someone else's, someone who is not related to me in any way, shape, or form. . . . The work that I do here is done for my family, but the problem is they are not close to me but are

far away in the Philippines. Sometimes, you feel the separation and you start to cry. Some days, I just start crying while I am sweeping the floor because I am thinking about my children in the Philippines. Sometimes, when I receive a letter from my children telling me that they are sick, I look up out the window and ask the Lord to look after them and make sure they get better even without me around to care after them. [*Starts crying.*] If I had wings, I would fly home to my children. Just for a moment, to see my children and take care of their needs, help them, then fly back over here to continue my work.

The children of migrant workers also suffer an incalculable loss when a parent disappears overseas. As Ellen Seneriches,[13] a twenty-one-year-old daughter of a domestic worker in New York, says:

There are times when you want to talk to her, but she is not there. That is really hard, very difficult. . . . There are times when I want to call her, speak to her, cry to her, and I cannot. It is difficult. The only thing that I can do is write to her. And I cannot cry through the e-mails and sometimes I just want to cry on her shoulder.

Children like Ellen, who was only ten years old when her mother left for New York, often repress their longings to reunite with their mothers. Knowing that their families have few financial options, they are left with no choice but to put their emotional needs aside. Often, they do so knowing that their mothers' care and attention have been diverted to other children. When I asked her how she felt about her mother's wards in New York, Ellen responded:

Very jealous. I am very, very jealous. There was even a time when she told the children she was caring for that they are very lucky that she was taking care of them, while her children back in the Philippines don't even have a mom to take care of them. It's pathetic, but it's true. We were left alone by ourselves and we had to be responsible at a very young age without a mother. Can you imagine?

Children like Ellen do experience emotional stress when they grow up in transnational households. But it is worth emphasizing that many migrant mothers attempt to sustain ties with their children, and their children often recognize and appreciate these efforts. Although her mother, undocumented in the United States, has not returned once to the Philippines in twelve years, Ellen does not doubt that she has struggled to remain close to her children despite the distance. In fact, although Ellen lives only three hours away from her father, she feels closer to and communicates more frequently with her mother. Says Ellen:

I realize that my mother loves us very much. Even if she is far away, she would send us her love. She would make us feel like she really loved us. She would do this by always being there. She would just assure us that whenever we have problems to just call her and tell her. [*Pauses.*] And so I know that it has been more difficult for her than other mothers. She has had to do extra work because she is so far away from us.

Like Ellen's mother, who managed to "be there" despite a vast distance, other migrant mothers do not necessarily "abandon" their traditional duty of nurturing their families. Rather, they provide emotional care and guidance from afar.[14] Ellen even credits her mother for her success in school. Now a second-year medical school student, Ellen graduated at the top of her class in both high school and college. She says that the constant, open communication she shares with her mother provided the key to her success. She reflects:

We communicate as often as we can, like twice or thrice a week through e-mails. Then she would call us every week. And it is very expensive, I know. . . . My mother and I have a very open relationship. We are like best friends. She would give me advice whenever I had problems. . . . She understands everything I do. She understands why I would act this or that way. She knows me really well. And she is also transparent to me. She always knows when I have problems, and likewise I know when she does. I am closer to her than to my father.

Ellen is clearly not the abandoned child or social liability the Philippine media describe. She not only benefits from sufficient parental support—from both her geographically distant mother and her nearby father—but also exceeds the bar of excellence in schooling. Her story indicates that children of migrant parents can overcome the emotional strains of transnational family life, and that they can enjoy sufficient family support, even from their geographically distant parent.

Of course, her good fortune is not universal. But it does raise questions about how children withstand such geographical strains; whether and how they maintain solid ties with their distant parents; and what circumstances lead some children to feel that those ties have weakened or given out. The Philippine media tend to equate the absence of a child's biological mother with abandonment, which leads to the assumption that all such children, lacking familial support, will become social liabilities.[15] But I found that positive surrogate parental figures and open communication with the migrant parent, along with acknowledgment of the migrant parent's contribution to the collective mobility of the family, allay many of the emotional insecurities that arise from transnational household arrangements. Children who lack these resources have greater difficulty adjusting.

Extensive research bears out this observation. The Scalabrini Migration Center, a nongovernmental organization for migration research in the Philippines, surveyed 709 elementary-school-age Filipino children in 2000, comparing the experiences of those with a father absent, a mother absent, both parents absent, and both parents present. While the researchers observed that parental absence does prompt feelings of abandonment and loneliness among children, they concluded that "it does not necessarily become an occasion for laziness and unruliness." Rather, if the extended family supports the child and makes him or her aware of the material benefits migration brings, the child may actually be spurred toward greater self-reliance and ambition, despite continued longings for family unity.

Jeek Pereno's life has been defined by those longings. At twenty-five, he is a merchandiser for a large department store in the Philippines. His mother more than adequately provided for her children, managing with her meager wages first as a domestic worker and then as a nurse's aide, to send them $200 a month and even to purchase a house in a fairly exclusive neighborhood in the city center. But Jeek still feels abandoned and insecure in his mother's affection, he believes that growing up

without his parents robbed him of the discipline he needed. Like other children of migrant workers, Jeek does not feel that his faraway mother's financial support has been enough. Instead, he wishes she had offered him more guidance, concern, and emotional care.

Jeek was eight years old when his parents relocated to New York and left him, along with his three brothers, in the care of their aunt. Eight years later, Jeek's father passed away, and two of his brothers (the oldest and youngest) joined their mother in New York. Visa complications have prevented Jeek and his other brother from following— but their mother has not once returned to visit them in the Philippines. When I expressed surprise at this, Jeek solemnly replied: "Never. It will cost too much, she said."

Years of separation breed unfamiliarity among family members, and Jeek does not have the emotional security of knowing that his mother has genuinely tried to lessen that estrangement. For Jeek, only a visit could shore up this security after seventeen years of separation. His mother's weekly phone calls do not suffice. And because he experiences his mother's absence as indifference, he does not feel comfortable communicating with her openly about his unmet needs. The result is repression, which in turn aggravates the resentment he feels. Jeek told me:

> I talk to my mother once in a while. But what happens, whenever she asks how I am doing, I just say okay. It's not like I am really going to tell her that I have problems here. . . . It's not like she can do anything about my problems if I told her about them. Financial problems, yes she can help. But not the other problems, like emotional problems. . . . She will try to give advice, but I am not very interested to talk to her about things like that. . . . Of course, you are still young, you don't really know what is going to happen in the future. Before you realize that your parents left you, you can't do anything about it anymore. You are not in a position to tell them not to leave you. They should have not left us. (*Sobs.*)

I asked Jeek if his mother knew he felt this way. "No," he said, "she doesn't know." Asked if he received emotional support from anyone, Jeek replied,

"As much as possible, if I can handle it, I try not to get emotional support from anyone. I just keep everything inside me."

Jeek feels that his mother not only abandoned him but failed to leave him with an adequate surrogate. His aunt had a family and children of her own. Jeek recalled, "While I do know that my aunt loves me and she took care of us to the best of her ability, I am not convinced that it was enough. . . . Because we were not disciplined enough. She let us do whatever we wanted to do." Jeek feels that his education suffered from this lack of discipline, and he greatly regrets not having concentrated on his studies. Having completed only a two-year vocational program in electronics, he doubts his competency to pursue a college degree. At twenty-five, he feels stuck, with only the limited option of turning from one low-paying job to another.

Children who, unlike Jeek, received good surrogate parenting managed to concentrate on their studies and in the end to fare much better. Rudy Montoya, a nineteen-year-old whose mother has done domestic work in Hong Kong for more than twelve years, credits his mother's brother for helping him succeed in high school:

My uncle is the most influential person in my life. Well, he is in Saudi Arabia now. . . . He would tell me that my mother loves me and not to resent her, and that whatever happens, I should write her. He would encourage me and he would tell me to trust the Lord. And then, I remember in high school, he would push me to study. I learned a lot from him in high school. Showing his love for me, he would help me with my schoolwork. . . . The time that I spent with my uncle was short, but he is the person who helped me grow up to be a better person.

Unlike Jeek's aunt, Rudy's uncle did not have a family of his own. He was able to devote more time to Rudy, instilling discipline in his young charge as well as reassuring him that his mother, who is the sole income provider for her family, did not abandon him. Although his mother has returned to visit him only twice—once when he was in the fourth grade and again two years later—Rudy, who is now a college student, sees his mother as a "good provider" who has made tremendous sacrifices for his sake. This knowledge offers him emotional security, as

well as a strong feeling of gratitude. When I asked him about the importance of education, he replied, "I haven't given anything back to my mother for the sacrifices that she has made for me. The least I could do for her is graduate, so that I can find a good job, so that eventually I will be able to help her out, too."

Many children resolve the emotional insecurity of being left by their parents the way that Rudy has: by viewing migration as a sacrifice to be repaid by adult children. Children who believe that their migrant mothers are struggling for the sake of the family's collective mobility, rather than leaving to live the "good life," are less likely to feel abandoned and more likely to accept their mothers' efforts to sustain close relationships from a distance. One such child is Theresa Bascara, an eighteen-year-old college student whose mother has worked as a domestic in Hong Kong since 1984. As she puts it, "[My inspiration is] my mother, because she is the one suffering over there. So the least I can give back to her is doing well in school."

For Ellen Seneriches, the image of her suffering mother compels her to reciprocate. She explained:

Especially after my mother left, I became more motivated to study harder. I did because my mother was sacrificing a lot and I had to compensate for how hard it is to be away from your children and then crying a lot at night, not knowing what we are doing. She would tell us in voice tapes. She would send us voice tapes every month, twice a month, and we would hear her cry in these tapes.

Having witnessed her mother's suffering even from a distance, Ellen can acknowledge the sacrifices her mother has made and the hardships she has endured in order to be a "good provider" for her family. This knowledge assuaged the resentment Ellen frequently felt when her mother first migrated.

Many of the children I interviewed harbored images of their mothers as martyrs, and they often found comfort in their mother's grief over not being able to nurture them directly. The expectation among such children that they will continue to receive a significant part of their nurturing from their mothers, despite the distance, points to the conservative gender ideology most of them maintain.[16] But whether or not they see their mothers as martyrs, children of migrant women feel best cared for when their mothers make consistent efforts to show parental concern from a distance. As Jeek's and Ellen's stories indicate, open communication with the migrant parent soothes feelings of abandonment; those who enjoy such open channels fare much better than those who lack them. Not only does communication ease children's emotional difficulties; it also fosters a sense of family unity, and it promotes the view that migration is a survival strategy that requires sacrifices from both children and parents for the good of the family.

For daughters of migrant mothers, such sacrifices commonly take the form of assuming some of their absent mothers' responsibilities, including the care of younger siblings. As Ellen told me:

> It was a strategy, and all of us had to sacrifice for it. . . . We all had to adjust, every day of our lives. . . . Imagine waking up without a mother calling you for breakfast. Then there would be no one to prepare the clothes for my brothers. We are all going to school. . . . I had to wake up earlier. I had to prepare their clothes. I had to wake them up and help them prepare for school. Then I also had to help them with their homework at night. I had to tutor them.

Asked if she resented this extra work, Ellen replied, "No. I saw it as training, a training that helped me become a leader. It makes you more of a leader doing that every day. I guess that is an advantage to me, and to my siblings as well."

Ellen's effort to assist in the household's daily maintenance was another way she reciprocated for her mother's emotional and financial support. Viewing her added work as a positive life lesson, Ellen believes that these responsibilities enabled her to develop leadership skills. Notably, her high school selected her as its first ever female commander for its government-mandated military training corps.

Unlike Jeek, Ellen is secure in her mother's love. She feels that her mother has struggled to "be there"; Jeek feels that his has not. Hence, Ellen has managed to successfully adjust to her household arrangement, while Jeek has not. The continual open communication between Ellen and her mother has had ramifications for their entire family: in return for her mother's sacrifices, Ellen assumed

the role of second mother to her younger siblings, visiting them every weekend during her college years in order to spend quality time with them.

In general, eldest daughters of migrant mothers assume substantial familial responsibilities, often becoming substitute mothers for their siblings. Similarly, eldest sons stand in for migrant fathers. Armando Martinez, a twenty-nine-year-old entrepreneur whose father worked in Dubai for six months while he was in high school, related his experiences:

> I became a father during those six months. It was like, ugghhh, I made the rules. . . . I was able to see that it was hard if your family is not complete, you feel that there is something missing. . . . It's because the major decisions, sometimes, I was not old enough for them. I was only a teenager, and I was not that strong in my convictions when it came to making decisions. It was like work that I should not have been responsible for. I still wanted to play. So it was an added burden on my side.

Even when there is a parent left behind, children of migrant workers tend to assume added familial responsibilities, and these responsibilities vary along gender lines. Nonetheless, the weight tends to fall most heavily on children of migrant mothers, who are often left to struggle with the lack of male responsibility for care work in the Philippines. While a great number of children with migrant fathers receive full-time care from stay-at-home mothers, those with migrant mothers do not receive the same amount of care. Their fathers are likely to hold full-time jobs, and they rarely have the time to assume the role of primary caregiver. Of thirty children of migrant mothers I interviewed, only four had stay-at-home fathers. Most fathers passed the caregiving responsibilities on to other relatives, many of whom, like Jeek's aunt, already had families of their own to care for and regarded the children of migrant relatives as an extra burden. Families of migrant fathers are less likely to rely on the care work of extended kin.[17] Among my interviewees, thirteen of twenty-six children with migrant fathers lived with and were cared for primarily by their stay-at-home mothers.

Children of migrant mothers, unlike those of migrant fathers, have the added burden of accepting nontraditional gender roles in their families.

The Scalabrini Migration Center reports that these children "tend to be more angry, confused, apathetic, and more afraid than other children."[18] They are caught within an "ideological stall" in the societal acceptance of female-headed transnational households. Because her family does not fit the traditional nuclear household model, Theresa Bascara sees her family as "broken," even though she describes her relationship to her mother as "very close." She says, "A family, I can say, is only whole if your father is the one working and your mother is only staying at home. It's okay if your mother works too, but somewhere close to you."

Some children in transnational families adjust to their household arrangements with greater success than others do. Those who feel that their mothers strive to nurture them as well as to be good providers are more likely to be accepting. The support of extended kin, or perhaps a sense of public accountability for their welfare, also helps children combat feelings of abandonment. Likewise, a more gender-egalitarian value system enables children to appreciate their mothers as good providers, which in turn allows them to see their mothers' migrations as demonstrations of love.

Even if they are well-adjusted, however, children in transnational families still suffer the loss of family intimacy. They are often forced to compensate by accepting commodities, rather than affection, as the most tangible reassurance of their parents' love. By putting family intimacy on hold, children can only wait for the opportunity to spend quality time with their migrant parents. Even when that time comes, it can be painful. As Theresa related:

> When my mother is home, I just sit next to her. I stare at her face, to see the changes in her face, to see how she aged during the years that she was away from us. But when she is about to go back to Hong Kong, it's like my heart is going to burst. I would just cry and cry. I really can't explain the feeling. Sometimes, when my mother is home, preparing to leave for Hong Kong, I would just start crying, because I already start missing her. I ask myself, how many more years will it be until we see each other again?
> . . . Telephone calls. That's not enough. You can't hug her, kiss her, feel her, everything. You can't feel her presence. It's just words that

you have. What I want is to have my mother close to me, to see her grow older, and when she is sick, you are the one taking care of her and when you are sick, she is the one taking care of you.

Not surprisingly, when asked if they would leave their own children to take jobs as migrant workers, almost all of my respondents answered, "Never." When I asked why not, most said that they would never want their children to go through what they had gone through, or to be denied what they were denied, in their childhoods. Armando Martinez best summed up what children in transnational families lose when he said:

> You just cannot buy the times when your family is together. Isn't that right? Time together is something that money can neither buy nor replace. . . . The first time your baby speaks, you are not there. Other people would experience that joy. And when your child graduates with honors, you are also not there. . . . Is that right? When your child wins a basketball game, no one will be there to ask him how his game went, how many points he made. Is that right? Your family loses, don't you think?

Children of transnational families repeatedly stress that they lack the pleasure and comfort of daily interaction with their parents. Nonetheless, these children do not necessarily become "delinquent," nor are their families necessarily broken, in the manner the Philippine media depicts. Armando mirrored the opinion of most of the children in my study when he defended transnational families: "Even if [parents] are far away, they are still there. I get that from basketball, specifically zone defense." [He laughed.] "If someone is not there, you just have to adjust. It's like a slight hindrance that you just have to adjust to. Then when they come back, you get a chance to recover. It's like that."

Recognizing that the family is an adaptive unit that responds to external forces, many children make do, even if doing so requires tremendous sacrifices. They give up intimacy and familiarity with their parents. Often, they attempt to make up for their migrant parents' hardships by maintaining close bonds across great distances, even though most of them feel that such bonds could never possibly draw their distant parent close enough.

But their efforts are frequently sustained by the belief that such emotional sacrifices are not without meaning—that they are ultimately for the greater good of their families and their future. Jason Halili's mother provided care for elderly persons in Los Angeles for fifteen years. Jason, now twenty-one, reasons, "If she did not leave, I would not be here right now. So it was the hardest route to take, but at the same time, the best route to take."

Transnational families were not always equated with "broken homes" in the Philippine public discourse. Nor did labor migration emerge as a perceived threat to family life before the late 1980s, when the number of migrant women significantly increased. This suggests that changes to the gendered division of family labor may have as much as anything else to do with the Philippine care crisis.

The Philippine public simply assumes that the proliferation of female-headed transnational households will wreak havoc on the lives of children. The Scalabrini Migration Center explains that children of migrant mothers suffer more than those of migrant fathers because child rearing is "a role women are more adept at, are better prepared for, and pay more attention to."[19] The center's study, like the Philippine media, recommends that mothers be kept from migrating. The researchers suggest that "economic programs should be targeted particularly toward the absorption of the female labor force, to facilitate the possibility for mothers to remain in the family."[20] Yet the return migration of mothers is neither a plausible nor a desirable solution. Rather, it implicitly accepts gender inequities in the family, even as it ignores the economic pressures generated by globalization.

As national discourse on the care crisis in the Philippines vilifies migrant women, it also downplays the contributions these women make to the country's economy. Such hand-wringing merely offers the public an opportunity to discipline women morally and to resist reconstituting family life in a manner that reflects the country's increasing dependence on women's foreign remittances. This pattern is not exclusive to the Philippines. As Arjun Appadurai observes, globalization has commonly led to "ideas about gender and modernity that create large female work forces at the same time that cross-national ideologies of 'culture,' 'authenticity,' and national honor put increasing pressure on various communities to morally discipline working women."[21]

The moral disciplining of women, however, hurts those who most need protection. It pathologizes the children of migrants, and it downplays the emotional difficulties that mothers like Rosemarie Samaniego face. Moreover, it ignores the struggles of migrant mothers who attempt to nurture their children from a distance. Vilifying migrant women as bad mothers promotes the view that the return to the nuclear family is the only viable solution to the emotional difficulties of children in transnational families. In so doing, it directs attention away from the special needs of children in transnational families—for instance, the need for community projects that would improve communication among far-flung family members, or for special school programs, the like of which did not exist at my field research site. It's also a strategy that sidelines the agency and adaptability of the children themselves.

To say that children are perfectly capable of adjusting to nontraditional households is not to say that they don't suffer hardships. But the overwhelming public support for keeping migrant mothers at home does have a negative impact on these children's adjustment. Implicit in such views is a rejection of the division of labor in families with migrant mothers, and the message such children receive is that their household arrangements are simply wrong. Moreover, calling for the return migration of women does not necessarily solve the problems plaguing families in the Philippines. Domestic violence and male infidelity, for instance—two social problems the government has never adequately addressed—would still threaten the well-being of children.[22]

Without a doubt, the children of migrant Filipina domestic workers suffer from the extraction of care from the global south to the global north. The plight of these children is a timely and necessary concern for nongovernmental, governmental, and academic groups in the Philippines. Blaming migrant mothers, however, has not helped, and has even hurt, those whose relationships suffer most from the movement of care in the global economy. Advocates for children in transnational families should focus their attention not on calling for a return to the nuclear family but on trying to meet the special needs transnational families possess. One of those needs is for a reconstituted gender ideology in the Philippines; another is for the elimination of legislation that penalizes migrant families in the nations where they work.

If we want to secure quality care for the children of transnational families, gender egalitarian views of child rearing are essential. Such views can be fostered by recognizing the economic contributions women make to their families and by redefining motherhood to include providing for one's family. Gender should be recognized as a fluid social category, and masculinity should be redefined, as the larger society questions the biologically based assumption that only women have an aptitude to provide care. Government officials and the media could then stop vilifying migrant women, redirecting their attention, instead, to men. They could question the lack of male accountability for care work, and they could demand that men, including migrant fathers, take more responsibility for the emotional welfare of their children.

The host societies of migrant Filipina domestic workers should also be held more accountable for their welfare and for that of their families. These women's work allows First World women to enter the paid labor force. As one Dutch employer states, "There are people who would look after children, but other things are more fun. Carers from other countries, if we can use their surplus carers, that's a solution."[23]

Yet, as we've seen, one cannot simply assume that the care leaving disadvantaged nations is surplus care. What is a solution for rich nations creates a problem in poor nations. Mothers like Rosemarie Samaniego and children like Ellen Seneriches and Jeek Pereno bear the brunt of this problem, while the receiving countries and the employing families benefit.

Most receiving countries have yet to recognize the contributions of their migrant care workers. They have consistently ignored these workers' rights and limited their full incorporation into society. The wages of migrant workers are so low that they cannot afford to bring their own families to join them, or to regularly visit their children in the Philippines; relegated to the status of guest workers, they are restricted to the low-wage employment sector, and with very few exceptions, the migration of their spouses and children is also restricted.[24] These arrangements work to the benefit of employers, since migrant care workers can give the best possible care for their employers' families when they are free of care-giving responsibilities to their own families. But there is a dire need to lobby for more inclusive policies, and for employers to develop a sense of accountability for their workers' children. After all, migrant workers significantly help their employers to reduce *their* families' care deficit.

NOTES

1. Arlie Hochschild, "The Culture of Politics: Traditional, Post-modern, Cold Modern, Warm Modern Ideals of Care," *Social Politics*, vol. 2, no. 3 (1995): pp. 331–46.

2. While women made up only 12 percent of the total worker outflow in 1975, this figure grew to 47 percent twelve years later in 1987 and surpassed the number of men by 1995. IBON Facts and Figures, "Filipinos as Global Slaves," vol. 22, nos. 5–6 (March 15–31, 1999), p. 6.

3. Notably, Filipino women. . . also alleviate the care crisis plaguing hospitals and hospices in more developed nations by providing services as professional nurses. At the expense of the quality of professional care in the Philippines, nurses have sought the better wages available outside the country.

4. Gina Mission, "The Breadwinners: Female Migrant Workers," *WIN: Women's International Net Issue* (November 1998): p. 15A.

5. Hochschild and Machung, 1989. By "stalled revolution," Hochschild refers to the fact that the economic contributions of women to the family have not been met with a corresponding increase in male responsibility for household work.

6. Agence France-Presse, "Ramos: Overseas Employment a Threat to Filipino Families," *Philippine Inquirer* (May 26, 1995), p. 11.

7. Perfecto G. Caparas, "OCWs Children: Bearing the Burden of Separation," *Manila Times* (September 30, n.d.), pp. 1–2.

8. Susan Fernandez, "Pamilya ng OFWs maraming hirap" (Many hardships in the families of OFWs), *Abante* (January 27, 1997), p. 5.

9. Lorie Toledo, "Child Sexual Abuse Awareness," *People's Journal* (February 19, 1996), p. 4. Although incest is a social problem in the Philippines, its direct correlation to the emigration of mothers is an unproven speculation.

10. Lorie Toledo, "Overseas job vs. family stability," *People's Journal* (December 15, 1993), p. 4.

11. Bureau of Employment and Labor Statistics, "Remittances from Overseas Filipino Workers by Country of Origin Philippines: 1997–Fourth Quarter 1999," *Pinoy Migrants, Shared Government Information System for Migration,* http://emisd.web.dfa.gov.ph/~pinoymigrants/.

12. Rosemarie Samaniego is a pseudonym. This excerpt is drawn from Rhacel Salazar Parreñas, *Servants of Globalization: Women, Migration, and Domestic Work* (Stanford, Calif.: Stanford University Press, 2001).

13. Ellen Seneriches and the names of the other children whom I quote in this article are all pseudonyms.

14. Pierrette Hondagneu-Sotelo and Ernestine Avila, "'I'm Here, but I'm There': The Meanings of Latina Transnational Motherhood," *Gender and Society,* vol. 11, no. 5 (1997), pp. 548–71.

15. A two-part special report by Caparas, "OCWs Children," which appeared on the front page of the *Manila Times,* summarized the media's incredibly negative view on the plight of children in transnational families. It reported that children suffer from a "psychological toll," "extreme loneliness," "unbearable loss," "strained relations," "incest," and consequently delinquency, as indicated, for instance, by rampant "premature pregnancies." See also Caparas's "OCWs and the Changing Lives of Filipino Families," *Manila Times* (August, 29, n.d.), pp. 1, 5.

16. Similarly, I found that children use the corollary image of the struggling "breadwinner" father to negotiate the emotional strains of their transnational household arrangement.

17. Scalabrini Migration Center (SMC), *Impact of Labor Migration on the Children Left Behind* (Quezon City, Philippines: Scalabrini Migration Center, 2000).

18. SMC, 2000, p. 65.

19. SMC, 2000, p. 57.

20. SMC, 2000, p. 65.

21. Arjun Appadurai, "Globalization and the Research Imagination," *International Social Science Journal,* vol. 160 (June 1999), p. 231.

22. National Commission for the Role of Filipino Women, *Philippine Plan for Gender-Responsive Development, 1995–2025* (Manila, Philippines: National Commission for the Role of Filipino Women, 1995).

23. Marije Meerman, "The Care Chain," episode 42 of *The New World* (Netherlands: VPRO-TV); www.dnv.vpro. nl/carechain.

24. Policies in various receiving countries restrict the migration of workers' families. Such restrictions can be found both in countries, such as Singapore and Taiwan, that have illiberal policies and in those, like Canada, with liberal policies.

FORTY-FIVE

◆◆◆

Remotely Sensed (2002)
A Topography of the Global Sex Trade

Ursula Biemann

Ursula Biemann is a researcher at the Institute for Theory of Art and Design in Zurich. Her art, writings, and curatorial work focus on media, geography, and gender relations in the economy. Her award-winning video essays and installations have been widely shown at international exhibitions and museums including the Museum of Modern Art (MOMA) in New York.

It has become increasingly difficult to find a model of cultural representation that would live up to the complexity of the present discourse of gender and visual culture in the context of globalization. Over the last few years I have recognized the need to locate gender and other categories of identity, such as ethnicity and nationality, within the context of the wider transformations of the public sphere, particularly urban reality. In this endeavour, geography proves to be a useful and attractive arena to articulate questions of the moving subject in relation to space and location. Globalization is a very gendered process: an evergrowing proportion of migrant people looking for work are female. However, beyond a simple feminization of migration we notice that women's labour is being sexualized, that is to say, global processes actually address women directly in their sexuality. The worldwide migration of women into the sex industry or more specifically the burgeoning trafficking in women can be read as a structural part of pancapitalism. . . . I am using the theoretical framework of geography because it allows for an examination of female migrancy, mobility and routing in relation to specific sites, while at the same time permitting an integration of their psychological and material experience. In other words, I am interested in the practice of linking geo-politics to an understanding of how subjects are produced.

Geography is understood as a visual culture in this context. Satellite media and other geographic information systems are generating profuse quantities of topographic images to be interpreted for scientific, social and military use. Increasingly they make their way into our daily lives, inform the way we think about the world and code our concept of globality. I make it my project to explore how these satellite visions of globality are producing a sexual economy in which it has become thinkable to reorganize women geographically on a global scale.

Countergeographies

Spiralling down from an orbital view the video essay *Remote Sensing* takes an earthly perspective on the topography of the global sex trade. It is a project of countergeography that engages in migration and cross-border circuits, illegal and illicit networks as well as alternative circuits of survival, where women have emerged as key actors. The digital documents generated for the video essay trace the routes and reasons of women who travel across the globe to enter this gigantic Fordism [production line] of service that is the sex industry.

Trafficking hinges on the displacement of women, their costly transportation across topographies from one cultural arrangement to another, from one spatial organization to another, from one abandoned economy to a place of greater accumulations. It is the route that counts. The agents charge money for the vehicle and for the escort who knows the path and the border geography, the contacts and the bribes. Female bodies are the new cargo in these transactions across boundaries that generate massive amounts of footloose capital, abstract global capital that is nevertheless so physical for some. The travel money will go back into bonding women to do unpaid sex work for the trafficking ring. It is a common practice of debt-bondage that places women in the contexts of the historical spaces of the brothel and the colony.

There are numerous structural and political reasons why women move, and are being moved, into the global sex industry. The Mekong region [South East Asia] has traditionally been a burgeoning basin for the trafficking of women who criss-cross borders in all directions. . . . Thailand is no longer just a sending country, but has also become a country of transit and destination. While Thai women migrated in the 1970s to Europe and North America or have been promoted to the higher echelons of the sex industry catering to foreign tourists, there is a need to supply new women and girls to the lower class brothels in Thailand. This market segment draws on the young rural female population in neighbouring countries

like Burma, Laos, and Vietnam. China goes through a different predicament. The prolonged period under the one-child policy has caused a major gender disparity in the present generation. Many Chinese men who do not find wives will acquire them abroad. In Taiwan, on the other hand, women prefer a modern life in the city and male farmers have a hard time attracting a wife who wants to live a hardworking rural lifestyle. They also have to import females from the Philippines by the tens of thousands for unpaid agricultural labour and every year 100,000 South East Asian women are shipped into the Japanese entertainment industry, which equals Japan's defence budget in volume.

The commodification and displacement of female bodies in South East Asia generates impressive figures, but my work does not situate itself in the production of factual information. The questions I have to ask myself as an artist and video maker are: How can I dislocate and recontextualize a much belaboured question such as the marketability of women and the objectification of female sexuality? How can a video, rather than simply arguing against capitalism and affirming rigid gender identities, reflect and produce the expansion of the very space in which we write and speak of the feminine? There is a need to investigate the interplay between the symbolization of the feminine and the economic and material reality of women. To reproduce closed, privatized and restricted images of women is confining the feminine further. Some women take the route into sex work voluntarily, others not, it is true, but there is a large grey zone in between these two conditions, a vast field of negotiation, on which I focus my attention. The process of re-signification, which I undertake in my video practice, then, is not only an incessant struggle against the effacement of the diversification and differentiation of the feminine, it is also an analysis of the gendered dynamic inscribed in social and material landscapes. Of course I would like to see the space in which we write our lives, our bodies and sexuality as a heterogeneous one but in the course of creating this space, I am bound to look at the existing technologies and networks of knowledge that operate in delimiting and formalizing it.

Bandana Pattanaik (*Global Alliance Against Traffic in Women, GAATW*): I think seeing them as victims creates a lot of sympathy and therefore people find it easier to accept. If I'll say that I have been forced into prostitution, people say, oh poor thing, let's help her, she is in a really bad situation. But if somebody says I chose to become a prostitute that's very difficult to accept or to understand. Why would you choose to be a prostitute? So many times it's framed in this either/or debate. Either you are a victim or you are an agent. Either you have chosen to be a sex worker or you have been forced into prostitution. And I think there are such large grey areas in between.

While all of my videos to date elaborate on the relations of gender, technology and transnational capitalism, *Remote Sensing* engages maybe most explicitly in a critique of visualizing technologies, particularly the orbital omniscient view of satellite imagery. Taking up a feminist critique that has claimed the importance of the viewing structures and apparatuses for the power relations established by the gaze, there is a need to displace and interrogate the images and to reintroduce a situated way of seeing and knowing. Geographic information systems (GIS) propose an abstract and highly accurate view of the world from the top down. GIS are criticized by feminist scientists for applying binary and mutually exclusive categories that are unable to hold and interpret a great variety of conflicting information. They are also completely unable to think in relational terms and reveal the gendered meaning of data. Cartography is insufficient, then, to map the subjective path of people on the move.

A major objective of *Remote Sensing* is to propose a mode of representation that traces the trajectory of people in a pancapitalist world order wherein the space between departure and arrival is understood as a transnational one, i.e., a potentially subversive space which does not adhere to national rules, but nevertheless a complex material and social space that is formed by economic relations. All this is from a gendered perspective. Remotely gazed at from the orbital perspective, transnational sexuality comes into full sight. In this topography of the global sex trade, the female bodies get sensed and identified, evaluated and re-routed according to their assigned function. The moving women appear as data streams in the video, scans and X-rays portrayed over landscapes passing by, their anatomical and demographic data are recorded, their routes appear in electronic travel schedules on the screen. They are the embodiment of the abstract financial flows that feed the global economy.

Remote Sensing visualizes the multilayered meaning of geography where the mobilization and the sexualization of women is linked to the implementation of new technologies, often in contradictory ways. While the Internet facilitates the migration flow, particularly for women via the bride market, border reinforcement technologies on the other hand hinder and push it into the illegal sector.

Heat and movement sensors, infra-red and roentgen cameras, digital and genetic control mechanisms are developed and put to use along the . . . borders. Parallel to this, European migration politics are quite explicit in their practice of directing migrant women straight into the sex industry without giving them any future option to switch to another trade. For non-European female applicants, the Swiss government only issues "dancers' visas" which hinge on cabaret contracts. The automatic channelling of migrant women into sex work is an index of their status under national rule, but it also speaks of the place of sex in that national space where laws protect the flourishing sexual life of male citizens as a privilege and source of power. Two-thirds of the 500,000 women entering Europe's entertainment industry every year are from Eastern post-socialist countries. The social change in these sending countries since the 1990s and the migration politics of the receiving countries both impact the flow of women into the sex trade. Even though the official policy is to fight human trafficking and to help women getting out of the sex trade, the fact is that the number of trafficked women is steadily increasing. Technologies of marginalization always affect women, and particularly economically disadvantaged women, in their sexuality because powerful players like states, scientific complexes, and military institutions tend to create a sexuality that eroticizes hierarchies.

Aida Santos *(Women's Education, Development, Productivity and Research Organization, WEDPRO):* The history of the American involvement in prostitution and trafficking should not be missed. . . . In the 40s the Americans came and established their bases in the Philippines. The presence of the U.S. Army and Navy contributed dramatically to the rise in prostitution and trafficking, in the sense that when you have an institution like twenty-one military bases scattered all over the country in a situation of poverty and where women's status is very low, families are willing to send off their kids to work, and the elder daughters are bound by tradition to help their families and send their siblings to school, you've got very rich soil for exploitation. And that's what happened in the former U.S. baselands. The Marines are still coming here for training and when the big carriers dock in the harbour, 10,000 servicemen go on shore. In the small town near the Subic base of Olongapo, there are 6000 women registered [to work] in bars.

Since the infrastructure for the entertainment industry was already in place, many of the Rest and Recreation areas created for the U.S. soldiers during the war in Vietnam and Korea have been turned into sites of prostitution and sex tourism. Most of the women who came to the baselands expected to find restaurant jobs, but as it turns out, waitresses do not have a regular salary but work on a commission basis only. Unless they go out with the customers and provide personal entertainment and sexual services, they will not earn a living. Some of the former bases have been transformed into assembly plants for outsourced production paying wages that do not cover their living costs so that many women are bound to gain a complementary income by prostituting. Whether [through] . . . an offspring of military camps or a by-product of Western off-shore operations, women are displaced and drawn into the global economy through sexual labor. Sexual difference becomes a primary structural factor in understanding a migration-bound economy.

Another reason for the trafficking of women is that movements of exile, migration, and international business have created the need to supply "familiar" services abroad. So Filipinas are routed to Lagos in Nigeria to cater to Chinese businessmen; Thai women are trafficked to Paris to serve French-born Chinese and Cambodian immigrants; and girls from Nicaragua are dispatched to Southern California to supply camps of Mexican agricultural workers while others are kept in mobile trailer brothels that circulate in the Chicano suburbs of Los Angeles. The clandestine becomes an obscure form of living the locality of culture, a location that remains suspended and transitory. There is no arrival. The existence of these women is marked by a constant mobility, their time is scheduled, their space is confined, civil rights and sexual governance are suspended. The non-status of their existence speaks of a geographic ambivalence,

and it is not surprising that these bodies are usually suspended from the cartographic discourse even though they have become an important part of illicit border transactions and underground economic circuits and increasingly represent a major source of foreign currency for national households. The video makes an effort to track and register the movement of these women and to infuse meaning into the mapping of their trajectories. Why is it so important to trace their paths through space? I think because these very bodies are in fact the site of numerous conflicts. Clearly, they represent a phantasmatic femininity that has been ruled out from Western consciousness but continues to thrive in the a-national space in which the fleeing temporality of their presence and their non-adherence to a national program are major criteria. Their service needs to be secured materially but denied in the official ideology. While their civil status is suspended, their figurative representation reveals another phantasm deeply rooted in the bourgeois projections onto permanently seductive postcolonial places. Silk dresses and an Asian gentleness mask the drastic economic imbalance in which the hard bargain between the sexes takes place in capitalist society.

While the powerful players certainly lay the foundation for the global trafficking of women, we have to recognize that most trafficking operations are not conducted by mighty syndicates. They work in small units, relatives or acquaintances who recruit girls in slum neighbourhoods; frequently there are bi-national couples who have good contacts to the source country. Women often feel that these agents are not exploiting them but actually providing a valuable service in their desire to move to richer countries or to the cities for a modern and more exciting life, helping them to trade a slum existence for the glamour of a Bunny Club. And even if they feel lonely and exhausted, they are still able to send money home, not only supporting their family but generating hard cash for their governments.

Siriporn Skrobanek: We respect these women because many are illiterate, cannot speak a word of English but still have a strong will and encounter the whole world. And many of them can survive and struggle in their own way.

The video, *Remotely Sensing,* is available from Women Make Movies (www.wmm.com). A Web site includes images and text: www.geobodies.org/video/sensing/sensing.html

◆◆◆

Separation Anxiety: The Schisms and Schemas of Media Advocacy, or 'Where Are You Tonight, Langston Hughes?' (2005)

Paromita Vohra

Paromita Vohra is an award-winning independent filmmaker and writer. She directed *Work in Progress: At the WSF; Cosmopolis: Two Tales of a City; UnLimited Girls; A Short Film About Time; A Woman's Place;* and *Annapurna*. Her screenplays include *Khamosh Pani; If You Pause: In a Museum of Craft; A Few Things I Know About Her;* and *Skin Deep*. She teaches scriptwriting at Sophia Polytechnic (Mumbai) and is the India coordinator of A Woman's Place, a collective of women using media for social change.

'Theme for English B'
The instructor said:
Go home and write
a page tonight.
And let that page come out of you—
Then, it will be true.
I wonder if it's that simple?

. . .

It's not easy to know what is true for you or me
at twenty-two, my age. But I guess I'm what
I feel and see and hear, Harlem, I hear you:
hear you, hear me—we two—you, me, talk
    on this page.
(I hear New York too.) Me—who?
Well, I like to eat, sleep, drink, and be in
    love.
I like to work, read, learn, and understand
    life.
I like a pipe for a Christmas present,
    or records—Bessie, bop, or Bach.
I guess being coloured doesn't make me
    NOT like
the same things other folks like who are
    other races.
So will my page be coloured that I write?
Being me, it will not be white.
But it will be
a part of you, instructor.

. . .

Sometimes perhaps you don't want to be a
    part of me.
Nor do I often want to be a part of you.
But we are, that's true!
(Langston Hughes)[1]

When did they start to call political art media advocacy? I'm not sure, but possibly around the same time that the feminist movement began to be called the women's movement.

At some point we ceased to see art and media projects as expressions of our political ideas and came to regard them as receptacles—some sort of fast, cheap and convenient carriers of "content": disseminating tools.

Media for social change is a decades-old institution in India.[2] It is tied to the conception of nationhood, either to build or critique its practices, right from the paternal governmental vision of Doordarshan and All India Radio,[3] through to the left and liberal filmmakers of the 1970s and 1980s, the media collectives of the 1990s until today, where there is a growing diversity of alternative media initiatives. Media advocacy follows roughly three routes: the making of alternative media, for example documentary films, the critique of mainstream media, and the handing over of media tools to untrained groups in order to demystify the process and give them the power to tell their own stories.

With respect to the feminist movement in India, media advocacy has been of particular relevance. In part, this is because the media seemed like a very good way to combat the cultural attitudes that underpin patriarchy and prevent the success of organizational or developmental projects. In part, it is because video records of women's initiatives and experience overlapped so easily with the idea of oral history, as well as "the making public of the personal," hence rendering it political.

There have been important moments in this engagement, like the oft-noted Video Sewa experiment or the formation of Mediastorm, a women's documentary film collective in Delhi. But over the years, barring a few exceptions, much of this media work has remained at a sort of early stage.[4] While in more recent times the Indian documentary film movement has seen a proliferation of *styles* in feminist films, it has seen fewer new feminist approaches or narratives; there is a stronger tendency to clarify a position than to speak from it. In a sense there is an industrial strength replication of pre-established narratives with only the tiniest of modifications, a preference for sticking close to familiar modes. From being a philosophical political narrative, informed by the ideas of feminist thought and activism, a lot of women's media advocacy (and a lot of other social-issue advocacy as well) is example-oriented, a reiteration of known ideas, not a deepening or widening of the feminist discourse. Having established the importance of a woman's room, it is as if it stays there. . . . How did it all get to be so thoroughly domesticated?

"Women's Issues" Rather than Feminism

There is something to be learned from this trajectory of women's media advocacy, and it is crucially tied to the growth of feminism as a dynamic, meaningful philosophy. Much advocacy work has tended to circle around the idea of "women's issues" rather than feminist approaches to the world. This is in large part because there is, in fact, an industry around this—of funding and promotion—which considers women being on film sufficient, women picking up a camera empowering, women making movies an amazing achievement, and asks not much else of it. Funding for media advocacy often proceeds along these concretized lines. It is relatively easily available for a list of appropriate issues—say, women and housing, or adolescence, or violence. These have a programmatic nature and are illustrative rather than exploratory projects. The issue is seen as being quite clear, and it asks that the project have a result that is equally visible and unambiguous: something we can touch and see in our lifetimes. In government terms, it's what we call "implementation." As the industry expands, the work grows further away from the central ideology that it once radiated from, becoming a free-floating process of routine and, eventually, a dead metaphor. Those who become absorbed into it, do so by professional routes, carrying out the job rather than seeking to subvert these processes.

In effect, this approach also stems from a fixed, rather than evolving, delineation of what is political, and what are the problems of being an Indian woman. The tendency then is to speak of women primarily as examples of their socio-economic location, and only in terms of the problems they either experience or triumph over. At some primitivist level, it is as though women do not negotiate complex compromises or produce theory, or, heaven forbid, art. It is a pseudo-socialist aesthetic: where determined sameness is a metaphor for equality and the world of imagination is an exiled counter-revolutionary.

The new rhetoric of accessible technology makes this process even more pedestrian. Technology is seen as sufficient to counter the intensely ideological weight of cultural life, as if material access were the sole separator of the marginalized from the privileged. To suggest that there may be need to understand a medium aesthetically or semiotically, to explore the implications of form, is at best to be told, "Well, this is not an arty film, it's an issue-based video," or its variation, "We are not artists, we are activists." At worst, it is to be accused of being "brahminical" and "anti-people's media." It is a matter of unending wonder that the very people who underline the inequities born of language politics—the fact that education in English confers privilege—dismiss the language of media and art, deny that it has its own nuances and political weight, and effectively separate entire communities of artists and audiences from the alternative discussion of political life.

In a fundamental sense then, media advocacy has abandoned the very rich theoretical and political underpinnings of feminist thought, and domesticated itself into an industry. It has fallen into a cautious, conformist mode, using the most hackneyed conventions in self-justification—seeking not the poetry of felt observation, the creation of an alternative culture, but a mechanistic and essentially conservative approach.

It is certainly true that this concept of media advocacy has paralleled the rise of the NGO sector. But these same floating mechanics can be found outside the purview of the NGO film as well. For instance, another form popular with women has been the personal film. Born from the feminist idea that "the personal is political," it is now a shadow of that idea. It has become a diary form, akin to the slip-dress, where it is more a case of what is inside is outside, where it is enough just to speak of one's personal life or centralize the narratives of inspiring female relatives and imagine that it will translate into political meaning. But, sister, we are a long way from letting it all hang out and calling it a revolution. The magic of the phrase "the personal is political" was that it made sense backwards as well—"the political is personal"—and it is a suggestion that we render the personal political through something we do in expressing it.

Further, this malaise is deeply tied to a similar crisis within party or union politics. Within political movements, the prescriptive approach to media, or (let's face it) propaganda, has existed for a very long time. In terms of form and intent, it is not that different from the state's own didactic mechanisms, and it is often tied to moral lessons rather than ethical issues. More disturbingly, what leads from this is the inherent, implicit, but overwhelming hierarchy of issues. In this roster, feminist issues are just not considered that important, no matter what lip service is paid to them.

Obviously there has been a long journey from early denouncements of feminism as an elite, Western conspiracy to divide the people's movement, and the refusal to accept that patriarchy was a category by which power could be understood. At a quick glance, it seems that in a pervasively patriarchal understanding of the world, many—though by no means all—activists have (roughly) this order of important issues: communal conflict, defence policy and peace movements, land rights, indigenous people's movements, labor or allied economic issues, women's issues—preferably to be discussed around 8 March—and then, child rights. If there were a catalog, it would read: "Category: communalism,[5] Subcategory: women." In this automated perception, the issue connotes urgency, rather than the moment that the issue finds itself within.

When surrounded by this powerful but unarticulated environment, it becomes difficult to assert a more complex voice with confidence. For many women, it translates into a highly ambivalent relationship with being called "woman artist" or "feminist media practitioner" because it is seen as an apologist stream, a limited identity. The limitations exist equally in both domains that have now become so separate from each other—activism and art. While the romanticized figure of the radical male artist evinces a perspective that his work pertains to all, the woman artist is stereotypically seen as being grim or kooky, her concerns being herself and her fluids.

Isms, Schisms, and Schemas

This is a mind-set of schisms and schemas. Faced with this separation of feminism from the world, by its being recast as women's issues, media advocacy done by women flutters anxiously between addressing women's issues and experiences, and making tense, circuitous disclaimers about how their work is not just, well, "women's work."

It is all the more confusing because the doublespeak of caring about the "women's question" is the very thing that facilitates and gives space to so much of the work. But its boundaries are firmly drawn with invisible ink. Why is it so difficult to see that one needs more intuitive forms to counter this intuitively felt prejudice?

The schisms are binary. The separation is not only between women and the rest of the world, or feminism and women's issues, but just as strongly, and more fundamentally, between what is perceived as cultural/artistic, what is seen as theoretical and what is considered political. This approach sees art and culture in a fragmented way—as mere adjuncts to the real work of a society, as an illustration of social and historical moments. All media can be clearly identified via a schema, in which art or media work is commercial if it entertains, personal if it is expressive, and political if it is didactic and unambiguous. Everything that seems betwixt and between is problematic.

This suspicion of art is the same as the suspicion of feminism. Both approaches—of art and of feminism—undermine what has been the dominant tendency of academic and organizational thought: a strongly objectivist tendency, uncomfortable with the modes of intuitive observation and ambiguous responses. Both subvert the very structure of thought, not just a point or two in it, and so the anxiety of keeping them separate from the mainstream of *the alternative* is stubborn.

The Identikit and the Moment of Ambivalence

Several years ago, I was involved in a project called *A Woman's Place,* which was a cross-cultural exploration of how women strategically redefine power, around the world. It was a collaborative effort between filmmakers from India, South Africa and the U.S., meant for broadcast—an attempt to work in a mainstream format but with a greater focus on process, rather than just product. Predictably, funding for this was not easy to obtain, and I got quite used to wearing Indian dress to meetings with funders, as proof of my authenticity. Along the way we met with an established women's media network. We were told by its president that the only people entitled to tell the stories of women of a specific context were those women themselves, as indeed this group had facilitated in some places. For us to aspire to do so was to usurp their voices.

Almost a decade later I made a film, *UnLimited Girls,* in English, about feminism and varied people's responses to it; it was quite rooted in content and form within various urban contexts. At several screenings I was lectured about how I ought to be making films about rural and underprivileged women, and told that by speaking of my own and allied contexts, I was effectively silencing the women of rural India (I've met a few of these rural women and I can't remember speaking much in that encounter, but that's another story for another time). One person even sent me a four-page academic article about how my film was elitist, as was my persona. Therefore, by implication, the film could not be a valuable political document because after all the "real" India is in the villages and the rest is, I guess, *maya,* illusion.

Identity politics has its roots in a very important tenet of equal but different, not same; it resists the power structures of caste, class, and gender within progressive politics. In fact, it often seems to have become a peculiar form of wielding power: as if, now that your box has been recognized, you dare not leave it. A sense that we must forever work along the lines of what has been codified and ordained; blurring these lines is not permitted. It creates an effective medium of conservative caution—the focus is on what should be said and who should speak for whom. This process has a militaristic aesthetic, and it effectively disallows the most fundamental questions of form, essential both to feminism and art—now that we know what we want to speak of, *how* shall we speak of it? How do we join what is individual and human in us with the universal, the socio-economic common identity we each embody?

As importantly, if I am not permitted to speak of others' stories, does it mean by implication that I need never listen to them? Or that I tell them with a comfortable disclaimer, acquitting myself of responsibility? Optionally, if speaking of my own experiences is a political indulgence and so to be eschewed, then what am I? Someone set apart from the need for change and accountability? These questions and uncertainties are a natural corollary of change. But it seems to be enough to plug these anxieties rather than to use them as a means of developing a deeper conversation.

It is almost as though a checklist has been created on which you can tick off a set of identity representations, rather than plunge into the messy questions: how do we speak of heterosexuality without undermining same-sex relationships? How do we speak of Hindu identity without ignoring Muslim women's issues? When does anxiety about not speaking *for* others translate into not speaking *of* them? How do we find a way for the many identities within us to form a fluid whole; that there is a little of me in you and you in me, loved, hated, othered, that we imbue in each other?

How, in other words, do we find a new complex language rich with ideas and questions, as opposed to clarifying a prescribed understanding? If this is the room that media advocacy lives in, then we have to wonder: what exactly is it advocating? Like some great continental drift, as art separates from politics, theory from activism, intellect from emotion, how do we find a way to integrate these vital aspects of understanding, communication, ideas, and ways of knowing and doing?

Perhaps we need to return to an early lesson of feminism: that the thing we know intuitively has meaning. That, by articulating the intuitive, what we thought was a random personal inclination begins to form a map of larger political meaning: that it is not enough to articulate the intuitive, but necessary to join it with the experience of others, in order to find other ways of being.

When I was making a film on feminism for Sakshi, a Delhi-based NGO, I went through all the fears and anxieties I have outlined above. I was scared of not representing everyone, of not covering all the bases. Underneath it were all the things that had bothered me for years: that while the ideas of feminism had been very powerful for my life, the encounters with many feminists whose work I admired had left me with suppressed questions. Where was I to go to find a feminist history if I wasn't already "in the know"? Why in the discourse of empowerment did no one tell me that some of my choices would be so hard, and render me alone and confused? And now that I have found myself in that state how do I speak of it and find a new meaning for it? How can I purify my choices?

But my task was to make a film that would invite young women to rejoin the politics of feminism. If I were to speak of these confusions, would it not put these women off? Was it therefore not more strategic to tell a tale of achievements, and advertise all the advantages? Perhaps it may have been. We'll never know because in the end I made a film untidy with both doubt and certitude, moody with questions and answers in no particular progression. I had a great desire to speak to my audience; to do so, I had to let go of the anxiety about what they would go away with, after watching the film. I had to open myself up to the uncertainties of a conversation, choosing this form over the comfortable elevation of media advocacy. Conversation presumes knowledge, and it takes certain things for granted. It is an exploratory exercise of clarification in which we take the time to listen to each other. It has wit, and it is to be hoped, honesty rather than posturing. But it also has elements of performance that charm the listener, a persuasive statement of one's views—in other words, a deep concern with form. At its heart is the desire to be understood and to understand and then to seek, together, some answers.

In this, I believe I was true to what I think is the place of art. It is not the work of the artist to place strategy above ideas, truisms above honesty. Most of all, art is a place of honesty, where the nature of art—which is affective as much as explicit or intellectual, something that allows us to feel or sense as much as see or understand—allows for a certain arrangement of contradictions and dilemmas. The honesty and form can then, perhaps, lead to a slow resolving or acceptance of these contradictions. The creative endeavour is a constant reconsideration and refining of politics. It is a spontaneous form of politics but also vulnerable because of its openness. We cannot claim with art: "Don't shoot me, I'm only the messenger." We cannot claim an unassailability that the category of media advocacy purports to provide with its procedures and methodologies and/or politically indignant films. Nor does art ensure recognizable and unmistakable responses in a range of registers—outrage, opposition, sympathy, empathy, gratitude at being informed, and

the desire to act. These are time-honoured emotions and have their importance in the world, but . . . perhaps there are other ways? To take on more conversational or formal and creative approaches may mean accepting less definite responses, it may mean that we have to abandon the anxiety that our message needs to be crystal clear, that our stand should be perceived as unequivocal.

I found few of these cast iron responses to *UnLimited Girls.* Yet, to date, I feel this has been one of my most useful films, leading to few certain statements but perhaps many moments of questions. I have had the odd reassuring, definite response—"I always thought I am not a feminist although I believe in equal rights, but after seeing the film, I am proud to call myself one." But more often, there are the long exploratory discussions about the self, the world, feminism, feminists, men, women, parents, love, anger, violence, and change—interesting and involved but inconclusive. For audiences too, this is unfamiliar, not the know-it-all territory of a quiz. Yet every time I see an audience moving on from the straitjacket of that quiz to the liberated wanderings of saying what's in their heads, to a conversation, I think perhaps that honesty and openness are what films and art and the media in that form can spawn: they can build a culture of exchange and the desire to understand. Does that change people? Who can say for sure, but it does change the tone, shift the paradigm.

This is the place of art—to provide that moment of pausing, the moment when our audience does not say what we want to hear (although once in a while that feels good) but tries to listen to what it is telling itself; what the travel writer Robyn Davidson describes as "ambivalence—the space in which we can make up our own minds."[6] That moment of interiority is the potential moment of transformation: one we must learn to trust without anxiously searching for proof that the message has indeed reached the other end.

I Wonder If It's that Simple . . .

As any parent will tell us, it's all very well figuring things out for yourself but it's different when you have to make decisions for your children. So, as predictable as a parent, when I began working with a group of teenage girls, I found myself often falling back on traditional workshops about gender, media analysis, creating a personal diary, and so on. But as my colleague and I discovered in our work with the girls' media group, . . . girls are as canny at reproducing model versions of themselves as they are at replicating the cool images from MTV within a few days of learning to use a video camera. And despite our best efforts, the truth is that at the end of the first year, they did a little bit of just that.

With due respect to the people who pioneered the placing of technology in the hands of the under-privileged, we have to move on. It is still surprisingly in vogue to hand cameras to women, children, and other under-privileged groups as if they were a *tabula rasa*,[7] noble savages whose truth will automatically emerge.

But as Langston Hughes asked in the poem that I quoted at the beginning of this chapter: is it really that simple? Are people's truths so simple that a digital machine in their hands is enough to unravel them? There is no denying the first surge of power that comes from being able to write, draw, take a picture, or record a voice. Can we declare, though, that the beginning is the end, that the means are the ends, and then say that we've killed two birds with one stone? Can our process of change really be suspended forever in that poster moment? There seems to be a strange smell of charity to that act. Clearly the point of media advocacy is not to turn people into media practitioners. I would imagine that it is about mutually finding a new language for us to express the complexities within—the mutuality that is called conversation.

In the second year of working with the girls' media group, we abandoned much of our anxiety about how pedagogical we were being and whether we were addressing all the right feminist points even though we did so in an innovative way. We replaced most of the workshops with creative ones: open-ended, conversational, expressive. At the end of the year, it was quite clear that the work that emerged had a tremendous honesty in it, but, more importantly, a certain integrity and intelligence. Yet I cannot imagine going to a funder and describing the project as it played out in the second year and coming away with anything resembling a check.

One of the advantages of writing this chapter in the twenty-first century is that hindsight liberates us; we can simultaneously be loyal to a political idea or movement as well as sharply critical of parts

of it. The feminist movement both theoretically and politically opened up a rich space of subjective knowledge and ambiguous experience—declaring all these to be equally important ways of knowing. In a sense it provided a means to incorporate, seriously, the creative process as a fundamental part of the processes of political examination and growth. Along the way, it has allowed itself to be swept up by the anxieties that this is not enough, and scrambled to shore itself up with more conventional methods of academic proof or empirical administrative targets.

So perhaps from within it and without, it is time to start advocacy for media as an affirmation of this creative way of being political and to put our energies behind the idea that art, like the intuitive, experiential documentation of history, is not an inferior, less political record of life and thought.

When we produce media in an industrial fashion, along respectable, predictable, formulaic lines, we function as an establishment and we remove these artifacts from context, anxious to create a value-free, problem-free cultural product. But it is not the place of the alternative to become the mainstream, just as it is not feminism for women to become just like men or the other way round. We need to abandon the safety of justifying mechanistic, commercial, value-for-money approaches as mass media or media advocacy and push for the unverifiable veracities of creativity. Art becomes a meaningful political space only if it is emotionally viable to people—and it is so only if it is a place where they can make meanings of their own instead of merely consuming those that they are given. Moreover, it is a place where we allow nascent ideas to exist and slowly grow, a place of constant renewal and change, which should not be harnessed in an instrumentalist manner working against its very grain. As feminists, as political people and activists, we have to accept the responsibilities of art along with its delicacies and its particular ways of understanding reality. We need to allow it to fill us with a sense of possibility, the easier to imagine a "different world" and fantasize the details of how this world will be.

NOTES

1. L. Hughes (1951), *The Collected Poems of Langston Hughes*, © 1994 Estate of Langston Hughes (New York: Knopf and Vintage).

2. I address issues of art and advocacy from within the context of my life and work in India. However, there may well be resonances and reverberations of the schemas and schisms I describe in other parts of the world.

3. State-owned television and radio channels in India, respectively.

4. SEWA (the Self Employed Women's Association) is a trade union of over 250,000 poor women working in the non-formal sector in Gujarat, India. In 1984, 20 women in SEWA received training in videography techniques; today the Video Sewa project is a formal cooperative, providing information and communication services (<http://www.c4c.org/india.html>).

5. In other parts of the world, "communalism" or "communal conflict" would be called "fundamentalism."

6. R. Davidson (2000), 'Against travel writing', *Granta*, 72 (Overreachers), p. 249.

7. In the philosophy of John Locke, the seventeenth-century English philosopher, a young unformed mind, not yet affected by experience.

FORTY-SEVEN

◆◆◆

The Virtual Economy (2003)

V. Spike Peterson

V. Spike Peterson is a feminist scholar of international relations. Her books include *A Critical Rewriting of Global Political Economy: Integrating Reproductive, Productive and Virtual Economies*; *Gendered States: Feminist (Re)Visions of International Relations Theory*; and *Global Gender Issues* (with Anne Sisson Runyan). She is a Professor in the Department of Political Science at the University of Arizona.

. . . In terms of technology and material practices, the virtual economy resonates particularly with the electronics revolution and the instantaneous, worldwide communications it enables.[1] As so many have noted, globalization is most visible when we consider the transborder flow of information, symbols, and communication through electronic and wireless transmissions that defy territorial constraints. On the one hand, it has always been true that symbolic goods—abstractions, ideas, information— "cannot be constrained within geographical and temporal boundaries in the way that material goods can" (Waters 1995, 93). On the other hand, today's information and communication technologies have both dramatically reduced the costs of transmitting symbolic goods and exponentially increased the speed, volume, scope, and complexity of such transmissions.

Two key points emerge. First and obviously, analyses of the global economy must acknowledge and address the new scale and velocity of cross-border transactions. Second and less obviously, analyses must acknowledge and address the *nature* of these transactions and their effects on more conventional forms of exchange—and social relations. . . .

This [virtual] economy has grown in significance as information and communication technologies have compressed time-space, enabled the shift from material-intensive to knowledge-intensive industries, facilitated the expansion of services and the exchange of intangibles, and fueled tremendous growth in financial market transactions. Stated simply, the virtual economy features the exchange of symbols: primarily money in the context of global financial markets; but also information in the context of a "postindustrial," "informational," or "service economy"; and "signs" in the context of postmodern aesthetics, consumption, meaning, and culture. . . .

Introducing Three Modes of the Virtual Economy

In the context of global restructuring, the virtual economy is most familiar as a reference to the exchange of symbols associated with international monetary and financial markets. Global finance broadly defined is a reference to cross-border capital flows of credit (bonds, loans), money (currency exchange), and investment (equities, capital transfers)(Held et al. 1999, 190). And global finance *matters* because of the phenomenal growth in these flows and their relationship to the "real" economy of goods and services. Recall that after World War Two, capital flows were effectively *regulated* through the

Bretton Woods agreements that established a system of "fixed" exchange rates among national currencies. With the collapse of that system in the early 1970s, currencies "floated" against one another, their value being determined by market forces. Foreign exchange trading (in currency markets, i.e., making money from the movement in currency values) quickly grew to unprecedented levels. Other controls were gradually dismantled in the following decades, rendering capital "footloose" and relatively free to flow where market forces took it. The 1970s and 1980s thus marked a decisive shift toward "globalization" insofar as *de*regulation—marketization—meant fewer restrictions on capital movements worldwide and initiated phenomenal growth in cross-border capital flows.

The resulting growth in financial transactions is truly phenomenal. Whereas in 1973 the daily foreign exchange turnover was $15 billion, in 1995 it grew to $1.2 trillion, and in 1998 to $1.5 trillion—a *daily* amount "equal to around one-sixth of the annual output of the U.S. economy" (World Bank 2000, 71). In addition to this trade in currency markets, billions of dollars of financial investment assets are traded daily (Held et al. 1999, 189). The volume and velocity of these transactions and the amounts of money they entail make it difficult to grasp their meaning. But do so we must, because through their influence on prices, these flows link together "all of the other economic processes in the global marketplace" (Cerny 1994, 332). What transpires in global financial markets shapes the direction of investments (short-term or long-term; in trade, financial instruments, or human resources), the production of goods and services (material-based or knowledge-based; labor-intensive or capital- and technology-intensive) and the structure of labor markets (what types of labor, where located, with what compensation and under what conditions). In short, exchange rates and interest rates—which are key to business decision-making, public policy-making, and hence everyday lives worldwide—are increasingly determined by *financial* trading on world markets (Cerny 1996, 130; Held et al. 1999, 189).

Financial globalization is virtual in the sense of the symbolic nature of money, which is the object being traded. Of course money has always involved abstraction: as a means of exchange, store of wealth, or standard of value. But "world money"

circulating in today's financial markets defies traditional definitions and expectations because it is increasingly "decoupled" from the "real" economy of goods and services (Drucker 1986, 1997). To repeat Strange's racecourse analogy: "it is the opinions [of participating bettors] not the objective prowess of the horse that moves the prices" (Strange 1997, 111). Similarly, world money (prices determined by the *subjective* opinions of the bettors) has an ambiguous and only indirect relationship to the "real" economy (the objective prowess of the horses). The role of subjective opinions in financial matters is hardly new, though (beyond a narrow construction of "rationality") it has rarely been a focal point of liberal and/or positivist analyses. Because financial markets now "drive" the global economy, our analyses of them must be improved, and that involves taking the subjective aspects seriously. In short, it is not only the scale but the elusive—symbolic, subjective, even irrational—character of financial markets that renders them simultaneously so potent yet so opaque.

. . . We need to think more productively about: the world as the economic unit, information and signs as what is exchanged, and the meaning and value of exchanges that are virtual but systemically consequential. At the same time, we need to be able to link the exchange of symbols and intangibles to expectations, identities, and practices of the virtual economy and relate these to the productive and reproductive economies.

Whereas financial markets feature the exchange of money, the second, informational mode of the virtual economy features the exchange of knowledge, information or "intellectual capital" (Dunning 2000, 8). . . . Insofar as information and knowledge are symbolic goods, they are not subject to the same time and space constraints associated with material commodities. Like the electronic signals moving money around the world, the electronic transmission of knowledge knows no territorial boundaries—hence its global tendencies, not only because information and communication technologies are global but also because the information and services associated with flexibilized production are global.

Moreover . . . , information is inherently conceptual and hence cultural; its commodification thus entails a fusion of culture and economy that disrupts conventional economic analyses. We cannot just "add" informational goods to existing theories, as if the number of commodities in circulation has simply increased. The unique features of informational goods mean they are not only different from widgets and weapons but affect what we know about, how we produce, and how and why we value widgets, weapons, and virtual commodities. Hence, informational goods link *all* social relations and all three of my economies.

The third mode of the virtual economy emphasizes symbolic goods in consumerist and more postmodern terms, as a political economy of signs. I refer here to the aesthetic content—music, design, "branding," sign value—that is also, and increasingly, a value-determining component of goods being exchanged. Hence, specifying the virtual economy involves not only the exchange of money/finance and information/knowledge, but also the exchange and consumption of signs/symbols as cultural codes. . . .

In one sense, the economy of signs is familiar as an aspect of "consumer culture" in its most glaring forms. While the desire for and attempt to consume more than one "needs" is a hallmark of capitalism (and no doubt precedes it), the second half of the twentieth century signals a marked expansion of consumerism as the pursuit of hedonistic ("unnecessary") goods. Consumerism on a large scale requires the abundance of commodities made possible by industrialized production and the production of desires made possible by mass marketing. In advanced industrial countries these conditions were realized under Fordist production relations after World War Two.

In a second but less familiar sense, the economy of signs is a reference to more interpretive concerns that I will ultimately link to how we valorize money, goods, and workers. On the one hand, interpretive, postmodern approaches offer the most illuminating accounts of "sign value" and the significance of codes. The economy of signs here is less about commodities/products (material, informational or monetary) being exchanged than about symbolic codes and sign values that are invested in the product as an object of exchange (Luke 1989, 32). On the other hand, interpretive and especially semiotic accounts are crucial for comprehending the valorization of exchanges throughout the global political economy. The key issue here is how fundamentally value is determined not by any inherent measure of labor inputs or material needs but by reference to positioning within a *system* of signs/values.

Of course symbolic and cultural coding has never been absent from the production of commodities and promotion of consumption. Today however it assumes a new significance as the production of desire and rapidly changing tastes are key to surplus accumulation. In an important sense, capital focuses less on producing consumer goods than on producing consumer *subjectivities* and a totalizing "market culture" that sustain consumption. Like the exchange of money and the exchange of information, the exchange of signs has expanded and appears increasingly decoupled from the conventional economy. Once again, we are challenged to make analytical sense of this counterintuitive dynamic. . . .

Technologies Shaping Dematerialization and Deterritorialization

Information and communication technologies afford an unparalleled increase in the speed and scale of transmitting "pure information," which effectively collapses time and space in favor of dematerialized and deterritorialized exchanges. Exchanges are *dematerialized* insofar as electronically and digitally coded information—rather than material goods—constitute what is produced, circulated, and exchanged. Exchanges are *deterritorialized* insofar as coded information moves instantaneously through frictionless—rather than material, territorial—space. The *global* in globalization is perhaps best captured by reference to how these technologies cross previously less permeable borders that deeply structured social relations. Not only spatial distance but conceptual and organizational boundaries (the meaning and uses of money, commercial versus investment banking, "real" and virtual economies) are collapsed or reconstituted. The political significance of geography/space is not eliminated but reconfigured, as power is concentrated in old and new nodes of networking circuits (e.g., global cities).

Most obviously, the information revolution has transformed the scale, scope, and complexity of electronic and wireless transmissions. Continuous innovation accelerates the speed and decreases the costs of these transmissions, altering who undertakes them and for what purposes. . . . First, the resources—material infrastructure, intellectual capital, education and training—required for advanced technologies are unevenly distributed, managed, and controlled. This shapes who the key players are and whose rules dominate in the global economy. Second, the information, images and ideologies circulating in the global economy are selective. Media and marketing become politically strategic as key transmitters of information that in turn shapes valorization—of ideas, goods, identities, and practices.

Identities and Subjectivities in the Virtual Economy

The power-wielding players in the virtual economy are those most in control of monetary, financial, informational, and media activities, who variously operate at local, corporate, national, and global "levels." People everywhere are agents in the virtual economy through their consumption, savings, and investment activities. The mass of world consumers primarily respond to but through their responses also shape virtual economy practices; like workers more generally, consumers are not simply passive "receivers" but active agents. At the same time (like capitalism more generally), power to set the agenda and influence whose interests are served is concentrated in corporate, national, and global elites. These elites are significant for their role in shaping the dominant cultural coding of valued economic practices: neoliberalism and flexibilization as a global strategy, and consumerism as an individual and global ethic.

Among the elite are national, international, and global policy-makers; financial and investment firm executives; investment strategists of global firms; globe-trotting technical and "knowledge" experts; media moguls; and advertising and marketing agents with global reach. In spite of obvious variation in the roles they play (policy-making compared to financial trading), we can assume that these elites share a commitment to the premises of neoliberal capitalism. This commitment need not be homogenous or total. But the prevailing "rules of the game" suggest that in the absence of such commitment, one is unlikely to succeed and hence unlikely to be among the high-end power wielders. At the same

time, and not unrelated, the embodied elite agents of the virtual economy mirror structural hierarchies. While the international level includes some ethnic/racial and national diversity, Anglo-European elites tend to dominate the most influential financial and policy-making arenas, and women more generally are hardly to be seen.

Identities and subjectivities favored in the "commanding heights" of global finance are those of national and international elites, and especially professionals and executives. Some studies indicate that these elites exhibit a global consciousness less dominated by traditionally conceived national identities. In Cerny's (1996, 630) words, "Today, business men and women, business schools, the financial press, and international elite gatherings and organizations, however nationally rooted they remain in many ways, proclaim the virtues of global management styles and transnational profit-making strategies and see the problems of capitalism—as well as of their own firms and sectors—in global terms." Such shared ways of thinking are an aspect of "transnational epistemic communities" (Haas 1992; Helleiner 1994) with increasing power to shape international policy and practice.[1]

According to *The Economist*, the symbol of the influential global player has shifted from the "Chatham House Man" to the "Davos Man." Chatham House is the home of the Royal Institute of International Affairs and traditionally associated with political strategists and inter-state affairs. Davos (Switzerland) is the site of annual meetings of today's global decision-makers—businessmen, bankers, officials, intellectuals.[2] While predominately but not exclusively male, these decision-makers are characterized by the admiring authors in masculinist terms: "[they] hold university degrees, work with words and numbers, speak some English and share beliefs in individualism, market economics and democracy. They control many of the world's governments, and the bulk of its economic and military capabilities" (*The Economist*, 1 February 1997, 18). This image situates Davos Man far from the mundane activities of the family/household and associated stereotypes of voluntary, altruistic, and unskilled (feminized) labor. It is hardly less at odds with the factory site of waged workers who organize to improve local working conditions and participate in activities that shape labor and management relations. In spite of these apparent "distances," activities undertaken by

Davos Man are both shaped by and decisively affect identities, activities, and resources in both the reproductive and productive economies. All individuals and households—through their consumption and investment practices—are inextricably linked to financial networks that determine the availability and "price" of credit, and to production networks that determine the desires, goods, and employment conditions of everyday life.

While the most influential players are top decision-makers, we are all subject to, and complicit with, the increasing power of the virtual economy to shape our individual and collective lives. . . .

The International Financial System

> The heart of globalization is abstract: it is a finance market made up of shares, currencies and derivatives which every day . . . are speculatively moved around on dealers' computer screens in email time. *(Wichterich 2000, viii)*

More than any other sector of the economy, information technology has revolutionized monetary and financial activities. This is due in part to the role of time-space compression in money markets (where mere seconds can determine the profit—or loss—of vast sums) and in part to the symbolic and informational nature of money (so readily accommodated by electronic transmission of "pure information"). Global financial transactions since the 1980s have not only increased exponentially but also altered the terrain of monetary and financial decision-making. Most frequently noted is the sheer scale of transactions and the volume of money traded. Also important are the pervasive social effects. In *Mad Money,* Strange examines technological innovations and then observes "the sheer size of these [financial] markets, the volumes traded, the variety of possible deals to be done, the number of new financial centers, the men and women employed directly or indirectly in the business of international finance. There is, in short, more of everything, including potential victims, the involuntary gamblers in the casino. Their number too has grown" (Strange 1998, 9). Given the scale and significance of global finance, it is somewhat surprising to realize it is a relatively neglected area of study, and poorly understood. Reasons for this

neglect include academic divisions of labor and the challenges posed by technological innovations and their multiple effects. On the one hand, specialization and disciplinary commitments continue to impede the study of globally *integrated* financial markets. Macroeconomic theory has traditionally assumed the nation-state as its unit of analysis, though the study of finance has expanded to the global level. In their preoccupation with the labor process and working-class welfare, most Marxists have overlooked the politics of banking and monetary management. Among theorists of the international economy, those who study trade have been privileged over those who study monetary relations, producing a neglect both of the latter and its relationship to the former. IR [international relations] theorists have traditionally focused on state and military power, relegating the study of domestic and international economics to others. Even theorists of international political economy have only recently taken up the challenge of analyzing global financial markets.

On the other hand, analyses are also hampered by the newness and strangeness of today's global finance. While cross-border activities regarding banking securities and derivatives have a long history, they were extended and transformed by technologies specific to the late twentieth century. The challenges posed by technological innovations complicate accurate data collection and comprehensive research. Communication and information technologies increase the number of players and new ways of playing. As financial transactions expanded, innovative and sophisticated instruments were developed to maximize profits and to hedge against risks; the proliferation of instruments complicates both the documentation and interpretation of transactions.

In an important sense, efforts to "map" the ever-changing financial terrain are always already outpaced by innovations. Thus, the accelerated speed and expanded scale of transactions, in addition to the proliferation of financial instruments, pose new challenges to existing theories. Moreover, the speed and anonymity of electronic transfers permits secrecy and systemic complexities. Finally and as alluded to earlier, analyzing the global financial system is complicated by its apparent delinking from the "real economy" of goods and services. Drucker in 1986 identified "the emergence of the 'symbol' economy—capital movements, exchange rates and credit flows—as the flywheel of the world economy, in place of the 'real' economy—the flow of goods and services. The two economies seem to be operating increasingly independently" (Drucker 1986, 782). Theorists are now challenged to understand financial markets as "the strategic, dominant network of the new economy" (Castells 2000, 156).

The complexities of the subject afford no obvious organizing device or simple way to explicate global finance. We know that global finance is key to rewriting GPE [global political economy] because of its phenomenal scale, and that deregulation and securitization are key to this growth. As the discussion makes clear, these are entwined in practice. Separating them analytically, however, affords an organizational device for elaborating significant trends[:] deregulation—"freeing" money from state-imposed regulatory constraints [and] securitization—"freeing" investment money from banking controls. . . .

With reference to agency in the world economy, it is now a commonplace to observe that power shifts from national governments to market authorities. The precise nature, or even existence, of this shift is the object of considerable research and debate. I simply note here that the integration of national financial markets in important ways constrains the macroeconomic policy autonomy of individual states due to the unholy trinity discussed earlier. In sum, the dictates of interdependent global financial *markets* increasingly shape the policy options and hence *politics* of territorially bounded nation-states. Related to these issues, but only noted briefly here, is the emergence of what Gill (1992, 1995b) calls "disciplinary neo-liberalism" in which government by nationally elected officials is displaced by that of non-elected international agencies. Insofar as the latter tend to represent private rather than public interests, this shift resonates with domestic patterns of increasing private over public power.

The allure of financial trading exacerbates the devalorization of manufacturing. . . . Capital necessary to finance housing, small business, and community services is redirected from local banks to finance investment in global securities. Capital necessary for long-term investment in public works, educational infrastructure, production facilities and job creation is directed instead to the speculative interests of financial traders and the borrowing needs of global corporations.

The apparent ease and expectation of higher profits in the financial sector put pressure on the manufacturing sector in an additional sense. As quicker and higher profits become the general *expectation*, management can use that consciousness to further justify cutting wages and worker benefits (Sassen 1993, 65). In effect, inflated capital and shareholder expectations are valorized over the interests of workers in realizing a more equitable portion of the profits generated by their productivity. Given these conditions, and the problematic but seductive ideologies that accompany them, it is not surprising that trade in virtual money is dwarfing trade in "real" products. Hence, the wildfire growth in financial markets is structurally linked to the shift from manufacturing jobs and Fordist practices to less secure work associated with flexibilization. These labor market dynamics entail not only differently valorized activities but differently gendered, raced, and classed identities. . . .

Power is also reconfigured spatially. Decentralization of production, as evidenced by informalization, flexibilization, home work, and "the global assembly line," expands even as decision-making and monitoring remains centralized. For many industries, distance is no longer an issue, because workers can be monitored (telemarketing, data entry), assembled parts can be cheaply transported (microchip industries), or the product itself is information (airline reservations, over-the-counter trading). Low-wage worksites may be globally dispersed (or out in the suburbs) and simply linked to the center via communications technologies. But in Sassen's words, "the territorial dispersal of current economic activity creates a need for expanded central control and management" (Sassen 1991, 4). We observe this in relation to corporate strategies that "outsource" production and marketing even as they increase the centralization of financial and investment decision-making. Similarly, Thrift argues that while the number of international centers that "count" is understood to have decreased since the 1980s, those "that are left in contention have become more important. In other words, the interdependent connectedness of disembedded electronic networks promotes dependence on just a few places like London, New York, and Tokyo where representations can be mutually constructed, negotiated, accepted and acted upon" (Thrift 1996, 232). Here again, the effects of globalization and the virtual economy are uneven: some cities and regions gain prominence while others become marginalized; rural areas tend to lose both jobs and people to urbanization; overvalorized sectors (knowledge-based management, finance, professional jobs) enjoy high-quality benefits while devalorized sectors (manufacturing, low-wage services) struggle to make ends meet; and women and immigrants participate in the labor force but typically under low-wage "dead-end" conditions.

In summary, money is not neutral, "a lubricant with no influence of its own, one that merely simplifies transactions in an economy based on the exchange of goods" (Henwood 1998, 11). Rather, money is a form of social power that has assumed new forms with the expansion, integration, and transformation of financial markets. The flow of capital in these markets increasingly determines the fate of national economies and hence their domestic populations. At the same time, these flows of symbolic money are increasingly delinked from the "real" (material, productive) economy of goods and services. Global finance thus systemically affects the "real" economy, but the value of financial investments is determined by making money from money, not by growth or productivity in the economy of goods and services. The result is a "virtual" economy, where the vast preponderance of value in the global economy—which affects the entire system—is determined less by "objective" than subjective factors.

The Informational Economy

Whereas financial markets feature the exchange of symbolic money, the second, informational mode of the virtual economy foregrounds the exchange of symbols in the form of information, knowledge, or intellectual capital. All goods and production processes involve informational/knowledge content; the difference here is of degree and centrality. In one sense, what distinguishes this mode is that information/knowledge is the key or constitutive component of the good's value. In a second sense, the informational economy refers to the cognitive content of commodities, and knowledge as a commodity itself.

Points raised here resonate with work on "post-industrial" society and the transition that term captures: from material-intensive (industrial or Fordist) production centered on manufacturing to information- or knowledge-intensive (post-industrial or post-Fordist) production featuring services. Because globalization is uneven, material production (primary commodities and manufactured goods) continues to dominate in developing countries. In this sense, post-industrialism is more specific to developed economies where the social and technological forms of informationalism have permeated social relations (Castells 2000, 20–21). Worldwide, however, the role of information and intellectual capital has expanded to such a degree and in such a way that it transforms more material production, defies conventional practices of production and exchange, and requires attention in its own right.

The central claim here is that informational or cognitive content has become an increasingly dominant feature of production, exchange, and consumption. "Data-intensive management techniques, robotized materials processing, numerically controlled tools, aesthetically intensified marketing tactics, and the telecommunication of images all are used now to add value in the production process" (Luke 1989, 11). Hence, in addition to the familiar factors of production—land, labor and capital—we must now recognize knowledge itself as a value-adding factor. More specifically, in post-industrial society "the informational mode of production is more than just a method of production in which information is applied to production: it is one in which the production of knowledge/information itself has become the dominant sector of the economy" (Hoogvelt 2001, 111).

The shift to post-industrial or informational society has important (but limited) parallels with the shift . . . from agriculture to manufacturing. In both cases, the transition is enabled by technological innovations and marked by profoundly altered production processes and their social relations. What changes is not just the numbers of people engaged in particular kinds of work but the nature of work itself and which kinds of work (and workers) are valorized. In the informational economy, "white-collar service jobs replace blue-collar industrial ones" (Strange 1994, 131).[3] And just as the industrial revolution devalorized the work of primary producers, the information revolution is devalorizing the work of industrial producers. Privileged instead are "knowledge workers" or "symbolic analysts": those who produce, own, work with, control, improve, manipulate, and transmit knowledge/information.

Several patterns . . . are relevant here. First, down-graded manufacturing means a decline in skilled, middle-income, unionized employment in favor of un- or semi-skilled, low-wage, non-unionized jobs. Second, the proportion of service employees increases and service employment tends to be polarized. Third, flexibilization relies on and fuels this polarization: it requires decision-makers at the top who are innovative, well-educated, and effective information manipulators, and service providers at the bottom who are less empowered to resist (or demand more from) flexibilization insofar as they lack competitive skills that are attributed to elites.

In short, the shift to information-based production and the increase in services reorders production processes, reconfigures labor markets, and under present conditions tends to exacerbate the polarized gap between haves and have-nots. . . .

Characteristic Features of Information/Knowledge-Based Goods

What makes the informational economy analytically challenging is not only that we have increasingly more goods that are increasingly more information/knowledge-based but that the symbolic (virtual) nature of these goods alters production, exchange, and consumption—and how we think. . . . In the informational economy, . . . information *is* the commodity: ideas, codes, concepts, knowledge are what is being exchanged. Because information is inherently conceptual and is a pervasive feature of human thought and practice, its function as a commodity uniquely fuses culture and economy. The informational economy then entails both changes in thinking about production and exchange, etc., and more complex transformations in thinking itself. The important claim here is that the informational economy *necessarily* involves a transformation not only of goods but also of minds.

A number of related points support and clarify these claims. First, what characterizes the electronics revolution is the application of knowledge to the knowledge generation and information processing/communication devices, in a cumulative feedback loop between innovation and the uses of innovation. . . . [D]iffusion of technology endlessly amplifies the power of technology, as it becomes appropriated and re-defined by its users. New information technologies are not simply tools to be applied, but processes to be developed. . . . For the first time in history, the human mind is a direct productive force, not just a decisive element of the production system. *(Castells 2000, 31)*

Second, as suggested in this description, rapid and unceasing innovation is a hallmark of the information economy. As one effect, the relatively quick obsolescence of products alters how products are valorized, and reinforces the drive toward constant innovation and the "imperative of acceleration." As Jessop writes (1994, 277), flexibility is not new, but has changed the "way flexibility is shaped and enhanced by a new techno-economic paradigm which institutionalized the search for permanent innovation."

Third, the symbolic and interactive features of information technology mean that the product/commodity is not simply operated or consumed. Instead, owners can appropriate, manipulate, and transform the product itself through their "use" of it. Fourth, and similarly, knowledge/information is unlike traditional forms of capital where exclusivity of use and/or possession is central to claiming effective ownership or benefits. Rather, the "same" information/knowledge can be sold to multiple buyers, and still be retained by the seller. And knowledge may actually increase in value when it is "shared" with others, or when it is combined with other units of knowledge to generate a new "product."[4]

In this sense, the informational economy, fifth, defies the conventional rule of "diminishing" returns and instead offers "increasing" returns: "Knowledge is a factor of production that . . . increases its value by being used" (Hoogvelt 2001, 111). For example, while the first fax machine had little value, the expansion of users increased the value of all fax machines. The success of products is less a matter of sales *per se* than achieving a critical mass of users and securing a market niche. This alters production, marketing, and accumulation objectives. Because "'prevalence' is all important to the law of increasing returns, the 'locking in' of the market (creating a network effect) is the driving business strategy associated with the knowledge economy. Microsoft's 'locking in' of internet access through its Windows software is a classic example" (Hoogvelt 2001, 111).

Sixth, . . . the informational economy marks a profound shift in the relationship of conceptual and material production, as information/knowledge becomes not just an aspect but the objective of production. Hence, information is both the product and key to the production process, and because information is a pervasive feature of human thought and action, information technologies act upon and link all domains of human activity. "There is therefore a close relationship between the social processes of creating and manipulating symbols (the culture of society) and the capacity to produce and distribute goods and services (the productive forces)" (Castells 2000, 31).

This close integration of culture and economy, or "minds and machines," fundamentally alters how we live because the new technological system "has its own, embedded logic, characterized by the capacity to translate all inputs into a *common information system,* and to process such information at increasing speed, with increasing power, at decreasing cost, in a potentially ubiquitous retrieval and distribution network" (Castells 2000, 31–32, my emphasis; also Mitchell 1995; Postman 1993, 111). All elements, actions, and agents are linked, and deeply affected by the increasing salience of virtual products and processes.

In brief, the informational economy has unique characteristics: its self-transforming feedback loop, the imperative of accelerating innovation, the defiance of exclusive possession, the capacity to increase in value through use, and the intrinsic dissolution of cultural-economic distinctions. Because the informational economy is so fluid, dynamic, and transformative it is hard to specify; by its very nature it is always changing. For similar reasons, its power relations are difficult to map, not least because they involve *subjective* assessments of credibility and authority more than objective assessments of material volume or quality (Strange 1994, 119). Yet the activities and effects of this economy are so pervasive and powerful that we must try to specify the most important issues.

To contextualize the power investments of the informational economy and their relation to structural hierarchies I consider three vantage points: the process and politics of digitization, the social and conceptual context within which digitization is operationalized and privileged, and the politics of the informational economy in practice.

Digitization as Process and Politics

What is common to this "common information system" is computer-based digitization. In effect, computerization involves the translation (reduction) of symbolic and material goods—images, data, information, knowledge, designs, models, literature, music, prototypes, machines—into a binary code of 1s and 0s that can be "read," manipulated, and communicated by information and communication technologies. The reduction of so many diverse goods to a "universal" code that can be electronically transmitted worldwide is the revolutionary aspect of ICT and the informational economy. Digitization permits traditionally disparate and experientially dense phenomena—the textures of a tapestry, the violence of war, the multiple sensory dimensions of seduction—to be converted into a binary code available to anyone with the relevant "reading" capacity. Not only are these many and diverse phenomena reduced to a common, universal code but in coded form they are available around the world, virtually without the constraints of time and space.

Why is digitization such a revolutionary development? In a positive sense, it is precisely the reduction of vastly disparate phenomena to a binary code that enables us to make this coded information globally available, almost irrespective of traditional physical, temporal, spatial, cultural, and linguistic barriers. It is as if we finally developed a truly "universal" (not culturally specific but disembedded from all cultures) language that transcends old barriers, eliminating the demands of cultural and linguistic translation. In this sense, digitization offers revolutionary potential as a universal code that enhances cross-cultural *communication.* It may also break down barriers of difference and facilitate democratization, which are now familiar claims about the internet.[5]

Moreover, digitization offers revolutionary potential as a universal solvent that objectifies disparate and complex phenomena. It does so by reducing them to a single binary code that enables them to be valued and exchanged according to a common reference system: disparate phenomena are translated into digitized objects/products. For example, the information revolution vastly extends the "range of human transactions (mainly services) that can be made 'tradable' and thus be subject to market transactions and pricing" (Hoogvelt 2001, 111). Never before has so much been so easily reduced to communicable "bits" that are so easily shared, transmitted, exchanged, bought, and sold.

In a negative sense, it is precisely the translation of vastly disparate phenomena into a binary code that reduces and implicitly *impoverishes* our knowledge about and experience of those phenomena. The traditional richness, complexity, and texture of physical, temporal, spatial, cultural, and linguistic differences are rendered irrelevant and hence "lost" in the coding process. It is as if we finally abandoned the quest for understanding of difference in relation to context in favor of abolishing difference and ignoring context. Reading the "positive" depiction through a critical lens, digitization offers more disturbing revolutionary potential as a universal code that enhances not communication but *domination,* as everything and everyone is disciplined by the binary code. "Reality" is reduced to that which conforms to "an oppositional rather than a relational dialogic system"—"there is no code for maybe" (Eisenstein 1998, 95, 96). Similarly, this universal code objectifies all phenomena, rendering them objects/commodities that are tradable. Never before has so much been so easily reduced to "bits" that are so at odds with subjective, embodied, complex, differentiated, culturally- and contextually-specific, lived experience. Never before has so much of the life world been subject to commodification or colonization.

In short, while the revolutionary "force" of informational technologies is undeniable, evaluating its effects is obviously contentious. In the rich north we are encouraged—by our consumption of cheap products, the convenience of appliances, and the discourse of mainstream media—to applaud the benefits of technology. The real and perceived benefits of technology also figure significantly—and increasingly—in the cultural worldview of developing countries. It seems appropriate, therefore, to consider some of the less positive and indeed less obvious issues raised by informational technologies.

First and foremost, not all information/knowledge is deemed worthy of digitization or incorporation in networks of communication. A selection process is at work, and it is structured by familiar exclusions. It is thus a politically consequential distortion to claim that digital coding is decontextualized and not culture-specific. While globalization does not merely homogenize culture but also celebrates novelty and the local, decision-making power over what is selected for valorization or disapprobation is quite globally concentrated. The choice of what is included and to what effect is inherently a political one, informed by the cultural preferences and political-economic interests of those with greater ownership and control of relevant media. "Receivers" *do* variously interpret, disrupt, and resist "intended" messages; "alternative" sources of information do exist; and the internet—with its dispersed users and relatively uncontrolled networking—affords a different concentration of power than the telecoms industry or media conglomerates. But for most of the planet most of the time, participation in communications media is that of *relatively* passive consumers: all of us hearing/watching/reading/absorbing/responding to what "the media" selectively choose to broadcast. The point is not to deny individuals and audiences agency, but to situate them in relation to networks of power. The power at issue here is no less than who gets to most effectively represent and hence create "reality" and "common sense."

Second, the effects of "totalizing commodification" are difficult to discern clearly and hence to assess "fairly." Objectification is a dimension of conceptual ordering and hence unavoidable; and not all objectifying practices are pernicious. But like reductionism, objectifying always involves a loss: of differences, complexity, meaning. The extent of digital objectification in today's world has massive effects. In a significant sense, informational technologies render that which cannot or does not conform to the digital code irrelevant. In Holmes's (1997a, 15) words, "computer-based technologies effectively displace the real by revealing it only according to grids translatable into digital code." Existence "outside of the code" may mean, at best, marginalization, or at worst, elimination. Increasingly, what does not conform to the informational codes and economy does not count, is not valorized.

Third, there is the additional and perennially fraught question of how to interpret commodification of the life world. Is it inevitable and worth the trade-offs, as enthusiasts are inclined to believe? Is it unnecessary and inherently harmful, as critics protest? How do we distinguish between commodification that is equalizing and liberating from that which debases intimacy, bodies, and "meaningful" social relations? These difficult questions are of course at the core of debates regarding globalization and capitalism, as well as complex theoretical, normative, ideological, and political debates spanning modernity and postmodernity.

Fourth and related, there is the role of commodification as establishing a system of valorization based on vendibility, which effectively assigns value to disparate phenomena on the basis of competitive pricing. In other words, once incorporated as a commodity, or understood to be commodifiable, the value of any information, product, or experience is subject to determination by market forces. This is another sense in which we observe closer integration of the symbolic and material: like food and shelter, lived experience and cognitive processes are now reduced to a code that permits them to be commodified and priced, thus integrated in one seamless system of exchange and capital accumulation. The real becomes virtual, as the virtual system of pricing appropriates "reality."

The Politics of Conceptual Codes

These points begin to clarify (and complicate) our understanding of a "common information system." But the "system" within which binary coding is operationalized and prospers requires further specification. Digitization is not just an effect of technological developments but of historically specific norms and practices. Commitments to rationalism, objectivism, and instrumentalism are the conceptual hallmarks of modernity. This is the historical context and cultural milieu within which digitization was developed and privileged. It is also the context and milieu of modern capitalism and its commitments to expanding commodification. Digitization is thus embedded in social practices and conceptual commitments that have a politics: one that critics argue privileges objectivism as a way of thinking and objectification as a way of ordering social life.

Objectivism is associated with the hierarchical binaries of fact–value, objective–subjective, and mind–body; these dichotomies underpin positivist

commitments and their categorical separations are the target of interpretive and postmodernist critiques. *Objectification* is associated with the binaries of self–other, civilized–primitive, and masculine–feminine; these dichotomies underpin modernist commitments and their stratifying differentiations are the target of marxist, postcolonial, and feminist critiques. In this sense, digitization is continuous with modernity and replicates its ideological commitments and power relations.

At the same time, the unique characteristics of the informational economy—its feedback effects, constant innovation, and fusion of mind and matter—are hallmarks of postmodernity. In this sense, the informational economy is both a product of modernity and a self-transforming process that disrupts—even as it assumes—modernity's givens. These paradoxical claims are frustrating (if not maddening) to modernists and positivists, and preoccupying to postmodernists. They underlie the current impasse between what are constructed or construed as opposing, rather than related, positions. . . . Here I raise these points as background for the following section, which considers the structure and diffusion of power in the informational economy.

The Politics of Information in Practice

The conceptual and ideological commitments of digitization and the informational economy are inextricable from the embodied practices of this economy, which are the focus of this section. We have already touched on the politics of selecting what information/knowledge is privileged, stored, and communicated. Power relations are further illuminated when we ask the following questions.

Whose history, stories, lives, language, music, dreams, beliefs, and culture are documented, much less celebrated? Who is accorded credibility and authority: as religious or political leader, economic expert, marketing genius, financial guru, scientific expert, objective journalist, leading scholar, art critic, futurist, technological wizard, "average American," "good mother," "man on the street"? Who is empowered to speak on behalf of their identity group, who on behalf of "others"? Who benefits and how from English as the global *lingua franca*? Whose inquiries are endorsed and published? Who determines what information is publicized—witnessed, replicated, published, disseminated, broadcast?

These questions raise multiple issues, but the power of communications media (in the broadest sense) is again salient. This power is increasingly concentrated in a small number of global multimedia conglomerates that integrate, and shape the ideological content of, what were previously separate media domains (e.g., television, radio, films, music, art, and print media). The cultural and political significance of this control cannot be overstated, for it ultimately shapes what most of us know about "reality" beyond our personal, embodied experience. More to the point: even our personal experience of reality is shaped by the cultural coding of mass media.[6] News reporters, politicians, and advertisers know that the media powerfully shape what we have knowledge of, believe in, hope for, and work toward; they create and direct consumer desire as well as social consciousness and political understanding.

Related to the power of media to control what we know "in general" is the issue of access to and control of more specifically "valuable" information/knowledge. For example, there is the power of who knows first and/or most about the design, operation, and timing of publicly significant events: new product releases, health and environmental risks, welfare reform policies, political scandals, military agendas. Or the power of those with "insider" information—about stock market movements, interest rate hikes, military targets. Or the economically decisive power to attribute credit-worthiness (accurately or inaccurately) to states, firms, or individuals. In reference to economic theory, an orthodox assumption is that markets are efficient because information is freely available; yet in the real world, information is always selective and selectively available.

Of particular relevance to themes of this text is the political economy of research and development. On the face of it, resources, access to, and control over research facilities and their output are decisive factors; we have already noted their uneven distribution. But much more is involved. The politics of knowledge information include whose questions are pursued, whose concerns are silenced,[7] whose health needs are prioritized,[8] whose methods are authorized, whose paradigm is presumed, whose project is funded, whose findings are publicized, whose intellectual property is protected.[9] There are the additional issues of human

capital development and deep infrastructural support: educational systems that engender effective learning and research proficiency; technological systems that enable sophisticated procedures and effective dissemination; and ideological systems that promote instrumental, scientific orientations. The implications seem obvious: those individuals and institutional actors with more social and infrastructural resources are more likely to be competitive. In the case of developing countries, "catching up"—even with the benefit of large capital investments—is hard to do because of the time required to build appropriate cultural coding, educational facilities and faculty, and technological infrastructure.

These points suggest how conventional distributions of power and their related structural hierarchies are reflected in and tend to be reproduced by the informational economy. At the same time, and crucially, the unique characteristics of this economy do not conform to conventional accounts of power. In the new global economy power is *diffused* as much, if not more than, it is concentrated in particular groups or at particular sites. It is diffused in cultural and informational codes and global networks and ultimately in people's minds (Castells 1997, 359). In important respects, this observation is the counterpart of the paradoxical claims above: the informational economy in practice both reproduces the hierarchical structures of modernity and transforms the way power operates and where (actually, whether) it is concentrated.

New technologies have transformed the "mass media" (delivering standardized messages) to the "new media" (delivering customized messages to segmented audiences). For example, Walkmans, video players, and cable television offer consumers more individual choice, and encourage producers to diversify their products and target increasingly differentiated audiences. While the concentration of media ownership continues to be the case, the programs and messages they offer are diverse and constantly changing. Castells (2000, 370) captures it in these words: "While the media have become indeed globally interconnected, and programs and messages circulate in the global network, *we are not living in a global village, but in customized cottages globally produced and locally distributed.*" Both familiar and new power dynamics paradoxically merge.

Like money, information is not neutral. It carries, conveys, and confers power in multiple ways, with diverse effects. Adequate analysis of the informational economy requires taking the politics of cultural coding seriously. Because the exchange of informational commodities does not conform to the rules operating with material-based goods, orthodox economic theories are inadequate. The informational fusion of concept and product, culture, and economy disrupts conventional binaries and habitual modes of analysis. It forces us to rethink not just the nature of products but the nature of production, marketing, exchange, and consumption. . . .

The Consumer Society and the "Economy of Signs"

Reality becomes more code-intensive, embracing whatever can be stylized, modeled, simulated, gamed, designed.   *(Luke 1989, 42)*

The third mode of the virtual economy features the exchange of aesthetic or cultural signs/symbols. On the one hand, this involves a discussion of the *consumer* economy/society, the creation of a social imaginary of particular tastes and desires, and the extensive commodification of tastes, pleasure, and leisure. Aesthetics figure prominently here, as the value-added component of goods is less a function of information/knowledge and more a production of ephemeral, ever-changing tastes, desires, fashion, and style. On the other hand, the third mode involves a discussion of the *political economy* of signs in the explicit sense of how *power* operates through symbols, signs, and codes to determine meaning and hence value. The basic argument is that commodities do not have value in and of themselves but as a function of the social codes/context within which they have significance. To understand how commodities are valued then requires attention to how they are invested with value by signs/symbols/codes. For this, an interpretive approach is necessary—understanding that all meaning depends on signifying codes and any particular meaning/value depends upon its relational position within a system of codification/signification.[10] This approach enables us both to link the valorization processes of the financial, informational, and consumer/aesthetic dimensions of the virtual economy and to relate these to the reproductive and productive economies.

Earlier economic neglect of consumption has changed with the advent of the informational or post-industrial "consumer society." The commodification of consciousness associated with Fordist mass production both continues and takes on new meaning in the context of postmodern culture, where the fusion of culture and commodity enables deeper—and more subtle—commodification of the lifeworld. What distinguishes the third mode is a focus on cultural symbols. The consumer economy emphasizes not the material aspects of objects exchanged but the signs, symbols, codes that invest these commodities with (cultural) meaning and value. (For example, it is not the durability of the jeans but the visibility of the designer brand-name that matters.) But the emphasis here is on the centrality of design, aesthetics, or style to the commodity's value; what matters is what the commodity culturally symbolizes (signifies). We observe this "not only in the proliferation of objects which possess a substantial aesthetic component (such as pop music, cinema, leisure, magazines, video and so on), but also in the increasing component of sign-value or image embodied *in* material objects," such as design-intensive goods and designer "branding" (Lash and Urry 1994, 4).

The Fusion of Culture and Commodity

The consumer economy exemplifies how flexibilization and time-space compression associated with the electronics revolution increasingly pervade culture and erode any lingering boundary between production/material/commodities/work/"the economic" on the one hand and consumption/nonmaterial/tastes/culture/"the social" on the other. This is succinctly captured by Amin, who identifies the "aestheticization of commodities" and the "commodification of aesthetics" as

> two aspects of the emerging age which serve to blur the traditional distinction between economic and cultural activity. The first refers to the embellishment of products, artifacts, buildings, workplaces, infrastructure and so on, as a means of enlivening everyday life at the same time as legitimating consumerism and social acceptance of the imperatives of capitalism. The second refers to the increasing transformation of culture and cultural activity, especially

leisure and recreation, into cultural industries, that is, commodities sold in the market to individual consumers who, in turn, increasingly identify cultural gratification with consumption, rather than as an independent activity, geared towards, say, creative learning.

(Amin 1994, 31, citing Urry 1990)

The character of consumption changes as commodification penetrates into all aspects of culture, of personal and public life. Speed, fluidity, mobility are key. "If taste is the only determinant of utility then that utility is ephemeral and subject to whim . . . mass-mediated images . . . are lost the moment that they are consumed. Insofar as images have no past and no future, human experience becomes compressed in an overwhelming present" (Waters 1995, 57). These observations suggest how the consumer economy is associated (for many) with a sense of ephemerality, fragmentation, and dislocation. The artifice of constructed tastes and fleeting fashions is disorienting and may induce feelings of loss—loss of an "authentic" self, of historically specific particularity and what meaning it affords—as past and future disappear into only the fragmented present moment of consumption.

> The traditional forms of both individuality and society collapse under these conditions. . . .
> Real human needs exist, but their forms of articulation, experience, and satisfaction are actualized within a market culture that constrains individuals to realize their needs in mass-produced material packages and professionally approved behavioral scripts. Capital produces consumers, simultaneously constructing a total culture of market-dominated subjectivity for them.   *(Luke 1989, 35)*

Commodification makes capitalism and its profit motive the primary "business" of not only markets but everyday life. As private activities are penetrated by commodification and public life is reduced to "consumer choice," the market becomes "the only locus of legitimation in society. That is, any idea, movement, or even culture can maintain itself only by translating its images, expressions, or messages into marketable commodities. There is no other basis for justifying or validating a claim, in contemporary postmodern culture, than finding a market for it" (Firat 1994, 218).

The Politics of Producing Consumption

Because demand for ephemeral, specialized, aestheticized products cannot be assumed it must be continuously created. This requires the production of tastes and desires in line with always changing commodities; it is a never-ending, expensive, and elaborate project in which consumers variously collaborate. In this sense, the consumer economy entails a constant reworking of what we might call the social imaginary: cultivating a consumerist ideology and aesthetic, and in effect commodifying subjectivity itself. An ideology of consumption involves relentless subjection to media images, enticements, and directives, all aimed at promoting consumption as a positive, vital, pleasurable, identity-conferring and rewarding activity.

I identify three interacting themes in the big business of promoting, sustaining, and expanding the ideology and practice of consumer capitalism. First, consumers are encouraged to believe that consumption—even hedonistic, conspicuous, and excessive consumption—is *natural*. This is consistent with, and draws upon, modernist models of human nature (read: elite male nature) as competitive, self-interested, and acquisitive. It is especially visible in advertising and television media, which are key to "naturalizing" (depoliticizing) the consumer economy. Advertisements, news stories, and entertainment programs illustrate how contemporary western culture admires "the rich," perhaps increasingly so, and even at the expense of admiring traditional political and military leaders. Global media circulate these images and cultivate a sense of consumption and accumulation as not only natural but *desirable*. This "common sense" underpins both the acceleration of consumption and perpetuation of structural hierarchies.

Second, a particular *aesthetic* must be cultivated among consumers, leading them to recognize and respond positively to the symbols invested in ever-changing products. The print media, especially magazines, play an important role in intensifying awareness of the coding system. They first of all add to the proliferation of advertisements, but also extend consumer exposure to claims about products through evocative images and storyboards, informational essays, cultural reviews, "how to" reports, personal narratives, and stories of the rich and famous. These media encourage consumers to perceive/experience a "lack" or inadequacies in their own lives (their well-being, bodies, relationships, pleasures, jobs) that can be—miraculously—corrected by the appropriate commodity consumption. Advertisements and marketing strategies blend the local and global: they make use of cultural variations to enhance local purchasing and further the accumulation processes of transnational firms. The consumer aesthetic promoted by global media reflects the culture and interests of western ownership and control. While critics of and resistance to westernization ("westoxification") complicate claims of hegemony or homogenization, the power of global media to shape consumer consciousness worldwide is formidable.

Third, consumers must *participate.* Few of us escape the deluge of images, advertising, and marketing lures, especially in cities and advanced industrialized economies. But consumers must go beyond awareness and desire to the actual buying of commodities. This requires not only that consumers have money (or acquire it, so credit issues are key) but also that they take the time to shop and make a commitment to purchase.[11] Appadurai (1996) characterizes debt as "income expansion by other means," and in the face of declining real incomes and inflated buying expectations, debt is increasingly the means by which consumption is made possible. Technologies enable quick and easy access to cash and credit through electronically coded cards and automated teller machines. Technologies also facilitate shopping and buying (online, by fax, mail-order) and by ready access to one-stop convenience stores and climatically controlled shopping malls.

While consumption in the broadest sense occurs across a variety of spaces/places, the economy of signs emphasized here is concentrated in urban and suburban areas. . . . A rich literature is now available on cities in relation to globalization dynamics and especially as privileged sites of consumption (e.g., Sassen 1991, 1998). We know that global cities are key to the management and reproduction of global finance, that major cities everywhere are hubs of flexibilized production and its worldwide coordination, and that all cities enjoy more infrastructure and technology than rural areas. . . .

Not only malls, but theme parks, marinas, arts centers, museums, entertainment areas—all are designed to foster consumption and have us think of it as culture. While individuals, families, and small social groups are welcome, there is little room for building community: the point is to further private consumption not public/civic interaction. While some celebrate cities as sites of pleasure, consumption, and cultural pluralism, others note the polarization of incomes and lifestyles, the surveillance and exclusion of non-consumers, and the erosion of civic intentions in the design of today's public spaces.

Ideologies, Linkages, and a Political Economy of Consumption

We can easily overstate the extent to which consumerism has become a way of life (or lifestyle). For most of the world's inhabitants most of the time, consumer activities are less an aesthetic experience than a necessary effort; for too many of the world's people, getting enough to eat is a daily struggle. But the commodification of culture is pervasive in advanced economies and significantly shapes identities, expectations, and everyday lives. And it has effects worldwide on how people think (due to the global, though always locally mediated, exposure to advertising and marketing messages), what resources they have (due to naturalizing the ideology of elite consumption), and what work they do (due to production processes driven by northern consumption). Therefore, while affluent consumption is the privilege of only a small percentage of the world's population, it shapes the choices (and valorization) of those without affluence. In short, there is a political economy of consumption, with pervasive but extremely uneven effects. Specifying this unevenness links themes threading throughout this text, some of which have been treated in earlier discussions.

First and foremost are the effects of consumerism as an ideology that becomes "common sense." Even where goods or the resources to buy them are not available, the desire for them is fueled by pervasive advertising and global media. While consumerism takes many forms, with a range of positive and negative effects, the problematic core assumption is that self- and social expression are primarily achieved through the consumption of goods. One effect of this ideology is to marginalize alternative ways of thinking about and practicing meaningful lives (e.g., spiritual/ethical development, building egalitarian and sustainable communities). The ideology of consumption then works at the micro level, in terms of advertising and marketing aimed at individuals and individuals engaging in consumption practices; and at the macro level, in terms of collective expectations, worldviews, or a "common sense" that consumption is natural, desirable, and key to the meaning of individual and collective life. Of course consumption as a way of life is not the only historical or contemporary option. But believing it is has tremendously powerful material (and normative) implications.

Second and paralleling points made above, there is a political economy of consumption as ideology *in practice*. Whose consumption is being privileged? Whose needs are met and whose interests served? Whose are ignored, obscured, denied, or manipulated and for what purpose, and to whose benefit? Who determines what we think we "need" or simply "want," and what warrants being produced, where, by whom, and for whom? Whose bodies and environments are devalorized in pursuit of consumerism and the neoliberal commitment to growth (rather than redistribution) that fuels it? The messages of global media (determined by corporate sponsors) are again central to understanding these power dynamics, coupled with the implications of intensive, expensive, and sophisticated advertising and marketing campaigns.

Gender and the reproductive economy are central to the political economy of consumption, primarily due to gendered stereotypes and divisions of labor that continue to identify women/housewives as the primary consumers. This raises a number of issues: advertising is disproportionately targeted at women (and tends to depend on and reproduce heteronormative stereotypes); constructions of "femininity" are arguably more dependent on market/consumer ideologies and the aesthetics they promote than are constructions of "masculinity"; women must learn and use particular (but typically unacknowledged) skills as informed and competent consumers; women/housewives exercise varying forms of power as consumers, especially within the household but also as investment decision-makers; masculinist paradigms tend to neglect consumption "work" (and skills); and masculinist and productivist paradigms have been slow to recognize the economic role of consumption in today's economy.[12]

The informational economy involves a politics of knowledge—who decides what we "know" and with what effects—that is largely implicit: assuming unquestioned beliefs in science, technology, and instrumental paradigms. The consumer economy involves a politics of advertising—who decides what we "want" and with what effects—that is explicitly about manipulating consciousness. In the latter case, power dynamics are closer to the surface, but not necessarily easier to "see through" or resist. Indeed, insofar as the consumer economy manipulates desire, aesthetics, and cultural consciousness (subjective factors), its psychological and psycho-social effects are especially opaque to conventional (objectivist) modes of analysis.

Third, the consumer economy is pre-eminently about "finance." The availability of money/credit to engage in consumption is inextricable from the financial and informational economies and their role in creating an environment where "unnecessary" consumption is expected and borrowing money is seductive and encouraged. Access to and control over money and credit continue to be powerfully shaped by structural hierarchies. The patterns are familiar whenever access to credit is at stake, whether for personal loans in cities or rural villages, or national loans by the IMF. In short, class and (national) economic development clearly differentiate those currently most empowered to consume; for individuals and nations, control over credit resources and the rules regarding who has access to credit are powerful determinants of "who has, and who can get more." As a result, access to credit (and on what/whose terms) structures inclusions and exclusions in global circuits of capital.

Fourth, there is a politics of consumption in the broadest sense of commodifying the lifeworld: what trade-offs are involved and how do we evaluate (valorize) them? And there is a politics of consumption in the narrower sense of threats posed by specific consumption practices. On the face of it, consumers have an interest in protecting themselves against harm due to inappropriate, fraudulent, ill-designed, dangerous, inadequately tested, substandard, unhealthy, and/or toxic goods. "Consumer rights" movements recognize such threats and engage in diverse strategies to secure protections, disseminate information, curb egregious practices, and cultivate more responsibility and accountability on the part of corporate and government decision- and policy-makers. At a more complicated level, the "rights" or interests of diverse consumers are often in tension (e.g., the benefits of easy access to goods for some may be costs—polluting conditions or inferior access—for others). This surfaces especially in relation to environmental costs (who should pay soonest and greatest) as environmental problems generated in the production/consumption cycle are spatially and socio-culturally differentiated.

In sum, consumption is neither neutral nor banal. It involves power in multiple ways, with diverse effects. Most of the patterns of unevenness are familiar, as they derive from and reproduce deeply stabilized hierarchies of access to and control over symbolic and material resources. These patterns are embodied and exemplified in major cities worldwide, where a polarization of skills, resources, and lifestyles is becoming the norm. But they are globally manifested in the pervasive effects of consumerist ideology, the political economy of credit, and the organization of production to serve consumerist lifestyles. . . .

NOTES

1. Particularly important at the global level are managerial elites who form new transborder communities and through organizational fora (e.g., International Accounting Standards Committee, Trilateral Commission) are (re)shaping the "rules of the (trans-national business) game" (Scholte 1997, 438). Others posit an emerging transnational class, shaped by international networking (Gill 1990) or cast as a global bourgeoisie (van der Pijl 1997). Bakker refers to "a high priesthood" (Bakker 2001, 5). Young (2001, 41) distinguishes a "money society" of transnational power wielders and a "work society" of territorially bound others. Hooper (2000) describes the "new man" of jet-setting, post-industrial global relations and (2001) "globalization" as a masculinized space. Thrift (1996, 236–239) details the gentlemanly order of London's banking community, and McDowell (1997) examines masculine identities in London's financial sector. Mayhall (2002) examines the role of gendered identities in shaping who the financial operators are and how social identities can affect the movement of markets themselves (e.g., by encouraging excessive risk-taking and speculation).

2. My depiction relies on the discussion and citations in Benería 1999a.

3. The whiteness is noteworthy, as a reference to both collars and job holders. For it is not all services that offer attractive jobs and are well compensated. What are regarded as knowledge workers and well rewarded are those in white-collar jobs, especially the producer, business, or advanced services. Due in large part to the educational and cultural qualifications expected in these jobs, they have conventionally favored economically advantaged workers, which in the north translates primarily into elite, "white" males.

4. Specialist knowledge requires combination with other forms of information/knowledge to realize its potential. Recent growth in virtual corporations (*Business Week* 1993), alliance capitalism, and e-commerce exemplify both flexibilization and the fusion of formerly discrete inputs and entities. Information and communication technologies enable the cheap, easy, and instantaneous transmission of information itself (data, designs, conversations) as dematerialized/symbolic goods. They also, interactively, generate further demand for informational goods (e.g., computer software and hardware, cell phones, ICT infrastructure) and for more informational services (e.g., computer support, instruction).

5. Most familiar is the use of the internet to publicize resistance movements, as in Afghanistan, Chiapas, China, and Serbia. While some hail the internet for its democratizing potential, others decry its reproduction of familiar dominations. Any simplistic generalization is pointless because the net is inherently complex, contradictory, fluid, dynamic, and unpredictable. That is not to say that patterns, and especially patterns of power, are absent; only that they are manifested in both familiar (e.g., whose programs and search engines dominate, who has access to and makes most use of the net), and unfamiliar ways (e.g., absence of centralized control, novel applications).

6. In Castells's (2000, 362) words, "The media, particularly radio and television, have become the audiovisual environment with which we interact endlessly and automatically." While the extent of media "immersion" varies, television especially has a significant presence worldwide.

7. Consider the differential access to and support for research on collective ownership of enterprises, alternative energy sources, conflict resolution, communal living, redistributing global assets, long-term and community-involved economic planning, or the elimination of hatred, homophobia, racism, and sexism.

8. The benefits of improved health care are especially structured by reference to sex/gender, socio-economic status, occupational risks, sexual practices, and geopolitical location. Consider the different populations most vulnerable to breast cancer, prostate cancer, heart disease, tuberculosis, HIV-AIDS, sickle-cell anemia, malaria, schistosomiasis, and river blindness.

9. The literature on intellectual property rights expands as the stakes mount in the global economy. Hoogvelt argues that the protocol relating to Trade-Related Intellectual Property Rights (TRIPS) "strengthens the international property rights of foreign investment and it extends international patent protection to . . . for example, genetic material collected by agribusinesses or pharmaceutical companies," in ways that favor transnational capital over the interests of developing countries (Hoogvelt 2001, 150).

10. Luke's (1989, 5) characterization of semiotics is helpful: "a conceptual means for examining the exchange of messages, the systems of signing or coding that anchor them, and the nature of the social relations that frame the production, exchange, and interpretation of their meaning."

11. Mies (1998, 126–127) observes an increase in "consumption work" among women, especially as service personnel disappear from stores and consumers themselves locate, weigh, and price merchandise. Consumption work increases as an effect of informalization and "do it yourself" activities required to complete the production process, and as self-expressive artisan-craftwork expands in an attempt to counteract the effects of "meaningless consumption."

12. In addition, "considerable evidence across diverse cultures and income groups" indicates that consumption patterns differ between men and women, with women more likely to "spend on goods that benefit children and enhance their capacities" (Çağatay, Elson and Grown 1995, 1830). This links women's decision-making in the household with macro issues of long-term growth as a function of investment in human resources (1995, 1830).

REFERENCES

Amin, A. 1994. Post-Fordism: Models, fantasies and phantoms of transition. In *Post-Fordism: A Reader*, ed. Ash Amin. Oxford: Blackwell. Pp. 1–39.

Appadurai, A. 1996. Disjuncture and Difference in the Global Economy. *Public Culture* 2, 2.

Bakker, I. 2001. *Who Built the Pyramids? Engendering the New International Economic and Financial Architecture.* Paper presented to the International Studies Association Annual Meeting, Chicago.

Benaría, L. 1999. Globalization, Gender and the Davos Man. *Feminist Economics* 5, 3: 61–83.

Business Week. 1993. Cover Story: The Virtual Corporation. 8 February: 99–102.

Çağatay, N., D. Elson, and C. Grown. 1995. Introduction. *World Development* 23, 11 (November): 1827–1836.

Castells, M. 1997. *The Power of Identity.* Oxford: Blackwell.

———. 2000. *The Rise of the Network Society.* Cambridge: Blackwell.

Cerny, P.G. 1994. The Dynamics of Financial Globalization: Technology, Market Structure, and Policy Response, *Policy Sciences* 27:319–342.

———. 1996. What Next for the State? In *Globalization: Theory and Practice,* ed. Eleonore Koffman and Gillian Youngs. London: Pinter. Pp. 123–137.

Drucker, P. 1986. The Changed World Economy. *Foreign Affairs* 64, 4: 768–791.

Dunning, J. H. 2000. Regions, Globalization, and the Knowledge Economy: The issues stated. In *Regions, Globalization, and the Knowledge-Based Economy,* ed. John H. Dunning. Oxford: Oxford University Press. Pp. 7–41.

Eisenstein, Z. R. 1998. *Global Obscenities: Patriarchy, capitalism, and the lure of cyberfantasy.* New York: New York Press.

Firat, A. F. 1994. Gender and Consumption: Transcending the feminine? In *Gender Issues and Consumer Behavior,* ed. Janeen Arnold Costa. Provo, UT: Association for Consumer Research. Pp. 205–228.

Gill, S. 1990. *American Hegemony and the Trilateral Commission.* Cambridge: Cambridge University Press.

———. 1992. Economic Globalization and the Internationalization of Authority: Limits and contradictions. *Geoforum* 23, 3: 269–283.

———. 1995. Globalization, Market Civilization, and Disciplinary Neoliberalism. *Millenium* 24, 3: 399–423.

Haas, P. 1992. Introduction: Epistemic communities and international policy coordination. *International Organization* 46 (Winter): 1–35.

Held, D., A. A. G. McGrew, D. Goldblatt, and J Perraton. 1999. *Global Transformations: Politics, economics, and culture.* Stanford, CA: Stanford University Press.

Helleiner, E. 1994. *States the Re-emergence of Global Finance.* Ithaca, N.Y.: Cornell University Press.

Henwood, D. 1998. *Wall Street: How it works and for whom.* London and New York: Verso.

Holmes, D. 1997a. Introduction. In *Virtual Politics: Identity and community in cyberspace,* ed. David Holmes. London: Sage. Pp 1–25.

———. ed. 1997b. *Virtual Politics: Identity and community in cyberspace,* ed. David Holmes. London: Sage.

Hoogvelt, A. 2001. *Globalization and the Postcolonial World: The new political economy of development.* 2nd ed. Baltimore: Johns Hopkins University Press.

Hooper, C. 2000. Disembodiment, Embodiment and the Construction of Hegemonic Masculinity. In *Political Economy, Power and the Body: Global Perspectives,* ed. Gillian Youngs. London: MacMillan. Pp. 31–51.

———. 2001. *Manly States: Masculinities, international relations, and gender politics.* New York: Columbia University Press.

Jessop, B. 1994. Post-Fordism and the State. In *Post-Fordism: A Reader,* ed. Ash Amin. Oxford: Blackwell. Pp. 251–279.

Lash, S. and J. Urry. 1994. *Economies of Signs and Space.* London: Sage.

Luke, T. M. 1989. *Screens of Power: Ideology, domination, and resistance in informational society.* Urbana and Chicago: University of Illinois Press.

Mayhall, S. 2002. Riding the Bull/Wrestling the Bear. Dissertation. Toronto: York University.

McDowell, L. 1997. *Capital Culture: Gender at work in the city.* Oxford: Blackwell.

Mitchell, W. 1995. *City of Bits.* Cambridge, MA: MIT Press.

Postman, N. 1993. *Technopoly: The surrender of culture to technology.* New York: Vintage.

Sassen, S. 1991. *The Global City: New York, London, Tokyo.* Princeton, NJ: Princeton University Press.

———. 1993. Economic Globalization. In *Global Visions: Beyond the new world order.* Boston: South End Press. Pp. 61–66.

———. 1998. *Globalization and Its Discontents.* New York: New Press.

Scholte, J. A. 1997. Global Trade and Finance. In *The Globalization of World Politics: An introduction to international relations,* ed. John Baylis and Steve Smith. Oxford: Oxford University Press. Pp. 430–447.

Strange, S. 1994. *States and Markets.* 2nd ed. London: Pinter.

———. 1997. *Casino Capitalism.* Manchester: Manchester University Press.

———. 1998. *Mad Money.* Manchester: Manchester University Press.

Thrift, N. 1996. *Spatial Formations.* London: Sage.

Urry, J. 1990. *The Tourist Gaze.* London: Sage.

van der Pijl, K. 1997. The History of Class Struggle: From original accumulation to neoliberalism. *Monthly Review* 49, 1: 28–44.

Waters, M. 1995. *Globalization.* London: Routledge.

Wichterich, C. 2000. *The Globalized Woman: Reports from a future of inequality.* London: Zed Books.

World Bank. 2000. *World Development Report 1999/2000: Entering the 21st Century.* Oxford: Oxford University Press.

Young, B. 2001. Globalization and Gender: A European perspective. In *Gender, Globalization, and Democratization,* eds. Rita Mae Kelly, Jane H. Bayes, Mary E. Hawkesworth, and Brigitte Young. Lanham, MD: Rowman and Littlefield. Pp. 27–47.

FORTY-EIGHT

◆◆◆

Building Water Democracy (2004)
People's Victory Against Coca-Cola in Plachimada
Vandana Shiva

Vandana Shiva directs the Research Foundation for Science, Technology and Natural Resource Policy in India, where she is also involved in Naydanya, a movement for biodiversity conservation and farmers' rights. She is a recipient of the Right Livelihood Award (an alternative to the Nobel Prize). Her many books include *Staying Alive: Women, Ecology and Development; Water Wars: Privatization, Pollution, and Profit;* and *Earth Democracy: Justice, Sustainability and Peace.*

Two years ago, adivasi[1] women in a small hamlet, Plachimada, in Palghat, Kerala, started a movement against Coca-Cola. Today, the Coca-Cola plant in Plachimada has been shut down. The victory of the Plachimada movement is a major step in reversing corporate hijacking of our precious water resources. It provides both inspiration and lessons for building water democracy in other parts of India and in the rest of the world.

The Coca-Cola plant in Plachimada was commissioned in March 2000 to produce 1,224,000 bottles of Coca-Cola, Fanta, Sprite, Limca, Thums Up, Kinley Soda, and Maaza. The Panchayat[2] was issued a conditional license for installing a motor for drawing water. However, the company started to illegally extract millions of litres of clean water from more than 6 bore wells installed by it using electric pumps in order to manufacture millions of bottles of soft drink.

According to the local people, Coca-Cola was extracting 1.5 million litres per day. The water level started to fall, going from 150 feet to 500 feet. Not only did Coca-Cola "steal" the water of the local community, it also polluted what was left. The company is also pumping wastewater into dry bore wells within the company premises for disposing of solid waste.

Earlier it was depositing the waste material outside the company premises, and during the rainy season it spread into paddy fields, canals, and wells, causing serious health hazards.

As a result of this, 260 bore wells which were provided by public authorities for drinking water and agriculture facilities have become dry. Complaints were also being received from tribals and farmers that storage of water and sources of water were being adversely affected by indiscriminate installation of bore wells for tapping ground water, leading to serious consequences for crop cultivation in the area on which residents of the Panchayat depend for their living: e.g., maintenance of traditional drinking water sources, preservation of ponds and water tanks, maintenance of waterways and canals, and shortage of drinking water. When the Panchayat asked for details, the company failed to comply.

The Panchayat therefore served a show cause notice and cancelled the license. Coca-Cola tried to bribe the Panchayat President A. Krishnan with Rs. 300 million, but he refused to be corrupted and coopted. In 2003, the district medical officer informed the people of Plachimada their water was unfit for drinking.

The women already knew their water was toxic. Instead of drawing water from the wells in their homes they had to walk miles. Coca-Cola had created a water scarcity in a water abundant region. And the women of Plachimada were not going to allow this "hydropiracy." They started a "dharna" (sit-in) at the gates of Coca-Cola. On Earth Day 2003, they invited me to celebrate one year of their agitation.

On 21st September, 2003, a huge rally was organized to give an ultimatum to Coca-Cola. On 21st and 22nd of January, 2004 a World Water Conference brought global activists like Jose Bove and Maude Barlow to Plachimada to support the local activists.

A movement started by local adivasi women had unleashed a national and global wave of people's energy in their support. On 17th February, 2004, the Kerala Chief Minister, under pressure of the growing movement and the aggravation of the water crisis because of a drought, ordered closure of the Coke plant. The victory of the movement in Plachimada was the result of creating broad alliances and using multiple strategies.

The rainbow alliances, beginning with the local women and activists like Veloor Swaminthan, Convenor of the anti Coca-Cola task force in Plachimada, grew to include the local Gram Panchayat and its members Girija Devi, Geetha Mohandas, Sheeba Radhakrishnan, Aruchamy K, Sivakam, Subbayyan, MK Arumugham, K Varathara, A Krishnan, President, K Parthan, Presitha Mohandas, M Shanmugham, G Ponnukkuttam, N Chellankutty, C Murughan.

The local Panchayat used its constitutional rights to serve notice to Coca-Cola. The Perumatty Panchayat also filed a public interest litigation in the Kerala High Court against Coca-Cola.

The courts supported the women's demands. In an order given on 16th December, 2003, Justice Balakrishnana Nair ordered Coca-Cola to stop pirating Plachimada's water. As the Honorable Justice stated:

> The Public Trust Doctrine primarily rests on the principle that certain resources like air, sea waters and the forests have such a great importance to the people as a whole that it would be wholly unjustified to make them a subject of private ownership. The said resources being a gift of nature, they should be made freely available to everyone irrespective of the status in life. The doctrine enjoins upon the government to protect the resources for the enjoyment of the general public rather than to permit their use for private ownership or commercial purpose. . . .
>
> Our legal system—based on English common law—includes the public trust doctrine as part of its jurisprudence. The State is the trustee of all natural resources, which are by nature meant for public use and enjoyment. Public at large is the beneficiary of the seashore, running waters, airs, forests and ecologically fragile lands. The State as a trustee is under a legal duty to protect the natural resources. These resources meant for public use cannot be converted into private ownership. . . .
>
> In view of the above authoritative statement of the Honourable Supreme Court, it can be safely concluded that underground water belongs to the public. The State and its instrumentalities should act as trustees of this great wealth. The State has got a duty to protect ground water

against excessive exploitation and the inaction of the State in this regard is tantamount to infringement of the right to life of the people, guaranteed under Article 21 of the Constitution of India.

The Apex Court has repeatedly held that the right to clean air and unpolluted water forms part of the right to life under Article 21 of the Constitution. So, even in the absence of any law governing ground water, I am of the view that the Panchayat and the State are bound to protect ground water from excessive exploitation. In other words, the ground water, under the land of the 2nd respondent, does not belong to it.

Even assuming the experts' opinion that the present level of consumption by the 2nd respondent is harmless, the same should not be permitted for the following reasons:

The underground water belongs to the general public and the 2nd respondent has no right to claim a huge share of it and the Government have no power to allow a private party to extract such a huge quantity of ground water, which is a property, held by it in trust.

If the 2nd respondent is permitted to draw such a huge quantity of ground water, then similar claims of the other landowners will also have to be allowed. The same will result in drying up of the underground aqua-reservoirs.

Accordingly, the following directions are issued:

The 2nd respondent shall stop ground water for its use after one month from today.

The Panchayat and the State shall ensure that the 2nd respondent does not extract any ground water after the said time limit. This time is granted to enable the 2nd respondent to find out alternative sources of water.

The alliance grew to include people like Veerandra Kumar of Mathrubhumi and me. And we mobilized our networks to offer our full support to the local movement. The January conference was co-organised with the local Panchayat. It brought on one platform every political party, and the leader of the opposition V.S. Achuthanandan who kept up the pressure in the Kerala Assembly to translate the Court decision into Executive action.

The literary movement provided leadership through Dr. Sukumar Azhikode. And global support came in the presence of Jose Bove, Maude Barlow, European Parliamentarians and activists from across the world. The women's protest, the heart and soul of the movement, got support through legal action, parliamentary action and scientific research. This pluralism and diversity in support of local action was the secret of the victory of people against Coke in Plachimada.

This is the strength of our multiplicities and complementarities; we have to mobilize in other parts of India where Coke and Pepsi are mining and stealing people's water resources. The Plachimada Declaration issued at the World Water conference of 21st–23rd January, 2004 states:

Plachimada Declaration

Water is the basis of life; it is the gift of nature; it belongs to all living beings on earth.

Water is not a private property. It is a common resource for the sustenance of all.

Water is the fundamental right of man. It has to be conserved. Protected and managed. It is our fundamental obligation to prevent water scarcity and pollution and to preserve it for generations.

Water is not a commodity. We should resist all criminal attempts to marketise, privatize and corporatise water. Only through these means we can ensure the fundamental and inalienable right to water for the people all over the world.

The Water Policy should be formulated on the basis of this outlook.

The right to conserve, use and manage water is fully vested with the local community. This is the very basis of water democracy. Any attempt to reduce or deny this right is a crime.

The production and marketing of the poisonous products of the Coca-Cola, Pepsi Cola corporates lead to total destruction and pollution and it also endangers the very existence of local communities.

The resistance that has come up in Plachimada, Pududdery and in various parts of the world is the symbol of our valiant struggle against the devilish corporate gangs who pirate our water.

We, who are in the battlefield in full solidarity with the Adivasis who have put up resistance against the tortures of the horrid commercial forces in Plachimada, exhort the people all over the world to boycott the products of Coca-Cola and Pepsi Cola.

Coca-Cola—Pepsi Cola: "Quit India".

EDITORS' NOTES

1. *Adivasi* means "original inhabitants" in Sanskrit, or indigenous people, who have a distinct identity and culture. They have been marginalized within India, often brutally, starting with the British colonial administration, which opened up Adivasi areas for timber and developed these lands as estates. Adivasis continue to struggle for autonomy, control over resources, and restoration of traditional rights. Access to land is a major issue for Adivasis of Kerala.

2. *Panchayat* is the local community in tribal areas, recognized under the 1996 Provision of the Panchayats Act as the highest form of authority in matters of culture, resources, and conflict resolution. Village communities retained the power to approve or reject development plans and programs (Shiva 2002).

9

Women, Crime, and Criminalization

The number of women who are serving time in U.S. jails and prisons, on probation, or otherwise caught up in the "correctional" system has increased dramatically in the past twenty-five years. Criminalization is one of the most dramatic ways in which gender, race, and class position shape women's lives, and it is essential for students of women's studies to understand the processes whereby women become defined as criminals. Many of us are shielded from this reality because incarcerated women are literally locked away, behind bars, and out of sight.

The societal assumptions that justify and reinforce this separation between "inside" and "outside" are that these are bad women, perhaps foolishly involved with criminal men, maybe crazy from drink, drugs, or the pain of their lives, but that they must have done something *very wrong* to end up in prison. This chapter examines the experiences of incarcerated women, processes of criminalization, assumptions about criminality, and theoretical frameworks for understanding the increase in women's imprisonment. In this discussion we draw on points made in previous chapters concerning women's economic insecurity (Chapter 7), and the effects of economic globalization on U.S. women's opportunities (Chapter 8). The arguments for community solutions to violence against women rather than increasing reliance on the criminal justice system are also relevant here (see Chapter 6: Readings 31 and 34).

This chapter was originally written by Barbara Bloom, MSW, Ph.D., a criminal justice consultant and researcher specializing in the development and evaluation of programs serving girls and women under criminal justice supervision; it has been edited, adapted, and updated by Gwyn Kirk and Margo Okazawa-Rey.

The National Context: "Get Tough on Crime"

As discussed by Nancy Kurshan in Reading 49, "prisons serve the same purpose for women as they do for men": they are instruments of social control. However, Kurshan argues, the imprisonment of women must be seen against "a backdrop of patriarchal relationships." She traces European roots of women's incarceration from medieval times when unwanted daughters and wives were forced into convents, followed by sixteenth- and seventeenth-century witch hunts in Europe and the United States. With industrialization and urbanization came the development of prisons, including custodial prisons for women as well as reformatories that purported to "improve" the character of the women confined there. Kurshan shows how racism was built into this system, with more Black women and men serving custodial sentences, and more white women sent to reformatories. The latter were more "benign" physically but "insidiously patriarchal." More recently, Kurshan argues, the conditions of women's imprisonment resemble that of men, though still "replete with sexist ideology and practices."

The number of people imprisoned in the United States has been growing for the past thirty-five years. Approximately 330,000 people were in custody in 1972. The incarceration rate increased rapidly during the 1990s mainly due to mandatory minimum sentences for drug offenses introduced in 1986. By December 2006, the total number of people incarcerated in U.S. correctional facilities was at an all time high, with 1,570,861 people in state and federal prisons—where people convicted of felony charges and serving more than a one-year sentence are held—and another 766,010 in local jails—where people are held before trial and when convicted of a misdemeanor with a sentence of less than one year (Sabol, Couture, and Harrison 2007, pp. 1, 4). Journalist Adam Liptak (2008) reported that the United States leads the world "in producing prisoners"; it has less than 5 percent of the world's population but almost one quarter of the world's prisoners. In 2006 the incarceration rate was 751 per 100,000 population (Sabol, Couture, and Harrison 2007, p. 4). Over 5 million more women and men were on probation—a period of supervision in the community following a conviction, and 798,202 were on parole—a period of conditional supervised release following

a prison term (Bureau of Justice Statistics 2007). According to organizer and writer Anannya Bhattacharjee (2002), "The entire apparatus of law enforcement in the United States has expanded dramatically, becoming more punitive, highly integrated, heavily funded, and technologically sophisticated" (p. 1). The criminalization of women must be understood in this pro-punishment context.

In the 1988 presidential election, the Republican candidate George Bush used the case of Willie Horton, a Black inmate from a Massachusetts prison who committed murder while out of prison on the state's furlough program, to establish street crime—burglary, auto theft, mugging, murder, and rape committed by strangers—as one of the most important national issues. This tactic implied that Black men were the ones to fear most. Since then, politicians and the media have reinforced that view by promoting and reporting on legislation such as the "three-strikes-you're-out" law, which requires a life sentence without parole for three-time felons, and by continually publicizing crime stories, particularly high-profile cases such as those involving murder and abduction of children. People are led to believe that no one is safe from street crime anywhere, but especially around African American and Latino men, and that everyone labeled "criminal" is an incorrigible street tough or "gangsta." Contrary to this rhetoric, the facts show that many crime rates have decreased. Violent crime rates reached the lowest level ever recorded in 2005 (U.S. Department of Justice 2005b). Women are least safe in their own homes or with men they know (as we argued in Chapter 6). Moreover, the greatest economic losses from crime do not happen on the street. According to Alexander Lichtenstein and Michael Kroll (1996), "Society's losses from 'white collar crime' far exceed the economic impact of all burglaries, robberies, larcenies, and auto thefts combined" (p. 20). Nonetheless, high-income criminals who commit such crimes as fraud and embezzlement are not only less likely to be incarcerated but also less likely to be considered hardened criminals; rather, they may be regarded as people who used bad judgment or went "off track" (Sherrill 1997). The year 2002 saw an unprecedented number of corporate scandals, most notably Enron, but also including Adelphia Communications, Rite Aid, and Martha Stewart. Dozens of corporate executives, financial analysts, regulators, and politicians are criticized for conflicts of interest and the possibility of fraud. Fewer are investigated, and fewer still are convicted.

According to Human Rights Watch (1999a), U.S. "get tough on crime" policies, which have enjoyed significant public support, have become the vehicle for constitutional rights violations, documented by international human rights monitors. Although the United States regards itself highly in the area of human rights, "Both federal and state governments have nonetheless resisted applying to the U.S. the standards that, rightly, the U.S. applies elsewhere" (Human Rights Watch 1999a, p. 1). Since the attacks on the World Trade Center and the Pentagon on September 11, 2001, Congress has passed two far-reaching pieces of legislation with regard to civil rights. The Uniting and Strengthening America by Providing Appropriate Tools Required to Intercept and Obstruct Terrorism Act (USA PATRIOT Act) became law on October 26, 2001, and was reauthorized in 2005. It greatly increased the government's powers, including measures that

- allow for indefinite detention of noncitizens who are not terrorists on minor visa violations;

- minimize judicial supervision of federal telephone and Internet surveillance by authorities;

- expand the government's powers to conduct secret searches;

- give the Attorney General and the Secretary of State the power to designate domestic groups as terrorist organizations and deport any noncitizens who belong to them;

- give the FBI access to business records about individuals without having to show evidence of a crime;

- lead to large-scale investigation of U.S. citizens for "intelligence" purposes. (American Civil Liberties Union 2002b)

The Homeland Security Act, signed into law on November 25, 2002, involved the creation of a new Department of Homeland Security that includes the functions of the former INS, now Immigration and Customs Enforcement (ICE). Among its sweeping provisions, the act authorized the collection of data on individuals and groups from databases that combine personal, governmental, and corporate records, including

e-mails and Web sites viewed. It also allowed more latitude for government advisory committees to meet in secret if deemed "national-security related" (Chaddock 2002).

Earlier, we discussed aspects of U.S. immigration law and policy (Chapter 3) and increasing migration as a characteristic of the globalizing world (Chapter 8). We noted that some people have freedom to move and others are forced to do so, often for work or because of conflict or war. The wider "get tough on crime" context has affected U.S. policy towards migrants, including refugees and asylum seekers. The number of detainees held by Immigration and Customs Enforcement (ICE) rose 41 percent from 2005 to 2006, mainly people from Mexico and the Central American nations of El Salvador, Guatemala, and Honduras (Sabol, Couture, and Harrison 2007, p. 9). According to the National Immigrant Justice Center (2007), the problems of isolation, inhumane conditions, and lack of access to health care or legal counsel that characterize immigration detention are particularly problematic for women. This includes medical conditions for pregnant and nursing mothers, sexual assault, separation from children, and lack of treatment for abuse and trauma.

Asylum seekers, including families with young children, are held in prison-like detention while they wait for their cases to be decided. The U.S. Asylum Program provides protection to qualified refugees who have been persecuted or fear that they will be persecuted on account of their race, religion, nationality, membership in a particular social group, or because they hold a particular political opinion. Testifying before the Inter-American Commission on Human Rights, Michelle Brané of the New York–based Women's Commission for Refugee Women and Children argued that such punitive conditions violate U.S. standards as well as international treaty obligations (Reading 52).

Women in the Criminal Justice System

I stood with my forehead pressed as close as possible to the dark, tinted window of my jail cell. The window was long and narrow, the foot-deep wall that framed it made it impossible to stand close. The thick glass blurred everything outside. I squinted and focused, and I concentrated all my attention on the area where my mother said the family would stand and wave. . . . It would be good to see my grandparents and my mother, but it was my daughter I really wanted to see. My daughter who would be two years old in two months.

A couple of minutes passed, and in that small space of time, I rethought my entire life and how it had come to this absurd moment, when I became a twenty-one-year-old girl in jail on a drug charge, a mother who had to wait for someone to bring my own daughter to glimpse me. I could not rub my hands across her fat, brown cheeks, or plait her curly hair the way I like it.   *(Gaines 1994, p. 1)*

In December 2006, there were 112,498 women in prison, 7.2 percent of the total prison population compared to 6.7 percent in 2000 (Sabol, Couture, and Harrison 2007, p. 3). Historically, women offenders were ignored by researchers and media reports because their numbers were small in comparison with those of men. During the 1990s, however, the rate of growth in women's imprisonment far outstripped that of men's, and a growing literature of firsthand accounts documents women's experiences of incarceration (e.g., Gaines 1994; Lamb and the Women of New York Correctional Facility 2003; Richie 1996; Rierden 1997; Ross 1993; Serna 1992; Stein 1991; Watterson 1996). Marilyn Buck (2004) discussed how incarcerated women cope with idle time—literally "doing time"—and prison work, which is a means of punishment as well as the only way to earn "a pittance . . . to buy items of personal hygiene, a candy bar . . . any material we might want to use for our own human productivity. . . . as well as for telephone calls to our families, children, and friends with whom we desperately seek to maintain some level of attachment" (p. 454). In Reading 50, she describes the daily routine of her prison life.

The dramatic increase in the imprisonment of women has been driven primarily by "the war on drugs" and mandatory sentencing for drug offenses, with drug use seen as a criminal matter rather than a public health issue. The majority of female arrests are for drug offenses, such as possession and dealing, and crimes committed to support

a drug habit, particularly theft and prostitution, sometimes referred to as drug-related crimes. About half of the women confined in state prisons had been using drugs, alcohol, or both at the time of the offense for which they were incarcerated (Bureau of Justice Statistics 2000). Almost 30 percent of women in state prisons have been convicted of drug-related offenses (Sabol, Couture, and Harrison 2007, Appendix Table 10). Criminologist Stephanie Bush-Baksette (1999, p. 223) argued that the war on drugs targeted women intentionally. The sentencing guidelines, mandatory nature of the imprisonment laws, focus on first-time offenders, and mandatory minimum sentences for persons with prior felony convictions all brought more women into the criminal justice system and led to a tremendous increase in the number of incarcerated women.

Under current punishment philosophies and practices, women are also increasingly subject to criminalization of noncriminal actions and behaviors. For example, poor and homeless women—many of them mothers—are subject to criminalization as many cities pass ordinances that prohibit begging and sleeping in public places. Another disturbing trend has been the criminalization of HIV-positive women and pregnant drug-addicted women. For example, in 1992, a woman in North Carolina, allegedly HIV-positive, became entangled in the criminal justice system when she went to a public health facility for a pregnancy test. The test was positive, and she was arrested and prosecuted for "failure to follow public health warning." Her crimes were not advising her sexual partners of her HIV status and not using condoms whenever she had sexual intercourse (Cooper 1992; Seigel 1997). Although this may seem an extreme example, it was part of a growing trend. Pregnant women using illegal drugs are characterized as "evil women" and "bad mothers," willing to endanger the health of their unborn children in pursuit of drug-induced highs. There also has been a trend to arrest and prosecute these women for "the 'delivery' of controlled substances to their newborns; their alleged mode of 'delivery' to the newborn is through the umbilical cord between birth and the time the cord is cut" (Cooper 1992, p. 11). Law professor Kaaryn Gustafson (2005) noted that welfare rules have become more punitive with explicit links to law enforcement, as mentioned in

Chapter 7. Law enforcement officials may access information in welfare files. Women wanted by law enforcement officials for a felony or for violating the terms of parole or probation—which may be as little as missing a meeting—cannot receive government benefits. Anyone found guilty of a drug-related felony is banned from receiving benefits for life. In addition, states can require drug tests, fingerprints, and photographs for those applying for benefits.

Characteristics of Incarcerated Women

Women prisoners have a host of medical, psychological, and financial problems and needs. Poverty, unemployment, physical and mental illness, substance abuse, homelessness, and a history of physical and sexual abuse often propel women into a revolving cycle of life inside and outside jails and prisons.

The median age of women in prison is approximately 35 years; the majority are high school graduates. They are predominantly single heads of households, and 70 percent have children under the age of 18. A Bureau of Justice special report estimated that about 200,000 children under 18 had incarcerated mothers, and that 1.5 million children had a parent behind bars (Mumola 2000). African American children were nearly nine times, and Latino children three times more likely to have a parent in prison than white children (Mumola 2000). More recently, public school teacher and administrator Cynthia Martone (2005) estimated that 2.3 million children had a parent in prison. Public policy analysts Erika Kates and Paige Ransford (2005) emphasized the criminal justice system's lack of recognition of incarcerated women's role as mothers. They identified a range of factors that prevent regular contact between these mothers and their children: isolated locations of prisons served by poor or nonexistent public transport; restrictive policies governing visits and phone calls; the removal of infants born to women in prison (about 9 percent of women are pregnant when incarcerated); speedy termination of child custody for incarcerated women; restrictive welfare policies that make it difficult for families to

Sexual Abuse of Women Inmates and Detainees

- Sexual abuse of women inmates by male staff is common. This includes insults, harassment, rape, voyeurism in showers and during physical exams, and touching women's breasts and genitals during pat-downs and strip searches (Amnesty International 2000). A public hearing on Sexual Violence in Immigration Detention Facilities brought to light the prevalence of sexual assault in immigration detention (National Immigrant Justice Center 2007).

- In 2000, the (then) Immigration and Naturalization Service (predecessor to ICE) developed 36 standards to ensure "safe, secure, and humane treatment" of detainees. They do not address sexual assault or rape (National Immigrant Justice Center 2007).

- The Prison Rape Elimination Act became federal law in 2003. It provided for data

collection with public hearings, research conducted in prisons, and policy recommendations. It required the National Institute of Corrections to train and educate officials at all levels to prevent sexual abuse in prisons and to punish offenders, whether inmates or guards. Critics are skeptical that the Department of Justice can carry out meaningful research on this sensitive subject and question the need for more research on a topic about which so much is already known (Prison Activist Resource Center 2003).

- The United States is a party to international laws that require governments to protect incarcerated women from violence, including the Convention Against Torture and Other Cruel, Inhuman or Degrading Treatment or Punishment, and the Declaration on the Elimination of Violence Against Women.

be reunited; and women's repeated periods in custody. They outlined a Family Connections policy framework to support and strengthen relationships between incarcerated women and their children, who are often the key motivating factor for women to try to get their lives back on track. The majority of those children live with relatives, primarily grandparents, and approximately 10 percent of them are in foster care, a group home, or other social service agency. Despite the difficulties, sociologist Sandra Enos (2001) found that some mothers tried a variety of means to mother their children from prison; other researchers have emphasized the enormous "collateral consequences" of mass imprisonment, which decimates families and communities (e.g., Martone 2005; Mauer and Chesney-Lind 2002).

Some women come to prison pregnant; others become pregnant in prison. Few receive prenatal care, and pregnant prisoners suffer a high rate of miscarriage as a result. Congress has banned the use of federal funds for abortion in prison; women who can pay for an abortion themselves may be able to get one at a clinic, but they will need to convince prison authorities to get them there. Women who carry their pregnancies to term are often treated inhumanely, denied prompt medical attention, and may be forced to undergo labor and childbirth in shackles (Liptak 2006).

Incarcerated women used more serious drugs and used them somewhat more frequently than did incarcerated men (Bureau of Justice Statistics 2000). Also the rate of HIV infection is higher for women prisoners than for men prisoners (Bureau of Justice Statistics 2000). Legal researchers and activists Cynthia Chandler and Carol Kingery (2002) noted that women imprisoned in the United States were more likely to be HIV-positive than free people, and that once imprisoned, "HIV-positive women face serious medical neglect and discrimination" (also see Boudin 2007).

Offenses Committed by Women and Patterns of Arrest

In 2006, 34 percent of women were imprisoned for violent crimes, 31 percent for property crimes, and 29 percent for drug offenses (Sabol, Couture, and Harrison 2007, Appendix Table 10).

Studies have consistently shown that women generally commit fewer crimes than men and that their offenses tend to be less serious, primarily nonviolent property offenses such as fraud, forgery, and theft, as well as drug offenses (Bloom, Chesney-Lind, and Owen 1994; Honderich 2003). Violent offenses committed by women continue to decline. When women do commit acts of violence, these are usually in self-defense against abusive spouses or partners. Art professor and artist Carol Jacobsen describes her video documentary work that tells the stories of such women incarcerated in Michigan (Reading 51; see also Jones 1980; Rennison 2003; Ritchie 1996).

Race and Class Disparities

Most women in the U.S. criminal justice system are marginalized by race and class. Poor women are pushed into the "underground economies" of drugs, prostitution, and theft as a way of supporting themselves and their children. Analyzed by race/ethnicity, 35 percent of women in state or federal prisons in 2004 were white and 65 percent were women of color (Sabol, Couture, and Harrison 2007, Table 8). For those sentenced to more than a year, the incarceration rate for white women was 48 per 100,000 population, compared to 148 for Black women and 81 for Latinas. This follows historical disparities based on race, noted by Nancy Kurshan (Reading 49). According to writers and organizers Jael Silliman and Anannya Bhattacharjee (2002), "For the same offense, Black and Latina women are respectively eight and four times more likely to be incarcerated than white women" (p. xv). White women are more likely to be placed on probation than women of color. Many crimes committed on Native American reservations are classified as federal offenses, and lawbreakers are held in federal prisons, usually in remote places long distances away from home and hard to get to by public transportation, two factors that increase the isolation of such prisoners (Ogden 2006).

Racial bias is a factor in arrests, pretrial treatment, and differential sentencing of women. Professor of criminal justice Coramae Richey Mann (1995) documented disparity in prison sentences by comparing arrest rates with sentencing rates of women offenders in California, Florida, and New

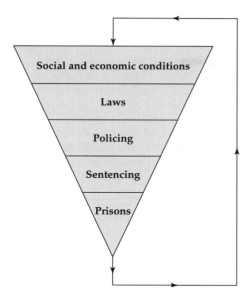

FIGURE 9.1 The Funnel of Injustice
(*Source:* Honderich 2003, p. 10.)

York. She found that, in all three states, women of color, particularly African Americans, were disproportionately arrested. The few studies that report race-specific differences indicate more punitive treatment of women of color. Economist Kiaran Honderich (2003) described this channeling of poor women of color into the criminal justice system in terms of a "funnel of injustice" (see Figure 9.1). Differential sentencing for cocaine use is a case in point. Currently sentences for possession of 500 grams of powder cocaine, mainly used by middle- and upper-middle-class white people, are set at a minimum of five years. Possession of any amount of crack cocaine, mainly used by poor people of color, carries a mandatory minimum sentence of five years.

The "war on drugs," initiated by the Reagan administration in the 1980s, has been aggressively pursued in poor urban neighborhoods, especially poor African American and Latino communities, and in countries of the global South, despite the fact that white people make up the majority of U.S. drug users and traffickers. Proponents justified massive government intervention as necessary to quell the drug epidemic, gang violence, and

"narco-terrorism." However, critics charged that "Blacks, Latinos, and third world people are suffering the worst excesses of a program that violates . . . civil rights, human rights, and national sovereignty" (Lusane 1991, p. 4). Julia Sudbury takes up this issue in Reading 54, in her analysis of economic globalization and the criminalization of women of color.

The declared intention to get rid of drugs and drug-related crime has resulted in the allocation of federal and state funding for additional police officers on the streets, more federal law-enforcement officers, and more jails and prisons, rather than for prevention, rehabilitation, and education. Poor women of color have become the main victims of these efforts in two ways: They are trying to hold their families and communities together while so many men of color are incarcerated, and they are increasingly incarcerated themselves. As author, activist, and scholar Clarence Lusane (1991) observed "The get-tough, mandatory-sentencing laws are forcing judges to send to prison first-time offenders who a short time ago would have gotten only probation or a fine. . . . It is inevitable that women caught selling the smallest amount of drugs will do time" (p. 56). As argued in Chapter 8, the international drug trade must be understood at the global level, as one way producer countries earn hard currency to repay foreign debt. Mandatory minimum prison sentences are not cost effective according to some policy analysts and appear to have had a negligible effect on the drug trade in this country.

Girls in the Criminal Justice System

When people think of juvenile crime they often think of boys, but in the 1990s roughly two-thirds of incarcerated women were first arrested as juveniles, and about half of them spent time in detention when they were minors (Siegal 1995). African American girls are much more likely to be held in detention than white girls or Latinas. There are fewer options for girls as compared with boys in terms of rehabilitation and housing, so girls spend more time in detention awaiting placement. The great majority of girls in the criminal justice system have been physically or sexually abused; many have learning disorders; many use drugs and alcohol (Chesney-Lind and Pasko 2003, 2004). According to journalist Nina Siegal (1995), "Probation officers, counselors, and placement staffers prefer to work with boys because they say girls' problems are more complex and more difficult to address" (p. 16). Girls express more emotional needs than boys. "Middle-class girls with the same problems might end up in therapy, treatment programs, boarding schools, or private hospitals. But girls in Juvenile Hall have fallen through the system's proverbial safety net" (p. 17) or lack of safety net.

In 2004, girls were 29 percent of juveniles arrested, up from 23 percent in 1990; girls' arrests for assault, however, increased 41 percent from 1992 to 2003 (Leach 2004). Researchers question whether this is because girls are more unruly than previously or whether policy changes and greater media attention are responsible for the increase. Journalist Susan L. Leach (2004) reported three changes that may account for part, if not all of this increase. In some areas, running away from home, truancy, scuffling with family members, or repeated discipline problems have been reclassified as offenses. Zero-tolerance policies in schools have turned relatively minor offenses that used to be addressed informally into crimes. Policy makers and media reporters are paying much more attention to girls' offenses than in the past when they assumed juvenile justice meant boys.

Dating from the 1890s, the early juvenile justice system held to the principle of rehabilitation, but the "get tough on crime" policy has meant that many states have changed their approach to an explicitly punitive one. California, for example, has reduced the age at which minors can be tried as adults from 16 to 14 for 24 different crimes. The state has also changed the law on confidentiality so that the names of juvenile offenders can become public knowledge.

Women Political Prisoners

A small but significant group of women in federal prisons is there as a result of political activities, including members of the Puerto Rican Socialist Party, supporters of Native American sovereignty movements, and participants in Black revolutionary movements in the United States and abroad. Silvia Baraldini, an Italian citizen, was given a forty-year sentence after being arrested on conspiracy charges arising out of political activities in solidarity with national liberation movements, including assisting in the escape of Black activist Assata Shakur. Like Marilyn Buck, Susan Rosenberg, and Laura Whitehorn, she was active in the women's movement and the anti-Vietnam War movement, and was a supporter of African, African American, and Puerto Rican national liberation movements. From 1986 to 1988, Silvia Baraldini and Susan Rosenberg were held in the "High Security Unit" (HSU), a specially built underground prison for political prisoners in Lexington, Kentucky. Although this sixteen-bed prison housed no more than six women at a time, it became the center of intense scrutiny by national and international human rights organizations, including Amnesty International. As a result of sustained political pressure from activists and the Italian government, Silvia Baraldini was released to Italian authorities in 1999 so that she could return to Italy because of serious complications associated with cancer. Susan Rosenberg and Laura Whitehorn were released in 1999 having served sixteen- and fourteen-year sentences, respectively. Marilyn Buck is still in prison, serving an eighty-year sentence. In her account of daily life, she describes the many constraints on prisoners' lives that deprive them of virtually all autonomy. She worries about becoming "inured to the casual cruelty that prevails. It lures us into becoming the very creatures the prison system advertises us to be and robs us of our humanity. I worry about succumbing, losing my will to resist dehumanization, and ultimately, losing my own sense of who I am as a human being" (Reading 50).

Since about the mid-1950s, the federal government has operated "counter-insurgency programs," to track, undermine, and destroy left-wing political organizations it deemed radical and militant and to imprison or kill activists. The Federal Bureau of Investigation (FBI) in its Counter Intelligence Programs (COINTELPRO) launched campaigns against the Communist Party in 1954 and, subsequently, against the Socialist Workers Party, the Puerto Rican independence movement, the Black Power Movement, particularly the Black Panther Party, and the American Indian Movement (AIM) (Churchill 1992). Mumia Abu-Jamal,

Leonard Peltier, and Geronimo Pratt were all convicted of murder, although they all claim to have been framed by the FBI. Geronimo Pratt was freed in 1997 after more than twenty-five years in prison. A judge ruled that the evidence used to convict him had been tampered with, as Pratt and prison rights activists had argued all along (Booth 1997). Angela Davis, an internationally known scholar and activist, was imprisoned for two years on murder, conspiracy, and kidnapping charges but later acquitted.

First-wave feminists were jailed in the early 1900s for peacefully picketing the White House in their campaign for votes for women. In 1917, for example, hundreds of suffragists, mainly white, middle-class women, organized pickets around the clock. At first they were ignored by the police. By June they began to be arrested, and in August they received thirty-day and sixty-day sentences for obstructing traffic. A number of those who were jailed went on hunger strikes; they were forcibly fed and threatened with transfer to an insane asylum. They were released the following year by order of President Wilson, and the Washington, D.C., Court of Appeals ruled that their arrests, convictions, and imprisonment were illegal (Gluck 1976). This kind of political action was very different from that of revolutionary organizations committed to self-defense and armed struggle if necessary. But, like the sentences of political women prisoners active in the 1970s and 1980s, suffragists received disproportionately long sentences and harsh treatment, clearly intended to discourage this kind of determined opposition to government policy.

Another example of politically motivated incarceration was the internment of thousands of Japanese Americans in remote camps following the bombing of Pearl Harbor by Japanese troops in 1941 (see, e.g., Daniels, Taylor, and Kitano 1991; Iwamura 2007; Tateishi 1984; Yoo 2000). Most of these people were U.S. citizens living in West Coast states. They were forced to leave their homes, farms, and businesses, and most were kept in the camps for the duration of U.S. involvement in World War II. Researcher Rita Takahashi (1998) commented that although the U.S. constitution "prohibits deprivation of life, liberty, or property without due process of law," these constitutional guarantees "were suspended in this case, and the Government was able to implement this massive program with few questions asked," though there was no evidence that these Japanese Americans were in any way "disloyal" to the United States (p. 362). In a similar move, authorities arrested some 1,500 men, mostly Arabs, after the attacks of September 11, 2001. In addition, various officials and private citizens committed acts of violence and harassment against Arab Americans, South Asians, and "people who look like Muslims." In one instance, Samar Kaukab, a U.S. woman of Pakistani descent, was detained at Chicago's O'Hare International Airport in November 2001 and subjected to an unjustified, illegal, and degrading search by airport security personnel. The American Civil Liberties Union filed suit and the matter was settled through a confidential agreement in 2004. In Reading 53, Suad Joseph and Benjamin D'Harlingue present their analysis of negative media coverage of Arabs and Arab Americans, a factor in creating a climate of opinion whereby racial profiling, preemptive arrests and detentions, abuse and humiliation of those detained, and suspension of their constitutional rights can be justified and supported in the name of "national security." In November 2002, a "Special Registration" program required males over 16 years of age from twenty-five mainly Arab and Muslim countries to be fingerprinted, photographed, and questioned about terrorism. This program lasted eighteen months with devastating impact on these communities (Nguyen 2005). Several thousand men were detained and an unknown number deported though few, if any, of those arrested were charged or found to have any connection to terrorism. Japanese Americans were among the first to speak out against these detentions, recognizing the similarity with what had happened to their own community sixty years earlier (Kim 2001; Leung and Chow 2002).

A current example of criminalization during military conflict concerns prisoners of war, mainly men, held at the Guantanamo Bay Naval Base (Cuba), military prisons in Afghanistan and Iraq, and in other countries. Public debate in this country has centered on the legality of interrogation methods, definitions of torture, the role of professional psychologists in supporting torture, and U.S. obligations to international human rights laws, such as the Geneva Conventions (see, e.g., Greenberg 2006;

Lifton 2004; Maran 2006). Another factor concerns the way gender has been deployed to humiliate detainees, for example through military women's participation in human rights violations at Abu Ghraib prison. We take up this issue in the following chapter.

Theories of Women and Crime

Until recently there has been a lack of research specifically on women in conflict with the law in the United States. This is partly because far fewer women than men were incarcerated and also because it is difficult for researchers to obtain access to women in prison. Official data collected by the Bureau of Justice are limited and often date back several years by the time they are published, a limitation of the data cited in this chapter.

Early theories of women's criminality either attempted to explain it in individual terms or used theories developed to explain male criminality and applied them to women. Theories that emphasized individual behavior applied stereotypical assumptions about the "female psyche" that are blatantly sexist and without much evidence to support their claims. They included biological arguments—for example, that women commit crimes as a result of premenstrual syndrome (PMS)—and psychological notions—that "hysterical" women behave criminally, or that women are conniving and manipulative, and so resort to using poison rather than a gun to kill. The second type included theories of *social learning* (crime is learned), *social process* (individuals are affected by institutions such as the family, school, and peers), *social structure* (individuals are shaped by structural inequalities), and *conflict theory*, a specific social structure theory, which generally claims that the law is a weapon of social control used by the powerful against the less powerful (Turk 1995).

An increase in female crime in the 1960s and 1970s prompted new theories attributing female criminality to the women's liberation movement. The female offender was identified as its "dark side" (Chesney-Lind 1986). The phenomenon of girls in gangs has also been blamed on the women's movement (Chesney-Lind and Pasko 2004; Chesney-Lind and Shelden 1992). Sociologist Freda Adler (1975), for example, proposed that

women were committing an increasing number of violent crimes because the women's movement had created a liberated, tougher class of women, a view that became known as the "masculinity thesis." Similarly, criminologist Rita Simon (1975) developed an "opportunity thesis," arguing that a rise in women's involvement in property crimes, such as theft, embezzlement, and fraud, was due to women entering previously male occupations, such as banking and business, and to their consequent exposure to opportunities for crime that were previously the preserve of men. Neither of these theses is supported by much empirical evidence.

A third theory, the "economic marginalization thesis," posited that it is the absence, rather than the availability, of employment opportunity for women that appears to lead to increases in female crime (Giordano, Kerbel, and Dudley 1981; Naffine 1987). Proponents of this view argue that most crime committed by women is petty property crime, such as theft, a rational response to poverty and economic insecurity. The increasing numbers of single women supporting dependent children mean that more women may risk the benefits of criminal activity as supplements or alternatives to employment (Rafter 1990). Noting that the majority of female offenders were low-income women who committed non-employment-related crimes, rather than middle- and upper-middle-class professional women who committed employment-related crimes, proponents of economic marginalization theory argued that the feminization of poverty, not women's liberation, was the social trend most relevant to female criminality.

Some feminist scholars saw the cause of female crime as originating in male supremacy and in men's efforts to control women sexually. They attempted to show how physical and sexual victimization of girls and women could be underlying causes of criminal behavior (Chesney-Lind 1995; Owen and Bloom 1995). They argued that the exploitation of women and girls caused some to run away from home or to begin abusing drugs at an early age, which often led to criminal activity.

Other feminists viewed gender inequality as stemming from the unequal power of women and men in a capitalist society (Connell 1990; Messerschmidt 1986). They traced the origins of gender differences to the development of private property and male domination over the laws of inheritance, asserting that within the current economic system, men control women economically as well as socially. Such theorists argued that women commit fewer crimes than men because women are isolated in the family and have fewer opportunities to engage in white-collar crimes or street crimes. Because capitalism renders women relatively powerless both in the home and in the economic arena, any crimes they commit are less serious, nonviolent, self-destructive crimes such as theft, drug possession, and prostitution. Moreover, women's relative powerlessness also increases the likelihood that they will be the target of violent acts, usually by men.

Yet other feminist scholars have foregrounded racism in explaining the disproportionately high incarceration rates for people of color (e.g., Davis 1998; Silliman and Bhattacharjee 2002; Smith 2005). They focus on community experiences of state violence, including police brutality and women's struggles to keep their families and communities intact in the face of arrests, harassment, and raids by the police.

In Reading 54, ethnic studies professor Julia Sudbury takes an intersectional approach to explain the upsurge in women's incarceration. She asks: "Who benefits when more women are imprisoned? What are the processes by which certain actions are labeled criminal and others are not, and how are women channeled into these actions and thus into conflict with the criminal justice system?" Sudbury explores three macro- and global-level factors—the effects of globalization on national economies, the expansion of the prison industry as a profit-making business, and the war on drugs—to account for women's imprisonment. She discusses the experiences of three individual women, one from Canada, one from Colombia, and one from the United States, to illustrate her argument. She critiques feminist criminology on two counts: first, for focusing on women's behavior, assuming a connection between punishment and crime, to explain their incarceration. Rather, Sudbury contends, "we should look at the shifting action of the state as it seeks to control poor communities and populations of color." Secondly, she argues, feminist criminologists have focused on gender at the expense of race and class. Advocates, policy makers, and theorists who seek to understand and explain

the criminal justice system must, as Sudbury puts it, "engage meaningfully with the significance of race."

Is Equal Treatment Fair Treatment?

There has been extensive debate among feminist legal scholars about whether equality under the law is necessarily good for women (see, e.g., Chesney-Lind 1995; Chesney-Lind and Pasko 2004; K. Daly 1994). On the one hand, some argued that the only way to eliminate the discriminatory treatment and oppression that women have experienced in the past is to push for continued equalization under the law. Though equal treatment may hurt women in the short run, in the long run it is the only way to guarantee that women will be treated as equal partners economically and socially. By contrast, legal scholars Deborah Labelle and Sheryl Pimlott Kubiak (2004) explored how "the legal right to 'substantially equivalent' treatment and facilities for female prisoners was jeopardized by an administrative interpretation of the policy as gender neutral" (p. 417). In the situation they investigated, "female and male prisoners were treated identically—based on the male prisoner model" (p. 418). This meant that no allowances were made for physical contact on prison visits, such as women kissing, hugging, or even touching their children. Male guards were assigned to women's housing units, thus "subjecting women prisoners to twenty-four-hour male supervision—while showering, dressing, and performing basic bodily functions" (p. 419). This compounded incarcerated women's sense of powerlessness, especially as many had been sexually assaulted as girls or as adults. These scholars concluded that equal treatment should not mean gender neutrality, which "is not appropriate in circumstances in which there are real differences in gender socialization and social conditions" (p. 424).

Gender-neutral sentencing reforms have aimed to reduce gender-based disparities in sentencing by punishing like crimes in the same way. This emphasis on parity, the utilization of a male standard, and gender-blind mandatory sentencing statutes, particularly for drug-law violations, have all contributed to the rising numbers of women in prison. A Phoenix, Arizona, sheriff proudly boasted, "I don't believe in discrimination," after he established the first female chain gang in the United States, where women, whose work boots are chained together, picked up trash in downtown Phoenix (In Phoenix chain gangs for women 1996). This is what Lahey (1985) called "equality with a vengeance."

Another effect of the equalization approach has been in the types of facilities women are sentenced to. For example, boot camps have become popular with prison authorities as an alternative to prison. New York, for instance, operates a boot camp for women that is modeled on those for men. This includes uniforms, shorn hair, humiliation for behaviors considered to be disrespectful of staff, and other militaristic approaches.

Twenty years ago, criminologist Pat Carlen (1989) argued that equality with men in the criminal justice system meant more punitive measures applied to women. Instead, she advocated the supervision of women in noncustodial settings in their communities, where they could remain connected with their children and families. She called for reducing the number of prison beds for women and using nonprison alternatives for all but the most dangerous offenders. She based her argument on the fact that most women commit nonviolent crimes and are often victims of physical, sexual, and emotional abuse. Therefore, she claimed, programs that support women's emotional needs would be more appropriate than punitive measures. Currently, advocates working to reduce rates of women's imprisonment use similar arguments.

The "Prison Industrial Complex"

Some critics and commentators have described the expansion and privatization of the prison system, with prison services provided by private firms and prisoners working for corporations, as the "prison industrial complex" (Browne 1996; Davis 1997; Walker 1996). Borrowing from the term "military industrial complex," coined by President Dwight Eisenhower, the phrase "prison industrial complex" refers to the increasingly interconnected relationships among private corporations, the public prison system, public investment, and public interests. The Corrections Corporation of America manages many prisons in this country. The construction and servicing of prisons and jails have

become big business—as argued in Reading 54. Profits are being generated by architecture firms designing prisons, security companies supplying equipment, food distribution companies providing food service, and also, by the direct and indirect exploitation of prisoners. For example, TWA and Best Western (the international motel chain) use prisoners to take calls from customers during times when there is an overflow, such as before holidays and certain vacation periods. Microsoft, Victoria's Secret, and Boeing also use low-cost prison labor (Parenti 1999), as does Starbucks and Nintendo (Barnett 2002). Hundreds of prison-generated products end up attached to well-known labels like No Fear, Lee Jeans, and Trinidad Tees (Levister 2006). After deductions, Chris Levister (2006) reported that many prisoners "earn about $60 for an entire month of nine-hour days." Nancy Kurshan noted that hiring out prison labor has a long history (Reading 49). Today, prisoners are the ultimate in a flexible and dependable work force; they do not have to be paid minimum wage, provided with health benefits or vacation time, or covered by workers' compensation (a tax employers must pay for regular employees), and they cannot unionize (Lichtenstein and Kroll 1996). Telephone companies also profit because people outside jails and prisons are not allowed to call prisoners directly; prisoners are allowed only to call collect, which is one of the most expensive ways of making telephone calls. In August 2005, in *Byrd v. Goord,* a federal trial court ruled in favor of friends and family members of incarcerated prisoners in New York state who were "bearing an unlegislated tax" in inflated phone charges for collect calls to speak with their loved ones (Center for Constitutional Rights 2005). The court ruled that the 60 percent "commission" which the New York State Department of Corrections received from MCI's profits on the inmate phone system was unconstitutional. However, it upheld two other charges: the restriction of calls to collect only and the limitations of statewide service to one provider, MCI.

Most state budgets are currently in crisis as a result of economic recession and changes in federal allocations to states. Their colossal investment in new jails and prisons has eaten up a growing portion of states' resources nationwide, in direct competition with other state investments like higher education (see Box for details). Because of budget constraints Julie Falk (2003) noted that education, training, and rehabilitation for prisoners have been cut back severely; overcrowding is getting worse; inmates are being kept in their cells for longer periods to reduce the wage bill for guards; and some prisoners are required to pay for health care as well as room and board. Susan Tucker and Eric Cadora (2003) note the failures of what they called "prison fundamentalism." They challenged the logic of current policy that expects people released from prison with no new skills to return to the same impoverished communities and make a go of their lives. They argued, instead, for

Comparable Costs: Education, Drug Treatment, and Imprisonment

- Research shows consistently that education is needed to compete in today's workforce and to secure jobs that pay decent wages and benefits. Many people in prison or on probation do not have high school or equivalent level of educational achievement.

- Prisons and higher education compete for budget dollars from a state's General Fund. Throughout the 1980s and 1990s, state spending on prisons, on average, grew at six times the rate of higher-education spending. Forty-five states increased spending on prisons by more than 100 percent; eighteen states by over 200 percent; and the top five (Colorado, Idaho, Oregon, Pennsylvania, and Texas) by over 300 percent (Justice Policy Institute 2002, Table 5). In Maryland, for example, the prison budget increased by $147 million, while the university budget fell by $29 million. In the decade 1988–1998, New York spent $762 million more on corrections while spending on state colleges and universities dropped by $615 million (Justice Policy Institute 2002, p. 3).

- It costs as much or more to send someone to prison as to university. The estimated cost per inmate in California state prisons was $30,929 for fiscal year 2003–2004, or $27,167 in Alameda county jail. Stanford University fees were $40,591 per year, including room, board, books, and fees, while U.C. Berkeley (in-state tuition) amounted to $6,730 (Urban Strategies Council 2004).

- Research on the Drug Treatment Alternative-to-Prison Program, carried out in Brooklyn, New York, in the 1990s, showed that participants in this program had lower re-arrest and re-conviction rates compared to those who were incarcerated for similar offenses. Two years after leaving the program, graduates were 67 percent less likely to have been re-convicted as opposed to those in the comparison group two years after leaving prison. Graduates were three-and-a-half times as likely to be employed compared to before their arrest (26 percent were employed on arrest; 92 percent were employed two years after completing the program). These results were achieved at half the average cost of incarceration (National Center for Addiction and Substance Abuse 2003, p. ii). Despite these findings, for every $100 the state of New York spent on substance abuse in 1998, only $5.81 went to fund prevention, treatment, and research; the rest paid for building and upkeep of prisons, incarceration of drug offenders, and probation and parole services (National Center for Addiction and Substance Abuse 2003, p. 12).

- Close to half the 2 million people incarcerated in the United States are African American (Justice Policy Institute 2002, p. 8). Between 1980 and 2000, 38 states and all federal prisons added more African American men to prison populations than to enrollment in state colleges and universities (Justice Policy Institute 2002, Table 6). Texas added more than four times the number of African American men to its prison system (54,500) than to its colleges and universities (12,163)—the highest discrepancy nationwide.

"justice reinvestment" in poor communities for education, healthcare, job creation, and job training. Others advocate for measures that will help women return to their communities after incarceration. Especially needed are safe affordable housing, transitional income, and employment (e.g., Sentencing Project 2007). The enormous costs of mandatory minimum sentences and three-strikes laws have caused some states to reassess their policies and to expand parole and early release, to close prisons and develop alternative sentencing programs—the very reforms that anti-prison advocates want to see (Falk 2003; Miller 2005).

Inside/Outside Connections

Women who have never been incarcerated can be allies to incarcerated and formerly incarcerated women by supporting organizations and activities involving former prisoners and advocates. Examples of organizations that support women in prison include Aid to Inmate Mothers (Montgomery, Ala.); California Coalition for Women Prisoners (San Francisco); Chicago Legal Advocacy for Incarcerated Mothers; Justice Now (Oakland); Legal Services for Prisoners with Children (Oakland); Let's Start (St. Louis, Mo.); Michigan Women's Justice and Clemency Project (Ann Arbor); National Women's Prison Project (Baltimore); and A New Way of Life Reentry Project (Los Angeles). *Women and Prisons: A Site for Resistance* is a web space for prisoners, those previously incarcerated, activists, students, and teachers that makes visible women's experiences in the criminal justice system (http://womenandprison.org). Women on the outside are working with women prisoners in literacy classes and creative writing, providing books (Women's Prison Book Project, Minneapolis), and undertaking theater productions with incarcerated women (The Medea Project, San Francisco; also see Fraden 2001; Troustine 2001). AIDS awareness programs for people in prison are sponsored by the ACLU National Prison Project (Washington, D.C.) and the AIDS in Prison Project (New York). Women in a maximum-security prison have organized HIV peer education (Members of the AIDS Counseling and Education Program of the Bedford Hills Correctional Facility 1998). Films by and about women who killed abusive partners include *Defending Our Lives* (Cambridge Documentary Films), which tells the story of Battered Women Fighting Back!, a group of inmates at a prison in Framingham, Massachusetts. *From One Prison . . .* (Michigan Women's Justice and Clemency Project) was produced in collaboration with women at a Michigan prison who are serving life or long-term sentences for killing their batterers, as discussed by video artist, Carol Jacobsen (Reading 51).

Advocates press for health care, drug treatment, and educational, therapeutic, and life-skills programs for incarcerated women. They also critique funding priorities of successive administrations that give a higher priority to building jails and prisons than to education, social services, and welfare; they urge a fundamental redirection of these resources. The Rocky Mountain Peace and Justice Center's Prison Moratorium Project (Boulder, Colo.) challenges the idea that prisons can solve social problems based on poverty and inequality. It seeks to halt prison expansion and redirect resources toward the development of alternative sentencing, prevention, and treatment programs, as does the nationwide Critical Resistance network (see Critical Resistance 2005; Magnani 2006). The nonprofit Justice Policy Institute (2002) argued for repealing mandatory sentencing, reforming drug laws to direct offenders into treatment programs, restructuring sentencing guidelines, and reforming parole practices—where high numbers of parolees currently are returned to custody not for committing new crimes but for technical violations of their parole orders (see Davis 2003; Silliman and Battacharjee 2002). In Reading 54, Julia Sudbury examines arguments for prison reform, de-carceration, and prison abolition.

Criminalization is a major source of insecurity for poor women and their families, especially African Americans and Latinas. There is a wide gap between organizations working on behalf of women in the criminal justice system and the broader U.S. women's movement. Data presented in this chapter give grounds for more effective coalition efforts across lines of race and class to address the needs of formerly incarcerated women and those currently in custody.

Questions for Reflection

As you read and discuss this chapter, consider these questions:

1. Why is there such attention by politicians and the media to street crimes?

2. Where is the prison nearest to where you live? Are men, women, or both incarcerated there? Who are they in terms of class, race, and age?

3. Note the official language of "corrections" or the "correctional system." What is being corrected? Why? How? And corrected to what?

4. How do you define security and for whom? How does women's incarceration contribute to security—at micro, meso, macro, and global levels? Does it undermine security? If so, how and for whom?

Finding Out More on the Web

1. Research the work of organizations cited in this chapter. How are they working to support women in the criminal justice system? Try to find organizations that are active in your city or state.

2. Use your search engine to find out the financial and human costs each year of white-collar crime in the United States.

3. What is the relationship between state spending on the criminal justice system and spending on higher education in your state?

Taking Action

1. Analyze the way the news media report crime, or analyze the portrayal of criminals in movies and TV shows. How are women who have committed crimes portrayed? Pay particular attention to issues of race and class.

2. Find out about the daily conditions for women in the jail or prison nearest to you.

3. Find out about activist groups in your area that support incarcerated women. What can you do on behalf of women in prison?

4. The USA PATRIOT Act allows law enforcement agencies access to information on students and to student records. Find out what steps your college or university has taken to provide information under the terms of this act.

◆◆◆

Behind the Walls (1996)
The History and Current Reality of Women's Imprisonment

Nancy Kurshan

Nancy Kurshan was a founder of the Youth International Party (whose members were nicknamed Yippies) and participated in the first demonstration against the Vietnam War in 1965. She worked for many years to free political prisoners such as Sundiata Acoli and Geronimo Pratt. She was a founding member of the Committee to End the Marion Lockdown, a Chicago-based prisoners' rights group, which has been organzing to abolish control-unit prisons since 1985. She worked for 20 years as a social worker in the Chicago public schools.

Prisons serve the same purpose for women as they do for men; they are instruments of social control. However, the imprisonment of women, as well as all the other aspects of our lives, takes place against a backdrop of patriarchal relationships.... Therefore, the imprisonment of women in the United States has always been a different phenomenon than that for men; the proportion of women in prison has always differed from that of men; women have traditionally been sent to prison for different reasons; and once in prison, they endure different conditions of incarceration. Women's "crimes" have often had a sexual definition and been rooted in the patriarchal double standard. Furthermore, the nature of women's imprisonment reflects the position of women in society....

As long as there has been crime and punishment, patriarchal and gender-based realities and assumptions have been central determinants of the response of society to female "offenders." In the late Middle Ages, reports reveal differential treatment of men and women. A woman might commonly be able to receive lenient punishment if she were to "plead her belly"; that is, a pregnant woman could plead leniency on the basis of her pregnancy. On the other hand, women were burned at the stake for adultery or murdering a spouse, while men would most often not be punished for such actions. Such differential treatment reflected ideological assumptions as well as women's subordinate positions

within the family, church, and other aspects of society. Although systematic imprisonment arose with industrialization, for centuries prior to that time unwanted daughters and wives were forced into convents, nunneries, and monasteries. In those cloisters were found political prisoners, illegitimate daughters, the disinherited, the physically deformed, and the mentally "defective."

A more general campaign of violence against women was unleashed in the witch hunts of sixteenth- and seventeenth-century Europe, as society tried to exert control over women by labeling them as witches. This resulted in the death by execution of at least tens of thousands and possibly millions of people. Conservative estimates indicate that over 80 percent of all the people killed were women. Here in the United States, the witchcraft trials were a dramatic chapter in the social control of women long before systematic imprisonment. Although the colonies were settled relatively late in the history of European witch hunts, they proved fertile ground for this misogynist campaign. The context was a new colonial society, changing and wrought with conflicts....

Hundreds were accused of witchcraft during the New England witchcraft trials of the late 1600s, and at least 36 were executed. The primary determinant of who was designated a witch was gender; overwhelmingly, it was women who were the objects of witch fear. More women were charged with witchcraft, and women were more likely than men to be convicted and executed. In fact, men who confessed were likely to be scoffed at as liars. But age, too, was an important factor. Women over 40 were most likely to be accused of witchcraft and fared much worse than younger women when they were charged. Women over 60 were especially at high risk. Women who were alone, not attached to men as mothers, sisters, or wives were also represented disproportionately among the witches. Puritan society was very hierarchal, and the family was an essential aspect of that hierarchy. According to Carol Karlsen, the Puritan definition of woman as procreator and "helpmate" of man could not be ensured except through force. Most of the witches had expressed dissatisfaction with their lot, if only indirectly. Some were not sufficiently submissive in that they filed petitions and court suits, and sometimes sought divorces. Others were midwives and had influence over the well-being of others, often to the chagrin of their male competitors, medical doctors. Still others exhibited a female pride and assertiveness, refusing to defer to their male neighbors.

Karlsen goes on to offer one of the most powerful explanations of the New England witchcraft trials. She argues that at the heart of the hysteria was an underlying anxiety about inheritance. The inheritance system was designed to keep property in the hands of men. When there were no legitimate male heirs, women inheritors became aberrations who threatened the orderly transmission of property from one male generation to the next. Many of the witches were potential inheritors. Some of them were already widowed and without sons. Others were married but older, beyond their childbearing years, and therefore no longer likely to produce male heirs. They were also "disposable" since they were no longer performing the "essential" functions of a woman, as reproducer and, in some cases, helpmate. Many of the witches were charged just shortly after the death of the male family member, and their witchcraft convictions meant that their lands could easily be seized. Seen in this light, persecution of "witches" was an attempt to maintain the patriarchal social structure and prevent women from becoming economically independent. These early examples of the use of criminal charges in the social control of women may be seen as precursors to the punitive institutions of the 1800s. Up until this time, there were few carceral institutions in society. However, with the rise of capitalism and urbanization come the burgeoning of prisons in the United States. It is to those initial days of systematic imprisonment that we now turn.

The Emergence of Prisons for Women

The relatively few women who were imprisoned at the beginning of the nineteenth century were confined in separate quarters or wings of men's prisons. Like the men, women suffered from filthy conditions, overcrowding, and harsh treatment. In 1838 in the New York City Jail (the "Tombs"), for instance, there were 42 one-person cells for 70 women. In the 1920s at Auburn Penitentiary in New York, there were no separate cells for the 25 or so women serving sentences up to 14 years. They were all lodged together in a one-room attic, the windows sealed to prevent communication with men. But women had to endure even more. Primary among these additional negative aspects was sexual abuse, which was reportedly a common occurrence. In 1826, Rachel Welch became pregnant while serving in solitary confinement as a punishment, and shortly after childbirth she died as a result of flogging by a prison official. Such sexual abuse was apparently so acceptable that the Indiana state prison actually ran a prostitution service for male guards, using female prisoners.

Women received the short end of even the prison stick. Rather than spend the money to hire a matron, women were often left completely on their own, vulnerable to attack by guards. Women had less access to the physician and chaplain and did not go to workshops, mess halls, or exercise yards as men did. Food and needlework were brought to their quarters, and they remained in that area for the full term of their sentence.

Criminal conviction and imprisonment of women soared during and after the Civil War. In the North, this is commonly attributed to a multitude of factors, including men's absence during wartime and the rise of industrialization, as well as the impact of the dominant sexual ideology of nineteenth-century Victorianism. The double standard of Victorian morality supported the criminalization of certain behaviors for women but not for men. In New York in the 1850s and 1860s, female "crimes against persons" tripled while "crimes against property" rose 10 times faster than the male rate.

Black people, both women and men, have always been disproportionately incarcerated at all times and all places. This was true in the Northeast and Midwest prisons before the Civil War. It was also the case in the budding prison system in the western states, where Blacks outstripped their very small percentage of the population at large. The only exception was in the South, where slavery, not imprisonment, was the preferred form of control of African-American people. Yet while the South had the lowest Black imprisonment rate before the Civil War, this changed dramatically after the slaves were freed. This change took place for African-American women as well as men. After the Civil War, as part of the re-entrenchment of Euro-American control and the continuing subjugation of Black people, the post-war southern states passed infamous Jim Crow laws that made newly freed Blacks vulnerable to incarceration for the most minor crimes. For example, stealing a couple of chickens brought three to ten years in North Carolina. It is fair to say that many Blacks stepped from slavery into imprisonment. As a result, southern prison populations became predominately Black overnight. Between 1874 and 1877, the Black imprisonment rate went up 300 percent in Mississippi and Georgia. In some states, previously all-white prisons could not contain the influx of African-Americans sentenced to hard labor for petty offenses.

These spiraling rates in both the North and South meant that by mid-century there were enough women prisoners, both in the North and South, to necessitate the emergence of separate women's quarters. This practical necessity opened the door to changes in the nature of the imprisonment of women. In 1869, Sarah Smith and Rhoda Coffin, two Indiana Quakers, led a campaign to end the sexual abuse of women in that state's prison, and in 1874 the first completely separate women's prison was constructed. By 1940, 23 states had separate women's prisons. . . .

On the one hand, there were custodial institutions that corresponded by and large to men's prisons. The purpose of custodial prisons, as the name implies, was to warehouse prisoners. There was no pretense of rehabilitation. On the other hand, there were reformatories that, as the name implies, were intended to be more benevolent institutions that "uplifted" or "improved" the character of the women held there. These reformatories had no male counterparts. Almost every state had a custodial women's prison, but in the Northeast and Midwest the majority of incarcerated women were in reformatories. In the South, the few reformatories that existed were exclusively white. However, these differences are not, in essence, geographical; they are racial. The women in the custodial institutions were Black whether in the North or the South, and had to undergo the most degrading conditions, while it was mainly white women who were sent to the reformatories, institutions that had the ostensible philosophy of benevolence and sisterly and therapeutic ideals.

The Evolution of Separate Custodial Prisons for Women

In the South after 1870, prison camps emerged as penal servitude and were essentially substituted for slavery. The overwhelming majority of women in the prison camps were Black; the few white women who were there had been imprisoned for much more serious offenses, yet experienced better conditions of confinement. For instance, at Bowden Farm in Texas, the majority of women were Black, were there for property offenses, and worked in the field. The few white women who were there had been convicted of homicide and served as domestics. As the techniques of slavery were applied to the penal system, some states forced women to work on the state-owned penal plantations but also leased women to local farms, mines, and railroads. Treatment on the infamous chain gangs was brutal and degrading. For example, women were whipped on the buttocks in the presence of men. They were also forced to defecate right where they worked, in front of men.

An 1880 census indicated that in Alabama, Louisiana, Mississippi, North Carolina, Tennessee, and Texas, 37 percent of the 220 Black women were leased out whereas only 1 of the 40 white women was leased. Testimony in an 1870 Georgia investigation revealed that in one instance "There were no white women there. One started there, and I heard Mr. Alexander (the lessee) say he turned her loose. He was talking to the guard; I was working in the cut. He said his wife was a white woman, and he could not stand it to see a white woman worked in such places." Eventually, as central penitentiaries were built or rebuilt, many women were shipped there from prison farms because they were considered "dead hands" as compared with the men. At first, the most common form of custodial confinement was attachment to male prisons; eventually, independent women's prisons evolved out of these male institutions. These separate women's prisons were established largely for administrative convenience, not reform. Female matrons worked there, but they took their orders from men.

Like the prison camps, custodial women's prisons were overwhelmingly Black, regardless of their location. Although they have always been imprisoned in smaller numbers than African-American or Euro-American men, Black women often constituted larger percentages within female prisons than

Black men did within men's prisons. For instance, between 1797 and 1801, 44 percent of the women sent to New York state prisons were African-Americans as compared to 20 percent of the men. In the Tennessee state prison in 1868, 100 percent of the women were Black, whereas 60 percent of the men were of African descent. The women incarcerated in the custodial prisons tended to be 21 years of age or older. Forty percent were unmarried, and many of them had worked in the past.

Women in custodial prisons were frequently convicted of felony charges; most commonly for "crimes" against property, often petty theft. Only about a third of female felons were serving time for violent crimes. The rates for both property crimes and violent crimes were much higher than for the women at the reformatories. On the other hand, there were relatively fewer women incarcerated in custodial prisons for public order offenses (fornication, adultery, drunkenness, etc.), which were the most common in the reformatories. This was especially true in the South, where these so-called morality offenses by Blacks were generally ignored, and where authorities were reluctant to imprison white women at all. Data from the Auburn, New York, prison on homicide statistics between 1909 and 1933 reveal the special nature of the women's "violent" crimes. Most of the victims of murder by women were adult men. Of 149 victims, two-thirds were male; 29 percent were husbands, 2 percent were lovers, and the rest were listed as "man" or "boy" (a similar distribution exists today). Another form of violent crime resulting in the imprisonment of women was performing "illegal" abortions.

Tennessee Supreme Court records offer additional anecdotal information about the nature of women's violent crimes. Eighteen-year-old Sally Griffin killed her fifty-year-old husband after a fight in which, according to Sally, he knocked her through a window, hit her with a hammer, and threatened to "knock her brains out." A doctor testified that in previous months her husband had seriously injured her ovaries when he knocked her out of bed because she refused to have sex during her period. Sally's conviction stood because an eye-witness said she hadn't been threatened with a hammer. . . .

Southern states were especially reluctant to send white women to prison, so they were deliberately screened out by the judicial process. When white women were sent to prison, it was for homicide or sometimes arson; almost never did larceny result in incarceration. In the Tennessee prison, many of the African-American property offenders had committed less serious offenses than the whites, although they were incarcerated in far greater numbers. Frances Kellor, a renowned prison reformer, remarked of this screening process that the Black female offender "is first a Negro and then a woman—in the whites' estimation." A 1922 North Carolina report describes one institution as being "so horrible that the judge refuses to send white women to this jail, but Negro women are sometimes sent." Hundreds of such instances combined to create institutions overwhelmingly made up of African-American women.

The conditions of these custodial prisons were horrendous, as they were in prisons for men. The southern prisons were by far the worst. They were generally unsanitary, lacking adequate toilet and bathing facilities. Medical attention was rarely available. Women were either left totally idle or forced into hard labor. Women with mental problems were locked in solitary confinement and ignored. . . .

Generally speaking, the higher the proportion of women of color in the prison population, the worse the conditions. Therefore, it is not surprising that the physical conditions of incarceration for women in the custodial prisons were abysmal compared to the reformatories (as the following section indicates). Even in mainly Black penal institutions, Euro-American women were treated better than African-American women.[1]

Early Twentieth Century: Female Reformatories

Reformatories for women developed alongside custodial prisons. These were parallel, but distinct, developments. By the turn of the century, industrialization was in full swing, bringing fundamental changes in social relations: shifts from a rural society to an urban one, from a family to market economy; increased geographic mobility; increased disruption of lives; more life outside the church, family, and community. More production, even for women, was outside the home. By 1910, a record high of at least 27 percent of all women in New York state were "gainfully" employed. Thousands of women worked in the New York sweatshops under abominable conditions.

There was a huge influx of immigration from Southern and Eastern Europe; many of these were Jewish women who had come straight from Czarist Russia and brought with them a tradition of resistance and struggle. The division between social classes was clearly widening and erupted in dynamic labor struggles. For example, in 1909, 20,000 shirt-waist makers, four-fifths of whom were women, went on strike in New York. Racism and national chauvinism were rampant in the United States at the turn of the century in response to the waves of immigrants from Europe and Black people from the South. The Women's Prison Association of New York, which was active in the social purity movement, declared in 1906 that

> if promiscuous immigration is to continue, it devolves upon the enlightened, industrious, and moral citizens, from selfish as well as from philanthropic motives, to instruct the morally defective to conform to our ways and exact from them our own high standard of morality and legitimate industry. . . . Do you want immoral women to walk our streets, pollute society, endanger your households, menace the morals of your sons and daughters . . .? Do you think the women here described fit to become mothers of American citizens? Shall foreign powers generate criminals and dump them on our shores?[2]

Also at the turn of the century various currents of social concern converged to create a new reform effort, the Progressive movement, that swept the country, particularly the Northeast and Midwest, for several decades. It was in this context that reformatories for women proliferated. Reformatories were actually begun by an earlier generation of female reformers who appeared between 1840 and 1900, but their proliferation took place during this Progressive Era as an alternative to the penitentiary's harsh conditions of enforced silence and hard labor. The reformatories came into being as a result of the work of prison reformers who were ostensibly motivated to improve penal treatment for women. They believed that the mixed prisons afforded women no privacy and left them vulnerable to debilitating humiliations.

Indeed, the reformatories were more humane and conditions were better than at the women's penitentiaries (custodial institutions). They did eliminate much male abuse and the fear of attack. They also resulted in more freedom of movement and opened up a variety of opportunities for "men's" work in the operation of the prison. Children of prisoners up to two years old could stay in most institutions. At least some of the reformatories were staffed and administered by women. They usually had cottages, flower gardens, and no fences. They offered discussions on the law, academics, and training, and women were often paroled more readily than in custodial institutions. However, a closer look at who the women prisoners were, the nature of their offenses, and the program to which they were subjected reveals the seamier side of these ostensibly noble institutions.

It is important to emphasize that reformatories existed for women only. No such parallel development took place within men's prisons. There were no institutions devoted to "correcting" men for so-called moral offenses. In fact, such activities were not considered crimes when men engaged in them and therefore men were not as a result imprisoned. A glance at these "crimes" for women only suggests the extent to which society was bent on repressing women's sexuality. Despite the hue and cry about prostitution, only 8.5 percent of the women at the reformatories were actually convicted of prostitution. More than half, however, were imprisoned because of "sexual misconduct." Women were incarcerated in reformatories primarily for various public order offenses or so-called "moral" offenses: lewd and lascivious carriage, stubbornness, idle and disorderly conduct, drunkenness, fornication, serial premarital pregnancies, keeping bad company, adultery, venereal disease, and vagrancy. A woman might face charges simply because a relative disapproved of her behavior and reported her, or because she had been sexually abused and was being punished for it. Most were rebels of some sort.

Jennie B., for instance, was sent to Albion reformatory for five years for having "had unlawful sexual intercourse with young men and remain[ing] at hotels with young men all night, particularly on July 4, 1893." Lilian R. quit school and ran off for one week with a soldier, contracting a venereal disease. She was hospitalized, then sentenced to the reformatory. Other women were convicted of offenses related to exploitation and/or abuse by men. Ann B. became pregnant twice from older men, one of whom was her father, who was sentenced to prison for rape. She was convicted of "running around" when she was seven months pregnant. One woman who claimed to have miscarried and disposed of the fetus had been convicted of murdering her illegitimate child. There was also the increasing practice of abortion that accounted for at least some of the rise in "crime against persons."

As with all prisons, the women in the reformatories were of the working class. Many of them worked outside the home. At New York State's Albion Reformatory, for instance, 80 percent had, in the past, worked for wages. Reformatories were also overwhelmingly institutions for white women. Government statistics indicate that in 1921, for instance, 12 percent of the women in reformatories were Black while 88 percent were white.

Record keeping at the Albion Reformatory in New York demonstrates how unusual it was for Black women to be incarcerated there. The registries left spaces for entries of a large number of variables, such as family history of insanity and epilepsy. Nowhere was there a space for recording race. When African Americans were admitted, the clerk penciled "colored" at the top of the page. African-American women were much less likely to be arrested for such public order offenses. Rafter suggests that Black women were not expected to act like "ladies" in the first place and therefore were reportedly not deemed worthy of such rehabilitation.

The program of these institutions, as well as the offenses, was based on patriarchal assumptions. Reformatory training centered on fostering ladylike behavior and perfecting housewifely skills. In this way it encouraged dependency and women's subjugation. Additionally, one aspect of the retraining of these women was to isolate them, to strip them of environmental influences in order to instill them with new values. To this end, family ties were obstructed, which is somewhat ironic since the family is at the center of the traditional role of women. Letters might come every two months and were censored. Visits were allowed four times a year for those who were on the approved list. The reformatories were geographically remote, making it very difficult for loved ones to visit. Another thorn in the rosy picture of the reformatory was the fact that sentencing was often open-ended. This was an outgrowth of the rehabilitative ideology. The incarceration was not of fixed length because the notion was that a woman would stay for as long as it took to accomplish the task of reforming her.

Parole was also used as a patriarchal weapon. Ever since the Civil War, there was a scarcity of white working-class women for domestic service. At the same time, the "need for good help" was increasing because more people could afford to hire help. It was not an accident that women were frequently paroled into domestic jobs, the only ones for which they had been trained. In this way, vocational regulation went hand-in-hand with social control, leading always backwards to home and hearth, and away from self-sufficiency and independence. Additionally, independent behavior was punished by revoking parole for "sauciness," obscenity, or failure to work hard enough. One woman was cited for a parole violation for running away from a domestic position to join a theater troupe; another for going on car rides with men; still others for becoming pregnant, going around with a disreputable married man, or associating with the father of her child. And finally, some very unrepentant women were ultimately transferred indefinitely to asylums for the "feeble-minded."

Prison reform movements have been common; a reform movement also existed for men. However, all these institutions were inexorably returned to the role of institutions of social control. Understanding this early history can prepare us to understand recent developments in women's imprisonment and indeed imprisonment in general. Although the reformatories rejected the more traditional authoritarian penal regimes, they were nonetheless concerned with social control. Feminist criminologists claim that in their very inception, reformatories were institutions of patriarchy. They were part of a broad attack on young working-class women who were attempting to lead somewhat more autonomous lives. Women's sexual independence was being curbed in the context of "social purity" campaigns. As more and more white working-class women left home for the labor force, they took up smoking, frequenting dance halls, and having sexual relationships. Prostitution had long been a source of income for poor women, but despite the fact that prostitution had actually begun to wane about 1900, there was a major morality crusade at the turn of the century that attacked prostitution as well as all kinds of small deviations from the standard of "proper" female propriety.

Even when the prisons were run by women, they were, of course, still doing the work of a male supremacist prison system and society. We have seen how white working-class women were punished for "immoral behavior" when men were not. We have seen how they were indoctrinated with a program of "ladylike" behavior. According to feminist criminologists such as Nicole Hahn Rafter and Estelle Freedman, reformatories essentially punished those who did not conform to bourgeois definitions of femininity and prescribed gender roles. The prisoners were to embrace the social values, although, of course, never to occupy the social station of a "lady." It is relevant to note that the social stigma of imprisonment was even greater for women than men because women were supposedly denying their own "pure nature." This stigma plus the nature of the conditions of incarceration served as a warning to all such women to stay within the proper female sphere.

These observations shed some light on the role of "treatment" within penal practice. Reformatories were an early attempt at "treatment," that is, the uplifting and improvement of the women, as opposed to mere punishment or retribution. However, these reforms were also an example of the subservience of "treatment" to social control. They demonstrate that the underlying function of control continually reasserts itself when attempts to "improve" people take place within a coercive framework. The reformatories are an illustration of how sincere efforts at reform may only serve to broaden the net and extend the state's power of social control. In fact, hundreds and hundreds of women were incarcerated for public order offenses who previously would not have been vulnerable to the punishment of confinement in a state institution were it not for the existence of reformatories.

By 1935, the custodial prisons for women and the reformatories had basically merged. In the 1930s, the United States experienced the repression of radicalism, the decline of the progressive and feminist movements, and the Great Depression. Along with these changes came the demise of the reformatories. The prison reform movement had achieved one of its earliest central aims, separate prisons for women. The reformatory buildings still stood and were filled with prisoners. However, these institutions were reformatories in name only. Some were administered by women, but they were women who did not even have the progressive pretenses of their predecessors. The conditions of incarceration had deteriorated miserably, suffering from cutbacks and lack of funding.

Meanwhile, there had been a slow but steady transformation of the inmate population. Increasingly, the white women convicted of misdemeanors were given probation, paroled, or sent back to local jails. As Euro-American women left the reformatories, the buildings themselves were transformed into custodial prisons, institutions that repeated the terrible conditions of the past. As custodial prison buildings were physically closed down for various reasons, felons were transferred to the buildings that had housed the reformatories. Most of the women were not only poor but also were Black. African-American women were increasingly incarcerated there with the growth of the Black migration north after World War I. These custodial institutions now included some added negative dimensions as the legacy of the reformatories, such as the strict reinforcement of gender roles and the infantilization of women. In the end, the reformatories were certainly not a triumph for the women's liberation. Rather, they can be viewed as one of many instances in which U.S. institutions are able to absorb an apparent reform and use it for continuing efforts at social control. . . .

Prison Resistance

One topic that has not been adequately researched is the rebellion and resistance of women in prison. It is only with great difficulty that any information was found. We do not believe that is because resistance does not occur, but rather because those in charge of documenting history have a stake in burying this herstory. Such a herstory would challenge the patriarchal ideology that insists that women are, by nature, passive and docile. What we do know is that as far back as 1943 there was a riot in Sing Sing Prison in New York, which was the first woman's prison. It took place in response to overcrowding and inadequate facilities.

During the Civil War, Georgia's prison was burned down, allegedly torched by women trying to escape. It was again burned down in 1900. In 1888, similar activity took place at Framingham, Massachusetts, although reports refer to it as merely "fun." Women rebelled at New York's Hudson House of Refuge in response to excessive punishment. They forced the closing of "the dungeon," basement cells and a diet of bread and water. Within a year, similar cells were reinstituted. The story of Bedford Hills is a particularly interesting one. From 1915 to 1920 there were a series of rebellions against cruelty to inmates. The administration had refused to segregate Black and white women up until 1916, and reports of the time attribute these occurrences to the "unfortunate attachments formed by white women for the Negroes." A 1931 study indicated that "colored girls" revolted against discrimination at the New Jersey State Reformatory.

Around the time of the historic prison rebellion at Attica Prison in New York State, rebellions also took place at women's prisons. In 1971, there was a work stoppage at Alderson simultaneous with the rebellion at Attica. In June of 1975, the women at the North Carolina Correctional Center for Women staged a five-day demonstration "against oppressive working atmospheres, inaccessible and inadequate medical facilities and treatment, and racial discrimination, and many other conditions at the prison." Unprotected, unarmed women were attacked by male guards armed with riot gear. The women sustained physical injuries and miscarriages as well as punitive punishment in lockup and in segregation, and illegal transfers to the Mattawan State Hospital for the Criminally Insane. . . .

This short exposition of the rebellions in women's prisons is clearly inadequate. Feminist criminologists and others should look towards the need for a detailed herstory of this thread of the women's experience in America.

Conclusion

We began this research in an attempt to understand the ways that patriarchy and white supremacy interact in the imprisonment of women. We looked at the history of the imprisonment of women in the United States and found that it has always been different for white women and African-American women. This was most dramatically true in the social control of white women, geared toward turning them into "ladies." This was a more physically benign prison track than the custodial prisons that contained Black women or men. But it was insidiously patriarchal, both in this character and in the fact that similar institutions did not exist to control men's behavior in those areas. We also saw that historically the more "Black" the penal institution, the

worse the conditions. It is difficult to understand how this plays out within the walls of prisons today since there are more sophisticated forms of tracking. That is, within a given prison there are levels of privileges that offer a better or worse quality of life. Research is necessary to determine how this operates in terms of white and African-American female prisoners. However, we can hypothesize that as women's prisons become increasingly Black institutions, conditions will, as in the past, come more and more to resemble the punitive conditions of men's prisons. . . .

Although the percentage of women in prison is still very low compared to men, the rates are rapidly rising. And when we examine the conditions of incarceration, it does appear as if the imprisonment of women is coming more and more to resemble that of men in the sense that there is no separate, more benign, track for women. Now more than ever, women are being subjected to more maximum-security, control units, shock incarceration; in short, everything negative that men receive. We thus may be looking at the beginning of a new era in the imprisonment of women. One observation that is consistent with these findings is that the purpose of prisons for women may not be to function primarily as institutions of patriarchal control. That is, their mission as instruments of social control of people of color generally may be the overriding purpose. Turning women into "ladies" or "feminizing" women is not the essence of the mission of prisons. Warehousing and punishment are now enough, for women as well as men.

This is not to suggest that the imprisonment of women is not replete with sexist ideology and practices. It is a thoroughly patriarchal society that sends women to prison; that is, the rules and regulations, the definition of crimes are defined by the patriarchy. This would include situations in which it is "okay" for a husband to beat up his wife, but that very same wife cannot defend herself against his violence; in which women are forced to act as accessories to crimes committed by men; in which abortion is becoming more and more criminalized. Once in prison, patriarchal assumptions and male dominance continue to play an essential role in the treatment of women. As discussed previously, women have to deal with a whole set of factors that men do not, from intrusion by male guards to the denial of reproductive rights. Modern day women's imprisonment has taken on the worst aspects of the imprisonment of men. But it is also left with the sexist legacy of the reformatories and the contemporary structures of the patriarchy. Infantilization and the reinforcement of passivity and dependency are woven into the very fabric of the incarceration of women.

The imprisonment of women of color can be characterized by the enforcement of patriarchy in the service of the social control of people of color as a whole. This raises larger questions about the enormous attacks aimed at family life in communities of color, in which imprisonment of men, women, and children plays a significant role. However, since this area of inquiry concerns the most disenfranchised elements of our society, it is no wonder that so little attention is paid to dealing with this desperate situation. More research in this area is needed as there are certainly unanswered questions. But we must not wait for this research before we begin to unleash our energies to dismantle a prison system that grinds up our sisters.

NOTES

1. Estelle B. Freedman, *Their Sisters' Keepers: Women's Prison Reform in America, 1830–1930* (Ann Arbor: University of Michigan Press, 1981). Ch. 4, note 44.
2. Nicole Hahn Rafter, *Partial Justice: Women in State Prisons 1800–1935* (Boston: New England University Press, 1985), pp. 93–94.

FIFTY

◆◆◆

Prison Life: A Day

Marilyn Buck

Marilyn Buck describes herself as a political prisoner, activist, poet, and artist. Currently serving an eighty-year sentence in the Federal Correctional Institution, Dublin (California), she has completed her bachelors degree in psychology from prison, as well as becoming an accomplished potter. Recipient of the 2001 PEN Prison Writing Program poetry prize, she is involved in cultural and educational activities for women prisoners.

Don't let your throat tighten with fear. Take sips of breath all day and night. Before death closes your mouth.—Jalaluddin Rumi

The seemingly normal routine life behind the walls is more than sufficiently punishing and corrosive. When I awake, I do not shudder with fear to face another day of extreme measures; instead, I worry more about becoming more inured to the casual cruelty that prevails. It lures us into becoming the very creatures the prison system advertises us to be and robs us of our humanity. I worry about succumbing, losing my will to resist dehumanization, and ultimately, losing my own sense of who I am as a human being.

What is normal and routine about this world would be a nightmare to one who has not had to experience such indignity and lack of control over one's self. Prison is a parallel world to the "outside." Only if one has lived in a Black community, under martial law in Puerto Rico (or in other parts of the world), survived military invasions, or been held as a virtual hostage in an abusive, battering relationship, might one have an idea of what it is like to live in conditions where your every word and action is subject to censorship, control, punishment, and even possible torture by guards hired to watch and secure you. Most new prisoners walk around in a state of shock, fear, and uncertainty. The new prisoner is alternatively on the verge of tears or filled with rage at the way she is treated by the guards and "administrators." She cannot believe that she has so few rights and that there is no due process when a guard tells her that she must do as he or she says or suffer the consequences. Even to be transferred to another prison causes a similar, though less intense, response. One must learn to negotiate the unfamiliar minefield—the personalities and boundaries of the prison guards as well as those of the prisoners, each of whom is arduously negotiating each day.

At 5:30 I rise, still tired from being awakened during the night by flashlights in my eyes during three "morning-shift" counts. After the 5:00 count, I finally stumble out of bed into the cold dankness of the cell, three steps to the toilet. I move to the sink to wash my face, trying to open the metal locker without great screeching (so as not to wake my cellmates), both women younger than my own children would be. One moans at the sound of the flushing toilet, the creaking locker, and the water dripping into the sink. Already I feel anxiety, knowing that I am disrupting her sleep and that she will jump up in a moment exasperated and frustrated. I know how it feels not to be able to sleep because of constant intrusions—loud voices, metal doors clanging, and cellmates who live on a different schedule.

I am fortunate that both my cellmates are considerate; we all get along in this space built for one prisoner. But the constant attention to consideration creates a tension—an artificial politeness—as well as the vigilance of constantly moving out of each other's way, predicting the next move, like playing in a championship tennis tournament and trying to determine where the ball will land.

At 6:00 AM the officer begins screeching over the loudspeaker. Names and commands blare out. My ears strain to hear whether my name is being called. I am on constant alert; I feel like Pavlov's dog waiting for a bell—or an electrical shock. Even though I am aware of the phenomenon and resist it, I am subject to it. Every interaction— conversation, reading, even thinking—is subject to this harsh intrusion. Concentration flees. The act of being on alert—hypervigilant—almost 24 hours per day wreaks havoc on my nervous system.

I make a phone call. The person on the line stops, aware that I am distracted—the guards are calling out names. I have to ask my caller to speak louder so that I can hear over the constant din of voices and background noise. Morning is the quietest time; I have managed to work in the afternoons and evenings in order to have some moments of relative quiet in which I might concentrate and read or write.

Thinking is a luxury. Most of my thought processes have retreated below the conscious level. Someone is hollering that the iron is dirty, and who is the trifling @#%^* who messed it up? Oh, to be like Buddha beneath the tree becoming enlightened. But he did not have to function in this world. He had the choice to get up at any moment.

I sit down to write; I look for what I need in a pile of papers. There is no place to store materials or books. We are permitted by policy to have five books. An hour of intermittent silence; the loud speaker intrudes only once. The fire alarm goes off at 9:05 AM. I sigh and hurriedly grab a book, water, and jacket. Is this one more false alarm set off by someone smoking, or is it to be a unit shakedown in which we will be exiled to the yard for hours and hours? (I'm glad I am dressed, a habit of mine to be prepared, not to be caught off guard.) The guard announces, "Clear the unit!" Another comes banging on doors, "Everyone outdoors! Now!"

Women file out doors opened only in emergencies. Many are still in their nightclothes. They are among those who have contrived to sleep their days away. Most are very young, 20–25 years old. We stand outside in the chill wind. The alarm continues to blare, raking my eardrums. The smokers light up. I move further away from the crowd to avoid the press of bodies. Lieutenants stride purposefully through the crowd into the building.

Ten minutes pass. No order to leave the area. Relief. Today will not be a shakedown. Today I will not have to spend hours reorganizing my pitiful few possessions. I might still get something accomplished before work.

The Lieutenant walks out the door screaming, "You must stand behind the yellow line!" Two sisters who are deaf and mute remain standing where they were along with several others who do not understand English and have not been here long enough to know that until everyone moves across the plain yellow line we will be forced to remain standing. Another woman, closer to the "offenders" goes and pulls them gently across the line. I am irritated at the whole show. I also realize that I'm irritated at those women who don't move. I am irritated at myself for being exasperated at the other women even though I understand that some have not moved as their own personal act of rebellion. I, too, have done that and may do so in some other situation in order to retain some modicum of my own power. Six more minutes pass. Everyone is now behind the line. The Lieutenant strides out through the crowd, ignoring us. Resentment hovers over us. Finally, a guard walks out to say, "You can return now."

At 10:45 AM women come speed walking by from UNICOR, on their way to lunch.[1] By 11:30–11:45, my unit is released to lunch. We are "out last" this week because we were ranked last in the sanitation and safety inspection. One of the orderlies/workers did not have her steel-toed boots on when cleaning labels off plastic bottles with a toothbrush and bucket of water. A collective punishment for a petty procedural offense.

I have stood waiting at the front door to get out of the unit among the first in order not to stand long in the line. Even so, as I stand in line, ten women come racing by to cut. I say something to the woman who cuts in front of me. She swings her hair and moves in front of her friend, looking back at me, a challenge in her eyes. It's not worth the energy—but I am exasperated. I never get used to such lack of regard among the women. The lines are long, but we're all anxious not to spend one minute longer than necessary in any given line.

Once inside, before I can get into the line there, the Lieutenant stops me, "Button your shirt! Take off your sunglasses!" I button my shirt perturbed by the ridiculousness of the rule. But it is a direct order. After all, I am wearing a tee shirt beneath my uniform shirt. I do not look provocative. . . I do not remove my sunglasses, telling the Lieutenant that they are prescription lenses. He already knows that, but says, "Let me see your eyes!" I sigh; do I really want to eat? I have made it this far.

I get my tray. Before me is a scene not unlike Times Square at rush hour. Too many people in too little space. The women on the serving line are all ill humored by this time; the vegetables are steamed beyond recognition, and the cantaloupe is gone. Only apples, the ever present last year's apples. I look out on the floor. Against a low wall stand a number of the suited administrators: warden, bureaucrats, and department heads. Their policy is to be available to the prisoner population to listen to requests, problems. Most carry a small notebook into which they may write the prisoner's name, then smile and say, "We'll look into it." I move into the fray. There is a line to get water, a line to get soup, a free-for-all to get a few wilted salad greens already picked over. If one waits for the salad bar to clear out, one will never get anything. She who gets there first gets the tomato or the potato salad. I move off to find a place to sit, jockeying with my tray in order not to end up with it in my chest or on someone else. There are 300–400 women in this area. Some have left, thank goodness. Others could not face the dining room today.

I eat then juggle my way out carefully. I avoid getting pat searched—a daily gauntlet to run, which is done ostensibly to prevent women from taking even a slice of bread from the dining room. I do not have any "contraband," but recoil at being patted down—felt up—by some female or even male guard. Eighteen years in prison has not inured me to the invasive violations of hands that assert the right to paw on my body.

Now I must hurry back to the unit to pick up my work materials and a bottle of water, which is, I hope, less toxic than that in the tap. Off to work. The loudspeaker sounds, "The yard is closed. Return to your work site." We have ten minutes on the half hour to move from one area to another. A Lieutenant is yelling at some woman across the yard to turn around and return to wherever she came from. The woman is pleading her case. I hurry and make it across without an encounter. The Education Department is a relatively safe place to work unless the "suits" or a guard brings a tour through—new guard recruits, visiting prison officials (like the officials from the People's Republic of China who were escorted through proudly a few years ago by higher-ranking U.S. Bureau of Prison officials). We go about our business. We are not anxious to engage in conversation with tour-types. We are not saleswomen for the criminal justice system.

I work as the correspondence clerk in the Vocational Training area (where computer training is given). I work with those few women who are able to pay for college correspondence courses, or other distance-learning courses and take care of the "paperwork" involved in documenting prisoner activities for my supervisor. Both the supervisors in VT are interested in women gaining skills in order to get work that will sustain them economically once they are released. That interest is rare inside prison walls. One can feel nearly like an efficacious human being here, except of course for the endemic male supremacy. A main perk of working here is that, as in the rest of the Education Department, the loudspeaker does not penetrate. It is usually quiet.

At 3:30 PM, we wait for the last students to leave so that we, the prisoner clerks may also return to the units for the nationwide, official 4:00 PM standing count.[2] Back to the unit. The guard is yelling on the loudspeaker, "Clear the unit, go to your rooms." I try to get a cup of hot water for coffee before the unit is cleared. Success. I exhale and whisper-chat with one cellmate; the other is lying down. A few minutes later the loudspeaker blares, "Stand up for the count." We strain to hear which unit they will count first. If we can't discern the distorted sounds clearly, we sit tensely, waiting to leap up at the sound of approaching keys, or we stand, waiting for 15–20 minutes.

After the count, there is a visible lessening of tension. Most of the "suits" are gone. Even the evening shift guards are somewhat less tense. The loudspeaker continues to invade, haranguing someone to go somewhere—all evening long, incessantly. "Mail call" is the one welcome announcement. Since we are "out last," we must wait nearly an hour before being released from the unit to pursue evening duties, activities, and have dinner. It is our unit's day to go to commissary. At last the door does open, and the mad rush begins. "No running!" Women stop running to walk fast. Do I have time to eat before my number is called? Yes, I rush to the dining hall, get through the line relatively quickly, and gulp down my food. I do not want to miss my number. I need soap and tea. I rush out to find my number hasn't been called yet. Relief. Now, how much longer? I have to go back to work, so I'm feeling pressed. Finally I shop and hurry back to my unit to drop off my commissary, hoping no one decides to come into my cell and make off with my bag. I don't have time to put it away. Off to work. At 8:30 VT closes.

I rush back to the unit to sign up for laundry—it's our tier's evening to sign up for the next day, an improvement from years of dashing at 5:30 AM to try to get a space. I get a wash time when I can actually wash. Now I dash to try to get a shower before the 9:15 PM call for count. Fortunately, only one woman stands in line before me. On my way back to my cell from the shower, I check to see whether a phone call will be possible. No, a line there too.

Once we are locked in for the count, I do not leave the cell again. I lay down to read the news from several days earlier. I try to relax and go to sleep. Hopefully, after 10:00 PM, the loudspeaker will fall silent. Barring a fire alarm or a guard waking me to give a urine sample, I will get a full night's rest.

NOTES

1. UNICOR is the acronym for Federal Prison Industries. It is a highly profitable set of factories from data processing to furniture-making, military supplies, etc. Prisoners are paid "third-world" wages, $1.10/hour is the highest wage. Women compete to work there, as it is the only source of income for most prisoners. With this small wage, they can sustain themselves and perhaps send some money home to their families.

2. Every prisoner must be standing upright at this count unless one has the proper medical approval not to do so.

FIFTY-ONE

◆◆◆

Creative Politics and Women's Criminalization in the United States (2008)

Carol Jacobsen

Carol Jacobsen is an award-winning artist whose works in video and photography address issues of women's criminalization and censorship. Her work has been exhibited and screened at prestigious venues worldwide and by many U.S. grassroots organizations. She teaches art and women's studies at the University of Michigan and directs the Michigan Women's Justice and Clemency Project, a nonprofit organization that seeks freedom for women incarcerated for killing their abusers in self-defense.

I began working on issues of women's criminalization in the early 1980s when I made the connection between my own sense of shame, stigma, and guilt about my past and so many women's experiences—abortion, rape, lesbian identity, and prostitution—that were punished by the state. I had been discouraged, even ridiculed, in graduate school for my efforts to combine art and politics. But after spending a year in Europe, I was electrified by the creative politics of Greenham Common Women's Peace Camp outside London (Jacobsen 1986).[1] I had visited the camp around the North Atlantic Treaty Organization (NATO) base and sat through jaw-dropping trials of women being prosecuted for disturbing the peace. They were like scenes out of Monty Python: the women on trial ruled over the blustering, white-wigged men who could not control the courtrooms. . . . Returning to the United States, I was anxious to work with artists and writers in other politically active communities, so I joined Political Artists Documentation and Distribution (PADD), Heresies, Window Peace, Ceres, and other groups in New York where I felt my work could expand and contribute to a larger cultural conversation.

When my grassroots documentaries on street workers in Detroit caught the attention of a prisoners' advocate in the late 1980s, I was asked to produce a short film on the women's prison in Michigan.[2] I was both eager and apprehensive to go inside and continue my work on prostitutes' rights. But once inside, I was stunned. I discovered who the so-called murderers were in our U.S. women's prisons; many, if not most, were women who had acted in self-defense against an abuser (see Browne 1987, 10–11).

At age seventeen, I, too, had married a batterer and had broken the law (some would call it murder) to get out alive. I'd had an illegal abortion. I was lucky: I did not die, and I was not arrested or prosecuted for my crime. I had friends and family who hid me for months until the batterer's stalking ended. And so, inside the prison, in the faces and stories of these women, I saw myself.

In the prison, I also saw vividly the crushing domination that extends from the domestic to the criminal justice sphere, from individual men to the sexualized violence of the punishment industry, and realized it had only suppressed these women's resistance, not killed it.[3] Like the sex workers I'd been working with, these inmates were survivors: women who had saved their own, and often their children's, lives. They were not heroines, but they were not vigilantes either. I was determined to make a film that would bring them close up, face-to-face with public audiences. I wanted those audiences to feel what I felt and to see and hear, as I did, women narrating their own social critiques of the systems that failed them—that fail us all (*From One Prison* . . . 1994).

I knew from raw experience that it could be me sitting in prison alongside these women. Historically, wife beating was not illegal, and police and courts are still unwilling to hold batterers responsible for their violent acts (Gillespie 1989, 22; Schneider 2000, 181; Buel 2003, 229–35). Judges, prosecutors, defense attorneys, and jurors all bring to any trial an astonishing degree of incompetence, as well as myths and stereotypes about battered women, that prevent individual women from receiving fair trials based on the facts of their cases (Buel 2003, 217–23). Battered women who were tried prior to the early 1990s were rarely allowed to present evidence of abuse at all.[4]

Growing up in Jackson, Michigan, in the shadow of the world's largest walled prison also alerted me to the horror that, today, we all live in the shadow of a prison in the world's most incarcerated country (International Centre for Prison Studies 2005). The punishment industry is a toxic consequence of the mutual complicity between politicians and the corporate media, which have traded on public fear for their own elections and profits, as both Joseph Hallinan (2001, xvi–xvii) and Meda Chesney-Lind (1997, 6–9) have pointed out. In the war on crime and drugs, women have suffered disproportionately despite the fact that there has been no dramatic shift in women's share of violent crime (Chesney-Lind 1997, 118–19). And through an endless recycling of mythologies disconnected from context, mainstream news and documentaries have demonized human beings who are in prison, yet the reality is very different, especially for women (Chesney-Lind 1997, 151; Zimmerman 2000).

Fully 70–80 percent of women in prison are single heads of households serving time for nonviolent, poverty-induced crimes (Chesney-Lind 1997, 158, 179; ACLU n.d.). Two-thirds are women of color, although they do not commit more crimes than white women, and most are poor, although they do not commit more crimes than those of the middle or upper classes (ACLU n.d.). They are struggling to support their children, their dreams, and their habits the best they can in an unequal and unjust society, and their economic circumstances deny them access to effective, paid defense attorneys (Chesney-Lind 1997, 6–9; Buel 2003). Most come from backgrounds of incest or other physical and/or sexual abuse and attribute their incarceration to their association with a batterer (Chesney-Lind 1997, 3, 108–11; Schneider 2000, 265 n. 8; Buel 2003, 219). Many would not be there at all if they were men because far fewer drug treatment, tether (electronic monitoring devices placed on ankles to track persons rather than incarcerate them), and halfway-house programs are available to women and because gender-based crimes (e.g., prostitution or bad checks written to support children whose fathers are not held accountable by the law) provide easy arrests for police who are manipulating the system (Pearl 1987; Chesney-Lind 1997, 149–52, 169). Once in prison, women face more abuse: sexual assault by guards, medical neglect, and harassment and retaliation for filing complaints against staff (Chesney-Lind 1997, 4; Human Rights Watch 1998; Amnesty International 1999).

In 1991 Susan Fair, an activist and former prisoner, founded the Michigan Battered Women's Clemency Project. She guided me through the bureaucracy of the Department of Corrections so that I could interview and film again inside Michigan's two facilities for women. The women trusted me because they trusted Susan, and over the years I built many strong and lasting relationships with them. But the work has not been without costs and controversies. Petty censors threatened to end the filming on a regular basis: guards jumped in front of the camera and made me erase shots; deputies threatened to kick me out for asking questions about corruption; a warden seized my footage and sent it to the state; the state refused my requests for public information on the basis that I was a "controversial figure"; and the Department of Corrections demanded to see my first film before it was finished (I ignored the letter on advice from the American Civil Liberties Union). I gathered as many hours of footage as quickly as I could during those years before I began editing and distribution. . . .

By the mid-1990s, Michigan's governor had issued a media ban and severe visitor restrictions on all Michigan prisons; cameras and taping devices were not allowed inside at all. I continued to go inside, however, as a legal assistant, since I work on women's cases and write clemency petitions, and I have found other ways to visually document the stories and the human rights abuses occurring inside, which remain largely invisible to the general public. In 2000 I made a film with a woman who had spent months chained down in the segregation unit at Scott Prison (*Segregation Unit* 2000). She sued the State of Michigan for torture and won a settlement. She gave me (and NBC, Court TV, and Senator John Conyers) the video footage that was

shot by guards of her repeated chaining and being gassed with pepper spray, and she narrated the film. The footage is terrifying, and she has continued to speak out courageously about the cruelties of four-point chaining (Whitcomb 1999; *Segregation Unit* 2000).

The media blackout was the result of investigations of human rights violations in Michigan's women's prisons by Amnesty International, the U.S. Justice Department, Human Rights Watch, and the United Nations, and also of lawsuits filed by courageous women inmates. The reports and lawsuits documented rampant abuse: sexual assault, harassment and retaliation by male guards, medical neglect, chaining, and other atrocities.[5]

Since 1995 I have directed the Clemency Project, working together with Fair, feminist attorneys Lynn D'Orio and Lore Rogers, and many skilled volunteers. My films, installations, and photography serve as organizing, recruiting, and public education tools for the project. They are also shown in traditional art venues such as galleries, museums, and theaters. They are narrated by the women inmates, my voice in theirs, theirs in mine. The process of filmmaking becomes a commitment to speak publicly, together, for the promise of justice that was denied them and so many others. Visually, the works combine portraits, mug shots, voices, original court and police documents, and texts, often in black and white (*Convicted: A Prison Diary* 2006).

The Clemency Project has repeatedly presented, revised, and resubmitted petitions for twenty-six women and has also filed appeals, supported paroles, protested human rights violations, and consulted and represented many more women in and out of court. Over the years, several women have died, and one committed suicide. In 1998–99 we freed two women from life sentences through motions for relief from judgment in court.[6] Those victories were sweet, though too few. We have filed similar motions for more women, but without success. We have assisted a number of women in obtaining paroles on their earliest possible release date, a small victory in a state where the parole board is noted for its history of denying paroles and feeding the bloated prison industry.[7] We have more than seventy-five women on our waiting list, more than one hundred in our rejected file, and another hundred needing research. Many cases deserve attention but cannot be directly linked to domestic violence.

While clemency remains the last hope of redress for many battered women, recent studies have shown that the number of clemencies has declined across the country as governors have become more cowardly about taking actions that do not promote their own political interests (Kobil 2003). However, after almost two decades, we are seeing signs of change in the parole board's pattern of denial and in the governor's appointment of a new clemency board. It is, ironically, the near bankruptcy of our state that is forcing these actions, though we will celebrate every woman's release no less when it comes.

The frustration of banging my head against the seemingly immutable walls of a closed system that is built on so much cruelty and corruption cannot be measured. Yet walking away is not an option. Not when I know the dirty details and indignities that are thrust upon women in the courts and prisons every day. And not when I can imagine, as Angela Davis does, that a system so (white-wigged and) obsolete must one day give way to the power of humanity and compassionate alternatives (Davis 2003). In recent efforts the Clemency Project submitted twelve petitions to Michigan Governor Jennifer Granholm, consulted on several current cases awaiting trial, documented and protested a number of torture incidents (four-point chaining of the mentally ill, sexual assault, serious injuries, and other cruelties) at Scott Prison, and published a three-year study showing bias against battered women homicide defendants in one Michigan county.[8] We are also researching and working on other strategies to challenge violence and gender subordination in the criminal-legal system, which includes developing legislation similar to California's habeas corpus law that would allow battered women prisoners to apply for parole and altering sentencing guidelines to mitigate the sentences of women whose crimes are precipitated by domestic violence (Adams 2004). We continue to hold rallies at the state capitol each fall; organize campaigns each spring; collaborate with legislators, judges, reporters, nonprofit organizations, and policy makers; and give lectures, hold screenings, and distribute films narrated by women prisoners that reach audiences worldwide. As a teacher, I find that students are eager to know about women's criminalization and prison politics, so it is exciting to integrate these topics into my art and women's studies and human rights courses. As an artist, making issues of women's criminalization, past and present, visible in emotionally arresting ways to ever-widening audiences is a necessary antidote to my howling rage at such persistent injustice. Ultimately, the rewards of sharing passion and work and hope for change with so many indomitable feminists situated on both sides of the law are immeasurable, too.

NOTES

I wish to gratefully acknowledge my colleagues, Joanne Leonard, Peg Lourie, and Lora Lempert, for their contributions to this essay, and my partners in this struggle, Lynn D'Orio, Susan Fair, and Lore Rogers.

1. Women from all over the world occupied camps encircling the NATO base at Greenham Common for about a decade in protest against nuclear weapons. The British government bulldozed their campsites over and over to get rid of them. In 1982, four hundred women appeared in court with affidavits declaring Greenham their home and demanded the right to vote there. They were awarded residency.

2. For a filmography, see http://www.umich.edu/~iinet/cics/humanrights/PDFs/jacobsen-filmograpy.pdf.

3. Angela Y. Davis discusses the use of sexualized violence as a means of social control (2005, 15). Contrary to popular belief, battered women engage in a range of resistance behaviors within the oppressive structures that shape their choices, from calming the batterer to calling police or leaving (Schneider 2000, 83–86).

4. In a study of one urban county in Michigan during the late 1980s, the Clemency Project found that victims of domestic violence who had killed their abusers received higher conviction rates and longer sentences than all other homicide defendants (Jacobsen, Mizga, and D'Orio 2007). In the early 1990s a number of states passed laws allowing evidence and expert testimony on battered woman's syndrome (first identified in Walker 1979) to be presented at trial. In Michigan, the Court of Appeals ruled that this evidence would be allowed at trial in *People v. Wilson,* 487 N.W. 2d 822, 825 (Mich. Ct. App. 1992).

5. See Human Rights Watch 1998; Amnesty International 1999; *Nunn v. Michigan Department of Corrections,* Civil Action No. 96-CV-71416-DT, U.S. District Court for the Eastern District of Michigan; *United States of America v. State of Michigan, et al.,* Civil Action No. 97-CV-71514, U.S. District Court for the Eastern District of Michigan Southern Division.

6. Violet Allen was freed after serving twenty-two years for shooting her husband in defense of her baby, and Juanita Thomas had served nineteen years for the stabbing death of her violent boyfriend. For a discussion of the legal investigation in the campaign to free Thomas, see Lyon, Hughes, and Thomas (2001). The Clemency Project has not gained any releases through clemency.

7. Michigan spends the highest proportion of its general fund on corrections of any state in the nation: 21.5 percent (National Association of State Budget Officers 2006, 60).

8. See Jacobsen, Mizga, and D'Orio 2007; letter to U.S. Justice Department, September 17, 2006, on file with the author; and summaries of the women's cases currently represented by the Clemency Project at http://www.umich.edu/~clemency.

REFERENCES

Adams, Jill E. 2004. "Unlocking Liberty: Is California's Habeas Law the Key to Freeing Unjustly Imprisoned Battered Women?" *Berkeley Women's Law Journal* 19(1):217–45.

ACLU (American Civil Liberties Union). n.d. "Women in Prison: An Overview." http://www.aclu.org/womens-rights/violence/25829res20060612.html.

Amnesty International. 1999. *Not Part of My Sentence: Violations of the Human Rights of Women in Custody.* Washington, DC: Amnesty International.

Browne, Angela. 1987. *When Battered Women Kill.* New York: Free Press.

Buel, Sarah M. 2003. "Effective Assistance of Counsel for Battered Women Defendants: A Normative Construct." *Harvard Women's Law Journal* 26 (Spring): 217–350.

Chesney-Lind, Meda. 1997. *The Female Offender: Girls, Women, and Crime.* Thousand Oaks, CA: Sage.

Convicted: A Prison Diary. 2006. Directed by Carol Jacobsen. Independently produced.

Davis, Angela Y. 2003. *Are Prisons Obsolete?* New York: Seven Stories.

———. 2005. *Abolition Democracy: Beyond Empire, Prisons, and Torture.* New York: Seven Stories.

From One Prison. . . . 1994. Directed by Carol Jacobsen. Independently produced.

Gillespie, Cynthia K. 1989. *Justifiable Homicide: Battered Women, Self-Defense, and the Law.* Columbus: Ohio State University Press.

Hallinan, Joseph T. 2001. *Going up the River: Travels in a Prison Nation.* New York: Random House.

Human Rights Watch. 1998. "Nowhere to Hide: Retaliation against Women in Michigan State Prisons." Human Rights Watch Reports 10(2). http://www.hrw.org/reports98/women/.

International Centre for Prison Studies. 2005. "Entire World: Prison Population Rates per 100,000 of the National Population." International Centre for Prison Studies, King's College, University of London. http://www.kcl.ac.uk/depsta/rel/icps/home.html.

Jacobsen, Carol. 1986. "Peace by Piece: The Creative Politics of Greenham Common Women's Peace Camp." *Heresies* 6(20):60–64.

Kobil, Daniel T. 2003. "How to Grant Clemency in Unforgiving Times." *Capital University Law Review* 31(2):219–41.

Lyon, Andrea D., Emily Hughes, and Juanita Thomas. 2001. "The People v. Juanita Thomas: A Battered Woman's Journey to Freedom." *Women and Criminal Justice* 13(1):27–64.

National Association of State Budget Officers. 2006. "2005 State Expenditure Report." Washington, DC: National Association of State Budget Officers. http://www.nasbo.org/Publications/PDFs/2005%20State%20Expenditure%20Report.pdf.

Pearl, Julie. 1987. "The Highest Paying Customers: America's Cities and the Costs of Prostitution Control." *Hastings Law Journal* 38(4):769–800.

Schneider, Elizabeth M. 2000. *Battered Women and Feminist Lawmaking.* New Haven, CT: Yale University Press.

Segregation Unit. 2000. Directed by Carol Jacobsen. Independently produced.

Walker, Lenore E. 1979. *The Battered Woman.* New York: Harper & Row.

Whitcomb, Jamie. 1999. "Former Female Inmate Talks about What It Was Like in Prison" (online interview). *CourtTV Online.* http://www.courttv.com/talk/chat_transcripts/WIP1.html.

Zimmermann, Patricia R. 2000. *States of Emergency: Documentaries, Wars, Democracies.* Minneapolis: University of Minnesota Press.

FIFTY-TWO

Testimony on Family Detention by U.S. Immigration and Customs Enforcement (2007)

Michelle Brané

Attorney **Michelle Brané** directs the Detention and Asylum Program of the Women's Commission for Refugee Women and Children, a New York–based nonprofit organization that works to improve the lives and defend the rights of refugee women and children, including the internally displaced, returnees, and asylum seekers. She has twenty years of experience working on immigration and human rights issues in the United States and internationally.

Good Morning and thank you for the opportunity to testify before you today.[1] My name is Michelle Brané with the Women's Commission for Refugee Women and Children. I will be focusing on the use of family detention by the United States Immigration and Customs Enforcement (ICE).

There are currently two major family detention facilities in the U.S.: the Berks county facility in Pennsylvania and the unlicensed T. Don Hutto facility in Texas, which opened in 2006 and was supposed to serve as a model for future facilities. The Women's Commission visited both facilities and wrote a report on our findings, which was submitted to the commission. The practice of detaining families, most of whom are asylum seekers, and the prison-like conditions of this detention violate several provisions of U.S. standards as well as international treaty obligations, including the *American Declaration of the Rights and Duties of Man.*

While there are many procedural and structural differences between these two facilities, both are overly restrictive settings in which children and families are subject to inhumane and inappropriate treatment. The facilities are based on a criminal prison model. At Hutto, families, including young children and babies in cribs, sleep in concrete prison cells. Hutto is particularly problematic because it is a former prison, complete with prison cells, gates, barbed wire, and control rooms and because it is run by a private prison corporation. This was reflected in many of the practices at the facility such

as children and babies wearing prison uniforms, no freedom of movement within the facility and no contact visits. Dominica, a pregnant asylum seeker, slept with her two children in the same single prison bed rather than have her children sleep alone in another cell. She was lucky; in most cases children over six years old have no choice but to be separated at night.

At the time of our visit detainees, including children, received only one hour of education and one hour of recreation a day. Both facilities are equipped with cameras that monitor detainees' movements 24 hours a day.

Families are subject to harsh and disproportionate disciplinary practices, including threats of separation. When I asked how the discipline worked, one nine-year-old girl said that if you do not behave "they send you away from your mom." Families are frequently threatened with separation if they complain or if the children do not keep quiet and behave. Children were punished for crying, asking for more food, and for being too loud or active. In one case, a child who was crying because he was not allowed by a guard to take a picture he had colored into his room was separated from his father for several days after his father complained to the guard for yelling at the child.

We heard repeatedly from mothers that their children were losing weight. Even a guard expressed concern during our tour and asked me "off the record" to look into the food situation because, "These children are hungry." Families in Hutto received no more than twenty minutes to go through the cafeteria line and feed their children and themselves. For those at the end of the line, this could mean less than five minutes to eat.

Medical care is also a concern. Children and pregnant women were receiving grossly inadequate care. One pregnant woman we spoke to arrived at Hutto with a five-month-old child. She is a victim of trafficking who is applying for asylum. After being at the facility for a few months, she fainted and was taken to the hospital. She was told that she had a kidney infection and was told to drink lots of water; she was not given any antibiotics. The situation of her young daughter is perhaps even more disturbing. Lily arrived at Hutto at five months. In the time that she was at Hutto, she actually lost several pounds. While losing a few pounds is not such a big deal for an adult, for a child—especially a child under one year old—it is dangerous. This should not be happening to children who are in U.S. physical custody.

Some families with young children have been detained in these facilities for as long as two years, and the majority of children we observed appear to be under the age of 12.

Access to counsel is extremely limited due to the remote location. None of the family facilities have formal know-your-rights presentations. The submission by the University of Texas outlines some issues related to the obstruction of access to counsel. I would add that the facility in Pennsylvania has no arrangements for presentation or access to pro bono counsel, and the vast majority of the families there have inadequate or no legal representation.

No alternatives to detention are in place for families. My colleague will speak more of alternative programs. However, I want to stress that alternatives would be particularly appropriate for families.

At the Berks facility we met a woman who had been detained with her 15-year-old son. She had left behind her U.S. citizen infant son with a neighbor, thinking that she would only be away for one day. When we last spoke with her she had not seen her baby in over one year. The child was still with the neighbor. This situation of U.S. citizen children being separated from their parents and left in precarious situations is unnecessary and can be avoided with programs that already exist.

This approach of using a penal model and deterring by detaining has resulted in a situation in which the U.S. government is violating its own standards for care and custody as well as its obligations under international law including the *American Declaration of the Rights and Duties of Man,* which is binding on the U.S. by virtue of its membership in the O.A.S. [Organization of American States].

The University of Texas submission to the Commission outlines specifically several of the articles that are violated by the current system. These include Articles VI, VII, XI, XV, and XXVII.

- *The family detention model strips parents of their role as arbiter and architect of the family unit.*

Article VI: Right to a family and to protection thereof; Article VII: Right to protection for mothers and children; Article XI: Right to the preservation of health and to well-being

- *It places families in settings modeled on the criminal justice system.*

Article VI: Right to a family and to protection thereof; Article VII: Right to protection for mothers and children; Article XI: Right to the preservation of health and to well-being; Article XV: Right to leisure time and to the use thereof.

- *There are no licensing requirements and no standards for family detention, but both facilities violated the Flores settlement agreement outlining standards for children and Immigration and Customs Enforcement Detention Standards.*[2]

Article VI: Right to a family and to protection thereof; Article VII: Right to protection for mothers and children; Article XI: Right to the preservation of health and to well-being; Article XV: Right to leisure time and to the use thereof; Article XXVII: Right of asylum.

- *The current approach fails to take into consideration both Congress's directive to explore alternatives and the reality that alternatives exist.* We understand that the government has to secure its borders, but detention is not necessary in all cases. Alternatives exist that can take into account public safety and appearance at hearings. Such alternatives are less costly to the taxpayer while complying with American and international human rights standards.

Article XI: Right to the preservation of health and to well-being; Article XV: Right to leisure time and to the use thereof; Article XXVII: Right of asylum.

In conclusion, through the course of our research, we became deeply concerned about the physical and emotional well-being of families in detention. The families we spoke with—the large majority of them women asylum seekers with young children—all expressed signs of depression, particularly the children. Children who have been released from Hutto have suffered from continued weight loss, nightmares, and bedwetting. Almost every woman we spoke with cried when describing the conditions of detention. These facilities are not "the least restrictive setting" appropriate for the children's age, and policies and procedures fundamentally compromise normal parent-child interaction. There has been a disturbing lack of transparency on the part of the U.S. government with respect to detention facilities in general and particularly with the Hutto facility. In June of 2007, the U.N. Special Rapporteur on the Rights of Migrants was denied entry. . . . However, detainees tried to communicate the gravity of the situation to us as best they could. As we were touring this facility, a little girl ran up to us and pressed a note into the hand of my colleague that read, "Help us and ask us questions."

NOTES

1. The author presented this testimony to the Inter-American Commission on Human Rights on behalf of the Women's Commission for Refugee Women and Children, October 12, 2007, Washington, D.C. See www.cidh.org/DefaultE.htm for information on the IACHR.

2. Stipulated Settlement Agreement, *Flores v Reno,* Case No CV85-4554-RJK (C.D. Cal. 1996) and U.S. Immigration and Customs Enforcement, *Detention Operations Manual.* http://www.ice.gov/partners/dro/opsmanual/index.htm

◆◆◆

Media Representations and the Criminalization of Arab Americans and Muslim Americans (2005)

Suad Joseph and Benjamin D'Harlingue

Suad Joseph is Director of the Middle East/South Asia Studies Program and Professor of Anthropology and Women's Studies at the University of California, Davis. She is general editor of the *Encyclopedia of Women and Islamic Cultures* and editor of *Gender and Citizenship in the Middle East.*

Benjamin D'Harlingue is a Ph.D. candidate in Cultural Studies at the University of California, Davis, where he has also taught Introduction to Women and Gender Studies. His primary research focus is on cultural geographies of contemporary ghost tourism in the United States.

Arab Americans and Muslim Americans are heterogeneous peoples from all over the world. They come from different countries, have different histories, belong to different cultures, and use different languages. Arabs, for example, are highly diverse, and include large numbers of Christians and Jews who consider themselves Arab. The total world Arab population is over 300 million (Arab American Anti-Discrimination Committee 2004). By contrast, there are about 1.3 billion Muslims in the world. The majority of Muslims are neither Arab nor Middle Eastern. Over 50 percent of the world's Muslims are from South Asia—India, Pakistan, Bangladesh, and Afghanistan. From the nineteenth century to the middle of the twentieth century, the overwhelming majority of immigrants to the United States from the Arab region were Christian. It was not until the 1960s and 1970s that Muslim immigrants from the Arab world began to outnumber Christian Arab immigrants. The first Muslims in the United States were African slaves. Estimates indicate that 30 to 40 percent of Muslims in the United States are African American; 25 to 30 percent are South Asian Americans; and 12 to 15 percent are Arab American (Ibish 2002).

Despite this wide diversity, however, U.S. media and popular culture tend to portray Arab Americans and Muslim Americans as if they are all the same. This erasure of differences makes it easier for government and the wider society to treat them the same and to make them all, collectively, different from "us." The "us" is the West, the United States—that is, the imagined United States, a white Christian nation that does not include Arabs and Muslims. As Nadine Naber (2000) has argued, Islam has been essentialized and racialized in the U.S., particularly in the politics of citizenship. Persons from Muslim countries and U.S. citizens from Muslim regions are represented in terms of their religion before any of their other multiple identities. Their actions are invariably characterized as "Muslim" regardless of their nature and intent. By prioritizing Islam as their overriding identity, the popular media portray every act of violence or incivility committed by a Muslim as a Muslim act.

Samar Kaukab with her ACLU lawyer (see p. 451).

In our examination of representations of Arab Americans, Muslim Americans, and Muslims in *New York Times* articles from 2000 to 2004, we found a predominantly negative representation of Islam. In article after article, Islam is presented as reactionary, violent, oppressive, anti-American, and incomprehensible to the "Western mind." Muslim leaders are represented as dangerous fanatics rather than respected spiritual leaders, and Muslim places of worship as sites of insurgencies rather than sites of the sacred. One article captured this image explicitly in its headline, "Seeing Islam as 'Evil' Faith, Evangelicals Seek Converts" (Goodstein 2003). Reporter Laurie Goodstein comments, "At the grass roots of evangelical Christianity, many are now absorbing the antipathy for Islam that emerged last year with the incendiary comments of ministers like Franklin Graham, Jerry Falwell, Pat Robertson, and Jerry Vines, the former president of the Southern Baptist Convention. Franklin Graham called Islam 'a very evil and wicked religion,' and Mr. Vines

called Muhammad, Islam's founder and prophet, a 'demon-possessed pedophile'" (Goodstein, 2003, 1). By not questioning these Christian leaders' views of Islam, the reporter, perhaps inadvertently, endorses and reinforces this prevailing negative view.

In the name of the nation and its security, Arab Americans and Muslim Americans have become increasingly racialized and targeted for discriminatory policies and practices by the government. The demonization of Arabs and Muslims reached a new level after 9/11/01 (Abdelkarim 2002, Cainkar 2002, Gonzaga 2002, *Middle East Reports* 2002). The profile of a "terrorist" was made equivalent to "looking" "Middle Eastern" or "Arab" or "Muslim." A U.S. Congressman of Arab background was detained at an airport because he fit this profile (Akram and Johnson 2002). A white, male, Christian U.S. citizen killed a Sikh U.S. citizen because he looked "Arab" or "Muslim," although Sikhs are neither Arab nor Muslim. Over 1,200 legal residents (mostly Arab and Muslim) were detained without charges or access to attorneys; many were deported without public hearings even though none were found to have direct links with supposedly terrorist organizations (Akram and Johnson 2002, 331). A number of the 5,000 men (mostly Arab and Muslim, 18–33 year olds) were arrested after they responded to an invitation by the Justice Department and the Federal Bureau of Investigation (FBI) for "voluntary" interviews, despite the fact that their visas were in order and they were living in this country legally.

After the bombing of the U.S. federal building in Oklahoma City in 1995, then Attorney General Janet Reno made comments that implied the involvement of Arabs or Muslims in the bombing, as did the media. The FBI focused its investigation on Arabs and Muslims in this country. Congress passed the Anti-Terrorism and Effective Death Penalty Act in 1996, which targets Arab and Muslim U.S. and non-U.S. citizens as suspects of terrorism (Akram and Johnson 2002, 346). Hate crimes against Arab and Muslim U.S. citizens continued well after the identification, arrest, and conviction of white, Christian U.S. citizens responsible for the Oklahoma City terrorist attack.

Yet, when a Christian person acts, their action is not represented as "Christian." Timothy McVey, who bombed the federal building in Oklahoma City, was not described in media reports as committing a Christian act, even though fundamentalist

Christianity was part of his worldview. Immediately after the September 11, 2001, bombing of the World Trade Center, the Reverend Jerry Falwell commented that the attacks were the wrath of God brought upon us by gays, lesbians, and feminists. Newspaper reports did not refer to these comments as Christian statements even though Reverend Falwell presents himself as speaking in a Christian voice. The killings of the Ku Klux Klan are not described as Christian although the Christian cross is central to their symbolism. When domestic abuse occurs in Christian homes the media do not look to the Bible to explain domestic abuse. Historians do not try to analyze what it is about Christianity that gives rise to dictators and tyrants such as Hitler, Mussolini, or Franco. In the dominant discourse, however, Muslims are defined by their religion and constructed as "alien," while the normative "we" is defined by economics and politics.

The U.S. government, popular media, TV and radio news, and print journalism often represent Arab Americans and Muslim Americans as uncertain, problematic, or suspect citizens (Joseph 1999). This began long before 9/11/01 (Abraham and Abraham 1983, Aswad 1974, Leonard 2003, Suleiman 1999). In 1914, an immigrant by the name of George Dow was denied U.S. citizenship based on the 1790 statute, which defined citizens as "free white persons" (*Dow v. United States et al.*, No. 1345. 4th Cir. 1915). As a "Syrian of Asiatic birth," (probably a Lebanese Christian), George Dow was not considered to be a "free white person" and therefore ineligible for citizenship. The decision was later appealed and reversed on the basis that Syrians were Semitic, even part Jewish, and therefore white—a clear example of the social construction of race. This case is emblematic of the on-going ambivalence in U.S. citizenship laws and practices towards U.S. citizens of Arab or Muslim origin (Cainkar 1999, Naff 1985, Suleiman 1999). By definition, to be a U.S. citizen was to be white. But, as Mary Ramadan (1996) has pointed out, white was understood to mean not only European but also Christian. Arabs and Muslims are not only "not quite white" as Nadine Naber argued (2000), Muslims are not Christians, and the majority of Arabs are Muslims. Arabs and Muslims are not the same as each other, as argued above, nor with the imagined U.S. white, Christian citizen. Arab and Muslim U.S. citizens embody this contradiction; they continue to be seen as against the grain of the nation (Joseph 1999), as not quite white (Naber 2000, Saliba 1999, Samhan 1999), and, despite legal citizenship, not quite citizens.

Law professors Susan Akram and Kevin Johnson (2002, 337) have observed that ". . . the current treatment of Arabs and Muslims is more extralegal than the internment" of Japanese Americans during World War II.

> No Executive Order authorizes the treatment of Arabs and Muslims; nor has there been a formal declaration of war. Moreover, nationality, which is more objective and easier to apply than religious and racial classifications, is not used as the exclusive basis for the measures. Rather, the scope of the investigation is broad and amorphous enough to potentially include all Arabs and Muslims, who may be natives of [many] countries. *(Akram and Johnson 2002, 337)*

However, the government does have plans for detaining Arab-Americans in internment camps as exposed in 1991 by Norman Mineta, then a U.S. Representative and later Secretary of Transportation under President George W. Bush. In an article entitled, "Questioning of Arab-Americans Protested" (Mecoy 1991), a story carried in *The Sacramento Bee* but in few other news media, Mineta "pointed to a 1987 contingency plan the FBI and the Immigration and Naturalization Service drew up to detain Arab-Americans at an internment camp in Oakdale, Louisiana, in the event of war with certain Arab states. Mineta said that plan could still be initiated to 'round up' Arab-Americans" (Mecoy 1991). Moreover, during the 1991 Gulf War, many incidents of violence and harassment were committed against Arab and Muslim U.S. citizens by fellow U.S. citizens in various regions of the country.

Postcolonial theorist Gayatri Spivak showed in her discussion of British rule in India that colonial ideology often seeks to justify colonialist domination as being in the interests of women, constructing imperial intervention in terms of "white men saving brown women from brown men" (Spivak 1988, 297). More recently, anthropologist Lila Abu-Lughod has argued that the U.S. war on terrorism has taken on such a tenor. She points out that First Lady Laura Bush's November 17, 2001, address to the nation linked the "fight against terrorism" to the fight for women's rights, and thus "enlisted women to justify American bombing and intervention in Afghanistan and to make a case for the 'War on Terrorism' of which it was allegedly a part" (Abu-Lughod 2002, 784). Bombing Afghans was thus made to seem as though it was in the service of Muslim women, even though many Afghan women's organizations opposed U.S. intervention. When they cover Arab or Muslim women, U.S. news media tend to represent them as silent, passive, oppressed, inaccessible, and mysterious. The voices of Arab or Muslim women are rarely represented, and most print news sources portray them as in need of rescue. It is inconceivable that women might willingly embrace Islam if one relied on these stories. Abu-Lughod points to the imperial and racist presuppositions of savior discourses: "Projects of saving other women depend on and reinforce a sense of superiority by Westerners, a form of arrogance that deserves to be challenged" (Abu-Lughod 2002, 789). How do discourses about saving Muslim women support forms of state violence such as war and sexism?

The veil (*burka, abayya*) (a pre-Islamic African tradition) and clitoridectomy (a pre-Islamic ritual practiced more in non-Arab than Arab countries and not practiced by the overwhelming majority of Muslims) are pervasively represented as signature Islamic practices in the U.S. press. A *New York Times* article entitled "Behind the Veil: A Muslim Woman Speaks Out" is an example (Simons 2002, A4). The article discusses Ayaan Hirsi Ali's activism against domestic violence, sexual abuse, and genital cutting in Muslim communities in the Netherlands and internationally. The reporter asserts that "[t]he theme of injustice toward Muslim women in Islamic countries has become common in the West." The title of the article stands as a metaphor for practices that the article sympathetically quotes Ali as calling "backwards." According to Lila Abu-Lughod (2002), using the veil as a symbol of sexism elides the complex historical and political dynamics that produce differences amongst women. She stresses that rather than intervene in other communities, it would be better to ask how imperial policies and our social locations as U.S. citizens might contribute to the life conditions of people in other communities and to support demands from within those communities to make women's and men's lives better.

The veil, mobilized as a sign of backwardness or sexism, has underwritten the criminalization of Muslims in the war on terror. In a *New York Times* article entitled "A Little Late, But a Stand Against Hate,"

Clyde Haberman lauded a group called the Progressive Muslim Union of North America for supposedly acting as a "counterweight to the 'oppressive or dysfunctional practices' that have come to define Islam for many people" (Haberman 2004, B1). "Islam," Haberman asserts, "had become grim, cramped, exclusionary and—no getting around it—all too often death-embracing." As Haberman reports this group's stand against "treating women as barely human"—implying that sexism is the norm amongst Muslims—he notes: "Not a headscarf or beard was in sight" in the room when he interviewed the group. This narrative implies a link between headscarves, beards, and sexist practices. He also links religiosity to sexism, asserting, "No imam need apply" to this group. Finally, Haberman criticizes the Progressive Muslim Union of North America: "Is it possible to talk about Islam in the post–9/11 world without a single reference to the dread T-word? Nowhere in the group's mission statement or in the members' remarks was terrorism mentioned. Why is that?" For Haberman, whether they are for or against sexism, all Muslims must be suspected of terrorism.

Trinh Minh-ha (1989) has noted that colonialist strategy—through law, policy, military and police activity, and media representations—homogenizes the "other" as a way of creating an oppositional binary that defines the other as enemy. President George W. Bush relied on popularly held stereotypic binaries in his designation of an "axis of evil" which included two Muslim countries, Iraq and Iran, fostering further demonization of Muslims in the U.S. media and popular opinion. The United States is waging a war based on the construction of binary opposites. President Bush's statement, "You are either with us or you are with the terrorists," comes out of a history of control based on the construction of difference.

The impact of the targeting of Arabs and Muslims through media discourse and public policy has been to control both Arab and non-Arab, Muslim and non-Muslim U.S. citizens. Fear mongering has affected the majority of U.S. citizens, particularly people of color, as more repressive measures are implemented in the name of "national security." What is at stake for Arab and Muslim U.S. citizens in the aftermath of 9/11/01 is not simply their home, but the home of all U.S. citizens. The exclusions and inconsistencies of citizenship applied to Arab and Muslim Americans can be used to justify the abuse of the citizenship rights of others. Just as oppression against Native Americans, African Americans, Asian Americans, and Latino Americans laid the groundwork for discriminations toward Arab and Muslim Americans, so do the exclusions and inconsistencies practiced toward Arab and Muslim Americans add bricks to a house heated by fear. Moreover, stereotypical and negative portrayals of Arabs, Arab Americans, and Muslim Americans in the news media are integral to the construction of these diverse people as intrinsically suspect, a key step in the process of their criminalization.

REFERENCES

Abdelkarim, R.Z. 2002. American Muslims and 9/11: A Community Looks Back . . . and to the Future." *Washington Report on Middle East Affairs.* Vol. XXI, No. 7, pp. 82 (Oct. 31).

Abraham, Sameer Y. and Nabeel Abraham, eds. 1983. *Arabs in the New World: Studies on Arab-American Communities.* Detroit: Wayne State University Center for Urban Studies.

Abu-Lughod, Lila. 2002. Do Muslim Women Really Need Saving? Anthropological Reflections on Cultural Relativism and Its Others, *American Anthropologist.* Vol. 104, No. 3, pp. 783–790.

Akram, S. M. and K. Johnson. 2002. Race, Civil Rights, and Immigration Law After September 11, 2001: The Targeting of Arabs and Muslims, *New York University Annual Survey of American Law,* Vol. 58.

American Arab Anti-Discrimination Committee. 2004. *Facts about Arabs and the Arab World.* http://www.adc.org/index.php?id5248 (accessed: 22 July 2004).

Aswad, Barbara C., ed. 1974. *Arabic Speaking Communities in American Cities.* New York: Center for Immigration Studies.

Cainkar, Louise. 1999. The Deteriorating Ethnic Safety Net Among Arab Immigrants in Chicago. In *Arabs in America: Building a New Future,* edited by Michael Suleiman. Philadelphia: Temple University Press, pp. 192–206.

———. 2002. No Longer Invisible: Arab and Muslim Exclusion After September 11, *Middle East Report* 224 (Fall).

Gonzaga, Russell Reza-Khaliq. 2002. One Nation Under Allah: Islam Is the Fastest Growing Religion in America, But It Still Fits the Profile of the "Other." *Colorlines.* Vol 5. No. 3, p. 27 (Oct 31).

Goodstein, Laurie. 2003. Seeing Islam as "Evil" Faith, Evangelicals Seek Converts, *The New York Times,* Section A, pp. 1, 22, May 27.

Haberman, Clyde. 2004. A Little Late, But a Stand Against Hate, *The New York Times* (Late Edition, East Coast). November 16, p. B1.

Ibish, Hussein. 2002. *Post 9/11 Anti-Arab Discrimination in American Immigration Policy and Practice.* Presented at the Middle East Studies Association Meeting, Washington, D.C., November.

Joseph, Suad. 1999. Against the Grain of the Nation—The Arab. In *Arabs in America: Building a New Future,* edited by Michael Suleiman. Philadelphia: Temple University Press, pp. 257–271.

Leonard, Karen Isaksen. 2003. *Muslims in the United States: The State of Research.* New York: Russell Sage.

Mecoy, Laura 1991. Questioning of Arab-Americans Protested, *The Sacramento Bee.* 24 January, p. A9.

Middle East Report. 2002. Arabs, Muslims and Race in America (Special Issue). No. 224. Fall.

Minh-ha, Trinh. 1989. *Woman, Native, Other: Writing Postcoloniality and Feminism.* Bloomington: Indiana University Press.

Naber, Nadine. 2000. Ambiguous Insiders: An Investigation of Arab American Invisibility, *Ethnic and Racial Studies.* Vol. 23. No. 1 (Jan.), pp. 37–61.

Naff, Alexa. 1985. *Becoming American: The Early Arab Immigrant Experience.* Carbondale, Il.: Southern Illinois University Press.

Ramadan, Mary. 1996. *Anti-Arab Racism and Arab-American Response.* Paper presented at the Association of Arab-American University Graduates Convention. Anaheim, CA., October.

Saliba, Therese. 1999. Resisting Invisibility: Arab Americans in Academia and Activism. In *Arabs in America: Building a New Future,* edited by Michael Suleiman. Philadelphia: Temple University Press, pp. 304–319.

Samhan, Helen Hatab. 1999. Not Quite White: Race Classification and the Arab-American Experience. In *Arabs in America: Building a New Future,* edited by Michael Suleiman. Philadelphia: Temple University Press, pp. 209–226.

Simons, Marlise. 2002. Behind the Veil: A Muslim Woman Speaks Out: [Biography], *The New York Times* (Late Edition, East Coast). November 9, p. A4.

Spivak, Gayatri Chakravorty. 1988. Can the Subaltern Speak? In *Marxism and the Interpretation of Culture,* edited by Cary Nelson and Lawrence Grossberg. Urbana: University of Illinois Press, pp. 271–313.

Suleiman, Michael, ed. 1999. *Arabs in America: Building a New Future.* Philadelphia: Temple University Press.

◆◆◆

FIFTY-FOUR

Women of Color, Globalization, and the Politics of Incarceration (2003)

Julia Sudbury

Scholar and activist **Julia Sudbury** is Professor of Ethnic Studies at Mills College. Editor of *Global Lockdown: Race, Gender and the Prison-Industrial Complex,* her work focuses on women of color, women's activism, globalization and the transnational prison-industrial complex. Other books include *Activist Scholarship: Antiracism, Feminism and Social Change* (co-editor) and *Outsiders Within: Writings on Transracial Adoption* (co-editor).

In November 1999, 40,000 people came together in an explosion of street activism to protest the policies of the World Trade Organization and to highlight the impact of neoliberal globalization on the global south and poor communities in the global north. . . . Labor, environmental, human rights, housing, antiracist, and feminist activists came to Seattle out of a common understanding that problems such as sweatshop working conditions, toxic dumping in black neighborhoods, and cutbacks in welfare, housing, and health care are all rooted in a global capitalist system that values corporate interests and freedoms over human needs for decent wages, shelter, food, and health care. At the Seattle protests, . . . activists used puppets, banners, and flyers to link the struggle against global capital with opposition to the current criminal justice system. Activists challenged police brutality, racial profiling, the death penalty, and the prison industrial complex, arguing that dramatic increases in prison populations have occurred as a result of globalization.

While these connections are being made at the street level, feminist criminologists have had little to say about what connections, if any, may be made between women's imprisonment and the rise of global corporate capital that has occurred in the past two decades. Such an analysis would need to stray beyond the boundaries of what has traditionally been considered within the scope of criminology to examine the broader socioeconomic context of women's criminalization and incarceration. . . . [I] argue that

the explosion in women's incarceration is the hidden face of globalization and cannot be understood without reference to three overlapping phenomena. The first is the restructuring of national economies and social welfare provision that has occurred as a result of the globalization of capital. The second . . . is the emergence and subsequent global expansion of what has been labeled a "prison industrial complex" made up of an intricate web of relations between criminal justice institutions, politicians, and . . . corporations. The third is the . . . U.S.-led war on drugs that has crossed national borders to become a global phenomenon.

The Boom in Women's Imprisonment

The past 25 years have witnessed dramatic increases in the use of incarceration in the United States, leading to a prison building boom as federal and state governments rush to keep up with demand for prison beds. Although there are more men in prison than women, the rate of women's imprisonment is spiraling upward at a greater rate than that of men. . . . Similar patterns have occurred in Canada, Europe, and Australasia. In Britain, for example, the number of women in prison doubled between 1985 and 1998. . . .

Statistics that look at gender but not race underrepresent the impact of the prison boom on women of color and indigenous women. In all the countries just mentioned, oppressed racialized groups are disproportionately targeted by the criminal justice system. For example, in the United States, Latinas and African American women make up 60 percent of the prison population. And despite their small numbers in the population, Native Americans are 10 times more likely than whites to be imprisoned.[1] In New South Wales, Australia, where all women's imprisonment increased by 40 percent in five years, aboriginal women's incarceration increased by 70 percent in only two years.[2] In Canada, aboriginal people comprise 3 percent of the general population and

12 percent of federal prisoners, a figure that increases to over 60 percent in . . . Saskatchewan and Alberta.[3] African Canadians are also disproportionately policed, prosecuted, and incarcerated.[4] Finally, 12 percent of women prisoners in England and Wales are British citizens of African Caribbean descent compared to 1 percent of the general population.[5] In addition, British prisons hold numerous women from West Africa, the Caribbean, and Latin America, either as immigration detainees or serving sentences for drug importation. The crisis of women's prisons can therefore be read as a crisis for women of color and indigenous women worldwide.

Explaining the Prison Boom

How can we explain this explosion in the population of women prisoners? In the 1970s, "emancipation theorists" put forward a possible explanation for an upward trend in women's incarceration. In her influential study, Freda Adler suggested that the women's liberation movement had opened up new opportunities for women, both in the legitimate and in the criminal worlds.[6] Thus women who were now working in white-collar jobs could commit crimes such as fraud and embezzlement, which previously would have been inaccessible to them. Women's liberation was also credited with giving women a more assertive stance and enabling them to engage in violence, burglary, and organized crime, acts that were previously the domain of men.

Subsequent studies challenged Adler's findings; they contested her claim that there had been a rise in women's offending and suggested that any increase could in fact be explained by social factors such as an increase in women's poverty.[7] Despite vigorous challenges to Adler's claims, subsequent work by feminist criminologists has failed to shift the debate around women and crime in two important ways. First, it perpetuates the commonsense equation between crime and punishment that is at the core of both Adler's work and mainstream criminology. This equation leads us to look to women's behavior for explanations of increases in women's incarceration. If more women are being arrested, prosecuted, and punished, this argument goes, it must be because they are committing more crimes. Sociologists working within a radical framework make a different argument. Rather than looking to women's behavior, we should look at the

shifting actions of the state as it seeks to control poor communities and populations of color. Rather than women's criminality, the focus of study should be the role of the state in labeling, prosecuting, and punishing women—that is, women's criminalization. Our search for an explanation for the prison boom must therefore ask: Who benefits when more women are imprisoned? What are the processes by which certain actions are labeled criminal and others are not, and how are women channeled into these actions and thus into conflict with the criminal justice system?

The second limitation of feminist criminology is its unwillingness to engage meaningfully with the significance of race in the criminal justice system, choosing to view women first as gendered beings and only secondly as having a social class, national, or racialized identity. . . . Rather than talking about "woman" as a unitary category, as if all women's experiences were fundamentally the same, feminists of color argue that we must always be explicit about the ways that racism and racial privilege intersect with class location and gender to create unique experiences for diverse women. Intersectionality may produce unexpected outcomes. In some instances, for example, women of color may have as much in common with men of color as they do with middle-class white women. Deploying an intersectional approach to explain women's criminalization therefore requires us to pay as much attention to racial profiling and racialized discrepancies within the criminal justice system as we do to gender disparities. It also requires us to examine the feminization of poverty, the impoverishment and surveillance of communities of color, and global inequalities between third- and first-world nations as causal factors behind the growing criminalization of women.

1. Globalization and the Racialized Feminization of Poverty

. . .

Both urban "ghettos" and small rural towns have been hard hit by the downsizing of manufacturing since the 1970s, suffering high unemployment and a decline in tax revenues. For inner-city residents, especially African Americans and Latinos, these declines have meant underfunded schools, dirty streets, insufficient public housing, and poor health care facilities. Neighborhoods have been taken over by liquor stores, crack houses, and prostitution as supermarkets and department stores relocate to more profitable locations. Women bear the brunt of this social dislocation, because they tend to be the primary caretakers of children and elderly relatives and are responsible for providing adequate food, shelter, medicine, and clothing. For working-class women of color in the inner cities, the globalization of capital translates into few opportunities for a living wage, food and clothing that is expensive and of poor quality, and inadequate day care and schooling for their children.

Rural areas have also been affected by the radical restructuring signaled by globalization. Faced with global commodities markets that set the price for meat, milk, or grain according to the lowest price that can be obtained internationally, small farmers have been unable to compete and have been forced to sell their land or contract to sell their produce to large farming corporations.[8] The emergence of agribusiness as the primary supplier of the nation's food has led to a rise in rural poverty as farm workers, particularly immigrant workers, are forced to work for low wages in insecure, seasonal jobs. Small rural towns that relied on car, munitions, and other industries have also been hit as factories have relocated abroad or closed as a result of a decline in cold war–era military investment. . . .

This newfound mobility has given corporations the ability to pack up and move to a new location if they find that policies and legislation governing workers' rights, wages, and environmental protections are not to their liking. Thus, national governments within the global capitalist economy have seen their policy options narrowed if they wish to remain attractive to corporate capital. The 1990s, therefore, witnessed a shift toward neoliberal policies being pursued by conservative and liberal governments alike. These policies aim to create a liberal environment for corporate profit making and financial speculation. . . .

The global spread of neoliberal social and economic policies is underpinned by two international institutions. The World Trade Organization (WTO) was established as the global headquarters for the drafting and policing of international trading rules. In the past decade, the WTO has come under criticism by activists who claim that by enforcing rules that benefit corporate profit while ignoring the exploitation of child laborers, the use of sweatshops, and environmental destruction by those same corporations, it is complicit in these exploitative practices.[9] The International Monetary Fund (IMF) is an organization

with 184 member countries that promotes international monetary exchange and trade and provides loans and economic guidance to impoverished countries. The IMF has been criticized for imposing economic policies on formerly colonized countries that generate immense poverty and suffering. Governments have been forced to cut back public expenditure. In Jamaica, for example, policies introduced since the mid-1980s by the Jamaican Labour Party working closely with the IMF have led to cuts in public-sector employment; the scaling back of local government services in health and education; increases in the cost of public utilities as state-owned companies are sold to the private sector; and a dramatic decline in real wages. Such cuts hit working-class Jamaican women particularly hard because they carry the burden of caring for children and sick or elderly relatives. This disproportionate impoverishment of third-world women is referred to as the racialized feminization of poverty.

At the same time that the Jamaican state has cut back its role in social welfare, it has stepped up its role in subsidizing foreign and domestic capital. Free trade zones established in Kingston, Montego Bay, and elsewhere offer foreign garment, electronic, and communications companies factory space and equipment, tax exemptions, a cheap female workforce, and for the busy foreign executive, weekends of sun, sea, and sand.[10] Foreign-owned agribusiness and mining companies have also been encouraged, displacing traditional subsistence farming and causing migration from rural areas to the cities, which now account for 50 percent of the Jamaican population. As the economy has shifted, women working in the informal economy as farmers and higglers[11] find themselves unable to keep up with the rising costs of survival. Whereas younger women may find employment in the tourist industry as maids, entertainers, or prostitutes, or within the free trade zones assembling clothes or computers for Western markets, working-class women in their 30s and older have fewer options. Even where these women do find employment, low wages—driven down by multinational corporations in search of ever greater profit margins and kept low by governments unwilling to set a living minimum wage for fear of losing foreign investment—mean that women cannot earn a sufficient income to support their families. The failure of the legal economy to provide adequate means for women's survival then becomes a key incentive for Jamaican women who enter the drug trade as couriers and are subsequently incarcerated in British, Canadian, and U.S. prisons. . . .

2. The Prison Industrial Complex

Why has the racialized feminization of poverty under neoliberal globalization led to an explosion in the imprisonment of women? In other words, how can we explain the current state response to the increase in poverty among working-class women and women of color, a response that deploys criminalization and punishment rather than poverty relief or empowerment? Scholars, activists, and former prisoners seeking to explain this problem . . . [rely on] the concept of the prison industrial complex.[12] Joel Dyer argues that three components make up the "perpetual prisoner machine" that transforms criminalized populations in the United States into fodder for the prison system.[13] The first are the large media corporations, like CNN and NBC, that rely on violent and crime-oriented content to grab ratings. The disproportionate airtime dedicated to crime-related news, dramas such as *NYPD Blue* and *Law and Order*, and real-life shows such as *America's Most Wanted* and *Cops* have created a dramatic rise in the fear of crime in the U.S. population at large.[14] These shows provide stereotypical representations of communities of color, from the black drug dealer to the Latino "gangbanger," that fuel a racialized fear of crime. The second is the use of market research by politicians to align their platforms with popular views about policy areas. Since the voting population tends to believe that criminal penalties are too soft and that "criminals" are unlikely to serve adequate prison sentences, politicians can win votes by appearing to be "tough on crime." Although Republicans have traditionally positioned themselves as tougher on crime than Democrats, it is only by positioning themselves as equally punitive that liberals can achieve power. Thus the unfounded assumption that building more prisons and jails and incapacitating more people for longer periods will solve deep-rooted social problems, such as drug use, poverty, and violence, remains unchallenged by both major parties. . . .

The third component is the intervention of private prison corporations such as Wackenhut Corporation and Corrections Corporation of America, which have generated millions for their shareholders by designing, constructing, financing, and managing prisons, jails, and detention centers. The mutually profitable relationship between private corporations and public criminal justice systems enables politicians to mask the enormous cost of their tough-on-crime policies. Instead of allocating millions for new prison construction in their annual budgets, politicians can simply reallocate revenue funds from welfare, health, or education into contracts with privately run for-profit prisons. . . .

. . . Although the prison industrial complex emerged in the United States, the past 15 years have witnessed its transformation into a transnational phenomenon. . . . U.S.-based prison corporations and their subsidiaries now manage prisons in Britain, Canada, New Zealand, Puerto Rico, Australia, and South Africa; and in all these locations, prison populations are rising. The prison industrial complex incorporates diverse interest groups, all of which stand to profit from the global prison boom. State and national politicians, correctional officer unions, media and corporate executives, and shareholders all benefit in very direct ways from the growth in women's imprisonment.

3. The Global War on Drugs

The third factor implicated in the explosion in women's imprisonment is the global war on drugs. The contemporary war on drugs was announced by U.S. president Ronald Reagan in the early 1980s and formalized in the 1986 Anti Drug Abuse Act. The act made a critical break with the concept of drug users as a medical population in need of treatment and instead targeted them as a criminal population. It also utilized the erroneous assumption that users would be deterred from their habit and dealers and traffickers incapacitated by extensive use of penal sanctions. It was assumed that by removing those involved in the criminalized drug trade from the streets for long periods of time, syndicates would be severely damaged in their ability to get drugs to the streets.[15] Since "liberal" judges could not be trusted to hand down sufficiently severe sentences to deter and incapacitate those involved in the drug trade, the act removed judicial discretion and imposed mandatory minimum sentences.

Thus, treatment programs and community service were effectively barred in cases involving drugs, and sentence length related not to the role of the defendant in the offense, but to the weight and purity of drugs involved. In the United States, African American women and Latinas are disproportionately affected by mandatory minimums for reasons that are both gendered and racialized. The only way a lesser sentence can be given is in cases in which the defendant provides "substantial assistance" in the prosecution of another person. However, women, who tend to be in subordinate positions within drug syndicates and thus have little access to information, are usually unable to make such a deal. The crack-cocaine disparity also feeds the disproportionate impact on women of color. The mandatory minimum sentence for cocaine is one hundred times harsher for crack than for powder cocaine. Thus, being caught with 500 grams of powder cocaine is equivalent to being caught with only 5 grams of crack, itself a derivative of powder cocaine. Since crack is cheaper and has flooded poor inner city neighborhoods, African Americans and Latinos and Latinas receive disproportionate sentences when compared with powder cocaine users and dealers, who are much more likely to be white.

Although the war on drugs has had a dramatic impact on U.S. communities of color, it has reached far beyond U.S. borders. From the mid-1980s, the war on drugs increasingly played a key role in U.S. foreign policy decisions as the Reagan and Bush administrations pushed a U.S. drug agenda on the global community. . . . Whereas the domestic war on drugs is fought primarily by the police, beyond the borders of the United States it has become a military war justifying U.S. military interventions throughout Latin America. By the mid-1990s, Canada, Australia, New Zealand, Taiwan, South and Central America, the Caribbean, and African countries including Nigeria and South Africa were full-fledged partners in the U.S.-driven global war on drugs.

Inside the Transnational Prison Industrial Complex: Three Women's Stories

Accounts of structural economic and political processes are important if we are to understand the reasons behind the boom in women's imprisonment. However, by putting these macrolevel processes in the foreground, we risk losing sight of women's agency. Indeed, in such accounts, women, especially women of color and third-world women,

are often reduced to faceless victims while corporations, governments, and supranational bodies such as the IMF and World Bank take center stage. In order to move women of color from the margin to the center, I have chosen to highlight three women's stories. These stories reflect the lives of women incarcerated in three national locations: Britain, Canada, and the United States. Looking beyond the borders of the United States enables us to examine the ways in which globalization, the transnational prison industrial complex, and the global war on drugs lead to the criminalization and incarceration of women of color and third-world women.

Narrative One: Militarization, Displacement, and the War on Drugs

Teresa is a Colombian woman in her early 40s.[16] As a single mother, she struggled to support her three children. Carrying Class A drugs (cocaine) between Colombia and England enabled her to supplement her meager income. She was arrested at Heathrow airport in England and was given a five-year sentence. . . . She does not know what has become of her three children and has not been able to contact them since she was arrested. Her fear is that they will be homeless since she did not leave any emergency funds for them. Teresa's story challenges us to rethink common sense ideas about dangerous Latin American "drug traffickers" flooding the United States and Europe with cocaine. In common with many drug "mules" from developing countries, Teresa was pushed into trafficking drugs by desperation. In her words:

> Cargamos drogas porque lo necessitamos; porque tenemos situations de financia. Somos de Colombia, de paises del tercer mundo, que son pobres. La situacion en lo que viven, por eso lo hicemos.
>
> We carry drugs because we need to, because we have financial difficulties. We come from Colombia, the third world, which are poor countries. The conditions we live in, that's what pushed us.

Colombia is a country shackled by foreign debt, political and social dislocation, violence, war, and kidnappings. As a leading harvester of the coca leaf, estimated to produce 80 percent of the world's cocaine, Colombia has been a key target of U.S. anti-drug interventions. Instead of alleviating horrendous social, political, and economic conditions for women in Latin America, U.S. financial assistance is targeted at building military forces that participate in the war on drugs. These forces have been used to carry out counterinsurgency wars against revolutionary groups like the FARC (Revolutionary Armed Forces of Colombia) and ELN (National Liberation Army) that have spearheaded the struggle for indigenous and poor people's rights. The U.S. military alleges that such groups have received millions of dollars per annum for protecting coca plantations, drug trafficking routes, and airstrips. By identifying these revolutionary groups as "narco-terrorists," the U.S. administration is able to justify providing military expertise and assistance to Colombia, despite its poor human rights record and evidence of collusion between the military and right-wing paramilitary death squads.[17] . . .

In tying aid to military gains against the FARC, the United States finances a four-decade-old civil war in which at least 35,000 people have died and two million have been internally displaced or forced to emigrate. The displacement of peasants and indigenous people is further exacerbated by the use of herbicides and organic toxins that affect large areas of rain forest and groundwater and create health problems for local people in addition to destroying the coca.[18] Women bear the brunt of this atmosphere of violence and instability as displaced landless peasants, as primary caretakers seeking to feed their children, and as spouses of men killed in the fighting. Ironically, the very conditions that pushed Teresa to risk importing Class A drugs are caused in part by the war on drugs. She, like many other foreign nationals in U.S. and European prisons, will be deported after serving a long sentence to a homeland where she has no house, no income, and no social security. In the meantime, she will be replaced by any of the millions of impoverished and desperate women in Latin America, the Caribbean, and Africa who become drug mules each year.

Narrative Two: Racialization, Labeling, and Exclusion

Camille is a 21-year-old African Canadian woman. Camille's mother, an immigrant from Jamaica, brought her up in public housing in the declining West End of Toronto. As a young girl, Camille was in constant conflict with her mother's expectations. She experienced difficulties at school, was labeled as having attention deficit hyperactive disorder (ADHD), and was sent to a school for children with special needs:

> They always told me I was bad, but you know kids. They said I had attention deficit disorder. I went to a couple of behavior schools, after that my mum switched us to Catholic school. I was going there for a while, then grade 2, me and the teacher got into something. I think I hit the teacher. They sent me to another behavior school for a couple of years.

At age 11, Camille was sent by her mother to a group home; this move started a pattern of disruption as she was shuttled between group homes and her mother's apartment. Raising two girls in the racist and often dangerous environment of the inner city, Camille's mother attempted to impress rigid gender roles on her daughters, encouraging them to limit themselves to the domestic sphere. African Caribbean women in Canada are located within a racially gendered capitalist economy in which black femininity is constructed as simultaneously a sign of hard labor and sexual availability.[19] Fearing the racialized sexual subordination of their Canadian-born children, many immigrant women seek to enforce strict sexual mores and harsh discipline. Such attempts can lead to generational conflicts that are sometimes interpreted as a culture gap but in fact arise out of the survival strategies engendered by the experience of migration. Camille resisted her mother's attempts to "protect" her by curtailing her freedom:

> I was a tomboy. Me and my brother always used to do stuff. But then he got older, he didn't want to hang out with me no more. He always got to go outside, and she's always telling me I'm a girl and I can't do this and that. She was always beating me. But I always did my own thing.

On leaving school with few qualifications, Camille found herself unemployed and living with her mother with no source of income. When she was approached by a male friend who asked her if she was interested in earning $5,000 in a week by importing cocaine from Jamaica, she accepted. After being detained by customs at Toronto airport, she was sentenced to two years and four months . . .

Unlike Teresa, Camille did not have children to support, and her mother paid for her basic needs. However, her situation is indicative of the problems facing young black Canadians who have been failed by an underfunded educational system that is unwilling to deal with the diverse needs of a multiracial population. Rather than places of education, inner-city schools have become locations where young black people are warehoused and, increasingly, policed. Unfamiliar with the Canadian school system, immigrant parents are ill equipped to challenge the labeling of their children as educationally subnormal or suffering from ADHD. Rather than dealing with working-class black children's needs, schools and child psychiatrists treat difficult behavior as medical problems, thus justifying notions of inherent (racialized) mental incapacity. Camille emerged from the school system with few skills and qualifications into a racially and gender stratified labor market that offers, at best, minimum-wage jobs to young women of color. In the context of a North American youth culture that defines personal value via consumerism, Camille's lack of legitimate access to money, or routes to better earning power, is a significant motivation for her involvement in drug importation.

. . . When funding for prisons and additional policing is squeezed from the budget of a government committed to making tax cuts, further cuts in social spending become inevitable. Youth programs, shelters for women and teens, schools, black community projects, and social workers are all affected. As social workers are forced to raise minimum intervention levels, families with problems that are not considered urgent are left without support. Underfunded social programs are limited to crisis intervention rather than prevention. As schools are forced to operate on limited budgets, the incentive to exclude children who behave in difficult ways is increased. The pattern of Camille's life, dotted with family conflict and violence, school exclusions, and unemployment, is evidence of an absence of appropriate social support. By redirecting tax monies from social programs into the prison industrial complex and by promoting a low-wage, "flexible"[20] labor market, the state exacerbates this trend and ensures that there will be a pool of young women from Ontario's inner-city projects willing to risk their lives by importing drugs.

Narrative Three: Gender Entrapment and the Crack Cocaine Disparity

Kemba Smith was a middle-class African American student at Hampton College, a traditionally black college in Virginia. She became involved with a young man, Khalif Hall, who, unknown to her, was a key figure in a large drug operation. When Hall began to abuse Kemba and threatened to kill her, she did not leave him because she was afraid for her family and herself and because she had become pregnant. Shortly before the drug ring was apprehended, Hall was shot and killed. Kemba pleaded guilty to conspiracy to distribute crack cocaine, but hoped Hall's intimidation would be taken into account. Instead, she was held responsible for the full 255 kilos involved in the offense—although she personally was not found to have handled the drugs—and was sentenced to 24.5 years in prison. Kemba's case has been adopted by activists who oppose the war on drugs, including Families Against Mandatory Minimums, the Kemba Smith Justice Project, and the Million Woman March.[21] . . . The 24.5-year sentence Kemba received is not indicative of a particularly unsympathetic judge but of a series of laws and policies introduced since the mid-1980s that have targeted users and street-level retail sales, highlighting crack cocaine as a particular threat. As Kemba argues:

> While laws should be designed to protect our communities from drug kingpins, instead, low level offenders with little or no involvement in the sale of drugs are being locked up for 15, 25, 30 [years], or 13 life sentences. In fact, I know a 30 year old Black woman, mother of two girls who was sentenced to 13 life sentences.[22]

Under the Anti Drug Abuse Act, Kemba's knowledge of her boyfriend's drug dealing was sufficient for her to receive a mandatory minimum sentence. However, her lack of involvement in the drug ring prevented her from providing information that might have reduced her sentence.

Kemba's case also illustrates what Beth Richie calls the "gender entrapment of battered black women": the high levels of male violence and abuse experienced by African American women entering the criminal justice system.[23] Many women are incarcerated as a direct result of a coercive and violent male figure. The woman's situation may have been caused by involvement in criminal activities, such as prostitution and drug dealing, in which the male is profiting from her; alternatively, her incarceration may be because of self-defense against a violent male partner. Feminist activists have organized around the cases of women incarcerated for killing their abusive partners, but there has been less awareness of the role of male violence—from early childhood sexual abuse to domestic violence—in the lives of women incarcerated for other types of offenses. In this sense, the psychological, physical, and sexual abuse that women are subjected to in prison is just one aspect of a continuum of violence in incarcerated women's lives. Women of color who live in emotionally and economically vulnerable positions in relation to men may be pressured by them to serve as free or cheap labor in the drug business. Although the women's movement has attempted to reduce women's dependence on men, welfare reforms and cutbacks in funding for women's shelters and day care under the Clinton and Bush administrations in the United States have further limited the choices of working-class women in particular. Kemba's case demonstrates that mandatory minimums and heightened police surveillance of communities of color, when combined with women's dependence on and coercion by male family members, create the conditions under which increasing numbers of women of color have been criminalized and turned into fodder for the prison industrial complex. As Kemba argues:

> With the entering of the New Year, I want to give you the gift of vision, to see this system of Modern Day Slavery for what it is. The government gets paid $25,000 a year by you (taxpayers) to house me (us). The more of us that they incarcerate, the more money they get from you to build more prisons. The building of more prisons create more jobs. The federal prison system is comprised of 61% drug offenders, so basically this war on drugs is the reason why the Prison Industrial Complex is a skyrocketing enterprise.[24]

Conclusions and Reflections on Abolitionism

This . . . [article] has described an exponential increase in women's imprisonment internationally and has suggested a new set of questions for feminist researchers and criminologists who wish to explain this phenomenon. . . .

· · ·

At a time when increasing numbers of women are being incarcerated, families separated, and communities devastated, any discussion of women, crime, and punishment must end with proposals for change. There are three possible approaches for those wishing to challenge the status quo regarding women's imprisonment: reform, decarceration, and abolition. *Reformers* focus on producing suggestions for change that are practical within the existing system. Feminist reformers have proposed women-centered prison regimes, for example, that require female prison officers, introduce programs on domestic violence and rape, or provide therapists working within a framework of women's empowerment. Feminist reformers have also proposed reforms to the law, legalizing prostitution, for example, or removing status offenses from the criminal law.

There are three problems with reformism. First, . . . reform tends to be incorporated into the prison and used as justification for its expansion. For example, in Canada, demands for women-centered prison regimes led to the construction of five new federal prisons, thus increasing the number of women behind bars. In Britain, the provision of a mother and baby unit led judges to feel more comfortable with sentencing pregnant women to prison. Second, reformers tend to work with the system, thus enabling the stigmatization of those with more radical proposals as idealist and unrealistic. Finally, reformers frequently fail to question why and whether women should be imprisoned in the first place and instead focus on reducing the pains of imprisonment. They are therefore ill equipped to oppose the explosion in women's imprisonment.

The second possibility is *decarceration*. This strategy goes a step further than reform by pushing for laws that will lead to people being released from prison. For example, decarceration strategies emphasize alternative forms of punishment, including fines and community service, as well as rehabilitation and reeducation programs in the free world, such as sex offender training and anger management. . . . A first step toward decarceration is the establishment of a prison moratorium, whereby states are petitioned to pass a resolution preventing the construction of any new prisons. If no new prison beds are made available, the argument goes, officials will have to find other ways to deal with men and women in conflict with the law. Decarceration is an important political strategy that challenges the constant expansion of the prison industrial complex and seeks to reduce the profit motive in prison growth. However, decarceration policies are vulnerable to political swings, and a moratorium can swiftly be reversed.

The third possibility is *abolition*. Prison abolitionists use this term to identify the prison as a fundamentally unjust institution that, like slavery, cannot be reformed.[25] They argue that prisons do not work, fail to reduce crimes, and fail to make vulnerable populations—including women and people of color—safer. Abolitionists also argue that prisons are incapable of rehabilitating people; instead, they brutalize prisoners and return them to their communities ill equipped to survive by legitimate means. Abolitionists point out the huge economic costs of imprisonment, and they argue that public funds could more effectively be spent preventing social problems by creating jobs with a living wage, providing women's shelters, creating youth programs, and developing high-quality education. They also point out the social costs of incarcerating two million people in the United States, with a devastating impact on their families and communities, particularly communities of color.

Abolitionism is the only strategy that requires a fundamental rethinking of the way in which justice is delivered. It requires that we look for the *root causes* of antisocial acts, such as assault, burglary, or domestic violence, and look for alternatives that address these root causes. Abolitionism has not been viewed with great enthusiasm by many feminists, however. After spending years campaigning for the criminal justice system to take rape, domestic violence, and child abuse seriously, many feminists have seen abolitionism as a mechanism that will remove valuable legal protections from women. Feminist abolitionists have dealt with this problem in two ways. First, some have called for the abolition of women's prisons only, arguing that women are imprisoned for very different reasons than men and therefore need different treatment.[26] This argument is, however, unsustainable in the light of calls for equal treatment of women under the law. Second, others have challenged the idea that "the nonsolution of imprisonment" makes women safe and have

argued that, in fact, an overreliance on punitive strategies prevents a more fundamental challenge to the patriarchal gender roles—and the institutions that support them—that are at the root of male violence against women.[27]

Reform *in isolation of a broader strategy for social change* serves to legitimize and even expand the prison industrial complex, and decarceration is only a stopgap measure. In contrast, abolitionism . . . offers a radical critique of the punitive approach to women's survival strategies. Abolitionism is the only strategy that removes the profit motive from the criminal justice system and the only approach that challenges the belief that prison works. Although it does not offer an immediate solution, it does provide a *critical framework* within which proposed legislation, campaigns, and activism can be assessed. By working together within an abolitionist framework, scholars, activists, prisoners, and their families are building a movement for lasting social change and for a safe and just global community.[28]

NOTES

1. Patricia Macias Rojas. 1998. Complex Facts, *Colorlines*, Fall.

2. Parliament of New South Wales, Select Committee on the Increase in Prisoner Population, www.parliament.nsw.gov.au, accessed July 4, 2000.

3. Canadian Criminal Justice Association. 2000. *Aboriginal Peoples and the Criminal Justice System*, Ottawa.

4. Commission on System Racism in the Ontario Criminal Justice Sytem. 1994. *Racism Behind Bars*, Toronto: Queens Printers.

5. Mike Elkins, Carly Gray, and Keith Rogers. 2001. *Prison Population Brief: England and Wales April 2001.* London: Home Office Research Development Statistics.

6. Freda Adler, 1975. *Sisters in Crime: The Rise of the New Female Criminal.* New York: McGraw-Hill.

7. Carol Smart. 1979. The New Female Offender: Reality or Myth, *British Journal of Criminology* 19(1): 50–59.

8. William Grieder. 2000. "The Last Farm Crisis," *The Nation*, November 20.

9. Manning Marable. 2000. Seattle and Beyond: Making the Connection in the 21st Century, *Dialogue and Initiative*, Fall.

10. "As Jamaica gets ready to go global and sticks to liberal policies, international investors need look no further than this Caribbean island to find opportunities which they won't regret." Quoted from *Jamaica: Island of Opportunity*, www.vegamedia.com/jamaica/jamaica.html, accessed January 20, 2002.

11. Higglers are traders, often women, who buy and resell cheap clothing, food, and other low-cost products in Jamaica's informal economy.

12. Angela Y. Davis. 1998. Race and Criminalization: Black Americans and the Punishment Industry. In *The Angela Y. Davis Reader*, ed. Joy James. Malden, MA: Blackwell.

13. Joel Dyer. 2000. *The Perpetual Prisoner Machine: How America Profits from Crime.* Boulder, CO: Westview.

14. Mark Fishman and Gray Cavender, eds. 1998. *Entertaining Crime: Television Reality Programs.* New York: Aldine DeGruyter.

15. This has not been the case; instead, criminalization and targeting by law enforcement artificially inflate the price of drugs, so that manufacturing, trafficking, and selling them become immensely profitable and increasingly associated with violence. This mutually profitable relationship between law enforcement and the drug trade has been labeled the "international drug complex" (Hans Van Der Veen. 2000. *The International Drug Complex.* Amsterdam: Center for Drug Research, University of Amsterdam).

16. Pseudonyms have been used to protect the identities of the first two interviewees. The case of Kemba Smith has reached national prominence due to the clemency granted her by president Bill Clinton at the end of his term in office. I have therefore used her real name.

17. Human Rights Groups Criticize Clinton over Aid to Colombian Military. 2000. *San Francisco Chronicle,* August 29.

18. US Sprays Poison in Drug War. 2000. *Observer,* July 2.

19. Dionne Brand. 1999. Black Women and Work: The Impact of Racially Constructed Gender Roles on the Sexual Division of Labour. In *Scratching the Surface: Canadian Anti-Racist Feminist Thought.* ed. Enakshi Dua and Angela Robertson. 1999. Toronto: Women's Press.

20. Corporations prefer a workforce that can be hired and fired according to seasonal fluctuations in demand. This "flexible" workforce is thereby denied stable, permanent employment and adequate compensation for being laid off.

21. For information on the campaigns on behalf of Kemba Smith, see www.geocities.com/CapitolHill/Lobby/8899. These groups were largely responsible for bringing about the pardoning of Kemba Smith in the last days of the Clinton administration in 2000. Kemba has continued to campaign on behalf of the thousands of low-level, drug-involved prisoners who remain incarcerated for obscenely long terms of imprisonment.

22. Kemba Smith, From the Desk of Kemba Smith, www.geocities.com/CapitolHill/Lobby/8899/pen.html, December 13, 1999.

23. Beth Richie. 1996. *Compelled to Crime: The Gender Entrapment of Battered Black Women.* London and New York: Routledge.

24. www.geocities.com/CapitolHill/Lobby/8899.

25. Jim Thomas and Sharon Boehlefeld. 1991. Rethinking Abolitionism: "What Do We Do with Henry?" *Social Justice* 18(3): 239–25.

26. Pat Carlen. 1998. *Sledgehammer: Women's Imprisonment at the Millennium.* Basingstoke and London: MacMillan.

27. Fay Honey Knopp. 1993. On Radical Feminism and Abolition. In *We Who Would Take No Prisoners: Selections from the Fifth International Conference on Penal Abolition,* ed. Brian D. MacLean and Harold E. Pepinsky, p. 55. Vancouver: Collective Press.

28. Organizations working within this framework include Critical Resistance http://www.criticalresistance.org and the International Conference on Penal Abolition (ICOPA) http://www.interlog.com/~ritten/icopa.html

10

♦♦♦

Women and the Military, War, and Peace

In the United States most people grow up with pride in this country, its wealth, its power, and its superior position in the world. We learn the Pledge of Allegiance, a sense of patriotism, and that our way of life is worth fighting and perhaps dying for. Most families have at least one member who has served in the military. The United States is number one in the world in terms of military technology, military exports, and military expenditure. It accounts for half of world military spending, equal to that of the next fifteen countries combined (China, Russia, Britain, France, Japan, Germany, Saudi Arabia, South Korea, India, Brazil, Italy, Australia, Canada, Indonesia, and the Netherlands), most of which are U.S. allies (War Resisters League 2008). The largest proportion of our federal budget, $1,449 billion for fiscal year 2009 or 54 percent, supports current and past military operations, including the upkeep of over four hundred bases and installations at home and one thousand of those abroad, the development and maintenance of weapons systems, pensions for retired military personnel, veterans benefits,

and interest on the national debt attributable to military spending (War Resisters League 2008). From 2002 to 2009 military operations in Afghanistan and Iraq cost another $10 billion per month on average (Center of Arms Control and Non-proliferation 2008). Major companies with household names like Westinghouse, Boeing, and General Electric research and develop weapons systems and military aircraft. War movies are a film industry staple, portraying images of manly heroes, with movies like *Private Benjamin* (1980) and *G.I. Jane* (1997) presenting female military heroes. Many best-selling video games involve violent scenarios. "Full Spectrum Warrior," a video game set in an apparently Arab city, was developed with $4 million from the U.S. Army as a training tool for recruits (Ahn and Kirk 2005). The Army also has its own video game, America's Army, as a recruitment tool (www.americasarmy.com). Toy manufacturer Mattel markets a female colleague for G.I. Joe, a helicopter pilot dressed in a jumpsuit and helmet and armed with a 9mm Beretta. Even Barbie is in uniform.

The military shapes our notions of patriotism, heroism, honor, duty, adventure, and citizenship. President Clinton's avoidance of military service as a young man was heavily criticized by his detractors in the 1992 and 1996 election campaigns, the suggestion being that this was unpatriotic and not fitting for a president of the United States, who is also the commander in chief of the armed forces. Psychologist Stephen Ducat (2004) discussed the importance of "the wimp factor" in U.S. politics. In the 2008 race for Democratic party presidential candidate, neither Hillary Clinton nor Barack Obama, the main contenders, had military experience, and at times both presented themselves as tough candidates who would not be "soft on defense."

Politically, economically, and culturally, the military is a central U.S. institution. This is more explicit since the attacks on the World Trade Center and Pentagon on September 11, 2001, and the Bush administration's declaration of an open-ended "war on terrorism." Under the banner of patriotism, young people enlisted in the military and parents were encouraged to support them. By 2008, over four thousand U.S. troops had been killed in Iraq; thousands more had been seriously injured or were suffering from trauma. Some had gone AWOL (absent without leave) or sought conscientious objector status. Others had committed suicide. In Reading 56, Anuradha Kristina Bhagwati gives thumbnail sketches of her experiences in boot camp and later of her participation in a peace rally after serving in Iraq. Military recruiters are falling behind in their targets as the war in Iraq continues, despite an increased number of recruiters and bigger sign-up bonuses. The No Child Left Behind Act concerning education also requires high schools to provide the Department of Defense with a directory of all juniors and seniors (names, addresses, and phone numbers) or risk losing federal funding. Parents must be notified; if they object to having their child's information released to military recruiters, the onus is on them to write to the school administration and say so. As part of the global "war on terrorism" the Bush administration called on the Hollywood film industry to make more pro-war movies. The Walt Disney Corporation distributed a State Department ad nationwide, "Can you trust your neighbor?" that urged people to report any "suspicious" activity to the police. Political scientist Cynthia Enloe shows that many aspects of U.S. culture have become militarized and notes specific ways that culture is deployed in the service of militarism (Reading 55). There are "G.I. Jane Boot Camp" fitness programs. Toy manufacturer Ever Sparkle Inc. has a bombed-out dollhouse where grenades replace salt and pepper shakers, ammunition boxes litter the kitchen, and G.I. Joe, armed with a bazooka, is on the balcony ready for action. High-fashion designers are promoting the "military look" and camouflage chic. Backpacks, cell phone covers, baby clothes, and condoms all come in "cammo."

The Need for Women in the Military

Although the vast majority of U.S. military personnel have always been male, the military has needed and continues to need women's support and participation in many capacities (see, e.g., D'Amico and Weinstein 1999; Enloe 1983, 2000a; Isakson 1988; Weinstein and White 1997). It needs mothers to believe in the concept of patriotic duty and to encourage their sons, and more recently their daughters, to enlist or at least to support their desire to do so. It needs women nurses to heal the wounded and the traumatized. It needs wives and girlfriends back home, the prize waiting at the end of war or a period of duty overseas, who live with veterans' trauma or who mourn loved ones killed in action.

During World War II, white women and women of color symbolized by Rosie the Riveter were needed for the war effort working in shipyards and munitions factories while men were drafted for active service overseas (Denman and Inniss 1999). Currently the military needs women to work in electronics and many other industries producing weapons components, machine parts, tools, uniforms, household supplies, and foodstuffs for military contracts. It needs women working in nightclubs, bars, and massage parlors near foreign bases and ports providing R and R, rest and relaxation, for military personnel, or, as it is sometimes called, I and I, intoxication and intercourse (Enloe 1993a, 2000a; Sturdevant and Stoltzfus 1992). And the military needs women on active duty, increasingly trained for combat as well as performing more traditional roles in administration, communications, intelligence, or medicine.

Having women in the military in significant numbers is a relatively new phenomenon. In 1972, near the end of the Vietnam War, women were only 1.2 percent of military personnel. The following year, after much debate, Congress ended the draft for men, though young men are still required to register for the draft when they turn 18. Many left the services as soon as they could, causing a manpower shortfall that has been made up by recruiting women, especially women of color. In 2004 women were 15 percent of all military personnel (in the Army, Air Force, Navy, Marine Corps, and Coast Guard). Almost half the women in the Army's enlisted ranks were Black (46 percent), compared to 31 percent in the Navy and 28 percent in the Air Force. African American women, Asian American women, Native American women, and Latinas made up 63 percent of enlisted women in the Army, 52 percent in the Navy, and 40 percent in the Air Force. By contrast, 64 percent of women officers in the Army were white, 75 percent of the women officers in the Navy were white, and 76 percent of women officers in the Air Force were white (Women's Research and Education Institute 2002). As part of the long process of accommodating women, all service branches have had to design uniforms for them, including for pregnant soldiers, and to specify rules for hairstyles and make-up (see Box).

Army Regulations on Hair and Cosmetics

Military uniforms are the subject of detailed regulations and protocols. Uniform committees have long deliberated over appropriate dress for women—seeking to balance the soldier (read male) with the feminine. Nowadays women's uniforms emphasize practicality; they include pants, for example. Maternity uniforms have been introduced for pregnant servicewomen. The emphasis is on uniformity and professionalism, with precise rules governing all aspects of appearance, including fingernails and scrunchies, as shown in this excerpt from Army Regulation 670-1 (AR 670-1) Wear and Appearance of Army Uniforms and Insignia:

(3) Female haircuts will conform to the following standards.

(a) Females will ensure their hair is neatly groomed, that the length and bulk of the hair are not excessive, and that the hair does not present a ragged, unkempt, or extreme appearance. Likewise, trendy styles that result in shaved portions of the scalp (other than the neckline) or designs cut into the hair are prohibited. Females may wear braids and cornrows as long as the braided style is conservative, the braids and cornrows lie snugly on the head, and any hair-holding devices comply with the standards in 1-8a(3)(d) below. Dreadlocks (unkempt, twisted, matted individual parts of hair) are prohibited in uniform or in civilian clothes on duty. Hair will not fall over the eyebrows or extend below the bottom edge of the collar at any time during normal activity or when standing in formation. Long hair that falls naturally below the bottom edge of the collar, to include braids, will be neatly and inconspicuously fastened or pinned, so no free-hanging hair is visible. This includes styles worn with the physical fitness uniform/improved physical fitness uniform (PFU/IPFU).

(b) Styles that are lopsided or distinctly unbalanced are prohibited. Ponytails, pigtails, or braids that are not secured to the head (allowing hair to hang freely), widely spaced individual hanging locks, and other extreme styles that protrude from the head are prohibited. Extensions, weaves, wigs, and hairpieces are authorized; however, these additions must have the same general appearance as the individual's natural hair. Additionally, any wigs, extensions, hairpieces, or weaves must comply with the grooming policies set forth in this paragraph.

(c) Females will ensure that hairstyles do not interfere with proper wear of military headgear and protective masks or equipment at any time [see1-8a(1)(a), above]. When head-gear is worn, the hair will not extend below the bottom edge of the front of the headgear, nor will it extend below the bottom edge of the collar.

(d) Hair-holding devices are authorized only for the purpose of securing the hair. Soldiers will not place hair-holding devices in the hair for decorative purposes. All hair-holding devices must be plain and of a color as close to the soldier's hair as is possible or clear. Authorized devices include, but are not limited to, small, plain scrunchies (elastic hair bands covered with material), barrettes, combs, pins, clips, rubber bands, and hair bands. Devices that are conspicu-ous, excessive, or decorative are prohibited. Some examples of prohibited devices in-clude, but are not limited to, large, lacy scrunchies; beads, bows, or claw clips; clips, pins, or barrettes with butterflies, flowers, sparkles, gems, or scalloped edges; and bows made from hairpieces.

b. Cosmetics.

(1) General. As with hairstyles, the require-ment for standards regarding cosmetics is necessary to maintain uniformity and to avoid an extreme or unmilitary appearance.

Males are prohibited from wearing cosmet-ics, to include nail polish. Females are au-thorized to wear cosmetics with all uniforms, provided they are applied conser-vatively and in good taste and complement the uniform. Leaders at all levels must exer-cise good judgment in the enforcement of this policy.

(a) Females may wear cosmetics if they are conservative and complement the uniform and their complexion. Eccentric, exagger-ated, or trendy cosmetic styles and colors, to include makeup designed to cover tattoos, are inappropriate with the uniform and are prohibited. Permanent makeup, such as eyebrow or eyeliner, is authorized as long as the makeup conforms to the standards out-lined above.

(b) Females will not wear shades of lipstick and nail polish that distinctly contrast with their complexion, that detract from the uni-form, or that are extreme. Some examples of extreme colors include, but are not limited to, purple, gold, blue, black, white, bright (fire-engine) red, khaki, camouflage colors, and fluorescent colors. Soldiers will not ap-ply designs to nails or apply two-tone or multi-tone colors to nails.

For many of these women, the military offers much better opportunities than the wider society: jobs with better pay, health care, pensions, and other benefits, as well as the chance for education, travel, and escape from crisis-torn inner cities in the United States or economically depressed small towns and rural areas. It enhances women's self-esteem and confers the status of first-class citizenship attributed to those who serve their country. Military recruiters emphasize security, professionalism, empowerment, adventure, patriotism, and pride. In noting the bene-fits of army life in the early 1950s, Jean Grossholtz (1998) included medical services, expanded opportu-nities for learning and growth, a ready-made com-munity of women, and a sense of self-worth and accomplishment. Margarethe Cammermeyer served

as a military nurse for twenty-six years, in the Army, the Army Reserves, and the National Guard; she was the highest-ranking officer to challenge military pol-icy on homosexuality before being discharged in 1992 on the basis of sexual orientation. Her autobiography emphasized the professionalism, structure, and disci-pline she experienced in military life and her keen sense of patriotism and duty (Cammermeyer 1994). Some women who have been stationed in Iraq have commented that the physical and mental challenges of serving in a war zone and engaging in combat gave them a sense of agency and accomplishment. In Reading 56, Anuradha Kristina Bhagwati suggests her intense sense of belonging to the military, or at least people she describes as "the good ones I used to know," despite deep contradictions. Her word sketches raise questions about who can belong, what it takes and what it means to belong, and what one belongs to.

As we argued in Chapter 7, the U.S. labor market has changed markedly over the past forty years through automation and the movement of jobs overseas. In addition to a loss of jobs, there are few sources of public funding for working-class women's (and men's) education. Government funding for education and many welfare programs was cut back during the 1980s and 1990s, but the military budget has been maintained at high levels and is increasing. Women who enter the military are thus going where the money is. Their very presence, however, exposes serious dilemmas and contradictions for the institution, which we explore in the next section. Another contradiction of this situation is the fact that massive government spending on the military diverts funds that could otherwise be invested in civilian job programs, education, and community services.

Limitations to Women's Equal Participation in the Military

Support for women's equality within the military is based on a liberal feminist belief in women's right to equal access to education, jobs, promotion, and authority in all aspects of society, and to the benefits of first-class citizenship. Women's rights organizations, such as the National Organization for Women, have campaigned for women to have equal opportunity with men in the military, as have women military personnel, military women's organizations like the Minerva Center (Pasadena, Md.) and the Pallas Athena Network (New Market, Va.), and key members of Congress like former representative Pat Schroeder, who was on the Armed Services Committee for many years. In 2001, in the military, as in the civilian job market, most enlisted women were doing "women's work," including support and administration (34 percent), health care (15 percent), service and supply (10 percent), and communications and intelligence (10 percent). Among officers this was also true: 41 percent worked in health care, 12 percent as administrators, and 10 percent in supply and logistics (Women's Research and Education Institute 2002) and this overall pattern still holds.

After years of pressure, women who served in Vietnam were honored with a memorial in Washington, D.C. This advocacy and recognition, together with women's changing position in society, have also affected social attitudes. In 1991, in the Persian Gulf War, for example, military women were featured in headline news stories around the country. Saying good-bye to their families as they prepared to go overseas, they were portrayed as professional soldiers as well as mothers. Also, the Department of Defense has paid more attention to the needs of military families than formerly, including posting couples with both partners in the military to the same locations.

Women's equal participation in the military has been limited in several ways, however, including limits on combat roles; limited access to some military academies; the effects of a general culture of racism, sexism, and sexual harassment; and the ban on being openly lesbian.

Women in Combat Roles

Women served in the U.S. military during World War II, the Korean War, and the Vietnam War. They were generally designated as auxiliary, according to political scientist Mary Katzenstein (1993), despite the fact that they performed a wider range of tasks than is usually recognized—as transport pilots (Cole 1992), mechanics, drivers, underground reconnaissance, nurses (Camp 1997), and administrators. The influx of women into the military since the mid-1970s and the question of whether to train women for combat exposed a range of stereotypical attitudes toward women on the part of military commanders, Pentagon planners, and members of Congress, depending on the degree to which they believed that combat is male. From the late 1980s through the 1990s, countless news reports, magazine articles, editorials, and letters to the editor took up this issue. Many argued that women are not physically strong enough, are too emotional, and lack discipline or stamina. They would be bad for men's morale, it was said, and would disrupt fighting units because men would be distracted if a woman buddy was hurt or captured. The country was not ready for women coming home in body bags.

Women in the military perform their jobs well. Military planners faced a dilemma. They needed

Are we willing to sacrifice one or
two of the children for oil?

women to make up the shortfall in personnel; at the same time, they held sexist or condescending notions about women. Many of their stereotypes were confounded by women's skills, professionalism, focus, endurance, strength, and loyalty. Debate continues on other grounds, such as whether it is appropriate for mothers to go to war. Restricting women from combat roles was a way of limiting their career advancement because senior positions often require combat experience (Franke 1987; Stiehm 1989). Political scientists Francine D'Amico and Laurie Weinstein (1999) commented that the "military must camouflage its reliance on *woman*-power in order to maintain its self-image as a quintessentially *masculine* institution" (p. 6). It has done this by marginalizing women through sexual harassment, professional disparagement, and distinctions between combatant and noncombatant. What counts as combat in modern warfare is not as simple as it might seem, however, and definitions of "the front" and "the rear" have changed with developments in military technology. Communications and supply, defined as noncombat areas where women work, are both likely targets of attack.

Media attention on women's participation in the 1991 Persian Gulf War showed that many performed combat roles similar to those of men, and this led to changes in laws and regulations that had previously kept women out of combat assignments (Muir 1993; Peach 1997; Sadler 1997; Skaine 1998). In 1993, the combat exclusion law was repealed, and some women began to train for combat roles.

In 2008, close to 90 percent of military jobs were open to women, to fly helicopters and fighter jets, work on combat ships, or command military police units. Women are still not permitted to engage in "direct ground combat" or work on submarines.

During the war against Iraq, "traditional front lines were virtually obliterated, and women were tasked to fill lethal combat roles more routinely than in any conflict in U.S. history" according to *Chicago Tribune* reporter Kirsten Scharnberg (2005). She described a mission just south of Baghdad where

> a young soldier jumped into the gunner's turret of an armored Humvee and took control of the menacing .50-caliber machine gun. She was 19 years old, weighed barely 100 pounds and had a blond ponytail hanging out from under her Kevlar helmet.
>
> "This is what is different about this war," Lt. Col. Richard Rael, commander of the 515th Corps Support Battalion, said of the scene at the time. "Women are fighting it. Women under my command have confirmed kills. These little wisps of things are stronger than anyone could ever imagine and taking on more than most Americans could ever know."
>
> *(Scharnberg 2005)*

Scharnberg reported that female troops returning from Iraq "appear more prone to post-traumatic stress disorder, or PTSD, than their male counterparts." The Veterans Affairs Department launched a $6 million study of PTSD among female veterans, the first VA study to focus exclusively on female veterans. A preliminary finding suggested that "female military personnel are far more likely than their male counterparts to have been exposed to some kind of trauma or multiple traumas before joining the military or being deployed in combat," including physical assault, sexual abuse, or rape, factors that can trigger PTSD (Scharnberg 2005). Research on Vietnam War veterans conducted by psychologist Rachel MacNair (2002) found that troops who had killed—or believed they had killed—suffered significantly higher rates of PTSD than those who had not. A Defense Department study of combat troops returning from Iraq found that many soldiers and Marines suffering from PTSD and readjustment problems were concerned about the stigma attached to appearing weak. They feared "their commanders and fellow troops would treat them differently and lose confidence in them if they sought treatment for their problems" (Scharnberg 2005). Recognizing that many service women are not adequately cared for by Veterans Administration health programs, the Service Women's Action Network (SWAN) was founded in 2007 to create support for military service women and to offer women veterans alternative options for healing and transitioning back into the civilian world. They plan to utilize a combination of therapies consistent with women's needs and preferences in this many-layered process.

Officer Training: Storming the Citadel

In 1975 Congress mandated that the three military academies were to admit women. Researching the experiences of the first women to enter the U.S. Military Academy at West Point, Janice Yoder (1989) noted the severe pressure on these women to do well. They were a highly visible, very small minority, tokens in what had been constructed as an exclusively male institution. They faced tough physical tests designed for men; they were out of the loop in many informal settings and were routinely subjected to sexist notions and behavior by male cadets who did not accept them as peers (Campbell with D'Amico 1999). As a result, for the first four years at least, the dropout rate for women was significantly higher than it was for men, a fact that could be used by policy makers to justify exclusionary practices. Yoder concluded, however, that these women were not competing on equal terms with men, and she argued for changes in evaluation criteria and the overwhelmingly male culture of the Academy, an increase in the number of women entering the Academy, and greater commitment to women's full participation at an institutional level. Since then, women have entered other private military academies like the Citadel and the Virginia Military Institute (VMI) with similarly mixed success. In January 1997, two of the first four women at the Citadel withdrew because of intolerable harassment (Applebome 1997). The other two became the first female cadets to graduate from the Citadel in 1999. Two women also completed their training at the VMI in the same year. In 2002 the first class of Black women graduated from the Citadel.

Sexism and Misogyny

Added to this chilly climate for women are overt sexual harassment and sexual abuse. Many women in the military experience sexual harassment, even though the Department of Defense has had a "specific policy prohibiting sexual harassment of military personnel for over fifteen years," summed up as "zero-tolerance" (Guenter-Schlesinger 1999, p. 195). A 1995 Department of Defense survey reported that 4 percent of all female soldiers said they had been the victim of a completed or attempted rape during their military service, and 61 percent said that they had been sexually harassed in the Army (High 1997). Ninety percent of women in a Veterans Administration study reported harassment, and a third said they had been raped by military personnel (*STAMP Newsletter* 1998/99). Paula Coughlin, a helicopter pilot, went public with her experiences of sexual assault at the 1991 Tailhook naval aviators' convention at the Las Vegas Hilton, where women were subjected to sexual harassment, indecent assault, and indecent exposure. She testified that she endured relentless harassment from colleagues afterward and had since resigned her commission as a Navy lieutenant (Noble 1994). More than eighty other women filed complaints, and a few also filed civil lawsuits.

After hearing testimony from servicewomen in 1992, a Senate Committee estimated that as many as 60,000 women had been sexually assaulted or raped while serving in the U.S. armed forces. Senator Dennis DeConcini commented, "American women serving in the Gulf were in greater danger of being sexually assaulted by our own troops than by the enemy" (Walker 1992, p. 6). In 1996 this issue surfaced publicly again, when women at the Aberdeen Proving Grounds Ordnance Center in Maryland complained of being sexually harassed and raped by drill sergeants during training. As part of its investigations into these allegations, the Army set up a toll-free hotline, which took four thousand calls in the first week relating to harassment at many military facilities (McKenna 1996/1997). *Time* magazine reporter Elizabeth Gleick (1996) described this issue as an abuse of power by superiors, threatening "to undermine the thing that many in the military hold sacred: the chain of command" (p. 28). As the investigation spread, military commanders did their best to attribute any misconduct to "a few bad apples," a comment that officials also made in connection with widespread sexual harassment reported by women cadets at the U.S. Air Force Academy in Colorado Springs in 2003. More than 1,000 incidents of sexual misconduct throughout the military were reported in 2003 (Smith 2004). A growing outcry caused Congress to require the Department of Defense to report on sexual assault in the military each year. Department of Defense policy emphasizes that sexual assault harms military readiness, that education about sexual assault policy needs to be increased and repeated, and that responses to sexual assault must be improved to encourage victims to report assaults (Cohn 2006). According to official statistics, in 2007, 181 out of 2,212 service members investigated for sexual assault—including 1,259 reports of rape—were referred to courts-martial, the military equivalent of a criminal prosecution. Another 218 cases were handled by nonpunitive administrative action or discharge, and 201 offenders were disciplined through "nonjudicial punishment" (Department of Defense 2008, pp. 15–19).

Congresswoman Jane Harman, Chair of the House Homeland Security Subcommittee on Intelligence, contended that nonjudicial punishment means being confined to quarters, assigned extra duty, or "a similar slap on the wrist" (Harman 2008). She added that in nearly half of the cases investigated, the chain of command took no action. According to law professor Marjorie Cohn (2006), commands can reject complaints if they decide they are not credible, and women who come forward have limited protection against retaliation from perpetrators, colleagues, or superiors. Women who report sexual abuse often find themselves interrogated and intimidated by skeptical officers. Some are disciplined themselves for drinking or wearing civilian clothes at the time of the assaults. Others say they have been given a medical discharge or otherwise "hounded out" of the military (Cohn 2006; National Women's Law Center 2003; Shumway 2004). Many women simply do not report such incidents. Cohn (2006) reports statements made by Col. Janis Karpinksi regarding several women who died of dehydration in Iraq because they stopped drinking liquids after 3 or 4 PM. "They were afraid of being assaulted or even raped by male soldiers if they had to use the women's latrine after dark" (Karpinski, quoted by Cohn 2006).

In the past decade more women have undertaken scholarly research on sexism as ingrained in military culture (Burke 2004; D'Amico 1998; Guenter-Schlesinger 1999; Morris 1999; Pershing 2003), initiated internal proceedings or lawsuits concerning sexual abuse (Woodman 1997), opened up these issues to a wider audience by writing about their personal experiences (e.g., Dean 1997), and organized to change military protocols, regulations, practices, and culture. Survivors Take Action Against Abuse by Military Personnel (STAAMP, Fairborne, Ohio), for example, grew out of women's anger and frustration with the lack of accountability for sexual harassment and abuse of women in the armed forces by their colleagues and superiors. Despite the existence of policies against sexual harassment and assault and an increase in sensitivity training for military personnel, entrenched military culture has blocked the systematic implementation of such policies.

Racism

The military prides itself on being an "equal opportunity" employer with a much more diverse workforce than many civilian businesses. The armed services were officially integrated in 1948, decades before desegregation in the southern states. Nevertheless, racism, like sexism, occurs between individuals and at an institutional level. Hall (1999) noted that a 1994 House Armed Services Committee report found that service members of color perceived racial discrimination, sometimes subtle, in opportunities for career-enhancing assignments, training, and promotions. Much Department of Defense information does not employ an intersectional analysis; data given by race may not be broken down by gender, which makes discrimination difficult to track.

The 1994 report uncovered serious problems with institutionalized racism throughout the armed forces and warned about skinhead and other extremist activity on four military bases visited by investigators. In December 1995, two African American civilians were shot, apparently at random, and killed by three white servicemen from the Army's 82nd Airborne Division at Fort Bragg, North Carolina (Citizen Soldier 1996). A year later, two African American airmen at Kelly Air Force Base (San Antonio, Texas) talked to news reporters about a racist incident in which they were taunted by men wearing pillowcases resembling Ku Klux Klan hoods. The airmen said that they were dissatisfied with the Air Force response to their complaints (2 Black airmen 1996). During the late 1990s, high-ranking officials regularly included declarations against racial discrimination in speeches and news briefings on behalf of the Department of Defense (e.g., Department of Defense 1996, 1997; Hamre 1998). Like incidents of sexual assault, racist incidents are likely to be underreported.

The preponderance of people of color in the enlisted ranks, mentioned earlier, shows the institutionalized racism of the wider society (Hall 1999; Moore 1996). Currently, military recruiters "target" high school students of color, including Spanish-language ads aimed at Latino youth and their families. Also racism plays a key part in the dehumanization of "enemies," a point we return to later in this chapter.

Sexual Orientation

A final area of limitation for women—and men—in the military concerns sexual orientation. The Pentagon considers homosexuality incompatible with military service, and a series of regulations have precluded lesbians and gay men from serving openly, despite their continuing presence as officers and enlisted personnel (Scott and Stanley 1994; Webber 1993). Jean Grossholtz (1998) pinpointed the contradiction implicit in this policy: The military is based on male bonding, yet homosexuality is banned. Thousands of gay men and lesbians have been discharged over the years in what she refered to as "purges." Research from the Center for the Study of Sexual Minorities in the Military (University of California, Santa Barbara) found that of the 6,300 people discharged between 1998 and 2003 the majority were active duty enlisted personnel in the early stages of their careers (Fouhy 2004). They included linguists, nuclear warfare experts, and other job specialties requiring years of training and expertise. The Army was responsible for 41 percent of these discharges, even though it was down on its recruitment targets and had invoked a "stop loss" order to stop soldiers from retiring or leaving if they were deployed to Iraq or Afghanistan. Women were 30 percent of those discharged, though they made up only 15 percent of active duty personnel. During

fiscal year 2006, the Pentagon dismissed 612 service members, the fewest annual discharges since 1993, perhaps applying its discharge policy more lightly given severe personnel shortages in a time of war.

During his first presidential election campaign, Bill Clinton promised to lift the ban on gays in the military when he came into office in 1992. Concerted opposition from the Pentagon and many politicians made this impossible, however, and some argue that current policy, summed up as "Don't Ask, Don't Tell, Don't Pursue," is not much different than before. "Homosexual conduct," defined as homosexual activity, trying to marry someone of the same sex, or acknowledging one's homosexuality is grounds for discharge. A number of lesbians and gay men have challenged this policy in court. Organizations, like the National Gay and Lesbian Task Force and Gay, Lesbian, and Bisexual Vets of America, continue to raise this issue as an example of lesbians' and gay men's second-class citizenship.

Reports of anti-gay harassment—including verbal abuse, beatings, death threats, and apparent killings—more than doubled in the late 1990s, increasing from 182 violations documented in 1997 to 400 in 1998 (Servicemembers Legal Defense Network 1999a). Military policy expressly forbids such harassment, but in April 1998, five years after the "Don't Ask, Don't Tell, Don't Pursue" law was enacted, the Pentagon acknowledged that the service branches had not instructed commanders on how to investigate those who make anti-gay threats. In August 1999, the Department of Defense issued an updated policy requiring mandatory training on anti-harassment guidelines for all troops, beginning in boot camp. In March 2000, Pentagon officials conceded that there was a "disturbing" level of gay harassment in the military (Richter 2000) and this continues. The Servicemembers Legal Defense Network (2002) urged Pentagon officials and service members to uphold the Anti-Harassment Action Plan published in 2000, and argued that "forcing lesbian, gay and bisexual service members to hide, lie, evade and deceive their commanders, subordinates, peers, families and friends breaks the bonds of trust among service members essential to unit cohesion" (p. 6). This network has continued to campaign for the repeal of the "Don't Ask, Don't Tell" law and reported that 79 percent of those polled in a 2007 CNN/Opinion Research Corporation poll were in favor of repealing this legislation (Servicemembers

Legal Defense Network 2007). The Netherlands was the first nation to end its ban on gays and lesbians in the military in 1972; other European countries gradually followed this lead, including Britain, which lifted its ban in 2000 (Neumann 2007).

Military Wives

Military wives have been the subject of a number of studies (e.g., D'Amico and Weinstein 1999; Enloe 1983, 2000a; Weinstein and White 1997). The model military wife is a staunch supporter of her husband's career. She learns to manage the moves from base to base, the disruption of family life, and interruptions in her own work. Increasingly, she may be in the military herself. Kristin Henderson (2004, 2006), a writer who is married to a Navy chaplain, interviewed U.S. military wives whose husbands had been deployed to Iraq. She noted the strains on personal relationships and family life and the wide gaps in the military's family policy that military wives attempt to fill on a voluntary basis as they also hold down paid employment and care for their children. In addition, they are a crucial source of emotional support, via phone and e-mail, for husbands thousands of miles away.

Wives and children of military families also suffer abuse at the hands of servicemen husbands and fathers, as discussed by anthropologist Catherine Lutz in Reading 57. She found that "the immediate pre- and post-deployment periods are the most dangerous for women: their partners fear losing control as they prepare to leave and attempt to reassert it when they return." She notes that "war always comes home, even when it seems safely exported." "Even in the best of times," she comments, "rates of domestic violence are 3 to 5 times higher in military couples than in comparable civilian ones." This finding is corroborated by Deborah Tucker, executive director of the National Center on Domestic and Sexual Violence, who also co-chaired the Department of Defense Task Force on Domestic Violence (Gettelman 2005; also see Houppert 2005a, 2005b). Women abused by military spouses are often fearful of reporting incidents because of a combination of lack of confidentiality and privacy; limited victim services; lack of training and assistance on the part of military commanders; and disruption caused by moving from base to base. As in civilian families,

estimates of domestic violence in military families are undoubtedly underestimates.

A made-for-TV documentary, "The War at Home," which first aired on *60 Minutes* in January 1999 and again in September 2002, helped to make this issue more public. The Miles Foundation (Waterbury, Conn.) and Survivors in Service United have taken up the issue of violence within military families (Hansen 2001). In 2000, President Clinton appointed a Defense Task Force on Domestic Violence, comprising twelve high-ranking military members and twelve civilian members (domestic violence experts and legal practitioners), to assist in improving the military's response to domestic violence. In November 2001, Deputy Secretary of Defense Paul Wolfowitz issued an official memorandum stating that domestic violence would not be tolerated and calling on all commanders to update and standardize education and training programs, to increase protection for victims, to improve coordination between military and civilian agencies that respond to incidents of domestic violence, and to provide information to personnel on local services and resources. Meanwhile, this issue hit the headlines in the summer of 2002 when, within six weeks, the wives of three soldiers who had served in Afghanistan were killed at Fort Bragg (N.C.), allegedly by their husbands, discussed by Catherine Lutz (Reading 57). Two of the soldiers killed themselves as well. Three of the four men were in the Special Forces, considered the toughest and most aggressive unit in the Army. The Special Operation command said it would study the stress wartime deployments may be adding to already-shaky marriages. Soldiers would be screened for psychological problems before they leave Afghanistan and commanders would watch out for symptoms of depression and anxiety among their troops. Also in 2002, a bipartisan effort by elected officials and activists was successful in getting increased funding for domestic violence services in the Defense Appropriation Act for Fiscal Year 2003. Moreover, the 2002 Armed Forces Security Act provided for the enforcement of civilian court protective orders. These efforts, however, do not address systemic issues. Catherine Lutz notes that "there is no workplace more supportive of a masculine identity centered in power, control, and violence"; "there is little institutional incentive to rid the service of men who batter, since the military puts its war-making mission above all others." "Moreover, the military attempts to retain soldiers despite their crimes when they see them in terms of training costs that can range from $100,00 to $500,000 and more per person" (Reading 57).

The Impact of the U.S. Military on Women Overseas

The worldwide superiority of the United States—in political, economic, and military terms—is sustained by a global network of U.S. bases, troops, ships, submarines, and aircraft. Since the Bush administration declared war on terrorism after the attacks of September 11, 2001, U.S. bases have been established at thirteen locations in nine countries around Afghanistan; U.S. troops have returned to the Philippines; and base expansion is underway in Eastern Europe, Latin America, and Africa. This U.S. presence relies on agreements with each particular government. In return the military may pay rent for the land it occupies. Some local people may be employed directly on the bases; many others work in nearby businesses patronized by U.S. military personnel. U.S. military policies and bases abroad affect women in several ways, for example, through militarized prostitution, women's responsibility for mixed-race children fathered by U.S. service personnel, crimes of violence committed by U.S. troops, and the direct effects of war.

Militarized Prostitution

As a way of keeping up the morale of their troops, military commanders have long tolerated, and sometimes actively encouraged, women to live outside military camps to support and sexually service the men. With U.S. bases positioned strategically around the globe, especially since World War II, militarized prostitution has required explicit arrangements between the U.S. government and the governments of the Philippines, Japan (Okinawa), Thailand, and South Korea, for example, where many women work in bars and massage parlors, "entertaining" U.S. troops (Enloe 1990, 1993a, 2000a; Sturdevant and Stoltzfus 1992). As a way of protecting the men's health, women who work in bars must have regular medical exams, on the assumption that they are the source of sexually transmitted infections (Moon 1997). If the bar women fail such tests, they are quarantined until they pass. They usually earn better money than they can make in other ways, though this may be much harder as they grow older. By creating a class of women who are available for sexual servicing, the governments attempt to limit the sexual demands of U.S. military personnel to specific women and specific locations.

Occupational dangers for the women include psychological violence, rape, and beatings from some of their customers; health risks from contraceptive devices, especially IUDs; abortions; HIV/AIDS and other sexually transmitted infections; drug use; and a general lack of respect associated with this stigmatized work. Currently, most women working in bars around U.S. bases in South Korea and Okinawa are recruited from the Philippines, due to the weakness of the Philippine economy. Women displaced due to the collapse of the former Soviet Union and subsequent transition to a market economy also work in bars around U.S. bases overseas. Militarized prostitution is an integral part of the global sex trade, as mentioned by Ursula Biemann (see Reading 45).

Crimes of Violence Against Women

The behavior of U.S. troops in other countries is governed by agreements between the U.S. government and the host government, called Status of Forces Agreements (SOFAs). Usually U.S. military personnel who commit crimes against civilians are dealt with, if at all, through military channels rather than the local courts. In many cases, U.S. troops are not held responsible for crimes they commit. Sometimes they are simply moved to another posting. This is a highly contentious issue, especially for those who do not support the U.S. military presence in their countries. In Reading 57, Catherine Lutz mentions the work of the National Campaign for Eradication of Crime by U.S. Troops in Korea, which collects information about crimes committed against Korean civilians by U.S. military personnel and seeks redress for victims. In Reading 58, Suzuyo Takazato, cofounder of Okinawa Women Act Against Military Violence, reports on the long history of crimes of violence committed by U.S. troops against women and girls in Okinawa (see also Fukumura and Matsuoka 2002).

Takazato contends that the 65-year U.S. military presence in Okinawa constitutes an ongoing occupation with serious consequences for local communities. U.S. troops based in Okinawa have trained for combat in the Korean War, the Vietnam War, the Persian Gulf War (1991), and the war in Iraq.

The Effects of War

The many direct effects of wars on human beings include the killing of soldiers—mainly younger men—and of noncombatants—mainly women, children, and elders; the trauma of experiencing or witnessing destruction, torture, or rape; physical injuries and disabilities and post-traumatic stress disorders; the chaos of everyday life, with hunger and loss of home, family, and livelihood; and the trauma of being forced to flee from home and live as refugees. Other effects include contaminated water, broken sewers, power outages, environmental devastation, and the prevalence of weapons. Economic collapse resulting from war causes shortages of food, water, and basic supplies; exorbitant prices; destruction of farms and gardens, factories, and other workplaces; endless queuing for necessities; and having to go without. This situation impacts women severely as they try to care for children and sustain their families and communities. An Iraqi woman, who took the name Riverbend (2005, 2006), gave outsiders a rare window into the daily effects of war and occupation through her blog reports from Baghdad. She wove descriptions of her family's experiences—of raids, queuing, cuts in water and electricity services, the noise of helicopters, explosions at night—together with her analysis of news reports and current events (www.riverbendblog.blogspot.com). Her voice is clear, engaging, sarcastic, angry, fearful, and also generous, as she explains what many readers outside Iraq were not learning through mainstream media reporting (see Reading 59 for several early postings).

Perhaps one of the most far-reaching effects of war is the normalization of violence in everyday life, including violence against women by family members, acquaintances, or strangers as well as police officers, prison guards, and military personnel. News reports of U.S. military women raped or sexually assaulted by U.S. troops or contract personnel trickled into the U.S. news during 2007 and 2008. There have been far fewer accounts of sexual abuse of Iraqi women by U.S. troops, whether in prison or in their homes and neighborhoods (see L. Harding 2004). Sexual abuse and torture committed by U.S. military personnel and contractors against Iraqi prisoners in Abu Ghraib prison shocked the world in 2004 and introduced a grim new twist on sexualized military violence, where race and nation "trumped" gender. White U.S. women were among the perpetrators (taking on the masculinist role); Iraqi men were violated (forced into the feminized role). Seeing women engaged in torture turned upside down "deeply gendered presumptions" (Enloe 2007, p. 100) of militarized sexual abuse as a crime against women by men, and challenged theorists to explain it (see McKelvey 2007). Some feminist scholars emphasized the process of feminization—"imposing allegedly feminine characteristics on a person . . . or a group or a kind of activity" often with the goal of lowering their status—at the heart of these atrocities (Enloe 2007, p. 95). U.S. women captors were deployed strategically to shame and humiliate Iraqi men. However, the power they wielded derived from their national affiliation as members of the United States military and from their whiteness as well as their gender.

As a weapon of war, rape of women involves a complex intertwining of gender and race/ethnicity and is a strategic and systematic way of dishonoring and attacking enemy men. In World War II, Korean and Chinese "comfort women" were forced to provide sexual services for the Japanese Imperial Army (Hicks 1994; Kim-Gibson 1999; Sajor 1998). In the 1990s, armies conducted systematic rapes in the Balkans (Cockburn 1998; Kesic 2000; Walsh 2001) and in Rwanda (Newbury and Baldwin 2001; Rehn and Sirleaf 2002). More recently, pro-government militias have raped women and girls in the Darfur region of Sudan (Kristof 2005; Lacey 2004). "International Criminal Tribunals for the former Yugoslavia and Rwanda raised the standards of accountability for crimes of sexual violence against women" (Rehn and Sirleaf 2002, p. 96). Rape is explicitly listed among crimes against humanity, which can occur in war or in peacetime.

Health Effects of Environmental Contamination

Militaries create more pollution than other institutions, but unlike industry, military pollution is governed by fewer regulations, monitoring programs, and controls (Seager 1993). Routine military operations involve the use of highly carcinogenic materials, including fuels, oils, solvents, and heavy metals that are regularly released, affecting the land, water, air, and ocean, as well as the health of people living around U.S. bases or training areas, as mentioned by Mililani Trask in Reading 65 (also see Institute for Policy Studies 2000; Kirk 2008; Zamora-Olib 2000). The U.S. nuclear weapons industry has caused long-term environmental destruction in this country and overseas (Birks and Erlich 1989; Lindsay-Poland 2003; Seager 1993; Shulman 1990), with serious effects on people's health. In the 1950s and early 1960s the United States military, as well as those of Britain and France, undertook a series of atomic tests in the Pacific that irradiated whole islands and contaminated soil and water for generations to come. Micronesian women gave birth to children with severe illnesses or disabilities caused by radiation, including some "jellyfish babies" without skeletons who lived only a few hours (de Ishtar 1994; Dibblin 1989). Pacific Island women and men have contracted several kinds of cancer as a result of their exposure to radioactive fallout. Given the long-lasting effects of atomic materials in the food chain and people's reproductive systems, these disabilities and illnesses are likely to last for generations. Environmental destruction in the 1991 Persian Gulf War included the burning of oil wells, contamination of water, and use of depleted uranium (see, e.g., Bloom et al. 1994; Seager 1992; Tashiro 2001). The environmental health effects of more recent wars against Afghanistan and Iraq are still to be assessed.

Women's Opposition to the Military

Activist organizations oppose the presence and impact of U.S. military bases in many countries, including those mentioned earlier. This opposition is sometimes based on nationalism, sometimes on arguments for greater self-determination, local control of land and resources, with more sustainable economic development. Women often play a key role in these groups.

Early Women's Peace Organizations in the United States

In the United States, too, although many women have supported and continue to support the military in various ways, there is a history of women's opposition to militarism and war with roots in Quakerism and the nineteenth-century suffrage and temperance movements (Alonso 1993; Washburn 1993). Julia Ward Howe, for example, remembered as the author of the Civil War song "The Battle Hymn of the Republic," was involved in the suffrage movement as a way of organizing women for peace. In 1873 she initiated Mothers' Day for Peace on June 2, a day to honor mothers, who, she felt, best understood the suffering caused by war. Howe's *Mother's Day Proclamation,* written in 1870, calls on women to oppose war (Reading 60). Women's peace festivals were organized in several U.S. cities, mainly in the Northeast and Midwest, with women speakers who opposed war and military training in schools. During the 1890s many women's organizations had peace committees that were active in the years before U.S. entry into World War I. The Philadelphia Peace Society was still organizing in this way as late as 1909 (Alonso 1993). In 1914 the Women's Peace Party was formed under the leadership of Carrie Chapman Catt and Jane Addams.

Despite difficulties of obtaining passports and wartime travel, over one thousand women from twelve countries, "cutting across national enmities," participated in a Congress of Women in the Hague, Holland, in 1915, calling for an end to World War I. The congress sent delegations to meet with heads of state in fourteen countries and influenced press and public opinion (Foster 1989). A second congress at the end of the war proposed an ongoing international organization: the Women's International League for Peace and Freedom (WILPF), which is active in thirty-seven countries today and maintains international offices at the United Nations and in Geneva, Switzerland. Among the participants at the second congress were Mary Church Terrell, a Black labor leader from the United States, and Jeanette Rankin, the first U.S. congresswoman and the only member of Congress to vote against U.S. involvement in both world wars. Felicity Hill and Mikele Aboitiz (2002) reported on a WILPF-sponsored initiative in 2000, that resulted in the U.N. Security Council adopting Resolution 1325, which addresses the disproportionate impact of armed conflict on women. It recognizes the undervalued contributions that women make to conflict prevention, conflict resolution, and peace building and stresses the importance of women's equal and full participation as active agents in peace and security. These authors discussed the significance of this resolution for women in Afghanistan (Reading 73).

From World War I onward, U.S women's peace organizations opposed U.S. involvement in successive wars, especially the Vietnam War, and also opposed the nuclear arms race with the (then) Soviet Union (see, e.g., Adams 1991; Swerdlow 1993).

Feminist Antimilitarist Perspectives

Women's opposition to militarism draws on a range of theoretical perspectives, which we discuss briefly below. In any particular organization several of these perspectives may provide the basis for activism, but it is useful to look at them separately to clarify different and sometimes contradictory positions.

Women's Peaceful Nature   Although some women— and men—believe that women are "naturally" more peaceful than men, there is no conclusive evidence for this. Differences in socialization, however, from infancy onward, lead to important differences in attitudes, behavior, and responsibilities in caring for others. Many who oppose the military see the current division of labor in society between men's and women's roles as a fundamental aspect of military systems, whereby men (and now a few women) "protect" women, children, and older people. They ask: Can we afford this dichotomy? Where does it lead? Those who support women's equal access to social institutions argue that everyone should have the opportunity to join the military and take on roles formerly reserved for men. Opponents contend that the abolition of war is dependent on changing this division of labor, with men taking on traditional women's roles and caring for infants and small children, the elderly, and the sick (Dinnerstein 1989; Ruddick 1989). In U.S. electoral politics more women than men have opposed high military budgets and have supported socially useful government spending, giving rise to a **gender gap** in voting patterns (see Abzug 1984; Ducat 2004; Gallagher 1993).

Maternalism   Some women see their opposition to war mainly in terms of their responsibility to protect and nurture their children; they want to save the lives of their own children and the children of "enemy" mothers. In the early 1980s, for example, when the U.S. and Soviet militaries were deploying nuclear weapons in Europe, Susan

Lamb, who lived near USAF Greenham Common in England, a nuclear base, put it this way:

> I've got two young children, and I've taken responsibility for their passage into adulthood. Everyone tells me they are my responsibility. The government tells me this. It is my responsibility to create a world fit for them to grow up in. I can't say I'm responsible for my children not catching whooping cough and not responsible for doing anything about the threat of annihilation that hangs over them every minute of the day.
>
> *(Quoted in Cook and Kirk 1983, p. 27)*

Although this approach can sentimentalize motherhood, it is also powerful because mothers are behaving according to conventional roles and it is difficult for the state to suppress them. They expose contradictions: that the state, through militarism, does not let them get on with their job of mothering.

Diversion of Military Budgets to Socially Useful Programs   Another argument put forward by peace activists—women and men—concerns government spending. Organizations like Women's Action for New Directions (WAND) and the Women's International League for Peace and Freedom (WILPF, U.S. section) argue for reductions in military expenditures and redistribution of those funds to provide for social programs that benefit women and their families. Cuts in funding for nuclear weapons, chemical and biological weapons, and U.S. troops, ships, and aircraft carriers around the world, they argue, could fund job-training programs, public housing, education, urban development, environmental cleanup, and AIDS research, for example. Former legislative and executive director for WILPF (U.S. section) Jane Midgley (2005) analyzed the federal budget process and presents gender-sensitive ways of thinking about the bloated military budget and alternative people-centered budgets. When tax dollars are diverted from civilian programs like education and health care, where many women are employed, military spending is also at the expense of women's jobs. Economist and director of Employment Research Associates Marion Anderson (1999) noted that "every $1 billion transferred from the Pentagon to these civilian expenditures generates a net gain of about 6,800 women's jobs" (p. 248).

Human and Financial Costs of War

- Since 1900 there have been more than 250 wars. The civilian casualty rate in World War I was 5 percent, compared to 90 percent of war casualties in 1990, most of whom were women and children. This change is due in part to "deliberate and systematic violence against whole populations" (Swiss and Giller 1993, p. 612).

- There are approximately 50 million uprooted people around the world due to war—refugees who have sought safety in another country and people displaced within their own country. Between 75 and 80 percent of them are women and children who have lost their homes, farms, and sources of livelihood (UN High Commission for Refugees 2002).

- Women are subjected to widespread sexual abuse in wartime. In the 1990s in Bosnia and Rwanda, rape and forced impregnation were deliberate weapons of war.

- World military spending has been increasing since 1998 after an eleven-year period of reductions (1987–98). In 2006, it amounted to an estimated $1,204 billion, of which the United States was responsible for 46 percent (SIPRI—Stockholm International Peace Research Institute 2008). In 2002, SIPRI estimated that approximately $200 billion would allow all nations to provide decent housing, health care, and education for everyone; this amount was one-quarter the sum then invested in militaries (quoted in Rehn and Sirleaf 2002, 123). A change in budget priorities could provide resources for all those services and amenities, as well as develop renewable energy, clean up environmental contamination, address climate change, disarm nuclear weapons, and rid the world of land mines.

- U.S. taxpayers paid $15.1 billion for nuclear weapons in 2007. The same amount of money could have paid the salaries of 248,265 elementary school teachers or built 1,108 elementary schools. In 2007, U.S. taxpayers paid $137.6 billion for the cost of the war against Iraq. This could have provided scholarships for over 21 million university students for one year (National Priorities Project: www.nationalpriorities.org/tradeoffs).

- The cost of one multiple launcher rocket system loaded with ballistic missiles (a long-range self-propelled artillery weapon widely used in the 1991 Persian Gulf War), at $29 million, could have supplied one year's basic rural water and sanitation services for 2 million people in developing countries (Sivard 1996).

The Military as a Sexist and Racist Institution
Opposition to the military also turns on the argument that, by its very nature, the military is profoundly antifeminist and racist and based on the objectification of "others" as enemies. Its effectiveness depends on people's ability to see reality in oppositional categories: us and them, friends and enemies, kill or be killed (Reardon 1985). To this end it is organized on rigidly hierarchical lines, demanding unquestioning obedience to superiors. Although the military uses women's labor in many ways, it does so strictly on its own terms. The military environment fosters violence against women, as discussed earlier. Moreover, rape is used as a weapon of war (Peterson and Runyan 1993; Rayner 1997; Tétreault 1997).

Militarism is a system of investments, institutions, values, and practices that is much broader than a specific war or military operation. The Women's Pentagon Action, for example, identified militarism as a cornerstone of the oppression of women and the destruction of the nonhuman world. Thousands of women surrounded the Pentagon in November 1980 and 1981. They protested massive military budgets; the fact that militaries cause more ecological destruction than any other institutions; the widespread, everyday culture of violence manifested in war toys, films, and video games; the connection between violence and sexuality in pornography, rape, battering, and incest; and the connections between militarism and racism. This was no routine demonstration but a highly creative action organized in four stages: mourning, rage, empowerment, and defiance, culminating in the arrest of many women who chose to blockade the doors of the Pentagon (King 1983). The Unity Statement of the Women's Pentagon Action is included as Reading 61. These activists saw crucial connections between personal violence and international violence, both based on the objectification of others. Psychologist Stephen Ducat (2004) discussed the development of male identity "in a culture that disparages the feminine and insists that the boundaries between masculine and feminine remain unambiguous and impermeable" (p. 5). He argued that in most patriarchal cultures "the most important thing about being a man is *not being a woman*" (p. 6) and emphasized men's fear of feminization and the liability for men in public life of "the wimp factor." Political scientist Cynthia Enloe's (1990, 1993b) concept of a constructed **militarized masculinity** fits in here, an ideal of manhood that involves individualistic heroism of physical strength, emotional detachment, the capacity for violence and killing, and an appearance of invulnerability. She also emphasizes the role masculinity plays in national foreign policy making (Enloe 2000b). Other scholars argue that the nation-state, which the military is said to protect, is a patriarchal, heterosexist institution (Allen 2000; Peterson 2000; Plumwood 1993). Thus, women in combat roles, for example, threaten the manliness of war and the very nature of militarism as male.

Women who oppose militarism have very different perspectives from those who enter the military. They may also have different class positions and more opportunities for education and employment. Liberal feminists have criticized feminist peace activists as classist and racist in their condemnation of the military as an employer when working women, especially women of color, have few employment options. While liberal feminists call for women's equality within the military, the Unity Statement of the Women's Pentagon Action argues against participation in the military by women or men. Peace activists also argue that the military is no place for gay men and lesbians. Jean Grossholtz (1998) wrote that, ironically, it was her involvement in the military, seeing casualties of the Korean War, that changed her views and led her to become a peace activist later in life. Professor of sociology and activist Barbara Omolade (1989) noted the contradictions of militarism for people of color in the United States, many

DO YOU HAVE A FEMALE *ACTION FIGURE* THAT SPEAKS OUT AGAINST *DISCRIMINATION AND WAR!?*

of whom support the military because it provides opportunities that are lacking in civilian society. At the same time, military personnel of color fight for the United States, a country where they are oppressed. Since World War II, the people they have fought against and are trained to kill are other people of color in various parts of the world—Vietnam, Grenada, Libya, Panama, and Iraq—to take examples from the past several decades.

Globalization and Militarism   The military system is a core element in the global economy. Colonial expansion and the quest for control of strategic locations and scarce resources have been a major justification and impetus for military intervention for centuries. In the current war on Iraq, a key issue is access to oil supplies. Steven Staples, Chair of the International Network on Disarmament and Globalization (Vancouver, Canada), argued that

> globalization and militarism should be seen as two sides of the same coin. On the one side, globalization promotes the conditions that lead to unrest, inequality, conflict, and, ultimately war. On the other side, globalization fuels the means to wage war by protecting and promoting the military industries needed to produce sophisticated weaponry. This weaponry, in

turn, is used or is threatened to be used to protect the investments of transnational corporations and their shareholders.

(Staples 2000, p. 18)

Nation-states, militaries, and corporations are increasingly intertwined as military functions are privatized and outsourced (Ferguson and Turnbull 2004). As far back as 1961, President Dwight Eisenhower warned against the power of the "military industrial complex" in a speech on leaving office. Political scientist Spike Peterson has used the term "military industrial congressional academic media complex" to refer to these institutional interconnections which include "revolving-door job opportunities" among the higher echelons of government, military, and corporations. Former Secretary of State Condoleeza Rice is one of the few women in this loop—formerly a political science professor, administrator, and Provost of Stanford University, she was also on the board of Chevron oil company. Military contractors, like Lockheed Martin and Haliburton, provide substantial campaign contributions and receive government contracts valued in billions of dollars. Staples (2000, p. 19) argued that the large U.S. military budget "is for all practical purposes a corporate subsidy" siphoning public money into private hands and protected under Article XXI of the General Agreement on Tariffs and Trade (GATT), which allows "governments free reign for action taken for national security interests."

The international arms trade, especially trade in smaller arms, is a central part of the global economy because it is an earner of hard currency and a way for many countries to repay foreign debt. Major bombing and missile strikes function like giant bazaars for arms manufacturers as war-tested planes and munitions command a price double or triple that of weapons without such testing. Jostling for contracts to rebuild Iraq was well under way before the war was started, as reported on the business pages and in the financial press.

Redefining Security

Since the attacks of September 11, 2001, and the Bush administration's immediate decision to take military action, many people have questioned whether the military and militarism—as a system of values and operations—can provide everyday human security or even national security. This open-ended war on terrorism has generated new feminist research and analysis and new energy for established organizations like Women's International League for Peace and Freedom (Philadelphia), Women's Action for New Directions (WAND, Arlington, Mass.), Women in Black (New York and other cities), and Women Against Military Madness (Minneapolis). It has also given rise to many new groups and networks, including Code Pink (San Francisco and other cities), Mothers Acting Up (Boulder, Colo.), Gather the Women, the Lysistrata Project, Racial Justice 911, and Women United for Peace, with an emphasis on organizing in a decentralized way, often via the Internet. Global Women's Strike, adopted the slogan "Invest in Caring, Not Killing," with participating groups from over thirty countries. The Women of Color Resource Center (Oakland, Calif.) held an antimilitary fashion show, "Fashion Resistance to Militarism," in 2005, highlighting—and critiquing—the upsurge of "camouflage chic" referred to earlier (see Euloe 2007, ch. 6).

Families for Peaceful Tomorrows came together in 2001 soon after the attacks of September 11 around their belief, "Our grief is not a cry for war." Military Families Speak Out, formed in 2002, is an organization of people who oppose the war in Iraq and who have relatives or loved ones in the military. Gold Star Families for Peace came to prominence in the summer of 2005, when Cindy Sheehan and members of other families who had lost loved ones in the war in Iraq camped outside the Bush family ranch in Crawford (Tex.), asking the president to explain why her son had died. The Central Committee for Conscientious Objectors counsels military personnel who want to leave, and the Youth and Militarism project of the American Friends Service Committee provides information for young people considering enlistment. The Service Women's Action Network publishes a leaflet, *What Every Girl Should Know About the U.S. Military,* warning young women about myths and realities of military life.

On the international level, in 2005, one thousand women were recognized and honored for their enormous and varied peace-making work worldwide. This project had two components: nominating a group of outstanding women from over 150 countries for the 2005 Nobel Peace Prize and creating a permanent record of their work. Choosing a thousand was symbolic—a way of saying that one cannot make peace alone. Although these remarkable women did not win the Nobel Prize, the documentation of their work through video, photography, and writing continues to spread knowledge of their contributions to peacemaking (1000 Women for the Nobel Peace Prize, 2005; see also Cockburn 2007; Porter 2007).

A significant tool for women's peace work was provided by the UN Security Council, which adopted Resolution 1325 on women, peace, and security in October 2000, as mentioned earlier. Although not binding on governments, Resolution 1325 sets a new standard of inclusiveness and gender sensitivity in peace negotiations and provides leverage for women's efforts to influence policy in post-conflict reconstruction (Lynes and Torry 2005).

Based on data and readings presented in this chapter, we argue that genuine security is not created by militarism. The UN Development Program lists four basic requirements for human security:

- The environment in which we live must be able to sustain human and natural life.
- People's basic survival needs for food, clothing, shelter, health care, and education must be met.
- People's fundamental human dignity, agency, and cultural identities must be honored.
- People and the natural environment must be protected from avoidable harm.

This view includes security for the individual— a major reason why women in the United States are drawn to enlist in the military—but also involves security at the meso, macro, and global levels.

◆◆◆

Questions for Reflection

As you read and discuss this chapter, think about these questions:

1. What purposes does the military serve in this society?

2. Who joins the military? Why?

3. What types of agency do women have in armed conflict, as combatants or as civilians? What is their agency based on? How is it complicated by oppression and abuse of women in various forms?

4. What is your idea of security—at all levels of analysis?

5. What can you do to improve your sense of safety/security in different settings?

6. How do you understand the "war on terrorism"?

◆◆◆

Finding Out More on the Web

1. Compare the proportion of the federal budget that is spent on education, social services, health, and foreign aid with that spent on the military. How much does your state contribute to the military budget? How much do you contribute? Use the following Web sites:

   Center for Defense Information: **www.cdi.org**

   National Priorities Project: **www.nationalpriorities.org**

   Stockholm International Peace Research Institute: **www.sipri.org**

   War Resisters League: **www.warresisters.org**

2. Find out more about the organizations mentioned in this chapter. What are their strategies and activities?

Additional websites for military women include:

Military Spouse Resource Center: www.milspouse.org

Military Woman: www.militarywoman.org

Service Women's Action Network: www.servicewomen.org

Taking Action

1. Think about the ways you usually resolve conflicts or serious differences of opinion with your family, friends and peers, teachers, and employers. What are the dynamics involved in each case? Do you cave in without expressing your opinion? Do you insist that you are right? Does violence play a part in this process? If so, why? What, if anything, do you want to do differently about resolving conflicts in the future?

2. List all the kinds of service you can imagine, as an alternative to military service, that would improve security at micro-, meso-, macro-, and global levels.

3. Analyze the representation of armed conflict and war in the news media or popular culture. Compare various U.S. news reports with those from other nations.

4. Using the information about federal spending you found on the Web, make a budget to provide for genuine security.

5. Research the Women of Color Resource Center's anti-military fashion show (www.coloredgirls.org) and create your own anti-military fashion show on campus or in your community.

FIFTY FIVE

Sneak Attack (2002)
The Militarization of U.S. Culture

Cynthia Enloe

Cynthia Enloe is Research Professor in International Development and Women's Studies at Clark University. Her many books include *Globalization and Militarization: Feminists Make the Links; The Curious Feminist: Searching for Women in the New Age of Empire,* and *Maneuvers: The International Politics of Militarizing Women's Lives.* She travels widely to lecture and serves on the editorial boards of several scholarly journals.

Things start to become militarized when their legitimacy depends on their associations with military goals. When something becomes militarized, it appears to rise in value. Militarization is seductive.

But it is really a process of loss. Even though something seems to gain value by adopting an association with military goals, it actually surrenders control and gives up the claim to its own worthiness.

Militarization is a sneaky sort of transformative process. Sometimes it is only in the pursuit of *de*militarization that we become aware of just how far down the road of complete militarization we've gone. Representative Barbara Lee (D.-Calif.) pulled back the curtain in the aftermath of the September 11 attacks when she cast the lone vote against giving George W. Bush carte blanche to wage war. The loneliness of her vote suggested how far the militarization of Congress—and its voters back home—has advanced. In fact, since September 11, publicly criticizing militarization has been widely viewed as an act of disloyalty.

Whole cultures can be militarized. It is a militarized U.S. culture that has made it easier for Bush to wage war without most Americans finding it dangerous to democracy. Our cultural militarization makes war-waging seem like a comforting reconfirmation of our collective security, identity and pride.

Other sectors of U.S. culture have also been militarized:

- **Education.** School board members accept Jr. ROTC programs for their teenagers, and social studies teachers play it safe by avoiding discussions of past sexual misconduct by U.S. soldiers overseas. Many university scientists pursue lucrative Defense Department weapons research contracts.

- **Soldiers' girlfriends and wives.** They've been persuaded that they are "good citizens" if they keep silent about problems in their relationships with male soldiers for the sake of their fighting effectiveness.

- **Beauty.** [In 2002] the Miss America Pageant organizers selected judges with military credentials, including a former Secretary of the Navy and an Air Force captain.

- **Cars.** The Humvee ranks among the more bovine vehicles to clog U.S. highways, yet civilians think they will be feared and admired if they drive them.

Then there is the conundrum of the flag. People who reject militarization may don a flag pin, unaware that doing so may convince those with a militarized view of the U.S. flag that their bias is universally shared, thus deepening the militarization of culture.

The events of post–September 11 have also shown that many Americans today may be militarizing non-U.S. women's lives. It was only after Bush declared "war on terrorists and those countries that harbor them" that the violation of Afghan women's human rights took center stage. Here's the test of whether Afghan women are being militarized: if their well-being is worthy of our concern only because their lack of well-being justifies the U.S.'s bombing of Afghanistan, then we are militarizing Afghan women—as well as our own compassion. We are thereby complicit in the notion that something has worth only if it allows militaries to achieve their missions.

It's important to remember that militarization has its rewards, such as new-found popular support for measures formerly contested. For example, will many Americans now be persuaded that drilling for oil in the Alaskan wilderness is acceptable because it will be framed in terms of "national security"? Will most U.S. citizens now accept government raids on the Social Security trust fund in the name of paying for the war on terrorism?

Women's rights in the U.S. and Afghanistan are in danger if they become mere by-products of some other cause. Militarization, in all its seductiveness and subtlety, deserves to be bedecked with flags wherever it thrives—fluorescent flags of warning.

FIFTY-SIX

◆◆◆

Belonging (2008)

Anuradha Kristina Bhagwati

Anuradha Kristina Bhagwati is a former Captain in the Marine Corps. She has a Masters in Public Policy from Harvard University. She is currently writing and teaching yoga in New York City.

Unwrapped

The twelve of us are crawling on our hands and feet. I have long since stopped feeling my arms. Not

feeling helps me to keep inching my feet forward. My head down, I see a large pair of black boots in front of me. In seconds, I am hauled into the air like a ragdoll and tossed over a wide set of shoulders. Bristol has removed me from my squad and proceeds to parade me around them.

Straight out of a Marvel comic strip, Bristol is the size of Godzilla. His nose is still crooked from years of fighting. His skin is cracked, his voice smooth and deep but weathered. I am one-third of his mass.

Bristol is a master manipulator. I am wary of letting him in, this beast of a man. The first woman he ran through this course was hazed, several hours a day for six weeks, in the heat of summer. Bristol's minions told him it was dangerous and unfair. Bristol uses pepper spray and pain to reinforce one's desire to succeed. He gave her more of it, but finally let her pass. I am his second experiment. I am too proud for this shit. In what way will he penetrate my pride?

Bristol's war stories are private affairs, but he will reveal information if it serves his purpose. Bristol and I share many things in common, and he will use these details to draw me in and spit me out at will. Bristol lets me know he's a cultured man. He can get away with this because he knows it's true. Why waste his poetry on the likes of thugs? Bristol will wax poetic with me because he'll know I'm listening.

We've circled my squad three times now. For all I know, they have no idea I'm being strutted around them like some giant girl trophy. Bristol is concerned that the third woman in his experiment is failing miserably. It is my job to make sure she gets through. She's not in my squad, so what do I care? I am trying to breathe as his shoulder blade cuts into my gut. Upside down, I see them still inching forward. I can't stand that I'm getting a break now. I have to earn my respect. Goddamnit, put me down.

The last time he wanted to prove I was different, he grabbed my hair, hard. "See, this is what they'll do to you if they really get their hands on you." Never flinch before the master. Why don't you say it, sir, say what they'll really do to me. Or are you scared I might cry and call daddy.

My knee went on strike before I arrived here. Flew out of the socket because I was hauling packs filled with sand and people twice my size for three straight weeks. The damn thing still wobbles around in a pool of jelly and reminds me of my fallibility and pride with every movement I make. It reinforces my inferior size and strength and boils the essence of this fight down to will. At the end of each day, I can barely walk without going numb. I fall asleep on several tablets of Naproxyn and bags of ice melting in between my legs. I have to prove I can make it on my own. Every time someone says to take it easy, I want to stab them.

Two weeks later and these nights have turned into longer days. Bristol appears and disappears, without notice. I see him now in my sleep. I am armed, moving through woods with bayonet. His eyes are everywhere to reinforce my vulnerabilities. The woods have no exit. His voice has no bottom. I feel it will snap into insanity if I ever wake up. I must keep him calm.

Bristol calls me into his office this week to tell me I'm not cutting it. He says something is missing. I'm disappointing. I am lulled into his throat again. Bristol has found it, finally, the son of a bitch. Goddamn spooks and operatives think they're masters of the universe and all of its minds. Bristol's playing dad. On the inside I tell him to go fuck himself. I'd rather take another blown leg than this psychodrama bullshit. I won't let him do this again.

Boredom

We are stripped down to t-shirts and trousers. It's as far as we can go without breaking regulations. Everyone has something to sport: tattoos encircling bulging biceps and forearms, cut-up pecs, and by the end of the afternoon, chafed and sunburned skin.

In this business of making riflemen, the peanut gallery shows no mercy. Everyone uprange is a loser, a boot. When our man hits too low, the berm crackles into hundreds of particles of dirt that tumble down over our heads and cake against our soaked shirts. When he hits too high, someone echoes the sound of a plane crashing. And while the shooters shift windage and measure their breaths in time with the pull of the trigger, we get bored.

Sergeant Mac wants some action. He finds an unsuspecting bug walking along the concrete, among cigarette stubs and Wonder Bread crumbs. It's got long thread-like legs, long enough for Mac to easily snatch him up.

It's a preying mantis. *Mac, what the hell is that?* Mac doesn't hear anyone. Just surveys the curves of the insect's legs, fully admiring its anatomy.

We're changing targets from 200 to 300 yards. Mac is still stroking his trophy. The creature doesn't seem to mind its newfound attention. And then Mac has an idea. With one hand wrapped around the bug, he reaches for the stickers we use to mark up a bullet-ridden target. Black and white one-inch-by-one-inch squares. Mac pulls down the target and places the bug smack in the center of the bulls-eye. Taking six stickers, he tapes the bug down by each leg.

No one notices this. If they do, they're unimpressed.

The bug is squirming on its canvas. Immobilized, it is now detached from the hands that found it. The bug misses Mac.

Mac is proud. Without batting an eye, he proclaims, "If you make it out alive, I'll let you go." Mac is convinced his idea is utterly original. Directly addressing his trainee, and with the utmost confidence, Mac really doesn't need an audience to affirm his self-worth.

Thirty 556 rounds from 300 yards away is a hell of a lot of racket for a bug on a target. But he stands a chance. He's got those fine, spindly legs, which means there's less of him to hit. And our shooter's been having a rough day. Hitting black only gets harder the further back he goes. All bets are on Mac's bug.

On "targets up," Mac raises our target to the sky. There's always a five second pause before the first shooter gets his round off. When it comes crackling through that giant piece of paper, the bug starts flipping out. He's struggling to unpin himself as rounds streak by him on both sides. Ten seconds later, they subside, and we pull the target down. Mac checks for six legs, and before the thing has time to breathe, Mac sends him up again for a second round.

I lose count as I watch Mac and the bug in their game of Russian roulette. Like a proud trainer, Mac is delighted that the bug's made it so far.

And then it happens. *Pow!*

Faces glance over for only a second. Mac brings down the target. He counts five and a half legs. The bug is in hysterics.

"Not bad, little man." Generous in doling out praise when it is due, Mac has become this bug's ringside coach.

As Mac raises the target for the bug's last dance, he bets with pride that the bug won't crack. And then it starts, the rapid fire. A deafening hail of three or four shots on target, then down and up again for more thunder, so many times, up and down, that I wonder if this bug knows which way is heaven and which way is hell.

Finally, a way out. A man of honor, Mac keeps his word and releases the bug from the canvas. Numb again, Mac grabs a cigarette.

Camouflage

Camouflage has mutated over the years. In order to survive, it has adapted with the times. It used to be about wanting to be all that you can be. The mystery of the jungle: its vines and darkness, the unexpected bayonet. Today, it has taken on the character of its hosts. In the personality, it is harder to detect as its own species.

Sexy brown women with six packs and glistening skin sport camouflage bikinis, bandanas, and combat boots in hip hop videos. Teenagers on the street wear cammies baggy and low just to own the uniform. Others wear it ripped and washed too many times to state that they'll never be what the government wants them to be. Camouflage has taken on all the colors of the rainbow. Orange and green or blue and gray camouflage means you can be part of the system and against it. You can recognize its vices and virtues, or maybe you don't have to recognize it at all.

I find a rich white college kid in a coffee shop one evening talking about himself to his father. Recruit Tommy is sporting a light pink shirt with a solid black print of an Apache helicopter, over blue jeans.

Instant analysis of the weaponry: This version of the helicopter has been hand-crafted. Another mutation. No hellfire, no tanks, no napalm. Neither sound, nor fury. It's Apache Lite. But Tommy takes the game of softening the warrior too far. This pink is the one parents choose to make their little girls look like dolls. Real GQ men choose harder versions. Tommy will never survive.

Men in Uniform

It is October in Boston, Massachusetts, and there are 2,000 of us gathered on the Common. It has begun to snow lightly. I am about to never look back again.

Seven white kids in their twenties are holding signs that say "Support the Troops" and "Hippies Smell." I recognize these counter-protesters from an anti-war rally on campus. I approached them intent to understand why they were there. My favorite patriot told me she was there because she "loved America." I told her to sign up. Today she and her friends are barricaded by a stretch of riot police. She's being lectured by some of the older peace veterans, their fingers pointing through shields and helmets to drive home the point. Her red, white and blue balloons are no match for their words.

I find a couple of guys in camouflage jackets, and they take me to see Jose. He is standing by a small table with a picture of a tank in the desert. He's blowing air into his hands and slowly swaying from side to side. He is underdressed and out of camouflage.

Jose is 31 and speaks like an older man who knows the bottom of things. He reminds me of the good ones I used to know, but there is no instinct to impress left in him. Jose tells me that somewhere between meditation and education he determined he didn't want to kill anyone. Jose still worries about his buddies, but he will refuse to participate. Jose is a conscientious objector.

I'm listening to a series of activists from around the globe decry the administration's war. They are a haze of brown—Filipino, Haitian, Colombian, Liberian. The United States has screwed them all. None of them reach me till the thirty-something black man gets up to perform his verse. It is eerie to recall desert duty in this bitter cold. He's a Gulf War infantryman, who reenacts his fixation to kill Saddam in rhythmic repetition, like a prayer and a promise, like cadence. I feel the tingle again, the reminder that this man and I are linked by virtue of our understanding the permanent influence of the institution on our psyche. This performance art goes straight to the heart of our experience. I wonder if anyone else knows.

He is followed by families of the war dead. The Puerto Rican father who killed the Marine messenger and tried to burn himself alive after being told his son had died overseas, the sister who watched her brother tormented by memories of combat finally kill himself, and Cindy Sheehan, the mother I'd heard about who made everyone believe accountability counted for something.

We march through Boston, somewhere towards the end of the pack of socialists and anarchists and peaceniks and pissed-offniks.

Watching Jose I remember why that pull into proud immersion still lays there, deep in my gut. God, I miss it so. This Staff Sergeant I could have used. Even-tempered and in full control, seeing the whole field as he addresses each member of his

society as if they were the one. Resting his hand on the shoulders of those who fought before, Jose invites the Vietnam generation to walk side by side with ours.

We pass a group of seven skinheads dressed mostly in black, protesting the rally with signs that say "AIDS cures Fags" and "Commies are Scum." All the vets start laughing, which jars the skinheads. Andy almost starts talking to the one with the pointy beard, but we tug him back. I feel the pull again to watch and protect. No one will touch these boys, or over my dead body.

Up ahead on our right we see the Park Street Armed Forces Recruiting Station. Outside the building are three Marine recruiters dressed in camouflage. GI Joe and his minority sidekicks: one white man, one black man, and one Latina—a picture of diversity for urban youth. I am reminded that Marines once took pride in not being allowed to wear camouflage utilities in the civilian world. Only the nasty Army could walk around off base in their utilities, as if they were no different than civilians. Regulations changed a few months ago, when the Commandant realized he'd have to switch tactics to get the teenagers to sign up for war. No more bling-bling and polished belt buckles for these Marines. It would be all about combat. Urban combat.

As we pass the station, no one speaks. There is a gulf between us and them as we observe one another watching. A few steps beyond, the conversation starts up again, but not about the recruiters. In the world of "been there, done that, so shut the fuck up," I wonder if these three give more thought to us than we do to them.

It begins to snow now, hard, and true to spirit, we get prouder. I waltz around gleefully documenting the throngs on the streets, the cops in riot gear and the endless parade of people too pissed off to be quiet ever again. When the band passes a riot squad in front of Macy's, we witness a cop on the sidewalk staring into the crowd.

Firmly nodding his head he says, "Goddamn right, bring the troops home."

FIFTY-SEVEN

Living Room Terrorists (2004)

Catherine Lutz

Catherine Lutz is a professor at the Watson Institute for International Studies and Department of Anthropology, Brown University. Her books include *The Bases of Empire: The Global Struggle Against U.S. Military Posts; Homefront: A Military City and the American 20th Century; Reading National Geographic* (co-author); and *Local Democracy Under Siege: Activism, Public Interests, and Private Politics* (co-editor).

War always comes home, even when it seems safely exported. We now have indications that the new wars of preemption and empire building are bleeding back already onto our shores. The evidence is not just in the thousands of ill and mangled soldiers returning from combat but in troubling new clusters of domestic violence in the military as well as ongoing efforts to shield military batterers from justice. Just as individuals, families, public infrastructure, and the international reputation of the United States will be paying the price of the ongoing debacles in Iraq and Afghanistan for decades, women partnered with soldiers will face increased rates and levels of violence far down the road.

The spotlight was focused on this problem during 2002, when the bodies of five women, each the current or recently separated wife of a soldier at the army's Fort Bragg, were discovered in Fayetteville, North Carolina. Shalamar Franceschi had her throat slit; Marilyn Griffin was stabbed seventy times and her trailer set on fire; Teresa Nieves and Andrea Floyd were shot in the head; and Jennifer Wright was strangled. They are only a few of the hundreds of women who have been killed or permanently disabled by soldiers—often their husbands or partners—in recent years around the approximately 1,600 domestic and overseas U.S. military bases. Even in the best of times, rates of domestic violence are three to five times higher among military couples than among comparable civilian ones. Yale University researchers reported their finding that male veterans who had been in combat (a relatively small subset of all veterans) were more than four times as likely as other men to have engaged in domestic violence (Prigerson, Maciejewski, and Rosenheck 2002).

Despite the prevalence of such crimes, the murders in North Carolina became objects of intense media attention: reporters and film crews flew in from all over the country and from as far afield as Japan and Denmark. The attention was in part because the killings were clustered tightly together, but also because several of the killers had recently returned from the war in Afghanistan. But the media have now moved on to other things, and the many murders and murderous assaults around the country that have followed those at Fort Bragg have been ignored.

Many in the general public and media wondered if the murders might have resulted from combat trauma suffered by the perpetrators. Army brass immediately suggested that the stress of deployment was to blame, particularly because it created what the army called marital problems. This argument had the advantage of supporting the army's requests to Congress for more money for a larger military, while also maintaining the hygienic fiction about combat required if one is to reach recruitment goals. In both media and military accounts, the soldier was the victim, and his murdered wife in one sense was the sign of his sacrifice and pain. After the murders, army officials ordered an investigation. Its conclusions: the couples suffered from marital discord and family stress. At most, gender appeared briefly in the analysis when it was noted that soldiers . . . have difficulty "asking for help" from service providers available on installations like Fort Bragg.

In an earlier formal directive to military commanders, Deputy Secretary of Defense Paul Wolfowitz had said that "domestic violence is an offense against the institutional values of the Military" (2001, 1). But from the ritualized abuse at the navy's Tailhook convention to the ubiquitous and virulent misogyny of everyday "humor" in the military to the . . . public testimony of dozens of women cadets raped at the Air Force Academy (fifty-six rapes are currently under investigation there), all the instances indicate that domestic and other forms of violence against women are not anomalies. Rather, they are at the center of the rationale and methods of war. The military as an institution promotes the idea of heterosexual male supremacy, glorifies power and control or discipline, and suggests that violence is often a necessary means to one's ends. Taking a life already requires that soldiers violate the most basic precept of human society. In a military increasingly forced or even willing to bend international codes of conduct in prosecuting wars, soldiers may absorb an attitude that they are above the law at home as well.

Alternatively, more adequate explanations come from those who work daily to provide services to women attacked or threatened by their partners and from the battered women themselves. They focus on what should be obvious—there is no workplace more supportive of a masculine identity centered in power, control, and violence; there is little institutional incentive to rid the service of men who batter, since the military puts its war-making mission above all others; and the military's toxic effects on rates of violence against women continue apace in "peacetime" as well as in wartime. Moreover, the military attempts to retain soldiers despite their crimes when they see them in terms of training costs that can range from $100,000 to $500,000 and more per person.

The Miles Foundation and STAAMP (Survivors Take Action Against Abuse by Military Personnel) are the two organizations working most visibly on the issue of military domestic violence at the national level, while virtually every domestic violence shelter and service provider in the country deals with women who have been assaulted by active-duty soldiers or veterans. These groups know that the immediate pre- and post-deployment periods are the most dangerous for women: their partners fear losing control as they prepare to leave and attempt to reassert it when they return. Christine Hansen of the Miles Foundation has said that her group could "tell what units were being deployed from where, based on the volume of calls [for help] we received from given bases" (personal communication with author). She notes that soldiers may also attempt to exert control at home in response to their workday experiences—they are among the most supervised and tightly controlled workers in the United States.

The military has worked hard to learn of, count, and root out same-sex, private sexual behavior in the services, but for some reason it is stymied when it comes to the much more visible problem of domestic violence. In 2000 the army reported that 1,213 domestic violence incidents had been recorded by their military police during that year. This figure is a drastic undercounting of the actual incidence of this crime given the strong disincentives to report it. Victims fear retaliation by the perpetrator, of course, but many also believe that reporting the crime will "destroy his career" or, paradoxically and apparently much more realistically, that it will not be taken seriously. Of the more than 1,200 cases, the army reported that only 29 resulted in court-martial or civilian court prosecution of the accused. They have no record of what happened in 81 percent of the military police reports or in any of the 12,068 violent incidents reported to the post's family services that same year.

An investigative report in the *Denver Post* by Amy Herdy and Miles Moffeit (2003) that examined military and civilian documents, including hospital, police, and court records, showed that all branches of the military have systematically ignored the problems of domestic violence and rape. They have failed to investigate or prosecute offenders, failed to provide protection to the women involved, and in fact often intimidated or even prosecuted the victim herself. Batterers are often given light administrative punishments, such as anger management classes, and go on eventually to be promoted and given honorable discharges.

Even men who murder their partners have not been pursued. When Tabitha Croom was killed and her body found at Fort Bragg in 1999, investigators had strong probable cause that her special forces boyfriend, Forest Nelson, was the perpetrator. (He was the last person seen with her before she disappeared; a neighbor saw him load a large sheet-covered object in his trunk that night; he failed a polygraph test; and he had a previous history of attacks on her and on a former wife.) But Sergeant Nelson continued to work in a psychological operations battalion for the next two-and-a-half years, at which point he separated from service. The case was closed mere months after the multiple Fort Bragg murders and after assurances that domestic violence prevention was a key army goal. Croom's case was only reopened after the attention brought to it by the *Denver Post,* and murder charges were finally filed against him in 2004. Nelson's military unit works under the banner "Win the Mind, Win the Day," which is clearly the military's strategy not only for engaging the "enemy without" but the "enemy within." That enemy is any woman (or anyone else) who threatens the recruitment, "unit cohesion," and budget goals of the U.S. military.

The Department of Defense has consistently failed to respond to congressional directives meant to deal with domestic violence, a problem that has been evident for several decades now. In 1988, for example, the department was told to report crimes committed by soldiers to the FBI; it has not yet complied. Even after the Fort Bragg murders, the Pentagon continues to stonewall efforts to raise awareness about the problem of domestic violence in the military and its cover-up.

Domestic violence in this country typically is defined by the boundary of the heterosexual family, although as conceptions of family and appropriate sexuality have shifted in most parts of society, that boundary has expanded to include intimate partners. The military, however, lags behind in this area. During my visits to U.S. military base communities in several Asia-Pacific countries over the last several years, women activists in these communities told me about the problems of prostitution, rape, and other forms of violence, and about the local government's and the U.S. military's tolerance or support of it. The intent of this complicity, Suzuyo Takazato of Okinawan Women Act against Military Violence told me, has been to deflect violence from "good" local women onto the "bad" ones who, as a result of poverty and other forms of coercion, become prostitutes (see Reading 58). In 1992, however, hundreds of thousands of Koreans rallied in protest around the Internet-circulated image of the desecrated body of a woman prostitute, Yoon Kum-I, who had been killed by a GI. Since then, the National Campaign for the Eradication of Crime by U.S. Troops in Korea has kept a list of offenses perpetrated by members of the U.S. military, although it does not categorize assaults on women by their relationship to the man who attacked or killed them.

In the United States, we find that desperately underfunded civilian public services—from shelters for victims of domestic violence to courts and hospital emergency rooms—do not have the money to deal with the injured and dead women or the returning troops. The military adventure in Iraq has created further problems for women in at least three ways: it has taken funds away from prevention and treatment of domestic violence; it has increased the demand for such services in the ways just mentioned and through a general militarization and masculinization of the culture; and it continues to legitimate a huge military and an atrophied sense of the public interest—something further exacerbated when the military siphons off several million, often working-class men and women who receive the health and educational benefits that a more fully socialized system of public care would provide for all.

Since the *Denver Post* articles, there have been yet more calls for reform of the military's methods for preventing and handling domestic violence and for more congressional hearings. Virginia Republican John Warner held hearings of the Senate Armed Services Committee in 2004 but restricted them to the problem of rape at the Air Force Academy. An aide to a key member of that committee claimed that hearings after the Fort Bragg murders had established that in those cases, "there were problems in the marriage either before he left or while he was gone that served as a catalyst [for murder] rather than him just coming home and freaking out," repeating the army's findings that the murders were not part of a pattern of masculine control and militarized abuse. With every failed attempt to get justice for the victims of violence, however, more people may recognize that the problem is in fact war itself and the system of patriarchy and profit it is meant to defend.

The catchphrase "Support our troops" is on many lips these days, and the courage and endurance of military family members are widely celebrated. Few in government or media, though, suggest that this notion means anything more than beaming them all good feelings. The Bush administration has cut back on some veterans' benefits, while the tangible and often violent costs of being in a military family continue apace. Like earthquakes, however, moments of tectonic social change often expose buried objects as the ground shifts and opens. The unprecedented level of military mobilization and interventionism that has gone on in the last several years has suddenly revealed the problem of "normal" military violence against women. It is especially striking that it began to garner that attention in 2002 and 2003, when the issue to which our attention seemed fixed was official state-sanctioned violence in mortal contest with unsanctioned nonstate violence or "terror." But terror is a homegrown tactic of patriarchy; its victims are not random at all but our sisters, mothers, and friends. Tens of thousands of these women are working bravely against such terror every day.

ACKNOWLEDGMENTS

This chapter first appeared in the *Women's Review of Books*, 2004, 21(5): 17–18.

REFERENCES

Herdy, Amy, and Miles Moffeit. 2003. "Betrayal in the Ranks." *Denver Post*, November 16, 17, and 18. http://extras.denverpost.com/justice/tdp_betrayal.pdf (accessed April 1, 2007).

Prigerson, Holly G., Paul K. Maciejewski, and Robert A. Rosenheck. 2002. "Population Attributable Fractions of Psychiatric Disorders and Behavioral Outcomes Associated with Combat Exposure among U.S. Men." *American Journal of Public Health* 92(1): 59–63.

Wolfowitz, Paul. 2001. "Memorandum for Secretaries of the Military." November 19. http://www.ncdsv.org/images/Att5LetterfromWolfowitz.pdf (accessed March 10, 2007).

FIFTY-EIGHT

♦♦♦

Report from Okinawa (1997)
Long-Term U.S. Military Presence and Violence Against Women

Suzuyo Takazato

A prominent feminist activist and opinion leader in Okinawa (Japan), **Suzuyo Takazato** is co-facilitator of Okinawa Women Act Against Military Violence, the first women's anti-militarist organization in Okinawa. She has worked as a social worker, particularly concerned with violence against women, and was elected to the Naha City Assembly as an independent candidate for four terms.

In the mid-1990s, thanks to the concerted efforts of women organizers and activists, UN conferences began to address military violence against women in war and armed-conflict situations as a human-rights issue. The Vienna Declaration, adopted at the World Conference on Human Rights, June 1993, focused on mass rape and forced impregnation of women as strategies of "ethnic cleansing" in Bosnia-Herzegovina:

> Violations of the human rights of women in situations of armed conflict are violations of the fundamental principles of international human rights and humanitarian law. In particular, it is essential to effectively engage in addressing all forms of human rights violations, including murder, systematic rape, sexual slavery and forced impregnation.
> *(Vienna Declaration and Program of Action, No. 38)*

The Beijing *Platform for Action,* adopted by the UN Fourth World Conference on Women, 1995, built on the Vienna Declaration, stated that "Rape in the conduct of armed conflict constitutes a war crime," and urged the necessity to "take all measures required for the protection of women and children from such acts" and to

> undertake a full investigation of all acts of violence against women committed during war, including rape, in particular systematic rape, forced prostitution and other forms of indecent assault and sexual slavery, prosecute all criminals responsible for war crimes against women and provide full redress to women victims.
> *(Beijing Platform for Action, article 233)*

Clearly, cases such as the Japanese military system of sexual slavery during World War II, mass rapes in Bosnia-Herzegovina, and many circumstances of armed conflict are instances in which the violent nature of military power has been directed

This information was presented to the International Conference on Violence against Women in War and Armed Conflict Situations, which reported to the UN Special Rapporteur on Violence Against Women. Tokyo, Oct. 30–Nov. 3, 1997. This article was translated by Carolyn Bowen Francis, and edited by Gwyn Kirk.

against women. Today, as in the past, women and children become entangled in wars whenever and wherever armed conflict breaks out.

Military violence against women also occurs in many other situations, such as military occupation, colonial domination, military political control, and even UN military forces' peacekeeping activities. This reality, and policies to address it, are not included in the Beijing *Platform for Action*. Human rights violations which occur as a result of a foreign military presence must be understood and addressed from a gender perspective. Even when women are not at the battle-site, as in Asian countries during the Vietnam War, wherever U.S. troops were stationed or a "Rest and Relaxation" ("R&R") site established, violence against women occurred. This is the case with the long-term U.S. military presence in Okinawa (Japan).

Okinawa's Unique Situation

Okinawa, the southern-most prefecture of Japan, is situated midway between Tokyo and Manila, and has been called the "keystone of the Pacific" by military planners because of its strategic location. Currently, some 59,000 U.S. troops are stationed in Japan, including 12,000 Navy personnel of the Seventh Fleet based at Yokosuka. Seventy-five percent of the U.S. military presence in Japan is in Okinawa, although Okinawa is only 0.6 percent of the land area. There are 39 U.S. bases and military installations in Okinawa, roughly 30,000 troops, and 22,500 family members.

Okinawa's situation in regard to U.S. bases differs from other parts of Japan in three ways. In 1945, Okinawa was the site of a fierce, three-month land battle between U.S. and Japanese forces, in which Okinawa citizens became entangled. The Battle of Okinawa resulted in the death of one-fourth of the Okinawan population—more than 200,000 people. The battlefield also became the site of violence against women. Second, the most productive land—where Okinawan people had long secured their livelihood—was requisitioned to build vast U.S. bases. Okinawans, displaced by the battle, were not allowed to return to their land until after the military had selected sites for new bases. Okinawa was under total U.S. military control for 27 years after World War II, during which

period the U.S. military in Okinawa was directly involved both in the Korean War and the Vietnam War. Third, administrative control of Okinawa was returned to Japan in 1972 while the Vietnam War was still in process, resulting in continued escalation of U.S. military crime and violence against Okinawan women. Today, 27 years after Okinawa's reversion to Japan, a huge U.S. military presence continues to be located in highly-congested Okinawa, which still serves as the site of U.S. Marine Corps battlefield simulation drills conducted on a regular basis. Many Okinawans oppose this U.S. presence and are also bitter that successive Japanese governments have allowed Okinawa to bear the major burden of U.S. troops and bases in the country (Japan Coalition on the U.S. Military Bases 1998).

Military Endorsement and Support of Violence Against Women

In general, the extent of military violence against women depends on a number of factors: the attitude of the host government and host country regarding the status of women and respect for their human rights; the legal system that is in place to protect their status; the treaties and agreements between the sending country and the receiving country regarding human rights; and the adequacy of the arrangements to prevent crimes. The larger the economic gap existing between the country deploying the military presence and the country receiving the military presence, the more military personnel look down on women in the host community, view women's sexuality as a commodity to be purchased, and contribute to the growth of military prostitution.

The U.S. military system is overwhelmingly male-dominated, . . . (Enloe 1995; Reardon 1993). Troops engage in daily training exercises to hone their skills in killing and wounding to maintain a constant state of readiness that will enable them to be deployed to a conflict situation on a moment's notice. Military bases in Okinawa are located next to, or within, Okinawan residential areas. U.S. troops are allowed to move freely outside the base, and their violent training overflows into the Okinawa community. The U.S. forces stationed in Okinawa were deployed to the Korean War in the 1950s, the Vietnam War in the 1960s and '70s, and the Persian Gulf War in 1991.

The warriors returned to Okinawa on each occasion carrying their pent-up battlefield aggression, which they released on women in the vicinity of military bases.

To promote "morale," U.S. military operations include routine "Rest and Relaxation" sites in Asian countries (Sturdevant and Stoltzfus 1992). Prostitution and rape are the military system's outlets for aggression, and its way of maintaining control and discipline—the target being local women, as well as women in the military or U.S. military families. Prostitution and rape is viewed as a reward—for example, in "R&R"—and serves to bolster a sense of masculinity. After the rape of a 12-year-old Okinawan girl by three U.S. military personnel in 1995 (discussed later in this article), Admiral Richard Macke, Commander of the Asia-Pacific Forces and a veteran of the Vietnam War, declared, "What fools! . . . for the price they paid to rent the car, they could have had a girl" (Schmitt 1995 p. 6Y). He was removed from his position for this remark, a revealing comment on military attitudes to prostitution.

Today, former U.S. military women are denouncing military violence and sexual harassment. Both the U.S. Army and Navy admit the existence of sexual violence within those organizations, including violence in U.S. military families (Kelly 1998).

History of Military Prostitution and Sexual Violence in Okinawa

Between 1943 and 1945, Korean women were brought to Okinawa by the Japanese Imperial Army and were moved throughout the islands, where they were forced to serve as sexual slaves to Japanese troops stationed in Okinawa to defend the Japanese mainland. There were 130 Japanese military brothels established in Okinawa. Some Okinawan women were also made to serve as Japanese "comfort women."

April, 1945–49: The Battle of Okinawa and the Period of Postwar Chaos

Following the U.S. forces' landing on Okinawa, women were frequently abducted from their homes in areas under U.S. military control and raped by military personnel. Rapes occurred at random, including the rape of a nine-month-old baby girl (*The Okinawa Times* 1949). Some of these rapes resulted in the impregnation of Okinawan women and the birth of many children, posing a threat to the harmony of postwar Okinawa society. To prevent rape of the civilian population, brothels were established in each local area to service U.S. troops. At the internment camp in Chinen Village, a solitary house was repainted and turned into a U.S. military brothel. According to Okinawan women who laundered U.S. military uniforms they searched the pockets for unused condoms, which they returned to the U.S. military before washing the uniforms.

June 1950: Okinawa Bases Become Launching Sites to the Korean War

One portion of land returned by the U.S. military in September 1950 was turned into a brothel area in an attempt to address the frequent rapes perpetuated by soldiers in residential areas and the spread of sexually-transmitted diseases. In an attempt to safeguard U.S. military personnel from sexually-transmitted diseases, women serving U.S. troops were required to undergo periodic checkups. The military established the "A-sign" system (with an "Approved" sign awarded to establishments passing the health inspection conducted by U.S. military officials), and the "Off-limits" system (which restricted military personnel from unapproved bars). In the meantime, as Okinawa bases became launching sites to the Korean war, frequent military air crashes and traffic accidents resulted in the deaths of Okinawan citizens.

1965–73: The Vietnam War

B-52's from Kadena Air Base, on the main island of Okinawa, took off for bombing raids over North Vietnam, and Okinawa bases served as personnel deployment, command, training, weapons storage, and "R&R" sites. The brothel areas flourished. Women serviced 20–30 customers a day and were fined for taking time off during their menstrual periods or to care for children or other family members. Women who worked in clubs and bars under a system of controlled prostitution endured heavy debts and sexually-transmitted diseases, as well as suffered brutality at the hands of soldiers returning from Vietnam. Many women working as prostitutes were killed, and many cases of rape-related strangulation occurred. It was said that going to the (outside) toilet alone was a suicidal act, because a woman would likely be raped. According to a survey conducted in 1969, one out of every 50 women was involved in prostitution . . . one out of 30 to 40 for women in their 20s and 30s.

May 1972–1995: The Post-Reversion Period

In 1972, Okinawa reverted to Japan after 27 years of U.S. military administration. In 1973, the U.S. draft system changed from military conscription to voluntary enlistment. At the same time, the Japanese *yen* strengthened against the dollar, and U.S. troops in Japan no longer had superior buying power. During this period, the number of military personnel stationed in Okinawa remained virtually unchanged, although the prostitution areas experienced a sharp decline as U.S. troops could no longer afford to patronize them. Meanwhile, the number of Okinawan junior-high and high-school girls who were victims of sexual violence increased. Philippine women began working in bars and clubs around military bases in Okinawa, entering Japan on short-term "entertainer" visas. They endured inferior working conditions and severe human rights violations. In fact, in 1983, two Philippine women working in a club near a base burned to death in a fire as a result of unsafe working conditions (*Okinawa Times* 1983). Children fathered by U.S. military personnel and problems related to these men acknowledging paternity and paying child support increased during the post-reversion period. For instance, one woman attorney handled 30 of these cases in a two-year period (*Asahi Shinbun*). In 1991, U.S. bases in Okinawa were once again launching sites for war. This time, U.S. troops were deployed to the Persian Gulf War.

1995–1999: The Rape of a 12-Year-Old Girl

At 8.30 p.m. on September 4, 1995, a 12-year-old girl was returning home from a neighborhood shop in an area near a U.S. base when she was abducted in a car. She was hit and had her eyes and mouth covered. Her body was bound with duct tape. She was raped and then dumped out of the car and left on the side of the road. Her three U.S. military assailants had rented the car inside the military base, purchased duct tape and condoms, and left the base for the purpose of abducting a woman and committing rape. The assailants' statements during their trial made clear their motives for committing the crime. Brothels are drab and reminded them of their poverty-stricken childhoods (personal testimony). Japanese women do not carry weapons such as guns or knives with which to defend themselves, so even if they resist, there is little chance of danger. Japanese people are not able to distinguish U.S. military personnel on the basis of their appearance. Colleagues had committed rape without being caught, so they felt that their victim would not press charges. Thus, they drove around bustling shopping areas and residential neighborhoods for several hours, targeting several women, but failing to accomplish their goal. Finally, they attacked the young girl.

What especially shocked Okinawan citizens was that exactly 40 years before, a six-year-old girl had been abducted, raped, and murdered by U.S. troops (*Ryukyu Shinpo*). This recent incident was merely the latest in a long string of similar incidents that have continued throughout the postwar period. But this case resulted in an outpouring of activity for several reasons. First, the young girl pressed charges. Second, the rape occurred during the Beijing Women's Conference where violence against women was declared a violation of human rights and this inspired confidence in Okinawan women activists returning from Beijing who quickly organized to protest the rape, and U.S. military violence in general. Third, the rape occurred during the 50th anniversary of the end of the war, a time of reflection concerning Okinawa's 50-year-long military presence. Parents, teachers, and citizens were shocked and were forced to recognize that the age of the girl made it very clear that such violence reaches out to claim its victims without distinction. Okinawans' perceptions of U.S. military personnel have changed over the years. Nowadays, they move about freely, compared to the Vietnam War period and are perceived not as military personnel but as American citizens.

Limitations in the Status of Forces Agreement

The stationing of U.S. forces in Okinawa is governed by treaties and agreements between the U.S. and Japanese governments (Status of Forces Agreements). But these agreements treat military crimes lightly, especially crimes against women, and make possible the acceptance of military "R&R." There are several severe limitations to the Status of Forces Agreement from the perspective of Okinawan communities.

No Policy for Preventing the Violation of Women's Human Rights

The freedom of activity of U.S. military forces stationed in Okinawa is guaranteed, but policies to prevent crimes or support victims of crimes committed by U.S. troops have never even been discussed. There is no systematic data on U.S. military crimes. U.S. authorities proclaimed that the rape of the wife or daughter of a U.S. serviceman would result in the death penalty for the assailant. In contrast, punishments for U.S. military crimes were light. In many cases, because the suspect was returned to the U.S., the trial verdict was never known. Until 1972, U.S. military crimes were handled by military courts-martial, and only after Reversion were trials held under the Japanese legal system. During the 27 years of U.S. military control there was no accurate report of the results of military courts-martial. Even today, there is no complete report of the total number of incidents and how they are dealt with. Some cases are adjudicated through the Japanese courts; while crimes committed inside U.S. bases that result in a court-martial are tried entirely separately.

This situation arose partly due to limitations in Japan's legal system, which judges crimes of rape more lightly than robbery (sentences for robbery result in prison sentences of five to 15 years, while rape results in prison sentences of six months to seven years). Published crime statistics in Okinawa have not itemized rape separately from other felonies like murder, burglary, and arson, another factor which indicates that rape is not taken seriously, and which makes it difficult to organize around this issue. Rape victims are looked down upon by society, and police treatment of rape victims is like enduring a "second rape." Because of women's deeply-rooted mistrust and apprehension toward the Japanese police and the legal system, the number of women reporting a rape represents the tip of the iceberg.

Responsibility for Children Fathered by U.S. Troops Is Not Addressed

The Status of Forces Agreement between the U.S. and Germany makes recommendations concerning the recognition of paternity of a child fathered by U.S. military personnel and the father's responsibility for child support. Whether the father is transferred to a third country or back to the U.S., he can be traced and requested to pay child support. In contrast, there has never been any discussion of this matter in relation to the Status of Forces Agreement between Japan and the U.S.

Do U.S. Citizens Know About the Activities of U.S. Troops in Okinawa?

In the case of the rape of a 12-year-old girl, the U.S. Consul and the U.S. Ambassador in Japan, as representatives of the sending country, issued apologies, followed by the Japanese government. But to what extent are American citizens aware that such crimes occur on a regular basis? For the past 50 years, since the end of World War II, the United States has seen itself as the world's policeman. Even after the end of the Cold War, the U.S. has intervened in regional conflicts throughout the world and continues to maintain the world's largest military operation. What do U.S. citizens know of military endorsement and support for prostitution and rape? Do they know that crimes committed by U.S. military personnel in Okinawa continue to be treated more lightly than crimes committed by members of the civilian community?

Working to Eliminate U.S. Military Violence Against Women

Okinawan women activists came together to protest the rape of the 12-year-old girl immediately upon their return from the Beijing Conference,

September 1995, a few days after the rape had occurred. Seventy-one women from Okinawa had gone to Beijing to make connections with other Asian women and to share their experiences of living with U.S. bases. Seven of the eleven workshops they presented concerned militarism and peace. Their preparation for the Beijing conference, as well as the inspirational and energizing effect of this momentous gathering, served them well upon their return. They organized a 12-day street vigil in downtown Naha, the capital, drawing worldwide attention to the rape of this girl and, more generally, the many incidents of violence against women by U.S. troops in East Asia. They played a central role in organizing a major demonstration attended by some 85,000 people (out of a total population of one million). They started a new organization, Okinawa Women Act Against Military Violence, to focus on the impact of U.S. military operations on women and children.

Okinawan women are working on this issue in three main ways: developing their own local organizing; uncovering what has happened in the past through conversations, workshops, drama, and historical research; and making international connections through regional and international networks. We have organized vigils, protests, and public demonstrations in Okinawa (Zielenziger 1996). We have sent many petitions and letters to the governments of Okinawa, Japan, and the United States, and have undertaken speaking engagements in Japan, the United States, and as participants in The Hague Appeal for Peace, May 1999 (Burress 1996; Kang 1998). We are engaged in research to ascertain the reality and full extent of military violence against women and the way that cases have been handled. Starting in 1945, we have details of 92 incidents so far, taken from historical records, police reports, newspaper articles, and individual testimony.

When Okinawan women went to the U.S. as part of the American Peace Caravan (Jan–Feb, 1996), the following five demands were issued to U.S. citizens, the U.S. government, and members of Congress:

- We demand the investigation of all past crimes committed by U.S. military personnel in Okinawa, especially those that constitute human rights violations against women and girls;
- We demand the establishment of a concrete plan for the reduction and ultimate removal of all U.S. military personnel from Okinawa, especially the Marines;
- We demand that the U.S. military strengthen its orientation and continuing-education program to sensitize all personnel overseas, and their dependents, to respect and uphold the basic human rights of the citizens of the country in which they are stationed, especially its women and children;
- We demand that the governments of Japan and the United States: (a) implement the *Platform for Action (PFA)* approved at the UN Fourth World Conference on Women, (b) revise the Status of Forces Agreement, and (c) reexamine the Japan–U.S. Security Treaty to ensure that these two documents are in accord with the *PFA;*
- We demand that experts on such issues as the violation of women's human rights and the destruction of the environment be dispatched to Okinawa to investigate and evaluate the actual situation existing today.

We appeal to related governments and international agencies to review treaties including the U.S.–Japan Status of Forces Agreement and the new Defense Guidelines, as well as other international agreements, in order to bring them in line with the proposals of the Beijing *Platform for Action* and a gender perspective. We appeal for the revision of laws in order to prevent violence against women and to protect women's and children's human rights.

We are working to promote an international network, support system, and campaign to actualize the goals of the statement approved at the International Conference on Militarism and Human Rights held in Okinawa, May 1997 (Kirk and Okazawa-Rey 1998).

REFERENCES

Asahi Shinbun. May 3, 1997: 31.
Burress, C., "Okinawan Base Protesters Bring Cause to Bay Area." *San Francisco Chronicle* 5 Feb. 1996: A15
Enloe, Cynthia. *The Morning After: Sexual Politics at the End of the Cold War.* Berkeley, CA: University of California Press, 1993.
Japan Coalition on the U.S. Military Bases. "It's Time to Bring the U.S. Marines Home!" *New York Times* 23 November 1998: A17.

Kang, Connie, "Okinawans Bring Drive to L.A." *Los Angeles Times* 7 October 1998: A3.

Kelly, R. J. "Assault Reports Distress Pacific's Leading Admiral." *Pacific Stars and Stripes* 13 May 1998: 1.

Kirk, Gwyn and Margo Okazawa-Rey. "Making Connections: Building an East Asia-U.S. Women's Network against U.S. Militarism." *Women and War Reader.* Eds. J. Turpin and L. A. Lorentsen. New York: New York University Press, 1998: 308–322.

Okinawa Times. September 15, 1949.

Okinawa Times. November 12, 1983.

Reardon, Betty A. *Sexism and the War System.* New York: Teachers College Press, Columbia University, 1985.

Ryukyu Shinpo. September 11, 1955.

Schmitt, E., "Admiral's Gaffe Pushes Navy to New Scrutiny of Attitudes." *New York Times* 19 Nov. 1995: 6Y.

Sturdevant, Saundra and Brenda Stoltzfus. *Let the Good Times Roll: Prostitution and the U.S. Military in Asia.* New York: New Press, 1992.

Zielenziger, Michael, "Women Finding a Voice." *San Jose Mercury News* Sept. 12, 1996: 1A.

◆◆◆

FIFTY-NINE

Baghdad Burning: Girl Blog from Iraq (2003–04)—Excerpts

Riverbend

Riverbend is an Iraqi woman blogger who posted reports of the U.S. attack on Baghdad and subsequent war and occupation from August 2003 to September 2007 when her family left for Syria (www.riverbendblog.blogspot.com). She described herself as an Iraqi raised abroad during childhood, who returned to Baghdad in her early teens. In her first posting she wrote, "I'm female, Iraqi, and 24. I survived the war. That's all you need to know. It's all that matters these days anyway" (Riverbend 2005, p. 5).

My New Talent

Suffering from a bout of insomnia last night, I found myself in front of the television, channel surfing. I was looking for the usual—an interesting interview with one of the council, some fresh news, a miracle . . . Promptly at 2 AM, the electricity went off, and I was plunged into the pitch black hell better known as "an August night with no electricity in Iraq." So I sat there, in the dark, trying to remember where I had left the candle and matches. After five minutes of chagrined meditation, I decided I would "feel" my way up the stairs and out onto the roof. Step by hesitant step, I stumbled out into the corridor and up the stairs, stubbing a toe on the last step (which wasn't supposed to be there).

(For those of you who don't know, people sleep up on the roof in some of the safer areas because when the electricity goes off, the houses get so hot it feels like you are cooking gently inside of an oven. The roof isn't much better, but at least there's a semblance of wind.)

Out on the roof, the heat was palpitating off of everything in waves. The strange thing is that if you stand in the center, you can feel it emanating from the walls and ground toward you from all directions. I stood there trying to determine whether it was only our area or the whole city, that had sunk into darkness.

A few moments later, my younger brother (we'll call him E.) joined me—disheveled, disgruntled, and half asleep. We stood leaning on the low wall enclosing the roof watching the street below. I could see the tip of Abu Maan's cigarette glowing in the yard next door. I pointed to it with the words, "Abu Maan can't sleep either . . ." E. grunted with the words, "It's probably Maan." I stood staring at him like he was half wild or maybe talking in his sleep. Maan is only 13 . . . how is he smoking? How can he be smoking?

"He's only 13," I stated.

"Is anyone only 13 anymore?" he asked.

I mulled the reality of this remark over. No, no one is 13 anymore. No one is 24 anymore . . . everyone is 85, and I think I might be 105. I was too tired to speak, and in spite of his open eyes, I suspected E. was asleep. The silence was shattered a few moments later by the sound of bullets in the distance. It was just loud enough to get your attention but too far away to be the source of any real anxiety. I tried to determine where they were coming from . . .

E: How far do you think that is?

Me: I don't know . . . 'bout a kilometer?

E: Yeah, about.

Me: Not American bullets—

E: No, it's probably from a . . .

Me: Klashnikov [Kalishnikov].

E (impressed): You're getting good at this.

No—I'm getting great at it. I can tell you if it's "them" or "us."

. . .

I can tell you how far away it is. I can tell you if it's a pistol or machine gun, tank or armored vehicle, Apache or Chinook . . . I can determine the distance and maybe even the target. That's my new talent. It's something I've gotten so good at, I frighten myself. What's worse is that almost everyone seems to have acquired this new talent . . . young and old. And it's not something that anyone will appreciate on a resume . . .

I keep wondering . . . will an airplane ever sound the same again? **Posted by River @ 3:15 PM, Thursday, August 21, 2003.**

We've Only Just Begun

Females can no longer leave their homes alone. Each time I go out, E. and either a father, uncle, or cousin has to accompany me. It feels like we've gone back fifty years ever since the beginning of the occupation. A woman or girl out alone, risks anything from insults to abduction. An outing has to be arranged at least an hour beforehand. I state that I need to buy something or have to visit someone. Two males have to be procured (preferably large) and "safety arrangements" must be made in this total state of lawlessness. And always the question: "But do you have to go out and buy it? Can't I get it for you?" No you can't, because the kilo of eggplant I absolutely have to select with my own hands is just an excuse to see the light of day and walk down a street. The situation is incredibly frustrating to females who work or go to college.

Before the war, around 50 percent of the college students were females, and over 50 percent of the working force was composed of women. Not so anymore. . . . Before the war, I would estimate (roughly) that about 55 percent of females in Baghdad wore a hijab—or headscarf.

I am female and Muslim. Before the occupation, I more or less dressed the way I wanted to. I lived in jeans and cotton pants and comfortable shirts. Now, I don't dare leave the house in pants. A long skirt and loose shirt (preferably with long sleeves) has become necessary. A girl wearing jeans risks being attacked, abducted, or insulted by fundamentalists who have been . . . liberated!

The whole situation is alarming beyond any description I can give. Christians have become the victims of extremism also. Some of them are being threatened; others are being attacked. A few wannabe Mullahs came out with a "fatwa," or decree, in June that declared all females should wear the hijab, and if they didn't, they could be subject to "punishment." Another group claiming to be a part of the "Hawza Al Ilmia" decreed that not a single girl over the age of fourteen could remain unmarried—even if it meant that some members of the Hawza would have to have two, three, or four wives. This decree included females of other religions. In the south, female UN and Red Cross aides received death threats if they didn't wear the hijab. This isn't done in the name of God—it's done in the name of power. It tells people—the world—that "Look—we have power, we have influence."

Don't blame it on Islam. Every religion has its extremists. In times of chaos and disorder, those extremists flourish. Iraq is full of moderate Muslims who simply believe in "live and let live." We get along with each other—Sunnis and Shi'a, Muslims and Christians, and Jews and Sabi'a. We intermarry, we mix and mingle, we live. We build our churches and mosques in the same areas; our children go to the same schools . . . it was never an issue.

Someone asked me if, through elections, the Iraqi people might vote for an Islamic state. Six months ago, I would have firmly said, "No." Now I'm not so sure. There's been an overwhelming return to fundamentalism. People are turning to religion for several reasons. The first and most prominent reason is fear. Fear of war, fear of death, and fear of a fate worse than death (and yes, there are fates worse than death). If I didn't have something to believe in during this past war, I know I would have lost my mind. If there hadn't been a God to pray to, to make promises to, to bargain with, to thank—I wouldn't have made it through.

Encroaching Western values and beliefs have also played a prominent role in pushing Iraqis to embrace Islam. Just as there are ignorant people in the Western world (and there are plenty—I have the emails to prove it . . . don't make me embarrass you), there are ignorant people in the Middle East. In Muslims and Arabs, Westerners see suicide bombers, terrorists, ignorance, and camels. In Americans, Brits, etc., some Iraqis see depravity, prostitution, ignorance, domination, junkies, and ruthlessness. The best way people can find to protect themselves, and their loved ones, against this assumed threat is religion.

Finally, you have more direct reasons. 65% of all Iraqis are currently unemployed for one reason or another. There are people who have families to feed. When I say "families" I don't mean a wife and 2 kids . . . I mean around 16 or 17 people. Islamic parties supported by Iran, like Al-Daawa and SCIRI, are currently recruiting followers by offering "wages" to jobless men (an ex-soldier in the army, for example) in trade of "support." This support could mean anything—vote when the elections come around, bomb a specific shop, "confiscate," abduct, hijack cars (only if you work for Al-Chalabi . . .).

So concerning the anxiety over terror and fundamentalism—I would like to quote the Carpenters—worry? "We've only just begun . . . we've only just begun . . ." **Posted by River @ 6:20 PM, Saturday, August 23, 2003.**

About Riverbend

A lot of you have been asking about my background and the reason why my English is good. I am Iraqi—born in Iraq to Iraqi parents, but was raised abroad for several years as a child. I came back in my early teens and continued studying in English in Baghdad—reading any book I could get my hands on. Most of my friends are of different ethnicities, religions, and nationalities. I am bilingual. There are thousands in Iraq like me—kids of diplomats, students, expatriates, etc.

As to my connection with Western culture . . . you wouldn't believe how many young Iraqi people know so much about American/British/French pop culture. They know all about Arnold Schwarzenegger, Brad Pitt, Whitney Houston, McDonalds, and M.I.B.s . . . Iraqi tv stations were constantly showing bad copies of the latest Hollywood movies. (If it's any consolation, the Marines lived up to the Rambo/Terminator reputation which preceded them.)

But no matter what—I shall remain anonymous. I wouldn't feel free to write otherwise. I think Salam and Gee are incredibly brave . . . who knows, maybe one day I will be too. You know me as Riverbend; you share a very small part of my daily reality—I hope that will suffice.

Will Work for Food

Over 65% of the Iraqi population is unemployed. The reason for this is because Bremer made some horrible decisions. The first major decision he made was to dissolve the Iraqi army. That may make sense in Washington, but here, we were left speechless. Now there are over 400,000 trained, armed men with families that need to be fed. Where are they supposed to go? What are they supposed to do for a living? I don't know. They certainly don't know.

They roam the streets looking for work, looking for an answer. You can see perplexity and anger in their stance, their walk, their whole demeanor. Their eyes shift from face to face, looking for a clue. Who is to answer for this mess? Who do you think?

. . .

The story of how I lost my job isn't unique. I'm a computer science graduate. Before the war, I was working in an Iraqi database/software company located in Baghdad as a programmer/network administrator (yes, yes . . . a geek). Every day, I would climb three flights of stairs, enter the little office I shared with one female colleague and two males, start up my PC and spend hours staring at little numbers and letters rolling across the screen. It was tedious, it was back-breaking, it was geeky, and it was . . . wonderful.

I loved my job. At 8 A.M. I'd walk in lugging a backpack filled with enough CDs, floppies, notebooks, chewed-on pens, paperclips, and screwdrivers to make Bill Gates proud. I made as much money as my two male colleagues and got an equal amount of respect from the manager. . . .

What I'm trying to say is that no matter *what* anyone heard, females in Iraq were a lot better off than females in other parts of the Arab world (and some parts of the Western world—we had equal salaries!). We made up over 50 percent of the working force. We were doctors, lawyers, nurses, teachers, professors, deans, architects, programmers, and more. We came and went as we pleased. We wore what we wanted (within the boundaries of the social restrictions of a conservative society).

During the first week of June, I heard my company was back in business. It took several hours, seemingly thousands of family meetings, but I finally convinced everyone that it was necessary for my *sanity* to go back to work. They agreed that I would visit the company (with my two male bodyguards) and ask them if they had any work I could possibly take home and submit later on or through the Internet.

One fine day in mid June, I packed my big bag of geeky wonders, put on my long skirt and shirt, tied back my hair, and left the house with a mixture of anticipation and apprehension.

We had to park the car about a hundred meters away from the door of the company because the major road in front of it was cracked and broken with the weight of the American tanks as they entered Baghdad. I half-ran, half-plodded up to the door of the company, my heart throbbing in anticipation of seeing friends, colleagues, secretaries . . . just generally something familiar again in the strange new nightmare we were living.

The moment I walked through the door, I noticed it. Everything looked shabbier somehow—sadder. The maroon carpet lining the hallways was dingy, scuffed, and spoke of the burden of a thousand rushing feet. The windows we had so diligently taped prior to the war were cracked in some places and broken in others . . . dirty all over. The lights were shattered, desks overturned, doors kicked in, and clocks torn from the walls. Everyone was standing around, looking at everyone else. The faces were sad and lethargic and exhausted. And I was one of the only females . . .

I continued upstairs, chilled to the bone, in spite of the muggy heat of the building which hadn't seen electricity for at least two months. My little room wasn't much better off than the rest of the building. The desks were gone, papers all over the place . . . but A. was there! I couldn't believe it—a familiar, welcoming face. He looked at me for a moment, without really seeing me, then his eyes opened wide and disbelief took over the initial vague expression. He congratulated me on being alive, asked about my family, and told me that he wasn't coming back after today. Things had changed. I should go home and stay safe. He was quitting—going to find work abroad. Nothing to do

here anymore. I told him about my plan to work at home and submit projects . . . he shook his head sadly. I stood staring at the mess for a few moments longer, trying to sort out the mess in my head, my heart being torn to pieces. My cousin and E. were downstairs waiting for me—there was nothing more to do, except ask how I could maybe help? A. and I left the room and started making our way downstairs. We paused on the second floor and stopped to talk to one of the former department directors. I asked him when they thought things would be functioning; he wouldn't look at me. His eyes stayed glued to A.'s face as he told him that females weren't welcome right now—especially females who "couldn't be protected." He finally turned to me and told me, in so many words, to go home because "they" refused to be responsible for what might happen to me.

Ok. Fine. Your loss. I turned my back, walked down the stairs and went to find E. and my cousin. Suddenly, the faces didn't look strange—they were the same faces of before, mostly, but there was a hostility I couldn't believe. . . . I cried bitterly all the way home—cried for my job, cried for my future and cried for the torn streets, damaged buildings and crumbling people.

I'm one of the lucky ones . . . I'm not important. I'm not vital. Over a month ago, a prominent electrical engineer (one of the smartest females in the country) named Henna Aziz was assassinated in front of her family—two daughters and her husband. She was threatened by some fundamentalists from Badir's Army [a Shi'a extremist group] and told to stay at home because she was a woman, she shouldn't be in charge. She refused—the country needed her expertise to get things functioning—she was brilliant. She would not and could not stay at home. They came to her house one evening: men with machine guns broke in and opened fire. She lost her life—she wasn't the first; she won't be the last. **Posted by River @ 11:33 PM, Sunday, August 24, 2003.**

Shari'a and Family Law

On Wednesday our darling Iraqi Puppet Council decided that secular Iraqi family law would no longer be secular—it is now going to be according to Islamic Shari'a. Shari'a is Islamic law, whether from the Quran or quotes of the Prophet or interpretations of modern Islamic law by clerics and people who have dedicated their lives to studying Islam.

The news has barely been covered by Western or even Arab media and Iraqi media certainly aren't covering it. It is too much to ask of Al-Iraqiya [the Pentagon-funded Iraqi TV station] to debate or cover a topic like this one—it would obviously conflict with the Egyptian soap operas and songs. This latest decision is going to be catastrophic for females—we're going backwards.

Don't get me wrong—pure Islamic law according to the Quran and the Prophet gives women certain unalterable, nonnegotiable rights. The problem arises when certain clerics decide to do their own interpretations of these laws (and just about *anyone* can make themselves a cleric these days). The bigger problem is that Shari'a may be drastically different from one cleric to another. There are actually fundamental differences in Shari'a between the different Islamic factions or "methahib." Even in the same methahib, there are dozens of different clerics who may have opposing opinions. This is going to mean more chaos than we already have to deal with. We've come to expect chaos in the streets . . . but chaos in the courts and judicial system too?!

This is completely unfair to women specifically. Under the Iraqi constitution, men and women are equal. Under our past secular family law (which has been in practice since the '50s), women had unalterable divorce, marriage, inheritance, custody, and alimony rights. All of this is going to change. I'll give an example of what this will mean. One infamous practice brought to Iraq by Iranian clerics was the "zawaj muta'a," which when translated by the clerics means "temporary marriage." The actual translation is "pleasure marriage"—which is exactly what it is. It works like this: a consenting man and woman go to a cleric who approves of temporary marriage, and they agree upon a period of time during which the marriage will last. The man pays the woman a "mahar," or dowry, and during the duration of the marriage (which can be anything from an hour, to a week, a month, etc.) the man has full marital rights. Basically, it's a form of prostitution that often results in illegitimate children and a spread of STDs.

Sunni clerics consider it a sin and many Shi'a clerics also frown upon it . . . but there are the ones who will tell you it's "halal" and Shari'a, etc. Secular Iraqi family law considers it a form of prostitution and doesn't consider a "pleasure marriage" a legitimate marriage. In other words, the woman wouldn't have any legal rights, and if she finds herself pregnant—the child, legally, wouldn't have a father . . . .

Another example is in marriage itself. By tribal law and Shari'a, a woman, no matter how old, would have to have her family's consent to marry a man. By Iraqi law, as long as the woman is over eighteen, she doesn't need her family's consent. She can marry in a court, legally, without her parents. It rarely happened in Iraq, but it *was* possible. According to Iraqi secular law, a woman has grounds to divorce her husband if he beats her. According to Shari'a, it would be much more difficult to prove abuse.

Other questions pose themselves—Shari'a doesn't outlaw the marriage of minors (on condition they've hit puberty). Iraqi secular law won't allow minors to marry until the age of at least sixteen (I think) for women and the age of eighteen for men.

By Iraqi civil law, parents are required to send their children to complete at least primary school. According to Shari'a, a father can make his son or daughter quit school and either work or remain at home. So what happens when and if he decides to do that? Does Shari'a apply or does civil law apply?

Women are outraged . . . this is going to open new doors for repression in the most advanced country on women's rights in the Arab world! Men are also against this (although they certainly have the upper hand in the situation) because it's going to mean more confusion and conflict all around.

During the sanctions and all the instability, we used to hear fantastic stories about certain Arab countries like Saudi Arabia, Kuwait, Oman, and Qatar to name a few. We heard about their luxurious lifestyles—the high monthly wages, the elegant cars, sprawling homes and malls . . . and while I always wanted to visit, I never once remember yearning to live there or even feeling envy. When I analyzed my feelings, it always led back to the fact that I cherished the rights I had as an Iraqi Muslim woman. During the hard times, it was always a comfort that I could drive, learn, work for equal pay, dress the way I wanted, and practice Islam according to my values and beliefs without worrying whether I was too devout or not devout enough.

I usually ignore the emails I receive telling me to "embrace" my new-found freedom and be happy that the circumstances of all Iraqi women are going to "improve drastically" from what we had before. They quote Bush (which in itself speaks volumes) saying things about how repressed the Iraqi women were and how, now, they are going to be able to live free lives.

The people who write those emails often lump Iraq together with Saudi Arabia, Iran, and Afghanistan, and I shake my head at their ignorance but think to myself, "Well, they really need to believe their country has the best of intentions—I won't burst their bubble." But I'm telling everyone now—if I get any more emails about how free and liberated the Iraqi women are *now* thanks to America, they can expect a very nasty answer. **Posted by River @ 7:55 PM, Thursday, January 15, 2004.**

S I X T Y

Mother's Day Proclamation (1870)

Julia Ward Howe

Julia Ward Howe (1819–1910) is known for her Civil War poem, *The Battle Hymn of the Republic,* championing freedom for all men and women. She published many poems, plays, and travel books and played a prominent role in several women's suffrage organizations. She saw the devastation of the war through her work with widows and orphans on both sides of the Civil War and called for women to oppose war in all its forms.

Arise then . . . women of this day!
Arise, all women who have hearts!
Whether your baptism be of water or of tears!
Say firmly:
"We will not have questions answered by irrelevant agencies,
Our husbands will not come to us, reeking with carnage,
For caresses and applause.
Our sons shall not be taken from us to unlearn
All that we have been able to teach them of charity, mercy and patience.
We, the women of one country,
Will be too tender of those of another country
To allow our sons to be trained to injure theirs."
From the voice of a devastated Earth a voice goes up with
Our own. It says: "Disarm! Disarm!

The sword of murder is not the balance of justice."
Blood does not wipe out dishonor,
Nor violence indicate possession.
As men have often forsaken the plough and the anvil
At the summons of war,
Let women now leave all that may be left of home
For a great and earnest day of counsel.
Let them meet first, as women, to bewail and commemorate the dead.
Let them solemnly take counsel with each other as to the means
Whereby the great human family can live in peace . . .
Each bearing after his own time the sacred impress, not of Caesar,
But of God—
In the name of womanhood and humanity, I earnestly ask
That a general congress of women without limit of nationality,
May be appointed and held at someplace deemed most convenient
And the earliest period consistent with its objects,
To promote the alliance of the different nationalities,
The amicable settlement of international questions,
The great and general interests of peace.

SIXTY-ONE

Unity Statement (1980)

Women's Pentagon Action

> In 1980 and 1981, some 2,000 women mainly from the northeastern United States encircled the Pentagon to express their opposition to war through theater and ritual—the **Women's Pentagon Action.** They utilized weaving as a metaphor for women's power against institutions, weaving the doors to the Pentagon shut with brightly colored yarns.

We are gathering at the Pentagon on November 16 because we fear for our lives. We fear for the life of this planet, our Earth, and the life of the children who are our human future.

We are mostly women who come from the north-eastern region of our United States. We are city women who know the wreckage and fear of city streets, we are country women who grieve the loss of the small farm and have lived on the poisoned earth. We are young and older, we are married, single, lesbian. We live in different kinds of households: in groups, families, alone, some are single parents.

We work at a variety of jobs. We are students, teachers, factory workers, office workers, lawyers, farmers, doctors, builders, waitresses, weavers, poets, engineers, homeworkers, electricians, artists, blacksmiths. We are all daughters and sisters.

We have come here to mourn and rage and defy the Pentagon because it is the workplace of the imperial power which threatens us all. Every day while we work, study, love, the colonels and generals who are planning our annihilation walk calmly in and out the doors of its five sides. They have accumulated over 30,000 nuclear bombs, at the rate of three to six bombs every day. They are determined to produce the billion-dollar MX missile. They are creating a technology called Stealth—the invisible, unperceivable arsenal. They have revised the cruel old killer, nerve gas. They have proclaimed Directive 59 which asks for "small nuclear wars, prolonged but limited." The Soviet Union works hard to keep up with the United States' initiatives. We can destroy each other's cities, towns, schools and children many times over. The United States has sent "advisors,"

money and arms to El Salvador and Guatemala to enable those juntas to massacre their own people.

The very same men, the same legislative committees that offer trillions of dollars to the Pentagon have brutally cut day care, children's lunches, battered women's shelters. The same men have concocted the Family Protection Act which will mandate the strictly patriarchal family and thrust federal authority into our home life. They are preventing the passage of ERA's simple statement and supporting the Human Life Amendment which will deprive all women of choice and many women of life itself.

We are in the hands of men whose power and wealth have separated them from the reality of daily life and from the imagination. We are right to be afraid.

At the same time, our cities are in ruins, bankrupt; they suffer the devastation of war. Hospitals are closed, our schools deprived of books and teachers. Our Black and Latino youth are without decent work. They will be forced, drafted to become the cannon fodder for the very power that oppresses them. Whatever help the poor receive is cut or withdrawn to feed the Pentagon which needs about $500,000,000 a day for its murderous health. It extracted $157 billion last year from our own tax money, $1,800 from a family of four.

With this wealth our scientists are corrupted; over 40 percent work in government and corporate laboratories that refine the methods for destroying or deforming life. The lands of the Native American people have been turned to radioactive rubble in order to enlarge the nuclear warehouse. The uranium of South Africa, necessary to the nuclear enterprise, enriches the white minority and encourages the vicious system of racist oppression and war.

The President has just decided to produce the neutron bomb, which kills people but leaves property (buildings like this one) intact. There is fear among the people, and that fear, created by the industrial militarists, is used as an excuse to accelerate the arms race. "We will protect you . . . " they say, but we have never been so endangered, so close to the end of human time.

Carrying large puppets symbolizing mourning, rage, empowerment, and defiance, women protested against militarism at the Pentagon, November 1980.

We women are gathering because life on the precipice is intolerable. We want to know what anger in these men, what fear, which can only be satisfied by destruction, what coldness of heart and ambition drives their days. We want to know because we do not want that dominance which is exploitative and murderous in international relations, and so dangerous to women and children at home—we do not want that sickness transferred by the violent society through the fathers to the sons.

What is it that we women need for our ordinary lives, that we want for ourselves and also for our sisters in new nations and old colonies who suffer the white man's exploitation and too often the oppression of their own countrymen?

We want enough good food, decent housing, communities with clean air and water, good care for our children while we work. We want work that is useful to a sensible society. There is a modest technology to minimize drudgery and restore joy to labor. We are determined to use skills and knowledge from which we have been excluded—like plumbing or engineering or physics or composing. We intend to form women's groups or unions that will demand safe workplaces, free of sexual harassment, equal pay for work of comparable value. We respect the work women have done in caring for the young, their own and others, in maintaining a physical and spiritual shelter against the greedy and militaristic society. In our old age, we expect our experience, our skills, to be honored and used.

We want health care which respects and understands our bodies. Physically challenged sisters must have access to gatherings, actions, happy events, work. For this, ramps must be added to stairs, and we must become readers, signers, supporting arms. So close, so many, why have we allowed ourselves not to know them?

We want an education for children that tells the true story of our women's lives, which describes the earth as our home to be cherished, to be fed as well as harvested.

We want to be free from violence in our streets and in our houses. One in every three of us will be raped in her lifetime. The pervasive social power of the masculine ideal and the greed of the pornographer have come together to steal our freedom, so that whole neighborhoods and the life of the evening and night have been taken from us. For too many women the dark country road and the city alley have concealed the rapist. We want the night returned: the light of the moon, special in the cycle of our female lives, the stars and the gaiety of the city streets.

We want the right to have or not to have children—we do not want gangs of politicians and medical men to say we must be sterilized for the country's good. We know that this technique is the racists' method for controlling populations. Nor do we want to be prevented from having an abortion when we need one. We think this freedom should be available to poor women as it always has been to the rich. We want to be free to love whomever we choose. We will live with women or with men, or we will live alone. We will not allow the oppression of lesbians. One sex or one sexual preference must not dominate another.

We do not want to be drafted into the army. We do not want our young brothers drafted. We want *them* equal with us.

We want to see the pathology of racism ended in our time. It has been the imperial arrogance of white male power that has separated us from the suffering and wisdom of our sisters in Asia, Africa, South America and in our own country. Many North American women look down on the minority nearest them: the Black, the Hispanic, the Jew, the Native American, the Asian, the immigrant. Racism has offered them privilege and convenience; they often fail to see that they themselves have bent to the unnatural authority and violence of men in government, at work, at home. Privilege does not increase knowledge or spirit or understanding. There can be no peace while one race dominates another, one people, one nation, one sex despises another.

We must not forget the tens of thousands of American women who live much of their lives in cages, away from family, lovers, all the growing-up years of their children. Most of them were born at the intersection of oppressions: people of color, female, poor. Women on the outside have been taught to fear those sisters. We refuse that separation. We need each other's knowledge and anger in our common struggle against the builders of jails and bombs.

We want the uranium left in the earth and the earth given back to the people who tilled it. We want a system of energy which is renewable, which does not take resources out of the earth without returning them. We want those systems to belong to the people and their communities, not to the giant corporations which invariably turn knowledge into weaponry. We want the sham of Atoms for Peace ended, all nuclear plants decommissioned and the construction of new plants stopped. That is another war against the people and the child to be born in fifty years.

We want an end to the arms race. No more bombs. No more amazing inventions for death.

We understand all is connectedness. We know the life and work of animals and plants in seeding, reseeding and in fact simply inhabiting this planet. Their exploitation and the organized destruction of never to be seen again species threatens and sorrows us. The earth nourishes us as we with our bodies will eventually feed it. Through us, our mothers connected the human past to the human future.

With that sense, that ecological right, we oppose the financial connections between the Pentagon and the multinational corporations and banks that the Pentagon serves. Those connections are made of gold and oil. We are made of blood and bone, we are made of the sweet and finite resource, water. We will not allow these violent games to continue. If we are here in our stubborn thousands today, we will certainly return in the hundreds of thousands in the months and years to come.

We know there is a healthy, sensible, loving way to live and we intend to live that way in our neighborhoods and our farms in these United States, and among our sisters and brothers in all the countries of the world.

11

◆◆◆

Women and the Environment

Place is a fundamental element in our lives whether we live in a spacious suburb; a vibrant—maybe overcrowded—downtown area; an old, established inner-city neighborhood; or on a farm, a ranch, or a reservation (Anderson 1991; Barnhill 1999; Williams 1992). Places change over time so that a formerly Polish American or Italian American community may now be home to African Americans or Vietnamese immigrants; a poorer neighborhood may become gentrified as middle-class people move in and push up property values. Neighborhood facilities—churches, temples, synagogues, schools, stores, restaurants, parks, community centers—reflect the interests and concerns of people who live there. The quality of some local services and the physical space also reflect the standing of a particular community in the wider society. In general, middle-class and upper-middle-class communities have better school buildings, more sports facilities, more doctors' offices and banks, more open space, and a wider range of stores, cafes, and restaurants than poorer neighborhoods. They are also farther from factories, oil refineries, power plants, sawmills, stockyards, railway terminals, highways, garbage dumps, and other sources of pollution, bad smells, and noise.

This chapter is concerned with impacts of the physical environment on women's lives and with women's activism around environmental issues. It assumes that there is an ethical dimension to living in any location—that we care for the environment for its own sake and for the sake of future generations. As with other topics in this book, environmental issues are experienced at the micro- and meso-levels, but also have macro- and global-level dimensions. The lenses of gender, race, class, and nation are also tools of analysis in this chapter. In addition to the readings in this chapter, other articles touch on environmental issues: the health effects of a toxic waste incinerator (Reading 28), cleanup of former military bases in the Philippines (Reading 16), and a campaign to stop the Coca-Cola company from excessive use of water in south India (Reading 48).

Many people contribute to safeguarding our physical environment. Federal legislation such as the Clean Air Act and regulatory agencies like the Environmental Protection Agency were established to limit toxic emissions from factories, homes, and vehicles. Cities or counties provide services like potable water, garbage disposal, street cleaning and repair, snow clearance, stop signs and traffic lights, town parks, and recreation centers. National environmental organizations have lobbied for the preservation of wilderness areas as national parks, for the protection of endangered species, and for stronger environmental regulation of industry. Community organizations clear trash from highways and vacant lots or work in community gardens. Individuals mow lawns, trim trees, sweep the

sidewalk, recycle reusable materials, compost organic matter, and buy "green" or environmentally
safe products like paper goods from recycled paper
or biodegradable soaps and detergents. Women are
very involved in many of these efforts, especially at
household and community levels. Important as
they are, these activities cannot keep up with the
scale and pace of environmental degradation,
which requires major change at macro- and global
levels.

Over the past forty years or so, many people in
the United States have become increasingly concerned with environmental issues. Hazardous industrial production processes have affected the
health of workers and people who live near or
downwind of industrial areas. Industrial pollutants, chemical pesticides and fertilizers, and
wastes from nuclear power plants and uranium
mines are seeping into the groundwater in many
parts of the country, as exemplified in feature films
like *A Civil Action* and *Erin Brockovich*. Homes and
schools have been built on land once used for toxic
dumps (Gibbs 1995, 1998). Deforestation, global
warming, and the disappearance of hundreds of
species are also hallmarks of vast environmental
destruction worldwide. Most United States environmental activists probably agree that the greatest
threat to environmental security worldwide comes
from the waste-producing, industrialized, militarized countries of the global North, especially the
United States, Canada, Europe, and Japan.

Environmental crises affects men as well as
women, of course, but in terms of environmental
health, women and children show the effects of
toxic pollution earlier than men do, either because
of low body weight or because women's bodies
become what some have termed "unhealthy environments" for their babies (Reading 68; Kettel 1996;
Nelson 1990; Steingraber 2001). A significant number of babies without brains have been born to
women on both sides of the Rio Grande, a river polluted by U.S.-controlled *maquiladora* industries on
the Mexican side (Kamel and Hoffman 1999).
(Working conditions in these *maquiladoras*, or sub-
assembly plants, are described in more detail in
Chapter 8.) Contact with pesticides has led to poor
health for many women farmworkers in the United
States and to chronic illnesses or severe disabilities
for their children (Chavez 1993; Moses 1993). Several firms have tried to keep women of childbearing

age out of the most noxious production processes—
often the highest paid—or to insist that they be sterilized, lest women sue them later for fetal damage
(Gottlieb 1993). Women who work in computer
manufacturing, chicken processing, the dairy industry, and housecleaning are all exposed to chemicals as part of their work, as are manicurists and
farm workers.

Environmental writer Florence Williams (2005)
noted: "If human breast milk came stamped with an
ingredients label, it might read . . . 4 percent fat,
vitamins A, C, E, and K, lactose, essential minerals,
growth hormones, proteins, enzymes and anti-
bodies." In addition, some women also pass traces
of DDT, PCBs, dioxin, mercury, lead, benzene,
arsenic, or flame retardants to their nursing babies.
The Akwesasne Mothers' Milk project in upstate
New York, founded by midwife Katsi Cook, was
one of the first community projects to explore the
toxicity of breast milk in response to Native American
mothers' concern that breast-feeding, supposedly
the best way to nurture infants, could expose them
to pollutants (LaDuke 1999; Boswell-Penc 2006). As
biological scientist Sandra Steingraber argues in
Reading 62, it is difficult to know how even relatively low chemical levels will affect the development of a fetus or infant. During the sixth month of
her pregnancy she studied fetal brain development
and, in the excerpt reprinted here, discusses the
effects of lead on this highly complex and delicate
process. She believes that environmental policy and
regulations do not protect our health adequately.
She argues for the **precautionary principle,** defined
by an international group of scientists, government
officials, lawyers, and labor and grassroots environmental activists who met at Wingspread (Racine,
Wis.) in January 1998, as follows:

> When an activity raises threats of harm to hu-
> man health or the environment, precautionary
> measures should be taken even if some cause
> and effect relationships are not fully estab-
> lished scientifically. In this context the propo-
> nent of an activity, rather than the public,
> should bear the burden of proof.
> *(Rachel's Environment and Health Weekly 1998, p. 1)*

An international covenant banning lead-based paint
in 1925, mentioned by Steingraber, was operating on
a precautionary principle. But this covenant was
not adopted in the United States at the time due to

the influence of the lead industry, which dismissed relevant scientific findings as "anti-lead propaganda."

Many household products contain chemicals associated with health hazards. Stacy Malkan (2007), communications director with Health Care Without Harm and a media strategist for the Campaign for Safe Cosmetics, argues that toxic chemicals are widespread in beauty products. She discusses the five-year campaign by environmental and health groups to pressure the $35 billion cosmetics industry, unregulated for many years, to use safer ingredients. Asian Communities for Reproductive Justice has established POLISH, the Participatory Research, Organizing, and Leadership Initiative for Safety and Health to research the degree to which Asian women and girls and nail salon workers are exposed to toxic chemicals through both personal use and professional occupation. The Environmental Working Group has a Skin Deep project that provides a safety assessment of ingredients in personal care products (www.ewg.org).

Many more women than men are involved in campaigning on behalf of environmental issues at a grassroots level, though women are less active than men concerning environmental issues at the national level (Mohai 1997). We do not see women as somehow closer to nature than men, as is sometimes argued, or as having an essentially nurturing, caring nature. Rather, we see women's environmental activism as an extension of their roles as daughters, wives, and mothers, caring for families and communities. Women have a long-standing history of involvement in community organizing: campaigning against poor housing conditions, high rents, unsafe streets, lead in gasoline, toxic dumps, and so on, described by sociologist Nancy Naples (1998) as "activist mothering." Ideally, taking care of children and other family members should be everyone's responsibility, including government and corporations, and would involve safeguarding and restoring the environment.

Theoretical and Activist Perspectives

As we argued in Chapter 2, theories grow out of and inform experience. Women who are concerned about environmental degradation draw on several theoretical and activist perspectives, particularly deep ecology and bioregionalism, ecofeminism, and environmental justice. These are not unitary perspectives, though here we emphasize points of comparison between them rather than their internal variations.

Environmentalism

Over the past forty years, successive U.S. Congresses have passed a number of environmental laws, for example, to improve air and water quality or to protect wilderness areas and endangered species. This is largely due to the work of dedicated environmentalists like Rachel Carson (1962;

Dorsey and Thormodsgard 2003; Hynes 1989) and to concerted public education and lobbying by major environmental organizations such as the Sierra Club, the Natural Resources Defense Council, and the Environmental Defense Fund. Limitations of such efforts are that they are slow and invariably compromised by corporate interests. These hard-earned gains rolled back by President Bush's environmental policy that included the weakening of existing environmental legislation and the role of the Environmental Protection Agency, opening up national forests to commercial interests, allowing exemptions from environmental law for military training and maneuvers, abandoning the international treaty on global warming (the Kyoto Treaty), and an energy plan with a heavy emphasis on fossil fuels, including the proposal to drill for oil in the Alaska Arctic National Wildlife Refuge.

Deep Ecology and Bioregionalism

The term *deep ecology* was coined by Norwegian philosopher Arne Naess and taken up in the United States by ecological philosophers Bill Devall and George Sessions (1985). It is premised on two fundamental principles: self-realization for every being and a "biocentric" equality among species. Many environmental activists in the United States who are drawn to deep ecology are critical of the more mainstream environmental organizations mentioned above, which have a human-centered focus. Earth First! is an activist network that exemplifies principles of deep ecology in practice. It gained public recognition through direct action, particularly in opposition to the logging of old-growth forests in the Pacific Northwest and northern California (J. Davis 1991; Hill 2000; List 1993).

At its worst, deep ecology has been reduced to a rather simplistic view of the world in which nature is "good" and people are "bad." Deep ecologists argue for reducing human population, reducing human interference in the biosphere, and reducing human standards of living. As its name implies, Earth First! has been more interested in saving the earth than in safeguarding the human population. This led to arguments that, for example, if AIDS didn't exist it would have had to be invented, or that starving people in Africa should be left to die so that the human population can be brought back into balance with the carrying

capacity of the land (Thropy 1991). A related argument concerns opposition to immigration into the United States on the grounds that additional people will overburden the resource base (Lindsley 2004; Urban 2008). Typically, such arguments are cast in terms of "overpopulation" rather than focusing on consumption, and draw on ideologies of racism.

Deep ecologists value the preservation of nature in and of itself rather than for any benefit such preservation affords to humans. Nature is often seen in romantic terms: The virgin, feminized wilderness is vulnerable, innocent, and weak, and protecting "her" draws on old macho, militaristic iconography (King 1987). Wilderness is not thought of as the homeland of indigenous people but as a special place where people (at least athletic, nondisabled people) can get close to an "experience" of nature. Critics of deep ecology oppose its people vs. nature stance and argue, for example, that "if we believe that we are in essence bad for nature we are profoundly separated from the natural world" (Starhawk 2002a, p. 161). Nature is not something far away, to be encountered on weekend hikes or occasional camping trips. Everyone is connected to the natural environment in the most mundane but profound way: through the air we breathe, the water we drink, and the food we eat, as embodied human beings in a continuum of life. Ecofeminist writer and activist Starhawk (2002a) also noted that a "humans-as-blight" view is self-defeating for organizing around environmental issues, as people "don't act effectively out of feeling bad, guilty, wrong, and inauthentic" (p. 161).

In the 1980s and 1990s, people who tried to stop logging, for example, especially in old-growth forests of western states, often found themselves up against loggers who were dependent on timber companies for their livelihood. Feminist and Earth First! strategist and activist Judi Bari, who had been a union organizer, has been credited with helping to forge alliances among Earth First!, labor unions, and other social justice organizations. In urban areas, too, industrial jobs are often set against a cleaner environment. Corporations argue that they cannot afford to clean up their operations or that cleaning up would be at the expense of jobs. An alliance between environmentalists and labor organizers is essential. People need a livelihood as well as good environmental conditions, and the two are not mutually exclusive (Goodstein 1999; Pulido 1996; Schwab 1994; Alliance for Sustainable Jobs and the Environment, Portland, Ore.).

Thinking of one's home area as a bioregion is a way of foregrounding interconnections among plant, animal, and human communities. Bioregions are often defined by ecological boundaries, like a watershed for example, and must be large enough to maintain the integrity of the region's ecosystems and habitats. Human intervention in the use and management of land and water should support ecological sustainability—or work toward this goal. Bioregions may be largely self-sufficient in food, products, and services. Their boundaries usually differ from political borders of counties, states, or nations. A humans-as-nature view prevails within the bioregional movement, which emphasizes decentralization, small-scale projects, agricultural and economic self-sufficiency within bioregions, and a strongly developed attachment to place (e.g., Andruss et al. 1990; Berg 1993; Sale 1985). Indigenous people invariably emphasize the importance of connection to the land for their communities, as discussed by lawyer, legal scholar, and Hawaiian sovereignty activist Mililani Trask (Reading 65; also see Allen 1986; LaDuke 1999). This point is taken up by Starhawk (2002a) from the perspective of earth-centered spirituality. Vandana Shiva (2002), director of the Research Foundation on Science, Technology, and Ecology, focuses on **relocalization,** as opposed to globalization, which places an enormous economic and environmental burden on countries of the global South. She argues that "what can be grown and produced locally should be used locally" rather than exported, and, further, that "relocalization everywhere—in the South and in the North—would conserve resources, generate meaningful work, fulfill basic needs and strengthen democracy" (p. 249). Crucially important for ecofeminists and environmental justice activists is that these localized systems also include a commitment to anti-racist principles, women's liberation, and economic justice.

Ecofeminism

The creation of the term **ecofeminism** is usually attributed to a group of French feminists who founded the Ecology-Feminism Center in 1974, based on their analysis of connections between masculinist social institutions and the destruction of the physical environment (d'Eaubonne 1994). A few years later, groundbreaking work in the United States by poet and essayist Susan Griffin (1978) and environmental historian Carolyn Merchant (1980) articulated a central insight of ecofeminism: the connection between the domination of women and the domination of nature. These authors pointed to the ways in which Western thought and science has seen nonhuman nature as wild and hostile, so much matter to be mastered and used. Francis Bacon, a seventeenth-century English statesman, philosopher, and champion of modern science, was an early exponent of this view and a powerful influence on the development of Western science. He wrote:

> For you have to but follow and . . . hound nature in her wanderings, and you will be able when you like to lead and drive her afterward to the same place again. . . . Neither ought a man make scruple of entering and penetrating into these holes and corners, when the inquisition of truth is his whole object.
> *(Quoted in Merchant 1980, p. 168)*

In Western thought, nature is often feminized and sexualized through imagery such as "virgin forest," "the rape of the earth," and "penetrating" the wilderness. Shiva (1988) noted that in the Western model of development, *sources,* living things that can reproduce life—whether forests, seeds, or women's bodies—are turned into *resources* to be objectified, controlled, and used. As resources, they count as productive in economic terms. In this view, a forest that is not logged, a river that is not fished, or a hillside that is not mined, is unproductive (Waring 1988).

A core point in ecofeminist analysis involves the concept of dualism, where various attributes are thought of in terms of oppositions: culture/nature, mind/body, male/female, civilized/primitive, sacred/profane, subject/object, self/other. Philosopher Val Plumwood (1993) argued that these dualisms are mutually reinforcing and should be thought of as an interlocking set. In each pair, one side is valued over the other. Culture, mind, male, civilized, for example, are valued over nature, body, female, primitive, which are thought of as "other" and inferior. Plumwood argued that dualism is the logic of hierarchical systems of thought—colonialism, racism, sexism, or militarism, which rely on the idea of otherness, enemies, and inferiority to justify superiority and domination. Ecofeminist ideas involve the transcendence of dualistic thought and valuing cultural and ecological diversity. Ynestra King (1998) argued that for ecofeminists "Modern Western science and technology . . . capitalism and Eurocentric masculinist culture together pose a threat to the continuation of life on earth" (p. 207; Reading 63). Ecofeminism is intrinsically about intersectionality, and has the potential to link opposition to racism, economic exploitation, militarism, and colonialism with opposition to the domination of women and nature (see Hawthorne 2002; Kirk 1997a, 1997b, 1998; Mies and Shiva 1993; Shiva 1988).

Such a broad approach is open to many interpretations and ideas for activism and organizing. The first ecofeminist conference in the United States, titled "Women for Life on Earth," was held in Amherst, Massachusetts, as a response to the near-meltdown at the Three Mile Island nuclear power plant in 1980, as discussed by Ynestra King (Reading 63). One outcome of the conference was the Women's Pentagon Action, a major demonstration against militarism in the early 1980s, mentioned in Chapter 10 (see Reading 61). Ecofeminism has been explored and developed through newsletters and study groups, college courses, animal rights organizing, and long-term women's land projects (see, e.g., Adams 1999; Diamond and Orenstein 1990; Gaard 1993; King 1988, 1993b; Sturgeon 1997; Warren 1994, 2000). Some ecofeminist writers and researchers have worked with local activist groups or have contributed to national and international debates. Examples include the National Women's Health Network's research and organizing around industrial and environmental health (Nelson 1990), critiques of reproductive technology and genetic engineering by the Feminist Network of Resistance to Reproductive and Genetic Engineering (Mies and Shiva 1993), and the Committee on Women, Population, and the Environment, which has critiqued simplistic overpopulation arguments that focus only on countries of the South rather than also addressing the overconsumption of the North (Bandarage 1997; Hartmann 1995; Mello 1996; Silliman and King 1999; also see Urban 2008). The Women's Environment and Development Organization (WEDO) is an educational and advocacy organization and a co-author of Reading 67 on

gender and climate change. This article comes out of transnational feminist collaboration on environmental issues using opportunities offered through the United Nations Framework Convention on Climate Change to introduce a gender perspective into climate change policies, research, and theorizing.

Ecofeminist writer Charlene Spretnak (1990) embraced the eclectic nature of U.S. ecofeminism and noted its varied roots in feminist theory, feminist spirituality, and social ecology. This diversity in ecofeminist approaches raises the question of whether there is a sufficiently consistent, intellectually coherent ecofeminist perspective, and many academics have claimed that there is not. Some women of color argued that, as with much U.S. feminism, ecofeminism emphasizes gender over race and class; others contend that it focuses on abstract ideas about women and nature rather than on practical issues grounded in everyday reality (Davis 1998; Smith 1997; Taylor 1997). Left-wing radicals, some environmentalists, and many academics reject ecofeminism as synonymous with goddess worship or on the grounds that it assumes women are essentially closer to nature than men. Geographer Joni Seager (1993), for example, undertook a feminist analysis of environmental issues but did not use the term *ecofeminism* to describe her work. At present, U.S. ecofeminism is very much the preserve of writers and scholars, albeit those who are often on the margins of the academy. Although this may lead to an activism of scholarship—by no means insignificant—it does not often connect directly with the reality of daily life for many women organizing around environmental issues (also see Epstein 1993; Kirk 1997a, 1997b; MacGregor 2006; Sachs 1996). We argue that an ecological feminism can, and should, integrate gender, race, class, and nation in its analyses and that its powerful theoretical insights can, and should, translate into practice.

Environmental Justice

The people most affected by poor physical environments in the United States are women and children, particularly from communities of color. Many women of color and poor white women are active in hundreds of local organizations campaigning for healthy living and working conditions in their communities, which are disproportionately affected by

Women's environmental activism includes caring for home and community gardens or gathering herbs for medicinal uses.

pollution from incinerators, toxic dumps, fertilizers, pesticides, and hazardous working conditions in industry and agriculture (see, e.g., Adamson, Evans, and Stein 2002; Bullard 1990, 1993; Hofrichter 1993; LaDuke 1999; Quintero-Somaini and Quirindongo 2004; Spears 1998; Stein 2004; Szasz 1994). Data show a strong correlation between the distribution of toxic wastes and race, which has been termed **environmental racism** (Lee 1987).

The theory of environmental racism and the movement for **environmental justice** draw on concepts of civil rights, under which all citizens have a right to healthy living and working conditions. Organizationally, too, the environmental justice movement has roots in civil rights organizing, as well as in labor unions, Chicano land-grant movements, social justice organizations, and Native American rights organizations. Its tactics include demonstrations and rallies, public education, research and monitoring of toxic sites, preparing and presenting expert testimony to government agencies, reclaiming land through direct action, and maintaining and teaching traditional agricultural practices, crafts, and skills. Examples of local organizations include the Asia Pacific Environmental Network (Oakland, Calif.), the Mothers of East Los Angeles (see Pardo 1990), the Newtown Florist Club (Gainesville, Ga.), the Southwest Network for Environmental and

Economic Justice (Albuquerque, N.M., and Austin, Tex.), and West Harlem Environmental Action (New York; see Miller 1993).

Local organizations embrace different issues depending on their memberships and geographic contexts. Some are primarily concerned to stop the location of toxic waste dumps or incinerators in their neighborhoods, an approach sometimes dubbed the Not-In-My-Back-Yard (NIMBY) syndrome. Most groups are quick to see that it is not enough to keep hazards out of their own neighborhoods if this means that dumps or incinerators will then be located in other poor communities. This has led to coordinated opposition on a local, regional, and national level. The First National People of Color Environmental Leadership Summit in Washington, D.C. in 1991 adopted "Principles of Environmental Justice," included here (Reading 64). These principles are remarkable for their vision, breadth, and timelessness. They affirm the interdependence of all species and mandate the ethical, balanced, and responsible use of land and renewable resources in the interest of a sustainable planet for humans and other living things. They refer to people's rights to self-determination, to participation in making public policy, and to compensation for environmental injustice. Furthermore, they consider government acts of environmental injustice to be violations of international law. The principles do not mention gender even though the majority of those who attended this summit were women, and women have played a major part in sustaining grassroots organizing for environmental justice. Following the summit, several major grassroots networks were formed, such as the African American Environmental Justice Action Network, the Indigenous Environmental Network, and the Farmworkers Network for Economic and Environmental Justice, committed to building a multicultural, multiracial movement. Twenty years after its original study, *Toxic Wastes and Race in the United States* (Lee 1987), and following two decades of activism and advocacy on this topic nationwide, the United Church of Christ published a new study, using a more sophisticated methodology, that showed "racial disparities in the distribution of hazardous wastes are greater than previously reported" (Bullard et al. 2007, p. x). An egregious example of environmental racism was the official response to the impact of Hurricane Katrina on communities of color in New Orleans and the Gulf coast. Beverly Wright, professor of Environmental Studies at Dillard University, initiated the *A Safe Way Back Home* project to educate residents on what they could do about the toxins in the soil and in their homes after the flooding (Reading 71; also see Jones-DeWeever 2007; Pastor et al. 2006).

Besides opposing hazardous conditions, the environmental justice movement also has a powerful reconstructive dimension involving sustainable projects that intertwine ecological, economic, and cultural survival. Examples include Tierra Wools (northern New Mexico) where a workers' cooperative produces high-quality, handwoven rugs and clothing and organically fed lamb from its sheep (Pulido 1993); the Native American White Earth Land Recovery Project in Minnesota, which produces wild rice, maple sugar, berries, and birch bark (LaDuke 1993, 1999); and many inner-city community gardening projects producing vegetables for local consumption (e.g., Bagby 1990; Hynes 1996; Warner 1987).

Although very few local environmental issues are exclusively the concern of women, women form the majority of environmental justice activists at local level. As noted earlier, women have a history of community organizing. This activism may be given special impetus if they have sick children or become ill themselves. Illnesses caused by toxics are sometimes difficult to diagnose and treat because they affect internal organs and the balance of body functioning, and symptoms can be mistaken for those of other conditions. Women have been persistent in raising questions and searching for plausible explanations for such illnesses or tracing probable sources of pollution affecting their neighborhoods, sometimes discovering that their communities have been built on contaminated land, as happened at Love Canal, New York, for example, (Gibbs 1995, 1998; Kaplan 1997). They have publicized their findings and taken on governmental agencies and corporations responsible for contamination. In so doing they have been ridiculed as "hysterical housewives" by officials and reporters and their research trivialized as emotional and unscholarly. By contrast, Nelson (1990), for example, honored this work as kitchen table science. In October 1991, women were 60 percent of the participants at the First National People of Color Environmental Leadership Summit. Many urban gardeners in northern cities are elderly African American women (e.g., Bagby 1990). On the west coast, Latino and Asian immigrants continue the gardening traditions of their homelands. In rural areas, women work on family subsistence garden plots, planting, harvesting, and processing fruits and vegetables for home use (Sachs 1996). Some know the woods or backcountry areas in great detail, as ethnobotanists, because they go there at different seasons to gather herbs for medicinal purposes. Among Mexican Americans, for example, *curanderas*—traditional healers—continue to work with herbal remedies and acquire their knowledge from older women relatives (Perrone, Stockel, and Krueger 1989). Others attest to the healing and redemptive power of gardening and caring for plants. Catherine Sneed, for example, who founded the Garden Project for prisoners and former prisoners, wrote: "we're not just growing plants—we're growing people" (Sneed 2000, p. 27; see also Gross 1992; Hynes 1996).

When women become involved with environmental justice organizing, they become politicized (Gibbs 1995, 1998; Krauss 1993; Zeff, Love, and Stults 1989). They are caught up in attending meetings, maybe traveling to other towns and cities and staying away from home overnight. They spend much more time, and money, on the phone than before. They are quoted in the local papers or on the TV news. They often face new challenges, balancing family responsibilities, perhaps struggling with their husbands' misgivings about their involvement, or facing the tensions of being strong women in male-dominated communities.

Women active in the environmental justice movement generally see themselves and their communities in terms of race and class and "have remained wary of a 'feminist' label" (Gottlieb 1993, p. 234). Indeed, most environmental justice organizations do not draw on a gender analysis, even though many grassroots participants are women. By contrast, ecofeminists have tended to emphasize gender at the expense of race and class and have been less effective in linking theory and practice in a sustained way. Robert Gottlieb (1993), professor of urban and environmental policy, noted that the U.S. environmental movement as a whole has been unable to respond to the question "What constitutes an agenda and organizing style that incorporates women's experiences?"(p. 234). Given the crucial importance of the environment in a more secure and sustainable world, there is a great need for a theoretical framework that integrates gender, race, class, nation, and environmental issues and that generates broad-based activist efforts.

Sustainability and Connectedness

The idea of sustainability is often invoked but means very different things to different people. For corporate economists, for example, it means sustained economic growth that will yield ongoing profits; for ecologists it involves the maintenance of natural systems—wetlands, forests, wilderness, air and water quality; for environmentalists it means using only renewable resources and generating low or nonaccumulating levels of pollution (Pearce, Markandya, and Barbier 1990). Many concerned with environmental economics note the contradiction between the linear expansionism of capitalist economies and long-term sustainability (Daly and Cobb 1989; Henderson 1991; O'Connor 1994). Ecological relationships are circular not linear, like the water cycle, the oxygen cycle, and the rotting of compost which fertilizes the ground for new growth. In the early 1990s, scholar and writer Maria Mies (1993) noted that for countries of the South to follow the development model of the industrial North there would need to be two more worlds: one for the necessary natural resources and the other for the waste. Since then, this estimate has been revised drastically as consumption continues to increase. Current estimates assume the need for between two and seven planets for the South to consume at the same rate as the global North.

A more sustainable future for both North and South means rethinking current cultural and economic systems and priorities, as argued by scholar and writer H. Patricia Hynes (Reading 66). She uses the concept **ecological footprint** to refer to the amount of energy, land, water, minerals, and other natural resources required by varying lifestyles and levels of development (see Figure 11.1). This tool can be used to analyze and measure levels of consumption and to evaluate changes in consumption patterns. Reducing our consumption might include reusing and recycling materials, driving much less, wearing used clothing, bartering with others for things we need, engaging in socially responsible shopping and investing, and buying directly from farms and craftspeople. Hynes notes that "green consumerism" is *still* consumerism and involves the cultivation of "needs" as with any major business. She argues for meso-, macro-, and global-level changes that go beyond individual decisions to live more simply. She asks:

> what insights and efforts can a woman-centered analysis bring to the issue of consumption in order to further the goals of redistributing and humanizing our use of natural resources?

Briefly, we discuss three interrelated issues—food security, water security, and climate change—in light of this question.

Food Security

Food security means that families, communities, and nations have reliable year-round access to adequate supplies of nourishing food. Some people grow much of what they eat, and women shoulder the work of subsistence farming in many countries, especially in Asia and Africa, as mentioned in Reading 67.

Food insecurities have many causes. Agribusiness has developed factory farming methods that require chemical pesticides and fertilizers, and that

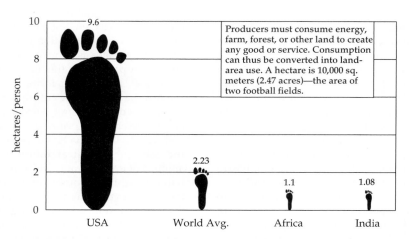

FIGURE **11.1 Comparative Consumption of Environmental Resources, 2003 (in hectares per person).** (*Sources:* Bill Bigelow and Bob Peterson [eds.], *Rethinking Globalization* [Milwaukee, Wis.: Rethinking Schools Press, 2002.] Reprinted by permission of Rethinking Schools Press and World Wide Fund for Nature, 2006. *Living Planet Report 2006,* Table 2. Gland, Switzerland: WWFN. Accessed at www.panda.org/news_facts/publications/living_planet_report/index.cfm.)

focus on monoculture—growing large fields of one crop such as soybeans or corn. In the 1950s and 1960s proponents of a so-called "green revolution" exported this model of chemically dependent agriculture to poorer countries on the argument that it would end world hunger. More recently, similar claims have been made for genetically modified organisms (GMOs). Experience has shown that chemically dependent agriculture is not sustainable over the long term. It requires increasing amounts of chemical "inputs," which farmers have to buy and results in declining yields and impoverished soils. Monoculture makes plants more vulnerable to pests and diseases that can wipe out a whole crop. Industrialized food production provides "cheaper" foods in the United States because U.S. agriculture is subsidized. These foods are not cheaper, however, if one adds costs to the environment, the cost of oil, and costs to people's health. As consumers in the United States, we have become accustomed to even-sized, waxed fruits selected as much for their long shelf life and ability

to withstand being transported over long distances, as for their flavor or nutritional value. Indeed, a major cost of food is transportation. Communities in Canada have introduced the concept of food-miles to underscore this point. Fresh produce from Chile and New Zealand, countries in the southern hemisphere where summer coincides with the northern winter, is imported into the United States, so that we can eat apples year round. Tea, coffee, and tropical fruits are imported from countries of the global South, where they compete with subsistence crops for land, labor, and water. They earn hard currency; in addition, agricultural exports are required under World Bank and IMF Structural Adjustment Programs to increase market profitability, as mentioned in Chapter 8.

Free trade agreements are another factor affecting the availability and price of food in many producer countries. Rice grown in the United States, which is subsidized under the U.S. Farm bill, is sold in South Korea, a rice-producing country, at half the cost of Korean-grown rice. In 2008, a new phase of the North American Free Trade Agreement (NAFTA) came into effect, opening up the Mexican market for U.S.-grown corn. Also, the development of biofuels based on corn has sent corn prices skyrocketing as corporations buy up corn stocks and take them out of the food supply. Food riots in many poorer nations hit the headlines in 2008. Food crises were sparked by several factors, including increased oil prices, drought, crop failure, and competition from cash crops and biofuels. Farmers in India and South Korea, to name but two examples, have killed themselves in despair over the devastating economic circumstances of farming in their countries.

In reality, food is not scarce, as argued over twenty years ago by Frances Moore Lappé and Joseph Collins (1986, 1998), founders of Food First: Institute for Food and Development Policy. As they demonstrated, the food industry is a for-profit business, increasingly dominated by a few transnational corporations like Monsanto and Cargill. Food security requires sustainable forms of food production that rely on biofertilizers and pesticides, subject to community control. Food security is enhanced through direct connections between producers and consumers, as with U.S. farmers' markets or community-supported agriculture schemes (see, e.g., Winne 2008). The Community Food Security Coalition (Venice, Calif.) links people involved in small-scale organic production, farmers' markets, schoolyard gardens, hospital food services, food banks, and food pantries. Eating locally produced food supports local growers, cuts down on transportation costs and the need for oil, and provides better nutrition because produce is fresher. This is what Vandana Shiva (2002) advocates as relocalization. Women are playing a key role in this movement for food security, as growers and as consumers caring for their families (see, e.g., Bollinger 2007).

In the United States, access to nourishing food is linked to race and class. Low-income neighborhoods lack supermarkets that carry a full range of fresh fruit and vegetables, a factor in the increase in obesity, as we noted in Chapter 5 (see also, e.g., Gonzalez 2008; Shaffer and Gottlieb 2007). Government food stamps and the Women, Infants, and Children (WIC) Program provide some support for low-income families to buy food, and in some states these can be exchanged at farmers' markets. Local government agencies and nonprofit organizations run food pantries and food banks for low-income

families, and these are well used, especially at the end of the month. Drawing on an intersectional analysis that emphasizes race and class inequalities, the food security movement in the United States provides a forum for learning, research, advocacy on food policy, and support for farmers' markets and other community-based food projects.

Water Security

Access to adequate supplies of uncontaminated water has become a major issue worldwide, exacerbated by the fact that, increasingly, water supplies are owned and managed by transnational corporations (see Box). Water has long been assumed to be part of the Commons—the wealth of natural resources available to all to fulfill our basic needs. "Companies like Coca-Cola are fully aware that water is the real thirst quencher and are jumping into the bottled water business" together with Pepsi, Nestlé, and others (Shiva 2002, p. 99). Bottled water is a fast-growing business worldwide, consumed by many people in the global North, as well as elites and middle classes in the South. Again, structural adjustment programs are implicated, as indebted countries are pressured by international financial institutions to allow the privatization of publicly owned and managed water supplies.

Bottled water is marketed as pristine, and in the United States many women have assumed that bottled water is safer than tap water. Research shows, however, that this is not so (e.g., Morrison 2007; Natural Resources Defense Council 1997; Steingraber 2001). Indeed, some bottled water *is* tap water. In fact, big city tap water is tested for some bacteria at least 100 times a month, whereas the FDA requires bottlers to test only once a week (Morrison 2007). Bottled water is convenient, however, especially since public water fountains may have been removed or no longer function.

In various countries of the global South, water supplies are polluted, which can have serious effects on people's health; and thousands of infants and children die each day from preventable diseases like diarrhea. Moreover, women are responsible for providing water for home and garden use—from piped supplies, wells, lakes, and rivers—and may have to carry it each day, sometimes over long distances.

The Water Business

- Water is essential. There are no alternatives. We die without it.

- Most of the earth's surface is water, but almost all of it is salt water or glaciers. Less than 1 percent is freshwater that is potentially available for human use.

- The World Bank has estimated the potential water market at $1 trillion (Shiva 2002).

- In Bolivia, the World Bank pressured the government to privatize water in the city of Cochabamba as a condition of receiving new development loans. The Bechtel corporation raised water prices there by 300 percent (Caplan 2004).

- Two French water companies, Vivendi Environment and Suez Lyonnaise des Eaux, operate in 120 countries. The Spanish company Aguas de Barcelona dominates in Latin America. British conglomerates, Biwater and Thames, have operations in Asia, South Africa, and the Americas (Shiva 2002).

- Transnational corporations like Coca-Cola (Dasani) and Pepsi (Aquafina) are making massive profits out of bottled water. Other well-known brands include Perrier, Evian, and Poland Spring. Norway and Fiji export drinking water.

- Annually, at least 1.5 million tons of plastics and 1.5 million barrels of oil go into the production of bottles. The manufacturing process releases toxics such as nickel, ethylbenzene, ethylene oxide, and benzene. Most bottles end up in landfills (Caplan 2004).

- It takes 174 gallons of water to produce 1 pound of wheat; 5,100 gallons for one pound of beef (Hiller et al. 2005).

- It takes 25 liters of water to manufacture 1 liter of Coca-Cola and 250 liters of water to irrigate the sugar cane that sweetens it (Glantz 2007).

Investing in community-controlled water systems is key to water security and involves cleaning up local supplies, not substituting bottled water for those who can afford it. Problems related to a community's water supply are public meso- and macrolevel issues and cannot be addressed by private micro-level actions. There are many examples of people in India, in Cochabamba (Bolivia), in Europe, and the United States who are standing up to corporate control of water and working for what Vandana Shiva (2005) calls "water democracy." Coca-Cola, Nestlé, and Pepsi have all been sued by local communities for excessive use of water supplies. One case, in Plachimada (southern India), led to a court ruling against Coca-Cola (see Reading 48). In the United States, too, communities are organizing to resist water privatization, as shown in the film *Thirst*. The Graywater Guerillas, a group of women who co-authored the zine, *The Guerilla Graywater Girls Guide to Water,* underscore the enormous waste of water in this country. They urge reuse of water, the development of alternative systems, and watershed restoration (Woelfle-Erskine et al. 2007).

Gender and Climate Change

Climate changes, caused by increased carbon emissions affecting the entire planet, are under way. These changes have led to the melting of glaciers and ice caps, changing rain patterns, and greater extremes of weather, including both droughts and heavy storms. Members of European women's environmental groups and the Women's Environment and Development Organization (based in New York City) are using the United Nations Framework Convention on Climate Change to introduce a gender perspective into research and policy making on this topic (Reading 67). Once considered a marginal issue, climate change has broken through barriers of ignorance, disinterest, and denial on the part of U.S. elected officials and the general public in the past few years. These authors argue, however, that a gender dimension to this issue has been largely overlooked.

They note that women tend to be more vulnerable to disasters linked to climate change, such as the Asian tsunami, Hurricane Mitch in Central America, and Hurricane Katrina in the United States. Older women in Europe have died as a result of abnormally high temperatures. With the expansion of cash crop production in countries of the global South, communities have been forced to fell trees that would have anchored the soil during heavy rains. Women have been pushed to farm more marginal land, like steep hillsides, which has increased the likelihood of flooding. In the United States, structural factors like the development of low-density suburbs, urban planning and zoning laws, and poor public transportation all mean that many people have to drive on a regular basis, thus generating carbon emissions. More women than men use public transportation and often make several short trips in a day, including household errands, picking up children from school, and so on.

Women's daily experiences in the global North and South must be part of policy making about this issue. These authors note that women organized effectively to safeguard their families during Hurricane Mitch in 1998. For over twenty years, the Kenyan Women's Green Belt movement has planted millions of trees that provide firewood, stabilize and nourish the soil, and generate a modest income for women who tend tree nurseries and teach others about this issue (Brownhill 2007; Maathai 2006). Their work has inspired women in other nations, mainly in Africa, to do the same. It is part of an integrated approach to self-provisioning and food sovereignty that claims farmers have the right "to feed themselves and their communities, and to be free from pressures to commercialize production to the exclusion of food security" (Brownhill 2007, p. 36). The work of the Kenyan Women's Green Belt shows solutions to problems of food security, water security, and climate change are interconnected. In 2007, the Canadian magazine, *Women and Environments*, published a special issue on gender and climate change, an early feminist resource on this topic.

Environmentalists, development agencies, nonprofit organizations, farmers, and gardeners endorse some age-old sustainable technologies and have developed many innovations including biological methods to restore soil and increase its fertility, the use of plants to clean contaminated water, and the use of mushrooms to clean toxic soil. They have devised solar cookers and low fuel stoves for use in rural areas of the global South. They have formed seed banks that collect and distribute fertile seed, rather than buy non-fertile hybrid seeds produced by corporate agribusiness. They are cultivating home gardens, teaching about nutrition, and urging people to avoid junk food, which is high in fats and sugars but has very little food value. Cuba, a small Caribbean nation which has been isolated economically by a U.S.-imposed embargo for decades, has made a spectacular transition from oil- and chemical-based agriculture to intensive organic farms and gardens based on the principles of agro-ecology and permaculture and has much to teach other nations about how to do this.

The writers and activists mentioned in this chapter all seek to maintain or remake connections between people and the natural world. Together such projects and movements draw on alternative visions and strategies for sustainable living, however small scale and fragile they may be at present. At root, this is about taking on the current economic system and the systems of power—personal and institutional— that sustain and benefit from it, working to transform relationships of exploitation and oppression. Vandana Shiva (2005) writes of the natural world as a living economy in contrast to corporate economies of destruction. She notes that women are guardians of life-centered cultures through their caring work for children, families, and communities. The examples cited above all contribute to life-centered cultures; but clearly, much more needs to be done to develop sustainable ways of living, especially at macro- and global-levels.

A sustainable future implies local control over transnational corporations, reduction of poor countries' foreign debt, and making money available for development that is ecologically sound, as we suggested in Chapter 8. At a local level in the United States it implies support for community gardens, farmers' markets, credit unions, and small-scale, worker-owned businesses and markets, mentioned in Chapter 7. It means valuing women's unpaid domestic and caring work, a key aspect of sustaining home and community life (Mellor 1992; Waring 1988). Sociologist Mary Mellor notes that this caring work is geared to biological time. Children need feeding when they are hungry; sick people need care regardless of what time of day it is; gardens need planting in the right season. She argued that, given a gendered division of labor, "women's responsibility for biological time means that men have been able to create a public world that largely ignores it," a world "no longer rooted in the physical reality of human existence" (pp. 258–59). A sustainable future must be based in biological time and will require emotional as well as physical and intellectual labor.

Novels provide an effective way of showing the possibilities—positive and negative—of particular philosophies and societal arrangements, and they can help us to imagine different futures (e.g., Butler 1993; Hogan 1997; Kingsolver 2000; Piercy 1976; Silko 2000; Starhawk 1993). Environmental artists are working on reclamation and recycling projects that are both practical and beautiful, using natural materials and natural settings.

To create such a future will also mean changing current definitions of wealth that emphasize materialism and consumerism. A broader notion of wealth includes everything that has the potential to enrich a person and a community, such as health, physical energy and strength, safety and security, time, skills, talents, wisdom, creativity, love, community support, a connection to one's history and cultural heritage, and a sense of belonging. This is not a philosophy of denial or a romanticization of poverty, though it does involve a fundamental **paradigm shift,** or change of worldview, in a country so dominated by material consumption and wealth. Vandana Shiva (2005) calls this process "earth democracy." Writers included in this chapter all implicitly or explicitly argue for a profound change in attitudes, in which human life and the life of the natural world are valued, cared for, and sustained.

Questions for Reflection

As you read and discuss this chapter, ask yourself these questions:

1. What does it mean to you to be part of an interconnected chain of life?

2. What are the main environmental issues in your area?

3. How far are you away from farming—in terms of geographical distance and generations of your family? Are there community gardens in your area?

4. Do you have access to a compost pile or worm box?

5. What are the main illnesses in your area? Are they linked to environmental causes?

6. Think about the practical projects mentioned in this chapter. What resources were used by the people involved? What worldviews are implicit in their actions?

7. What is your vision of a sustainable future?

Finding Out More on the Web

1. Find out more about the organizations mentioned in this chapter. Evaluate their strategies and activities. The following are women's organizations or those where women are prominent:

Association for Women's Rights in Development: www.awid.org

Center for Health, Environment, and Justice: www.chej.org

Committee on Women, Population, and the Environment: www.cwpe.org

Community Food Security Coalition: www.foodsecurity.org/farm_to_college.html

Student Environmental Action Coalition: www.seac.org

Tierra Wools: www.tierrawools.com

White Earth Land Recovery Project: www.welrp.org

Women's Earth Alliance: www.womensearthalliance.org

Women's Environment and Development Organization: www.wedo.org

2. In Reading 63, Ynestra King gives data for nuclear warheads and toxic dumps. What are the current figures?

3. In Reading 65, Mililani Trask refers to contamination and destruction of land by military operations at Kahoolawe Island and Johnston Island. What has happened at these places? Find out more about the environmental effects of military activities. A useful place to start is Global Green USA: www.globalgreen.org.

4. Find out about pollution in your community at www.scorecard.org.

Taking Action

1. Find out about environmental organizations and environmental justice organizations in your area. What are their goals and perspectives? What projects are they currently working on? How could you participate in or support their work?

2. Find out about the people who used to live where you live now. What happened to the Native American people who lived on this land? Are there other groups who used to live here? How did they support themselves? Why did they move? Where are they now? How are they living now?

3. Calculate your ecological footprint at Redefining Progress: www.rprogress.org/index.htm. Work out how to make it smaller.

SIXTY-TWO

Rose Moon (2001)—Excerpt

Sandra Steingraber

Sandra Steingraber is a biological scientist, award-winning science writer, teacher, cancer survivor, and expert on environmental links between cancer and reproductive health. Author of *Living Downstream: An Ecologist Looks at Cancer and the Environment, Having* *Faith: An Ecologist's Journey to Motherhood,* and *Post-Diagnosis,* a volume of poetry, she was *Ms.* magazine's 1997 Woman of the Year and has held academic appointments at several universities and colleges.

Editors' note: In *Having Faith,* Sandra Steingraber names the months of her pregnancy according to traditional names given to each month's full moon in the agricultural calendar. Rose moon is the sixth month. At the end of a semester as visiting professors in Illinois, Steingraber and her husband drive back to their home in Somerville, near Boston. This excerpt refers to their conversations and to Steingraber's ongoing research into fetal development.

. . . In its narration of life in the womb, the popular literature waxes eloquent over a completely different set of milestones than do the academic texts to which I'm more accustomed. The textbooks devote most of their pages to the complicated early events of organogenesis, with all their origami-like precision. The writing perks up again at the end with the avalanche of hormonal changes that triggers labor and delivery. But the discussion of fetal changes during the second and third trimesters is swift and almost dismissive: growth of body parts, fat deposition, refinement of features. . . .

By contrast, the popular media pass swiftly over the treacherous early months—except to mention morning sickness and symptoms of imminent miscarriage—and hit their rhetorical stride during the months of mid- and late pregnancy. These periodicals dote lovingly on such achievements as growth of the eyebrows (well developed by month six!), the secretion of waxy *vernix* (protects the skin from chapping), and the growth of *lanugo* (fine downy hair that holds the vernix in place). What mother-to-be can resist these endearing details, this special language, which resembles the vocabulary of a Catholic Mass? ("Vernix" is Latin for varnish, "lanugo," for wool). From the popular books, I learn that a six-month-old fetus is about thirteen inches long and weighs a little more than a pound. I learn that the top of my uterus has risen above my belly button and that the fetus, now pressed directly against the wall of the uterus, is affected by the womb's various squeezings.

. . .

What the popular books and magazines do not talk much about are environmental issues. Even the March of Dimes publication, *Mama,* which is devoted to the prevention of birth defects, does not mention solvents or pesticides or toxic waste sites or Minamata or Vietnam. There is some kind of disconnect between what we know scientifically and

what is presented to pregnant women seeking knowledge about prenatal life. At first, I assumed the silence around environmental threats to pregnancy might be explained by the emerging nature of the evidence. Perhaps the writers of public educational materials choose to present only the dangers for which the data are iron-clad and long-standing. All the books and periodicals include a standard discussion of rubella, for example, and urge pregnant smokers to quit.

But the more I read, the more I realize that scientific certainty is not a consistent criterion by which reproductive dangers are presented to pregnant mothers. For example, pregnant women are urged to drink no alcohol. The guidebooks and magazines are unanimous about this. While fetal alcohol syndrome is a well-described and incontrovertible phenomenon . . . no one knows if an occasional glass of wine is harmful. Nevertheless, caution dictates—and again I wholeheartedly agree—that in the absence of information to the contrary, one should assume no safe threshold level. One of the pregnancy books in my collection, *Life Before Birth,* even quotes Voltaire on this issue: "In ignorance, abstain."

Yet this same principle is not applied to nitrates in tap water. Here we assume we *can* set safe thresholds—in this case ten parts per million—even though these thresholds have never been established for fetuses and even though almost nothing is known about transplacental transfer of nitrates or about how nitrate-inactivated hemoglobin in the mother's blood might interfere with oxygen delivery to the fetus. What's more, we allow 4.5 million Americans to drink water with nitrate levels above this arbitrary limit. Four and a half million people surely includes a lot of pregnant women. We also presume we can set safe limits on pesticide residues, solvents, and chlorination byproducts in drinking water—and yet none of these thresholds has ever been demonstrated to protect against fetal damage. In fact, plenty of evidence exists to the contrary. When it comes to environmental hazards, not only do we dispense with the principle of "In ignorance, abstain," we fail to inform pregnant women that the hazards even exist. . . .

The more I read, the more contradictions I see. A recent scientific report summarizing the reproductive effects of chemical contaminants in food reaches a strong conclusion: "The evidence is overwhelming:

certain persistent toxic substances impair intellectual capacity, change behavior . . . and compromise reproductive capacity. The people most at risk are children, pregnant women, women of childbearing age. . . . Particularly at risk are developing embryos and nursing infants."

By comparison one of the most popular guidebooks to pregnancy opens a discussion of this same topic with a complaint about that kind of bad news: "Reports of hazardous chemicals in just about every item in the American diet are enough to scare the appetite out of anyone. . . . Don't be fanatic. Though trying to avoid theoretical hazards in food is a commendable goal, making your life stressful in order to do so is not."

Of course, the don't-worry-be-happy approach does not apply to smoking and drinking; the authors take a very stern, absolutist position on these topics.

I look over at my [husband] who's been singing louder and louder.

"Hey, Jeff?"

"Mmm."

"I'm trying to figure something out."

"What's that?" He turns down the radio.

"Not a single one of these pregnancy magazines encourages mothers to find out what the Toxics Release Inventory shows for their own communities."

"You did it though, right?"

"Yeah, I looked it up on the Internet."

"And?"

"And McLean County is one of the top counties in Illinois for airborne releases of reproductive poisons."

I detail for him the results of my research. The biggest emissions of fetal toxicants are hexane from the soybean processing plant and toluene from the auto plant. My list also includes glycol ethers and xylene. All are solvents.

"Jesus," says Jeff.

"I also found out that the university uses six different pesticides on their grounds and fields. So I looked up their toxicology profiles. Two of them are known to cause birth defects in animals." . . .

"So what are you trying to figure out?"

"Two things. One, why is there is no public conversation about environmental threats to pregnancy?"

"What's the other thing?"

I quote Voltaire: "In ignorance, abstain." "Why does abstinence in the face of uncertainty apply only to individual behavior? Why doesn't it apply equally to industry or agriculture?"

"Okay, let me think for a minute." Jeff turns the radio back on. And then turns it off again. "I think the questions overlap. Pregnancy and motherhood are private. We still act like pregnant women are not part of the public world. Their bodies look strange. They seem vulnerable. You are not supposed to upset them. If something is scary or stressful, you shouldn't talk about it."

"But pregnant women are constantly being told what to do. No coffee. No alcohol. No sushi. Stay away from cat feces."

"That's still private. Industry and agriculture are political, public. They exist outside one's own body, outside one's own house. You can't do something immediately about them within the time period of a pregnancy. So it seems unmanageable."

"It's pregnant women who have to live with the consequences of public decisions. We're the ones who will be raising the damaged children. If we don't talk about these things because it's too upsetting, how will it ever change?"

Jeff throws me a look.

"You're the writer. Can you find a language to manage it? Break the taboo?"

Now I have to think for a while.

. . .

Back in our Somerville neighborhood, with its views of Bunker Hill and low-lying, wealthier Cambridge, I forget the expanses of Illinois. Up in our third-floor apartment in this most densely populated city in North America (or so claims the Somerville newspaper on a regular basis), Jeff and I spend a few days bumping into each other and reacquainting ourselves with car alarms and Indian take-out food. In the evenings, we sit out on the balcony and wait for an ocean breeze. The neighbor who shares the balcony with us has planted morning glories and tomatoes, which are already twining up the latticework. In the mornings, I walk the dog to the park, sharing the sidewalk with caravans of strollers pushed by pouty teenagers and muttering grandmothers. I never noticed how many babies lived in my neighborhood. Up and down the block, rhododendrons are blooming in tiny cement yards, and vines of purple wisteria wrap the porches of shingled triple-deckers. Underwear flaps on a hundred clotheslines. From the park's old locust trees hang panicles of fragrant white flowers. It is Somerville's finest season.

With the public library only two blocks away, I resume my research. What interests me now is the sine qua non of pregnancy's sixth month: fetal brain development.

Trying to understand the embryological anatomy of the vertebrate brain nearly unhinged me two decades ago. It was some of the most difficult biology I had ever encountered—and the most beautiful. It was like watching a rose bloom in speeded-up time. Or like spelunking in an uncharted cave. My embryology professor, Dr. Bruce Criley, used to drill us by flashing slides of fetal brain sections on a huge screen while we sat in the darkened lab trying to keep our bearings. "Okay, where are we now?" he would demand, whacking a pointer against an unfamiliar structure. Prosencephalon, rhombencephalon, mesencephalon—ancient-sounding names identified rooms in a continuously morphing cavern.

Both the brain and the spinal cord are made up of the same three layers. The brain then adds a fourth layer when cells migrate from the inside out to form the cortex. It's what happens during and after this migration that is so dazzlingly disorienting. Indeed, in order to explain it all, the language of human brain development borrows its vocabulary from botany, architecture, and geography. There are lumens, islands, aqueducts, and isthmuses. There are ventricles, commissures, and hemispheres. There are roofs and floors, pyramids and pouches. There are furrows called sulci and elevations called gyri. Structures are said to balloon, undulate, condense, fuse, and swell. They pass by, flatten, overgrow, and bury each other. They turn, grow downward, turn again, grow upward.

Some structures are formed from tissues derived from two completely different locations. The pituitary gland, for example, is at the place where an upgrowth from a valley near the mouth meets a downgrowth from the forebrain. Meanwhile, the twelve cranial nerves go forth like apostles to make contact with the far-flung, newly developing eyes, ears, tongue, nose, etc. It was all enough to make us mild-mannered, high-achieving biology majors reel with panic. It also was enough to make us feel, once the lights went on again, that we had just emerged from a secret temple, the likes of which we had never seen before.

On a microscopic scale, the story is a bit simpler—although this may only be because we know so little about what actually goes on at the cellular level. All embryological structures are created through migration. But brain cells travel like spiders, trailing silken threads as they go.

There are two kinds of threads: dendrites and axons. Dendrites are fine and short. They receive messages from other nearby cells. Axons are ropy and long. They send out messages, often over great distances. Of the two, axons develop first. They grow out from the body of the brain cell along a specific pathway and in a specific direction. In this they are guided by proteins called cell adhesion molecules. The dendrites are spun out later. In fact, the peak period of dendrite growth doesn't even begin until late in the third trimester, and it continues until at least a year after birth.

Despite these differences, axons and dendrites have a lot in common. Both types of fibers branch after they elongate so that connections can be made with many other cells. These connecting points—the synapses—continue to increase in number throughout the first two years of life. Both axons and dendrites transmit messages by sending electrochemical signals down their lengths. Sometimes, these signals can also fly between fibers. But in most cases, in order to continue a message from one nerve cell to the next, chemicals have to diffuse across the synaptic space. These are the neurotransmitters, with their role call of familiar names: acetylcholine, dopamine, serotonin.

Fetal brain mysteries abound. Chief among them is the role of the neuroglia, whose name means nerve glue. These are brain cells that do not themselves conduct messages but that apparently exert control over the cells that do. They are far more than glue. In some cases they act as coaches to the neurons' athletes—wrapping their axons in ace-bandage layers of fat and thereby speeding the passage of electricity. They also appear to alter the neurons' diets, for example, by modulating the amount of glucose available. And they provide signals and pathways for migration. In this last capacity, they work in tandem with early-migrating neurons. That is to say, the brain cells that are the first to make the journey to the cortex provide essential cues—along with those of the neuroglia—that help later migrants find their way. But no one knows exactly how these trails are blazed, maps are drawn, and bread crumbs scattered.

Once you understand how the embryonic brain unfolds, chamber after hidden chamber, and how its webs of electricity all get connected up, you can easily see why neurological poisons have such profound effects in utero. Exposures that produce only transient effects in adult brains can lay waste to fetal ones. This happens through a variety of pathways. Neurotoxins can impede synapse formation, disrupt the release of neurotransmitters, or strip off the fatty layers wound around the axons. Neurotoxins can also slow the outward-bound trekking of migrating fetal brain cells. Because the earliest-maturing brain cells erect a kind of scaffolding to help their younger siblings find their way, a single exposure at the onset of migration can irretrievably alter the brain's architecture. A fetus also lacks the efficient detoxification systems that already-born human beings carry around within their livers, kidneys, and lungs. And, until they are six months old, fetuses and infants lack a blood-brain barrier, which prevents many blood-borne toxins from entering the brain's gray matter.

As if all this weren't enough, fetal brains are made even more vulnerable by lack of fat in the fetal body. The brain is 50 percent fat by dry weight, and after birth, body fat competes with the brain in attracting fat-soluble toxic chemicals. But throughout most of pregnancy, the fetus is lean, plumping up only during the last month or so. In fetuses, toxic chemicals that are fat-soluble—and many of them are—do not have other fat depots in which to be sequestered, and so they have disproportionately greater effects on the brains of fetuses than on the brains of the rest of us.

More than half of the top twenty chemicals reported in the 1997 Toxics Release Inventory are known or suspected neurotoxins. These include solvents, heavy metals, and pesticides. And yet our understanding of brain-damaging chemicals is vague and fragmentary. Part of the problem is that animal testing is of limited use in trying to figure out how a human baby might be affected by exposure to a particular neurotoxin. Humans are born at a much earlier stage of fetal brain development than, for example, monkeys. Rhesus monkeys' brains are closer to their final form when the monkeys are born, and the young are upright and walking before they are two months old, whereas the average age of human walking is thirteen months. Certain structures within rodent brains, on the

other hand, are less well developed at birth than ours. For example, cells in the human hippocampus, the seat of memory, are finished being produced at the time of birth, whereas in rodents, they are not formed until well into postnatal life. These kinds of differences between species mean that extrapolating from animal studies to humans is tricky. The windows of vulnerability are different. And obviously, conducting controlled experiments on human embryos and fetuses is not permissible.

Unhappily, plenty of human fetuses have been exposed to brain-damaging chemicals anyway—not through controlled experiments but through unintended exposures. There is much we can learn by studying their various deficits. However, this kind of research did not begin in earnest until the last few decades. According to the old thinking, either a chemical killed the fetus or it didn't. Either a chemical could produce an obvious structural deformity like anencephaly (no brain) or it couldn't. Not until the 1960s and '70s did fetal toxicologists recognize that certain low-level exposures can elicit functional abnormalities in the brain. That is, the brain *looks* fine—it has all the necessary structures—but it doesn't *act* fine. Once researchers tested children who had had low-level exposures to toxicants on cognitive and motor performance, subtle problems became apparent. The same was true for animals. As soon as laboratory testing of neurotoxicants was expanded to include not just birth defects but also behavioral problems (learning, memory, reaction time, the ability to run a maze), myriad other problems became evident. In both cases, researchers began to see that toxicants can affect brain functioning at much lower levels of exposure than they had previously imagined.

Unfortunately, this epiphany in brain research happened long after the establishment of environmental regulations governing toxic chemicals. Many of these regulations are based on pre-World War II assumptions about neurological development, not on the findings of recent studies. When it comes to fetal neurotoxicants, instead of following the admonition "In ignorance, abstain," we adhere to the principle "In ignorance and disregarding emerging science, proceed recklessly."

The sixth month of pregnancy is a joyful one. My round belly elicits smiles and happy comments from postal workers, dog walkers, and fellow subway riders, who compete to be the first to surrender a seat to me.

Meanwhile, the random fetal movements of last month have evolved into a predictable and reassuring choreography. And as the weeks go by, I begin to notice something else about the baby's movements: they are often generated *in response* to something that I do. When I take a warm bath, she begins to squirm and shimmy, as if she were bathing as well. When I curl up to Jeff at night, my belly pressing against his back, she kicks—with enough force that Jeff can feel it, too. If I roll over in bed, she sometimes rolls over. If police cars or fire trucks suddenly blare down the street, she becomes very still, and I know I won't hear much from her for a while. I pat my belly and try to comfort her. "It's okay, baby; it's just a siren." In these moments, I realize that I am beginning to perceive her as a sentient being—as a child—and myself more and more as her mother.

. . .

A commonly held belief is that natural substances are less toxic to the human body than synthetic ones. Like a lot of folk biology, this idea is both true and misleading at the same time. It all depends on what you mean by "natural."

Consider lead, the element that occupies square number eighty-two in the periodic chart. It is indeed present in the earth's crust. But lead is not really part of nature in the sense that it has no function in the world of living organisms. While abundant in the geological world, it does not naturally inhabit the ecological one. A normal blood lead level in a human being—or any other animal—should be zero. And even in the inanimate world of rocks, the soft, dense, silvery substance we know as lead cannot really be said to exist. Elemental lead has to be roasted and smelted out of other minerals. In this sense, a lead fishing weight is as much a synthetic creation as polyester, plastic wrap, or DDT.

There is no doubt that lead is a remarkable material. Its Latin name *plumbum* (abbreviated Pb by chemists) hints at its usefulness. Think plumbing. Essentially uncorrodible, it has long been used to line water pipes. For the same reason, it has found a place in roofing. Lead salts make excellent pigments, thus lead paint. Tetraethyl lead stops engine knocking, thus leaded gasoline. Lead also has handy electrical properties. Its largest use now is in the manufacture of lead-acid storage batteries, especially the ones used in cars.

Lead is also a formidable destroyer of human brains. This property has been recognized for at least 2,000 years. Once called plumbism, lead poisoning causes capillaries in the brain to erode, resulting in hemorrhage and swelling. Its symptoms include irritability, abdominal spasms, headache, confusion, palsy, and the formation of a black line across the gums. Prenatal transfer of lead across the placenta is also old news. In 1911, women working in the white-lead factories of Newcastle noticed that pregnancy cured plumbism. They were right: by passing lead on to their fetuses, workers lowered their own body burdens and thereby alleviated their symptoms of lead poisoning. Of course, most of their babies died. We now know that lead, once it gains entry into the adult female body, settles into bones and teeth. During the sixth month of pregnancy, when the fetal skeleton hardens, placental hormones free up calcium from the mother's bones and direct it through the placenta. Whatever stores of lead lay in the bones are also mobilized and follow calcium into the fetal body. In this way, a developing baby receives from its mother *her* lifetime lead exposure.

Our understanding about lead's toxicity changed radically in the 1940s. Before then, victims of acute lead poisoning who escaped death were presumed to enjoy a complete recovery. But soon a few observant physicians began to notice that child survivors often suffered from persistent nervous disorders and were failing in school. In the 1960s, behavioral changes were noted in experimental animals exposed to low doses of lead. Then, in the early 1970s, children living near a lead smelter in El Paso, Texas, were found to have lower IQ scores than children living farther away. By the 1980s, studies from around the world documented problems in lead-exposed children who had never exhibited any physical symptoms of acute poisoning. These included short attention spans, aggression, poor language skills, hyperactivity, and delinquency. We now know that lead can decrease mental acuity at levels one sixth those required to trigger physical symptoms. The new thinking is that no safe threshold exists for lead exposure in children or fetuses.

Fetal neurologists have also shed new light on the various ways by which lead wrecks brain development. At levels far lower than required to swell the brain, lead alters the flow of calcium in the synapses, thereby altering neurotransmitter activity. It also prevents dendrites from branching, and it interferes with the wrapping of fat around axons. But it doesn't stop there. Lead affects the adhesion molecules that guide the growth of these axons, thereby altering the architecture of the entire electrical web. It also poisons the energy-generating organelles (mitochondria) within the neuronal bodies and so lowers overall brain metabolism. In laboratory rats, lead inhibits a receptor known to play a key role in learning and memory. The adult brain can fend off some of these problems, thanks both to its blood-brain barrier and to an ability to bind lead to protein and so keep it away from the mitochondria. Fetal brains lack these defenses. This is why early lead exposures have life-changing consequences.

On its surface, the story of lead seems like a story of science triumphing over ignorance. Lead paint was banned in the United States in 1977, the year I graduated from high school, and leaded gas was phased out soon after, finally banned in 1990. With paint and gasoline as the two biggest sources of human lead exposure, the decisions to prohibit—and not just regulate—these products is a shining victory for public health. In their wake, the average blood lead levels in American children have fallen dramatically—75 percent between 1976 and 1991.

But there is another story about lead, told by historians and toxicologists who fought long and hard to banish lead from the human economy. It's a story about the willful suppression of science by industry. It's a story that helps explain why one in twenty American children still suffers from lead poisoning in spite of everything we know. It helps explain why lead, never outlawed for use in cosmetics, can still be found in some lipsticks and hair dyes. And it helps explain why the soil in my neighborhood in Somerville is so full of lead that we are still advised not to grow vegetables in our gardens.

Consider lead paint. Its production was halted in this country in the late 1970s. But in 1925, an international covenant had already banned lead-based paints for interior use in much of the rest of the world. This agreement acknowledged that lead was a neurotoxin and that lead paint in the homes produced lead dust, which is easily ingested when crawling babies put their hands in their mouths or chew on toys. But the United States was not a signatory to this agreement. In fact, the same industry trade group that prevented the United States from adopting the convenant also succeeded in blocking restrictions on lead in plumbing. The lead industry—which owned at least one paint company outright—treated the emerging science on low-level lead poisoning as a public relations problem, dismissing objective research as "anti-lead propaganda."

As has been meticulously documented by two public health historians, Gerald Markowitz and David Rosner, the manufacturers of lead pigments went on the offensive after the 1925 agreement. They reassured the American public that lead fears were unfounded. They even promoted lead paint for use in schools and hospitals. Most wickedly, they employed images of children in advertising. The most famous of these was the Dutch Boy, a cartoon character dreamed up by the National Lead Company. With his requisite haircut, overalls, and wooden shoes, the little Dutch Boy cheerfully sloshed buckets of paint labeled "white lead" in ad campaigns throughout the midcentury. The implicit message was that lead paint was safe for children to handle. . . .

The industry also fought labeling requirements that would warn buyers not to use lead paint on children's toys, furniture, or rooms. Many a nursery was painted with lead by pregnant women eagerly awaiting the birth of their babies. Those questioning the safety of such practices were repeatedly reassured by Lead Industry Associates that a link between lead paint exposure and mental deficiencies has never been proved. And up until the 1970s, this was true—in no small part because the lead industry was the main source of funding for university research on the health effects of lead. Researchers with other opinions and other funding sources were condemned as hysterical and sometimes threatened with legal action. Only when the U.S. government became a major funder of lead research did the case against lead began to mount.

When the truth eventually became undeniable, the industry shifted tactics. Instead of denying lead's powers to damage children's brains, it blamed inner-city poverty and unscrupulous landlords who, the argument went, had allowed paint to peel in their tenement buildings. And the neglected children living there, with nothing better to do, ate it. At one point, recalls a leading toxicologist deeply involved in the lead wars, an industry representative actually suggested that the problem was not that eating lead paint chips made children stupid but rather that stupid children ate paint. All these arguments finally collapsed under the weight of emerging scientific evidence. But decades were wasted in denials, obfuscations, deflections of responsibility, counter-accusations, intimidation of scientists, and attempts to tranquilize a legitimate public concern. The result is that any home built and painted before 1978 probably contains lead paint, and all children and pregnant women living in such buildings continue to face risks from it. And since I live in a century-old building listed on Somerville's historical registry, I am now such a woman. It is a problem that continues to vex landlords and homeowners alike, as removing the lead is expensive and is itself a health menace. It is a problem that could have been solved in 1925.

Now consider leaded gas. In 1922, General Motors discovered that adding lead to gasoline helped alleviate its tendency to "knock," to burn explosively under high compression. Solving this problem meant that automobile engines could be made bigger, and cars could go faster. Ethanol, which can be distilled from corn, also worked well as an antiknock additive but could not be patented and was therefore not as profitable to the oil companies. In 1923 leaded gas went on sale for the first time. This development immediately attracted the attention of public health officials, who raised urgent questions about the effects of broadcasting lead-laced fumes into public air space. At about the same time, serious health problems began afflicting refinery workers whose jobs involved formulating the lead additive. Several died and many others suffered hallucinations. The tetraethyl lead building at one plant was even nicknamed the House of Butterflies because so many employees who worked in it saw imaginary insects crawling on their bodies.

Then a remarkable thing happened. In 1925, a meeting was convened by the U.S. Surgeon General to address the issue of lead dust. And a moratorium was declared. The sale of leaded gas was banned on the grounds that it might well pose a public health menace. It was a perfect expression of the principle "In ignorance, abstain"—what is now popularly called the precautionary principle. Unfortunately for us all, the moratorium did not hold. After the

prohibition took effect, the lead industry funded a quick study that showed no problems with lead exposure. Over the objection that lead was a slow, cumulative poison and that such a study could not possibly reveal the kind of human damage researchers were worried about, the ban was subsequently lifted. The production of leaded gas resumed.

It continued for almost seventy years. By the time it was banned again, this time for good, more than 15.4 billion pounds of lead dust had been released into the environment. Much of this has sifted down into the topsoil. As a metal, lead is not biodegradable and is considered absolutely persistent. In other words, it is not going away anytime soon. It is tracked into homes on the bottoms of shoes. It is absorbed from soil into plant roots. This is why, in high-traffic urban areas such as my neighborhood in Somerville, we cannot grow and eat carrots.

The irony of our gardening situation is that lead in gasoline was finally removed on the basis of a landmark 1979 study showing significant IQ changes among first- and second-graders in response to environmental lead exposures. And the children investigated lived here in Somerville.

Should you ever find yourself in Boston, you may wish to pay a visit to the Old North Church in the North End. It's the one-if-by-land-two-if-by-sea church made famous by Paul Revere. If you go, take a look at the pale violet walls inside the sanctuary. Jeff painted them. Well, he and a crew of men that he supervised. Restoration work and decorative painting are specialties of his; these skills have helped to fund a lot of art projects over the years and paid a lot of rent. Elegant old homes up and down Beacon Hill and on Cambridge's Brattle Street contain his handiwork, as do buildings at Harvard University. Jeff is more at ease with a paintbrush and a sander in his hands than anyone else I have ever met, which is one reason (among others) I fell in love with him.

Now we lie awake on a summery night, reggae drifting into the window from the street below, and discuss whether or not he should continue this work. His blood lead levels are more than double that of the average American male. One physician actually congratulated him for this. Given that his line of work puts him in direct contact with old, lead-based paint, she expected they would be much higher. Jeff is very careful. But even when he changes clothes at the job site and leaves his work pants out on our fire escape, he still comes home covered in dust and paint. He's paying the price for reckless decisions made three generations ago.

But we would like to ensure that our daughter doesn't. Almost nothing is known about how lead exposures in fathers affect their unborn children. "Lower lead levels have not been well studied for their possible effects on the male reproductive system or on pregnancy in the partners of exposed males."

In ignorance, abstain. But can we afford to? With a baby coming? In the end, we decide that Jeff should fold his business. And as soon as the baby is crawling, we'll move out of our apartment. We know there is lead paint under the many layers of latex—our landlord has confirmed it—and we know that painting over lead paint is not considered a safe method of containment. We also know that our neighbors around the corner discovered very high lead levels in the soil in their back yard. Nevertheless, a home lead detector kit has revealed no lead on the surface of our interior walls, in the cupboards, or in the dusty corners behind the radiators. For now, we'll stay put. . . .

"Don't grow our own root vegetables. Quit a job I like. How come we're always the ones that have to do the abstaining?" Jeff wants to know.

And that is my question exactly. . . .

NOTES

550 Quotation by Voltaire: P. W. Nathanielsz, *Life Before Birth: The Challenges of Fetal Development* (New York: W. H. Freeman, 1996), pp. 158. The literal translation of the original quotation is "Abstain from an action if in doubt as to whether it is right or not" (from "Le Philosophe Ignorant," in *Mélanges de Voltaire* [Paris: Bibliothèque de la Pléiade, Librairie Gallimard, 1961], p. 920). Thanks to Dr. James Matthews, a French scholar, of Illinois Wesleyan University for tracking down the original source.

550 Standards for nitrates in drinking water not shown safe for fetuses: Committee on Environmental Health, American Academy of Pediatrics, *Handbook of Pediatric Environmental Health* (Elk Grove Village, Ill.: AAP, 1999), p. 164; National Research Council, *Nitrate and Nitrite in Drinking Water* (Washington, D.C.: National Academy Press, 1995), p. 2.

550 4.5 million Americans drink water with elevated nitrate levels: AAP, *Handbook of Pediatric Environmental Health*, p. 164.

550–551 Quote from scientific report: International Joint Commission, *Ninth Biennial Report on Great Lakes Water Quality* (Ottawa, Ont.: International Joint Commission, 1998), p. 10.

551 Quote from popular guidebook: A. Eisenberg et al., *What to Expect When You're Expecting* (New York: Workman, 1996), pp. 129–32.

551 Toxic releases in McLean County: Data on toxic emissions are measured and sent by the industries in question to the U.S. Environmental Protection Agency. These are disseminated on the Internet in a user-friendly format by the Environmental Defense (www.scorecard.org).

551 University's use of pesticides: According to the director of the grounds crew, pesticides used in 1999 include mecoprop and bromoxynil. As of 2001 they are no longer used. Thanks to my student, Sarah Perry, for investigating this issue.

551 34 million pounds of reproductive toxicants released in Illinois in 1997: Toxics Release Inventory (www.scorecard.org).

552 Description of fetal brain development, gross anatomy: B. M. Carlson, *Human Embryology and Developmental Biology,* 2d ed. (St. Louis: Mosby, 1999) pp. 208–48; England, *Life Before Birth,* pp. 51–70.

552–553 Description of fetal brain development, cellular anatomy: D. Bellinger and H. L. Needleman, "The Neurotoxicity of Prenatal Exposure to Lead: Kinetics, Mechanisms, and Expressions," in H. L. Needleman and D. Bellinger, eds., *Prenatal Exposure to Toxicants: Developmental Consequences* (Baltimore: Johns Hopkins University Press, 1994), pp. 89–111; Carlson, *Human Embryology,* pp. 208–48; England, *Life Before Birth,* pp. 51–70; Victor Friedrich, "Wiring of the Growing Brain," presentation at the conference Environmental Issues on Children: Brain, Development, and Behavior, New York Academy of Medicine, New York City, 24 May 1999; Nathanielsz, *Life Before Birth,* pp. 38–42; T. Schettler et al., *In Harm's Way: Toxic Threats to Child Development* (Cambridge: Greater Boston Physicians for Social Responsibility, 2000), pp. 23–28.

552 Neuroglia modulate available glucose: Nathanielsz, *Life Before Birth,* p. 16.

552 Later brain cells follow early-migrating neurons: K. Suzuki and P. M. Martin, "Neurotoxicants and the Developing Brain," in G. J. Harry, ed., *Developmental Neurotoxicology* (Boca Raton: CRC Press, 1994), pp. 9–32.

553 Mechanisms of fetal neurotoxicity: G. J. Harry, "Introduction to Developmental Neurotoxicology," in Harry, *Developmental Neurotoxicology,* pp. 1–7.

553 More than half of TRI chemicals are neurotoxins: U.S. releases of neurotoxins into air, water, wells, and landfills totaled 1.2 billion pounds in 1997. These chemicals include heavy metals such as lead and mercury as well as methanol, ammonia, manganese compounds, chlorine, styrene, glycol ethers, and a variety of solvents, such as toluene and xylene (Schettler, *In Harm's Way*, pp. 103–5).

553 Interspecific differences in brain development: E. M. Faustman et al., "Mechanisms Underlying Children's Susceptibility to Environmental Toxicants," *EHP 108*(2000, sup. 1): 13–21; P. M. Rodier, "Comparative Postnatal Neurologic Development," in Needleman and Bellinger, *Prenatal Exposure to Toxicants*, pp. 3–23.

553 When testing expanded to include behavior: Harry, "Introduction to Developmental Neurotoxicology"; H. L. Needleman and P. J. Landrigan, *Raising Children Toxic Free: How to Keep Your Child Safe from Lead, Asbestos, Pesticides and Other Environmental Hazards* (New York: Farrar Straus & Giroux, 1994), pp. 11–15.

554 Historical awareness of lead poisoning: Bellinger and Needleman, "The Neurotoxicity of Prenatal Exposure to Lead: Kinetics, Mechanisms, and Expressions"; Suzuki and Martin, "Neurotoxicants and the Developing Brain."

554–555 Lead's migration into fetal body: Bellinger and Needleman, "The Neurotoxicity of Prenatal Exposure to Lead."

554 Awareness in the 1940s: AAP, *Handbook of Pediatric Environmental Health*, pp. 131–43; H. L. Needleman, "Childhood Lead Poisoning: The Promise and Abandonment of Primary Prevention," *Am. J. of Public Health* 88(1998): 1871–77; Needleman and Landrigan, *Raising Children Toxic Free*, pp. 11–15.

554 Lowering of IQs in El Paso: Described in Needleman and Landrigan, *Raising Children Toxic Free*, pp. 11–15.

554 Studies from around the world: AAP, *Handbook of Pediatric Environmental Health*, pp. 131–43.

554 Lead levels required to affect mental acuity: Suzuki and Martin, "Neurotoxicants and the Developing Brain."

554–555 Mechanisms by which lead wrecks brain development: Bellinger and Needleman, "The Neurotoxicity of Prenatal Exposure to Lead"; M. K. Nihei et al., "*N*-Methyl-D-Aspartate Receptor Subunit Changes are Associated with Lead-Induced Deficits of Long-Term Potentiation and Spatial Learning," *Neuroscience* 99(2000): 233–42; Suzuki and Martin, "Neurotoxicants and the Developing Brain."

555 Vulnerability of fetus to lead: The elderly are also at risk. As bone demineralizes with age, blood lead levels can rise. In seniors, even slight elevations can have adverse cognitive effects (Bernard Weiss, University of Rochester, personal communication).

555 Life-changing consequences: New research suggests that these consequences include a propensity to violent behavior, as well as a lowered IQ. See, for example, R. Nevin, "How Lead Exposure Relates to Temporal Changes in I.Q., Violent Crime, and Unwed Pregnancy," *Environmental Research* 83(2000): 1–22.

555 Public health triumph of lead bans: AAP, *Handbook of Pediatric Environmental Health*, pp. 131–43.

555 75 percent decline: Nevin, "How Lead Exposure Relates to Temporal Changes."

555 One in twenty children: G. Markowitz and D. Rosner, "'Cater to the Children': The Role of the Lead Industry in a Public Health Tragedy, 1900–1955," *Am. J. of Public Health*, 90(2000): 36–46.

555 Lead not outlawed in cosmetics: T. Schettler et al., *Generations at Risk: Reproductive Health and the Environment* (Cambridge: MIT Press, 1999), p. 273.

555 Lead paint: Markowitz and Rosner, "'Cater to the Children"; E. K. Silbergeld, "Protection of the Public Interest, Allegations of Scientific Misconduct, and the Needleman Case," *Am. J. of Public Health* 85(1995): 165–66; Schettler et al., *Generations at Risk*, pp. 52–57.

555–556 A leading toxicologists remembers: Herbert Needleman, "Environmental Neurotoxins and Attention Deficit Disorder," presentation at the conference Environmental Issues on Children: Brain, Development, and Behavior, New York Academy of Medicine, New York, N.Y., 24 May 1999.

556 Leaded gas: J. L. Kitman, "The Secret History of Lead," *The Nation* 270(20 March 2000): 11–41; Needleman, "Childhood Lead Poisoning"; H. L. Needleman, "Clamped in a Straitjacket: The Insertion of Lead into Gasoline," *Environmental Research* 74(1997): 95–103; D. Rosner and G. Markowitz, "A 'Gift of God'?: The Public Health Controversy over Leaded Gasoline During the 1920s," *Am. J. of Public Health* 75(1985): 344–52; Silbergeld, "Protection of the Public Interest."

556 1979 study of Somerville children: Needleman, J. Palca, "Lead Researcher Confronts Accusers in Public Hearing," *Science* 256(1992): 437–38.

557 Quote on lower lead levels in men: Schettler et al., *Generations at Risk*, p. 57.

◆◆◆

SIXTY-THREE

The Ecofeminist Imperative (1983)

Ynestra King

Ynestra King is a writer and activist focusing on environmental, feminist, and disability issues. Co-author of *Dangerous Intersections: Feminist Perspectives on Population, Environment, and Development,* she has taught at the New School for Social Research and has been a Visiting Scholar at several academic institutions, including Rutgers University and Columbia University.

In the one year since the Conference on Women and Life on Earth (held in Amherst, Massachusetts, in March 1980) our movement has burgeoned. The Conference grew out of hope and fear—out of a fear for life and the awesome powers of destruction arrayed against it and out of a hope—a hope for women's power to resist and create. We came together following the meltdown at Three Mile Island. We talked of our sisters we knew by name and reputation through the mythology of our own movement and of what together we might be, and we decided to call sisters to a conference on Women and Life on Earth.

We are both a beginning and a continuation. We are a beginning for this decade but we continue the work of the many brave and visionary women who have gone before us. There was Ellen Swallow, the founder of ecological science. There was Rachel Carson, who wrote *Silent Spring* [in 1962], sounding a warning about chemicals and pesticides which was not heeded until many years later. There were the women of the Women's Strike for Peace and the Ban the Bomb movements of the fifties, mailing their babies' teeth to Congressmen as a reminder of future generations. And there are the brave women scientists who have spoken out more recently, and the women who have been at the forefront of antinuclear struggles, peace movements, struggles against toxic wastes and for occupational health and safety. There are those who have helped us to imagine the world as it could be: artists, poets, writers and dreamers who have given us new visions of culture, health, technology, community and politics. And there are our sisters the world over, with

us in the creation of a planetary movement. We are shaking the world.

Over ten years ago this wave of the feminist movement began. We said then that "the personal is political," that the denial of our selfhood was systemic and political, that masculine society even had a name: "patriarchy."

Many more women now see their oppression as political, not individual. Over the past ten years women have begun to rediscover our history, and to name and work to end violence against women in all its forms, demand equal rights, the right of every woman to decide when and if to bear children, and to express her sexuality freely.

But as we have gained in consciousness and numbers the devastation of the planet has accelerated. Every day brings new disasters, some irrevocable. The story of Love Canal where a school and homes were built on a hazardous waste site is a warning of things to come. Three to six nuclear bombs are produced each day. The Pentagon nuclear arsenal now numbers over 30,000 warheads and it is growing. There are thousands of toxic waste dumps around the country that will not be discovered until observant women notice a common birth defect or sickness in their neighborhood. The coastlines are deteriorating, and the Amazon forest, the source of much of earth's oxygen, is being rapidly defoliated. Each day a whole species of life becomes extinct, never to be seen on this earth.

Ecofeminism is about connectedness and wholeness of theory and practice. It asserts the special strength and integrity of every living thing. For us, the snail darter is to be considered side by side with a community's need for water, the porpoise side by side with appetite for tuna. . . . We are a woman-identified movement, and we believe that we have special work to do in these imperilled times. We see the devastation of the earth and her beings by the corporate warriors, and the threat of nuclear annihilation by the military warriors, as feminist concerns. It is the same masculinist mentality which would deny us our right to our own bodies and our own sexuality, and which depends on multiple systems of dominance and state power to have its way.

At the same time as we have been making the connections between feminism, ecology, and militarism, the New Right has been making those very same connections. They are actively opposing women's reproductive freedom, attacking lesbians and gay men, undermining battered women's shelters and efforts to introduce anti-sexist and anti-racist curricula in schools. The Family Protection Act, now being introduced in Congress piecemeal, is explicit about its intention to shore up patriarchal authority in every aspect of our lives. They want to be sure that strong, angry women do not stand in their way, as the carnivorous appetite of the military gobbles up food stamps, Aid for Dependent Children, Medicaid, schools, legal aid and more. We are beginning to have an understanding of ourselves about how these concerns are intertwined and to act on them as we develop an imaginative, transformative women's movement.

Why women? Because our present patriarchy enshrines together the hatred of women and the hatred of nature. In defying this patriarchy we are loyal to future generations and to life and this planet itself. We have a deep and particular understanding of this both through our natures and through our life experience as women.

We have the wisdom to oppose experiments which could permanently alter the genetic materials of future generations. As feminists we believe that human reproduction should be controlled by women not by a male-dominated medical establishment. We insist on the absolute right of a woman to an abortion. We support the life-affirming right of women to choose when and if to bear children.

We oppose war and we recognize its terrible force when we see it, undeclared but all around us. For to us war is the violence against women in all its forms—rape, battering, economic exploitation and intimidation—and it is the racist violence against indigenous peoples here in the U.S. and around the world, and it is the violence against the earth.

We recognize and respect the beauty of cultural diversity as we abhor racism. Racism divides us from our sisters, it lines the pockets of the exploiters and underlies the decimation of whole peoples and their homelands. The imperialism of white, male, western culture has been more destructive to other peoples and cultures than any imperialist power in the history of the world, just as it has brought us to the brink of ecological catastrophe.

We believe that a culture against nature is a culture against women. We know we must get out from under the feet of men as they go about their projects of violence. In pursuing these projects, men deny and dominate both women and nature. It is time to reconstitute our culture in the name of that nature, and of peace and freedom, and it is women who can show the way. We have to be the voice of the invisible, of nature who cannot speak for herself in the political arenas of our society, of the children yet to be born and of the women who are forcibly silenced in our mental institutions and prisons. We have been the keepers of the home, the children and the community. We learn early to observe, attend and nurture. And whether or not we become biological mothers, we use these nurturant powers daily as we go about our ordinary work. No one pays us to do this. If the children are born deformed or go hungry, if the people in homes built on a dumping site or near a nuclear weapons factory have terrible sickness, we are the ones who care for them, take them to the doctor, console survivors and soothe the terrified. And it is women who have begun to confront government agencies, politicians and corporations. As the deadly sludge of our political system encroaches on every aspect of our most intimate lives, all of us know that life cannot go on this way. The political and the personal are joined: the activities of women as feminists and anti-militarists, and the activities of women struggling in our neighborhoods and communities for survival and dignity are the same struggle.

And with the same attentiveness we give consideration to the kinds of jobs people do. Many people in this society are compelled to accept jobs which contribute to the destruction of life. In the workplace women particularly are saddled with menial tasks and meaningless work. We oppose such "jobs" and propose instead that work must involve free self-expression and an execution which is playful, not drudgerous. Demands for full employment which ignore the ecological and social devastation daily wrought in the process of ordinary work are dangerously shortsighted. This technological society offers finally the possibility of a materially abundant society with meaningful work for everyone. It is this potential we must claim for ourselves—that these capacities be used for our needs and desires in an appropriately scaled, ecologically aware manner. To create such a web of life is a precondition for freedom. The creation of work that is not merely a job, or worse yet a perpetuation of the kind of machines which daily destroy both the biosphere and the worker, must be a feminist priority. To this end we propose that women begin to use the powers of imagination and creativity we possess as builders, engineers, scientist-alchemists and artists to develop the ways of livelihood and life which fulfil this promise.

In all our workings, we believe in the philosophy of nonviolence—that no person should be made into an "other" to despise, dehumanize and exploit. As women we have been an "other" but we are refusing to be the "other" any longer and we will not make anyone else into an "other." Sexism, racism, class divisions, homophobia and the rape of nature depend on this process of objectification. Men's fear of female sexuality has led them to pile up institutions which limit women's options. These keep us obligated to men and unaware of alternatives to traditional women's roles and compulsory heterosexuality. It is in the interest of all women to support lesbian women. We oppose anything which prevents women from loving each other freely in whatever way we choose.

We are building a feminist resistance movement in the tradition of the militant suffragists of the last wave of feminism, from whom Gandhi and Martin Luther King drew their inspiration. We believe in and practice direct action. By direct action we do not mean activity which is necessarily either legal or illegal, but intentional activity which does not even recognize these governmental sanctions. We mean the creation of a tradition which demands that we act directly, in all matters which concern us, that we do not recognize a higher authority whom we call upon to act for us. If we believe a parking lot should be a garden we might just dig it up and plant a garden. If we believe that there should be vigils of community women against militarism and violence . . . we go out and vigil. If we believe that there should be women's speakouts against violence in every community we will speak. If we believe that women should be safe walking the streets at night we will take back the night.

As ecofeminists the locus of our work is with women in our own communities, in small groups based on personal affinity, shared concerns and a sense of connectedness to our own landscape. But we are joining together regionally, nationally and internationally to confront systems of dominance that go beyond our communities and neighborhoods. Women all over the world are engaging in imaginative direct action to stop the war machine, and to assert our right to our own bodies and our own sexuality and to a poison-free, fruitful earth. Our feminist embrace must come to enfold all these women struggling in our respective communities.

We are the repository of a sensibility which can make a future possible. Feminists must exemplify this in our ideas, our relationships to each other, our culture, politics and actions. It is by necessity that we are feminist utopians. We look backwards to women-centered societies based on respect for life and life cycles. We look forward to new possibilities of reconstituting a culture which is non-hierarchical, which has not only the primitive respect for life and sense of interconnectedness but also those modern technologies which further peace and liberation. Peace is more than the absence of war, as freedom is more than the absence of coercion. They mean more than putting down the gun, taking off the shackles, or even just hearing and remembering. They are both ongoing processes which must be constantly attended to, criticized and expanded upon. Our movement is a process without end, much as life itself is a process without end.

◆◆◆

SIXTY-FOUR

Principles of Environmental Justice (1991)

The First National People of Color Environmental Leadership Summit

The First National People of Color Environmental Leadership Summit was convened by the United Church of Christ's Commission on Racial Justice and held in Washington, D.C., in 1991. Over 1,000 national and international environmental activists gathered, establishing the "Principles of Environmental Justice."

Preamble

We, the people of color, gathered together at this multinational People of Color Environmental Leadership Summit, to begin to build a national and international movement of all peoples of color to fight the destruction and taking of our lands and communities, do hereby re-establish our spiritual interdependence to the sacredness of our Mother Earth; to respect and celebrate each of our cultures, languages and beliefs about the natural world and our roles in healing ourselves; to ensure environmental justice; to promote economic alternatives which would contribute to the development of environmentally safe livelihoods; and, to secure our political, economic and cultural liberation that has been denied for over 500 years of colonization and oppression, resulting in the poisoning of our communities and land and the genocide of our peoples, do affirm and adopt these Principles of Environmental Justice:

1. *Environmental justice* affirms the sacredness of Mother Earth, ecological unity and the interdependence of all species, and the right to be free from ecological destruction.

2. *Environmental justice* demands that public policy be based on mutual respect and justice for all peoples, free from any form of discrimination or bias.

3. *Environmental justice* mandates the right to ethical, balanced and responsible uses of land and renewable resources in the interest of a sustainable planet for humans and other living things.

4. *Environmental justice* calls for universal protection from nuclear testing, extraction, production and disposal of toxic/hazardous wastes and poisons and nuclear testing that threaten the fundamental right to clean air, land, water, and food.

5. *Environmental justice* affirms the fundamental right to political, economic, cultural and environmental self-determination of all peoples.

6. *Environmental justice* demands the cessation of the production of all toxins, hazardous wastes, and radioactive materials, and that all past and current producers be held strictly accountable to the people for detoxification and the containment at the point of production.

7. *Environmental justice* demands the right to participate as equal partners at every level of decision-making including needs assessment, planning, implementation, enforcement and evaluation.

8. *Environmental justice* affirms the right of all workers to a safe and healthy work environment, without being forced to choose between an unsafe livelihood and unemployment. It also affirms the right of those who work at home to be free from environmental hazards.

9. *Environmental justice* protects the right of victims of environmental injustice to receive full compensation and reparations for damages as well as quality health care.

10. *Environmental justice* considers governmental acts of environmental injustice a violation of international law, the Universal Declaration on Human Rights, and the United Nations Convention on Genocide.

11. *Environmental justice* must recognize a special legal and natural relationship of Native Peoples to the U.S. government through treaties, agreements, compacts, and covenants affirming sovereignty and self-determination.

12. *Environmental justice* affirms the need for urban and rural ecological policies to clean up and rebuild our cities and rural areas in balance with nature, honoring the cultural integrity of all our communities, and providing fair access for all to the full range of resources.

13. *Environmental justice* calls for the strict enforcement of principles of informed consent, and a halt to the testing of experimental reproductive and medical procedures and vaccinations on people of color.

14. *Environmental justice* opposes the destructive operations of multi-national corporations.

15. *Environmental justice* opposes military occupation, repression and exploitation of lands, peoples and cultures, and other life forms.

16. *Environmental justice* calls for the education of present and future generations which emphasizes social and environmental issues, based on our experience and an appreciation of our diverse cultural perspectives.

17. *Environmental justice* requires that we, as individuals, make personal and consumer choices to consume as little of Mother Earth's resources and to produce as little waste as possible; and make the conscious decision to challenge and reprioritize our lifestyles to ensure the health of the natural world for present and future generations.

SIXTY-FIVE

◆◆◆

Native Hawaiian Historical and Cultural Perspectives on Environmental Justice (1992)

Mililani Trask

Mililani Trask is an attorney and a founder of Na Koa Ikaika o Ka Lahui Hawai'i, an organization working for Hawaii sovereignty. She is a founding member of the Indigenous Women's Network. She served as Pacific Representative to the U.N. Permanent Forum on Indigenous Issues (2002–2005) and helped author the U.N. Declaration on the Rights of Indigenous Peoples.

When you ask a Hawaiian who they are, their response is "Keiki hanau o ka aina, child that is borne up from the land." I am a Native Hawaiian attorney. I also have the great honor and distinction, and the great burden and responsibility, of being the first elected Kia'Aina of Ka Lahui Hawai'i, the sovereign nation of the Native Hawaiian people, which we created ourselves in 1987.

It's a great pleasure and honor for me to be here to address a group such as yourselves, such a momentous occasion, the first time that the people of color will gather to consider the impacts on our common land base.

I thought I would begin by giving a little bit of history about Hawaii Nei because many people are

This paper was presented at the First National People of Color Environmental Leadership Summit, October 24–27, 1991, Washington, D.C.

not aware of the crisis there and the status of the Native Hawaiian people. As we approach the United Nations' celebration of the discoverers, we are celebrating not only the arrival of Columbus but also of Cortez and Captain Cook. In Hawaii Nei we are celebrating 500 years of resilient resistance to the coming of the "discoverers."

In 1778 Captain James Cook sailed into the Hawaiian archipelago. He found there a thriving Native community of 800,000 Native people, living in balance on their lands, completely economically self-sufficient, feeding and clothing themselves off the resources of their own land base. Within one generation, 770,000 of our people were dead—dead from what is called "mai haole, the sickness of the white man," which Cook brought: venereal disease, flu, pox, the same tragic history that occurred on the American continent to Native American Indians and the Native people of Central and South America.

In 1893 the United States Marines dispatched a group of soldiers to the Island of Oahu for the purpose of overthrowing the lawful kingdom of Hawaii Nei. Prior to 1893, Hawaii was welcomed into the world family of nations and maintained over 20 international treaties, including treaties of friendship and peace with the United States. Despite those international laws, revolution was perpetrated against our government, and our lawful government over-thrown. . . .

In 1959, Hawaii was admitted into the Union of the United States of America. There were great debates that occurred in Washington, DC that focused on the fact that people were afraid to incorporate the Territory of Hawaii because it would become the first state in the union in which white people would be a minority of less than 25 percent. That was the reason for the concern when those debates were launched. In 1959, when Hawaii became a state, something happened that did not happen in any other state of the union. In all of the other states, when the U.S. admitted that state into the union, America set aside lands for the Native people of those states, as federal reserves. Today there is a policy that provides that Native Americans should be self-governing, should be allowed to maintain their nations, should be allowed to pass laws, environmental and otherwise, to protect their land base. That did not occur in the State of Hawaii. In the State of Hawaii in 1959, the federal government gave our lands to the state to be held in trust, and gave the Native Hawaiian people, of which there are 200,000, the status of perpetual wardship. We are not allowed to form governments if we are Native Hawaiian; we are not allowed to control our land base. To this day our lands are controlled by state agencies and utilized extensively by the American military complex as part of a plan designed by Hawaii's Senator Daniel Inouye.

In 1987 we decided to exercise our inherent rights to be self-governing. The Hawaii Visitors Bureau declared 1987 the Year of the Hawaiian for a great tourist and media campaign. We took a look at our statistics: 22,000 families on lists waiting for land entitlements since 1920; 30,000 families dead waiting for their Hawaiian homelands awards; 22,000 currently waiting. We thought to ourselves, how are *we* going to celebrate 1987? And we decided that the time had come to convene a constitutional convention to resurrect our nation and to exert our basic and inherent rights, much to the dismay and consternation of the state and the federal government, and certainly to the shock of Senator Inouye.

We have passed a constitution that recognizes the right and the responsibility of Native people to protect their land base and to ensure water quality, because Western laws have been unable to protect the environment. We decided to lift up and resurrect

our nation in 1987, passing our constitution, and we are proceeding now to come out, to announce that we are alive and well, and to network with other people.

I have come to announce that a state of emergency exists with regards to the natural environment of the archipelagic lands and waters of Hawaii, and also a state of emergency exists with regards to the survival of the Native people who live there and throughout the Pacific basin. We have many environmental injustices and issues that need to be addressed; most of them have dire global consequences. The expansion of the United States military complex presents substantial threats to our environment.

Right now on the Island of Hawaii and on the Island of Kauai, Senator Inouye is pressing for what he calls the "space-porting initiative," which we all know to be Star Wars. It will distribute large amounts of toxic gases, it will scorch the earth beyond repair and, most importantly and offensive to us, the lands that have been chosen are lands set aside by the Congress in 1920 for the homesteading of Hawaiian people. These are the lands that are pursued on the Island of Hawaii.

Our response to that is "kapu Ka'u." Ka'u is the district; kapu is the Hawaiian way for saying, "It is taboo." We cannot allow desecration of sacred lands, desecration of historic properties that are the cultural inheritance of our people to be converted for the military complex and for the designs of those who would further the interests of war against others. It is an inappropriate use of Native lands.

Other Threats

The United States Navy continues its relentless bombing of Kahoolawe Island. [This was discontinued in 1990, but the land was not returned to the State of Hawaii until 1994.] Not only have they denuded the upper one-third of that island, but as they have blasted away the lands, trees and shrubs, all that silt has come down to the channels between Kahoolawe and Maui Islands, the channels that are the spawning grounds of the whales that migrate every year to Hawaii Nei.

We now have information coming from Lualualei on the Island of Oahu that there is a very high incidence of leukemia and other cancers among the Hawaiian children who live there. We believe that this is due to electromagnetic contamination. In Lualualei the United States military is taking control of 2,000 acres of Hawaiian homelands, lands set aside by the Congress to homestead our people. These lands were taken over and converted for a nuclear and military storage facility. Ten years ago, in 1981, they issued a report saying that there's electromagnetic radiation there. After the report was issued all the military families were moved out of the base, but nobody told the Hawaiian community that lives in the surrounding area. We have taken it to the Western courts, we have been thrown out, because the court ruled that Native Hawaiians are wards of the state and the federal government. Therefore, Native Hawaiians are not allowed standing to sue in the federal courts to protect our trust land assets. We are the only class of Native Americans, and the only class of American citizens, that are not allowed access to the federal court system to seek redress of grievances relating to breach of trust.

Ka Lahui Hawai'i is pleased and proud to join all of the other Pacific Island nations in opposing the federal policy which is being perpetrated by Mr. Bush and Senator Inouye identifying the Pacific region as a national sacrifice area. What is a national sacrifice area? I did some legal research and I found out that national sacrifice areas usually occur on Indian reservations or in black communities. They are areas that the nation identifies primarily for the dumping of toxic wastes. As the Greens celebrate in Europe what they perceive to be an environmental victory in forcing America to remove its nuclear and military wastes from Europe, we in the Pacific region have been told that Johnston Island and other Pacific nations have been targeted for storage and dumping. We will not allow that and we will continue to speak out against it.

Tourist Evils

Tourism and its attendant evils continue to assault our island land base. Hundreds of thousands of tourists come to Hawaii every year. They are seeking a dream of paradise. They drink our water, they contaminate our environment. They are responsible for millions of tons of sewage every year, which is deposited into the Pacific Ocean. And, in addition, they are taking lands from our rural communities.

Tourism perpetuates certain Western concepts of exclusive rights to land. Tourists don't like to see other people on their beaches. Tourists don't like to allow Native people to go and fish in the traditional ways. And, because of toxification of the ocean due to release of sewage in Hawaii, there are many places where you can no longer find the reef fish. You cannot go there and take the opihi, the squid, or take the turtle, because they're gone now. So in the few remaining areas where there are fish, the state and federal governments have imposed public park restrictions to prevent Native people from going there to lay the net and take the fish. If the fish are taken out, what will the tourists see when they put on their snorkels? Native people are not allowed to fish so that tourists can view through their goggles what remains of the few species we have because their own tourist practices destroyed all the rest of the bounty of our fisheries.

Tourists need golf courses; golf courses need tons of pesticides, herbicides and millions of tons of water. Hawaii is an island ecology, we do not get fresh water from flowing streams. All the water that falls from the rain in Hawaii is percolated through the lava of the islands and comes to rest in a central basal lens underneath our island. As the rains percolate down they bring with them all the herbicides and pesticides that have been used for years by agribusiness: King Cane, Dole Pineapple, United States military. Already on the island of Oahu we have had to permanently close two of our drinking wells because of toxification. Nobody in the State of Hawaii or the Hawaii Visitors Bureau is going to tell you that at the present time there are 30 contaminants in the drinking water in the State of Hawaii.

The specter of geothermal development lays heavily upon our lands. For 25 years the United States and its allies have been developing geothermal energy in Hawaii. It is destroying the last Pacific tropical rain forest on the Island of Hawaii, Wao Kele o Puna Forest, sacred to the lands of Tutu Pele, our Grandmother Pele, who erupts and gives birth to the earth. This is her home, yet this is the place where they are developing geothermal. And as it proceeds, Native people are denied their basic right to worship there. We have taken this case to the United States Supreme Court. It was struck down along with the Native American freedom of religion cases because the court ruled that religious worship in America must be "site-specific."

If you take the Akua, if you put God in the building, American courts will understand. But if you take God and say, "The earth is the Lord's and the fullness of it, the Black Hills of South Dakota, the lands and forests of Tutu Pele," American courts do not understand. . . .

International fishing practices, gill netting and drift netting, are genocide in the sea. As a result of these practices, the Native fisheries are diminished and depleted. In some areas our marine fisheries are depleted to the point that we can no longer harvest that resource.

What is the appropriate response to this environmental and human outrage? In Hawaii Nei we have undertaken to address these things through sovereignty and the basic exertion of the rights of Native people to govern and control their own land base. These are political issues, certainly. But they spring from a very ancient source, a source within our heart, a source that all Natives and people of color understand: our relationship in the global context. As Hawaiians say, "Keiki hanau o ka aina, child that is borne up from the land," understanding that there is an innate connection to the earth as the Mother. We are called upon now as the guardians of our sacred lands to rise up in the defense of our Mother. You don't subdivide your Mother, you don't chop her body up, you don't drill, penetrate and pull out her lifeblood. You protect and nurture your Mother. And the Hawaiian value for that is aloha ai'na, love for the land, malama ai'na, care and nurturing for the land. It is reciprocal. It gives back to the Native people. Our people know that the Akua put us here on this earth to be guardians of these sacred lands. It is a God-given responsibility and trust that a sovereign nation must assume if it is to have any integrity. And so we in Ka Lahui have undertaken this struggle. Environmental racism is the enemy. The question is, What is our response? What really is environmental justice? I'll tell you one thing I learned in law school at Santa Clara. Do you know how they perceive and teach justice, the white schools of this country? A blind white woman with her eyes covered up by cloth, holding the scales of justice. And if you look at it, they're not balanced.

The Native scale and the environmental scale are outweighed by other priorities.

Well, environmental justice is not a blindfolded white woman. When I saw the woman with the scales of justice in law school, I thought to myself, "You know, if you blindfold yourself the only thing you're going to do is walk into walls." You are not going to resolve anything. And that's where we are with Western law. I know that there are many attorneys here and others who are working on environmental cases. I support them. We have received a great deal of support from attorneys working in environmental law. But do not put your eggs in the basket of the blind white lady. We must try other approaches.

In closing, I would like to say in behalf of myself and the Hawaii delegation that we are very renewed in coming here, and that when we return to Hawaii in two or three days we will have good news to share with our people, that we have come ourselves these many thousands of miles, that we have looked in the faces of people of color, that we have seen there, in their hearts and in their eyes, a light shining, a light of commitment, a light that is filled with capacity and a light that is filled with love for the Mother Earth, a light that is the same that we have in our hearts.

I try to do one thing whenever I finish speaking. I try to leave the podium by telling people what the motto of Ka Lahui Hawai'i is, the motto of our nation that we're forming now. I find it to be very applicable to the situations that we are in. We are facing a difficult struggle. Every bit of commitment and energy is needed to save our Mother Earth and to ensure the survival of our people and all of the species of the earth. It is a difficult row to hoe. There is going to be a great deal of strife and a great deal of pain. But we must proceed; we have no alternative. This is the same position that the native people of Hawaii Nei found themselves in 1987 when we committed to resurrecting our national government. And at the time that we passed that constitution we also adopted a motto. It is a motto that I think you might want to live by as we proceed in this environmental war that we are waging. That motto is: "A difficult birth does not make the baby any less beautiful."

◆◆◆

SIXTY-SIX

Consumption (1999)
North American Perspectives

H. Patricia Hynes

Environmental engineer **H. Patricia Hynes** is Professor of Environmental Health at the Boston University School of Public Health where she works on urban environmental issues, environmental justice, and feminist perspectives on health. Her books include *A Patch of Eden: America's Inner-City Gardeners; The Recurring Silent Spring;* and *Urban Environmental Health: Readings in the Social, Built and Physical Environments of U.S. Cities.*

. . . The consumption of resources by individuals, by governments and ruling elites, by semi-autonomous and secretive institutions such as the military, and by macroeconomic systems is embedded within the matrix of political economy and cultural values [see Figure 1]. Yet consumption . . . has been reduced to a mere empirical, per capita phenomenon, as if it were detached from those structural and ideological forces that result in wealth-building for some and impoverishment and poor health for others. . . .

What, then, is the content of recent North American critiques of consumption and consumerism? What are their strengths and weaknesses? What core elements of a woman-centered analysis can we bring to them?

. . . A handful of analyses and practice-based responses have emerged to characterize, critique, and provide alternatives to consumption patterns and consumerist ideology in industrialized countries. Among the chief prototypes are three approaches: the "demographics of consumption," movements to simplify life and make consumer choices that are less environmentally damaging, and the computation of the ecological footprint.

Demographics of Consumption

Asking the question "How much is enough?" Worldwatch Institute researcher Alan Durning has amassed quite a stunning picture of the explosion in the consumption of consumer goods and services in the United States and worldwide.[1] He traces the origins of "consumer society" in the United States to the 1920s, with the emergence of name brands, the entrée of packaged and processed foods, the rise of the car as the popular symbol of American upward mobility, and the birth of mass marketing through advertising. Consumerism was stymied by the Depression and World War II, but it picked up enormous momentum in the United States after the war and was rapidly disseminated worldwide, under the gospel of development and the democratization of consumerism, to gain markets for expanding U.S. industries. To cite a few supporting statistics on the radical change in post–World War II consumption: People in the United States own, on the average, "twice as many automobiles, drive two and a half times as far, use 21 times as much plastic, and cover 25 times as much distance by air as their parents did in 1950."[2]

Durning's data on the growth in household appliance ownership over time embody the triumph of the central message of mass marketing: Greater purchasing power and growing choice in the marketplace guarantee a better (and happier) life. Popular culture advertising underpins the macroeconomic maxim: An expanding economy—with rising per capita income and consumer spending—is a healthy economy.

Comparing global patterns of consumption leads Durning to a deeper inquiry into the qualitative differences in consumption among peoples in the world. He asks what kinds of resources people consume on a day-to-day basis and structures his answer around a comparison of consumption by diet, transport, and principal type of materials used. The result is three classes of consumption, the latter two being of much sounder environmental quality than the first, which has no sustainable characteristics.

The primary focus of this tripartite view of consumption in the world—emerging from Worldwatch

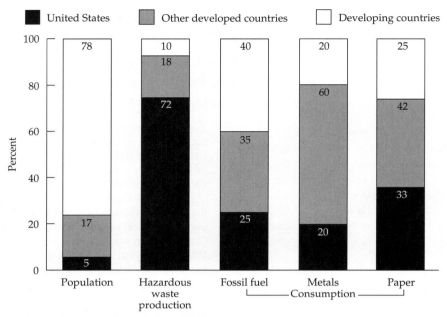

FIGURE 1 **Share of Population, Hazardous Waste Production, and Natural Resource Consumption in the United States, Developing, and Developed Regions, 1990s.** (*Source:* Natural Resources Defense Council, in Lori S. Ashford, *New Perspectives on Population: Lessons from Cairo. Population Bulletin* [Washington, D.C.: Population Reference Bureau, Inc.], Vol. 50, No. 1 [March 1995], 30.)

Institute and a number of liberal environmental, economic, and alternative-lifestyle circles in the United States—is the plight of the consumer class in the United States. Economist Juliet Schor points out that people in the United States work more hours today in their jobs than they did two decades ago, even though we are twice as productive in goods and services as we were in 1948. Why, instead of working more and having less leisure, do we not work less and enjoy more leisure, she queries. Describing the pitfalls of consumerism and the manufacture of discontent that keep middle-class people locked into a work-and-spend cycle, she calls for overcoming consumerism, revaluing leisure, and rethinking the necessity of full-time jobs.[3]

Both Schor and Durning hinge a key part of their prescription—that people rethink and modify their consumerist work- and lifestyles—on the question of happiness. National polls conducted since the 1950s show no increase in the percentage of people who report being "very happy," despite the fact that people now purchase almost twice the number of consumer goods and services they did in the 1950s. Time spent enjoying two of the classic sources of happiness—social relations and leisure—has diminished as people work more to purchase more nondurable, packaged, rapidly obsolete, nonvital goods and services.

Durning advocates that the consumer class be wary of the estimated 3,000 advertising messages that bombard us per day cultivating consumer taste and needs, and that we climb a few rungs down the consumption ladder by choosing durable goods, public transportation, and low-energy devices. In other words, he points to the consumption patterns of the 3.3 billion "middle consumer class" people in Table 1 as more sound and sustainable for the environment.

Table 1 World Consumption Classes, 1992

CATEGORY OF CONSUMPTION	CONSUMERS (1.1 BILLION)	MIDDLE (3.3 BILLION)	POOR (1.1 BILLION)
Diet	meat, packaged food, soft drinks	grain, clean water	insufficient grain, unsafe water
Transport	private cars	bicycles, buses	walking
Materials	throwaways	durables	local biomass

Source: Alan Durning, *How Much Is Enough?* (New York: W. W. Norton, 1992), 27.

Voluntary Simplicity Movement

Arising from these same cultural observations, the voluntary simplicity, or new frugality, movement offers a new road map for those of the consumer class who wish to live better with less . . . this movement was given a high profile by the best-selling book *Your Money or Your Life,* a pragmatic self-help approach to living securely on less money in order to spend one's time in more meaningful social, personal, spiritual, and environmentally sustaining ways.[4]

In this movement, people learn to assess their real financial needs (with generous distinctions made between "needs" and "wants"), how to budget and invest to achieve financial independence on a substantially reduced income, and how to calculate the impacts of their lifestyle on the environment through household audits of energy, products, and waste. More than 300,000 people have developed "new road maps" for their future lives, based on core values they have identified in the process of rethinking what ultimately matters to them. Most reduce their cost of living by 20 percent immediately and, eventually, by even more; many "retire" from careers and full-time jobs to pursue personal and social interests.

If It's Good for the Environment and Good for the Person, What's the Problem?

How can we fault the appeal to happiness and to core values that these critiques of the consumerist culture make? They result in people living "more softly" on the Earth. They reach deeper into a person's self than the green consumer movement, which redirects, but does not necessarily reduce or challenge, consumerism. How many green products are designed for durability and marketed as such? The majority of green product manufacturers employ mass marketing techniques, including the cultivation of "need," and use shallow appeals to feel-good environmentalism to sell their products. Green consumers get locked into seesaw debates over plastic versus paper, for example, never learning that the debate is a foil that deters deeper questions of product durability and necessity. At its best, says Durning, green consumerism outpaces legislation and uses market tactics to reform the market; at its worst, it is "a palliative for the conscience of the consumer class, allowing us to continue business as usual while feeling like we are doing our part."[5]

The primary shortcoming of the "consumer treadmill" critique is that it is socially and politically underdeveloped. Focusing on average per capita consumption, Durning and others make little distinction among the highly disparate economic classes of people within the United States. While our society as a whole is locked into meat, packaged food, soft drinks, and throwaways—with a McDonald's on every corner—the gap between the poorest fifth and richest fifth of the United States begs for an environmental policy that is based on "a hunger and thirst for justice" as well as national concern about global climate change and the decline of personal happiness. The prescriptions to live on less, to get out of the rat race and enjoy more leisure, to examine one's personal values and organize one's life by those values, may not necessarily result in a more equitable or humanistic society.

Those who choose voluntary simplicity, durables, and bicycles may live happily and stress-free across town from the angry (or depressed) involuntary poor, with no more empathy, solidarity, or insight into undoing social injustice. (Alternatively, of course, by choosing to live on less, people may end up in less expensive mixed-income neighborhoods, join their neighborhood associations, and, in so doing, meet and collaborate with the involuntary poor on neighborhood betterment.)

The focus on the cultivation of need by mass marketing and the lack of personal fulfillment, when di-

vorced from an inquiry into the patterns and structures that reward the well-off and punish the poor, creates islands of better-living and more personally satisfied people without necessarily generating a sense of a new social movement or new society. "Twelve-step" programs to break the consumer habit offer good techniques borrowed from self-fulfillment and self-control support-group settings, but they are no substitute for social responses to persistent poverty, to misogyny that sells women as sex to be consumed, to child labor and sweatshops, to the consumption engine of militarism and military spending that siphons the life force out of societies, and to all oppressions of "the other."

Social consciousness within the environmental movement on the other hand, speaks to people's civic and humanistic being, to their quest for a connectedness with others and the earth, to their desire to make the world more just and humane, as well as to the stressed, overworked, and seemingly optionless plight of individuals caught on the work-and-spend treadmill of late-twentieth-century industrial life. Taming consumption through a personal, spiritual quest is part of the answer, but not the whole one.

The Ecological Footprint

The intriguing epithet "ecological footprint" is shorthand for an analysis that more successfully integrates the calculation of consumer impact on the earth with the responsibilities of government, the right of every human to a fair and healthful share of the Earth's resources, and a deep concern for not overloading or degrading global ecosystems.[6] Here, too, the focus is primarily the North American consumer lifestyle and an accounting of its impacts on the environment. However, the goal is to calculate the size of the Canadian and U.S. ecological footprint compared with that of others in lesser-industrialized and nonindustrialized countries and to determine how the oversized North American footprint can be reduced through better regional planning, more ecologically conscious consumption, and the restructuring of industrial technology and economics.

This ecological accounting tool, as geographer Ben Wisner points out so well, inverts "carrying capacity" to ask: Given nearly six billion people in the world, how should we live so as to enable all to live within the limits of the biosphere?[7] The premise of the ecological footprint is that although half the world lives in cities (and by 2020 an estimated two-thirds of people will), we live in a biosphere much larger than the physical boundaries of our cities and towns when we buy goods that are grown or made from resources outside our municipality or region and when we dispose of our wastes in the global atmosphere and marine environments. The ecological footprint is calculated by translating key categories of human consumption—food, housing, transport, consumer goods and services—into the amount of *productive land* needed to provide these goods and services and to assimilate their resultant waste.

Using assumptions about biomass substitutes for fossil fuels and so on, the authors of this method, Mathis Wackernagel and William Rees, calculate that the amount of land needed to support the average Canadian's present consumption, or ecological footprint, is 4.8 hectares [Table 2].

In their calculations of ecologically productive land, Wackernagel and Rees estimate that an average of 1.6 hectares of land per capita is available worldwide for goods and services. In other words, the average Canadian uses three times as much of the earth's capacity as is available to every person; in other words, the average Canadian's ecological footprint is three times the size it ought to be, since everyone deserves a fair share of the global commons. Correspondingly, the average Indian ecological footprint is 0.4 hectare per person.

The average per capita consumption in Canada, as in every country, is a composite of the consumption of the rich, poor, and middle consumption classes.

Table 2 The Ecological Footprint of the Average Canadian, in Hectares per Capita

	ENERGY	BUILT ENVIRONMENT	AGRICULTURAL LAND	FOREST	TOTAL
Food	0.4		0.9		**1.3**
Housing	0.5	0.1		0.4	**1.0**
Transport	1.0	0.1			**1.1**
Consumer Goods	0.6		0.2	0.2	**1.0**
Resources in Services	0.4				**0.4**
TOTAL	**2.9**	**0.2**	**1.1**	**0.6**	**4.8**

Source: Mathis Wackernagel, *How Big Is Our Ecological Footprint?* (Vancouver: University of British Columbia, 1993), 3.

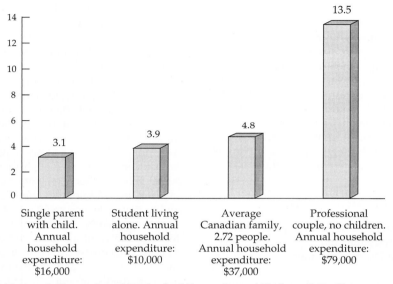

FIGURE 2 Examples of Ecological Footprints of Various Canadian Households, in Hectares per Capita. (*Source:* Mathis Wackernagel, *How Big Is Our Ecological Footprint?* [Vancouver: University of British Columbia, 1993], 3.)

Thus, Figure 2 compares the ecological footprints of various Canadian households in order to show where the extremes of consumption lie and whose consumer lifestyle inordinately appropriates the carrying capacity of the Earth.

Three aspects of this analysis are particularly laudable. First, its starting point is the assumption that every human being has the same claim on nature's productivity and utility. Thus, it is inequitable and undesirable for North Americans to appropriate others' share of the global commons. Second, it promotes an urban and regional planning strategy that would reduce North Americans' footprint on the global environment by reversing sprawl through integrating living, working, and shopping; promoting bike paths and public transportation; and favoring the local economy. Third, it calls for a massive reform of industrial society to free up the ecological space needed by the poor to raise their standard of living, while enabling the well-off to maintain their high material standards.[8] Wackernagel and Rees's recommendations for restructuring industrialism to achieve a smaller ecological footprint on the world include reforms that

are simultaneously being advocated by radical environmental economists:

- Shift taxes from income to consumption and include the full costs of resources and pollution in consumer products through environmental taxes and fees. Including true environmental costs in the full cost of products will motivate industry to make cleaner products and consumers to buy them; it will favor reuse, repair, and reconditioning of products.

- Invest in research into energy- and material-efficient technologies to achieve the "four- to ten-fold reduction in material and energy intensity per unit of economic output" needed in industrial countries to reduce the ecological footprint to a sustainable size.

- Invest the anticipated economic gains from the enhanced efficiency in remediating and restoring critical ecosystems.[9]

Even with a more structural approach to macroeconomic systems and the socially conscious goal of commonweal, certain footprints, in this analysis, remain invisible. Women have much less stake in the global economy than men—by virtue of having little political and economic power, as well as by holding different economic priorities, in many instances, from men. Thus, women have a smaller individual and structural footprint than men and male institutions. The economic and political institution of the military, for example ([which has an] extreme impact on economies, cultures, and ecosystems), arises from patriarchal concepts of power and methods of conflict resolution.

What insights and efforts can a woman-centered analysis bring to the issue of consumption in order to further the goals of redistributing and humanizing our use of natural resources, consumer goods, and services, and of mitigating and reversing our pollution impacts on ecosystems?

Conclusion

. . . Why are more than a billion women and girls consigned to spending hours daily collecting wood and biomass and ingesting smoke when the dissemination of technologies such as more efficient cook stoves and solar cookers would ease their lives; save their health; and conserve woodlands, soil, water, and biomass in critical ecosystems? Authors Kammen and Dove have identified a bias in science against "research on mundane topics" in energy, agriculture, public health, and resource economics. . . .[10] Their analysis of the fallacies that underlie the inattention to labor-, time-, health- and environment-saving technologies is consonant with feminist critiques of science culture and science values.[11] According to the canon of science, the premier scientific work is basic research, uncontaminated by the needs of real people and characterized by objective and detached thought. The potential of "breakthrough discoveries" charges the rarefied atmosphere of science research and relegates revisiting old, unsolved, human-centered problems to second-tier science. In this first-order science, abstract theory, mathematical modeling, speed, distance, and scale are privileged over social benefits,

qualitative methods, and the local and small-scale applications of "mundane" science. . . .

Social goodness and community health, as the "ecological footprint" analysis affirms, are requisites and indices of a sustainable community. In our effort to reduce overconsumption through distinguishing genuine needs and consumerist wants, we must confront the consumption of so-called goods and services that are based on the sexual exploitation of women and girls and are often a consequence of war and environmental degradation, such as prostitution, pornography, and mail-order brides. The impeccable logic of environmental justice—that poor communities of color have been systematically exploited by polluters and industry by reason of race, and suffer disproportionately from poor health—holds for women as well. Like racial justice, a sexual justice that seeks to eliminate the sexual exploitation of women is fundamental to environmental justice, to community health, and to social goodness.

NOTES

1. Alan Durning, *How Much Is Enough?* (New York: W. W. Norton, 1992).

2. Ibid., 30.

3. Juliet Schor, *The Overworked American: The Unexpected Decline of Leisure* (New York: Basic Books, 1991).

4. Joe Dominguez and Vicki Robin, *Your Money or Your Life* (New York: Viking, 1992).

5. Durning, *How Much Is Enough?* op. cit., 125.

6. Mathis Wackernagel and William Rees, *Our Ecological Footprint: Reducing Human Impact on the Earth* (Gabriola Island, British Columbia, and Philadelphia: New Society Publishers, 1996).

7. Ben Wisner, "The Limitations of 'Carrying Capacity,'" *Political Environments* (Winter–Spring 1996), 1, 3–4.

8. Wackernagel and Rees, *Our Ecological Footprint,* op. cit., 144.

9. Ibid., 144–45.

10. Daniel M. Kammen and Michael R. Dove, "The Virtues of Mundane Science," in *Environment*, Vol. 39, No. 6 (July/August 1997), 10–15, 38–41.

11. See Sue V. Rosser, *Female-Friendly Science* (New York: Teacher's College Press, 1990).

◆◆◆

Gender Aspects of Climate Change (2005)

ENERGIA International Network on Gender and Sustainable Energy, LIFE/Women in Europe for a Common Future, the World Conservation Union, and the Women's Environment and Development Organization

Karachi, Pakistan. August 2007. A woman removes floodwaters from her house after heavy rainstorms.

Climate change is an environmental problem with a strong political and development component. The impacts of global climate change are not only physical and economic (for instance, in the form of natural disasters) but also social and cultural, jeopardizing environmentally-based livelihoods in many areas of the world.

As predicted by the Intergovernmental Panel on Climate Change (IPCC), "climate change impacts will be differently distributed among different regions, generations, age classes, income group, occupations, and genders" (IPCC, 2001). The IPCC also notes: "the impacts of climate change will fall disproportionately upon developing countries and the poor persons within all countries, and thereby exacerbate inequities in health status and access to adequate food, clean water, and other resources." People living in poverty are more vulnerable to environmental changes. The gender-poverty links show that 70 percent of the poor in the world are women, and their vulnerability is accentuated by race, ethnicity, and age. When natural disasters and environmental change happen, women and men are affected differently because of traditional, socially-based roles and responsibilities.

Most climate change issues, policies, and programs are not gender neutral. In light of this, several areas deserve attention, specifically: gender specific resource-use patterns; gender-specific effects of climate change; gender aspects of mitigation and adaptation; gender and decision-making on climate change; women's capacity to cope with climate change; and gender-related patterns of vulnerability.

It is widely recognized that industrial countries bear the main responsibility for greenhouse gas emissions, but the impacts are felt most severely in developing countries. It is therefore relevant to analyze the gender aspects of climate change in developed countries from the angle of emissions and to also consider mitigation strategies from a gender perspective. But so far, the critical issues of who is responsible for CO_2 emissions and through what activities, of how social, political, and planning conditions affect emission reduction, and of the role played by gender in increasing or curbing emissions, have scarcely been identified, much less debated.

The Issues At Stake

Climate change has many gender-specific characteristics: (i) women are affected differently, and more severely, by climate change and natural disasters because of social roles, discrimination, and poverty,

(ii) women are still underrepresented in decision-making about climate change, greenhouse gas emissions, and adaptation/mitigation, and (iii) there are gender biases in carbon emissions. They should be included not only because they are most vulnerable but also because they have different perspectives and expertise to contribute. Gender is a significant dimension to take into account when understanding environmental change. Perspectives, responses, and impacts related to disaster events are different for men and women, as men and women have different social responsibilities, vulnerabilities, capabilities, and opportunities for adjustment and unequal assets and power relations; they experience environmental change and disasters differently.

Women Are Affected Differently and More Severely

The effects of climate change manifested in the increase of extreme weather conditions such as hot summers, droughts, storms, or floods impact women more severely than men, both in developing and in developed countries. For example, the 20,000 people who died in France during the extreme heat wave in Europe in 2003 included significantly more elderly women than men.

In natural disasters that have occurred in recent years, both in developing and in developed countries, it is primarily the poor who have suffered—and all over the world, the majority of the poor are women, who at all levels earn less than men. In developing countries, women living in poverty bear a disproportionate burden of climate change consequences. Because of women's marginalized status and dependence on local natural resources, their domestic burdens are increased, including additional work to fetch water or to collect fuel and fodder. In some areas, climate change generates resource shortages and unreliable job markets, which lead to increased male out-migration and more women left behind with additional agricultural and household duties. Poor women's lack of access to and control over natural resources, technologies, and credit mean that they have fewer resources to cope with seasonal and episodic weather and natural disasters. Consequently traditional roles are reinforced, girls' education suffers, and women's ability to diversify their livelihoods (and therefore their capacity to access income-generating jobs) is diminished.

Climate change, which reduces crop yields and food production, particularly in developing countries, affects women's livelihood strategies and food security, and therefore, their right to food. Women are responsible for 70–80 percent of household food production in sub-Saharan Africa, 65 percent in Asia, and 45 percent in Latin America and the Caribbean. Traditional food sources may become more unpredictable and scarce as the climate changes. Droughts and flooding can be detrimental to women who keep livestock as a source of income and for security. Women's knowledge and experience of maintaining biodiversity through the conservation and domestication of wild edible plant seeds and food crop breeding is key to adapting to climate change more effectively.

Both in developing and in developed countries women are primary caregivers, combining the care for children and the elderly with their domestic and income-earning activities. These additional responsibilities place additional burdens on women that impact their ability to work outside the home and to deal with the effects generated by environmental changes caused by global warming. . . .

In traditional societies women are even more vulnerable to the impacts of climate change because they are often not allowed to participate in the public sphere and are therefore less likely to receive critical information for emergency preparedness. They are also less mobile due to strict and gendered codes of social behavior and have fewer chances to escape from affected areas.

Climate protection instruments may affect women and men differently because of their differing economic status. Financial support of technical measures to protect the climate likewise tends to be more in favor of men's interests. Measures necessary

An Oxfam report (March 2005) on the impact on women of the 2005 Asia Tsunami raised alarms about gender imbalances since the majority of those killed and among those least able to recover were women. In Aceh, for example, more than 75 percent of those who died were women, resulting in a male-female ratio of 3:1 among the survivors. As so many mothers died, there have been major consequences with respect to infant mortality, early marriage of girls, neglect of girls' education, sexual assault, trafficking in women, and prostitution. These woes, however, are largely neglected in the media coverage.

Rebenacq, France. May 2007. A woman removes mud and water from her house following storms and flash floods.

to produce changes in behavior do not receive a similar level of recognition and support. As reported by the gender disaster workshop in Ankara (2001):

> Women's human rights are not comprehensively enjoyed throughout the disaster process. Economic and social rights are violated in disaster processes if mitigation, relief, and reconstruction policies do not benefit women and men equally. The right to adequate health care is violated when relief efforts do not meet the needs of specific physical and mental health needs throughout their life cycle, in particular when trauma has occurred. The right to security of persons is violated when women and girls are victims of sexual and other forms of violence while in relief camps or temporary housing. Civil and political rights are denied if women cannot act autonomously and participate fully at all decision-making levels in matters regarding mitigation and recovery.[1]

Women Are Underrepresented in Decision-Making

Women's role in communities is not formally recognized or accounted for in mitigation, adaptation, and relief efforts. Women's knowledge about ecosystems and their strategies, experiences, and skills for coping with natural disasters and water shortages are often ignored. Strategies and policies to cope with climate change are neglecting the gender dimensions of climate change and the current gender–climate change agenda. Women are poorly represented in planning and decision-making processes in climate change policies, limiting their capacity to engage in political decisions that can impact their specific needs and vulnerabilities. Vulnerability and mitigation are part of the 1988 UN International Panel on Climate Change agenda, but gender perspectives have still not been incorporated in its work.

The level of women's participation in planning and decision-making on climate protection is very low even in industrialized countries, and this is linked above all to the heavily technical nature and male dominance in key areas of work: energy, transport, town planning. Consequently, it is generally men who profit more from the newly emerging jobs in these areas, be it renewable energies or emissions trading.

At both international and national levels, it remains difficult for women to gain recognition in the field of climate protection. While there is now a small and growing group of committed women and men in policy forums advocating for gender to be taken into account, response to the issues remains limited. At the national level, the picture is not much better. The integration of gender appears most likely to succeed at the regional and local levels but even here it is the exception rather than the rule.

Gender Biases in Carbon Emissions

In some instances, responsibility for emissions appears related to the gender-specific division of labor, economic power, and the different consumption and leisure habits of men and women. For example, emissions connected with mobility have a clear gender component. In Europe, in both the work and leisure contexts, women travel by car less frequently and over shorter distances, use smaller, energy-saving cars, and fly considerably less frequently than men.

Women are over-represented as heads of low-income households and under-represented in high-income groups. In this respect, income levels play a role in CO_2 emissions: the higher the income, the higher the emissions from larger houses with more electrical equipment, bigger cars, and so on; the lower the income, the less the household's ability to use energy-efficient appliances, build energy-saving houses, or purchase electricity and heat produced from renewables. These differences must be addressed in climate change mitigation policies. Lack of technical education also has an effect since behavioral changes, including consumption patterns, cannot be made without knowledge of the challenges and options for reducing CO_2 emissions.

Women and men perceive the cause of climate change (including CO_2 emissions) differently. In Germany, more than 50 percent of women compared to only 40 percent of men rate climate change brought about by global warming as extremely or very dangerous. Women also believed very firmly that each individual can contribute toward protecting the climate through his/her individual actions. However, policy planning does not reflect these perceptions in any way.

Lessons Learned

Women at the international level have organized to influence climate change negotiations and national policies, and important international networks promoting the role of women in energy and climate change have been established, including the Gender and Climate Change Network established by LIFE, WECF, SAGEN, and ENERGIA during COP-9 [Milan 2003] (see www.gencc.net/policy/conference/cop9.html).

A concept for integrating the gender perspective in UN climate protection negotiations has been drawn up by women's networks in Germany supported by women's groups worldwide. Entry points for incorporating a gender perspective as well as strategies and possible alliances are identified. Initial

steps toward implementation are planned for COP-11 at the end of 2005, including a strategy workshop, a women's caucus, and a "Climate Talk" to present the issues to high-level representatives. A workshop, to be organized jointly with the IPCC, will aim to close, in the medium term, the considerable gaps in research.

At the local level, women provide particular kinds of social capital for mitigation, adaptation, and coping with environmental change, actively organizing during and after disasters to help their households and community.

In those situations where climate change programs and policies have recognized gender differences within the same community, household, or stakeholder groups, there have been several benefits. For instance, unlike many other communities in Honduras, La Masica reported no deaths after Hurricane Mitch in 1998; six months earlier, a disaster agency had provided gender-sensitive community education on early warning systems and hazard management. The community decided to involve women and men

Climate Program 2004–2008, Lower Austria

The government of the Austrian federal state of Lower Austria has applied gender mainstreaming to its newly established climate protection program. Five . . . measures have been drafted and assigned to the over 200 climate protection measures to be taken into consideration during implementation. Resistance was substantial, which is why at the end of the agreement process only five GM measures remained although there had originally been double that number. These are as follows:

- Representation of women in decision-making positions
- Equality of opportunity in planning, organization, and promotions
- Promotion of women in technical occupations
- Inclusion of gender aspects in training
- Inclusion of gender aspects in PR work.

Inuit women in Northern Canada have always had a deep understanding of weather conditions because they were responsible for assessing hunting conditions and preparing the hunters accordingly. During a drought in the small islands of the Federal States of Micronesia, it was local women, knowledgeable about island hydrology as a result of land-based work, who were able to find potable water by digging a new well that reached the fresh-water lens.

equally in all hazard management activities, and women took over from men the abandoned task of continuously monitoring the early warning system. As a result, the municipality was able to evacuate the areas promptly when Hurricane Mitch struck.

Tapping women's interest in disaster mitigation and preparedness has led to improved community welfare during and after disasters. Ensuing strategies, including gender-sensitive target group analysis, identification, and preparation of safe areas for villagers to escape floods; the establishment of local early cyclone warning, monitoring, and communication systems; research on indigenous resilience practices; and the creation of women-accessible emergency loan funds help the poor reduce their risks in natural disasters.

Through improved access to resources, technologies, and finance, women have been more likely to increase efficiency in their use of renewable energy and mitigate climate change. More secure access to resources from forests and protected areas has resulted in less deforestation and maintenance of carbon sinks, and improved access to safe water for humans and animals has enabled dry-land women to have more time for livelihood and subsistence activities.

Women are able to map their risks and vulnerabilities from their own standpoint and to play an important role in early warning. Women's knowledge in adaptation (traditional and community-specific) could be used as an important resource.

Since 1996, Costa Rica has been implementing the Program to Pay for Environmental Services (Programa de Pago por Servicios Ambientales) to promote and encourage conservation, reforestation, carbon emission mitigation and its greenhouse effect, and the sustainable management of Costa Rica's natural resources. The program offers economic rewards to landowners who don't cut back the forests on their land. The problem also encompasses ownership issues since most landowners are men, and women have little access. To help resolve this problem, FONAFIFO (Fondo Nacional de Financiamiento Forestal), the national institution in charge of implementing the program as well as promotion of gender equity, imposes a fee to ensure that a certain amount of the gains goes to supporting women to become landowners.

Improvements in family income have reduced the need for males to migrate to urban and other areas, thereby increasing rural labor availability for anti-desertification and reclamation practices (for example, soil and water conservation, cut-and-carry fodder systems, intensive agro-forestry systems) and enabling traditional ecosystem management practices to be passed on by both women and men.

Gender-sensitive methods of problem analysis, situation description, and impact assessment will have to be developed for climate change contexts. Instruments such as gender impact assessment can already be applied and can be developed further during the process of application. For all instruments and measures relevant to climate protection, in local areas and regions as well as at the national and international level, an impact analysis should be conducted regarding the situation of women and men and how gender justice and climate protection can be mutually reinforcing. Questions include: What is the socio-economic situation forming the backdrop to these measures? Is care work and its requirements recognized and taken into account? How is this reflected in the general situation (for example, financial aid, information, supportive measures)?

Toolkit: "Climate for Change—Gender Equality and Climate Change Policy"

The Climate Alliance of European Cities conducted its first gender project between 2003 and 2005. In cooperation with 10 cities in four European countries, the situation of women in municipal climate protection bodies was examined, and instruments were discussed with a view to increasing the proportion of women in decision-making positions.

Discussions also touched on ways that increasing the proportion of women would contribute to climate protection and whether a more gender-sensitive climate protection policy could automatically be expected as a result. Even though the questions were left unanswered, there was interest to continue working on them in the future.

Seven Principles for Engendered Relief and Reconstruction: "Nothing in Disaster Work Is Gender Neutral"

- Think big: Gender equality and risk reduction principles must guide all aspects of disaster mitigation, response and reconstruction.
- Get the facts: Gender analysis is not optional or divisive but imperative to direct aid and planning for full and equitable recovery.
- Work with grassroots women: Women's community organizations have insights, information, experiences, networks, and resources vital to increasing disaster resilience.
- Work with and develop the capacities of existing women's groups.
- Resist stereotypes: Base all initiatives on knowledge of difference and specific cultural, economic, political, and sexual contexts, not on false generalities.
- Take a human rights approach: Democratic and participatory initiatives serve women

and girls best. Women and men alike must be assured of the conditions needed to enjoy their fundamental human rights, as well as to simply survive.

- Respect and develop the capacities of women: Avoid overburdening women with already heavy workloads and family responsibilities.

(Gender and Disaster Network, 2005)

Conclusion

There is a need to refocus the thinking and the debate on energy and climate change to include a human rights perspective. Integrating a rights-based approach to access to sustainable and affordable energy is an approach that will recognize and take into account women's specific needs and women's human rights. Current economic models based primarily on privatization strategies do not include accountability in terms of meeting people's basic needs.

Women must be recognized as agents of change who have a significant role to play in creating sustainable models for energy consumption and production and in responsible climate change mitigation and adaptation efforts. There is an urgent need to include gender equality and involvement of women at all environmental planning and decision-making levels. Empowerment through capacity building and technical training will increase women's capacity to effectively participate in energy policy-making and decision-making bodies.

Finally, addressing the absence of the gender dimension in the UNFCCC [UN Framework Convention on Climate Change] and the scarcity of research focusing on the gender aspects of climate change will also help to build a more consistent and solid approach regarding climate change policies.

NOTES

This paper has been developed through joint contributions by ENERGIA International Network on Gender and

Sustainable Energy (www.energia.org), LIFE/Women in Europe for a Common Future (www.wecf.org), IUCN-The World Conservation Union (http://cms.iucn.org), and Women's Environment and Development Organization (www.wedo.org) in consultation with women's organizations throughout the world.

1. Division for the Advancement of Women and UN International Strategy for Disaster Reduction, "Environmental Management and the Mitigation of Natural Disasters: A Gender Perspective" Report of the Expert Group Meeting, Ankara, Turkey, 6–9 November 2001.

REFERENCES

Intergovernmental Panel on Climate Change. 2001. *Climate Change 2001: Third Assessment report.* Geneva: IPCC.

Kandaswamy, D. 2005. Media Forgets Female Face of Tsunami. *WomensENews,* July 22. www.womensenews.org/article.cfm/dyn/aid/2390/context/archive.

OXFAM. 2005. The Tsunami's Impact on Women. Briefing Note, March. www.oxfam.org.uk/resources/policy/conflict_disasters/index.html.

12

◆◆◆

Creating Change
Theory, Vision, and Action

In the last one hundred years, women in the United States have won the right to speak out on public issues, to vote, to own property in their own names, to divorce, and to have increased access to higher education and the professions. Developments in birth control have allowed women to have fewer babies, and family size is much smaller than it was in the early years of the twentieth century. Improved health care and better working conditions mean that women now live longer than ever before. Women are freer to choose whether to marry or not. Women's wage rates are inching closer to men's. Issues like domestic violence, rape, sexual harassment, and women's sexual freedom are public matters. Overall, women in the United States are more independent—economically and socially—than ever before.

Although women have broken free from many earlier limitations, this book also shows how much still needs to be done. As we argue in previous chapters, many aspects of women's lives are subject to debate and controversy as **contested terrains.** These controversial issues include women's sexuality, reproductive freedom, the nature of marriage and family relationships, the right to livelihood independent of men, and the right to affordable health care. Gains have been made and also eroded, as conservative politicians aided by conservative religious leaders and media personalities have organized to limit or reverse women's progress.

It is easy to review the details of U.S. women's experiences of discrimination and to come away feeling angry, depressed, hopeless, and disempowered. The interlocking systems that keep women oppressed can seem monolithic and unchangeable. Major U.S. social movements of the past one hundred years—for the rights of working people; the civil rights of peoples of color; women's liberation; disability rights; gay, lesbian, bisexual, and transgender rights—have all made significant gains and also seen those gains challenged and attacked.

In this final chapter we consider what is needed to tackle the problems we have identified throughout the book. How can this be done in ways that address underlying causes as well as visible manifestations? How can women and men build relationships, systems of work, local communities, and a wider world based on sustainability and real security?

Each person needs to find meaning in his or her life. Knowing a lot of facts may be an effective way of doing well on tests and getting good grades, but this kind of knowledge does not necessarily provide meaning. Knowing what matters to you means that you can begin to take charge of your own life and begin to direct change. This process involves examining your own life, as suggested through the questions included in each chapter. Unless you do this, you will be absent from your own system of knowledge. The article by Abra Fortune Chernik provides an excellent example of this (Reading 68). She examines her struggle with an eating disorder and the process of overcoming it. Moving beyond her own experience, she asks, "Why society would reward my starvation and encourage my vanishing?" She examined psychological, sociological, and feminist theories for answers to this question. Other writers in this collection also start by examining their own lives but go beyond micro-level explanations as we noted in Chapter 3. Examples include articles by Christina Leaño (Reading 16), Aurora Levins Morales (Reading 32), Ann Filemyr (Reading 37), and Marilyn Buck (Reading 50).

How Does Change Happen?

The process of creating change requires a combination of theoretical insights and understandings, visions of alternatives, and action. This involves using your head, heart, and hands in ways that reinforce one another. The readings in this chapter include a blend of these three aspects.

Using the Head: Theories for Social Change

As we pointed out in Chapter 2, doing something about an issue or a problem requires us to have a theory, an explanation, of what it is. The theory we create directly shapes what we think ought to be done. Thus *how* we theorize is a key first step in creating change. If we examine only certain specifics of an issue, examine issues separately, or use a limited analytical framework, we will end up with limited understandings of women's lives. For a fuller picture we need to analyze issues individually and together, looking for commonalities and patterns, recognizing differences, and using frameworks that illuminate as many parts as possible. Our theoretical ideas, which run through the previous chapters— sometimes explicit, sometimes implicit—are summarized here:

- A social-constructionist perspective allows us to see how social and political forces shape our lives and our sense of ourselves. It encourages us to focus on the specificity of experience and also the diversity of experiences among people. It allows us to see that situations and structures are not fixed for all time but are changeable under the right circumstances.

- How an issue is defined and framed will affect how we think about the problem, where we look for probable causes, our ideas about what ought to be done about it, and who is likely to become involved in working to change it.

- It is necessary to analyze social situations in terms of micro, meso, macro, and global levels and to understand how these levels affect one another. Strategies for change need to address all of these levels.

- Many women's activist organizations and projects are working on the issues discussed in this book.

- Efforts to create equal opportunities for women and equal access to current institutions have made a difference for many women, but by themselves they cannot achieve a genuinely secure and sustainable world because these are not the goals of most institutions.

Using the Heart: Visions for Social Change

Vision is the second ingredient needed to create social change—some idea of a different way of doing things, a different future for humankind, framed by explicit principles around which human relations ought to be organized. Otherwise, as the saying goes, "If you don't know where you're going, any road will get you there."

Visions are about values, drawing from inside ourselves everything we value and daring to think big. The many demands of our busy lives leave most people with little time or opportunity to envision alternatives. In school and college, for example, students are rarely asked to think deeply about their hopes and dreams for a more truly human world in which to live. Much of what we do is guided not by our own visions but in reaction to the expectations of others and outside pressures. Social issues, too, are framed in reactive and negative terms. People talk about "antiracism," for instance, not about what a truly multicultural society would be like.

Some people scorn this step as time-wasting and unrealistic. What matters, they say, is to come up with "realistic" ideas that people feel comfortable with, that businesses will want to invest in, or that fit government programs and guidelines. Tackle something small and specific, something winnable. Don't waste time on grandiose ideas.

Because most of us are not encouraged to envision change, it may take a while to free ourselves from seemingly practical ideas. Our imaginations are often limited to what we know, and that makes it difficult to break out of our cramped daily routines and habits of thought. Envisioning something different also means putting on hold the voice inside your head that says: Are you *crazy?* This will never work! Who do you think you are? Where will you *ever* get the money?

Go ahead. Envision the multicultural society, the women's health project, the community play/read/care program for elders and children, the Internet information business run by inner-city teenagers, the women's taxi service, the intimate relationship of your dreams, your blossoming sexuality. Envision it in as much detail as you can. Think it, see it, taste it, smell it, sing it, draw it, and write it down. Share it with others who you think will be sympathetic to it. This is where you're headed. Now all you need is to create the road. The projects we mention throughout this book, like this book itself, all started this way, as somebody's dream.

Using the Hands: Action for Social Change

The third essential ingredient for change is action. Through action, theories and visions are tested, sharpened, and refined to create even more useful theories and more creative visions. In Chapter 2 we referred to philosopher Alan Rosenberg's (1988) distinction between *knowing* and *understanding.* Rosenberg further argued that understanding compels us to action, even though we may not initially want to change our habitual ways of thinking and being. When you understand something, you

find that [your] world becomes a different world and that [you] must generate a new way to be in the new world. Since each person's

way of being in the world is relatively fixed— and serves as protection against the anxieties of the unknown—integration is extremely hard. To give up a world in which one's life makes sense means undergoing great loss. Yet without the readiness to risk that loss we cannot hope to pursue understanding. *(p. 382)*

In previous chapters we mentioned many activist projects, which are all relevant to this discussion. In this chapter, Amy Jo Goddard argues for the importance of cultural work to social movements (Reading 69). Barbara Ransby focuses on grassroots women's organizing in New Orleans in the aftermath of Hurricane Katrina (Reading 71). Cindy Lewis highlights education, training, and networking by Mobility International USA with women from many countries (Reading 72). Peggy Antrobus summarizes the origins and characteristics of the global women's movement (Reading 74).

Here we suggest a range of avenues for trying to implement your visions. Some will be more appropriate than others, depending on your goals and theoretical perspectives. Some of the activities we list below may be impossible for students, who need to concentrate on getting degrees, to participate in. Progressive social change is a long-term project; there will be plenty to do after you graduate (see Naples and Bojar 2002).

- Think of yourself as someone with something valuable to say, who can take the initiative and start something you think is important. Think about what you want to do after college, how to live your values and ideals.

- Express your ideas: talk to others; write 'zines, poems, leaflets, speeches, letters to newspaper editors and politicians; put up flyers or posters; organize a film series; paint murals, dance, sing, or perform your ideas.

- Be a conscious shopper. Support fair-trade products; boycott products made in sweatshops, for example. Buy directly from farmers' markets or craft producers. Spend your money where it will support your values.

- Support women's organizations, environmental groups, antiracist organizations, or gay/lesbian/bisexual/transgender groups by letting them know you appreciate their work, letting others know these groups exist, attending

events, donating money or something the group needs, volunteering your time, proposing ideas for projects, working as an intern for college credit.

- Work for institutional change. Within your family you may want to stop others from telling sexist or racist jokes, create greater understanding between family members, or develop more egalitarian relationships. At school you may want to set up study groups to work together, support teachers who help you, point out glaring gaps in the curriculum or college services to teachers and administrators, challenge racism or sexual harassment.

- Participate in direct action. This includes interrupting, keeping silent, organizing groups of women to walk together at night, defending clinics where abortions are performed, participating in demonstrations and rallies, boycotts, picketing, rent strikes, tax resistance. Whatever the setting, take back the Nike slogan. Just Do It!

- Get involved in grassroots organizing. Meet with others and decide what you can do together to tackle some issue of shared concern.

- Participate in coalitions. Consider joining with other groups on an issue of shared concern so as to be more visible and effective.

- Learn about local and national issues, and let your representatives at city, state, and national levels know your opinions. Urge them to pass appropriate laws and to speak out in public situations and to the media. Use your vote. Help to elect progressive candidates. Support them

if they get into office, and hold them accountable to their election promises.

- Learn more about international networks and organizations working on issues that concern you. Consider participating in an international meeting and bringing the knowledge you gain there to your organizing work back home.

A range of factors help us in taking action: a sense of hope and conviction that women's lives can be improved, anger at current inequalities and injustices, reliable allies, well-thought-out strategies, and help from parents, partners, neighbors, friends, children, or total strangers who may make a crucial contribution, which allows us to be involved.

Overcoming Blocks to Effective Action

Political action does not always work; that is, a chosen course of action may not achieve our original goals. There are many possible reasons for this: inadequate theoretical understandings and analysis of the issues; choosing inappropriate or ineffective strategies; not following through on the course of action; not being able to get enough people involved for this particular strategy to be effective; wrong timing; the failure of the group to work together well enough; the failure of people whom you thought were allies to come through when needed; and so on. The other major reason, of course, is that the opposition—whether this is your sexist uncle, your boss, the university administration, the city school board, the opposing political party, or the U.S. Congress—was simply more powerful.

Feeling that an action has failed is disheartening and may lead people to give up, assuming that creating change is hopeless. But action *always* accomplishes something, and in this sense it always works. At the very least, activism that does not meet your goals teaches you something important. In hindsight, what may seem like mistakes are actually valuable ways to learn how to be more effective in the future. This is what we called "socially lived" theory in Chapter 2. Always evaluate what you did after some activity or event, personally and with the group. If it worked as you hoped, why did it work? What have you learned as a result? If it did not work, why? What will you do differently next time?

Personal blocks to activism may include practical factors like not having enough time or energy, or needing to focus on some other aspect of life. Emotional blocks include guilt—a paralyzing emotion that keeps us stuck—and cynicism—a frustrated idealism that has turned hopeless and bitter. Anger can be a very useful, high-octane fuel if you can channel it in a constructive direction. Overextending yourself is not a sign of your commitment to your ideals, and trying to do more than you can is one sure way to burn out quickly. Activism for progressive social change needs patience, humor, creativity, a range of skills and resources, an ability to talk to other people, a willingness to listen and to change, a willingness to be reflective, refining your ideas and your visions.

Theorists of social change usually see it as an interplay between individual agents or groups and the social and political structures that form the larger context of our lives and often restrict us. Some emphasize what English professor Ellen Messer-Davidow (1991) called "agent-centered models of change" that represent powerful people and a passive system (p. 293). This is the view of those who characterize the U.S. political system as open and responsive to pressure from organized groups. "Social-system models of change represent powerful systems and passive people" (Messer-Davidow 1991, p. 294). This is the view of those who point to the central role money plays in determining who can run for office and, in many cases, who has access to them once they are in power. A third of all eligible voters appear to hold this view, as they are not registered to vote, even though many of these same people may be very active in their churches, synagogues, temples, or other community organizations.

We see a key role for individuals, as change agents, working with others to envision alternatives and bring them into being through collective action: through identity-based politics, feminist organizing, electoral politics, and broad-based coalitions and alliances. We explore these forms of activism in the next section.

Women and Political Activism

Politics involves the use of power. What is it? Who has it? How is it used? Who does it benefit, and who is disadvantaged? Sociologists and political scientists define **power** as the ability to influence others. This may be by persuasion, charisma, law, political activism, or coercion (Andersen 2000). As we argue throughout this book, individuals and groups have power and influence based on a range of attributes, such as race, class, gender, age, and education, that are valued in this society. Many people focus on the ways in which others exert power over us or on the fact that they have more power than we have. We generally pay less attention to the ways in which we have more power than others. This is true especially for people in subordinated groups, such as women and men of color in the United States, where some fundamental aspect of our existence, if not our identity, is predicated on being "the powerless" in many settings.

Poet and essayist Audre Lorde writes of women's personal power (Reading 18, Chapter 4), and several writers in this book refer to the importance of personal empowerment. People exercise power through institutions such as education, religion, corporations, the media, the law, the military, and all aspects of government. Sometimes this happens regardless of individual intent or knowledge of its existence. Power is also expressed in the values and practices of institutions that compel people to think and behave in specific ways. For example, the heterosexist values embedded in our culture and its institutions define the family as a heterosexual couple, legally bound by marriage, and their children. The value and legitimacy attached to this institution is a powerful influence on everyone and is in itself a pressure to marry. Higher education operates out of values that are overwhelmingly Eurocentric, middle class, and masculinist. These values uphold particular ways of learning, certain kinds of discourse, and the use of a specific language. To succeed in college, a student must work within these parameters even if they do not subscribe to these values.

Power operates at the community, macro, and global levels. Political scientists have focused on formal political organizations, especially the U.S. Congress, where there are relatively few women. As a result, past studies of women's political power have seriously underestimated it. Feminist researchers have pointed out that women's political participation includes active membership in a wide range of local, state, and national organizations including women's clubs, parent-teacher associations (PTAs), and labor unions, working in support of candidates for political office, organizing fund-raising events, circulating petitions, participating in letter-writing and call-in campaigns, as well as voting (see Freeman 2008; Naples 1997, 1998; Swers 2001; West and Blumberg 1990). Several articles in this collection give details of women's organizing: how they draw in participants; strategize about goals, priorities, and activities; and use their knowledge, personal connections, and links to institutions (e.g., Readings 28, 33, 34, 35, 48). In this chapter, Amy Jo Goddard emphasizes cultural work as an effective form of activism and popular education (Reading 69). Other writers focus on details of organizing in the United States and across national borders (Readings 72, 73, and 74).

Identity-Based Politics

Throughout this book many contributors write about identity. Some mention the difficulties of coming to terms with who they are, the complexities of their contradictory positions, or breaking the silence surrounding taboo subjects, thoughts, and feelings. They also comment that coming to new understandings about themselves and being able to speak from a place of personal identity and self-knowledge is profoundly empowering.

Identity politics is, literally, a politics that puts identity at the center, based on, for example, age, race, ethnicity, or sexual orientation. It usually involves the assumption that this particular characteristic is the most important in the lives of a specific identity group and that the group is not differentiated according to other characteristics in any significant way. Identity politics is concerned with wider opportunities—maybe greater visibility and recognition in society, equality, justice, even liberation for ourselves and our group. Our authoritativeness comes from our shared identity, some common ground of experience that allows a group to say "we." This is the foundation for many student organizations, community groups, religious groups, national networks, and major social movements. Thus, identity can be an effective springboard for action.

At the same time, identity politics has serious limitations. Groups tend to remain separate, focused on their own issues and concerns, often competing with each other for recognition and resources. The language of identity politics gives voice to people's discrimination and oppression. It does not encourage us to think about identity in a more complex way, as a mix of privilege and disadvantage. In Chapter 3 we noted that most people occupy multiple positions and that salient aspects of identity may vary significantly depending on the context. An African American graduate student who is about to receive her Ph.D., for example, may be highly respected by her teachers and peers, regardless of their race or hers. A white man walking past her in the street may insult her because she is Black.

Understanding this notion of multiple positionality helps us to see how our personal and group identities are political and how the various identity groups fit together in the wider society. The specific context is crucial. In public discourse about immigration, for example, there is a fear on the part of white people—usually hinted at rather than stated directly—of being "overrun" by Asians. When the context shifts to a discussion of peoples of color in the United States, however, Asian immigrants and Asian Americans become the "model minority," the standard against which African Americans or Latinos are compared unfavorably. Understanding one's identity involves a recognition of the ways in which one is privileged as well as the ways in which one is disadvantaged, and the contradictions that this raises, as noted by several authors in this collection (see, e.g., readings by Melanie Kaye/Kantrowitz, Veronica Chambers, and Ann Filemyr). With this more nuanced perspective, one not only focuses on the circumstances and concerns of one's own group, but also can use the complexity of one's identity to make connections to other groups. Thus, a white, middle-class woman with a hearing disability can take all of these aspects of her identity and understand her social location in terms of privilege as well as disadvantage. This is important for building effective alliances with others, which we discuss in more detail later. We make a distinction between a narrower identity politics, discussed above, and **identity-based politics,** which has a strong identity component and also a broader view that allows people to make connections to other groups and issues. Melanie Kaye/Kantrowitz (Reading 14), Christina Leaño (Reading 16), Combahee River Collective (Reading 5), Leslie Feinberg (Reading 23), and Amy Jo Goddard (Reading 69) all exemplify this more connective, identity-based

politics. Feminist movements grow out of identity-based politics. Movements call forth the energies, passions, and visions of many people, often in ways that are life-changing for the participants, as we discussed in Chapter 1. They inspire and make space for groundbreaking projects and alternative institutions. Some women have created change through grassroots organizing, and by providing services and supports that did not exist before. Others focused on the need for laws and public policy to change women's lives and set their sights on elected office.

Women in Electoral Politics

Women who seek political office invariably do so because they want to make a difference in people's lives. Those who work hard to support women candidates argue that a critical mass of women in elected office will be able to change public policy and legislation to provide for women's needs. This includes local offices like parent-teacher associations (PTAs), city council seats, statewide offices, and the U.S. Congress. Together with male allies in Congress, women elected officials and their staffs have worked long and hard to pass legislation to ensure better

opportunities for women, including, for example, Title IX of the 1972 Education Act, which requires schools and colleges that receive federal funding to provide equal opportunities for male and female students (see the Box on page 591), the Family and Medical Leave Act, and the Violence Against Women Act. They have also worked for improvements in women's wages, the availability of affordable child care, the opening of military combat roles to women, and so forth.

In 1990 women were 5.6 percent of congressional representatives. At the slow rate women's participation was growing, it would have taken another fifty years before there was equality in state legislatures and at least another three hundred years before there were equal numbers of women and men in Congress. The proportion of women elected to political office has increased since then, though the United States has fewer women in office than many other countries (see Table 12.1). In 2008 women held 87 (16.3 percent) of the 535 seats in the U.S. Congress: 16 percent of the 100 seats in the Senate and 71 (16.3 percent) of the 435 seats in the House of Representatives. Of the 1,746 women state legislators nationwide, 20 percent were women of color (Center for American Women and Politics 2008). Sociologist Margaret Andersen (2000) noted

Table 12.1   Women's Representation in National Legislatures

COUNTRY	% WOMEN IN LOWER OR SINGLE HOUSE	COUNTRY	% WOMEN IN LOWER OR SINGLE HOUSE
Rwanda	48.8	Poland	20.2
Sweden	47.0	North Korea	20.1
Cuba	43.2	United Kingdom	19.5
Denmark	38.0	Venezuela	18.6
Costa Rica	36.8	Nicaragua	18.5
Spain	36.3	France	18.2
Mozambique	34.8	Uzbekistan	17.5
South Africa	33.0	United States of America	16.3
Germany	31.6	Panama	16.7
Peru	29.2	Dominican Republic	16.1
Switzerland	28.5	Republic of South Korea	13.7
Australia	26.7	Ireland	13.3
Vietnam	25.8	Ghana	10.9
Iraq	25.5	Malaysia	10.8
Mexico	23.2	Japan	9.4
Tunisia	22.8	India	9.1
Lithuania	22.7	Turkey	9.1
Pakistan	22.5	Algeria	7.7
Canada	21.3	Iran (Islamic Republic of)	2.8
China	21.3	Kuwait	1.5
Croatia	20.9	Saudi Arabia	0.0
Philippines	20.5		

Source: Inter-Parliamentary Union. Women in National Parliaments (30 April 2008) www.ipu.org/wmn-e/classif.htm.

the impediments that limit women who want to run for political office: voter and media prejudice against women candidates, lack of support from party leaders, lack of access to extensive political networks, and lack of money. At the same time, women seeking office and organizations like Emily's List, the Fund for a Feminist Majority, the National Women's Political Caucus, and the White House Project are working to overcome these limitations (Burrell 1994; Ford 2002; Norris 1997; Thomas and Wilcox 1998; Woods 2000). Feminist historian and writer Jo Freeman (2008) examined U.S. women's contributions to electoral politics, including running for the highest elected office. Senator Margaret Chase Smith ran for Republican nomination for President in 1964; Shirley Chisholm

(Dem.) was the first African American woman to run for the Democratic Presidential nomination (1972); Patsy Mink was the first Asian American woman named on a Democratic presidential primary ballot (1972); Pat Schroeder (Dem.) raised money but dropped out after a short exploratory campaign (1988); Elizabeth Dole (Rep.) raised even more money but dropped out early (2000); Carol Mosely Braun (Dem.) dropped out after the first primary (2004). Hillary Rodham Clinton was the first woman to compete as a major contender for the Democratic presidential nomination (2008).

As elected officials and as voters, women are more likely than men to hold liberal views and to support the Democratic party. For example, more

Title IX

Title IX ("title nine") of the 1972 Education Act was a landmark piece of civil rights legislation requiring educational institutions that receive federal funding to provide equal opportunities for male and female students in academics, athletics, financial assistance, and resources like student health and housing. Indeed, Title IX is a key reason that girls and women have made such gains in higher education, particularly in sports. In 1971, 294,015 girls participated in high school athletics compared to over 2.7 million girls in 2001—an 847 percent increase (U.S. Department of Education, quoted in Nelson 2002, p. 33), and there are now many more opportunities and facilities at the college level also.

A college must meet one of the following three standards to comply with the law. It must have roughly the same proportion of women among its varsity athletes as it has in its undergraduate student body; it must have a "history and continuing practice" of expanding opportunities for women; or it must demonstrate that it is "fully and effectively accommodating the interests and abilities" of its women students (Suggs 2002). Detractors have argued that increased resources for women have resulted in fewer opportunities for men, and some athletics departments have achieved parity by cutting opportunities for male students rather than increasing those for women. A General Accounting Office report released in March 2001, found a net gain in men's teams from 1982 to 1999, and many more opportunities for men than for women (Nelson 2002). Several Ivy League colleges and state universities have been forced to comply with the law, as women sued them for discrimination.

In March 2005, with no notice given or public input, the Department of Education Office of Civil Rights (OCR) posted a letter to its Web site clarifying the regulations for Title IX compliance. The letter stated that there can be considerable inequality between women's and men's athletic opportunities, and a school can still be in compliance unless there is

1. "unmet interest sufficient to sustain a varsity team in the sport(s)";

2. "sufficient ability to sustain an intercollegiate team in the sport(s)"; and

3. "reasonable expectation of intercollegiate competition for a team in the sport(s) within the school's normal competitive region" (OCR 2005).

This "clarification" does not require schools to look broadly and proactively at whether they are satisfying women's interests in sports. The burden of proof is not on the schools but on students or OCR to show that the institution is discriminating against women.

In March 2005, the U.S. Supreme Court decided that individuals who protest sex discrimination may sue to challenge retaliation if their schools punish them as a result (*Jackson v. Birmingham Board of Education*), a significant re-affirmation of rights provided under Title IX. Moreover, the Court held that for effective enforcement of Title IX, retaliation against those who come forward to report discrimination must be prohibited.

---

women than men support gun control, a national health-care system, government funding for social programs, tougher sentences for perpetrators of sexual assault and domestic violence, and workplace equality as well as issues like women's right to abortion and LGBT rights. This gender gap can be significant in two ways: getting more liberal candidates—women and men—elected and giving greater focus to liberal issues once such candidates are in office (Abzug 1984; Ducat 2004; Gallagher 1993; Norris 1997; Smeal 1984).

By the mid 1990s a growing bipartisan Congressional Women's Caucus served as a focus for women's concerns on Capitol Hill. Janet Reno was appointed as the first woman U.S. attorney general in the nation's history, and Madeleine Albright the first woman secretary of state. Bush administration "firsts" include the appointment of Condoleeza

Rice as the first woman national security adviser, and later Secretary of State. When the 108th Congress convened in January 2003, Nancy Pelosi, the new minority leader of the House, was the first woman to lead either political party and the highest-ranking woman in the history of Congress. She broke new ground for women when she became speaker of the house in 2007. More women also hold high office at the state level, whether as governors, attorneys general, state treasurers, chief educational officers, and so on.

Many women are on committees concerned with health, education, and social services, and they bring their support for women and knowledge of women's experiences to their work. Those in high positions are doubtless constrained by political considerations. In the Clinton administration, Secretary of State Madeleine Albright, for example, was very vocal about women's oppression in Afghanistan, but, following U.S. government policy, she did not push for an end to economic sanctions against Iraq—a step that would have saved the lives of thousands of people, especially women and children.

Political scientist Michele Swers (2001) reviewed data on the effects of women in public office. She found that at the state and national levels women legislators "do bring different policy priorities to the legislative agenda, particularly in the area of women's issues" (also see Carroll 2001). Whether or not elected women can make a significant difference in public policy that is still overwhelmingly dominated by masculinist and corporate interests is an open question. There are still too few women in elected office to know whether women can change national level policy and legislation significantly in favor of women.

In the second half of the nineteenth century, the activism of women, and their male allies, succeeded in winning the vote for all U.S. women in 1920, and the strength of women's organizing in the 1970s and 1980s made it possible for increasing numbers of women to become elected officials. Nevertheless, current public policy and budget priorities, together with a worsening economy, are having disastrous effects on women. Restrictions on the availability of welfare, the erosion of *Roe v. Wade* and affirmative action policies, major tax cuts for the richest citizens, and enormous military spending have all taken resources away from women. Women's organizations and elected officials who seek to improve women's lives currently face a

hard road ahead, where a hallmark of success will be holding on to previous gains. This will require strategic thinking, clear focus, hard work, and acts of personal courage, such as that of Congresswoman Barbara Lee, who voted against authorizing military force in response to the attacks of September 11, in a historic 420–1 House vote on September 14, 2001.

In the 2008 election cycle, voters endorsed a change in the White House and the U.S. Congress, with the election of Barack Obama and an increased majority for Democrats in both the House and Senate. Earlier in 2008, a group of influential feminist leaders met informally to discuss the facile and divisive media characterization of the contest for the Democratic presidential nomination between Senators Barack Obama and Hillary Rodham Clinton (Reading 70). These veteran organizers and scholars were united in their concern regarding the "race-gender split" that dominated much mainstream theorizing and reporting of this historically unprecedented campaign. They referred to splits along race lines during nineteenth-century suffrage campaigns when some white feminists refused to support Black men's right to vote before women—including white upper-class, educated women—gained this right. Remembering this history, these feminists argued that it had generated "racial resentment and rift that weakened feminism throughout much of the twentieth century," as we noted in Chapter 1. Regardless of the election outcome, they argued, it would be vital to continue to work in coalition across lines of race and class on bedrock feminist concerns such as discrimination, domestic violence, the disruptions of war, human trafficking, child poverty, and the effects of a worsening national economy.

Building Alliances for the Twenty-First Century

The many inequalities among women, mentioned throughout this book, often separate us and make it difficult to work together effectively. Those with power over us know this and often exploit differences to pit one group against another. Progressive social change is a slow process that needs sustained action over the long haul. Effective alliances are necessary for long-term efforts, as well as coalition work where the important thing is to stand together on a specific issue regardless of other differences. Alliances across lines of difference are both a means and an end. They provide both the process for moving toward, and some experience of, multicultural society. Melanie Kaye/Kantrowitz (Reading 14) and Ann Filemyr (Reading 37) offer insights for alliance building, especially across lines of race and class.

Some Principles for Alliance Building

Alliances may be personal, campus-wide, city-wide, national, or transnational in scope. Regardless of scale, some basic principles of alliance building include the following points:

- Know who you are, what is important to you, what are your non-negotiables. Know your strengths and what you bring to a shared venture.

- Decide whether you want to be allies with a particular person or group. What are their values? What are they interested in doing in terms of creating social change? Are they open to the alliance? What is the purpose for coming together? Are you coming together as equals? In solidarity with another group?

- Check out the person or the group as the acquaintance grows. Are they who they say they are? Do you have reason to trust them to be there for you? Judge them by their track records and what actually happens, not by your fears, hopes, or expectations based on previous experiences.

- Commit yourself to communicate. Listen, talk, and listen more. Be committed to the process of communication rather than attached to a specific position. Communication may be through conversations, reading, films, events and meetings, or learning about one another's communities. Work together on projects and support one another's projects. Go into one another's settings as participants, observers, guests. All these activities are part of learning to understand in the sense of folding this knowledge into our own moral frameworks as Alan Rosenberg (1988) argued (see Chapter 2).

- Share your history. Talk about what has happened to you and to the people of your group.

- Be patient. Wanting to understand, to hear more, to stay connected requires patience from the inside. Allow one another room to explore ideas, make mistakes, be tentative. Hold judgment until you understand what's going on.

- Honesty is most important. Be authentic and ask for authenticity from others. If this is not possible, what is the alliance worth?

- Keep the process "clean." Call one another on bad things if they happen—preferably with grace, teasing maybe, firmly but gently, so that the other person does not lose face. Don't try to disentangle difficulties when it is impossible to do so meaningfully, but don't use externals (too late, too tired, too busy, too many other items on the agenda) to avoid this.

- Be open to being called on your own mistakes, admitting when you're wrong, even if it is embarrassing or makes you feel vulnerable. Tell the other person when his or her opinions and experiences give you new insights and help you to see things differently.

- Do some people in the group take up a lot of time talking about their own concerns? Are they aware of it? How does privilege based on gender, race, class, nation, sexuality, disability, age, culture, or language play out in this relationship or alliance? Can you talk about it openly?

- What is the "culture" of your group or alliance? What kinds of meetings do you have? What is your decision-making style? If you eat together, what kind of food do you serve? What kind of music do you listen to? Where do you meet? What do you do when you are together? Does everyone in the group feel comfortable with these cultural aspects?

- Work out the boundaries of your responsibilities to one another. What do you want to do for yourself? What do you need others to help with? When? How?

- Look for the common ground. What are the perspectives, experiences, and insights we share?

Overcoming Impediments to Effective Alliances

Many sincere and committed attempts at building alliances have been thwarted, despite the best of intentions. Be aware of several common impediments to creating effective alliances, including the following beliefs and behaviors, which apply at meso, macro, and global levels of interaction and analysis.

Internalized Oppression   This is a learned mindset of subservience and inferiority in oppressed peoples. It includes the acceptance of labels, characteristics, prejudices, and perceptions promoted by the dominant society. Specific behaviors include self-hatred and dislike, disrespect for, and hatred of others of the same group.

Internalized Domination   This is a mind-set of entitlement and superiority among members of dominant groups. Always speaking first in group discussions, being unconscious of the large amount of physical and social space one takes up, and automatically assuming leadership roles are some manifestations of internalized domination.

Operating from a Politics of Scarcity   This results from a deeply held, sometimes unconscious, belief that there is not enough of anything—material things as well as nonmaterial things like power, positive regard, popularity, friendship, time—and, more important, that however much there is, it will not be shared equally. In this view, inequality is simply a given that cannot be changed. It also justifies individualism and competition.

Subscribing to a Hierarchy of Oppression   This involves the placement of one oppressed group in relation to another so that one group's experiences of discrimination, prejudice, and disadvantage are deemed to be worse or better than another's.

Not Knowing One Another's History   Ignorance about other persons' backgrounds often results in drawing incorrect conclusions about their experiences. This prevents us from recognizing the complexity of women's experiences and can hide the ways our experiences are both different and similar.

Transnational Women's Organizing

Alliances have been central to women's movements in the United States and around the world, as mentioned by Peggy Antrobus (Reading 74). Several readings in this collection focus on transnational feminist efforts, such as the International Community of Women Living with HIV/AIDS (Reading 29), Mobility International USA (Reading 72), and Sixteen Days of Activism Against Gender Violence, November 25–December 10, initiated by Center for Women's Global Leadership (Chapter 6).

Historian Bonnie Anderson (2000) examined international connections among feminists from Britain, France, Germany, Italy, Sweden, and the United States in the mid-nineteenth century. Her research findings astonished her because she had assumed that international alliances first developed in the twentieth century with the aid of phones, faxes, e-mail, and air travel. She found that in the nineteenth century, women shared tactics and ideas through letters, personal visits, and by reading published writings. Anderson argued that these early feminists relied upon each other for support, inspiration, and practical help and that feminist organizing in these countries "occurred within the matrix of a feminism which transcended national boundaries." Nowadays feminist work across national boundaries, facilitated by e-mail and air travel, involves many coordinated campaigns and activities.

Conferences under the auspices of the United Nations have provided one avenue for international networking, consolidating shared understandings and solidarity as argued by Peggy Antrobus (Reading 74). Although the world headquarters of the United Nations is in New York City, it is a long way from most people's awareness in the United States. Many women's groups and organizations around the world, particularly outside the U.S., have come to see the U.N. as a potential ally in their struggles for women's rights and have been using its various instruments as catalysts and tools for improving the conditions women face. Perhaps one of the most widely known is CEDAW (Convention on the Elimination of All Forms of Discrimination against Women). Since its adoption by the U.N. General Assembly in 1979, CEDAW has been used to pressure individual countries to implement laws, policies, and services to advance women's economic, political, and social status in that society. Other examples of U.N. conventions include: the International Covenant on Economic, Social, and Cultural Rights; the Convention on Rights of the Child; and the Framework Convention on Climate Change, of which the Kyoto Protocol is well known. Women's NGOs from western Europe and the United States are active in seeking to introduce an awareness of gender into U.N. work on climate change (see Reading 67).

In September 1995, more than thirty thousand women from virtually every country in the world gathered in Huairou, China, to discuss the many issues and problems faced by women and girls. This was an NGO forum with nearly five thousand workshops listed in the schedule and the largest meeting of women in history. A two-hour bus ride away at the official U.N. Fourth World Conference on Women in Beijing, some five thousand delegates discussed what their governments were doing to improve women's lives, and they negotiated an official U.N. document, the *Platform for Action.* The U.N. Fourth World Conference was the culmination of over twenty years of meetings, proposals, position papers, and discussions by women activists, government delegates to the U.N., and U.N. staff, starting with International Women's Year in 1975. The U.N. Security Council Resolution 1325 on Women, Peace, and Security was adopted in 2000 and grew out of the Beijing *Platform for Action.* This was the first time the Security Council addressed the disproportionate impact of armed conflict on women. It recognized the undervalued contributions that women make to conflict prevention, conflict resolution, and peace building and stressed the importance of women's equal and full participation as active agents in peace and security. Although not binding on governments, Resolution 1325 set a new standard of inclusiveness and gender sensitivity in peace negotiations and provides leverage for women's efforts to influence policy in post-conflict reconstruction (Reading 73: Lynes and Torry 2005).

Individual governments must ratify United Nations conventions and resolutions for them to become accepted as national law and policy. Even if governments do not ratify them—and the U.S. has not ratified several U.N. conventions—they are still useful for activists in their attempts to hold governments accountable and to show what others have pledged to do for women and girls. Speaking of the *Platform for Action,* Nobel laureate Wangari Maathai, coordinator of Kenyan Women's Green Belt, commented:

> It's very hard to push governments on issues that affect all aspects of society, let alone those that affect women. But the U.N. document has given us a tool with which to work. Now it's up to the women to push their issues into the boardrooms where political and economic decisions are made by those who did not. . . come to Beijing. *(Quoted in Morgan 1996, p. 18)*

Major changes in international laws and standards with regard to women's lives include: defining violence against women as a violation of women's human rights, defining rape committed in war as a war crime, and recognizing women's vulnerability in armed conflicts and women's right to participate in peace negotiations and post-conflict activities, as mentioned earlier.

In March 2005, the U.N. Commission on the Status of Women affirmed the Beijing *Platform for Action,* adopted at the Fourth U.N. World Conference on Women held ten years earlier. Delegates reported on the progress—or in many cases, the lack of progress—governments have made to create opportunities for women and to safeguard their health, well-being, and overall security. In contrast to the congratulatory reports of many governments, the New York–based Women's Environment and Development Organization published a scathing report concluding that, in the main, "governments have failed to turn the platform into action, and that, despite well-meaning intentions, many women in all regions are actually worse off than they were ten years ago" (Lederer 2005; WEDO 2005).

Although activists from many countries are engaged in these kinds of international efforts, they do so recognizing the constraints and problems associated with them. There is widespread recognition that the U.N. and its Universal Declaration of Human Rights were established in a specific political, economic, and social context just after World War II. The U.N. framework focuses on relationships among nation-states and assumes equality among nations, which is not current reality. The General Assembly, comprising all 192 member countries, is the chief deliberative, policy-making, and representative organ of the United Nations, but the Security Council is the center of power. Its membership consists of five permanent members and ten other members who serve according to a two-year rotation. The permanent members are China, France, the Russian Federation, the United Kingdom, and the United States, with the U.S. dominating this body since the beginning.

U.N. Millennium Development Goals

The United Nations articulated eight Millennium Development Goals to be achieved by 2015 that respond to the world's main development challenges. These goals were drawn from actions and targets contained in the Millennium Declaration adopted by 189 nations and signed by 147 heads of government during the U.N. Millennium Summit in September 2000. The Millennium Development Goals exemplify the constructive nature of United Nations' efforts that oppose global trends. They generate an alternative discourse that is hopeful and human centered.

- Goal 1: Eradicate extreme poverty and hunger

- Goal 2: Achieve universal primary education
- Goal 3: Promote gender equality and empower women
- Goal 4: Reduce child mortality
- Goal 5: Improve maternal health
- Goal 6: Combat HIV/AIDS, malaria, and other diseases
- Goal 7: Ensure environmental sustainability
- Goal 8: Develop a Global Partnership for Development

Source: United Nations, http://www.undp.org/mdg/basics.shtml

The vision for the United Nations came out of a liberal framework, explored in Chapter 2, and our discussion of cultural relativism in that chapter is pertinent to working with U.N. standards. There is a tension between the notion of the universality of human rights standards and cultural specificities, especially given the inequalities that exist among and within nations. Some activists and commentators have asked: Is it meaningful to talk of universal human rights and universal women's rights? How can specific cultural values and norms be respected and women protected in cases where those values and practices violate their rights and dignity? Who decides?

Chandra Talpade Mohanty (2003) critiques transnational organizing efforts that reproduce parallel inequalities that define relations between rich and poor nations. As mentioned in Chapter 2, Mohanty embraces transnational multicultural feminism, by which she means a theory and practice that is "noncolonized," and anchored in equality and respect. This would avoid false universalisms and involve ethical and caring dialogue across differences, divisions, and conflicts. From very different social locations, women would define "common contexts of struggle." These are laudable goals. They require good intentions, knowledge, and awareness as well as determination, creativity, trust, and considerable patience to tackle, let alone sur-

mount, structural inequalities between women from richer and poorer nations. These inequalities include the fact that most women do not have reliable Internet access; interpretation and translation services are necessary to include women who do not speak a common language; there are disparities in fundraising opportunities; the unequal purchasing power of national currencies is problematic; difficulties of travel must be solved, including the need for women to take time away from home and work responsibilities; women from poorer countries face difficulty securing visas to travel to meetings in the global North; organizational styles and cultures vary greatly; and last, but certainly not least, differences in political perspectives abound. Similar inequalities exist in working across class and race lines within nations.

Providing services to women in the United States and reforming existing institutions to make them more responsive to those who are excluded are crucially important in the overall work of progressive social change and have made a difference to generations of women. The challenge for the future is to continue to expand this work. Given the many insecurities of life for women and for men, and the growing threat to the planet itself from increasing industrialization, militarization, and ecological devastation, what sense does it make for women to seek an equal piece of what ecofeminist activist and writer Ynestra King (1993b, p. 76) has called this "rotten and carcinogenic" pie?

Women's movements are shared endeavors. There are many overlapping movements constructed around issues and identities, with links to other progressive movements such as the antiglobalization movement and the antimilitarist movement. Given that corporations control more and more of the world and that women's rights are under serious attack in this country, we need to work together to address interconnected issues: economic survival, reproductive rights, all forms of violence including state violence, criminalization and incarceration, immigrant rights, and so on, as argued by Labaton and Martin (2004). These vibrant, broadbased efforts draw on our creativity, our emotions, our spirituality, and our sense of justice, strengthening connections between people and communities. There is great accumulated experience and insight about how to work on multi-issue politics, and also much to learn. Grace Lee Boggs, a long-time activist in Detroit, noted that this is both an exciting and a daunting time in human history. She urged: "For our own well-being, for the health and safety of our communities, our cities and our country, we need to accept the awesome responsibility of creating new ways of . . . living" (1994, p. 2).

This book is about U.S. women's lives and the kind of world we need to create for women's empowerment, development, and well-being. This world will be based on notions of genuine security and sustainability. The project of human development—for both women and men—is one that has been in process for a very long time. It is our challenge to take the next steps in this process. How can we settle for anything less?

Activism is not issue-specific
It's a moral posture that, steady state, propels you
*   forward, from one hard hour to the next.*
Believing that you can do something to make things
*   better, you do*
Something, rather than nothing.
You assume responsibility for the privilege of your
*   abilities.*
You do whatever you can.
You reach beyond yourself in your imagination, and
*   in your wish for*
Understanding, and for change.
You admit the limitations of individual perspectives.
You trust somebody else.
You do not turn away.   *(June Jordan)*

Questions for Reflection

As you read and discuss this chapter, think about these questions:

1. What are your assumptions about how people and societies change? What do you think needs changing, if anything? How is knowledge related to social change?

2. Have you ever been involved in a social-action project or electoral politics? What was your experience like? If you have not, why not?

3. Have you tried to establish and maintain an ongoing relationship, friendship, or working partnership with someone from a background very different from your own? What happened? What did you learn from that experience? What would you do differently another time, if anything?

4. If you have had such a relationship, why did you become involved in the first place? Was this a good enough reason? Why or why not? If you never have, why not?

5. What do you know about the history of the various groups you are a member of? What do you know about groups that are not your own? How does knowing this history help, and how does not knowing it hinder you in making alliances across lines of difference? How can you learn what you don't know?

6. What is your vision of a secure and sustainable personal relationship? Community? Society? World?

7. Assuming you had time, energy, resources, and support, what kind of an organization would you create to work for changes in women's lives, and why do you think it would be effective?

Finding Out More on the Web

1. Research the work of women's organizations cited in this chapter. What are their strategies and visions? Who do they speak to? These are additional resources:

Guerilla Girls, a group of women intent on exposing patterns of sexism, racism, and censorship in the art world: www.guerillagirls.com

African Women's Development and Communication Network: www.femnet.or.ke

Articulacion Feminista Marcosur: www.mujeresdelsur.org.uy

International Community of Women Living with HIV/AIDS: www.icw.org

Isis International-Manila: www.isiswomen.org

Public Leadership Education Network (PLEN): www.plen.org

Women Against Violence Europe: www.wave-network.org/start.asp?ID=22650

Working Group on Girls: www.girlsrights.org

Women Living Under Muslim Laws: www.wluml.org/english/index.shtml

Taking Action

1. List all the ways you are an activist. Review the suggestions for taking action at the end of each chapter. Commit yourself to continuing to involve yourself in issues that matter to you.

2. Think about how aspects of your identity can help you to make alliances with others. Support campus or community groups that are working together on an issue of shared concern.

3. Where do your elected officials (at the city, state, and national levels) stand on issues that matter to you? What is their voting record on these issues? Write to thank them for supporting issues you care about (if they do), or urge them to change their positions. Present them with information from your course materials or other sources to make a strong case.

4. Many of the issues discussed in this book have implications at the global level. What can you do that will have an impact at that level?

SIXTY-EIGHT

The Body Politic (1995)

Abra Fortune Chernik

> **Abra Fortune Chernik** is a writer who speaks frequently about eating disorders in schools and to women's organizations. She has optioned her first screenplay, *Portrait of an Invisible Girl.*

My body possesses solidness and curve, like the ocean. My weight mingles with Earth's pull, drawing me onto the sand. I have not always sent waves into the world. I flew off once, for five years, and swirled madly like a cracking brown leaf in the salty autumn wind. I wafted, dried out, apathetic.

I had no weight in the world during my years of anorexia. Curled up inside my thinness, a refugee in a cocoon of hunger, I lost the capacity to care about myself or others. I starved my body and twitched in place as those around me danced in the energy of shared existence and progressed in their lives. When I graduated from college crowned with academic honors, professors praised my potential. I wanted only to vanish.

It took three months of hospitalization and two years of outpatient psychotherapy for me to learn to nourish myself and to live in a body that expresses strength and honesty in its shape. I accepted my right and my obligation to take up room with my figure, voice and spirit. I remembered how to tumble forward and touch the world that holds me. I chose the ocean as my guide.

Who disputes the ocean's fullness?

Growing up in New York City, I did not care about the feminist movement. Although I attended an all-girls high school, we read mostly male authors and studied the history of men. Embracing mainstream culture without question, I learned about womanhood from fashion magazines, Madison Avenue and Hollywood. I dismissed feminist alternatives as foreign and offensive, swathed as they were in stereotypes that threatened my adolescent need for conformity.

Puberty hit late; I did not complain. I enjoyed living in the lanky body of a tall child and insisted on the title of "girl." If anyone referred to me as a "young woman," I would cry out, horrified, "Do not call me the *W* word!" But at sixteen years old, I could no longer deny my fate. My stomach and breasts rounded. Curly black hair sprouted in the most embarrassing places. Hips swelled from a once-flat plane. Interpreting maturation as an unacceptable lapse into fleshiness, I resolved to eradicate the physical symptoms of my impending womanhood.

Magazine articles, television commercials, lunchroom conversation, gymnastics coaches and write-ups on models had saturated me with diet savvy. Once I decided to lose weight, I quickly turned expert. I dropped hot chocolate from my regular breakfast order at the Skyline Diner. I replaced lunches of peanut butter and Marshmallow Fluff sandwiches with small platters of cottage cheese and cantaloupe. I eliminated dinner altogether and blunted my appetite with Tab, Camel Lights, and Carefree bubble gum. When furious craving overwhelmed my resolve and I swallowed an extra something, I would flee to the nearest bathroom to purge my mistake.

Within three months, I had returned my body to its preadolescent proportions and had manipulated my monthly period into drying up. Over the next five years, I devoted my life to losing my weight. I came to resent the body in which I lived, the body that threatened to develop, the body whose hunger I despised but could not extinguish. If I neglected a workout or added a pound or ate a bite too many, I would stare in the mirror and drown myself in a tidal wave of criticism. Hatred of my body generalized to hatred of myself as a person, and self-referential labels such as "pig," "failure" and "glutton" allowed me to believe that I deserved punishment. My self-hatred became fuel for the self-mutilating behaviors of the eating disorder.

As my body shrank, so did my world. I starved away my power and vision, my energy and inclinations. Obsessed with dieting, I allowed relationships, passions and identity to wither. I pulled back from the world, off of the beach, out of the sand. The waves of my existence ceased to roll beyond the inside of my skin.

And society applauded my shrinking. Pound after pound the applause continued, like the pounding ocean outside the door of my beach house.

The word "anorexia" literally means "loss of appetite." But as an anorexic, I felt hunger thrashing inside my body. I denied my appetite, ignored it, but never lost it. Sometimes the pangs twisted so sharply, I feared they would consume the meat of my heart. On desperate nights I rose in a flannel nightgown and allowed myself to eat an unplanned something.

No matter how much I ate, I could not soothe the pangs. Standing in the kitchen at midnight, spotlighted by the blue-white light of the open refrigerator, I would frantically feed my neglected appetite: the Chinese food I had not touched at dinner; ice cream and whipped cream; microwaved bread; cereal and chocolate milk; doughnuts and bananas. Then, solid sadness inside my gut, swelling agitation, a too-big meal I would not digest. In the bathroom I would rip off my shirt, tie up my hair, and prepare to execute the desperate ritual, again. I would ram the back of my throat with a toothbrush handle, crying, impatient, until the food rushed up. I would vomit until the toilet filled and I emptied, until I forgave myself, until I felt ready to try my life again. Standing up from my position over the toilet, wiping my mouth, I would believe that I was safe. Looking in the mirror through puffy eyes in a tumescent face, I would promise to take care of myself. Kept awake by the fast, confused beating of my heart and the ache in my chest, I would swear I did not miss the world outside. Lost within myself, I almost died.

By the time I entered the hospital, a mess of protruding bones defined my body, and the bones of my emaciated life rattled me crazy. I carried a pillow around because it hurt to sit down, and I shivered with cold in sultry July. Clumps of brittle hair clogged the drain when I showered, and blackened eyes appeared to sink into my head. My vision of reality wrinkled and my disposition turned mercurial as I slipped into starvation psychosis, a condition associated with severe malnutrition. People told me that I resembled a concentration camp prisoner, a chemotherapy patient, a famine victim or a fashion model.

In the hospital, I examined my eating disorder under the lenses of various therapies. I dissected my childhood, my family structure, my intimate relationships, my belief systems. I participated in experiential therapies of movement, art and psychodrama. I learned to use words instead of eating patterns to communicate my feelings. And still I refused to gain more than a minimal amount of weight.

I felt powerful as an anorexic. Controlling my body yielded an illusion of control over my life; I received incessant praise for my figure despite my sickly mien, and my frailty manipulated family and friends into protecting me from conflict. I had reduced my world to a plate of steamed carrots, and over this tiny kingdom I proudly crowned myself queen.

I sat cross-legged on my hospital bed for nearly two months before I earned an afternoon pass to go to the mall with my mother. The privilege came just in time; I felt unbearably large and desperately wanted a new outfit under which to hide gained weight. At the mall, I searched for two hours before finally discovering, in the maternity section at Macy's, a shirt large enough to cover what I perceived as my enormous body.

With an hour left on my pass, I spotted a sign on a shop window: "Body Fat Testing, $3.00." I suggested to my mother that we split up for ten minutes; she headed to Barnes & Noble, and I snuck into the fitness store.

I sat down in front of a machine hooked up to a computer, and a burly young body builder fired questions at me:

"Age?"

"Twenty-one."

"Height?"

"Five nine."

"Weight?"

"Ninety-nine."

The young man punched my statistics into his keyboard and pinched my arm with clippers wired to the testing machine. In a moment, the computer spit out my results. "Only ten percent body fat! Unbelievably healthy. The average for a woman your age is twenty-five percent. Fantastic! You're this week's blue ribbon winner."

I stared at him in disbelief. *Winner? Healthy? Fantastic?* I glanced around at the other customers in the store, some of whom had congregated to watch my testing, and I felt embarrassed by his praise. And then I felt furious. Furious at this man and at the society that programmed him for their ignorant approbation of my illness and my suffering.

"I am dying of anorexia," I whispered. "Don't congratulate me."

I spent my remaining month in the hospital supplementing psychotherapy with an independent examination of eating disorders from a social and political point of view. I needed to understand why society would reward my starvation and encourage my vanishing. In the bathroom, a mirror on the open door behind me reflected my backside in a mirror over the sink. Vertebrae poked at my skin, ribs hung like wings over chiseled hip bones, the two sides of my buttocks did not touch. I had not seen this view of myself before.

In writing, I recorded instances in which my eating disorder had tangled the progress of my life and thwarted my relationships. I filled three and a half Mead marble notebooks. Five years' worth of: *I wouldn't sit with Daddy when he was alone in the hospital because I needed to go jogging; I told Derek not to visit me because I couldn't throw up when he was there; I almost failed my comprehensive exams because I was so hungry; I spent my year at Oxford with my head in the toilet bowl; I wouldn't eat the dinner my friends cooked me for my nineteenth birthday because I knew they had used oil in the recipe; I told my family not to come to my college graduation because I didn't want to miss a day at the gym or have to eat a restaurant meal.* And on and on for hundreds of pages.

This honest account of my life dissolved the illusion of anorexic power. I saw myself naked in the truth of my pain, my loneliness, my obsessions, my craziness, my selfishness, my defeat. I also recognized the social and political implications of consuming myself with the trivialities of calories and weight. At college, I had watched as classmates involved themselves in extracurricular clubs, volunteer work, politics and applications for jobs and graduate schools. Obsessed with exercising and exhausted by starvation, I did not even consider joining in such pursuits. Despite my love of writing and painting and literature, despite ranking at the top of my class, I wanted only to teach aerobics. Despite my adolescent days as a loud-mouthed,

rambunctious class leader, I had grown into a silent, hungry young woman.

And society preferred me this way: hungry, fragile, crazy. *Winner! Healthy! Fantastic!* I began reading feminist literature to further understand the disempowerment of women in our culture. I digested the connection between a nation of starving, self-obsessed women and the continued success of the patriarchy. I also cultivated an awareness of alternative models of womanhood. In the stillness of the hospital library, new voices in my life rose from printed pages to echo my rage and provide the conception of my feminist consciousness.

I had been willing to accept self-sabotage, but now I refused to sacrifice myself to a society that profited from my pain. I finally understood that my eating disorder symbolized more than "personal psychodynamic trauma." Gazing in the mirror at my emaciated body, I observed a woman held up by her culture as the physical ideal because she was starving, self-obsessed and powerless, a woman called beautiful because she threatened no one except herself. Despite my intelligence, my education, and my supposed Manhattan sophistication, I had believed all of the lies; I had almost given my life in order to achieve the sickly impotence that this culture aggressively links with female happiness, love and success. And everything I had to offer to the world, every tumbling wave, every thought and every passion, nearly died inside me.

As long as society resists female power, fashion will call healthy women physically flawed. As long as society accepts the physical, sexual and economic abuse of women, popular culture will prefer women who resemble little girls. Sitting in the hospital the summer after my college graduation, I grasped the absurdity of a nation of adult women dying to grow small.

Armed with this insight, I loosened the grip of the starvation disease on my body. I determined to re-create myself based on an image of a woman warrior. I remembered my ocean, and I took my first bite.

Gaining weight and getting my head out of the toilet bowl was the most political act I have ever committed.

I left the hospital and returned home to Fire Island. Living at the shore in those wintry days of my new life, I wrapped myself in feminism as I hunted seashells and role models. I wanted to feel proud of my womanhood. I longed to accept and honor my body's fullness.

During the process of my healing, I had hoped that I would be able to skip the memory of anorexia like a cold pebble into the dark winter sea. I had dreamed that in relinquishing my obsessive chase after a smaller body, I would be able to come home to rejoin those whom I had left in order to starve, rejoin them to live together as healthy, powerful women. But as my body has grown full, I have sensed a hollowness in the lives of women all around me that I had not noticed when I myself stood hollow. I have made it home only to find myself alone.

Out in the world again, I hear the furious thumping dance of body hatred echoing every place I go. Friends who once appeared wonderfully carefree in ordering late-night french fries turn out not to eat breakfast or lunch. Smart, talented, creative women talk about dieting and overeating and hating the beach because they look terrible in bathing suits. Famous women give interviews insulting their bodies and bragging about bicycling twenty-four miles the day they gave birth.

I had looked forward to rejoining society after my years of anorexic exile. Ironically, in order to preserve my health, my recovery has included the development of a consciousness that actively challenges the images and ideas that define this culture. Walking down Madison Avenue and passing emaciated women, I say to myself, *those women are sick.* When smacked with a diet commercial, I remind myself, *I don't do that anymòre.* I decline invitations to movies that feature anorexic actors, I will not participate in discussions about dieting, and I refuse to shop in stores that cater to women with eating-disordered figures.

Though I am critical of diet culture, I find it nearly impossible to escape. Eating disorders have woven their way into the fabric of my society. On television, in print, on food packaging, in casual conversation and in windows of clothing stores populated by ridiculously gaunt mannequins, messages to lose my weight and control my appetite challenge my recovered fullness. Finally at home in my body, I recognize myself as an island in a sea of eating disorder, a sea populated predominantly by young women.

A perversion of nature by society has resulted in a phenomenon whereby women feel safer when starving than when eating. Losing our weight boosts self-esteem, while nourishing our bodies evokes feelings of self-doubt and self-loathing.

When our bodies take up more space than a size eight (as most of our bodies do), we say, *too big.* When our appetites demand more than a Lean Cuisine, we say, *too much.* When we want a piece of a friend's birthday cake, we say, *too bad.* Don't eat too much, don't talk too loudly, don't take up too much space, don't take from the world. Be pleasant or crazy, but don't seem hungry. Remember, a new study shows that men prefer women who eat salad for dinner over women who eat burgers and fries.

So we keep on shrinking, starving away our wildness, our power, our truth.

Hiding our curves under long T-shirts at the beach, sitting silently and fidgeting while others eat dessert, sneaking back into the kitchen late at night to binge and hating ourselves the next day, skipping breakfast, existing on diet soda and cigarettes, adding up calories and subtracting everything else. We accept what is horribly wrong in our lives and fight what is beautiful and right.

Over the past three years, feminism has taught me to honor the fullness of my womanhood and the solidness of the body that hosts my life. In feminist circles I have found mentors, strong women who live with power, passion and purpose. And yet, even in groups of feminists, my love and acceptance of my body remains unusual.

Eating disorders affect us all on both a personal and a political level. The majority of my peers—including my feminist peers—still measure their beauty against anorexic ideals. Even among feminists, body hatred and chronic dieting continue to consume lives. Friends of anorexics beg them to please start eating; then these friends go home and continue their own diets. Who can deny that the millions of young women caught in the net of disordered eating will frustrate the potential of the next wave of feminism?

Sometimes my empathy dissolves into frustration and rage at our situation. For the first time in history, young women have the opportunity to create a world in our image. But many of us concentrate instead on re-creating the shape of our thighs.

As young feminists, we must place unconditional acceptance of our bodies at the top of our political agenda. We must claim our bodies as our own to love and honor in their infinite shapes and sizes. Fat, thin, soft, hard, puckered, smooth, our bodies are our homes. By nourishing our bodies, we care for and love ourselves on the most basic level. When we deny ourselves physical food, we go hungry emotionally, psychologically, spiritually and politically. We must challenge ourselves to eat and digest, and allow society to call us too big. We will understand their message to mean too powerful.

Time goes by quickly. One day we will blink and open our eyes as old women. If we spend all our energy keeping our bodies small, what will we have to show for our lives when we reach the end? I hope we have more than a group of fashionably skinny figures.

SIXTY-NINE

◆◆◆

Staging Activism: New York City Performing Artists as Cultural Workers (2008)

Amy Jo Goddard

Amy Jo Goddard is a writer, playwright, filmmaker, performing and visual artist, and professional sexuality educator and trainer. She teaches about sexuality in schools, community-based organizations, and colleges and is an advocate for comprehensive sexuality education. She co-authored *Lesbian Sex Secrets for Men*; directed the documentary film, *At Your Cervix*; and wrote and hosted a women's sexuality program *Fresh Advice* on Pseudo.com's women's sexuality site CherryBomb.

To examine the impact of artists and cultural workers who are influencing social change, I might start by asking: What if as a middle-class, queer, white girl growing up in the United States, I had learned about the fluid and transformational nature of gender through creative, mind-provoking male cross-dressing performances? What if I had seen a Caribbean cultural activist talk to an audience about current events I never heard about on the 6:00 nightly news? What if I saw an out Argentine butch lesbian play a male monarch, commenting on social class, religion, and homophobia? How would my world have been shaped differently had I been exposed to performing artists such as Diyaa MilDred Gerestant, Imani Henry, and Susana Cook, whose performances and activism establish them as cultural workers?

Imani Henry, Susana Cook, and Diyaa MilDred Gerestant are performing artists based in New York City that produce original work addressing cultural themes related to sexual, gender, ethnic, and class identities. These three artists have been strongholds in many of New York City's alternative performance spaces, such as The Kitchen, La Mama, WOW Café Theater, Brooklyn Arts Exchange, and Dixon Place, to name a few. In these spaces, audiences can anticipate thought-provoking work that often challenges established theater norms. Audiences comprised of social activists, gender and sexual minorities, outsiders, and people with low or fixed income are, unsurprisingly, drawn to the work of these artists since it reflects their worlds. These worlds are different from the typical upwardly mobile status quo that many mainstream performing arts programs and Broadway theaters highlight in content and/or form. I will consider these three performing artists as activists and cultural workers who persistently create political work in an artistic environment where many cultural institutions and alternative arts spaces struggle to keep their leases and maintain low ticket prices.

The work of each artist/performer reveals their mulitiplicitous identities and explores and gives voice to racial, national, class, gender, and sexual identities that are not the dominant norm in the U.S. Such intersections of multiple identities make their bodies of work unique and allow audience members who share those identities to see images of themselves that rarely get front and center stage. Moreover, the artists' positions as cultural workers allow them to bridge activist movements and communities that might not otherwise form alliances. Besides the creative work itself, their activism extends to the creative processes in their work, touring with their work, as well as other aspects of their lives.

Susana Cook, a self-avowed butch lesbian from Argentina, celebrates butch/femme lesbian identities and exposes class structures that exclude the working class from resources and power. She plays male roles to reveal and dissect the incongruence and instability of masculine identities. Using humor and ironic representation, her performances challenge the status quo. Diyaa MilDred Gerestant, a Haitian-American, queer[1] performing artist, made her name as Drag King Dred. Her sophisticated blend of styles raised the bar of expectation and anticipation for drag king performances. She dons gender from many corners of the spectrum, creating confusion in often unsuspecting audiences who are not keen to drag. Gerestant educates her audiences by elucidating her own potential to unmask gender and has begun to produce full-length plays that explore her own personal transformational path through gender, drag king performance, and spirituality. Imani Henry identifies as a queer, Caribbean, female-to-male transsexual activist and creates characters that express masculine gender identities in his plays, ranging from butch women to playing himself. He does not use gender in a playful way, as Gerestant or other drag kings might, but rather explores real stories through characterization. Henry finds creative ways to bring the attention of his audience members to current real-world situations that demand action. All three produce provocative work that asks audiences to actively engage with the material.

Each artist has consistently inspired me, and I continue to admire and support their work. This led to my desire to speak with them about their perspectives on their work, how it functions as activism, and its place in New York City's downtown queer performance communities. Consider this article an invitation to acquaint yourself with three artists who have provoked my thinking and who may, in turn, challenge you in positive ways. A section on each artist begins with an interview, followed by a discussion section that addresses the intersections of performance, identity, and activism. Themes include how performers work toward social change by using performance as a tool

of visibility and connection to raise consciousness; the participatory process that enhances the activism of performance; risks in exploring personal identities through performance; and self-identifying as a cultural worker, with an exploration of that term as it is used in a contemporary context.

Trans, Butch, and King: The Gender Lens of Three Activist Artists

I conducted face-to-face, in-depth interviews about art and social change with Imani Henry, Susana Cook, and Diyaa MilDred Gerestant, New York City–based performing artists and writers. Each is nationally or internationally known for a distinctive artistic style in work that is seen as a catalyst for social change. As artists with varying levels of outsider status—that is, outside the North American mainstream—their perspectives on the dominant culture and the current state of affairs are valuable to understanding oppression, power, sexuality, and political structures where dominant privilege may be taken for granted. Additionally, all are educated, accomplished mid-career artists, and people of color who identify as queer or lesbian.

Since audience members commit at least an hour to listen to what an artist has to say, performance becomes fertile ground for activating social change. These interviews focus on art and social change through the following questions and expand into territory organically produced in the interview process: How do these artists define themselves? What is the role of the artist who works for social change? How do these artists use their performance to encourage, inspire, or incite activism for social change, and what effects have they observed? Why are sexuality, nationality, gender, class, and race important subject matter? How do working class, communities of color, gay and lesbian, and queer communities intersect? I also draw upon my own experiences as a performance artist in this context.

In 1999, Susana Cook regularly produced and directed shows at the WOW Café Theater. One of the best-established women's theaters in the world, it is collectively run and has ensemble casts of mostly people of color. Cook asked three performers with whom she had not previously worked, Diyaa MilDred Gerestant, Imani Henry, and myself, to perform in a second run of the highly successful play, *Hot Tamale.* I had known Gerestant before as Dred, a preeminent drag king in New York City, and a regular at Club Casanova, the first weekly drag king performance night in the country. Highly regarded as a performer, she was one of the kings who had inspired me to perform male drag myself. Imani Henry, in the midst of his own gender transition, had recently relocated to New York City and was eager to get involved with New York's downtown theater scene. Cook's play facilitated our first meeting.

As a playwright and performer who came out of the spoken word boom of the 1990s, I found drag kinging to be an important bridge between my work with text and work that incorporates the body. "Kinging" is a term Judith Halberstam (1998) uses to describe the performance of masculinity. Drag kings bring masculinity into the theater as a spectacle, particularly through humor, and challenge the idea that male masculinity is unquestionable, authentic, and non-performative. When masculine roles are parodied or disassembled in a drag king performance, the idea that masculinity belongs solely to men is destabilized, and the performance provides, for lesbians in particular, "the rare opportunity to expose the artificiality of all genders and all sexual orientations" (*Ibid.*: 240). The electric nature of spaces such as Club Casanova gave rise to subcultures within the lesbian community, creating more freedom around gender, especially to explore, play with, and make humorous masculine gender expression. This freedom grew not only in performance spaces where drag kings were central and lesbians were the primary audience, but also in terms of greater acceptance of queer masculine gender identities, such as bois and female-to-male transsexuals (transmen or FTMs).[2]

Gender identity is complex. Each artist identifies with gender differently, with each having a relationship to a masculine identity on some level. Diyaa MilDred Gerestant is a drag king and "gender illusionist" who aims to expose the artificiality and illusory nature of gender. Imani Henry identifies as a transman and is strongly connected to the transgender community. Susana Cook identifies as a butch lesbian, an often misunderstood or misrepresented identity. As a butch, she expresses her masculinity and is at the same time comfortable being a woman. As Halberstam (1998) has noted, butch—or what she calls "transgender

butch"—is not a preamble to an FTM identity, but has a rich history within lesbian communities and is its own identity.

Since I am a white woman writing about three people of color with complex identities, throughout this article I am conscious of honoring their voices and words, where possible, over mediation through my own interpretation. Each section on a given artist begins and ends with quotes from the artists to privilege their own words and thoughts about their work. During the article's development, each artist received a copy for feedback, dialogue, and inclusion in the process. The reader should gain a real sense of Henry, Cook, and Gerestant on their own terms. This format was used in an attempt to dismantle the traditional paradigm of a white, privileged researcher who writes about other cultural groups and may inappropriately represent their real experiences through a skewed lens of dominant cultural privilege.

Imani Henry

In the U.S. there needs to be a clear understanding that we are cultural workers—like in Cuba. This is our work and there needs to be health benefits. The "starving artist" thing is so capitalist. It is unbelievably damaging and disrespectful how racist and sexist the oppression of queer folks plays out as artists; how commercial marketability is valued under capitalism over the merit of someone's expression, craft, or point of view.

Imani Henry, a self-defined Caribbean, FTM transsexual activist, writer, and performer, promotes himself as a "cultural worker," knowing the importance of identifying his work as a meaningful societal contribution and, as such, deserving of support and economic compensation. Frustrated with the few and narrow roles that existed for him as an actor, he began to create his own work, knowing well the limitations for a queer actor of color who was often recruited to play thugs, prostitutes, and other stereotypical roles.

Henry made his "home" at the Brooklyn Arts Exchange, where he created and produced three plays during his artist residency from 2002 to 2004. He is a slam poet champion and is often featured as a performance poet or speaker at political rallies and events. Political activism and performance are intrinsically connected in his work. "Art can be a form of resistance under capitalism," he says, noting that when disenfranchised, multinational voices make art, it is an act of resistance because it disrupts and challenges the notion that art can be accessed only by the elite, as stories of people who do not have the same access as those with economic privilege, artistic training, and/or ethnic and gender privilege are told.

Henry expresses his work as an activist through his plays. Two of them actually feature a political demonstration. He brings his multiple personal identities into his work and says, "All of those identities mean something to me. To represent them is a big deal." Asked about the importance of visibility for identities that fall outside the dominant norm, he says that "visibility is everything." When Henry performs butch or other transgender characters, or when he travels and meets people who have never met a trans person, he gives visibility to those identities and the real life experiences that go with them. On and off stage representation allows him to do the thing he values most as "an out radical activist," which is to build coalitions and solidarity, since building solidarity requires working to understand the struggles of others.

B4T (Before Testosterone), Henry's first play, has functioned in this way. He calls it an "ode to butch blackness."

> *A woman looking like a man*
> *looking for a woman*
> *who likes women*
> *who look like men.*
>
> *Now, ain't that some shit?. . .*
>
> *You ask me what it is to be Black, Butch and Lesbian. Words, names, I have never claimed for myself. It was given and now I can only remember before there was words, before there were names, before I could, would, say it out loud. . .*
>
> *I am only telling you because it needs to be said. I am only saying it because it lays too heavy, cuts too deep, runs like water bursting from a dam*
> *(Henry, 2002).*

This passage from *B4T* (2002) speaks to the complex issues around identity: who has the right to name us, the power of words, and how having a word for something can give us comfort, or alternately, disturb us. The act of identifying oneself allows for the development of communities around common experience, and education across lines of difference.

In 1999, Henry began his gender transition, while participating as an activist within the antiwar and Millions for Mumia movements in New York City. The latter developed to support Mumia Abu-Jamal, a journalist accused of killing a police officer in Philadelphia in 1981. Abu-Jamal has since served 22 years as a political prisoner and is currently on death row. Henry, a leader in this movement, says: "People have gone through that [gender] transition process with me inside a larger political movement. I look different. People respected my pronoun changes." One of Henry's great achievements was spearheading Rainbow Flags for Mumia and connecting the struggles of the lesbian/gay/bisexual/transgender/queer (l/g/b/t/q) community with those of political prisoners like Mumia Abu-Jamal. He worked to build solidarity between these two movements and was instrumental in the large l/g/b/t/q turnout for Mumia demonstrations and events. Within these movements, he has seen the transformation of homophobia or transphobia on a personal level, as people have been able to see him as a brother in the struggle. Though he has had many positive experiences, he acknowledges that unlike other transgender individuals, such as transwomen or effeminate men, he has the ability to be more invisible because he more easily "passes" as a man.

Indeed, within a larger movement of people working publicly for change, another level of change happens among activists on an interpersonal level. At an antiracism or anti-police brutality demonstration, as people of color make the connection that queer people are fighting for the same issues, many are forced to think about the connections between racial, gender, and sexual justice. Research has shown that one way homophobia is healed is by knowing someone personally who is gay, lesbian, or bisexual. According to Poynter and Talbot (2006: 276), "personal contact is a significant event in the development as an ally to GLB people." Henry works hard to bridge connections and build coalitions across lines of difference, within his performances and as a cultural worker. Human connection is a fundamental component for coalition building within social justice movements. Henry speaks passionately on this issue:

Social justice and change happens by the living, breathing struggle. You can't learn it in a book. Solidarity is what happens in the streets—you have to work with people. You can do trainings, but what is it to go to an anti-police brutality demonstration? What is it to stand in solidarity with a family whose house has been firebombed by the Klan? You can't learn solidarity any other way.

Henry echoes Bernice Johnson Reagon's (1983) statement that "coalition work is not work done in your home. Coalition work has to be done in the streets." Indeed, many activists enter political movements with high ideals about justice and human rights, but personal growth occurs when we learn to work effectively with people who speak different languages, have different customs, or look different. The difficult work of coalescing with others is the real work, especially in situations where the people involved experience different levels of dominant privilege, and in which privilege and oppression beg to be examined.

During his performances, coalescence happens as Henry intentionally breaks the fourth wall[3]—the accepted barrier between the actors onstage and the audience—exploiting the intimacy of theater and including his audience to the point where he actually makes the audience part of his pieces. In *B4T*, Henry stationed his co-actor in the audience; in his second show, *The Strong Go Crazy,* he created a living room out of the theater and had a TV party where the audience was encouraged to talk back to the television along with him in a group cultural critique, resulting in lines being added to his script that came directly from audience members. After he welcomed everybody and passed out popcorn, he would stand outside the theater, listening:

> people are talking and making their own jokes or comments and just being together. And I love it. People who didn't know each other came for a night of theater, and they're just laughing with each other. I thought it was brilliant—beyond what I've ever seen in theater. People organically became connected to each other and became part of the show.

The structure for audience members encourages and supports connection and coalescence with one another, and to Henry as performer. Some of his characters are fictional and others are based on real people; at times he weaves his own stories into the fibers of his work. Whether audience members attribute those stories to him personally, they experience an intimacy with him onstage that functions as a connecting force.

Henry is a sought-after performer on U.S. college campuses and has seen his work affect thousands of students and university communities. Audience members may not necessarily attend a march for l/g/b/t/q equality or a demonstration against violence toward young people of color, but they will come to see a play. His work functions as activism in myriad ways, reaching students who would never decide to attend his show if it were not for the extra credit offered by professors. Many of his predominantly white, heterosexual, student audience members are compelled to write academic papers about race, gender, and sexual identity after seeing his show. Additionally, various student groups have built coalitions and worked together to raise money to bring Henry to their campus. Student groups on one campus worked for three years to bring Henry's show to their school. Student groups of color collaborated with student groups working around sexual identity. The students were compelled to connect their struggles.

Henry has a class-consciousness that pervades his approach to politics and artistic work. He attests that in a capitalist system, where making money is the primary goal, art that serves other purposes such as raising awareness, creating visibility for noncommercial stories, or activating people is not going to bring in big money. Rather, it becomes a form of resistance. Much of Henry's energy is spent supporting and engaging in such acts of resistance. He states:

> If art is political, it discusses issues meant to be silent. When we create art that is political in any shape or form, or when we as oppressed peoples stand up and talk about our truth or experience—if a woman talks about what it's like to be sexually assaulted or abused, that's political. Capitalism would say "be silent, don't talk about that."

Susana Cook

I am your Hot Tamale baby.
Come sweet señorita, you know you can't resist our
full lips and curvaceous bodies . . .

Let's dance colonizer
I am for civilization and progress
I am your colonized stereotype of the
    Latino-macho-catholic fatalism
I am an insatiable sex machine. . . . Market me baby
I love you my democratic enlightened post-modern
    one
on the basis of this confrontation with this exotic
    other
I am your significant other. . . . Do you want to
    know what I signify?
Do you want to taste my exotic Passion. . . . with
    beans. . . .
Chew my uncivilized, primitive, barbarian second-
    class identity, while I drink your bold superior
    fully shaped identity of the one. . . .
Let's walk half naked under the sun eating tortilla
    and mango
I was recently brought into civilization
I could never fully overcome the fact of carrying
    primitiveness in my blood
I arrived late to the capitalist fiesta. . . but I run
I am your Speedy Gonzales baby
I am your bandit. . . your papi chulo
Sit back, look pretty and let the immigrant do the
    work (Cook, 1999)

In this classic Susana Cook opening monologue, all of the Argentine, butch, lesbian, New York City–based performing artist's signature elements are there: seducing the audience through clever poetics, using shameless humor that forces the audience into an uncomfortable place of self-reflection, pointedly poking fun at U.S. establishments and the privileged classes, and bringing her multiplicitous identities to center stage. Other elements from a Susana Cook performance to expect are unabashed butches and femmes, quick-fire dialogue with her ensemble cast made up of lesbian and queer women of color, music scored by her son Julian, and playful choreography. Cook's shows are community in the making, a dynamic, at times disjointed cultural experience for audience members and performers alike, due to the often nonlinear structure.

Cook's life experience significantly affected her creative work and career moves. Since 1991, she has participated in the New York City performing arts scene and continues to write and direct all of her own work as one of the most prolific artists to grace many a downtown stage. At age 16, Cook joined a theater group run by political Jewish artists in Argentina. It was 1976, the year the Argentine dictatorship began. The Internet was not yet a tool of global connection and Las Madres de Plaza de Mayo (Mothers of the Disappeared) started what became a political movement in Buenos Aires. As the government abducted people, the Mothers of the Disappeared searched for their sons and daughters in hospitals, jails, police stations, and morgues, finding each other and organizing themselves. The Madres had a significant impact on Cook. "Somehow my theater and activism came together out of this," she explains. When I interviewed her in her quirky house in the Bronx, she spoke with effusive pride about the Madres, whose images were depicted in large framed pictures on her walls.

For Cook, it is important to have images that represent her politics, images with which she, and others like her, can relate. This visibility is a central political force in her work and she becomes frustrated if the impact of her work is minimized because of what may be perceived as a limited audience of converts.

> I love preaching to the converted. The "norm" has a whole culture preaching to them—every magazine, movie, TV program is preaching to them and we have a couple of lesbian cultural events, and [critics say], 'Oh, they're preaching to the converted.' It's not enough to convert, you also need to create a culture we can identify with, to help us reflect on our communities.

As a teen, Cook did not see images of lesbians in Buenos Aires. When she came to New York City and discovered women's bookstores and women's theater, her life experience and her own struggles with hiding parts of herself were validated by knowing that there were other lesbians like her and community spaces where she could find them. She became involved with the WOW Café Theater, a (predominantly lesbian-run) women's theater, which has since changed its mission to include trans people, marking a challenging shift within the WOW collective. Learning of the disproportionately high suicide rates of l/g/b/t youth (Garofalo et al., 1998; D'Augelli et al., 2001), it became critical for Cook to place lesbian women and butch identities at the epicenter of her work.

"Masculinity is not the monopoly of men," she says about her identity in a time when butches are being eclipsed in queer communities by various transgender and gender-variant masculine identities, such as transmen, bois, and gender queer people. She echoes what has been called a "butch phobia" that impedes many women from identifying as butch (Halberstam, 1998: 244).

> Many women think the associations or the stereotype of a butch are so negative. It's a whole idea that butches are imitating men. Also, butches are identified with the working class, which is seen as a negative thing. That they were working class and supposedly imitating patriarchal values gave butches a bad rap.

Cook takes great pride in her butch identity and her own embodiment of masculinity. Because she has made it a central and positive place from which to create artistic work, exploring the butch/femme identities and "energy" in lesbian relationships, she has encouraged and made a space for many others to claim their butch identities. Since it is not tied to male privilege, she rejects the compulsory abnegation of butch identities that views them as dated or as a limited form of masculinity. Indeed, because she creates an affirming space and positively encourages butch identifications, many of her cast members have come out as butch after working on her plays.

Like Henry, Cook identifies herself as a "Creator of Culture" or "Worker of Culture." Having produced 16 plays between 1991 and 2006, she sees her role as a person who likes to read, develop political analysis, and cull it into something explored onstage through humor for people who do not read or follow the news. Given her subject matter of politics, war, class struggles, and homophobia, she often grapples with how to make her shows funny. She believes her cultural role as an artist is to "create culture that will support the values or counter-values that we think are important."

Since the 2000 election debacle in the U.S., Cook has focused on making connections between the Argentine dictatorship and current U.S. politics. In *The Values Horror Show* (2005), Cook ends her trademark monologue by saying,

> I grew up during the dictatorship in Argentina, for example, and now I am sharing this one with you. I am not going to tell you the horrors we went through in Argentina; you have your own horrors to deal with. We are horror sisters and brothers. This is like a *deja vu* to me. But I am not going to tell you the end; I am not gonna ruin your movie.

Currently, she is exploring how nationalism and religion have been used in the U.S. to promote homophobia. Her most recent show, *The Idiot King* (2006), mocks the stupid, vacuous monarch who kills in the name of religious nationalism, again connecting current U.S. politics to Argentina's dictatorship. As the king, Cook (who dons a gold and red rubber crown from which her long hair steals out, and a tattered jacket adorned with gold braided rope and insignia on the shoulders) is surrounded onstage by the nurse, several advisors, and the queen. In a campy moment, the queen invites a gang comprised of gender queer people wearing pink bandanas to visit, thinking they will be reformed by seeing how royalty lives. Illuminating a blatant collapsing of the church with the nation-state, the king discusses parts of the Bible that should be modified or removed, and then addresses some homophobic concerns with his Christian God.

> King—Hi God. Yes, I called you. I wanted to talk to you about the pearly gates, the walls of alabaster, and the floors made of gold. Suddenly I realized that it might look pretty gay in heaven. Yes, of course it is up to you, the decoration. Yes, I want to go to heaven. I just had the disturbing thought of Saint Peter with a pearly keyholder. I can't stop thinking about the pearly, pearly gates. . . (2006).

Her political positions are evident in her work and in her choices about how and what to produce. Disturbed by what she calls the "worship" of the rich and celebrities, Cook aims to expose the economic and political forces that support such worship. Cook says she is not interested in being a part of U.S. corporations or Broadway. "I'm a butch. I have an accent. I didn't have what they wanted." And, she sees value in the aesthetic of the underground. In her casts, she highlights the experiences of the working class, women of color, and sexual minorities. She consciously brings her work to downtown audiences, where she can "preach to the converted," keep ticket prices low, and her art accessible. Cook carefully considers what to expose, and who and what to make visible in her work, knowing that each decision expresses her values and is part of her political practice.

> Even if you don't want to be political, you are being political. If you are not saying anything, then in a way you make a political choice of complying with the general discourse. The place where you choose to perform, the price of tickets, the people you put in your show, everything is a choice where you are showing something onstage—the winners, the losers, the minorities—this whole system is based on a certain set of values.

Diyaa MilDred Gerestant

I, Diyaa MilDred Gerestant, aka Drag King/Gender-Illusionist Dred, am a multi-spirited, Haitian-American, gender-illusioning, black, shaved, different, Goddess, anti-oppression, open, nontraditional, self-expressed, blessed, gender-bending, drag-kinging, fluid, ancestor-supported, and—after all that—non-labeling woman! (Gerestant, 2006)

Diyaa MilDred Gerestant describes her childhood self as shy, lonely, and sad, and as someone who had difficulty with self-expression. Like Henry, Gerestant grew up connected to the church and questioned the homophobic preachers who articulated hatred in their sermons as if it were God's word. She found this inauthentic, and her spiritual path has taken her to a very different and powerful spirituality that connects to her many genders and identities. "Performance is a spiritual tool. Everything I do is a spiritual tool. . . . My performance has definitely helped me open up to my spirit."

Her life transformation mirrored what she expresses in her drag king performances. For many years, Gerestant stormed stages from New York to London to Rio in sophisticated male cross-dressing performances as Drag King Dred, dancing and lip-syncing as she brought to life dynamic characters such as Shaft or Superfly, and paid homage to Marvin Gaye, Grace Jones, P. Diddy, and Busta Rhymes. She would shape-shift from one character into another with onstage costume and prop changes that allow her audiences to be insiders in her transformational process. Over the last few years, Gerestant has taken the stage as herself, merging those dynamic

drag performances with her own personal voice to talk about the story behind Dred. Doing so brought her full-circle, with a new confidence and ability to celebrate her multifaceted self. She reflects on her life in a deeply honest way with her audiences, and her candor imbues her audience with the strength of feeling connected to someone's struggle. She says,

> A lot of us are under a cloud or shadow of something keeping us from seeing who we really are. I can only share that from my own life experience, because most of my life was like that. I went through a lot of abuse and teasing; I didn't have any kind of self-worth. For a while, Dred was someone I was hiding behind. Dred was my male character. I had to really look at that and face those demons—like I wasn't worthy of just being myself as MilDred.

That spirit and her ability to "speak from a truthful place," she believes, contribute to social change; she hopes this will "inspire others to do the same for themselves."

Gerestant never thought she would be a performer. In 1995, though, she attended a drag king show at the Pyramid in the East Village, just as the pulse of the New York City drag king scene was starting to thump. Performances by soon-to-be notorious kings such as Busta Hymen and Mo B. Dick empowered her: "They were free of any particular gender box and I was like a little kid in a candy store." Gerestant's first transformation into what would become Dred preceded hundreds of women she would similarly inspire over the next 10 years. It was expressed in her first play in 2006,

> Looking in the mirror, I couldn't believe my transformation. I wondered, "Where did that handsome man come from?" I couldn't believe that I was looking at another side of me, that this side existed. It's still incredible each time I do it.

Gerestant's life was transformed by her introduction to kinging in a way she never anticipated. Over the years, the style of her character Dred solidified into a performance of a medley of songs and characters, climaxing with Aretha Franklin's "Natural Woman," and stripping down from her final male drag king costume into a sexy red bikini top and miniskirt, full with a bulge, and her facial hair still intact. At the pinnacle of the medley, she reaches into her skirt in a typical male gesture, revealing a shiny red apple that she bites into, reflecting her power as a woman and referencing Eve's transgression in the Garden of Eden. She has been one of the most inspiring contemporary drag kings, claiming a trademark masculinity—a political flip of the stereotypical macho man into one who did not need to denigrate women to be powerful. This is part of the reason drag kinging can be so stalwart; the way a woman interprets masculinity need not rely on sexism, but rather, on exposing the gimmicks that create a sexist persona, revealing how gender, specifically, masculinity, is manufactured.

Gerestant's strength lies in her exploration of her gender before an audience. As a gender illusionist, she challenges the internalized belief systems of audiences regarding gender. To say her performances make people think differently is to put the power of her transformation delicately. They have pushed people's boundaries in over 20 countries, each with its own set of gender norms. One of the most well-known drag kings in the world, many people find themselves attracted to her and approach her after her shows. In the presence of a person with a womanly body and a goatee, the conflicted desire becomes wholly complex, as audience members are forced to think about what they are attracted to and why. A heterosexual man will be attracted to her "from the neck down" and struggle to rectify her hairy face; someone else's attraction may be based on the belief that she is transitioning from a male into a woman—that her facial hair is "real" and her breasts are implants. Each scenario forces a person to consider how desire can be bound to ideas or expressions of gender, rather than to a real person. She aims to break down all of these illusions and get people to question what makes a man or a woman, and at the core, the nature of what is "real." In those intimate exchanges between audience member and performer, how does her joy in her whole self, with all her levels of gender expression, affect those who watch her?

"I'm very much into opening people's eyes up to [the question], 'are they really living as who they want to be or is it just something they've been trained to do?'" she asserts. Now able to more fully have Dred and Diyaa MilDred co-exist onstage, she uses storytelling, singing, and drag to speak her truths and inspire her audiences.

The man, or the yang in me, really empowered the woman, the yin. The male in me broadened and empowered the woman I was born as and integrated all that I am. . . . That's where true wholeness, I'm realizing, comes in, and accepting all of who you are.

In her first full-length play, she tells the story of competing in a "Superfly Look-Alike Competition" sponsored by a mainstream hip-hop and R&B radio station in New York City, where,

I wore a red velour suit, black ribbed turtleneck, thick black platforms, gold chains, a gold tooth engraved with the peace symbol, a fake black fur coat with a bright yellow lining draped over my shoulder, dark shades, and a big, sweet black hat with a feather glued to the top, tilted over my right eye.

She embodies that character, oozing confidence, as she pays homage to Superfly, the blaxploitation character, and honors her culture. At the Superfly competition, the women were crazy for her and she took second place, at which point she, wishing to express the full scope of her act, took the microphone. In her feminine voice, she told the audience she is a woman who performs as a drag king, at which point the crowd of 1,500 fell silent. For an audience she describes as "nowhere near queer," this jolt calls many assumptions into question and positions her in the middle of a bold activist move. Most people in such an audience have never seen a drag king and may have never heard of the concept. She thus simultaneously expresses her yin and yang, the flow of power between her genders in the context of her performance, and she undoubtedly sends many viewers home thinking in new ways about gender and desire.

Gerestant believes all of what we do is performance, and all of it is drag in one form or another. Social change through performance, for her, is summed up in one idea: acceptance.

From all different cultures where I've been asked to perform, whether it's Germany, or Korea, or Croatia, Australia . . . the one thing everyone really got was wanting to be accepted for who they are—I think that's the base of everything whether it's dealing with race, religion, sexuality, spirituality, gender, whatever it is, people just want to be who they are. . . . All cultures get that.

Activist Performance Art Is Cultural Work

For each artist, creating connections across lines of difference is a critical aim, and their cultural work functions as activism on multiple levels. Henry, Cook, and Gerestan use participatory processes of audience engagement. Connecting the collaborative process of activist artists to the process of public participation, Nina Felshin (1995:12) explains: "Such participation is a critical catalyst for change, a strategy with the potential to activate both individuals and communities, and takes many forms." The tactic of breaking the fourth wall makes audience members a constitutive part of a production; for example, Henry's *The Strong Go Crazy* (2003) dismantles the fabricated fissure between what is "real" and what is "just play." With that dismantling, the issues hit closer to home and there is less illusion that performance is something simply to watch and enjoy, then forget, as audience members quickly go back to their "real" lives. These artists' audiences are activated in classrooms and schoolwork, personal exploration of cross-dressing, community organizing, and decisions about claiming sexual identities, to name a few.

These artists have taken great risks in their work and by exposing their personal selves through performance to dispense their messages. From their own cultural perspectives, each addresses and analyzes issues of race and ethnicity. Cook and Henry depict masculine gender identities—butch and transman respectively—that they live every day, whereas Gerestant performs gender as drag, but does not identify in her daily life with a masculine gender identity. A critical component of their work is that each artist challenges a gender binary and gender roles. As descendents of the feminist artists of the 1970s "that made creative use of feminist methodologies to grapple with issues of self-representation, empowerment, and community identity" (Felshin, 1995: 19), these three artists continue to change the dialogue about social issues and assumptions about people's identities and place within communities. Claiming an identity makes possible communities based on common experience. Each performer appeals to queer or lesbian communities, artist communities of color, and many political communities; they create community within their shows, facilitating a deepening of the experience and connections made during a production.

Independent artists that connect and explore issues, invite audience involvement, and create community through theater productions perform the role of cultural workers and cultural activists. Brian Wallis (1990: 8) defines *cultural activism* as "the use of cultural means to try to effect social change." For all three artists, the activist/performer nexus is built into their role as cultural workers or creators of culture through their performances, where ethnic, gender, and sexual identities, as well as conversations regarding identity, are invoked. If, as George and Trimbur (2004: 2) argue, culture includes "social institutions, patterns of behavior, systems of belief, and . . . popular entertainment that create the social world in which people live," then Cook, Henry, and Gerestant's work on and off the stage of translating, critiquing, and participating in these cultural elements for the public can be deemed cultural work. Henry writes for *Worker's World* and organizes protests and community events; Cook teaches theater and dreams of creating a "School for the Revolution"; and Gerestant plans to open an alternative healing center and teaches drag king workshops around the world. Each act creates culture, explores and expands belief systems, creates literary texts and art, culls current events into critical analysis, facilitates critical thought and dialogue, builds communities around common values, and generates community-based institutions and organizations.

Performance is, by nature, a political tool of visibility in which the artisan has the power to give voice to the stories and perspectives they wish to value. The manipulation of language and the creation of images manufacture power by establishing a presence. These artists put power into the hands of the underrepresented and the disenfranchised, making important those lesser-heard stories. The meaning of gender shifts as an audience gets to know a gender variant character's inner thoughts and struggles with his or her place in society, observes lesbians expressing the norms of their community, or watches a handsome man win a contest only to find out that he is a biological woman. For mainstream audiences unaccustomed to such gendered performances, or who do not typically question gender roles believed to be axiomatic, these performances may mean a shift in consciousness. Yet an audience of similarly disenfranchised individuals may experience empowerment by seeing stories with which they can relate.

Henry, Gerestant, and Cook cite many instances of the impact their work has had on individuals and communities. A young lesbian thanked Cook for validating or giving voice to her experience, Gerestant's drag king workshops helped young women explore gender expression, while students on college campuses connected to these issues and to one another due to Henry's work. Gerestant brings it back to human connection, live performance's strength over non-live media:

> When you treat others as yourself, or when you realize we are all connected, you won't want to bomb someone in Iraq, you won't want to abuse somebody, you won't want rape to be happening, you won't want somebody homeless on the street. We're all connected and to me that's the basis of social change.

Engaging audiences "every single time" he performs, Henri leaves political literature on the theater seats and talks afterwards about what people can do next. In a mobilization effort, he educates people about little-known cases of injustice. Cook and Gerestant also engage audiences with question-and-answer periods following performances, so that conversation and critical analysis of issues raised in their work can continue dialogue with all in the room. These acts are ways of creating community and solidarity around issues and between people, both of which are necessary for effective activism.

Sociopolitical movements require consciousness-raising art. Because burnout is common, activist movements need to celebrate identities, laugh, and find humor in the dire issues they face. Political art and theater are creative outlets for activists, and the presence of a larger social movement allows artists such as Henry, Cook, and Gerestant to tell the stories people need to hear.

Interviews with these performing artists reveal a commitment to using the stage to involve and speak with audiences. Important aspects of Imani Henry's activism encompass the visibility of identities, including as a cultural worker, supporting acts of resistance, and coalition and solidarity building. Susana Cook's activist work cites issues of represen-

tation and visibility, creating images with which to identify, and her choices and political practice concerning her performance. Diyaa MilDred Gerestant's activism is based on challenging illusions surrounding gender and desire, and spotlighting transformational processes for growth as ways of creating wholeness and acceptance among people. Since performance can create contexts for new understanding through the dynamic relationship of these artists to their audiences, action is encouraged and the possibility for shifting consciousness is expanded. In New York and on their tours, they are making a meaningful contribution to activist movements working toward social change.

NOTES

1. Queer has been used derogatorily for gay, lesbian, bisexual, and transgender people and has, over the last decade, been adopted as an identity by many members of these communities to deconstruct and dismantle its aspersive power. Although queer does not necessarily mean gay, many gay, lesbian, transgender, or bisexual people, as well as heterosexuals whose sexuality does not fit into the cultural standard of monogamous heterosexual marriage, have adopted the label "queer" as an act of resistance, since it indicates being outside dominant sexual norms and expectations. Queer theory has been built around many of these ideas, with resistance acting as a central component for queer identities (Hall, 2003; Wikholm, 1999).

2. Transmen, FTMs, and bois are individuals who may have been assigned a female gender at birth and socialized accordingly, but whose identity and gender expression become masculinized. This may or may not include taking testosterone to assist the development of male secondary sex characteristics or having surgery to alter the body to appear more masculine. Many people clearly distinguish between identifying as a transman or as a boi, and each is its own masculine gender identity. FTM has been widely used, but can be seen as offensive for a person of trans experience, and transman is more appropriate (Gender Identity Project, 2006). As ideas about the multiplicity of gender identities continue to develop, individual identities are expanding. *Gender queer* is a term some use to resist established gender norms and to challenge the traditional gender binary. I say this to give the reader who may be unfamiliar with these terms some understanding of what is being discussed, but do not wish to imply that it is at all simple. See the work of Judith Halberstam, Kate Bornstein, and Leslie Feinberg for more analysis of gender identity specifically in transgender individuals. Not much has been written on the identity boi, but a mainstream article was featured in *New York Magazine* in 2004 (Levy, 2004).

3. The ritual breaking of the fourth wall to address the audience directly is generally attributed to Bertolt Brecht's *epic theater;* however, Brecht's exploration of this method was based on his research of *the alienation effect* in Chinese theater (Brecht, 1992: 136; Brockett, 1991: 523). The alienation effect has been used onstage and in cinema as an intentional jolt for the viewer, reminding them that they are watching something unreal and to allow for more objective analysis of what they are watching.

REFERENCES

Brecht, B. 1992. *Brecht on Theater: The Development of an Aesthetic.* J. Willett (ed. and trans.). New York: Hill and Wang. (Original work published in 1957.)

Brockett, O. 1991. *History of the Theater* (sixth edition). Needham Heights, MA: Allyn and Bacon.

Cook, S. 2006. *The Idiot King.* Unpublished play.
————— 2005. *The Values Horror Show.* Unpublished play.
————— 1999. *Hot Tamale.* Retrieved on June 28, 2006, from *http://susanacook.com/words2.htm#hot.*

D'Augelli, A.R., S.L. Hershberger, and N.W. Pilkington. 2001. "Suicidality Patterns and Sexual Orientation-Related Factors Among Lesbian, Gay, and Bisexual Youths." *Suicide and Life Threatening Behavior* 31: 250–264.

Felshin, Nina 1995. "Tailor-Made." *Art Journal* 54, 1, *Clothing as Subject* (Spring): 7–16.
—————1995. *But Is It Art? The Spirit of Art As Activism.* Editor. Seattle: Bay Press.

Garofalo, R., R.C. Wolf, S. Kessel, J. Palfrey, and R.H. DuRant. 1998. "The Association Between Health Risk Behaviors and Sexual Orientation Among a School-Based Sample of Adolescents." *Pediatrics* 101:895–902.

Gender Identity Project. 2006. *Trans-Care.* Training presented at the Lesbian, Gay, Bisexual and Transgender Community Center Y.E.S. Program. New York, NY (November).

George, D. and J. Trimbur (eds.). 2004. *Reading Culture: Contexts for Critical Reading and Writing.* Fifth edition. New York: Pearson Longman.

Gerestant, M. 2006. "Exposures of a Multi-Spirited, Haitian-American, Gender-Harmonizing Woman." Robin Bernstein (ed.), *Cast Out: Queer Lives in Theater.* Michigan: University of Michigan Press.

Halberstam, J. 1998. *Female Masculinity.* Durham, NC: Duke University Press.

Hall, D. (ed.). 2003. *Queer Theories (Transitions).* United Kingdom: Palgrave Macmillan.

Henry, I. 2004. *Living in the Light.* Unpublished play.
—————2003. *The Strong Go Crazy.* Unpublished play.
—————2002. *B4T.* Unpublished play.

Levy, A. 2004. *Where the Bois Are.* Retrieved on November 12, 2006, from *http://nymag.com/nymetro/news/features/n_9709/index.html.*

Poynter, K. and D. Talbot. 2006. *Heterosexual Allies in Higher Education: The Development of a Model.* Retrieved July 5, 2006, from *www.duke.edu/~kpoynter/Heterosexual Allies%20(Jan06).doc.* Manuscript submitted for publication.

Reagon, B.J. 1983. "Coalition Politics: Turning the Century." Barbara Smith (ed.), *Home Girls: A Black Feminist Anthology.* New York: Kitchen Table Press: 356–368.

Wallis, B. (ed.). 1990. *Democracy: A Project by Group Material.* Seattle: Bay Press: 8.

Wikholm, A. 1999. *Words: A Glossary of the Words Unique to Modern Gay History.* Retrieved April 29, 2005, from *www.gayhistory.com/rev2/words/queer.htm.*

S E V E N T Y

◆◆◆

Morning in America: A Letter from Feminists on the Election (2008)

Two days after the Texas debate between Hillary Clinton and Barack Obama, a group of old friends broke out the good china for a light breakfast of strong coffee, blueberry muffins, and fresh-squeezed orange juice. We were there to hash out a split that threatened our friendship and the various movements with which we are affiliated. In some ways it was a kaffeeklatch like a million others across America early on a Saturday morning—but for the fact that this particular group included Gloria Steinem, a co-founder of the National Women's

Political Caucus; Beverly Guy-Sheftall, director of the Women's Research and Resource Center at Spelman College; Johnnetta Cole, chair of the board of the JBC Global Diversity and Inclusion Institute; British-born radio journalist Laura Flanders; Kimberlé Crenshaw, professor of law at Columbia and UCLA; Carol Jenkins, head of the Women's Media Center; Farah Griffin, professor of English and comparative literature at Columbia; Eleanor Smeal, president of the Feminist Majority; author Mab Segrest; Kenyan anthropologist Achola Pala Okeyo;

management consultant and policy strategist Janet Dewart Bell; and Patricia Williams, Columbia law professor and *Nation* columnist.

It was a casual gathering but one that settled down to business quickly. We were all progressives but diverse nonetheless. We differed in our opinions of whether to vote for Hillary Clinton or Barack Obama—our goal was not an endorsement. Rather, the concern that united us all was the "race-gender split" playing out nationally, in which the one is relentlessly pitted against the other. We did not want to see a repeat of the ugly history of the nineteenth century, when the failure of the women's movement to bring about universal adult suffrage metastasized into racial resentment and rift that weakened feminism throughout much of the twentieth century.

How, we wondered, did a historic breakthrough moment for which we have all longed and worked hard, suddenly risk becoming marred by having to choose between "race cards" and "gender cards"? By petty competitiveness about who endures more slings and arrows? By media depictions of white women as the sole inheritors of the feminist movement and black men as the sole beneficiaries of the civil rights movement? By renderings of black women as having to split themselves right down the center with Solomon's sword in order to vote for either candidate? What happened, we wondered, to the last four decades of discussion about tokenism and multiple identities and the complex intersections of race, gender, sexuality, ethnicity, and class?

We all worried that the feminist movement's real message is not being heard, and we thought about how to redirect attention to those coalitions that form the bedrock of feminist concern: that wide range of civil rights groups dedicated to fighting discrimination, domestic violence, the disruptions of war, international sex and labor trafficking, child poverty, and a tattered economy that threatens to increase the number of homeless families significantly.

We thought of all that has happened in just seven short but disastrous years of the Bush Administration, and we asked: How might we position ourselves so we're not fighting one another? Our issues are greater than any disagreement about either candidate. We all know that there is simply too much at stake.

On the one hand, we celebrate the unprecedented moment in which a black person and a female person have risen to the lead in the Democratic race for President of the United States. On the other hand, both of them are constantly pressed to deny their race or gender, to "transcend" it, to prove by their very existence that misogyny and racism no longer exist. This, even as both are popularly and reductively caricatured in perniciously stereotypical ways. Clinton as a woman with balls, Obama as "unqualified" and "grandiose," Chelsea Clinton being "pimped" by her mother while Bill O'Reilly declares that Michelle Obama should be "lynched."

How do we resist such a toxic Punch and Judy show of embattled identity, to the degree that many women feel that a vote for Obama "cheats" Clinton of her chance to break the glass ceiling, and many blacks feel that a vote for Clinton is a betrayal of the chance to break the race barrier?

We agreed that everyone needs to refocus on the big picture. All of us know that another Republican presidency would effectively bury the gains of both the civil rights and the feminist movements of the past fifty years. Judicial nominations alone could upend decades of hard work.

How, therefore, to reclaim a common purpose, a truly democratic "we": we women of all races, we blacks of all genders, we Americans of all languages, we immigrants of all classes, we Latinas of all colors, we Southerners of all regions, we families of all ages, we parents working three jobs without healthcare, we poor who sleep on the streets, we single mothers whose homes are being repossessed, we displaced New Orleanians whose . . . epic of displacement has yet to be resolved.

"Can't we all just get along?" could have been the mantra of this power breakfast—though certainly not forever, nor for all purposes. Just long enough to roust the Republican rascals: the oil barons and Enron fraudsters and pre-emptive warmongers and sadistic torture-masters and trigger-happy antiabortionists and Blackwater mercenaries and the tribal extremists of various religious stripes who seem to look forward to Armageddon finally segregating humanity into true believers and recalcitrant, disposable trash.

In the confusion of this triumphalist but precarious moment, therefore, it is important that the alliance between a now global feminism and a now global civil rights movement not be turned against itself and ultimately defeated. Obama and Clinton, each a complex archetypal "role model," represent, at their best, a new kind of American possibility. If we could get over our fixation on a fantasy that many of us hoped to see realized in our lifetimes, maybe we could finally turn to the issues that each of them brings to the table. We cannot remain tangled by stereotypes that demean with their sweeping divisiveness and historical cliché.

As we gathered up the empty plates, we recommitted ourselves to further joint discussions about how to attain that collective better future, however many early mornings, late nights, and urns of coffee into the future that may take. We hope women across America will choose to do the same.

S E V E N T Y - O N E

◆◆◆

Katrina, Black Women, and the Deadly Discourse on Black Poverty in America (2006)

Barbara Ransby

Barbara Ransby is a historian, writer, and political activist whose biography of civil rights leader Ella Baker, *Ella Baker and the Black Freedom Movement: A Radical Democratic Vision,* has won many awards. She is Associate Professor of History and African American Studies at the University of Illinois/Chicago. She serves on editorial and advisory boards, consults on film and radio projects, and works closely with The Public Square, a Chicago-based nonprofit organization that facilitates public dialogue on contemporary issues.

Most observers, even some of the most conservative and purportedly color-blind observers, have conceded the overwhelmingly racial character of the social disaster that followed in Hurricane Katrina's wake. Journalists covering the story could not help but acknowledge that those left behind to endure nature's wrath, and for whom little help and few resources were provided in the critical days following the hurricane, were disproportionately poor and Black. What does not often get added is that by most accounts those hardest hit and least able to rebound from it were also women: poor Black women who waded through chest-high water with sick and elderly parents, with young children on their hips, and meager belongings in tow. This should not be surprising given the correlation between gender, race, and poverty. Black single mothers are more likely to be poor than any other demographic group, and New Orleans was no exception to the rule. In fact, a study by the Institute for Women's Policy Research points out that the percentage of women in poverty in New Orleans before the storm was considerably *higher* than in other parts of the country: more than half of the poor families of the city were headed by single mothers, and the median income for African American women workers in New Orleans before the storm was a paltry $19,951 a year (DeWeever 2005).

The effect of the hurricane on African American women was not merely a consequence of demographics; it was also fueled and framed by the rabid anti-poor discourse that has cast Black single mothers as unworthy of public aid or sympathy. In this paper, I will discuss several aspects of the gendered nature of the disaster: the effect of government inaction on Black women in New Orleans after the hurricane, the pre-Katrina discourse on Black female poverty that set the stage for that inaction, and how Black women activists have responded. Even though this was clearly a regional crisis, the various contradictions came together with particular vividness in New Orleans, so I focus my observations on that city alone.

Women in Katrina's Wake

When Katrina slapped New Orleans, she slapped everyone hard, but she slapped women especially hard. The impact is not simply measured in the number of injuries, deaths, and the amount of property loss, but in the kind of human currency that is difficult to measure. Women were more encumbered and less mobile. One gets a window into how women's lives were turned upside down by this crisis by looking at what women did and where women were situated in the community in ordinary times. As a number of commentators and experts have pointed out, there was a social crisis in New Orleans that had been fueled by the widespread prevalence of poverty and the absence of resources long before meteorologists sighted a category five hurricane bearing down on the Gulf Coast. There was already a 40 percent poverty rate among single mothers in the city. A state-by-state breakdown of poverty statistics ranked Louisiana number forty-seven out of fifty-one, and forty-third in terms of health-care insurance coverage. And 13 percent of Louisiana's children live in extreme poverty, which is defined as a family of four surviving on less than $10,000 a year.[1] A large percentage of New Orleans' poor single mothers also lived in the historic Ninth Ward, the low-lying area of the city most vulnerable to flooding. So, as in any crisis, those with few assets, little money, and even less maneuverability were hard-pressed to get out of the path of the storm and further compromised in their ability to recover after the blow.

Oral Histories

The impact of Katrina on women of African descent in New Orleans is best reflected in the stories and anecdotes that emerged from the storm. Our understanding of this tragedy and its aftermath is aided by the plethora of oral history projects that have emerged in response to the situation.[2] Some of them are an extension of pre-existing archival or public history projects, and some are grassroots interventions by students, artists, historians, and activists determined to document what actually happened and provide an outlet for those who want to tell their stories. The narratives, testimonies, and profiles of real flesh and blood people are the best rebuttal to one-dimensional stereotypes. One very powerful story, collected by *Alive in Truth: The New Orleans Disaster Oral History and Memory Project*, tells of the experience of a woman named Clarice B. (later identified as Clarice Butler), who describes her life before and after Katrina. "I worked all my life," she explains:

> I worked all my life for Metropolitan Homecare for 28 years: home care, nurse's assistant. I took care of a lot of people in my life, a lot

of people. I was good at my job, oh, yeah. It's not a clean job, and it's not no dirty, dirty job. But no job is clean all the time, but it's a job. And I did good. I had to go to school: I went to school and wound up working in a nursing home.

Here is how she describes her ordeal after the levee broke and she found herself stranded on the interstate highway with thousands of others:

> And you want me to tell you the truth, my version of it? They tried to kill us. When you keep somebody on top of the Interstate for five days, with no food and water, that's killing people. And there ain't no ands, ifs, or buts about it, that was NOPD [New Orleans Police Department] killing people. Four people died around me. Four. Diabetes. I am a diabetic and I survived it, by the grace of God, but I survived it. . . . Look, I was on top of the Interstate. Five days, okay? Helicopters at night shining a light down on us. They know we was there. Policemen, the army, the whole nine yards, ambulance passing us up like we wasn't nothing. Drove by and by all day. At night when they got ready to pull out, they pulled out and left us in darkness. We was treated worse than an animal. People do leave a dog in a house, but they do leave him food and water. They didn't do that. . . .

Clarice goes on to recall the trauma of leaving her home:

> And of course I had to leave my birds and my dog. Of course I didn't want to. But I didn't have no other choice. Didn't have a choice. So I brought my dogs and my bird to as far as I could bring them. And I left them there upstairs. And I'm hoping I can retrieve them. I'm hoping. I have to call the SPCA [Society for the Prevention of Cruelty to Animals] or somebody. I left them upstairs on the deck, and I think if they was captured I should get them back. I'm hoping, anyway. I had a little Chihuahua. He was 9 months old. I had five birds. Two parakeets and two cockatiels. And my cockatiels just had a baby bird which was five weeks old. So you know I'm heartbroken. But again, my life was more important at that moment.

Finally, she wonders aloud:

> Now why our Mayor and government did this I'll never understand it. I never would understand what happened to New Orleans. That is really a disaster. Nobody would never believe it until you get into that situation. I go to bed one night with everything that I needed, and wake up the next morning with nothing.[3]

There was another woman's story that made a powerful impression on me, and which I could not get out of my mind for weeks after I saw it on *CNN*. The scene was of a middle-aged Black woman, dirty, desperate, and crying. She looked into the camera and said to the viewers, "We do not live like this."[4] She repeated it over and over again. Contradicting the image of slovenly, hapless, poor folk, this woman's face reflected not simply fatigue and hunger but humiliation as well. Most poor people spend a lot of time and attention making sure their homes and their children are as neat and clean as possible so that they will not be straight-jacketed into the stereotypes associated with poverty. And here this seemingly hard-working woman was left with nothing, not even her dignity.

Whatever circumstances led to poor Black women's lives being battered and devastated by this storm, as Clarice's story so painfully recounts, the real unforgivable disaster is the fact that they were abandoned by those whose job it was to intervene and help in such situations. The local government was paralyzed, and the federal government looked the other way. Despite the tens of millions of dollars spent on the various apparatuses of the Office of Homeland Security (OHS), no one seemed to have spent much time worrying about the widely predicted hurricane that terrorized the Gulf Coast region or the security of those who were its victims. There was no plan to help those who could not help themselves, and even after the failure of FEMA and the OHS to aid and coordinate relief efforts, the President's silence and the federal government's inaction for days after the crisis occurred left tough veteran journalists dumbfounded, angry, and sometimes even in tears. Initially, President Bush seemed not to take the crisis and human suffering seriously. Perhaps his mother spoke for the family when she visited displaced families forced to flee to Houston. During that visit she made the following disturbing comment: "So many of the people in the area here, you know, were underprivileged anyway, so this, this is working very well for them."[5] In her mind, those poor families really didn't need to have real homes or familiar communities; instead, like animals, they just needed basic shelter and food, no matter under what conditions.

On one level, many of us could not help but be surprised by the level of disregard for the collective well-being of New Orleans' Black poor, white poor, its elderly and infirm. However, when we zero in on the plight of Black women, again, the stage was set long before the scandalous treatment they received after Katrina. The dismantling of welfare for the poor in 1996, which climaxed with President Clinton's Personal Responsibility Act, was surrounded by a public discourse that dehumanized and denigrated the Black poor, charging them as the main culprits in their own misfortune. Black women were implicitly deemed lazy, promiscuous, and irresponsible; hence, the withdrawal of public aid was ostensibly designed to jolt them into the labor force and into more responsible sexual behavior. Never mind that there were shrinking jobs for applicants with few skills and little education, and never mind that the president himself was breaking the very same sexual moral code that he was so mightily imposing on single mothers. Still, the problem was defined as that of Black women having babies out of the confines of heterosexual marriages, rather than the low pay and lack of jobs and affordable housing that marked their condition and compromised the future of their children.

Post-Katrina pundits continued the "blame the Black poor" rhetoric even as the blame clearly lay elsewhere. Six weeks after Katrina wreaked havoc on the Gulf Coast region, Mona Charen, columnist and former staffer for President Ronald Reagan, wrote: "Still it is true as the aftermath of Katrina underlined that parts of the black community remain poor and dysfunctional" (Charen 2005). The word *dysfunctional* is usually offered to modify *family,* and the association Charen is making is clear. The rest of her article goes on to make the case that the biggest problem facing the Black poor before and after Katrina is that of single-mother families. But Charen was just one of many making this argument. Conservative pundit Rich Lowry of the *National Review* argued that "If people are stripped of the most basic social support—the two parent family . . . they will be more vulnerable in countless ways" in times of crisis. He went on to propose government programs that "include greater attention to out of wedlock births" (Lowry 2005). Liberals such as *New York Times* columnist Nicholas Kristof even jumped on the bandwagon, giving a positive nod to Lowry's proposal (Kristof 2005).

Black Conservatives Weigh In

The attack on Black mothers did not stop with journalists such as Kristof and Lowry. Black conservatives weighed in with a vengeance. In a gush of patriarchal nostalgia, Reverend Jesse Lee Peterson, founder of the Los Angeles–based Brotherhood Organization of a New Destiny (BOND), blamed Black people and the absence of strong Black men in charge: "Prior to 40 years ago, a pathetic performance by the Black community in a time of crisis would have been inconceivable. The first response would have come from Black men. They would take care of their families, bring them to safety, and then help the rest of the community" (Peterson 2005a). Even more bluntly, Peterson wrote: "it was the lack of moral character and dependence on government that cost Blacks when Hurricane Katrina hit New Orleans, not President Bush or racism" (Peterson 2005b). If Peterson were an irrelevant voice on the far-right fringe he could be ignored. However, his voice has been cited, invoked, and amplified by various conservative organizations, publications, and websites.

Syndicated columnist George Will (2005) was one of the most outrageous in his slander of the Black women of New Orleans. He first contended that there was too much obsession about race. In his words: "America's always fast-flowing river of race-obsessing has overflowed its banks," in discussions about Katrina. Those who are poor are poor because they don't follow the rules, Will insists, and those rules mean conforming to his code of sexual and social behavior. He offered "three not-at-all recondite rules for avoiding poverty: Graduate from high school, don't have a baby until you are married, don't marry while you are a teenager. Among people who obey those rules, poverty is minimal." If only things were so simple. Will drives the ill-conceived argument home, however, by making an even more explicit point:

> . . . it is a safe surmise that more than 80 percent of African American births in inner-city New Orleans—as in some other inner cities—were

to women without husbands. That translates into a large and constantly renewed cohort of lightly parented adolescent males, and that translates into chaos in neighborhoods and schools, come rain or come shine. (Will 2005)

So, in Will's view, the chaos of Katrina was an extension of the self-inflicted chaos created by homes without strong father figures. These are the distorted realities that conservatives have to craft for themselves in order to sleep at night, I suppose. The reality on the ground is of course quite different, as the stories of Clarice B. and others illustrate so compellingly.

A powerful hurricane ravaged the lives of poor Black women and their families and neighbors, not because the women did not have wedding bands on their fingers, nor because their sons lacked strong paternal figures in the home to enforce curfew. To suggest as much is another way of devaluing the suffering and strivings of these families. Putting the issue in an international context, writer and activist Ritu Sharma, who works with the Washington-based advocacy group *Woman's Edge* (the Coalition for Women's Economic Development and Global Equity), writes that "women are the vast majority of the world's poor and money is the great protector" (Sharma 2006). Those who have little or none are more vulnerable than others to hurricanes, tsunamis, and all other forms of natural disasters that quickly escalate into human and social disasters.

Women Take Action after the Storm

While they may have little else, poor Black women are creative and resilient. They have to be in order to survive in such difficult and challenging times. So, if one part of this story is what happened to African American women after Katrina hit, the other half of the story is how they responded. And if part one is depressing and disturbing, part two is uplifting and encouraging. African American women have responded to the crisis as individuals and in groups. One individual response was that of long-time New Orleans resident and organizer Diane "Momma D." Frenchcoat, an older resident, who became a self-appointed relief worker after the storm. In the weeks following the hurricane, each day she would collect food, pile it in her cart, and navigate the flooded and filthy streets to deliver meals to hungry and isolated neighbors. She eventually recruited others to help in her efforts, dubbing them the "Soul Patrol." When asked by a newspaper reporter why she did not evacuate the city for safer ground, she replied: "Why would I leave now? Why would I leave my people when so many of them are still here and suffering?" The reporter described her in this way: "Graying dreadlocks flowed down the nape of her neck, spilling over her sturdy, sloping shoulders as she spoke of a city she hopes will be reborn" (Lee 2005).

Another inspiring story of determination against the odds is that of Beverly Wright, initiator of the volunteer-driven *A Safe Way Back Home* project. A professor of Environmental Studies at Dillard University and a lifelong New Orleans resident, Dr. Wright's project has educated New Orleans residents about the toxins still prevalent in the soil and in their homes. She was particularly concerned about the lawns of contaminated homes. With advice from the Environmental Protection Agency (EPA) and donations from several foundations, *A Safe Way Back Home* has provided equipment, information, and protective gear for dozens of residents to skim off toxic topsoil and replace it with healthy sod. The coalitions that Wright was able to forge were an interesting and important aspect of the project. Based on her past research and consulting for national labor unions about environmental dangers in the workplace, she was able to enlist the United

Steelworkers Union to help train volunteers and to provide tools and equipment for the project. College students were recruited, and the National Black Environmental Justice Network, to which Wright belongs, lent its support and resources as well. A creative team effort of some unlikely allies is making a difference in the lives of dozens of families.

On the surface, a very masculine and muscular image of relief workers dominates popular images. Men are pictured lifting boxes, operating heavy equipment, and toting guns, ostensibly to keep the peace. However, women are working tirelessly and courageously in the trenches, as has so often been the case. Even within the larger coalitions and community-based organizations such as the *People's Hurricane Relief Fund and Oversight Coalition* (PHRFOC), women are important actors, leaders, and contributors. The PHRFOC even has a women's caucus to highlight and make visible the work of women, providing a forum where women can support one another within the larger effort. The work of Diane Frenchcoat, Beverly Wright, and the women of the PHRFOC are but three examples of African American women taking initiative, being imaginative, and acting boldly. These real stories stand in stark contrast to what the George Wills and Rich Lowrys of the world would have us believe.

A sober read of the situation in New Orleans nearly one year after the storm hit is still worrisome. Some biased and shortsighted city builders are trying to push Black women and children out of the picture altogether, to reconfigure a city without what must be perceived as the burden of the Black poor. PHRFOC and others have fought this scheme by demanding the right to return and by insisting upon voting rights for displaced citizens. A number of scholars and activists have referred to this period of rebuilding and remapping of this southern subregion as another "Reconstruction." At stake today, as they were in the years following the Civil War, are land rights, voting rights, control of the military, accountability, jobs, and the reconstitution of families and communities. Wherever New Orleans is headed in the future, hardworking Black women with big hearts and steel-willed determination will be a part of the picture. They have needs and problems to be sure, but their presence adds to rather than detracts from the strength and vitality of a remarkable American city.[6]

New Orleans resident and organizer Diane "Momma D." Frenchcoat testifies on Capitol Hill before the House Select Bipartisan Committee to Investigate the Preparation for and Response to Hurricane Katrina (December 6, 2006).

NOTES

1. Statistics from DeWeever (2005).

2. A few of the projects that are attempting to document the stories of hurricane survivors include: the I-10 Witness Project (www.i10witness.com), which emerged out of a group of artists, teachers, and activists; the Story Corps radio project; projects hosted by the Center for Cultural Resources in Baton Rouge (www.hurricanestories .org); and projects initiated by the University of Southwestern Mississippi and the Mississippi Humanities Council.

3. Oral history collected by AliveinTruth.org, and posted at www.alternet.org on October 29, 2005.

4. Claudette Paul was also quoted in the *New York Times* as saying that "We need help. We don't live like this in America" (Appleborne et al., 2005).

5. Barbara Bush interviewed on Marketplace, *National Public Radio (NPR)*, September 5, 2005.

6. Thanks to Joseph Lipari for his assistance with the research for this essay.

REFERENCES

Appleborne, P., C. Drew, J. Longman, and A. Revkin. 2005. A Delicate Balance Is Undone in a Flash. *New York Times*, September 4, A25.

Charen, M. 2005. No More Marches, <http://Townhall .com> October 14. (accessed May 25, 2006).

DeWeever, A. J. 2005. The Women of New Orleans and the Gulf Coast: Multiple Disadvantages and Key Assets for Recovery, Part I. Washington, D.C.: Institute for Women's Policy Research, October 11, 2005. www.iwpr.org/pdf/ D464.pdf (accessed May 25, 2006).

Kristof, N. 2005. The Larger Shame. *New York Times*, September 6, A27.

Lee, T. D. 2005. Momma's Mission. *Times-Picayune*, September 18, Metro Section. At www.nola.com (accessed May 25, 2006).

Lowry, R. 2005. The Coming Battle Over New Orleans. *National Review Online*, September 2. www.national review.com (accessed September 4, 2005).

Peterson, J. L. 2005a. Moral Poverty Costs Blacks in New Orleans. *Worldnetdaily.com*, September 21. www. worldnet daily.com (accessed May 25, 2006).

—————. 2005b. Truth: Solution to Black America's Moral Poverty. *Worldnetdaily.com*, October 7. www. world netdaily.com (accessed May 25, 2006).

Sharma, R. 2006. Disasters Dramatize How Women's Poverty Is Lethal. *Women's eNews*, January 5. www.women senews.org (accessed May 25, 2006).

Will, G. 2005. Poverty of Thought. *Washington Post*, September 14, A27.

SEVENTY-TWO

◆◆◆

Meeting the Leadership Challenges of Women with Disabilities
Mobility International USA

Cindy Lewis

Director of Programs at Mobility International USA (MIUSA), **Cindy Lewis** specializes in the empowerment of women and girls with disabilities through international exchange and leadership training. She is co-author and producer of educational and organizing materials for MIUSA and also co-authored the ground-breaking resource, *Building an Inclusive Development Community: A Manual on Including People with Disabilities in International Development Programs*, sponsored by the U.S. Agency for International Development.

Since 1981, Mobility International USA (MIUSA) has collaborated with women with disabilities from every region of the world through international exchange programs emphasizing leadership training and disability rights. MIUSA specializes in leadership programs for women with disabilities, including the International Symposium on Issues of Women with Disabilities preceding the Fourth U.N. World Conference on Women in Beijing (1995), the International Symposium on Microcredit by and for Women with Disabilities (1998), Global Options for Women with

Disabilities in Leadership and Employment (2000), and Loud, Proud, and Prosperous: Microcredit By and For Women with Disabilities in Southern Africa (2000–2003). MIUSA's three International Women's Institutes on Leadership and Disability (1997, 2003, and 2006) included women from Albania, Argentina, Armenia, Australia, Belarus, Brazil, Canada, Cambodia, Chile, Colombia, Dominican Republic, Ecuador, Egypt, El Salvador, Fiji, France, Gambia, Georgia, Guatemala, Guyana, Haiti, Honduras, India, Indonesia, Jamaica, Kenya, Kosovo, Korea, Kyrgyzstan, Lebanon, Lesotho, Mali, Malaysia, Malawi, Mauritius, Mexico, Moldova, Nepal, Nicaragua, Nigeria, West Bank/Gaza, Pakistan, Panama, Palau, the Philippines, Peru, Romania, Russia, Rwanda, Somalia, Syria, Thailand, Turkey, Uganda, Uzbekistan, Vietnam, Zambia, Zimbabwe, and the U.S.

Mobility International USA's women's leadership programs are guided by lessons learned from women with disabilities over the past 25 years:

- Women and girls with disabilities experience challenges to leadership and leadership development based on gender and disability-based discrimination.

- In spite of obstacles, women with disabilities around the world are nevertheless taking leadership: directing organizations, running businesses, heading families, assuming political offices, and advocating for their rights.

- Hands-on experiences of inclusion and accessibility are powerful catalysts for strengthening leadership capacity of women with disabilities. New experiences create visions; visions spark ideas that become action for change and empowerment.

- Women with disabilities gain valuable insights by sharing the challenges and solutions lived by women from diverse circumstances. International, cross-disability, cross-cultural exchange programs offer a rich pool of resources for learning and creating solutions.

Women's Institutes on Leadership and Disability (WILD)

Mobility International USA's WILD programs are built around MIUSA's trademark curriculum, a combination of practical workshops with dynamic, hands-on activities. WILD participants share experiences, advice, and ideas in workshops on such issues as microenterprise, education and literacy, violence prevention, HIV/AIDS and reproductive health, and the development of skills such as proposal writing and use of the media. Challenge and cultural activities provide opportunities for risk taking, team building, leadership practice, and development of "disability pride." Each participant creates individual as well as collaborative action plans to address issues of women with disabilities in their home communities.

"When we began our women's programs, there were so few women with disabilities in leadership positions," said Susan Sygall, MIUSA CEO. "In 1997, WILD participants were just beginning to see the potential of women with disabilities, of themselves, as leaders. The discussions at that time were about how to start disabled women's groups, whether and how to break away from disability organizations that were completely controlled by men. We focused on basic leadership skills, looking for solutions and developing confidence and pride in ourselves as women with disabilities."

Over the years, the experience and leadership needs of the participants has shifted. "Now, WILD women already understand the importance of leadership and women's solidarity, and they are more confident in their skills. Their concerns today are practical: how to tap into the development programs that are working—but not including women with disabilities—in their communities, to address the survival issues of women with disabilities: poverty, lack of education, violence, disease," said Sygall.

Gender, Disability, and Development Institute

During WILD 2003 and WILD 2006, representatives of leading U.S.-based international development organizations joined WILD participants for a five-day Gender, Disability, and Development Institute (GDDI), coordinated by MIUSA. During this intensive "think tank," WILD women and international development professionals worked together to identify issues that impact participation of women with disabilities in development efforts, strategize solutions, and create collaborative plans to promote inclusion of women with disabilities in development programs. International development organizations at the 2003 and/or 2006 GDDI included American Friends Service Committee, the Association for the Rights of Women in Development (AWID), CBM, the Global Fund for Women, the Hesperian Foundation, Holt International, Mercy Corps, Trickle Up Program, Women Pushing Forward, and Whirlwind Wheelchair International.

Important outcomes of the Gender, Disability, and Development Institute activities include new avenues of communication and relationships between disabled women leaders and development professionals. All participants agreed that disabled women's organizations often do not have experience or information necessary to effectively approach development NGOs, while NGOs are not equipped with accurate information about the issues and capacity of disabled women to respond effectively. Formal GDDI activities provided opportunities for participants on both sides to identify common interests, to gain insight into different perspectives, and to more accurately understand the constraints, goals, and resources of women with disabilities and development program implementers.

Gender, Disability, and Development Institute participants met over the course of the Institute in sector-specific work groups, to articulate issues, identify obstacles, and generate strategies to ensure that women with disabilities are included and more effectively served in micro finance, health, education, civil society, and refugee assistance programs. In one particularly powerful exercise, WILD women were assigned the roles of development organization staff, while development professionals played leaders of disability organizations. Each side presented and deliberated requests from the other, for inclusion, funding, assistance with outreach, etc. WILD women and participants from development organizations each recounted valuable and often surprising insights gained from the exercise, including feedback on how they were perceived by the other side.

Sharing of unstructured time also gave all participants unprecedented opportunities to establish relationships and deepen the dialogues begun in structured seminars. Relaxed, informal settings, small group activities, and opportunities for individual consultations resulted in personalized advice and enabled delegates to make connections with people who hold potential for valuable information and resources. Simple adaptations made by the owners of the rustic retreat center where the

GDDI took place, such as small homemade ramps, a bathroom door replaced by a curtain, and a mattress raised by boards, were also eye opening for all participants.

While discussion focused on how development organizations can reach out and make programs accessible to women with disabilities, Susan Sygall, MIUSA CEO, also urged women with disabilities to take initiative by reaching out to international development organizations in their communities. A brainstorming session on recommendations for disability-led organizations to approach development NGOs more effectively incorporated suggestions from development professionals and WILD women. These included:

- Do your homework. Know the goals and mission of the development organization, and be sure that your request is compatible with that mission. Be able to explain how your organization's goals fit with the overall mission of the development organization. Learn the development vocabulary used by the organization, and use it.

- Be prepared to explain the mission of your organization and the key points of your request as concisely as possible. Practice expressing your main idea in one sentence, then making a brief explanation of your idea.

- Be specific about exactly what your organization wants from the international development organization. For example, "we want women with disabilities to participate in your microcredit program" is more effective than "women with disabilities need economic empowerment."

- Be prepared to counter stereotypes about women with disabilities. Emphasize the capabilities of women with disabilities rather than focusing only on their problems. Emphasize that women with disabilities are not interested in handouts but want the opportunity to show what they are capable of.

- Be polite, positive, and persistent. If an international development organization is resistant on the first approach, try again (and again!).

- Make an offer. Ask how you can assist the organization, for example with recruitment efforts, ideas, and contacts for making adaptations, accessible meeting space, etc., or support the NGO in meeting its goals in some other way.

Results

The impact of Mobility International USA's women's leadership programs is clear. MIUSA's women's program alumni today include a government minister and an elected representative to national Parliament; founders, directors, and officers of national and international organizations; Fulbright scholars and Fellowship recipients. MIUSA's alumni have created opportunities for countless other women with disabilities, initiating microcredit programs, business training, health projects, accessible transportation systems, and empowerment programs for disabled girls. Our alumni from all over the world credit MIUSA women's leadership programs with giving them the skills, resources, and confidence to step up as leaders in their communities and countries.

Our development program partners have also been affected. One participant reports that her experience at the Institute has led her to change the focus of development projects involving people with disabilities from "provision of care services" to "services to promote rights and empowerment." Another organization reports that the experience of working side by side with blind women made her understand very concretely what had previously been an abstract concept: the need for accessible format materials. All NGO participants noted that the opportunity to spend time with disabled women as colleagues had brought home the importance of providing access, and all have incorporated accessibility considerations into the regular project planning process.

As an organization, MIUSA has also greatly benefited from the WILD trainings. By bringing women together, MIUSA learns from the experts about the critical, real life issues that affect women with disabilities, and so is better prepared to advocate and provide technical assistance and information to promote inclusive development practice. "WILD helps us learn concretely what we often talk about in theory," said Sygall. "We are able to speak more accurately about the issues that women face throughout the world. In the same way, listening to dialogues between women with disabilities and development practitioners has enabled us to understand more practically the kind of issues that development organizations face as they work to include women with disabilities."

The Women's Institutes on Leadership and Disability program can be adapted and replicated anywhere in the world, by bringing cross-disability groups of women together to build confidence and skills as leaders, facilitating discussions between disabled women and development organizations, and focusing on solutions. "We want other people to do this," said Sygall. "We encourage our WILD participants to take our framework and adapt it to work in their own community. Or make up something new—anything that works to tap into the power of women with disabilities to contribute to international development."

NOTES

For more information and resources by MIUSA, including *Loud, Proud and Passionate*®: *Including Women with Disabilities in International Development Programs; Loud, Proud and Passionate*® Video (available in open-captioned format and in English, Spanish, Arabic, Russian, and French); and *Loud, Proud and Prosperous*®: *A Video Documentary* (available in open-captioned format and in English, Spanish, French, and Arabic), as well as recommendations for women with disabilities and international development organizations for inclusive development programs, see MIUSA's website: www.miusa.org

A version of this article is available at http://www.miusa.org/publications/freeresources/mti/chapter3

◆◆◆

Women Are Opening Doors (2003)
Security Council Resolution 1325 in Afghanistan

Felicity Hill and Mikele Aboitiz

Felicity Hill directed the Women's International League for Peace and Freedom, U.N. Office, New York (1997–2001). She created a web portal (www.Women WarPeace.org) on the impact of conflict on women after adoption of the U.N. Security Council Resolution on Women, Peace, and Security. She works for the Medical Association for Prevention of War (Australia). **Mikele Aboitiz** is a former Program Associate at WILPF's U.N. office. She works in nonprofit and public policy sectors, specializing in project management, strategic planning, evaluation, and organizational development.

After September 11, 2001, the world became aware of the suffering of women in Afghanistan. Women's nongovernmental organizations (NGOs) around the world had been trying to raise awareness for years, but only after September 11 did these women appear so prominently in the *New York Times*, the *Washington Post*, and on CNN and similar high-profile news media. Only then did women appear on the radar screen of international policy makers. International media attention focused on the Taliban's war on Afghan women, with less attention given to the need for women to be present at the peace table.

As the U.S.-led war in Afghanistan developed, women's organizations around the world saw an opportunity to turn a terrible situation into a positive outcome. It was not enough that the Taliban were pushed out of Afghanistan; it was not enough that the United States and the international community spoke about women's issues. It was time to let women speak for themselves and decide their future.

WILPF and the NGO Working Group on Women, Peace, and Security

At the Women's International League for Peace and Freedom (WILPF),[1] the process of empowering women to find peace started a long time ago.

WILPF is an old and well-established organization, dating back to 1915, when its founders and leaders outlined a new and compassionate concept of human security. That year some 1,300 women from Europe and North America gathered in The Hague, the Netherlands. These women originated both from countries at war with each other and from countries that were neutral. All came together in a congress of women to protest the killing and destruction wrought by the war raging in Europe. They envisioned a security that does not rest on military strength but rather lies in equitable and sustainable economic and social development.

These 1,300 women issued 20 resolutions; some were of immediate importance, while others aimed at reducing conflict and preventing war by establishing the foundation for a permanent peace among the world's nations. Neutral governments were called on to press warring nations to stop fighting and settle their differences by negotiations that would be held within the borders of neutral countries. Grievances and remedies would be voiced and met with impartiality.

This vision translates into an equal distribution of resources to meet the basic needs of all people and guarantees full and equal participation of men and women in all levels of society, including in its decision making. The women organized "envoys" to carry these resolutions to both neutral and belligerent states in Europe and to the president of the United States. Jane Addams, having been elected president of the congress and of the International Women's Committee (the beginning of WILPF), met with President Woodrow Wilson, who, according to government records, said that the congress's resolutions were by far the best formations for peace that had been put forward to date.[2] Again, according to the records, Wilson "borrowed" some of their ideas for his own peace proposals. In total, the congress had small delegations that visited fourteen countries during May and June of 1915. WILPF was founded as an international organization to work globally.

Two of WILPF's original founders, Jane Addams and Emily Greene Balch, received the Nobel Peace Prize, in 1931 and 1946, respectively, for their peace efforts and international views and work.

Women's voices are needed not only at the negotiating tables but also in the larger political institutions that generate and dictate security policy. The utter failure of current conceptions of security, largely defined by men, suggests the need for new approaches by new people. The full and equal participation of women at all levels of national and international life would undoubtedly contribute to addressing the current human security vacuum. Women are still suffering disproportionately in situations of armed conflict, but as more women participate in decision making and negotiating peace and security issues, the hope is that armed conflict will no longer be a tolerable solution and that preparation for armed conflict will not be confused with security.

With this concept in mind, WILPF has organized rallies, lobbied politicians, and pushed members of the United Nations (UN) to find solutions to inequalities as a means of solving all armed conflicts. In 2001 WILPF joined Amnesty International, the Hague Appeal for Peace, International Alert, International Peace Research Association, and the Women's Commission for Refugee Women and Children, and created the NGO Working Group on Women and International Peace and Security. This working group seized a window of opportunity and pushed for a thematic debate in the United Nations Security Council after Ambassador Anwarul Karim Chowdhury of Bangladesh, president of the Security Council, made a ground-breaking statement on March 8, 2000, linking equality, development, peace, and the need for women's urgent involvement in these matters. The combination of contributions from the Namibian presidency of the Security Council, the NGO Working Group, the Division for the Advancement of Women (DAW), and the United Nations Development Fund for Women (UNIFEM) helped to identify and bring the experiences and expertise of civil society into the sacred and once-exclusive realm of the Security Council.

Besides creating a list of experts and NGOs that would speak to the issues in the Security Council, members of the working group lobbied and debated with every Security Council member. Furthermore, they compiled packets of relevant documents with summaries that they hand-delivered to all Security Council members and undertook media strategy to maximize attention on this issue. Synergy among NGOs, UN departments, and governments brought together the strengths of each segment and ensured success. Representatives of WILPF expressed hope and relief that issues so long ignored were at last being registered at the highest levels.

Security Council Resolution 1325

It was a profoundly moving and historic moment when women at last filled the public gallery of the Security Council on October 24, 2000, applauding and cheering. After fifty-five years of efforts on the part of the United Nations to end the scourge of war, women's perspectives on war and peace had finally been acknowledged in the Security Council. Women from Sierra Leone, Guatemala, Somalia, Tanzania, and international NGOs had spoken to members of the Security Council in an Arria Formula meeting[3] the previous day. Arria Formula meetings offer an opportunity for NGO experts to brief the ambassadors on specific topics. These meetings focused on the suffering of women in war, their undervalued and underutilized work to prevent conflict and build peace, and the leadership they demonstrate in rebuilding wartorn societies.

As a result, on October 31, 2000, Security Council members unanimously passed Resolution 1325, which calls for:

- The participation of women in decision-making and peace processes
- Gender perspectives and training in peace-keeping
- The protection of women
- Gender mainstreaming in UN reporting systems and programmatic implementation mechanisms.

Resolution 1325 provides a tool for women because it requires gender sensitivity in all UN missions including peacekeeping, women's equal participation at all negotiating tables, and the protection of women and girls during armed conflict. The last paragraph of this resolution notes that the Security Council "decides to remain actively seized of the matter." This resolution provides an important tool in shifting the UN system from words to action.

SC 1325 in Action: Afghanistan

On the surface, Resolution 1325 might seem like empty words that may never be implemented, but for women's groups involved in peace building in conflict zones worldwide, it is a historic statement with significant implications that can be quoted and used in related contexts. Moreover, as a Security Council resolution, it is binding international law that for the first time officially endorses the inclusion of civil society groups, notably women, in peace processes and in the implementation of peace agreements. Women finally have a tool they can use to become part of the planning for the future of their country. Afghan and non-Afghan women have used this resolution to demand that Mr. Lakhdar Brahimi, the secretary-general's special representative for Afghanistan, meet with five Afghan women immediately after he was appointed.

The United Nations strongly supported the inclusion of women at the Bonn meetings in December 2001. Because of the prioritization of this issue, a few women did participate in the Bonn negotiations. However, the presence of a mere three women as delegates and two as advisors is not enough. Women's involvement in these matters cannot be restricted to a small number of token individuals who are supposed to represent all women. Three people cannot represent so many others, especially when the population they represent is as disparate as Afghan women.

However, acknowledging that there is much room for improvement does not by any means diminish the importance and historic achievement of the participation of women at Bonn. Considering that women are usually absent at high decision-making levels and virtually invisible from negotiations on cease-fires, peace agreements, and postconflict reconstruction, women activists for peace did feel some sense of accomplishment in the participation of five women at the Bonn negotiations. Years of activism, raising awareness, and conferences organized by women in New York, Berlin, and all over the world played a major part in that achievement. We regard it as a turning point and an important benchmark along the road to full and equal participation for women in all aspects and at all levels of governance.

Women rarely participate in negotiating cease-fires and drafting treaties because they do not occupy leadership positions in governments or other armed groups. Women are not leading warring parties. Rather, women constitute the majority of those executed, enslaved, impoverished, and damaged. Ultimately, however, women must be involved in the peace process not only because they suffer disproportionately, or because they have previously been excluded, but because of their contribution to the world is invaluable.

If the importance of the resolution is recognized, it will have profound implications for change. It has the potential to be an effective tool in the hands of the United Nations, NGOs, and governments. In order to ensure collaboration and coordination, Secretary-General Kofi Annan established a task force on women, peace, and security, composed of representatives from fifteen UN entities. This task force is developing an action plan on the implementation of the resolution and will produce a comprehensive report on the role of the United Nations within the year.

UNIFEM also appointed two independent experts who will produce a report with recommendations to the United Nations, governments, and NGOs. The Office of the Coordination of Humanitarian Affairs (OCHA) launched its fund-raising appeal immediately after the resolution was passed to benefit women in conflict zones. The Department for Disarmament Affairs produced a series of briefing papers showing the connections between gender and the full range of disarmament issues, land mines, small arms, weapons of mass destruction, and the peace movement. These developments are only a few examples of the shifting climate within the United Nations.

A Look into the Future

Since the passage of this momentous Resolution, reports on UN peace-keeping operations, such as those on Afghanistan (S/2000/1106), the Democratic Republic of Congo (S/2001/128), Western Sahara (S/2001/148), and other countries, have included material on gender and the situation of women in their countries. The gender unit in East Timor is outstanding in the kinds of reports and information it has produced for the Department of Peace Keeping Operations and the Security Council. It has shown concretely that the efforts of the United Nations on gender, while difficult to establish at first, have enhanced the effectiveness and the sense of integrity of the United Nations in the field. The training that has taken place through the Gender Unit in East Timor will enable women to occupy key positions in the new government. The technical assistance and guidance given to the NGOs trying to navigate the sometimes intimidating UN system should not be underestimated.

Men still disproportionately dominate all of the formal governing bodies of peace and security. Let's face it—they have totally and utterly failed in their efforts. Wars continue to rage everywhere. The fragility of the most militarily powerful nation on earth is exposed. And the result of militarizing countries—arming, training, and paying thugs—turns out to be the formula for antisecurity.

To pressure their governments to take action, women's groups must be made aware of treaties and laws that have been agreed on by their governments to address gender concerns. Nongovernmental organizations can support and sustain women's efforts using the tools provided in Resolution 1325 by:

- Pressing governments to increase the numbers of senior women in the United Nations
- Contributing women's names to rosters for these positions
- Pressing for greater involvement of national and international negotiators in conflict zones and monitoring their actions
- Ensuring that local civil society groups are integrated into all levels and aspects of conflict prevention, resolution, and management
- Lobbying governments to contribute funds for gender training of peacekeepers
- Ensuring gender training in armies
- Monitoring and lobbying for increased civil society involvement in the design and implementation of humanitarian assistance programs in refugee camps
- Collecting gender-sensitive data and testimonies to provide greater accuracy and understanding of the needs of refugees and internally displaced persons
- Monitoring the implementation of Resolution 1325 at national and international levels
- Lobbying for greater consultation with UN agencies in follow-up processes and reports.

A WILPF project in the works will help women monitor progress and share news, campaigning tools, and contact details. Our new website (www.peacewomen.org) aims to pull together the efforts of women working for peace in conflict zones. We wish to make it impossible for the world, especially the United Nations, to ignore the peacebuilding work of women. We exist to support women in their efforts to attain peace and justice, abolish oppression, and to challenge colonialism, discrimination, aggression, occupation, and foreign domination.

One section of the site gathers a comprehensive database of women's organizations in every country to facilitate networking and resourcing. Another section provides a collection of resources, including annotated bibliographies of books, articles, NGO reports, and tools for organizational building that feed critical thinking on sexism and militarism and enable women's groups to proceed in their work better informed. The third part translates the UN resolution into understandable language, focusing on war, peace, and security, and highlighting UN efforts that pertain particularly to women affected by war. The final section features campaigns and news of women who are working for peace and justice around the world.

The words of Security Council Resolution 1325 have translated into action and must continue to do so. The people who comprise the United Nations must ensure that women are included at every level of peace and security, from local communities to international criminal tribunals for countries coming out of conflict.

The doors were open just wide enough for women to squeeze into the peace negotiations in Afghanistan. They came with the knowledge that war is a gendered activity. Now, concerned women and men must use the words of Resolution 1325 to force the doors permanently open, to enter *all* rooms where peace agreements are negotiated and where peacekeeping operations are planned. Afghanistan must be the testing ground for the implementation of Resolution 1325.

NOTES

1. WILPF has offices in New York City and Geneva
2. Gertrude Bussey and Margaret Tims, *Pioneers for Peace, Women's International League for Peace and Freedom: 1915–1917* (Oxford, U.K.: Alden Press, 1980), p. 21.
3. Informal, off-the-record exchanges between security council members and NGOs, often used to provide expert testimony on specific issues, particularly humanitarian concerns.

SEVENTY-FOUR

The Global Women's Movement (2004)
Definitions and Origins

Peggy Antrobus

Peggy Antrobus is an economist, teacher, researcher, consultant, and organizer whose work focuses on women in development. She set up the Women and Development Unit at the University of the West Indies in 1987 and was a founding member of the Caribbean Association for Feminist Research and Action (CAFRA). She was a founding member of DAWN, the network of Third World women promoting Development Alternatives with Women for a New Era, and the International Gender and Trade Network.

. . . This [article] attempts to answer the questions: Is there a global women's movement? How can we understand such a movement? How can it be defined, and what are its characteristics? My conclusion is that there is a global women's movement . . . different from other social movements and . . . defined by diversity, its feminist politics and perspectives, its global reach and its methods of organizing.

Definitions

Many authors admit that this movement does not conform to conventional definitions of a "movement" lacking as it does common objectives, continuity, unity and coordination. Yet this should not surprise us, nor should it be taken as a sign of deficiency. . . . Only a few activists take the view that the objectives of the women's movement are similar to those of labor, human rights and student groups, which seek justice for their members. Many see the objectives of women's groups as broader, seeking changes in relationships that are more varied and complex. At the same time it is sometimes difficult to identify clear objectives; worse, the objectives articulated by some groups seem to contradict those of others. The following quotes from [a] Nigerian case study illustrate the problem:

The Nigerian women's movement is an unarmed movement. It is non-confrontational. It is a movement for the progressive upliftment of women for motherhood, nationhood and development.[1]

And again:

When African women demand equality, we are only asking for our rights not to be tampered with, and the removal of laws that oppress and dehumanize women. We are not asking for equality with our husbands. We accept them as the bosses and heads of the family.[2]

The confusion and contradictions captured in these statements reflect the complexity of a movement that is caught in the tension between what is possible and what is dreamed of, between short-term goals and long-term visions, between expediency and risk-taking, pragmatism and surrender, between the practical and the strategic. Most of all, there is understandable ambivalence surrounding challenging and confronting relationships that are intimate and deeply felt. But the confusion also reflects a lack of clarity about definitions of what groups might be considered part of a "women's movement."

Many activists, including Nigerian activists who identify themselves with a women's movement, would question definitions of the objectives of their movement in terms of the "upliftment of women for motherhood, nationhood and development." They would argue that this instrumentalizes women, while being in complete accord with patriarchal definitions of women's traditional role.

It seems to me that the continuing confusion about what defines women's movements relates not so much to the fact that this movement does not conform to a conventional definition of a movement, but rather to lack of clarity about objectives in contexts that differ widely.

One way of clarifying these apparent contradictions is to recognize two mutually reinforcing tendencies within women's movements—one focused on gender identity (identity politics) and the other concerned with a larger project for social transformation. There are two entry points to concerns about a larger social project. One is recognition of the centrality of the care and nurture of human beings to the large social project, and that to address this, given the primacy of women's gendered role in this area, requires addressing gender relations in all the complex interplay of their economic, social, political, cultural and personal dimensions. It also involves locating gender inequality within other forms of inequality that shape and often exacerbate it.

Another entry point is recognition that women cannot be separated from the larger context of their lived experience and that this includes considerations of class, race/ethnicity and geographic location, among other factors. This means that the struggle for women's agency must include engagement in struggles against sources of women's oppression that extend beyond gender.

The larger social project would therefore include transforming social institutions, practices and beliefs so that they address gender relations along with other oppressive relationships, not simply seeking a better place within existing institutions and structures. For this reason, women's movements in countries where the majority of women are marginalized by class, race or ethnicity must be concerned with the larger social project. This is often a point of tension between women's movements in the context of North–South relations, as well as in the context of struggles against oppression on the basis of class, race and ethnicity.

I believe that confusion about definitions of women's movements is also caused by failure to make distinctions between women's organizations as part of a wide spectrum of non-governmental organizations (NGOs) or civil society organizations (CSOs), and those that might be better understood as part of a politically oriented social movement.

Similarly, the term "women's movements" is sometimes used interchangeably with "feminist movements," an error that confuses and misrepresents both feminism and the broad spectrum of women's organizations.

In the final analysis, it seems to me that the identification of feminist politics as the engine of women's movements may help to clarify some of the confusion around women's organizing . . . as well as to focus the answer to the central question: Can women's movements make a difference in the struggle for equity, democracy and sustainability in today's globalized economy? It is the combination of struggles for gender justice with those for economic justice and democracy that enables women's movements to make a difference to the larger social project for transformation of systems and relationships.

An important segment of women's movements is composed of the associations that work to incorporate a feminist perspective into their theoretical, analytical, professional and political work. In academia, most disciplines now have feminist associations—Anthropology, Economics, Political, Social and Natural Sciences and Theology, among others. Moreover, within these disciplines—whether women are organized into feminist associations or not—women in the academies are doing important theoretical and empirical work that deepens our understanding of women's realities and produces the analyses and insights that strengthen the work of activists.

In the professions there are also women's associations—doctors, nurses, midwives, social workers, teachers, lawyers, bankers, etc.—that are challenging patriarchal patterns and relationships, raising new questions and changing the practices and methods by which their professions operate.

Many women's organizations, even those that focus on traditional concerns of home and family, are nevertheless important participants in women's movements. Among these are grassroots women's organizations of various kinds—Women's Institutes, Federations of Women, the YWCA, and many worldwide organizations identified with strong advocacy on behalf of women's rights, although they may not describe themselves as feminist.[3]

Finally, a definition of a women's movement must include those individual women who would never join an organization, nor define themselves as feminists, but whose lives and actions nevertheless serve to advance the liberation of women in their community and beyond.

All of these women must be seen as part of, or at least contributing to, women's movements. They are all part of the diversity and richness of a movement that seeks change in the relationships of superiority and inferiority, domination and subordination between women and men in a patriarchal world.

The following statements summarize my own views on women's movements:

- A women's movement is a *political* movement—part of the broad array of social movements concerned with changing social conditions . . .

- A women's movement is grounded in an understanding of women's relations to *social conditions*—an understanding of gender as an important relationship within the broad structure of social relationships of class, race and ethnicity, age and location.

- A women's movement is a *process,* discontinuous, flexible, responding to specific conditions of perceived gender inequality or gender-related injustice. Its focal points may be in women's organizations, but it embraces individual women in various locations who identify with the goals of feminism at a particular point in time.

- Awareness and *rejection of patriarchal privilege* and control are central to the politics of women's movements.

- In most instances, the "movement" is born at the moments in which individual women become aware of *their separateness as women,* their alienation, marginalization, isolation or even abandonment within a broader movement for social justice or social change. In other words, women's struggle for agency within the broader struggle is the catalyst for women's movements.

bell hooks describes this process of *conscientization* thus:

> Our search leads us back to where it all began, to that moment when an individual woman . . . who may have thought she was all alone, began a feminist uprising, began to name her practice, indeed began to formulate theory from lived experience.[4]

Women from across the world who identify themselves as part of an international and global women's movement are to be found participating in international meetings organized by feminist associations, networks and organizations such as the International Inter-disciplinary Congress, the Association for Women's Rights and Development (AWID) and UN conferences.[5] They celebrate annual special "days" such as International Women's Day (IWD) on 8 March and International Day Against Violence Against Women on 25 November. They are in constant communication with each other through the Internet, where they sign petitions and statements in solidarity with women around the world, formulate strategies and organize campaigns and meetings.

The movement has important resources:

- resource centers such as the International Women's Tribune Centre (IWTC), set up following the 1975 International Women's Year (IWY) Conference in Mexico City;

- media, such as feminist radio stations like the Costa Rica–based FIRE (Feminist International Radio Endeavor); news services like WINGS (Women's International News Gathering Service) and Women's Feature Services (WFS), supported initially by UNESCO;

- websites;

- publishers and women's presses;

- artists . . . —filmmakers, musicians, dancers, painters, writers, poets and playwrights;

- women's funds started by individual philanthropists and organizations that support women's projects, organizations and networks.

Characteristics

Diversity

Experience of the past thirty years points to the pitfall of starting with an assumption of a "global sisterhood," especially when that "sisterhood" is defined by a privileged minority. The emergence of a global movement has indeed depended on the emergence of new and different voices challenging hegemonic tendencies and claiming their own voice and space, and the acceptance of differences within the movements.

Diversity is now recognized as perhaps the most important characteristic of women's movements. Nevertheless, many of the tensions among women in their movements can be related to differences of race/ethnicity, nationality/culture and class, although, as Audre Lorde points out:

> [I]t is not those differences between us that are separating us. It is rather our refusal to recognize [them] and to examine the distortions which result from our misnaming them and their effects upon human behaviour and expectation.[6]

She also reminds us, "There is no such thing as a single-issue struggle because we do not live single-issue lives."[7] Women understand that each of us has multiple identities and that at any point in time one or other may be more important than others. Insistence on focusing on gender in isolation from issues like race, ethnicity and class has often been more divisive than the inclusion of these issues in the agendas of the various movements. It is indeed impossible and even counterproductive to separate the varied forms of oppression because of the systemic links between them. Thus in many countries of the South women have had to confront colonialism, imperialism or racism before they could confront patriarchy.

Feminist Politics

It may be useful to identify feminism as a specific politics, grounded in a consciousness of all the sources of women's subordination, and with a commitment to challenge and change the relationships and structures which perpetuate women's subordinate position, in solidarity with other women. The consciousness of sexism and sexist oppression is the essence of feminist politics, and it is this politics that energizes women's movements, whether or not the word "feminist" is used. It is possible then to identify feminist politics as a specific element within a broader universe of women's organizations, women's movements and other social movements.

Feminists have worked with and within other social movements—especially those on peace, racism, the environment, indigenous peoples and the poor. These initiatives have served both to broaden and redefine the issues of concern to women, as well as to refocus the agendas of these movements.

In addition, there are feminists within institutions and agencies who recognize the ways in which the ideology of patriarchy constrains and diminishes the achievement of laudable goals and objectives, and who engage in the struggle to challenge it.

Feminist politics can also be identified within bureaucratic initiatives and institutional arrangements established for the improvement of the condition and position of women, enabling them to contribute to the movement for gender justice. These include women's bureaus, desks, commissions, special units and gender focal points within mainstream institutions.

Global Reach

Our understanding of the diversity within women's movements that has led us to speak more often of a multiplicity of "movements" would lead many to question the concept of a single global women's movement. However, I would argue, as others have done, that despite the rich diversity of experience, grounded in specific local struggles, women have been able to transcend these to become a movement of global proportions, with a global agenda and perspective.

Here I want to distinguish between an international women's movement and a global women's movement.[8] Although, as Uta Ruppert has pointed out, local or national women's movements have never viewed their activities as "simply crossing the borders of nation states,"[9] I would conceptualize an "international" movement as one in which the national and cultural differences between women were recognizable and paramount. Indeed, this was characteristic of women's movements at the international level in the mid-1970s, at the launching of the UN Decade for Women (1975–85), and to some extent throughout most of the Decade. However, as women established their separate identities along the prevailing axes of North–South, East–West, they discovered commonalities that moved them increasingly towards greater coherence and even common positions in the policy debates around issues of environment, poverty, violence and human rights. At the same time, as these issues became increasingly "global" (as reflected in the themes and agendas of the global conferences of the 1990s), women's movements converged in these global arenas to negotiate and articulate common agendas and positions. As Ruppert puts it:

The political process of international women's movements has been shaped by the insight that international politics does not simply take place at the inter-nation-state level, but also encompasses multicentric and multilevel processes. Thus the movement's multidimensional political understanding, which is sensitive to differences, almost predestined it to become the most global of social movements of the 1990s.[10]

She goes on to identify:

[A] second component . . . essential for the women's movement to become an effective global actor, [which] was the movement's shift toward aiming for "globality" as a main objective. Even though there has never been an explicit discourse along these lines, the movement's political practice suggests a conceptual differentiation between three different political approaches on the global level: criticizing and combating globalization as a neoliberal paradigm; utilizing global politics, or rather global governance, as tools for governance under the conditions of globalization; and specifically creating "globality,"[11] which the women's movement has aimed for and worked towards as an important factor in women's global politics.[12]

Methods of Organizing

It is widely understood that a characteristic of a global women's movement is the linking of local to global, the particularities of local experience and struggles to, as Ruppert says, "the political creation and establishment of global norms for world development and global ethics for industrial production, such as (social and gender) justice, sustainability and peace, based on the creation of globally valid fundamental human rights."[13] However, few have related this to the particular methods of feminist organizing.

Although . . . this practice has not been the subject of an explicit discourse, it has nevertheless been based on conscious decisions to involve women from different backgrounds and regions in the search for "globality." These decisions have been the result of an understanding of the ways in which global events, trends and policies impact on local experience, and in particular on the experiences of poor women in the global South.

While Ruppert and others cite women's organizing around the 1992 UN Conference on Environment and Development (UNCED) and the 1993 International Conference on Human Rights as the first signs of this kind of organizing, I would refer to the experience of the network of Third World women, DAWN,[14] in their preparations for the Forum of the 1985 Third World Conference on Women. It was here that a conscious attempt was made to bring together local and regional experiences as the beginning of a process for the preparation of a platform document for a global event.

. . . The starting point was a meeting at which women were invited to reflect on their experience of development over the course of the Decade for Women—from the perspective of poor women living in the economic South. In this way the final document reflected regional differences, even as it reached for a framework that revealed the linkages between these experiences. This process—which starts with testifying to local, regional, or even individual experiences ("telling our stories," "speaking our truths"), leading to the negotiation of differences and finally to the articulation of a position that attempts to generalize, synthesize or "globalize" the diversity of experience—was repeated in the processes leading to the global conferences on environment, human rights and population. . . .

This methodology, clearly related to that of feminist consciousness-raising and Freirian *conscientization*[15] (combining reflection on personal experience with socio-political analysis to construct and generate global advocacy) has been a powerful tool for the global women's movement. Like *conscientization*, which takes specific realities "on the ground" as the basis for social analysis that can lead to action, it is a *praxis* (process of reflection and action) that has helped to mobilize women to challenge neoliberal and fundamentalist state policies at national and global levels. This praxis has also been a powerful tool in feminist theorizing.

To drive home one of the differences between international women's movements and a global women's movement, I want to compare this feminist method of globalizing to the process of regional meetings and consultations used by the UN in the preparation of their international conferences. The documents that feed into and emerge from these processes have to be screened and sanctioned by governments and, by their very nature, are limited in the degree to which they are able to reflect the realities of women. While the plans and platforms of action that emerge from the conferences contain many recommendations and resolutions that accord with the advocacy of women's movements, they often lack the coherence and clarity of the platforms produced by a movement unrestrained by the conventions of international diplomacy. Moreover, without the vigilance and political activism of women's movements, especially at local or national, but also at global, levels, these recommendations are meaningless to women.

This brings me to another aspect of the links between global and local—the ways in which local actors organize to defend themselves against global threats. Recognizing the relationship between global trends and local realities, women are organizing around the defence of their bodies, their livelihoods and their communities. The word "glocality" has been coined to highlight the ways in which global trends affect local experience. This recognition of a "politics of place" poses new challenges to a global women's movement. While organizing in the defence of "place" has the potential to be the most powerful and effective form of organizing,[16] local groups clearly need information and analysis on the broader policy frameworks that are affecting their lives. A global women's movement also needs links to this level of organizing to retain its relevance and to legitimize its advocacy.

The global women's movement is very aware that action at global level must have resonance at local, national and regional levels if it is to be meaningful to women. In this sense we need to see the global women's movement as made up of many interlocking networks. Many of the global networks have worked to strengthen their links to activities at regional, national and local levels.

A second method of organizing . . . is networking. Some may say that women's movements invented networking! Networking is the method used to make the vertical (local-global) as well as the horizontal (inter-regional as well as issue-specific) links that generate the analysis and the organizing underlying global action.

A third is the linking of the personal to the political, the ways in which gender identification and recognition of common experience can short-circuit difference to create a sense of solidarity. This often makes it easier for women who are strangers to each other to work together.

Symbols and Images

In the final analysis, words may not be enough to enable us to understand the complexity of a global women's movement made up of such a diversity of movements. . . . I have often been struck by the ways in which images and symbols capture the shape and structure of a global women's movement. The images and symbols that come to mind are those of the spiral, the wheel, the pyramid, the web and the patchwork quilt.

A spiral is an open-ended circle. As an adjective it is a "winding about a centre in an enlarging or decreasing continuous cone." As a noun, "a plane or three-dimensional spiral curve" (*Concise Oxford Dictionary*, 1990). In both cases it captures images of continuity and change, depth and expansion—something that is identifiable yet varied.

. . . A spiral is open-ended, continuous, ever enlarging our understanding of events, our perspectives. The global women's movement can be thought of as a spiral, a process that starts at the centre (rather than at the beginning of a line) and works its way outwards, turning, arriving at what might appear to be the same point, but in reality at an expanded understanding of the same event.

A spiral is also dialectic, allowing for the organic growth of a movement of women organizing—a movement in a state of on-going evolution as consciousness expands in the process of exchanges between women, taking us backwards (to rethink and reevaluate old positions) and forwards (to new areas of awareness).

As a number of interlocking networks, a global women's movement might also be likened to pyramids, webs and wheels. In a study of two campaigns, the campaign against breast-milk substitutes in Ghana, and against child labor in the carpet industry in India, the New Economics Foundation (NEF) identified

> three structures for organizing constructive collaboration: the pyramid, the wheel, and the web. Pyramids have a coordinating secretariat who disseminates information through the

campaign; wheels have one or more focal points for information exchange, but information also flows directly among the members; in the web, no focal point exist, so information flows to and from all the members in roughly equal quantities.[17]

The pyramid, the wheel and the web underline the fluidity of the global women's movement, comprised as it is of interlocking networks that come together as appropriate, even as each continues to focus on its specific area of interest.

The movement can also be understood as a patchwork quilt, full of color and different patterns, discontinuous and defying description, but nonetheless an identifiable entity made up of units that have their own integrity. A quilt, an art form peculiarly developed by women, uses whatever material is available to make something both beautiful and functional. It represents ingenuity, creativity, caring and comfort. A global women's movement can have no better symbol as it seeks to create a world in which people might find beauty, comfort and security.

Origins

Since the concept of a global women's movement conceals the actors who make it possible, I turn now to consider some of the contexts that energized the local struggles out of which a global movement was formed. Reference is often made to "three waves" of the women's movement: the first wave of the late 19th–early 20th century, the second covering the mid-20th century, and the third, the late 20th century. Although these waves are often depicted as distinct, it is instructive to look at the connections between them because, as Gita Sen points out:

> They delineate in an early form potential strengths as well as tensions that characterize the international women's movement right until today. The presence of multiple strands from early on has made for a movement that is broad and capable of addressing a wide range of issues. But the potential tensions between prioritizing economic issues (such as control over resources and property) or women's personal autonomy or bodily integrity existed then and continue to exist now.[18]

Conclusion

It is clear that, despite the lack of clear and common objectives, continuity, unity and coordination, . . . there is nevertheless an identifiable movement enriched by its diversity and complexity, sustained by the depth of its passions and enduring commitment to its causes, and strengthened by the apparent lack of coordination and spontaneity of its strategizing.

Varied experiences highlight the complexity of women's struggles, the interplay between race, class and gender and the need to distinguish between the material and the ideological relations of gender.

There are many roads to the awareness that manifests as involvement in a women's organization or identification as part of a women's movement. There are still more steps towards a feminist consciousness, which would transform involvement in a women's organization into a political struggle for gender equity and equality, often within a broader project for social transformation. Many of the women involved in women's organizations, or movements, were influenced by leftist politics, and discovered their own marginalization within the processes of these struggles. Others began the journey to feminist consciousness through personal experiences; still others through their work experience. A characteristic of many of those involved in women's movements is the process of personal transformation which they undergo as they become aware of gender subordination. At the same time, this essentially individualistic experience seems to engender a connection to the wider universe of injustice in a way that leads to a better understanding of the link between different forms of oppression and builds life-long commitments to the struggle against injustice.

Given these histories, there is no doubt that there is a global women's movement, recognizable in its understanding of how "common difference"[19] links us all in a political struggle for recognition and redistributive justice. Its difference from other social movements lies not only in the absence of homogeneity . . . but in the value it places on diversity, its commitment to solidarity with women everywhere, its feminist politics and its methods of organizing. . . . as an important global actor in the struggles for a more equitable, humane, sustainable and secure world.

NOTES

1. Interview with representatives of the National Commission for Women, Abuja, 2 February 1993, Amrita Basu (ed.) *The challenge of local feminism: Women's movements in global perspective.* Boulder: Westview Press. (1995), p. 211.

2. Interview with Obiageli Nwankwo, project coordinator, International Federation of Women Lawyers, Enugu, 1993, Basu (1995), p. 212.

3. However, there may be self-defined feminists among their members.

4. bell hooks, 1994. *Teaching to transgress.* New York: Routledge, p. 75.

5. Although UN conferences are also attended by women and organizations that are opposed to advances in women's human rights, as was seen at the Five-Year-Review of the Fourth World Conference on Women, when the call went out from right-wing religion-based organizations for women to come to New York to "defend" women against that "dangerous" document, the Beijing *Platform for Action.*

6. Audre Lorde, *Sister outsider: Essays and speeches by Audre Lorde.* Freedom, Calif.: Crossing Press. p. 115.

7. Ibid., p. 138.

8. In thinking about this distinction I have found Uta Ruppert's analysis extremely helpful in M. Braig and S. Wolte (eds.) 2002. *Common ground or mutual exclusion? Women's movements and international relations.* New York: Zed Books.

9. Ibid., p. 148.

10. Ibid., p. 149.

11. Ruppert defines *globality* as "everything global politics or global governance should be based on or directly accompanied by" (ibid., p. 151).

12. Ibid.

13. Ibid.

14. The Network of Third World women promoting Development Alternatives with Women for a New Era. www.dawn.org.fj.

15. The combination of consciousness and action, "praxis," introduced by Brazilian educator, Paolo Freire, to enable oppressed groups to gain an understanding of the forces impinging on their world, the sources of their oppression.

16. Examples abound. The work of the Chipko movements and of the Self-Employed Women's Association (India) come to mind because they are so well-documented; however, there are examples of this kind of organizing in every region.

17. Jennifer Chapman. 2001. What makes international campaigns effective? Lessons from India and Ghana. In *Global citizen action,* edited by M. Edwards and J. Gaventa, Boulder: Lynne Rienner Publishers, pp. 263–64.

18. Gita Sen. 2003. The politics of the international women's movement. In *Claiming global power: Transnational civil society and global governance,* edited by Srilatha Batliwala and David Brown. Kumarian Press.

19. Gloria Joseph and Jill Lewis. 1986. *Common differences: Conflicts in Black and White feminist perspectives.* Boston: South End Press.

Glossary

GLOSSARY OF TERMS IN COMMON USE

This glossary contains key concepts found in this book. The first time the concept is used in the text it is shown in **bold.** Refer to the definitions here to refresh your memory when you come across the terms again later.

able-bodyism—Attitudes, actions, and institutional practices that subordinate people with disabilities.

adultism—Attitudes, actions, and institutional practices that subordinate young people on the basis of their age.

ageism—Attitudes, actions, and institutional practices that subordinate elderly persons on the basis of their age.

alliance—Working with others as a result of a deepening understanding of one another's lives, experiences, and goals.

analytical framework—A theoretical perspective that allows one to analyze the causes and implications of a particular issue, rather than simply describing it.

anti-Arabism—Attitudes, actions, and institutional practices that subordinate Arabs and Arab Americans.

anti-Semitism—Attitudes, actions, and institutional practices that subordinate Jewish people. (The term *Semite* is used also to refer to some Arabs.)

assimilation—The process by which a minority group adopts the customs, values, and attitudes of the dominant culture.

biological determinism—A general theory holding that a group's biological or genetic makeup shapes its social, political, and economic destiny. This view is used to justify women's subordination or the subordination of peoples of color on the argument that they are biologically or genetically different from, and usually inferior to, men or white people, respectively.

Black nationalism—A radical redefinition of Black national identity that challenges mainstream African American identities; opposes white racism; promotes economic, political, social, and cultural independence for African Americans; and promotes various African-based forms of culture, models of learning, and so on for the African diaspora in the United States. Black nationalism is often male-dominated in its theorizing and practice.

blame the victim—An analysis or recommended course of action that attributes responsibility for a problem to those who experience it. An example is to urge women not to be out alone at night, for their safety, rather than to curb male violence against women.

Bretton Woods Agreements—In 1944, delegates from 44 allied nations who met at Bretton Woods

(New Hampshire) agreed to the formation of international financial institutions such as the World Bank and International Monetary Fund for rebuilding and regulating the international economic system after World War II.

capital—Money and property invested in manufacturing, communications, agricultural, or financial ventures.

capitalism—An economic system in which most of the **capital**—property, raw materials, and the means of production (including people's labor)—and goods produced are owned or controlled by individuals or groups—capitalists. The goal of all production is to maximize profit making. Also referred to as **free market system.**

classism—Attitudes, actions, and institutional practices that subordinate working-class and poor people on the basis of their economic condition.

coalition—Usually a short-term collaboration of organizations in which the strategy is to stand together to achieve a specific goal or set of goals around a particular issue, regardless of other differences among the organizations.

commodification—The process of turning people into things, or commodities, for sale; an example is the commodification of women's bodies through advertising and media representations.

comparable worth—A method of evaluating jobs that are traditionally defined as men's work or women's work—in terms of the knowledge and skills required for a particular job; the mental demands or decision making involved; the accountability or degree of supervision involved; and working conditions, such as how physically safe the job is—so as to eliminate inequities in pay based on gender.

conscientization—A methodology for understanding reality, or gaining a "critical consciousness," through group dialogue, critical analysis, and examination of people's experiences and conditions that face them, which leads to action to transform that reality (Freire 1989).

contested terrain—An area of debate or controversy, in which several individuals or groups attempt to impose their own views or meanings on a situation.

criminalization—The process of turning people's circumstances or behaviors into a crime, such as the criminalization of homeless people or mothers with HIV/AIDS.

cultural appropriation—Taking possession of specific aspects of another group's culture in a gratuitous, inauthentic way, as happens, for example, when white people wear their hair in "dreads" or when nonindigenous people use indigenous people's names and symbols or adopt indigenous people's spiritual practices without being taught by indigenous practitioners. A particularly egregious form of cultural appropriation involves using another group's culture to make money. This is routine in the tourist industry, and it also occurs in the "New Age" spirituality movement, for example.

culture—The values, symbols, means of expression, language, and interests of a group of people. The **dominant culture** includes the values, symbols, means of expression, language, and interests of people in power in this society.

discrimination—Differential treatment against less powerful groups (such as women, the elderly, or people of color) by those in positions of dominance.

ecofeminism—A philosophy that links the domination of women with the domination of nature.

ecological footprint—The amount of land and energy required by various lifestyles and levels of consumption; calculated by estimating the amount of productive land needed to provide food, housing, transport, and consumer goods and services, and to absorb the waste that results from these processes; expressed in hectares or acres.

emigrate—The process of leaving one's native country to settle in another.

environmental racism—The strong correlation between the distribution of environmental pollution and race; the movement for **environmental justice** draws on concepts of civil rights, whereby all citizens have a right to healthy living and working conditions.

epistemology—A theory about knowledge, including its sources, structure, validity, and limits. This includes who can know, under what circumstances, and the researcher's values and choices about how to carry out their inquiry.

essentialism—The view that people have some inherent essence, or characteristics and qualities, that define them. Some people argue, for example, that women are essentially more caring and nurturing than men.

eugenics—The belief that the human race can be "improved" through selective breeding; linked to racism and able-bodyism.

feminization of poverty—Women and children constitute the majority of poor people in the United States and throughout the world, a result of structural inequalities and discriminatory policies.

fertility rate—The number of children born to women between 15 and 44, considered by official census reports to be the childbearing years.

first-wave feminism—Organizations and projects undertaken by suffragists and women's rights advocates from the 1830s to the 1920s.

First World—Countries grouped together according to political alliances and economic status: western Europe, Japan, Australia, New Zealand, Canada, and the United States. This is often contrasted with the **Third World,** which includes most of Asia, Latin America, Africa, and the Caribbean.

free market system—An ideological term used to describe a capitalist economic system with an emphasis on transnational trade and freedom from government regulation. In reality, this system has both government regulation of and support for businesses.

gender bending—Adopting clothing, body language, or behavior that challenges and undermines conventional gender norms and expectations.

gendered division of labor—A division of duties between men and women under which women have the main responsibility for home and nurturing and men are mainly active in the public sphere. Also referred to as **gender roles.**

gender gap—A significant difference between the political attitudes and voting patterns of women and men.

gender socialization—The process of learning the attitudes and behaviors that are considered culturally appropriate for boys or girls.

glass ceiling—An unseen barrier to women's promotion to senior positions in the workplace. Women can see the senior positions in their company or field, but few women reach them because of negative attitudes toward senior women and low perceptions of their abilities and training. This barrier may also be based on race/ethnicity.

globalization—Contemporary form of cultural and economic integration facilitated by electronic media, international financial institutions, trade agreements, and national immigration policies.

global level—A term used to describe and analyze the connections among people, institutions, and issues as viewed from a worldwide perspective.

glocalization—Emphasis on the overlap of local and global. Transnational corporate decisions made according to rules established by international financial institutions affect local economies (nations, cities, and neighborhoods) that may be thousands of miles away from those who make these decisions.

hegemony—A dominant organizing principle or the permeation throughout society of the ruling elite's values, attitudes, beliefs, and morality. To the extent that people internalize this prevailing consciousness, it appears natural.

heteronormativity—Portrayal of the institution of heterosexuality, its norms and practices, as natural and inevitable; also "compulsory heterosexuality" (Rich 1986a).

heterosexism—Attitudes, actions, and institutional practices that subordinate people on the basis of their gay, lesbian, bisexual, or transgender orientation and identification.

identity-based politics—Activism and politics that have a strong identity component but also a broader view that allows people to make connections to other groups and issues.

identity politics—Activism and politics that put identity at the center. This usually involves the assumption that a particular characteristic, such as race, ethnicity, or sexual orientation, is the most important in the lives of group members and that the group is not differentiated according to other characteristics in a significant way.

ideology—Ideas, attitudes, and values that represent the interests of a group of people. The dominant ideology comprises the ideas, attitudes, and values that represent the interests of the dominant group(s). The ideological role of the idealized nuclear family, for example, is to devalue other family forms.

immigrate—The process of moving to and settling in another country.

imperialism—The process of domination of one nation over other nations that are deemed inferior for the purpose of exploiting their human and natural resources, to consolidate its power and wealth. An empire is able to draw resources from many nations and to deploy those governments and territories in its interest. Examples include the Roman empire, the British empire, and the current U.S. empire.

internalized oppression—Attitudes and behavior of some oppressed people that reflect the negative, harmful, stereotypical beliefs of the dominant group directed at them. An example of internalized sexism is the view of some women that they and other women are inferior to men, which causes them to adopt attitudes and behaviors that reinforce the subordination of women.

international—Relationships among nation states.

international division of labor—A division of work between rich and poor countries under which low-waged workers in the global South do assembly, manufacturing, and office work on contract to companies based in the global North.

intersectionality—An integrative perspective that emphasizes the intersection of several attributes, for example, gender, race, class, and nation.

liberal feminism—A philosophy that sees the oppression of women as a denial of equal rights, representation, and access to opportunities.

liberalism—A political theory about individual rights, freedom, choice, and privacy with roots in seventeenth-century European ideas (e.g., the writings of political philosopher John Locke).

macro level—A term used to analyze the relationships among issues, individuals, and groups as viewed from a national institutional perspective.

marginality—The situation in which a person has a deep connection to more than one culture, community, or social group but is not completely able to identify with or be accepted by that group as an insider. For example, bisexual, mixed-race/mixed-culture, and immigrant peoples have connections with different groups and may find themselves caught between two or more social worlds.

marginalization—Attitudes and behaviors that relegate certain people to the social, political, and economic margins of society by branding them and their interests as inferior, unimportant, or both.

matrix of oppression and resistance—The interconnections among various forms of oppression based on gender, race, class, nation, and so on.

These social attributes can be sources of disadvantage or privilege. Negative ascriptions and experiences may be the source of people's resistance to oppression.

medicalization—The process of turning life processes, like childbirth or menopause, into medical issues. Thus, menopause becomes an illness to be treated by medical professionals with formal educational qualifications and accreditation. By the same token, experienced midwives are considered unqualified because they lack these credentials.

meso level—A term used to analyze the relationships among issues, individuals, and groups as viewed from a community, or local, perspective.

micro level—A term used to analyze the connections among people and issues as seen from a personal or individual perspective.

militarism—A system and worldview based on the objectification of "others" as enemies, a culture that prepares for, invests in, and celebrates war and killing. This worldview operates through specific political, economic, and military institutions and actions.

militarized masculinity—A masculinity constructed to support militarism, with an emphasis on heroism, physical strength, lack of emotion, and appearance of invulnerability (Enloe 1990, 1993a).

misogyny—Woman-hating attitudes and behavior.

neocolonialism—Economic, political, and cultural domination by which a nation maintains or extends its control and influence over other nations, creating new forms of colonialism.

neoliberal/neoliberalism—Economic philosophy and policies that call for the freedom of business to operate with minimal interference from governments, international organizations, or labor unions. Basic tenets include the rule of the market, free trade, economic deregulation, privatization of government-owned industries, reduction of social welfare spending, and belief in individual responsibility rather than valuing community and the public good. Termed "neo" liberal because it calls for a revival of the free-market philosophy that prevailed in the U.S. through the 1800s and early 1900s prior to the enhanced role of government that gained legitimacy during the Depression (1930s), culminating in the "War on Poverty" and other "Great Society" programs of the 1960s.

objectification—Attitudes and behaviors by which people are treated as if they were "things." One example is the objectification of women through advertising images.

objectivity—A form of understanding in which knowledge and meaning are believed to come from outside oneself and are presumably not affected by personal opinion or bias.

offshore production—Factory work or office work performed outside the United States—for example, in Mexico, the Philippines, or Indonesia—that is done for U.S.-based companies. Sales and support jobs are also outsourced.

oppression—Prejudice and discrimination directed toward whole social groups and promoted by the ideologies and practices of all social institutions. The critical elements differentiating oppression from simple prejudice and discrimination are that it is a group phenomenon and that institutional power and authority are used to support prejudices and enforce discriminatory behaviors in systematic ways. Everyone is socialized to participate in oppressive practices, either as direct and indirect perpetrators or passive beneficiaries, or—as with some oppressed peoples—by directing discriminatory behaviors at members of one's own group or another group deemed inferior. See **internalized oppression.**

paradigm shift—A complete change in one's view of the world.

patriarchy—A family, social group, or society in which men hold power and are dominant figures. Patriarchal power in the United States plays out in the family, the economy, the media, religion, law, and electoral politics.

peer marriage—An intentionally egalitarian marriage with an emphasis on partnership, cooperation, and shared roles that are not highly differentiated along gender lines.

positivism—A version of empirical science to be applied to social as well as physical phenomena. French philosopher August Comte believed that the only authentic knowledge is scientific knowledge and that such knowledge can only come from positive affirmation of theories through strict scientific method.

postcolonial feminism—A perspective that critiques Western imperialism and imperialist tendencies of Western feminism and emphasizes historically defined colonial power relations that provide a foundational context for women's lives and struggles for change.

postmodern feminism—A type of feminism based on ideas of the fluidity of social categories depending on historical time, place, and cultural context. An analysis of subjectivity is central, meaning "the ways we understand ourselves as subjects positioned by discourses or ideologies" (Stacey 1993, p. 64) and constrained by power structures and institutions.

poverty level—An income level for individuals and families that officially defines poverty.

power—The ability to influence others, whether through persuasion, charisma, law, political activism, or coercion. Power operates informally and through formal institutions and at all levels (micro, meso, macro, global).

power elite—A relatively small group—not always easily identifiable—of key politicians, senior corporate executives, the very rich, and opinion makers such as key media figures who influence political and economic decisions in the country. Although this group shifts over time and according to the issue, it is relatively closed.

praxis—Reflection and action upon the world in order to transform it; a key part of socially lived theorizing.

precautionary principle—The view that when an activity raises threats of harm to human health or the environment, precautionary measures should be taken even if some cause and effect relationships are not fully established scientifically. Those proposing the activity should bear the burden of proof rather than the public.

prejudice—A closed-minded prejudging of a person or group as negative or inferior, even without personal knowledge of that person or group and often contrary to reason or facts; unreasonable, unfair, and hostile attitudes toward people.

privilege—Benefits and power from institutional inequalities. Individuals and groups may be privileged without realizing, recognizing, or even wanting it.

productive economy—Characterized by monetary exchanges through trade, the organization of work, distribution and marketing of goods, contracts, negotiation of wages and salaries, and so forth.

public versus private dichotomy—The view that distinguishes between the private and personal (dating, marriage, sexual habits, who does the housework, relationships between parents and children) and the public (religion, law, business). Although these two spheres affect each other, according to this view they are governed by different rules, attitudes, and behavior.

racism—Racial prejudice and discrimination that are supported by institutional power and authority. In the United States, racism is based on the ideology of white (European) superiority and is used to the advantage of white people and the disadvantage of peoples of color.

radical feminism—A philosophy that sees the oppression of women in terms of patriarchy, a system of male power and authority, especially manifested in sexuality, personal relationships, and the family, and carried into the male-dominated world of work, government, religion, media, and law.

relativism—The view that all "authentic" experience is equally valid and cannot be challenged by others. For example, White Supremacist views of Ku Klux Klan members are seen to be equally as valid as those held by antiracist activists. There are no external standards or principles by which to judge people's attitudes and behaviors.

relocalization—Emphasis on local production and use of goods, crops, and media productions rather than on production for export. "Relocalization would conserve resources, generate meaningful work, fulfill basic needs, and strengthen democracy" (Shiva 2002, p. 249).

reproductive economy—This domestic labor includes biological and social reproduction, mainly done by women, to maintain daily life, raise children, care for elders, and so on. It is often considered unproductive because it is unwaged, but it is fundamental to the ability to do waged work.

reproductive justice—A perspective that links health and reproductive rights to broader issues of social and economic justice. It offers a view of wellness for individuals, communities, and the wider society based on the eradication of inequality, oppression, and injustice.

second shift—Responsibilities for household chores and child care mostly by women after having already done a full day's work outside the home.

second-wave feminism—Feminist projects and organizations from the late 1960s to the mid-1980s that campaigned for women's equality in all spheres of life and, in some cases, that argued for a complete transformation of patriarchal, capitalist structures. See **liberal feminism, radical feminism, socialist feminism.**

separatism—The process of creating a separate life-space, often for political purposes, such as white lesbian separatists in the 1970s who chose to live in community with other women, to work with women, and to support women's projects. Some people of color may also advocate separatism from white people, institutions, values, and culture and decide to put their energies only in support of other people of color.

sexism—Attitudes, actions, and institutional practices that subordinate individuals because of their gender.

situated knowledge—Knowledge and ways of knowing that are specific to a particular historical and cultural context and life experiences.

social capital—Recognition, knowledge, and connections based on family, community, and institutional ties that provide potential or actual resources for individuals or groups in seeking jobs, access to education, media coverage, or other opportunities.

social constructionism—The view that concepts that appear to be immutable and often solely biological, such as gender, race, and sexual orientation, are defined by human beings and can vary, depending on cultural and historical contexts. On this view, for example, heterosexuality is something learned—socially constructed—not innate. The "normalcy" of heterosexuality is systematically transmitted, and appropriate attitudes and behaviors are learned through childhood socialization, life experiences, and reinforced through institutional norms, policies, and law.

social control—Attitudes, behaviors, and mechanisms that keep people in their place. Overt social controls include laws, fines, imprisonment, and violence. Subtle ones include ostracism and withdrawal of status, affection, and respect.

social institutions—Institutions such as the family, education, the media, organized religion, law, and government.

socialist—Someone who believes that work should be organized for the collective benefit of workers rather than the profit of managers and corporate owners, and that the state should provide for human needs.

socialist feminism—A view that sees the oppression of women in terms of their subordinate position in a system defined as both patriarchal and capitalist.

social location—The social features of one's identity incorporating individual, community, societal, and global factors such as gender, class, ability, sexual orientation, age, and so on.

speciesism—Attitudes, actions, and institutional practices that subordinate nonhuman species; usually used in discussions of environmental and ecological issues.

standpoint theory—The view that different social and historical situations give rise to very different group experiences and theories about those experiences. See **situated knowledge.**

state—Governmental institutions, authority, and control. This includes the machinery of electoral politics, lawmaking, government agencies that execute law and policy, law enforcement agencies, the prison system, and the military.

sticky floor—Structural limitations for women in low-paid, low-status jobs that block them from moving up. Also see **glass ceiling.**

subjectivity—A form of understanding in which knowledge and meaning are grounded in people's lived experiences; also being the subject rather than an object of theorizing. Since powerless

groups have historically been treated as objects of "objective" knowledge production, feminist assertions of subjectivity are also assertions of the previously objectified groups' claims to the subject position (that of actor and agent of action), their ability to create their own knowledge, and, therefore, their agency in knowledge production.

subjugated knowledge—Knowledge generated from positions of subordination.

sustainability—The ability of an ecologically sound economy to sustain itself by using renewable resources and generating low or nonaccumulating levels of pollution. A more sustainable future means rethinking and radically changing current production processes, as well as the materialism and consumerism that support excessive production and waste.

theory—An explanation of how things are and why they are the way they are; a theory is based on a set of assumptions, has a perspective, and serves a purpose.

third-wave feminism—Feminist perspectives adopted in the 1990s, often by younger women, with an emphasis on personal voice and multiple identities, intersectionality, ambiguity, and contradictions.

transnational—Relationships, organizations, or movements that connect individuals or groups across national boundaries. These boundaries are not erased but are greatly reduced as barriers. Emphasis is on activities that transcend national boundaries, such as transnational corporations or transnational feminist organizing.

References

1000 Women for the Nobel Peace Prize. 2005. *1000 Peace-women across the Globe.* Zurich: Scalo.

Abbey, S., and A. O'Reilly, eds. 1998. *Redefining motherhood: Changing identities and patterns.* Toronto: Second Story Press.

Abramovitz, M. 1996. *Regulating the lives of women.* Rev. ed. Boston: South End Press.

Abramson, W., E. Emanuel, V. Gaylord, and M. Hayden. 2000. *Impact: Special issue on violence against women with developmental or other disabilities* 13(3). Minneapolis: The Institute on Community Integration, University of Minnesota. Available online at http://ici.umn.edu/products/impact/133.

Abzug, B. 1984. *Gender gap: Bella Abzug's guide to political power for American women.* Boston: Houghton Mifflin.

Adair, V. 2004. Reclaiming the promise of higher education: Poor single mothers in academe. *On Campus with Women* 33(3–4), Spring/Summer.

———, and S. Dahlberg. 2003. *Reclaiming class: Women, poverty, and the promise of higher education in America.* Philadelphia: Temple University Press.

Adams, C. J. 1999. *The sexual politics of meat: A feminist-vegetarian critical theory.* 10th anniversary ed. New York: Continuum.

Adams, J. P. 1991. *Peacework: Oral histories of women peace activists.* New York: Twayne.

Adamson, J., M. M. Evans, and R. Stein, eds. 2002. *The environmental justice reader: Politics, poetics and pedagogy.* Tucson: Arizona University Press.

Adler, F. 1975. *Sisters in crime: The rise of the new female criminal.* New York: McGraw-Hill.

Agosín, Marjorie, ed. 2001. *Women, gender, and human rights: A global perspective.* New Brunswick, N.J.: Rutgers University Press.

Ahn, C., and G. Kirk. 2005. Why war is all the rage. *San Francisco Chronicle,* May 29, p. D5.

Albelda, R., and C. Tilly. 1997. *Glass ceilings and bottomless pits: Women's work, women's poverty.* Boston: South End Press.

Albrecht, G. H. 2004. *Hitting home: Feminist ethics, women's work, and the betrayal of "family values."* New York: Continuum.

Alcoff, L. 1988. Cultural feminism versus post-structuralism: The identity crisis in feminist theory. *Signs: Journal of Women in Culture and Society* 13(3): 405–36.

Alexander, J. M., and C. T. Mohanty, eds. 1997. *Feminist genealogies, colonial legacies, democratic futures.* New York: Routledge.

Allen, D., R. R. Rush, and S. J. Kaufman, eds. 1996. *Women transforming communications: Global intersections.* Thousand Oaks, Calif.: Sage.

Allen, H. 2000. Gender, sexuality and the military model of U.S. national community. In *Gender ironies of nationalism: Sexing the nation,* ed. Tamar Mayer, 306-27. New York: Routledge.

Allen, P. G. 1986. *The sacred hoop: Recovering the feminine in American Indian traditions.* Boston: Beacon Press.

Alonso, H. H. 1993. *Peace as a women's issue: A history of the U.S. movement for world peace and women's rights.* Syracuse, N.Y.: Syracuse University Press.

Alterman, Eric. 2003. *What liberal media? The truth about bias and the news.* New York: Basic Books.

American Civil Liberties Union. 2002. *The USA Patriot Act.* Accessed online at http://www.aclu.org.

American Heritage Dictionary. 1993. 3d ed. Boston: Houghton Mifflin.

Amnesty International USA. 2000. *United States of America: Breaking the chain. The human rights of women prisoners.* New York: Amnesty International USA.

Amott, T. 1993. *Caught in the crisis: Women and the U.S. economy today.* New York: Monthly Review Press.

———, and J. Matthaei. 1996. *Race, gender, and work: A multicultural economic history of women in the United States.* Rev. ed. Boston: South End Press.

Anderlini-D'Onofrio, Serena, ed. 2003. *Women and bisexuality: A global perspective.* New York: Haworth Press.

Andersen, M. 2000. Women, power and politics. In *Thinking about women: Sociological perspectives on sex and gender,* 5th ed., 290–322. Boston: Allyn and Bacon.

Anderson, B. 2000. *Joyous greetings: The first international women's movement. 1830–60.* New York: Oxford University Press.

Anderson, L., ed. 1991. *Sisters of the earth: Women's prose and poetry about nature.* New York: Vintage Books.

Anderson, M. 1999. A well-kept secret: How military spending costs women's jobs. In *Gender camouflage,* ed. F. D'Amico and L. Weinstein, 247–52. New York: New York University Press.

Andre, J. 1988. Stereotypes: Conceptual and normative considerations. In *Racism and sexism: An integrated study,* ed. P. S. Rothenberg. New York: St. Martin's Press.

Andruss, V., C. Plant, J. Plant, and S. Mills. 1990. *Home!: A bioregional reader.* Philadelphia: New Society.

Angwin, J. 1996. Pounding on the glass ceiling. *San Francisco Chronicle,* 24 November, p. C3.

Antrobus, P. 2004. *The global women's movement: Origins, issues and strategies.* New York: Zed Books.

Anzaldúa, G. 1987. *Borderlands la frontera: The new mestiza.* San Francisco: Spinsters/Aunt Lute.

———. 2002. Now let us shift . . . the path of conocimiento . . . inner work, and public acts. In *This bridge we call home,* ed. Gloria Anzaldúa and Analouise Keating, pp. 540–78. New York: Routledge.

Applebome, P. 1997. Citadel's president insists coeducation will succeed. *New York Times,* 14 January, p. A1.

Arcana, J. 1994. Abortion is a motherhood issue. In *Mother journeys: Feminists write about mothering,* ed. M. Reddy, M. Roth, and A. Sheldon, 159–63. Minneapolis: Spinsters Ink.

———. 2005. *What if your mother.* Goshen, Conn.: Chicory Blue Press.

Arditti, R., R. D. Klein, and S. Minden, eds. 1984. *Test-tube women: What future for motherhood?* Boston: Pandora Press.

———, and T. Schreiber. 1998. Breast cancer: The environmental connection—A 1998 update, in *Resist Newsletter.* May/June.

Associated Press. 2005. Bush rallies abortion foes in annual protest. *USA Today,* January 25, 2A.

Avery, B. 1990. Breathing life into ourselves: The evolution of the Black women's health project. In *The Black women's health book,* ed. E. White, 4–10. Seattle: Seal Press.

Bagby, R. 1990. Daughter of growing things. In *Reweaving the world: The emergence of ecofeminism,* ed. I. Diamond and G. Orenstein, 231–48. San Francisco: Sierra Club.

Baird-Windle, P., and E. J. Bader. 2001. *Targets of hatred: Anti-abortion terrorism.* New York: Palgrave.

Baker, B. 1993. The women's convergence for national health care. *The Network News,* July/August, pp. 1, 3.

Baldwin, James. 1984. On being white and other lies, *Essence* (April).

Bandarage, A. 1997. *Women, population and global crisis: A political-economic analysis.* London and New Jersey: Zed Books.

Barboza, D. 2006. China drafts law to boost unions and end labor abuse. *New York Times.* October 13. www .nytimes.com/2006/10/13/business/worldbusiness/ 13sweat.html?_r=1&oref= slogin Accessed May 23, 2008.

Barnett, E. 2002. Prison coffee and games: Starbucks and Nintendo admit their contractor uses prison labor. *Prison Legal News* 13(3): 12–13.

Barnett, R., and C. Rivers. 1996. *She works, he works: How two-income families are happier, healthier, and better-off.* New York: HarperSanFrancisco.

Barnhill, D. L., ed. 1999. *At home on the earth: Becoming native to our place.* Berkeley: University of California Press.

Barr, D. A. 2008. *Heath disparities in the United States: Social, class, race, ethnicity and health.* Baltimore: Johns Hopkins University Press.

Bart, P., and P. O'Brien. 1993. *Stopping rape: Successful survival strategies.* New York: Teachers College Press.

Bartlett, J. 1994. *Will you be a mother? Women who choose to say no.* London: Virago.

Bass, E., and L. Davis. 1988. *The courage to heal.* New York: Harper & Row.

Baumgardner, J., and A. Richards. 2000. *Manifesta: Young women, feminism, and the future.* New York: Farrar, Straus and Giroux.

Baxandall, R., and L. Gordon, eds. 2000. *Dear sisters: Dispatches from the women's liberation movement.* New York: Basic Books.

Beasley, M., and D. Thomas. 1994. Violence as a human rights issue. Pp. 323–46 in *The public nature of private violence: The discovery of domestic abuse,* edited by M. A. Fineman and R. Mykitiuk. New York: Routledge.

Beauboeuf-Lafontant, T. 2007. "You have to show strength": An exploration of gender, race, and depression. *Gender and Society.* 21(1): 28–51.

Belenky, M. F., B. M. Clinchy, N. R. Goldberger, and J. M. Tarule. 1997. *Women's ways of knowing: The development of self, voice, and mind.* 10th anniversary ed. New York: Basic Books.

Belkin, L. 2007. The feminine critique. *New York Times.* November1. www.nytimes.com/2007/11/01/fashion/ 01WORK.html?pagewanted=2&_r=1&ei=5070&en=91feaf 95fabced83&ex=1194580800 Accessed April 26, 2008.

Bell, D., and R. Klein, eds. 1996. *Radically speaking: Feminism reclaimed.* North Melbourne, Australia: Spinifex Press.

Benard, C., and E. Schlaffer. 1997. "The man in the street": Why he harasses. In *Feminist frontiers IV,* ed. L. Richardson, V. Taylor, and N. Whittier, 395–98. New York: McGraw-Hill.

Bennett, K. 1992. Feminist bisexuality: A both/and option for an either/or world. In *Closer to home: Bisexuality and feminism,* ed. E. R. Weise, 205–31. Seattle, Wash.: Seal Press.

Benston, M. 1969. The political economy of women's liberation. *Monthly Review* 21(4): 13–27.

Berg, P. 1993. Growing a life-place politics. In *Radical environmentalism: Philosophy and tactics,* ed. J. List. Belmont, Calif.: Wadsworth.

Bernstein, R., and S. C. Silberman, eds. 1996. *Generation Q.* Los Angeles: Alyson.

Bethel, T. 2005. The gender gyp. *AARP Bulletin Online,* August 9. www.aarp.org/bulletin/socialsec/the_ gender_gyp Accessed on August 9, 2005.

Bhattacharjee, A. 2002. Private fists: Pubic force: Race, gender, and surveillance. In *Policing the national body: Sex, race, and criminalization,* ed. J. Silliman and A. Bhattacharjee, 1–54. Cambridge, Mass.: South End Press.

Bianchi, S., M. Milkie, L. Sayer, and J. Robinson. 2002. Is anyone doing the housework? Trends in the gender division of household labor. In *Workplace/women's place,* 2d ed., ed. P. Dubeck and D. Dunn, 174–87. Los Angeles: Roxbury.

Bigelow, B., and B. Peterson, eds. 2002. *Rethinking globalization: Teaching for justice in an unjust world.* Milwaukee, Wis.: Rethinking Schools.

Bird, C. 1995. *Lives of ours: Secrets of salty old women.* New York: Houghton Mifflin.

Birks, J., and A. Erlich, eds. 1989. *Hidden dangers: The environmental consequences of preparing for war.* San Francisco: Sierra Club Books.

Black Women's Health Project. 1995. *Reproductive health and African American women. Issue brief.* Washington, D.C.: Black Women's Health Project.

Blakely, M. K. 1994. *American mom: Motherhood, politics, and humble pie.* Chapel Hill, N.C.: Algonquin Books.

Blank, H., ed. 2001. *Zaftig: Well-rounded erotica.* San Francisco: Cleis Press.

Blauner, R. 1972. *Racial oppression in America.* New York: Harper & Row.

Bleier, R. 1984. *Science and gender: A critique of biology and its theories on women.* New York: Pergamon Press.

Bleyer, J. 2004. Cut-and-paste revolution: Notes from the girl zine explosion. In *The fire this time: Young activists and the new feminism,* ed. Vivien Labaton and Dawn Lundy Martin, 42–60. New York: Anchor Books.

Bloom, B., M. Chesney-Lind, and B. Owen. 1994. *Women in California prisons: Hidden victims of the war on drugs.* San Francisco: Center on Juvenile and Criminal Justice.

Bloom, S., J. Miller, J. Warner, and P. Winkler, eds. 1994. *Hidden casualties: Environmental, health and political consequences of the Persian Gulf War.* Berkeley: North Atlantic Books.

Boggs, G. L. 1994. Fifty years on the left. *The Witness,* May, 8–12.

Bohmer, C., and A. Parrot. 1993. *Sexual assault on campus: The problem and the solution.* New York: Lexington Books/Macmillan.

Bollinger, H. 2007. *Women of the harvest: Inspiring stories of contemporary farmers.* Osceola, Wis.:Voyageur Press.

Boonstra, H. D. 2007. The case for a new approach to sex education mounts: Will policymakers heed the message? *Guttmacher Policy Review,* 10(2). www.guttmacher.org/pubs /gpr/10/2/gpr100202.html Accessed March 28, 2008.

Booth, W. 1997. Ex-Black Panther freed. *Washington Post,* 11 June, p. A1.

Bordo, S. 1993. *Unbearable weight: Feminism, Western culture, and the body.* Berkeley: University of California Press.

Borjesson, Kristina, ed. 2002. *Into the buzzsaw: Leading journalists expose the myth of a free press.* Amherst, N.Y.: Prometheus Books.

Borkovitz, D. K. 1995. Same-sex battering and the backlash. *NCADV Voice,* Summer, 4.

Bornstein, K. 1995. *Gender outlaw: On men, women, and the rest of us.* New York: Vintage/Random House.

———. 1998. *My gender workbook: How to become a real man, a real woman, the real you, or something else entirely.* New York: Routledge.

Boston Women's Health Book Collective. 2005. *Our bodies ourselves: A new edition for a new era.* New York: Simon and Schuster.

Boswell, J. 1994. *Same-sex unions in premodern Europe.* New York: Villard Books.

Boswell-Penc, M. 2006. *Tainted milk: Breastmilk, feminisms, and the politics of environmental degradation.* Albany.: State University of New York Press.

Boudin, K. 2007. Stories from the inside: Prisoners and HIV. In *Stories of illness and healing; Women write their bodies,* ed. Sayantani Das Gupta and Marsha Hurst. Kent, Ohio: Kent State University Press.

Boxer, M. 1998. *When women ask the questions: Creating women's studies in America.* Baltimore: Johns Hopkins University Press.

Boylan, J. F. 2003. *She's not there: A life in two genders.* New York: Broadway Books.

Braveman, P. 2006. Health disparities and health equity: Concepts and measurements. *Annual Review of Public Health,* 27: 167–194.

Breitbart, J, and A. Nogueira. 2004. An independent media center of one's own: A feminist alternative to corporate media. In *The fire this time: Young activists and the new feminism,* ed. Vivien Labaton and Dawn Lundy Martin, 19–41. New York: Anchor Books.

Brennan, S., J. Winklepleck, and G. MacNee. 1994. *The resourceful woman.* Detroit: Visible Ink.

Brenner, J. 1996. The best of times, the worst of times: Feminism in the United States. In *Mapping the women's movement,* ed. M. Threlfall, 17–72. London: Verso Books.

Brice, Carleen. 2003. *Age ain't nothing but a number: Black women explore midlife.* Boston: Beacon Press.

Bright, S, ed. 2000. *The best American erotica.* New York: Simon & Schuster.

Bright, S. ed. 2000. *The best American erotica.* New York: Simon and Schuster.

Browne, C. 1998. *Women, feminism, and aging.* New York: Springer.

Browne, J. 1996. The labor of doing time. In *Criminal injustice: Confronting the prison crisis,* ed. E. Rosenblatt. Boston: South End Press.

Brownell, K. D., and K. B. Horgen. 2004. *Food fight: The inside story of the food industry, America's obesity crisis, and what we can do abut it.* Chicago: Contemporary Books.

Brownhill, L. 2007. Gendered struggles for the commons: Food sovereignty, tree-planting and climate change, *Women and Environments,* 74/75: 34–37.

Brownmiller, S. 1975. *Against our will: Men, women, and rape.* New York: Simon & Schuster.

Bruce, C., ed. 2001. *Best bisexual women's erotica.* San Francisco: Cleis Press.

Brumberg, J. J. 1997. *The body project: An intimate history of American girls.* New York: Random House.

Buchwald, E., P. Fletcher, and M. Roth, eds. 2005. *Transforming a rape culture,* Rev. ed. Minneapolis: Milkweed.

Buck, M. 2004. Women in prison and work. *Feminist Studies,* 30(2): 451–455.

Bulhan, H. A. 1985. *Frantz Fanon and the psychology of oppression.* New York: Plenum Books.

Bullard, R. D. 1990. *Dumping in Dixie: Race, class, and environmental quality.* Boulder, Colo.: Westview Press.

———. ed. 1993. *Confronting environmental racism: Voices from the grassroots.* Boston: South End Press.

———, P. Mohai, R. Saha, and B. Wright. 2007. *Toxic waste and race at twenty 1987–2007: Grassroots struggles to dismantle environmental racism in the United States.* Cleveland, Ohio: United Church of Christ.

Bullough, V. L., and B. Bullough. 1993. *Cross dressing, sex, and gender.* Philadelphia: University of Pennsylvania Press.

Bunch, C. 1987. *Passionate politics: Essays 1968–1986.* New York: St. Martin's Press.

———, and R. Carillo. 1991. *Gender violence: A human rights and development issue.* New Brunswick, N.J.: Center for Women's Global Leadership, Rutgers University.

———, and N. Reilly. 1994. *Demanding accountability: The global campaign and Vienna Tribunal for women's human rights.* New Jersey: Center for Women's Global Leadership, Rutgers University; New York: UNIFEM.

Bureau of Justice Statistics. 1995. *Violence against women: Estimates from the redesigned survey.* Washington, D.C.: U.S. Department of Justice.

———. 2000. *Women offenders.* Washington, D.C.: U.S. Department of Justice.

———. 2007. *One in every 31 U.S. adults was in a prison or jail or on probation or parole at the end of last year.* Press release, December 5. www.ojp.usdoj.gov/bjs/pub/press/ p06ppus06pr.htm Accessed April 29, 2008.

Burke, C. 2004. *Camp all-American, Hanoi Jane, and the high- and-tight: Gender, folklore, and changing military culture.* Boston: Beacon Press.

Burnham, Linda. 2001. *The wellspring of Black feminist theory.* Oakland: Women of Color Resource Center. www .coloredgirls.org

Burrell, B. 1994. *A woman's place is in the House: Campaigning for Congress in the feminist era.* Ann Arbor: University of Michigan Press.

Burton, N. 1998. Resistance to prevention: Reconsidering feminist antiviolence rhetoric. In *Violence against women: Philosophical perspectives,* ed. S. French, W. Teays, and L. Purdy, 182–200. Ithaca, N.Y.: Cornell University Press.

Bush, Melanie E. L. 2004. *Breaking the code of good intentions: Everyday forms of whiteness.* Lanham, Md.: Rowman and Littlefield.

Bush-Baksette, S. R. 1999. The "war on drugs" a war against women? In *Harsh punishment: International experiences of women's imprisonment,* ed. S. Cook and S. Davies. Boston: Northeastern University Press.

Butler, J. 1990. *Gender trouble: Feminism and the subversion of identity.* New York: Routledge, Chapman, & Hall.

Butler, O. 1993. *The parable of the sower.* New York: Warner Books.

Byerly, C. M. and K. Ross. 2006. *Women and media: A critical introduction.* Malden, Mass.: Blackwell.

Calasanti, T. M. and K. F. Slevin, eds. 2006. *Age matters: Realigning feminist thinking.* New York: Taylor and Francis.

Califia. P. 2000. *Public sex: The culture of radical sex.* San Francisco: Cleis Press.

Cammermeyer, M. 1994. *Serving in silence.* New York: Viking.

Camp, L. T. 1997. *Lingering fever: A World War II nurse's memoir.* Jefferson, N.C.: McFarland and Co.

Campbell, D., with F. D'Amico. 1999. Lessons on gender integration from the military academies. In *Gender camouflage: Women and the U.S. military,* ed. F. D'Amico and L. Weinstein, 67–79. New York: New York University Press.

Cancian, F. M., D. Kurz, A. S. London, R. Reviere, and M. C. Tuominen. 2002. *Child care and inequality: Rethinking carework for children and youth.* New York: Routledge.

Caplan, P., ed. 1987. *The cultural construction of sexuality.* London: Tavistock.

Caplan, R. 2004. *Thirst: A guide to the film for teachers and discussion leaders.* San Francisco: Sierra Club Water Privatization Task Force.

Caputi, J., and D. E. H. Russell. 1990. "Femicide": Speaking the unspeakable. *Ms.,* September/October, 34–37.

Carilli, T., and J. Campbell, eds. 2005. *Women and the media: Diverse perspectives.* Lanham, Md.: University Press of America.

Carlen, P. 1989. Feminist jurisprudence, or womenwise penology. *Probation Journal* 36(3): 110–14.

Carroll, S. J., ed., 2001. *The impact of women in public office.* Bloomington: Indiana University Press.

Carson, R. 1962. *Silent spring.* Boston: Houghton Mifflin.

Catalano, S. 2008. *Intimate partner violence in the United States.* Bureau of Justice Statistics. Washington, D.C.: U.S. Department of Justice. www.ojp.usdoj.gov/bjs/homicide/intimates.htm#intimates Accessed February 19, 2008.

Catalyst. 2007. *Census of women board directors of the Fortune 500,* Appendix 5. www.catalyst.org/knowledge/titles/title.php?page=cen_WBD_07 Accessed March 15, 2008.

Cavin, S. 1985. *Lesbian origins.* San Francisco: Ism Press.

Center for American Women and Politics. 2008. *Women office holders.* www.cawp.rutgers.edu/Facts.html#color Accessed May 25, 2008.

Center for Arms Control and Non-Proliferation. 2008. *Total Iraq and Afghanistan supplemental war funding to date.* Washington D.C.: CACNP. www.armscontrolcenter.org/policy/securityspending/articles/supplemental_war_funding/ Accessed May 3, 2008.

Center for Constitutional Rights. 2005. *Federal judge rules on constitutionality of kickback in contract between NY state prisons and MCI,* Center for Constitutional Rights, New York, Press Release, August 30.

Centers for Disease Control and Prevention. 2007a. *HIV/AIDS among women.* www.cdc.gov/hiv/topics/women/resources/factsheets/women.htm#3 Accessed February 14, 2008.

———. 2007b. *Trends in reportable sexually transmitted diseases in the United States, 2006.* www.cdc.gov/std/stats/pdf/trends2006.pdf Accessed on February 14, 2008.

Chaddock, G. R., 2002. Security act to pervade daily lives. *Christian Science Monitor,* November 21. http://www.csmonitor.com/2002/1121/p01s03-usju.html Accessed 17 January 2003.

Chalker, R. 1995. Sexual pleasure unscripted. *Ms.,* November/December, 49–52.

Chandler, C., and C. Kingery. 2002. Speaking out against state violence: Activist HIV-positive women prisoners redefine social justice. In *Policing the national body: Race, gender and criminalization,* ed. Jael Silliman and Anannya Bhattacharjee, 81–99. Cambridge, Mass.: South End Press.

Chang, G. 2000. *Disposable domestics: Immigrant women workers in the global economy.* Cambridge, Mass.: South End Press.

———, and K. Kim. 2007. Reconceptualizing approaches to human trafficking: New directions and perspectives from the field(s). *Stanford Journal of Civil Rights and Civil Liberties,* III(2): 317–344.

Chavez, C. 1993. Farm workers at risk. In *Toxic struggles: The theory and practice of environmental justice,* ed. R. Hofrichter, 163–70. Philadelphia and Gabriola Island, B.C.: New Society.

Chernin, K. 1994. *The obsession: Reflections on the tyranny of slenderness.* New York: Harper Perennial.

Chesler, P. 1972. *Women and madness.* New York: Avon.

Chesney-Lind, M. 1986. Women and crime: A review of the literature on the female offender. *Signs: Journal of Women in Culture and Society* 12(1): 78–96.

———. 1995. Rethinking women's imprisonment: A critical examination of trends in female incarceration. In *Women, crime, and criminal justice,* ed. B. R. Price and N. Sokoloff. New York: McGraw-Hill.

———, and L. Pasko. 2004. *The female offender: Girls, women and crime.* Second ed. Thousand Oaks, Calif.: Sage.

———. eds. 2003. *Girls, women and crime: Selected readings.* Thousand Oaks, Calif.: Sage.

———, and R. G. Shelden. 1992. *Girls, delinquency and juvenile justice.* Pacific Grove, Calif.: Brooks/Cole.

Chiawei O'Hearn, Claudine, ed. 1998. *Half and half: Writers on growing up biracial and bicultural.* New York: Pantheon.

Children's Defense Fund. 2005. *Child care basics.* www.childrensdefense.org Accessed August 6, 2005.

———. 2008. *Poor children in 2006.* www.childrensdefense.org/site/PageServer?pagename=research_family_income Accessed May 16, 2008.

Chodorow, N. 1978. *Reproduction and mothering: Psychoanalysis and the sociology of gender.* Berkeley: University of California Press.

Churchill, W. 1992. Introduction: The Third World at home. In *Cages of steel: The politics of imprisonment in the United States,* ed. W. Churchill and J. J. Vander Wall. Washington, D.C.: Maisonnueve Press.

Citizen Soldier. 1996. *Newsletter.* New York: Citizen Soldier.

Cockburn, C. 1998. *The space between us: Negotiating gender and national identities in conflict.* London and New Jersey: Zed Books.

———. 2007. *From where we stand: War, women's activism and feminist analysis.* London: Zed Press.

Cohen, Elliot D., ed. 2005. *News incorporated: Corporate media ownership and its threat to democracy.* Amherst, N.Y.: Prometheus Books.

Cohn, M. 2006. Military hides cause of women's soldiers deaths. *Truthout.* January 30. www .truthout.org/cgi-bin/artman/exec/view.cgi/57/17327/printer Accessed May 3, 2008.

Cole, J., and B. Guy-Sheftall. 2003. *Gender talk: The struggle for women's equality in African American communities.* New York: Ballantine.

Cole, J. H. 1992. *Women pilots of World War II.* Salt Lake City: University of Utah Press.

Colligan, S. 2004. Why the intersexed shouldn't be fixed: Insights from queer theory and disability studies. In *Gendering Disability,* ed. B.G. Smith and B. Hutchinson, pp. 45–60. New Brunswick, N.J.: Rutgers University Press.

Collins, J. 2003. *Threads: Gender, labor, and power in the global apparel industry.* Chicago: University of Chicago Press.

Collins, L. 2008. Pixel perfect: Pascal Dangin's virtual reality. *The New Yorker.* May 12. www.newyorker.com/reporting/2008/05/12/080512fa_fact_collins Accessed on May 23, 2008.

Collins, P. H. 1990. *Black feminist thought: Knowledge, consciousness, and the politics of empowerment.* Boston: Unwin Hyman.

———. 1997. Comment on Hekman's 'Truth and method: feminist standpoint revisited': Where's the Power? *Signs: Journal of Women in Culture and Society* 22(2): 375–81.

———. 2004. *Black sexual politics: African Americans, gender, and the new racism.* New York: Routledge.

Commonwealth Fund. 1997. *The Commonwealth Fund survey of the health of adolescent girls: Highlights and methodology.* New York: The Commonwealth Fund.

Condry, I. 2006. *Hip-hop Japan: Rap and the paths of cultural globalization.* Durham: Duke University Press.

Connell, R. W. 1990. The state, gender, and sexual politics: Theory and appraisal. *Theory and Society* 19(4): 507–44.

Cook, A., and G. Kirk. 1983. *Greenham women everywhere: Dreams, ideas, and actions from the women's peace movement.* Boston: South End Press.

Coontz, S. 1997. *The way we really are: Coming to terms with America's changing families.* New York: Basic Books.

Cooper, E. 1992. When being ill is illegal: Women and the criminalization of HIV. *Health/PAC Bulletin,* Winter, 10–14.

Cooper, F. and A.L. Stoler, eds. 1997. *Tensions of empire: Colonial cultures in a bourgeois world.* Berkeley: University of California Press.

Corea, G. 1985. *The mother machine: Reproductive technologies from artificial insemination to artificial wombs.* New York: Harper & Row.

———. 1987. *Man-made women: How reproductive technologies affect women.* Bloomington: Indiana University Press.

Cornell, D., ed. 2000. *Feminism and pornography.* New York: Oxford University Press.

Counts, C. E. 2007. Let's talk about sex: SisterSong conference. *Teen Voices Online.* www.teenvoices.com/issue_current/aotm_sistersong.html Accessed May 12, 2008.

Cox, T. 1999. *Hot sex: How to do it.* New York: Bantam Books.

Crenshaw, K. 1993. The marginalization of sexual violence against Black women. Speech to the National Coalition Against Sexual Assault, 1993 Conference, Chicago. http://www.ncasa.org/marginalization.html

Critical Resistance. 2005. *Instead of prisons: A handbook for abolitionists.* Oakland, Calif.: AK Press.

Cromartie, S. P. 2007. Labor force status of families: A visual essay. *Monthly Labor Review,* 130(7, 8): 35–41.

Croteau, D., and W. Hoynes. 1997. *Media/society: Industries, images, and audiences.* Thousand Oaks, Calif.: Pine Forge Press.

Cruickshank, Margaret. 2003. *Learning to be old: Gender, culture, and aging.* Lanham, Md.: Rowman and Littlefield.

Daly, H. E., and J. B. Cobb Jr. 1989. *For the common good: Redirecting the economy toward community, the environment, and a sustainable future.* Boston: Beacon Press.

Daly, K. 1994. *Gender, crime, and punishment.* New Haven, Conn.: Yale University Press.

Daly, M. 1976. *Gyn/ecology: The metaethics of radical feminism.* Boston: Beacon Press.

D'Amico, F. 1998. Feminist perspectives on women warriors. In *The women and war reader,* ed. L. A. Lorentzen and J. Turpin, 119–25. New York: New York University Press.

D'Amico, F., and L. Weinstein, eds. 1999. *Gender camouflage: Women and the U.S. military.* New York: New York University Press.

Daniels, R., S. C. Taylor, and H. H. L. Kitano, eds. 1991. *Japanese Americans from relocation to redress.* Seattle: University of Washington Press.

Danquah, M. 1998. *Willow weep for me: A Black women's journey through depression.* New York: W. W. Norton.

Darling, M., and J. Tyson. 1999. The state: Friend or foe? Distributive justice issues and African American women. In *Dangerous intersections: Feminist perspectives on population, environment, and development,* ed. J. Silliman and Y. King, 214–41. Cambridge, Mass.: South End Press.

das Dasgupta, S., and S. DasGupta. 1996. Public face, private space: Asian Indian women and sexuality. In *"Bad girls"/"good girls": Women, sex, and power in the nineties,* ed. N. Bauer Maglin and D. Perry, 226–43. New Brunswick, N.J.: Rutgers University Press.

Davis, A. 1983. Racism, birth control, and reproductive rights. In *Women, race, and class.* New York: Vintage Books.

———. 1997. A plenary address. Paper presented at conference, Frontline Feminisms: Women, War, and Resistance, 16 January, at University of California, Riverside.

———. 1998. Masked racism: Reflections on the prison industrial complex. *Color Lines,* Fall.

———. 2001. The color of violence against women. *Sojourner: The Women's Forum,* October, 12–13.

———. 2003. *Are prisons obsolete?* New York: Seven Stories Press.

Davis, B. 2004. Will debt move backfire on Argentina? *Asian Wall Street Journal,* November 29, A6.

Davis, F. 1991. *Moving the mountain: The women's movement in America since 1960.* New York: Simon & Schuster.

Davis, J., ed. 1991. *The Earth First! reader: Ten years of radical environmentalism.* Salt Lake City: Peregrine Smith Books.

Dean, D. 1997. *Warriors without weapons: The victimization of military women.* Pasadena, Md.: The Minerva Center.

d'Eaubonne, F. 1994. The time for ecofeminism. In *Ecology,* edited by C. Merchant. Atlantic Highlands, N.J.: Humanities Press.

de Ishtar, Z. 1994. *Daughters of the Pacific.* Melbourne, Australia: Spinifex Press.

D'Emilio, J. 1984. Capitalism and gay identity. In *Powers of desire: The politics of sexuality*, ed. A. Snitow et al., 100–13. New York: Monthly Review Press.

———, and E. Freedman. 1997. *Intimate matters: A history of sexuality in America*. 2d ed. Chicago: University of Chicago Press.

Denman, J. E., and L. B. Inniss. 1999. No war without women: Defense industries. In *Gender camouflage: Women and the U.S. military*, ed. F. D'Amico and L. Weinstein, 187–99. New York: New York University Press.

Department of Defense. 1996. *DoD news briefing: Mr. Kenneth H. Bacon*. www.defenselink.mil/transcripts/transcript .aspx?transcriptid=571 Accessed May 4, 2008.

———. 1997. *DoD news briefing: Secretary of Defense William S. Cohen*. www.defenselink.mil/transcripts/transcript .aspx?transcriptid=419 Accessed May 4, 2008.

———. 2008. *FY07 report on sexual assault in the military*. Washington, D.C.: DoD.

Devall, B., and G. Sessions. 1985. *Deep ecology: Living as if nature mattered*. Salt Lake City: Smith Books.

Diamond, I., and G. F. Orenstein, eds. 1990. *Reweaving the world: The emergence of ecofeminism*. San Francisco: Sierra Club Books.

Diamond, L. M. 2008. *Sexual fluidity: Understanding women's love and desire*. Cambridge: Harvard University Press.

Dibblin, J. 1989. *The day of two suns: U.S. nuclear testing and the Pacific Islands*. New York: New Amsterdam Books.

Dicker, R., and A. Piepmeier, eds. 2003. *Catching a wave: Reclaiming feminism for the 21st century*. Boston: North-eastern University Press.

Digby, T., ed. 1998. *Men doing feminism*. New York: Routledge.

Dinnerstein, D. 1976. *Sexual arrangements and the human malaise*. New York: Harper & Row.

———. 1989. Surviving on earth: Meaning of feminism. In *Healing the wounds*, ed. J. Plant. Philadelphia: New Society.

Dollars and Sense. 2005. Rich and poor in the global economy: Interview with Bob Sutcliffe. no. 258, March/April, pp. 13–15.

Donchin, A., and L. M. Purdy. 1999. *Embodying bioethics: Recent feminist advances*. Lanham, Md.: Rowman and Littlefield.

Doress-Worters, P., and D. L. Siegal. 1994. *The new ourselves, growing older*. New York: Simon & Schuster.

Dorsey, E., and M. Thormodsgard. 2003. Rachel Carson warned us. *Ms.*, December 2002/January 2003, 43–45.

Dougherty, A. 2007. No media, no progress, *Women's Review of Books*, 24(6): 25.

Douglas, S. J., and M. W. Michaels. 2004. *The mommy myth: The idealization of motherhood and how it has undermined women*. New York: Free Press.

Duberman M. B., M. Vicinus, and G. Chauncey Jr. 1989. *Hidden from history: Reclaiming the gay and lesbian past*. New York: New American Library.

Ducat, S. J. 2004. *The wimp factor: Gender gaps, holy wars, and the politics of anxious masculinity*. Boston: Beacon Press.

Duff, K. 1993. *The alchemy of illness*. New York: Pantheon.

Duggan, L., and N. Hunter. 1995. *Sex wars: Sexual dissent and political culture*. New York: Routledge.

Dujon, D., and A. Withorn, eds. 1996. *For crying out loud: Women's poverty in the United States*. Boston: South End Press.

Dula, A. 1996. An African American perspective on repro-ductive freedoms. Panel on Reproduction, Race, and Class at the Third World Congress of Bioethics, Feminist Approaches to Bioethics, November, San Francisco.

DuPlessis, R. B., and A. Snitow, eds. 1998. *The Feminist Memoir Project: Voices from women's liberation*. New York: Three Rivers Press.

Duran, J. 1998. *Philosophies of science/feminist theories*. Boulder, Colo.: Westview Press.

Dworkin, A. 1987. *Intercourse*. New York: Free Press.

———. 1993. *Letters from a war zone*. Chicago: Chicago Review Press.

Earnest, L. 2005. Made in LA, for now. *Los Angeles Times*, January 16, C1.

Echols, A. 1989. *Daring to be bad: Radical feminism in America 1967–1975*. Minneapolis: University of Minnesota Press.

Economic Policy Institute. 2006. The *State of working America 2006–07*. Ithaca: Cornell University Press.

Edison, L. T., and D. Notkin. 1994. *Women en large: Images of fat nudes*. San Francisco: Books in Focus.

Ehrenreich, B. 2001. *Nickel and dimed: On (not) getting by in America*. New York: Henry Holt/Metropolitan Books.

———. 2005. *For her own good: Two centuries of the experts' advice to women*. Garden City, N.Y.: Anchor/Doubleday.

———, and D. English. 1972. *Witches, midwives, and nurses: A history of women healers*. Old Westbury, N.Y.: Feminist Press.

———, and A. R. Hochschild, eds. 2003. *Global woman: Nannies, maids, and sex workers in the new economy*. New York: Henry Holt.

Ehrenreich, B., E. Hess, and G. Jacobs. 1986. *Remaking love: The feminization of sex*. New York: Anchor/Doubleday.

Eisenstein, Z. R. 1979. *Capitalism, patriarchy, and the case for socialist feminism*. New York: Monthly Review Press.

———. 1981. *The radical future of liberal feminism*. New York: Longman.

———. 1998. Socialist feminism. In *The reader's companion to U.S. women's history*, ed. W. Mankiller, G. Mink, M. Navarro, B. Smith, and G. Steinem, 218–19. Boston: Houghton Mifflin.

Ekins, R. 1997. *Male femaling: A grounded theory approach to cross-dressing and sex-changing*. New York: Routledge.

Elam, H., and K. Jackson, eds. 2005. *Black cultural traffic: Crossroads in global performance and popular culture*. Ann Arbor: University of Michigan Press.

Eng, D., and A. Y. Hom, eds. 1998. *Q & A: Queer in Asian America*. Philadelphia: Temple University.

Enloe, C. 1983. *Does khaki become you? The militarization of women's lives*. Boston: South End Press.

———. 1990. *Bananas, beaches and bases: Making feminist sense of international politics*. Berkeley: University of California Press.

———. 1993. *The morning after: Sexual politics at the end of the cold war*. Berkeley: University of California Press.

———. 1995. The globetrotting sneaker, *Ms.*, March/April, pp. 10–15.

———. 2000a. *Maneuvers: The international politics of militariz-ing women's lives*. Berkeley: University of California Press.

———. 2000b. Masculinity as foreign policy issue. *Foreign Policy in Focus* 5(36). www.fpif.org/briefs/vol5/v5n36masculinity_body.html Accessed May 17, 2008.

———. 2007. *Globalization and militarism: feminists make the links*. Lanham, Md.: Rowman and Littlefield.

Enos, S. 2001. *Mothering from the inside: Parenting in a women's prison.* Albany: State University of New York Press.

Ensler, E. 1998. *The vagina monologues.* New York: Villard/Random House.

Epstein, B. 1993. Ecofeminism and grassroots environmentalism in the United States. In *Toxic struggles: The theory and practice of environmental justice,* ed. R. Hofrichter, 144–52. Philadelphia and Gabriola Island, B.C.: New Society.

Eridani. 1992. Is sexual orientation a secondary sex characteristic? In *Closer to home: Bisexuality and feminism,* ed. E. R. Weise. Seattle, Wash.: Seal Press.

Evans, S. 1980. *Personal politics.* New York: Vintage Books.

Facts on the global sweatshop. 1997. *Rethinking Schools: An Urban Education Journal* 11(4): 16.

Faderman, L. 1981. *Surpassing the love of men: Romantic friendship and love between women from the Renaissance to the present.* New York: William Morrow.

Falcón, S. 2006. "National security" and the violation of women: Militarized border rape at the US-Mexico border. In *Color of violence: The Incite! anthology,* ed. Incite! Women of Color Against Violence, 119–129. Cambridge: South End Press.

Falk, J. 2003. Fiscal lockdown, *Dollars and Sense,* July/August, pp. 19–23, 45.

Faludi, S. 1991. *Backlash: The undeclared war against women.* New York: Crown.

Family Violence Prevention Fund. 1998. *Domestic violence is a serious, widespread social problem in America: The facts.* Available from the Family Violence Prevention Fund, 383 Rhode Island Ave., San Francisco, CA 94103.

Fausto-Sterling, A. 1993. The five sexes: Why male and female are not enough. *The Sciences,* March/April, 20–24.

———. 2000b. The five sexes, revisited. *Sciences,* July/August 40(4):18. www.neiu.edu/lsfuller/5sexesrevisited.htm Accessed May 11, 2008.

Featherstone, L. 2002. *Students against sweatshops: The making of a movement.* New York, Verso.

———. 2004. Will labor take the Wal-Mart challenge? *The Nation,* June 28.

Feinberg, L. 1996. *Transgender warriors: Making history from Joan of Arc to RuPaul.* Boston: Beacon Press.

———. 1998. *Trans liberation: Beyond pink or blue.* Boston: Beacon Press.

Feldt, G. 2004. *The war on choice: The right wing attack on women's rights and how to fight back.* New York: Bantam.

Feminist Anti-Censorship Task Force. 1992. *Caught looking: Feminism, pornography, and censorship.* East Haven, Conn.: Long River Books.

Ferguson, K., and P. Turnbull. 2004. Globalizing militaries. In *Rethinking globalism,* ed. M. B. Steger, 79–91. Lanham, Md.: Rowman and Littlefield.

Fiduccia, B. W., and M. Saxton. 1997. Disability feminism: A manifesto. *New Mobility: Disability Culture and Life-style* 8(49): 60–61.

Findlen, B., ed. 1995. *Listen up: Voices from the next feminist generation.* Seattle, Wash.: Seal Press.

Fineman, M. A., and R. Mykitiuk, eds. 1994. *The public nature of private violence: The discovery of domestic abuse.* New York: Routledge.

Finger, A. 1990. *Past due: A story of disability, pregnancy, and birth.* Seattle, Wash.: Seal Press.

Firestone, S. 1970. *The dialectics of sex: The case for feminist revolution.* New York: Morrow.

Fisher. B., F. Cullen, and M. Turner. 2000. *The sexual victimization of college women.* Washington, D.C.: U.S. Department of Justice and the National Institute of Justice.

Flanders, L. 1997. *Real majority, media minority: The costs of sidelining women in reporting.* Monroe, Maine: Common Courage Press.

Flax, J. 1986. Gender as a social problem: In and for feminist theory. *Amerikastudien/American Studies* 31: 193–213.

Folbre, N. 2001. *The invisible heart: Economics and family values.* New York: New Press.

Foo, L. J. 2007. *Asian American women: Issues, concerns, and responsive human and civil rights advocacy.* 2nd ed. New York: National Asian American Women's Forum, iUniverse.

Ford, L. E. 2002. *Women and politics: The pursuit of equality.* Boston: Houghton Mifflin.

Foster, C. 1989. *Women for all seasons: The story of W.I.L.P.F.* Athens: University of Georgia Press.

Fouhy, B. 2004. Gay, patriotic and banished. *San Francisco Examiner,* June 21, p. 1.

Fox-Genovese, E. 1994. Beyond individualism: The new Puritanism, feminism, and women. *Salmagundi* 101(2): 79–95.

Fraden, R. 2001. *Imagining medea: Rhodessa Jones and theater for incarcerated women.* Chapel Hill: University of North Carolina Press.

Franke, L. B. 1987. *The gender wars in the military.* New York: Simon and Schuster.

Frankenberg, R. 1993. *White women, race matters: The social construction of whiteness.* Minneapolis: University of Minnesota Press.

Freeman, C. 2000. *High tech and high heels in the global economy: Women, work and pink-collar identities in the Caribbean.* Durham: Duke University Press.

Freeman, J. 2008. *We will be heard: Women's struggles for political power in the United States.* Lanham, Md.: Rowman and Littlefield.

Freire, P. 1989. *Pedagogy of the oppressed.* New York: Continuum.

Friedan, B. 1963. *The feminine mystique.* New York: W. W. Norton.

Frye, M. 1992. *Willful virgin: Essays in feminism 1976–1992.* Freedom, Calif.: The Crossing Press.

Fuchs, L. 1990. The reaction of Black Americans to immigration. In *Immigration reconsidered,* ed. V. Yans-McLaughlin. New York: Oxford University Press.

Fukumura, Y., and M. Matsuoka. 2002. Redefining security: Okinawa women's resistance to U.S. militarism. In *Women's activism and globalization: Linking local struggles and transnational politics,* ed. Nancy Naples and Manisha Desai, 239–263. New York: Routledge.

Fuss, D., ed. 1991. *Inside out: Lesbian theories, gay theories.* New York: Routledge.

Gaard, G., ed. 1993. *Ecofeminism: Women, animals, nature.* Philadelphia: Temple University Press.

Gage, S., L. Richards, and H. Wilmot. 2002. *Queer.* New York: Thunder's Mouth Press.

Gaines, P. 1994. *Laughing in the dark: From colored girl to woman of color—a journey from prison to power.* New York: Anchor Books.

Gallagher, N. W. 1993. The gender gap in popular attitudes toward the use of force. In *Women and the use of military force,* ed. R. Howes and M. Stevenson, 23–37. Boulder, Colo.: Lynne Rienner.

Garber, M. 1992. *Vested interests: Cross-dressing and cultural anxiety.* New York: HarperPerennial.

Geller, J. 2001. *Here comes the bride: Women, weddings, and the marriage mystique.* New York: Four Walls Eight Windows.

George, S. 1988. Getting your own back: Solving the Third World debt crisis. *New Statesman & Society,* 15 July, 20.

Gettelman, E. 2005. The Pentagon v. abuse: An interview with Deborah Tucker. *Mother Jones,* June 28.

Gibbs, L. 1995. *Dying from dioxin: A citizens' guide to reclaiming our health and rebuilding democracy.* Boston: South End Press.

———. 1998. *Love canal: The story continues.* Gabriola Island, B.C.: New Society.

Ginsburg, F. D., and R. Rapp. 1995. *Conceiving the new world order: The global politics of reproduction.* Berkeley: University of California Press.

Giordano, P., S. Kerbel, and S. Dudley. 1981. The economics of female criminality. In *Women and crime in America,* ed. L. Bowker, 15–82. New York: Macmillan.

Girshick, L. B. 2002. *Women-to-women sexual violence.* Boston: Northeastern University Press.

Glantz, A. 2007. Coke faces new charges in India, including "greenwashing." *One World,* June 7. http://us.oneworld .net/section/us/current Accessed May 26, 2008.

Gleick, E. 1996. Scandal in the military. *Time,* 25 November, 28–31.

Glenny, M. 2008. *McMafia: A journey through the global criminal underworld,* New York: Alfred A. Knopf.

Gluck, S. 1976. *From parlor to prison: Five American suffragists talk about their lives.* New York: Vintage Books.

Gold, J., and S. Villari, eds. 2000. *Just sex: Students rewrite the rules on sex, violence, activism, and equality.* Lanham, Md.: Rowman and Littlefield.

Goldstein, N., and J. L. Manlowe, eds. 1997. *The gender politics of HIV/AIDS in women.* New York: New York University Press.

Gonzalez, D. 2008. The lost supermarket: A breed in need of replenishment. *New York Times.* May 5. www.nytimes.com /2008/05/05/nyregion/05citywide.html?_r=1&oref=slog in Accessed May 26, 2008.

Goodstein, E. 1999. *The trade-off myth: Fact and fiction about jobs and the environment.* Washington, D.C.: Island Press.

Gordon, L. 1988. *Heroes of their own lives: The politics and history of family violence, Boston 1880–1960.* New York: Viking.

———. 1997. Killing in self-defense. *The Nation,* 24 March, 25–28.

Gore, A. 2004. *The essential* Hip Mama: *Writing from the cutting edge of parenting.* Seattle: Seal Press.

Gore, A., and B. Lavendar. 2001. *Breeder: Real life stories from the new generation of mothers.* Seattle, Wash.: Seal Press.

Gottlieb, R. 1993. *Forcing the spring: The transformation of the American environmental movement.* Washington, D.C.: Island Press.

Gozemba, P., K. Kahn, and M. Humphries. 2007. *Courting equality: A documentary history of America's first legal same-sex marriages.* Boston: Beacon Press.

Grady, D. 2000. Study backs hormone link to cancer for women. *New York Times,* 27 January, p. A17.

Grahn, J. 1984. *Another mother tongue: Gay words, gay worlds.* Boston: Beacon Press.

Greenberg, K. J., ed. 2006. *The torture debate in America.* New York: Cambridge University Press.

Greenhouse, S. 1997. Nike shoe plant in Vietnam is called unsafe for workers. *New York Times,* 8 November, p. A1.

Greider, W. 1997. *One world ready or not: The manic logic of global capitalism.* New York: Simon & Schuster.

Griffin, S. 1971. Rape: The all-American crime. *Ramparts* 10(3): 26–35.

———. 1978. *Woman and nature: The roaring inside her.* San Francisco: Harper Colophon.

———. 1999. *What her body thought: A journey into the shadows.* San Francisco: Harper San Francisco.

Gross, J. 1992. A jail garden's harvest: Hope and redemption, *New York Times,* 3 September.

Grossholtz, J. 1983. Battered women's shelters and the political economy of sexual violence. In *Families, politics, and public policy: A feminist dialogue on women and the state,* ed. I. Diamond, 59–69. New York: Longman.

Grossman, R. 1998a. Can corporations be accountable? (Part 1). *Rachel's Environment and Health Weekly,* 30 July, 1–2.

———. 1998b. Can corporations be accountable? (Part 2). *Rachel's Environment and Health Weekly,* 6 August, 1–2.

Guenter-Schlesinger, S. 1999. Persistence of sexual harassment: The impact of military culture on policy implementation. In *Beyond zero tolerance,* ed. M. Katzenstein and J. Reppy, 195–212. Lanham, Md.: Rowman and Littlefield.

Gullette, M. M. 2004. *Aged by culture.* Chicago: University of Chicago Press.

Gustafson, K. 2005. *To punish the poor: Criminalizing trends in the welfare system.* Oakland: Women of Color Resource Center.

Guttmacher Institute. 2008a. *An overview of abortion laws.* www.guttmacher.org/statecenter/spibs/spib_OAL.pdf Accessed February 14, 2008.

———. 2008b. *Facts on induced abortion in the United States.* www.guttmacher.org/pubs/fb_induced_abortion.html Accessed February 14, 2008.

Guy-Sheftall, Beverly, ed. 1995. *Words of fire: An anthology of African-American feminist thought.* New York: The New Press.

Haines, S. 1999. *The survivor's guide to sex: How to have an empowered sex life after childhood sexual abuse.* San Francisco: Cleis Press.

Halberstam, J. *Female masculinity.* Durham, N.C.: Duke University Press.

———. 2005. *In a queer time and place.* New York: New York University Press.

———, and D. L. Volcano. 1999. *The drag king book.* London: Serpent's Tail.

Hall, G. M. 1999. Intersectionality: A necessary consideration for women of color in the military? In *Beyond zero tolerance,* ed. M. Katzenstein and J. Reppy, 143–61. Lanham, Md.: Rowman and Littlefield.

Hall, K. Q., ed. 2002. *NWSA Journal,* special issue: Feminist Disability Studies.

Hamer, D., and B. Budge. 1994. *The good, the bad and the gorgeous: Popular culture's romance with lesbianism.* London: Pandora.

Hamilton, B. E., J. A. Martin, and S. J. Ventura. 2006. *Births: Preliminary data for 2005.* Health E-Stats. November 21. www.cdc.gov/nchs/products/pubs/pubd/hestats/ prelimbirths05/prelimbirths05.htm Accessed February 14, 2008.

————. 2007. Births: Preliminary data for 2006. *National Vital Statistics Reports* 56(7). Washington, D.C.: Centers for Disease Control and Prevention.

Hamilton, C. 1993. Coping with industrial exploitation. In *Confronting environmental racism: Voices from the grassroots,* ed. R. Bullard. Boston: South End Press.

Hamilton, J. T. 2004. *All the news that's fit to sell: How the market transforms information into news.* Princeton, N.J.: Princeton University Press.

Hammonds, E. 1995. Missing persons: African American women, AIDS, and the history of disease. In *Words of fire: An anthology of African-American feminist thought,* ed. B. Guy-Sheftall, 443–49. New York: New Press.

Hamre, J. 1998. *Racial, gender bias will not be tolerated.* Speech to World-Wide Equal Opportunity Conference, July 26. www.defenselink.mil/speeches/speech.aspx?speechid57 22 Accessed May 3, 2008.

Hansen, C. 2001. A considerable service: An advocate's introduction to domestic violence and the military. *Domestic Violence Report* 6(4): 49, 50, 60–64.

Harding, L. 2004. Focus shifts to jail abuse of women. *Guardian,* May 12.

Harding, S. 1988. *Feminism and methodology: Social science issues.* Bloomington.: University of Indiana Press.

————., ed. 2004. *The feminist standpoint theory reader: Intellectual and political controversies.* New York: Routledge.

Harman, B. 1996. Happy ending. In *"Women in the trees": U.S. women's short stories about battering and resistance, 1839–1994,* ed. S. Koppelman, 286–90. Boston: Beacon Press.

Harman. J. 2008. Rapists in the ranks: Sexual assaults are frequent, and frequently ignored, in the armed services. *Los Angeles Times.* March 31. www.latimes.com/news /opinion/commentary/la-oe- harman31mar31,0, 5399612.story Accessed May 3, 2008.

Harne, L., and E. Miller, eds. 1996. *All the rage: Reasserting radical lesbian feminism.* New York: Teachers College Press.

Hartmann, B. 1995. Dangerous intersections. *Political Environments,* no. 2 (summer): 1–7. Publication of the Committee on Women, Population and the Environment, Hampshire College, Amherst, Mass.

Hartmann, H. 1981. The unhappy marriage of Marxism and feminism: Towards a more progressive union. In *Women and revolution: A discussion of the unhappy marriage of Marxism and feminism,* ed. L. Sargent. Boston: South End Press.

Hartsock, N. 1983. *Money, sex, and power: Toward a feminist historical materialism.* New York: Longman.

Hawthorne, S. 2002. *Wild politics: Feminism, globalization, bio/diversity.* Melbourne, Australia: Spinifex.

Hays, S. 1996. *The cultural contradictions of motherhood.* New Haven, Conn.: Yale University Press.

————. 2004. *Flat broke with children: Women in the age of welfare reform.* New York: Oxford University Press.

Healey, S. 1997. Confronting ageism: A MUST for mental health. In *In our own words: Readings on the psychology of women and gender,* ed. M. Crawford and R. Unger, 368–76. New York: McGraw-Hill.

Heise, L. 1989. Crimes of gender. *World Watch,* March/April, 12–21.

————, J. Pitanguy, and A. Germain. 1994. *Violence against women: The hidden health burden.* World Bank Discussion Papers #255. Washington, D.C.: The World Bank.

Hemmings, C. 2002. *Bisexual spaces: A geography of sexuality and gender.* New York: Routledge.

Henderson, H. 1991. *Paradigms in progress: Life beyond economics.* Indianapolis: Knowledge Systems.

Henderson, K. 2004. The siege. *Washington Post,* October 10.

————. 2006. *While they're at war: The true story of American families on the homefront.* New York: Houghton Mifflin.

Hennessy, R., and C. Ingraham, eds. 1997. *Materialist feminism: A reader in class, difference, and women's lives.* New York: Routledge.

Henshaw, S. K. 2003. Abortion incidence and services in the United States, 2000. *Family Planning Perspectives,* 35(1), Jan/Feb.

Herman, J. 1992. *Trauma and recovery.* New York: Basic Books.

Hernández, A. 1975. *Equal Opportunity Commission and the women's movement (1965–1975).* Unpublished paper for the Symposium on the Tenth Anniversary of the U.S. EEOC, sponsored by Rutgers University Law School, November 28–29.

————. 2002. *In pursuit of equality: The ups and downs in the struggle for inclusion.* Available from Aileen C. Hernández Associates, 818 47th Ave., San Francisco, CA 94121.

Hernández, R., and B. Flory. 2005. The label is Justicia! *Quaker Action,* 86(1): 7, Winter.

Hesse-Biber, S. J. 1996. *Am I thin enough yet?* New York: Oxford University Press.

Heymann, J. 2006. *Forgotten families: Ending the growing crisis confronting children and working parents in the global economy.* New York: Oxford University Press.

Heywood, L., and J. Drake. 1997. *Third wave agenda: Being feminist, doing feminism.* Minneapolis: University of Minnesota Press.

High, G. 1997. Combating sexual harassment. *Soldiers* 52(2): 4–5.

Hill, F., and M. Aboitiz. 2002. Women are opening doors: Security Council Resolution 1325 in Afghanistan. In *Women for Afghan women: Shattering myths and claiming the future,* ed. Sunita Mehta, 156–165. New York: Palgrave/Macmillan.

Hill, J. B. 2000. *The legacy of Luna: The story of a tree, and a woman, and the struggle to save the Redwoods.* San Francisco: Harper San Francisco.

Hiller, L., L. Gates, N. Munger, N. Douttiel, E. Ehrlich-Walsh, and M. Zepernick. 2005. *Save the water: A curriculum study guide.* Philadelphia: Women's International League for Peace and Freedom.

History Project. 1998. *Improper Bostonians: Lesbian and gay history from the Puritans to Playland.* Boston: Beacon Press.

Hite, S. 1994. *Women as revolutionary agents of change: The Hite Report and beyond.* Madison: University of Wisconsin Press.

Hochschild, A. R. 1989. *The second shift: Working parents and the revolution at home.* New York: Viking.

————. 1997. *The time bind: When work becomes home and home becomes work.* New York: Henry Holt.

Hofrichter, R., ed. 1993. *Toxic struggles: The theory and practice of environmental justice.* Philadelphia and Gabriola Island, B.C.: New Society.

Hogan, L. 1997. *Solar storms.* New York: Scribner.

Hondagneu-Sotelo, P. 2001. *Doméstica: Immigrant workers cleaning and caring in the shadows of affluence.* Berkeley: University of California Press.

Honderich, K. 2003. *The real cost of prison for women and their children.* Washington, D.C.: The Real Cost of Prisons Project/The Sentencing Project.

hooks, b. 1984a. *Feminist theory: From margin to center.* Boston: South End Press.

———. 1984b. Feminist movement to end violence. In *Feminist theory: From margin to center,* ed. b. hooks, 117–31. Boston: South End Press.

———. 1993. *Sisters of the yam: Black women and self recovery.* Boston: South End Press.

———. 1994. Seduced by violence no more. In *Outlaw culture: Resisting representations,* ed. b. hooks, 109–13. New York: Routledge.

———. 2000. *Feminism is for everybody: Passionate politics.* Cambridge, Mass.: South End Press.

Houppert, K. 2005a. Base crime. *Mother Jones,* July/August.

———. 2005b. *Home fires burning: Married to the military—for better or worse.* New York: Ballantine.

Howe, F., ed. 2000. *The politics of women's studies: Testimony from 30 founding mothers.* New York: The Feminist Press at the City University of New York.

Hubbard, R. 1989. Science, facts, and feminism. In *Feminism and science,* ed. N. Tuana. Bloomington: Indiana University Press.

———. 1990. *The politics of women's biology.* New Brunswick, N.J.: Rutgers University Press.

Hübinette, T. 2006. From orphan trains to babylifts: Colonial trafficking, empire building, and social engineering. In *Outsiders within: Writing on transracial adoption,* ed. Jane Jeong Trenka, Julia Chinyere Oparah, and Sun Yung Shin, 139–149. Cambridge: South End Press.

Human Rights Watch. 1999a. *World report 1999. United States: Human rights developments.* New York: Author.

———. 1999b. No guarantees: Sex discrimination in Mexico's maquiladora sector. In *The maquiladora reader: Cross-border organizing since NAFTA,* ed. R. Kamel and A. Hoffman, 31–35. Philadelphia: American Friends Service Committee.

Humphrey, S., and A. Kahn. 2000. Fraternities, athletic teams and rape: Importance of identification with a risky group. *Journal of Interpersonal Violence,* 15(12): 1313–22.

Hutchins, L., and L. Kaahumanu. 1991. *Bi any other name: Bisexual people speak out.* Boston: Alyson.

Hynes, H. P. 1989. *The recurring silent spring.* New York: Pergamon Press.

———. 1996. *A patch of Eden.* White River Junction, Vt.: Chelsea Green.

Indigo, Susannah. 2000. *Blow jobs and other boring stuff: Teens have casually redefined what used to be called sex.* http://www.salon.com/sex/feature/2000/12/14/teens/print.html Accessed July 21, 2005.

Ingraham, C. 2004. *Thinking straight: The power, promise, and paradox of heterosexuality.* New York: Routledge.

In Phoenix chain gangs for women. 1996. *New York Times,* 28 August, p. C1.

Institute for Policy Studies. 2000. *International grassroots summit on military base cleanup conference report.* Washington, D.C.: Institute for Policy Studies.

International Organization for Migration. 2007. *About migration.* www.iom.int/jahia/Jahia/lang/en/pid/3 Accessed May 23, 2008.

Isakson, E., ed. 1988. *Women and the military system.* New York: St. Martin's Press.

Iwamura, J. M. 2007. Critical faith: Japanese Americans and the birth of a new civil religion. *American Quarterly* 59(3): 937–968.

Jacob, K. 2002. *Our choices, our lives: Unapologetic writings on abortion.* Minneapolis: Writers Advantage.

Jaggar, A. M. ed. 1994. *Living with contradictions: Controversies in feminist social ethics.* Boulder, Colo.: Westview Press.

Jaimes, A., and T. Halsey. 1986. American Indian women at the center of indigenous resistance in contemporary North America. In *The state of Native America: Genocide, colonization, and resistance,* ed. A. Jaimes, 311–44. Boston: South End Press.

Jeffreys, Sheila. 1997. *The idea of prostitution.* North Melbourne, Australia: Spinifex.

———. 2003. *Unpacking queer politics: A lesbian feminist perspective.* New York: Blackwell.

Jetter, A., A. Orleck, and D. Taylor, eds. 1997. *The politics of motherhood: Activist voices from left to right.* Hanover, N.H.: University Press of New England.

Joffe, C. 1995. *Doctors of conscience: The struggle to provide abortion before and after* Roe v. Wade. Boston: Beacon Press.

Johnson, A. G. 2005. *The gender knot: Unraveling our patriarchal legacy.* Philadelphia: Temple University Press.

Johnson, M. L. 2002. *Jane sexes it up: True confessions of feminist desire.* New York: Four Walls, Eight Windows.

Jones, A. 1980. *Women who kill.* New York: Holt, Rinehart, and Winston.

———. 1994. *Next time, she'll be dead: Battering and how to stop it.* Boston: Beacon Press.

Jones-DeWeever, A. A. 2007. *Women in the wake of the storm: Examining the post-Katrina realities of the women of New Orleans and the Gulf coast.* Washington, D.C.: Institute for Women's Policy Research.

Jong, E. 1998. Ally McBeal and *Time* magazine can't keep the good women down. *New York Observer,* 13 July, p. 19.

Justice Policy Institute. 2002. *Cell blocks or classrooms?* Washington, D.C.: Justice Policy Institute. www.justicepolicy.org/article.php?id=3 Accessed September 2, 2005.

Kadi, J. 1996. *Thinking class: Sketches from a cultural worker.* Boston: South End Press.

Kamel, R. 1990. *The global factory: Analysis and action for a new economic era.* Philadelphia: American Friends Service Committee.

———, and A. Hoffman, eds. 1999. *The maquiladora reader: Cross-border organizing since NAFTA.* Philadelphia: American Friends Service Committee.

Kamen, P. 2000. *Her way: Young women make the sexual revolution.* New York: New York University Press.

Kaplan, L. 1995. *The story of Jane: The legendary underground feminist abortion service.* New York: Pantheon Books.

Kaplan, T. 1997. *Crazy for democracy: Women in grassroots movements.* New York: Routledge.

Kaschak, E., ed. 2002. *Intimate betrayal: Domestic violence in lesbian relationships.* New York: Haworth Press.

Kates, E., and P. Ransford with Carol Cardozo. 2005. *Women in prison in Massachusetts: Maintaining family connections—A research report.* Boston: Center for Women in Politics and Public Policy, McCormack Graduate School of Public Policy, University of Massachusetts.

Katz, J. N. 1995. *The invention of heterosexuality.* New York: Plume.

Katzenstein, M. F. 1993. The right to fight. *Women's Review of Books* 11(2): 30–31.

Katz Rothman, B. 1986. *Tentative pregnancy: Prenatal diagnosis and the future of motherhood.* New York: Viking.

Kaufman, M., C. Silverberg, and F. Odette. 2003. *The ultimate guide to sex and disability: For all of us with disabilities, chronic pain and illness.* San Francisco: Cleis Press.

Kawachi, I., N. Daniels, and D. Robinson. 2005. Health disparities by race and class: Why both matter, *Health Affairs,* 24(2): 343–352.

Kaysen, S. 1994. *Girl interrupted.* New York: Vintage Books.

Kearney, M. C. 2006. *Girls make media.* New York: Routledge.

Kempadoo, K., and J. Doezema, eds. 1998. *Global sex workers: Rights, resistance and redefinition.* New York: Routledge.

Kerr, J., ed. 1993. *Ours by right: Women's rights as human rights.* London: Zed Books.

Kesic, V. 2000. From reverence to rape: An anthropology of ethnic and genderized violence. In *Frontline feminisms: Women, war, and resistance,* ed, Marguerite Waller and Jennifer Rycenga. New York: Garland Publishing.

Kettel, B. 1996. Women, health and the environment. *Social Science Medicine* 42(10): 1367–79.

Kich, G. K. 1992. The developmental process of asserting a biracial, bicultural identity. In *Racially mixed people in America,* ed. M. P. Root, 304–17. Newbury Park, Calif.: Sage.

Kilbourne, J. 1999. *Deadly persuasion: Why women and girls must fight the addictive power of advertising.* New York: Free Press.

Kilty, K. M., and E. A. Segal, eds. 2006. *The promise of welfare reform: Political rhetoric and the reality of poverty in the twenty-first century.* Philadelphia: Haworth Press.

Kim, R. 2001. Japanese Americans fight backlash. *San Francisco Chronicle,* October 2.

Kim-Gibson, D. S. 1999. *Silence broken: Korean comfort women.* Parkersburg, IA: Mid Prairie Books.

Kimmel, M. 1993. Clarence, William, Iron Mike, Tailhook, Senator Packwood, Spur Posse, Magic . . . and us. In *Transforming a rape culture,* ed. E. Buchwald, R. Fletcher, and M. Roth, 119–38. Minneapolis: Milkweed Editions.

———. 2000. *The gendered society.* New York: Oxford University Press.

———, and M. Messner. 1998. *Men's lives.* 3d ed. Boston: Allyn & Bacon.

———, and T. Mosmiller, eds. 1992. *Against the tide: Pro-feminist men in the United States, 1776–1990.* Boston: Beacon Press.

Kincaid, J. 1988. *A small place.* New York: Penguin/Plume.

King, Y. 1983. All is connectedness: Notes from the Women's Pentagon Action, USA. In *Keeping the peace,* ed. L. Jones. London: The Women's Press.

———. 1987. Letter to the editor. *The Nation,* 12 December, 702, 730–31.

———. 1988. Ecological feminism, *Z Magazine,* July/August, 124–27.

———. 1993a. The other body. *Ms.,* March/April, 72–75.

———. 1993b. Feminism and ecology. In *Toxic struggles: The theory and practice of environmental justice,* ed. R. Hofrichter, 76–84. Philadelphia and Gabriola Island, B.C.: New Society.

———. 1998. Ecofeminism. In *The reader's companion to U.S. women's history,* ed. W. Mankiller, G. Mink, M. Navarro, B. Smith, and G. Steinem, 207. Boston: Houghton Mifflin.

Kingsolver, B. 2000. *Prodigal summer.* New York: Harper Collins.

Kirk, G. 1997a. Ecofeminism and environmental justice: Bridges across gender, race, and class. *Frontiers: A Journal of Women's Studies* 18(2): 2–20.

———. 1997b. Standing on solid ground: Towards a materialist ecological feminism. In *Materialist feminism: A reader in class, difference, and women's lives,* ed. Rosemary Hennessy and Chrys Ingraham, 345–63. New York: Routledge.

———. 1998. Ecofeminism and Chicano environmental struggles: Bridges across gender and race. In *Chicano culture, ecology, politics: Subversive kin,* ed. D. G. Peña, 177–200. Tucson: University of Arizona Press.

———. 2008. Environmental effects of U.S. military security: Gendered experiences from the Philippines, South Korea, and Japan. In *Gender and globalization in Asia and the Pacific: Method, practice, theory,* edited by K. E. Ferguson and M. Mironesco. Honolulu: University of Hawaii Press.

Klein, R., and L. J. Dumble. 1994. Disempowering midlife women: The science and politics of hormone replacement therapy (HRT). *Women's Studies International Forum* 17(4): 327–43.

Kline, C. B., ed. 1997 *Child of mine: Writers talk about the first year of motherhood.* New York: Hyperion.

Koedt, A., E. Levine, and A. Rapone, eds. 1973. *Radical feminism.* New York: Quadrangle Books.

Kohl, H. 1992. *From archetype to zeitgeist: Powerful ideas for powerful thinking.* Boston: Little Brown.

Komesaroff, P., P. Rothfield, and J. Daly, eds. 1997. *Reinterpreting menopause: Cultural and philosophical issues.* New York: Routledge.

Koppleman, S. ed. 2004. *"Women in the trees": U.S. Women's short stories about battering and resistance, 1839–2000.* New York: Feminist Press at CUNY.

Koser, K. 2007. *International migration: A short introduction.* Oxford: Oxford University Press.

Koss, M. P. 1988. Hidden rape: Sexual aggression and victimization in a national sample of students in higher education. In *Rape and sexual assault,* expanded ed., ed. A. W. Burgess, 3–25. New York: Garland.

———, E. T. Dinero, and C. A. Seibel. 1988. Stranger and acquaintance rape: Are there differences in the victim's experience? *Psychology of Women Quarterly* 12: 1–24.

———, L. Goodman, A. Browne, L. Fitzgerald, G. P. Keita, and N. F. Russo. 1994. *No safe haven: Male violence against women at home, at work, and in the community.* Washington, D.C.: American Psychological Association.

———, C. A. Gidycz, and N. Wisiewski. 1987. The scope of rape: Incidence and prevalence of sexual aggression and victimization in a national sample of higher education students. *Journal of Consulting and Clinical Psychology* 55(2): 162–70.

Koyama. E. 2003.The transfeminist manifesto. In *Catching a wave: Reclaiming feminism for the 21st century,* ed. Rory Dicker and Alison Piepmeier, 244–259. Boston; Northeastern University Press.

Krauss, C. 1993. Blue-collar women and toxic-waste protests: The process of politicization. In *Toxic struggles: The theory and practice of environmental justice,* ed. R. Hofrichter, 107–17. Philadelphia and Gabriola Island, B.C.: New Society.

Kuhn, T. 1962. *The structure of scientific revolutions.* Chicago: University of Chicago Press.

Kurshan, Nancy. 1996. Behind the walls: The history and current reality of women's imprisonment. In *Criminal injustice: Confronting the prison crisis,* ed. E. Rosenblatt. Cambridge: South End Press.

Labaton, V., and D. Lundy Martin, eds. 2004. *The fire this time: Young activists and the new feminism.* New York: Anchor/Random House.

Labelle, D., and Kubiak, S. P. 2004. Balancing gender equity for women prisoners. *Feminist Studies* 30(2), Summer: 416–26.

LaDuke, W. 1993. A society based on conquest cannot be sustained: Native peoples and the environmental crisis. In *Toxic struggles: The theory and practice of environmental justice,* ed. R. Hofrichter. Philadelphia and Gabriola Island, B.C.: New Society.

———. 1999. *All our relations: Native struggles for land and life.* Cambridge, Mass.: South End Press.

Lahey, K. 1985. Until women themselves have told all they have to tell. *Osgoode Hall Law Journal* 23(3): 519–41.

Lake, C. 2005. The polls speak: Americans support abortion. *Ms.* XV(2), Summer: 37, 39.

Lamb, W., and the Women of New York Correctional Facility. 2003. *Couldn't keep it to myself: Testimony from our imprisoned sisters.* New York: ReganBooks.

Lamm, N. 1995. It's a big, fat revolution. In *Listen up: Voices from the next feminist generation,* ed. Barbara Findlen, 85–94. Seattle: Seal Press.

Lancaster, R. N., and M. di Leonardo, eds. 1997. *The gender/sexuality reader: Culture, history, political economy.* New York: Routledge.

Larkin, J., and K. Popaleni. 1997. Heterosexual courtship violence and sexual harassment: The private and public control of young women. In *In our own words: Readings on the psychology of women and gender,* ed. M. Crawford and R. Unger, 313–26. New York: McGraw-Hill.

Lasch, C. 1977. *Haven in a heartless world: The family besieged.* New York: Basic Books.

LaVeist, T. A. 2005. *Minority population and health: An introduction to health disparities in the U.S.* San Francisco: Jossey-Bass.

Leach, S. L. 2004. Behind the surge in girl crime. *Christian Science Monitor.* September 15. www.csmonitor.com/2004/0915/p16s02-usju.html Accessed April 29, 2008.

Lederer, E. 2005. Women said worse off now than 10 years ago. *Associated Press,* March 4.

Lee, C. 1987. *Toxic wastes and race in the United States.* New York: New York Commission for Racial Justice United Church of Christ.

Lefkowitz, B. 1997. *Our guys: The Glen Ridge rape and the secret life of the perfect suburb.* Berkeley: University of California Press.

Leidholdt, D., and J. Raymond. 1990. *The sexual liberals and the attack on feminism.* New York: Pergamon.

Leong, L. C. P. 2004. Virulent virginity: "Abstinence-only" sex ed programs are putting youth at risk. *Color Lines* 7(4): 36–37.

Leong, R., ed. 1996. *Asian American sexualities: Dimensions of the gay and lesbian experience.* New York: Routledge.

Lerman, H. 1996. *Pigeonholing women's misery: A history and critical analysis of the psychodiagnosis of women in the twentieth century.* New York: Basic Books.

Le Sueur, M. 1982. *Ripening: Selected work.* 2d ed. New York: Feminist Press at the City University of New York.

Leung, A., and A. Chow. 2002. Mass organizing continues around detainees. *Asian Week,* March 1–7.

Levister, C. 2006. *A sweatshop behind bars.* www.alternet.org/story/41481/ Accessed May 2, 2008.

Lichtenstein, A. C., and M. A. Kroll. 1996. The fortress economy: The economic role of the U.S. prison system. In *Criminal injustice: Confronting the prison crisis,* ed. E. Rosenblatt. Boston: South End Press.

Lifton, R. J. 2004. Doctors and torture. *New England Journal of Medicine,* 315:415–416.

Lindsay-Poland, J. 2003. *Emperors in the jungle: The hidden history of the U.S. in Panama.* Durham: Duke University Press.

Lindsley, S. 2004. Bearing the blame: Gender, immigration, reproduction, and the environment. In *The fire this time: Young activists and the new feminism,* ed. Vivien Labaton and Dawn Lundy Martin, 220–253. New York: Anchor/Random House.

Liptak, A. 2006. Prisons often shackle pregnant inmates in labor. *New York Times.* March 2. www.nytimes.com/2006/03/02/national/02shackles.html?_r=3&oref=slogin&oref=slogin&oref=slogin Accessed May 2, 2008.

———. 2008. Inmate count in U.S. dwarfs other nations'. *New York Times.* April 23. www.nytimes.com/2008/04/23/us/23prison.html? pagewanted=3&_r=2&hp Accessed April 29, 2008.

List, P. C., ed. 1993. *Radical environmentalism: Philosophy and tactics.* Belmont, Calif.: Wadsworth.

Litt, J. S., and M. K. Zimmerman. 2003. Global perspectives on gender and carework: An introduction. *Gender and Society* 17(2): 156–65.

Lopez, I. 1997. Agency and constraint: Sterilization and reproductive freedom among Puerto Rican women in New York City. In *Situated lives: Gender and culture in everyday lives,* ed. L. Lamphere, H. Ragone, and P. Zavella pp. 157–74 New York: Routledge.

Lorber, J. 1994. *Paradoxes of gender.* New Haven, Conn.: Yale University Press.

Lorde, A. 1996. *The cancer journals.* San Francisco: Aunt Lute Books.

Lovejoy, M. 2001. Disturbances in the social body: Differences in body image and eating problems among African American and White women. *Gender and Society* 15(2): 239–61.

Lowy, J. 1999. Gay adoption backlash growing. *San Francisco Examiner,* 7 March, p. A20.

Lublin, N. 1998. *Pandora's box: Feminism confronts reproductive technology.* Lanham, Md.: Rowman and Littlefield.

Luebke, B. F., and M. E. Reilly. 1995. *Women's studies graduates: The first generation.* New York: Teachers College Press.

Lusane, C. 1991. *Pipe dream blues: Racism and the war on drugs.* Boston: South End Press.

Lynes, K. and G. Torry. 2005. *From local to global: Making peace work for women. Security Council Resolution 1325 five years on.* New York: NGO Working Group on Peace and Security.

Maathai, W. 2006. *The green belt movement: Sharing the approach and the experience.* Rev. ed. New York: Lantern Books.

MacGregor, S. 2006. *Beyond mothering earth: Ecological citizenship and the politics of care.* Vancouver: University of British Columbia Press.

Mack-Canty, C. 2004. Third-wave feminism and the need to reweave the nature/culture duality. *NWSA Journal* (16)83, Fall: 154–79.

Mackinnon, C. 1991. From practice to theory, or what is a white woman anyway? *Yale Journal of Law and Feminism* 4(13–22): 1281–1328.

MacNair, R. 2002. *Perpetration-induced traumatic stress: The psychological consequences of killing.* Westport, Conn.: Praeger.

Magnani, L. and H. L. Wray. 2006. *Beyond prisons: A new interfaith paradigm for our failed prison system.* Minneapolis: Fortress Press.

Maher, F. A., and M. K. T. Tétreault. 1994. *The feminist classroom.* New York: Basic Books.

Mahoney, M. 1994. Victimization or oppression? Women's lives, violence, and agency. In *The public nature of private violence: The discovery of domestic abuse,* ed. M. A. Fineman and R. Mykitiuk, 59–92. New York: Routledge.

Mainardi, P. 1992. The politics of housework. *Ms.,* May/June, 40–41.

Malkan, S. 2007. *Not just a pretty face: The ugly side of the beauty industry.* Gabriola Island, B.C.: New Society.

Mairs, N. 1996. *Waist-high in the world: A life among the nondisabled.* Boston: Beacon Press.

Mann, C. R. 1995. Women of color and the criminal justice system. In *The criminal justice system and women,* ed. B. R. Price and N. J. Sokoloff. New York: McGraw-Hill.

Maran, R. 2006. Detention and torture at Guantanamo. *Social Justice,* 33(4):151–175.

Marcus, S. 2005. Queer theory for everyone: A review essay. *Signs: Journal of Women in Culture and Society* 31(1): 191–218.

Martin, C. E. 2007. *Perfect girls, starving daughters: The frightening new normalcy of hating your body.* New York: Simon and Schuster.

Martinez, E. 1998. *De colores means all of us: Latina views for a multi-colored century.* Boston: South End Press.

Martinson, K., and J. Strawn. 2003. *Built to last: Why skills matter for long-run success in welfare reform.* Washington, D.C.: Center for Law and Social Policy.

Martone, C. 2005. *Loving through bars: Children of parents in prison.* Santa Monica, Calif.: Santa Monica Press.

Marx, F. 2002. Grassroots to graduation: Low-income women accessing higher education. *Final Report: Evaluation of the Women in Community Development Program, Women's Institute for Housing and Economic Development.* Boston: Center for Research on Women, Wellesley College.

Mauer, M., and M. Chesney-Lind, eds. 2002. *Invisible punishment: The collateral consequences of mass imprisonment.* New York: The New Press.

May, L. 2005. *Transgenders and intersexuals: Everything you ever wanted to know but couldn't think of the question.* Bowden, South Australia: Fast Lane.

McCarthy, C., and W. Crichlow, eds. 1993. *Race, identity, and representation in education.* New York: Routledge.

McChesney, R. W. 2004. *The problem of the media: US communications politics in the 21st century.* New York: Monthly Review Press.

McClintock, A. 1995. *Imperial leather: Race, gender, and sexuality in the colonial context.* New York: Routledge.

McIntosh, P. 1988. *White privilege and male privilege: A personal account of coming to see correspondences through work in women's studies.* Wellesley, Mass.: Center for Research on Women, Wellesley College.

McKelvey, T., ed. 2007. *One of the guys: Women as aggressors and torturers.* Emeryville, Calif.: Seal Press.

McKenna, T. 1996/1997. Military culture breeds misogyny. *Women Against Military Madness,* December/January, 1.

Mello, F. V. 1996. Population and international security in the new world order. *Political Environments,* 3(Winter/Spring):

25–26. Publication of the Committee on Women, Population and the Environment, Hampshire College, Amherst, Mass.

Mellor, M. 1992. *Breaking the boundaries: Towards a feminist green socialism.* London: Virago Press.

Members of the AIDS Counseling and Education Program of the Bedford Hills Correctional Facility. 1998. *Breaking the walls of silence: AIDS and women in a New York State maximum security prison.* Woodstock, N.Y.: Overlook Press.

Mendez, J. B. 2002. Creating alternatives from a gender perspective: Transnational organizing for maquila workers' rights in Central America. In *Women's activism and globalization: Linking local struggles and transnational politics,* ed. Nancy A. Naples and Manisha Desai, 121–141. New York: Routledge.

Merchant, C. 1980. *The death of nature: Ecology and the scientific revolution.* San Francisco: Harper & Row.

Messer-Davidow, E. 1991. Know-how. In *(En)gendering knowledge: Feminists in academe,* ed. J. E. Hartman and E. Messer-Davidow, 281–309. Knoxville: University of Tennessee Press.

Messerschmidt, J. W. 1986. *Capitalism, patriarchy, and crime: Toward a socialist feminist criminology.* Totowa, N.J.: Rowman and Littlefield.

Messner, M. 1992. *Power at play: Sports and the problem of masculinity.* Boston: Beacon Press.

Meyers, D. T. 2001. The rush to motherhood—pronatalist discourse and women's autonomy. *Signs: Journal of Women in Culture and Society* 26(3): 735–73.

Midgley, J. 2005. *Women and the U.S. budget: Where the money goes and what you can do about it.* Gabriola, B.C.: New Society Publishers.

Mies, M. 1993. The need for a new vision: The subsistence perspective. In *Ecofeminism,* ed. M. Mies and V. Shiva. London: Zed Books.

———, and V. Shiva, eds. 1993. *Ecofeminism.* London: Zed Books.

Miller, P. 1993. *The worst of times: Illegal abortion—survivors, practitioners, coroners, cops, and children of women who died talk about its horrors.* New York: HarperCollins.

Miller, S. 2005. California prison boom ends, signaling a shift in priorities. *Christian Science Monitor,* June 20.

Miller, V. D. 1993. Building on our past, planning our future: Communities of color and the quest for environmental justice. In *Toxic struggles: The theory and practice of environmental justice,* ed. Richard Hofrichter, 128–135. Philadelphia and Gabriola Island, B.C.: New Society.

Millett, Kate. 1990. *The loony bin trip.* New York: Simon & Schuster.

Mills, R. J., and S. Bhandari. 2003. Health insurance coverage in the United States: 2002. *Current Population Reports,* Washington, D.C.: U.S. Census Bureau.

Mink, G. 1998. Feminists, welfare reform, and welfare justice. *Social Justice* 25(1): 146–57.

———. 2002. Violating women: Rights abuses in the welfare police state. In *Lost ground: Welfare, poverty, and beyond,* ed. R. Albelda and A. Withorn, 95–112. Cambridge, Mass.: South End Press.

Mitchell, T. ed. 2001. *Global noise: Rap and hip hop outside the USA.* Middletown, Conn.: Weslyan University Press.

Mohai, P. 1997. Men, women, and the environment: An examination of the gender gap in environmental concern and activism. In *Women working in the environment*, ed. C. Sachs, 215–39. New York: Taylor and Francis.

Mohanty, C. T. 2003. *Feminism without borders: Decolonizing theory, practicing solidarity*. Durham, N.C.: Duke University Press.

Moon, K. 1997. *Sex between allies: Military prostitution in U.S.–Korea relations*. New York: Columbia University Press.

Moore, B. 1996. From underrepresentation to overrepresentation: African American women. In *It's our military too! Women and the U.S. military*, ed. J. H. Stiehm, 115–35. Philadelphia: Temple University Press.

Moraga, C., and G. Anzaldúa. 1981. *This bridge called my back: Writings by radical women of color*. New York: Kitchen Table/Women of Color Press.

Moraga, C. and G. Anzaldua. 1981. *This bridge called my back: Writings by radical women of color*. New York: Kitchen Table/Women of Color Press.

Morell, C. M. 1994. *Unwomanly conduct: The challenge of intentional childlessness*. New York: Routledge.

Morgan, L. M., and M. Michaels. 1999. *Fetal subjects: Feminist positions*. Philadelphia: University of Pennsylvania Press.

Morgan, R. 1996. Dispatch from Beijing, *Ms.* January/February, 12–15.

Morgen, S. 2002. *Into our own hands: The women's health movement in the United States, 1969–1990*. Piscataway, N.J.: Rutgers University Press.

Morland, K., S. Wing, A. D. Roux, and C. Poole. 2002. Neighborhood characteristics associated with the location of food stores and food service places. *American Journal of Preventive Medicine* 22(1): 23–29.

Morris, M. 1999. In war and peace: Incidence and implications of rape by military personnel. In *Beyond zero tolerance: Discrimination in military culture*, ed. M. F. Katzenstein and J. Reppy, 163–94. Lanham, Md.: Rowman and Littlefield.

Morrison, A., R. White, E. Van Velsor, and the Center for Creative Leadership. 1992. *Breaking the glass ceiling: Can women reach the top of America's largest corporations?* Reading, Mass.: Addison-Wesley.

Morrison, P. 2007. Hey, why not try the tap sometime? *San Francisco Examiner*, August 6, p. 11.

Morrison, T., ed. 1992. *Race-ing, justice, en-gendering power: Essays on Anita Hill, Clarence Thomas, and the construction of reality*. New York: Pantheon.

Morrow, L. 1999. Folklore in a box. In *Readings in mass communication: Media literacy and culture*, ed. K. B. Massey, 22–26. Mountain View, Calif.: Mayfield.

Moses, M. 1993. Farmworkers and pesticides. In *Confronting environmental racism: Voices from the grassroots*, ed. R. Bullard, 161–78. Boston: South End Press.

Movement for a New Society. 1983. *Off their backs . . . and on our own two feet*. Philadelphia: New Society.

Mudrick, N. R. 1988. Disabled women and the public policies of income support. In *Women with disabilities: Essays in psychology, culture, and politics*, ed. M. Fine and A. Asch. Philadelphia: Temple University Press.

Muir, K. 1993. *Arms and the woman*. London: Hodder and Stoughton.

Mullings, L. 1997. *On our own: Race, class, and gender in the lives of African American women*. New York: Routledge.

Mumola, C. J. 2000. *Incarcerated parents and their children*. Bureau of Justice Statistics special report, August. Washington, DC: U.S. Department of Justice.

Murphy, E., and E. J. Graff. 2005. *Getting even: Why women don't get paid like men—and what to do about it*. New York: Touchstone.

Muscio, I. 1999. *Cunt: A declaration of independence*. Seattle, Wash.: Seal Press.

Nadasen, P. 2005. *Welfare warriors: The welfare rights movement in the United States*. New York: Routledge.

Naffine, N. 1987. *Female crime: The construction of women in criminology*. Boston: Allen & Unwin.

Nagel, J. 1997. *Whores and other feminists*. New York: Routledge.

Naidus, B. 1993. *One size does not fit all*. Littleton, Colo.: Aigis Publications.

Namaste, V. K. 2000. *Invisible lives: The erasure of transsexual and transgendered people*. Chicago: University of Chicago Press.

Naples, N., ed. 1997. *Community activism and feminist politics: Organizing across race, class, and gender*. New York: Routledge.

———. 1998. *Grassroots warriors: Activist mothering, community work, and the war on poverty*. New York: Routledge.

———, and K. Bojar, eds. 2002. *Teaching feminist activism: Strategies from the field*. New York: Routledge.

National Center for Addiction and Substance Abuse. 2003. *Crossing the bridge: An evaluation of the Drug Treatment Alternative-to-Prison Program (DTAP)*. New York: NCASA at Columbia University.

National Center for Health Statistics. 2007. *Health, United States 2006*. www.cdc.gov/nchs/data/hus/hus06 .pdf#027 Accessed February 14, 2008.

National Committee on Pay Equity. 2007. *The wage gap over time: In real dollars, women see a continuing gap*. www.pay-equity.org/info-time.html Accessed March 15, 2008.

National Council for Research on Women. 2004. *Missing: Information about women's lives*. New York: NCRW.

National Immigrant Justice Center. 2007. Briefing paper to U.N. special rapporteur on the rights of migrants. www.immigrantwomennetwork.org/Resources/ Briefing%20Paper_Women%20in%20Detention_UN%20S pecial%20Rapporteur%202007%2004%2017%20FINAL.p df Accessed May 2, 2008.

National Women's Law Center. 2003. *Air Force must face systemic problems to address sexual assaults at Academy*, press release, February 28. www.nwlc.org/details.cfm?id= 1331&section=newsroom Accessed May 10, 2005.

———. 2004. *Slip-sliding away: The erosion of hard-won gains for women under the Bush administration and an agenda for moving forward*. Washington, D.C.: National Women's Law Center.

Nelson, J. 2003. *Women of color and the reproductive rights movement*. New York: New York University Press.

Nelson, K. P. 2006. Shopping for children in the international marketplace. In *Outsiders within: Writing on transracial adoption*, ed. Jane Jeong Trenka, Julia Chinyere Oparah, and Sun Yung Shin, 89–104. Cambridge: South End Press.

Nelson, L. 1990. The place of women in polluted places. In *Reweaving the world: The emergence of ecofeminism*, ed. I. Diamond and G. Orenstein. San Francisco: Sierra Club Books.

Nelson, M. B. 2002. And now they tell us women don't really like sports? *Ms.*, December 2002/January 2003, 32–36.

Nestle, J., C. Howell, and R. Wilchins. 2002. *Genderqueer: Voices from beyond the sexual binary*. Los Angeles: Alyson.

Neumann, C. E. 2007. United Kingdom lifts ban on gays and lesbians in the military. In *Gay, lesbian, bisexual, transgender* events 1848–2006, vol 2, ed. Lillian Faderman, Horacio Roque Ramírez, Yolanda Retter, Stuart Timmons, and Eric C. Wat, 669–671. Pasadena, Calif.: Salem Press.

Newbury, C. and H. Baldwin. 2001. Confronting the aftermath of conflict: Women's organizations in post-genocide Rwanda. In *Women and civil war: Impact, organizations, and action*, ed. K. Kumar. Boulder, Colo: Lynne Reinner.

Nguyen, T. 2005. *We are all suspects now.* Boston: Beacon Press.

NiCarthy, G. 1987. *The ones who got away: Women who left abusive partners.* Seattle, Wash.: Seal Press.

———. 2004. *Getting free: You can end abuse and take back your life.* Expanded ed. Seattle, Wash.: Seal Press.

Nicholson, L. J., ed. 1990. *Feminism/postmodernism.* New York: Routledge.

Nimoy, L. 2007. *The full body project.* Brooklyn, N.Y.: Five Ties.

Noble, K. 1994. Woman tells of retaliation for complaint on Tailhook. *New York Times,* 5 October, p. A10.

Norris, P., ed. 1997. *Women, media, and politics.* New York: Oxford University Press.

Norsigian, J. 1996. The women's health movement in the United States. In *Man-made medicine: Women's health, public policy, and reform,* ed. K. L. Moss, 79–97. Durham, N.C.: Duke University Press.

Nowrojee, S., and J. Silliman. 1997. Asian women's health: Organizing a movement. In *Dragon ladies: Asian American feminists breathe fire,* ed. S. Shah, 73–89. Boston: South End Press.

NWSAction. 2004. Feminist uses of science and technology. College Park, Md.: National Women's Studies Association.

Ochs, Robyn, and Sarah F. Rowley, eds. 2005. *Getting bi: Voices of bisexuals around the world.* Boston: Bisexual Resource Center.

O'Connor, M., ed. 1994. *Is capitalism sustainable? Political economy and the politics of ecology.* New York: Guilford Press.

Office of Justice Programs. 2007. *Rape and sexual violence.* U.S. Department of Justice. www.ojp.usdoj.gov/nij/topics/crime/rape-sexual-violence/welcome.htm Accessed March 9, 2008.

Ogden, S. 2006. Pomo woman, ex-prisoner, speaks out. In *The color of violence* ed. INCITE! Women of Color Against Violence, 164–169. Cambridge: South End Press.

Ogur, B. 1996. Smothering in stereotypes: HIV-positive women. In *Talking gender: Public images, personal journeys, and political critiques,* ed. N. Hewitt, J. O'Barr, and N. Rosebaugh. Chapel Hill: University of North Carolina Press.

Okazawa-Rey, M. 1994. Racial identity development of mixed race persons: An overview. In *Diversity and human service education,* ed. J. Silver-Jones, S. Kerstein, and D. Osher. Council of Standards in Human Service Education Monograph Series, No. 4.

Oliver, R. 2007. All about "green" shopping. *CNN.com/World Business,* December 24. http://edition.cnn.com/2007/BUSINESS/12/23/eco.shopping/index.html#cnnSTC Accessed May 16, 2008.

Olson, R. 2008. *This is who i am: Our beauty is all shapes and sizes.* New York: Artisan/Workman.

Omolade, B. 1986. *It's a family affair: The real lives of Black single mothers.* New York: Kitchen Table: Women of Color Press.

———. 1989. We speak for the planet. In *Rocking the ship of state: Toward a feminist peace politics,* ed. A. Harris and Y. King. Boulder, Colo.: Westview Press.

———. 1994. Ella's daughters. In *The rising song of African American women.* New York: Routledge.

O'Reilly, B. 1991. Cooling down the world debt bomb. *Fortune,* 20 May, 123.

Orlando, L. 1991. Loving whom we choose. In *Bi any other name: Bisexual people speak out,* ed. L. Hutchins and L. Ka'ahumanu, 223–32. Boston: Alyson.

O'Shea, K. 1998. *Women and the death penalty in the United States, 1900–1998.* Westport, Conn.: Praeger.

O'Toole, L., and J. Schiffman. 1997. *Gender violence: Interdisciplinary perspectives.* New York: New York University Press.

Owen, B., and B. Bloom. 1995. Profiling women prisoners. *The Prison Journal* 75(2): 165–85.

Oxfam International. 2004. *Trading away our rights: Women working in global supply chains.* Oxford, UK: Oxfam.

Paasonen, S., K. Nikunen, and L. Saarenmaa, eds. 2008. *Pornification: Sex and sexuality in media culture.* Oxford, U.K.: Berg.

Page, S. 1988. *If I'm so wonderful, why am I still single? Ten strategies that will change your love life forever.* New York: Viking.

Paglia, C. 1990. *Sexual personae: Art and decadence from Nefertiti to Emily Dickinson.* New Haven, Conn.: Yale University Press.

Paley, G. 1998. The illegal days. In *Just as I thought,* 13–20. New York: Farrar, Straus, Giroux.

Pardo, M. 1990. Mexican American women grassroots community activists: "Mothers of East Los Angeles." *Frontiers: A Journal of Women's Studies* 11(1): 1–7.

Parenti, C. 1999, September. The prison industrial complex: Crisis and control. *Corporate Watch.* San Francisco: Transnational Resource and Action Center.

Parreñas, R. S. 2001. *Servants of globalization: Women, migration, and domestic work.* Stanford, Calif.: Stanford University Press.

Pastor, M., R. Bullard, J. Boyce, A. Fothergill, R. Morello-Frosch, and B. Wright. 2006. *In the wake of the storm: Environment, disaster, and race after Katrina.* New York: Russell Sage Foundation.

Peach, L. J. 1997. Behind the front lines: Feminist battles over combat. In *Wives and warriors: Women and the military in the United States and Canada,* ed. L. Weinstein and C. White, 99–135. Westport, Conn.: Bergin & Garvey.

Pearce, D., A. Markandya, and E. B. Barbier. 1990. *Blueprint for a green economy.* London: Earthscan.

Perez, B. E. 2003. Woman warrior meets mail-order bride: Finding an Asian American voice in the women's movement. *Berkeley Women's Law Journal* 18:211–36.

Perrone, B., H. H. Stockel, and V. Krueger. 1989. *Medicine women, curanderas, and women doctors.* Norman: University of Oklahoma Press.

Pershing, J. 2003. Why women don't report sexual harassment: A case study of an elite military institution. *Gender Issues* 21(4): 3–30.

Petchesky, R. 1990. *Abortion and woman's choice: The state, sexuality, and reproductive freedom.* Rev. ed. Boston: Northeastern University Press.

———. 1997. Fetal images: The power of visual culture in the politics of reproduction. In *The gender/sexuality reader,* ed. R. Lancaster and M. di Leonardo, 134–50. New York: Routledge.

Petersen, B. 1991. *Dancing with Daddy: A childhood lost and a life regained.* New York: Bantam Books.

Peterson, V. S. 2000. Sexing political identity/Nationalism as heterosexism. In *At home in the nation? Gender, states and nationalism,* edited by Sita Ranchod-Nilson and Mary Ann Tétreault. Pp. 54-80. New York: Routledge.

Peterson, V. S., and A. S. Runyan. 1993. *Global gender issues.* Boulder, Colo.: Westview Press.

Pharr, S. 1988. *Homophobia: A weapon of sexism.* Inverness, Calif.: Chardon Press.

Phillips, L. 2000. *Flirting with danger: Young women reflect on sexuality and domination.* New York: New York University Press.

Piercy, M. 1976. *Woman on the edge of time.* New York: Fawcett Crest.

Plath, S. 1971. *The bell jar.* New York: Harper and Row.

Plumwood, V. 1993. *Feminism and the mastery of nature.* New York: Routledge.

Polikoff, N. 1993. We will get what we ask for: Why legalizing gay and lesbian marriage will not "dismantle the legal structure of gender in every marriage." *Virginia Law Review* 79: 1535–50.

Porter, E. 2007. *Peacebuilding: Women's international perspectives.* Routledge: New York.

Portes, Alejandro. 1997. *Los Angeles in the context of the new immigration.* Los Angeles: UCLA, Lewis Center for Regional Policy Studies, Working Paper, no. 18.

Postman, N., and S. Powers. 1992. *How to watch TV news.* New York: Penguin Books.

Poverty Guidelines. 2005. *Federal Register,* February 18, 70(33): 8373–75.

Pozner, J. L. 2006. The tax on being female, *Women's Review of Books* 23(3): 5.

Pratt, M. B. 1984. Identity: Skin blood heart. In *Yours in struggle: Three feminist perspectives on anti-semitism and racism,* E. Bulkin, M. B. Pratt, and B. Smith, 9–63. Brooklyn, N.Y.: Long Haul Press.

Prilleltensky, O. 2003. A ramp to motherhood: The experience of mothers with physical disabilities. *Sexuality and Disability,* 21: 21–47.

Prison Activist Resource Center. 1997. *Women in prison.* Fact sheet prepared by Prison Activist Resource Center, Berkeley, Calif.

Project for Excellence in Journalism. 2005. *The gender gap: Women are still missing as sources for journalists.* www.journalism.org/resources/research/reports/gender/default.asp Accessed July 5, 2005.

Prokosch, M., and L. Raymond, eds. 2002. *The global activist's manual: Local ways to change the world.* New York: Thunder's Mouth Press/Nation Books.

Pulido, L. 1993. Sustainable development at Ganados del Valle. In *Confronting environmental racism: Voices from the grassroots,* ed. R. Bullard. Boston: South End Press.

———. 1996. *Environmentalism and economic justice: Two Chicano struggles in the Southwest.* Tucson: University of Arizona Press.

Queen, Carol. 2002. *Real live nude girl: Chronicle of sex positive culture.* San Francisco: Cleis Press.

Quintero-Somaini, A., and M. Quirindongo. 2004. *Hidden danger: environmental health threats to the Latino community.* New York: Natural Resources Defense Council.

Rachel's Environment and Health Weekly. 1998. *The precautionary principle. Feb 19, 586.* www.monitor.net/rachel/r586.html Accessed September 4, 2005.

Radical Women. 2001. *The radical women manifesto: Socialist feminism theory, program, and organizational structure.* Seattle: Red Letter Press.

Rafter, N. 1990. *Partial justice: Women, prisons and social control.* New Brunswick, N.J.: Transaction.

Ragone, H., and F. W. Twine, eds. 2000. *Ideologies and technologies of motherhood: Race, class, sexuality and nationalism.* New York: Routledge.

Raphael, J., and R. Tolman. 1997. *Trapped in poverty, trapped by abuse: New evidence documenting the relationship between domestic violence and welfare.* Project for Research on Welfare, Work, and Domestic Violence. A collaboration between Taylor Institute and University of Michigan Development Center on Poverty, Risk, and Mental Health.

Rayner, R. 1997. Women in the warrior culture. *New York Times Magazine,* 22 June, 24–29, 40, 49, 53, 55–56.

Reagan, L. J. 1997. *When abortion was a crime: Women, medicine, and law in the United States 1867–1973.* Berkeley: University of California Press.

Reardon, B. A. 1985. *Sexism and the war system.* New York: Teachers College Press.

Reaves, S., J. B. Hitchon, S.-Y. Park, and G. W. Yun. 2004. If looks could kill: Digital manipulation of fashion models. *Journal of Mass Media Ethics* 19(1): 56–71.

Rehn, E., and E. J. Sirleaf. 2002. *Women, war, peace: The independent experts' assessment.* New York: UNIFEM.

Rennison, C. M. 2002. *Rape and sexual assault: Reporting to police and medical attention, 1992–2000.* Bureau of Justice Statistics, selected findings. Washington, D.C.: U.S. Department of Justice.

———. 2003. *Intimate partner violence, 1993–2001.* Bureau of Justice Statistics, Crime Data Brief. Washington, D.C.: U.S. Department of Justice.

Renzetti, C. M. 1992. *Violent betrayal: Partner abuse in lesbian relationships.* Newbury Park, Calif.: Sage.

Reti, I., ed. 1992. *Childless by choice: A feminist anthology.* Santa Cruz, Calif.: Her Books.

Rhodes, J. 2005. *Radical feminist writing and critical agency: From manifesto to modern.* Albany, N.Y.: SUNY Press.

Rich, A. 1986a. Compulsory heterosexuality and lesbian existence. In *Blood, bread, and poetry.* New York: W. W. Norton.

———. 1986b. *Of woman born: Motherhood as experience and institution.* 10th anniversary ed. New York: W. W. Norton.

———. 1986c. Notes towards a politics of location. In *Blood, bread, and poetry,* 210–31. New York: W. W. Norton.

Richie, B. 1996. *Compelled to crime: The gender entrapment of battered Black women.* New York: Routledge.

Richter, P. 2000. Armed forces find "disturbing" level of gay harassment. *Los Angeles Times,* 25 March, p. A1.

Rierden, A. 1997. *The farm: Inside a women's prison.* Amherst: University of Massachusetts Press.

Risman, B. J. 1998. *Gender vertigo: American families in transition.* New Haven, Conn.: Yale University Press.

Ristock, J. 2002. *No more secrets: Violence in lesbian relationships.* New York: Routledge.

Ritz, D., ed. 2001. *Defying corporations, defining democracy.* New York: Apex Press.

Ritzer, G. 1993. *The McDonaldization of society: An investigation into the changing character of contemporary social life.* Thousand Oaks, Calif.: Pine Forge Press.

Riverbend. 2005. *Baghdad burning: Girl blog from Iraq.* New York: Feminist Press of the City University of New York.

———. 2006. *Baghdad burning II: More girl blog from Iraq.* New York: Feminist Press of the City University of New York.

Roberts, D. 1997. *Killing the Black body: Race, reproduction, and the meaning of liberty.* New York: Pantheon.

Roberts, M. M., and T. Mizuta, eds. 1993. *The reformers: Socialist feminism.* London: Routledge/Thoemmes Press.

Rodríguez, J. M. 2003. *Queer latinidad: Identity practices, discursive spaces.* New York: New York University Press.

Roediger, D. R. 1991. *The wages of whiteness: Race and the making of the American working class.* New York: Verso.

Roiphe, K. 1993. *The morning after: Sex, fear, and feminism.* Boston: Little Brown.

Root, M. P., ed. 1996. *The multiracial experience: Racial borders as the new frontier.* Thousand Oaks, Calif.: Sage.

Rose, Tricia. 2003. *Longing to tell: Black women talk about sexuality and intimacy.* New York: Farrar, Straus & Giroux.

Rosen, R. 2000. *The world split open: How the modern women's movement changed America.* New York: Viking.

Rosenberg, A. 1988. The crisis in knowing and understanding the Holocaust. In *Echoes from the Holocaust: Philosophical reflections on a dark time,* ed. A. Rosenberg and G. E. Meyers. Philadelphia: Temple University Press.

Rosenberg, H. H. 1998. *How to get married after thirty-five: The game plan for love.* New York: HarperCollins.

Rosenblum, B. 1997. Living in an unstable body. In *Staring back: The disability experiences from the inside out,* ed. K. Fries, 93–104. New York: Penguin/Plume.

Ross, A., ed. 1997. *No sweat: Fashion, free trade, and the rights of garment workers.* New York: Verso.

Ross, L. 1993. Major concerns of imprisoned American Indian and White mothers. In *Gender: Multicultural perspectives,* ed. J. Gonzalez-Calvo. Dubuque, Iowa: Kendall Hunt.

Ross, L. J. 1993. African-American women and abortion: 1800–1970. In *Theorizing black feminisms: The visionary pragmatism of black women,* ed. S. M. James and A. P. A. Busia, pp. 141–59. New York: Routledge.

———, S. L. Brownlee, D. D. Diallo, L. Rodriquez, and the SisterSong Women of Color Reproductive Health Project. 2002. Just choices: Women of color, reproductive health and human rights. In *Policing the national body: Race, gender, and criminalization,* ed. J. Silliman and A. Bhattacharjee, 147–74. Cambridge, Mass.: South End Press.

Roth, B. 2003. *Separate roads to feminism: Black, Chicana and white feminist movements in America's second wave.* New York: Cambridge University Press.

Rubin, G. 1984. Thinking sex: Notes for a radical theory of the politics of sexuality. In *Pleasure and danger: Exploring female sexuality,* ed. C. S. Vance, 267–319. Boston: Routledge and Kegan Paul.

Ruddick, S. 1989. *Maternal thinking: Toward a politics of peace.* Boston: Beacon Press.

Russell, B. 1935. *In praise of idleness and other essays.* New York: W. W. Norton.

Russell, D. 1995. *Women, madness, and medicine.* Cambridge, England: Polity Press.

Russell, D. E. H. 1975. *The politics of rape: The victim's perspective.* New York: Stein and Day.

———. 1990. *Rape in marriage.* Rev. ed. Bloomington: Indiana University Press.

———. 1993. *Making violence sexy: Feminist views on pornography.* New York: Teachers College Press.

Sabol, W. J., H. Couture, and P. M. Harrison. 2007. *Prisoners in 2006.* Washington, D.C.: U.S. Department of Justice, Office of Justice Programs. www.ojp.usdoj.gov/bjs/pub/press/p06ppus06pr.htm Accessed April 29, 2008.

Sachs, C. 1996. *Gendered fields: Rural women, agriculture, and environment.* Boulder, Colo.: Westview Press.

Sachs, S. 2000. Sexual abuse reported at an immigration center. *New York Times,* 5 October, p. A20.

Sacks, K. B. 1976. The class roots of feminism. *Monthly Review* 27(9).

Sadler, G. C. 1997. Women in combat: The U.S. military and the impact of the Persian Gulf War. In *Wives and warriors,* ed. L. Weinstein and C. White, 79–97.

Sahadi, J. 2007. CEO pay: 364 times more than workers. *CNNMoney.com,* August 29. http://money.cnn.com/2007/08/28/news/economy/ceo_pay_workers/index.htm Accessed May 16, 2008.

Sajor, I. ed. 1998. *Common grounds: Violence against women in war and armed conflict.* Quezon City, Philippines: ASCENT.

Sale, K. 1985. *Dwellers in the land, the bioregional vision.* San Francisco: Sierra Club Books.

Sampson, R. 2002. *Acquaintance rape of college students.* Washington, D.C.: U.S. Department of Justice, Office of Community Oriented Policing Services.

Sanders, B., and M. Kaptur. 1997. Just do it, Nike. *The Nation,* 8 December, 6.

Sarah, R. 2006. *Single mom seeking: Playdates, blindates, and other dispatches from the dating world.* Emeryville, Calif.: Seal Press.

Saxton, M. 1995. Reproductive rights: A disability rights issue, *Sojourner.* July.

Scharnberg, K. 2005. Female GIs hard hit by war syndrome. *Chicago Tribune,* March 24.

Schneir, M. 1994. *Feminism: The essential historical writings.* New York: Vintage Books.

Scholinski, D. 1997. *The last time I wore a dress.* New York: Riverhead Books.

Schultz, A. J. and L. Mullings. 2005. *Gender, race, class and health: Intersectional approaches.* San Francisco: Jossey-Bass.

Schur, L. 2004. Is there still a "double handicap"? Economic, social and political disparities experienced by women with disabilities. In *Gendering disability,* ed. B. G. Smith and B. Hutchison, 253–71. New Brunswick: Rutgers University Press.

Schwab, J. 1994. *Deeper shades of green: The rise of blue-collar and minority environmentalism in America.* San Francisco: Sierra Club Books.

Schwartz, P. 1994. *Love between equals: How peer marriage really works.* New York: Free Press.

Scott, J. W. 1988. Deconstructing equality-versus-difference: Or, the uses of poststructuralist theory for feminism. *Feminist Studies* 14(1): 33–50.

———. 1993. The evidence of experience. In *The lesbian and gay studies reader,* ed. Henry Abelove, Michele Aina Barale and David M. Halperin, 397–415. New York: Routledge.

Scott, W. J., and S. C. Stanley. 1994. *Gays and lesbians in the military: Issues, concerns, and contrasts.* Hawthorne, N.Y.: Aldine de Gruyter.

Scott-Dixon, K., ed. 2006. *Trans/forming feminisms: Transfeminist voices speak out.* Toronto: Sumach Press.

Seager, J. 1993. *Earth follies: Coming to feminist terms with the global environmental crisis.* New York: Routledge.

Seager, Joni. 1992. Operation desert disaster: Environmental costs of the war. In *Collateral Damage: The 'New World Order' at home and abroad,* ed. Cynthia Peters. Boston: South End Press.

Sedgwick, E. K. 1990. *Epistemology of the closet.* Berkeley: University of California Press.

Segal, L. 1994. *Straight sex: Rethinking the politics of pleasure.* Berkeley: University of California Press.

Segrest, M. 1994. *Memoir of a race traitor.* Boston: South End Press.

Seigel, L. 1997. The pregnancy police fight the war on drugs. In *Crack in America: Demon drugs and social justice,* ed. C. Reinarman and H. G. Levine, 249–59. Berkeley: University of California Press.

Sentencing Project. 2007. *Women in the criminal justice system: Barriers to re-entering the community.* www.sentencingproject .org/PublicationDetails.aspx?PublicationID5586 Accessed April 29, 2008.

Serano, J. 2007. *Whipping girl: A transsexual woman on sexism and the scapegoating of femininity.* Emeryville, Calif.: Seal Press.

Serna, I. 1992. *Locked down: A woman's life in prison.* Norwich, Vt.: New Victoria.

Servicemembers Legal Defense Network. 1999. *Conduct unbecoming. Fifth annual report on "Don't ask, don't tell, don't pursue."* http://www.sldn.org/scripts/sldn.ixe?page?pr _03_15_99.

———. 2002. *Conduct unbecoming: The eighth annual report on "Don't ask, Don't tell, Don't pursue, Don't harass."* Washington, D.C.: SLDN.

———. 2007. *New poll shows 8 out of 10 Americans favor repealing "Don't ask don't tell."* Press Release. www.sldn.org/ templates/press/record.html?section=2 & record=4099 Accessed May 4, 2008.

Shaffer, A., and R. Gottlieb. 2007. Filling in 'food deserts.' *Los Angeles Times,* November 5. www.latimes.com/news/ opinion/la-oe-gottlieb5nov05,0,7040113.story?coll= la-opinion-rightrail Accessed May 26, 2008.

Shanley, M. ed. 2004. *Just marriage.* New York: Oxford University Press.

Shannonhouse, R. 2003. *Out of her mind: Women writing on madness,* Expanded ed. New York: Modern Library.

She, P. and G. A. Livermore. 2006. *Long-term poverty and disability among working-age adults.* Washington, D.C.: Cornell University Institute for Policy Research.

Sherrill, R. 1997. A year in corporate crime. *The Nation,* 7 April, 11–20.

Shih, E. 2007. Spirits in traffic: Transient community formation in opposition to forced victimization. In *Shout out: Women of color respond to violence,* ed. María Ochoa and Barbara K. Ige, 86–100. Emeryville, Calif,: Seal Press.

Shin, A. 1999. Testing Title IX. *Ms.,* April/May, 32–33.

Shiva, V. 1988. *Staying alive: Women, ecology and development.* London: Zed Books.

———. 1993. *Monocultures of the mind: Perspectives on biodiversity and biotechnology.* London and New Jersey: Zed Books.

———. 2002a. Relocalization not globalization. In *Rethinking globalization: Teaching for justice in an unjust world,* ed. B. Bigelow and B. Peterson, 248–49. Milwaukee, Wis.: Rethinking Schools.

———. 2002b. *Water wars: Privatization, pollution, and profit.* Cambridge, Mass.: South End Press.

———. 2005. *Earth democracy: Justice, sustainability, and peace.* Cambridge: South End Press.

Showalter, E. 1987. *The female malady: Women, madness, and English culture, 1830–1980.* London: Virago.

Shugar, D. R. 1995. *Separatism and women's community.* Lincoln: University of Nebraska Press.

Shulman, S. 1990. Toxic travels: Inside the military's environmental nightmare. *Nuclear Times,* Autumn, 20–32.

Shumway, C. 2004. Violence against female soldiers ignored. *The New Standard,* June 16.

Sidel, R. 1996. *Keeping women and children last: America's war on the poor.* New York: Penguin Books.

Siegal, N. 1995. Girl trouble. *San Francisco Bay Guardian,* 29 November, pp. 16–18.

———. 1998. Women in prison. *Ms.,* September/October, 64–73.

Sigler, H., S. Love, and J. Yood. 1999. *Hollis Sigler's breast cancer journal.* New York: Hudson Hills Press.

Silko, L. M. 2000. *Gardens in the dunes.* New York: Simon and Schuster.

Silliman, J., and A. Bhattacharjee, eds. 2002. *Policing the national body: Sex, race, and criminalization.* Cambridge, Mass.: South End Press.

———, M. G. Fried, L. Ross, and E. R. Gutiérrez. 2004. *Undivided rights: Women of color organize for reproductive justice.* Cambridge: South End Press.

———, and Y. King, eds. 1999. *Dangerous intersections: Feminist perspectives on population, environment, and development.* Cambridge, Mass.: South End Press.

Simon, R. 1975. *Women and crime.* Lexington, Mass.: Lexington Books.

Simon, R. J., and R. M. Roorda. 2000. *In their own words: Transracial adoptees tell their stories.* New York: Columbia University Press.

Sivard, R. L. 1996. *World military and social expenditures 1996.* 16th ed. Washington, D.C.: World Priorities.

Skaine, R. 1998. *Women at war: Gender issues of Americans in combat.* Jefferson, N.C.: McFarland and Co.

Slater, L. 1998. *Prozac diary.* New York: Random House.

Slugocki, L. A., and E. C. Wilson. 2000. *The erotica project.* San Francisco: Cleis Press.

Smeal, E. 1984. *Why and how women will elect the next president.* New York: Harper & Row.

Smith, A. 1991. To all those who were Indian in a former life. *Ms.,* November/December, 44–45.

———. 2001. The color of violence: Violence against women of color. Conference report. *Meridians: Feminism, Race, Transnationalism* 1(2): 65–72.

———. 2002. Better dead than pregnant: The colonization of Native women's reproductive health. In *Policing the national body: Race, gender, and criminalization,* ed. J. Silliman and A. Bhattacharjee, 123–46. Cambridge, Mass.: South End Press.

———. 2005a. Beyond pro-choice versus pro-life: Women of color and reproductive justice. *NWSA Journal* 17(1): 119–40.

———. 2005b. *Conquest: Sexual violence and American Indian genocide.* Cambridge: South End Press.

Smith, B. 1998. *The truth that never hurts: Writings on race, gender, freedom.* New Brunswick, N.J.: Rutgers University Press.

Smith, B. G., and B. Hutchison, eds. 2004. *Gendering disability.* New Brunswick, N.J.: Rutgers University Press.

Smith, J. 2004. Sexual assaults in army on rise. *Washington Post,* June 3.

Smith, M. 1997. When violence strikes home. *The Nation,* 30 June, 23–24.

Smith, S. 2005. *Women and socialism: Essays on women's liberation.* Chicago: Haymarket Books.

Sneed, C. 2000. Seeds of change, *Yes: A journal of positive futures,* Fall, no. 15.

Snitow, A., C. Stansell, and S. Thompson, eds. 1983. *Powers of desire: The politics of sexuality.* New York: Monthly Review Press.

Solinger, R. 1994. *The abortionist: A woman against the law.* New York: Routledge.

———. 1998. *Abortion wars; A half century of struggle, 1950–2000,* Berkeley: University of California Press.

———. 2000. *Wake up little Susie: Single pregnancy and race before Roe v. Wade.* New York: Routledge.

———. 2005. *Pregnancy and power: A short history of reproductive politics in America.* New York: New York University Press.

Spears, E. G. 1998. *The Newtown story: One community's fight for environmental justice.* Gainesville, GA: Center for Democratic Renewal and Newtown Florist Club.

Spelman, E. V. 1988. *Inessential woman: Problems of exclusion in feminist thought.* Boston: Beacon Press.

Spivak, G. C. 1988. *In other worlds: Essays in cultural politics.* New York: Routledge.

Sprague, J. 2005. *Feminist methodologies for critical researchers: Bridging differences.* Walnut Creek, Calif.: AltaMira Press.

Spretnak, C. 1990. Ecofeminism: Our roots and flowering. In *Reweaving the world: The emergence of ecofeminism,* ed. I. Diamond and G. Orenstein. San Francisco: Sierra Club Books.

Springer, K. 2005. *Living for the revolution: Black feminist organizing, 1968–1980.* Durham: Duke University Press.

Stacey, Jackie. 1993. Untangling feminist theory. In *Thinking feminist: Key concepts in women's studies,* ed. D. Richardson and V. Robinson, 49–73. New York: Guilford Press.

Stacey, Judith. 1996. *In the name of the family: Rethinking values in the postmodern age.* Boston: Beacon Press.

Stan, Adele. 1995. *Debating sexual correctness.* New York: Delta.

Stanworth, M. ed. 1987. *Reproductive technologies.* Cambridge, England: Cambridge University Press.

Staples, S. 2000. The relationship between globalization and militarism. *Social Justice: A Journal of Conflict and World Change* 27(4): 18–22.

Starhawk. 1993. *The fifth sacred thing.* New York: Bantam Books.

———. 2002a. Our place in nature. In *Webs of power: Notes from the global uprising,* 160–68. Gabriola Island, B.C.: New Society.

———. 2002b. *Webs of power: Notes from the global uprising.* Gabriola Island, B.C.: New Society.

Stefan, S. 1994. The protection racket: Rape trauma syndrome, psychiatric labeling, and law. *Northwestern Law Review* 88(4): 1271–1345.

Stein, A. 1997. Sisters and queers: The decentering of lesbian feminism. In *The gender sexuality reader,* ed. R. Lancaster and M. di Leonardo, 378–91. New York: Routledge.

Stein, D., ed. 1991. *From inside: An anthology of writing by incarcerated women.* Minneapolis: Honor Press.

Stein, R., ed. 2004. *New perspectives on environmental justice: Gender, sexuality, and activism,* New Brunswick, N.J.: Rutgers University Press.

Stein, R. 2007. Plan B use surges, and so does controversy. *Washington Post,* July 13, p. A1.

Steinem, G. 1983. *Outrageous acts and everyday rebellions.* New York: Holt, Rinehart, & Winston.

Steingraber, S. 2001. *Having faith: An ecologist's journey to motherhood.* Cambridge, Mass.: Perseus.

Stewart, N. A. 2007. Transform the world: What you can do with a degree in women's studies, *Ms.* Spring: 65–66.

Stiehm, J. H. 1989. *Arms and the enlisted woman.* Philadelphia: Temple University Press.

Stockholm International Peace Research Institute. 2006. *The fifteen major spenders in 2006.* www.sipri.org/contents/milap/milex/mex_trends.html Accessed May 3, 2008.

Stoller, E. P., and R. C. Gibson, eds. 1994. *Worlds of difference: Inequality in the aging experience.* Thousand Oaks, Calif.: Pine Forge.

Stone, P. 2007 *Opting out? Why women really quit careers and head home.* Berkeley: University of California Press.

Stonequist, E. V. 1961. *The marginal man: A study in personality and cultural conflict.* New York: Scribner & Sons.

Storr, M., ed. 1999. *Bisexuality: A critical reader.* New York: Routledge.

Strossen, N. 2000. *Defending pornography: Free speech, sex, and the fight for women's rights.* New York: New York University Press.

Stryker, S., and S. Whittle, eds. 2006. *The transgender reader.* New York: Routledge.

Sturdevant, S., and B. Stoltzfus. 1992. *Let the good times roll: Prostitution and the U.S. military in Asia.* New York: New Press.

Sturgeon, N. 1997. *Ecofeminist nature: Race, gender, feminist theory and political action.* New York: Routledge.

Suggs, W. 2002. Title IX at 30. *Chronicle of Higher Education,* 21 June, pp. A38–41.

Sullivan, N. 2003. *A critical introduction to queer theory.* New York: New York University Press.

Swerdlow, A. 1993. *Women strike for peace: Traditional motherhood and radical politics in the 1960s.* Chicago: University of Chicago Press.

Swers, M. 2001. Research on women in legislatures: What have we learned, Where are we going? *Women and Politics* 23: 167–85.

Swiss, S., and J. Giller. 1993. Rape as a crime of war: A medical perspective. *Journal of the American Medical Association* 27: 612–15.

Szasz, A. 1994. *Ecopopulism, toxic waste and the movement for environmental justice.* Minneapolis: University of Minnesota Press.

Tadiar. N. 2003. *Fantasy production: Sexual encounters and other Philippine consequences for the new world order.* Hong Kong: Hong Kong University Press.

Takahashi, R. 1998. U.S. concentration camps and exclusion policies. In *Women's lives: Multicultural perspectives,* ed. Gwyn Kirk and Margo Okazawa-Rey, 362–68. Mountain View, Calif.: Mayfield.

Takaki, R. 1987. *Strangers from a different shore: Perspectives on race and ethnicity in America.* New York: Oxford University Press.

Tanenbaum, L. 2000. *Growing up female with a bad reputation.* New York: HarperCollins.

Tarrant, S., ed. 2007. *Men speak out: Views on gender, sex and power.* New York: Routledge.

Tashiro, Akira. 2001. *Discounted casualties: The human cost of depleted uranium.* Hiroshima, Japan: Chugoku Shimbun.

Tateishi, J. 1984. *And justice for all: An oral history of the Japanese American detention camps.* New York: Random House.

Taylor, D. E. 1997. Women of color, environmental justice, and ecofeminism. In *Ecofeminism: Women, culture, nature,* ed. K. Warren, 38–81. Bloomington: Indiana University Press.

Teays, W., and L. Purdy. 2001. *Bioethics, justice, and health care.* Belmont, Calif.: Wadsworth.

Tenenbein, S. 1998. Power, beauty, and dykes. Pp. 155–60 in *Looking queer,* edited by D. Atkins. Binghampton, N.Y.: Harrington Park Press.

Tétreault, M. A. 1997. Accountability or justice? Rape as a war crime. In *Feminist frontiers IV,* ed. L. Richardson, V. Taylor, and N. Whittier, 427–39. New York: McGraw-Hill.

Thomas, S., and C. Wilcox, eds. 1998. *Women and elective office: Past, present, and future.* New York: Oxford University Press.

Thompson, B. W. 1994. *A hunger so wide and so deep.* Minneapolis: University of Minnesota Press.

Thornhill, R., and C. T. Palmer. 2000. *A natural history of rape: Biological bases of sexual coercion.* Cambridge: MIT Press.

Thropy, M. A. 1991. Overpopulation and industrialism. In *Earth First! reader,* ed. J. Davis. Salt Lake City: Peregrine Smith Books.

Trenka, J. J., J. C. Oparah, and S. Y. Shin, eds. 2006. *Outsiders within: Writing on transracial adoption.* Cambridge: South End Press.

Troustine, J. 2001. *Shakespeare behind bars: The power of drama in a women's prison.* New York: St. Martin's Press.

Trujillo, C., ed. 1991. *Chicana lesbians: The girls our mothers warned us about.* Berkeley, Calif.: Third Women Press.

Tuana, N., ed. 1989. *Feminism and science.* Bloomington: Indiana University Press.

Tuominen, M. C. 2003. *We are not babysitters: Family care providers redefine work and care.* Piscataway, N.J.: Rutgers University Press.

Turk, A. T. 1995. Transformation versus revolutionism and reformism: Policy implications of conflict theory. In *Crime and public policy: Putting theory to work,* ed. H. Barlow. Boulder, Colo.: Westview Press.

2 black airmen allege racial discrimination. 1996. *San Francisco Chronicle,* 4 December, p. A9.

U.N. High Commissioner for Refugees. 2002. Refugee Women. http://www.worldrefugeeday.info/men2.html Accessed May 1, 2003.

UNICEF. 2007. *The state of the world's children 2008: Child survival.* New York: UNICEF. www.unicef.org/publications/index_42623.html Accessed May 12, 2008.

University of Maryland. 2007. *J-school administrators overwhelmingly white and male, survey finds.* Press release, August 14. www.journalism.umd.edu/newrel/07newsrel/jmcsurvey03.html Accessed April 10, 2008.

Urban, J. L. 2008. *Nation, immigration, and environmental security.* New York: Palgrave MacMillan.

Urban Strategies Council. 2004. *Community Safety and Justice,* special issue, July. Oakland, Calif.: Urban Strategies Council. www.urbanstrategies.org/program/csj/news/2004/2004-07-01.html Accessed September 2, 2005.

U.S. Department of Health and Human Services. 2008. *The 2008 HHS poverty guidelines.* http://aspe.hhs.gov/poverty/08poverty.shtml Accessed March 15, 2008.

U.S. Department of Justice. 1997. *Violence-related injuries treated in hospital emergency departments.* Michael R. Rand. Washington, D.C.: Bureau of Justice Statistics.

———. 2008. *National teen dating violence awareness and prevention week,* February 4–8, 2008 www.ovw.usdoj.gov Accessed March 9, 2008.

U.S. Department of Labor, Bureau of Labor Statistics, 2007. *Data on unions,* Table 2. www.bls.gov/news/release/union2.t02.htm Accessed March 15, 2008.

U.S. Department of Labor, Women's Bureau. 2005. *Fact sheets.* Washington, D.C.: U.S. Department of Labor.

Ussher, J. 1991. *Women's madness.* Hemel Hempstead, England: Harvester Wheatsheaf.

Uttal, L. 2002. *Making care work: Employed mothers in the new childcare market.* New Brunswick, N.J.: Rutgers University Press.

Vance, C., ed. 1984. *Pleasure and danger: Exploring female sexuality.* Boston: Routledge and Kegan Paul.

Wade-Gayles, G. 1993. *Pushed back to strength: A Black woman's journey home.* Boston: Beacon Press.

Walker, J. 1996. The prison industrial complex. *RESIST Newsletter* 5(9): 4–6.

Walker, L. 1979. *The battered woman.* New York: Harper & Row.

———. 1984. *The battered woman syndrome.* New York: Springer.

Walker, M. 1992. Sex attacks "rife" on U.S. servicewomen. *London Guardian,* 2 July, p. 6.

Walker, R. 1995a. Lusting for freedom. In *Listen up: Voices of the next generation,* ed. Barbara Findlen, 95–101. Seattle: Seal Press.

———. 1995b. *To be real: Telling the truth and changing the face of feminism.* New York: Anchor/Doubleday.

———. 2001. *Black, white, and Jewish: Autobiography of a shifting self.* New York: Riverhead Books.

Wallach, L., and M. Sforza. 2000. *The WTO: Five years of reasons to resist corporate globalization.* New York: Seven Stories Press.

———, and P. Woodall. 2004. *Whose trade organization? A comprehensive guide to the World Trade Organization.* New York: New Press.

Walters, B., and H. Downs. 1996. *20/20,* November 15. New York: American Broadcasting Company.

Walters, S. D. 2001. *All the rage: The story of gay visibility in America.* Chicago: Chicago University Press.

Waring, M. 1988. *If women counted: A new feminist economics.* New York: Harper & Row.

Warner, S. B. 1987. *To dwell is to garden: A history of Boston's community gardens.* Boston: Northeastern University Press.

War Resisters League. 2008. *Where your income tax money really goes.* www.warresisters.org/piechart.htm Accessed March 9, 2008.

Warren, K. J., ed. 1994. *Ecological feminism.* New York: Routledge.

———. 2000. *Ecofeminist philosophy: A western perspective on what it is and why it matters.* Lanham, Md.: Rowman and Littlefield.

Washburn, P. 1993. Women and the peace movement. In *Women and the use of military force,* ed. R. Howes and M. Stevenson, 135–48. Boulder, Colo.: Lynne Rienner.

Wasserman, C. 1992. FMS: The backlash against survivors. *Sojourner: The Women's Forum,* November, 18–20.

Watterson, K. 1996. *Women in prison.* Rev. ed. Boston: Northeastern University Press.

Webber, W. S. 1993. *Lesbians in the military speak out.* Northboro, Mass.: Madwoman Press.

Weedon, C. 1987. *Feminist practice and poststructuralist theory.* New York: Blackwell.

Weinstein, L., and C. White, eds. 1997. *Wives and warriors: Women and the military in the United States and Canada.* Westport, Conn.: Greenwood Press.

Weise, E. R., ed. 1992. *Closer to home: Bisexuality and feminism.* Seattle, Wash.: Seal Press.

West, G., and R. L. Blumberg, eds. 1990. *Women and social protest.* New York: Oxford University Press.

Whisnant, R., and C. Stark. 2004. *Not for sale: Feminists resisting prostitution and pornography.* North Melbourne, Australia: Spinifex.

White, E. 2002. *Fast girls: Teenage tribes and the myth of the slut.* New York: Penguin.

White, E. C. 1985. *Chain, chain, change: For Black women dealing with physical and emotional abuse.* Seattle, Wash.: Seal Press.

———, ed. 1990. *The Black women's health book: Speaking for ourselves.* Seattle, Wash.: Seal Press.

———. 1991. Unhealthy appetites: Large is lovely, unless you're unhappy overeating and unable to lose weight. *Essence,* September, 28.

White, J. 1988. *The obsidian mirror: An adult healing from incest.* Seattle, Wash.: Seal Press.

Wilchins, R. A. 1997. *Read my lips: Sexual subversion and the end of gender.* Ithaca, N.Y.: Firebrand.

Wilkerson, A. 2002. Disability, sex radicalism, and political agency. *NWSA Journal* 14(3), Fall: 33–57. Special issue: Feminist Disability Studies.

Williams, F. 2005. Toxic breast milk? *New York Times Magazine,* 9 January.

Williams, J. 2000. *Unbending gender: Why family and work conflict and what to do about it.* New York: Oxford University Press.

Williams, K. with M. E. Straub, 2005. *Love my rifle more than you: Young and female in the U.S. army.* New York: Norton.

Williams, T. T. 1992. *Refuge: An unnatural history of family and place.* New York: Vintage.

Wilson, M. 1993. *Crossing the boundary: Black women survive incest.* Seattle, Wash.: Seal Press.

Wingspan Domestic Violence Project. 1998. *Abuse and violence in same-gender relationships: A resource for lesbian, gay, bi, and transgendered communities.* Tucson, Ariz.: Wingspan Domestic Violence Project.

Winne, M. 2008. *Closing the food gap: Resetting the table in the land of plenty.* Boston: Beacon Press.

Winterich, J. A. 2007. Review of "age matters" edited by T. M. Calasanti and K. F. Slevin. *Gender and Society* 21(5): 783–86.

Withorn, A. 1999. Temp work: "A devil's bargain" for women. *Sojourner: The Women's Forum,* October, 9.

Woelfle-Erskine, C., J. O. Cole, L. Allen, and A. Danger. 2007. *Dam nation: Dispatches from the water underground.* Brooklyn, N.Y.: Soft Skull Press.

Wolf, N. 1991. *The beauty myth.* New York: Doubleday.

———. 1997. *Promiscuities: The secret struggle for womanhood.* New York: Ballantine.

Women and Environments. 2007. special issue on Gender and Climate Change. no. 74/75.

Women's Foundation. 2002. *Failing to make ends meet: The economic status of women in California.* San Francisco: The Women's Foundation.

Women's Research and Education Institute. 2002. *Women in the military.* Washington, D.C.: WREI. http://www.wrei.org/projects/wiu/wim/index.htm Accessed January 3, 2003.

Woodman, S. 1997. An officer and a . . .? *Ms.,* March/April, 19–22.

Woods, H. 2000. *Stepping up to power: The political journey of American women.* Boulder, Colo.: Westview Press.

Worcester, N. 2004. Hormone replacement therapy: Getting to the heart of the politics of women's health? *NWSA Journal* 16(3), Fall: 56–69.

Working Group on the WTO. 1999. *A citizens' guide to the World Trade Organization.* New York: Apex Press.

World Bank. 2004. *Global debt finance.* Washington, D.C.: World Bank.

World Health Organization. 1946. *Preamble to the constitution of the World Health Organization,* adopted by the International Health Conference, New York, 19–22 June.

Yancey, A. K., J. Leslie, and E. K. Abel. 2006. Obesity at the crossroads: Feminist and public health perspectives. *Signs: Journal of Women in Culture and Society* 31(2): 425–43.

Yans-McLaughlin, V., ed. 1990. *Immigration reconsidered.* New York: Oxford University Press.

Yen, M. 1989. Refusal to jail immigrant who killed wife stirs outrage. *Washington Post,* 10 April, p. A3.

Yoder, J. 1989. Women at West Point: Lessons for token women in male-dominated occupations. In *Women: A feminist perspective,* ed. J. Freeman. Mountain View, Calif.: Mayfield.

Yoo, D. K. 2000. *Growing up Nisei: Race, generation and culture among Japanese Americans of California, 1924–1949.* Urbana-Champagne: University of Illinois Press.

Young, M. E., M. A. Nosek, C. A. Howland, G. Chanpong, and D. H. Rintala. 1997. Prevalence of abuse of women with physical disabilities. *Archives of Physical Medicine and Rehabilitation* 78: S34–S38.

Young, W. A. 1997. Women and immigration. Unpublished manuscript produced for Women's Commission for Refugee Women and Children, Washington, D.C.

Zambrano, M. Z. 1985. *Mejor sola que mal accompanda: For the Latina in an abusive relationship.* Seattle, Wash.: Seal Press.

Zamora-Olib, O. A., ed. 2000. *Inheritors of the earth: The human face of the U.S. military contamination at Clarke Air Base, Pampanga, Philippines.* Quezon City, Philippines: People's Task Force for Bases Cleanup.

Zeff, R., M. Love, and K. Stults, eds. 1989. *Empowering ourselves: Women and toxics organizing.* Falls Church, Va.: Citizens Clearinghouse for Hazardous Wastes.

Zepernick, M. 1998a. The sovereign people are stirring. *The Cape Cod Times,* 27 November, p. A15.

———. 1998b. A lesson in democracy. *The Cape Cod Times,* 11 December, p. A15.

Zernike, K. 2003. Many women gleeful at old friend's encore. *New York Times,* March 7, A16.

Zimmerman, L. 2003. Where are the women? The strange case of the missing feminists. When was the last time you saw one on TV? *The Women's Review of Books* XXI(1): 5–6.

Zimmerman, M., J. Litt, and C. Bose. 2006. *Gender and care work in global perspective.* Palo Alto, Calif.: Stanford University Press.

Zinn, H. 1995. *People's history of the United States: 1492–present.* Rev. and updated ed. New York: HarperPerennial.

Zita, J., ed. 1997. Special issue: Third wave feminisms. *Hypatia: A Journal of Feminist Philosophy* 12(3) (Summer).

Credits

Readings, Text, Cartoon, and Line Art Credits

Chapter 1: Page 18 From THE SACRED HOOP by Paula Gunn Allen. Copyright © 1986, 1992 by Paula Gunn Allen. Reprinted by permission of Beacon Press, Boston. **Page 30** "The Combahee River Collective Statement" © Zillah Eisenstein, from Capitalist Patriarchy and the Case for Socialist Feminism. Copyright © 1979 by MR Press. Reprinted by permission of Monthly Review Foundation. **Page 35** "Asian Pacific American Women and Feminism" by Mitsuye Yamada as appeared in THIS BRIDGE CALLED MY BACK by Cherie Moraga and Gloria Anzaldua, 1984. **Page 38** Thompson, Becky, "Multi-Racial Feminism: Recasting the Chronology of Second Wave Feminism" was originally published in FEMINIST STUDIES, Volume 28, Number 2 (Summer 2002): 337–360, by permission of the publisher, Feminist Studies, Inc.

Chapter 2: Page 63 "The Social Construction of Gender" from THE PARADOXES OF GENDER (1994). New Haven: Yale University Press. Used by permission of Yale University Press. **Page 68** From "Patriarchy, the System: An It, Not a He, a Them or an Us" from THE GENDER KNOT: UNRAVELING OUR PATRIARCHAL LEGACY by Allan G. Johnson. Used by permission of Temple University Press. Copyright © 2005 by Allan G. Johnson. All Rights Reserved. **Page 76** "Black Feminist Thought: Knowledge, Consciousness and the Politics of Empowerment" by Patricia Hill Collins. Reprinted by permission of the author. **Page 81** "Genealogies of Community, Home, and Nation," in FEMINISM WITHOUT BORDERS: DECOLONIZING THEORY, PRACTICING SOLIDARITY, pp. 124–136. Copyright, 2003, Duke University Press. All rights reserved. Used by permission of the publisher.

Chapter 3: Page 104 "Perspectives of Native American Women on Race and Gender" from CHALLENGING RACISM & SEXISM: ALTERNATIVES TO GENETIC EXPLANATIONS, copyright © 1994 by Ethel Tobach and Betty Rosoff, by permission of the Feminist Press at the City University of New York, www.feministpress.org. **Page 112** "A Question of Class" by Dorothy Allison, from SISTERS, SEXPERTS, QUEERS by Arlene Stein, copyright © 1993 by Arlene Stein. Used by permission of Dutton Signet, a division of Penguin Putnam Inc. **Page 119** "Jews in the U.S.: The Rising Costs of Whiteness" by Melanie Kaye/Kantrowitz from NAMES WE CALL HOME, ed. by Becky Thompson and Sangeeta Tyagi, pp. 121–137 (Routledge/Taylor & Francis Books). Reprinted by permission by Routledge/Taylor & Francis Group, LLC and the author. **Page 130** "Optional Ethnicities: For Whites Only?" by Mary C. Waters from ORIGINS AND DESTINIES: IMMIGRATION, RACE AND ETHNICITY IN AMERICA edited by Sylvia Pedraza and Ruben G. Rumbaut. Copyright © 1996. Rerpinted with permission of Wadsworth, a part of Cengage Learning, Inc. Reproduced by permission. www.cengage.com/permissions. **Page 138** "Listening to the Voices of My Spiritual Self" by Christina Leano. Reprinted by permission of the author. **Page 140** Adapted from an excerpt from *Once Upon a Quinceañera: Coming of Age in the USA*. Copyright © 2007 by Julia Alvarez. Published in paperback by Plume, an imprint of Penguin Group (USA), and originally in hardcover by Viking. Reprinted by permission of Susan Bergholz Literary Services, New York, NY and Lamy, NM. All rights reserved.

Chapter 4: Page 152 "Thought Frequency as Pie Charts" by Jennifer Berman. Copyright © Jennifer Berman. Reprinted by permission. **Page 153** By R. Piccolo as appeared in MS Magazine, March/April 1998. **Page 156** © Marian Henley. Reprinted by permission of the artist. **Page 161** "Uses of the Erotic: The Terotic as Power" reprinted from SISTER OUTSIDER: ESSAYS AND SPEECHES by Audre Lorde. Freedom, CA: The Crossing Press. Copyright © 1984 Audre Lorde. Used with permission of the publisher. **Page 164** Copyright © 1996 by Sandra Cisneros. From GODDESS OF THE AMERICAS/LA DIOSA DE LAS AMERICAS: Writings on the Virgin de Guadalupe, ed. by Ana Castillo. Copyright © 1996 by Ana Castillo. Riverhead Books, New York. Reprinted by permission of Susan Bergholz Literary Services, New York. All rights reserved. **Page 167** "If It's Not On, It's Not On—Or Is It?" by Nicola Gavey, Kathryn McPhillips and Marion Doherty from GENDER & SOCIETY, Vol. 15, No. 6, December 2001. Copyright © 2001. Reprinted by permission of Sage Publications, Inc. **Page 178** "The All-American Queer Pakistani Girl." Used with permission of the author. She is an Associate Analyst at Political Research Associates, a think tank and research center that monitors authoritarian, anti-democratic movements. She has contributed to the BOSTON PHOENIX, SOJOURNER, the WASHINGTON BLAD, GAY COMMUNITY NEWS, and the HARVARD GAY AND LESBIAN REVIEW, among other publications. **Page 180** Excerpts from "Popular Culture and Queer Representation" by Diane Raymond from GENDER, RACE, AND CLASS IN MEDIA: A Text-Reader, edited by Gail Dines and Jean M. Humez, © 2003, pp. 98–110. Reprinted by permission of Sage Publications, Inc. **Page 187** "We Are All Works in Progress" from TRANS LIBERATION by Leslie Feinberg. Copyright © 1998 by Leslie Feinberg. Reprinted by permission SLL/Sterling Lord Literistic, Inc. **Page 192** "The Brandon Archive" by Judith Halberstam from IN A QUEER TIME AND PLACE, pp. 22–46. Reprinted by permission of the author.

Chapter 5: Page 212 NON SEQUITUR © 2003 Wiley Miller. Dist. By UNIVERSAL PRESS SYNDICATE. Reprinted with permission. All rights reserved. **Page 218** © Viv Quillin. Reproduced by permission. **Page 224** "Feminist Theory, the Body and the Disabled Figure" by Rosemarie Garland-Thomson from DISABILITY STUDIES READER, ed. by Lennard Davis, pp. 279–292. Reprinted by permission of Routledge/Taylor & Francis Group, LLC and Rosemarie Garland-Thomson. **Page 231** Reprinted and edited with the permission of The Free Press, a Division of Simon & Schuster Adult Publishing Group, from DEADLY PERSUASION: Why Women and Girls Must Fight the Addictive Power of Advertising by Jean Kilbourne. Copyright © 1999 by Jean Kilbourne. All rights reserved. **Page 239** "Three Generations of Native American Women's Birth Experience" by Joy Harjo from Ms. Magazine, 1991. Reprinted by permission of Joy Harjo. **Page 243** "Reproductive Justice: Vision, Analysis, and Action for a Stronger Movement" reprinted by permission. **Page 245** "Reproductive Justice: Vision, Analysis, and Action for a Stronger Movement" reprinted by permission. **Page 246** "Reproductive Justice: Vision, Analysis, and Action for a Stronger Movement" reprinted by permission. **Page 247** "Understanding Positive Women's Realities" by Emma Bell and Luisa Orza from EXCHANGE ON HIV/AIDS, Sexuality and Gender, Autumn 2006, pp. 1–4. Reprinted by permission of the authors. **Page 250** "Living to Love" by bell hooks from SISTERS OF THE YAM, pp. 97–111. Copyright © 1993. Reprinted by permission of South End Press.

Chapter 6: Page 259 Source: Asian Women's Shelter, adapted from Domestic Abuse Intervention Project, Duluth, MN. Used with permission. **Page 261** With kind permission of Jacky Fleming. **Page 274** "Sexual Violence and American Indian Genocide" by Andrea Smith. Reprinted by permission of the author. **Page 283** "Radical Pleasure: Sex and the End of Victimhood" by Aurora Levins Morales from MEDICINE STORIES, pp. 117–119. Reprinted by permission of South End Press. **Page 285** "I am not a rapist! Why college guys are confronting sexual violence" by John Stoltenberg from INTERNATIONAL JOURNAL OF SOCIOLOGY AND SOCIAL POLICY (1997, Vol. 17, No. 1). Copyright © Emerald Group Publishing Limited. Reprinted by permission. **Page 291** "Creative Interventions to Violence: Barbara's Story." Used by permission of Creative Interventions, stories@creative-interventions.org, www. creative-interventions.org, StoryTelling & Organizing Project. **Page 297** International Committee for the Peace Council and Center for Health and Social Policy. Reprinted by permission.

Chapter 7: Page 303 By Kirk as appeared in MS Magazine, May/June 1997, p. 5. Copyright © 1994 by Kirk. **Page 307** Baby Blues Partnership. King Features Syndicate. **Page 317** "Since When Is Marriage a Path to Liberation?" by Paula J. Ettelbrick. Reprinted by permission of the author. **Page 320** "Loving across the Boundary." Copyright © 1995 Ann Filemyr. Reprinted by permission of the author. **Page 327** Excerpt from HITTING HOME: Feminist Ethics, Women's Work and the Betrayal of "Family Values" by Gloria H. Albrecht. © 2004. Reprinted by permission of The Continuum International Publishing Group. **Page 337** "The Mommy Tax" (pp. 87–109) from THE PRICE OF MOTHERHOOD by Ann Crittenden, © 2001 by Ann Crittenden. Reprinted by permission of Henry Holt and Company, LLC. **Page 338** Copyright Nicole Hollander. Reprinted by permission. **Page 346** "Circumventing Discrimination: Gender and Ethnic Strategies in Silicon Valley" by Johanna Shih from GENDER & SOCIETY, Vol. 20, No. 2, April 2006, pp. 177–206. Reprinted by permission of SAGE Publications via Copyright Clearance Center. **Page 362** "To Whom Much Is Given, Much Is Expected: Successful Women, Family, and Responsibility" from HAVING IT ALL? BLACK WOMEN AND SUCCESS by Veronica Chambers, copyright © 2003 by Veronica Chambers. Used by permission of Doubleday, a division of Random House, Inc.

Chapter 8: Page 373 From CAFRA NEWS, March–May 1990, p. 9. Reprinted by permission. **Page 376** Herri/Mujeres en Accion. **Page 383** "Supply chain pressures create precarious employment" from OXFAM INTERNATIONAL (2004, 5). Reprinted by permission. **Page 384** Source: http://www.werner-newtwist.com,

Volume 3, May 18, 2007. **Page 392** "The Homeland, Aztlan," from BORDERLANDS/LA FRONTERA: The New Mestiza. Copyright © 1987, 1999 by Gloria Anzaldua. Reprinted by permission of Aunt Lute books. **Page 399** "Shilling Love" by Shailja Patel. Reprinted by permission. **Page 401** "The Care Crisis in the Philippines: Children and Transnational Families in the New Global Economy" by Rhacel Salazar Parrenas from GLOBAL WOMAN: Nannies, maids and sex workers in the new economy, edited by Barbara Ehrenreich and Arlie Hochschild, pp. 39–54. Reprinted by permission of Rhacel Salazar Parrenas. **Page 410** "Remotely Sensed: A Topography of the Global Sex Trade" by Ursula Biemann from FEMINIST REVIEW (70) 2002, pp. 75–88. Reprinted by permission of Palgrave Macmillan. **Page 414** "Separation anxiety: The schisms and schemas of media advocacy, or `Where are you tonight, Langston Hughes?'" by Paromita Vohra from DEFENDING OUR DREAMS edited by Wilson et al., © 2005. **Page 414** Reprinted by permission of Zed Books. **Page 420** "The virtual economy'" by V. Spike Peterson from A CRITCAL REWRITING OF GLOBAL POLITICAL ECONOMY, © 2003. **Page 438** "Building Water Democracy: People's Victory Against Coca-Cola in Plachimada" by Vandana Shiva from ZNet Commentary, May 13, 2004.

Chapter 9: Page 448 The Funnel of Injustice by Kiaran Honderich 2003, p. 10. Reprinted by permission of the author. **Page 458** Behind the Walls: The History and Current Reality of Women's Imprisonment by Nancy Kurshan. Reprinted by permission of the author. **Page 466** "Women in Prison and Work" by Marilyn Buck was originally published in FEMINIST STUDIES, Volume 30, Number 2 (Summer 2004): 451–455, by permission of the publisher, Feminist Studies, Inc. **Page 469** "Creative Politics and Women's Criminalization in the United States" by Carol Jacbosen from SIGNS, Vol. 33, No. 2, 2008. Reprinted by permission of The University of Chicago Press. **Page 474** "Testimony on Family Detention by U.S. Immigration and Customs Enforcement" 2007, by Michelle Brane. Women's Commission for Refugee Women and Children. Reprinted by permission. **Page 476** "Media Representations and the Criminalization of Arab Americans and Muslim Americans" by Suad Joseph and Benjamin D'Harlingue. Reprinted by permission. **Page 481** Excerpts from "Women of Color, Globalization and the Politics of Incarceration" by Julia Sudbury from THE CRIMINAL JUSTICE SYSTEM AND WOMEN, ed. by Barbara Raffel Price and Natalie Sokoloff, pp. 219–234. Reprinted by permission of The McGraw-Hill Companies.

Chapter 10: Page 498 © 2005 P.S. Mueller—Used by permission. **Page 508** Cartoons by bulbul—www.bulbul.com, P.O. Box 4100, Mountain View, CA 94040. Reprinted by permission. **Page 511** "Sneak Attack: The Militarization of U.S. Culture" by Cynthia Enloe from MS Magazine, December/January 2002. Reprinted by permission of MS Magazine, © 2002. **Page 512** "Belonging" by Anuradha Kristina Bhagwati. Reprinted by permission of the author. **Page 516** "Living Room Terrorists" by Catherine Lutz, 2004. Reprinted by permission of the author. **Page 519** "Report from Okinawa: Long-Term U.S. Military Presence" by Suzuyo Takazato from Canadian Woman Studies/Les Cahiers de la Femme, Vol. 19, No. 4, pp. 42–47. **Page 525** Riverbend, excerpts from BAGHDAD BURNING: GIRL BLOG FROM IRAQ. Copyright © 2005 by Riverbend. Reprinted with the permission of The Feminist Press at the City University of New York, www.feministpress.org. **Page 530** "Mother's Day Proclamation—1870" by Julia Ward Howe. **Page 531** "Unity Statement" by Women's Pentagon Action.

Chapter 11: Page 537 © M. Wuerker **Figure 11.1, p 544** Source: Bill Bigelow and Bob Peterson [eds.], *Rethinking Globalization* [Milwaukee, Wis.: Rethinking Schools Press, 2002.] Reprinted by permission of Rethinking Schools Press. World Wide Fund for Nature, 2006. *Living Planet Report, 2006,* Table 2. Gland, Switzerland: WWFN. Accessed at www.panda.org/news_facts/publications/living_planet_report/index.cfm. **Page 549** Excerpt from "Rose Moon" from HAVING FAITH by Sandra Steingraber. Copyright © 2001 by Sandra Steingraber. Reprinted by permission of Da Capo Press, a member of Perseus Books, L.L.C. **Page 559** "The Ecofeminst Imperative" by Ynestra King. Reprinted by permission. **Page 562** "Principles of Environmental Justice" from The First National People of Color Environmental Leadership Summit. **Page 563** "Native Hawaiian Historical and Cultural Perspectives on Environmental Justice" from RACE, POVERTY AND THE ENVIRONMENT, Vol. 3, No. 1, Spring 1992. For inquiries, call (415) 561-3331. Used with permission of Urban Habitat Program and the author. **Page 567** "Consumption: North American Perspectives" from DANGEROUS INTERSECTIONS: FEMINIST PERSPECTIVES ON POPULATION, ENVIRONMENT, AND DEVELOMENT, edited by Ynestra King and Jael Silliman. Boston: South End Press, 1999, pp. 189–201. Used by permission. **Page 568** Source: Natural Resources Defense Council, in Lori S. Ashford, NEW PERSPECTIVES ON POPULATION: LESSONS FROM CAIRO and POPULATION BULLETIN (Washington, DC: Population Reference Bureau, Inc.), Volume 50, No. 1 (March 1995), p. 30. **Page 570** Reprinted by permission of Stephanie McMillan. **Page 572** Source: Mathis Wackernagel, HOW BIG IS OUR ECOLOGICAL FOOTPRINT? (Vancouver: University of British Columbia, 1993), 3. **Page 574** "Gender Aspects of Climate Change" from www.wedo.org. Reprinted with permission by the Women's Environment and Development Organization.

Chapter 12: Page 586 With kind permission of Jacky Fleming. **Page 589** By Yang as appeared in MS Magazine, January/February 1993, p. 30. **Page 590** Source: http://www.ipu.org/wmn-e-classif.htm. Reprinted by permission of Inter-Parliamentary Union. **Page 595** UN Millenium Development Goals from www.undp.org. Reprinted by permission. **Page 599** "The Body Politic" from LISTEN UP: VOICES FROM THE NEXT FEMINIST GENERATION, edited by Barbara Findlen. Copyright © 1995 by Barbara Findlen. Reprinted by permission of Seal Press, a member of Perseus Books Group. **Page 603** "Staging Activism: New York City Performing Artists as Cultural Workers" by Amy Jo Goddard from SOCIAL JUSTICE, Vol. 34, No. 1, 2007. Reprinted by permission. **Page 614** "Morning in America: A Letter from Feminists" by Various Authors from the March 17, 2008 issue of THE NATION. Reprinted with permission from the March 17, 2008 issue of THE NATION. For subscription information, call 1-800-333-8536. Portions of each week's Nation magazine can be accessed at http://www.thenation.com. **Page 616** "Katrina, Black Women, and the Deadly Discourse on Black Poverty in America (2006)" by Barbara Ransby from DU BOIS REVIEW 2006, Vol. 3, No. 1, pp. 215–222. NY: Cambridge University Press. **Page 621** Meeting the Leadership Challenges of Women with Disabilities: Mobility International USA, Cindy Lewis. Reprinted by permission of the author. **Page 625** "Women Are Opening Doors: Security Council Resolution 1325 in Afghanistan" by Felicity Hill and Mikele Aboitiz from Sunita Mehta, ed., Women for Afghan Women (Palgrave Macmillan, 2003), and is reprinted by permission of Palgrave Macmillan. **Page 629** Excerpts from "The Global Women's Movement: Definitions and Origins" by Peggy Antrobus from THE GLOBAL WOMEN'S MOVEMENT: Origins, Issues and Strategies, © 2004, pp. 9–25. Reprinted by permission of Zed Books Ltd.

Photo Credits

pp. 2, 29, © Bettmann/Corbis; p. 50, Doug Menuez/PhotoDisc/Getty Images; p. 90TL, © Rick Reinhard; p. 90TR, © Royalty-Free/Corbis; p. 90BL, Hoby Finn/PhotoDisc/Getty Images; pp. 90BR, 98, © Rick Reinhard; p. 148TL, © Bettmann/Corbis; p. 148TR, © Underwood & Underwood/Corbis; p. 148BL, © Albert Ferreira/Corbis; p. 148BR, © Philippe Petit-Mars/Corbis; p. 158, © JupiterImages/ThinkStock; p. 192, Courtesy Everett Collection; p. 206, © David Sherman/NBAE/Getty Images; p. 209, © Reuters NewMedia Inc./Corbis; p. 228, © Brenda Prager; p. 256, Created by Southpaw (www.southpaw.org) for the Commission on the Status of Women in San Francisco; p. 287, Courtesy Men Stopping Violence Against Women, Atlanta, GA; p. 300TL, © Andersen Ross/PhotoDisc/Getty Images; p. 300TR, © Geoff Manasse/PhotoDisc/Getty Images; p. 300BL, © Studio M/Jupiter Images; p. 300BR, © Geoff Manasse/PhotoDisc/Getty Images; p. 302, © Walter Hodges/Corbis; p. 304, © Barbara Seyda; p. 305, © Owen Seumptewa; p. 370, © Reuters NewMedia, Inc./Corbis; p. 382, "Remote Sensing" © Ursula Biemann; p. 386, © Michael S. Yamashita/Corbis; p. 492, Scott Braley (www.scottbraley.com) for Critical Resistance; pp. 477, 592, © AP/Wide World Photos; p. 532, Courtesy of the War Resisters League; p. 534, © Peter Beck/Corbis; p. 541, © Jim Cummins/Corbis; p. 574L, © Rizwan Tabassum/AFP/Getty Images; p. 574R, © Alain Guilhot/AFP/Getty Images; p. 582, © Alex Wong/Getty Images; p. 616, © AP/Wide World Photos

Name Index

Index